ADVERTISING & PROMOTION

An Integrated Marketing Communications Perspective

Sixth Canadian Edition

Michael A. Guolla
University of Ottawa

George E. Belch
San Diego State University

Michael A. Belch
San Diego State University

McGraw Hill Education

Advertising & Promotion
An Integrated Marketing Communications Perspective
Sixth Canadian Edition

ISBN-13: 978-1-25-927230-1
ISBN-10: 1-25-927230-3

2 3 4 5 6 10 WEB 22 21 20 19 18

Printed and bound in Canada.

Portfolio and Program Manager: Karen Fozard

Product Manager: Sara Braithwaite

Executive Marketing Manager: Joy Armitage Taylor

Product Developer: Amy Rydzanicz

Senior Product Team Associate: Marina Seguin

Supervising Editor: Jessica Barnoski

Photo/Permissions Editor: Monika Schurmann

Copy Editor: Laurel Sparrow

Plant Production Coordinator: Michelle Saddler

Manufacturing Production Coordinator: Emily Hickey

Cover Design: Dianne Reynolds

Cover Images: Mobile phone: d3sign/Getty Images; Dundas Square: Photographed by Dan Cronin—Toronto, Canada/Getty Images

Interior Design: David Montle

Composition: Aptara, Inc.

Page Layout: SPi Global

Printer: Webcom

BRIEF CONTENTS

CONTENTS

Preface

ADVERTISING AND PROMOTION

Advertising and other forms of promotion influence people even though they might not realize it or admit it. Organizations in both the private and public sectors frequently demonstrate that communicating effectively and efficiently with their target audiences is critical to their success. Advertising and other types of promotional messages known as marketing communication are used to sell goods and services, promote causes and individuals, and influence attitudes and behaviour to resolve societal problems. In fact, it would be impossible to find an organization that does not communicate externally to its constituents to achieve its mandate, and marketing communication usually contributes in achieving objectives consistent with what an organization intends to accomplish.

In today's complex world, an organization communicating effectively—the right message to the right audience at the right time—is a critical and difficult task for promotional planners to achieve efficiently. A marketer's audiences are current customers, potential customers, and external stakeholders and all of these groups require a customized message to be accepted. The message design is informational and/or transformational and usually communicated with creativity to convince the audiences. And there are myriad media for message delivery—broadcast (TV networks, specialty TV, radio), print (newspaper, magazines), out-of-home (outdoor, transit, place-based), and Internet (websites, content publishers, social media)—that are strengthened with sales promotions, events, sponsorships, and public relations.

Moreover, the Internet's interactive characteristics strengthen (and possibly weaken) an organization's image or reputation due to consumers' brand-related online activities. Watching brand-related videos, reading brand-related information on social networking sites, commenting on brand-related blogs, and uploading brand-related pictures/images potentially influences an organization's audiences. These activities are prompted directly by a brand's communication, and are also a manifestation of attitudes established over time yet initiated by motives we are only beginning to uncover as marketers. In either case, promotional planners must take a broad and all-encompassing view of marketing communication if they are to be successful in their decision making.

This text introduces students to advertising and promotion with an integrated marketing communications (IMC) perspective. IMC calls for a "big picture" approach to planning promotion programs and coordinating the communication tools described above to positively enhance a brand. To make effective promotional decisions, a promotional planner must decide how the IMC tools will work individually and collectively so that the organization can achieve its goals efficiently.

SIXTH CANADIAN EDITION ADVANTAGES

This sixth Canadian edition accomplishes the task of showing students how to devise and construct an IMC plan better than any other product on the market. Its numerous advantages include:

- **IMC Perspective**—Advertising and promotion is approached with an integrated marketing communications perspective to attain communication and behavioural objectives for multiple target audiences. The importance of specific communication objectives for each target audience and the importance of unique messages that resonate for each target audience are developed throughout. This approach shows promotional planners how to establish a unique brand position for each target audience while maintaining the overall market position of the brand.

- **Canadian Practice**—Canadian ads and uniquely Canadian examples are featured to give a comprehensive look at the most innovative marketing communications occurring in our country. The text has approximately 500 references from sources such as *Marketing Magazine, Strategy,* the *National Post, The Globe and Mail,* and others to illustrate uniquely Canadian stories so that future promotional planners can see what successful marketing communication looks like. The 53 new perspectives and vignettes are additional stories representing approximately 200 new articles.

- **Canadian Data**—Statistical information presented in tables, charts, and figures appears throughout the text. There are about 230 figures, of which a substantial portion describe the Canadian marketing communication environment. Much of these data occur in the media chapters, the most thorough coverage of media by anyone's standards.

- **Decision Oriented**—Chapter 1 summarizes a planning framework and identifies the content of an IMC plan. This framework is followed closely throughout the text as major parts are organized and given a title that corresponds to the steps in the IMC plan. A distinction is made between the type of decision that an advertiser makes and the information used to formulate the decision. This approach helps students to understand the key decisions that need to be made for a successful IMC plan.

- **Internet Focus**—Internet media and tools occur throughout the text where they appear most relevant. The majority of the opening vignettes and chapter perspectives highlight the use of websites or other digital tools. A balance between Internet media and other media reinforces the importance of IMC decision making.

- **Mobile**—Marketing communication through mobile technology has taken on a greater focus in the sixth edition as consumer adoption has grown. It is featured in many chapter openers and vignettes, and considerable usage statistics are presented in the media chapters.

- **Social Media Planning**—Internet media coverage is expanded considerably in Chapter 17 with the inclusion of a major section on social media. An application of how it can be used as "owned, paid, earned media" to achieve a brand's objectives is developed and the scope of social media is shown with its numerous media classes and vehicles.

- **Current Theory**—Extensive updating of academic references from the *Journal of Advertising* and the *Journal of Advertising Research* and others occurred independently by the Canadian author over the past four editions. The text references about 400 journal articles to give students a resource for further understanding of how marketing communication works and to demonstrate that the material presented is credible.

- **Visual Balance**—The number of figures and exhibits stands at just over 500 visuals for the fifth and sixth editions, up from just over 400 in the fourth edition and up from just over 300 in the first edition. As part of this process, paragraphs have been carefully edited and text has been concisely summarized.

ORGANIZATION OF THIS TEXT

The sixth Canadian edition is divided into five parts. In Part 1, "Understanding Integrated Marketing Communications," we provide background in the areas of IMC planning, consumer behaviour, and communication. Chapter 1 provides an overview of advertising and promotion and an IMC planning model shows the steps in the promotional planning process. This model provides a framework for developing the IMC program and is followed throughout the text. In Chapter 2, we describe the role of ad agencies and other firms that deliver promotional services. Chapter 3 explains how managers use an understanding of buyer behaviour to develop effective communication that is directed to specific target audiences. Chapter 4 examines communication models of how consumers respond to advertising messages and other forms of marketing communication.

In Part 2, "Articulating the Message," we consider how firms develop objectives for their IMC programs and how to translate those objectives into meaningful messages. Chapter 5 stresses the importance of setting objectives for advertising and promotion and the different types of marketing, communication, and behavioural objectives Based on models of consumer responses to marketing communication, this approach is applied for advertising and all other facets of IMC. Chapter 6 explores how advertisers position their brands through effective marketing communication to persuade target audiences. Chapter 7 describes the planning and development of the creative strategy and advertising campaign. In Chapter 8, we illustrate ways to execute the creative strategy and identify criteria for evaluating creative work. Like the objectives chapter, these three chapters are applicable for brand positioning and message development for any aspect of marketing communication. Chapter 9 discusses how to measure the effectiveness of promotional messages of an IMC program.

For Part 3, "Delivering the Message," we explore how to direct the message through media to the target audience in Chapters 10 through 13. Chapter 10 introduces the principles of media planning and strategy, and examines how a media plan is developed for all IMC tools. We have also included in this chapter methods for determining and allocating the promotional budget across all IMC tools. Chapter 11 discusses the strengths and limitations of broadcast media, as well as issues regarding the purchase of radio and TV time and audience measurement. Chapter 12 considers the same issues for the print media (magazines, newspapers). Chapter 13 presents similar material for out-of-home (outdoor, transit, place-based) and support media (promotional products, product placement).

In Part 4, "Strengthening the Message," we examine other promotional tools with a continued IMC emphasis. Chapter 14 covers sales promotion, including both consumer promotions and programs targeted to the trade (retailers, wholesalers, and other intermediaries). Chapter 15 reviews the role of public relations in IMC. Chapter 16 looks at direct marketing and the importance of databases that allow companies to communicate directly with target audiences through various media. Chapter 17 describes how Internet media deliver promotional messages and how social media is an important part of an IMC plan.

The text concludes with Part 5, "Advertising and Society," which contains Chapter 18 on the regulatory, social, ethical, and economic issues for advertising and promotion.

CHAPTER FEATURES

The following features in each chapter enhance students' understanding of the material as well as their reading enjoyment.

Learning Objectives

Learning objectives are provided at the beginning of each chapter to identify the major areas and points covered in the chapter and to guide the learning effort. The objectives are tagged throughout the chapter and summarized at the conclusion of each chapter.

Chapter Opening Vignettes

Each chapter begins with a new vignette that describes an exciting example of the effective use of integrated marketing communications by a company or ad agency, bringing current industry issues into focus as they pertain to the chapter.

IMC Perspectives

These boxed items feature descriptions of interesting issues related to the chapter material or the practical application of integrated marketing communication. Many of these stories integrate aspects of digital technology, social media, or mobile media, as technology is used universally within marketing as an integral part of all marketing communication.

IMC Planning

Each chapter includes an IMC Planning section illustrating how chapter content relates to integrated marketing communication. It provides guidance on how a manager can use the conceptual material to make better practical decisions.

Learning Objectives Summaries

These synopses provide a quick review of the key topics covered and serve to illustrate how the learning objectives have been achieved. Each summary corresponds exactly to the learning objective at the start of the chapter.

Review and Applied Questions

Questions at the end of each chapter give students an opportunity to test their understanding of the material. These questions can also serve as a basis for class discussion or assignments. The applied questions provide students with the opportunity to apply what they have learned within the chapter. Each numbered review question and applied question corresponds to the similarly numbered learning objective of the chapter.

MARKET LEADING TECHNOLOGY

Learn Without Limits

McGraw-Hill Connect® is an award-winning digital teaching and learning platform that gives students the means to better connect with their coursework, with their instructors, and with the important concepts that they will need to know for success now and in the future. With Connect, instructors can take advantage of McGraw-Hill's trusted content to seamlessly deliver assignments, quizzes, and tests online. McGraw-Hill Connect is a learning platform that continually adapts to each student, delivering precisely what they need, when they need it, so class time is more engaging and effective. Connect makes teaching and learning personal, easy, and proven.

Connect Key Features:

SmartBook®

As the first and only adaptive reading experience, SmartBook is changing the way students read and learn. SmartBook creates a personalized reading experience by highlighting the most important concepts a student needs to learn at that moment in time. As a student engages with SmartBook, the reading experience continuously adapts by highlighting content based on what each student knows and doesn't know. This ensures that he or she is focused on the content needed to close specific knowledge gaps, while it simultaneously promotes long-term learning.

Connect Insight®

Connect Insight is Connect's new one-of-a-kind visual analytics dashboard—now available for instructors—that provides at-a-glance information regarding student performance, which is immediately actionable. By presenting assignment, assessment, and topical performance results together with a time metric that is easily visible for aggregate or individual results, Connect Insight gives instructors the ability to take a just-in-time approach to teaching and learning, which was never before available. Connect Insight presents data that helps instructors improve class performance in a way that is efficient and effective.

Simple Assignment Management

With Connect, creating assignments is easier than ever, so instructors can spend more time teaching and less time managing.

- Assign SmartBook learning modules.
- Instructors can edit existing questions and create their own questions.
- Draw from a variety of text specific questions, resources, and test bank material to assign online.
- Streamline lesson planning, student progress reporting, and assignment grading to make classroom management more efficient than ever.

Smart Grading

When it comes to studying, time is precious. Connect helps students learn more efficiently by providing feedback and practice material when they need it, where they need it.

- Automatically score assignments, giving students immediate feedback on their work and comparisons with correct answers.
- Access and review each response; manually change grades or leave comments for students to review.
- Track individual student performance—by question, by assignment, or in relation to the class overall—with detailed grade reports.
- Reinforce classroom concepts with practice tests and instant quizzes.
- Integrate grade reports easily with Learning Management Systems including Blackboard, D2L, and Moodle.

Instructor Library

The Connect Instructor Library is a repository for additional resources to improve student engagement in and out of the class. It provides all the critical resources instructors need to build their course.

- Access instructor resources.
- View assignments and resources created for past sections.
- Post your own resources for students to use.

Instructor Resources:

- **Instructor's Manual.** The instructor's manual includes chapter overviews, learning objectives, chapter and lecture outlines, teaching suggestions, answers to review and applied questions, and additional discussion questions and answers (not shown in text).

- **PowerPoint® Presentation and Digital Assets.** These incorporate a high-quality photo and art program, including figure slides, product shots, and advertisements.
- **Computerized Test Bank.** This test bank contains over 3,000 questions categorized by topic and level of learning (definitional, conceptual, or application). The instructor-friendly format allows easy selection of questions from any part of the text, boxed materials, and cases. The program allows you to select any of the questions, make changes if desired, or add new questions—and quickly print out a finished set customized to your course.
- **Video Case Studies.** A unique series of contemporary advertising cases is available on Connect.

SUPERIOR LEARNING SOLUTIONS AND SUPPORT

The McGraw-Hill Education team is ready to help instructors assess and integrate any of our products, technology, and services into your course for optimal teaching and learning performance. Whether it's helping your students improve their grades, or putting your entire course online, the McGraw-Hill Education team is here to help you do it. Contact your learning solutions consultant today to learn how to maximize all of McGraw-Hill Education's resources.

For more information, please visit us online: http://www.mheducation.ca/he/solutions

ACKNOWLEDGEMENTS

Many colleagues provided detailed and thoughtful reviews that helped immensely. I would like to thank the following reviewers who provided valuable feedback to guide the content of the sixth Canadian edition: Derek Barnes, *Sheridan College*, Mary-Ann Cipriano, *Concordia University*, Mary Dellar, *McGill University*, Lori Futterer, *George Brown College*, Robyn Pettapiece, *St. Clair College*, Pallavi Sodhi, *York University*, Teresa Sturgess, *NAIT*, Claire Tsai, *University of Toronto*, and Jayne Van Dusen, *Algonquin College*. It is impossible to make everyone happy, but I assure you that I thoughtfully read all the suggestions many times to figure out how to make the book better within the time allotted.

I would like to recognize the cooperation I received from people in the business, advertising, and media communities. The sixth Canadian edition contains additional ads, illustrations, charts, and tables published by advertisers and/or their agencies, trade sources, and other advertising and industry organizations. Many individuals provided materials and gave permission to use them. A special thanks to all of you for helping us teach students with up-to-date examples and information. A marketing book cannot exist without the assistance of marketing people!

A successful book like this happens because of the publisher's exceptional work. Talented individuals at McGraw-Hill Education who contributed to this project over the past 18 months have made the final product look fantastic. My portfolio and program manager, Karen Fozard, encouraged a complete revision with the goal of making a strong book even better. A special thanks goes to Amy Rydzanicz, my product developer, for her tremendous effort and high expectations to stay on schedule and to produce a meticulously prepared manuscript. I want to acknowledge the exceptional work of Monika Schurmann for obtaining permissions for the Canadian content that appears throughout the book; the task for this edition was magnified substantially due to digital publication rights. I'd also like to recognize Laurel Sparrow for her splendid copy editing and proofreading skills that improved the text. Thank you to Jessica Barnoski for managing the production process. Thanks also to other members of the production team for their hard work on this edition.

I have taught marketing communication to many students over the years; it has been gratifying to see students enjoy my teaching and apply their knowledge attained within my advertising course, within other marketing courses, and in winning case competitions. So many former students from the Telfer School of Management of the University of Ottawa have achieved great marketing success, and I hope that learning how to make effective promotion decisions proved useful in their career. To my current students, I hope you enjoy reading the book, and achieve great success after graduating like your predecessors. To students beyond my classroom, I wish you success as well after reading this material. Please thank your professor for selecting this book, and thereby demonstrating their great insight!

On a personal note, my children, Louise, Daniel, and Nicholas, have been supportive during the time-consuming and involving process of finding, researching, writing, editing, and organizing the material for this text. All my love and gratitude goes to my wife, Teresa, since I disappeared to my offices for hours on end to produce this sixth edition.

Michael Guolla

ABOUT THE AUTHOR

Michael Guolla is an assistant professor at the Telfer School of Management of the University of Ottawa. He completed his Ph.D. in Business Administration with a concentration in Marketing at the Stephen M. Ross School of Business of the University of Michigan (Ann Arbor) and received his Honours in Business Administration from the Richard Ivey School of Business at the University of Western Ontario. Dr. Guolla has published articles in academic journals, proceedings of scholarly conferences, and management journals.

© David Dow/NBAE via Getty Images

CHAPTER ONE

Integrated Marketing Communications

LEARNING OBJECTIVES

LO1 Describe the importance of marketing communication within the marketing mix.

LO2 Identify the tools of the promotional mix—advertising, sales promotion, public relations, direct marketing, Internet marketing, and personal selling—and summarize their purpose.

LO3 Illustrate the concept of integrated marketing communications (IMC) by distinguishing its evolution, renewed perspective, and importance.

LO4 Explain the IMC planning process model and express the steps in developing a marketing communications program.

LO5 Identify how the IMC planning process is continued throughout all chapters.

Raptors' "We the North" Captures Canada

For Toronto Raptors fans across Canada, April 2014 will be memorable for many years as the team's message "We the North" ignited their passion just before the NBA playoffs began. As a rallying cry for all, the direction for Canada's only basketball team signalled a new era to celebrate a national following of the only team north of the border. A few weeks earlier, the creative agency Sid Lee proposed the message to Raptors communication managers as an approach to celebrate the team's 20th anniversary for the 2015–2016 season, eight months in the future. However, the powerful idea struck the managers so significantly that they stepped up the schedule and immediately launched the campaign. With the Toronto Blue Jays' baseball season starting slowly and only one Canadian team in the NHL playoffs, the Raptors capitalized on the open strategic window and captivated sports fans from coast to coast to coast!

Sid Lee recorded the 60-second commercial in two days after casting for local basketball players. They shot numerous scenes throughout many parts of Toronto and spliced the images with highlight sequences from Raptors games. The imagery attained the goal of giving the team a new identity to go with the planned revision of the logo and uniforms. Moreover, the 86-word spoken copy portrayed the team as distinctively Canadian, with phrases like "In many ways we're in a league of our own" along with "And far from the east side. Miles from the west side. Nowhere near the south side. We are the north side." The final visual of a black and white flag swaying in the wind flashed "We the North" to go along with the audio of "Let's go Raptors" chanted by the fans.

The team placed the video in social media and attained 500,000 views in two days, just prior to the first playoff game. It also placed the full 60-second version on TV, rather than a shortened 30-second version. Immediately, fans waved their own "We the North" flags as they cheered the team on, and the players loved the imagery and got pumped up. However, the exuberant momentum could not carry onto the courts as the Raptors went down in defeat. One commentator noted that the national excitement for "We the North" seemed like Molson Canadian's "The Rant" 20 years earlier when the NBA first hatched the Raptors.

Launching the campaign quickly paid off financially. Tickets sold out for preseason games in Vancouver and Montreal, a great signal that the goal of appealing to all Canadians worked. Season ticket sales rose by 4,000 seats and merchandise sales doubled. The team followed up with three new executions to launch the next season. The team handed out numerous "We the North" T-shirts for the 2014 home opener to carry on the excitement a few months later. Copycats emerged to show great flattery; the Montreal Canadiens started "Oui the North" and Canadian golfer Mike Weir used "Weir the North."

Sources: Emily Wexler, "She the North," *Strategy*, December 2014, p. 26; Rachel Brady, "How the Raptors Redefined Their Brand—and Took Toronto by the Throat," *The Globe and Mail*, October 28, 2014; Kirstin Laird et. al., "I Made the List of Marketers," *Marketing Magazine*, January 15, 2015.

Question:

1. What suggestions do you have for the Raptors to maintain the initial momentum of the "We the North" campaign?

As the opening vignette illustrates, companies use advertising, websites, direct marketing, sales promotion, public relations, and social media to communicate something about their products, prices, or availability. In fact, finding the right combination of marketing communication tools is a critical decision for small and large firms, private and public organizations, and those that market goods, services, or ideas. In response, many companies use *integrated marketing communications* to link or connect their promotional tools and communicate with their current and prospective customers. Companies develop their marketing communication plans such that each promotional tool retains its unique communication effect and that the combination of promotional tools contributes to the overall communication effect of the brand or organization.

This opening chapter sets the direction for the entire book as it highlights the marketing context for advertising and promotion. First, it describes the importance of marketing communication. It then briefly defines the different promotional or marketing communication tools available for marketers. Next, it illustrates the idea of integrated marketing communications and indicates why it is so important. Finally, it explains the content of an integrated marketing communications (IMC) plan as a way of orienting the perspective and organization of this text.

LO1   Marketing Communication

In this opening section we describe the importance of marketing communication within an organization's overall marketing effort. We begin by reviewing the definition of marketing to understand the importance of marketing communication in delivering value to consumers. We then explore examples of the content of marketing communication plans to illustrate their many different purposes.

MARKETING

Historically, the American Marketing Association (AMA), the organization that represents marketing professionals in the United States and Canada, defined marketing as *the process of planning and executing the conception, pricing, promotion, and distribution of ideas, goods, and services to create exchanges that satisfy individual and organizational objectives.*[1] This definition focused on **exchange** as a central concept in marketing and the use of marketing activities to create and sustain relationships with customers.[2] For exchange to occur, there must be two or more parties with something of value to one another, a desire and ability to give up that something to the other party, and a way to *communicate* with each other. Marketing communication plays an important role in the exchange process by informing consumers of an organization's product and convincing them of its ability to satisfy their needs or wants. Exhibit 1-1 communicates an important characteristic about A&W's chicken sandwich. Consumers may conclude that this product would be a healthier choice, and better able to meet their dietary needs, than a competitor's sandwich.

The marketing function in an organization facilitates the exchange process by examining the needs and wants of consumers, developing a product that satisfies these needs, offering it at a certain price, making it available through a distribution channel, and developing a marketing communication program. These four Ps—product, price, place (distribution), and promotion (marketing communication)—are elements of the **marketing mix**. The main purpose of the marketing function is to combine these four elements into a marketing program that facilitates the potential for exchange with consumers in the marketplace. The remainder of this section describes how the marketing mix decisions of product, price, and distribution (Figure 1-1) are often the primary content of marketing communication messages with the ultimate objective of delivering value.

Exhibit 1-1   A&W's guarantee potentially reassures consumers that their chicken sandwich is a healthy option for a meal.

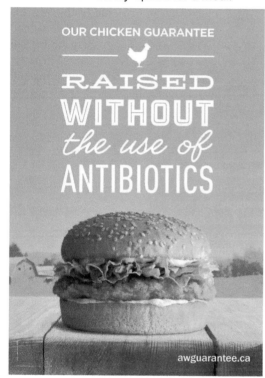

Hand-out/A&W RESTAURANTS/Newscom

Figure 1-1   Examples of typical marketing decisions

Product Decisions	Price Decisions	Distribution Decisions
Product Type	Price Level	Channel Type
Features or Attributes/Benefits	Price Policy	Channel Policy
Corporate Name/Identification	Discount	Type of Intermediary or Reseller
Brand Name/Identification	Allowance	Type of Location/Store
Package Design	Flexibility	Service Level

COMMUNICATING PRODUCT

Each of the product facets listed in Figure 1-1 can be the focus of marketing communication. This section shows how marketing messages can communicate the product type, the importance of salient attributes or benefits, and the identity of the brand or organization, in order to assist with brand equity development.

Product Type   An organization exists because it offers a product to consumers, generally in exchange for money. This offering may be a physical good (such as a soft drink, pair of jeans, or car), a service (banking, air travel, or legal assistance), a cause (United Way, March of Dimes), an idea (don't drink and drive), or even a person (political candidate). The product is anything that can be marketed and that, when consumed or supported, gives satisfaction to the individual. When we use the term *product* in this book, it refers to any one or a combination of these five product types which are not always independent. When eating at a restaurant, consumers enjoy the food but also enjoy the service by not having to prepare the meal, or by eating food they may not have the culinary skill to make. Thus, whatever the product type, marketing communication attempts to show how the product offering fulfills a consumer's needs.

Product Attributes/Benefits   Every product has fairly objective attributes that characterize what it is; a chocolate bar can have varying types of chocolate (e.g., milk, dark) and different kinds of ingredients (e.g., nuts, wafers). Marketing communication can take the simple role of identifying the composition of a good. For example, ads for Prime Chicken, produced by Maple Leaf Foods, stated that it was 100 percent all-vegetable grain-fed poultry in its original message. Notice how the Montblanc ad in Exhibit 1-2 highlights attributes of the watch regarding the watch face and functions. Moreover, organizations use marketing communication to educate consumers on service delivery. For instance, WestJet ads demonstrate the personal attentiveness the airline's staff provides to customers, while The Keg Steakhouse ads focus on the ambiance of the restaurant as well as the food.

Consumers typically view a product as an offering of a benefit or a bundle of benefits. Advertising and other marketing communication tools draw attention toward these benefits and make claims about them. Benefits can be communicated as functional via the product's attributes, as seen in the above examples. Benefits are also subjectively claimed through the performance of the product (e.g., convenience). Finally benefits are communicated by feelings or emotions associated with the experiential consumption of a product. These positive (e.g., contentment) or negative emotions (e.g., fear) can be psychologically based (e.g., pride) or socially based (e.g., jealousy).

Exhibit 1-2   Quality attributes are identified for the Montblanc watch.

Montblanc TimeWalker Chronograph Automatic
Automatic chronograph movement, 43 mm stainless steel case, sapphire crystal case back, fine silver dial.
SWISS MADE BY MONTBLANC.

MONTBLANC BOUTIQUE
800-995-4810
WWW.MONTBLANC.COM

© Montblanc Inc.

Prime Chicken changed its message to show that the convenience of the brand brought families together to create lasting memories, using vignettes of families enjoying their dinner together. The company intended for consumers to connect with the brand on an emotional level by highlighting the enjoyment people have with food at dinner time.[3] Thus, managers decide which benefits to emphasize or how to portray the benefits in a message, and the best way to deliver that message across many different time periods. BMW's advertising emphasized the emotion experienced in driving its vehicle by showing an "expression of joy" in a print ad that did not show the product, but rather depicted the car's tire marks in colour as if they were painted upon a canvas.[4]

Brand Identity   A brand or corporate name and its identification through its logo, symbol, or trademark represent critical product decisions. Marketers use brand names that communicate product concepts clearly, such as Air Canada (airlines) and Seadoo (water craft). The symbol of any automobile company illustrates the importance of selecting an appropriate visual representation of a brand. One primary purpose of marketing communication is to present the brand and its identification in favourable locations, situations, or time frames that allow consumers to think or feel more positively toward the brand. The ad in Exhibit 1-3 clearly shows the Heineken brand identity. The identification of a trademark in an ad is critical, as evidenced by a legal battle between Victoria's Secret PINK brand and the luxury shirt brand Thomas Pink on the use of the colour in its brand identity.[5] Figure 1-2 identifies the best Canadian brands as compiled by Interbrand.

Brand identity is reinforced by the tagline or slogan appearing in any form of marketing communication. IKEA's slogan "Long Live the Home" encapsulates the essence of the brand succinctly by connecting the brand name to the products it sells. Executives suggest that the tagline is very relevant since it "communicates a brand position or brand benefit." For example, Swiss Chalet returned to a previously successful tagline, "Always so good for so little," after making many changes over the years. Firms that offer many types of goods and services use an audio logo as one way of connecting brand messages across multiple media and IMC tools, much like a visual logo. For example, the Rogers audio logo can be heard for many of its services, including wireless and cable. Continuity and consistency in the promotional message across IMC tools—television, radio, wireless, interactive displays, Internet, podcasts—makes simple reminders of brand identification a key part of the brand experience.

Packaging provides functional benefits such as economy, protection, and storage, which can be the main purpose of a marketing communication message. However, since the package is associated so closely with the brand by giving it a distinctive look, its identity is the focal point of a marketing communication message. For example, the main point of an ad can be to show the packaging of the product, since this influences consumer choice (as in the case of perfume, Exhibit 1-4). Other characteristics of packaging, like its being fully biodegradable, are a concern for marketers and have become the focal message for marketing communication.[6]

Brand Equity   The culmination of marketing communication messages of product type, product attributes/benefits, and brand identification assists with brand equity, either creating, maintaining, or enhancing this important marketing outcome. **Brand equity** is the differential effect of brand knowledge on consumer responses to the marketing of the brand.[7] By extension, it is an intangible asset added to a product due to the favourable image, impressions of differentiation, or strength of consumer attachment toward a company name, brand name, or trademark. Brand equity provides the company with a competitive advantage by allowing its product to earn greater sales volume and/or higher margins than it could without the name. The vehicle shown in Exhibit 1-5 looks really nice, yet the Maserati brand name certainly conveys something greater than a stylish sedan.

Exhibit 1-3   Heineken ensures that its brand identification is prominently displayed.

© ton koene / Alamy Stock Photo

Figure 1-2   Best Canadian brands

1	TD
2	RBC Financial Group
3	Thomson Reuters
4	Scotiabank
5	Tim Hortons
6	Bell
7	Shoppers Drug Mart
8	Rogers
9	Lululemon
10	Telus

Source: Based on data from Best Canadian Brands 2014, Interbrand.

Exhibit 1-4   Showing a product's packaging is often a focus of ads.

Image courtesy of "Christian Dior Parfums"

Conceptually, IMC planning and the subsequent marketing communication decisions are expected to strongly generate brand equity.[8] The growing interest in this particular brand effect has led to organizations reporting different ways to view and measure brand equity. Figure 1-3 highlights the top 10 most valuable Canadian brands as determined by Brand Finance.[9] The differences in this and the earlier table in Figure 1-2 show the challenge in consistently measuring effects like brand equity. In both cases, these organizations use financial data and surveys of consumers of Canadian-based brands. In contrast, Ipsos Reid uncovers the most influential brands from any country with Canadian survey panelists' attitudes only, and finds Google, Microsoft, Facebook, Apple, and YouTube in its top five.[10] Interbrand's rankings (Figure 1-2) lack Canadian technology firms, one reason why the strength of the top Canadian brands is weaker with the decline of noteworthy brands (e.g., BlackBerry, Nortel).[11]

Beyond brand equity as a strategic initiative, marketers are interested in other aspects with views like brand experience, brand attachment, and brand love. Brand experience involves receiving marketing communication messages, shopping behaviour, product use, and consumption, leading to one view that it includes sensory, affective, intellectual, and behavioural dimensions.[12] Brand attachment is the strength of the bond between a brand and one's self and comprises brand–self connection and brand prominence.[13] Brand love is a more abstract notion reflecting seven more concrete aspects: passion-driven behaviours, self–brand integration, emotional attachment, anticipated separation distress, long-term relationship view, positive attitude, and confidently held attitude.[14] From these definitions we conclude that marketing communication is important for achieving any type of brand-based consumer response. While brand equity is currently a dominant one, these ideas provide direction for new routes.

Exhibit 1-5 This Maserati ad contributes to its brand equity.

© Maserati North America, Inc.

Figure 1-3 The top 10 most valuable Canadian brands

Rank 2015	Brand
1	RBC
2	TD
3	Bell
4	Scotiabank
5	Bank of Montreal
6	Rogers
7	CIBC
8	TELUS
9	Enbridge
10	McCain Foods

Source: Based on data from The Most Valuable Canadian Brands of 2015, The Brand Finance Group.

Sport Chek worked with its agency of record, Sid Lee, as it devoted 25 percent of its budget to building its brand. Research indicated that the product-specific communication no longer resonated with a younger consumer who spent considerable time online. The advertising went in a new direction with the "Your Better Starts Here" campaign featuring Sidney Crosby in TV spots and out-of-home ads near and in gyms that showed the determination of the NHL star as he worked out while on the road to recover from an injury. The campaign also included extensive digital messages featuring Blue Jay Brett Lawrie on YouTube and Twitter.[15]

COMMUNICATING PRICE

The price of a product, usually expressed in a dollar amount, is a signal of a consumer's economic cost to purchase a product in exchange for receiving its combined benefits. Price planning involves decisions concerning the level, policy, adjustments through discounts or allowances, and flexibility when facing competition. Marketing communication plays a role in reinforcing a consumer's belief that the product's benefit or quality accurately reflects the price. One historical study regarding price, product quality, and advertising expenditures concluded that pricing and advertising strategies go together. High relative ad expenditures should accompany premium prices, and low relative ad expenditures should be tailored to low prices.[16]

Price is also a key piece of information conveyed in marketing communication messages. For example, car dealerships and manufacturers focus on price and price discounts in TV and newspaper ads. Internet ads focus on price offers that attempt to influence consumer price beliefs; competitors advertise mortgage rate information in many media and specialized websites like RateHub.ca.[17] The information on websites offering deals is predominantly price related (e.g., RedTag.ca). A main purpose of the billboard ad in Exhibit 1-6 is to communicate price. Research concludes that price comparison advertising plays a key role in consumers' reference price for products when determining the value of a product.[18] Other research finds that communicating price information is critical for influencing consumers who are in the process of deciding to buy a product.[19]

Exhibit 1-6   Ads may feature price information as their primary message, as shown in this McDonald's example.

© BirchTree / Alamy Stock Photo

COMMUNICATING DISTRIBUTION

Marketing channels, the "place" element of the marketing mix, are "sets of interdependent organizations involved in the process of making a product available for use or consumption."[20] Consumer product companies distribute through **indirect channels** using a network of wholesalers and/or retailers, or through **direct channels** such as the Internet and do not use any channel intermediaries to sell to customers. In either case, marketing communication provides information as to where and how to purchase a product.

For example, sporting goods companies with different quality and price levels might communicate which brands and models are at different types of retailers. Alternatively, different service levels might be available within the distribution network and be the focus of marketing communication. For instance, particular locations for cosmetics products offer customized beautifying services, while others are self-serve. Also, extensive marketing communication occurs to direct consumers to organizational websites for online purchases. As these examples demonstrate, the importance of communicating in a multi-channel environment, along with a multi-media universe, makes the development of brand equity within distribution decisions a compelling management task.[21]

COMMUNICATING VALUE

The AMA's earlier definition of marketing highlighted a company's offering via the marketing mix, a useful view for easy reference. More recently, the AMA renewed its definition of marketing as *the activity, set of institutions, and processes for creating, communicating, delivering, and exchanging offerings that have value for customers, clients, partners, and society at large.*[22] The earlier elements of the marketing mix remain implied and the importance of value within the exchange is now very prominent.

The idea of value is elusive across academic disciplines and within managerial uses of the term, however the relative balance or ratio of what consumers "receive" for what they "give" is a view that is well appreciated by researchers and decision makers. From a "give" standpoint, consumers pay for products via the price as mentioned but also incur time, physical effort, social, and psychological costs while shopping and/or consuming. For example, one could simply pay a premium price and ask a travel agent to book a vacation, or one could spend time online searching for the best price; each option clearly has its own unique costs. Thus, marketing communication takes on a significant role to signal to consumers the benefit they will accrue for the total costs they incur. Consumers' opportunity to shop physically and virtually anywhere, in any way, at any time, opens the door for marketing communication decisions to be one of the most important management decisions for an organization so that its customers and potential customers understand a brand's value offering.

 LO2   # The Promotional Mix

Promotion is the coordination of all seller-initiated efforts to set up channels of information and persuasion to sell goods and services or promote an idea.[23] While implicit communication occurs through the other elements of the marketing mix, most of an organization's communication with the marketplace occurs as part of a carefully planned and controlled promotional program. The tools an organization uses in a promotional program are referred to as the **promotional mix** (Figure 1-4). While either *promotion* or *marketing communication* is a suitable term, many marketers use the latter since the tools are often connected. For example, a television commercial can direct viewers to a website, or a brand may use the same type of message in its radio and print ads. We now define each of the tools and summarize their purpose.

Figure 1-4   Tools of the promotional mix

ADVERTISING

Advertising is defined as any paid form of nonpersonal communication about an organization, product, service, or idea by an identified sponsor.[24] The *paid* aspect of this definition reflects the fact that the space or time for an advertising message generally must be bought. An occasional exception to this is the public service announcement (PSA), whose advertising space or time is donated by the media.

The *nonpersonal* component means advertising involves mass media (e.g., TV, radio, magazines, newspapers) that can transmit a message to large groups of individuals, often at the same time. The nonpersonal nature of advertising means there is generally no opportunity for immediate feedback from the message recipient (except in direct-response advertising). Therefore, before the message is sent, the advertiser must consider how the audience will interpret and respond to it.

Canadian advertisers spend more than $14 billion annually to reach their audiences, and there are several reasons why advertising is such an important part of many marketers' promotional mixes.

Cost-Efficiency   Advertising can be a very cost-efficient method for communicating with large audiences. For example, during a television season, prime-time network television reached 85 percent of Canadians on a daily basis. The most-watched TV show each week attracts an audience of about 3 million English-speaking viewers. The average top-10 show audience is about 2.4 million viewers, while the average audience for the top 11 to 20 shows is about 1.7 million viewers.[25] One study quotes media experts who estimate the cost per thousand reached at $25 for a top 10 show and $20 for a top 11–20 show. To reach an audience for Canadian-produced television shows costs $16 per thousand; specialty channel audiences cost $8 per thousand.[26]

Cost-Effectiveness   Assuming that a majority of the viewers actually watched a TV ad, paid attention during the airing, and remember something about the message, then advertising can be seen as a very cost-effective form of marketing communication for many brands. In general, advertising can be a cost-effective method for allowing potential customers to know something about a brand and have a positive attitude toward the brand prior to, during, or after purchasing a product.

Brand Communication Effects   Advertising is a valuable tool for brand communication as it is a powerful way to provide consumers with information as well as to influence their attitudes. Advertising can be used to create favourable and unique images and associations for a brand, which can be very important for companies selling products that are difficult to differentiate on the basis of functional attributes. Brand image and brand reputation play an important role in the purchase of many goods and services, and advertising remains a recommended approach to building a brand.[27] Empirical research also finds that advertising directly and indirectly leads to greater firm value due to intangible assets (e.g., brand communication effects).[28]

Brand Interaction   Advertising in media such as television, print, and outdoor is employed to encourage consumers to interact with the brand online. For example, a Broil King campaign created the fictitious journalist Rob Liking, who interviewed people grilling on their barbecues. Executives identified research showing that consumers researched their purchase online prior to a store visit, thus leading to a primary objective of influencing consumers' behaviour in the form of visiting the company's website.[29]

Flexible Tool   Advertising is a flexible tool that can be used for many industries (e.g., cars or soft drinks), market situations (e.g., new product launch or market development for established product), channel members (e.g., consumers or retailers), and target audiences (e.g., new customers or loyal customers). New products entering the Canadian market use some form of advertising, and *Marketing Magazine* annually recognizes outstanding ads. Vaseline Spray and Go ran a series of 15 video ads showing how quickly a woman could moisturize and get dressed. The creatively entertaining demonstration illustrated the key product benefits of ease and speed of application for new customers to understand perfectly.[30]

Multiple Domains   Different types of advertising occur in many domains. Canadian marketers of goods and services advertise to consumer markets with national or regional brand messages, and in some cases with messages to particular international consumer markets. Alternatively, local retailers and other goods and services providers use advertising for many communication purposes in order to achieve sales objectives. Also, industry associations, like the Dairy Farmers of Canada, advertise extensively to consumer markets as do all levels of government and non-governmental organizations like Canadian Blood Services. Shoppers Drug Mart, Canada's number one pharmaceuticals retailer, advertised to celebrate its 50th anniversary with a "Fabulous 50" campaign featuring its largest media buy ever to support all of its marketing communication. Its "red gift box" messaging and imagery emphasized health, beauty, and convenience.[31]

Business-to-business advertising is directed to those who buy or influence the purchase of goods or services for their organization. Exhibit 1-7 shows an example of how General Electric communicates to other organizations in the solar energy market. Professional advertising directed to those with specific designations is found in many industries such as health, management, government, and technology. Finally, advertising directed to channel members like wholesalers, distributors, and retailers is found in all industry sectors around the world.

SALES PROMOTION

Sales promotion is defined as marketing activities that provide extra value or incentives to the salesforce, distributors, or the ultimate consumer and can influence their behaviour to stimulate sales. Sales promotion is generally broken into two major categories: consumer-oriented and trade-oriented activities.

Consumer sales promotion is targeted to the ultimate user of a product and includes coupons, samples, premiums, rebates, contests, and events. These promotional tools encourage consumers to make an immediate trial or repeat purchase, participate in a brand activity like attending the Red Bull Crashed Ice competition, or be more involved with the organization's marketing communication by uploading a video to a social media site celebrating one's consumption of a brand. Exhibit 1-8 is an example of a coupon offer within an ad that encourages parents to switch to a new brand of snack for their children. Shoppers Drug Mart celebrated its anniversary with a contest offering 50 grand prizes and attracted more than 900,000 entrants.

Trade sales promotion is targeted toward marketing intermediaries such as wholesalers, distributors, and retailers. Promotional and merchandising allowances, price deals, sales contests, and trade shows are examples of the promotional tools used to encourage the trade to stock and promote a company's products. Some trade promotions benefit consumers since they receive information contained in a display or receive discounted prices that are passed along to them from the retailer. Retail personnel at Shoppers Drug Mart liked the specialized celebration point-of-purchase material so much that they avoided dismantling it even after the party was over.

Exhibit 1-7   Business-to-business marketers use advertising to build awareness and brand identity.

© GE

Exhibit 1-8   Dare combines its sales promotion with its advertising.

© Dare Foods Limited

PUBLIC RELATIONS

Public relations (PR) occurs when an organization systematically plans and distributes information in an attempt to control and manage its image. **Public relations** is defined as "the management function which evaluates public attitudes, identifies the policies and procedures of an individual or organization with the public interest, and executes a program of action to earn public understanding and acceptance."[32] Public relations uses a variety of tools—including special publications, participation in community activities, fundraising, sponsorship of special events, and public affairs activities—to enhance an organization's image. Many organizations make PR an integral part of their predetermined marketing and promotional strategies. Exhibit 1-9 shows how sponsorship of artistic displays is part of the public relations activities for major corporations. Scotiabank and many others supported Nuit Blanche, a sunset-to-sunrise, free, contemporary art event. There are other examples. Cisco and the CBC, two key drivers of the "One Million Acts of Green" program, recruited Tim Hortons to their cause through the promotion of a 10-cent discount for each hot drink purchased and consumed with a reusable travel mug.[33] Shoppers Drug Mart sponsored the Toronto International Film Festival and featured its imagery with the red carpet entry of the celebrities.

Publicity refers to nonpersonal communications regarding an organization, product, person, or idea not directly paid for by an identified sponsorship. The message reaches the public in the news media as a story or editorial. Like advertising, publicity involves nonpersonal communication to a mass audience, but unlike advertising, publicity is not directly paid for by the organization. The organization encourages the media to cover a favourable story by using tools like news releases, press conferences, feature articles, and media.

Exhibit 1-9   Scotiabank supported the Nuit Blanche along with other sponsors.

© Valentino Visentini / Alamy Stock Photo

An advantage of publicity is its credibility; consumers tend to be less skeptical toward favourable information about a product when it comes from a source they perceive as unbiased. For example, movie reviews from film critics may be viewed by moviegoers as an objective evaluation. Another advantage of publicity is its low cost, since the company is not paying for time or space in a mass medium. While costs in developing public relations items to foster publicity occur, these expenses will be far less than advertising.

DIRECT MARKETING

Direct marketing occurs when organizations communicate directly with target audiences to generate a response and/or a transaction. Direct marketing tools are used by companies that distribute their products to consumers directly and by companies that distribute their products through traditional distribution channels or their own salesforce. Direct marketing tools include telemarketing and call centres, direct mail, mail-order catalogues, Internet-order websites, and direct-response ads in media. Direct marketing is an important component of a firm's marketing communication program since it is connected to other aspects of marketing communication. Direct marketing is used to distribute product samples and promotional products. Extensive direct marketing activities occur with the administration of loyalty programs designed to reward frequent purchasing customers. Direct marketing can also be used as part of a public relations program by sending relevant information. Shoppers Drug Mart revamped its Optimum points program while celebrating its 50th anniversary, which translated into a 20 percent growth in its membership.

In order to communicate directly, companies develop and maintain databases containing contact information (e.g., address, phone number, email), customer profiles, purchase history, and media preferences of present and/or prospective customers. Marketers use this information to target either audience through many tools. They use telemarketing to call customers directly and attempt to sell products and services or qualify them as sales leads. Call centres are used to respond to customer inquiries. Marketers send out direct-mail pieces ranging from simple letters to detailed brochures, catalogues, and DVDs to give potential customers information about their products. Finally, marketers use **direct-response advertising**, whereby a product is promoted through an ad (e.g., television or print) that encourages the consumer to purchase directly via the phone or Internet (Exhibit 1-10).

Exhibit 1-10   Under Armour uses direct-response advertising to promote its products.

© Under Armour

INTERNET MARKETING

We are experiencing a dynamic change in marketing through interactive media, delivered via the Internet. **Interactive media** allow for a back-and-forth flow of information where users participate in and modify its form and content instantly. The interactive media characteristics of the Internet allow users to receive, alter, and share information and images, experience all forms of marketing communication, make inquiries, respond to questions, and make purchases. Approximately 6 percent of all Canadian retail sales occur with online shopping.[34] Thus, the Internet is a multifaceted marketing communication tool with advertising and other IMC capabilities that we focus on in this book and now briefly introduce.

The Internet is an advertising medium much like any other, since brands pay a fee to place a video ad, various styles of display ads that look like a print ad, or an audio ad virtually anywhere, such as on content publishing websites like TSN or social media sites like Facebook or YouTube. Search engine ads are another paid advertising opportunity as are messages on classified/directory websites. In total, Canadian companies spent almost $4 billion on these forms of Internet advertising in 2014, and many of the points about advertising raised earlier are applicable here.

Websites provide current and potential customers with information about the company's products and activities. Other firms develop websites to entertain or communicate emotionally with their clientele. In either case, these branded websites are "owned media" much like other marketing collateral material such as catalogues. Of course, the interactive media characteristics of a brand's website alter a consumer's experience considerably.

Social media facilitates interaction and communication among its members to create, share, and exchange information, experiences, perspectives, and media. Social media like Facebook, YouTube, Twitter, and Instagram are means for marketers to reach consumers as each allows a brand to create a group (Facebook) or channel (YouTube) for all kinds of marketing communication activities. Since these types of social media do not charge a brand to set up an account, a brand's presence is much like "owned media" as a brand's personnel (or agency personnel) construct the message and style much like what is found on a brand's website. As we shall see later in Chapter 17, social media players offer additional features for a fee to enhance a brand's marketing communication, thereby easily moving toward "paid media" that might make the advertising message not necessarily look like advertising from the point of view of a consumer.

The interactive features of social media that facilitate communication among users provide a powerful means of brand influence. Positive communication about a brand is referred to as "earned media" by marketing practitioners. This terminology gained stronger notoriety as social media matured, however the idea existed previously in the domain of public relations for decades and with managers interested in tracking consumers' verbal word-of-mouth communication. Marketers are very active with online postings to stimulate conversations among consumers with the hopes of generating peer or group influence. At other times, brand managers contract special agencies that will financially arrange for an influential blogger to endorse a brand by posting their consumption via a picture or video.[35] So while the blogger's post might look like "earned" media to a consumer, it is in fact "paid" media.

The Internet is a medium to execute all elements of the promotional mix beyond advertising-like messages via paid, owned, and earned media. Marketers offer sales promotion incentives such as coupons and contests online, and they use the Internet to conduct direct marketing and public relations activities effectively and efficiently. For example, Exhibit 1-11 shows the many ways a consumer can interact with the Naked Juice brand on the Internet that share characteristics of all elements of the promotional mix. In fact, a brand can implement a completely digital IMC program that includes advertising, sales promotion, events, public relations, and social media interaction online. For example, BMW's Smart Car used Internet media with a dedicated microsite, a customized Facebook page, and YouTube to demonstrate the car's big interior despite its being small on the outside.[36]

Access to websites, social media, interactive experiences, and all facets of marketing communication

Exhibit 1-11   Naked Juice used a creative Facebook application to promote its new recyclable bottle.

© Naked Juice Company

is prevalent with mobile media devices like smart phones and tablets. These devices and accompanying applications open the door for marketers to adapt and invent ways of implementing marketing communication. For example, while walking down the street a person could receive a message with an incentive to turn back and eat at a restaurant she had just passed by. Although consumers access online marketing communication similarly (mobile vs. non-mobile), the portability of receiving brand messages or interacting with a brand, or a peer, makes this a new frontier for IMC planners, who need to consider how existing promotional decisions will be adapted to fit with or influence consumer behaviour. For example, a Starbucks app allows customers to pay for purchases, find locations, obtain nutritional information, and manage their rewards account, all on a smart phone.

Although the Internet has been an increasingly popular medium over the past 20 years, offering many media delivery options for marketing communication as shown above, the ultimate role of advertising and promotion and the content of the message remain essentially unchanged. According to two noted marketing writers, promotional planners still try to achieve brand communication effects by delivering a relevant message with the ultimate goal of achieving a marketing objective, such as selling more of a product.[37] While feedback of digital message delivery is virtually instantaneous with media like Twitter, considerable planning is required by a promotional manager for initial digital message delivery, much like what has existed for nearly a century since the advent of radio advertising. Supporting this view is research that compares the direct and indirect communication effects of digital and broadcast media.[38]

PERSONAL SELLING

The final promotional mix element is **personal selling**, a form of person-to-person communication in which a seller assists and/or persuades prospective buyers to purchase the company's good or service or to act on an idea. Personal selling involves direct contact between buyer and seller, either face-to-face or through telecommunications. This interaction gives the marketer communication flexibility; the seller can see or hear the potential buyer's reactions and tailor the message to their specific needs or situation. We do not cover personal selling in this book, as many decisions pertaining to this topic are the responsibility of a sales manager.

PARTICIPANTS IN THE PROMOTIONAL PROCESS

Thus far we have identified the major promotional tools that marketers use. To understand the context in which promotional decisions are made, we identify the participants of the promotional process (Figure 1-5). Overall, there are five major groups: advertiser, advertising agency, media organizations, specialized marketing communication services, and collateral services. Each group has specific roles in the promotional process.

Figure 1-5   Participants in the promotional process

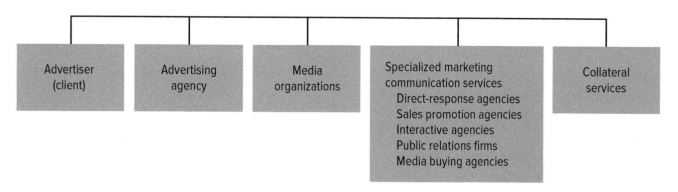

Advertisers have the goods, services, causes, ideas, or persons to be marketed, and they provide the funds that pay for advertising and promotions. Advertisers assume major responsibility for developing the marketing program and making the final decisions regarding the marketing communication program. An organization may perform most of these efforts itself, either through its own advertising department or by setting up an in-house agency.

Advertising agencies are outside firms that specialize in the creation, production, and placement of promotional messages, and possibly provide other support services. Advertisers are referred to as **clients** if they retain the services of advertising agencies. Large advertisers retain the services of a number of agencies, particularly when they have multiple products. An ad agency acts as a partner with an advertiser and assumes more responsibility for developing the marketing and promotional programs.

Media organizations provide information or entertainment to their subscribers, viewers, or readers. Media provide an editorial or program content environment for the firm's promotional planner to deliver the marketing communication message. While the media perform many functions that help advertisers understand their markets and their customers, a medium's primary objective is to sell its time or space so companies can effectively reach their target audiences with their messages (Exhibit 1-12). Media companies in Canada have grown significantly through acquisition of different formats and provide considerable integration options for advertisers. For example, Rogers offers customers virtually all media opportunities and its staff has a strong integration orientation when selling packages to clients.[39]

Specialized marketing communication services include direct marketing agencies, sales promotion agencies, interactive agencies, public relations firms, and media buying agencies who provide services in their areas of expertise. A direct-response agency develops direct-marketing programs. Sales promotion agencies develop contests, premium offers, or sampling programs. Interactive agencies develop websites, social media activities, or other types of Internet ads. Public relations firms generate and manage publicity for a company and its products, and also focus on its relationships with relevant publics. Media buying agencies work with clients and the media organizations for optimal placement of advertisers' messages. IMC Perspective 1-1 describes how Ubisoft communicates with its target audiences with new IMC approaches and works with digital IMC agencies.

Exhibit 1-12   CityTV promotes its value to advertisers.

© ValeStock / Shutterstock.com

Collateral services include marketing research companies, package design firms, consultants, photographers, printers, video production houses, and event marketing services. These individuals and companies perform specialized functions that the other participants (advertisers, agencies, media organizations, and specialized marketing communication services) use in planning and executing the IMC plan.

IMC PERSPECTIVE 1-1

UBISOFT GAMES ITS WAY TO NEW ADVERTISING

Ubisoft Montreal is the Canadian division of the video game conglomerate based in France. Its Canadian studio is one of the world's largest programming outfits and is responsible for developing its biggest titles, like *Assassin's Creed, Watch Dogs, Far Cry, Just Dance* and the *Tom Clancy* series. And the Canadian marketing communication of these video games proved to be equally successful with extensive use of expected IMC tools like TV advertising and the innovative use of IMC tools like video game apps, stunts, events, and

© AP Photo/Jae C. Hong

sponsorships across all of its brands. Headed by Lucile Bousquet, director of marketing, Ubisoft faces stiff competition as the industry transforms from niche markets with thousands of developers to a mainstream market with a few major players like Electronic Arts, Nintendo, and Sony. With declining market sales for a period of time, Ubisoft improved sales with 18 percent growth.

For *Watch Dogs*, Ubisoft built anticipation by releasing a free video game app months prior to the actual game launch. The app allows users to act like a "hacker" and outwit other hackers by hitting geo-targeted landmarks, much like using Foursquare. The virtual hacking included targets like hospitals, night clubs, and police stations. The app rewarded successful hacks with data, money, and skills that helped move the contestant up the scoreboard. Frequent users received additional rewards as well. Total downloads hit 200,000, culminating in 8.7 million hacks. Experts see this "gamification" as a new way of encouraging consumers to interact with a brand, however, in many cases such as this one it is essentially a sales promotion (sample with contest). As for stunts, Ubisoft coordinated surprising activities like blowing up a car in and dispensing money from an ATM; video recordings of these stunts circulated digitally for enjoyment and yielded 500,000 YouTube views. Another stunt worked well for the *Assassin's Creed* title when Ubisoft placed a flag from the game near a competitor's office; subsequent forwarding of the picture appeared in many social meeting vehicles.

Just Dance, another popular video game mostly played by young females, requires continued marketing support that includes event sponsorships such as the MuchMusic Video Awards to go along with celebrity endorsements. A recent "POPtimism" campaign allowed consumers to insert images of themselves into viral videos. Supported with the Garnier brand, *Just Dance* videos featured extensive branded imagery, and exclusive choreography and music. Connection with celebrities like Justin Bieber gives Ubisoft the opportunity to repurpose recorded footage with original online messages that garner significant views. For university and college aged young females, the *Just Dance* marketers created a contest inviting dance teams to compete after finding market research that indicated students used the video game to relieve exam stress. Teams applied to be contestants based on the support of their fellow student fans who posted images and videos of their dance moves.

Key planning activities unique to Ubisoft Montreal, compared to Ubisoft's American operations, include its marketing communication team working on IMC plans for all games, in contrast to dedicated teams for each game. The Canadian division's promotional planners learn from one brand and apply their knowledge to another brand. Ubisoft reflected this approach in its digital marketing, with only one Facebook page compared to multiple pages for each game title; this permitted improved awareness and stronger cross-sales of other game brands. This approach grew followers fivefold over the course of 18 months. Social media monitoring and postings moved from external agencies to two internal staff members and ensured a consistent tone and quality of marketing messages.

Sources: Jennifer Horn, "Gamification Is Everywhere," *Strategy*, June 2015, p. 16; Tanya Kostiw, "Getting in on the Action," *Strategy*, June 2015, p. 20; Jennifer Horn, "Lucile Bousquet Shows Her Game Face," *Strategy*, December 2013/January 2014, p. 47; Megan Haynes, "Ubisoft Taps the Everyday Hacktivist," *Strategy*, September 2013, p. 22; "Ubisoft Shifts Its Focus to Fans on Campus," *Strategy*, April 2013, p. 16.

Question:

1. Why would these marketing communication tools be a useful approach for the gaming industry?

 # Integrated Marketing Communications

Most large companies understand that the wide range of promotional tools must be coordinated to communicate effectively and present a consistent image to target audiences. In turn, even smaller-scale marketers have followed suit and are moving to a more comprehensive perspective of marketing communication. We now illustrate the topic of integrated marketing communications by distinguishing its evolution, renewed perspective, and importance.

THE EVOLUTION OF IMC

During the 1980s, companies moved toward **integrated marketing communications (IMC)** as the need for strategic planning and integration of their promotional tools intensified. Marketers subsequently asked their advertising agency to coordinate the use of all promotional tools and looked to employ other promotional specialists to develop and implement other parts of their promotional plans. At this point in time, the American Association of Advertising Agencies defined IMC as planning that recognizes the added value of a comprehensive program that evaluates the strategic roles of all communication disciplines and combines them to provide clarity, consistency, and maximum communications impact.[40]

By the 1990s, IMC represented an improvement over the traditional method of treating the promotional tools as virtually separate activities as all agencies contributed to the IMC planning for their clients.[41] IMC became one of the "new-generation" marketing approaches used by companies to better focus their efforts in acquiring, retaining, and developing relationships with customers and other stakeholders.[42] With this change, IMC faced criticism that it primarily relied on the tactical coordination of communication tools with the goal of making them look and sound alike.[43] Others criticized it as an "inside-out" marketing approach that simply bundles promotional mix elements together so they have one look and speak with one voice.[44] As IMC evolved, both academics as well as practitioners suggested a renewed perspective that viewed the discipline from a strategic perspective.

A RENEWED PERSPECTIVE OF IMC

A renewed understanding of IMC later viewed it as a strategic business process that identifies the most effective persuasive brand communications program over time with customers, prospects, employees, associates and other targeted relevant external and internal audiences to build and maintain relationships and achieve financial goals.[45]

IMC is now seen by promotional planners as an ongoing strategic business process where a number of relevant audiences require specific marketing communication programs. This approach reflects the increasing emphasis on accountability and measurement of the *outcomes* of marketing communication programs as well as marketing in general. Thus, a renewed perspective suggests that IMC has four general characteristics:[46] unified communication for consistent message and image, differentiated communication to multiple customer groups, database-centred communication for tangible results, and relationships fostering communication with existing customers.

Today, marketers and marketing communication agencies embrace IMC within their marketing and business practices. In fact, it is hypothesized that IMC is now critically connected to a firm's market and brand orientation.[47] Research reports higher use of IMC leading to higher levels of sales, market share, and profits.[48] Academics and practitioners have questioned whether IMC is just another "management fashion" whose influence will be transitory.[49] Critics of IMC argue that it merely reinvents and renames existing ideas and concepts and question its significance for marketing and advertising thought and practice.[50]

Despite these concerns, one major marketing organization significantly moved toward IMC. While the debate over the value and relevance of IMC is likely to continue, proponents of the concept far outnumber the critics as IMC is proving to be a permanent change that offers significant value to marketers.[51] We will now discuss reasons for the importance of IMC.

IMPORTANCE OF IMC

A successful IMC program requires that a firm find the right combination of promotional tools, define their role and the extent to which they can or should be used, and coordinate their use. This perspective becomes important for the organization because of the many audiences it communicates with, the vast number of messages consumers receive from many brands, the emergence of strong marketing relationships, consumer adoption of technology and media, and improved managerial planning.

Audience Contacts   Marketers use the promotional mix elements to communicate with current and/or prospective customers as well as other relevant audiences such as employees, suppliers, community, and government. Companies take an *audience contact* perspective whereby they consider all the potential ways of reaching their target audience and presenting the message of the company or brand in a favourable manner. In terms of customers, for example, marketers identify how their loyal buyers interact with a company or brand. This contact ranges from seeing or hearing an ad to actually using or experiencing a brand at a company-sponsored event. Moreover, this idea is extended to non-customers and all other potential audiences the company or brand may choose as targets of its marketing communication.

Figure 1-6 shows how target audiences come into contact with a company or brand. Marketers determine how valuable each contact tool is for communicating with their target audience and how they are combined to form an effective IMC program. This is generally done by starting with the target audience and determining which IMC tools will be most effective in reaching, informing, and persuading them and ultimately influencing their behaviour. Canadian banks rely on this approach to their marketing communication. Each has a broad strategic approach conveyed to all audiences and seen in the slogan used for all IMC tools for all audiences. For example, RBC shows its Arbie mascot and says that it has "Advice you can bank on," while Scotiabank claims that "You're richer than you think." However, banks market to both current customers and new customers on a regular basis and do this for many different products. Scotiabank's audience contacts are very much focused on hockey and movie themes, with its sponsorship of the NHL and partnership with Cineplex in its Scene promotion. In contrast, RBC's mascot might signal "old-school" and "blue-blood" banking, but RBC also uses innovative digital marketing tools directed to young consumers. It produced three two-minute fake movie trailers entitled *The Mortgage*—one each in the romantic comedy, science fiction, and horror genres—and obtained 1.7 million YouTube views in a few short months after their launch.[52]

Figure 1-6   IMC audience contact tools

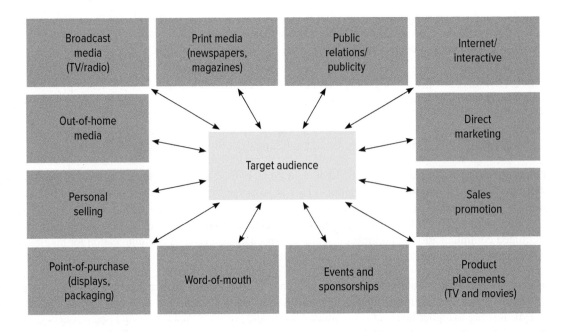

Consumer's Point of View   It is important for marketers to distinguish between concepts in order to better communicate with colleagues or other organizations when making decisions. For example, when planning a sales promotion, refer to it as a *sales promotion* so that everyone involved can discuss its merits appropriately and allocate the sales promotion expenditure within the correct budget. What is the right sales promotion (e.g., coupon versus bonus pack)? Is the incentive strong enough to encourage the target audience to switch to our brand? Consumers, on the other hand, receive many exposures from many different brands, each using many different promotional tools. In fact, consumers receive so many exposures that they often refer to any promotional tool as "advertising." Given this situation, planning with an IMC perspective becomes imperative. All the elements of the promotional campaign have to be carefully linked so that the message is clear and the brand is represented well, as seen in the following example.

Faced with many food myths that had dogged the largest quick service restaurant, McDonald's Canada launched its "Our Food. Your Questions." digital marketing communication program to articulate how its food is made and presented. The premise hinged on answering consumer questions, like "Does your Egg McMuffin use real eggs?" The food quality message and focus on unique attributes was critically important as the brand experienced pressure from high-end burger shops and breakfast menu items in other restaurants (e.g., Tim Hortons).

Consumers asked their questions at McDonalds.ca/YourQuestions when also logged into their Facebook or Twitter account. Visitors viewed the profiles of the questioners to gauge their source credibility and observed real people, not advertising personnel! A preliminary YouTube clip directed consumers to the website to ask a question. Initial communication of the answers posted on YouTube occurred in a TV commercial, wild postings, video projections on buildings, and transit dominations in key markets. After one year, the chain had answered 19,000 questions and website visitors stayed an average of 4.5 minutes and read 12 questions. McDonald's Canada answered all questions and addressed some of them with a video posted on the company's YouTube channel. One of the most watched videos (with 8,000,000 viewings by year-end) featured Hope Bagozzi, who took consumers through an astonishing journey that explained why a hamburger looked different in ads versus what consumers saw when they opened the packaging in the restaurant.[53]

Relationship Marketing   Marketers may seek more than a one-time transaction and concentrate on relationships with their customers.

Relationship marketing involves creating, maintaining, and enhancing long-term relationships with individual customers as well as other stakeholders for mutual benefit.[54] The banking industry focuses on relationship marketing successfully; the extensive personal and financial information banks collect allows them to serve people's financial needs through financial products (e.g., mortgages) and advice (e.g., financial advisers).

A relationship focus is generally profitable since it is often more cost-effective to retain customers than to acquire new ones, since these retained customers tend to buy more products or expand their purchases to other products that an organization offers. Marketers, like in the bank example above, calculate the *lifetime value* of a customer, which tallies the increased revenue and minimized costs of an individual customer over time. Studies have shown that reducing customer defections by just 5 percent, or maintaining loyalty at 95 percent each year, can increase future profit by as much as 30–90 percent.[55]

In order to facilitate the relationship, companies build databases containing customer names; geographic, demographic, and psychographic profiles; purchase patterns; media preferences; credit ratings; and other characteristics. Marketers use this information to target loyal customers through a variety of IMC tools, thereby enhancing the relationship. With so many tools, and since their customers are involved so closely with the firm, the need for consistency and coordination becomes even more critical.[56]

Consumer Adoption of Technology and Media   The expanded use of integrated marketing communications is critical due to consumer adoption of technology and media. For example, TV audiences are fragmented with the increased number of channels available. TV advertising now reaches smaller and more selective audiences, requiring brands to place their messages in other media or other IMC tools like sponsorship, or to use TV adverting to direct consumers to their website or social media. Consumers are watching "TV shows" while on the Internet as broadcasters offer new services as digital technology continues to expand. Portable devices allow promotional planners to consider new methods, time frames, and situations to communicate with consumers with advertising or interaction over social media.

Marie-Josée Lamothe is the chief marketing officer of L'Oréal, Canada's leading beauty brand (with 31 different skincare, makeup, and hair brands and an estimated one-third of the beauty industry). L'Oréal's strategic direction was to "digitize everything," with presence in all facets of the electronic universe. Combined with innovation toward community-building campaigns, high-profile sponsorships, and a unique partnership with Rogers, L'Oréal increased its market share considerably. Digitally, the international fashion brand established a Canadian-specific Facebook page for more than 20 brands and attained a fan base of more than 1.5 million. In particular, the brand L'Oréal Paris offered extensive on-location video of its sponsorship of the Toronto International Film Festival (TIFF) and Toronto Fashion Week through its social media page. With Rogers, L'Oréal sponsored the web series *Canada's Best Beauty Talent,* a competition for Canada's leading stylists and beauticians with five of its brands.[57]

Planning Efficiency and Effectiveness   A final reason for IMC importance is that marketers understand the value of strategically integrating the communication functions; by coordinating their marketing communications efforts, companies can avoid duplication, take advantage of synergy among promotional tools, and develop more efficient and effective marketing communications programs. Advocates of IMC argue that it is one of the easiest ways for a company to maximize the return on its investment in marketing and promotion.[58] Empirical research supports this contention, as strong IMC capability leads to campaign effectiveness and stronger market and financial performance.[59] Exhibit 1-13 shows a marketing effort where planning is paramount for the managers of both brands identified in the promotion, Air Wick and Parks Canada. Much of Shoppers Drug Mart's success in its "Fabulous 50" campaign hinged on a dedicated 30-person cross-functional team in charge of the IMC plan who ensured consistency across all audience contact points.

Exhibit 1-13   Two brands featured in this promotional offer demonstrate the importance of planning.

Hand-out/Air Wick Canada/Newscom

Integrated Marketing Communications Planning

IMC planning is a process to conceive, develop, implement, and control the promotional mix elements to communicate effectively with target audiences. An IMC planning process model is shown in Figure 1-7. The marketer decides which promotional tools to use, the role and function of each element of the promotional mix, and how to combine them to achieve IMC objectives. The resulting **IMC plan** provides the framework for managing all of an organization's marketing communication. The remainder of this chapter explains the planning model and describes the steps in developing an IMC program.

Figure 1-7   An integrated marketing communications planning model

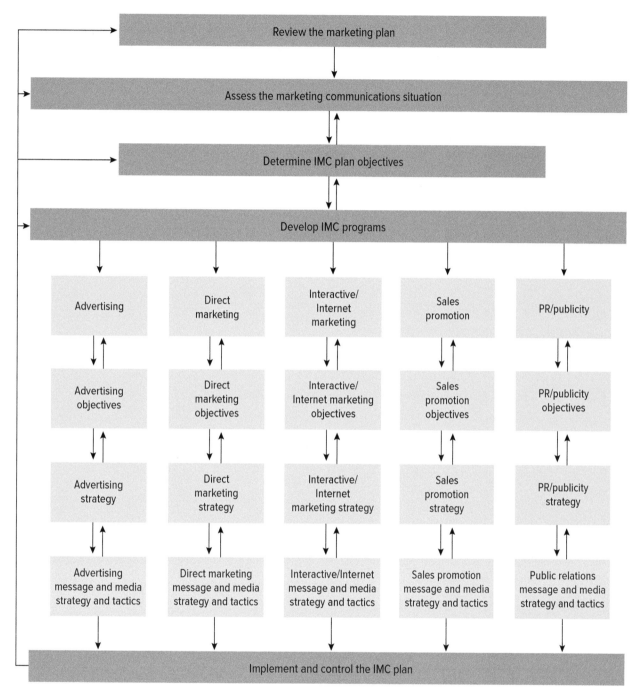

[Continued on next page]

[Figure 1-7 continued]

Review the Marketing Plan
Focus on market, company, consumer, competitive, and environmental information
Examine marketing objectives, strategy, and programs
Understand role of promotion within marketing plan

Assess the Marketing Communications Situation
Relative strengths and weaknesses of products/services
Previous promotional programs
Brand image
Promotional organization and capabilities
Consumer behaviour analysis
Competitive analysis
Environmental analysis
Market analysis

Determine IMC Plan Objectives
Establish IMC communication objectives
Establish IMC behavioural objectives

Develop IMC Programs
For advertising, sales promotion, public relations, direct marketing, and Internet marketing:
    Set specific communication and behavioural objectives for each IMC tool
    Determine budget requirements
    Develop relevant message strategy and tactics
    Select suitable media strategy and tactics
Investigate integration options across all five programs

Implement and Control the IMC Plan
Design all promotional materials internally or with agencies and buy media space/time
Measure promotional program results/effectiveness and make adjustments

REVIEW THE MARKETING PLAN

The starting point for a promotional planner is the **marketing plan**, a written document that describes the overall marketing strategy and programs developed for an organization, a particular product line, or a brand. With this, promotional planners understand where the company (or the brand) has been, its current position in the market, where it intends to go, and how it plans to get there. Marketing plans generally include five basic parts: situation analysis (market, company, consumer, competition, and environment), marketing objectives that provide a mechanism for measuring performance, marketing strategy that includes selection of target market(s) and decisions for the marketing mix elements, implementation program (tasks to be performed and responsibilities), and control program (monitor and evaluate performance to make strategic or tactical revisions).

ASSESS THE MARKETING COMMUNICATIONS SITUATION

The promotional plan is developed similarly to the marketing plan and uses its detailed information to understand the situation. Some IMC strategy decisions require more specific information or additional analysis of the existing information, thus necessitating a unique situation analysis for marketing communication. It is important to note the significance of the preceding sentence. A situation analysis compiles relevant information, and makes conclusions or derives implications from the information. The content generally concerns consumer, competition, market, company, and environment information and interpretation, as shown in Figure 1-8.

Figure 1-8   Areas covered in the situation analysis

Company analysis

What are the product strengths and weaknesses?

How strong is the firm or brand image?

What is the performance of past promotional programs?

What are the firm's promotional capabilities?

Competitive analysis

Who are our direct and indirect competitors?

What key benefits and positioning are used by our competitors?

What is our position relative to the competition?

How big are competitors' promotion budgets?

What promotion strategies are competitors using?

Consumer behaviour analysis

How is the purchase decision made?

Who assumes what role? (e.g., decider, influencer)

What does the consumer buy? What needs must be satisfied?

Why do consumers buy a particular brand?

Where do they go or look to buy the product?

When do they buy? Are there any seasonality factors?

What social, lifestyle, or demographic factors influence the purchase decision?

Environmental analysis

What current trends or developments affect the promotional program?

Market analysis

What is the size, growth, and profitability, of national, regional and city markets?

Are there changes in product formats, styles, or applications?

Detailed consideration of consumers' characteristics (e.g., demographics, psychographics) and buying patterns, their decision processes, and factors influencing their purchase decisions are relevant to making effective decisions. Often, marketing research studies are needed to answer these questions. The attractiveness of different market segments must be evaluated and the segments to target identified.

A situation analysis examines both direct and indirect competitors. Focus is on the firm's primary competitors' strengths and limitations; segmentation, targeting, and positioning strategies; and promotional strategies and tactics. The size and allocation of competitors' promotional budgets, media strategies, and message strategies should all be considered. IMC Perspective 1-2 describes both marketing strategy and marketing communication decisions by McCain while facing significant competitive forces, in addition to other situational analysis factors.

IMC PERSPECTIVE 1-2

HEALTHY FROZEN FOODS BY McCAIN

Within its frozen food portfolio of products, McCain faced considerable indirect competition from fresh food used for cooking "from scratch." Increased consumer interest toward wholesome or natural foods appeared to decrease the sales of frozen food as consumers viewed the latter as less healthy. Moreover, consumer beliefs in the freshness and healthfulness of frozen food continued to decline. The trend appeared even more confusing as one research firm projected the overall Canadian frozen food market declining by 4 percent over the next five years,

© Sipa via AP Images

while another saw the market growing by 2 percent per year.

Movement in a new direction began years ago with the "It's all good" slogan and strategic change as McCain reconfigured its recipes by removing ingredients that appeared unfamiliar or unpronounceable, to signal the naturalness of products to consumers. One recent marketing strategy decision to carry on the initial momentum included a redesign of the logo and packaging to bring a more positive emotional connection to the brand. The new package, introduced initially on all of McCain's potato products, featured a rising sun with a farmer's field in the foreground. According to the director of marketing, "The redesign brings to life those cues of naturalness and wholesomeness and that connection to the field and land and the potato."

Research indicated low levels of consumer awareness of McCain's many options for frozen potato products (e.g., variations of the standard french fry). Furthermore, Canadians on average eat potatoes 105 times per year, but only eat frozen potatoes 15 times per year on average. The advertising strategy called for communicating many different meal occasions for consuming fries, with an emphasis on small households. Research showed that 60 percent of all households had one or two persons, and that 50 percent of those households did not buy within the frozen potato product category. The change from family focused ads to singles and couples marked a new direction to refocus those consumers' views from their past experiences as children or young adults. The IMC tools used to convey the new approach included TV advertising, in-store promotions, and online messaging. McCain moved toward digital communication for the first time, to reach younger consumers who are in the smaller households.

While this trend appeared very good on paper, critics offered suggestions for improving McCain's business. One praised the repackaging and new advertising emphasis but cited the need for McCain to launch new frozen products that address consumer tastes for ethnic and fusion styles. Another argued for McCain to move toward products that celebrate the ritual of cooking rather than avoid it. And a third suggested McCain focus on raising product quality through improved taste of all of its products. In contrast, executives at McCain saw their frozen products as natural and healthy as the manufacturing used fresh and ripe ingredients just prior to freezing. Nevertheless, many saw certain product categories facing difficult marketing communication issues as consumer interests are evolving. For example, canned fruits and vegetables faced a similar consumer obstacle much like frozen foods with consumers desiring freshness. In either case, prepared foods required careful planning and usage of well thought out situation analyses for both new marketing strategies and new marketing communication strategies to grow their businesses.

Sources: Susan Krashinsky, "McCain Aims to Bring Warmth Back to the Frozen Food Aisle," *The Globe and Mail,* August 6, 2015; Susan Krashinsky, "OCAD Students Sink Their Teeth Into Pizza Pocket Ad Campaign," *The Globe and Mail,* August 6, 2015; "Brand Doctor – Patient: McCain Foods," *Marketing,* September 2014, p. 38; Kristin Laird, "Warming Up a Brand," *Marketing,* September 2014, pp. 8–9.

Question:

1. What advertising and marketing communication suggestions can be made to assist McCain to build sales?

The market analysis examines a number of factors like market size, growth, and profitability that can be investigated nationally, regionally, or locally using a census metropolitan area (CMA) basis. Emerging submarkets may be identified as potential sources of new revenue. Trends with respect to product formats or styles along with new product developments may be relevant. Environmental analysis factors can vary according to industry, but generally concern technology, economic, social, and government/regulatory factors that constrain promotional decisions or offer marketing communication opportunities. Concluding how a brand can address its environmental uncertainty is a planner's priority.

The company analysis assesses the relative strengths and limitations of the product; the product's unique selling points, attributes, or benefits; and its packaging, price, and design. This information is important to the creative personnel who must develop the brand's advertising message and communicate aspects of the brand.

The strengths and limitations of the firm image or brand image will have a significant impact on the way it can advertise and promote itself as well as its products and services. For example, Starbucks has an outstanding image due to the quality of its coffee and other products and its reputation as a socially responsible company. The company is recognized as a good citizen in its dealings with communities, employees, suppliers, and the environment. Starbucks understands that being identified as a socially responsible company is an important part of its success, which guides the selection of its promotional decisions. For example, Starbucks publishes a Corporate Social Responsibility Annual Report that describes the company's social, environmental, and economic effects in the communities it serves (Exhibit 1-14).

Since the firm is devising a new promotional plan, past promotional objectives, budgets, strategies, and tactics of all elements should be reviewed to understand their strengths and limitations. Information from marketing research that tracked the results of previous programs should be examined closely to determine what promotional decisions should be retained, revised, or withdrawn.

Reviewing the capabilities of the firm and its ability to develop and implement a successful promotional program, as well as the organization of the promotional department, the analysis may indicate that the firm is not fully capable of planning and implementing the

Exhibit 1-14   Starbucks has a very strong brand image and reputation as a socially responsible company.

© Starbucks

promotional program. If true, the planners should seek assistance from a marketing communication agency. If the organization is using an agency, the focus will be on the quality of the agency's work and the results achieved by past and/or current campaigns.

DETERMINE IMC PLAN OBJECTIVES

An important part of this stage of the promotional planning process is establishing relevant and appropriate objectives. In this text, we stress the importance of distinguishing among different types of objectives that are generally decided during the planning of different strategies.

Marketing objectives refer to what is to be accomplished by the overall marketing program. They are often stated in terms of sales, market share, or profitability and are determined when the marketing plan is constructed. Precise definition of marketing objectives and their time frame is important to give guidance on what is to be accomplished in the marketing communication plan. With the re-launch of Tourism BC, the government looked to increase tourism revenue by 5 percent over a five-year time period.[60]

Communication objectives refer to what the firm seeks to accomplish with its IMC program. They are often stated in terms of the nature of the message to be communicated or what specific communication effects are to be achieved, such as awareness. The promotional planner must think about the process consumers will go through in responding to marketing communications. Tourism BC needed to improve its image as visits declined while tourism gained in other provinces. **Behavioural objectives** in terms of trial purchase or repeat purchase, among others, may be defined along with the communication objectives. Tourism BC sought to increase the number of visitors from Ontario, presumably many for the first time, to achieve impressive revenue growth. Communication and behavioural objectives should be the guiding force for the IMC strategy and for each promotional tool. Exhibit 1-15 shows an ad where the call to action encourages the reader to visit Beau's Internet site. Brands like Canon run video ads shown on TV and in theatres to encourage consumers to see the full length version online to spark consumer interest.

While determining these objectives, two questions are asked to tentatively set the budget: (1) What will the promotional program cost? and (2) How will these monies be allocated? Ideally, the amount a firm spends on promotion should be determined by what must be accomplished to achieve communication and behavioural objectives. Tourism BC decided to spend $52 million for 2012, down from the $65 million it spent in 2009.

Exhibit 1-15   Beau's invites readers to learn more about its craft beer online by visiting its website.

© Courtesy of Beau's All Natural Brewing Co.

DEVELOP IMC PROGRAMS

As Figure 1-7 shows, each promotional mix element has its own set of objectives, overall strategy, message and media strategy and tactics, and a budget. For example, the advertising program will have its own set of objectives, usually involving the communication of a message or appeal to a target audience. A budget will be determined, providing the advertising manager and the agency with an idea of how much money is available for developing the ad campaign and purchasing media to disseminate the ad message.

Two important aspects of the advertising program are development of the message and the media strategy. Message development, often referred to as *creative strategy,* involves determining the basic message the advertiser wishes to convey to the target audience. This process, along with the ads that result, is to many students the most fascinating aspect of promotion. The Special K ad shown in Exhibit 1-16 creatively displays the brand's new sour cream and onion flavour.

Media strategy involves determining which communication channels will be used to deliver the advertising message to the target audience. Decisions must be made regarding which types of media will be used (e.g., newspapers, magazines, radio, TV, billboards) as well as specific media selections (e.g., a particular magazine or TV program). This task requires careful evaluation of the media options' strengths and limitations, costs, and ability to deliver the message effectively to the target audiences.

A similar process and set of decisions occur for *all* other elements of the IMC program as objectives are set, an overall strategy is developed, and message and media strategies are determined. If a firm decides to include a sales promotion, it might decide to use a specific message and media strategy and tactics to communicate information about the sales promotion, in addition to whatever advertising decisions that have been recommended.

Furthermore, if a firm considers using multiple tools for its complete plan, it must decide which ones best fit together to solve a particular marketing communication problem. For example, Taco Bell's Canadian national launch (excluding Quebec) of the Doritos Locos Taco attempted to increase same store sales by 7 percent. The campaign evolved over 12 months with multiple IMC tools and media, resulting in substantial online popularity and higher than expected sales (Figure 1-9).[61]

Exhibit 1-16 Special K uses a creative visual to communicate its new flavour.

© Kellogg Company. Used with permission.

Figure 1-9   Taco Bell: Doritos Locos Taco Launch

Budget	$1 million to $2 million
Time Frame	June 2013 to May 2014
Target	Light/Medium Users
Strategic Message	Eat Your Words
Tactical Message	Ambiguous and mysterious pre-launch teaser messages in social media
Social Media	Fan outreach on Facebook, Instagram, Snapchat, Twitter
Advertising Media	Television
Sales Promotion	Coupon (3 DLTs for $5), invited marketing event
Digital Media	YouTube channel, and pre-roll, micro-site counting down 1 million tacos eaten
Public Relations	Buzzfeed sponsored articles

IMPLEMENT AND CONTROL THE IMC PLAN

Once the message and media strategies have been determined for each tool, steps must be taken to implement them. Most large companies hire advertising agencies to plan and produce their messages and to evaluate and purchase the media that will carry their ads. However, most agencies work very closely with their clients as they develop the ads and select media, because it is the advertiser that ultimately approves (and pays for) the creative work and media plan. While the marketer's advertising agencies may be used to perform other IMC functions, they may also hire other communication specialists.

It is important to determine how well the promotional program is meeting communication and behavioural objectives and helping the firm accomplish its overall marketing objectives. The promotional planner wants to know not only how well the promotional program is doing but also why. For example, problems with the advertising program may lie in the nature of the message or in a media plan that does not reach the target audience effectively. The manager must know the reasons for the results in order to take the right steps to correct the program.

This final stage of the process is designed to provide managers with continual feedback concerning the effectiveness of the promotional program, which in turn can be used as input into the planning process. As Figure 1-7 shows, information on the results achieved by the promotional program is used in subsequent promotional planning and strategy development.

IMC Planning: Organization of Text

This book provides a thorough understanding of advertising and other elements of a firm's promotional mix and shows how they are combined to form a comprehensive marketing communications program with an IMC planning perspective. To implement this idea, we conclude each chapter of the book with an IMC planning section. Its purpose is to relate the chapter material to the content of an IMC plan and illustrate how to make IMC decisions. The final section of this chapter establishes this approach by illustrating how the entire book is organized into five major parts around the IMC planning perspective.

UNDERSTANDING INTEGRATED MARKETING COMMUNICATION

Part 1 comprises four chapters that define the topic of the book and provide the context for marketing communication decisions. This initial chapter introduces the IMC tools and how they relate to marketing. The chapter also gives a brief description of IMC and the content of a promotional plan.

We discuss how advertisers work with ad agencies and other firms that provide marketing and promotional services in Chapter 2. Agencies are an important part of the IMC planning process as they assist in the decision making with promotional planners and execute many of the decisions by creating promotional messages.

To plan, develop, and implement an effective IMC program, those involved must understand consumer behaviour and the communications process. We focus on consumer behaviour and target audience decisions in Chapter 3, and summarize many communication response models in Chapter 4. Combined, these two chapters establish a conceptual foundation for developing the subsequent decisions of an IMC plan.

ARTICULATING THE MESSAGE

Part 2 concerns a number of decisions that firms make to put together a persuasive marketing communication message and comprises five chapters. The ideas developed here are applicable for advertising and all other IMC tools. Sales promotion offers include a brand message, as do public relations activities. All brand-initiated communication in Internet media provides a clear message about the brand.

Chapter 5 explains how to set IMC objectives to achieve the desired effects. A general model is explained for setting behavioural and communication objectives that are universally applicable to all IMC tools.

Chapter 6 reviews the important decisions to construct a brand positioning strategy. This is the heart of marketing communication, where decisions regarding how brands compete with marketing communication messages are determined.

The most exciting aspects of IMC are presented in Chapters 7 and 8, where we illustrate creative strategy and creative tactics decisions that are reflected in the vibrant and exciting ads we all experience in every part of our daily living. Creative illustration of a brand is the pinnacle task of creative specialists and their work is central for building a brand.

Chapter 9 examines how to measure promotional message effectiveness. The research ideas presented in this chapter also set the stage for understanding how to assess the effects of all IMC tools found in later chapters.

DELIVERING THE MESSAGE

Part 3 comprises four chapters and explores the key media strategy, media tactics decisions, and budgeting for IMC, along with the use of six different media.

Chapter 10 provides the technical information for media planning. Media planning is an important advertising decision and this information is also used to implement other IMC tools. Scheduling and determining how many consumers should receive a message and how often is critical with Internet media like all other media. Similarly, the timing and media presentation of promotional offers assist in the success of their execution. The chapter also explores how to construct a budget and allocate the budget for advertising and all IMC tools.

Chapters 11, 12, and 13 describe the use and strengths and limitations of media choices that have been historically labelled as *mass media* (i.e., television, radio, magazines, newspapers, out-of-home, and support). Once again, background on these topics is useful for implementing advertising and for using these media in executing other IMC tools. Much of these mass media are used to direct consumers to different aspects of Internet media. There are QR codes on outdoor ads. TV and radio messages say "Facebook us" to carry on further communication. These media are also used for presentation of community activities designed to "give back" and foster goodwill among citizens.

STRENGTHENING THE MESSAGE

Our interest turns to the other areas of the promotional mix—sales promotion, public relations, direct marketing, and Internet marketing—in Part 4, "Strengthening the Message." Each tool is explored in its own chapter and related to communication objectives as was done in Part 3.

Chapter 14 investigates consumer and trade sales promotions that are often combined with advertising to influence behaviourally and from a communication standpoint. A multitude of options are available for planners to both stimulate sales and enhance brand equity.

Chapter 15 presents the topic of public relations and related topics of publicity through media and corporate advertising. Using other tools and building a corporate brand through IMC are important topics for fully understanding how to put together a complete IMC plan.

Chapter 16 covers direct marketing and direct-response media used to communicate with this particular IMC tool. Improved technology allows brands to communicate to individuals and vice versa. Methods for advertising and promoting directly are described in this chapter.

Chapter 17 examines the considerable options for interactive communication via the Internet. While continued growth makes it a challenge to remain current, the available options and how brands are built with electronic communication are developed to fulfill the need for a comprehensive IMC plan.

ADVERTISING AND SOCIETY

Part 5 concludes the book with one chapter that examines advertising regulation and the ethical, social, and economic effects of an organization's advertising and promotional program. Advertising is a very public and controversial part of any organization's activities and Chapter 18 explores the complexities of these points. Each topic is relevant at varying points of the earlier chapters and may be read when desired.

Learning Objectives Summary

 Describe the importance of marketing communication within the marketing mix.

Marketing combines the four controllable elements, known as the marketing mix, into a comprehensive program that facilitates exchange with a group of customers. The elements of the marketing mix are the product, price, place (distribution), and promotion (market communication). Advertising and other forms of promotion are an integral part of the marketing process in most organizations since these tools communicate the value consumers receive within the exchange. Marketing communication conveys elements of the product through benefit claims and brand identity with the hopes of building brand equity. Providing price and distribution information are two other important roles of marketing communication so that value is perceived by both customers and non-customers.

 Identify the tools of the promotional mix—advertising, sales promotion, public relations, direct marketing, Internet marketing, and personal selling—and summarize their purpose.

Promotion is accomplished through a promotional mix that includes advertising, sales promotion, public relations, direct marketing, Internet marketing, and personal selling. The inherent advantages and disadvantages of each of these promotional mix elements influence the roles they play in the overall marketing program. In developing the promotional program, the manager must decide which tools to use and how to combine them to achieve the organization's objectives. Many organizations assist promotional managers in developing or implementing their plans, including advertising agencies, media organizations, and specialized communication services firms like direct-response agencies, sales promotion agencies, interactive agencies, and public relations firms.

 Illustrate the concept of integrated marketing communications (IMC) by distinguishing its evolution, renewed perspective, and importance.

Historically, companies used mass-media advertising extensively in their promotional plans. Eventually, companies linked their promotional tools to achieve a more efficient and effective communication program. Managers referred to this practice as integrated marketing communications (IMC). Today, IMC is viewed as a strategic and comprehensive planning perspective for all facets of an organization's marketing communication.

An IMC perspective is important for decision making for a number of reasons. Most organizations need to communicate with multiple target audiences, requiring decisions on the consistency or uniqueness of messages to each member. When planning for IMC, managers have to consider how each promotional tool will communicate the brand effectively depending on who is receiving the brand message. The emergence of IMC has become even more important for organizations that communicate with different messages to current customers and prospective customers.

An IMC perspective also starts with the consumer's point of view in that much marketing communication is perceived as being very similar to advertising and is labelled as such. Moreover, an IMC perspective for promotional planning has become critical as audiences receive messages from competing brands across different IMC tools.

A movement toward building long-term relationships through strategies like relationship marketing has altered the communication perspective of many promotional planners. Customized communication to individual customers via extensive databases to enhance the lifetime value of customers makes IMC more critical.

Increased consumer adoption of technology and media provides marketers with far-reaching communication tools whose effects must be considered carefully. Finally, taking an IMC perspective has many advantages that make it a very effective way of planning for promotion that can lead to greater efficiencies.

Explain the IMC planning process model and express the steps in developing a marketing communications program.

IMC management involves coordinating the promotional mix elements to develop an integrated program of effective marketing communication. The model of the IMC planning process in Figure 1-7 contains a number of steps: (1) Review the marketing plan; (2) Assess the marketing communications situation; (3) Determine IMC plan objectives; (4) Develop IMC programs; and (5) Implement and control the IMC plan. This model is consistent with the more general marketing planning model, but is more specific to the context of marketing communication. It shows that individual marketing communication tools can be recommended to achieve multiple objectives so that the completely coordinated or integrated plan can build brand equity across multiple target audiences.

Identify how the IMC planning process is continued throughout all chapters.

The IMC planning process is an important perspective that is continually reinforced in every chapter. All chapter material for the rest of the book is presented with an approach to assist in decision making for every step.

Review Questions

1. Why is marketing communication important for communicating value to consumers?
2. How do smart phone brands use each marketing communication tool for communicating messages?
3. What are the reasons why marketers are taking an IMC perspective to their advertising and promotion programs?
4. What parts of the IMC planning model are similar to and different from a marketing planning model?
5. How is the structure of the book consistent with the content of an IMC plan?

Applied Questions

1. Consider how a university or college communicates value in its marketing communication to its prospective students and current students. In what ways are the two approaches similar or different?
2. Identify all the possible marketing communication tools that a favourite brand or performance artist is using. Try to explain why these tools were selected. In what ways did the tools support one another? How did they not support one another? Was each tool effective or ineffective?
3. Find one example where all promotional tools of a brand have the same look and feel, and find another example of a brand where the promotional tools have a different look and feel. Why did these decisions occur, based on relevant situation analysis variables?
4. Why is it important for those who work in the field of advertising and promotion to understand and appreciate all IMC tools, not just the area in which they specialize?
5. How does one of your favourite brands link or integrate its different IMC communication tools? Is it done effectively?

© Fancy Collection/SuperStock

CHAPTER TWO

Organizing for IMC: Role of Agencies

LEARNING OBJECTIVES

LO1 Identify the role of the advertising agency and the services it provides.

LO2 Describe methods for compensating and evaluating advertising agencies.

LO3 Contrast the role and functions of specialized marketing communication organizations.

LO4 Evaluate the perspectives on the use of integrated services across agencies or within one agency, and agency–client responsibilities and partnerships.

Leo Burnett Returns to the Top

It has been a long time coming, but Leo Burnett finally received the nod from *Strategy* for its Agency of the Year (AOY) Award for 2014. The agency received honourable mention for 2012 and 2013 and last won the prize in 1996. According to Judy John, chief executive officer and chief creative officer, the Toronto office received praise and recognition from colleagues of its 85 global offices for the past few years, culminating in winning the internal Leo Burnett Worldwide AOY Award in 2012. With excellent work for brands like Always, Earls Kitchen and Bar, Ikea, and Yellow Pages, the agency received numerous awards recently: Cannes Lions 2015 (one Grand Prix, one Titanium, one Glass, seven Gold, three Silver, and three Bronze), One Show's Most Awarded Canadian Agency, Gunn Report's #1 Canadian Agency, and Best of Show at the Bessies, to name a few.

Leo Burnett Canada's most recognized and awarded work is the "Like a Girl" campaign for P&G's Always brand. The Toronto office teamed up with the Chicago and London offices, and recorded video of girls, boys, women, and men reacting to the instructions "Run like a girl" and "Throw like a girl" along with them answering questions on what these phrases mean. Younger girls actually ran according to their ability or ran their fastest, while teens and young women ran and threw with an exaggerated feeble approach. The difference appeared to highlight the negative connotations of the phrase that young girls eventually learn, but are not aware of at a young age. The Always brand sought a unique emotional message for its brand to enhance the confidence of girls as they transitioned to puberty and started to need menstrual products. The video posted on YouTube and elsewhere obtained 76 million views and invited other digital communication on Facebook and other social media vehicles like Twitter and Instagram. Post-campaign purchase intent rose from 42 percent to 46 percent overall, and from 40 percent to 60 percent for teens.

For Earls, Leo Burnett invented the "Earls Steak Redemption" on social media where the restaurant invited disgruntled steak eaters for a free meal and recorded their experiences for a YouTube posting. Sales responded succulently with a 90 percent growth rate, and restaurant traffic grew by 7 percent. For Yellow Pages, Leo Burnett's message of "Highlight Your Hood" displayed on billboards and wall projections let Torontonians know about different businesses within a person's local area. Increased mobile visits to Yellow Pages increased by 21 percent, demonstrating strong success of the program, so it was extended elsewhere in Canada.

For Ikea, Leo Burnett explored residents' "house rules" by inviting them in a TV ad to share their rules online; in return, the retailer sent gifts that reflected their story. Rules included mundane things like "we must eat leftovers" and funny things like "there is no laughing when pets walk into screen doors," and the retailer organized the rules online visually by each room. General media advertising communicated many of the more popular "rules." Ikea also tweeted the "rules" during TV shows and encouraged participation in radio contests. Awareness jumped 10 percent as Ikea compiled almost 27,000 rules as visitors spent 3.5 minutes on the Internet site, giving it a store sales lift of 12 percent.

Sources: Jennifer Horn, "2014 Agency of the Year," *Strategy*, November 2014, p. 21; Tanya Kostiw, "Participation Is King," *Strategy*, June 2015, p. 31; Jennifer Horn, "Old Brands, New Tricks," *Strategy*, June 2015, p. 26; www.leoburnett.ca; "Grand Prix Gold Idea Canadian Tire Tests the Limit," *Strategy*, May 2015, p. 21.

Question:

1. What is significant about these campaigns that allowed Leo Burnett to win the award?

Developing and implementing an IMC program is usually a complex process involving the efforts of individuals from the marketing firm, the advertising agency, and often other types of agencies. Strong relationships with these agencies are important as their expertise in creative planning, media placement, new digital executions, and other activities contributes to successful brand development. Alternatively, brands also work with a full-service marketing communication agency capable of providing all services. This chapter explores how these agencies function, for those who may want to work in the marketing communication agency industry.

This chapter first identifies the characteristics of a full-service agency and its client relationship. It then describes how agencies are compensated and evaluated. Next, the chapter contrasts the role of specialized marketing communication organizations such as creative boutiques, media buying services, direct-response, sales promotion, and interactive agencies, and public relations firms. These organizations are increasingly involved in IMC planning and some are owned by large agencies which they work with considerably. Finally, the chapter evaluates whether marketers are best served by using the integrated services of one large agency or the separate services of multiple marketing communication specialists.

LO1 Advertising Agencies

Many different types of advertising agencies make the selection a unique decision for each advertiser. In this section we provide a general overview of advertising agencies; we review the agency decision, highlight the agency industry, and describe the activities of a full-service agency.

ADVERTISING AGENCY DECISION

Marketing organizations have a fundamental choice of whether a firm will have its own in-house agency or whether it will employ an external advertising agency. Interestingly, a trend exists where major corporations are employing both approaches and allowing the two types of agencies to collaborate. For example, Boeing's in-house agency works with multiple external agencies that are responsible for placement of messages in different media.[1] We now briefly discuss the relative merits and concerns of both options.

In-House Agency   An **in-house agency** is an advertising agency that is set up, owned, and operated by the advertiser. Some in-house agencies are essentially advertising departments, but in other companies they are given a separate identity and are responsible for the expenditure of large sums of advertising dollars. Research finds that about half of all companies use an in-house agency and that the likelihood of this occurring decreases with larger advertising budgets but increases with advertising intensity (i.e., advertising/sales ratio), technological intensity, and for creative industries.[2] Many companies use in-house agencies exclusively; others combine in-house efforts with those of outside agencies. For example, Target in the United States has an internal creative department that handles the design of its weekly circulars, direct-mail pieces, in-store displays, promotions, and other marketing materials. However, the retailer uses outside agencies to develop most of its branding and image-oriented ads and for specific TV and print assignments.[3] Joe Fresh, a key brand for Loblaw, moved its creativity in-house from an agency "to get our staff thinking about our brand" as it opened up stores in the United States. Coincidentally, that staff of 14 includes a couple of creatives from Target.[4]

A major reason for using an in-house agency is to reduce advertising and promotion costs. Companies with very large advertising budgets pay a substantial amount to outside agencies. An in-house agency can also provide related work—such as sales presentations and salesforce materials, package design, and public relations—at a lower cost than outside agencies. One study found that creative and media services were the most likely functions to be performed outside, while merchandising and sales promotion were the most likely to be performed in-house.[5] Time savings, bad experiences with outside agencies, and the increased knowledge and understanding of the market that come from continuously working on advertising and promotion for the product also support in-house agency use. Companies can also maintain tighter control over the process and more easily coordinate promotions with the firm's overall marketing program.[6] A limitation of an in-house agency is that personnel may grow stale while working on the same product line in comparison to an outside agency where creative specialists design campaigns for a variety of products. Furthermore, changes in an in-house agency could be slow or disruptive compared to the flexibility of hiring a new outside agency.

Advertising Agency   Many major companies use an advertising agency to assist them in developing, preparing, and executing their promotional programs. An ad agency is a service organization that employs highly skilled personnel and specializes in planning and executing advertising programs for its clients. An advertising agency's staff may include artists, writers, media analysts, researchers, and others with specific skills, knowledge, and experience who can help market the client's products. Agencies may specialize in a particular type of business and use their knowledge of the industry to assist their clients. For example, Mentus Inc. is an agency that specializes in the high-technology, ecommerce, and bioscience industries (Exhibit 2-1). Alternatively, the agency can draw on the broad range of experience it has gained while working on diverse marketing problems for assorted clients and apply that knowledge for new clients. For example, an ad agency handling a travel-related account may have had previous travel industry accounts or employ individuals with travel-related industry experience (e.g., airlines, cruise ships, travel agencies, hotels).

The Institute of Communications and Advertising offers a comprehensive document that acts as a guide for selecting the most appropriate agency. Using a "best practices" approach, the steps in the search process are diagrammed and explained so that both clients and agencies could benefit. The steps range from eight to 16 weeks and include preparation, expression of interest, choosing the short list, agency visits, capability presentation, work session, and final selection. In the end, the client and agency form a partnership where the responsibilities of each are recorded and agreed upon with the intention of a positive working relationship. The document also gives guidance on performance reviews and remuneration, two topics we address later in this chapter.[7]

Agency-of-record (AOR) is the term used to describe those situations where a client works with a primary agency for a number of years. It is the very foundation on which the advertising agency business exists—a service provider whose foremost interest is in building the client's brand. Examples of longstanding relationships include Taxi with Telus for 18 years and Marketel with Air Canada for 25 years.[8] Clients periodically put their account up for renewal and allow other agencies to make a sales pitch. Agencies decide how many and which accounts to attract; DDB is very selective on these decisions and its president estimates a 60 percent hit rate.[9] In the case of Taxi and Telus, the latter had not opened the account for others to pitch during the whole time.

At times, the AOR will subcontract work to other specialized agencies; however, the AOR will have considerable responsibility given its designation with the client. A trend is that advertisers do not have a specific AOR, but work with different agencies at once, or in succession, depending upon their communication needs. The agencies perform project-like work for a client by developing a short campaign or performing creative work only, or, a client can contract the creative work to an agency but rely on its own market research resources. Boeing contracted multiple AOY relationships and allowed each to work within a defined scope to make full use of each agency's expertise.

ADVERTISING AGENCY INDUSTRY

Exhibit 2-1   Mentus specializes in creating ads for bioscience companies.

© Mentus

The Canadian advertising agency industry features small and mid-sized domestic firms and large international organizations with domestic service providers. The strong presence of international ad agencies in Canada reflects a global trend of large agencies merged with or acquired by other agencies and support organizations that provide clients with IMC services worldwide. Mid-sized agencies were acquired by or forged alliances with larger agencies because clients wanted an agency with IMC capabilities, and their alignment with larger organizations permitted access to a network of agencies around the world. Currently, most major agencies offer specialized services in areas of interactive communications, direct marketing, PR, and sales promotion so that they can provide their clients with an ever-broader range of IMC services.[10] In fact, a larger multiservice firm is a **marketing communication agency**, making the term "advertising agency" somewhat obsolete for these situations. Global advertising campaigns are facilitated by using larger international agencies (Exhibit 2-2).

Figure 2-1 summarizes the five major international marketing communication conglomerates and their most noteworthy subsidiaries; the list was compiled by R3, an international consulting firm that assists agencies.[11] A major partially Canadian-based firm is MDC, which is ranked eighth at US$1.3 billion. Vision 7 International is a partially Canadian company, having recently forged a deal with BlueFocus in China.[12] Formerly known as Cossette, it retains this brand name for one division and its sales are not divulged at present. As expected, two major players (Omnicom and Interpublic) are based in New York, as is MDC to a degree; each one includes famous advertising agencies recognized for their creative talent. Additionally, the table includes two major European conglomerates, WPP and Publicis, which own established American advertising greats Ogilvy and JWT, and BBDO and DDB, respectively. Although Dentsu is based in London, much of its origin and one main division are Japan-based. Finally, the Ogilvy group within WPP is a good example of how an original advertising agency is more like a marketing communication agency since it features numerous services in all IMC disciplines with the Ogilvy brand. The sixth largest agency, Havas, continues to bring different disciplines together by amalgamating previously acquired agencies under the Havas name.[13] Although a trend toward international holding companies occurred over numerous decades, a study using American data concluded that the advertising services industry concentration levels are consistent with past decades, thereby providing a robust competitive market.[14]

Exhibit 2-2   TAG Heuer uses a global campaign featuring different celebrity ambassadors for various countries.

© Tag Heuer

Figure 2-1   Largest international marketing communication firms (US$ sales in billions, 2014)

WPP ($17.3)	Omnicom ($15.3)	Publicis ($8.3)	Interpublic ($7.5)	Dentsu Aegis ($5.9)
Ogilvy	BBDO	Burnett	Mediabrands	Canat
JWT	DDB	Saatchi & Saatchi	McCann	Dentsu Media
Taxi	TBWA	Starcom Media	Lowe	Isobar
Kantar	Omnicom Media	Zenithoptmedia	FCB	iProspect
Group M	FleishmanHilliard	MSL Group	CMG	Posterscope

Data from www.r3ww.com

Two agencies with strong Canadian roots developed internationally. Taxi won about 1,200 national and international awards and was named agency of the year five times by *Strategy*. Taxi expanded to the United States and Europe and is now a mainstay within WPP as the holding company phased out Young & Rubican after 80 years in Canada.[15] Sid Lee expanded to the same geographic locations and developed an international presence for Adidas in 100 countries, after Adidas hired the agency as the leader for its worldwide marketing communication. One development featured a mobile app where a shoe photo would direct the user to the closest store with the product available.[16] Individual Canadians who achieved success are also in demand internationally, finding top-level positions paying seven figures.[17] IMC Perspective 2-1 highlights the accomplishments of Canadian agencies.

Like any other industry, agencies in Canada carve out their own specialty or develop a particular reputation. Zulu Alpha Kilo is known as a brand transformation agency since it is drawn to clients who have brands that are in need of a major strategic or creative shift. It created the "Live Mas Fina" campaign for Corona, a distinctive Canadian message that doubled sales. It retooled Interac's imagery with the "Be in the Black" campaign to encourage consumers to use their debit card instead of their credit card. Low Roche aspires to be strategically and creatively smart as a teaching agency with its focus on health and wellness clients. The agency attracted awards for its "Make Health Last" campaign for the Heart and Stroke Foundation. Taxi sees itself as a purely creative agency since it has won 46 Canadian Advertising Success Story (CASSIES) awards over the past 20 years with clients such as Telus, Mini, and Boston Pizza. And Lg2 is a results agency with its work seemingly always attaining strong consumer involvement.[18] Successful Canadian agencies like these are often recognized. Canadian agencies (or agencies with a historical Canadian origin) on *Strategy* magazine's short list for agency of the year in 2014 were Cossette, John St., Rethink, Sid Lee, Taxi, Union, and Zulu Alpha Kilo. The non-Canadian contenders on the list were BBDO, DDB, JWT, Leo Burnett, Lg2, and Ogilvy.[19]

As an alternative to larger agencies, small and mid-sized agencies handle local and regional work throughout Canada, often with great success but on a smaller scale. *Marketing Magazine* featured up-and-coming new agencies in western Canada like Giant Ant Media (Creative Agency/Production Studio) with MEC as a key client, FCV (Interactive Agency) with Telus, Nike, and Scotiabank as key clients, and Smak (Experiential/Media Agency).[20] Across the country, these independent agencies offer an opportunity for students to pursue a career in the advertising industry. One smaller agency, Acart in Ottawa, continues to outbid other more dominant players as it secures many government advertising assignments.[21] And in the oldest city in North America, Target of St. John's continues to innovate as it listens to the "beat of a different drum" while enjoying the view of the Atlantic Ocean. Check out its creative "Weiner News Network" on YouTube![22]

IMC PERSPECTIVE 2-1

AGENCY OF THE YEAR FOR SID LEE

Sid Lee is an anagram for the agency's original name of *Diesel* to distinguish it from the stylish fashion producer. From its humble start in Montreal 25 years ago when the first owners had no advertising agency experience, Sid Lee ramped up to 550 employees and four more offices located in Toronto, Amsterdam, Paris, and New York. A Canadian advertising agency expanding to the international stage is almost unheard of historically, but Sid Lee proved it can be done. One international client, Adidas, recognized the talent and hired the agency on as the leader for its worldwide marketing communication. Senior management at Sid Lee attributed their success to the informal work culture, with relaxed dress and no hierarchy. A professional and organizational development program launched recently shows new employees the Sid Lee way of doing business.

Domestically, Sid Lee recently took a strategic approach to solving Sport Chek's marketing communication issues by asking about growth, brand, and business objectives. Together, Sport Chek and Sid Lee planned to completely alter the shopping experience for sporting goods consumers with extensive digital content throughout the store and

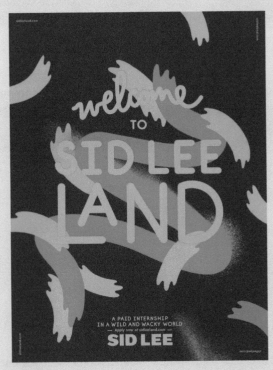

© Sid Lee

fresher brand concepts and images. Cirque du Soleil hired on with Sid Lee more than a decade ago and the innovative agency handled all decisions for some of Cirque's new shows, from brand identification to positioning to key messaging. The relationship blossomed so much that Cirque became a minor owner among 25 owners including Sid Lee's management staff. With Cirque's worldwide distribution and exposure, Sid Lee looked to leverage that experience for greater steps abroad.

Developing the agency in new directions parlayed greater success for Sid Lee. Each new entity retained the brand identity with a variation. Jimmy Lee is the production and art-buying partner for advertising and branded content, essentially the unit that makes the ads. Sid Lee Technologies has a digital focus, working on applications, social media, Internet sites, data projects, and ecommerce. Sid Lee Architecture is a design team that develops physical brand experiences. Sid Lee Entertainment specializes in production of events, shows, and exhibitions. Sid Lee Media is the media buying agency that includes placement of messages in broad areas of marketing communication. Sid Lee Labs delivers brand experiences that intersect physical and digital worlds. As all of these domains suggest, Sid Lee represents a full-service marketing communication agency that may be evolving into a type of organization for which we currently do not have a clear descriptive identification.

Other international key account wins include Disney, Coca-Cola, and Intel. And Sid Lee's longstanding relationship with Cirque strengthened with more experiential activities, including a major event at the Cannes International Festival of Creativity. But one of the most significant changes occurred when an international brand observed Sid Lee's direction and joined on once it understood the agency's philosophy. Absolut Vodka ended its long AOR relationship with TBWA, the agency that founded one of the greatest ad campaigns ever. A key motivator is Sid Lee's passion for developing experiential marketing for its clients. For example, it created video and other experiences with Icona Pop with Absolut Vodka.

As an agency moving in new experiential directions with sharable marketing content, Sid Lee offers the following suggestions. Content sharing still requires a paid media buy to start the momentum, and the paid media buy distributors should be partners in the development and execution of the IMC. Subsequent frequency after seeing the initial video message is needed for message reinforcement. For the Icona Pop video, additional events and media messages carried forth the initial idea behind the video.

Sources: Russ Martin, "An Absolutely Great Year," *Marketing Magazine*, January/February 2014, pp. 18–19, 21–22; "Prayer Is Not a Content Strategy," *Marketing Magazine*, January/February 2014, pp. 23–25; David Brown, "Sid Lee vs. The World," *Marketing Magazine*, January 16, 2012; Nicholas Van Praet, "Status Quo Sucks for Petite Sid Lee," *National Post*, February 24, 2012, sidlee.com.

Question:

1. In what new direction would you anticipate Sid Lee moving in the future?

FULL-SERVICE AGENCY

The services offered and functions performed vary depending upon the size of the agency. A **full-service agency** offers its clients a complete range of marketing, communication, and promotion services including planning, performing research, creating the message of the ad campaign, producing the advertising, and selecting media. A full-service agency may also offer non-advertising services, such as strategic market planning, sales promotions, direct marketing, interactive services, public relations and publicity, and package design. The full-service agency has departments led by a director that provide the activities needed to perform the advertising functions and serve the client, as shown in Figure 2-2. In this section we summarize these main characteristics.

Figure 2-2   Full-service agency organizational chart

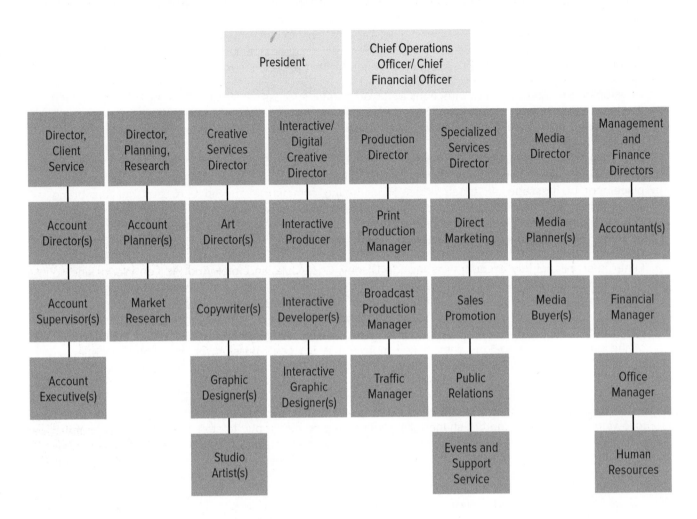

Account/Client Services   Account services, or client services, is the link between the ad agency and its clients. Depending on the size of the client and its advertising budget, one or more account executives serve as liaison. The **account executive** is responsible for understanding the advertiser's marketing and promotions needs and interpreting them to agency personnel. He or she coordinates agency efforts in planning, creating, and producing ads. The account executive also presents agency recommendations and obtains client approval. As the focal point of agency–client relationships, the account executive must know a great deal about the client's business and be able to communicate this to specialists in the agency working on the account. The ideal account executive has a strong marketing background as well as a thorough understanding of all phases of the advertising process.

Planning/Research Services   Most full-service agencies maintain a research department whose function is to gather, analyze, and interpret information as input for advertising decisions. Both primary research—where a study is designed, executed, and interpreted by the research department—and secondary (previously published) sources of information are relied upon. The research department also acquires studies conducted by independent syndicated research firms or consultants, interprets the findings, and disseminates the information to agency personnel working on that account. The research department may pretest the effectiveness of advertising with copy testing to determine how messages developed by the creative specialists are likely to be interpreted by the receiving audience. John St. is one example of an agency that embraced innovative ways of collecting and analyzing media data to demonstrate IMC effectiveness. For its client Mitsubishi, the agency found stronger responses for email messages versus display ads to those who had visited the company's Internet site.[23]

Research services may be augmented with services performed by account planners, who gather relevant information that can be used to develop the creative strategy and other aspects of the IMC campaign. Account planners work with the client and other agency personnel (including the account executives, creative team members, media specialists, and research department personnel) to collect information to better understand the client's target audience and the best ways to communicate with them. They gather and organize information about consumers, competitors, and the market to prepare the **creative brief**, which is a document that the agency's creative department uses to guide the development of advertising ideas and concepts.

Account planners may also be involved in assessing consumers' reactions to the advertising and other elements of the IMC program and providing the creative staff and other agency personnel with feedback regarding performance. Account planning is a very important function in many agencies because it provides the creative team, and other agency personnel, with more insight into consumers and how to use advertising and other IMC tools to communicate with them.[24] However, the account planning function is demanding with the increased number of marketing communication channels. Account planners interact with individuals from all marketing communication disciplines and require expertise in each area.

Creative Services   The creative services department is responsible for the creation and execution of advertisements. The creative team at the agency Innocean produced ads that put Hyundai on the map (Exhibit 2-3). The individuals who conceive the ideas for the ads and write the headlines, subheads, and body copy (the words constituting the message) are known as **copywriters**. They may also be involved in determining the message appeal and/or theme of the ad campaign and often prepare a rough initial visual layout of the print ad or television commercial.

While copywriters are responsible for what the message says, the art director, graphic designers, and studio artist are responsible for how the ad looks. For a print ad, they prepare a **layout**, which is a drawing that shows what the ad will look like and from which the final artwork will be produced. For a TV commercial, the layout is known as a **storyboard**, a sequence of frames or panels that depict the commercial in still form.

Members of the creative department work together to develop ads that will communicate the key points determined to be the basis of the creative strategy for the client's product or service. Writers and artists generally work under the direction of the agency's creative director, who oversees all the advertising produced by the organization. The director sets the creative philosophy of the department and may even become directly involved in creating ads for the agency's largest clients. The creative director's job is all the more demanding with the growth of digital media and client demands to be part of the decision making earlier in the creative process.[25]

Exhibit 2-3   The agency Innocean developed creative ads for Hyundai to build the car brand in North America.

© Hyundai Motor America

Digital Creative Services   Digital creative services share similarity with established creative departments with respect to copywriters and specialists with graphics skills. However, other personnel with computer technology skills are required for programming various interactive features of creative ads found in Internet media vehicles. Moreover, this newer genre of creativity includes an interactive producer to oversee all operations and to coordinate with creative work done in mass media. In order to grow this side of the business, full-service agencies purchase small or mid-sized independent interactive agencies.[26] With its president having a digital background, Zulu Alpha Kilo gravitated toward a higher percentage of its creative work being in this domain.[27]

Production Services   The ad is turned over to the production department once the copy, layout, illustrations, and mechanical specifications are completed and approved. Most agencies do not actually produce finished ads; they hire printers, engravers, photographers, typographers, and other suppliers. For broadcast production, the storyboard must be turned into a finished commercial. The production department may supervise the casting of people to appear in the ad, determine the setting for the scenes, and choose an independent production studio. The department may hire an outside director to turn the creative concept into a commercial. Specialists from all departments and client representatives may all participate in production decisions, particularly when large sums of money are involved.

Creating an advertisement often involves many people and takes several months. In large agencies with many clients, coordinating the creative and production processes is a major task. A **traffic department**, or traffic manager, coordinates all phases of production to see that the ads are completed on time and that all deadlines for submitting the ads to the media are met. The traffic department can be in production or may be a separate department or part of other service departments.

Media Services   The media department of an agency analyzes, selects, and contracts for space or time in the media that will be used to deliver the client's advertising message. The media department is expected to develop a media plan that will reach the target audience and effectively communicate the message. Since most of the client's ad budget is spent on media time and/or space, this department must develop a plan that both communicates with the right audience and is cost-effective and cost-efficient. Due to the potential to place any advertising format (e.g, video, print, audio) in virtually any media space, the global planning system at PHD/Touche revised its approach by organizing by format then media. For example, a video message could be placed out-of-home, on TV, in cinema, on social media, and on different video host sites.[28]

Media specialists must know what audiences the media reach, their rates, and how well they match the client's target audience. The media department reviews information on demographics, magazine and newspaper readership, radio listenership, and consumers' TV and Internet viewing patterns to develop an effective media plan. The media buyer implements the media plan by purchasing the actual time and space. Computerized decision support systems assist in this research, as demonstrated by OMD Canada's installation of the Annalect data management platform which aids in determining the optimal media purchase across all media types.[29] The media department is an important part of the agency business, as many large advertisers consolidate their media buying with one or a few agencies to improve media efficiency. An agency's strategic ability to negotiate prices and effectively use the vast array of media vehicles available is as important as its ability to create ads. Many full-service agencies see value in offering this service since media companies are competing against agencies by offering creative services. For example, *Metro* newspaper has a creative department that helps advertisers, like an agency does, to put together a print campaign.[30]

Specialized Services   Large, full-service agencies offer additional marketing services to their clients to assist in other promotional areas. An agency may have a sales promotion department, or merchandising department, that specializes in developing contests, premiums, promotions, point-of-sale materials, and other sales materials. It may have direct-marketing specialists and package designers, as well as a PR/publicity department. Bensimon and Byrne established Narrative PR within the agency, and its creative success makes the PR discipline the lead communication tool for some of its clients' IMC programs. Narrative grew its own client list and now provides leads to the advertising agency component.[31] Many agencies have developed interactive media departments to create websites or develop social media and email campaigns for their clients. Internet media growth initiated the opportunity for creative expression of brands and required agencies to organize additional creative departments. However, it is now so common that MEC agency disbanded its digital department on the grounds that personnel with this expertise are part of every client team since most campaigns involve digital and non-digital media.[32] In a completely new direction, Rethink and Sid Lee moved toward design services. Rethink involved itself tremendously with the new look in Freshco grocery stores. Sid Lee opened up its own architecture services as part of its design offering so that a consistent look is presented from both the retail and marketing communication perspectives.[33]

Organizational Structure   To provide superior service for its accounts, agencies use the **group system**, in which individuals from each department work together in groups to service particular accounts. In contrast to the **departmental system** we have been discussing thus far, each group is headed by an account executive or supervisor and includes media planners and buyers; a creative team, which includes copywriters, art directors, artists, and production personnel; and one or more account executives. The group may also include individuals from other departments such as marketing research, direct marketing, or sales promotion. The size and composition of the group varies depending on the client's billings and the importance of the account to the agency. For very important accounts, the group members may be assigned exclusively to one client. A group system is preferred because employees become very knowledgeable about the client's business and there is continuity in servicing the account.

 Agency Compensation and Evaluation

Agencies use a variety of compensation methods depending on the type and amount of service they provide to their clients. We review a number of methods, because there is no one method of compensation to which everyone subscribes. We also examine the related topic of performance evaluation and explore reasons why clients switch agencies.

COMMISSIONS FROM MEDIA

The historical method of compensating agencies is through a **commission system**, where the agency receives a specified commission (usually 15 percent) from the media on any advertising time or space it purchases for its client. This system provides a simple method of determining payments, as shown in the following example.

Assume an agency prepares a full-page magazine ad and arranges to place the ad on the back cover of a magazine at a cost of $100,000. The agency places the order for the space and delivers the ad to the magazine. Once the ad is run, the magazine will bill the agency for $100,000, less the 15 percent ($15,000) commission. The media will also offer a 2 percent cash discount for early payment, which the agency may pass along to the client. The agency will bill the client $100,000 less the 2 percent cash discount on the net amount, or a total of $98,300, as shown in Figure 2-3. The $15,000 commission represents the agency's compensation for its services.

Figure 2-3   Example of commission system payment

Media Bills Agency		Agency Bills Advertiser	
Costs for magazine space	$100,000	Costs for magazine space	$100,000
Less 15% commission	−15,000	Less 2% cash discount	−1,700
Cost of media space	$ 85,000	Advertiser pays agency	$ 98,300
Less 2% cash discount	−1,700		
Agency pays media	$ 83,300	Agency income	$ 15,000

Critics of the commission system argue that it encourages agencies to recommend high-priced media to increase their commission level. Another concern is that it ties agency compensation to media costs, allowing the agency to be disproportionately rewarded. Critics have argued that it provides an incentive for agencies to recommend mass-media advertising when other forms of communication might do a better job.[34]

Defenders of the commission system argue that it is easy to administer and it keeps the emphasis in agency competition on non-price factors like advertising quality. Proponents argue that agency services are proportional to the size of the commission, since more time and effort are devoted to the large accounts that generate high revenue for the agency. They also say the system is more flexible than it appears because agencies often perform other services for large clients at no extra charge, justifying such actions by the large commission they receive.

Agencies rely less on media commissions for their income as clients expand their IMC programs to include other forms of promotion and use less media advertising. A study of agency compensation conducted by the Association of National Advertisers (ANA) indicates that commission system usage ranged from 5 percent to 15 percent over the past 10 years.[35] Instead, advertisers used a **negotiated commission** system where commissions average 8–10 percent and are based on a sliding scale that becomes lower as clients' media expenditures increase. As the percentage of agency income from media commissions declines, a greater percentage is coming through other methods such as fees and performance incentives.

FEE ARRANGEMENT

There are two types of fee arrangement systems. In the straight or **fixed-fee method**, the agency charges a monthly fee for all of its services and credits to the client any media commissions earned. Agency and client agree on the specific work to be done and the amount the agency will be paid for it. Sometimes agencies are compensated through a **fee–commission combination**, in which the media commissions received by the agency are credited against the fee. If the commissions are less than the agreed-on fee, the client must make up the difference. If the agency does much work for the client in non-commissionable media, the fee may be charged over and above the commissions received.

Both types of fee arrangements require that the agency carefully assess its costs of serving the client for the specified period, or for the project, plus its desired profit margin. To avoid any later disagreement, a fee arrangement should specify exactly what services the agency is expected to perform for the client.

COST-PLUS AGREEMENT

Under a **cost-plus system**, the client agrees to pay the agency a fee based on the costs of its work plus an agreed-on profit margin (often a percentage of total costs). This system requires that the agency keep detailed records of the costs it incurs in working on the client's account. Direct costs (personnel time and out-of-pocket expenses) plus an allocation for overhead and a markup for profits determine the amount the agency bills the client. An agency can add a markup of percentage charges to various services the agency purchases from outside providers (e.g., market research, artwork, printing, photography).

Fee agreements and cost-plus systems are commonly used; the ANA survey reports that fee-based methods usage is at 81 percent.[36] The fee-based system can be advantageous to both the client and the agency, depending on the size of the client, advertising budget, media used, and services required. Clients prefer fee or cost-plus systems because they receive a detailed breakdown of where and how their advertising and promotion dollars were spent. However, these arrangements can be challenging for the agency, as they require careful cost accounting to estimate when bidding for an advertiser's business, and allow clients to see their internal cost figures. One complicating factor for agencies is that clients now hire procurement specialists from other industries who put pressure on the costs without fully understanding the advertising process.[37]

INCENTIVE-BASED COMPENSATION

Clients expect accountability from their agencies and link agency compensation to performance through an **incentive-based system**. The idea is that the agency's ultimate compensation level will depend on how well it meets predetermined performance goals. In Canada, the Performance by Results (PBR) system, initiated by the Institute of Communications and Advertising, highlights the importance of clearly identifying the objectives of the promotional plan and measuring the performance of the plan based on these objectives.[38] PBR defines an advertising remuneration process where the basic advertising agency fee is adjusted by a reward based on the degree of achieving mutually agreed upon objectives between the client and the agency. Overall, the remuneration is a part of a system of linking performance, its measurement, and reward within the client–agency relationship. The benefits of the PBR system are:

Greater efficiency and accountability	Stronger mutual understanding
Achievement of cost efficiencies	Improved retention of creative talent
Higher productivity	Increased agency strategic input
Fewer barriers of self-interest	Improved client–agency communication

Three general groups of performance measures are critical in the PBR system: overall business performance, marketing communication effectiveness, and agency process evaluation. Business measures include sales, market share, profitability, and margins. Marketing communication effectiveness measures include brand awareness, brand image ratings, and likability of advertising. This group also includes four objectives that are more behavioural: intent to purchase, trial, repeat purchase, and brand loyalty. The final group, agency process evaluation, concerns the services the agency provides and its overall management process.

Decisions regarding the first two groups are covered in later chapters, however, in general, the relative importance of each measure needs to be investigated for each brand and its marketing situation, and the measures should take into account the role of promotion in the marketing mix and how promotion contributes to business results for the brand and within the product category or industry. The ANA survey finds that over 50 percent of the clients reward agencies with a performance incentive with agency performance reviews, brand awareness, and sales being the highest, which corresponds to one measure from each group. Although the performance incentive added to the fee arrangement is relatively workable for both parties, agencies remain concerned that their compensation is not commensurate for situations when the IMC plan contributes to significant brand profit.[39]

EVALUATION OF AGENCIES

Regular reviews of the agency's performance are necessary. The agency evaluation process usually involves two types of assessments—one that is financial and operational, and another that is more qualitative. The **financial audit** focuses on how the agency conducts its business. It is designed to verify costs and expenses, the number of personnel hours charged to an account, and payments to media and outside suppliers. The **qualitative audit** focuses on the agency's efforts in planning, developing, and implementing the client's advertising programs and considers the results achieved.

The agency evaluation can be done on a subjective, informal basis, particularly in smaller companies where ad budgets are low or advertising is not seen as the most critical factor in the firm's marketing performance. Companies have developed formal, systematic evaluation systems, particularly when budgets are large and the advertising function receives much emphasis. As advertising costs continue to rise, the top managers of these companies want to be sure money is being spent efficiently and effectively.

As part of its mandate as an industry resource, the Institute of Communications and Advertising provides a Guide to Best Practice that includes information to facilitate agency evaluation (the Guide and PBR information identified earlier in the chapter can be found at www.icacanada.ca). The document provides guidelines on the client–agency relationship and includes many forms that can be used as a basis for evaluating an agency in all areas of performance, such as account management, creative, planning and research, production, media planning and buying, budget and financial, agency management, direct marketing, interactive marketing, and public relations.

One example of a formal agency evaluation system is that used by Whirlpool, which markets a variety of consumer products. Whirlpool management meets once a year with the company's agencies to review their performance. Whirlpool managers complete an advertising agency performance evaluation, part of which is shown in Figure 2-4. These reports are compiled and reviewed with the agency at each annual meeting. Whirlpool's evaluation process covers six areas of performance. The company and the agency develop an action plan to correct areas of deficiency.

Figure 2-4   Whirlpool's ad agency performance evaluation

CREATIVE SERVICES

Always	Often	Occasionally	Seldom	Never	NA	Marks Scored
4	**3**	**2**	**1**	**0**		

1. Agency produces fresh ideas and original approaches
2. Agency accurately interprets facts, strategies and objectives into usable advertisements and plans
3. Creative group is knowledgeable about company's products, markets and strategies
4. Creative group is concerned with good advertising communications and develops campaigns and ads that exhibit this concern
5. Creative group produces on time
6. Creative group performs well under pressure
7. Creative group operates in a businesslike manner to control production costs and other creative charges
8. Agency presentations are well organized with sufficient examples of proposed executions
9. Creative group participates in major campaign presentations
10. Agency presents ideas and executions not requested but felt to be good opportunities
11. Agency willingly accepts ideas generated by other locations/agency offices vs. being over-protective of its own creative product
12. Other areas not mentioned
13. Agency demonstrates commitment to client's business
14. Agency creative proposals are relevant and properly fulfill creative brief

---

Value–(marks)

Rating:	Excellent	90–100%	Total marks scored
	Good	80–89%	
	Average	70–79%	Total possible marks
	Fair	60–69%	
	Poor	below 60%	Score

[Continued on next page]

[Figure 2-4 continued]

ACCOUNT REPRESENTATION & SERVICE

Always	Often	Occasionally	Seldom	Never	NA	Marks Scored
4	**3**	**2**	**1**	**0**		

1. Account representatives act with personal initiative
2. Account representatives anticipate needs in advance of direction by client (ie: are proactive)
3. Account group takes direction well
4. Agency is able to demonstrate results of programs implemented
5. Account representatives function strategically rather than as creative advisors only
6. Account representatives are knowledgeable about competitive programs and share this information along with their recommendations in a timely manner
7. Account representatives respond to client requests in a timely fashion
8. Account group operates in a businesslike manner to control costs
9. Agency recommendations are founded on sound reasoning and supported factually, and appropriately fit within budget constraints
10. Agency is able to advise the client on trends and developments in technology
11. Account representatives demonstrate a high degree of professionalism in both written and oral communication
12. Agency presents ideas and executions not requested by felt to be good opportunities
13. Agency makes reasoned recommendations on allocation of budgets
14. Agency demonstrates commitment to client's business
15. There is a positive social relationship between client and agency

---

Value–(marks)

Rating:	Excellent	90–100%	Total marks scored
	Good	80–89%	
	Average	70–79%	Total possible marks
	Fair	60–69%	
	Poor	below 60%	Score

The evaluation process described above provides valuable feedback to both the agency and the client, such as indicating changes that need to be made by the agency and/or the client to improve performance and make the relationship more productive. Many agencies have had very long-lasting relationships with their clients; however. clients may eventually switch agencies for reasons summarized in Figure 2-5.[40] If the agency recognizes these warning signs, it can adapt to make sure the client is satisfied. Some of the situations identified are unavoidable, and others are beyond the agency's control. One study reports that a decline of market share in the immediate two quarters precedes an agency firing.[41] So despite doing everything in its power, an agency could feel the effect of weak performance in other marketing mix variables of the client's brand. Losing a major client can have a disastrous effect on a smaller agency, however, in the case of Grip Limited, the loss of Bell—accounting for one-quarter of revenue—allowed the upstart agency established with the help of Labatt to reinvent itself with a stronger focus toward interactive media and a more diversified client base.[42] Similar evaluations occur for major international corporations advertising worldwide (e.g., Exhibit 2-4), and the potential demise of a relationship such as this can be significant for an agency like Ogilvy & Mather.

Exhibit 2-4   IBM uses the agency Ogilvy & Mather for its global advertising.

HOW TO COMPETE IN THE ERA OF "SMART".

For five years, IBMers have been working with companies, cities and communities to build a Smarter Planet. We've seen enormous advances, as leaders have begun using the vast supply of Big Data to transform their enterprises and institutions through mobile technology, social business and the cloud.

Big Data has changed how these leaders work, how they make decisions and how they serve their customers. And the ability to harness Big Data is giving their enterprises a new competitive edge in today's era of "smart".

Police in Memphis used Big Data and analytics to verify patterns of criminal activity, which helped them change their strategy.

DECISIONS BASED ON ANALYTICS, NOT ON INSTINCT. Decision makers once viewed their intuition and experience as the keys to formulating strategy and assessing risk. But analytics increasingly helps them discern real patterns and anticipate events.

A decade ago, the Memphis Police Department developed an analytics platform that created multilayer maps to identify patterns of criminal

activity. The department then changed its patrolling strategy, reducing crime by 24 percent.

THE SOCIAL NETWORK IS THE NEW PRODUCTION LINE. In this knowledge economy, the exchange of ideas has become the new means of production. The advent of social and mobile technology is shifting the competitive edge from having workers who amass knowledge to having workers who impart it.

Cemex, a $15 billion cement maker, wanted to create its first global brand of concrete, which required a coordination of stakeholders from each country. Cemex didn't build

a new lab. It built a social business network. Employees in 50 countries formed one global active community whose collaboration helped launch its first global brand in a third of the anticipated time.

FROM YOU AS A SEGMENT TO YOU AS YOU.
The age of Big Data and analytics is revealing customers not as demographic "segments"

Effective marketing no longer aims publicity at broad demographic groups—it opens conversations with individuals.

but as individuals. And that's changing how companies serve customers. Call centers, once evaluated by how quickly they got callers off the phone, are training employees to engage *more* with customers by starting conversations and serving individuals.

Social networks shift value in the workplace from knowledge that people possess to knowledge that they can communicate.

FINDING SUCCESS ON A SMARTER PLANET.
An organisation that adopts these principles is a Smarter Enterprise. But using emerging technology is only part of the story. The real challenge now is to use these new insights to change entrenched work practices. To learn more about the new principles of the Smarter Enterprise, visit us at **ibm.com/smarterplanet/in**

LET'S BUILD A SMARTER PLANET.

IBM

IBM, the IBM logo, ibm.com, Smarter Planet and the planet icon are trademarks of International Business Machines Corp, registered in many jurisdictions worldwide. A current list of IBM trademarks is available on the Web at www.ibm.com/legal/copytrade.shtml. © International Business Machines Corporation 2013.

Courtesy of International Business Machines Corp.

Figure 2-5   Common reasons for agencies to lose clients

Performance Quality	The client is dissatisfied with the advertising and/or service.
Declining Sales	Advertising is blamed when the client's sales decline.
Communication	A poor working relationship and weak personal communication exist.
Demands	The client expects service beyond the compensation paid.
Conflict	Rapport is lacking among those working together.
Conflicts of Interest	A change in either business creates an unworkable situation.
Conflicting View	Disagreement arises over the level or method of compensation.
Size Change	Either the agency or the client outgrows the other.
Strategy Change	A client strategy change requires a new agency.
Personnel Change	New personnel prefer to work with established colleagues.
Policy Change	Either party reevaluates the importance of the relationship.

Specialized Services

Companies assign the development and implementation of their promotional programs to an advertising agency, but other agencies provide specialized services. Clients work with creative boutiques, media buying services, sales promotion agencies, public relations firms, direct-response agencies, and digital/interactive agencies to execute IMC programs. One survey found that PR firms and digital agencies posed the strongest threat to full-service agencies by offering similar research and creative services.[43] For example, the PR agency Veritas placed its glass-encased Growth & Innovation Lab in the centre of its office with the mandate to assist client teams.[44] Let us examine the functions these specialized marketing communication organizations perform.

CREATIVE BOUTIQUES

A **creative boutique** is an agency that provides only creative services. These specialized agencies have creative personnel but offer limited or no services in other areas (e.g., media, research, or account planning). Creative boutiques emerged in response to companies' desires to use only the creative services of an outside agency while managing the other functions internally. While creative boutiques work directly for clients, full-service agencies subcontract work to creative boutiques when they are busy or want to avoid adding full-time employees. Creative boutiques have been formed by members of the creative departments of full-service agencies who leave the firm and take with them clients who want to retain their creative talents.

Other creative boutiques have grown independently with tremendous success on their own. Red Urban is a notable Canadian agency operating as a creative boutique with clients such as VW, Porsche, and Rolling Rock. After seeing the awards won for its VW work, Porsche accepted Red Urban as its creative agency of record with the goal of attracting consumers who had not previously considered buying the sporty brand. [45] One organization refers to itself as this kind of agency; Lg2 Boutique, originally established in Quebec and now expanded to Toronto, has produced award-winning work, recognized both nationally and internationally.[46]

MEDIA BUYING SERVICES

Media buying services are independent companies that specialize in the buying of media. The task of purchasing advertising media is complex as specialized media proliferate, so media buying services achieved a niche by specializing in the analysis and purchase of advertising time and space. Agencies and clients usually develop their own media strategies and hire the media buying service to execute them, but the services do also help advertisers plan their media strategies. Because media buying services purchase large amounts of time and space, they receive large discounts and can save the small agency or client money on media purchases. Major agencies also divested their media departments to form independent media services

Exhibit 2-5   Initiative is one of the leading media specialist companies.

Courtesy of Initiative

companies that handle the media planning and buying for their clients and also offer their services separately to companies interested in a specialized approach to media planning, research, and/or buying. Advertisers have also unbundled agency services and consolidated media buying to get more clout from their advertising budgets. Exhibit 2-5 shows how Initiative, one of the largest media specialist companies, promotes its services.

Strategy magazine recognized MediaCom for its creative use of media and important organizational design changes as the agency emphasized a consumer-centric way of thinking for planning media for the agency's clients. As part of this, digital leaders reported directly to strategy leaders, which fostered stronger integration of IMC decision making. Furthermore, communications planning, research, and business sciences personnel remained in close contact with offices nearby to one another. As part of this improved service level, MediaCom innovated with extensive placement of TV-like video messages in many out-of-home locations, and anticipated placement of additional ads in the future on addressable TV. As well, MediaCom began to investigate the dissemination of passive audio fingerprinting technology to deliver ads to mobile devices when signals are picked up from media exposure from a CTV broadcast; the agency worked with Bell to develop the technology.[47] Touché is another media buying company at the forefront in Canada with its advanced use of data for decision making among other innovations, as described in IMC Perspective 2-2.

IMC PERSPECTIVE 2-2

TOUCHÉ'S STRATEGIC MEDIA DECISIONS PAY OFF

Touché started as a small media boutique 20 years ago in Montreal and, after a series of affiliations (Touché PHD, Touché OMD), it now resides as a key player within the Omnicom Group of agencies, in particular within Omnicom Media. With the resources of this big organization and its talented staff, *Marketing Magazine* recognized Touché as its Media Agency of the Year with its successful media strategies designed for Canadian Tire's "Ice Truck" and "We All Play for Canada" campaigns, a digital campaign for Red Bull, and a car safety message for Quebec's liquor control board (SAAQ).

© Touché

Canadian Tire's "Ice Truck" demonstrated the power of the MotoMaster Eliminator Ultra AGM battery. A team constructed an ice truck around an engine and chassis and inserted the frozen battery (at a temperature of minus 40 degrees Celsius), which showed its capability by starting the engine immediately. Touché arranged for the ad to be launched during the TV broadcast of the Winter Classic, a regular season NHL game played outdoors on or around New Year's Day each year. Touché also placed the ads for airing during the coldest days possible, of course to "feel" the battery's powerful effect when needed most! With digital and social media exposure, the ad achieved a total of 80 million earned media impressions.

The initial ad for the "We All Play for Canada" campaign featured a number of winter scenes with Canadians enjoying outdoor sports and activities. Along with the Internet site, WeAllPlayForCanada.ca, the messaging demonstrates Canadian Tire's commitment to helping all Canadians enjoy playing, no matter what the recreation. Another execution showed NHL star Jonathan Toews, and others who helped him in his career, coming together to form a Maple Leafs logo in the seats of a hockey arena. Touché's media strategy contribution naturally included the TV broadcast placement, but interestingly, the agency got the TV message placed in people's Facebook newsfeed a few minutes later. Other digital messaging included display ads, YouTube masthead dominations, and premium Facebook ad placement. Additional footage of Toews and company became a short documentary shown on CBC and online.

For Red Bull, Touché targeted messages in social media (Facebook, Twitter, LinkedIn, Foursquare) based on people's posts on New Year's resolutions. Using software that analyzed the emotional content of people's views, the agency targeted specific messages based on the type of emotion exhibited; essentially using mood as a micro segmentation variable. In this case, the media assisted greatly in the development of the message, a process not often followed in marketing communication. Touché prided itself on looking at technology and working with it to develop unique media opportunities. In this case, the idea took hold for other clients beyond Red Bull. For the SAAQ, Touché worked with Lg2 to develop a 3D projection of a person's ghost talking about the dangers of texting while driving or driving impaired. They installed the system at 39 university and college locations in Quebec so that when a student looked at the mirror, they perceived that someone who had perished in a car accident was actually speaking to them.

[Continued on next page]

[IMC Perspective 2-2 continued]

As these examples indicate, Touché remains at the forefront for new ideas and innovation in targeting audiences with relevant media options, something a good media planning agency does to contribute to an IMC program for a client. And in the future, it seems Touché will continue to be at the forefront with the increased online video messaging opportunity. Its research indicates that Canadians spend 15 percent of their media consumption time viewing online video, yet advertisers only spent 1 percent of their budgets on Internet video. And while there are different cost considerations for online versus broadcast that skews this data, it seems we will see Touché winning in the future with additional clever online media strategies.

Sources: Jeff Fraser, "Good Friends, Big Goals and a Little Extra Flair," *Marketing Magazine*, February/March, 2015, pp. 26–28, 30; Matthew Chung, "TJ Flood Scores an All-Star Strategy," *Strategy*, December 2014, p. 23; Matthew Chung, "Creating the Next Generation," *Strategy*, December 2014, p. 52.

Question:

1. Explain why a media agency is so critical for advertising.

SALES PROMOTION AGENCIES

Developing and managing sales promotion programs (such as contests and sweepstakes, refunds and rebates, premium and incentive offers) and sampling programs is a complex task. Most companies use a **sales promotion agency** to develop and administer these programs. Some large ad agencies have created their own sales promotion department or acquired a sales promotion firm. However, most sales promotion agencies are independent companies that specialize in providing the services needed to plan, develop, and execute a variety of sales promotion programs.

Sales promotion agencies often work in conjunction with the client's advertising and/or direct-response agencies to coordinate their efforts. Services provided by large sales promotion agencies include promotional planning, creative, research, tie-in coordination, fulfillment, premium design and manufacturing, catalogue production, and contest/sweepstakes management. Sales promotion agencies also develop direct/database marketing to expand their IMC capabilities. Circo de Bakuza, based in Montreal, is one promotional agency specializing in event marketing. It got its start organizing the Just for Laughs festival 10 years ago and has signed on clients like Bell, Cirque du Soleil, and UEFA Champions League since then while growing internally.[48] Sales promotion agencies are generally compensated on a fee basis.

PUBLIC RELATIONS FIRMS

Large companies use both an advertising agency and a PR firm. The **public relations firm** develops and implements programs to manage the organization's publicity, image, and affairs with consumers and other relevant publics, including employees, suppliers, shareholders, government, labour groups, citizen action groups, and the general public. The PR firm analyzes the relationships between the client and these diffuse publics, determines how the client's policies and actions relate to and affect these publics, develops PR strategies and programs, implements these programs using public relations tools, and evaluates their effectiveness. The activities of a public relations firm include planning the PR strategy and program, generating publicity, conducting lobbying and public affairs efforts, becoming involved in community activities and events, preparing news releases, performing research, promoting and managing special events, and managing crises. Companies look toward integrating public relations and publicity into the marketing communications mix to increase message credibility and save media costs.[49]

North Strategic received the inaugural nod from *Strategy* magazine for top PR firm. Started in 2011 by two experienced PR leaders, the small shop expanded to three offices serving major clients like FGL, RBC, Samsung, and Ubisoft. The agency strives creatively by inventing new approaches to generated publicity. For example, it surprised three pitchers of the Toronto Blue Jays with visits from their dads on Father's Day and publicized the event through TV sports channels and digitally. It also prides itself on working directly with senior managers of its client and by offering a unique method for billing based on the project's characteristics.[50] For Samsung, the agency invited media to an interactive fitness class to try out the Galaxy S5 and Gear Fit, a device that works with the smart phone while the wearer is working out. Additional follow-up interviews occurred with the fitness leader, Tracy Anderson, resulting in 225 featured media stories.[51]

DIRECT-RESPONSE AGENCIES

Direct marketing involves companies communicating with consumers through telemarketing, direct mail, television, the Internet, or any other direct-response media. As this industry has grown, numerous direct-response agencies have evolved that offer companies their specialized skills in both consumer and business markets. Many of the top direct-marketing agencies are subsidiaries of large agency holding companies (refer to Figure 2-1). However, there are also a number of independent direct-marketing agencies including those that serve large companies as well as smaller agencies that handle the needs of local companies.

Direct-response agencies provide a variety of services, including database management, direct mail, research, media services, and creative and production capabilities. A typical direct-response agency is divided into three main departments: account management, creative, and media. Agencies can also have a department whose function is to develop and manage databases for their clients. Database development and management is an important service as many companies use database marketing to pinpoint new customers and build relationships and loyalty among existing customers. The account managers work with their clients to plan direct-marketing programs and determine their role in the overall integrated marketing communications process. The creative department consists of copywriters, artists, and producers and is responsible for developing the direct-response message. The media department is concerned with its placement in the most appropriate direct-response media.

DIGITAL/INTERACTIVE AGENCIES

With the growth of the Internet, marketers needed services beyond historic advertising agency capabilities. Successful interactive marketing programs required expertise in technology, creativity, database marketing, digital media, and customer relationship management. Some existing advertising agencies established interactive capabilities, ranging from a few specialists to an entire interactive division, however **digital/interactive agencies** also emerged who specialized in developing interactive marketing tools such as websites, display ads, and social media applications. These agencies specialized and fostered their expertise in designing and developing digital/interactive tools as well as managing and supporting them. Currently, interactive agencies range from smaller companies that specialize (e.g., in website design or social media) to full-service interactive agencies that design and implement a complete digital/interactive marketing program through strategic brand consulting, creative and message development, and technical knowledge.

Both digital/interactive agencies and full-service agencies with digital capabilities are recognized with awards from industry players. *Strategy* recognized one in the latter group for its excellent work as digital agency of the year; Lg2 created a mobile pedometer for its fast-food client Valentine. After a meal, the Walk Off Your Poutine app counted the calories burned using GPS by measuring the speed and distance travelled. Interactive features included messages from Valentine and the option to link one's performance and experiences to Facebook. All told, 50,000 downloaded apps resulted in a total of 5,000 transactions and 300 million steps. Lg2 also installed motion triggered two-way mirrors in college/university washrooms that projected the story of ghosts (played by actors) who had perished after drinking and driving, on behalf of the Quebec government's automotive licensing branch. The agency posted recorded video of the interactive experiences on YouTube for a total of 220,000 views.[52]

 # IMC Planning: Agency Relationships

Currently, marketers can choose from a variety of organizations to assist them in planning, developing, and implementing an integrated marketing communications program. Companies must decide whether to use specialized organizations for each marketing communications function or to consolidate them with a large advertising agency that offers all of these services. In this final section, we discuss whether an advertiser would want to use an integrated services agency, assess the agency–client responsibilities for IMC, and summarize the current situation regarding the agency–client relationship in the context of an IMC environment.

INTEGRATED IMC SERVICES

Historically, marketing communication services were run as separate profit centres with each motivated to push its own expertise and pursue its own goals rather than develop truly integrated marketing programs. For example, creative specialists resisted becoming involved in sales promotion or direct marketing and preferred to concentrate on developing magazine ads or television commercials rather than designing coupons or direct-mail pieces. While agencies transitioned to full-service providers, proponents of the "one-stop shop" contend that these past problems are resolved and the individuals in the agencies and subsidiaries are working together.

Integrated services offer clients three benefits. First, clients maintain control of the entire promotional process and achieve greater synergy among the communications program elements. Second, it is more convenient for the client to coordinate all of its marketing efforts—media advertising, direct mail, special events, sales promotions, and public relations—through one agency. Third and finally, an agency with integrated marketing capabilities can create a single image for the client's brand and address everyone, from wholesalers to consumers, with one voice.

Some people feel that an advertising agency offering full services is neither sufficiently staffed to ensure complete integration, nor fully cognizant of multiple target audiences. Advertising agency personnel are trained in particular aspects of the process and are less inclined to consider many marketing variables in their decisions. Furthermore, they tend to consider only the end user or consumer rather than all the parties in the marketing process who are connected to the results of the communications plan. It is recommended that marketers ensure the agencies consider the needs of all (e.g., customer service staff, sales representatives, distributors, and retailers) in their communication plans.[53]

AGENCY–CLIENT RESPONSIBILITY

Surveys of advertisers and agency executives have shown that both groups believe integrated marketing communication is important to their organizations' success. However, marketers and agency executives have very different opinions regarding who should be in charge of the integrated marketing communications process. Many advertisers prefer to set strategy for and coordinate their own IMC campaigns, but most agency executives see this as their domain.[54]

While agency executives believe their shops are capable of handling the elements an integrated campaign requires, marketers historically preferred to allocate creative services to their advertising agency and use specialized service agencies or in-house departments for other IMC tools.[55]

On the one hand, agencies still view themselves as strategic and executional partners and are offering their clients a full line of services (e.g., interactive and multimedia advertising, database management, direct marketing, public relations, and sales promotion). On the other hand, marketers still want to set the strategy for their IMC campaigns and seek specialized expertise, more quality and creativity, and greater control and cost efficiency by using multiple providers.

AGENCY–CLIENT RELATIONSHIPS

Recent findings emerged from a survey of agencies and clients conducted by the Association of National Advertisers in the United States (current Canadian data was unavailable). The study investigated the strength of the relationship, the agency's role as a business partner, agency compensation, process management, and other factors. From the perspective of both parties, the relationships are positive, a long-term relationship is viewed strongly, and they trust one another. Figure 2-6 summarizes five areas in which there is noticeable disagreement between agency and client. In future, both agree on the importance of clients providing a better briefing process and on an agency's understanding of a client's business and situation.[56]

Figure 2-6   Agency–client relationship disagreement

Characteristic	Agency Agreement	Client Agreement
Compensation fairness	40%	72%
Clear assignment brief	27%	58%
Client approval process	36%	54%
Value of procurement	10%	47%
Work well with other agencies	88%	65%

One source of conflict contributing to an advertising agency's ability to work with another agency is partly a function of the growth of other types of agencies, especially digital agencies with the growth of the Internet. These types of agencies recruited many creative individuals from advertising agencies to enhance their ability to provide more complete marketing communications. Increasingly, all types of agencies see the creative decisions of the message, no matter how they are delivered, as being a key differentiating factor when a client is making an agency selection. While personnel from any type of agency may publicly say that working with other agencies is positive, behind the scenes is the fact that digital agencies and PR agencies are in competition with advertising agencies for clients; as a result some are hiring creative directors, a job usually seen in advertising agencies only.[57]

Learning Objectives Summary

 LO1   Identify the role of the advertising agency and the services it provides.

The development, execution, and administration of an advertising and promotion program involves the efforts of many individuals, both within the company and outside it. Firms have to decide whether they will hire an external advertising agency or use an in-house service to create their ads and purchase media. In-house agencies, while offering the advantages of cost savings, control, and increased coordination, have the disadvantage of less experience and flexibility. Many firms use advertising agencies to help develop and execute their programs. These firms offer the client a full range of services (including creative, account, marketing, and financial and management services). A full-service agency provides the services of highly skilled individuals and the objectivity to resolve the client's communication issues.

 LO2   Describe methods for compensating and evaluating advertising agencies.

Historically, clients compensated agencies through commission systems based on media sales, and fee- and cost-based systems. Increased emphasis on agency accountability has given rise to incentive-based compensation systems that tie agency compensation to performance measures such as sales and market share. Other more comprehensive measures include achievement of marketing communication objectives and how the agency operates and delivers services. Agencies are evaluated on both financial and qualitative measures that are formal in certain situations and less formal in others. Upon evaluation, a client may no longer require the service of the agency for a number of performance related issues. Some clients retain the services of an agency for a relatively long period of time and confer the status of "agency of record."

 LO3   Contrast the role and functions of specialized marketing communication organizations.

In addition to using ad agencies, marketers use the services of other marketing communication specialists, including creative boutiques and media buying services, direct marketing agencies, sales promotion agencies, public relations firms, and interactive agencies. Contracting out work to a specialized agency can enhance the creativity of the overall IMC plan with experts from specific fields. Moreover, while it may be more costly or time-consuming to work with other specialists, these organizations may reach the target audience more precisely, thus yielding a favourable return on investment. A marketer must decide whether to use a different specialist for each promotional function or to have all of its integrated marketing communications done by an advertising agency that offers all of these services under one roof. This latter idea allows an account team to know and control all aspects of the communication.

 LO4   Evaluate the perspectives on the use of integrated services across agencies or within one agency, and agency–client responsibilities and partnerships.

Studies have found that most marketers believe it is their responsibility, not the ad agency's, to set strategy for and to coordinate IMC campaigns. The lack of a broad perspective and specialized skills in non-advertising areas is seen as the major barrier to agencies' increased involvement in integrated marketing communications, and individual perspectives of clients and agencies will continue to adapt as the growth of IMC evolves.

Review Questions

1. How are the characteristics of a full-service agency contrasted with the characteristics of specialized marketing communication agencies?
2. Why is compensating with the performance by results approach optimal in comparison with other methods?
3. What are the similar and dissimilar functions of each of the specialized marketing communication agencies?
4. What are the issues of using one full-service agency versus multiple specialized agencies?

Applied Questions

1. The chapter distinguished between full-service and specialized agencies. Using Figure 2-1 as a guide for different agency names based in Canada, examine the websites of different full-service marketing communication agencies. Using the websites as the main source of information, identify which types of services each agency offers.
2. Which type of agency compensation system characterizes an environment where a young advertising graduate would most like to work?
3. Again, using Figure 2-1 as a guide for different agency names based in Canada, examine the websites of different specialized marketing communication agencies. Using the websites as the main source of information, identify which types of services each agency offers.
4. Given the evaluation of different agencies in the above questions, is the use of a full-service agency or the use of multiple specialized agencies the recommended approach for smart phone brands? for breakfast cereal brands? for energy drink brands?

CHAPTER THREE

Consumer Behaviour and Target Audience Decisions

LEARNING OBJECTIVES

LO1 Describe the consumer decision-making process and demonstrate how it relates to marketing communication.

LO2 Distinguish internal psychological processes, their influence on consumer decision making, and implications for marketing communication.

LO3 Contrast how the consumer decision-making process varies for different types of purchases and the effects on marketing communication.

LO4 Compare the similarities and differences of target market and target audience.

LO5   Identify the options for making a target audience decision for marketing communication.

 LO6   Express why a profile of the target audience is important for message, media, and IMC tool decisions.

The Foodie Lifestyle

San Pellegrino asks, "Are you a real foodie?" However, some might be asking, "What is a foodie?" One thought is that a foodie is an eater who has influence over food trends. Or perhaps it is someone who loves food and always talks about it. Maybe it is someone who eats exotic food or eats in a fashionable restaurant or location? On the other hand, suppose foodies are people who cook at home all the time and use new recipes or food products on a regular basis. No matter how many of these ideas might be true about foodies, it is clear that many consumers have activities, interests, and opinions surrounding food. How many are foodies is hard to say, although one research poll finds that 24 percent of all Canadians feel they have "serious culinary credibility," but we do know that virtually everyone in Canada eats food every day. Marketers other than the one selling Italian bubbly water in a green bottle are very keen on targeting this psychographic audience, including Loblaw, Metro, and Cracker Barrel.

San Pellegrino faced weaker brand awareness and diminished dining out sales so it revamped its "Live in Italy" slogan to target foodies by sending chefs to Italy for the first time in 14 years to participate in San Pellegrino's annual cooking competition. A film crew captured the stories of chefs and their cooking adventure for foodies to savour visually online. Subsequently, stories of other top Canadian chefs appeared the year after, online as well as in print and video ad messages, all with the purpose of enticing foodies to the brand with greater knowledge about the culture of food. Metro Inc. adopted a policy of buying from smaller Quebec based suppliers for that province's grocery stores. To communicate its new selection for foodies, its creative team produced video vignettes of the food producers and offered them for viewing in its social media channels and on daytime TV to go along with PR events and in-store promotions.

Loblaw moved toward the foodie crowd with its slogan "Crave More" to modernize its President's Choice (PC) brand, and to ward off a key food competitor in Walmart. According to a Loblaw senior VP, the new messaging is designed to move PC from a packaged goods food brand to a lifestyle brand. The initial launch ad showed how curiosity in food drove innovation, which would be the new direction of the PC brand: continued innovation in food to appeal to foodies. Executives believed that consumers had a passion for knowing more about where food comes from in addition to discovering new food. To address these foodie interests, Loblaw planned to monitor social media using Google software to adjust its food information and presentation. It also looked for additional exposure with product placement in Rogers owned media.

Cracker Barrel cheese created three TV spots with the slogan "Start With Cracker Barrel. End With Amazing."—with cooking reversed to break through the clutter of competing foodie ads. Each message showed the finished product initially and then backtracked the video to the beginning to reveal that the most important decision rested with the cheese selection. Executives saw the ad as targeting "culinary adventurers" who have a strong passion for food and are involved in its preparation. Past advertising highlighted the cheese's ingredients (Canadian milk, no antibiotics), but these ads showed the cheese in relation to other foods, with the cheese being the star. In a way, the reverse sequence and close-up shots made the commercial seem to take the food's point of view—something very enticing for foodies.

Sources: Megan Haynes, "Cracker Barrel's Cheesy Repositioning," *Strategy*, May 2015, p. 10; Megan Haynes, "Brands Tap Into Foodie Culture," *Strategy*, May 2015, p. 12; Susan Krashinsky, "Loblaw Targets Food-Savvy Canadians in Major Marketing Overhaul," *The Globe and Mail*, September 17, 2014.

Questions:

1. Is a foodie a legitimate lifestyle target for advertisers?

2. Are these advertisers actually targeting foodies?

The opening vignette reveals that effective marketing communication programs require knowledge of consumer behaviour. The resulting insight helps marketers to see how to encourage consumers to buy a product, what to emphasize in communication to specific audiences, where to target the marketing communication, and which types of IMC tools might be used. It is beyond the scope of this text to examine consumer behaviour in depth. However, promotional planners need an understanding of consumer decision making, factors that influence it, and how this knowledge assists in developing promotional strategies and programs.

This chapter describes the consumer decision-making process to demonstrate how marketers use this information for marketing communication decisions. In doing so, it distinguishes relevant psychological processes for each stage. Next, the chapter contrasts how the process varies for different types of consumer decision making. It then identifies the target audience options for marketing communication plans, and expresses the importance of identifying a detailed profile of the target audience.

 # LO1 Consumer Decision-Making Process

Consumer behaviour is the process and activities people experience when searching for, selecting, purchasing, using, evaluating, and disposing of products to satisfy their needs and desires. The conceptual model in Figure 3-1 is a framework for understanding the consumer decision-making process. It views the consumer as a problem solver and information processor who evaluates alternative brands and determines the degree to which they might satisfy the person's needs. We will describe what occurs at each of the five stages and demonstrate how advertising and promotion can be used to influence decision making. We also distinguish internal psychological processes that are prevalent at each stage, their influence on consumer decision making, and implications for marketing communication.

Figure 3-1 A basic model of consumer decision making

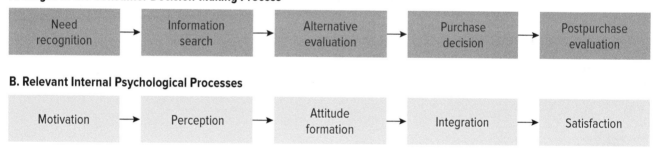

This model is a widely accepted representation of consumer decision making and is managerially useful for promotional planning purposes. Note, however, that the process is not always linear as the arrows indicate; consumers may backtrack to a previous stage as information is acquired. And there is implied continuity as postpurchase evaluation morphs into prepurchase anticipation at some point in time, which varies considerably by product category and by individual consumer. In fact, practitioners refer to the whole process as a *journey* since consumers express their thoughts and feelings at all stages across many digital and non-digital avenues leading to stronger or weaker levels of brand loyalty.[1] Mobile technology allows consumers to experience all stages anywhere and at any time across multiple advertising formats, as 65 percent bought something via online or mobile purchasing in the past month.[2]

NEED RECOGNITION

The first stage in the consumer decision-making process is **need recognition**, which occurs when the consumer perceives a need and becomes motivated to enter a decision-making process to resolve the felt need. Marketers are required to know the specific needs consumers are attempting to satisfy and how they translate into purchase criteria, since this knowledge allows them to accurately portray the need in promotional messages and place messages in an appropriate location.

Need recognition is caused by a difference between the consumer's *ideal state* and *actual state*. A discrepancy exists between what the consumer desires the situation to be like and what the situation is really like. A goal exists for the consumer, and this goal may be the attainment of a more positive situation from a neutral state. Or, the goal could be a shift from a negative situation, and the consumer wishes to be at a neutral state. A **want** is a felt need that is shaped by a person's knowledge, culture, and personality. Many advertised products satisfy consumer wants rather than their basic needs. Notice how the ad shown in Exhibit 3-1 associates its clothing product to those who desire the atmosphere of the beach.

The sources of need recognition can be internal or external, may be very simple or very complex, and arise from changes in the consumer's current and/or desired state. Advertising (i.e., external) may be used to help consumers crystallize their dissatisfaction with a currently used product. For example, the Oral B ad shown in Exhibit 3-2 helps users realize that its toothbrushes are superior. New needs arise quite simply with changes in one's financial situation, employment status, or lifestyle. For example, graduates from college or university may need a wardrobe change when starting a new professional career. Finally, the TaylorMade ad shown in Exhibit 3-3 identifies the product's improved features to support its claim as the number one driver on the market, allowing consumers to envision the end state of playing the game of golf at a higher level with improved tee shots. Need recognition is facilitated in social media with consumers seeing "wish lists," "likes," "check-ins," "bought by," and "pinned" depending on the source.[3]

Exhibit 3-1   Tommy Bahama clothing appeals to those who enjoy the beach.

Courtesy of Tommy Bahama

Exhibit 3-2   Oral B identifies reasons why consumers might be dissatisfied with their current toothbrushes in this ad.

© Oral B, Procter & Gamble

Exhibit 3-3   TaylorMade highlights the design features of its new driver.

Courtesy of TaylorMade Golf Company

CONSUMER MOTIVATION

The way a consumer perceives a purchase situation and becomes driven to resolve it will influence the remainder of the decision process. For example, one consumer may perceive the need to purchase a new watch from a functional perspective and focus on reliable, low-priced alternatives. Another consumer may see the purchase of a watch as part of a fashionable wardrobe and accessories and focus on the design and image. To better understand the reasons underlying consumer purchases, marketers extensively consider **motives**—that is, those factors that compel a consumer to take a particular action.

One approach for understanding consumer motivations is based on the classic theory of human motivation popularized by psychologist Abraham Maslow.[4] His **hierarchy of needs** theory postulates five levels of human needs, arranged in a hierarchy based on their importance. As shown in Figure 3-2, the five needs are (1) *physiological*—the basic level of primary needs for things required to sustain life, such as food, shelter, clothing, and sex; (2) *safety*—the need for security and safety from physical harm; (3) *social/love and belonging*—the desire to have satisfying relationships with others and feel a sense of love, affection, belonging, and acceptance; (4) *esteem*—the need to feel a sense of accomplishment and gain recognition, status, and respect from others; and (5) *self-actualization*—the need for self-fulfillment and a desire to realize one's own potential. For example, Columbia Sportswear Company focuses on the importance of personal protection when marketing its clothing and equipment (Exhibit 3-4).

Exhibit 3-4 Columbia shows the importance of the protection features of its outerwear.

© Columbia Sportswear

Maslow's needs hierarchy offers a framework for marketers to use in determining what needs their products satisfy. Advertising campaigns can be designed to show how a brand fulfills these needs for one or multiple segments of consumers. For example, a young single person may be attempting to satisfy social or self-esteem needs in purchasing a car, while a family with children will focus more on safety needs. The Jaguar ad in Exhibit 3-5 appears to address self-actualization. We will revisit the importance and an alternative view of motivation for marketing communication purposes in Chapter 6 when we present the topic of positioning.

Exhibit 3-5 Jaguar uses an appeal to self-actualization.

Copyright © 2012. Jaguar Land Rover North America, LLC. All Rights Reserved.

Figure 3-2 Maslow's hierarchy of needs

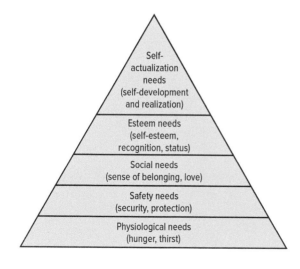

INFORMATION SEARCH

The second stage in the consumer decision-making process is *information search*. Once consumers perceive a need that can be satisfied by the purchase of a product, they begin to search for information needed to make a purchase decision. The initial search effort often consists of an attempt to scan information stored in memory to recall past experiences and/or knowledge regarding purchase alternatives.[5] This information retrieval is referred to as **internal search**. For many routine, repetitive purchases, previously acquired information that is stored in memory (such as past performance or outcomes from using a brand) is sufficient for comparing alternatives and making a choice.

If the internal search does not yield enough information, the consumer will seek additional information by an **external search**. External sources of information include:

- *Personal sources* (e.g., friends, relatives, or co-workers, face-to-face or via social media)
- *Marketer-controlled sources* (e.g., advertising, salespeople, displays, Internet)
- *Public sources* (e.g., articles in print media, reports on TV, Internet discussion boards)
- *Personal experience* (e.g., past use, actually handling, examining or testing the product)

Determining how much and which sources of external information to use involves the importance of the purchase decision, the effort needed to acquire information, the amount of relevant past experience, the degree of perceived risk associated with the purchase, and the time available. For example, the selection of a movie might entail talking to a friend (digitally or in person), checking the movie guide in the newspaper, or using a mobile app. A more complex vehicle purchase might use many information sources—perhaps a review of *Road & Track, Motor Trend,* or *Consumer Reports*; discussion with family and friends; and a dealer test-drive. The auto industry is the largest digital advertiser as two-thirds of all buyers rely on this media for their vehicle decision. Furthermore, compared to a couple of years ago, research finds that the time shopping is reduced to four weeks from five weeks, and buyers evaluate four brands versus 2.5 brands.[6] At this point in the purchase decision, the information-providing aspects of advertising are extremely important. In fact, one study concluded that Internet and non-Internet media are important for online purchases, with varying degrees depending on the level of Internet media experience and product type (e.g., utilitarian versus hedonistic). Surprisingly, those with high levels of Internet media experience thought more highly of non-Internet media sources![7]

Extensive qualitative and quantitative research commissioned by the Advertising Research Foundation (ARF) regarding digital and social media use during the consumer decision making process reported a number of findings.[8] Consumers in the information search stage are in "active shopping mode" and deliberately seek information (e.g., visit Internet sites, speak with friends, search for product reviews online), although in other stages like pre- or postpurchase, consumers are in "passive shopping mode" where they receive unsolicited information such as advertising and promotion messages or social media postings. The usage level of non-digital media information sources remains strong with the frequent use of digital information sources, and consumers do not necessarily differentiate among "paid," "owned," and "earned"—newer information sources. Finally, mobile access to digital information sources at all stages of the decision making process continues to grow.

PERCEPTION

Knowledge of how consumers acquire and use information from external sources is important in formulating communication strategies. Message and media decisions are dependent on (1) how consumers sense external information, (2) how they attend to different sources of information, (3) how this information is interpreted and given meaning, and (4) how the information is retained. These four processes are all part of **perception**, the process by which an individual receives, attends to, interprets, and stores information to create a meaningful picture of the world. Perception depends on internal factors such as a person's beliefs, experiences, needs, moods, and expectations. The perceptual process is also influenced by the characteristics of a stimulus (such as its size, colour, and intensity) and the context in which it is seen or heard. Selectivity occurs throughout the four stages of the consumer's perceptual process. Perception may be viewed as a filtering process in which internal and external factors influence what is received and how it is processed and interpreted. The sheer number and complexity of the marketing stimuli a person is exposed to in any given day requires that this filtering occur. **Selective perception** may occur within all four stages of the perceptual process, as shown in Figure 3-3.

Figure 3-3 The selective perception process

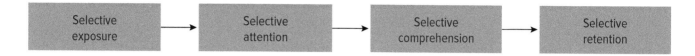

| Selective exposure | → | Selective attention | → | Selective comprehension | → | Selective retention |

Sensation   **Sensation** is the immediate, direct response of the senses (taste, smell, sight, touch, and hearing) to a stimulus such as an ad, package, brand name, point-of-purchase display, or mobile alert. Perception uses these senses to create a representation of the stimulus. Marketers plan certain marketing stimuli to achieve consumers' physiological reactions. For example, the visual elements of an ad must be designed so that consumers sense their existence. This is one reason why many TV ads start with a particular sound effect or visual movement. The ping of an email message from a favourite brand of shoes is also now used for sensation purposes.

Marketing communication with technology is facilitated at this stage. For example, Vidéotron, a Quebec telecommunications brand, installed a soundproof booth with an 85-inch HD screen and extensive multi-touch flat-screen countertops in its main downtown Montreal location. Similar units faced the exterior to interact with passersby and entice them into the store. Bell introduced similar interactive technology as part of its rebranding and delivery of comprehensive product and service information.[9]

Marketers try to increase the level of sensory input so that their advertising messages will get noticed. For example, marketers of colognes and perfumes often use strong visuals as well as scent strips to appeal to multiple senses and attract the attention of magazine readers. **Selective exposure** occurs as consumers choose whether or not to make themselves available to information. For example, a viewer of a television show may change channels or leave the room during commercial breaks. A non-user of perfume might decide not to open the scented strip to sample the aroma. Or, the smart phone user can decide to simply delete an unwanted email message from an unfamiliar brand.

Selecting Information   An individual's perceptual processes usually focus on elements of the environment that are relevant to his or her needs and tune out irrelevant stimuli. In a marketing communication context, two people may perceive the same stimuli (e.g., Intenet banner ad, sample offer) in very different ways because they select and attend to messages differently. Determinants of whether marketing communication stimuli will be attended to and how they will be interpreted include internal psychological factors such as the consumer's personality, needs, motives, expectations, and experiences.

Selective attention occurs when the consumer chooses to focus attention on certain stimuli while excluding others. In terms of advertising, promotional planners use the creative aspects of their ads to gain consumers' attention. For example, advertisers show their products with vibrant colours, such as the illuminating orange in the Tropicana ad (Exhibit 3-6). Notice that the contrasting deep green with the bright orange would also likely focus a consumer's eye on the message as a consumer turned the magazine page. Marketers also place ads in certain time slots or locations so that consumers will notice them more easily. For example, a consumer may pay more attention to a radio ad that is heard while alone at home than to one heard in the presence of friends, at work, or anywhere distractions may be present. Internet advertisers cleverly place their display ads on a page to encourage browsers to attend to their message; however, online ads have the lowest rates for gaining attention.

Exhibit 3-6 Tropicana uses colour to focus attention on orange juice.

Courtesy of PepsiCo

Interpreting the Information   The perceptual process focuses on organizing, categorizing, and interpreting the incoming information once a stimulus is attended to. This stage of the perceptual process is very individualized and is influenced by internal psychological factors. The interpretation and meaning an individual assigns to an incoming stimulus also depends in part on the nature of the stimulus. For example, many ads are objective, and their message is clear and straightforward. Other ads are more ambiguous, and their meaning is strongly influenced by the consumer's individual interpretation.

Even if the consumer does notice the advertiser's message, there is no guarantee it will be interpreted in the intended manner. Consumers may have **selective comprehension**, interpreting information on the basis of their own attitudes, beliefs, motives, and experiences. They often interpret information in a manner that supports their own position. For example, an ad that disparages a consumer's favourite brand may be seen as biased or untruthful, and its claims may not be accepted.

Retaining the Information   The final stage of the perceptual process involves the storage of the information in short-term or long-term memory. Consumers may make mental notes or focus on part of an advertising message to ensure that they will not forget, thus permitting easy retrieval during the information search stage. **Selective retention** means consumers do not remember all the information they see, hear, or read even after attending to and comprehending it. Advertisers attempt to make sure information will be retained in the consumer's memory so that it will be available when it is time to make a purchase. **Mnemonics** such as symbols, rhymes, associations, and images that assist in the learning and memory process are helpful. Energizer put pictures of its pink bunny on packages to remind consumers at the point of purchase of its creative advertising.

ALTERNATIVE EVALUATION

After acquiring information, the consumer moves to the **alternative evaluation** stage, where he or she compares the brands identified as being capable of satisfying the needs or motives that initiated the decision process. The brands identified as purchase options are referred to as the consumer's *evoked set.*

The evoked set is generally only a subset of all the brands of which the consumer is aware. The consumer reduces the number of brands to be reviewed during the alternative evaluation stage to a manageable level. The exact size of the evoked set varies from one consumer to another and depends on such factors as the importance of the purchase and the amount of time and energy the consumer wants to spend comparing alternatives.

The goal of most advertising and promotional strategies is to increase the likelihood that a brand will be included in the consumer's evoked set and considered during alternative evaluation. Marketers of strong or existing brands use advertising as a reminder to maintain *awareness* among consumers so that their brands are part of the evoked set of their target audiences. The ad in Exhibit 3-7 is an example of a brand with this objective. Marketers of new brands or those with a low market share need to gain awareness among consumers and break into their evoked sets.

Exhibit 3-7   L'Oréal's ads help contribute to high levels of awareness.

Liya Kebede @ Viva Paris for L'Oreal Paris

Once consumers have identified an evoked set and have a list of alternatives, they evaluate the brands by comparing the choice alternatives on specific and important criteria. **Evaluative criteria** are the attributes of a product that are used to compare different alternatives which can be objective or subjective. For example, in buying an automobile, consumers use objective attributes such as price, warranty, and fuel economy as well as subjective attributes such as image or styling.

Products are *bundles of attributes* and consumers also tend to think about products in terms of their consequences or *bundles of benefits*. Consequences are specific events or outcomes that consumers experience when they purchase and/or consume a product. **Functional benefits** are concrete outcomes of product usage that are tangible and objectively related to the purpose of the product. For example, a product placement message during *Canada's Amazing Race* stated that the Chevrolet Sonic subcompact car featured 10 air bags; many air bags in a small car exhibit functional utility of enhanced injury prevention for consumers who are in the market for buying a new small vehicle. **Performance benefits** are less tangible and more subjective product usage outcomes based on how the product attributes abstractly affect a consumer. For example, a personal care product may claim that it makes one more beautiful or handsome. **Experiential benefits** are related to how a product makes the consumer feel while consuming the product. These emotions can be psychologically based, such as feelings of happiness or joy which we see in car ads that show how consumers enjoy driving a particular brand on an open stretch of the highway, or socially based, such as feelings of pride which we also see in car ads that illustrate a driver passing by an admiring pedestrian.

Marketers distinguish between product attributes and benefits, because the importance and meaning consumers assign to an attribute are usually determined by its consequences for them. Moreover, advertisers communicate the link between a particular attribute and a benefit to enhance consumers' understanding. For example, the Pennzoil ad in Exhibit 3-8 focuses on how the motor oil protects the engine when driving fast. Product attributes and the benefits consumers think they will experience from a brand are very important, for they are often the basis on which consumers form attitudes and decide among their choice alternatives. Alternative evaluation is facilitated in social media with consumers seeing reviews, recommendations, discussion forum comments, blog posts, or tweets, and other communications depending on the nature of the social media.[10]

Marketing communication with technology is facilitated at this stage. For example, Wind Mobile implemented Microsoft's Surface technology with touch-screen features so that consumers can look through the details of its devices and service plans. Each unit amounted to $15,000, with newer versions pegged at half that cost, paving the way for much more efficient and wider distribution in the coming few years. Wall-mounted screens summarize consumer comments, reinforcing its "Power of Conversation" positioning. [11]

Exhibit 3-8 Pennzoil's ad conveys the engine protection of its motor oil.

© Pennzoil

ATTITUDES

Attitudes are learned predispositions to respond to an object, and represent one of the most heavily studied concepts in consumer behaviour.[12] Other perspectives view attitudes as a summary construct that represents an individual's overall feelings toward or evaluation of an object.[13] Consumers hold attitudes toward a variety of objects that are important to marketers, including individuals (endorsers like Sidney Crosby), brands (Cheerios), companies (Microsoft), product categories (beef, pork, tuna), retail stores (The Bay, Sears), or even advertisements.

Attitudes are important to marketers because they theoretically summarize a consumer's evaluation of an object (or brand or company) and represent positive or negative feelings and behavioural tendencies. Marketers' keen interest in attitudes is based on the assumption that they are related to consumers' purchase behaviour. Considerable evidence supports the basic assumption of a relationship between attitudes and behaviour.[14] The attitude–behaviour link does not always hold since other factors can affect behaviour.[15] Advertising and promotion are used to create favourable attitudes toward new products/ services or brands, reinforce existing favourable attitudes, and/or change negative attitudes. IMC Perspective 3-1 illustrates how advertising influences attitudes.

IMC PERSPECTIVE 3-1

WHAT WOMEN WANT IN ADVERTISING

What drives women away from a brand? According to one industry study, a brand should do the following if it wants to drive away half the population: avoid nutritional information on food labels, institute questionable business ethics, not practise what it preaches, ignore women as consumers, and objectify them as women. Consistent with these findings is a result that says women value health and wellness, relationships, morals and ethics, helping others, and fulfillment. Moreover, brand loyalty is driven by products that offer good value, meet expectations, make life easier, ensure family happiness, and positively affect well-being. When targeting

© Big Cheese Photo/SuperStock

women, advertisers look to other data and find that 56 percent of women visited YouTube in the past week. Of the 3.8 million Canadian Pinterest users, 66 percent of them are women. Women are more social on Facebook and are 18 percent more likely to follow a brand in that social media vehicle. Women tend to respond to emotional ads compared to men, who like light-hearted and humorous ads.

Given the above, we arrive at a key question for Dove's "Campaign for Real Beauty" as it hit its 10-year anniversary: Did the campaign change the way beauty product marketers advertise to women? At the time of the campaign's launch in 2004, many saw the messages as a radical departure for a personal care brand to focus on a different view of beauty that appeared contrary to stereotypical images of women in ads. The first print campaign showed images of everyday women, not models, with questions asking, "Wrinkled or wonderful?" or "Fat or fab?" to go along with a tick box to answer. A second print campaign supported the initial one with a spotlight on real women in the ads. The subsequent "Evolution" video captured the metamorphosis a model experiences for an advertising photo shot as well as the digital touch-ups thereafter, while the "Onslaught" video showed the sexualized advertising a young girl will experience as she matures. Support for the ads included workshops and activities to improve women's self-esteem.

Dove's implied message of natural beauty received numerous awards and seemed to resonate with women during the first six years. Experts cite many campaigns of the past five to seven years that show women portrayed more realistically and communicated to more truthfully. On the other hand, other experts believe that many decades of persistent social norms are difficult to change, and that many examples of showing women models in ads remain because of self-perception concerns. Dove moved the campaign in a different direction with tasks that challenged women to consider their self-perception. The "Sketches" video compared the drawings of an artist from a self-description versus from a friend's description. The "Patches" video revealed women's reaction after they discovered the beauty patch they had worn was a placebo, as many had thought the patch did in fact make them more beautiful. The "Choose Beautiful" video showed the women deciding which door to enter: beautiful or average.

These more recent videos raise another question. Do women approve of the campaign, or do aspects of the message and media go against what women want in advertising? Critics suggest that these newer messages are patronizing and manipulative, and have moved away from the original intent. Additionally, the message tone is condescending since it implies that women need to rise above the daily scrutiny of their appearance. One critic suggested the "Patches" video portrayed the women as victims for the story to work. Responding to the critics, Dove spokespersons highlight the 100 million views of the "Patches" video, reminding everyone that Dove continually listens to its customers, and that the company intended to spark a debate about women's relationship with beauty with the recent videos. Furthermore, they believed that if they did the right thing in their messaging, people would support the idea and good business results would emerge. However, from 2004 to 2013, Dove's global market share rose from 1.9 percent to 2.1 percent according to Euromonitor.

Sources: Susan Krashinsky, "Dove's Beauty Campaign," *Globe and Mail*, April 9. 2015; Kristin Laird, "The Real Impact of Real Beauty," *Marketing Magazine*, September 2014, pp. 20–23; Jennifer Horn, "Women by the Numbers," *Strategy*, November 2014, p. 9; "Understanding Women," *Strategy*, May 2014, p. 43.

Questions:

1. Is the criticism of the "Campaign for Real Beauty" warranted?
2. Has the "Campaign for Real Beauty" run its course and Dove should reconsider its message?

PURCHASE DECISION

At some point in the buying process, the consumer must stop searching for and evaluating information about alternative brands in the evoked set and make a *purchase decision*. As an outcome of the alternative evaluation stage, the consumer may develop a **purchase intention** or predisposition to buy a certain brand. Purchase intentions are generally based on a matching of purchase motives with attributes or characteristics of brands under consideration. Their formation involves many of the personal subprocesses discussed in this chapter, including motivation, perception, and attitude formation.

A purchase decision is not the same as an actual purchase. Once a consumer chooses which brand to buy, he or she must still implement the decision and make the actual purchase. Additional decisions may be needed, such as when to buy, where to buy, and how much money to spend. Often, there is a time delay between the formation of a purchase intention or decision and the actual purchase, particularly for highly involved and complex purchases such as automobiles, personal computers, and consumer durables. Marketing communication with technology assists in the purchase decision. For example, Adidas implemented a touch-screen interface where consumers can view all of its 8,000-plus shoes. Facial recognition technology customizes the display for males or females, allowing consumers a 3D view of their options. Links to social media provide access to what others thought or felt about the particular model. And if consumers find something they like, the whole system facilitates the transaction much like shopping online at home.[16]

For nondurable products such as consumer packaged goods, the time between the decision and the actual purchase may be short, as it occurs while in the store or while planning at home. Before leaving home, the consumer may make a shopping list that includes specific brand names because the consumer has developed **brand loyalty**—a preference for a particular brand that results in its repeated purchase. In this situation, marketers strive to maintain brand loyalty with reminder advertising to keep their brand names in front of consumers, prominent shelf positions and displays in stores, and periodic promotions to deter consumers from switching brands. Competitors also use many techniques to encourage consumers to try their brands and disrupt the loyalty of non-customers. In sum, marketers in many different product categories must continually battle to maintain their loyal consumers while replacing those who switch brands. A purchase decision is facilitated in social media with consumers seeing price comparison information, experiencing group purchases, reacting to "buy now" messages, and making use of promotions (e.g., coupons).[17]

INTEGRATION PROCESSES

A key part of the purchase decision stage is the way consumers combine information about the characteristics of brands. **Integration processes** are the way product knowledge, meanings, and beliefs are combined to evaluate two or more alternatives.[18] Analysis of the integration process focuses on the different types of *decision rules* or strategies consumers use to decide among purchase alternatives.

Consumers often make purchase selections by using formal integration strategies or decision rules that require examination and comparison of alternatives on specific attributes. This process involves a very deliberate evaluation of the alternatives, attribute by attribute. When consumers apply such formal decision rules, marketers need to know which attributes are being considered so as to provide the information the consumers require.

Sometimes consumers make their purchase decisions using more simplified decision rules known as **heuristics**. Heuristics are easy to use and are highly adaptive to specific environmental situations (such as a retail store). For familiar products that are purchased frequently, consumers may use price-based heuristics (buy the least expensive brand) or promotion-based heuristics (choose the brand for a price reduction through a coupon, rebate, or special deal).

One type of heuristic is the **affect referral decision rule**,[19] in which consumers make a selection on the basis of an overall impression or summary evaluation of the alternatives under consideration. This decision rule suggests that consumers have affective impressions of brands stored in memory that can be accessed at the time of purchase. Marketers selling familiar and popular brands may appeal to an affect referral rule by stressing overall affective feelings or impressions about their products. Market leaders, whose products enjoy strong overall brand images, often use ads that promote the brand as the best overall (Exhibit 3-9).

POSTPURCHASE EVALUATION

The consumer decision process does not end with the purchase. After consumption, the consumer assesses the level of performance of the product or service. The postpurchase evaluation process is important because the feedback acquired from actual use of a product will influence the likelihood of future purchases. Positive performance means the brand is retained in the evoked set and increases the likelihood it will be purchased again. Unfavourable outcomes may lead the consumer to form negative attitudes toward the brand, lessening the likelihood it will be purchased again or even eliminating it from the consumer's evoked set.

Exhibit 3-9   Market leaders such as Gatorade can appeal to consumer affect.

Courtesy of Gatorade, Inc.

Consumers explore a number of activities during the postpurchase evaluation process. They may seek out reassurance and opinions from others to confirm the wisdom of their purchase decision, lower their attitudes or opinions of the unchosen alternative, deny or distort any information that does not support the choice they made, or look for information that does support their choice. An important source of supportive information is advertising; consumers tend to be more attentive to advertising for the brand they have chosen.[20] Thus, it may be important for companies to advertise to reinforce consumer decisions to purchase their brands.

SATISFACTION

The most significant psychological concept during the postpurchase evaluation process is satisfaction. A leading expert in satisfaction research defined **satisfaction** as a judgment that consumers make with respect to the pleasurable level of consumption-related fulfillment.[21] The notion of fulfillment implies that a consumer's goal has been achieved (i.e., needs met), and that the fulfillment is "judged with reference to a standard." Thus, consumers make a comparison between the consumption outcome and another referent.

Consumers can make many comparisons. One is to compare the level of product performance to the expectations of the product that consumers had prior to purchase. Satisfaction can occur when the consumer's expectations are either met or exceeded, whereas dissatisfaction results when performance is below expectations. Consumers can also compare the product performance to an absolute standard of quality to perceive satisfaction or dissatisfaction.

Another aspect of satisfaction is **cognitive dissonance**, a feeling of psychological tension or postpurchase doubt that a consumer experiences after making a difficult purchase choice. Dissonance is more likely to occur in important decisions where the consumer must choose among close alternatives (especially if the unchosen alternative has unique or desirable features that the selected alternative does not have).

Marketers must recognize the importance of the postpurchase evaluation stage. Dissatisfied consumers not only are unlikely to repurchase the marketer's product but also may spread negative word-of-mouth information that deters others from purchasing the product or service. The best guarantee of favourable postpurchase evaluations is to provide consumers with a quality product or service that always meets their expectations. Marketers must be sure their advertising and other forms of promotion do not create unreasonable expectations their products cannot meet.

Marketers understand that postpurchase communication is important. Companies send follow-up letters or emails and brochures to reassure buyers and reinforce the wisdom of their decision. Companies use toll-free numbers, websites, and social media to allow for consumer feedback. Marketers also offer liberal return and refund policies and extended warranties and guarantees to ensure customer satisfaction.

Variations in Consumer Decision Making

We have reviewed the consumer decision-making process with respect to individual purchases. However, variations in this process arise depending upon the type of purchase and whether the individual is making the decision with other people. We now contrast these two variations in the consumer decision-making process and the effects on marketing communication.

TYPES OF DECISION MAKING

The general model of consumer decision making is a useful description; however, consumers do not always experience all five steps of the purchase decision process or proceed in the sequence presented. They may minimize or even skip one or more stages if they have previous experience in purchasing the product or service, or if the decision is of low personal, social, or economic significance. To develop effective promotional decisions, marketers need to understand the type of problem-solving processes their target consumers use to make purchase decisions.[22]

Many purchase decisions consumers make are based on a habit known as **routine problem solving** or routine response behaviour. For many low-priced, frequently purchased products, the decision process consists of little more than recognizing the need, performing a quick internal search, and making the purchase. The consumer spends little or no effort on external search or alternative evaluation.

Marketers of products characterized by a routine response purchase process want consumers to follow a routine choice process and continue to purchase their products. These marketers use relevant IMC tools to maintain high levels of brand awareness and positive brand attitude. Alternatively, marketers of new brands or those with a low market share face a different challenge. They must find ways to disrupt consumers' routine choice processes and get them to consider their brand by using IMC tools that encourage consumers to reconsider their habit or routine choice and switch brands. The Sun-Rype ad in Exhibit 3-10 tries this approach.

A more complicated decision-making process occurs when consumers have limited experience in purchasing a particular product or service and little or no knowledge of the brands available and/or the criteria to use in making a purchase decision. Consumers learn what attributes or criteria should be used in making a purchase decision and how the alternatives perform on these dimensions. For products or services characterized by **limited problem solving** or **extended problem solving**, marketers should make information available that will help consumers make a decision. Advertising that provides consumers with detailed information about a brand and how it can satisfy their purchase motives and goals is important.

Exhibit 3-10   The visual in Sun-Rype's ad invites consumers to reconsider their beverage choice.

It's like nectar of the gods. Assuming you worship raspberries.

© Sun-Rype Products Ltd.

Marketers may also want to give consumers information through other ways (e.g., displays, brochures, websites).

GROUP DECISION MAKING

A group is defined as "two or more individuals who share a set of norms, values, or beliefs and have certain implicitly or explicitly defined relationships to one another such that their behavior is interdependent."[23] Groups are one of the primary factors influencing learning and socialization, and group situations constitute many of our purchase decisions. For example, a woman's purchase of a dress for a party might be influenced by the type of party and who is attending.

A **reference group** is "a group whose presumed perspectives or values are being used by an individual as the basis for his or her judgments, opinions, and actions." Consumers use reference groups as a guide to specific behaviours, even when the groups are not present.[24] In the party example, peers—although not present—provided a standard of dress that referred the woman to her clothing selection. Likewise, friends, family, and co-workers, or even a group to which she aspires, may serve as referents, and consumption patterns will typically conform to the expectations of the groups that are most important to her.

Marketers use reference group influences in developing advertisements and promotional strategies; an *aspirational* reference group is a group to which we might like to belong, while a *disassociative* group is a group to which we do not wish to belong. Mattel presented an alternative view of Barbie in the global "Be Super" campaign that recognized the "super powers" in all girls. For the Canadian launch, girls signed up online to be on the "Super Squad" by demonstrating their super powers like kindness, creativity, or self-expression. Messaging encouraged "Super Squad" girls to be leaders by showing their heroism on a daily basis, and for other girls to emulate them. As part of this aspirational reference group development, Mattel donated $15,000 to four girl groups.[25]

Furthermore, the group may be involved more directly than just as a referent. Family members serve as referents to each other, or are involved in the purchase decision process—acting as an individual buying unit. The ad in Exhibit 3-11 shows how a parent may see the Golf Sportwagon as meeting the needs of all family members during the purchase of a new vehicle. As shown in Figure 3-4, family members can assume a variety of roles in the decision-making process.[26] There can be group interaction at every stage of the consumer decision-making process since members take on many roles throughout the process.

Exhibit 3-11 The Golf Sportwagon ad shows how all family members' needs may be fulfilled with its purchase.

© Volkswagen Canada

Figure 3-4   Roles in the family decision-making process

The initiator. The person responsible for initiating the purchase decision process; for example, the mother who determines she needs a new car.

The information provider. The individual responsible for gathering information to be used in making the decision; for example, the teenage car buff who knows where to find product information in specific magazines or collects it from dealers.

The influencer. The person who exerts influence as to what criteria will be used in the selection process. All members of the family may be involved. The mother may have her criteria, whereas others may each have their own input.

The decision maker(s). That person(s) who actually makes the decision. In our example, it may be the mother alone or in combination with another family member.

The purchasing agent. That individual who performs the physical act of making the purchase. In the case of a car, a couple may decide to choose it together and sign the purchase agreement.

The consumer. The actual user of the product. In the case of a family car, all family members are consumers. For a private car, only the mother might be the consumer.

Each role has implications for marketers. First, the advertiser must determine who is responsible for the roles in the decision-making process so that messages can be targeted at that person (or those people) and placed in the most appropriate and effective media. Second, understanding the decision-making process and the use of information by individual family members is critical to the design of messages and choice of promotional program elements. In general, to create an effective promotional program, a marketer must have an overall understanding of how the decision process works and the role that each group member plays. The ad in Exhibit 3-12 appeals to a gift-giver looking to buy a present for Mother's Day, a birthday, or an anniversary.

Exhibit 3-12   Roots targets the buyer in this ad for its handbags.

© Roots

Target Audience Decision

We reviewed the consumer decision-making process since marketers need to understand the behaviour they are attempting to influence through their promotional plans. Marketers try to understand consumers thoroughly since an IMC plan, IMC program (e.g., advertising campaign), or ad is directed to a target audience. Selection of a single target audience or multiple target audiences is a primary decision prior to other communication decisions such as message, media, or IMC tool, and the decision is derived from the segmentation and target market decisions of the marketing plan. In this section, we therefore review the marketing planning process to understand the context of this important promotional decision. Next, we summarize approaches for segmentation that are used for both target market and target audience selection, and then review the promotional planning process. Finally, we describe an approach for identifying options for the target audience decision.

MARKETING PLANNING PROCESS

The process of developing marketing and promotion decisions is summarized in Figure 3-5. The target market is an important focus of marketing effort; it is based on an extensive situation analysis and it provides direction for all marketing decisions, including the promotion decisions identified in Chapter 1. The **target market** is the group of consumers toward which an overall marketing program is directed. This decision is part of three steps: segment the market, select a target market, and determine the market positioning strategy. The marketing planner identifies the specific needs of groups of people (i.e., segments), selects one or more of these segments as a target, configures a positioning strategy for the selected market segment, and develops a marketing program.

Figure 3-5   Marketing and promotions process model

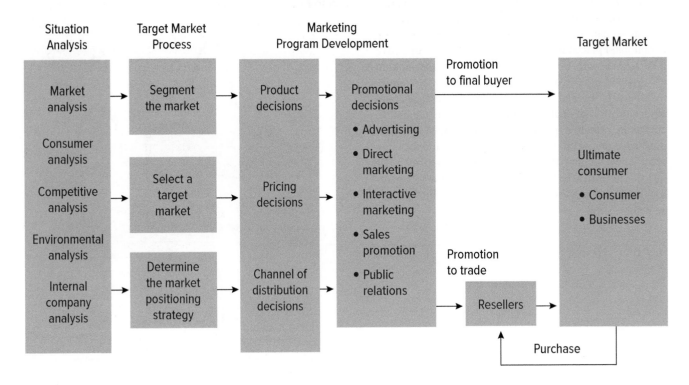

This approach involving segmentation is applicable in marketing for a number of reasons, including changes in the market (consumers are diverse in their needs, attitudes, and lifestyles); increased use of segmentation by competitors; and the fact that managers are trained in segmentation and realize the advantages associated with this strategy. Perhaps the best explanation comes back to the premise that marketing planners must understand consumers as much as possible to design marketing programs that meet their consumers' needs most effectively, as is demonstrated in IMC Perspective 3-2 regarding marketing to millennials. We now turn to the many ways in which to segment a market for decision making.

IMC PERSPECTIVE 3-2

TARGETING MILLENNIALS

Those born from 1980 to 2000 are often referred to as millennials, and marketing planners and marketing communication planners look to target this group with specific marketing strategies or marketing communication strategies. Research indicates that, compared to older generational cohorts (baby boomers, Generation X), millennials are more likely to shop for consumer goods, try new products, pay a premium for unique products, see brand as less important, and avoid brands that have a poor environmental reputation. However, one millennial who works in advertising suggests that "Millennials are more like everyone else than most marketers are willing to talk about," and questions whether this group is distinctly unique for targeting purposes. Nevertheless, a number of companies and brands attempt to sway this group with varying degrees of success, as shown with Birks and Diageo Canada.

©svetikd/iStock

Founded in 1879, Birks is a jewellery retailer that included over 200 stores at one time and retracted to 50 stores after a bankruptcy episode. Trying to rejuvenate itself and to retain its luxury image, the brand faced considerable competition from the introduction of luxury brands across many different product categories. A large portion of Birks' sales are for gifts which cut across many product categories, so the retailer now faces the likes of Saks and Nordstrom in addition to its house brand going up against Burberry, Prada, and Louis Vuitton. In short, the Birks brand no longer retained its exclusivity as a luxury brand.

In response, part of Birks' strategy to reclaim its lustre is to target a younger demographic in millennials, even though this group considered Birks as being too expensive and only 25 percent enjoyed buying jewellery compared to close to 50 percent for electronics. A primary first step involved a clearer placement of the Birks brand of jewellery in the store with a marketing communication emphasis of excellence and quality. Birks also extensively communicated that it sourced all its diamonds from Canadian mines, a key attribute it considered important to millennials. Although, one-third of Birks' sales are Rolex, management sought to increase the Birks branded jewellery percentage from 17 percent to 25 percent. The design division of Sid Lee marketing communication agency moved the in-store style away from a traditional jewellery store to one that is more appealing to a younger consumer, employing a modern design in which consumers can move about displays more enjoyably. Finally, the Birks brand took a stronger Canadian message both here and in its American division. It associated the Birks brand with Canadian imagery and identified its exclusivity at its stores; results from the United States indicated strong acceptance of this messaging.

The Canadian division of Diageo, a world-wide liquor producer, looks to millennials for spirited growth with its own Canadian advertising, contrary to other multinationals that repurpose their international messages and campaigns. The company markets 50 brands with 1,600 stock keeping units (SKUs) and regularly promotes half of the brands with active marketing communication campaigns. The cider, cooler, and refreshment category in Canada expanded by 10 percent in 2015, and Diageo looked at that as one avenue for further growth. For example, it brought the popular Jeremiah Weed Spiked Ice Tea up from the United States and promoted it with a grassroots campaign featuring an old-school van and brand reps handing out cool swag (e.g., Frisbees, T-shirts, etc.). Noting that Canadians switch brands in this category quite often, Diageo tried to keep the launch low key and avoid mass media to build awareness yet maintain a cool image with this new beverage offering, a key challenge to satisfying discerning millennials.

Sources: Maggie Windsor Gross, "On Being a Dinner-Date-Worthy Brand," *Strategy*, November 2014, p. 73; Megan Haynes, "Birks Regains Its Lustre," *Strategy*, December 2014, p. 14; Harmeet Singh, "Diageo's Domestic Plan, *Strategy*, July 2015, p. 15.

Question:

1. Do you agree that targeting millennials is a good decision for the two brands described?

SEGMENTATION VARIABLES

Figure 3-6 shows five approaches for segmentation—geographic, demographic, socioeconomic, psychographic, and behaviour—with each of these main dimensions averaging five variables. In total, all 25 variables can be applied for both marketing and marketing communication decisions, and both types of planners can use one or any combination of the variables for their respective decision-making. A marketing planner may begin to segment the market on the basis of benefits sought and then examine demographics and psychographic characteristics to describe and further understand this group. Applying these variables to the planning for ski boots, benefits may be sought depending on the level of skiing (low to high quality on responsiveness due to flexibility of the boot's plastic). The marketing planner might then consider age as an additional relevant demographic (younger beginners to older beginners) and add varying social classes (lower class to upper class). All this information will be combined to provide a complete profile of the skier.

Figure 3-6   Examples of market segmentation variables

Main Dimension	Segmentation Variables	Typical Breakdowns
Geographic	Region	West, Central, East
	City size	Under 10,000; 10,000–24,999; 25,000–49,999; 50,000–99,999; 100,000–249,999; 250,000–499,999; 500,000–999,999; 1,000,000 or more
	Metropolitan area	Census Metropolitan Area (CMA); etc.
	Density	Urban; suburban; small town; rural
Demographic	Gender	Male; female
	Age	Under 6 yrs; 6–11 yrs; 12–17 yrs; 18–24 yrs; 25–34 yrs; 35–44 yrs; 45–54 yrs; 55–64 yrs; 65–74 yrs; 75 yrs plus
	Race	Asian; Black; Hispanic; Indian; White/Caucasian; etc.
	Life stage	Infant; preschool; child; youth; collegiate; adult; senior
	Birth era	Baby boomer (1949–1964); Generation X (1965–1976); baby boomlet/Generation Y (1977–present)
	Household size	1; 2; 3–4; 5 or more
	Residence tenure	Own home; rent home
	Marital status	Never married; married; separated; divorced; widowed
Socioeconomic	Income	<$15,000; $15,000–$24,999; $25,000–$34,999; $35,000–$49,999; $50,000–$74,999; $75,000+
	Education	Some high school or less; high school graduate; some college or university; university/college graduate; etc.
	Occupation	Managerial and professional specialty; technical, sales, and administrative support; service; farming, forestry, and fishing; etc.
Psychographic	Values	Actualizers; fulfilleds; achievers; experiencers; believers; strivers; makers; strugglers
	Lifestyle	Activities, interests, opinions
	Personality	Gregarious; compulsive; introverted; aggressive; ambitious; etc.
	Culture	Ethnic; social
	Social class	Low middle class; upper middle class; etc.
Behaviour	Brand loyalty	Completely loyal; partially loyal; not loyal
	User status	Non-user; ex-user; first-time user; regular user
	Usage rate	Light user; medium user; heavy user
	Situation	Usage situation; purchase situation
	Benefits sought	Quality; service; price/value; convenience; prestige

As the skiing example implies, the more a marketing planner segments the market, the more precise is their understanding of it. But the more the market becomes divided, the fewer consumers there are in each segment. How far should one go in the segmentation process? An accurate answer to this question with the right kind of marketing strategy distinguishes good marketing decision makers. Another issue arises as to which segmentation variable is used first and which others are used as additional variables. A promotional planner, such as one working in an ad agency, faces similar questions when deciding upon an advertising program or other marketing communication activity, and relies on the same segmentation variables. We now identify these segmentation variables that are applicable for marketing strategy planners and marketing communication planners as they try to make effective decisions.

Geographic Segmentation   In the **geographic segmentation** approach, markets are divided into different geographic units. These units may include nations, provinces, states, counties, or even neighbourhoods. Consumers often have different buying habits depending on where they reside. To address this, advertisers use different IMC tools or advertising messages. Internet display ads are delivered geographically since the technology senses the location of the user. Out-of-home messaging relies extensively on geographic placements. Brands often face different penetration levels across markets and alter their sales promotions accordingly to stimulate trial purchases.

Demographic Segmentation   Dividing the market on the basis of a demographic variable such as gender, age, marital status, and household size is called **demographic segmentation**. Related variables that are socioeconomic such as income, education, and occupation are often viewed as being very similar to demographic. While demographic segmentation is a common method, it is important to note that other factors may be the underlying basis for homogeneity and/or consumer behaviour. The astute marketer will identify additional approaches for segmenting and will recognize the limitations of demographics. For example, one critique concluded that the use of birth era in marketing is exploitative, misleading, and condescending since it groups so many disparate people into one group; and this critique may be relevant for other demographic segmentation variables as well. Interestingly, the very definition of Generation X is inaccurate to a degree. The start of birth era as a segmentation variable originated with the fictional novel *Generation X,* which described the angst of those who were born in the late 1950s and early 1960s (final stage of baby boomers).[27] For now we kept it at the collective misbelief in Figure 3-6, but if a marketing or promotional planner intends to use a demographic variable, it is generally suggested to use it with other variables.

Psychographic Segmentation   Dividing the market on the basis of values and lifestyle, personality, culture, and social class is referred to as **psychographic segmentation**. Each of these variables can be the basis for segmentation.

Values and Lifestyle   The determination of lifestyles is usually based on an analysis of the activities, interests, and opinions (AIOs) of consumers that are obtained via surveys. These lifestyles are then correlated with the consumers' product, brand, and/or media usage. Lifestyle may be the best discriminator between use and non-use for many goods or services. Harley-Davidson motorcycles demonstrated this with a campaign that showed its customer base consists of virtually every conceivable variable. Its Facebook page boasts over 3 million fans, many of whom are younger and not the stereotypical boomer reliving his or her glory. The main discerning characteristic is the lifestyle of enjoying motorcycle riding.[28] As another example, notice how the ad for Fluevog in Exhibit 3-13 reflects the life of the target audience member. Taken from another perspective, our activities, interests, and opinions are reflective of our individual values. We highlight two major approaches that have developed these forms of segmentation with proprietary research methods.

Psychographic segmentation occurred with the advent of the values and lifestyles (VALS) program now offered by Strategic Business Insights. Developed in the late 1970s and refined a decade later, VALS is a method for applying segmentation based on values. The underlying premise of VALS is that psychological traits and demographics are

Exhibit 3-13   The target audience's lifestyle is reflected in this Fluevog ad.

UNIQUE SOLES
FOR
UNIQUE SOULS

SINCE 1970

JOHN FLUEVOG ♥ OTTAWA
61 WILLIAM ST (BY BEAVERTAILS IN BYWARD MARKET)   613·244·1970
FLUEVOG.COM

© John Fluevog Shoes

better predictors of behaviour than demographics alone. The VALS approach combines an estimate of the resources the consumer can draw on (education, income, health, energy level, self-confidence, and degree of consumerism) along with their motivation. This is used to identify eight different types of people to understand their consumption behaviour. This U.S. invention is now adapted to other cultures such as Japan, the United Kingdom, and Latin America.

PRIZM$_{NE}$, developed by Claritas, is another American lifestyle segmentation approach that has been adapted for the Canadian market through the two divisions of the research firm Environics (Research Group & Analytics). PRIZM C2 associates the lifestyle questions asked on the survey with demographic data from the federal government's census. The analysis provides 66 different lifestyle segments and 18 social groups based on whether the respondent is a pre-boomer, boomer, or post-boomer. PRIZM C2 claims that the segmentation system is useful for communication decisions like target audience profiling and media planning, and for many other marketing strategy decisions for virtually all industries. The data from the different lifestyle segments can also be aligned with other data sources such as media consumption and geography to allow more precise targeting for marketing decisions.

Personality   Borrowing from psychological theory, we are interested in consumers' personality traits—the relatively enduring characteristics of one's personality that lead people to respond in a reasonably consistent manner. Characteristics like social orientation (introvert versus extrovert), innovativeness (degree a person likes to try new things), materialism (emphasis placed on product ownership), and self-consciousness (projection of personal image to others) are examples of personality traits used to describe a group of consumers more precisely.[29] Notice how the ad for a pair of John Fluevog shoes in Exhibit 3-13 appeals to potential consumers who view themselves as unique individuals.

Culture   The broadest and most abstract of the external factors that influence consumer behaviour is **culture**, or the complexity of learned meanings, values, norms, and customs shared by members of a society. Cultural norms and values offer direction and guidance to members of a society in all aspects of their lives, including their consumption behaviour. Marketers must also be aware of changes that may be occurring in a particular culture since it could be the basis for effective segmentation.

While marketers recognize that culture exerts a demonstrable influence on consumers, they often find it difficult to respond to cultural differences in different markets. The subtleties of unique cultures are often difficult to understand and appreciate, but marketers must consider the cultural context in which consumer purchase decisions are made and adapt their advertising and promotional programs accordingly. For instance, Nissan devoted a sizable portion of its advertising budget to South Asians when its agency discovered that a car purchase represented an important first step for this group when arriving in Canada. The message concentrated on the in-vehicle technology and all-wheel-drive systems and reached consumers via TV, digital media, and social media to ensure strong top-of-mind awareness. In contrast to this approach, Rogers historically split its advertising resources across "mainstream" and "multicultural" media; however, it considered greater collaboration or integration as the notion of groups of different cultures appeared less relevant. [30] These examples show the need for good research for promotional decision making as cultural effects have varying importance depending on the product category.

Within a given culture are generally found smaller groups or segments whose beliefs, values, norms, and patterns of behaviour set them apart from the larger cultural mainstream. These **subcultures** may be based on age, geographic, religious, racial, and/or ethnic differences. A number of subcultures exist within Canada. These racial/ethnic subcultures are important to marketers because of their size, growth, purchasing power, and distinct purchasing patterns. Other types of subcultures are also targeted through promotional communication. For example, Print Measurement Bureau and other data showed Black consumers spending more on phone plans and beauty and personal care products, and being associated with faith-based organizations at higher levels. A factor complicating the development of specific advertising messages for this consumer group rested on the point that many Black consumers speak English, thereby limiting the perceived need for media organizations to create unique vehicles for customized reach. Additionally, experts believe that in reality a number of different Black consumer groups exist, rather than simply one. They cite differences among those from the Caribbean or from Africa, and those who have historical ties to Canada spanning three or four generations.[31]

Social Class   Virtually all societies exhibit a form of stratification whereby individuals can be assigned to a specific social category on the basis of criteria important to members of that society. **Social class** refers to relatively homogeneous divisions in a society into which people sharing similar lifestyles, values, norms, interests, and behaviours can be grouped. While a number of methods for determining social class exist, class structures in Canada are usually based on occupational status, educational attainment, and income. For example, sociologists generally agree there are three broad levels of social classes in North America: the upper (14 percent), middle (70 percent), and lower (16 percent) classes.[32]

Social class is an important concept to marketers, since consumers within each social stratum often have similar values, lifestyles, and buying behaviour. Thus, the social class groups provide a natural basis for market segmentation. Consumers in the different social classes differ in the degree to which they use products and services and in their leisure activities, shopping patterns, and media habits. Marketers respond to these differences through their products and service offerings, the media strategies they use to reach different social classes, and the types of advertising messages they develop. The ad in Exhibit 3-14 shows how a product attempts to appeal to the upper class in both copy and illustration.

Behaviouristic Segmentation   Dividing consumers into groups according to different actions is known as **behaviouristic segmentation**. These actions are measurable and generally observable from a research standpoint. The consumer behaviour that is most critical includes brand loyalty, user status, usage rate, situation, and benefit sought.

Loyalty   The degree of loyalty to the brand is a variable used considerably in marketing as programs are developed to retain current customers or attract consumers who purchase other brands. Loyalty status is often combined with demographic and/or psychographic criteria to develop profiles of audiences for specific communication. We will have more to say on this idea, because it is a critical variable in designing promotional messages. Its importance is easily seen; current brand users obviously are aware of the brand and have considerably stronger product knowledge, and they have some regular or irregular interaction with the brand. For example, loyal users of Nike shoes might be more likely to look at the Nike website to see the latest brands.

User Status   In the case of usage, the marketer assumes that non-purchasers of a brand or product who have the same characteristics as purchasers hold greater potential for adoption than non-users with different characteristics. A profile (demographic or psychographic) of the user is developed, which serves as the basis for promotional strategies designed to attract new users. For example, teenagers share certain similarities in their consumption behaviours. Those who do not currently own, say, a smart phone are more likely to be potential buyers than people in other age groups. In this case, the new users may view this purchase decision as a new experience requiring comparison shopping with limited problem-solving activities and are therefore more involved while reading ads or looking at websites or talking to friends online.

Another factor related to the previous two concerns how much of a product category is consumed. Most product categories and most consumers can be classified along the lines of light, medium, or heavy usage. With these groups in mind, and demographic or psychographic variables, advertisers can direct messages more appropriately. For example, men tend to consume fewer cosmetic products than women (yes, men's skin care is a big business), so ads can be designed to move the many light users to more medium users. The purpose of the ad in Exhibit 3-15 is to teach consumers that avocados can be used in salads, soups. and sandwiches, which would increase the usage rate of the product.

Exhibit 3-14   This Volvo ad appeals to the upper class.

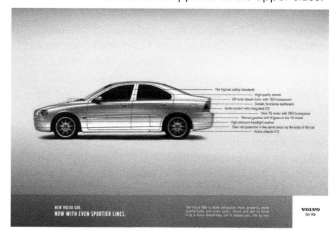

© Volvo Cars of North America, LLC

Exhibit 3-15   Avocados From Mexico educates consumers that its product has many uses.

Avocados From Mexico

Situation   Another way of viewing behaviouristic segmentation is to examine the situation in which consumers plan to use the product or brand since it directly affects their perceptions, preferences, and purchasing behaviours.[33] Two types of **situations** may be relevant: the specific usage situation and the purchase situation. *Usage situation* refers to the circumstance in which the product will be used. For example, purchases made for private consumption may be thought of differently from those that will be obvious to the public. Furthermore, purchases made for oneself versus for others as gifts offer another way to view consumer markets. The *purchase situation* more directly involves the environment operating at the time of the purchase. Time constraints, store environments, and other factors guide consumers' behaviour, which opens the door for inventive ways of segmenting the market.

Benefit Sought   In purchasing products, consumers are generally trying to satisfy specific needs and/or wants. They are looking for products that provide specific benefits to satisfy these needs. The grouping of consumers on the basis of attributes sought in a product is known as **benefit segmentation** and is widely used. Consider the purchase of a wristwatch. While some might buy a watch for particular benefits such as accuracy, water resistance, or stylishness, others may seek a different set of benefits. Watches are commonly given as gifts for birthdays, Christmas, and graduation. Certainly the same benefits are considered in the purchase of a gift, but the benefits the purchaser derives are different from those the user will obtain. Ads that portray watches as good gifts stress different criteria to consider in the purchase decision.

PROMOTIONAL PLANNING PROCESS

Promotional planners will refer to the segmentation approach used in the marketing plan. For example, the market segmentation may be based on demographics, so the target market could be men aged 18–24 or women aged 25–44. The selection of the target market has direct implications for advertising and promotion. As shown in Chapter 1, specific behavioural and communication objectives are derived and the promotional mix strategies are developed to achieve these objectives. Thus, different objectives may be established, different budgets may be used, and the promotional mix strategies may vary, depending on the market selected. And it is incumbent upon the promotional planner to gather more information or perform additional research to develop a more complete understanding of consumers in the targeted market, as suggested in Chapter 1.

When making decisions, promotional planners focus on a target audience. We make a careful distinction between target market and target audience since an advertising plan or IMC plan is one part of the overall marketing strategy. This approach is consistent with others regarding the topic of IMC planning.[34] The **target audience** is a group of consumers that a marketing communication program (i.e., advertising) is directed toward. And depending on the circumstances, the target audience decision is applicable for an entire IMC plan, an IMC program like advertising as mentioned, or a single advertising message.

Conceptually, the target market and target audience are interdependent, but their distinction allows promotional planners the ability to make more effective communication decisions with enhanced precision. The promotional planner must consider key questions. Is the target audience substantial enough to support individualized strategies? Can the target audience be reached with a communications program like advertising? Will a marketing communication program like sales promotion influence a target audience to switch brands? Is the target audience likely to participate in social media activities like creating user-generated content for the brand? As these questions illustrate, promotional planners are involved with determining the delivery of a message to a target audience who is a portion of the target market.

The difference between target audience and target market can also be seen when firms develop promotional programs that fit with an established target market that has a new cohort of consumers every couple of years. This occurs with products like Pogo (a breaded wiener on a stick), which has a clear demographic target market of teenage boys. Yet these boys grow older, so every few years there is a whole new group of teenage boys that Pogo directs marketing communication toward, and is therefore a new target audience (i.e., unaware of or unfamiliar with the brand experience). A fun marketing venture included Pogothons, street events, short flash TV ads of eight seconds, stickers delivered in skateboard parks, and so on, all with the intention to encourage website visits so that the new users—a new audience—could relate to the brand.[35] Of course, the promotional planners could realize that an alternative target audience exists for Pogo, and try to sway lapsed users like men in their thirties or forties to eat the product with their sons.

The difference between target audience and target market can also be seen when firms develop selective promotional programs beyond their target market. Promotional planners are concerned with activities like public relations, and the target audience may in fact be part of the general public, many of whom are not actual consumers. Alternatively, a promotional planner may be given direction or conclude from the situation analysis that the target audience is virtually identical to the target market. For example, a new brand entering an established product category may have no choice but to switch consumers from a competing brand. We now consider how to frame the target audience decision and see which segmentation variable a promotional planner should consider primary.

LO5   TARGET AUDIENCE OPTIONS

We turn to the Rossiter and Percy (R&P) perspective of identifying and selecting the target audience for0 promotional communication.[36] R&P state that the primary and most logical factor for initially defining a target audience is the current behaviour of consumers. This factor is critical since it is the individual decisions of customers to purchase a brand that add up to a firm's total sales. Furthermore, this behaviour is a manifestation of a consumer's attitude toward the brand. Thus, in setting the direction for any IMC plan or IMC program (i.e., advertising), the manager must have a clear idea if the target audience is customers (brand-loyal customers or favourable brand switchers) or non-customers (new category users, other brand switchers, or other brand loyal consumers). Targeting based on brand loyalty appears to be a sound idea; many research firms publish extensive findings indicating the challenges for companies to retain customers.[37] We now develop these five options for making the target audience decision for all marketing communication tool decisions.

Brand-Loyal Customers   Promotional planners have the opportunity to direct marketing communication to **brand-loyal customers** who regularly buy their firm's products. Marketing strategies (i.e., relationship marketing, discussed in Chapter 1) and communication strategies regularly focus on a firm's current customers to ensure that customers maintain their current purchasing and consumption behaviour. As we noted in Chapter 1, it is generally very profitable to maintain a stable core of current customers. From a communication standpoint, it suggests that we do not have to advertise as often or we do not have to have as many sales promotions. Part of the success with Tide is a stable group of loyal customers to whom the brand still often advertises (Exhibit 3-16).

Toyota demonstrated the importance of communicating to customers in the wake of its difficulties by having mass media messages, online video messages, specialized communications on safety, and a feel-good ad of customers enjoying the Corolla for decades.[38] While BlackBerry has had ups and downs over time, it recognized the importance of communicating to its current customer base to stay loyal and not defect to other brands.[39] This raises the question as to whether beer company ads should target their loyal customers and ensure future purchases by strengthening the loyalty with relevant messages, or target the remaining customers who claim they are not loyal to a specific beer.

Favourable Brand Switchers   The second customer group highlighted by R&P is **favourable brand switchers**. These customers buy the promotional planner's brand but also buy other brands within a given relevant time period for the product category. For certain product categories, consumers habitually purchase from a few favourites or those brands within their evoked set. These types of purchases may occur for many reasons. Consumers often face different purchase situations (e.g., own purchase versus gift). Sometimes certain moods influence brand choice. Whatever the motivation or external influencing factor, consumers adjust their

Exhibit 3-16   Tide often directs ads to its loyal customers.

Courtesy of The Procter & Gamble Company

Exhibit 3-17   Gain tries to sway consumers back to the brand by reminding them of the scent.

Courtesy of The Procter & Gamble Company

purchases accordingly. While a promotional planner would undoubtedly strive to have all customers be truly loyal, favourable brand switchers are an important source of purchases and are loyal to a degree. For these reasons, marketers would like to communicate directly with these consumers so that their brand remains in the evoked set. For example, the Gain ad in Exhibit 3-17 emphasizes its pleasant aroma to switch consumers back to the brand for their next purchase.

The importance of varying degrees of loyalty within a brand's customer base is a key topic. In a study of the cola market, the authors provide a decision-making framework for measuring varying degrees of customer loyalty and link these customers to varying levels of return on investment. The conclusions suggest that customer groups with different loyalty levels are predicated upon their beliefs toward the brand on the more salient attributes.[40]

The grocery store industry is one faced with considerable switching since it is unlikely that a household shops at one store for all of its food. In the face of competition from discount competitors like Walmart, Loblaw's message of "Crave More" for its PC brand captured the idea of attempting to sway switchers with its food innovations. As part of the switching emphasis, the campaign projected the PC brand as a lifestyle instead of its historic packaged goods approach. As part of this "foodie" lifestyle, the messages communicated where the food was sourced from and why, since more consumers are interested in such facts.[41]

New Category Users   Consumers that are not purchasing within the promotional planner's product category are within the non-customer group and are known as **new category users**. Exhibit 3-18 shows an ad for the electric Smart car; its most likely target audience is those currently using a gasoline car. Often, people become new category users because of life changes. For example, after graduating from college or university, many young adults begin to enter numerous categories partly because they have the income but also because they are at a stage of their life when new or latent needs emerge. Advertisers attempt to court this target audience since many of these consumers are potentially ready to make a purchase. Later on in life, consumers have different needs and move into a product category. Marketers believe that steady communication may entice these customers to their brand when the time comes for these consumers to actually purchase. Capital One, a financial services organization, attracted as new customers new Canadians (i.e., recent immigrants) who had not fully developed their credit history and who had minimal or no purchases with respect to banking products and services. To attract those who did not have a credit card, Capital One used "take-one" pads on signage of street cars that passed through Chinatown in Toronto, pre-movie ads shown before Bollywood films, and point-of-purchase ads in ethnic grocery stores.[42]

New category users also appear when brands try to attract new customers who might not perceive the product category as relevant for fulfilling their needs. Most people have entertainment needs that can be satisfied in many ways (e.g., dancing at a club, watching a movie at a theatre). Young people typically do not see the arts, such as ballet, as potentially fulfilling their entertainment needs, so the National Ballet of Canada faced an interesting communication challenge to attract new young consumers

Exhibit 3-18   Smart would like those using a gas engine car to consider their electric one.

© Mercedes-Benz Canada

to its production of *The Seagull*. The solution involved distributing an actual origami gull—5,000 of them, in fact—in Toronto bars, restaurants, and coffee shops. The unfolded gull displayed a flyer with key information and an opportunity to win tickets to the production.[43]

Other Brand Switchers   Another type of consumer that is in the non-customer group is **other brand switchers**. They are like the switchers in the customer group in that they purchase a few different brands within a category. However, from a promotional planner's perspective, they are fundamentally different because they are not purchasing their brand. This is a challenging target audience, as the brand needs to break into consumers' evoked set of the brands that these consumers are currently purchasing. It's a formidable task, but still the focus of a considerable amount of advertising and promotion. The ad in Exhibit 3-19 tries to encourage people to drink milk when eating their meals instead of other beverages.

The Gap targeted "millennials" with online videos of the denim design team living and working in Los Angeles with "street feel" imagery. While this initially appears to be demographic targeting, in fact it is closer to behavioural, as the fashionable brand that peaked in the 1990s looked to attract consumers who currently did not visit the store to replenish their wardrobe with the iconic brand's latest offerings.[44] Most clothing retailers try to attract non-customers to build sales and look to secondary variables like demographics to better profile the target audience, as this example suggests. Yet the strategy often is misinterpreted from the key targeting variable when news reports centre on the age factor instead of the behavioural one.

Other Brand Loyals   R&P's final non-customer group for target audience selection includes **other brand loyals**. As this label implies, these consumers purchase only one other brand. It is difficult to say how much in advertising and promotion expenditure is directed to these types of consumers across many industries. Logically, it would be very difficult to break the strongly held consumer behaviours. Nevertheless, this is still a potential target to which a firm may wish to deliver advertising and promotion. The tourism ad in Exhibit 3-20 encourages travellers to consider Canada as a destination to visit.

Exhibit 3-19   Quebec Milk Producers would like people to drink milk with meals.

© Quebec Milk Producers - AD - 2015

Exhibit 3-20   Travel Alberta and the Canadian Tourism Commission jointly try to attract visitors to Canada.

© Destination Canada

IMC Planning: Target Audience Profile

According to R&P, after prioritizing the target audience in terms of customer groups, other segmentation variables like lifestyle or demographics are used to develop a complete target audience profile. A complete profile of the target audience beyond the initial behavioural variable is necessary for direction of the remaining decisions in the promotional plan. Creative decisions involving the main message to be communicated require appropriate content so that consumers will attend to and understand the message. Effective media decisions require the promotional planner to match the consumer characteristics of the specific media with a complete target audience profile. Finally, more information about the target audience allows greater precision when assessing and choosing IMC tools to deliver the message. We now explore the planning implications of these three ideas.

PROFILE FOR MESSAGES

In later chapters, we will identify different aspects of constructing the main message a promotional planner would want to develop for its advertising or sales promotion or any other IMC tool like the Internet or public relations. For the message to be completely understood, the content of the message must be consistent with the background or experiences of the intended audience. For example, if the ad uses language or references to a lifestyle that is unfamiliar to the target audience, it is less likely to influence in the direction intended. Thus, a complete profile of the target audience will be useful when finalizing the body copy in a print ad or the scenes in a television commercial.

Many companies target a younger demographic. We may read in the press or in marketing trade publications that a firm is targeting an 18- to 24-year-old demographic. While this may be true, often there is an inherent behavioural variable implied. Sometimes it is more like a new category user, since young adults start to consume new categories of products as they mature. Other times, it is more like favourable brand switchers in an attempt to make these consumers exhibit stronger loyalty. Thus, a communication message has to resonate with the target audience based on their current behaviour, whether they buy the brand or not, and another variable like demographics.

One clever ad by Tide detergent illustrates this point from the other direction. The ad shows a child sitting in a highchair who has just finished eating a bowl of spaghetti. The picture clearly shows the child's face and the child is naturally very messy. The headline reads, "The day I switched to Tide," and there is no other text in the ad. It appears that this message is targeted toward other brand switchers or other brand loyals who are at a particular stage of the family life cycle. The ad represents the significant decision they undertook to finally stop consuming a current brand and move on to a presumably better brand. Had the ad shown an alternative picture, the additional profile variable would have been considerably different. For instance, the image of a young woman wearing athletic clothing who observes a stain or that the colours of her clothing are fading too quickly suggests an active lifestyle. This illustrates that any marketing segmentation variable can be used to further profile the behavioural variable.

PROFILE FOR MEDIA

Later in this text, we will also identify the different media decisions. For example, the promotional planner could select television or radio to deliver its message, or the promotional planner might consider newspapers or magazines or a multitude of other media. Each medium offers many avenues that also must be considered. For instance, would the promotional planner place the television commercial on a TSN sports event during the day, or on a CTV drama in the evening? A detailed profile of the target audience allows the message to be more precisely delivered in a medium that has a higher proportion of the target audience.

Critics contend that the advent of many different television channels leading to greater audience fragmentation has caused TV advertising to be less efficient, since an advertiser is required to place a commercial on more than one station to reach a larger audience. In contrast, the detailed target audience profile for media helps a promotional planner move toward greater effectiveness. With the possibility of offering a more customized message to different audiences, promotional planners can have one type of commercial oriented toward younger non-customers on one channel and another message to older current customers on a different channel. Or, with the extensive number of new television channels in languages other than the two official languages, advertisers can provide more customized messages on the respective channels.

Moving toward more interactive media for the purposes of building and maintaining relationships, brands could use certain kinds of media and media vehicles to communicate with different segments based on unique relationship variables that are within the firm's database.[45] This would allow more accurate exposure and more customized messages depending upon where the customer is within the relationship.

PROFILE FOR IMC TOOLS

Similarly, in a later part of the book we investigate the decisions involved for other IMC tools like sales promotion, public relations, direct marketing, and the Internet. Each of these represents additional avenues for reaching target audiences, and each represents a tool with a greater opportunity for building the brand. Like media, there is also the possibility of more closely aligning the use of a tool with a promotional planner's target audience, provided sufficient profiling is done.

Learning Objectives Summary

 LO1 **Describe the consumer decision-making process and demonstrate how it relates to marketing communication.**

Consumer behaviour is best viewed as the process and activities that people experience when searching for, selecting, purchasing, using, evaluating, and disposing of products and services to satisfy their needs and desires. A five-stage model of the consumer decision-making process consists of need recognition, information search, alternative evaluation, purchase, and postpurchase evaluation. The decision process model views consumer behaviour primarily from a cognitive orientation. Marketing communication plays a role in every stage as marketers adjust their messages and media along with IMC tools to influence appropriately so that consumers move from one stage to the other.

 LO2 **Distinguish internal psychological processes, their influence on consumer decision making, and implications for marketing communication.**

Internal psychological processes that influence the consumer decision-making process include motivation, perception, attitude formation and change, integration processes, and satisfaction. All of these are areas in which advertising attempts to influence. Most advertising reflects a particular purchase motive. Certain elements of an ad are designed to attract attention or ensure that the target audience retains the information or symbolic message. The body copy in a print ad, for example, can be written to influence the receiver's attitude, and allows certain ways of integrating the information. Finally, advertising is designed to suggest to consumers that they made the correct purchase so they feel satisfied.

 LO3 **Contrast how the consumer decision-making process varies for different types of purchases and the effects on marketing communication.**

Consumer decision making is classified along a continuum from routine problem solving to extended problem solving. Consumers generally spend more time and effort as they move from routine to extended problem solving. Some types of marketing communication are more relevant than others depending upon the type of behaviour expected. Consumer decision making moves from an individual decision to a group decision, and once again marketing communication must adjust its message, media, or IMC tool accordingly.

Compare the similarities and differences of target market and target audience.

This chapter also investigated how promotional planners make a target audience decision for any aspect of an IMC plan. To understand the context of this decision, the chapter examined the role of promotion in the overall marketing process, as shown in Figure 3-5. The process includes a situation analysis, target market process, and marketing program development, all directed toward a prescribed target market.

One of the key aspects pertains to the target marketing process, which includes segmenting the market, selecting a target market, and determining the market positioning strategy, as this process gives direction to the target audience decision. Accordingly, we reviewed how marketing planners and promotional planners segment the market, and explained how each made the target market and target audience decision, respectively.

 Identify the options for making a target audience decision for marketing communication.

The chapter identified a model to profile a target audience by considering the current purchase behaviour of the target audience with respect to the promotional planner's brand as the primary segmentation variable. Promotional messages can be directed to current customers, such as brand-loyal or favourable brand switchers. Alternatively, promotional messages could be targeted to non-customers, like new category users, other brand switchers, or other brand loyals.

 Express why a profile of the target audience is important for message, media, and IMC tool decisions.

Finally, the chapter concluded by expressing how other variables more accurately profile the audience in terms of lifestyle or psychographic variables after the initial direction is finalized. This descriptive profile becomes useful for all facets of the promotional plan (i.e., message, media, IMC tools).

Review Questions

1. What are the stages of the consumer decision-making process model? Why are they important for planning marketing communication?

2. What are the primary psychological processes associated with each stage of the consumer decision-making process model? How does marketing communication influence each stage?

3. How do the stages of the consumer decision-making process model differ with the three types of problem solving?

4. When defining a target audience for marketing communication, why is it a good idea to use consumer behaviour with respect to your brand as the primary variable before using other variables such as demographics or lifestyle?

5. What are the five customer groups? Explain in terms of a beverage product like soft drinks or beer.

6. Why is a complete profile of a target audience important for marketing communication?

Applied Questions

1. Explain the difference between functional, performance, and experiential benefits. Why might the messages recommended in an IMC plan for smart phones focus on each one separately or together?

2. How are ads or brand messages experienced in social media influenced by consumers' selective perception system?

3. Consider a group purchasing situation you have previously experienced, like going out for the evening. What role did each person play during prepurchase, purchase and consumption, and postpurchase?

4. In what situations are the target audience and the target market the same? In what situations is the size of the target audience larger or smaller than the target market?

5. Examine the ads in this chapter and identify the target audience each ad is directed toward using the model of five customer groups. Suggest other relevant segmentation variables to further profile the target audience. Also identify a relevant segmentation variable to pinpoint the target market.

6. Which segmentation variables are more useful or appropriate for profiling a target market for an automobile like the Mini? Similarly, which are more useful or appropriate for profiling the target audience for an automobile like the Mini?

CHAPTER FOUR

Communication Response Models

LEARNING OBJECTIVES

LO1 Explain the elements of the communication process and identify the role of marketing communication.

LO2 Contrast traditional communication response models and alternative response hierarchies.

LO3 Develop the response processes of receivers of marketing communication through two models of cognitive processing.

LO4 Illustrate a response model for managerial decision making.

LO5 Construct ideas on how the knowledge of response models can be used for IMC planning.

Walmart Canada's Evolving Message

Walmart Canada rolled into this country a couple of decades ago and celebrated its 20th anniversary in 2014. After purchasing 122 Woolco stores when it first started, it continually expanded its footprint a healthy 4 percent per year to hit 390 stores. Over the years, it withstood its Canadian-based competitors (e.g., Zellers, Consumers Distributing) and American-based competitors (e.g., Kmart, Target) with an ever changing assortment of messages and media. And now, facing competition from stronger Canadian retailers (e.g., Loblaw, Sobeys, Metro) and a very strong American online retailer in Amazon, Walmart Canada has entered its third decade with a new initiative to carve out a stronger position in the food retailing market in the face of many of the competitors pushing toward home delivery service, notably Amazon.

Canadians greeted Walmart's initial entry with skepticism and fear, worrying about the demise of Woolco and mistakenly thinking that it was a Canadian brand when in fact its longevity had erased its American heritage in our collective beliefs. Nevertheless, Walmart renovated its locations while remaining open, with signage and ads that proclaimed "We're working on it—becoming Walmart for you." Upon renovation completion, the message moved to educating consumers about Walmart's everyday low price, a foreign approach contrary to consumers' established habit of expecting high–low pricing tactics from retailers. In this case, the message moved toward customer testimonials—customers telling customers in ads—about this new way to view the prices of its products.

Results took time, as consumers maintained their regular behaviour of "stocking up" with their purchases, believing the price to be a temporary reduction. Enter "Smiley the rollback mascot" in 1996, which floated around demonstrating Walmart's low prices. For 10 years until Smiley's retirement, the iconic image helped brand Walmart as the low-price king. Seven years later, in 2013, Smiley returned to remind Walmart customers of its dedication to low prices once again, but this time the rollback featured food products. While in the past Smiley had occasionally appeared with a friend or gone beyond the "rollback" message, in the new round of ads Walmart Canada focused solely on the icon with an updated look and kept on point with the price emphasis.

Starting in 2008, Walmart emphasized its brand with a focus on fresh groceries and product selection with its employees speaking in its ads instead of consumers. The messages emphasized "Walmart Canada" to move from a functional approach to a more emotional approach to show how the brand is part of its customers' life. A more recent edition of this brand focus in 2013 returned to customers with different mom personas (e.g., enthused mom, on-a-mission mom) with Walmart as part of their life. At this time, Walmart Canada established a digital presence with its Facebook page and the beginnings of online shopping with the threat of Amazon and stronger Canadian retailers.

After its 20th anniversary celebrations, Walmart moved to the "Discover Another Side" message in 2015 to improve consumer awareness of its fresh food offerings. It doubled its organic produce selection, now carried more in-season locally grown produce when available, expanded its inventory of Canadian meat and Maple Leaf branded products, and emphasized the trio of produce, meat, and fresh baked goods in its marketing communication. IMC tools included enhanced in-store presentation, TV ads, digital banner ads, shareable content in the form of video and recipes, *Walmart Live Better* magazine, a stronger dedication to its 100 percent money back guarantee, and experiential sampling. As noted in the research, 86 percent of all Canadians shop at Walmart at least once per year, but not all purchase fresh foods, a trend that Walmart attempted to change as it continued to make inroads in the grocery market as the fastest growing retailer.

Sources: "Walmart Picks Up 13 Target Locations," *Marketing Magazine*, May 8, 2015; Megan Haynes, "Walmart: 20 Years of Turning Retail on Its Head," *Strategy*, June 2014; Harmeet Singh, "Walmart's Refresh," *Strategy*, May 28, 2015; Megan Haynes, "Walmart Brings Smiley Out of Retirement," *Strategy*, April 22, 2013.

Questions:

1. Why is it necessary for Walmart Canada to continually change its marketing communication message?
2. Is the fresh focus a compelling approach to ward off Amazon and Loblaw with their home delivery plans?

An organization's IMC strategy is implemented through the communication tools and messages it sends to current or prospective customers as well as other relevant publics. Organizations communicate in many ways, such as through advertisements, websites, press releases, sales promotion, and visual images. Those involved in the planning of an IMC program need to understand how consumers will perceive and interpret their messages and how these reactions will shape consumers' responses to the company and/or its product or service.

This chapter takes a historical perspective to illustrate how academics and practitioners have evolved in their thinking to understand how persuasion works in the context of marketing communication. We begin with a model to illustrate the complexity of the communication process. Next, we examine the response process of consumers that is explained by traditional models, alternative hierarchies, and cognitive processing of communication. Finally, we summarize with a framework that illustrates an IMC planning perspective.

 # A Model of the Communication Process

Communication has been defined as the passing of information, the exchange of ideas, or the process of establishing a commonness or oneness of thought between a sender and a receiver.[1] This definition suggests that for communication to occur, there must be common thinking between two parties and information must be passed from one person to another (or from one group to another). This section elaborates on this idea by explaining the elements of the communication process and identifying the role of marketing communication.

OVERVIEW OF THE MODEL

Communication is a complex process with success depending on the nature of the message, the audience's interpretation of it, and the environment in which it is received. The receiver's perception of the source and the medium used to transmit the message may also affect the ability to communicate, as do other factors. Words, pictures, sounds, and colours may have different meanings to different audiences, and people's perceptions and interpretations of them vary. Marketers must understand the meanings that words and symbols take on and how they influence consumers' interpretation of products and messages.

Over the years, a model of the communication process has evolved, as shown in Figure 4-1.[2] Two elements represent the major participants in the communication process: the sender and the receiver. Another two are the major communication tools: message and channel. Four others are the major communication functions and processes: encoding, decoding, response, and feedback. The last element, noise, refers to any extraneous factors in the system that can interfere with the process and work against effective communication.

Figure 4-1 A model of the communication process

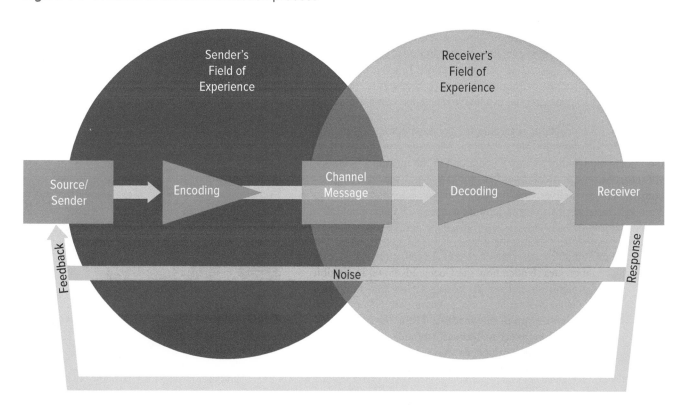

SOURCE/ENCODING

The sender, or **source**, of a communication is the person or organization that has information to share with another person or group of people. The source may be an individual (say, a salesperson or hired spokesperson, such as a celebrity who appears in a company's advertisements) or a non-personal entity (such as the brand or organization itself). Because the receiver's perceptions of the source influence how the communication is received, marketers must be careful to select a communicator the receiver believes to be knowledgeable and trustworthy or with whom the receiver can identify or relate in some manner.

The communication process begins when the source selects words, pictures, symbols, and the like to represent the message that will be delivered to the receiver(s). This process, known as **encoding**, involves putting thoughts, ideas, or information into a form that provides a meaningful message. For example, the Nestea ad in Exhibit 4-1 is constructed with multiple visual images and text information about the product and the promotions to allow unique meanings for individual receivers. The sender's ultimate goal is to encode the message in such a way that it will be understood by the receiver. This means using words, and pictures that are familiar to the target audience, as demonstrated in the Nestea ad. Companies also have highly recognizable symbols that are prominently shown in their ads—such as the McDonald's golden arches, the Nike swoosh, or the Coca-Cola trademark. So when these symbols are seen in ads, consumers instantly understand the message that is associated with the brand.

MESSAGE

The encoding process leads to development of a **message** that contains the information or meaning the source intends to convey. The message may be verbal or non-verbal, oral or written, or symbolic. Messages are put into a transmittable form that is appropriate for the channel of communication. In advertising, this may range from simply writing words or copy that will be read as a radio message to producing an expensive television commercial.

Marketers make decisions regarding the message content, structure, and design for optimal communication. **Message content** refers to the information and/or meaning contained in the message. **Message structure/message design** refers to the way the message is constructed to deliver the information or intended meaning. Message decisions are covered in more detail in Chapters 7 and 8.

For many products, it is not the actual words of the message that determine its communication effectiveness but rather the impression or image the ad creates. Notice how the Coach ad shown in Exhibit 4-2 uses only a picture to deliver its message. However, the brand name and picture help communicate a feeling of elegance and emphasize the classic design of the handbag. Using the meaning of products, brands, and symbols to represent brands, and the story implied about the brand, influences how consumers interpret messages—suggesting that careful consideration of the message is a critical task for promotional planners.[3]

Exhibit 4-1 The many elements in this ad require extensive decoding by consumers.

NESTEA® is a registered trademark of Société des Produits Nestlé S.A., Vevey, Switzerland.

Exhibit 4-2 The image projected by an ad often communicates more than words.

Courtesy of Coach, Inc.

CHANNEL

The **channel** is how the communication travels from the source or sender to the receiver. At the broadest level, channels of communication are of two types: nonpersonal and personal.

Nonpersonal Channels   Methods of communication that carry a message without interpersonal contact between sender and receiver are **nonpersonal channels**. These channels are generally referred to as the **mass media** or mass communication, since the message is sent to many individuals at one time. For example, a TV commercial broadcast on a prime-time show may be seen by a few million people. Nonpersonal channels of communication consist of three major types: print (e.g., newspapers, magazines), broadcast (e.g., radio and television), and out of home (e.g., outdoor, transit, place-based). For example, magazines provide a good channel for health messages encouraging people to take action (Exhibit 4-3). In this ad, the visual demonstrates the problem of taking medication for asthma for too long without any solution and indirectly invites consumers to call the phone number. While these media have existed for decades, innovation flourishes with technology. For example, holograms at events make a spectacular vision for spectators; Nissan Canada reflected 3D product images over water to simulate a lake-surface car chase on Canada Day. Laser-guided sound systems emit an audio message when people are within a specific distance or facing a public screen.[4]

Exhibit 4-3   Print media with clever visuals provide an opportunity to convey a message.

Hand-out/Association pulmonaire du Québe/Newscom

Automobile manufacturers continue to use nonpersonal channels extensively; Subaru targeted its BRZ to young men aged 30–35 who are tech-savvy driving enthusiasts by making it a "hot" new addition to the lineup with a super-slow-motion video showing the heat radiating off the car as it melted everything in the parking garage. It ended with customary close-up shots of its sleek styling and showcased its handling while accelerating with the joyful sounds of the engine roaring. Combined with the video, Subaru ignited the front cover of *Grid,* a free Toronto city magazine, with a hologram that looked like a regular cover until it was slightly tilted, when it showed an image of the BRZ burning through the page. Other media included ads in national newspapers and magazines showing similar images of the BRZ burning through the pages. A display on the streets of Montreal recreated the video effect with scorched street items like a mailbox and bike rack surrounding the BRZ. Wild postings permitted viewers to "tap or snap" with their smart phone to see a dedicated page for a full description.[5]

The Internet is a nonpersonal channel with both print and broadcast characteristics. We see display or video ads on many types of sites that publish content, such as TSN for sports information and Facebook or YouTube for social media postings. Thus, the Internet is nonpersonal as people consume information or entertainment content with no personal contact between them and the company (e.g., source) that disseminates the ad. And in many ways, a company's Internet site is an ad delivered to everyone and anyone, even though we often refer to its information and images as content. For Subaru's BRX, the brand placed its video ad on YouTube and used the same burning imagery in its banner ads.

Alternatively, the Internet is increasingly a form of personal communication, mediated through electronic devices, as consumers can interact with a company's personnel and share information, pictures, and video with other people. However, not all digital communication will be nonpersonal. Proximity- and time-based means of communication occur through data from consumers' smart phones and their use of social media. Finding patterns of routine behaviour, such as buying a daily coffee at one location and time, can be an impetus for targeting people to switch with an incentive or relevant message. Application of these kinds of algorithms produces substantially accurate results. Specialized shopping apps allow consumers to receive personalized information while roaming retail aisles.[6] Thus, while these methods appear to be directly communicated via technology, they remain nonpersonal media as there is no person-to-person communication.

Personal Channels   Direct interpersonal (face-to-face) contact with target individuals or groups is the hallmark of *personal channels* of communication. Salespeople serve as personal channels of communication when they deliver their sales message to a buyer or potential customer. With video and other capabilities of computers and the Internet, face-to-face contact with salespeople and customer service personnel can now be mediated through technology. A major advantage is that a customized message can be delivered to the audience, and immediate receiver feedback results in message adjustment from the source.

Social channels of communication such as friends, neighbours, associates, co-workers, and family members are also personal channels. They represent *word-of-mouth (WOM) communication,* a powerful source of information for consumers that has been researched for many decades.[7] For example, a sample of 70 product launches showed that only 10 percent produced 85 percent of the word-of-mouth communication. The majority of it occurred before the launch with traditional media expenditure for distinctive brands in ubiquitous product categories.[8] In turn, companies have always attempted to generate positive WOM for their brands. Knowing that the average consumer often listens to what others say about a brand, marketers will target specific groups of influential consumers such as trendsetters or loyal customers with influential messages or promotional incentives.[9]

Consumers communicate about brands within social media and use the Internet's networking features to send links to ads or other brand related content to whomever they choose. While there is no face-to-face contact in many of these instances, the interactive capabilities suggest it closely resembles a personal channel. Marketers use this as an opportunity to disseminate a message through the resulting WOM of these newfound personal channels of communication. This social media communication growth spawned research on social networks to understand influential participants within a social network. One finding suggests that one-fifth of a person's contacts actually influence a person's activity level on the site.[10] Another finding suggests that opinion leadership and opinion seeking both contribute to online forwarding and online chatting.[11] Finally, a third result concludes that electronic WOM yields greater shopping time overall and more time considering a recommended product.[12]

Furthermore, communication in social media like Twitter shares characteristics of a social channel where brand personnel interact with loyal customers. Continued messaging among Dove and its favourite followers who happened to be influential bloggers allowed the brand to recruit these women for a day-long beauty session that resulted in their being part of a cast of dancers in a rendition of *Singing in the Rain* to promote its Nourishing Oil Care line of shampoo shown on TV and Internet media. During their spa day, the women used social media to describe the experience for all to vicariously enjoy the moment.[13] Other examples of WOM and approaches for generating WOM are presented in subsequent chapters throughout the text.

One study conducted on the effects of a WOM campaign for a chain store examined the characteristics of the most successful "agents" so that firms could better understand whom to target with their marketing efforts.[14] They found that agents who were not loyal customers of the store were more effective at generating sales through WOM than were loyal customers. The explanation offered for these counterintuitive findings is that loyal customers have already told their friends and acquaintances about a product and are already generating positive WOM. Alternatively, non-loyal customers may be more responsive to marketing campaigns designed to encourage them to spread the word about a product. Other studies find that post-campaign WOM contributes to strengthening profitability through customer lifetime value calculations. and that advertising does lead to a measurable link to enhanced WOM.[15]

Although understanding online WOM is important for marketers, other research shows that 90 percent of conversations about products, services, and brands take place offline. Face-to-face interaction accounts for the vast majority of WOM (72 percent) about a brand, while phone conversations rank second (18 percent). Only 7 percent of WOM takes place through online channels such as email/instant messages, blogs, and chat rooms. The research also shows that nearly half the word-of-mouth conversations included references to the IMC tools used for a brand, including print and television ads, websites, and other marketing tools such as point-of-sale displays and promotions.[16] Additionally, WOM about a brand's advertising is significantly more likely to involve a recommendation to buy or try a brand when compared to other WOM induced discussions about brands. One-quarter of all consumer conversations involve a brand's advertising, with TV ads being most prevalent, and 75 percent communication occurs face-to-face.[17] While online and offline WOM appears critical, perhaps for different reasons, the authors of a review of electronic WOM studies conclude that understanding this digital version is paramount with expected future growth. They conclude that there are significant questions to consider such as: Why do people talk online? Why do people listen online? What happens to the sender? What is the WOM influence on the receiver?[18]

RECEIVER/DECODING

The **receiver** is the person(s) with whom the sender shares thoughts or information. Generally, receivers are the consumers in the target market or audience who read, hear, and/or see the marketer's message. The target audience may consist of individuals, groups, niche markets, market segments, or a general public or mass audience as discussed in the previous chapter. The ad in Exhibit 4-4 targets business administrators interested in learning more about payroll.

Exhibit 4-4   The Canadian Payroll Association attracts an audience from a niche market with its ad.

Hand-out/Canadian Payroll Association/Newscom

Decoding is the process of transforming the sender's message back into thought. This process is heavily influenced by the receiver's frame of reference or **field of experience**, which refers to the experiences, perceptions, attitudes, and values he or she brings to the communication situation. For effective communication to occur, the message decoding process of the receiver must match the encoding of the sender. Simply put, this means the receiver understands and correctly interprets what the source is trying to communicate. Exhibit 4-5 shows an ad where many ways of decoding might occur.

As Figure 4-1 showed, the source and the receiver each have a frame of reference (the circle around each) that they bring to the communication situation. Effective communication is more likely when there is *common ground* (i.e., overlap of circles) between the two parties. The more knowledge the sender has about the receivers, the better the sender can understand their needs, empathize with them, and communicate effectively.

While this notion of common ground between sender and receiver may sound basic, it often causes great difficulty in the advertising communications process. Marketing and advertising people often have very different fields of experience from the target audience with whom they must communicate in terms of age, education, and life experiences. Advertisers invest in research to understand the frames of reference of the target audiences and pretest messages to make sure consumers understand and decode them in the manner the advertiser intended prior to the launch. IMC Perspective 4-1 exemplifies the difficulty that comes with not communicating effectively.

Exhibit 4-5   This Corona ad allows for many interpretations in decoding.

Crown Imports, LLC

IMC PERSPECTIVE 4-1

VW CANADA HITS THE ROAD FOR MARKET SHARE

Peter Blackwell, director of marketing at Volkswagen Canada, has his hands on the wheel of innovative marketing communication activities as the Canadian division drives toward its 5 percent market share target by 2018, up from 3.7 percent. With eight different car models, and Jetta accounting for 50 percent of all sales, the competitive market called for unique messages to break through the "noise" of other imported brands in addition to the tough domestic ones as well. According to Blackwell, VW Canada suffered from expensive marketing communication budgets and a short-term project approach and needed to take a strategic direction rather than simply trying to move product in the next quarter. Overall, VW moved toward supporting all models continuously throughout the year rather than three times per year, in addition to working with North American messaging originating from the United States.

© Volkswagen Canada

In order to get the message and media right, VW Canada performed extensive data analysis to identify a more selective target audience for the Tiguan SUV. They looked at credit data, Internet search metrics, digital display ad results, and dealership data to understand who was mostly likely to purchase in the next 60 days and who also appeared to be predisposed to buy a Tiguan, and focused an information based message using Internet media to these potential customers. Their efforts were supported by a humorous TV ad where a man looking to buy a horse saw a Tiguan in a nearby barn stall and decided to switch his interest immediately when he heard the $25,000 price. The mass media assisted in building additional awareness and clarified the misconception of an expensive vehicle. This approach provided a 50 percent lift in sales for the latter half of 2013.

For VW's iconic Beetle, two distinct marketing communication initiatives proved that the Canadian division and its ad agency Red Urban could deliver with unique messages and media. The creative specialists worked with the band Walk Off the Earth and developed an 11-minute video featuring three versions of the same song with three different versions of the much loved car; playful, soulful, and powerful. According to Blackwell, the Beetle required a different approach than the Tiguan, more emotional, since it is more widely known and it is emblematic of the whole VW brand. The video received 1.2 million views and subsequent social media exposure. Additionally, the creative team put together the story of VIN 903847, a Beetle owned by Paul Loofs who drove it around the world three times. Initially shown on the Bravo and Discovery channels, an interactive version resides on the Internet for all to see. The remarkable video concentrated on the adventure and journey behind the car rather than the Beetle. These two messages saved considerable media costs as VW Canada invested more money in production value.

In contrast to these approaches, VW Canada's campaign for the Golf includes multiple executions demonstrating key features like its acceleration with VW's customary humorous situations and tactical "das auto" ending. The style of the message and approach is consistent in all ads, in addition to those for the Passat, Tiguan, and Jetta, especially the ad with the Jettas strung up on the wall at a butcher shop!

Sources: Rae Ann Fera, "Volkswagen The 567 Scroll," *Marketing Magazine*, October 2014, pp. 10–11; Megan Hayes, "The Next Wave of Branded Content," *Strategy*, April 2014; Megan Hayes, "Volkswagen Drives Into the Mainstream," *Strategy*, April 2014, www.adforum.com.

Question:

1. Do you agree with the strategy of VW to have some similarities and differences in its marketing communication across its multiple vehicle models?

NOISE

Throughout the communication process, the message is subject to extraneous factors that can distort or interfere with its reception. This unplanned distortion or interference is known as **noise**. Errors or problems that occur during message encoding or distractions at the point of reception are examples of noise. Perhaps the foremost distraction is advertising clutter, whereby the receiver is confronted with many competing messages. Noise may also occur because the fields of experience of the sender and receiver don't overlap. Lack of common ground may result in improper encoding of the message—using a sign, symbol, or words that are unfamiliar or have different meaning to the receiver.

RESPONSE/FEEDBACK

The receiver's set of reactions after seeing, hearing, or reading the message is known as a **response**. Receivers' responses can range from non-observable actions such as storing information in memory to immediate action such as visiting the brand's Facebook page after seeing an ad. Other responses can be emotional, where consumers enjoy or dislike messages they receive. Furthermore, responses such as stronger awareness of the brand or attitude to the brand may occur as well. The next section more thoroughly investigates consumers' responses to marketing communication.

Marketers are very interested in **feedback**, that part of the receiver's response that is communicated back to the sender. Feedback closes the loop in the communication flow and lets the sender monitor how the intended message is being decoded and received. While the ultimate form of feedback occurs through sales, it is often hard to show a direct relationship between marketing communication and purchase behaviour. So marketers use other methods to obtain feedback, including talking to customers, visiting stores, monitoring participation levels with promotions and within a brand's social media, and visiting Internet sites.

Trends in brand-related consumer-generated content and digital forwarding of ads or stories about products can be observed by planners as feedback from their audiences. However, after a few years of running contests or promotional events with user-generated content, brands began to exert control over their messages and appeared more cautious about encouraging further content growth.[19] Research now investigates the qualitative comments posted in social media after viewing consumer generated ads by mapping the response to understand the message's meaning along cognitive and emotional dimensions.[20] With research-based information similar to this regarding all aspects of a brand's digital communication, advertisers can determine reasons for success or failure in the communication process and make adjustments.

SUMMARY OF THE MODEL

The model has stood the test of time for decades to describe how advertising communicates through traditional media. Practitioners are debating how new digital channels and social media are affecting their marketing communication decisions. They appear to conclude that the fundamental tenets of a consistent brand strategy and understanding how that message is delivered through the new avenues is still a critical perspective within digital marketing communication.[21]

We can still conclude that successful communication is accomplished when the marketer selects an appropriate source, develops an effective message or appeal that is encoded properly, and then selects the channels or media that will best reach the target audience so that the message can be effectively decoded and delivered. So whether we are talking about delivering a message on television or through social media, the general communication principles are important to consider for effective decisions. Since these decisions must consider how the target audience will respond to the promotional message, the remainder of this chapter examines the process by which consumers respond to marketing communication.

 ## The Response Process

An important aspect of developing effective communication programs involves understanding the *response process* the receiver may go through in moving toward a specific behaviour and how the promotional efforts of the marketer influence consumer responses. To explain the response process, we now review two types of response hierarchy models—traditional and alternative.

TRADITIONAL RESPONSE HIERARCHY MODELS

A number of models have been developed to depict the process a consumer may pass through in moving from a state of not being aware of a company, product, or brand to actual purchase behaviour. Figure 4-2 shows three response models, which are known as hierarchy models since there is a prescribed order or defined steps the receiver experiences. While these response models may appear similar, they were developed for different reasons.

Figure 4-2   Models of the response process

	Models		
Stages	**AIDA model**	**Hierarchy of effects model**	**Information processing model**
Cognitive stage	Attention	Awareness	Presentation
			Attention
		Knowledge	Comprehension
Affective stage	Interest	Liking	Yielding
		Preference	
	Desire	Conviction	Retention
Behavioural stage	Action	Purchase	Behaviour

The **AIDA model** was developed to represent the steps a salesperson must take a customer through in the personal selling process.[22] The salesperson must first get the customer's attention and then arouse interest in the company's product or service. Strong levels of interest should create a desire to own or use the product. The action step in the AIDA model involves getting the customer to make a purchase commitment and closing the sale. When applying this idea to marketing communication, planners might design an ad with one of the stages in mind as a goal. The ad in Exhibit 4-6 likely sparks a desire to try one of the iced coffee products from Second Cup on a hot summer day. Brands try to encourage a behaviour other than purchase, such as participation in a contest, like Coca-Cola did with its "Cover" promotion where music-loving youth sang a song by a favourite artist and uploaded the recording (covers.muchmusic.com) to solicit votes to win.[23]

The **hierarchy of effects model** assumes a consumer passes through a series of steps in sequential order from initial awareness of a product to actual purchase.[24] A premise is that advertising effects occur over a period of time. Marketing communication may not lead to immediate behavioural response or purchase; rather, a series of effects must occur, with each step fulfilled before the consumer can move to the next step in the hierarchy. Xbox Kinect advertised and promoted its gaming console and received tremendous participation levels at its demonstration hubs set up in a few

Exhibit 4-6   Second Cup encourages consumers to try its iced coffee.

© The Second Cup Ltd.

major Canadian cities. With celebrities visiting the hubs, the events attracted many new users who eventually purchased, leading to stronger trial purchases down the road.[25]

The **information processing model** of advertising effects assumes the receiver in a persuasive communication situation like advertising is an information processor or problem solver.[26] The steps a receiver goes through in being persuaded constitute a response hierarchy that is similar to the hierarchy of effects sequence. However, this model includes a step not found in the other models: *retention,* or the receiver's ability to retain that portion of the comprehended information that he or she accepts as valid or relevant. This step is important since most promotional campaigns are designed not to motivate consumers to take immediate action but rather to provide information they will use later when making a purchase decision. In some ways, mobile apps are helping with future purchases. For example, Cineplex's app allows consumers to see schedules, read entertainment news, view movie trailers, and obtain promotional offers.[27] While the initial loading of the app and reading about the brand online did not make an immediate sale, the app certainly facilitates future repeat purchases.

IMPLICATIONS OF THE TRADITIONAL HIERARCHY MODELS

Implications for the response models are grouped into the individual steps within each of the models and the consistent stages across all three models.

Individual Steps   The hierarchy models of communication response are useful for promotional planners to make specific marketing communication decisions for each step. Potential buyers may be at different steps in the hierarchy, so the advertiser will face different sets of communication problems. For example, using the hierarchy of effects model, a company introducing an innovative product like the Microsoft Surface may use media advertising to make people aware of the product and its features and benefits (Exhibit 4-7). Microsoft provides product information in its ads but also encourages consumers to visit its retail stores and Internet site to learn more about its product. These consumers will progress through the response hierarchy and move closer to purchase more quickly than those who only see an ad, since they may like or prefer the brand more with greater exposure or experience with it.

Exhibit 4-7   Advertising for innovative new products such as the Microsoft Surface must make consumers aware of their features and benefits.

Microsoft's Surface tablet is an innovative new product. Photo by Alex Strohl

The steps within the hierarchy models are intermediate measures of communication effectiveness that guide communication decisions. The marketer needs to know where audience members are on the response hierarchy and then make the appropriate decision. For example, research may reveal that one target segment has low awareness of the advertiser's brand, and the communication task involves increasing the awareness level for the brand by increasing the number of ads. Another target segment may be aware of the brand and its attributes but have a low level of liking or brand preference, requiring the advertiser to develop a message that addresses the negative feelings.

Consistent Stages   As shown in Figure 4-2, the three models presented all consistently view the response process as involving movement through a sequence of three *stages,* even though the specific *steps* within a stage may be unique or defined with variation. The *cognitive stage* represents what the receiver knows or perceives about the particular product or brand. This stage includes awareness that the brand exists and knowledge, information, or comprehension about its attributes, characteristics, or benefits. The *affective stage* refers to the receiver's feelings or affect level (like or dislike) for the particular brand. This stage also includes stronger levels of affect such as desire, preference, or conviction. The *behavioural stage* refers to the consumer's action or behaviour toward the brand, such as purchase.

All models assume a similar ordering of the three stages. Cognitive development precedes affective reactions, which precede behaviour. One might assume that consumers become aware of and knowledgeable about a brand, develop feelings toward it, form a desire or preference, and then make a purchase. While this logical progression is often accurate, the response sequence does not always operate this way. Over the past decades, research in marketing, social psychology, and communications questioned the cognitive → affective → behavioural sequence, leading to other configurations of the response hierarchy.

ALTERNATIVE RESPONSE HIERARCHIES

Figure 4-3 relates two important consumer behaviour concepts: perceived product differentiation and product involvement. Perceived product differentiation is based on whether the receiver views competing *brands* within a product category similarly (b1 vs. b2), or views competing *product categories* similarly (pc1 vs. pc2). Involvement is based on the relevance with respect to the receiver's characteristics (e.g., needs), the message characteristics (e.g., source, content), and situational factors (e.g., time) across varying levels (pre-attention, focused attention, comprehension, and elaboration).[28] Figure 4-3 identifies the three alternative response hierarchies—the standard learning model, dissonance/attribution model, and low-involvement model—which result depending on high or low levels of differentiation and involvement.[29] Promotional planners would presumably alter their marketing communication plans depending on whether their target audience falls into one of the three hierarchies.

Figure 4-3   Alternative response hierarchies

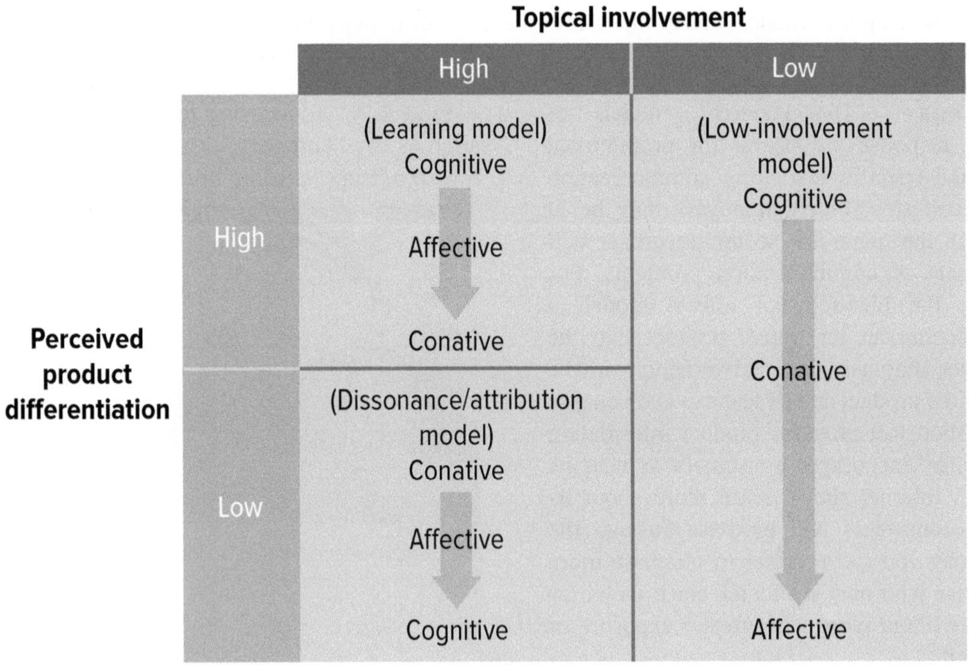

The Standard Learning Hierarchy   In many purchase situations, the consumer will go through the response process in the sequence depicted by the traditional communication models, identified as the **standard learning model** consisting of a learn → feel → do sequence. Information and knowledge acquired or *learned* about the brands is the basis for developing affect, or *feelings,* that guide what the consumer will do (e.g., actual trial or purchase). In this hierarchy, the consumer is viewed as an active participant in the communication process who gathers information through active learning.

The standard learning hierarchy likely occurs when the receiver of the message is highly involved in the purchase process and there is much differentiation among competing brands. High-involvement purchase decisions such as consumer durables (e.g., electronics, appliances, cars) are product categories where a standard learning hierarchy response process is likely for most consumers. Ads for these products and services are usually very detailed and provide consumers with information that can be used to evaluate brands and help them make a purchase decision (Exhibit 4-8). However, for a loyal customer who simply renews the lease or purchases the same brand of car over a few purchase occasions, the decisions are likely much less involving.

The Dissonance/Attribution Hierarchy   A second response hierarchy involves situations where consumers first behave, then develop attitudes or feelings as a result of that behaviour, and then learn or process information that supports the behaviour. This **dissonance/attribution model**, or do → feel → learn, occurs in situations where consumers must choose between two alternatives that are similar in quality but are complex and/or may have unknown attributes. The consumer may purchase the product on the basis of a recommendation by a non-media source and then attempt to support the decision by developing a positive attitude toward the brand and perhaps even developing negative feelings toward the rejected alternative(s). This reduces any *postpurchase dissonance* (as discussed in Chapter 3) that the consumer may experience resulting from doubt over the purchase. This is consistent with consumers' *selective perception* (as discussed in Chapter 3), where support reasons (i.e., attributions) for brand choice are relied upon. According to this model, attitudes develop *after* purchase, as does learning from the mass media. In these situations, the main effect of the mass media is not the promotion of original choice behaviour and attitude change but rather the reduction of dissonance by reinforcing the wisdom of the purchase or providing supportive information. For example, the ad shown in Exhibit 4-9 reinforces the consumer's decision to use Interac by providing reassurance to cardholders.

Critical marketers resist this view of the response hierarchy because they can't accept the notion that the mass media have no effect on the consumer's initial purchase decision. But the model doesn't claim the mass media have no effect—just that their major impact occurs after the purchase has been made. Marketing communications planners must be aware of the need for advertising and promotion efforts, not just to encourage brand selection but also to reinforce choices and ensure that a purchase pattern will continue. For example, one study found that advertising can lessen the negative effects of an unfavourable trial experience on brand evaluations when the ad is processed before the trial. However, when a negative trial experience precedes exposure to an ad, cognitive evaluations of the ad are more negative.[30] Other research showed that advertising can affect consumers' objective sensory interpretation of their experiences with a brand and what they remember about it.[31]

The Low-Involvement Hierarchy   For the **low-involvement hierarchy**, the receiver is viewed as passing from cognition to behaviour to attitude change. This learn → do → feel sequence characterizes situations of low consumer involvement in the purchase process. This hierarchy tends to occur when involvement in the purchase decision is low, there are minimal differences among brand alternatives, and mass-media (especially broadcast) advertising is important.

The notion of a low-involvement hierarchy is based on Herbert Krugman's theory explaining television advertising effects.[32] Krugman wanted to find out why TV advertising produced a strong effect on brand awareness and recall, but little change in consumers' attitudes toward the product. He hypothesized that TV is basically a low-involvement medium and the viewer's perceptual defences are reduced or even absent during commercials. In a low-involvement situation, the consumer does not compare the message with previously acquired beliefs, needs, or past experiences. The commercial results in subtle changes in the consumer's knowledge structure, however, particularly with repeated exposure. This knowledge change does not result in attitude change but is related to learning something about the advertised brand, such as a brand name, ad theme, or slogan. Subsequently, the knowledge may be sufficient to trigger a purchase when the consumer enters a purchase situation. The consumer will then form an attitude toward the purchased brand as a result of experience with it.

Exhibit 4-8   Ads for high-involvement decisions provide consumers with information to help them evaluate brands.

We made the best Civic even better.

© American Honda Motor Company

Exhibit 4-9   This ad reinforces the wisdom of the decision to use Interac Flash.

There's nothing you wouldn't do for your furry friend. From regular trips to the vet to buying the healthy dog food, you go to great lengths to protect the things you care about. That's why we go to great lengths to protect your money. With *Interac* Flash˚, you're protected with a $100 transaction limit, PIN verification after $200˚ and zero customer liability, so you won't pay for unauthorized purchases.

Interac Flash˚
The fast, secure way to use your own money.

© Interac Inc. and ACXSYS Corporation.

In the low-involvement hierarchy, the advertiser understands that passive or uninterested receivers may focus more on non-message elements like music, characters, symbols, and slogans or jingles rather than significant message content about the product or brand. Thus, advertisers of low-involvement products tend to repeat simple product claims such as a key copy point or distinctive product benefit and may use a non-message element (e.g., jingle) that is stored in the receiver's mind without active cognitive processing that becomes salient when entering an actual purchase situation. One study found that under low-involvement conditions, repetition of simple product claims increased consumers' memory of and belief in those claims.[33] Advertisers of low-involvement products might find it more profitable to pursue a heavy repetition strategy than to reach larger audiences with lengthy, more detailed messages. For example, Heinz has dominated the ketchup market by repeatedly telling consumers that its brand is the thickest and richest. Heinz has used a variety of advertising campaigns over the years, but they all repeat the same basic message and focus on the consistent quality of the brand (Exhibit 4-10).

IMPLICATIONS OF THE ALTERNATIVE RESPONSE MODELS

The three alternative response models show that the standard learning model, similar to the traditional hierarchy models, does not always apply. The notion of a highly involved consumer who engages in active information processing and learning and acts on the basis of higher-order beliefs and a well-formed attitude may be

Exhibit 4-10 Advertising promoting taste quality has helped Heinz dominate the ketchup market.

No one grows Ketchup like Heinz.

© H.J. Heinz Company, used with permission.

inappropriate for particular types of purchases. Sometimes consumers make a purchase decision on the basis of general awareness resulting from repetitive exposure to advertising, and attitude development occurs after the purchase, if at all. Thus, the objective of marketing communication may be to induce trial, so consumers can develop brand preferences primarily on the basis of their direct experience with the product.

From a promotional planning perspective, it is important that marketers examine the communication situation for their product and determine which type of response process is most likely to occur. They should analyze involvement levels and product/service differentiation as well as consumers' use of information sources and their levels of product experience. Once the manager has determined which response sequence is most likely to operate, the integrated marketing communications program can be designed to influence the response process in favour of the company's product or service.

For example, Cover Girl found itself in a precarious market position as high-end labels (e.g., Lancôme, Clinique) improved their penetration. Enter the Shade Brigade, a street team that went to high-traffic areas and helped the target select the right shade for her complexion and skin tone. After the consultation, the consumer was given a coupon indicating the correct shade to facilitate her purchase at a retail location. For those not reached by the team, in-store shade selectors assisted in decision making or acted as a key selling tool for beauty consultants, such as the ones in Shoppers Drug Mart. The turnaround moved overall market share up incrementally three years in a row to reach 17 percent.[34]

IMC Perspective 4-2 describes a new message for Cheerios cereal in which the response of the receiver would be subsequently measured to assess how it contributes positively to the brand.

IMC PERSPECTIVE 4-2

GENERAL MILLS GOES SOCIAL

General Mills turned its marketing communication approach toward socially significant directions for one of its main brands, Cheerios, and Cheerios brand extensions (regular, honey nut, multi-grain). The broad based change initially took time until senior management acceptance emerged, however once started, the momentum of moving beyond its healthy lifestyle messaging carried on until industry observers were praising the conglomerate. Impetus for the new approach began with General Mills establishing that it should communicate both its brand and what

© General Mills

the company cared about. Extensive and new research methods using social media for qualitative data collection instead of large-scale descriptive studies provided insight into consumer behaviour. Furthermore, market data indicated that brands connecting to social issues grew faster than those that did not.

First off, Multi-Grain Cheerios enlisted former Olympian Silken Laumann as a spokesperson for a message seemingly directed to her daughter, in which Silken pledged that she would from now on exclude the word "diet" from her vocabulary. The message concluded with an invitation to viewers to sign a petition (WorldWithoutDieting.ca) to show their commitment to eradicating the idea of dieting directed to young girls. General Mills planned to submit the petition once it gained 10,000 signatures to media companies to show that Canadians are concerned about "dietainment"—in other words, "unhealthy diet messages disguised as harmless entertainment." Although not stated, presumably the petition would encourage the media to minimize or eliminate their role in the "dietainment" dissemination. While it was a noble goal indeed, managers likely enjoyed the double-digit sales growth during the campaign.

An online marketing communication initiative entitled "The Cheerios Effect" tells the story of how Canadians connect and it also shows how the cereal connects: "Take two Os and drop them into a bowl of milk … see what happens? They're naturally drawn together. Scientists say the Cheerios Effect is the way small floating objects attract one another. That it has to do with fluid mechanics, surface tension, and buoyancy. We think it's about a lot more." Canadians volunteer their stories, which are all available for viewing (CheeriosEffect.ca), and a few are featured on YouTube and aired on TV. All of the stories have imagery of two Os moving together in a bowl of milk spliced between the scenes of the people in the story. The messages end with, "We all love to connect" followed by "That's the Cheerios Effect" written across the screen.

One message included a story of two gay Caucasian men adopting a young girl of a different ethnicity. The imagery is altered slightly with a third Cheerio joining a pair of Cheerios in the bowl, in addition to the men speaking and the child eating a few Cheerios. Marketing experts commenting on the Cheerios ad concluded that General Mills probably wanted to "reflect the reality of society today, rather than push a political agenda" with the story in its message. Consistent with this is that other Canadians' stories feature alternative ways of portraying the "Connect" theme. Another tells the story of a couple falling in love after the woman saw a man in a wheelchair singing in a band on TV. Melody and Parag's vignette illustrates their coming together even though they come from different backgrounds and did not speak each other's language. Two cousins living as sisters—one with hearing limitations—are the focus of another connection.

Across all these Canadian stories are characteristics not often seen in marketing communication messages: mixed race couples, homosexual couples, differently abled people, and non-traditional family

[Continued on next page]

[IMC Perspective 4-2 continued]

structures. However, many advertising executives see the General Mills advertising as part of a trend toward normalizing aspects of society that in the past may have seemed unusual. Echoing this is the CEO of the Canadian Centre of Diversity and Inclusion who suggests that car ads could show drivers with a disability who want to purchase a vehicle brand, rather than showing them in need of accommodation.

Sources: Russ Martin, "Stand Up and Say Something," *Marketing Magazine*, February/March 29, 2015; Tanya Kostiw, "Normalizing Today's Normal," *Strategy*, April 2015, p. 16; Tanya Kostiw, "Cheerios' Anti-Diet Mission," *Strategy*, July 2015, p. 9; https://cheerioseffect.ca.

Question:

1. Is the focus on social issues in advertising a good long-term message for building the Cheerios brand?

Cognitive Processing of Communications

For many years, research on the previous response models centred on identifying relationships between specific controllable variables (such as source and message factors) and outcome or response variables (such as attention, comprehension, attitudes, and purchase intentions). This approach appeared limited since it did not explain what caused the reactions.[35] In response, researchers attempted to understand the nature of cognitive reactions to persuasive messages. This section reviews two accepted approaches for understanding consumers' cognitive processing of advertising messages.

THE COGNITIVE RESPONSE APPROACH

One widely used method for examining consumers' cognitive processing of advertising messages is assessment of their **cognitive responses**, the thoughts that occur to them while reading, viewing, and/or hearing a communication.[36] These thoughts are usually measured by having consumers write or verbally report their reactions to a message. The assumption is that these thoughts reflect the recipient's cognitive processes or reactions and shape ultimate acceptance or rejection of the message.

Both academics and advertising practitioners use the cognitive response approach. Its focus has been to determine the types of responses evoked by an advertising message and how these responses relate to attitudes toward the ad, brand attitudes, and purchase intentions. Figure 4-4 depicts the three categories of cognitive responses—product/message, source-oriented, and ad execution thoughts—and how they may relate to attitudes and intentions.

Figure 4-4   A model of cognitive response

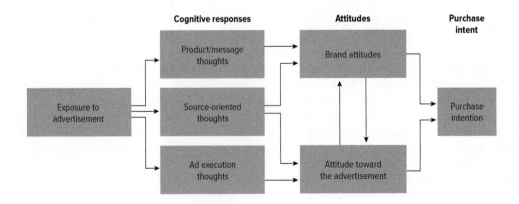

Product/Message Thoughts   The first category of thoughts comprises those directed at the product or service and/or the claims being made in the communication. Much attention has focused on two particular types of responses: counterarguments and support arguments.

Counterarguments are thoughts the recipient has that are opposed to the position taken in the message. For example, consider the ad for Shred-It shown in Exhibit 4-11. A consumer may express disbelief or disagreement by wondering why they should be concerned about being scammed. Other consumers may generate **support arguments**, or thoughts that affirm the claims conveyed in the message—"Ooohhh … I think I'd better take some action to protect my records and documents."

The likelihood of counterarguing is greater when the message makes claims that oppose the receiver's beliefs. For example, a consumer viewing a commercial that attacks a favourite brand is likely to mentally, and potentially verbally, disagree. These counterarguments relate negatively to message acceptance; the more the receiver counterargues, the less likely he or she is to accept the position advocated in the message.[37] Support arguments, on the other hand, relate positively to message acceptance. Thus, the marketer should develop ads or other promotional messages that minimize counterarguing and encourage support arguments.

Source-Oriented Thoughts   A second category of cognitive responses is directed at the source of the communication. One of the most important types of responses in this category is **source derogations**, or negative thoughts about the spokesperson or organization making the claims. Such thoughts generally lead to a reduction in message acceptance. If consumers find a particular spokesperson annoying or untrustworthy, they are less likely to accept what this source has to say.

Source-related thoughts are not always negative. Receivers who react favourably to the source generate favourable thoughts, or **source bolsters**. In general, most advertisers attempt to hire spokespeople their target audience likes so as to carry this effect over to the message. Considerations involved in choosing an appropriate source or spokesperson will be discussed in Chapter 7. How might consumers react to the model in Exhibit 4-12?

Ad Execution Thoughts   The third category of cognitive responses shown in Figure 4-4 consists of the individual's thoughts about the ad itself. Many of the thoughts receivers have when reading or viewing an ad do not concern the product and/or message claims directly. Rather, they are affective reactions representing the consumer's feelings toward the ad.[38] These thoughts may include reactions to ad execution factors such as the creativity of the ad, the quality of the visual effects, colours, and voice tones. **Ad execution-related thoughts** can be either favourable or unfavourable.[39] They are important because of their effect on attitudes toward the advertisement as well as the brand.

Exhibit 4-11   Consumers often generate support arguments in response to ads with extensive copy.

Hand-out/Shred-It/Newscom

Exhibit 4-12   The source in this ad could elicit both types of source thoughts.

Courtesy of Alberto-Culver Company

Attitude to Ad   Consumers' affective reactions to ads are an effect of cognitive responses, something not included in the previous models. **Attitude toward the ad** (A → ad) represents the receivers' favourable or unfavourable feelings toward the ad.[40] Advertisers are interested in consumers' reactions to the ad because they know that affective reactions are an important determinant of advertising effectiveness, since these reactions may be transferred to the brand itself or directly influence purchase intentions. One study found that people who enjoy a commercial are twice as likely as those who are neutral toward it to be convinced that the brand is the best.[41] Another study finds that those with more positive attitudes toward advertising in general result in stronger persuasion levels.[42]

Consumers' feelings about the ad may be just as important as their attitudes toward the brand (if not more so) in determining an ad's effectiveness.[43] The importance of affective reactions and feelings generated by the ad depends on several factors, among them the nature of the ad and the receiver's processing.[44] Many advertisers now use emotional ads designed to evoke feelings and affective reactions as the basis of their creative strategy. The success of this strategy depends in part on the consumers' involvement with the brand and their likelihood of attending to and processing the message.

THE ELABORATION LIKELIHOOD MODEL

Differences in the ways consumers process and respond to persuasive messages are shown in Figure 4-5, a simplified illustration of the **elaboration likelihood model (ELM)** of persuasion.[45] The ELM explains the process by which persuasive communications (such as ads) lead to persuasion by influencing *attitudes*. According to this model, the attitude formation or change process depends on the amount and nature of *elaboration,* or processing, of relevant information that occurs in response to a persuasive message.

Figure 4-5   Simplified elaboration likelihood model of persuasion

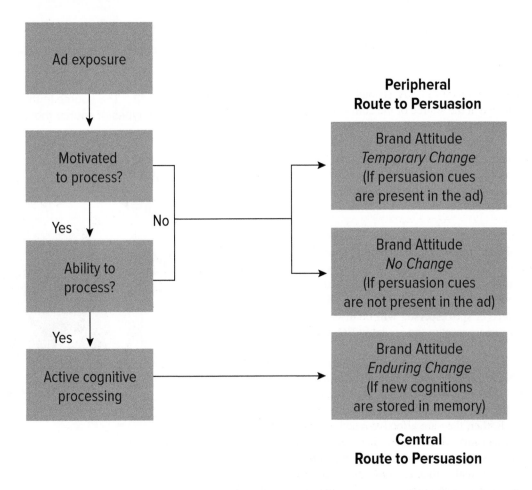

The ELM shows that elaboration likelihood is a function of two elements—motivation, and ability to process the message. *Motivation* to process the message depends on such factors as involvement, personal relevance, and the individual's needs and arousal levels. *Ability* depends on the individual's knowledge, intellectual capacity, and opportunity to process the message.

High elaboration (central route to persuasion) means the receiver carefully evaluates the information or arguments contained in the message. Low elaboration (peripheral route to persuasion) occurs when the receiver does not actively process the information but rather infers conclusions about the position being advocated in the message on the basis of simple positive or negative cues.

Central Route   Under the **central route to persuasion,** the receiver is viewed as a very active, involved participant in the communication process who has high ability and motivation to attend to, comprehend, and evaluate messages. When central processing of an advertising message occurs, the consumer pays close attention to message content and scrutinizes the message arguments. A high level of cognitive response activity or processing occurs, and the ad's ability to persuade the receiver depends primarily on the receiver's evaluation of the quality of the arguments presented. Predominantly favourable cognitive responses (support arguments and source bolsters) lead to favourable changes in cognitive structure, which lead to positive attitude change, or persuasion. Conversely, if the cognitive processing is predominantly unfavourable and results in counterarguments and/or source derogations, the changes in cognitive structure are unfavourable, resulting in negative attitude change. Attitude change that occurs through central processing is relatively enduring and should resist subsequent efforts to change it.

Peripheral Route   Under the **peripheral route to persuasion,** the receiver is viewed as lacking the motivation or ability to process information and is not likely to have detailed cognitive processing. Rather than evaluating the information presented in the message, the receiver relies on peripheral cues that may be incidental to the main arguments. The receiver's reaction to the message depends on how he or she evaluates these peripheral cues.

The consumer may use several types of peripheral cues or cognitive shortcuts rather than carefully evaluating the message arguments presented in an advertisement.[46] Favourable attitudes may be formed if the endorser in the ad is viewed as attractive and/or likable, or if the consumer likes certain executional aspects of the ad, such as the way it is made, the music, or the imagery. Notice how the ad in Exhibit 4-13 contains positive peripheral cues contained in the excellent visual imagery. These cues might help consumers form a positive attitude toward the brand even if they do not process the message portion of the ad.

Peripheral cues can also lead to rejection of a message. For example, ads that advocate extreme positions, use endorsers who are not well liked or have credibility problems, or are not executed well (such as low-budget ads for local retailers) may be rejected without any consideration of their information or message arguments. As shown in Figure 4-5, the ELM views attitudes resulting from peripheral processing as temporary. Therefore, favourable attitudes must be maintained by continual exposure to the peripheral cues, such as through repetitive advertising.

Explanation for ELM   One explanation for how the peripheral route to persuasion works lies in the idea of **classical conditioning**. Classical conditioning assumes that learning is an *associative process* with an already existing relationship between a stimulus and a response. This process is transferred to a **conditioned stimulus** that elicits a **conditioned response** resembling the

Exhibit 4-13   The colourful imagery in this ad acts as a peripheral cue.

Banking that fits your life.

CIBC Cube Design & "Banking that fits your life." are trademarks of CIBC.

Hand-out/CIBC/Newscom

original unconditioned reaction. Two factors are important for learning to occur through the associative process. The first is contiguity, which means the unconditioned stimulus and conditioned stimulus must be close in time and space. The other important principle is *repetition,* or the frequency of the association. The more often the unconditioned and conditioned stimuli occur together, the stronger the association between them will be.

Buyers can be conditioned to form favourable impressions of brands through the associative process. Advertisers strive to associate their products and services with perceptions and emotions known to evoke positive reactions from consumers. Products are promoted through image advertising, in which the brand is shown with an unconditioned stimulus that elicits pleasant feelings. When the brand is presented simultaneously with this unconditioned stimulus, the brand itself becomes a conditioned stimulus that elicits the same favourable response. The ad in Exhibit 4-14 shows an application of this strategy. Notice how this ad associates Chanel perfume with the playful behaviour of Gisele Bündchen.[47]

Implications of the ELM   The ELM has important implications for marketing communication since the most effective type of message depends on the route to persuasion the target audience follows. If the involvement level of the target audience is high, the message should contain strong arguments that are difficult for the receiver to refute or counterargue. If the involvement level of the target audience is low, peripheral cues such as music or images may be more important than detailed message arguments. For example, in the Casio ad in Exhibit 4-15 the cool skateboarder image and product images dominate the message, leaving someone in a low-involvement target audience group to not consider price or reliability attributes. Therefore, marketers of low-involvement products often rely on creative tactics that emphasize peripheral cues and use repetitive advertising to create and maintain favourable attitudes toward their brand.

An interesting test of the ELM showed that the effectiveness of a celebrity endorser in an ad depends on the receiver's involvement level.[48] When involvement was low, a celebrity endorser had a significant effect on

Exhibit 4-14   Chanel associates the product with the playfulness of its celebrity endorser.

© Lou Linwei / Alamy Stock Photo

Exhibit 4-15   This Casio watch ad emphasizes the cool skateboarder image, rather than price or reliability, likely influencing low-involvement audiences.

© Ovu0ng / Shutterstock.com

attitudes. When the receiver's involvement was high, however, the use of a celebrity had no effect on brand attitudes; the quality of the arguments used in the ad was more important. The explanation given for these findings was that a celebrity may serve as a peripheral cue in the low-involvement situation, allowing the receiver to develop favourable attitudes based on feelings toward the source rather than on engaging in extensive processing of the message. A highly involved consumer, however, experiences more detailed central processing of the message content. The quality of the message claims becomes more important than the identity of the endorser.

Response Model for Managerial Decision Making

In this section, we reconcile the models presented in this chapter and illustrate a response model relevant for managerial decision making. The first section concludes that traditional communication response models based on a hierarchy or adaptation of a hierarchy are limited in their ability to explain how advertising works. The subsequent sections summarize another part of the Rossiter and Percy perspective that is managerially oriented and will be used to set communication objectives and plan for creative messages in subsequent chapters.

IMPORTANCE OF A MANAGERIAL MODEL

A comprehensive literature review to better understand advertising effectiveness highlights the need for a response model that assists managerial decision making.[49] The authors concluded that although hierarchy models have been actively employed for nearly 100 years, there is little support for the temporal (i.e., time-based) sequence of the hierarchy of effects and that the models exclude product category and brand experiences.

As observed in the other models, the consumers' response process includes *cognition,* the "thinking" dimension of a person's response; *affect,* the "feeling" dimension; and *experience,* which is a feedback dimension based on the outcomes of product purchase and usage. However, as Figure 4-6 shows, there is no prescribed order or hierarchy. Each response can be a result of the audience's motivation and ability to process the message. Advertising, and other marketing communication, is mediated or filtered by factors that can change the individual's response. The implication is that promotional planners should focus on cognition, affect, and experience as critical responses that advertising may influence; however, they should not assume a particular sequence of response.

Figure 4-6   A framework for studying how advertising works

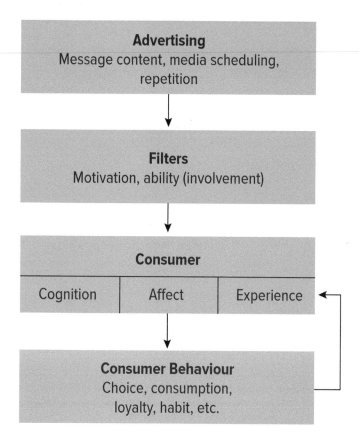

In contrast to the other models, the consumers' response process is significantly dependent on product category and brand experiences. They suggest that the effects of advertising should be evaluated using the cognition, affect, and experience dimensions, with intermediate variables being more important than others depending on factors such as the product category, stage of the product life cycle, target audience, and competition. Advertising and marketing communication have differing effects depending on whether the consumer currently uses the *product* or not when receiving the message. Furthermore, these differing effects also emerge when considering if a consumer currently uses the *brand* or not when receiving the message.

MANAGERIAL MODEL APPROACH

We introduced the Rossiter and Percy (R&P) perspective in Chapter 3 when identifying options for the target audience decision. This perspective suggests that promotional planners initially consider the message as being directed to either customers purchasing their brand or non-customers who have not purchased their brand. This managerial view starts with the consumer and is based on the consumer's previous brand experience and degree of brand loyalty, two critical factors that influence how motivated or involved the audience would be when responding to promotional messages.[50]

A continuation of the R&P perspective is a communication response model that takes a managerial view by identifying the responses in terms of the promotional manager's brand for any type of marketing communication decision. Figure 4-7 shows the initial processing stage, which highlights the immediate responses to any advertising message while receiving the ad exposure. This implies the psychological experiences that occur in the target audience's mind while watching a television commercial, for example. Communication effects refer to the lasting brand impressions that remain with the target audience after the target audience processes the message. This implies the target audience's memory of the brand that results after watching the television commercial.

Figure 4-7   Planning for processing and communication effects

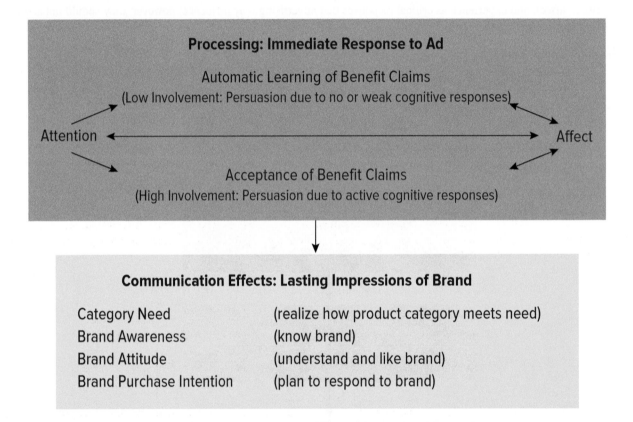

The example of processing and communication effects for a TV ad can be readily extended to all methods of marketing communication. Marketing communication professionals and researchers have called for an alternative model that accounts for consumer responses to all aspects of marketing communication.[51] The decision-making orientation of this model with a focus on brand building appears to address these requests.

PROCESSING OF MESSAGES

This notion of processing is consistent with all the features of the previous models. After attending to the ad, the target audience may have low or high involvement in terms of how much thought regarding the brand's benefit claims is generated while receiving the message. For example, as the ELM indicated, highly involved target audiences are more likely to have active cognitive responses. In addition, affect, or emotional responses, will influence and be generated as a result of these cognitive responses. Furthermore, pleasant or unpleasant emotional responses may occur while attending to the execution variables (e.g., music) of the message, and positive (or negative) emotional responses may focus greater (or less) attention to the message.

The seemingly simultaneous cognitive and emotional responses occurring while attending to a message are consistent with current views of marketing communication and how the brain works in psychology.[52] Anecdotal evidence of this is seen when one considers reactions to a Super Bowl ad (e.g., TV commercial) where both thinking and feeling something about the brand occurs. Furthermore, the temporal concern of the hierarchical models is diminished by considering the processing stage prior to the communication effects stage.

From an IMC planning perspective, managers need to design brand messages with the understanding of the target audience's processing. For instance, to attract new customers, the manager may consider brand messages that will support high-involvement processing. And, as we will see in the media chapters and the chapters relating to other communication tools, the manager may consider more involving avenues for delivering the message (e.g., social media).

Alternatively, companies often have programs to both attract and retain customers. This could require promotional planners to strategically evaluate the balance of their messages. Should messages that attempt to generate high involvement be primary or secondary in the overall message strategy? Analytical questions such as this emerge by considering the processing stage as a key precursor to planning for the communication effects stage.

COMMUNICATION EFFECTS OF MESSAGES

Figure 4-7 also distinguishes the brand communication effects that are established more permanently in the target audience's memory. Overall, R&P summarize four **communication effects** for the target audience.

Category Need   *Category need* involves the target audience's perception of requiring a specific product category to satisfy a particular need. This communication effect is relevant for a number of reasons. It supports the development of primary demand of a product category independent of the particular brand, something that certain industries and brands are considerably concerned about. Product factors are evident in the alternative hierarchy model where product differentiation affected consumer responses to messages, so a product category effect is especially important in most marketing communication situations. The start of the decision-making process is need recognition, so linking a product to a particular need is an ongoing marketing communication task for most brands.

Brand Awareness   *Brand awareness* involves the target audience's ability to recognize and/or recall the brand within the product category in sufficient detail to make a purchase. This communication effect is a strong form of consumer knowledge as the target audience needs to know extensive details about the brand to have confidence in the purchase selection. It also highlights the importance of distinguishing between knowledge that can be retrieved via brand recall and knowledge that is salient when given a prompt or cue via brand recognition.

Brand Attitude   *Brand attitude* involves the target audience's overall evaluation of the brand in relation to its ability to satisfy the reason why they want it. Brand attitude is a central communication effect where the target audience's evaluation includes both cognitive and affective components, acknowledging that each aspect is relevant for planning for all purchase situations. Other models represented the entire response process (i.e., cognition, affect, behaviour) as reflecting an attitude that occurred in various orders. This idea of brand attitude does not rely on any hierarchical order of the attitude components.

Brand Purchase Intention   Brand purchase intention involves the target audience's self-instruction to respond (shopping behaviour, purchase) to the brand. A mental activity predicated on the anticipation of participating in a behavioural action specifically directed to the brand is another indicator of the effects of marketing communication.

**LO5 IMC Planning:
Managerial Decision Making**

We suggest a few conclusions for managers in making advertising and promotion decisions based on the models presented regarding how advertising works in terms of consumer response; after all, academics will continue this investigation while managers still need to make decisions.

First, it appears that managers should consider and plan for both the cognitive and the affective responses of the receiver who is processing advertising or any promotional message. Receivers typically have both cognitive and emotional reactions to the messages they see all around them every day.

Second, managers are concerned with the resulting effects of the advertising or promotional message for a time period after the receiver has received and processed the message. As suggested in many of the models, managers want to know if their messages are improving awareness or attitudes.

Finally, the primary characteristic that influences communication success appears to be the receiver's previous brand experience. This implies managers should be cognizant of who exactly is the target of the message. As discussed in Chapter 3, the manager needs a detailed profile of the target audience to have an understanding to gauge communication success. Thus, managers require a decision framework that addresses these points.

The managerial approach suggested at the end of this chapter offers two important IMC planning considerations. One, there is an obvious and clear connection to the target audience's purchase of the promotional manager's particular brand. This is apparent with its reference to the brand in three communication effects. It is also seen in the connection to category need, which addresses the underlying reason why the target audience is motivated to buy the promotional manager's product, and where the target audience understands the brand fits in the market in relation to brands in other product categories.

Two, the managerial model can be applied for all aspects of an IMC program, as shown in Figure 4-8.[53] The managerial decisions (i.e., controllable variables), source, message, channel, and receiver (via target audience selection) are assessed in terms of resulting outcomes, exposure, processing, communication effects, and action. For example, ads with iPhone users (i.e., source) taking pictures or listening to music (i.e., message) shown on TV (i.e., channel) are directed to the target audience, who are likely to be users of iPhones. Promotional planners would undoubtedly be interested in four communication results listed for this execution. Furthermore, this logic could be extended for print ads or video-type ads placed on the Internet, either on a website or in social media.

Figure 4-8   IMC planning matrix

	Source	Message	Channel	Receiver
Exposure				
Processing (attention and comprehension)				
Communication Effects (yielding and retention)				
Action				

Similarly, the same approach applies for a whole advertising campaign over time. For example, Telus ads with multiple animals (i.e., source) behaving in a way to visually convey a product (i.e., message) across multiple media (i.e., channels) are directed to the target audience, who are likely to be users of other brands (e.g., Bell, Rogers). Across all aspects of this advertising, Telus promotional planners would concern themselves with all four communication results. Furthermore, this idea can be extended to other promotional tools like Telus's public relations activities.

The final implication of this is that all elements of an entire IMC program can be planned with a matrix, including any communication via the Internet and any kind of promotional event/activity or sales promotion. Any tool for communication retains the characteristics of the communication model in Figure 4-1. One revision would be situations where a receiver encounters a brand message from another consumer in social media; however, the other consumer is the sender in this respect, and the planning retains its characteristics. However, the brand is concerned with how it influenced the consumer who is the sender of the message. This is evident in many social media contexts where the brand encourages the development of user-generated content, or other forms of marketing communication from ordinary consumers.

The R&P model and the other communication response models will be revisited in the next chapter. Promotional planners use a communication response model to determine the communication objectives for advertising and other promotional tools. It is important to base marketing communication decisions on a model and translate them into specific objectives since promotional planners need clear guidance for the remaining marketing communication decisions.

Learning Objectives Summary

 LO1 Explain the elements of the communication process and identify the role of marketing communication.

The function of all elements of the promotional mix is to communicate, so promotional planners must understand the communication process. This process can be very complex; successful marketing communication depends on a number of factors, including the nature of the message, the audience's interpretation of it, and the environment in which it is received. For effective communication to occur, the sender must encode a message in such a way that it will be decoded by the receiver in the intended manner. Feedback from the receiver helps the sender determine whether proper decoding has occurred or whether noise has interfered with the communication process.

 LO2 Contrast traditional communication response models and alternative response hierarchies.

Promotional planning begins with the receiver or target audience, as marketers must understand how the audience is likely to respond to sources of communication or types of messages. Traditional response models provide an initial understanding of this process; however, limitations of these models led to more comprehensive approaches. Alternative response hierarchies imply modification of the traditional models due to the target audience's involvement and perceived product differentiation. Different orderings of the traditional response hierarchy include the standard learning, dissonance/attribution, and low-involvement models. The alternative response hierarchy postulated different ordering of cognition, affect, and behaviour depending upon the involvement and differentiation.

 LO3 Develop the response processes of receivers of marketing communication through two models of cognitive processing.

The cognitive processing of communication revealed two models: the cognitive response approach and the elaboration likelihood model. The former examines the thoughts evoked by a message in terms of product/message thoughts, source-oriented thoughts, and ad execution thoughts and how they shape the receiver's ultimate acceptance or rejection of the communication by influencing brand attitude and attitude to the ad. The elaboration likelihood model of attitude formation and change recognizes two forms of message processing, the central and peripheral routes to persuasion, which are a function of the receiver's motivation and ability to process a message. The model postulates that each route leads to varying degrees of attitude change.

 LO4 Illustrate a response model for managerial decision making.

Theoretical research concludes that there are three critical intermediate effects between advertising and purchase: cognition, affect, and experience. Those responsible for planning the IMC program should learn as much as possible about their target audience and how it may respond to advertising and other forms of marketing communications. A managerial view of the response process provides direction for understanding how promotional planners should determine their brands' communication strategies.

 LO5 Construct ideas on how the knowledge of response models can be used for IMC planning.

A more managerially useful approach for understanding how advertising works is included in this chapter. The model suggests that both cognitive and emotional processing responses are critical during the initial stages of receiving the message, such as while watching a TV ad or seeing an ad paid for by an advertiser in social media. Ads can be developed to invoke the anticipated content of the cognitive responses and the types of emotions experienced by the target audience. Furthermore, the model identifies lasting brand communication effects that promotional planners should strive to achieve with their ad messages and IMC tools.

Review Questions

1. Recall the elements of Figure 4-1 and identify them for all aspects of an IMC plan—advertising, sales promotion, direct marketing, public relations, and Internet marketing.
2. Explain why the three response models of Figure 4-2 are limited in planning for an IMC campaign.
3. Explain what is meant by a central versus a peripheral route to persuasion, and the factors that would determine when each might be used by consumers in response to an advertisement.
4. What are the key differences between traditional response models and the response model shown in Figure 4-7?
5. Why is it important to use a response model that is more applicable to managerial decision making?

Applied Questions

1. Consider ads found in social media like Facebook, Twitter, and YouTube, and assess whether the model in Figure 4-1 is useful for explaining how marketing communication works in these digital contexts.
2. Assume that you are the marketing communications manager for a brand of paper towels. Discuss how the low-involvement hierarchy could be of value in developing an advertising and promotion strategy for this brand.
3. Select an ad that would be processed by a central route to persuasion and one where peripheral processing would occur. Show the ads to several people and ask them to write down the thoughts they have about each ad. Analyze their thoughts using the cognitive and emotional responses discussed in the chapter.
4. Find an example of a print ad and evaluate it using the response model shown in Figure 4-7. Identify the specific types of cognitive and emotional responses that the ad might elicit from consumers and discuss why they might occur.
5. Red Bull has numerous IMC activities, including its TV advertising, events, and promotional activities. Check the Red Bull website and any other online material for background, and apply them to the matrix in Figure 4-8 to validate whether each activity assists in planning for an IMC.

CHAPTER FIVE

Objectives for the IMC Plan

LEARNING OBJECTIVES

LO1 Distinguish among marketing, behavioural, and communication objectives and identify the value of setting each type of objective.

LO2 Describe the historical approaches for setting communication objectives for advertising.

LO3 Evaluate the options for setting behavioural objectives and apply them when constructing a promotional plan.

LO4 Choose among the options for setting communication objectives and apply them when designing IMC recommendations.

LO5 Assemble the best combination of behavioural and communication objectives for each stage of the consumer decision-making process.

Boston Pizza Delivers Ads for Fans

With its 50th anniversary on the horizon, Boston Pizza's creative and memorable advertising and other marketing communications continually placed the brand at the forefront of everyone's mind as it carved out a 3.7 percent market share in the competitive full-service restaurant category. From its humble beginnings in Western Canada, Edmonton and Penticton in particular, the chain boasted over 360 restaurants across Canada, the United States, and Mexico by 2015. Early on, partners Jim Treliving and George Melville purchased the original company and grew it to one of Canada's iconic brands. Its strategy of balancing a big national brand within a local community paid off successfully over time.

Advertising always played a part in brand development during the early years, moving from flyers on car windshields, to newspaper ads, to radio ads with an Italian-themed jingle, but Boston Pizza's big break occurred during Vancouver's Expo 86, where people from the world over lined up to eat. The momentum gained with Expo 86 allowed Boston Pizza in the 1990s to expand its franchise base eastward and become a national company capable of launching national TV campaigns on TSN and Sportsnet. With a distinct Boston theme, this early '90s campaign communicated Boston Pizza as a restaurant and sports bar. One spokesperson was actor John Ratzenberger, who played Cliff on the TV show *Cheers,* which was set in Boston. Ads featured Ratzenberger speaking over the song "More Than a Feeling," which was recorded by the rock group Boston. Another campaign in the late '90s featured Canadian comedian Howie Mandel proclaiming "You're Among Friends," which became the main slogan for a message that gained notoriety and strong awareness in the eastern expansion regions.

Boston Pizza moved its advertising in a new direction over the past decade, with numerous creative approaches to continue to build its brand with a "Here to Make You Happy" slogan. One initiative, "Finger Cooking With Bill," targeted dads who preferred not to cook and emphasized Boston Pizza's online ordering for take-out and delivery, in addition to being a great sports bar for dads and dudes. Created by its agency, Taxi, the TV, digital, out-of-home, direct mail, and point-of-sale message provided Boston Pizza with a category unique message compared to others who were targeting women, moms, and families. The agency then launched the "Flatties and Drummies" campaign with the renowned and fictional chicken wings critic Carl Carlson, who humorously and eloquently spoke of Boston's Pizza's quality wings. The TV ads, combined with extensive social and Xbox media and promotional items, propelled the brand to win the fictitious Crystal Wingy Award for Best New Wing, much to the chagrin of fooled competitors who wondered why they did not win.

Carrying on with another character in its advertising beyond John, Howie, and Carl, Boston Pizza introduced a fake food inventor, Terry Peters, to launch its boneless wings. Again with the idea of appealing to dads and dudes, the message played in all sorts of vehicles including TV, radio, digital banners, and pre-rolls in Xbox media to go along with a fun avatar of Peters. After this, Boston Pizza continued to tie its brand advertising with product launches and produced ads of varying lengths with historical characters (e.g., a caveman, a Viking, a cowboy) who encouraged modern day dudes to eat one for them, with the one being Boston Pizza's new Pizzaburger (i.e., a burger wrapped in pizza dough). The ads produced significant brand communication effects and substantially assisted in improving burger sales. Another campaign featured "Ribnecks" characters from a rural southern family to advertise its ribs menu. A promotional item of a "Rib Stain Camo" T-shirt sold out immediately as the imagery of *Duck Dynasty* resonated with rib-lovers.

Boston Pizza's most recent entry, "We'll Make You a Fan," associated the Boston Pizza brand to sports and families more directly with images of children, men, and women playing sports and watching sports in the Boston Pizza locations. Citing statistics of high participation levels of children and adults playing sports, the brand looked to a new advertising avenue to build on its professional sports sponsorship of NHL teams and the Toronto Blue Jays.

Sources: Russ Martin, "Boston Pizza Promises to Turn Its Customers Into Fans," *Marketing Magazine*, February 20, 2015; "Boston Pizza's Epic Pizzaburger Launch," *Strategy*, February/March 2014; Tanya Kostiw, "Boston Pizza's Big 5-0," *Strategy*, April 2014; Susan Krashinsky, "Boston Pizza Ad Makes Man, Woman and Child a Fan," *Globe and Mail*, February 26, 2015.

Question:

1. Does the new approach retain the previous distinctiveness of past ads to ensure positive brand communication effects?

Promotional decision makers see objective setting as an important part of the IMC planning process. The task of setting objectives can be complex and difficult and it must be done properly, because specific goals and objectives are the foundation on which all marketing communication decisions are made and provide a standard against which performance can be measured.

This chapter examines the purpose of objectives and the role they play in the development, implementation, and evaluation of an IMC program. First, we distinguish among marketing, behavioural, and communication objectives. Then we describe the historical approaches of setting objectives for marketing communication based on the response models discussed in Chapter 4. We then present a comprehensive managerial framework for setting behavioural and communication objectives for each element of the IMC plan and for the overall IMC plan that we refer to in the remaining parts of the book.

LO1   Objective Setting

Setting specific objectives should be an integral part of the promotional planning process. However, companies can either fail to set marketing communication objectives or set ones that are inadequate for developing the promotional plan or measuring its effectiveness. This section discusses the value of objectives and distinguishes among marketing, behavioural, and communication objectives for optimal IMC planning.

VALUE OF OBJECTIVES

Perhaps one reason why companies do not set objectives for their IMC programs is a failure to see their value. Advertising and promotional objectives are needed for reasons such as communication function, planning and decision making, and measurement and evaluation.

Communication Function   Specific objectives for the IMC program facilitate coordination of the groups working on the campaign. One notable example is Hellmann's "Real Food Movement," designed to encourage Canadians to enjoy more real, local food. Led by its signature mayonnaise product with its all-natural Canadian ingredients of eggs, canola oil, and vinegar, Hellmann's portrayed its brand as a natural part of everyone's diet. The program featured urban gardens where residents received an allotment to grow fruits and vegetables. Extensive TV, newspaper, digital, direct, and in-store notification invited applicants to the program. Hellmann's worked with a chef who created real food recipes for TV ads and online videos, participated in a broadcast tour, and demonstrated how meal preparation with real food is fun and easy. The "Eat Real. Eat Local." phase featured a "family dinner" video that documented the state of Canada's food delivery system and emphasized the importance of eating local.[1] Promotional personnel involved in the planning and development of the IMC program include client personnel and numerous contracted agencies. All parties coordinated the program together, which required knowledge of what Hellmann's hoped to accomplish through the objectives of its IMC program. As another example, the ad in Exhibit 5-1 shows that RBC's involvement with the cause was dependent upon all promotional participants' understanding RBC's objectives.

Planning and Decision Making   Specific promotional objectives guide IMC plan development. All phases of a firm's promotional strategy should be based on the established objectives, including budgeting, creative, and media decisions as well as supportive programs. For example, to execute all the programs for its "Real Food Movement" campaign, Hellmann's retained agencies to coordinate public relations activities, digital tools, advertising, and in-store presentations, which all drove traffic to its Internet site. Meaningful objectives certainly helped guide the decision making of all partners that contributed to Hellmann's winning a Canadian Advertising Success Stories (CASSIES) Grand

Exhibit 5-1   The objective of this ad is to demonstrate RBC's support for a cause.

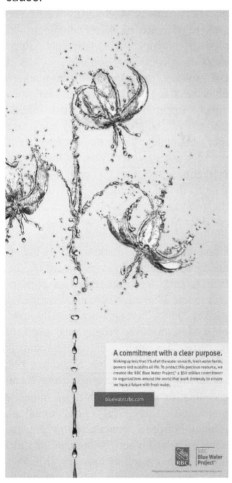

© Royal Bank of Canada

Prix for best overall IMC program. As this example shows, promotional planners face numerous strategic and tactical options in terms of creative themes, media, and budget allocation among promotional mix elements, and their choice should be based on how well a strategy matches the promotional objectives.

Measurement and Evaluation   Setting specific objectives provides a benchmark against which the effects of the promotional campaign can be measured. In the case of Hellmann's, sales growth averaged 7 percent per year over six years, which culminated in a market share of nearly 50 percent. Consumer belief that Hellmann's contained real and simple ingredients doubled to include nearly 50 percent of the population. As this indicates, good objectives are measurable, and they specify a method and criteria for determining how well the promotional program is working. Most organizations are concerned about the return on promotional investment; comparing actual effects against measurable objectives determines whether the return justifies the expense. With the explosion of digital communication in marketing, established procedures for measuring its effects are still undergoing development. Marketers are still trying to estimate the most appropriate methods and are not fully tracking all digital communication in comparison to established media.[2]

MARKETING OBJECTIVES

Marketing objectives are generally outlined in the firm's marketing plan and are statements of what is to be accomplished by the overall marketing program within a given time period. Marketing objectives are usually defined in terms of specific, measurable outcomes such as sales volume, market share, profit, or return on investment. Good marketing objectives are "smart" as they specifically delineate a target market, provide quantifiable measures, identify achievable and realistic levels of performance, and note the time frame for accomplishing the goal (often one year). For example, a copy-machine company may have as its marketing objective "to increase sales by 10 percent in the small-business segment of the market during the next 12 months."

The selection of the type of marketing objective is a function of market conditions. A company with a very high market share may seek to increase its sales volume by stimulating growth in the product category, perhaps by increasing consumption by current users or encouraging non-users to buy the product. A firm in a fast-growing market may have market share as its marketing objective since this reflects that it is growing more quickly than its direct competitors. In mature markets with limited growth, firms tend to focus on profit as the key marketing objective. Finally, a firm that faces unique consumer preferences across various geographic markets (e.g., Ontario versus Quebec) may in fact have a unique marketing objective for each region. The marketing objective guiding the ad in Exhibit 5-2 may be to increase sales volume, since the message attempts to sway users of other brands of tires to consider Michelin for its gas mileage and safety.

Upon reviewing the marketing plan, the promotional planner should understand the marketing objectives, the marketing strategy and tactics, and the importance and purpose of advertising and promotion. Marketing objectives defined in terms of sales, profit, or market share increases are usually not appropriate promotional objectives, however promotional planners may rely on marketing objectives for guiding the content and direction of the marketing communication objectives. Marketing objectives are for the entire marketing program, and achieving them depends on the proper coordination and execution of *all* marketing mix elements, not just promotion. Alternatively, promotional planners usually approach promotion from a communication perspective, where the purpose of advertising and other promotional mix elements is to communicate information or a selling message. IMC Perspective 5-1 identifies the importance of marketing and communication objectives in Canadian Tire's decisions. The debate between the use of sales objectives versus the use of communication objectives for promotion decisions is our next topic to explore.

Exhibit 5-2   Michelin stresses higher gas mileage, as well as safety, in its ads.

The MICHELIN® DEFENDER® tire allows you to stop up to 31 feet shorter[1] and drive up to 21,000 miles longer[2] than a leading competitor[2], and is backed by our 90,000-mile limited warranty.[4] Find out more at michelinman.com/defender

1 – Based on internal wet braking test results versus Goodyear® Assurance® ComforTred® Touring tire size 185/65R15. 2 – Based on commissioned third-party wear test results versus Continental® ProContact™ with EcoPlus Technology tire size 215/60R16. 4 – 90,000-mile limited warranty for H- and T-rated tires; 80,000-mile limited warranty for V-rated tires. See michelinman.com for warranty details. Copyright ©2013 Michelin North America, Inc. All rights reserved.

Courtesy of Michelin North America, Inc.

IMC PERSPECTIVE 5-1

CANADIAN TIRE IS CANADA'S STORE

Beyond its namesake retail store, Canadian Tire Corporation (CTC) includes PartSource, Gas+, FGL Sports (Sport Chek, Hockey Experts, Sports Experts, National Sports, Intersport, Pro Hockey Life, and Atmosphere), Mark's, Canadian Tire Financial Services, CT REIT, and Canadian Tire Jumpstart, a nationally registered charity dedicated to removing financial barriers so kids across Canada can participate in sports and physical activities. Across all these outlets, CTC transformed its marketing operations to achieve marketing objectives, and initiated IMC activities to clearly communicate and move it to the forefront of Canadian retailing.

© Valentino Visentini / Alamy Stock Photo

The inspiration for change began when the sponsorship car of three different retailers came to the starting line of a NASCAR race, with CTC senior executives and counterparts of each retailer completely unaware of the overlapping exposure. First off, CTC streamlined the organizational structure to improve communication across the retail units. Management moved toward clear brand identification by focusing on one consistent triangle logo after discovering that the company used over 70 variations. And CTC planned to be a leader in bringing digital shopping experiences to retail stores.

From a marketing standpoint, Canadian Tire retail reintroduced its ecommerce and created "The Canadian Way," a digital lifestyle site. The new approach offers social media features and lets consumers plan with their needs in mind along four domains: living, fixing, playing, and driving. Over the course of its initial eight months, the new site attracted 673,000 visitors who looked at 5.5 million pages. In Canadian Tire stores, in-aisle devices allow consumers to see the digital catalogue for enhanced shopping. Similarly, Sport Chek innovated with a new digital retail concept with 140 screens, digital tiles built into display tables, tablets attached to clothing racks, and many digital displays showing video and still messages. Sport Chek suppliers like Reebok installed customized shoe kiosks that allowed consumers to design their own shoe to be shipped weeks later. CTC saw Sport Chek's innovations as leading the way for similar changes for Canadian Tire retail.

And from a marketing communications standpoint, Canadian Tire retail produced over 30 television commercials, many with the same spokesperson, and identified the brand with a "Canada's Store" slogan. The executions focused on families and how Canadian Tire's product fit within the needs of this target audience. CTC signed sponsorship deals with the Canadian Olympic Committee and the NHL hockey ownership groups in Toronto and Ottawa, with an Ottawa arena being renamed as the Canadian Tire Centre. As part of this, CTC created a centralized sponsorship team to avoid mistakes like the NASCAR fiasco and to negotiate better deals across its over 70 sponsorship properties.

The ads associated with the Olympic sponsorship, "We All Play for Canada," inspired numerous Canadians as the campaign achieved 55 million media impressions. Advertising tracking measures improved in 2014 over 2013 in terms of prompted recall, brand effects, and message communication. Extensions of the "We All Play for Canada" message included exposure with other sports and a connection to Canadian Tire's Jumpstart program. An important feature of Jumpstart included the "Big Play" where children received tickets to a Team Canada game during the World Junior Championship. With heightened media exposure, awareness reached 95 percent and significant social media activity helped the charity to raise nearly $50,000.

Sources: Kristin Laird, "Acing the Test," *Marketing Magazine*, January/February 2014; Matthew Chung, "TJ Flood Scores an All-Star Strategy," *Strategy*, December 19, 2014; Jennifer Holt, "Cause Action Awards 2015," *Strategy*, April 2015, p. 22.

Question:

1. Do the digital innovations, sponsorship, and advertising appear to be good IMC strategy for Canadian Tire retail?

SALES OBJECTIVE DEBATE

Some managers believe that the only meaningful objective for their promotional program is sales, since the reason why a firm spends money on advertising and promotion is to sell its product or service. Promotional spending represents an investment of a firm's scarce resources that requires an economic justification like any other business decision. Managers generally compare investment options on a common financial basis, such as return on investment (ROI). Their position is that monies spent on advertising and other forms of promotion should produce measurable results, such as increasing sales or the brand's market share to assess the effectiveness of the expenditure decision.

One problem with a sales objective for promotion is that poor sales results can be due to other marketing mix variables, including product design or quality, packaging, distribution, or pricing. Advertising can make consumers aware of and interested in the brand, but it can't make them buy it, particularly if it is not readily available or is priced higher than a competing brand. Furthermore, unanticipated or uncontrollable environmental factors can devastate a firm's sales forecast even with a well communicated promotion program.

Another problem with a sales objective is that the effects of advertising often occur over an extended period. Advertising has a lagged or **carryover effect**; monies spent on advertising do not necessarily have an immediate impact on sales.[3] Advertising may create awareness, interest, and/or favourable attitudes toward a brand, but these feelings will not result in an actual purchase until the consumer enters the market later. A review of econometric studies that examined the duration of cumulative advertising effects found that for mature, frequently purchased, low-priced products, advertising's effect on sales lasts up to nine months.[4] Models have been developed to account for the carryover effect of advertising and to help determine the long-term effect of advertising on sales.[5]

The counterargument is that a sales objective is appropriate when these two factors are not relevant. If a marketer is certain that other marketing or environmental factors were not influencing sales and that the carryover effect was not occurring, then a sales objective could be plausible. In general, the likelihood of such conditions arising appears quite remote, which necessitates the use of behavioural and communication objectives as the primary approach for promotional planning purposes.

BEHAVIOURAL OBJECTIVES

When a firm sets a sales growth objective (e.g., increase sales by 10 percent) for a brand, the increased sales can arise from a greater number of purchases from current customers (e.g., brand loyals). Alternatively, higher sales can be gained from new customers who are currently not buying within the product category (i.e., new category users) or those currently buying within the product category, but not the firm's brand (e.g., other brand switchers). In all cases, achieving the sales growth is possible; however, the expected behaviour is fundamentally different. In the first case, the sales growth is due to a difference in the repurchase behaviour of current customers. In the latter two cases, the sales growth is due to trial behaviour by non-customers. Figure 5-1 shows examples of how marketing objectives can be attained through variations in the target audience and type of behaviour expected. We will define the behavioural objectives more exactly in a later section. Certainly, other opportunities are made possible by applying the concepts depending upon conclusions from a situation analysis.

Figure 5-1   Marketing objectives, audience, and behaviour

Marketing Objective	Target Audience	Behavioural Objective
Sales volume	New category users	Category and brand trial
Market share	Other brand switchers	Brand trial (switching)
Profit	Brand loyals	Repeat purchase (amount)
Return on investment	Favourable brand switchers	Repeat purchase (rate)

The distinction between repeat purchase versus trial purchase behaviour is critical as it provides direction for the communication objectives, which subsequently provide guidance for message development. For example, increasing the repeat purchasing rate of brand loyals might involve a message reminding these customers of the previous enjoyable consumption experiences, while a message to encourage trial from other brand switchers might require a comparative message to these non-customers showing the benefits of the competing brands. In these cases, the communication objectives are substantially different and are entirely derived from the target audience and the behavioural objective. The ad in Exhibit 5-3 is likely directed to consumers who have not used the services of 1-800-Got-Junk previously.

Exhibit 5-3   This ad encourages a trial purchase with its message of relief.

© 1-800-GOT-JUNK

COMMUNICATION OBJECTIVES

Communication objectives are statements of what the marketing communication will accomplish, and are usually based on one or more of the consumer response models discussed in Chapter 4. Each of these models identified a few communication effects a consumer receives from a brand message. Any of these effects can be the basis for establishing communication objectives. For example, brand awareness is an effect that most promotional planners would like to achieve, and they would probably establish a brand awareness objective on three levels.

First, an individual print ad is expected to increase the brand awareness, and the promotional planner will design the message and its presentation so the target audience will recall or recognize the brand when shopping. Second, a specific IMC tool is expected to strengthen brand awareness, and the promotional planner will select one (e.g., event sponsorship) to raise the profile of the brand to those in the target audience. Third and finally, all of the IMC tools within the overall IMC plan should contribute to improving brand awareness. In short, communication objectives are set for each of these aspects of promotional planning: individual element of an IMC tool, an IMC tool, and the overall IMC plan.

The Ford Escape ad shown in Exhibit 5-4 illustrates these three considerations with respect to attitudinal communication objectives. An ad for this vehicle would attempt to persuade non-users of hybrid vehicles of its fuel efficiency while reinforcing that it does not compromise on regular SUV performance. From an advertising campaign standpoint, the communication objective would be to ensure that an overall positive belief is established so that the target audience would visit the website or dealership. Finally, the IMC plan has other IMC tools with the objective of allowing consumers to believe that the Ford Escape SUV could fulfill all needs (safety, economy, performance).

Exhibit 5-4   The Ford Escape Hybrid attempts to influence non-hybrid users to consider this technology and brand.

© Photog2112/Dreamstime.com

Regardless of whether the communication objectives are for the IMC plan, a particular tool, or a specific ad, they should be based on the particular communication tasks required to deliver the appropriate messages to the specific target audience at a relevant point within the target audience's purchase decision-making process and consumption experience.

The promotional planner should see how integrated marketing communication fits into the marketing program and what the firm hopes to achieve through advertising and other promotional elements by reviewing the marketing plan. Managers must be able to translate a general marketing objective into a particular behavioural objective and specific communication objectives. The importance of setting communication objectives for a promotional plan is seen in Dove's famous "Campaign for Real Beauty." Clearly, the whole IMC campaign had certain esteem objectives. The advertising contributed to these IMC objectives, but also had more specific emotional effects. Finally, the sponsorship activities achieved their own behavioural change objective.

From Communication Response Models to Communication Objectives

A number of methods have been developed for setting communication objectives for advertising, related IMC tools, and complete IMC plans. We review two approaches from a historical perspective in this section. We begin with the DAGMAR model, which established the necessity for setting advertising objectives. Next, we consider managerial applications of the hierarchy of effects model and the information processing model.

DEFINING ADVERTISING GOALS FOR MEASURED RESULTS

In 1961, Russell Colley prepared a report for the Association of National Advertisers titled *Defining Advertising Goals for Measured Advertising Results*—colloquially known as **DAGMAR**,[6] it is a model for setting advertising objectives and measuring the results of an ad campaign. The major contribution of the DAGMAR model is its conclusion that communication effects are the logical basis for advertising goals and objectives against which success or failure should be measured.

Under the DAGMAR approach, an advertising goal involves a communication task that is specific and measurable. A **communication task**, as opposed to a marketing task, can be performed by, and attributed to, advertising rather than a combination of several marketing factors. The communication task should be based on a hierarchical model (similar to those in Chapter 4) of the communication process:

- *Awareness*—make consumers aware of the brand or company's existence.
- *Comprehension*—develop consumers' understanding of what the product is.
- *Conviction*—develop consumers' mental disposition to buy the product.
- *Action*—get consumers to purchase the product.

A primary advantage of DAGMAR is that the approach emphasized the value of using communication-based rather than sales-based objectives to measure advertising effectiveness and encouraged the measurement of relevant responses to assess a campaign's impact. This improved the advertising and promotional planning process by providing a better understanding of the goals and objectives toward which planners' efforts should be directed. A second contribution of DAGMAR to the advertising planning process was its definition of what constitutes a good objective; advertising objectives should specify a target audience, be stated in terms of concrete and measurable communication tasks, indicate a benchmark starting point and the degree of change sought, and specify a time period for accomplishing the objective(s).

Target Audience   A well defined target audience may be based on behavioural variables such as customer status (e.g., brand loyal users), usage rate, or benefits sought, as well as descriptive variables such as geography, demographics, and psychographics (on which advertising media selection decisions are based). This step is critical since the communication effect has to be interpreted from the perspective of the intended receiver, as discussed in Chapter 4.

Concrete, Measurable Tasks   The communication task specified in the objective should be a precise statement of what message the advertiser wants to communicate to the target audience. During the planning process, advertisers generally produce a document to describe their basic message that should be specific and clear enough to guide the creative specialists who develop the advertising message. The objective must be measurable to determine whether the intended message has been communicated properly. Other tasks beyond designing a message to influence attitudes are also required, as noted in Chapter 4.

Benchmark and Degree of Change Sought   To set objectives, one must know the target audience's present level concerning response variables (e.g., awareness) and then determine the degree to which consumers must be changed by the advertising campaign. Determining the target audience's present position regarding the response requires **benchmark measures**, often obtained from a marketing research study.

Establishing benchmark measures gives the promotional planner a basis for determining what communication tasks need to be accomplished and for specifying particular objectives. For example, a preliminary study for a brand may reveal that awareness is high but consumer perceptions and attitudes are negative. The objective for the advertising campaign must then be to change the target audience's perceptions of and attitudes toward the brand. Exhibit 5-5 shows an ad for Herbal Essences that is probably attempting to establish a positive attitude toward the brand's new Hydralicious formulation.

Quantitative benchmarks for communications goals and objectives are essential for determining campaign success, as they provide the standard against which the success or failure of a campaign is measured. An ad campaign that results in a 60 percent awareness level for a brand among its target audience cannot really be judged effective unless one knows what percentage of the consumers were aware of the brand before the campaign began. A 40 percent pre-campaign awareness level would lead to a different interpretation of the campaign's success than would a 20 percent level.

Specified Time Period   A final consideration in setting advertising objectives is specifying the time period in which they must be accomplished. Appropriate time periods can range from a few days to a year or more. Most ad campaigns specify time periods from a few months to a year, depending on the situation facing the advertiser and the type of response being sought.

For example, awareness levels for a brand can be created or increased fairly quickly through an intensive media schedule of widespread, repetitive advertising to the target audience. Repositioning of a product requires a change in consumers' perceptions and takes much more time. IMC Perspective 5-2 summarizes ideas on what marketers are doing to encourage action on the part of consumers.

Exhibit 5-5   A new Herbal Essences shampoo colourfully informs consumers of its moisturizing feature.

© Herbal Essences, Procter & Gamble

IMC PERSPECTIVE 5-2

MARKETERS ACHIEVING OBJECTIVES

Achieving objectives is the ultimate goal of any marketing or promotional manager looking to make effective decisions. *Strategy* recognized noteworthy marketers who reached their objectives and transformed their brands, such as Shannon Hosford (vice-president of marketing for Maple Leaf Sports and Entertainment), Connie Morrison (senior vice-president of marketing for Fresh Bakery at Maple Leaf Foods), Tony Matta (chief marketing officer at Kraft), and Oliver Walsh (chief marketing officer for Aritzia).

Shannon Hosford. Looking ahead to the Raptors' 20th anniversary in 2014–2015, Shannon Hosford and her team were charged with coming up with a new brand identity. They invited agencies to pitch with a specific goal in mind: "We wanted to be significant to 35 million people across Canada, not 8 million people in Toronto," says Hosford. "There's only one NBA team that sits outside of the States—how do we become Canada's team without saying, 'We're Canada's team'?" One of the agencies pitching was Sid Lee, which came to the table with an idea it called "We the North." "There wasn't even a question—we saw it, that was it," Hosford says. "It was a brand manifesto; it was never supposed to be seen by the consumer. It was a concept

© Eugene Gologursky/Getty Images

[Continued on next page]

[IMC Perspective 5-2 continued]

about what we had identified and what we wanted this brand to be. And we said, 'We need our fans to see this.'"

Connie Morrison. When she joined a baked goods titan in 2012, Connie Morrison decided to address bread myths and misconceptions head on. However, she knew that Canada Bread brands couldn't preach about the health benefits of wheat and grains on its own. "People would just think, 'Of course you would say that, Dempster's, you just want to sell more bread,'" says Morrison. The company needed the backing of the entire industry, from retailers to millers and even its biggest competitor, Weston Bakeries, which it approached, asking for its help in creating an institute to support the category. A scientific advisory council was formed, and the institute launched with facts promoting the health benefits of bread. The non-profit meets with dietitians and nutritionists and encourages them (using its science-backed research) to build wheat- and grain-based foods into their clients' meal plans. It has an educational website with healthy recipes and nutritional comparison charts and a social media presence. And now it's looking for funding to go direct to consumers with mass marketing. The institute has been such a success in Canada that Grupo Bimbo is looking to replicate the format in other countries in which it operates.

Tony Matta. It's almost too sweet to handle, but for Tony Matta, Kraft's chief marketing officer, it's a prime example of how the company has capitalized on finding the untapped emotional and cultural associations with some of its brands, something he says the old Kraft might not have considered. "We asked consumers to talk about their first memories of Kraft Peanut Butter and the most frequent image was of their grandmother," Matta says. "That's a very real emotional connection. There's not a lot of brands that have that kind of instant link to something so deep and personal. We'll probably sell 100,000 of those kits with very little marketing support, just through that latent demand."

Oliver Walsh. You'd be hard-pressed to find a fashionable Toronto woman who isn't familiar with Aritzia and its singular place on the retail landscape. It maintains a unique presence amid other higher-end mid-level players such as Banana Republic, Club Monaco, and J. Crew. Yet, until recently, the well known brand shied away from traditional marketing, and it didn't have an ecommerce platform or even a chief marketing officer. But the Canadian retailer has been making up for lost time, bursting onto the digital scene with what it believes to be the fashion industry's first fully responsive ecommerce platform and a series of digitally led initiatives, including its first integrated campaign. At the helm of this shift is Oliver Walsh, who became the brand's first chief marketing officer in September 2013. But Aritzia's foray into a brave new world of digital—and Walsh's charge of it—actually began before he was even technically part of the brand team.

Sources: Emily Wexler, "She the North," *Strategy*, December 2014; Jennifer Horn, "Connie Morrison Breaks Bread With Skeptics," *Strategy*, December 2014; Josh Kolm, "Krafting Icons," *Strategy*, December 2014; Tanya Kostiw, "Oliver Walsh Gives Aritzia a Digital Makeover," *Strategy*, December 2014.

Question:

1. Why is it important for promotional planners to consider specific communication tools at each stage of consumer decision making?

COMMUNICATION RESPONSE MODEL APPLICATIONS

In developing the response models, authors have suggested how they could be adopted for planning and setting communication objectives. We present an application of the hierarchy of effects model (Chapter 4) since for many years it has been used in analyzing the communication response of consumers and it has been a primary approach for setting communication objectives. We also present an application of the information processing model (Chapter 4) for measuring communication effects to illustrate the importance of feedback in the communication process.

Hierarchy of Effects Model   Figure 5-2 shows the steps in the hierarchy of effects model as the consumer moves from awareness to purchase. As consumers proceed through the steps, they are not expected to buy immediately; rather, advertisers realize they must provide relevant information and create positive predispositions toward the brand before trial or repurchase behaviour will occur. Figure 5-2 also shows the types of promotion or advertising relevant to each step. The ones listed are an illustration, as promotional planners will select the right tools for their brand depending on factors uncovered in the situation analysis. For example, Exhibit 5-6 shows a print ad designed to influence the target audience's behaviour by going to the website and participating in the contest.

Exhibit 5-6   Guylian Belgian Chocolates encourages consumers to visit the website and win the contest.

© Guylian

Figure 5-2   Application of the hierarchy of effects model

Response Stages	Examples of Relevant Messages	Examples of Relevant IMC Tools
Purchase	Value or minimize perceived risk copy	Point-of-purchase display
	Importance of buying now copy	Sales promotion incentive, loyalty program
Conviction	Closing copy	Take-away brochure
	Recapitulate all previous copy	Specialized digital app
Preference	Comparative or argumentative copy	Word-of-mouth communication
	Popularity appeal	Social networking brand fan (e.g., Facebook)
Liking	Imagery copy	Visually appealing media like video or print
	Positive emotional appeals	Blog, radio jingle
Knowledge	Long copy to fully understand offering	Brand's website
	Demonstration copy	Content community (e.g., YouTube)
Awareness	Copy to ensure consumers remember brand	Mass media and digital advertising
	Brand identity imagery such as logo or jingle	Event marketing or sponsorship

Setting communication objectives with this model is like building a pyramid over time by first accomplishing lower-level objectives, such as awareness and knowledge or comprehension. Subsequent tasks involve moving consumers who are aware of or knowledgeable about the product or service to higher levels in the pyramid (Figure 5-3). The initial levels, at the base of the pyramid, are easier to accomplish than those toward the top, such as trial and repurchase. Thus, the percentage of prospective customers will decline at the higher pyramid levels since the communication effect will not take hold on greater numbers of consumers. Actual brand data as illustrated in the exhibit requires a tracking study, proxies based on internal records of customer interactions, or research from a syndicated supplier like Nielsen.

Figure 5-3   Communication effects pyramid

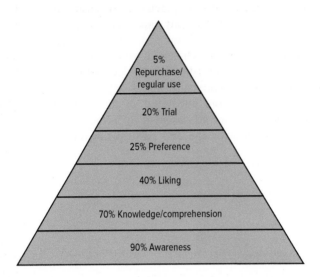

The communication effects pyramid guides promotional objective setting. The promotional planner determines where the target audience lies concerning the levels in the pyramid. If brand awareness and knowledge of its features and benefits are low, the communication objective should be to increase them. If these levels of the pyramid are already in place, but liking or preference is low, the advertising goal may be to change the target audience's image of the brand. As the illustrative numbers indicate, the campaign could focus on "liking" since there is a substantial drop in the number of consumers at this level from the previous level. Also, the drop-off from trial to repeat purchase suggests the marketing communication need to focus on continued buying. The varying levels of objectives could be due to many factors such as behaviour (e.g., brand loyalty segmentation) or regional differences (e.g., geographic segmentation).

Information Processing Model   The information processing model may be an effective framework for setting objectives and evaluating the effects of a promotional campaign. Figure 5-4 shows the steps of the model from exposure/presentation to purchase behaviour. For example, preliminary research might suggest to promotional planners that the target audience comprehends existing aspects of the brand, but does not accept a newer brand message. Thus, an objective of the marketing communication could be to enhance acceptance.

Figure 5-4   Methods of measuring feedback in the response process

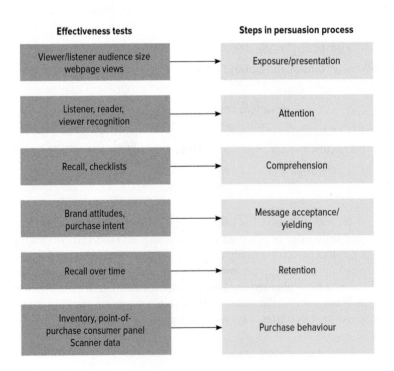

Also shown in Figure 5-4 are examples of research that can be measured at each step. The objectives can be the basis of research to assess whether the communication effects occurred as planned. This provides the advertiser with feedback regarding the effectiveness of promotional strategies tactics designed to move the consumer to purchase.

Extensive coverage of the research methods is provided in Chapter 9 to give a general direction for advertising. This understanding is then extended to measuring the effectiveness of individual IMC tools in their respective chapters later in the book. For example, investigating message acceptance is an important criterion for all aspects of marketing communication in which general approaches can be applied. However, each media and IMC tool is unique and requires specific investigation. The ad in Exhibit 5-7 would have multiple measures of effectiveness for the primary brand, Budweiser, and each of the other brands would have its own measures as well.

Application Conclusion   Decades of research has revealed mixed results when promotional planners apply the communication response model to set communication objectives. One study showed that most advertising agencies did not state appropriate objectives for determining advertising success.[7] A later study found that most advertisers did not set concrete advertising objectives, specify objective tasks, measure results in terms of stages of a hierarchy of effects, or match objectives to evaluation measures.[8] Finally, another later study measured the attitudes of executives, with the majority saying they did not know whether their advertising was working and fewer than 10 percent saying they thought it was working well.[9]

Clearly, the evidence suggests that a newer perspective with a stronger managerial point of view is warranted for enhanced adoption. We suggest the Rossiter and Percy (R&P) perspective as a worthy candidate that promotional planners should consider when setting behavioural and communication objectives.[10] We introduced their ideas in Chapter 3 when discussing the guidelines for target audience identification, selection, and profiling, and in Chapter 4 when summarizing communication response models. We include the R&P perspective since it attempts to resolve the limitations of other approaches for objective setting and provides guidelines for creative tactics (i.e., Chapter 8).

The R&P perspective has three distinguishing characteristics. First, it provides guidelines for specific behavioural objectives. Many of the models say something general, like *purchase* or *behaviour*, but promotional planners need to consider *particular kinds* of behaviour and purchases to make a connection to the marketing objectives. Second, it is consistent with the DAGMAR model by making a direct connection between the purchase decision and the communication task required for each target audience. Finally, it provides guidelines for communication objectives that are more managerially useful and that do not completely rely on a set hierarchy of effects. For example, the Air Transat ad in Exhibit 5-8 targets travellers who are likely at the need recognition stage of their decision making. Since it is trial behaviour, the ad attempts to encourage the target audience to consider this direct option instead of wasting time with connecting flights when visiting Europe.

Exhibit 5-7   Budweiser and its partners would set objectives based on their respective position in this multi-brand promotion.

© Labatt Breweries of Canada

Exhibit 5-8   This Air Transat ad encourages travellers who are non-customers to consider an alternative.

© Transat

LO3   Setting Behavioural Objectives for IMC

A clear behavioural objective for each target audience needs to be identified, since the individual purchasing behaviours of all customers add up to a firm's overall sales. As suggested earlier, the link between marketing objectives (i.e., sales) and communication objectives (i.e., attitude toward the brand) is behavioural objectives. Advertising and promotion can focus on influencing a particular form of behaviour based on the nature of the advertising message or IMC tool used. We now evaluate four options a manager has for setting behavioural objectives: trial purchase, repeat purchase, shopping, and repeat consumption.

TRIAL PURCHASE OBJECTIVES

A trial behaviour is one which the consumer has not previously incurred. A trial purchase objective pertaining to the target audience of a promotional planner's brand is contingent upon time, competition, and product category. To account for these three variables, we review four different trial objectives: brand trial, brand re-trial, category trial, and brand switching.

Brand Trial   A **brand trial purchase** is defined as a consumer's first purchase of a brand. For example, the brand trial purchase of most everyday products (e.g., soft drinks or snack food) occurred years ago for most consumers, and it is probably difficult to remember one's first soft drink purchase or the specific brand. However, producers of everyday products like soft drinks continue to have a **brand trial objective** as consumers enter the market when they attain a certain age or have income (i.e., allowance from parents). Generalizing this point, brand managers within all established product categories consider when a substantially large enough group of consumers may be entering their market and make a brand trial objective a priority in their plan. And while brand trial purchases are important for most firms throughout the year to generate sales, it is not necessarily the primary behavioural objective for all campaigns or all communication tools. Naturally, a brand trial objective is paramount for a product

Exhibit 5-9   Smart strives for a consumer trial purchase of its electric car.

© Mercedes-Benz Canada

launch as there are no consumers buying yet, but a brand trial objective may also be necessary for brand extensions. The message in the Smart car ad in Exhibit 5-9 suggests that brand trial is a primary objective since it highlights that the electric car does not burn gas. It reassures drivers of gasoline-powered cars that the Smart car is not deficient on speed for city driving.

Brand trial generally requires an extensive campaign. For example, with 76 percent of the Canadian coffee and baked goods market, Tim Hortons was a logical target for McDonald's to encourage coffee consumers to change their habit and try a new java with a unique brewing process. A free coffee giveaway launched the campaign and, combined with in-store communication, led the company to sell 1.3 million more cups of coffee. Things picked up with spectacular and very public creative executions a year later when the sample occurred once again. In Vancouver, a transit shelter filled with coffee beans slowly depleted for two weeks as a teaser for the campaign. Later, a giant coffee pot attached to a lamp post appeared, as if pouring coffee into an equally huge coffee cup. Visually, the lamp post acted as the stream of coffee poured into the cup that surrounded the post on the street corner. Nationally, TV, out-of-home, radio, and online advertising during the same two-week span built momentum, so all could recall the message, "Let's Start Fresh." These media highlighted the attributes of premium roast Arabica beans and full-bodied flavour.[11]

Brand Re-Trial   Alternatively, it is quite unlikely that consumers continue to purchase the same brand of soft drink as their first trial purchase. In fact, many people consume more than one brand of soft drink, and for whatever reason stop purchasing their initial brand. Many brand managers are faced with this dilemma of trying to recapture past customers who have not purchased the brand for a period of time (e.g., perhaps a year). The manager of such a brand would like these past customers to have a new trial experience of the brand. Thus, a **brand re-trial purchase** is defined as a consumer's first purchase of a brand after a time delay. The length of the delay to focus on when setting a **brand re-trial objective** is a decision the promotion manager makes. It depends upon the purchase frequency of the product, among other factors observed from the situation analysis. Brands like Coca-Cola constantly have a brand re-trial objective and set up tasting tents at events to reach lapsed consumers, as shown by the ad in Exhibit 5-10.

Category Trial   Now let's put the trial purchase in another perspective: consider the purchase of a smart phone, which many young adults currently own. The smart phone is a different kind of product and likely a somewhat involved purchase for many consumers. Despite this, phone companies and service providers had trial objectives as they attempted to attract consumers who did not own such technology. While this is obviously a brand trial purchase, it is also something broader. A **category trial purchase** is defined as a consumer's first purchase in a product category that the consumer has not purchased in previously. The ad in Exhibit 5-11 follows this idea as it attracts users of non-dandruff shampoo to try Head & Shoulders. Marketers of new products, such as the smart phone, have a dual challenge of attaining both **category trial objectives** and brand trial objectives. Of course, with significant smart phone adoption levels, a category trial objective is less relevant for marketers, but remains so with market segments with less adoption, such as older consumers perhaps.

Category trial is also possible in situations where a "purchase" does not occur. Each year, Canadian Blood Services recruits new donors, people who have never given blood. Its latest campaign tried to move the number of new donors from 85,000 to 90,000 with the message, "What if you needed blood?" The approach tried to shake people's usual complacency about giving blood by getting them to think that, at a certain point in their life, they may in fact need blood and should be part of the solution now.[12]

Brand Switching   A manager may plan for a brand trial or brand re-trial objective when consumers are purchasing another brand. A **brand-switching purchase** is defined as a consumer's purchase toward a brand from another competing brand. A brand-switching purchase occurs whereby the consumer makes a re-trial purchase of a brand and leaves the new favourite and returns to an old favourite. A brand-switching purchase also occurs when the consumer makes a trial purchase of a brand from a competing brand. Thus, brand trial or brand re-trial objectives are more specifically **brand-switching objectives** in certain planning situations. The Pellegrino ad in Exhibit 5-12 communicates to current bottled water users to consider a better-tasting alternative. Pepsi returned to its classic approach to switch Coca-Cola drinkers with its Taste Challenge, a taste test for consumers to demonstrate the brand they prefer while not knowing which brand is which. With a global 10 percent market share versus Coca-Cola's 25 percent, the popular idea launched nearly 40 years ago appeared as a viable alternative to stem the tide, and also keep sales afloat as soft drink consumption declined 18 percent from 2006 to 2010.[13]

REPEAT PURCHASE OBJECTIVES

In the age of relationship marketing and a focus on customer retention, this form of purchase behaviour is most critical. A **repeat purchase** is defined as a consumer's continued purchase of a brand within a specified time period. Again, the time factor

Exhibit 5-10   Coca-Cola desires brand re-trial from lapsed users who gravitated to other soft drinks for a while.

© Anton Gvozdikov / Shutterstock.com

Exhibit 5-11   Head & Shoulders wants non-dandruff shampoo users to consider using the product.

© The Advertising Archives / Alamy Stock Photo

Exhibit 5-12   Pellegrino tries to switch over users of other bottled water brands.

S.PELLEGRINO® is a registered trademark of Sanpellegrino S.p.A., Milano, Italy

for a **repeat-purchase objective** is at the discretion of the marketer, and it is contingent upon purchase frequency of the product or other factors derived from the situation analysis. Repeat purchasing can be an objective for loyal customers and those that switch between a brand and its competitor.

Brands can have a repeat-purchase objective for past customers as firms communicate with these potentially loyal consumers to maintain their positive attitude toward the brand and encourage continued purchasing. For example, direct marketing activities can be implemented where the identity of the consumer exists in a database from past transactions. Marketers request customer email addresses during transaction processes, ask permission to send text messages, and connect with consumers via social media to deliver product information. Direct mail or email is a common method to send reminder messages to visit the store or deliver a price promotion. Of course, communicating via mobile devices by alerting consumers on a regular basis is a growing opportunity.

Brands can also have a repeat-purchase objective for customers who habitually consume two or three brands continuously (i.e., favourable brand switchers). For instance, of 15 purchases 10 purchases might be of the brand, with the remaining five purchases spread across two other brands. While this consumer does not purchase the brand for every single occasion, the consumer is a consistent contributor to the firm's sales and a marketer would want to communicate appropriately to ensure future sales.

A repeat purchase objective pertaining to the target audience of a promotional planner's brand is contingent upon frequency (how often to purchase), amount (how much to purchase), and time (when to purchase). All of these objectives can be seen in the marketing activities of Cineplex, which leads its market with 66 percent. Its discounted price on Tuesdays guides purchasing timing. Its Scene card loyalty program, where enrolled members obtain points for movie ticket purchases that can be redeemed for movies or snacks, signals a purchase frequency objective. This program provides managers with an extensive database allowing them to target messages to guide repeat patronage.[14]

Purchase Frequency   The first alternative concerns the rate, or how often to purchase the brand. This implies that a marketer may set an objective pertaining to consumers purchasing its brand every week instead of every two weeks. This example shows an option where a manager may want to *increase* the rate of purchase from a "half" product per week to "one" product per week. A second managerial option is to *maintain* the rate of purchase. While this is a more conservative objective, it is still a viable option in very competitive environments. Finally, a manager may want to *decrease* the rate of purchase. This option may be viable in unique situations of high demand or with products that have potentially negative consequences (i.e., alcohol).

Purchase Amount   The amount or how much to purchase on each occasion is the second alternative. As this alternative implies, a marketer may set an objective where consumers purchase two products per occasion versus one per occasion. As above, this option is to *increase* the amount per occasion, but a marketer could still evaluate whether to *maintain* or *decrease* the amount per occasion. The McDonald's ad in Exhibit 5-13 encourages consumers to purchase multiple food products throughout the day. The extension makes the billboard act as a sundial showing when a consumer could consume each food type.

Purchase Timing   The final alternative is the timing, or when to purchase. Certain products are seasonal, have a peak in their sales, or can be easily stored. Marketers may have a behavioural objective to influence when consumers will make the purchase. For example, Wendy's restaurant advertises on television in the evening and communicates the fact that its drive-through service stays open late, thus prompting consumers to purchase at a certain time of day. Consistent with the other two alternatives, we can conceive three options: *maintain, accelerate,* and *delay.*

Exhibit 5-13   McDonald's reminds consumers to purchase multiple food products.

© McGraw-Hill Education/Christopher Kerrigan

As another example, retailers attempt to influence all three repeat purchase behaviours while consumers are shopping. Best Buy has an in-store app that provides deeper and richer information than what is found online that consumers obtain prior to the shopping stage. Indigo recommends books to its Plum Rewards members via email and online ads customized for communication when a membership card is swiped at the in-store kiosk. Digital in-store media networks offer specific and detailed video messages when consumers are browsing a product category, much more involved than what is found on 30-second television ads.[15]

SHOPPING OBJECTIVES

Often, communication is designed to encourage a consumer to progress through the decision-making process more smoothly. For example, most people find it imperative to visit a car dealership prior to buying a car. So the focus of parts of an IMC plan is to have consumers take action that will lead them one step closer to the final destination of a purchase. **Shopping behaviour** is an action consumers take that will lead to a higher probability of purchasing the brand. Many types of shopping behaviour exist, but in general most concern the consumer seeking information (e.g., visiting a website) about the brand or an experience with the brand (e.g., participating in an event, watching a demonstration, consuming a sample). Other terminology for this appeared historically (purchase facilitation, purchase related action), but a current view is to identify this as "shopper marketing" where brands foster brand experiences while consumers shop.[16]

Digital equivalents are prominent now as brands encourage website visits, interaction with other customers on Facebook, participation in Twitter, and viewing or posting of video or pictures in content communities. Accordingly, marketers can have many shopping behaviour objectives to know whether enough of the target audience is involved with the brand during the decision-making process. Firms can track the number of sales inquiries, requests for samples, or demonstrations to gauge how well the campaign is performing for the objective. It also can track the digital exposure and participation levels as all the interaction is electronically recorded. The ad in Exhibit 5-14 directs users of two-piece hockey sticks to consider a one-piece stick made by a Canadian manufacturer.

Exhibit 5-14   Combat directs consumers to its website and provides a QR code link.

© Combat Sports International

Another aspect of shopping behaviour is that consumers seek out the opinion of their friends and family, as discussed in the word-of-mouth topic section in Chapter 4. Young people aged 18–24 communicate this way extensively, with virtually 100 percent telling up to four of their friends when they have a positive brand experience.[17] Thus, brands now look to achieve specific word-of-mouth objectives as part of their plans, which guides the use of experiential marketing communication or more innovative and exciting digital activities.

REPEAT CONSUMPTION OBJECTIVES

Thus far we have considered repeat purchase as a behavioural objective. Related to this is repeat consumption as a behavioural objective. **Repeat consumption** is defined as the continued consumption of the brand once purchased. Marketers may have a **repeat-consumption objective** when communicating with their current customers who have previously purchased the brand and have the product at their home or work. This communication has an objective of modifying how often to consume the brand, how much to consume on each occasion, and when to consume.

Exhibit 5-15   California almonds are associated with a situational use to increase repeat consumption.

© Almond Board of California

To give an idea of a repeat-consumption objective in action, we will cite two common approaches. Often, food and drink products advertise through certain television commercials showing consumption visuals that may prompt consumers to snack or have another beverage. For example, dairy industry messages remind consumers to drink milk since it is often in people's homes on a regular basis. Also, research suggests that, for these kinds of product categories that have a well established market leader, a consumption intention is a better predictor of advertising success since goods are already in stock and a repeat purchase will not occur until the inventory is depleted.[18] Another approach is to show consumers how to enjoy the product for other uses, or in new or alternative situations. The California almonds ad in Exhibit 5-15 reinforces continued consumption by showing that the product can be taken from storage and used with vegetables for a family dinner. Its health benefits are made evident by the Health Check logo from the Canadian Heart and Stroke Foundation.

Reducing repeat consumption is a goal with products like electricity. Ads sponsored by PowerWise, the brand behind the provincial government's attempt to encourage the people of Ontario to consume less electricity, employed scientist and environmentalist David Suzuki as a spokesperson. In one execution, David explains to the homeowner, Bob, that his basement beer fridge uses lots of electricity and costs about $150 per year to operate. Bob quickly concludes that saving electricity means more beer and he humorously dashes throughout the house shutting off the TV, radio, and hair dryer (all, of course, while his family members are using the items). This and all other ads ended with the "You Have the Power" slogan and included a visual of the website address (PowerWise.ca). A number of website video illustrations by David Suzuki clearly taught consumers how to use less electricity or showed them how to change their behaviour for less electricity consumption. The website also allowed consumers to join and submit their own electricity-saving tips, and provided extensive resources so that consumers could make necessary adaptations.

The types of purchase and consumption behaviour that firms may try to influence are quite varied. If a firm has multiple target audiences to reach, quite likely it will have to carefully specify the type of behaviour associated with each target audience so that it can develop the most appropriate message and select the most relevant IMC tool. To assist a manager in making these subsequent decisions, it is important to set clear communication objectives.

Setting Communication Objectives for IMC

Earlier in this chapter, we saw how communication response models help formulate communication objectives. The R&P approach is similar since it translates their perspective of communication effects into options for managers to set communication objectives. We review the options for each of the four communication objectives that promotional planners may choose from to formulate their IMC plan, which also can be applied to one target audience or multiple target audiences.

The options for communication objectives can be universally applied for (1) a specific communication like one print ad or television commercial, (2) a specific campaign like advertising or sponsorship, and (3) a complete IMC program that includes all promotional tools. These communication objectives retain the characteristics set forth earlier for good objective setting (i.e., a specific benchmark with the degree of change sought within a specified time period). Finally, the R&P framework is flexible enough to apply all communication objectives to each stage of the buyer decision-making process for any target audience. We now turn to summarizing the options for each communication objective.

CATEGORY NEED

Category need pertains to whether the target audience believes that purchasing within a particular product category will fulfill the consumer's need. Smart phones are a clear product where consumers are users or non-users. A phone company may try to build demand by convincing new users of the benefits of owning a smart phone versus not owning one. This type of message is likely to be different from the type of message used to convince a current user to switch to another brand when the technology improves with new features. In this example, it is a question of whether the target audience believes their communication needs would be more fulfilled with the product or without it. The luxurious imagery of Exhibit 5-16 communicates to consumers how their air travel needs could be fulfilled with a superior class of services.

Another example of category need occurs with transportation. When thinking about buying a "car" upon graduation, a student's choice may in fact be a truck or a sport utility vehicle (SUV). In a broad sense, all vehicles can be used for transportation, but consumers have particular needs that are satisfied more easily with certain types or categories of vehicles than others. A marketer for SUVs may try to communicate in such a way that a target audience will feel the need for an SUV more strongly than the need for a sporty sub-compact, which might be the initial category of product that young consumers would gravitate toward. In this example, it is a question of which distinct yet related category fulfills the target audience's need more completely.

Exhibit 5-16   Singapore Airlines shows how business class can fulfill consumers' travel needs.

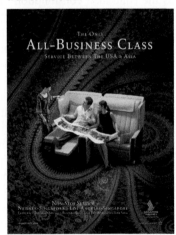

With water consumption growing and soft drink consumption declining, the need for flavouring water remained since consumers often desire variety or wish to avoid blandness. This opened the door for increased demand for the "water-additive" category, and Mio entered with style to pick up an impressive share with its quirky ads.[19] Beer continues its downward spiral as per capita consumption declines, forcing beer brands to compare certain formats to wine or spirits. One Molson executive claimed that "just a beer drinker" no longer existed and the brewer needed to expand its frame of reference to include other alcoholic beverages.[20]

Category Need Is Reminded   One obvious example of this is reminder advertising, where the brand is featured in the message and the need for the product is implicitly communicated or clearly illustrated. Often, the reminder option of category need is the focus of campaigns for lapsed users. For example, the ad for the Dairy Farmers of Canada in Exhibit 5-17 reminds consumers that cheese comes in a number of textures and tastes in addition to being made from Canadian milk.

Category Need Is Emphasized   The smart phone and vehicle examples above show two situations where we actively attempt to persuade the target audience to believe that the product category will fulfill a particular need. A category need objective is usually imperative when competing technologies or substitute products emerge on the market. thus creating two subcategories instead of one general category. However, market conditions discovered in a situation analysis can sway an established brand toward emphasizing category need in existing markets. With a trend toward healthier eating and drinking being seen especially among young consumers, Coca-Cola faced declining sales for its pop products. One factor is young people not entering the pop category at all or consuming other beverages along with significant levels of water.[21] Thus, emphasizing category need may be an important step in the famous brand's future, which may explain the inspiration for the "Share a Coke" campaign where loyal drinkers took the message to heart and gave a personalized can to a non-pop drinker who loved seeing their name in the famous Coke font.

Exhibit 5-17 Cheese ads remind consumers to purchase by highlighting the textures and taste.

© Dairy Farmers of Canada

BRAND AWARENESS

Brand awareness is a universal communication objective. This means that every single point of communication should contribute to a target audience's understanding and knowledge of the brand name. This understanding and knowledge should go even further, such that the target audience knows the category that the brand typically competes in when the consumer is in a position to make a purchase. This stronger interpretation of awareness is important for the brand to be considered in the decision-making process. There are two types of brand awareness that we now identify: brand recognition and brand recall. Naturally, if both forms of brand awareness are relevant, then a manager may have both as awareness objectives.

Brand Recognition   Recognition of the brand at the point of purchase based on past messages can be sufficient for brand consideration or purchase. The Corby ad in Exhibit 5-18 shows an example where the brand name and logo is prominent, which likely heightens the brand recognition effect. Boldly displaying awards the spirits have won assists consumers in remembering the high quality of the product. In a different product example, the "Design by Scotties" campaign raised awareness of this often forgotten facial tissue substantially versus Kleenex over a five-year period, as the message of the box being a complement to one's décor took hold.[22]

Brand Recall   If the target audience feels the need for a product but needs to remember what brands to consider away from the point of purchase, then recall becomes the focus of the campaign. Brand recall is often referred to as unaided brand awareness when measuring. McCain's "It's All Good" campaign increased recall of its brand for its Superfries (from 6 percent to 45 percent) and pizza (from 6 percent to 37 percent).[23]

Exhibit 5-18 Brand recognition for Corby's product is enhanced in this creative ad.

Hand-out/Corby Spirit and Wine Communica/Newscom

In defining brand awareness, we must be careful in distinguishing it from advertising awareness, which concerns itself with whether consumers are aware of a brand's television or print ads. While there is a logical connection between the two, they are not identical. For example, Activia established strong effects compared to industry norms with its "Vitality" message for unaided advertising recall (50 percent vs. 18 percent) and aided advertising recall (60 percent vs. 48 percent) levels.[24]

Shoppers Drug Mart's marketing communication tools, loyalty program, beauty magazine, advertising, and various sales promotions reinforce this objective since brand awareness sits at 98 percent. Recall is important, as consumers would often decide at home where to shop when in need of personal care, beauty, or other products that the store offers. Of course, recognition is important when consumers are driving by the store and see familiar signage that prompts need recognition for shopping in the product categories offered. Thus, even when a brand attains a strong level of awareness, it continues its effort to retain its strong position—such that Shoppers extended its presence with celebratory zeal with its 50th anniversary communication.[25]

BRAND ATTITUDE

Brand attitude is another universal communication objective. Like brand awareness, every aspect of a firm's IMC program or any particular element, such as a television commercial, should contribute to an aspect of the overall evaluation of the brand from the perspective of the target audience. A logical conclusion to this point is that there should be no such thing as an "awareness campaign," as every campaign should surely influence brand awareness and an aspect of brand attitude. Since brand attitude is such an important communication objective, prior understanding of the existing brand attitude is a critical guide for each option.

Establish Brand Attitude   A new target audience that has no awareness and therefore no prior attitude toward the brand generally requires extensive communication so that an attitude is created or established. The Roots ad in Exhibit 5-19 needs to establish a favourable brand attitude with its hand-crafted features.

Maintain Brand Attitude   Often, advertising is performed so that existing attitude levels will remain constant in order to ensure future sales. Stopping communication is one reason for declining sales that has been seen in many examples over time. In contrast, many major advertisers (e.g., Coca-Cola) consistently follow this approach to maintain sales. The Hyundai ad in Exhibit 5-20 reinforces the existing positive attitude its customers would have regarding the quality of its vehicles.

Increase Brand Attitude   Target audiences who are familiar with the brand and moderately favourable toward the brand can be influenced. For example, we can increase their brand attitude by getting the target audience to believe that the brand delivers better performance on a particular attribute or benefit. The beef ad in Exhibit 5-21 tries to increase consumers' already favourable attitude toward this source of nourishment. Looking at this from another point of view, brands that have "green" claims due to a benefit to the environment have difficulty achieving stronger brand attitudes since consumers are reluctant to pay a premium price or do not see the value to them as an individual. Research suggests that a grand "better for the environment" approach is less accepted for many mainstream consumers.[26]

Exhibit 5-19   Roots tries to establish a clear brand attitude with this visual ad.

© Courtesy of Roots Canada

Exhibit 5-20   Hyundai reminds consumers that its customers are very satisfied with vehicle quality.

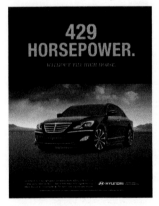

© Hyundai Motor America

Exhibit 5-21   Canadian Beef reinforces the belief that its product is a source of protein.

© Canadian Beef

Modify Brand Attitude   Similar to the previous option, if the target audience is moderately favourable, we still seek to improve their attitude. However, we modify the brand attitude if no increase is possible. In this option, marketers use a different point of reference in communicating the benefits. Typically, marketers focus on a new consumer motive for purchasing the brand that the target audience will be receptive toward. The tea ad in Exhibit 5-22 attempts to influence attitudes in a new direction. Mazda presents an interesting example since its sales are considerably lower than other Japanese brands. It is now pursuing a worldwide emphasis to put the brand in a premium niche, much like BMW did as it grew from humble origins during the 1970s.[27] Its future marketing communication could likely target users of other premium brands for them to switch, or target non-premium brand users to "trade up." In either case, innovative communication will be required to modify existing attitudes.

Change Brand Attitude   Negative attitudes are difficult to influence, but particular communication situations create the challenge of changing the brand attitude for a target audience. BC Hydro faced an uphill battle that illustrates a marketing communication problem that necessitated this kind of objective. According to executives, existing consumer attitudes tended to be negative since most pictured a high electrical bill when thinking of the brand. The challenge promised to be even more difficult with bills set to rise by one-third over the coming years as the utility upgraded its infrastructure. A message shift from "BC Hydro for Generations" to "BC Hydro Regeneration" attempted to ensure that British Columbians would feel more positively toward the provincial energy provider. Interestingly, this attitude existed despite a series of positive messages for its Power Smart conservation program, which garnered 33 awards for the agencies responsible for creating positive messages to use energy wisely.[28]

Exhibit 5-22   Nestea provides new reasons to consume its product.

NESTEA® is a registered trademark of Société des Produits Nestlé S.A., Vevey, Switzerland.

BRAND PURCHASE INTENTION

There are two fairly simple options for **brand purchase intention**.

Assume Brand Purchase Intention   In situations (i.e., low involvement) where the strength of an intention to purchase is consistent (i.e., highly correlated) with brand attitude, a marketer is not required to include this objective.

Generate Brand Purchase Intention   In contrast, managers need the target audience to have a plan to purchase a brand in situations of high involvement.

LO5   IMC Planning: Objectives for Buyer Decision Stages

In Chapter 3, we presented a model of consumer decision making that showed the stages typically experienced when making a purchase. We outlined several steps: need recognition, information search, alternative evaluation, purchase decision, and postpurchase evaluation. One important role of marketing communications is to help the target audience move through these stages. Marketers require specific communication tools and messages that will resonate with each target audience as they proceed through these stages. We assess this decision-making process for each target audience and make a conclusion as to which communication objectives are most relevant for each stage. Figure 5-5 illustrates how this works.

Figure 5-5   Assessing the consumer decision-making process

Analysis and Conclusions	Need Recognition	Information Search	Alternative Evaluation	Purchase Decision	Postpurchase Evaluation
Who? (roles)					
Where? (location)					

[Continued on next page]

[Figure 5-5 continued]

Analysis and Conclusions	Need Recognition	Information Search	Alternative Evaluation	Purchase Decision	Postpurchase Evaluation
When? (time, timing)					
How? (shopping behaviour)					
Why? (key motivator)					
Behavioural objectives					
Communication objectives					
Message options					
Communication tool options					

The analysis occurs in the first six rows, where the marketer includes the target audience information and makes a conclusion on the key communication objectives that need to be attained so that the target audience will continue to the next stage. We have addressed these ideas already. The first question (Who?) looks at the key participants in the decision. We highlighted these roles in Chapter 3. The next three questions are descriptors of where, when, and how the shopping behaviour will occur. This is based on market research, managerial experience, flashes of inspiration, and assumptions. The key point is that we need to make clear the behaviour that we are trying to influence.

After summarizing these questions, we determine which communication objectives are necessary to ensure that the consumer continues through all stages. For example, what aspect of brand attitude needs to be addressed at the need-recognition stage versus the alternative-evaluation stage? Is recall an awareness objective at the need-recognition stage, and recognition an awareness objective at the purchase-decision stage? We also need to determine the most relevant behavioural objective. For example, we may wish to encourage phone inquiries at the information-search stage. Or perhaps we may desire Internet visits to compare brands at the alternative-evaluation stage.

Once this assessment has been done, then the marketer can outline preliminary options concerning the types of messages and communication tools that would be most useful. Returning to the first question above, a marketer may decide to have a fun television commercial (e.g., communication tool option) that emphasizes the emotional attachment (e.g., brand attitude) to the product. It should be noted that, when identifying options, the marketer has not fully committed or recommended that this is exactly the plan, but rather has said that this is the template of analysis for making the final decision.

The rest of this book focuses on how to make IMC plan decisions that are based on the target audience, behaviour objectives, and communication objectives established at the start of the plan. Chapters 6 to 9 focus on the message, while Chapters 10 to 17 focus on the communication tools. As we noted at the start of this chapter, the contents of this framework become the key criteria for making all promotional decisions and the criteria by which the results are measured. While all firms may not be able to afford comprehensive studies to assess communication effects, they would benefit from the use of the framework because it provides disciplined thinking before investing in promotion.

Learning Objectives Summary

 LO1 Distinguish among marketing, behavioural, and communication objectives and identify the value of setting each type of objective.

Objectives guide promotional program development and provide a benchmark against which performance can be measured and evaluated. Objectives also serve a communication function for all participants in the planning process and direct all IMC program decision making. Objectives for IMC evolve from the organization's overall marketing plan and are based on the purpose of each promotional mix element within the marketing program. Managers use sales or a related measure such as market share as the basis for setting marketing objectives. Promotional planners believe the communication role of promotional mix elements is not directly connected with sales-based objectives. They use communication-based objectives like those in the response hierarchy as the basis for setting goals. These models suggest the importance of setting specific behavioural objectives (such as trial or repeat purchase) and appropriate communication objectives to direct the IMC strategy so that it contributes to the attainment of marketing objectives.

 LO2 Describe the historical approaches for setting communication objectives for advertising.

Historically, in setting objectives, traditional advertising-based views of marketing communication were emphasized. This originated from an application of basic response models like DAGMAR and the hierarchy of effects. DAGMAR established the principle that objectives should: specify a target audience; be stated in concrete and measurable communication tasks; indicate a benchmark starting point and the degree of change sought; and specify a time period for accomplishing the objectives. As an extension of this idea, the principles of the hierarchy of effects model, used in setting advertising objectives, could be applied to other elements in the promotional mix. The hierarchy of effects model suggested that unique promotional tools could be implemented in different stages of the response hierarchy. Managers would determine the location of a particular audience in the hierarchy and make appropriate decisions to move them closer to a trial and repeat purchase.

Adoption of communication models was limited, resulting in the need for a comprehensive managerial framework for setting behavioural and communication objectives for many IMC planning purposes, IMC plans, individual IMC tools (i.e., advertising), and specific elements (i.e., direct mail offer with coupon). Both types of objectives need to be established for any individual communication element, ranging from an activity at a sponsorship event to what is portrayed in a point-of-sale display. In short, all target audience contact points play a role in fulfilling IMC plan objectives and their expenditures can be accountable through achievement of their mandate. A complete plan requires direction through behavioural and communication objectives so that all tools and elements communicate accurately.

 LO3 Evaluate the options for setting behavioural objectives and apply them when constructing a promotional plan.

The comprehensive managerial framework identified options for behavioural objectives to guide the achievement of marketing objectives and to direct the formation of communication objectives. Behavioural objectives included brand trial, brand re-trial, brand switching, category trial, repeat purchase, shopping behaviour, and repeat consumption. Analysis of the target audience's decision-making process assists promotional planners in determining which ones to focus on in their IMC plan for each IMC tool.

 LO4 Choose among the options for setting communication objectives and apply them when designing IMC recommendations.

The comprehensive managerial framework also presented many options for setting communication objectives in terms of category need (i.e., omit, remind, emphasize), brand awareness (i.e., recognition and/or recall), brand attitude (i.e., establish, maintain, increase, modify, change), brand purchase intention (assume, generate), and brand purchase facilitation (omit, include). Similar to behavioural objectives, specific communication objectives can be attained for individual IMC tools so that the overall plan achieves each communication objective for a particular target audience. The end result enables managers to construct a multitude of IMC plans.

LO5   Assemble the best combination of behavioural and communication objectives for each stage of the consumer decision-making process.

The comprehensive managerial framework was then linked to the buyer decision-making model to show the connection between a consumer's behaviour and a particular brand's objectives. This application implies that as a consumer's decision-making progresses, managers can consider how objectives evolve at each stage in order to adjust the message, media, or IMC tool employed to communicate.

Review Questions

1. Discuss the value of setting objectives for the integrated marketing communications program. What important functions do objectives serve?

2. What are the strengths and weaknesses of using traditional hierarchy models for setting communication objectives?

3. Some claim that promotion is all about communication, so we should focus only on communication objectives and not worry about behavioural objectives. Convince them otherwise.

4. If a firm cannot afford large market research studies to quantitatively assess whether communication objectives have been achieved, why should the firm bother setting communication objectives?

5. A firm is running a campaign with advertising, sales promotion, and public relations. Why might it have different communication objectives for each IMC tool?

Applied Questions

1. In meeting with a client for an energy drink, you are informed that the only goal of advertising and promotion is to generate sales. As an account planner for a marketing communication agency, present reasons why communication objectives must also be considered.

2. Assess what the behavioural objectives would be for each ad in this chapter.

3. Assess what the communication objectives would be for each ad in this chapter.

4. After assessing the objectives for some of the ads of this chapter, check out the brand's Internet site or social media offerings and determine if the objectives are the same or different.

CHAPTER SIX

Brand Positioning Strategy Decisions

LEARNING OBJECTIVES

LO1 Identify the concepts of market positioning strategy and market position.

LO2 Apply the positioning concept in an advertising context by defining brand positioning strategy and brand position.

LO3 Illustrate how to formulate brand positioning strategy decisions.

LO4 Demonstrate brand repositioning strategy opportunities.

LO5 Interpret brand positioning strategy decisions in other contexts.

Samsung Moves to Consumer Brand Positioning

From its humble beginnings as a small South Korean trading company founded in 1938, Samsung has grown to an internationally dominant electronics brand. The Canadian vice-president of marketing saw the company as moving from a technology firm focused on communicating the features and specifications of its latest products to a consumer brand communicating consumer benefits on an emotional level. In another way, the company is no longer engineering a technology brand but rather a lifestyle and marketing brand. As part of this approach, the Canadian division opened "experience stores" to market its products to demonstrate how the functions of Samsung products create memorably positive consumption. With many new products over the past few years—such as a curved-screen TV, smart watch, and wearable tech clothing—the transformation in this direction will be more evident with its future communication. For example, communication objectives now focus on the brand ("I want a Samsung Galaxy") rather than the product category ("I want a smart phone").

As part of this approach, Samsung moved from its in-house agency of 40 years to using outside advertising agencies. One creative example of the success the Canadian division experienced is the work of its agency Cheil, which created the "What's Your Tabitat" video messages shown only on the Internet for the Galaxy 3 Tab. The theme of the three ads spoofed a nature documentary and classified three different tablet users for its three models: *Connecticus*, young socially active users looking for instant access; *Wanderus*, slightly older users on the go; and *Relaxicus*, middle-aged consumers using their tablet at home.

Another aspect of Samsung Canada's messages included a virtual line-up with personal avatars for the new Galaxy Smartphone S6. Targeted to younger consumers, those interested in moving up higher in the line could post social media messages or pictures that included the hashtag #S6lineup. Banking on research that indicated the importance of social influence as opposed to brand persuasion, Samsung's marketing team took this approach to drive favourable messages with resulting strong sales. Contests augmented the virtual line-up with prizes awarded to those in various places. Other communication featured a large digital display of the avatars at the intersection of Yonge and Dundas Streets in the heart of downtown Toronto.

Samsung Canada also contracted other agencies for other communication, including events. It marketed its household appliances to a younger cohort of consumers it hoped to win over by having its washing machines with a new Power Foam technology at Tough Mudder events, where contestants could clean their filthy, mud-soaked clothes after competing. The agency also set up an event for foodies and other influencers to test out Samsung's new refrigerators while they attended a swanky restaurant featuring food from a renowned chef.

These new Canadian advertising initiatives resulted in impressive numbers, as the Samsung brand preference and rankings rose meaningfully higher. Samsung product consideration for its smart phone and tablet products achieved respectable levels of 48 percent and 35 percent, respectively. Market share in Canada is currently at a level similar to Samsung's global level. The company planned to focus on the connectivity benefits of all of its products in future. Leading the way for this initiative is Samsung's Tizen software, which will act as an operating system as Samsung tries to be an international leader in connectivity among all of its products. And this may be in the offing, as Samsung emerged as the biggest exhibitor at the huge Las Vegas electronics show.

Sources: Matthew Chung, "Samsung Builds Up Its Street Cred," *Strategy*, October 2013; Susan Krashinsky, "Samsung Lets Your Avatar Do the Waiting," *The Globe and Mail*, March 27, 2015, p. B5; Jungah Lee, "Samsung to Target Smart Homes," *National Post*, January 5, 2015, p. FP 1.

Question:

1. Is the emotional and experiential approach for positioning logical for Samsung given its vast array of product lines?

As the opening vignette implies, advertising and all IMC tools that occur within a marketing strategy have a significant contribution toward the overall positioning of the product to selected target markets, or what is known as a market positioning strategy. However, advertising and each promotional activity has its own unique communication objectives to persuade a particular target audience. In this sense, we can examine how promotional tools and the whole promotional program influence the positioning of a brand to a designated target audience, or what is known as a brand positioning strategy.

Our investigation in this chapter—to understand positioning for both marketing strategy and marketing communication—is consistent with the distinction between target market and target audience (Chapter 3) and the importance of linking communication objectives and strategy with the marketing objectives and strategy (Chapter 5). First, we review market positioning strategy, define brand positioning strategy, and describe the brand positioning strategy decision process. We then define and illustrate the four decisions for developing a comprehensive brand positioning strategy. Finally, we explore opportunities for changing the brand positioning strategy, known as repositioning.

Positioning

In this section, we distinguish between positioning within the marketing strategy and positioning with marketing communication. We also highlight the difference between the decision a manager makes in terms of a positioning strategy and the resulting effects in terms of the position in which the target market or target audience perceives the firm or brand to be competing. We end the section with an overview of the decision-making process for a brand positioning strategy.

MARKET POSITIONING STRATEGY

Organizations intending to market their products or services successfully should have a **strategic marketing plan** to identify all marketing decisions and guide the allocation of resources. A strategic marketing plan evolves from an organization's corporate strategy and guides marketing programs and policies. In Chapter 1 we emphasized that promotional planners use the strategic marketing plan as an information source to plan marketing communication decisions. In particular, those creating promotional messages should be familiar with their client's or organization's market positioning strategy since it gives direction for how a brand should be positioned in the promotional program.

A **market positioning strategy** identifies the decision of the market(s) in which the firm plans to compete and the specific elements of the marketing mix that are designed to fulfill the respective needs of the market(s). This view of the positioning decision combines the target market(s) decision with the marketing mix decision that delivers the consumer benefit that is meaningfully distinct from competitors' offerings. For example, Smart cars compete in the electric car market and fulfill the need for those who desire to purchase a vehicle that is beneficial for the environment (Exhibit 6-1).With its new 767 airplanes and new international routes, Air Canada made its marketing strategy more global by competing against big international carriers like Air France and KLM for the more lucrative international travel market. It shifted a greater portion of its marketing budget in this direction and altered its slogan to "Your World Awaits" to signal a much different market positioning. [1] Sobeys rejuvenated its presence in the discount grocery market by changing the name of Price Chopper to FreshCo. A redesign of the store's interior and colour scheme provides a new market positioning strategy with a strong emphasis on an improved assortment of fresh goods.[2]

Typically, firms write a market positioning strategy statement into their marketing plan to accurately communicate this decision. This statement provides direction for the four decisions within the marketing program—product, price, distribution, and marketing communication—and the intended market(s) to be served. For example, different market segments in the personal computer (PC) industry include the home, education, science, and business markets, which can also be further divided. The business market consists of small companies and large corporations; the education market ranges

Exhibit 6-1   Smart cars compete in the electric car market.

>> Charge ahead with the surprisingly quick smart fortwo electric drive from only $26,990* before rebate.

Rebate
$3,000
smart discount*

thesmartcityproject.ca

smart – a Daimler brand

© Mercedes-Benz Canada

from elementary schools to colleges and universities. A clear market positioning strategy for a company that is marketing its products in the PC industry must decide which market segment it wishes to compete in, and assess the amount and nature of competition it will face to decide on its offering to the users in that market.

While considering its distinctive offering, the firm may evaluate combinations of product attributes with varying price levels across different retail outlets or online options. Alternatively, it could evaluate narrow product choices with very wide distribution and a mass advertising appeal. As these examples suggest, a firm considers as many feasible options as possible so that it does not miss a market opportunity. At this stage, the firm uses its market research and experience wisely to put together a "package of benefits" or "value offering" that will be acceptable to the target market selected. Currently, Canadian quick-service restaurants are evaluating whether they should add alcohol to their menu (as found in other countries), which would likely indicate a varied market positioning strategy.[3] With recycled battery parts as another example, Energizer may be creating a new market with its latest entry, or it may be offering a battery with greater value to a segment of the existing market; the market response will indicate which is true over time (Exhibit 6-2).

Exhibit 6-2 Energizer promoted its launch of a new battery with its familiar bunny.

© AP Photo/Jeff Roberson

Once the marketing programs are developed and implemented, organizations may find results at, above, or below expectations. For example, sales or market share objectives may or may not be obtained. The reactions of consumers may be very close to what the firm intended, or they could be quite different. We define this consumer response to be the **market position** of a firm. This distinction signifies that it is not the current or past market positioning strategy decided by the marketing managers, but rather the intended or unintended consumer beliefs caused by the organization's marketing efforts. In the case of Birks jewellery store, the revised store design, modified product line, altered distribution system, and advertising emphasis of Canadian sourced diamonds all resulted in promising sales levels, indicating that it successfully achieved a new market position.[4]

To expand on these ideas, we will use shampoo products as an example. Shampoo is a fragmented market, with over 30 brands measured by the Print Measurement Bureau (PMB). This research also reports 18 different characteristics of the product relating to the purpose of its use, like shining or thickening and anti-dandruff. The most-used brands in Canada, in order, are Head & Shoulders, Pantene Pro V, Herbal Essences, Dove, TRESemmé, and then salon-based brands. However, "other brand" is the most heavily used brand in PMB data. Ninety percent of the sample use shampoo on a weekly basis, 8 percent declined to answer the question, and 2 percent do not use shampoo.[5] We illustrate this market with a market position diagram, recognizing that alternative interpretations may be feasible (Figure 6-1). We graph two axes, cosmetic and therapeutic, with salon exclusivity and popular mainstream. The salon endpoint represents brands originating from a salon or a brand extensively used by salons.

Figure 6-1 Hypothetical illustration of a market position diagram for shampoo brands

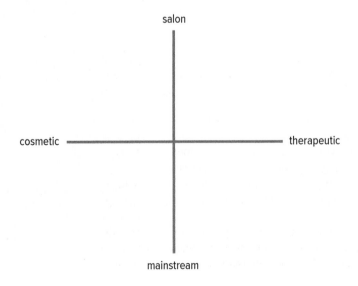

With a significant level of product category usage, it is not surprising to see that virtually every sector of this diagram would have brands competing, via brand name, ad imagery, product performance, packaging, and distribution location. We leave it to the reader to consider where each of the above brands may fit on these or other axes, but offer a couple of observations. Pantene Pro V implies that professionals use it, with the word *Pro* in the brand name. TRESemmé advertises that professionals use the product as the brand moved to the consumer market after establishing itself in the business market decades ago. Head & Shoulders originally claimed itself to be an anti-dandruff product but now claims benefits regarding how the shampoo makes the user's hair look and feel and has multiple formats and fragrances. Given this information, where do we think Dove and Herbal Essences would be located in this market position diagram?

The market position diagram, also known by its general term *perceptual map,* is a result of market research showing an accumulation of how all the respondents "see" the brands competing. It can also be a summary of how a manager believes consumer perceptions line up if market research is unaffordable. In conclusion, the market position diagram depends entirely upon clearly identifying and accurately defining the criteria for the two axes. Furthermore, multiple diagrams may be necessary if a planner desires to model three axes.

LO2 BRAND POSITIONING STRATEGY

It is tempting to believe that advertising and all other IMC tools define the market positioning strategy, because all these marketing communication exposures are so publicly visible. While this may be true in certain situations, in most cases advertising and IMC campaigns typically focus on a particular message that helps consumers understand the product in comparison to other brands *within* a specific product market or category. In fact, most ads or IMC tools speak to a very specific target audience, as observed in typical marketing communication done by a bank.

A bank can send a direct-mail piece to a current customer (i.e., brand loyal) to obtain a mortgage renewal and focus the message on the ease of continuity and the good follow-up service. Or it may run a TV ad with a message of attractive interest rates and specialized options directed to customers from competing banks (i.e, favourable brand switcher). Finally, it may develop a mobile app for young adults who are beginning to buy and use new financial products and services as they mature and earn money (i.e., new category users).

These examples identify different target audiences with different competitive reference points and suggest the need to use the positioning concept appropriately in a marketing communication context that is distinct from positioning in a marketing strategy context. This notion of positioning in marketing communication is the subject of a new direction in the marketing literature,[6] and we turn to it now.

Advertising practitioners consider positioning to be an important decision in establishing and maintaining a brand. In fact, managing a brand is so critical that the notion of branding is very topical with marketers these days; however, the original authors of the positioning concept remind us that branding cannot occur without positioning.[7] This original notion of positioning in an advertising context arose from Jack Trout and Al Ries, who distinguished between a marketer's decisions and the resulting effect in a consumer's knowledge structure.[8] Thus, in this text we use the term **brand positioning strategy** to mean the *intended* image of the product or brand relative to competing brands for a given competitive space as defined by certain product market or category characteristics.

A competitive space can be discovered with the market position diagram, as discussed previously. For example, the upper left quadrant is a space where brands like Pantene Pro V and TRESemmé may be challenging for consumers, and the battle may be on more specific characteristics like we saw in the PMB data that relate to desirable hair qualities: volume, thickness, strength, smoothness, shine, and so on. The relevant dimensions of competing within a space allow managers to determine the brand positioning strategy, a key decision prior to determining the most effective selling message of advertising or other IMC tools. Exhibit 6-3 identifies how SoBe competes for consumers in the specialized niche of the bottled water market.

Now consider consumer responses after being exposed to an entire IMC campaign. What do consumers feel and think about the brand after having experienced all of the messages? Do they have positive or negative feelings

Exhibit 6-3   SoBe competes in the enhanced water market.

© 2013 SoBe®

for the brand? What unique attributes or benefits come to mind when considering the brand? These questions pertain to the reactions consumers have to the marketing communication decisions implemented by the promotional planner. Thus, **brand position** refers to the target audience's overall assessment or image of the brand resulting from brand-related communication that tells the prospective buyer what the brand is, who it is for, and what it offers.[9]

We need to distinguish between the firm's intended brand image and the actual brand image, since these occur at different points in time and reside in different locations. The brand positioning strategy resides within the overall advertising or IMC plan, while the brand position exists within the target audience. The brand positioning strategy can be written annually or perhaps every few years depending on the company's direction. The brand position requires time, perhaps a few years, to take hold in a sufficient number of consumers before the planners will know whether the intended strategy worked. The importance of distinct vocabulary between brand positioning strategy (i.e., plan) and brand position (i.e., result) was implied by Trout and Ries many years ago and is consistent with others who have written on this topic.[10]

We now turn to our brand position diagram, where brands compete more directly in a competitive space. For this, we turn to the chocolate bar category. According to PMB data, this is a specific competitive space within the broader chocolate confectionery market that includes stand-up bags of wrapped chocolate, snack boxes, and bagged chocolate/candy. The broader chocolate confectionery market contains more than 100 brands, although there are duplicates with line extensions. Nevertheless, the chocolate bar category provides enough competing brands with varying characteristics such that brands manage their positioning strategy.

Chocolate bar brands actively compete and advertise on certain **salient attributes**. For this, we suggest three possible axes: (1) single-bar format–unique/multi-part format; (2) peanuts, almonds (nut-based)–nougat, caramel; and (3) layered wafers–solid bar. While a three-dimensional brand position diagram is feasible, Figures 6-2, 6-3, and 6-4 show the individual pairs to illustrate the possibilities more easily. According to PMB, the most frequently consumed, in order, are KitKat, Coffee Crisp, Aero, Caramilk, Mars, Reese's Peanut Butter Cups, and Oh Henry!, each of which can be placed on these axes accordingly based on their attributes. We suggest that soft-centre bars like Mars and Reese's would be in the middle of the layered wafers–solid bar axis.

Figure 6-2   Brand position by attributes—illustration A

Figure 6-3   Brand position by attributes—illustration B

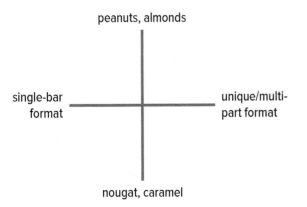

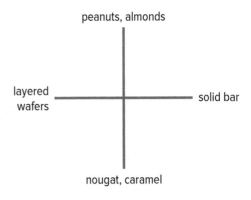

Figure 6-4   Brand position by attributes—illustration C

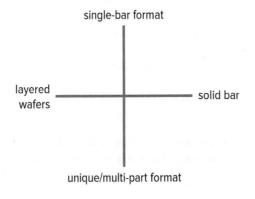

PMB data show that two-thirds of the sample consumed a chocolate confectionery product in the past six months, and 50 percent consumed one during the past week. Clearly, a brand could consider its distinctive attributes to encourage non-users to gravitate to the product category. The attribute-based brand position diagram helps identify what the competing brands might be and gives direction on how to emphasize the distinctiveness of the attributes. For example, both Reese's and Oh Henry! could target consumers who love peanuts but who do not eat chocolate bars, and specifics of the positioning are clearer if one knows which brand it is up against. Alternatively, the attribute brand position diagrams can assist the managers for the first four bars listed, since they all have a break-apart format. So if one brand tried to switch purchasers away from another brand on this feature, the approach for communicating the break-apart characteristic can be estimated more accurately. As these implications show, the brand position diagram visualizes how to consider the options for brand positioning strategy decisions, but this decision can instead be based on benefits, or a combination.

Chocolate bars also compete on certain **salient benefits**. For these, we again surmise three axes: (1) filling snack–indulgent treat; (2) individual pleasure–social sharing; and (3) pure chocolate taste–multi-flavour taste. The first axis is relatively self-explanatory as brands have competed on these aspects for decades. The individual pleasure–social dimension is relevant for the break-apart bars since the pieces can be shared, thereby signifying an interesting emotional benefit of belongingness along the lines of love for a particular consumer segment. Since one aspect of chocolate bar consumption is the flavour and sensory gratification, whether the resulting taste is mostly chocolate or a mix with others is another aspect brands may emphasize in their messages. Again, these axes are shown as three pairs in Figures 6-5, 6-6, and 6-7. Readers are encouraged to consider an alternative view and/or place the above brands accordingly to investigate the brand positioning strategy options for each brand.

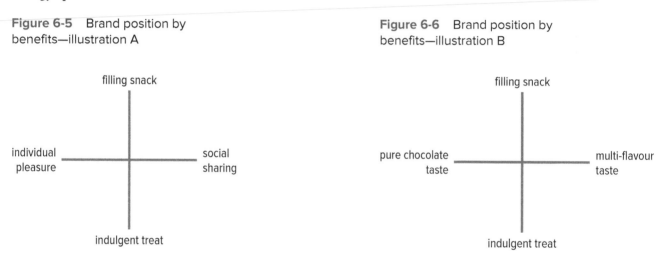

Figure 6-5   Brand position by benefits—illustration A

Figure 6-6   Brand position by benefits—illustration B

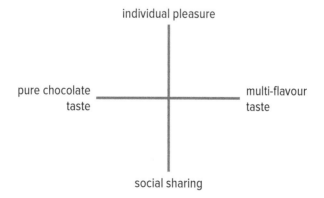

Figure 6-7   Brand position by benefits—illustration C

BRAND POSITIONING STRATEGY DECISION PROCESS

We present a five-step process for making the brand positioning strategy, adapted from other sources.[11] Chapter 1 briefly outlined this process, but here we investigate the actual steps in more detail to fully understand the brand positioning strategy decisions.

Develop a Market Partition   A useful approach for defining the market is to make it consistent with how consumers make a purchase decision. It is suggested that promotional planners view the market broadly as a general product category and subsequently divide the market into various subcategories until consumers perceive brands as being relatively similar. The criteria for market partitioning include the type of product, end benefit, usage situation, and brand name. Figures 6-8 to 6-11 show a basic partition of the car market for each of these four approaches, and these simple illustrations can be expanded or altered to the decision maker's requirements. This task is important for establishing the initial parameters for identifying the most important competitors to determine a unique positioning strategy that can be communicated. A change in premium brands, otherwise known as luxury brands, is the fact that their low-end models are now priced on par with more basic brands, calling into question how marketers will plan for marketing communication with extensive overlap not previously seen in the auto market.[12]

Figure 6-8   Partition of car market by product type

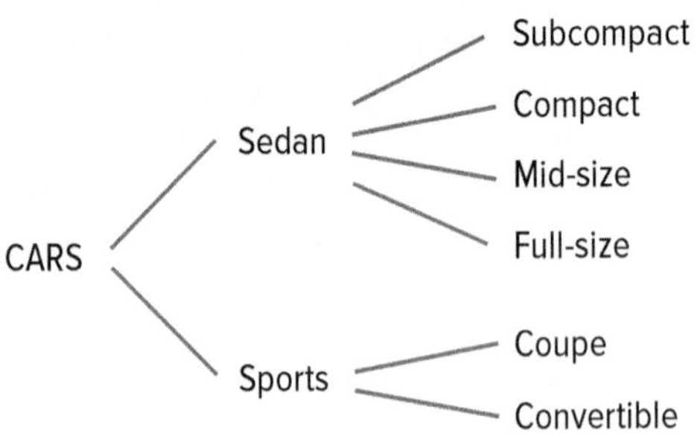

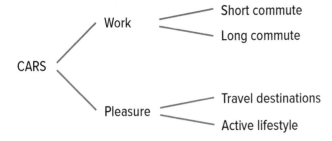

Figure 6-9   Partition of car market by end benefit

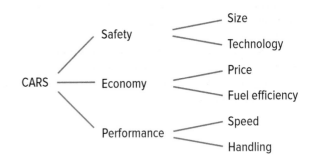

Figure 6-10   Partition of car market by usage situation

Figure 6-11   Partition of car market by brand

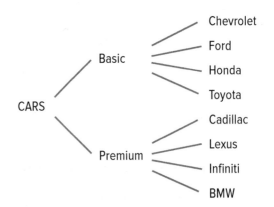

Assess Competitors' Position   Once we define the competitors through the market partition, we then determine their respective brand positions by assessing consumers' beliefs through new or existing consumer research. Often, survey research is performed to observe how consumers rate the competing brands on the relevant and important attributes and benefits that consumers use when evaluating a brand. The data from these types of surveys are used to formulate the brand position maps shown previously. Preliminary research may be necessary to identify new attributes or benefits that competitors are communicating to establish their brand position. For example, cars compete on numerous attributes and benefits, and over time new product characteristics may become important and need to be added to the usual competitive profiles to accurately assess the brand positions.

Assess Brand Position   Consumer research for the promotional planner's brand is used to assess how consumers currently perceive the brand. This research would be compared with the previously determined brand positioning strategy (e.g., last year, or the prior two to four years). If current efforts are not working, it may be time to consider an alternative strategy (Exhibit 6-4). Unless there is strong reason to believe a change in positioning is necessary, promotional planners are advised to maintain the current brand positioning strategy.

Determine Brand Positioning Strategy   Going through the first three steps should provide direction for where to establish a brand position; however, planners will often be faced with alternatives to select from. For example, Toyota previously positioned its trucks and SUVs as recreational, with messages like "I don't want to work all day," and "You belong outside." Promotional planners considered three positioning strategies along the idea of "tough" when evaluating options for change. The first involved a "work-tough" positioning by showing the Tacoma at work on Canadian oil fields and farms. A second, "recreation-tough," would show the Tacoma engaged in off-road activities. Finally, "international-tough" intended to demonstrate the Tacoma's use throughout the world. The final choice won, as the planners used live footage of Toyota trucks involved in delivering aid during international disasters to create the launch TV ad that carried the tagline "Never Quit."[13]

The remainder of this chapter presents a structure to make a well developed brand positioning strategy decision. Managers are faced with either performing research or using subjective judgments based on experience to make the final brand positioning strategy decision among identified alternatives. In making the decision, planners will assess whether the brand positioning strategy will be strong enough competitively and whether sufficient financial resources exist to establish the brand position over time. IMC Perspective 6-1 summarizes how McDonald's changed its brand positioning strategy.

Exhibit 6-4   V8 revitalizes its image.

You've tried trickery.
You've tried bribery.
But have you tried strawberry?

Kids not eating their veggies? Try *V8 V-Fusion*.* A full serving of fruit with a full serving of vegetables.* (But they only taste the fruit.)

© Campbell Soup Company

IMC PERSPECTIVE 6-1

WELCOME TO MCDONALD'S

Going beyond the success of its "Our Food. Your Questions." campaign, McDonald's Canada moved toward a "Welcome to McDonald's" theme. This next step took the story from behind the scenes restaurant activities to the front stage where consumers enjoy the food and interact while in the restaurant. While still retaining the "I'm Lovin' It" slogan, the new approach presented the stories of many consumers and heartwarming scenes of consumers within the restaurant. According to one commentator, the new positioning appeared to encourage current customers to visit McDonald's more frequently when selecting locations within the quick service restaurant category. Although McDonald's Canada remained as one of the strongest divisions within the multinational's empire, the declining corporate sales were a trend this division wanted to avoid by showing the human side of the brand.

© McGraw-Hill Education/John Flourno

A film crew travelled across the country to 35 locations, interviewed over 450 people, recorded 115 hours of video, and took more than 10,000 photographs. The main ads—entitled "Nicknames" and "A Place"—intended to show how consumers enjoy being at McDonald's and what the restaurant means to Canadians. The crew recorded unknowing customers for a realistic view, and obtained permission and paid them an honorarium for many of the scenes. The shots featured real people, without make-up, in regular light, doing regular restaurant activities. McDonald's also compiled numerous interview style

[Continued on next page]

[IMC Perspective 6-1 continued]

video messages where Canadians told their stories, some of which appeared in social media. Coinciding with the TV and online video messages, the campaign included extensive out-of-home media showing a photograph of a McDonald's customer, their name, and the location of the photo. In this case, the customers participated initially and posed for the picture.

The underlying meaning in all of these messages is that McDonald's is a place that Canadians rely on for a variety reasons, no matter who they are. Whether it is for a simple washroom break, or a new environment after being at the club, or a place to play before a child's nap time, McDonald's is a place to visit and enjoy when not at home or at work. All of the international divisions and their competitors heard the challenge by the head office co-CEO to be more than a fast food restaurant, but the Canadian division took it to heart and saw an opportunity to continue with its honest approach, as seen in the award winning campaign of 2012.

To extend the human side of the brand further, the messages included the stories of McDonald's employees and suppliers of McDonald's. For example, we meet Lorna from Fredericton who loves working and chats happily with customers, and we also meet Savin of Vancouver whose employment helps pay her way through school. In an out-of-home ad, Angelo and David from Grand Falls, New Brunswick, smile amid a pile of potatoes as they tell us that they grow the fries. Time will tell if the new positioning will take permanent root in the marketplace with the new entrants and changing consumer tastes, but the new store design in many locations may help make the message more believable for more Canadians over the next few years.

Sources: Russ Martin, "McDonald's Rolls Out the Welcome Mat With New Platform," *Marketing Magazine*, March 3, 2015; Susan Krashinsky, "McDonald's Canada Welcomes Customers With Candid Ad Campaign," *The Globe and Mail*, March, 3, 2015; Nicholas Misketi, "McDonald's Rebrands as Common Ground," *National Post*, March 23, 2015.

Question:

1. How effective is the brand positioning strategy for McDonald's?

Implement Brand Positioning Strategy   The content of the advertising message, its creative strategy, and creative tactics can be formulated once the brand positioning strategy is established. The implementation of other promotional communication tools also requires message and creativity development. For example, prior to launching a public relations or publicity campaign, a marketer would specify the positioning of its brand to its intended target audience before deciding upon the exact content of its message and how he or she would creatively present it.

Monitor Brand Positioning Strategy   After initial implementation of a new marketing communication campaign, a promotional planner would like to know if the resulting brand position is consistent with the intended brand positioning strategy. Alternatively, for a continuing marketing communication campaign, monitoring occurs to know how well the brand position is maintained. In either case, tracking studies measure the image of the brand over time, and changes in consumers' perceptions can serve as input for subsequent planning for future decisions. In the Toyota example, key communication effects improved substantially during the first seven months, indicating strong positioning. Brand awareness rose from 83 percent to 95 percent, advertising awareness rose from 5 percent to 19 percent, and purchase intention increased from 22 percent to 40 percent. Many consumer perception ratings rose significantly and surpassed competitors. For example, more than 70 percent of the consumers surveyed rated the Tacoma as high quality, dependable, well built, and trusted. Sales nearly doubled in a year, with market share moving to the 14–16 percent range. These remarkable results occurred with Chevrolet rebranding its S-10 to Colorado and the Dodge Dakota and Ford Ranger spending more money on advertising than the Tacoma.[14]

LO3   Brand Positioning Strategy Decisions

The essence of positioning the brand in the context of advertising is to clearly indicate where the brand is competing, with whom it is competing, how it is competing, and finally why consumers will purchase the brand. Each of these questions must be addressed through four decisions within the brand positioning strategy: market definition, differential advantage, target audience brand attitude, and consumer purchase motive.

MARKET DEFINITION

A primary decision for positioning is how the promotional planners define the market and where they intend for the brand to compete with its benefit claims. The market partition illustrations showed that brands compete against other brands on end benefits, brand name, usage situation, and product category. One purpose of advertising is to contribute to developing a perceived advantage over competing brands within the competitive space. Thus, each of these offers tremendous opportunity to communicate benefit claims and establish a perceived differential advantage.

Positioning by End Benefit   A common approach to positioning is setting the brand apart from competitors on the basis of its primary end benefit offered; a brand may be positioned on multiple benefits if necessary. The ad for Range Rover in Exhibit 6-5 exemplifies the driving experience to communicate the performance benefit. Marketers also attempt to identify salient attributes that are important to consumers and are the basis for making a purchase decision. In this case, the positioning focuses on these specific characteristics and the benefits are not directly claimed in the message. Advertisers require good research and reasons for justifying this kind of positioning recommendation, because moving toward a specific attribute or benefit precludes messages regarding other attributes and benefits.

In all of its marketing communication, Roots Canada sticks with the singular focus of being Canadian. All imagery and messaging reflects and reinforces this key attribute about the company. In fact, the brand takes pride in the fact that many of its products are produced in Canada, providing important support for this authentic attribute claim.[15] Alternatively, a pure benefit focus can be seen with Reebok Canada's effort as part of the global "Live With Fire" positioning. An ad with NHL stars John Tavares, Matt Duchene, and Maxime Talbot promoted the new Reebok Training collection of footwear and apparel. The direction of the campaign attempted to allow consumers to experience the "passion, intent, and purpose" benefits associated with using the new product line.[16] The 5-hour Energy ad in Exhibit 6-6 shows the product's positioning based on both its attributes (e.g. zero sugar, 4 calories) and benefits (e.g., quick, lasting energy), which are not directly connected.

While we refer to either attribute or benefit positioning in this discussion, marketers will also make a direct link between a particular attribute and the derived benefit, or they may highlight the attribute and allow the target audience to interpret the benefit. Activia's marketing communication highlighted the unique probiotic culture in its yogurt and the resulting vitality that continued consumption produced, with its interesting ads that featured boxed frames on people's stomachs as they danced and ate the product.[17]

Exhibit 6-5   The Range Rover ad captures the driving experience to demonstrate how it competes on performance.

© Lars A. Niki

Exhibit 6-6   Both attributes and benefits are communicated in this ad for 5-hour Energy.

This approach is often used in the car market, and is how the Lexus IS F competed in performance by showing extensive visuals of the engine in many forms of digital media.[18]

Positioning by Brand Name   Marketers use an emphasis on quality for a brand positioning strategy with ads that reflect the image of a high-end product where cost, while not irrelevant, is considered secondary to the benefits derived from using a quality brand. Premium or luxury brands tend to use this approach for positioning and one might speculate that much of Apple's advertising presumed a positioning by brand name with its innovative quality. Another way of brand name positioning is to focus on the quality offered by the brand at a competitive price (e.g., value-based). For example, Lands' End uses this strategy by suggesting that quality can be affordable. Remember that although price is an important consideration, the product quality must be comparable to competing brands for the positioning strategy to be effective.

Positioning by brand name is viable when its distinctive attribute or benefit is the message focus by associating it with the brand name which becomes the prominent approach for consumer evaluation. From an attribute standpoint, Canada Dry Ginger Ale rediscovered the importance of positioning by brand name as it reminded consumers that it contained ginger! While this obvious fact appears not to warrant advertising, the brand obtained good mileage as consumers looked at ginger as a healthy ingredient to consume in one's diet.[19] From a benefit view, we turn to Tassimo's "The Barcode Brews It Better" campaign designed to increase household penetration to 10 percent for its new coffee system. Tassimo wanted consumers to enter stores asking for "the one with the barcode" as the identification and association of that image became the key message to convey in the new brand positioning strategy. The creative solution featured a "live" barcode as people dressed in white or black like the bars in a barcode chatted about the technology in a light-hearted manner.[20]

The growth of craft beers raised the opportunity for new market entrants to emphasize their unique brand name. Upstart and independent Great Western Brewing Company tells the story behind its Original 16 premium ale, where the 16 refers to the number of employees who took ownership and rescued the small plant from being closed when Molson bought out the previous owner. Sixteen video messages on the company's Internet site captured the process, from the anxiety of closure to the celebration of ownership! The agency suggested the messages conveyed that the brand was "genuine" and "authentic" and allowed people beyond Saskatchewan to understand the history of the beer.[21]

Positioning by Usage Situation   Another way to communicate a specific image or position for a brand is to associate it with a specific use. Molson M distanced itself from mainstream beer advertising by positioning itself as premium beer for a sophisticated night out.[22] While this strategy is often used to enter a market based on a particular use, it is also an effective way to expand the situational usage of a product. For example, for its Kit Kat chocolate bars, Nestlé established a "take a break" positioning years ago and returned to it with a new campaign. The launch featured a TV ad showing break situations when people would want to eat a Kit Kat, as well as phone apps that call people automatically and give a fictitious and humorous reason for people to take a break, thus allowing people to get away with a "reason" instead of the truth.[23] Finally, empirical research suggests that marketing communication plays a strong role in consumers' adopting new uses.[24] The Intuit ad in Exhibit 6-7 advertises its specific use for small business owners.

Positioning by Product Category   Competition for a product comes from outside the product category and, rather than positioning against another brand, an alternative strategy is to position the brand against another product category. For example, Via Rail positioned itself as an alternative to airplanes, citing cost savings, enjoyment, and other advantages (Exhibit 6-8). V8 promotes drinking one's vegetables (Exhibit 6-9) to attract consumers who dislike or do not eat enough vegetables. Craft beers of Ontario made inroads toward the higher-end spirits with their placement in the provincial alcohol retailer. Extensive messaging from the Liquor Control Board of Ontario and the Ontario Craft Brewers Association looked beyond the beer market to carve out a niche and improve sales.[25] This result is all the more remarkable considering the decline of beer sales relative to other alcohol products, moving from 50 percent to 43 percent of

Exhibit 6-7   Intuit offers products for small business usage.

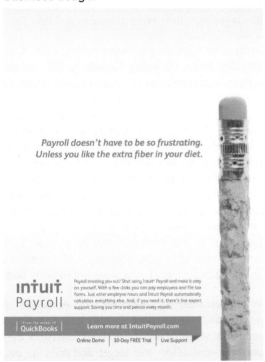

Payroll doesn't have to be so frustrating. Unless you like the extra fiber in your diet.

INTUIT. Payroll

From the maker of QuickBooks

Payroll stressing you out? Start using Intuit Payroll and make it easy on yourself. With a few clicks you can pay employees and file tax forms. Just enter employee hours and Intuit Payroll automatically calculates everything else. And, if you need it, there's live expert support. Saving you time and pencils every month.

Learn more at IntuitPayroll.com

Online Demo | 30-Day FREE Trial | Live Support

all alcohol sales.[26] Cereal brands have faced extensive sales decline over the past few years, and General Mills targeted men with its Peanut Butter Cheerios as data showed they frequently consumed breakfast outside of the home at fast food restaurants.[27] Dairy Queen, known as DQ these days, continually faces a message challenge in signalling its market definition, since the brand communicates its outlets as a destination for ice-cream treats while competing with similar kinds of venues, and as a location for eating fast food while competing with the big players like McDonald's. Its slogans over the years—"Fan Food, Not Fast Food," "So Good It's RiDQulous," and "Something Different"—reflect this difficult marketing challenge.[28]

DIFFERENTIAL ADVANTAGE

Brand benefit claims embodied in the positioning and represented in the ads contribute to the differential advantage for a brand. While it is generally expected that a brand positioning strategy should take a differential positioning approach and have a product benefit focus, we highlight situations where brands do not follow this pattern.

Differential vs. Central Positioning   In the previous section, we mentioned the importance of advertising contributing to the perceived differential advantage for the brand. This is true for most brands and the five major Canadian banks try to distance themselves from one another with their advertising.[29] For example, TD Canada Trust implemented its "Banking Can Be This Comfortable" in 1997 and symbolized it with a green leather armchair. TD evolved the idea to many dimensions of consumers' banking experience, such as an intuitive Internet site and stress-free retail environment. The success of this differentiation can be seen with its top ranking by Interbrand for two years in a row.

However, market circumstances allow brands to claim a central position within the product category. A central brand positioning strategy is possible when the brand can claim and deliver on the most salient benefits. This may be a function of the brand's being the market share leader, achieving success during the growth stage of the product life cycle, or having unique brand characteristics that essentially define the category. It could be suggested that Nike takes a central position for its messages across several product categories, especially with its slogan "Just Do It" (Exhibit 6-10). Similarly, one might conclude that Apple took a central position in its advertising for its new products over the past couple of decades. The house brand for Loblaw, President's Choice, continues to position it as a leader within the generic brand food category with its Insider's Report, product innovation ads, and new cooking shows.[30]

In another market context, being the first brand in a product category is a good start, but research suggests it is not a guarantee; in some categories, the second and third entries after the initial pioneer have also established strong positions. Yves Rocher, a pioneer in the plant-based skin-care category, lost its dominance as other brands claimed these ingredients as important in their ads (e.g., Aveeno). So the French brand ensured that its advertising, and all other marketing offers (e.g., store, spa, information lab), reflected its botanical roots to reconfirm its central position.[31] Finally, sometimes brands attempt to take a central position in a subcategory, as seen in Exhibit 6-11.

Exhibit 6-8   Via competes with other forms of transportation.

Hand-out/VIA Rail Canada Inc./Newscom

Exhibit 6-9   V8 positions itself as a drink that substitutes for vegetables.

© Campbell Soup Company

Exhibit 6-10   Nike likely takes a central positioning in much of its marketing communication.

© c43/Imaginechina/Zuma/ICON SMI/Newscom

Brand Benefit vs. User Positioning   We have thus far implied that most positioning decisions involve unique and differential benefit claims that the brand can deliver. The market partition and competitive analysis gives promotional planners the opportunity to identify and determine the most important ones to claim in advertising. For example, Lay's potato chip ads extol the virtues of using 100 percent Canadian potatoes.[32] The premise of the strategy focused on getting back to the core of the product, presumably to differentiate from other snacks with less pure ingredients. A focus on the product such as this is known as a **brand benefit positioning**, although it is generally referred to as a product focus. The Prada ad in Exhibit 6-12 is an example where its stylish looking handbags have a prominent focus.

While a brand benefit or product focus is a useful approach for many product categories and brands, **user positioning** is an alternative where the message benefit is expressed more personally. In this case, a brand is positioned by association with a particular user or group of users; an example is the Yodel ad shown in Exhibit 6-13. This campaign emphasizes identification or association with snowboarding enthusiasts. A user positioning strategy occurs where the individual is motivated for social or individual reasons, and the ads emphasize how the consumer positively feels while using the brand (Exhibit 6-14). Advertising for Samsung in Canada moved from a product focus to a user focus with its "Infinite Possibilities" messages as consumers became more accustomed to accepting the Android system.[33] Interestingly, Molson Canadian returned to ads with the "I Am Canadian" theme, signalling a user positioning while at the same time maintaining its more current brand benefit positioning "Made From Canada." Executives thought it feasible to introduce a dual positioning approach since the former lingered with consumers after its previous runs from 1994 to 1998, and 2000 to 2005.[34]

Exhibit 6-13   Yodel positions by product user.

Hand-out/YodelTECH Inc./Newscom

Exhibit 6-11   Smart establishes its brand in the ultra-small car category.

© geogphotos / Alamy Stock Photo

Exhibit 6-12   This positioning focuses on the benefit of looking stylish with colourful Prada handbags.

© Lou Linwei / Alamy Stock Photo

Exhibit 6-14   This positioning focuses on the product user.

Hilton Worldwide, Inc.

Gatorade's new marketing communication for the G Series likely suggests a central and product focus positioning. The G Series featured Prime, Perform, and Recover. Prime included carbs and B vitamins and was to be consumed prior to a workout. Perform represented the original Gatorade. Post-workout consumption included Recover, a protein- and carb-based drink. Executives saw the G Series as moving from a hydration brand to a sports nutrition brand. Key messaging to consumers employed MMA fighter Georges St-Pierre as a spokesperson. St-Pierre is an athlete with a colourful personality and a loyal social media following, and he has developed a celebrity-like persona that transcends the sport into popular culture. St-Pierre is rated highly on trust, sexiness, personality, and toughness—a powerful combination. "Georges epitomized what the brand stood for in terms of athleticism and the heart, hustle and soul of the brand," commented one G executive.[35]

TARGET AUDIENCE BRAND ATTITUDE

Previously in this chapter, we identified the concepts of salient attributes and salient benefits. This notion is based on the idea that consumers may hold a number of different beliefs about brands in any product or service category. However, not all of these beliefs are activated in forming an attitude. Beliefs concerning specific attributes or benefits that are activated and form the basis of an attitude are referred to as **salient beliefs**. Marketers should identify these salient beliefs and understand how the saliency varies among different target audiences, over time, and across different consumption situations. Marketers can use a specific model to develop persuasive brand positioning strategies since it guides which attributes and benefits to claim in advertising.

Brand Attitude Model   Consumer researchers and marketing practitioners use multiattribute attitude models to study consumer attitudes.[36] A **multiattribute attitude model** views an attitude object, such as a product or brand, as possessing a number of attributes that provide the basis on which consumers form their attitudes. According to this model, consumers have beliefs about specific brand attributes and attach different levels of importance to these attributes. Using this approach, an attitude toward a particular brand can be represented as

$$A_B = \sum_{i=1}^{n} B_i \times E_i$$

where A_B = attitude toward a brand

B_i = beliefs about the brand's performance on attribute i

E_i = importance attached to attribute i

n = number of attributes considered

For example, a consumer may have beliefs (B_i) about certain attributes of brands of toothpaste. One brand may be perceived as having fluoride and thus preventing cavities, tasting good, and helping control tartar buildup, while consumers may believe another brand performs well on other attributes such as freshening breath and whitening teeth. To predict attitudes, one must know how much importance consumers attach to each of these attributes (E_i). For example, parents purchasing toothpaste for their children may prefer a brand that performs well on cavity prevention, a preference that leads to a more favourable attitude toward the first brand. Teenagers and young adults may prefer a brand that freshens their breath and makes their teeth white and thus prefer the second brand.

In the case of Tim Hortons, the iconic Canadian brand competes on five benefits in its coffee marketing: quality (20 minute promise), popularity (Canada's Favourite Coffee), heart-warming emotion (True Stories), promotion (RRRoll Up the Rim to Win) and ethics (Fair Trade). Ads addressing these aspects typically focus on the delivery or importance of these beliefs.[37] As this suggests, the multiattribute model is applied for attribute- or benefit-based persuasion, depending on the promotional planner's strategic intention. IMC Perspective 6-2 takes a look at Cracker Barrel's brand positioning strategy.

IMC PERSPECTIVE 6-2

AN AMAZING CHEESE COMMERCIAL

Sliced havarti, grated mozzarella, and a block of old cheddar are featured at the end of three amazing cheese ads for Kraft's Cracker Barrel since they are what start three delicious treats; steak sandwich, lasagna, and a cheese board. Captioned with the slogan, "Start With Cracker Barrel. End With Amazing.", the ads show a close-up of the preparation of each food in reverse order! We start by seeing the juicy steak sandwich, the steaming dish of lasagna, or the elegantly decorated and designed cheese board, and then trace back through each preparation with a reverse recording, until we see that the whole thing started with Cracker Barrel. The video messages shown on TV and online accompanied similar photographs shown in magazines and in social media.

© baibaz/Shutterstock

The inspiration for the new ads flowed from consumer research. One conclusion suggested that consumers treated food as "convenient mindless stomach filler," and that consumers were "eating to live versus living to eat." Another finding reminded the decision makers that food preparation represented an expression of love that could be reflected in the ads. Furthermore, consumers saw cheese as a main ingredient in food preparation. Competitive research indicated that low-priced cheese, and cheese with price promotions, took a growing share of the marketing, giving Kraft the motivation to portray it as a higher end brand. Shoppers typically made their cheese purchase quickly, looking mainly at price without paying attention to quality.

To give importance to the quality angle, the ads used extensive food imagery with higher quality recording and photography, much like that found on cooking shows or in food magazines, to go along with the imagery found with gourmet brands. Cracker Barrel's agency, Leo Burnett, recruited experts from the food industry—an internationally acclaimed food stylist and a photographer with equal stature. The sandwich ad gives testament to the artistic presentation of each individual scene in reverse: biting, cutting in half, baking in the press, lifting the bread, watching greens rising, slicing the steak, cooking the steak, seasoning the steak, unravelling the red pepper, and finally starting with havarti. The ad makes you believe that you are there, eating and preparing the food!

Previous category ads, including those for Cracker Barrel, usually communicated messages of taste, convenience, and ingredients. Executives believed that Cracker Barrel's approach presented a more emotional experience and emphasized the brand more clearly to build stronger equity. They also felt that the ads did not target a specific gender or age demographic but resonated more with culinary adventurers, potentially seeing these consumers as a psychographic segment. With the first national campaign, Cracker Barrel simultaneously portrayed the brand in an entirely new way, and exhibited its messages in Quebec for the first time ever.

Sources: Megan Haynes, "Cracker Barrel's Cheesy Repositioning," *Strategy*, May 1, 2015; Susan Krashinsky, "Cracker Barrel Ads Aim to Solidify Reputation as Big Cheese of Quality," *The Globe and Mail*, April 24, 2015, https://www.youtube.com/channel/UCkDCbVD58DGYwHNfPAdFEOQ; http://www.kraftcanada.com/brands/cracker-barrel.

Question:

1. Compare the previous and the current brand positioning strategy decisions for Cracker Barrel cheese and comment on whether the new one will be effective.

Brand Attitude Persuasion   Multiattribute models help marketers diagnose the beliefs that underlie consumers' evaluations of a brand and the importance of attributes or benefits. This analysis guides communication strategies, like maintaining attitudes of current customers or changing attitudes of non-customers. A study demonstrated that research examining attribute ratings of customers and non-customers provided important direction for improving the marketing communication strategy for a European telecommunications firm.[38] Thus, the multiattribute model shows how marketers can influence attitudes of target audiences regarding brand characteristics they wish to emphasize.

Influence Attribute Belief   The first strategy is to identify an attribute or benefit that is important and communicate how well the brand performs. In situations where consumers do not perceive the marketer's brand as possessing an important attribute, where belief strength is to be improved to higher levels, or where the belief strength is low, advertising strategies may be targeted at changing the belief rating; this approach appears to be relevant for Tag Heuer in Exhibit 6-15. Even when belief strength is high, advertising may be used to increase the rating of a brand on an important attribute. The Harvey's campaign for grill-cooked hamburgers illustrates this approach. Other quick-service food retailers focused on fast drive-through or convenient locations, along with enhanced menus with healthier foods. Harvey's appeared disadvantaged in comparison and faced declining sales and a reduced number of franchises. The grill attribute positioning conjured both functional benefits (e.g., fresh, natural, healthy) and emotional benefits (e.g., outdoor BBQ, male bonding). The positioning succeeded, with unaided awareness moving from 13 percent to 22 percent, key brand attitude measures improving, purchase intention rising from 21 percent to 38 percent, and negative sales growth of 3 percent reversed to positive growth of 2 percent.[39] The Molson M example cited earlier focused on the new micro-carbonation and unique colour of the beer, an interesting combination of attributes to position on.

Exhibit 6-15   The Tag Heuer ad associates the internal drive of humans with the internal strength and quality of its watch.

© Lars A. Niki

Influence Attribute Importance   Marketers attempt to influence consumer attitudes by changing the relative importance of a particular attribute. This second strategy involves getting consumers to attach more importance to the attribute in forming their attitude toward the brand. Marketers using this strategy want to increase the importance of an attribute their particular brand has. The print ads for Jergens Ultra Care moisturizer highlight the importance to a woman of regularly applying lotion all over her body. The positioning was intended to demonstrate that moisturizing was as important as all the other beauty activities that women engage in every day. The main message suggested that women "Take Care of What You Wear Every Day" with a visual showing the lotion on a woman's body, and obviously associated a woman's skin with her wardrobe. The positioning was initiated in Quebec as the brand underachieved significantly compared to other parts of Canada. Research indicated that women from Quebec did not separate beauty and skin care from health. This insight suggested that new users could be attracted to the brand if the ads conveyed the sensuality of moisturized skin. A 50 percent increase in sales in Quebec allowed the brand's positioning to be extended in English rather than continuing with the planned U.S. ads.[40]

Add New Attribute Belief   The third strategy for influencing consumer attitudes is to add or emphasize a new attribute that consumers can use in evaluating a brand. Marketers do this by focusing on additional benefits or consequences associated with using the brand that have not been communicated previously. Exhibit 6-16 is an ad for Mott's Fruitsations, with enhanced nutrients for bone health. Wonder+, a line extension of

Exhibit 6-16   Mott's highlights the importance of strong bones via its Fruitsations brand.

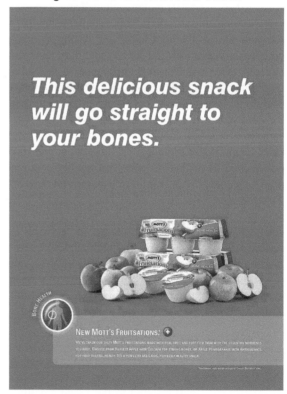

This delicious snack will go straight to your bones.

NEW MOTT'S FRUITSATIONS.

the famous Wonder bread, needed to communicate that it had the same great taste as the original, but that it had the nutrition of whole wheat bread. The new brand attempted to influence lapsed users of Wonder bread due to the perception that white bread was no longer healthy. Yet at the same time, managers knew that the message had to reinforce the attitude of loyal customers. Adding the health benefit worked, with clever imagery of twins eating both types of bread and believing that they both taste the same, yet one is now whole wheat. The positioning of this advertising produced significant gains for all communication effects and sales.[41]

Brands have innovated by adding new benefits to compete on with "green" or "environmental" messages. Molson Canadian's positioning with its "Made From Canada" slogan is a good example. According to one executive, "The land plays a pretty significant role in all of our advertising and things that we've done." And one of those things included cause-related activities entitled "Molson Canadian Red Leaf Project," where employees and citizens planted 100,000 trees and cleaned the shorelines and urban parks in 10 communities with assistance from Tree Canada, WWF, and Evergreen. The company rewarded participants with free tickets for a concert on the event date. Summing up the experience, one remarked, "If the land is that important to Canadians and it's that important to our brand and the quality of our beer, then we should be investing in making the land better."[42]

Influence Attribute Belief of Competitor Brand   A final strategy marketers use is to change consumer beliefs about the attributes of competing brands or product categories. This strategy has become much more common with the increase in comparative advertising, where marketers compare their brands to competitors' on specific product attributes. An example of this is the comparative ad shown in Exhibit 6-17. With a better understanding of health, Canadians are more concerned with health and food manufacturers responded with more emphasis on the ingredients of their products in terms of natural, authentic, and real. These healthier claims spawned growth in direct comparisons on an attribute by attribute basis in many categories.[43]

A battle between telecommunications firms demonstrates how brands compete this way. Rogers asked consumers to take the "Rogers Home Phone Challenge." Using a dual-coloured couch as a visual—red for Rogers and blue for Bell—the ads claimed price was the only difference in the services with quality being equal. Rogers entered the home phone market, a traditional Bell strength, and intended the ad as a suggestion for consumers to comparison shop. Bell shot back with the same imagery, and extended its end of the couch to defend the price claim. It also promoted its 3G network and HD channels and moved to defend its price and quality position with its own blue couch, with five blue cushions and one red cushion. The message was, "Get More Than Rogers for Less Than Rogers." Another battle emerged in the courts when Telus sued Rogers for the latter's claims of its wireless service

Exhibit 6-17   Kyocera tries to influence beliefs about competitor brands.

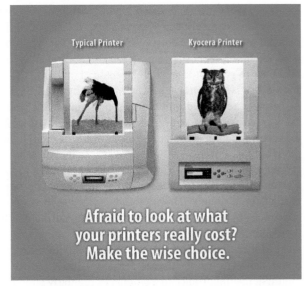

Courtesy of Kyocera Corporation

having "the fastest and most reliable network" and "Canada's fastest network: Two times faster than any other." A judge ordered Rogers to remove the "fastest" and "most reliable" claims on all of its marketing communication. As a result, Rogers discarded approximately $3 million worth of promotional material already produced and erected. Rogers switched its claim to "Canada's reliable network," dropping the word "most." At the same time, Rogers sued Bell for the latter's inaccurate claim of the "largest, fastest and most reliable" and "the best and most powerful" network—and subsequently won.[44]

CONSUMER PURCHASE MOTIVE

Since positioning involves presenting the brand's benefit claims to a target audience, the portrayal of the benefits influences how consumers will respond to the brand's delivery and whether the target audience perceives them as important. The portrayal of benefits is reflected by the purchase motivation associated with the brand. Thus, the purchase motivation of the target audience is another important decision for the brand positioning strategy.

Importance of Purchase Motives   As we suggested with the Harvey's attribute positioning, given the content of the ad, the underlying reason for enjoying a grilled hamburger appears to be the taste sensation. However, another perspective is that it could reflect healthier eating compared to fried hamburgers, since less fat is retained in the meat and consequently less fat is consumed, so consumers can feel better about their dietary choices. This connection between the cooking attribute and healthier eating could have been communicated with subtle changes in the ads of the current campaign. Thus, the attribute positioning still requires the right kind of motivation or reason for purchase demonstrated in the ad to be completely successful.

Keep in mind that the reasons for the Harvey's hamburger purchase are quite distinct: the sensory enjoyment of the hamburger versus the individual accomplishment of eating properly. We highlight these two ideas since they are two of eight basic consumer purchase motives that are more managerially useful to guide the brand positioning strategy decision within Rossiter and Percy's framework, which we have discussed previously. Figure 6-12 summarizes these motives into two types consistent with psychological theory.

Figure 6-12   Eight basic consumer purchase motives

Informational Motives	Transformational Motives
Problem removal	Sensory gratification
Problem avoidance	Intellectual stimulation or mastery
Incomplete satisfaction	Social approval
Mixed approach–avoidance	
Normal depletion	

Informational motives are negatively based since the consumer perceives their current consumption situation as a deficit in which the purchase of the product would minimize the shortfall and bring the consumer to a neutral or normal state. Exhibit 6-18 suggests an informational motive for non-users. **Transformational motives** imply that consumers perceive their consumption situation as requiring improvement from a neutral state. Negatively and positively oriented motives are consistent with psychological theories of motivation and are similar to Maslow's theory—however, there is no implied hierarchy.

Informational Motives   Problem-removal motives reflect consumption situations where consumers perceive a problem, for example dandruff, and seek a product that resolves the problem, like anti-dandruff shampoo. Many products in this category have emphasized this motive in their ads while attempting to highlight a unique attribute or benefit positioning. However, ads for Head & Shoulders currently in Canada have mentioned the problem while emphasizing how good one's hair feels after using their anti-dandruff shampoo, thus reflecting a different primary motive beyond the initial problem removal. This is the reason for connecting the purchase motive shown in the ad to the brand positioning strategy—it identifies the particular way to communicate effectively with a target audience that the brand has profiled in great detail. In contrast, problem avoidance motives occur when consumers anticipate a problem if they do not take pre-emptive action through the purchase of a product. Insurance advertising typically addresses this as a motive as the messages show the consequences of not having coverage, or not having the right type or amount of coverage.

Exhibit 6-18   WD-40 advertises the many uses of its product for solving problems.

Courtesy of the WD-40 Company

These two examples for removal and avoidance are fairly self-evident; their application to specific brands requires unique executions so that the idea of selling the category does not dominate and the brand effects are not achieved.

Incomplete satisfaction motives are based on the consumer perceptions that they are not fully satisfied with their current brand choice and are seeking a better product. With its expanded product offerings which allowed it to compete head-on against major banks, ING moved from its old "Save Your Money" approach to "It's Time to Stop Banking in the Past" as its ads portrayed its competitors as unreceptive and not very innovative.[45] Such a message conceivably resonates with disgruntled customers of other financial institutions. Similarly, Mobilicity aggressively pointed out the shortcomings of the "Big 3" mobile providers with executions from its "Now That's Smart" positioning.[46]

Mixed approach–avoidance motives are active for consumers in purchase situations where they enjoy some elements of a product but dislike other parts and are seeking alternative solutions. Van Houtte positions its brand as being a "Master Roaster Since 1919" and the Montreal-based gourmet coffee company released a series of educational videos on its blog and many social media vehicles. This historical and anthropological approach lends an air of authenticity to its beans and roasting skills, thereby potentially swaying consumers who may feel that other brands have less of these important characteristics.[47] Mr. Lube advertised to owners that they did not need to bring their vehicles to dealerships for all services, suggesting that the target audience might have mixed feelings about being completely loyal to a dealership.[48]

Consumers regularly require a product because they have none on hand, and so normal depletion as a reason for purchase is an almost-everyday situation; however, it is not a viable option for a primary brand positioning strategy. A message focusing on a reminder purchase when a consumer does not have the product is featured in seasonal purchases. For example, gardening products in the spring and school supplies in the fall are two obvious ad messages we commonly see. In essence, a normal depletion motive is not a long-term strategy; however, it is useful for short-term situations and reaching particular target audiences at a particular point in time to maximize total sales during a year.

Transformational Motives As the term implies, sensory gratification motives are predicated on the product's providing a positive experience via one of the five senses. The colourful imagery in Exhibit 6-19 makes consumers want to share in the fun and experience the Canadian Rockies. Clearly, this is a valuable approach for many types of products, but it is important to focus on the right aspect with the right reference point. Newfoundland and Labrador Tourism's "Find Yourself" campaign captured the sensory experience of being in the province through an exquisite portrayal of its landscape and culture, and garnered the CASSIES Grand Prix for 2012. The breathtaking scenery and delightful storylines brought a feeling of being there instantly, providing a prototypical example of communicating transformational motives.[49]

Intellectual stimulation or mastery is an individual motive linked to an element of self-improvement through the purchase of a product or brand. This mastery is driven by an innate human need to explore or learn. The marketing communication agency Sid Lee of Montreal, the global agency of record for Adidas, moved toward this motive in its messaging with the "All In" campaign. The wellness message associated with its sports gear encouraged consumers toward health, fitness, and achievement within the active sports community.[50] Curiously, Kraft Dinner used this kind of motivation to encourage adults to consume the product once again (e.g., lapsed users), with a nostalgic message that reminded them how much fun they experienced as a child when eating the cheesy noodles.[51]

Personal recognition is suggested with the social approval motive, whereby consumers are motivated to purchase certain products or brands because consumers aspire to be accepted in certain social groups; Exhibit 6-20 provides an example in the form of an unconventional hair colour. Women's fashion boutique Aritzia eschews traditional advertising, however its extensive use of public relations via influential bloggers, social media conversations, and celebrities wearing its fashions at store events all suggest a subtle connection to social approval. Its prominent placement of a flagship store on Fifth Avenue in New York City carries forth the boutique impression it strives to maintain in the market.[52]

Exhibit 6-19 Travel Alberta conveys the physical enjoyment of skiing in the Rockies.

Hand-out/TRAVEL ALBERTA/Newscom

Brand Repositioning Strategy

Exhibit 6-20   Splat gives its customers a cool new look to be proud of!

Courtesy of Developlus, Inc.

Developing a new brand positioning strategy for an established brand is referred to as *repositioning*, and the reasons for the change are discovered in the situation analysis. For example, marketing objectives such as sales or share may be below forecast, or advertising claims from competitors may threaten the current strategy. Repositioning is often difficult to achieve because of ingrained consumer understanding of market structure and established brand attitudes. The options for altering the brand positioning strategy typically focus on the four topics previously defined: market definition, differential advantage, target audience, and a salient motive. Each of these is applied subsequently after identifying the communication issue for a number of recent CASSIES winners. Further details of the examples provided in this section are available at Cassies.ca.

IMPORTANCE OF REPOSITIONING

The situational analysis in terms of consumer, competition, company, market, and environment may all signal the need for a brand moving from its existing brand positioning strategy to a new one. This analysis should reveal which of these are most critical and help identify the marketing communication issue the promotional plan will address. Figure 6-13 summarizes the origin of the repositioning strategy of the CASSIES winners that we now review.

Figure 6-13   Critical analysis guiding repositioning decisions

Competition	Company	Consumer	Market	Environment
Dove	Canadian 67	IKEA	Tetley Herbal Tea	Tourism
McDonald's	Cashmere	Subaru Outback	Reactine	Budweiser
Hospital for Sick Children	Ïögo	Oka	TD	Honda

Summarized from cases located on Cassies.ca

Competition   A brand's repositioning is often driven from competitive dynamics. Dove's research proved to managers that the brand appeared to be a "latecomer" to the personal care market, in which tremendous innovation had occurred in the preceding years from Procter & Gamble and other entrants like Nivea, Aveeno, and Jergens. While McDonald's invented the concept of a quick-service restaurant chain offering breakfast, it faced increased competition from other coffee shops offering similar breakfast sandwiches that appeared as copies of the original Egg McMuffin. McDonald's looked to invigorate the iconic breakfast sandwich and encourage more frequent purchases with a new repositioning. Toronto's Hospital for Sick Children faced increased competition for fundraising dollars during the Christmas season and required a new approach to encourage donations for its SickKids Foundation.

Company   Company-sourced factors can be an impetus for repositioning. While in some respects Molson introduced a new brand with Canadian 67, it replaced the previous Canadian Light and required the "re-launched" brand to develop a unique positioning distinctive from the popular Coors Light. Kruger Products (formerly Scott Paper) faced a difficult repositioning task when its licence from Kimberly-Clark ran out for the use of the highly successful Cottonelle brand in the bathroom tissue category. This looked even more challenging in the face of competition from Royale and Charmin, not to mention the expected "introduction" of Cottonelle after Kruger had put both the Cashmere and Cottonelle brand names on the package and ads for a period of time before the expiration. In a very unusual situation, Ultima Foods needed to completely reposition its marketing communication activities when the company learned that the licensing for its Yoplait brand expired. This required the company to launch a new brand, Ïögo, that would have to compete with its own previous brand as the original owners planned to centralize their operations and manage Yoplait's marketing.

Consumer   Brands like IKEA and Subaru saw declines in sales as consumers appeared to no longer gravitate to them, while Oka looked to its current customers in Quebec to expand sales. IKEA appeared to be a brand of choice for young consumers setting up their first or first few households, but they tended to move on to other brands once they reached the 35+ age range. Subaru Outback sales declined by over 50 percent during a seven-year time period; it repositioned the brand with its ad suggesting that consumers deserve to be outdoors more. For its home Quebec market, the famous Oka cheese encouraged its current customers to eat the artisan cheese every day for lunch and snacks to spark greater consumption frequency.

Market   Tetley saw a substantial decline in the herbal tea market at 2 percent per year with the growth of other types of tea when it repositioned by associating its flavours to different moods a consumer may have prior to consumption, thereby offering the perfect solution. Reactine needed to reposition its brand as the market shifted to increased use of other product formats. TD Bank's research indicated that the demand for mortgages would soften in the important spring season and repositioned its message to new home buyers who might be delaying entry into their first purchase.

Environment   The Canadian Tourism Commission and Newfoundland & Labrador Tourism both faced potential further declines in travel to Canada (from other countries) and to the province (from other provinces) during the 2008 recession and slow economic growth that followed, which necessitated new positioning strategies. Budweiser lost its sponsorship contract with the NHL when the league signed with Molson, and needed a new way to link its brand to the hockey fan experience. Honda believed it needed a push in a new direction during the spring so that car shoppers would consider the brand during their shopping for a new car.

MARKET DEFINITION

Markets are partitioned by end benefit, brand name, usage situation, and product category. One possibility for repositioning is that the brand defines its market within a new partition or reconstructs the partition favourably through its messaging so that consumers understand how brands are competing in an entirely different manner. We look at an example for each option derived from Figure 6-13.

End Benefit   Ïögo's launch partly suggests a repositioning by brand name with the slogan "Ïögo, a New Way to Say Yogurt," however the many ads for its individual brands (such as zip, moment, probio, geko, nano, and nomad) consistently portray the yogurt as a healthy alternative to existing brands since it has no gelatin or artificial flavours or colours, and contains all natural fruit and milk products (Exhibit 6-21).

Brand Name   Cashmere's dilemma of repositioning its product with a new brand name suggests it defined the marketing along this partition. The initial communication traced the evolution of the name change from Cottonelle to Cashmere. Subsequent ads connected the brand name of Cashmere to what cashmere material feels like. Maintaining the brand name out front in the positioning proved successful since the brand retained its strength when others might have faltered. In fact, the "new" Cashmere retained its leadership position after a few years and withstood the market entrance of the "new Cottonelle."

Usage Situation   Oka cheese tried to extend its growth in Quebec by moving away from a positioning of authentic artisan cheese produced by monks for generations to an entirely modern approach. A series of humorous ads showed

Exhibit 6-21   Ïögo yogurt repositioned itself away from its former brand name, Yoplait.

Hand-out/ULTIMA FOODS/Newscom

the many different ways in which the unique cheese could be eaten. In one execution, a man accidentally spills the breakfast he is trying to serve a woman after tripping over a nearby cat. Despite the calamity, the woman finds a piece of Oka cheese on her arm and pleasantly enjoys the taste as she thanks the man for being so thoughtful. Two other executions show people eating the cheese as a snack with a funny little twist in the story.

Product Category   Molson Canadian 67 encouraged those drinking other alcohol, wine, and mixed drinks to switch to the brand due to its much lower calorie content. The brand clearly positioned itself against another category with ads that showed how small other drinks would be if they had 67 calories (Exhibit 6-23). This is much different than the positioning of other light beers and the previous Canadian Light positioning that emphasized to current beer drinkers the benefits of drinking a light beer over regular beer. However, Molson Canadian 67 subsequently repositioned the beer once again with its "guyet" ads—humorous messages that showed how the beer fits within a *guy*'s di*et*—thereby suggesting another change of market definition in the direction end-benefit.

Exhibit 6-23   Drinks with 67 calories would be considerably smaller, unlike Molson Canadian 67 beer.

© Molson Coors Canada

DIFFERENTIAL ADVANTAGE

One possibility for repositioning is to move from differential to central or vice versa, or to move from a product focus to a user focus or vice versa. Most often, a brand looks for a differential element to claim in its messaging to carve out its initial positioning, and it is extremely difficult and rare to reposition centrally; nevertheless, it remains an option. It is much more common for brands to examine options on the product/user focus. We look at an example for each option derived from Figure 6-13.

Differential   McDonald's altered its coffee and used this as a springboard for repositioning its advertising for eating breakfast at the restaurant to those in the habit of eating at other quick-service outlets, notably Tim Hortons, which commanded a strong market share. McDonald's emphasized that its Egg McMuffin contained only 290 calories to defend its core business. It also claimed superior coffee since the beverage represented the number one drink purchased outside the home. Combined with eggs at number two, the pairing of both for morning consumption proved to be a key way of communicating its differential advantage. McDonald's used creative ads like the one in Exhibit 6-24 to defend its breakfast market.

Exhibit 6-24   Steaming cups of coffee appeared in public to entice consumers to McDonald's.

© samdcruz.com

Central   While Dove appeared to be a late entrant in the personal care market, the repositioning of the brand with its "Campaign for Real Beauty" attempted to define the market along the lines of "cosmetic beauty" and "real beauty," in which the brand would take a central position within the latter definition. Although alternative interpretations may be considered, the public relations and consumer reaction to the campaign indicate it changed the face of the market dramatically and unexpectedly. Continued messaging like the new beauty sketches likely supports this contention (Exhibit 6-25).

Brand Benefit Positioning   Honda communicated its affordability to consumers who generally believe that the brand's models are priced a little above their budget. Enter the promotional message that concentrated on the flexible payment options to finance a new Honda to those who would not normally consider the brand even though the consumers understood its dependability, quality, and reliability benefits. A series of TV and social media executions showed both perspectives of a pair of neighbours within a friendly rivalry as to how one could possibly afford a Honda.

User Positioning   Subaru extolled viewers of its ad to get out more often with its unusual approach of peeling the TV screen back with a crowbar. Follow-up print ads reminded consumers of the unique TV ad with the icon at the top of the page, as seen in Exhibit 6-26. An interactive website helped consumers plan their itinerary outdoors to support this user positioning.

Exhibit 6-25   Dove's ads contrast how women view themselves with how others view them.

Hand-out/DOVE/Newscom

Exhibit 6-26   Subaru Outback ads surprisingly showed viewers that life outdoors was better than sitting at home.

© Subaru

NEW TARGET AUDIENCE

As we saw in Chapter 3, organizations target advertising messages both to customers (such as brand loyals and favourable brand switchers) and to non-customers (such as new category users, other brand switchers, and other brand loyals). We now illustrate various repositioning strategies for each of these target audiences.

Brand-Loyal Customers   Budweiser beer created Bud Light ads, not to be confused with its Bud Lite beer, in which the main brand associated itself with hockey. The ads visualized the experience of fans watching a hockey game on TV and seeing "their" team score a goal with their own red light flash nearby just like at a real hockey game. Fans could order their own red light for their home and have it synchronized to flash to replicate the TV ad experience in their own home. Such a promotion and series of ads undoubtedly encouraged loyal Canadian customers to feel stronger affinity for the popular American beer.

Favourable Brand Switcher Customers   Ikea's research showed that each household operates in its own way, and its campaign to continue patronage of its customers once they reach their mid-thirties exemplified this idea. Canadians responded to Ikea's request for #houserules via social media, posting their own version of what was acceptable, such as "No tweeting during dinner" and many others that eventually became the message of outdoor ads (Exhibit 6-27) and messaging in other social media vehicles. The first commercial showed a variety of household compositions and images—all containing Ikea furniture, of course—inviting past customers to send a message, all while discreetly encouraging them to reconsider shopping at Ikea.

Exhibit 6-27   Ikea's #houserules campaign tried to reposition the brand toward lapsed customers.

© Used with the permission of Inter IKEA Systems B.V.

New Category Users   Mortgage selling involves getting consumers to renew a mortgage periodically (every one to five years), or encouraging people who do not own a home to take the risk and buy one. TD needed a fresh approach for encouraging new home buyers to evaluate the bank as an option for a mortgage, and—more importantly—to actually seriously evaluate purchasing a home for the very first time while the housing market appeared to be softening. Messages across multiple media focused on how TD's mortgage product had features that allowed new users to retain their financial flexibility, a key obstacle that research revealed many consumers believed.

Other Brand Loyals   Toronto's Hospital for Sick Children responded to the increased competition for fundraising dollars with a superhero theme in its ads that requested donations. The message portrayed children recovering from serious illnesses as everyday superheroes, much like we see in the movies. One execution featured a movie trailer where the actual child featured in the ad attended the movie with the audience giving him a standing ovation as a tribute to his achievement. Extensive media exposure showed different kids with their own effort at fighting off an illness, with an invitation for viewers and readers to contribute financially. The revenue exceeded the previous year's total by 20 percent, indicating that the campaign influenced those who had not contributed in the past.

Other Brand Switchers   A primary target audience for promotional messages for touring or travelling to other countries or regions of a country is generally consumers who visited other places and who are looking for new adventures. Nevertheless it is a challenge to get on the consideration list of those shopping around. Both tourism brands mentioned earlier focused their repositioning on potential customers who had travelled extensively elsewhere. The Canadian Tourism Commission targeted Canadians who typically planned to travel abroad but liked to travel to unique locations, so the "Locals Know" campaign revealed a side of Canadian travel not previously evaluated (Exhibit 6-28). Similarly, for Newfoundland and Labrador, the target attracted those who valued the idea of going in a new direction different from their past experiences.

PURCHASE MOTIVATION

A brand repositioning strategy through consumer purchase motivation implies a shift from one type of motive to another. The most significant shift would be moving from an informational motive to a transformational motive or vice versa. We present two examples to show successful repositioning through a new consumer purchase motivation.

Problem–Solution   Reactine's repositioning changed its motive considerably. Past approaches showed ways in which an allergy sufferer's distress and discomfort with symptoms did not accurately coincide with actual experience. Ads portrayed potential Reactine users in a humorous light without a clear rationale or reason for consumers to use the product category or brand. The repositioning took the problem more seriously and demonstrated the brand solving the problem in a favourable way.

Sensory Gratification   Tetley visually conveyed the consumption experience of drinking its herbal tea by connecting the mood of the consumer with the colour of the tea in an innovative use of social media (Exhibit 6-29). With the advertising visuals, the senses of consumption clearly portrayed the brand in a new light within the product category. Positionings of competitors lack the sensory experience, opening the door for a successful repositioning for Tetley.

Exhibit 6-28   The Canadian Tourism Commission's "Locals Know" campaign reminded Canadians to visit Canada.

© Destination Canada

Exhibit 6-29   Tetley's Herbal Tea campaign used colour to signify the emotion and sensory experience of drinking Tetley tea.

© Tetley Tea

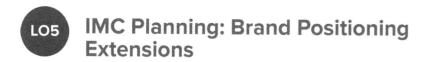

IMC Planning: Brand Positioning Extensions

From an IMC planning perspective, we can extend or adapt the concepts encompassing the brand positioning strategy decisions in three directions: multiple target audiences, buyer decision stages, and corporate brands. The idea is to work with the general model for the positioning decisions and modify it for different parts of the IMC plan.

MULTIPLE TARGET AUDIENCES

Throughout this chapter, we have examined the brand positioning strategy for a single target audience of end users. Many organizations target multiple audiences for their marketing communication for many reasons. For example, in Chapter 3 we described different customer and non-customer groups; brands in fact do have the opportunity to invest in marketing communication devoted to each group. This raises the question as to whether the brand should develop exactly the same positioning strategy for each target audience, or whether variation should exist. And if variation is necessary, what aspects of the brand positioning strategy need to be customized? A number of the examples in Chapter 3 implied this issue; however, after describing positioning strategy, we need to return to the opportunity for promotional planners to fully consider their options.

Although promotional planners could consider customizing all four brand positioning strategy decisions, the first two—market definition and differential advantage—would likely remain relatively constant across customer and non-customer groups. The specific messages to influence brand attitude and the purchase motive communicated offer greater opportunity for getting the right message at the right time. One IMC tool to execute this customized brand positioning strategy is the Internet. For example, automobile advertisers might consider consumers who visit websites to gather information while searching for a vehicle as more likely to be brand switchers, and will include messages that position the brand against its strongest competitor on specific benefits and portray those benefits along the lines of the target audience having dissatisfaction with their current brand. While this is just one example, promotional planners can look at all advertising options and all IMC tools for opportunities to deliver a more specific message to a particular target audience that reinforces a particular brand positioning strategy.

Another interpretation for multiple target audiences involves group decision making, another topic introduced in Chapter 3. For example, in traditional family situations an advertiser may attempt one brand positioning strategy for parents and a relatively different one for children. McDonald's has historically employed this approach with communication directed to children featuring Ronald McDonald and other characters, while parents received messages of the special time they could enjoy with their family. Additionally, automobile brands can use print ads to emphasize certain car features that appeal to men in magazines where men represent a higher proportion of the audience, and similarly for women.

BUYER DECISION STAGES

In the IMC planning section of Chapter 5, we noted that marketers could consider message and communication tool options for each stage of the consumer decision-making process. Various message options can be discerned from the brand positioning strategy decisions outlined in this chapter. First, promotional planners can decide which part of the brand positioning strategy would be most relevant or effective at each stage. Market definition and differential advantage may be more appropriate at the pre-purchase stage or need-recognition stage. For example, the marketing for the Mini in Canada used television advertising to signal that it competed against two markets: regular compact cars like the Honda Civic, and other smaller sports cars like the BMW 3 Series. It also emphasized its advantage of being small in size, but not *too* small.

CORPORATE BRANDS

Thus far we have defined brand positioning strategy and illustrated examples where the brand is at the product level. Corporate brands are also part of integrated marketing communications and are the focus of the public relations topics in Chapter 15. In this context, corporate brands often have varied target audiences, for example investors or members of a particular community.

Given the broader scope of the corporate brand, the initial positioning decision for market definition would concern brand name in most cases. Establishing a differential advantage from a corporate brand entails both differential and central positioning. For example, corporate brand-building activities for Honda suggest that it attempted to establish a central positioning concerning environmental responsibility. This would coincide with its marketing activities of introducing the first hybrid vehicle. Again, the organization-wide communication would imply that most corporate brand positioning would focus on brand benefit positioning over user positioning; however, "green marketing" efforts by companies suggest potential for the latter with an appropriate message that suggests altruistic feelings to the target audience.

All marketing communication decisions are or should be designed to influence target audience attitudes, so corporate brand attitude persuasion is entirely relevant. For example, organizations often involve themselves in sponsorship activities to signal that they are socially responsible, a key attribute to communicate to the general public or to future employees or other stakeholders. Finally, most corporate brand communication is intended along the lines of transformational motives; the clearest examples are television commercials with triumphant music and everlasting positive images.

Learning Objectives Summary

 Identify the concepts of market positioning strategy and market position.

The strategic marketing plan describes all marketing decisions, including promotion and the supporting analysis and justification. It typically includes the market positioning strategy, which summarizes the markets the organization is competing in (i.e., target market) and how the marketing mix fulfills the needs of this market. The resulting consumer perception of where the consumer believes the organization to be competing is known as the market position. Often, market research illuminates where consumers perceive an organization to be with respect to its competitors, which can be graphed on a market position diagram or perceptual map. Promotional planners rely on this document for all decisions, including the overall IMC direction, creative strategy, and creative tactics for advertising or any other IMC tool such as sales promotion, public relations, direct, or Internet.

 Apply the positioning concept in an advertising context by defining brand positioning strategy and brand position.

For many communication problems or opportunities, promotional messages are directed to target audiences. These audiences are a subset of the target market or an entirely different group, depending upon the communications situation. As discussed in Chapter 3, promotional planners require a detailed profile of the target audience with most appropriate segmentation variables, including whether the target is a customer or non-customer. Advertising or any other promotional message is guided by the brand positioning strategy, which specifies how it is intended to influence its target audience with a given product category or product market. The resulting target audience perception as to what the brand offers is known as the brand position. The flexibility of influencing a target audience's brand position through many IMC tools allows promotional managers to plan for unique brand positions for multiple target audiences.

 Illustrate how to formulate brand positioning strategy decisions.

The process for developing a brand positioning strategy in the context of marketing communications is similar to developing a positioning strategy for the overall marketing. However, it differs by evaluating or integrating very micro-level aspects of consumer behaviour in its planning by closely considering the nature of the purchase decision. The direction of the decision is much different, with the goal of finding the most appropriate message, media, or IMC tool versus determining optimal product design features.

The brand positioning strategy comprises four decisions: market definition, differential advantage, target audience brand attitude, and consumer purchase motive. The market definition decision allows the promotional planner to consider whether to define the market in which the brand is competing by benefits, brand name, usage situation, or product category. Differential advantage decisions include whether the brand takes a differential or central positioning and whether the brand focuses its positioning on its benefit claims or the user. Target audience attitude decisions consider how the message is expected to persuade existing beliefs to the desired beliefs about the brand. Finally, promotional planners decide what type of purchase motive should be associated with the brand.

 Demonstrate brand repositioning strategy opportunities.

In some communication situations—such as new competitors, changing consumer tastes, or poor brand performance—promotion planners need to reposition their brand. The repositioning can follow the same decisions as described above, where the promotional planner can consider an alternative market definition, communicate a new differential advantage, emphasize different benefit claims, or focus on another motivational option. Promotional planners can consider altering one or all four of these decisions to achieve moderate or very significant change in the current brand position.

 LO5   Interpret brand positioning strategy decisions in other contexts.

A brand positioning strategy can be augmented for any marketing communication purposes. Three relevant ones to consider are multiple target audiences, buyer decision stages, and corporate brand, to name a few. Organizations often face the dual task of communicating to long-time customers and newer customers, thereby requiring a more specific message for each and therefore raising the possibility of differences in the brand positioning strategy. Similarly, brands may alter their brand positioning strategy by emphasizing different benefits, for example, at varying stages of the consumer decision-making process. Finally, a corporate identity is of paramount importance and the decisions at the brand level are readily interpreted on a broader scale.

Review Questions

1. Describe how the market positioning strategy adopted for a brand would need to be supported by all other elements of the marketing mix.
2. Why is it useful to distinguish between brand positioning strategy and brand position?
3. What problems would a brand encounter if it communicated with an incorrect motive?
4. What factors would lead a marketer to use a repositioning strategy?
5. Why is it important to consider unique brand positioning decisions at each of the buyer decision stages? Is it feasible to implement this approach for all product categories?

Applied Questions

1. Explain how McDonald's market positioning strategy has changed with the new developments in its menu and outlets.
2. Examine the social media presence of a brand and assess whether it clearly identifies a brand positioning strategy.
3. Explain why a central positioning is feasible. Do any brands currently use this approach in their marketing communication?
4. Develop market partition diagrams for beverages. What repositioning options are available for any brand?
5. How can brand positioning decisions be applied to new category users and brand loyal users of smart phones?

CHAPTER SEVEN

Creative Strategy Decisions

LEARNING OBJECTIVES

LO1 Summarize the idea and importance of creativity in an advertising context.

LO2 Describe the creative strategy planning process.

LO3 Identify the approaches used for determining the creative theme that forms the basis of an advertising campaign.

LO4 Summarize the different types of message appeals that advertisers use to persuade their target audience.

LO5 Identify the source or communicator options a marketer has for a promotional message.

LO6 Apply source and message appeal options for different ad executions.

Creativity With the Molson Canadian Beer Fridge

Ten years after retiring the "I Am Canadian" slogan, Molson Canadian launched a new campaign with the same slogan for a limited period and just in time for Canada Day during 2013. The 90-second online ad and shortened 30-second TV ad showed a red Canadian fridge in public locations in the United Kingdom, France, and Belgium, with one catch: locals could not open the fridge unless they inserted a Canadian passport into a slot. Eventually a friendly Canadian appeared and opened the door to reveal Molson Canadian beer for everyone. According to a Molson executive, the ad and its red fridge with the white maple leaf symbolized Canadians' national pride.

While this user focused "I Am Canadian" campaign carried on throughout the summer, Molson Canadian continued to use its product focused advertising with the "Made From Canada" slogan. Nevertheless, a return of the previous slogan rejuvenated the patriotic culture of the brand, which probably never really ceased, as shown by constant requests for "I Am Canadian" merchandise. To carry on the momentum, Molson opened an online store to sell newer options, such as collectible T-shirts, sweaters, outdoor chairs, mugs, and temporary tattoos.

Molson followed up with a three-minute ad during the World Junior Hockey Championship broadcast on Boxing Day six months later. The ad showed two friends travelling from Ottawa to Indonesia with a similar red fridge as a gift to their friend living there who experienced difficulty in seeing hockey games. Molson selected this story after canvassing employees who knew of potential candidates. Success of the red fridge encouraged Molson to keep one in Canada House at the Sochi Olympics in early 2014. The brand offered other replica mini fridges signed by Team Canada athletes as prizes for contests.

Sales improved shortly after the release of these messages and Molson Canadian gained slightly from its 6.4 percent market share while the overall beer category declined in sales. Molson viewed the brand as competing in the premium beer category with a volume decline of 2.7 percent over five years, while the super-premium category grew 2.9 percent and the discount category remained flat over the same time period. Given this trend, Molson executives saw the investment in this creative as quite positive and carried on with the creative theme subsequently.

For Canada Day 2014, the beer fridge would open for Canadians who could sing a passable version of our national anthem. Set at a bar called the Great Canadian Cabin, in Ottawa's Byward Market, Molson's two-minute online video was displayed in multiple social media vehicles. A goal of the holiday messaging was to encourage consumers to believe that "this is the brand of beer to drink on Canada Day," such that it is almost unpatriotic to quaff any other kind of beer on that day.

For Canada Day 2015, the beer fridge would open for Canadians who could say the slogan in six languages, with the likely expectation that a group of friends would be teamed up to fulfill the request using Google's speech-to-text recognition software. The new fridge along with the others illustrated a trend of agencies using technology for their clients as part of the creative theme. Similarly, Molson made a modified interactive fridge for the Pan Am Games in Toronto so fans could take pictures and post them on social media.

Sources: Chris Powell, "Molson's Travelling Beer Fridge Comes Home for Canada Day," *Marketing Magazine*, June 23, 2014; Susan Krashinsky, "Cheers to a Winning Ad Campaign," *The Globe and Mail*, February 20, 2015, p. B7; Russ Martin, "Molson Brings Back 'I Am Canadian' for Canada Day," *Marketing Magazine*, June 24, 2013; Susan Krashinsky, "Molson's Newest Red Beer Fridge Touts Canada's Multicultural Side," *The Globe and Mail*, June 25, 2015; Susan Krashinsky, "Molson's Takes Online Beer Fridge Ads to Hockey Airwaves—and Points Beyond," *The Globe and Mail*, December 19, 2013.

Questions:

1. Why is an emotional connection to the Molson Canadian brand so important?
2. Why is it valuable for Molson Canadian to have two different creative themes at one time?

An important part of an IMC program is the advertising message, the means by which to tell consumers how the product can solve a problem or satisfy desires or achieve goals. Advertising messages create images or associations and establish a brand position as well as transform the experience of buying and/or using a product. Advertising messages play a leading role in the IMC program, and are crucial to the success of the brand's promotional effort. While most students may never design ads, everyone involved in marketing or promotion should understand the strategic decisions that underlie the development of advertising messages.

It is easy to see many ways to convey an advertising message while watching commercials on TV, seeing videos on the Internet, perusing print ads in a magazine, or witnessing advertising in out-of-home locations. Underlying these messages is a **creative strategy** that determines *what* the advertising message will communicate and **creative tactics** for *how* the message will be executed. In this chapter, we focus on three creative strategy decisions. First, we describe approaches to determining the idea of the creative theme, which provides direction for attention-getting, distinctive, and memorable messages. Second, we identify the message appeals that advertisers use to persuade consumers. Third, we focus on the key source characteristics that advertisers typically use to alter consumers' attitudes. Prior to these decisions, we summarize the process of planning for creative strategy. We also apply these latter two points in our IMC planning perspective.

Advertising Creativity

Upon determining the direction for the communications program, the advertising agency (or the department in the organization responsible for developing ads) focuses on finding an appropriate creative approach to communicating a message that reinforces the brand positioning strategy. Good advertising creativity can often be central to determining the success of a product as it clearly contributes to a strong brand position with its intended target audience. The essence of advertising is its creativity, and we now provide a working definition and demonstrate its importance.

DEFINITION OF ADVERTISING CREATIVITY

For many students, as well as many advertising and marketing practitioners, the most interesting aspect of advertising is the creative side. We have all at one time or another been intrigued by an ad and admired the creative insight that went into it. A great ad is a joy to behold and an epic to create, with the cost of producing a TV commercial potentially hitting $1 million. Conceiving an ad is such an exciting and enticing activity that a contest searching for the next top ad executive is run each year for university students by the DeGroote School of Business at McMaster University.[1] Many companies see money spent on advertising and other forms of marketing communication as good brand investment. They realize that the manner in which the advertising message is developed and executed is often critical to the success of the promotion, which in turn can influence the effectiveness of the entire marketing program. For example, BMW's creative messages over time firmly

Exhibit 7-1   Excellent advertising helps create an image for BMW automobiles.

JOY IS IN GOOD COMPANY.

JOY IS THE BMW 3 SERIES
COUPE AND CONVERTIBLE.

Courtesy of BMW of North America, LLC

planted the idea of Ultimate Driving Experience in Canada and Ultimate Driving Machine in other countries (Exhibit 7-1).

Creativity is a commonly used term in advertising. Ads are often called *creative*. The people who develop ads are known as creative specialists. These specialists work for ad agencies that develop ad campaigns or for marketers that handle their own advertising without the help of an agency. Perhaps the focus on creativity occurs because many people view the specific challenge for those who develop an advertising message as "to be creative." It is their job to turn all of the information regarding product features and benefits, marketing plans, consumer research, and communication objectives into a creative concept that will bring the advertising message to life. This begs the question: What is meant by *creativity* in advertising?

Advertising creativity is the ability to generate fresh, unique, and appropriate ideas that can be used as effective solutions to marketing communication issues (e.g., problems or opportunities). To be *appropriate* and *effective,* a creative idea must be relevant to the target audience.[2] Relevance, an important characteristic of creativity, has to instantly capture the target audience's attention and generate critical brand associations through specific cognitive and emotional responses. The relevance is even more critical when an advertiser takes into account the selective attention of the target audience. Moreover, the creativity has to crystallize the brand so that it is understood by the target audience, which is also experiencing selective comprehension when faced with many competing promotional messages. Extending this further, the relevance of the creativity to the target audience is critical to establishing an important link to the brand, its benefits, and why the target audience would purchase it. In other words, relevance clearly supports the brand positioning strategy. Reinforcing this view suggests two approaches: *ad to consumer relevance* and *brand to consumer relevance*.[3] *Ad to consumer relevance* involves ad characteristics that are meaningful to the target audience, such as the celebrity spokesperson or imagery. *Brand to consumer relevance* concerns the personal interest of the product to the target audience.

Appropriate and effective creativity should offer divergence as well, since the message must break through media clutter and attract the target audience's attention. *Divergence* is the extent to which an ad contains novel, different, or unusual characteristics.[4] Advertising creativity is divergent in terms of originality (e.g., rare or surprising ideas that are not common), flexibility (e.g., different ideas), elaboration (e.g., unexpected ideas that become intricate, complicated, or sophisticated), synthesis (e.g., normally unrelated ideas that are combined or connected), and artistic values (e.g., ideas expressed verbally or visually). Exhibit 7-2 shows an image from a very creative video message for Chipotle restaurant that won a Cannes award. The extremely original animated story elaborates upon the wholesome characteristics of the farms that Chipotle sources from.

Exhibit 7-2   Chipotle received international praise for its creative advertising.

"Back to the Start" Cannes Lions Film Grand Prix Winner 2012

The historic Absolut vodka ads demonstrate the relevance and divergence notions for good creativity. The original creative strategy for Absolut vodka showed the distinctive shape of its bottle and depicted it with visual puns and witty headlines that play with the Absolut name.[5] The agency and client jointly selected and customized the advertising campaign by tailoring the print ads for the audience of each magazine. The working relationship of creative specialists and others also demonstrated a model for working effectively. It is recognized as one of the most creative ad campaigns ever, and stood the test of time for over 20 years until sales eventually lagged. The new creative relies on thought-provoking imagery using the tagline "In an Absolut World" and plays off of the brand name to illustrate an imagined world where everything is as ideal as Absolut vodka. The creative strategy is an inspiring, humorous, and thought-provoking idea of what an Absolut world might look like, and challenges consumers to reflect on their own visions of the world. The ultimate goal of the campaign is to maintain the brand as a cultural icon.[6]

IMPORTANCE OF ADVERTISING CREATIVITY

Perspectives on what constitutes creativity in advertising differ. At one extreme are people who argue that advertising is creative only if it sells the product. An advertising message's or campaign's impact on sales counts more than whether it is innovative. At the other end of the continuum are those who judge the creativity of an ad in terms of its artistic or aesthetic value and originality. They contend creative ads can break through the competitive clutter, grab the consumer's attention, and have a positive communication effect. Both perspectives indicate the importance of advertising creativity as it either presents a good public exposure or contributes to a brand positioning strategy and ultimately sales.

The growth of brands has highlighted the importance of advertising creativity leading to renewed investigations.[7] Surveyed executives believe creativity has improved compared to the origin of modern-day advertising during the 1960s.[8] The Leo Burnett agency and *Contagious Magazine* conduct worldwide research to uncover the success of the most creative advertising in traditional and newer evolving media, while others present new or reconfigured ideas to define creativity.[9] In general, creative advertising messages help focus the receiver's attention, allowing deeper processing and stronger recall and recognition.[10]

Perspectives on advertising creativity often diverged along marketing and artistic lines, as shown in one study.[11] Product managers and account executives view ads as promotional tools whose primary purpose is to communicate favourable impressions to the marketplace. They believe a commercial should be evaluated in terms of whether it fulfills the client's marketing and communicative objectives. Alternatively, creative specialists view ads as an expression of their personal aesthetics and an opportunity to communicate their unique creative talent with the hopes of career advancement.

What constitutes creativity in advertising is probably somewhere between the two views. To break through the clutter and make an impression on the target audience, an ad often must be unique and entertaining, as demonstrated in Exhibit 7-3. Research has shown that a major determinant of whether a commercial will be successful in changing brand preferences is its "likability," or the viewer's overall reaction.[12] Advertising messages that are well designed and executed and generate emotional responses can create positive feelings that are transferred to the product or service being advertised.[13] Creative specialists believe this occurs if they are given considerable latitude in developing advertising messages, but purely creative ads might fail to communicate a relevant product message. In an attempt to resolve this discussion, research findings suggest that very creative advertising messages have additional positive brand communication effects (i.e., brand quality, brand interest) beyond recall and likability.[14]

However, the issue becomes less clear as one study found that the creative specialists themselves can disagree on the merits of creativity. A survey of art directors and copywriters found that the former are more concerned with visual creativity, while the latter more strongly believe in message delivery.[15] Finally, in the age of consumer-generated "advertising" messages, another study finds that perceptions of creativity differ among advertising professionals, students, and the general public.[16] Thus, it appears that everyone must keep a balanced perspective on the creativity of advertising messages.

Finally, studies conclude that advertising creativity impacts consumers' cognitive, affective, and behavioural responses to advertising messages.[17] Novel advertising requires consumer processing time, resulting in longer exposure and greater attention. Creative ads draw more attention to the advertised brand, and generate higher levels of recall, greater motivation to process the information, and deeper levels of processing.[18]

Exhibit 7-3   This colourful and creative ad captures people's attention when they are walking by.

© Alistair Laming / Alamy Stock Photo

Creative advertising positively impacts emotional reactions, including attitudes and purchase intentions.[19] Divergence is a particularly important component of advertising creativity; however, clients often favour relevance over divergence as they want their agencies to create ads that communicate pertinent information such as specific product features and benefits. Researchers suggest that clients should be less resistant to divergent approaches, and note that there is a fundamental need for divergent thinkers in the ad development process.[20] Considering that most advertising messages are seen and/or heard in a very cluttered media environment where marketers must compete for the attention of consumers, it is important that brand managers accept ads that are novel and divergent as well as relevant and meaningful.

Planning Creative Strategy

Creative specialists take all the research, creative briefs, strategy statements, communications objectives, and other input and transform them into an advertising message. Their job is to write copy, design layouts and illustrations, produce video messages, or program interactive digital tools that effectively communicate the central theme on which the campaign or IMC program is based. Rather than simply stating a product's features or benefits, they transform an advertising message into an approach that captures the audience's interest and makes the brand and the ad instantly memorable. In this section, we describe the creative challenge, illustrate the creative process, summarize the job of an account planner, identify forms of research for creative decision making, and summarize the end results—the creative brief and advertising campaign—when planning for creative promotional communication.

CREATIVE CHALLENGE

The job of the creative team is challenging because every marketing situation is different and each campaign or advertisement may require a different creative approach. Numerous guidelines have been developed for creating effective advertising.[21] Creative people follow proven formulas when creating ads because clients can feel uncomfortable with advertising that is too different. Bill Tragos, former chair of TBWA, says, "Very few clients realize that the reason that their work is so bad is that they are the ones who commandeered it and directed it to be that way. I think that at least 50 percent of an agency's successful work resides in the client."[22] Decades later, empirical research supports this practitioner's point of view.[23]

Exhibit 7-4   Residence Inn takes a very creative approach with its ads.

It's not a room. It's a Residence."

Reprinted with permission of Marriott International, Inc.

Creative people generally believe it is important for clients to take a risk if they want breakthrough advertising that gets noticed. One client taking a risk is Marriott International, as it launched the campaign theme "It's Not a Room. It's a Residence." to illustrate how the Residence Inn brand is positioned to meet the needs of long-term-stay guests. The ads spotlight Residence Inn's focus on providing ample room to work, relax, and maintain balance by creatively using a cast of animals. Two spots featured an elephant and giraffe demonstrating the spaciousness of the rooms by showing the animals going through the same routine that a human might follow while taking advantage of in-room amenities. One endearing ad featured a family of penguins marching into a Residence Inn suite and relaxing in the room by playing on the desk chairs, swimming in the bathtub, chilling out with frozen desserts, and unwinding by watching a movie about penguins (Exhibit 7-4). The use of animals showcased the features of the Residence Inn suites and diverged from the conventional approach of showing people within a hotel room.[24]

One agency that has been successful in getting its clients to take risks is Rethink, best known for its excellent creative work for Playland, Science World, A&W, and Solo Mobile. The agency's founders believe a key element in its success has been a steadfast belief in taking risks when most agencies and their clients have been retrenching and becoming more conservative. The agency can develop great advertising partly because its clients are willing to take risks and agree with the agency's approach of listening to their client and arriving at a creative solution for their marketing communication problem or opportunity. Empirical research concludes that risk taking agencies have an orientation to taking risks as a direction from senior management, a creative philosophy to enhance their creative reputation, and an acceptance of working with uncertainty.[25]

Not all agree that advertising has to be risky to be effective, however. Many marketing managers are more comfortable with advertising that simply communicates product or service features and benefits and gives the consumer a reason to buy. They see their ad campaigns as multimillion-dollar investments whose goal is to sell the product rather than to finance the whims of their agency's creative staff. They argue that creative people occasionally lose sight of advertising's bottom line: Does it sell?

CREATIVE PROCESS

Creativity in advertising can be viewed as a process, and creative success likely occurs when an organized approach is followed. James Webb Young, a former creative vice-president at the J. Walter Thompson agency, proposed the following five-stage approach that still remains a useful reference.[26]

- *Immersion.* Read background information regarding the problem.
- *Digestion.* Work the information over in one's mind.
- *Incubation.* Get away and let ideas develop.
- *Illumination.* See the light or solution with the birth of the idea.
- *Verification.* Study and refine the idea to see if it is a practical solution.

A model of the creative process is valuable to those working in the creative area of advertising, since it offers an organized way to approach an advertising problem. A model like Young's does not say much about how this information will be synthesized and used by the creative specialist, because this part of the process is unique to the individual. An investigation along these lines reveals four individual factors: orientation toward the creative work, approach to the communication problems, mindscribing (i.e., free-flow thinking), and heuristics (i.e., quick creative decision rules).[27] A study of advertising copywriters found that they work without guidance from any formal theories of communication. However, those interviewed claimed to use similar informal, implicit theories that guide them in creating ads. These theories are based on finding ways to break through the ad clutter, open the consciousness of consumers, and connect with them to deliver the message.[28]

However, advertising creativity is not the exclusive domain of creative specialists, as creative thinking is done by everyone involved when planning creative strategy. Agency people (such as account executives, media planners, researchers, and account planners) as well as those on the client side (such as marketing and brand managers) must all seek creative solutions to problems encountered in planning, developing, and executing an advertising campaign. It is also important that those working on the client side do not create a relationship with their agencies that inhibits the creative processes required to produce good advertising. Highly skilled creative specialists aspire to work with open-minded clients who are receptive to new ideas, and they note that some of the best creative work developed by agencies does not get used because clients are resistant to taking creative risks unless they are under pressure to perform.[29] Advertising agencies, as well as other IMC specialist organizations, thrive on creativity as it is at the heart of what they do and they must design an environment that fosters the development of creative thinking and creative advertising. Clients must also understand the differences between the perspectives of the creative personnel and marketing and product managers. While the client has ultimate approval of the advertising, the opinions of creative specialists must be respected when advertising ideas and content are evaluated.

ACCOUNT PLANNING

To facilitate the creative process, many agencies use **account planning**, which involves conducting research and gathering all relevant information about a client's product or service, brand, and consumers in the target audience. Jon Steel, a former vice-president and director of account planning, has written an excellent book on the process titled *Truth, Lies and Advertising: The Art of Account Planning.*[30] He notes that the account planner's job is to provide the key decision makers with all the information they require to make an intelligent decision. According to Steel, "Planners may have to work very hard to influence the way that the advertising turns out, carefully laying out a strategic foundation with the client, handing over tidbits of information to creative people when, in their judgment, that information will have the greatest impact, giving feedback on ideas, and hopefully adding ideas of their own."

Account planning plays an important role during creative strategy development by driving the process from the customer's point of view. Planners will work with the client as well as other agency personnel, such as the creative team and media specialists. They discuss how the knowledge and information they have gathered can be used in the development of the creative strategy as well as other aspects of the advertising campaign. Account planners are usually responsible for all the research (both qualitative and quantitative) conducted during the creative strategy development process. Account planning has evolved considerably over the past 20 years such that agencies and clients see it as part of the strategic creative process with a clear understanding of how to evaluate the performance of all personnel involved.[31] In the following section, we examine how research and information can provide input to the creative process of advertising.

RESEARCH IN THE CREATIVE PROCESS

The creative specialist first learns as much as possible about the product, the target audience, the competition, and any other relevant **research**. Much of this information would come from the marketing plan and advertising plan developed by the client. Alternatively, good clients will give proper direction to their agency by constructing a client brief that recapitulates their internal documents and adds additional information that would give the creative specialist an idea as to the direction of the brand positioning strategy. The Institute of Communications and Advertising produces a best practices document that shows brand managers how to construct a client brief that serves the needs of both parties, thus encouraging more creative marketing communication.

From this, the creative specialist can acquire additional background information in numerous ways:

- Read anything related to the product or market.
- Talk to people (e.g., marketing personnel, designers, engineers, consumers).
- Visit stores and malls.
- Use the product or service and become familiar with it.
- Work in and learn about the business.[32]

Creative people use both general and product-specific preplanning input. **General preplanning input** can include books, periodicals, trade publications, scholarly journals, pictures, and clipping services, which gather and organize magazine and newspaper articles on the product, the market, and the competition, including the latter's ads. Another useful general preplanning input concerns market trends and developments. Information is available from a variety of sources, including local, provincial, and federal governments, secondary research suppliers, and industry trade associations, as well as advertising and media organizations that publish research reports and newsletters. Those involved in developing creative strategy can also gather relevant and timely information by reading Canadian publications like *Marketing Magazine* or *Strategy,* and American publications like *Adweek* and *Advertising Age.*

Product/service-specific preplanning input is information that includes specific studies conducted on how consumers buy and consume the product/service and/or characteristics of the target audience regarding extensive consumer behaviour variables. **Quantitative research** includes attitude studies, market structure, and positioning studies such as perceptual mapping and psychographic or lifestyle profiles. As noted in Chapter 3, agencies or affiliated research companies conduct psychographic studies annually and construct detailed psychographic or lifestyle profiles of product or service users. Dove conducted one of the more significant research studies prior to launching the "Campaign for Real Beauty." The research involved numerous personal interviews and sampled women from many countries regarding their attitudes toward beauty with a survey methodology.

Qualitative research is used to gain insight into the underlying causes of consumer behaviour. Methods employed include in-depth interviews, projective techniques, association tests, and focus groups in which consumers are encouraged to bring out associations related to products and brands (see Figure 7-1). This research is often referred to as motivation research. In general, motivation research is considered important in assessing how and why consumers buy. Focus groups and in-depth interviews are valuable methods for gaining insights into consumers' feelings, and projective techniques are often the only way to get around stereotypical or socially desirable responses. Since motivation research studies typically use a low number of participants, a limitation is that findings are not generalizable to the whole population and may be discovering idiosyncrasies of a few individuals. Still, it is difficult to ignore motivation research since the resulting consumer insight inspires advertising messages aimed at buyers' deeply rooted feelings, hopes, aspirations, and fears.

Figure 7-1 Qualitative marketing research methods employed to obtain consumer insight

In-depth interviews

Face-to-face situations in which an interviewer asks a consumer to talk freely in an unstructured interview using specific questions designed to obtain insights into his or her motives, ideas, or opinions.

Projective techniques

Efforts designed to gain insights into consumers' values, motives, attitudes, or needs that are difficult to express or identify by having them project these internal states upon some external object.

Association tests

A technique in which an individual is asked to respond with the first thing that comes to mind when he or she is presented with a stimulus; the stimulus may be a word, picture, ad, and so on.

Focus groups

A small number of people with similar backgrounds and/or interests who are brought together to discuss a particular product, idea, or issue.

Focus groups are a prevalent research tool among the four methods at this stage of the creative process. **Focus groups** are a research method whereby consumers (usually 10 to 12 people) from the target audience are led through a discussion regarding a particular topic. Focus groups give insight as to why and how consumers use a product, what is important to them in choosing a particular brand, what they like and don't like about products, and any special needs they might have that aren't being satisfied. A focus group session might also include a discussion of types of ad appeals to use or might evaluate the advertising. Focus group interviews bring the creative people and others involved in creative strategy development into contact with the customers. Listening to a focus group gives copywriters, art directors, and other creative specialists a better sense of who the target audience is, what the audience is like, and to whom the creatives need to write, design, or direct in creating an advertising message.

Toward the end of the creative process, members of the target audience may be asked to evaluate rough creative layouts and to indicate what meaning they get from the ad, what they think of its execution, or how the ad makes them feel. The creative team can gain insight into how a TV commercial might communicate its message by having members of the target audience evaluate the ad in storyboard form. A **storyboard** is a series of drawings used to present the visual plan or layout of a proposed commercial. It contains a series of sketches of key frames or scenes along with the copy or audio portion for each scene (Exhibit 7-5).

Evaluating a commercial in storyboard form can be difficult because storyboards are too abstract for many consumers to understand. To make the creative layout more realistic and easier to evaluate, the agency may produce an **animatic**, a videotape of the storyboard along with an audio soundtrack. Storyboards and animatics are useful for research purposes as well as for presenting the creative idea to other agency personnel or to the client for discussion and approval. At this stage of the process, the creative team is attempting to find the best creative strategy before moving ahead with the actual production of the ad. The process may conclude with more formal, extensive pretesting of the ad before a final decision is made. Pretesting and related procedures are examined in detail in Chapter 9.

Exhibit 7-5   Marketers can gain insight into consumers' reactions to a commercial by showing them a storyboard.

VIDEO: A private Lear jet takes off during sunset as heat vapors rise from runway.

AUDIO: Sound of muffled cocktail music.

VIDEO: Close up of jet racing out of city as night falls over skyline.

AUDIO: Sound of jet engines.

VIDEO: Camera zooms in window to inside of plane. Close up of girl opening bottle of SKYY Blue and blowing mist from bottle.

AUDIO: Refreshing sound of bottle opening.

VIDEO: Camera pans down to woman sitting on modern jet refrigerator as she opens the door and man pulls out two bottles of SKYY Blue.

AUDIO: Sounds of bottles clanking.

VIDEO: Pan continues past couple as they put on a record on jet's high-tech turntable.

AUDIO: Classic cocktail music plays.

VIDEO: Pan continues past woman as she has straw inserted into her bottle.

AUDIO: Cocktail music plays.

VIDEO: Pan continues to close up of man wearing mirrored sunglasses looking out cabin window as clouds and a glimpse of sunlight reflect off sunglasses.

AUDIO: Cocktail music plays.

VIDEO: Man responds by opening another shade to let sunlight in as girl dances in aisle with SKYY Blue.

AUDIO: Cocktail music plays.

VIDEO: Jet zooms over a new city skyline with sun rising in background.

AUDIO: Muffled cocktail music. Jet engines.

Courtesy of Skyy Spirits, LLC

CREATIVE BRIEF

The written **creative brief** specifies the basic elements of the creative strategy and other relevant information. The creative brief may have other names depending upon the agency, such as creative platform, creative blueprint, creative contract, or copy platform. Essentially, it is a plan that summarizes the entire creative approach that is agreed upon by the creative team and the marketing managers. For example, the creative brief can be written by an agency's account representative or an account planner with the input from other specialists from all areas (e.g., creative, media, research, digital, etc.) and approved by the client's marketing communications or brand manager. Figure 7-2 shows a sample creative brief outline. Just as there are different names for the creative brief, there are variations in the outline and format used and in the level of detail included. The creative brief for the Tacori ad in Exhibit 7-6 called for a strategy of positioning the 18K925 brand as the ultimate expression of passion, with modern, accessible style and lasting quality.

The first three sections of the creative brief are derived from the marketing plan and prior communication between the creative specialists and brand managers. The planning framework of this text, shown in Chapter 1, also supports all sections of this creative brief illustration. Chapter 1 highlighted the importance of the marketing plan for promotional planning, which should provide sufficient background on the nature of the communication problem or opportunity. Chapter 3 described important aspects of consumer behaviour along with options for target audience selection and guidelines for a target audience profile. Combined, Chapters 4 and 5 explained the usefulness of response models and communication objectives that guide remaining decisions. Chapter 6 indicated different brand positioning options that creative specialists might propose as communication solutions. The rest of this chapter describes the creative strategy decisions that the creative specialists focus on when developing ad executions upon finalizing the creative brief. Finally, creative briefs may also include supporting information and requirements that should appear in any message to ensure uniformity across the ads used in a campaign.

At times, creative specialists experience communication problems among the participants of the creative process. Part of the problem is attributed to creative personnel not actually writing a creative brief. The creative process may be initially described in a series of notes or sketches, and as it evolves through the stages of the creative process some of the original participants may not be aware of all the changes. Alternatively, the lack of full description leads to misunderstanding of how the sequence of events, for example, would occur in a television commercial. And while it is important to have a written creative brief, it should be concise enough so that all participants could read it quickly and easily and still demonstrate the creativity of the advertising. In the end we can say that the creative brief should (1) be objective, (2) have proper vocabulary, spelling, and grammar, (3) demonstrate logical thinking, (4) be both creative and concise, (5) have specific recommendations, and (6) be viewed as a firm agreement.[33]

Exhibit 7-6   Tacori's positioning called for 18K925 to be the ultimate expression of passion.

© 2009 Tacori

Figure 7-2   Creative brief outline

1. Basic problem or opportunity the advertising must address
2. Target audience(s) and behaviour objective(s)
3. Communication objectives
4. Brand positioning strategy statement
5. Creative strategy (creative theme, message appeal, source characteristic)
6. Supporting information and requirements

ADVERTISING CAMPAIGN

An **advertising campaign** is a set of interrelated and coordinated marketing communication activities that centre on a single theme or idea. A campaign appears in different media and IMC tools across a specified time period. Advertising campaign plans are short-term in nature and, like marketing and IMC plans, are done on an annual basis. However, the campaign themes are usually developed with the intention of being used for a longer time period. Thus far we have referred to creativity as advertising creativity since this is the history and origin of creativity in marketing communication. But, creativity is an important facet in all aspects of promotion, even if there is not accompanying advertising in the campaign. Promotional elements like sponsorship of a good cause will often have supporting advertising. And digital communication, whether one classifies it as advertising or advertising-like, contains creativity—big time!

Multiple executions are required in order for a creative message to be considered a campaign. How many executions will depend on the creative specialists and clients before approval of a campaign occurs, but generally the creative idea driving the message needs at least three executions to tell the story. This notion is based on the "rule of three," where stories or jokes require three episodes for complete understanding; progression occurs as tension is created, built up, and then released with the unfolding of the message. This "rule" is more an observed pattern across many walks of life with respect to communication, rather than scientifically proven; however, it is consistent with how often a consumer needs to receive a message in media planning.

Success occurred with a trilogy of ads for the new Golf with the theme "Drive Until." The first showed a man driving around the block a few times trying to summon the courage to propose to his girlfriend. With only the music, the song "Just Like Honey" by Scottish alt-rockers The Jesus and Mary Chain, the mood is set for a continuation of the story. The end of the ad invites VW fans to submit their idea for the next sequence. Naturally the follow-up is a buddy road trip, which ends with the groom and three other guys arriving at the church in time with the song "Keep the Lights On" by Wave Machines. The story wraps up with the new husband leaving his home, clearly angry, and then returning with flowers and a smile, and welcomed back by his new bride. The song "When Your Love Is Safe" by Pat Grossi plays a role in communicating the theme and emotional connection to the brand. Each ad ended appropriately—"Drive Until Courage," "Drive Until Time," and "Drive Until Talk"—to signify the storyline and add meaning to the message.[34] With these ads, the "rule" works by telling a story across three executions, in this case with the input of consumers in this age of interactive media.

Scotiabank began its "Richer Than You Think" campaign in 2006, and included three phases. The first focused on getting a second opinion. The executions for this included three TV ads and two print ads, with supporting digital exposure. A later one in 2009 during the recession addressed people's financial concerns with 11 TV spots conveying a message of "making the most of what you have." A third wave occurred in 2012 when multiple messages looked at how consumers defined richness in their terms, which featured user-generated spots as part of Scotiabank's Richness Project.[35] This example demonstrates the requirement of multiple executions within a campaign, and how a campaign's message evolves over time.

 # Creative Theme

Determining the unifying theme around which the campaign will be built is a critical decision, as it often sets the tone for other forms of marketing communication that will be used, such as sales promotion or digital applications. Furthermore, the **creative theme** should be a strong idea since it represents the central message of a marketing communication program, reflects the market positioning strategy, and directly communicates the brand positioning strategy to its intended target audience. In this section, we describe four related decisions that comprise the creative theme. First, we identify ways to determine the creative theme. Then, we present the importance of slogans to reinforce brand positioning and/or creative theme. Next, we explore the issue of consistency of the creative theme across many parts of the promotional program. We conclude by exploring the importance of unique Canadian creative advertising and its success.

ORIGIN OF CREATIVE THEME

The creative team is provided with the challenge of deciding upon the strong or "big" idea of the creative theme that attracts the consumer's attention, gets a response, and sets the advertiser's product or service apart from the competition. Well known adman John O'Toole describes the *big idea* as "that flash of insight that synthesizes the purpose of the strategy, joins the product benefit with consumer desire in a fresh, involving way, brings the subject to life, and makes the reader or audience stop, look, and listen."[36] From another perspective, a theme arises from a story, and advertising creative is much like a storytelling process of the brand, its history, and its meaning that goes beyond the basic communication of product performance.[37] It is difficult to pinpoint the inspiration for a big idea or to teach advertising people how to find one. However, the following approaches can guide the creative team's search for a creative theme: unique selling proposition, brand image, inherent drama, and positioning.

Unique Selling Proposition The concept of the **unique selling proposition (USP)** was developed by Rosser Reeves, former chair of the Ted Bates agency, and is described in his influential book *Reality in Advertising*. Reeves noted three characteristics of unique selling propositions:

1. Each advertisement must make a proposition to the consumer. Not just words, not just product puffery, not just show-window advertising. Each advertisement must say to each reader: "Buy this product and you will get this benefit."

2. The proposition must be one that the competition either cannot or does not offer. It must be unique either in the brand or in the claim.

3. The proposition must be strong enough to move the mass millions, that is, pull over new customers to your brand.[38]

Reeves said the attribute claim or benefit that forms the basis of the USP should dominate the ad and be emphasized through repetitive advertising. An example of advertising based on a USP is the campaign for Colgate Total toothpaste (Exhibit 7-7). The brand has a unique, patented formula that creates a protective barrier that fights germs for 12 hours, which helps reduce and prevent gum disease.

For Reeves's approach to work, there must be a truly unique product or service attribute, benefit, or inherent advantage that can be used in the claim. The approach may require considerable research on the product and consumers, not only to determine the USP but also to document the claim.

Brand Image Competing brands in many product and service categories are so similar that it is a challenge to communicate a unique attribute or benefit. For example, packaged goods may be difficult to differentiate on a functional or performance basis and promotional planners look to a more intangible approach to creatively express product uniqueness. The creative theme used to communicate these products is based on the development of a memorable identity for the brand through **image advertising**.

David Ogilvy popularized the idea of brand image in his famous book *Confessions of an Advertising Man*. Ogilvy said that with image advertising, "every advertisement should be thought of as a contribution to the complex symbol which is the brand image." He argued that the image or personality of the brand is particularly important when brands are similar. Image advertising is designed to give a brand a unique association and create a certain feeling that is activated when a person consumes the brand. The key to successful image advertising is developing an image that will appeal to product users. For example the Bebe ad in Exhibit 7-8 gives the fashion brand a distinctive look for its line of clothing.

Image development often occurs through literary devices such as metaphors or analogies to create the symbolism. This involves both visual and copy elements of an ad that allow consumers to interpret the message by transferring meaning from another aspect to the brand. These metaphors can be concrete (e.g., direct, obvious) or abstract (e.g., indirect, interpretive). Selecting the right metaphor is sometimes difficult as consumers have difficulty discovering the references.[39] Simpler metaphors contribute toward higher levels of ad comprehension and ad appreciation compared to ads that do not have metaphors or ads with complex metaphors, giving support for advertisers to consider their usage.[40]

Exhibit 7-7 This Colgate Total ad uses a unique selling proposition.

Courtesy Colgate-Palmolive Company

Exhibit 7-8 Bebe uses advertising to build an image as a sexy and stylish brand.

Inherent Drama   Another approach to determining the creative theme is finding the **inherent drama** or characteristic of the product that makes the consumer purchase it. The inherent drama approach expresses the advertising philosophy of Leo Burnett, founder of the Leo Burnett Agency in Chicago. Burnett said inherent drama "is often hard to find but it is always there, and once found it is the most interesting and believable of all advertising appeals."[41] He believed advertising should be based on a foundation of consumer benefits with an emphasis on the dramatic element in expressing those benefits. Expression of the drama may take many forms, as the following examples illustrate. Manulife Financial continued the drama of the story in its TV ads by showing the conclusion on its Internet site, which motivated people to visit and spend more time viewing its messages.[42] Sport Chek's "My North"' advertising aligned itself with the NBA Raptors with a series of mini-documentaries of nine basketball neighbourhoods in Toronto to portray the brand in a new and dramatic light.[43] With the objective of increasing fundraising dollars, The Hospital for Sick Children in Toronto showed a unique and dramatic story of child's care for 45 days in a row on TV. One execution showed a surgeon repairing a heart defect.[44]

The ad in Exhibit 7-9 shows one moment of the story of a happy couple celebrating their love for one another. The woman's facial reaction that exudes surprise and happiness, along with her body language, provides a snippet of an emotional event in this dramatic expression of becoming engaged.

Positioning   Since advertising helps establish or maintain the brand position, it can also be the source of the creative theme. Positioning is often the basis of a firm's creative strategy when it has multiple brands competing in the same market. For example, Procter & Gamble markets many brands of laundry detergent—and positions each one differently. Positioning is done for companies as well as for brands. For example, the ad shown in Exhibit 7-10 is part of a GE campaign that is designed to position the company as an innovator in health care.

Trout and Ries originally described positioning as the image consumers had of the brand in relation to competing brands in the product or service category, but the concept has been expanded beyond direct competitive positioning.[45] As discussed in Chapter 6, products can be positioned on the basis of end benefit, brand name, usage situation, or product category. Any of these can spark a theme that becomes the basis of the creative strategy and results in the brand's occupying a particular place in the minds of the target audience. Since brand positioning can be done on the basis of a distinctive attribute, the positioning and unique selling proposition approaches can overlap.

CAMPAIGN SLOGANS

The theme for the advertising campaign is usually expressed through a **slogan or tagline** that reduces the key idea into a few words or a brief statement. The advertising slogan should serve as a summation line that succinctly expresses the brand positioning strategy, as well as the message it is trying to deliver to the target audience. The slogan usually appears in every advertisement and is often used in other forms of marketing communications to serve as a reminder of, and to reinforce, the marketer's branding message. IMC Perspective 7-1 tells the story of BioSteel and how its slogan arose from social media exposure of brand imagery.

Exhibit 7-9   The emotional expression of the woman conveys a dramatic point in a familiar story line.

Norman Wong/BIRKS GROUP INC./Newscom

Exhibit 7-10   GE positions itself as an innovative company in health care.

Courtesy of GE

What constitutes a good slogan? All of the following suggestions are not possible for a single slogan, but they offer guidance when making a final decision. Characteristics can pertain to the brand attitude objectives, include a key benefit, differentiate the brand, evoke positive feelings, reflect brand personality, and be believable and likable. Others pertain to brand awareness objectives: be memorable, and recall brand name. Additionally, slogans are oriented strategically, to be campaign-able and competitive. Finally, aesthetics are important as slogans should be original, simple, neat/cool, and positive.[46]

Canadian advertisers continually develop slogans, and it is interesting to examine new ones to figure out whether they meet these criteria. The Kobo electronic reader displayed, "For those who love reading above all else." Autotrader turned the phrase, "The better way to buy and sell cars." Corona sipped in, "Live the finer life." Hawaiian Punch returned to Canada with "Smashingly delicious." Tassimo, a maker of coffee machines, frothed up, "The barcode brews it better." Contiki Tours targeted youth with two slogans: "It's time to start living" and "One life, one shot, make it count." Canadian Tire is on its fourth slogan since 2001; the recent slogans are "Let's get started," "___ starts at Canadian Tire," "For days like today," and "Bring it on."[47] Finally, an empirical study that examined six variables concluded that shorter and long-lasting slogans that received high levels of media weight tended to produce higher levels of brand recall.[48]

IMC PERSPECTIVE 7-1

BIOSTEEL'S #DRINKTHEPINK

#drinkthepink and related imagery circulated social media to encourage consumers to seek out BioSteel's innovative high-performance sport drink, but before that, personal contacts and word-of-mouth encouraged professional athletes to try it. Sales occurred directly to professional sports teams since athletes requested it after receiving samples and seeing the effects. A big break for BioSteel occurred during the Stanley Cup playoffs broadcast in 2010 when Gary Roberts answered everyone's question: What was the pink drink the NHL players were consuming? People's seeing athletes drinking pink liquid, along with the social media communication, gave BioSteel an opportunity to expand.

© BioSteel Sports Nutrition Inc.

Inspired by the need for a natural drink that would pass NHL drug tests, a former Toronto Maple Leafs strength coach developed the product and teamed up with a business partner to bring it to market. The two saw it as filling the niche between sports and energy beverages like Gatorade and health or fitness supplements. Initially packaged as a powder which users would mix with water on their own, and distributed online for direct consumer purchases, BioSteel eventually made it into retailers like Loblaw, Sobeys, and Rexall, who placed BioSteel in the nutrition section to reinforce its price premium.

The company later introduced an individual ready-to-drink version with a portion of powder contained in the cap to go along with the bottle of water and distributed BioSteel more broadly in grocery and convenience stores right next to sports drinks. Retaining the powder format for the ready-to-drink version allowed the product to remain completely natural, free of preservatives and artificial flavours. In fact, BioSteel maintains its pink hue due to the red beet ingredient.

Another important promotional step occurred in 2011 when it hosted NHL players at a training camp, complete with practice jerseys with the BioSteel logo and extensive video recording for YouTube placement. Subsequently, NHL players used BioSteel in Gatorade bottles during the season. Of course this annoyed Gatorade, the official sponsor of the NHL, and BioSteel revised its training camps in order not to associate its brand identity with the players. Later on, athletes like Mike Cammalleri, Steven Stamkos, Carey Price, and Tyler Seguin endorsed the product through its use and appeared at branded events while receiving minimal remuneration.

More recently, BioSteel established a more formal relationship with sponsored athletes and began sponsoring high school basketball youth programs. BioSteel partnered with theScore Inc. for extensive distribution of branded messages. BioSteel implemented a contest on the media company's popular theScore app in which winners would receive a chance to see Tyler Seguin and Andrew Wiggins play and enjoy a meet-and-greet afterward. It also established branded messages featuring its sponsored athletes, and placed ads with its athletes in this digital media. Finally, BioSteel also launched a TV ad featuring Connor McDavid while he was still an undrafted Junior A player who later became the number one pick in the 2015 NHL draft. The message focused on his training and his use of the new ready-to-drink version of the product while the scene ends with the written and verbally stated (by Connor) slogan: #drinkthepink.

Sources: Chris Powell, "BioSteel Partners With theScore," *Marketing Magazine*, December 21, 2015; Josh Kolm, "BioSteel Goes Mass," *Strategy*, November 21, 2014; Grant Surridge, "BioSteel Plots Next Move," *Strategy*, September 24, 2012; John Lorinc, "Goodbye Gatorade: How BioSteel Is (Very Quietly) Taking Over the NHL," *Canadian Business*, April 2, 2015; Susan Krashinsky, "Drink Maker Tickled Pink With Start Endorsements," *The Globe and Mail*, May 15, 2014, p. B12.

Question:

1. Explain why #drinkthepink is a good slogan for BioSteel.

CREATIVE THEME CONSISTENCY

Consistency in promotional creativity is generally regarded as a key success factor so that the target audience retains the brand position. We explore examples of consistency in the creative theme across time, creative execution, advertising media, promotional tools, and products. The essential point is that when the target audience is exposed to a series of messages across different contexts, the creative theme should not change; thus there is a clear reinforcement of the brand positioning strategy. Deviation of the theme allows the possibility that the target audience will process the message alternatively and arrive at a different interpretation of the brand.

Consistency Across Time   Advertising or communication plans are generally done on an annual basis, thus the creative theme is often short-term in nature. However, the creative themes are usually developed with the intention of being used for a longer time period. While marketers might change their campaign themes often, a successful creative theme may last for years. A consistent creative theme across time builds on the established awareness of the brand's current customers by encouraging continued processing of future advertising messages. Moreover, the familiarity of the creative theme is recognizable to a brand's non-customers when they may be entering the product category or considering switching their purchases. The ad in Exhibit 7-11 for the Honda Odyssey is consistent with other ads showing the improved features of the new model.

After its initial launch, Koodo revised its creative theme but retained many characteristics so that the campaigns appeared continuous. They retained the same "fun, quirky and colourful characters"; however, they are no longer in spandex urging consumers to lose their bloated bills from other providers. Rather, the new characters articulate clever words like "textelation," "contractophobe," "fee-ectomy," and "bigbillification." The freshened campaign intended to keep the brand distinct from the campaign theme, as the message to consumers of other brands is to switch to this new discount provider.[49]

Consistency Across Creative Execution   As we noted above, an advertising campaign features a series of creative executions over time and it is important that marketers ensure all ads feature a similar "look and feel." Exactly what this entails is a matter of interpretation, but most advertisers and consumers would say they recognize it when they see it. And Telus TV ads of almost 20 years represent the best Canadian example of the most consistent set of messages.

Exhibit 7-11   Ads for the Honda Odyssey have used a similar format for many years.

© Honda

Nature became the canvas for Telus (named Clearnet at the time) when its advertising agency saw the simplicity of animals in its storytelling to deliver the proposition of "the future is friendly." Set to a white background with emotive music, the nature theme and critters help make the brand feel friendly, likeable, and approachable. Over time, we saw exotic birds (e.g., macaws), insects, colourful frogs, and lizards—until Telus took over, and began with a "disco duck" to celebrate the millennium and then moved on to penguins, monkeys, pot-bellied pigs, iguanas, bunnies, meerkats, hedgehogs, and fish, and back to exotic birds (flamingos, peacocks) once again. Pygmy goats danced to the hit "Jump Around" and Hazina the hippo made numerous appearances. According to experts, the characteristics associated with animals through stories (e.g., the cunning fox) act as a quick and simple reference that transfers to the advertised product. Furthermore, the feeling associated with the animal may also transfer to the product, so if someone likes Hazina they are more likely to feel positively toward Telus. And while the meaning of the animals is critical, the consistency of their use along with the key creative tactics makes Telus TV ads instantly recognizable with the near uniformity in style.[50]

Consistency Across Advertising Media   Often a successful creative theme is one that is amenable to more than one medium. For instance, the essence of creativity in a print ad is still captured in a follow-up radio ad. Or, the big idea found in a TV commercial transfers to an outdoor billboard. In both cases, the creativity of the initial media is seen in a supportive medium—one less central to the primary media, yet still important to continue exposing a similar idea to the target audience. Interestingly, this idea is difficult to convey with visual creative themes moving to radio. For a while, listeners heard a "friendly thought" from Telus that differed significantly from the nature theme portrayed in all visual media.

Consistency Across Promotional Tools   Using the advertising creative theme across the various promotional tools is an issue to be resolved. The argument for the same look and feel is pervasive. For example, Telus Mobility keeps its nature theme in all of its communications—from TV ads to promotional displays to its website and finally to its public relations and publicity. Actions such as this support the notion that the creative theme for the integrated marketing communication must support the broad market positioning and all brand positioning strategies for its many target audiences. This is also evident with Bud Light, which created the character Budd Light who appeared in all TV ads and was featured at promotional events. Representing the number-five beer in Canada, the fictional spokesperson embodies the spirit of the brand as he "keeps the good times going." This uniquely Canadian theme works with the target of fun-loving young men, yet spills over to women as well through other promotional activities like a contest to win a Caribbean cruise.[51]

Consistency Across Products   The same kind of use of a consistent theme across all IMC tools is evident in RBC Financial Group's "First" campaign; the theme pervades all of RBC's tools for all its products and services. And so the campaign's consistent theme works on multiple levels. It is positioning the overall firm as an innovative and forward-looking organization, yet the campaign adapts well to a variety of purchase and consumption situations for credit or investment products that can also be adjusted depending on whether the target audience is a loyal customer or a potential one that RBC Financial Group is attempting to switch. Consistency is also evident with RBC's message of "create" and its use of the financial adviser Arbie (i.e., R.B., for Royal Bank) who appears in messages across all IMC tools and products. Arbie is especially prominent in public relations activities, like the Olympic sponsorship, and for corporate advocacy issues such as water

Exhibit 7-12   Colourful ads are often used in Joe Fresh's product advertising.

Michael Crichton/Shoppers Drug Mart Corporation./Newscom

conservation.[52] Similarly, for its consumer products Joe Fresh has used a very similar design and colour scheme, especially orange, for many products advertised (Exhibit 7-12).

CANADIAN CREATIVE THEMES

We now present ideas regarding creative themes used in Canadian advertising and promotional communication. We begin with a perspective that supports the importance of unique ways of speaking to Canadian consumers. Since many brands are part of a North American or international marketing strategy, there is a tendency to standardize the message. We now highlight success stories as evidence of the importance of Canadian creativity in communication.

Importance of Canadian Creative Themes   The need for unique creative advertising can be found in the divergence of values between Canadians and Americans. Decades of consumer research by Environics researcher Michael Adams suggests that while the citizens of North America share similar aspects of society, the underlying values are quite distinct.[53] Since this groundbreaking revelation, Adams has continued the research and finds that the types of values are shifting but considerable differences remain.[54]

These unique Canadian values influence the motivation for consumption—Canadians buy products for what they can do for them, not what they say about them. Canadians favour experiences over possessions and are less inclined toward conspicuous consumption. For example, Canadians are more likely to believe that a car is basic transportation rather than a statement of personal style or image. Therefore, certain types of advertising messages are more palatable for Canadians since the underlying reasons for purchase are more accurately reflected in the dialogue of a commercial or the body copy of a print ad produced by Canadian advertisers.

Putting together a creative for Canada can be met with obstacles. Canadian managers who market U.S. brands in Canada often feel the pressure to run the same campaign in Canada that is being run in the United States. While this obviously saves on production costs of new ads, the money saving can be more than offset with lower sales due to messages not resonating with Canadian culture. Sometimes firms need to perform specific market research to demonstrate that a unique creative is warranted for the Canadian market. For example, Maytag required an entirely different positioning and creative in Canada when American messages focused on its made-in-the-U.S.A. claims. The Maytag repairman ventured north to shoot new ads that played during *Hockey Night in Canada* with a usage theme for cleaning hockey equipment, among others.[55]

Successful Canadian Creative Themes   Historically and recently, insightful and innovative Canadian creative themes demonstrate effective advertising and promotional communication. We take this opportunity to identify the Canadian organizations that recognize creative themes that have been truly outstanding. Specifically, we summarize the CASSIES, the trade magazine awards, the Bessies, and the Extra Awards. We also highlight Canada's performance at the prestigious Cannes competition held in France.

CASSIES   Awarded by the Institute of Communication Agencies (ICA), the Association of Creative Communications Agencies, and Association des professionels de la communication et du marketing, this recognition is perhaps the most significant in Canada. The CASSIES (Canadian Advertising Success Stories) awards identify Canadian advertising success stories. Initiated in Canada in 1993, the awards are based on a similar idea started during the 1980s in the United Kingdom. Originally awarded every second year from 1993 until 2001, the CASSIES are now an annual event.

The CASSIES recognize advertising and promotional campaigns that document a direct cause and effect relationship between the campaign and communication and business results. Entrants have to submit the details of their campaign in the form of a business case that summarizes the performance of the brand prior to the campaign and indicates the degree to which the performance has improved. The website, Cassies.ca, provides the complete entry requirements, identifies the winners, and contains the actual case history submitted. Newfoundland and Labrador Tourism won in 2012 when it showed spectacular and fascinating images of that province in ads across the country (Exhibit 7-13).

Exhibit 7-13   A breathtaking image of Gros Morne National Park captivated Canadians in this award-winning campaign.

The world can't weigh you down when you're standing on top of it.

Newfoundland Labrador

Trade Magazines   Two awards given out annually and sponsored by different trade magazines—*Strategy* and *Marketing Magazine*—identify the top Canadian creative communication launched each year in a number of categories. For example, there is an overall winner for best multimedia campaign, a winner for best single ad and campaign across all major media, and awards for nontraditional media, point-of-purchase, and public service announcements.

Bessies   These awards are given by the Television Bureau of Canada (TVB), an organization whose members comprise television stations, networks, and specialty services. The TVB promotes the use of television as an effective medium and has an important role as an information resource for its members. The Bessies recognize the best in English TV advertising each year and have been doing so since the early 1960s, shortly after the invention of television (an equivalent award for French TV advertising is awarded at La Fête de la Pub).

Extra Awards   Newspapers Canada is similar to the TVB but for daily newspapers. Its Extra Awards recognize outstanding creative advertising in this medium by giving ads a gold, silver, bronze, or merit award in nine product categories and types of ads (i.e., local ad, local campaign, national campaign, small-space ad).

Cannes   On a global level and inspired by the movie industry's more famous Cannes Film Festival, the Cannes Lions International Festival of Creativity is widely considered the most prestigious awards competition for advertising and all types of marketing communication. The Cannes competition receives entries from agencies around the world hoping to win Lions (the name of the award) in major categories—film (television, cinema, and Web film ads), press and poster (print and outdoor ads), cyber advertising (online marketing and ads for websites), media planning/buying, and direct marketing. The competition recently added the Titanium Lion for innovative work across integrated media. Over the years, Canadian advertising agencies' work performed very well by receiving awards in many categories.

Message Appeals

The **message appeal** refers to the approach used to influence consumers' attitude toward the product, service, or cause. As shown in Chapter 5, we are also concerned with influencing a target audience's attitude toward a brand (e.g., maintain or increase), so an accurate message appeal is important for marketing communication effectiveness. Numerous message appeals are possible, and we summarize five broad appeals: rational appeals, emotional appeals, fear appeals, humour appeals, and combined rational and emotional appeals. In this section, we focus on ways to use these appeals as part of a creative strategy and consider how they can be combined in developing the advertising message.

RATIONAL APPEALS

Rational appeals focus on the consumer's practical, functional, or utilitarian need for the product or service and emphasize features of a product or service and/or the benefits or reasons for owning or using a particular brand. Rational-based appeals tend to be informative by educating consumers with logical facts, and advertisers using them generally attempt to convince consumers that their product or service has a particular attribute or provides a specific benefit that satisfies their needs. Their objective is to persuade the target audience to buy the brand because it is the best available (e.g., provides a stronger sensory gratification motive) or does a better job of meeting consumers' needs (e.g., addresses incomplete satisfaction motive). For example, the ad shown in Exhibit 7-14 uses a rational appeal to promote the performance of Bridgestone tires. Weilbacher[56] identified several rational advertising appeals—feature, comparative, price, news, and product/service popularity—and we add reminder appeal to this list.

Feature Appeal   Ads that use a *feature appeal* focus on the dominant traits of the product or service. These ads tend to present the customer with a number of important product attributes or features that will lead to favourable attitudes and can be used as the basis for a rational purchase decision. Technical and high-involvement products often use message appeal. Exhibit 7-15 shows an ad for Red Bull energy drink that focuses on the benefits of its contents.

Exhibit 7-14   A rational appeal is used to promote the safety features of Bridgestone tires.

Courtesy of Bridgestone Americas, Inc.

Comparative Appeal   Ads that practise a *comparative appeal* either directly or indirectly identify competitors and compare the brands (or products) on one or more specific attributes or benefits.[57] Studies show that recall is higher for comparative than noncomparative messages, but comparative ads are generally not more effective for other response variables, such as brand attitudes or purchase intentions.[58] Advertisers must also consider how comparative messages affect credibility. Users of the brand being attacked in a comparative message may be especially skeptical about the advertiser's claims.

Comparative appeals may be particularly useful for new brands, since they allow a new market entrant to position itself directly against the more established brands and to promote its distinctive advantages. Direct comparisons can help position a new brand in the evoked, or choice, set of brands the customer may be considering.

Comparative appeals are often used for brands with a small market share. They compare themselves to an established market leader in hopes of creating an association and tapping into the leader's market. Market leaders, on the other hand, often hesitate to use comparison ads, as most believe they have little to gain by featuring competitors' products in their ads.

Price Appeal   An ad with a price offer as the dominant point of the message may be known as a *price appeal*. Price appeal advertising is used most often by retailers to announce sales, special offers, or low everyday prices. Fast-food chains have made price an important part of their marketing strategy through promotional deals and "value menus" or lower overall prices. Advertisers for vehicles and electronics use price appeals as part of their IMC strategy as well. For example, the Hewlett-Packard advertisement shown in Exhibit 7-16 promotes the affordability of the HP Officejet Pro printer for business use. The ad copy explains how it can print in colour at a cost that is up to 50 percent less per page than a laser printer and consumes less energy. The visual portion of the ad also uses vivid colours to represent the number 50 and deliver a message regarding the quality of the colour printing capabilities of the Officejet Pro.

News Appeal   When an announcement about the product, service, or company dominates the ad, advertisers are using a *news appeal*. This type of appeal can be used for a new product or to inform consumers of significant modifications, such as we see with new smart phone models. This appeal works best when a company has important news that it wants to communicate. For example, airlines sometimes use news appeals when beginning to offer service to new cities or opening new routes as a way of informing consumers as well as generating media exposure that results in publicity.

Popularity Appeal   Ads with a *popularity appeal* stress the popularity of a product or service by pointing out the number of consumers who use the brand, the number who have switched to it, the number of experts who recommend it, or its leadership position in the market. The main point of this advertising appeal is that the wide use of the brand proves its quality or value and other customers should consider using it. The ad shown in Exhibit 7-17 uses a popularity appeal by noting that TaylorMade drivers are used the most by PGA Tour professionals. Ads such as this are used to implement TaylorMade's marketing strategy, which focuses on innovation, the technological superiority of its golf equipment, and the popularity and use of its clubs by tour professionals who exert a strong influence on the purchase decisions of amateur golfers.

Reminder Appeal   When the objective of the ad is to build or maintain awareness, an advertiser might use a *reminder appeal*. Well known brands and market leaders with frequently used products often use a reminder appeal, which is often referred to as reminder advertising. Exhibit 7-18 shows a street ad, probably near shoe stores, reminding consumers to smile and to consider Ecco shoes when shopping. Products and services that have a seasonal pattern to their consumption also use reminder advertising, particularly around the appropriate period. For example, marketers of candy products often increase their media budgets and run reminder advertising around Halloween, Valentine's Day, Christmas, and Easter.

Exhibit 7-15   Red Bull uses a feature appeal to promote its benefits to students.

Exhibit 7-16   HP advertises the affordability of colour printing to businesses that use the Officejet Pro.

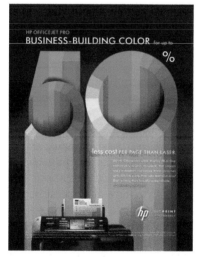

Courtesy of HP

EMOTIONAL APPEALS

Emotional appeals relate to the customer's social and/or psychological needs for purchasing a product or service. Consumers' motives for their purchase decisions contain strong emotions, and their feelings about a brand can be very important compared to knowledge of its features or attributes. Advertising appeals to consumers' emotions can be useful for brands that are similar to competing brands, since rational differentiation is a difficult communication effect to achieve.[59] The ad for Old Spice captured the emotion of consuming men's products with humour (Exhibit 7-19). Virtually every single Coca-Cola ad is dedicated to positive emotions associated with drinking the product, and when the beverage brand teamed up with Google to put digital software in dispensing machines that let consumers "buy" a Coke for someone else in the world, the joy spread exponentially.[60] Long versions of brand messages that become mini-films of emotional stories are a trend due to the growth of online video. with examples such as the Maddie execution for Chevrolet, the protective father for VW, and the love story for Cornetto ice cream in the United Kingdom.[61]

The choice between rational and emotional appeal requires careful consideration, to ensure that the advertising resonates with the target audience and evokes relevant processing responses connected to the purchase decision or consumption experience. Surprisingly, Google employed an emotional appeal in many ads to market its new array of products. When addressing the campaign, a Google executive even exclaimed, "It's about emotion, which is bizarre for a tech company."[62] Despite being a self-described tech company, Google's product is used and enjoyed on a daily (minute-by-minute?) basis, so how could there *not* be emotion with something involved so often in people's lives?

Hamish Pringle and Peter Field documented the effectiveness of emotion-based appeals in their book *Brand Immortality*.[63] They analyzed 880 case studies of successful advertising campaigns submitted for the United Kingdom–based Institute of Practitioners in Advertising Effectiveness Award competition over the past three decades and included campaigns from the United Kingdom as well as international competitions. Their analysis compared advertising campaigns that relied primarily on emotional appeals with those that used rational persuasion and information. A key finding is that advertising campaigns with purely emotional content produce nearly double the profit gains of rational content campaigns. One reason why emotional campaigns work so well is that they reduce price sensitivity and strengthen the ability of brands to charge a price premium, which contributes to profitability. Cereal manufacturers faced a declining market over the past decade and re-launched previously discontinued brands (e.g., Trix) and product extensions (e.g., Special K Protein) with emotional appeals along the lines of nostalgia with the hope of rekindling interest in lapsed users willing to pay high-margined prices.[64] Similarly, Kraft peanut butter experienced a sales decline and tried to rejuvenate the brand to millennials who are not eating the product category with a heartwarming story of a person's life from childhood to adulthood featuring the iconic Kraft teddy bear.[65]

Kamp and MacInnis note that commercials often rely on the concept of *emotional integration,* whereby they portray the characters in the ad as experiencing an emotional benefit or outcome from using a product or service.[66] Marketers use emotional appeals in hopes that the positive feeling they evoke will transfer to the brand and/or company. Research

Exhibit 7-17   TaylorMade promotes the popularity of its drivers among golf professionals.

Exhibit 7-18   This ad reminds consumers to associate Ecco shoes with happiness.

© Megapress / Alamy Stock Photo

Exhibit 7-19   This Old Spice ad uses an emotional appeal.

Courtesy Cannes Lions International Advertising Festival. Cannes Lions 2010 Grand Prix Winner

shows that positive mood states and feelings created by advertising can have a favourable effect on consumers' evaluations of a brand.[67] Ads using lifestyle, humour, sex, and other appeals that are very entertaining, arousing, upbeat, and/or exciting can affect the emotions of consumers and put them in a favourable frame of mind. For example, Second Clothing, a Montreal-based premium denim brand, demonstrated the feeling women have when first trying on a pair of yoga jeans. With very sensual images, sexy music, and the sound of an amorous woman "cooing," one presumes the experience lives up to the tagline: "Feel Good. Real Good."[68]

Many feelings can serve as the basis for advertising appeals designed to influence consumers on an emotional level, as shown in Figure 7-3. Relying on considerable research over time, this taxonomy identifies core negative and positive emotions. Moreover, the table indicates the origin of the emotion, which demonstrates the core subjective meaning of the emotion and the action consequences of someone experiencing the emotion.[69] These additional descriptions of the emotion are important as they give direction as to the content and authenticity of the emotion for planning this emotional message appeal; advertisers that miss the mark on emotional accuracy are quickly rejected. For example, the ad in Exhibit 7-20 accurately portrays the pride a longstanding car owner feels after using Quaker State oil for many years.

Each of these core emotions embodies nuances. Contentment might include things like happiness, joy, nostalgia, and sentiment. Elements of pride may be seen in recognition, status, acceptance, and approval. Canadians' feeling of pride toward their county is an emotion resurging in advertising message for brands like Tim Hortons and Molson Canadian. With hockey as a backdrop, the ads show Canadians as being more assertive and confident, reflecting research that indicates a change in how Canadians perceive themselves.[70] Other emotions appear to cross more than one emotion; for example, excitement is likely part of the first four positive emotions. We now review one negative and one positive emotional appeal commonly used in message delivery.

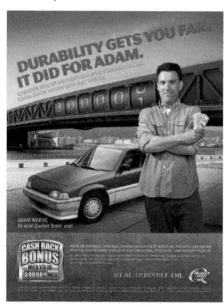

Exhibit 7-20 This Quaker State oil ad demonstrates the pride of long care ownership.

Figure 7-3 Basis for emotional appeals

Negative Emotion	Origin	Action
Anger	Offence against self	Restore justice, hold individuals responsible
Contempt	Other violates role, duty, obligation	Lower the reputation of perpetrator
Disgust	Contact with impure object or action	Push away
Embarrassment	Self has transgressed a social convention	Apologize
Envy	Other is superior to self	Reduce status of other
Fear	Imminent threat to self	Flee, reduce uncertainty
Guilt	Self has violated moral standard regarding harm	Remedy harm
Jealousy	Other threatens source of affection	Protect source of affection from others
Sadness	Irrevocable loss	Acquire new goods
Shame	Self has transgressed aspiration or ideal	Hide, avoid scrutiny

[Continued on next page]

[Figure 7-3 continued]

Positive Emotion	Origin	Action
Contentment	Pleasing stimulus	Savouring
Enthusiasm	Reward likely	Goal approach
Love	Perceived commitment	Affection
Sexual desire	Sexual cue or opportunity	Sexual release
Compassion	Undeserved suffering	Pro-social approach
Gratitude	Unexpected gift	Promote reciprocity
Pride	Self-relevant achievement	Status display
Awe	Self is small vs. something vast	Devotion, reverence
Interest	Novel opportunity	Exploration
Amusement	Recognize incongruity	Play
Relief	Cause of distress ends	Signal safety

Based on Dacher Keltner and Jennifer S. Lerner, "Emotion," *Handbook of Social Psychology*, ed. Susan T. Fiske, Daniel T. Gilbers, and Gardner Lindzey, 2010, John Wiley & Sons.

FEAR APPEALS

Fear is an emotional response to a threat that expresses or at least implies danger. Ads sometimes use **fear appeals** to invoke this emotional response and arouse individuals to take steps to remove the threat. Some, like anti-smoking ads, stress physical danger that can occur if behaviours are not altered. Others—like those for deodorant, mouthwash, or dandruff shampoos—threaten disapproval or social rejection.

Before deciding to use a fear appeal–based message strategy, the advertiser should consider how fear operates, what level to use, and how different target audiences may respond. One theory suggests that the relationship between the level of fear in a message and acceptance or persuasion is curvilinear, as shown in Figure 7-4.[71] This means that message acceptance increases as the amount of fear rises—to a point. Beyond that point, acceptance decreases as the level of fear rises.

Figure 7-4 Relationship between fear levels and message acceptance

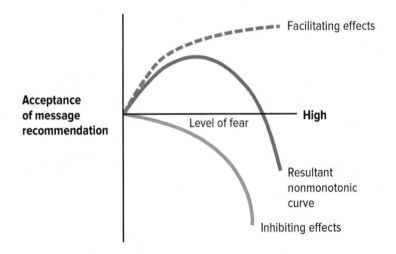

This relationship between fear and persuasion can be explained by the fact that fear appeals have both facilitating and inhibiting effects.[72] A low level of fear can have facilitating effects; it attracts attention and interest in the message and may motivate the receiver to act to resolve the threat. Thus, increasing the level of fear in a message from low to moderate can result in increased persuasion. High levels of fear, however, can produce inhibiting effects; the receiver may emotionally block the message by tuning it out, perceiving it selectively, or denying its arguments outright. Figure 7-4 illustrates how these two countereffects operate to produce the curvilinear relationship between fear and persuasion.

A study by Anand Keller and Block provides support for this perspective on how fear operates.[73] Their study indicated that a communication using a low level of fear may be ineffective because it results in insufficient motivation to elaborate on the harmful consequences of engaging in the destructive behaviour (smoking). However, an appeal arousing high levels of fear was ineffective because it resulted in too much elaboration on the harmful consequences. This led to defensive tendencies such as message avoidance and interfered with processing of recommended solutions to the problem.

Another approach to the curvilinear explanation of fear is the protection motivation model.[74] According to this theory, four cognitive appraisal processes mediate the individual's response to the threat: appraising (1) the information available regarding the severity of the perceived threat, (2) the perceived probability that the threat will occur, (3) the perceived ability of a coping behaviour to remove the threat, and (4) the individual's perceived ability to carry out the coping behaviour. This model suggests that ads using fear appeals should give the target audience information about the severity of the threat, the probability of its occurrence, the effectiveness of a coping response, and the ease with which the response can be implemented.[75] For example, the ad shown in Exhibit 7-21 uses a mild fear appeal for Seagate Technology's Replica product designed to back up computer hard drives. The ad uses playful illustrations in a graphic style to communicate what can happen if a computer crashes and all files are lost. The ad offers a solution to the threat by showing the ease of using the Replica product and the resulting peace of mind.

Exhibit 7-21   Seagate uses a mild fear appeal that alerts consumers to a problem and offers a solution.

Courtesy of Seagate Technology LLC

In reviewing research on fear appeals, Herbert Rotfeld has argued that the studies may be confusing different types of threats and the level of potential harm portrayed in the message with fear, which is an emotional response.[76] He concludes that the relationship between the emotional responses of fear or arousal and persuasion is not curvilinear but rather is monotonic and positive, meaning that higher levels of fear do result in greater persuasion. However, Rotfeld notes that not all fear messages are equally effective, because different people fear different things. Thus they will respond differently to the same threat, so the strongest threats are not always the most persuasive. This suggests that marketers using fear appeals must consider the emotional responses generated by the message and how they will affect reactions to the message.

HUMOUR APPEALS

Humorous ads are often the best known and best remembered of all advertising messages. Humour is usually presented through audio and video messages, as these media lend themselves to the execution of humorous messages. However, humour is occasionally used in print media, as seen in the ad for car safety testing in Australia and New Zealand (Exhibit 7-22). Often, humour fits with products like food, beverages, and household goods; however, advertisers are moving toward using it for personal care products that might have used a fear appeal in the past, which shows that the context and audience dictate the suitability of its use. For example, a maker of incontinence products paired up with Just for Laughs by suggesting that it was okay to laugh since its product would work. Winners of a contest would go to a Just for Laughs festival in Toronto, Montreal, or Chicago.[77]

Advertisers use **humour appeals** for many reasons. Humorous messages attract and hold consumers' attention. They enhance effectiveness by putting consumers in a positive mood, increasing their liking of the ad itself and their feeling toward the product or service. And humour can distract the receiver from counterarguing against the message.[78] Critics argue that funny ads draw people to the humorous situation but distract them from the brand and its attributes. Also, effective humour can be difficult to produce and attempts are too subtle for mass audiences. Finally, practitioners and researchers use the term *humour appeal*, which corresponds to amusement as the basic emotion, as shown in Figure 7-3.

Clearly, there are valid reasons both for and against the use of humour in advertising. Not every product or service lends itself to a humorous approach.[79] A number of studies have found that the effectiveness of humour depends on several factors, including the type of product and audience characteristics.[80] For example, humour has been more prevalent and more effective with low-involvement, feeling products than high-involvement, thinking products.[81] An interesting study surveyed the research and creative directors of the top 150 advertising agencies.[82] They were asked to specify which communications objectives are facilitated through the appropriate situational use of humour in terms of media, product, and audience factors. The general conclusions of this study are shown in Figure 7-5.

Exhibit 7-22   A clever ad shows how humour can be executed in print media.

Courtesy of Australasian New Car Assessment Program (ANCAP)

Figure 7-5   Advertising executives' experience with humour

Humour can:

Aid in gaining attention.

Assist with comprehension and yielding (i.e., cognitive responses).

Create a positive mood that enhances persuasion (i.e., emotional responses).

Aid name and simple copy registration (i.e., brand awareness).

Not aid persuasion in general (i.e., brand attitude), but does occur.

Generally not encourage consumer action, but does occur.

Enhance persuasion to switch brands.

COMBINED RATIONAL AND EMOTIONAL APPEALS

One decision facing the creative specialist is not whether to choose an emotional or a rational appeal, but rather how to combine the two approaches. Noted copywriters David Ogilvy and Joel Raphaelson eloquently argued many years ago that most products have both rational and emotional emotions associated with their use and purchase. One can experience happiness with clean clothes all due to a functional product like laundry detergent, and one can find joy that accompanies the high-involvement purchase of a new car that requires careful consideration of many facts.[83] Exhibit 7-23 appeals rationally and emotionally with the text of the ad and the compelling visuals.

MasterCard's "Priceless" campaign combined rational and emotional appeals when it lagged behind Visa and American Express. The brand repositioning challenge looked to create an emotional bond between consumers and MasterCard while retaining the brand's functional appeal. The campaign theme is that good spenders use credit cards to acquire important things that enrich their daily lives. The creative execution involved showing a shopping list of items that could be purchased for a certain dollar amount and one key item that could not and thus was deemed "Priceless." The tagline "There are some things money can't buy. For everything else there's MasterCard."

Exhibit 7-23   Advertising for Arrowhead water appeals rationally and emotionally.

Born Better.

Nestle Waters North America

positions the card as the way to pay for everything that matters. MasterCard built an entire international IMC program around the "Priceless" theme and won numerous creative awards. Exhibit 7-24 shows one of the print ads from the campaign. A new promotional element launched elsewhere to encourage greater usage came to Canada in the form of a video execution that featured the stories of people who use the card and then receive unexpected priceless surprises from former NHL hockey players like ticket upgrades.[84]

A unique example of combining rational and emotional appeals is the use of **teaser advertising**. Advertisers introducing a new product or new advertising campaign use teaser advertising, which is designed to build curiosity, interest, and/or excitement about a product or brand by talking about it but not actually showing it. Kia Canada's "Peer Into Your Soul" campaign launched the new urban crossover passenger car to unsuspecting TV viewers with three unbranded teaser ads over the course of three weeks. For 15 seconds, viewers watched mysterious characters staring back toward them and then saw the web address PeerIntoASoul.ca—inspiring enough curiosity for 180,000 visits before three branded ads for the Kia Soul appeared on TV. Picking up on the idea that people often stare into new cars parked on the street, Kia emulated this little nugget of consumer behaviour. The three executions spoofed different types of films. A "buddy" movie is seen in "Well," where a guy stuck in a well has his friend run for help only to get distracted by Kia's new vehicle. In a gangster style, "Mob" shows a couple of tough guys letting their hostage get away while they peer into a Soul. Finally, a horror flick emerges with "Cabin," as the intended victims awaken to find their would-be attacker fell asleep after staring at the uniquely styled car.[85]

Exhibit 7-24   MasterCard's "Priceless" campaign created an emotional bond with consumers.

The Duchess of Cambridge

Her Royal Highness Princess William

The Countess of Strathearn

George's Mum: Priceless®

Congratulations Kate on your most important title yet.

Courtesy of MasterCard Worldwide, created by McCann Erickson Worldwide

LO5   Source Characteristics

The third creative strategy decision is the source of the message appeal. We use the term **source** to mean the person involved in communicating a message appeal, either directly or indirectly. A *direct source* is a spokesperson who delivers a message and/or demonstrates a product or service. An *indirect source* (e.g., a model) doesn't actually deliver a message but draws attention to and/or enhances the appearance of the ad. Some ads use neither a direct nor an indirect source; the source is the brand or organization with the message to communicate. Since most research focuses on individuals as a message source, our examination follows this approach. Companies carefully select individuals to deliver their message appeal due to the costs involved and the fit with their brand positioning strategy. To understand this decision, we rely on a model that identifies three source attributes: credibility, attractiveness, and power.[86] This section looks at the first two characteristics in the context of advertising. Source power is omitted, as the compliance effect due to power is not really possible in most promotional communication.

SOURCE CREDIBILITY

Credibility is the extent to which the recipient sees the source as having relevant knowledge, skill, or experience and trusts the source to give unbiased, objective information, implying that there are two important dimensions to credibility: *expertise* and *trustworthiness*. A communicator seen as knowledgeable—someone with expertise—is more persuasive than one with less expertise. But the source also has to be trustworthy—honest, ethical, and believable. The influence of a knowledgeable source will be lessened if audience members think he or she is biased or has underlying personal motives for advocating a position (such as being paid to endorse a product).

One of the most reliable effects found in communications research is that expert and/or trustworthy sources are more persuasive than sources who are less expert or trustworthy.[87] Information from a credible source influences beliefs, opinions, attitudes, and/or behaviour through a process known as **internalization**, which occurs when the receiver adopts the opinion of the credible communicator since he or she believes information from this source is accurate. Once the receiver internalizes an opinion or attitude, it becomes integrated into his or her belief system and may be maintained even after the source of the message is forgotten.

Expertise   Because attitudes and opinions developed through an internalization process become part of the individual's belief system, marketers want to use communicators with expertise. Spokespeople are often chosen because of their knowledge of or experience with a particular product or service. Endorsements from individuals or groups recognized as experts, such as doctors or dentists, are also common in advertising (Exhibit 7-25). The importance of using expert sources was shown in a study which found that the perceived expertise of celebrity endorsers was more important in explaining purchase intentions than their attractiveness or trustworthiness. One implication is that celebrity spokespeople are most effective when they are knowledgeable, experienced, and qualified to talk about the product they are endorsing.[88]

Trustworthiness   While expertise is important, the target audience must also find the source (e.g., celebrities or other figures) to have a trustworthy image. For certain brands, options for selecting a trustworthy spokesperson may be limited. Alternatively, trustworthy public figures hesitate to endorse products because of the potential impact on their reputation and image.

A way of finding an appropriate trustworthy source is to use the company president or chief executive officer as a spokesperson in the firm's advertising. The use of this source is the ultimate expression of the company's commitment to quality and customer service. Research suggests that the use of a company president or CEO can improve attitudes and increase the likelihood that consumers will inquire about the company's product or service.[89] Companies are likely to continue using their top executives in their advertising, particularly when they have celebrity value that helps enhance the firm's image. However, there is a risk if CEO spokespeople become very popular and get more attention than their company's product/service or advertising message. Perhaps the most prolific corporate leader acting as the advertising spokesperson is Frank D'Angelo, who promotes his beer and energy drink brands. Loblaw returned to using its president in advertising, something the retailer originated during the 1970s. Owners or presidents of medium or small sized firms and local businesses rely on this approach for source trustworthiness, as seen in Exhibit 7-26.

Limitations of Credible Sources   Studies have shown that a high-credibility source is not always an asset, nor is a low-credibility source always a liability. High- and low-credibility sources are equally effective when they are arguing for a position opposing their own best interest.[90] A very credible source is more effective when message recipients are not in favour of the position advocated in the message.[91] However, a very credible source is less important when the audience has a neutral position, and such a source may even be less effective than a moderately credible source when the receiver's initial attitude is favourable.[92]

Another reason why a low-credibility source may be as effective as a high-credibility source is the **sleeper effect**, whereby the persuasiveness of a message increases with the passage of time. The immediate impact of a persuasive message may be inhibited because of its association with a low-credibility source. But with time, the association of the message with the source diminishes and the receiver's attention focuses more on favourable information in the message, resulting in more support arguing. However, studies have failed to demonstrate the presence of a sleeper effect.[93] Advertisers may hesitate to count on the sleeper effect since exposure to a credible source is a more reliable strategy.[94]

Exhibit 7-25   Dove promotes the fact that it is recommended by experts in skin care.

Courtesy of Unilever Home and Personal Care-USA

Exhibit 7-26   The trustworthiness of the Chapman family is emphasized in this ad.

© Chapman's

SOURCE ATTRACTIVENESS

A source characteristic frequently used by advertisers is **attractiveness**, which encompasses similarity, familiarity, and likability.[95] *Similarity* is a supposed resemblance between the source and the receiver of the message. *Likability* is an affection for the source as a result of physical appearance, behaviour, or other personal traits. Even when the sources are not famous, consumers often admire their physical appearance, talent, and/or personality. *Familiarity* refers to knowledge of the source through exposure. We describe these three characteristics and see how they operate via celebrity endorsers and decorative models in this section.

Source attractiveness leads to persuasion through a process of **identification**, whereby the receiver is motivated to seek a relationship with the source and thus adopts similar beliefs, attitudes, preferences, or behaviour. Maintaining this position depends on the source's continued support for the position as well as the receiver's continued identification with the source. If the source changes position, the receiver may also change. Unlike internalization, identification does not usually integrate information from an attractive source into the receiver's belief system. The receiver may maintain the attitudinal position or behaviour only as long as it is supported by the source or the source remains attractive. Exhibit 7-27 is an ad in which source attractiveness may be working effectively.

Exhibit 7-27   The model in this Tropez ad is an example of source attractiveness.

Markwins Beauty Products 2008, National Ad Campaign for Tropez Cosmetics, Designed by Jane Hjellum.

Similarity   Research findings suggest that people are more likely to be influenced by a message coming from someone with whom they feel a sense of similarity.[96] If the communicator and receiver have similar needs, goals, interests, and lifestyles, the position advocated by the source is better understood and received. Similarity can be used to create a situation where the consumer feels empathy for the person shown in the commercial. In a slice-of-life commercial, the advertiser usually starts by presenting a predicament with the hope of getting the consumer to think, "I can see myself in that situation." This can help establish a bond of similarity between the communicator and the receiver, increasing the source's level of persuasiveness. Many companies feel that the best way to connect with consumers is by using regular-looking, everyday people with whom the average person can easily identify.

The A&W manager represents the typical man trying to do a good job every day, while the younger Gen-Y slacker is along to resonate with today's youth in a humorous way.[97] The men's clothing retailer Harry Rosen returned to its roots of using regular businessmen for its print ads after using more famous names in the past 15 years. Moving from very familiar faces from the entertainment, sports, and business fields toward the more similar everyday manager gives a fresh look to the largely rational messages located in many newspapers.[98]

Likability   As noted in the above definition, a likable source in an ad is derived from virtually any characteristics the advertiser would like to draw attention toward in the message. Presumably, promotional planners would select a characteristic that reinforces the brand. For example, marketers of a facial skin care product would select a person who has a very good complexion so that physical characteristic would be noticed and associated with the brand name. Often, beverage brands will use likable sources with personality characteristics that emerge in the story of the ad to develop the brand personality.

Advertisers often feature a physically attractive person who serves as a passive or *decorative model* rather than as an active communicator. Research suggests that physically attractive communicators generally have a positive impact and generate more favourable evaluations of both ads and products than less attractive models.[99] The gender appropriateness of the model for the product being advertised and his or her relevance to the product are also important considerations.[100] IMC Perspective 7-2 illustrates Canadian-based Joe Fresh employing fashion models in its advertising as it expands the brand globally.

IMC PERSPECTIVE 7-2

JOE FRESH'S CANADIAN COOL

International consumers thinking about cool Canadian clothes probably could name Canada Goose and Lululemon, and now we might add Joe Fresh to the mix due to its significant global expansion. With plans to open 225 stores across 29 countries by 2019, the brand is taking its strength as one of Canada's leading apparel brands to destinations such as South Korea and Saudi Arabia. Starting out as a private label brand for Loblaw in 2006, the brand established its presence with 340 Canadian supermarkets, 16 stand-alone Canadian stores, six similar stores in the United States, and a distribution agreement with American retailer JCPenney that eventually fizzled. With a focus on

© Tupungato / Shutterstock.com

"offering great style at a great price," Loblaw looked to create an international iconic value brand offering a colourful selection of basic fashionable clothes.

Implementing the creative strategy across different countries proved to be a new experience for Joe Fresh. As a first step, Joe Fresh entered an international market with a set creative strategy for its displays, signage, and imagery for all consumer touch points. Essentially, it transported its well established minimalistic esthetic that appeals to many consumers with many cultural backgrounds. In the initial stages, the brand contracted a local agency to augment the creative strategy to fit the locale. While the core creative strategy remained consistent, necessary adjustments occurred with the teamwork of Joe Fresh Canada, the local marketing team, and the hired agency. The initial U.S. expansion proved useful when going global as Joe Fresh executives realized they had to learn and adapt to the market, and transferred that way of thinking as the company moved to Asian, European, and African countries.

One creative strategy decision that appears to resonate across all countries is Joe Fresh's employment of world famous models from many countries. A model recently highlighted in its ads and catalogues was Karlie Kloss. Other prominent models of the past few years included Andres Velencoso Segura, Liya Kebede, Joan Smalls, and Sean O'Pry, but it is Karlie who became the face of Joe Fresh in much of the imagery. In the past, Karlie Kloss graced the cover of fashion magazines such as *Elle*, *Vogue*, and *Glamour*, modelled for many high designers during their fashion shows, and represented other brands such as Marella, Kurt Geiger, Liu-Jo, L'Oréal, Chanel, and Versace in their advertising.

For the Canadian launch of Karlie Kloss's imagery, Joe Fresh partnered with *Flare* magazine to promote its capsule apparel collection. Subscribers received a special "unzip" cover where they had to open it like an article of clothing to reveal the full cover design that featured Karlie Kloss wearing Joe Fresh fashion. The issue included a four-page feature article about the success of Joe Fresh to go along with the Joe Fresh gatefold ads inside the front cover. Other communication involved publicity on other Rogers media such as TV with programs like *BT* and *CityLine* to go along with digital messaging like #joefreshxflare to direct users to Flare.com and JoeFresh.ca/Flare. With the excitement surrounding Karlie Kloss on the cover, executives expected online communication to peak significantly with the launch of the new fashion collection.

Sources: Kristin Laird, "Joe Goes Global," *Marketing Magazine*, July 2014, pp. 12–13; Canadian Press, "Joe Fresh Founder Steps Down," *Marketing Magazine*, March 16, 2015; Canadian Press, "Joe Fresh Getting Major International Expansion," *Marketing Magazine*, February 21, 2014; Kristin Laird, "Joe Fresh Appoints New President," *Marketing Magazine*, July 21, 2014; Kristin Laird, "Karlie Kloss to Be the Face of Joe Fresh/*Flare* Partnership," *Marketing Magazine*, August 5, 2015; Katie Underwood, "Behind the Brand: Joe Fresh," *Chatelaine*, January 16, 2015.

Question:

1. Does the use of internationally known models fit with the positioning of Joe Fresh?

Some models draw attention to the ad but not to the product or message. Studies show that an attractive model facilitates recognition of the ad but does not enhance copy readership or message recall. Thus, advertisers must ensure that the consumer's attention will go beyond the model to the product and advertising message.[101] Marketers must also consider whether the use of highly attractive models might negatively impact advertising effectiveness. Studies have shown that women may experience negative feelings when comparing themselves with beautiful models used in ads and the images of physical perfection they represent.[102]

To address this, Unilever's Dove developed the "Campaign for Real Beauty" (Exhibit 7-28), which portrayed typical women and girls in its messages, in contrast to the use of supermodels or decorative models. In essence, Dove relied on source similarity with the use of everyday women; however, their unexpected use in the beauty category quite possibly produced a degree of source likability due to the issues identified above. Thus, while there is often a primary source effect, a strong secondary effect may occur with creative campaigns. The campaign included many types of ads, extensive public relations, and a website (CampaignForRealBeauty.ca) where women discussed beauty-related issues. And, according to experts and the awards it won, the initiative appeared successful from a social standpoint, but less so financially.[103] More recently, the campaign received criticism for its "Patches" and "Choose Beautiful" executions, which showed typical women being misled or manipulated with a condescending or patronizing tone, which may question the viability of the original source effect.[104]

Familiarity   Familiarity through exposure from another context can provide a strong source. Essentially, advertisers hope the characteristics associated with the source from which the audience knows the original context carry over to the brand. This connection is often reinforced with the creative theme of the ad, so the two strategic variables work in tandem. Without question, familiarity often occurs through using famous endorsers, which we discuss subsequently, but it also occurs naturally in other ways. Familiarity is used with prototypical (and sometimes stereotypical) or representative images of a familiar person or persons from a well understood context. For example, familiarity is shown with a common situation that is known to occur within the target audience's use of the product.

Celebrity Endorsers   Advertisers understand the value of using spokespeople who are admired: TV and movie stars, athletes, musicians, and other popular public figures. Why do companies spend huge sums to have celebrities appear in their ads and endorse their products? These celebrities are clearly very likable due to their professional achievements and anticipated physical attractiveness, and they are generally very familiar given their media exposure. While the use of celebrities seems pervasive, they are seen in only about 10 percent of all TV and print ads. Furthermore, in the case of U.S. magazine ads, celebrities are shown within select product categories (e.g., cosmetics, fashion, food, media) and found in certain magazine vehicles (e.g., sports, teen, women's fashion).[105] Marketers expect that these celebrity characteristics draw consumer attention to advertising messages and favourably influence consumers' feelings, attitudes, and purchase behaviour. For example, a well known former athlete like David Beckham still adds lustre to a high end brand such as Breitling (Exhibit 7-29).

When selecting a celebrity, marketers are encouraged to follow a clear and formal process to avoid any problems, and to consider the celebrity's congruence with the audience, product/service or brand, overall image, specific source characteristics, profession, popularity, availability, and cost.[106] Celebrity endorsement is also a two-way street where the endorser evaluates the brand. Steve Nash, two-time Most Valuable Player of the National Basketball Association, acts as a spokesperson for brands that support his charitable causes like the Steve Nash Foundation, which provides

Exhibit 7-28   Dove's "Campaign for Real Beauty" uses everyday women rather than supermodels in its ads.

Courtesy of Unilever Home and Personal Care-USA

Exhibit 7-29   David Beckham is featured in this Breitling ad.

Image courtesy of Breitling. © Anthony Mandler

funds to children for health and education.[107] Other endorsers are quite strong in their beliefs by only endorsing products that they use or support. Four critical factors for a promotional planner include overshadowing the product, overexposure, the target audience's receptivity, and risk.

Overshadowing the Product   How will the celebrity affect the target audience's processing of the advertising message and their overall attitude toward the brand? Consumers may potentially focus their attention on the celebrity and fail to notice the brand. Advertisers should select a celebrity spokesperson who will attract attention and enhance the brand and its message, not the celebrity. Furthermore, the message should make a clear connection between the celebrity and the brand for a more positive brand attitude effect, otherwise the celebrity effect takes hold more strongly.[108] Canadian actor William Shatner has been Priceline.com's celebrity endorser for 20 years and appears not to overshadow the product. In fact, the U.S. creative expanded internationally with uniquely Canadian creative proving the celebrity–brand connection worked.[109]

Overexposure   Consumers may be skeptical of endorsements because they know the celebrities are being paid.[110] This problem is particularly pronounced when a celebrity endorses too many brands and becomes overexposed. Advertisers can protect themselves against overexposure with an exclusivity clause limiting the number of products a celebrity can endorse. However, such clauses are usually expensive, and most celebrities agree not to endorse similar products anyway. Many celebrities try to earn as much endorsement money as possible, yet they must be careful not to damage their credibility by endorsing too many products.

Target Audience's Receptivity   One of the most important considerations in choosing a celebrity endorser is how well the individual matches with and is received by the advertiser's target audience. Consumers who are particularly knowledgeable about a product or service or have strongly established attitudes may be less influenced by a celebrity than those with little knowledge or neutral attitudes. One study found that college-age students were more likely to have a positive attitude toward a product endorsed by a celebrity than were older consumers.[111]

Risk for Advertiser   A celebrity's behaviour may pose a risk to a company.[112] Entertainers and athletes have been involved in activities that embarrass the companies whose products they endorsed, and potentially negatively affect their brand (e.g., Lance Armstrong, see Exhibit 7-30). Marketers know that celebrity endorsers can be a very expensive and high-risk strategy because what the celebrities do in their personal lives (e.g., Tiger Woods) can impact their brand image. To avoid problems, companies often research a celebrity's personal life and background and include a morals clause in the contract allowing the company to terminate the endorsement if controversy arises. However, marketers should remember that adding morals clauses to their endorsement contracts only gets them out of a problem; it does not prevent it from happening. A summary of celebrity endorser studies concluded that the strongest impact on advertising effectiveness was negative information about the celebrity; it had almost twice as strong a negative effect compared to positive effects of source credibility and source attractiveness.[113]

Exhibit 7-30   Lance Armstrong caused significant difficulty for his brand sponsors because of his doping scandal.

© Spencer Platt/Getty Images

The Meaning of Celebrity Endorsers   Advertisers must try to match the product or company's image, the characteristics of the target audience, and the personality of the celebrity.[114] An interesting perspective on celebrity endorsement was developed by Grant McCracken.[115] He argues that credibility and attractiveness don't sufficiently explain how and why celebrity endorsements work and offers a model based on meaning transfer (Figure 7-6).

According to this model, a celebrity's effectiveness as an endorser depends on the culturally acquired meanings he or she brings to the endorsement process. Each celebrity contains many meanings, including status, class, gender, and age as well as personality and lifestyle. At Stage 1, the characteristics associated with the celebrity from their public exposure in movies and so on extend to their persona. Celebrity endorsers bring their meanings and image into the ad and transfer them to the product they are endorsing in Stage 2. In the final stage, the meanings the celebrity has given to the product are transferred to the consumer. This final stage is complicated and difficult to achieve. The way consumers take possession of the meaning the celebrity has transferred to a product is probably the least understood part of the process.

Figure 7-6   Meaning movement and the endorsement process

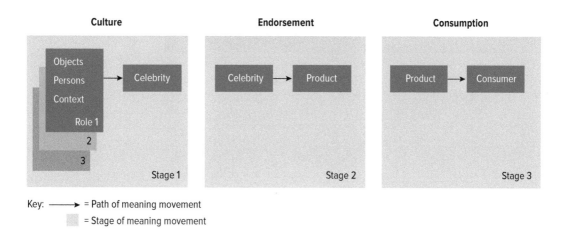

Key: ———▶ = Path of meaning movement
░░░ = Stage of meaning movement

For example, Electrolux employed Kelly Ripa for its premium line of stylish, high-performance appliances in an IMC campaign that capitalizes on her image. The campaign portrays the multitalented Ripa in her busy life—including scenes of her working, entertaining at home, and interacting with her children (Exhibit 7-31). She is an effective endorser for the brand since she represents the quintessential do-it-all woman who has an endless to-do list but who gets it all done. Electrolux delivers a brand idea that its appliances are designed to help women who are already doing amazing things in their lives to be even more amazing. To help deliver this message, Electrolux shows Ripa in TV and print ads and has also created an entertaining short film for its website.

The meaning transfer model implies that marketers must first decide on the image or symbolic meanings important to the target audience,

Exhibit 7-31   Kelly Ripa helps create the impression that Electrolux appliances are designed for the "do-it-all" woman.

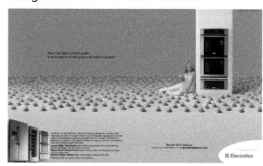

Courtesy of Electrolux

and then determine which celebrity best represents the meaning or image to be projected. An advertising campaign must be designed that captures that meaning in the product and moves it to the consumer. Marketing and advertising personnel often rely on intuition in choosing celebrity endorsers for their companies or products, but companies conduct research studies to determine consumers' perceptions of celebrities' meaning. Marketers may also pretest ads to determine whether they transfer the proper meaning to the product. When celebrity endorsers are used, the marketer should track the campaign's effectiveness by assessing whether the celebrity continues to communicate the proper meaning to the target audience.

LO6 IMC Planning: Message and Source Combinations

As noted at the outset of this chapter, the creative strategy comprises decisions regarding the creative theme, message appeal, and source characteristics. In the creative theme section, we noted that promotional planners determine the degree to which there is creative consistency across time, executions, media, promotional tools, and products. In this IMC planning section, we present a table that allows promotional planners to consider various combinations of message and source decisions.

Figure 7-7 summarizes the possible combinations of all message and source decisions. Essentially any ad or IMC tool has one of these 15 combinations. Promotional planners can consider using certain combinations for certain parts of the IMC plan. For example, a brand may select a more credible source with a rational appeal for its print communication, and possibly consider a familiar source with an emotional appeal for its television commercials. As noted in the creative consistency section, Telus has used a different message appeal and source on television and radio. Television ads feature likable critters with emotional appeals, while radio ads feature a trustworthy source with rational appeals.

While a number of combinations exist—and we have shown two examples where brands have adapted the source and message across IMC tools or media—promotional planners can certainly decide to keep the same source and message appeal for all their tools and media.

Figure 7-7   Possible combinations for message and source decisions

	Rational Appeal	Emotional Appeal	Combined Appeal
Credible			
Trustworthy			
Similar			
Likable			
Familiar			

Learning Objectives Summary

LO1   Summarize the idea and importance of creativity in an advertising context.

The creative development and execution of the advertising message are a crucial part of a firm's integrated marketing communications program. The creative specialist or team is responsible for developing an effective way to communicate the marketer's message to both customers and non-customers and reinforce the brand positioning strategy. Creativity is often difficult to articulate, but consumers and advertising people all know it when they see it. The challenge facing the writers, artists, and others who develop ads is to be creative and come up with fresh, unique, and appropriate ideas that can be used as solutions to marketing communication issues that may be problems or opportunities.

LO2   Decribe the creative strategy planning process.

Marketers often turn to ad agencies to develop, prepare, and implement their creative strategy, since these agencies are specialists in the creative function of advertising. Creativity in advertising is a process of several stages, including preparation, incubation, illumination, and verification. Various sources of information are available to help the creative specialists determine the best creative strategy. Creative strategy is guided by marketing goals and objectives and is based on a number of factors, including the basic problem the advertising must address; the target audience, behavioural, and communication objectives the message seeks to accomplish; and key benefits the advertiser wants to communicate as reflected in the brand positioning strategy. These factors and the creative strategy decisions are generally stated in a copy platform, which is a work plan used to guide development of the ad campaign.

LO3   Identify the approaches used for determining the creative theme that forms the basis of an advertising campaign.

An important part of creative strategy is determining the creative theme of the campaign. Often, a big idea strikes the creative specialist while embarking upon the creative process, which becomes the source of the creative theme. There are several approaches to discovering this big idea, including using a unique selling proposition, creating a brand image, looking for inherent drama in the brand, and positioning. In general, the creative theme guides much of the advertising campaign or IMC program. Consistency, originality, and its ability to effectively communicate are three key strengths of a good creative. The creative theme acts as a brand story to give it uniqueness compared to competitors.

Summarize the different types of message appeals that advertisers use to persuade their target audience.

A message appeal, the second decision of the creative strategy, is the central message used in the ad to elicit cognitive and emotional processing responses and communication effects from the target audience. A message appeal reveals the intended persuasion of the brand. Appeals can be broken into two broad groups—rational and emotional. Rational appeals focus on consumers' practical, functional, or utilitarian need for the product or service. Emotional appeals relate to social and/or psychological reasons for purchasing a product or service. Numerous types of appeals are available to advertisers within each group, and it is important for the client to clearly specify its intended message as accurately as possible.

Identify the source or communicator options a marketer has for a promotional message.

Selection of the appropriate source or communicator to deliver a message is the third creative strategy decision. The message source is the approach to deliver the message appeal. Three important attributes are source credibility, attractiveness, and power. Marketers enhance message effectiveness by hiring communicators who are experts in a particular area and/or have a trustworthy image. The use of celebrities to deliver advertising messages has become very popular; advertisers hope they will catch the receivers' attention and influence their attitudes or behaviour through an identification process. The chapter discusses the meaning a celebrity brings to the endorsement process and the importance of matching the image of the celebrity with that of the company or brand.

Apply source and message appeal options for different ad executions.

The chapter concluded by outlining options for IMC planning and suggesting that different combinations of source and message appeal could be constructed for different media or different IMC tools. Promotional planners can apply combinations depending on the context of the media such as TV, print, or social media. Furthermore, promotional planners might consider different combinations for specific IMC tools compared to what is shown in advertising.

Review Questions

1. Television commercials can use unusual creativity that has very little to do with the product being advertised. Explain why creative specialists would recommend such ads and why the brand managers would approve the production and placement.

2. Describe the types of general and product-specific preplanning input one might evaluate when assigned to work on an advertising campaign for a new brand of bottled water.

3. What is your opinion of advertising awards, such as the Cannes Lions, that are based solely on creativity? If you were a marketer looking for an agency, would you take these creative awards into consideration in your agency evaluation process? Why or why not?

4. Assume that a government agency wants to use a fear appeal to encourage college and university students not to drink and drive. Explain how fear appeals might affect persuasion and what factors should be considered in developing the ads.

5. What are source characteristics? What types are there? How do they affect processing of a message and the communication effects of the message?

6. How is it possible that an IMC program could have multiple sources for the message using both rational and emotional appeals?

Applied Questions

1. Find an example of a print ad that is very creative and an ad that is dull and boring. Select each element of the ad and figure out how it is contributing to the creativity or lack of creativity.

2. The chapter outlined a few campaigns; use the Internet to research and identify the most successful Canadian campaign in recent years.

3. Find an example of an ad or campaign that you think reflects one of the approaches used to develop a creative theme, such as unique selling proposition, brand image, inherent drama, or positioning. Discuss how the creative theme is used in this ad or campaign.

4. Describe how a few of the negative emotions conveyed in Figure 7-3 could be used in a campaign for car insurance. Describe how a few of the positive emotions conveyed in Figure 7-3 could be used in a campaign for smart phones.

5. Find a celebrity who is currently appearing in ads for a particular company or brand, and use McCracken's meaning transfer model (shown in Figure 7-7) to analyze the use of the celebrity as a spokesperson.

6. Actors portraying doctors in ads are often used for rational appeals. In what situation might it make sense to have a doctor for an emotional appeal? What type of emotional appeal would be most logical from Figure 7-3?

© Leo Burnett Toronto

CHAPTER EIGHT

Creative Tactics Decisions

LEARNING OBJECTIVES

LO1   Analyze the creative execution styles that advertisers can use and the situations where they are most appropriate.

LO2   Explain different types of message structures that can be used to develop a promotional message.

LO3   Express design elements involved in the creation of print, video, and audio messages.

LO4   Apply a planning model for making creative tactics decisions.

LO5   Illustrate how clients evaluate the creative work of their agencies and discuss guidelines for the evaluation and approval process.

#LikeAGirl

Procter & Gamble's feminine hygiene product Always followed the path of Dove with a social message associated with the brand. The three-minute video message featured people's physical response to the instructions "run like a girl" or "throw like a girl" as part of a disguised situation in which the participants believed they were part of a research panel or a casting call for a TV show. Young girls acted accordingly by performing the age-specific skill level, while others imitated stereotypical behaviours that clearly differed from the young girls'. Dubbed a "social experiment" by P&G executives, the creative approach garnered numerous advertising awards such as at Cannes, and continued with another execution one year later.

As noted, Dove's "Campaign for Real Beauty" altered the landscape for advertising with its social message approach that hit its 10-year anniversary in 2014. Other more recent executions include Nike ads showing how female athletes overcame discrimination when beginning their training. Pantene ads reflected on stereotypes of women being bossy. And while this innovative execution style is a growing trend, some are concerned that it actually perpetuates the very problem it seeks to eradicate. For example, Karen Howe, senior vice-president and creative director of One Advertising, commented, "There is a collective mining of women's insecurities. I wonder if, in their intent to empower, they are actually reinforcing some of these messages."

One motivation for creating a longer video message for online viewing is the belief that consumer segments seek out messages of interest and are more willing to view a longer message if it significantly matters to them. Coupled with the social message, these ads are now more relevant for a growing number of consumers. In the case of Always, 76 percent of women in the targeted 16–24 age range believed the message changed how they viewed the "like a girl" phrase. Over the course of the first year, about 80 million views occurred online, which led the brand to seek greater exposure. P&G created a 30-second version of the "like a girl" message for TV and saw so much potential that it aired it during the Super Bowl broadcast for a cost of $4.5 million to reach 115 million people in the United States, and they reached 9 million people in Canada with a separate media buy.

The follow-up execution showed girls providing examples of when they were told not to do something because they are a girl. The girls wrote about their experiences on cardboard boxes, and the video concluded with them kicking or striking the boxes. Research cited during the launch claimed that most girls aged 16–24 felt pressure to conform to the way they're supposed to feel and act. The video attempted to highlight the impact society's limitations have on girls' confidence and to empower them to be unstoppable. After the ads had been up and running for over a year, the majority of girls did not see the phrase "like a girl" as an insult.

Sources: Chris Powell, "From Social to Summits: Why #Likeagirl Is Unstoppable," *Marketing Magazine*, August 10, 2015; Susan Krashinsky, "Taking the Advertising World on Like a Girl," *The Globe and Mail*, July 4, 2015, p. B6; Susan Krashinsky, "P&G's Super Bowl Risk Pays Off," *The Globe and Mail*, February 3, 2015, p. B7; Susan Krashinsky, "Throw Run Fight Swing Punch Like a Girl," *The Globe and Mail*, July 4, 2014, B5; Susan Krashinsky, "Always Focuses on Female Confidence in Like a Girl Follow-Up," *The Globe and Mail*, July 7, 2015.

Question:

1. Explain why young women would want to see a longer video message regarding social issues from a brand of personal care products.

In the previous chapter, we identified and described the three creative strategy decisions. This chapter focuses on the three main creative tactics decisions. It examines execution styles that can be used to develop the ad, the important message structure choices available, and the elements involved in the design and production of effective advertising messages. We also present a framework for guiding the creative tactics decisions. We conclude by presenting guidelines marketers can use to evaluate the creative recommendations they need to approve to effectively communicate their brand positioning strategy.

Creative Execution Style

An important creative tactic decision is the **creative execution style**, defined as the way a message appeal is presented. While it is obviously important for an ad to have a meaningful message appeal to communicate to the consumer, the manner in which the ad is executed is very critical for achieving processing and communication effects. We now identify 11 commonly seen execution styles and provide examples of each. Two or three of these styles can be combined to present the message appeal.

STRAIGHT SELL

One basic creative execution style is the straight sell, which relies on a clear and direct presentation of information. This creative execution style is often used with rational appeals, where the focus of the message is the brand or specific product attributes and/or benefits. Straight-sell executions are commonly seen in print ads where a picture of the product occupies part of the ad, and the factual copy takes up the remaining space. They are used in TV ads, with an announcer generally delivering the sales message while the product/service is shown on the screen. Ads for high-involvement consumer products and business-to-business products generally use this format. Internet media ads may use a straight sell to encourage consumers to visit a brand's website or social media vehicles. The ad for the Gillette Mach3 shown in Exhibit 8-1 is an excellent example of a straight-sell execution style.

SCIENTIFIC/TECHNICAL EVIDENCE

In a variation of the straight sell, scientific or technical evidence is presented in the ad. Advertisers often cite technical information, results of scientific or laboratory studies, or endorsements by scientific bodies or agencies to support their advertising claims. The ad for Kinerase skin care treatment shown in Exhibit 8-2 uses this execution style by noting how the product has been clinically proven to reduce signs of aging.

DEMONSTRATION

Demonstration is designed to illustrate the key advantages of the product by showing it in actual use or in a staged situation. Demonstration executions can be very effective in convincing consumers of a product's utility or quality and of the benefits of owning or using the brand. TV is particularly well suited for demonstration executions, since the product benefits can be shown visually. Although perhaps a little less dramatic than TV, demonstration ads can also work in print. The Samsung ad shown in Exhibit 8-3 uses this style to demonstrate the ultra-thin feature and elegant design of its HD TV.

Exhibit 8-1 The ad for the Gillette Mach3 uses a straight-sell execution style.

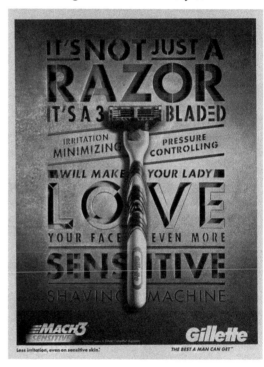

Courtesy of Procter & Gamble

Exhibit 8-2 Kinerase promotes how clinical test results support the product performance claim.

Courtesy of Kinerase. Kinerase is a registered trademark of Valeant Pharmaceuticals International.

COMPARISON

A comparison execution style—direct, indirect, or visual—is popular among advertisers. Direct brand comparisons are the basis for advertising executions to communicate a competitive advantage or to position a new or lesser-known brand with industry leaders. For example, computer manufacturers use direct comparisons to demonstrate superior performance claims. Although previous research found little support for the effectiveness of comparative ads, one study found positive results for the situation where a challenger brand compares itself to a category leader.[1] One unusual indirect comparison execution style occurred with ads for the Subaru Outback that compared life outdoors with the car against life indoors with a Snuggie blanket. The ad begins as a Snuggie ad that becomes a Subaru ad after a virile man uses a crowbar to symbolically pry open the television screen so that the viewer can see the car in the wilderness. Although a tactical consideration, this element clearly reinforces the brand positioning in terms of the target, motive, and key benefits the car offers.[2]

TESTIMONIAL

An advertiser may prefer to have its messages presented by way of a testimonial, where a person praises the product or service on the basis of his or her personal experience with it. Testimonial executions can have ordinary satisfied customers discuss their own experiences with the brand and the benefits of using it. This approach can be very effective when the person delivering the testimonial is someone with whom the target audience can identify or who has an interesting story to tell. The testimonial must be based on actual use of the product to avoid legal problems, and the spokesperson must be credible. The bicycle rider in Exhibit 8-4 acts as an indirect testimonial support for the "Ride to Conquer Cancer" fundraising activity. Testimonials can be particularly effective when they come from a recognizable or popular person.

SLICE OF LIFE

A widely used advertising format, particularly for packaged-goods products, is the slice-of-life execution. Slice-of-life executions are criticized for being unrealistic and irritating to watch because they are often used to remind consumers of problems of a personal nature, such as dandruff, bad breath, body odour, and cleaning problems. These ads can be perceived as contrived, silly, phony, or even offensive to consumers. However, advertisers prefer this style for certain marketing communication requirements because they believe it effectively presents a reasonably realistic consumer situation to communicate a product feature or benefit.

Execution is critical in using the technique effectively, as these ads are designed to be dramatizations of a supposedly real-life situation that consumers encounter. Getting viewers to identify with the situation and/or characters depicted can be challenging. Since the success of slice-of-life ads depends on how well the actors execute their roles, professional actors are often used to achieve credibility and to ensure that the commercial is of high quality. Advertisers with low production

Exhibit 8-3   This ad demonstrates the ultra-thin feature of Samsung's TV.

Photo and Ad by Arnell

Exhibit 8-4   The image of the rider suggests a testimonial executional style.

© ValeStock / Shutterstock.com

budgets may not be able to afford to hire the talent or to pay for the production quality needed to effectively create slice-of-life spots. One alternative gaining ground is the growth of user-generated executions.

Scotiabank tried its hand with this approach as an offshoot of its highly successful "You're Richer Than You Think" ads. In newer executions, the definition of *richer* moved toward how people felt rich in their lives during important life events like having a baby. With a consumer focus, the Scotiabank messages explored the meaning of moments of people's lives that matter to them. Some of these new executions used consumer-generated content across the TV ads, in branch material, and in digital ads. One such execution, entitled "Conversation," concerned the thoughts of parents of a new baby with video shots obtained from a friend of a Scotiabank employee.[3]

Marketers use the slice-of-life approach since it typically addresses a problem or issue and offers a solution. For example, Listerine used this executional style effectively to introduce a new Natural Citrus flavour of its popular mouthwash. The message addresses the problem that consumers have with the intense taste of the original flavour of the product. The ad opens with a mother returning home with a favourite dessert and Listerine; however, her husband and two kids hide when they see the mouthwash! The mother then tells them it is Natural Citrus Listerine, which tastes less intense. The humorous ad ends with the pots and pans dangling as one of the boys climbs down from the top of the kitchen island and the voiceover says, "You can handle it. Germs can't." (See Exhibit 8-5.)

Exhibit 8-5   Listerine uses a slice-of-life execution to introduce a new flavour.

Makers of Listerine

ANIMATION

With animation, scenes are drawn by artists or created on the computer, and cartoons, puppets, or other types of fictional characters may be used. Cartoon animation is especially popular for commercials targeted at children for products like toys and cereal; however, we also see it elsewhere. Nike created 100,000 customized animated films, one for each member of its Nike+ community of fitness members. They emailed the finished product, which told the personal story of each individual's training experience. Data derived from the community membership provided the content of the story. Each story showed familiar landmarks from the individual's training regime and encouraged the runner to achieve higher goals for the coming year.[4] In banking, RBC moved to numerous animated ads on TV and other media with its news spokesperson, Arbie. The friendly financial adviser finds himself in all sorts of situations showing how helpful RBC can be for consumers who want to create various things in their lives.

PERSONALITY SYMBOL

Another advertising execution involves developing a central character or personality symbol that can deliver the advertising message and with which the product or service can be identified. Dos Equis gained notoriety by creating "the most interesting man in the world," who accomplishes numerous feats prior to drinking the product (Exhibit 8-6). One study finds positive brand attitude effects through the use of spokescharacters.[5] Koodo's El Tabador is a new player on the scene. The Taxi 2 creative team invented him while brainstorming and ended up with the idea of a "freedom fighter" representing the little guy (e.g., consumer) who wants low prices and no contracts for the phone. According to a team member, "He is a bit of a ladies' man. He is sly and confident. We wanted him to be tough and not too cute but with a bit of self-deprecating sense of humour that would hit on the toy Barbie doll." The team pitched Telus with this one and only idea, and in the first year of ads the little guy starred in 11 executions.[6]

And it seems this industry can't get enough of personality symbols, as Mobilicity entered the market with a tandem of aliens—a green male and pink female. One executive claimed that, "Aliens tend to be seen as more advanced, forward-thinking, technologically advanced and a higher life form with better decision-making skills."[7] IMC Perspective 8-1 describes other example of brands using personality symbols in a variety of ways.

Exhibit 8-6   Dos Equis invented "the most interesting man in the world" as part of the brand's identity.

© Ethan Miller/WireImage/Getty Images

IMC PERSPECTIVE 8-1

PERSONALITY SYMBOLS FOR BRANDS

For decades, cereal brands have employed personality symbols, such as Snap, Krackle, and Pop for Rice Krispies, Tony the Tiger for Frosted Flakes, and Toucan Sam for Froot Loops. And we've seen symbols used in other product categories for many years as well, like Mr. Clean, the Jolly Green Giant, and the Pillsbury Doughboy. More recently, Travelocity featured a travel gnome in its ads and promotions like *The Amazing Race* sponsorship, and even created a Travelocity Gnome Twitter account! Of course, the list is fairly long over time and across many product categories, and spans Canada, the United States, and other countries, but the question remains as to why companies continue to use such approaches and how inventive they can be in the future.

© Stars and Stripes / Alamy Stock Photo

Research suggests that they are a tactical element in the creative message to ensure awareness. For example, two-thirds of Canadians recognize the Travelocity gnome and associate the character with the brand accurately. The advertising agency's inspiration of the gnome originated with a series of pranks in Australia 30 years ago, when people received a photo of their stolen garden gnome from far away destinations. Data from social media conversations found the Pillsbury Doughboy mentioned 22 percent of the time, with second place going to the Aflac Duck at 12 percent.

While not at the top of the list, the Maytag repairman hit 50 years old in 2017 and the famous appliance brand worked its way through five different actors over that span, sort of like the James Bond character. Originally cast as the goofy, lovable, woebegone, lonely repairman, Maytag recently updated his image with a more attractive and slimmer actor and portrayed him as more actively involved in customer service rather than waiting around for a call to fix a broken machine. The executives believed that the character should reflect the brand more accurately, with a masculine man who looked like he had strength and experience. As part of the mascot revision, the uniform became more tailored with a darker blue material and he obtained his own Twitter account, like the Travelocity gnome.

Closer to home, the CIBC introduced Percy the Penguin as part of its "Banking That Fits Your Life" campaign. Ads featured Percy and his family for the launch of the Aventura rewards program and then in messages for the edeposit of their bank accounts where cheques could be deposited with a digital photograph. In the first message, the ads showed real penguins, while the follow-up ad showed an animated penguin. CIBC planned to use a "real-life" Percy (i.e., a man in a penguin suit) to make visits to events and branch activities. The big Percy launch coincided with the Pan Am Games, in which CIBC acted as a lead partner.

A Toronto agency, Anomaly, introduced a talking beer tap in the likeness of the Wedgehead image found on the label of Labatt's Shock Top brew. Unsuspecting patrons in Toronto and Montreal interacted with the remote controlled animatronic creation, who wisecracked his way through many types of conversations. Messages ended with the ironic "It speaks for itself" slogan. Video recordings of the conversations found their way to social media. Executives in the United States watched the success of this Canadian launch with interest. Looking to expand the brand's awareness beyond 40 percent, they claimed the creative idea for a Super Bowl 50 ad as the first broadcast TV ad for the brand. The ad featured comedian TJ Millar trading humorous barbs with the Wedgehead character; score another international coup for Canadian ad creatives!

Sources: Harmeet Singh, "CIBC's Strategy to Stand Out," *Strategy*, May 25, 2015; Russ Martin, "Shock Top and Anomaly Toronto Head to the Super Bowl," *Marketing Magazine,* January 28, 2016; Russ Martin, "Shock Top Surprises Consumers With Talking Beer," *Marketing Magazine*, July 9, 2014; Susan Krashinsky, "The Power of Mascots," *The Globe and Mail,* June 25, 2014, p. B5; Susan Krashinsky, "The Maytag Man Made for 2014," *The Globe and Mail*, January 9, 2014, p. B3.

Question:

1. Why is it relevant that so many of the personality symbols are manifested in different formats: person, person in costume, animal, animation, object, or creation?

IMAGERY

Some ads contain little or no information about the brand or company and are almost totally visual. These advertisements use imagery executions whereby the ad consists primarily of visual elements such as pictures, illustrations, and/or symbols rather than information. An imagery execution is used when the goal is to encourage consumers to associate the brand with the symbols, characters, and/or situation shown in the ad. Imagery ads are often the basis for emotional appeals that are used to advertise products or services where differentiation based on physical characteristics is difficult.

An imagery execution may be based on **usage imagery** by showing how a brand is used or performs and the situations in which it is used. For example, advertising for trucks and SUVs often shows the vehicles navigating tough terrain or in challenging situations such as towing a heavy load. The San Pellegrino ad shown in Exhibit 8-7 uses the imagery of an Italian restaurant to convey the usage of its sparkling water. This type of execution can also be based on **user imagery**, where the focus is on the type of person who uses the brand. Ads for cosmetics often use very attractive models in the hope of getting consumers to associate the model's physical attractiveness with the brand (see Exhibit 8-8). Image executions rely heavily on visual elements such as photography, colour, tonality, and design to communicate the desired image to the consumer.

Exhibit 8-7 San Pellegrino water is enhanced with the Italian restaurant imagery.

S.PELLEGRINO® is a registered trademark of Sanpellegrino S.p.A., Milano, Italy

Marketers who rely on image executions have to be sure that the usage or user imagery with which they associate their brand evokes the right feelings and reactions from the target audience.

DRAMATIZATION

Another execution technique particularly well suited to television is dramatization, where the focus is on telling a short story with the product as the star. Dramatization is akin to slice-of-life execution, but it uses more excitement and suspense in telling the story. The purpose of using drama is to draw the viewer into the action it portrays. Advocates of drama note that when it is successful, the audience becomes lost in the story and experiences the concerns and feelings of the characters.[8] For instance, an Apple ad with a Christmas theme showed a family enjoying the holiday, playing in the snow, walking, tobogganing, skating, baking, decorating, etc., along with a young teen seemingly not enjoying himself. The message ends with him connecting his phone to the TV and playing a short montage of the day, eliciting smiles and tears from all family members. The ad, filmed in Alberta, won a significant creative award in the United States and critics claimed it meant Apple had regained its creative stride.[9] The ad in Exhibit 8-9 conveys a story of a family returning from vacation to find their long-parked car running smoothly and easily due to usage of the remote start feature a few moments earlier.

Exhibit 8-8   This Bebe ad uses an attractive model to create a favourable image for the brand.

Exhibit 8-9   The Buick Enclave commercial uses a dramatic execution style.

Courtesy of General Motors and Leo Burnett Detroit

HUMOUR

Like comparison, humour was discussed in Chapter 7 as a type of message appeal, but this technique can also be used as a way of presenting other message appeals. Old Spice continued with its humorous approach by interrupting a Bounce ad; both products are Procter & Gamble brands. Former NFL player Terry Crews crashed through the wall of the home of a very surprised woman in her laundry room. He then went on about the brand's body spray.[10] A rational message appeal occurred for both brands as a simple product characteristic is communicated; however, the whole execution of the appeal is certainly funny (for most people).

Skittles candy used humour as an execution style while going beyond TV or print media. In 2010, Skittles candy advertising showed what would happen were someone to "touch the rainbow," with characters turning anything into Skittles by simply touching it. In 2011, Skittles wanted its consumers to actually experience touching the rainbow by placing and holding their finger on a screen and watching five successive online commercials where their finger had the starring role. In one scene a cat and a human-like cat licked the finger; other scenes featured a car crashing into the finger, and a woman with a Skittles face complaining about having a finger pointed at her. Communication about the video went to bloggers and was posted on other social media. Within the time frame of the campaign, the ads garnered 6 million views, attained 11,000 fans on the candy's YouTube channel, and were featured extensively on other video outlets and social media. The campaign achieved 60 million media exposures and sales increased by 78 percent. The unique execution attained even greater stature by winning two Gold Lions at Cannes during the summer of 2011 for Film and Cyber.[11]

To understand the difference between the appeal and the execution with respect to humour, one could consider Boston Pizza's campaign with the fictitious Carl Carlson, president of the Flatties and Drummies Association, who expounds about the nibs and nubs of each chicken wing. The execution style uses a personality symbol, and the delivery of the message appeal is all sardonic humour.[12] Taken from a research view, one study concluded that humour with low complexity (e.g., one silly scene) is used within an execution style to garner attention without any direct brand linkage and is not persuasive, while more complex humour (e.g., amusement within the main message) with direct brand linkages is persuasive.[13]

 ## Message Structure

Marketing communication usually consists of a number of message points that the communicator wants to convey, as advertising messages have an important information provision characteristic. Extensive research has been conducted on how the structure of an advertising message can influence its persuasive effectiveness, including order of presentation, conclusion drawing, message sidedness, and verbal/visual balance. These first three message structure points mostly focus on the written words of a print message or the announcer in a video or audio message, while the last addresses the importance of visuals to deliver the message.

ORDER OF PRESENTATION

One consideration in the design of a persuasive message is the arguments' order of presentation. Should the most important message points be placed at the beginning of the message, in the middle, or at the end? Research on learning and memory generally indicates that items presented first and last are remembered better than those presented in the middle (see Figure 8-1).[14] This suggests that a communicator's strongest arguments should be presented early or late in the message but never in the middle.

Figure 8-1   Ad message recall as a function of order of presentation

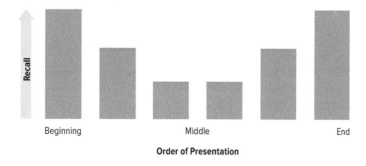

Presenting the strongest arguments at the beginning of the message assumes a **primacy effect** is operating, whereby information presented first is most effective. Putting the strong points at the end assumes a **recency effect**, whereby the last arguments presented are most persuasive. With the advent of multiple media, the presentation of the main message at the end may be to experience the additional messages online. For example, brands encourage Internet site visits at the end of a TV commercial so consumers will obtain additional information. Manulife took this in a different direction by finishing the commercial online. Viewers saw the first 15 seconds on TV as a preroll, and then had to see the remainder of the story on the company's Internet site. Consumers stayed on the site three times longer, with 60 percent of the visits arising from online links.[15]

Whether to place the strongest selling points at the beginning or the end of the message depends on several factors. If the target audience is opposed to the communicator's position, presenting strong points first can reduce the level of counterarguing. Putting weak arguments first might lead to such a high level of counterarguing that strong arguments that followed would not be believed. Strong arguments work best at the beginning of the message if the audience is not interested in the topic, so they can arouse interest in the message. When the target audience is predisposed toward the communicator's position or is highly interested in the issue or product, strong arguments can be saved for the end of the message. This may result in a more favourable opinion as well as better retention of the information.

The order of presentation can be critical when a long, detailed message with many arguments is being presented. For short communications, such as a 15- or 30-second TV or radio commercial, the order may be less critical. However, many product and service messages are received by consumers with low involvement and minimal interest. Thus, an advertiser may want to present the brand name and key selling points early in the message and repeat them at the end to enhance recall and retention. One study strongly concludes that the brand name should be identified at the start of a TV ad to enhance its persuasive ability.[16]

CONCLUSION DRAWING

Marketing communicators must decide whether their messages should explicitly draw a firm conclusion or allow receivers to draw their own conclusions. Research suggests that, in general, messages with explicit conclusions are more easily understood and effective in influencing attitudes. However, other studies have shown that the effectiveness of conclusion drawing may depend on the target audience, the type of issue or topic, and the nature of the situation.[17]

More highly educated people prefer to draw their own conclusions and may be annoyed at an attempt to explain the obvious or to draw an inference for them. But stating the conclusion may be necessary for a less educated audience, who may not draw any conclusion or may make an incorrect inference from the message. Marketers must also consider the audience's level of involvement in the topic. For highly personal or ego-involving issues, message recipients may want to make up their own minds and resent any attempts by the communicator to draw a conclusion. One study found that open-ended ads (without explicit conclusions) were more effective than closed-ended arguments that did include a specific conclusion—but only for involved audiences.[18]

Whether to draw a conclusion for the audience also depends on the complexity of the topic. Even a highly educated audience may need assistance if its knowledge level in a particular area is low. Does the marketer want the message to trigger immediate action or a more long-term effect? If immediate action is an objective, the message should draw a definite conclusion. When immediate impact is not the objective and repeated exposure will give the audience members opportunities to draw their own conclusions, an open-ended message may be used. Drawing a conclusion in a message may make sure the target audience gets the point the marketer intended. But many advertisers believe that letting customers draw their own conclusions reinforces the points being made in the message. The ad for the Hyundai Tucson in Exhibit 8-10 makes a clear conclusion on how the CUV fulfills the needs of the target audience.

Exhibit 8-10   This Hyundai Tucson ad makes a direct conclusion.

BREAK FREE.

THE ALL-NEW 2016 *Tucson*

Escape the endless repetition of eat, sleep, work, repeat. Break free from th everyday with a powerful and efficient 1.6 litre Turbocharged engine and all-wheel drive performance*. The all-new 2016 Tucson has arrived; prepare yourself to experience a CUV that will exceed your every expectation. This is th H-Factor.

hyundaicanada.com

WHEN EQUIPPED WITH AVAILABLE AUTONOMOUS EMERGENCY BRAKING
For more information visit www.iihs.org

TM/® The Hyundai names, logos, product names, feature names, images and slogans are trademarks owned by Hyundai Auto Canada Corp. *Available features.

© Hyundai Auto Canada Corp.

MESSAGE SIDEDNESS

Another message structure decision facing the marketer involves message sidedness. A **one-sided message** mentions only positive attributes or benefits. A **two-sided message** presents both good and bad points. One-sided messages are most effective when the target audience already holds a favourable opinion about the topic. They also work better with a less educated audience.[19]

Two-sided messages are more effective when the target audience holds an opposing opinion or is highly educated. Two-sided messages may enhance the credibility of the source.[20] A better-educated audience usually knows there are opposing arguments, so a communicator who presents both sides of an issue is likely to be seen as less biased and more objective. A meta-analysis of the research conducted on the effects of one- versus two-sided advertising messages showed that the persuasive impact of message sidedness depends on factors such as the amount and importance of negative information in the ad, attribute quality, placement of the negative information, the correlation between negative and positive attributes, and whether the advertiser discloses negative information voluntarily or because it is required to do so.[21]

Most advertisers use one-sided messages since they are concerned about the negative effects of acknowledging a weakness in their brand or don't want to say anything positive about their competitors. However, there are exceptions, such as when advertisers compare brands on several attributes and do not show their product as being the best on every one, or when a company acknowledges its shortcomings and communicates how it has improved. For example, Domino's admitted that its pizza did not taste very good, and its ads documented how the company transformed its ingredients and preparation in its messages (Exhibit 8-11).

Exhibit 8-11   Domino's two-sided message effectively introduced its reformulated pizza.

Domino's Pizza LLC

In certain situations, marketers may focus on a negative attribute as a way of enhancing overall perceptions of the product. For example, W.K. Buckley Limited became one of the leading brands of cough syrup by using a blunt two-sided slogan: "Buckley's Mixture. It tastes awful. And it works." Ads for the brand poke fun at the cough syrup's terrible taste but also suggest that the taste is a reason why the product is effective. The brand moved from number 10 in the mid-1980s to number one in 1992 with the launch of the message. In 2011, the Marketing Hall of Legends inducted Frank Buckley, the company spokesperson for many years and W.K.'s son.[22]

A special type of two-sided message is known as a **refutation**. The communicator presents both sides of an issue and then refutes the opposing viewpoint. Since this tends to "inoculate" the target audience against a competitor's counterclaims, refutation is more effective than one-sided messages in making consumers resistant to an opposing message.[23] Refutational messages may be useful when marketers wish to build attitudes that resist change and must defend against attacks or criticism of their products or the company. Market leaders, who are often the target of comparative messages, may find that acknowledging competitors' claims and then refuting them can help build resistant attitudes and customer loyalty.

VERBAL/VISUAL BALANCE

Thus far our discussion has focused on the information, or verbal, portion of the message. However, the nonverbal, visual elements of an ad are also very important. Many ads provide minimal amounts of information and rely on visual elements to communicate. Pictures are commonly used in advertising to convey information or reinforce copy or message claims. Advertisers will design ads where the visual image supports the verbal appeal to create a compelling impression. The ad in Exhibit 8-12 relies on the visual to communicate the ease and nutritional value of the appetizer.

Both the verbal and visual portions of an ad influence the way the advertising message is processed.[24] Consumers may develop images or impressions based on visual elements such as an illustration in an ad or the scenes in a TV commercial. The visual portion of an ad may reduce its persuasiveness, since the processing stimulated by the picture may be less controlled and consequently less favourable than that stimulated by words.[25]

Pictures affect the way consumers process accompanying copy. A study showed that when verbal information was low in imagery value, the use of pictures providing examples increased both immediate and delayed recall of product attributes.[26] However, when the verbal information was already high in imagery value, the addition of pictures did not increase recall. For very involved target audiences, a verbal message can be quite effective for persuading consumer attitudes; however, pure text still often requires supporting visuals to heighten motivation.

Advertisers may use a different approach designing ads in which the visual portion is incongruent with or contradicts the verbal information presented. The logic behind this idea is that the use of an unexpected picture or visual image attracts consumers' attention and gets them to have more effortful or elaborative processing.[27] A number of studies have shown that the use of a visual that is inconsistent with the verbal content leads to more recall and greater processing of the information presented.[28]

The "Deflate the Elephant" ads by the Liquor Control Board of Ontario designed to prevent drinking and driving used the visual of an elephant appearing in social gatherings to symbolize the awkwardness people experience when they feel compelled to speak to someone who has consumed too much alcohol. While most people in the over-35 target audience know they should not drink and drive, once in a while they slip up and drink more than planned. Their sober friends know they should speak up but suffer in a social grey zone of not knowing what to say. Hence, the elephant becomes a handy reference to give people courage and address the situation with light-hearted humour.[29]

Exhibit 8-12　The images in this Egg Farmers of Ontario ad show how easy it is to make a nutritious appetizer with eggs.

Hand-out/Egg Farmers of Ontario/Newscom

 ## Design Elements for IMC Tools

The design and production of advertising messages involves a number of activities, including writing copy, developing illustrations and other visual elements of the ad, and bringing all of the pieces together to create an effective message. In this section, we examine the verbal and visual elements of an ad and discuss tactical considerations in creating print, video, and audio messages. We use general terminology of print, video, and audio as these basic design elements can be applied to any print, video, or audio media distributed through advertising or other IMC tools.

DESIGN FOR PRINT MESSAGES

The elements of a print message are the headline, the body copy, the visual or illustrations, and the layout. The headline and body copy are the responsibility of the copywriters; artists, often working under the direction of an art director, are responsible for the visual presentation. Art directors also work with the copywriters to develop a layout, or arrangement of the above elements. We briefly examine the three design elements and explain how they are coordinated. These elements pertain to virtually all print messages that can be found in any media.

Headlines   The **headline** is the words in the leading position of the ad—the words that will be read first or are positioned to draw the most attention.[30] Headlines are usually set in larger, darker type and are often set apart from the body copy or text portion of the ad to give them prominence. The GE ads in Exhibit 8-13 effectively use two colours in the headline and ask a question to gain the reader's attention. Most advertising people consider the headline the most important part of a print ad.

Exhibit 8-13   GE innovates with headlines by asking a question after stating a product fact.

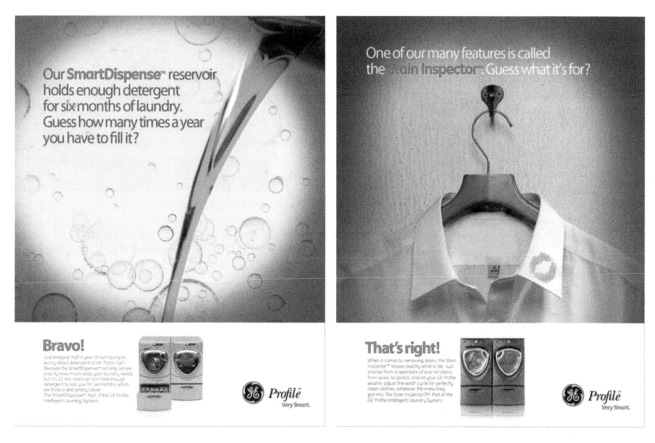

GE Appliances/MABE Canada

The most important function of a headline is attracting readers' attention and interesting them in the rest of the message. While the visual portion of an ad is obviously important, the headline often shoulders most of the responsibility of attracting readers' attention. Research has shown that the headline is generally the first thing people look at in a print ad, followed by the illustration. Only 20 percent of readers go beyond the headline and read the body copy.[31] So in addition to attracting attention, the headline must give the reader good reason to read the copy portion of the ad, which contains more detailed and persuasive information about the product or service. To do this, the headline must put forth the main theme, appeal, or proposition of the ad in a few words. Some print ads contain little if any body copy, so the headline must work with the illustration to communicate the entire advertising message.

Headlines also perform a segmentation function by engaging the attention and interest of consumers who are most likely to buy a particular product or service. Advertisers begin the segmentation process by choosing to advertise in certain media vehicles (e.g., fashion magazine, national newspaper, out-of-home). An effective headline goes even further in selecting good prospects for the product by addressing their specific needs, wants, or interests.

Types of Headlines   Numerous possibilities exist for headlines. The type used depends on several factors, including the creative strategy, the particular advertising situation (e.g., product type, media vehicle(s) being used, timeliness), and its relationship to other elements of the ad, such as the illustration or body copy. Headlines can be categorized as direct and indirect.

Direct headlines are straightforward and informative in terms of the message they are presenting and the target audience they are directed toward. Common types of direct headlines include those offering a specific benefit, making a promise, or announcing a reason why the reader should be interested in the product or service. For example, the headline in the ad shown in Exhibit 8–14 attracts attention by noting that one of the benefits of using an American Express credit card is being able to get tickets before the general public or, as the ad states, "before the ink's dried."

Indirect headlines are not straightforward about identifying the product or service or getting to the point. But they are often more effective at attracting readers' attention and interest because they provoke curiosity and lure readers into the body copy to learn an answer or get an explanation. Techniques for writing indirect headlines include using questions, provocations, how-to statements, and challenges.

Indirect headlines rely on their ability to generate curiosity or intrigue so as to motivate readers to become involved with the ad and read the body copy to find out the point of the message. This can be risky if the headline is not provocative enough to get the readers' interest. Advertisers deal with this problem by using a visual appeal that helps attract attention and offers another reason for reading more of the message.

While many ads have only one headline, it is also common to see print ads containing the main head and one or more secondary heads, or **subheads**. Subheads are usually smaller than the main headline but larger than the body copy. They may appear above or below the main headline or within the body copy. Subheads are often used to enhance the readability of the message by breaking up large amounts of body copy and highlighting key sales points.

Body Copy   The main text portion of a print ad is referred to as the **body copy** (or just *copy*). While the body copy is usually the heart of the advertising message, getting the target audience to read it is often difficult. The copywriter faces a dilemma: The body copy must be long enough to communicate the advertiser's message yet short enough to hold readers' interest. The ad in Exhibit 8-15 presents a creative use of the body copy as it mirrors the headline.

Body copy content often flows from the points made in the headline or subheads, but the specific content depends on the type of advertising appeal and/or execution style being used. For example, straight-sell copy that presents relevant information, product features and benefits, or competitive advantages is often used with the various types of rational appeals discussed earlier in the chapter. Emotional appeals often use narrative copy that tells a story or provides an interesting account of a problem or situation involving

Exhibit 8-14   This ad uses a direct headline in colour that motivates copy reading.

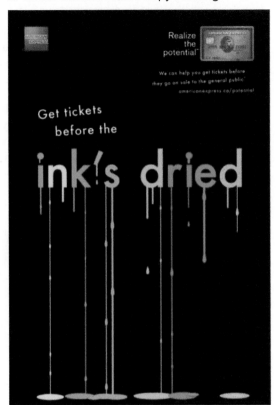

© American Express

Exhibit 8-15   The Crest Whitestrips ad uses the body copy in a creative way to support the headline.

© Procter & Gamble

the product. Advertising body copy can be written to go along with any message appeal or execution style. Furthermore, copywriters select body copy that is appropriate for the creative strategy (i.e., theme, message appeal, source) and supports the creative tactics like the message structure and other design elements.

Visual   The third major element of a print ad is the visual. The illustration is often a dominant part of a print ad and plays an important role in determining its effectiveness. The visual portion of an ad must attract attention, communicate an idea or image, and work in a synergistic fashion with the headline and body copy to produce an effective message. In some print ads, the visual portion of the ad is essentially the message and thus must convey a strong and meaningful image. The Quebec Milk Producers ad shown in Exhibit 8-16 contains important visual elements like the delicious treats that are more enjoyable when drinking a cool glass of milk.

Many decisions have to be made regarding the visual portion of the ad: what identification marks should be included (brand name, company or trade name, trademarks, logos); whether to use photos or hand-drawn or painted illustrations; what colours to use (or even perhaps black and white or just a splash of colour); and what the focus of the visual should be. Even the number of pages of visual ads is critical, as in the case of fashion products or automobiles. One study finds that advertisers should use fewer pages (e.g., 4 to 6) versus longer pages (e.g., 8 to 10) and insert the ads more frequently.[32] Exhibit 8-17 shows an ad where the visual is very important to support the copy and the call to action.

Layout   While each individual element of a print ad is important, the key factor is how these elements are blended into a finished advertisement. A **layout** is the physical arrangement of the various parts of the ad, including the headline, subheads, body copy, illustrations, and any identifying marks. The layout shows where each part of the ad will be placed and gives guidelines to the people working on the ad. For example, the layout helps the copywriter determine how much space he or she has to work with and how much copy should be written. The layout can also guide the art director in determining the size and type of photos.

Many layouts are standard poster format shown in a portrait orientation, although landscape formats do occur. Sometimes there are vertical or horizontal splits, with the latter being a separation between the visual and body copy. An optimal layout is an artistic expression of the brand as it achieves balance among the space, visuals, and colours.

DESIGN FOR VIDEO MESSAGES

Video messages contain the elements of sight, sound, and motion that are combined to create an unlimited number of advertising appeals and executions. Video messages occur in instances beyond television, as they are seen at theatres, in place-based locations, and online. Historically across much of these media, the viewer does not control the rate at which the message is presented, providing no opportunity to review key points of interest that are not communicated clearly. However, technological change places stronger control in the hands of viewers, allowing multiple views or skipping messages entirely. Nevertheless, the goal of capturing and maintaining a viewer's

Exhibit 8-16   The delicious imagery of the treats gives a good reason to enjoy drinking a glass of milk.

Exhibit 8-17   This ad uses a clever visual image to suggest readers visit the Internet site.

attention remains important in creating a video message since receivers may be doing other activities or may be exposed to multiple messages at the same time. The design decisions of these messages include video and audio elements to go along with careful planning of their production.

Video   The video elements of a commercial are what the consumer sees on the screen. The visual portion generally dominates the presentation, so it must attract viewers' attention and communicate an idea, message, and/or image. A number of visual elements may have to be coordinated to produce a successful ad. Decisions have to be made regarding the product, the presenter, action sequences, demonstrations, and the like, as well as the setting(s), the talent or characters who will appear in the commercial, and such other factors as lighting, graphics, colour, and identifying symbols.

Video messages can be expensive due to production personnel, equipment, location fees, video editing, sound recording and mixing, music fees, and talent. Acting talent certainly adds to the cost since good acting is an important characteristic for effective message delivery. Marketers are especially careful in selecting the presenters and actors for a video message, since incorrect associations may be processed if viewers recognize the actor from another message. At the heart of the matter is that the brand creates its own identity in the message to ensure brand awareness. While there are exclusivity clauses where actors cannot be in ads for products in the same category, advertisers are concerned about overexposure of the face. However, if one looks closely, one can see many familiar ones across a spectrum of ads.[33]

For Maxwell House, Kraft stripped down the production of its TV ads and plainly showed the product, thus saving a couple hundred thousand dollars per execution. The message mentioned this, and asked where the savings should be donated. Viewers responded with ideas on the Maxwell House website, and money eventually went toward Habitat for Humanity, children's music programs, and guide dog training—certainly good deeds reinforcing the tagline, "Brew Some Good."[34] Maxwell House continued with the low-cost approach with its "Optimism Breaks," where consumers would upload snippets of their good behaviour directed to others with a "cup half full" outlook on life.[35] With the growth of consumer-generated ads, brands moved toward using reality-type filming of actual customers in purchase and consumption situations. Production costs are notably less and the reality style is fashionably accepted by viewers.[36] Kokanee's new campaign after retiring its park ranger featured a point-of-view style that followed a man's everyday activities like personal care, sports, and meeting women at a party while drinking the beer.[37] Research suggests that user-generated ads influence brand loyal customers who are not capable of scrutinizing the message and who are given information about the ad creator.[38]

Another design consideration concerns interactive ads as seen on Microsoft's natural user-interface ads (NUads) placed on its Xbox Live network. An ad is launched by hand, voice, or controller via an ad square on the dashboard and Xbox's 360 Kinect sensor. Subway tested the new format with an ad for its Tuscan Chicken Melt sandwich. Subway provided the ad and Microsoft seamlessly incorporated the ad with the technology so it could be shown on the TV screen. The interactive results allow users to see what others are saying about the ad, while Subway can obtain instant campaign feedback. Subway interactively asked, "Where will you eat your Tuscan Chicken Melt?" with four different options for a response. Results indicated that 37 percent of the viewers explored the interactive feature, and 71 percent of those answered the poll question. One media expert commented that the 37 percent rate looked favourable compared to the 5–10 percent response rates for most digital applications.[39]

A longer version of video messages emerged due to social media and the sharing of video messages online. Known as microfilm advertising, this message format originates from an identified sponsor; is used to motivate online viewing, discussion, and distribution without further payment; and is intended to persuade. Results of the first ever empirical study concluded that enjoying the story is the only motivator for people to forward the message, however the enjoyment does lead to stronger brand attitude.[40] Related to this is the trend of video messages becoming more entertaining with interesting storylines and visual imagery. One important study concluded that the level of entertainment has an inverted U-shaped relationship with purchase intent, and the entertainment placed after brand identification influences purchase intent, but does not when placed prior.[41]

In contrast, low-budget online digital messages emerged as well. Surprisingly, one tactic of recording someone writing something down or doing a simple task has taken off on the Internet. Local businesses that use TV commercials are financially restricted to very simple production methods, such as a customer testimonial or demonstration from the owner. With Canada's smaller population relative to the United States, by comparison it is difficult to achieve economies of scale for lavish or high-cost productions. Creative executions and the accompanying video are designed with lower costs in mind. However, quality video everywhere may emerge as digital recording technology costs become more economical in future. IMC Perspective 8-2 describes another trend of video messages using prank jokes to communicate their point.

IMC PERSPECTIVE 8-2

EXECUTING PRANK VIDEO ADS

Did you get pranked? *Just for Laughs* and *Pranked* are two TV shows where someone plays a practical joke on an unsuspecting person. Often set in a real situation, the fun lies in seeing the disbelief during and the relief after the unfolding event. With a long history dating back to the *Candid Camera* TV show of the 1940s, the approach has remained a staple of entertainment over time in a variety of ways. So it is no surprise to see the idea applied to TV commercials and video messages shown online in social media and other media vehicles. From a historical perspective, one of the more memorable prank ads featured the Energizer bunny interrupting a subsequent fake ad after the original Energizer ad. With its long lasting battery message "keeps going and going..." the bunny continued from one ad to the next and disrupted the action with everyone wondering what was occurring.

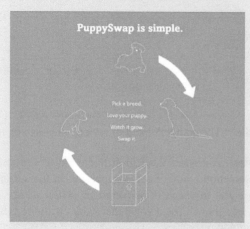

© Toronto Humane Society

One recent example of a prank ad is the effort by the Toronto Humane Society to make people understand that adopting a pet involves a lifetime commitment. The ad showed an easy to use app called "Puppy Swap" where people could trade in their older dog for a cute little puppy. At the conclusion, the ad provided statistics about the pet abandonment problem and said people need to consider the choice as a permanent one. Comments on YouTube indicated that the creative indeed pranked the viewers, especially pet owners who ultimately approved the message. The Humane Society's media relations manager felt that the ad worked since the emotional response to the prank caused viewers to seriously consider the message.

Plan Norway wanted to raise awareness about the problem of children being forced into marriage with an adult and created a message where a young girl prepared for a wedding. Ultimately she refused when asked by the presiding religious leader and received cheers from those in attendance. The conclusion displayed supers indicating the importance of the problem and action the general public could take.

Newcastle Brown Ale took its prank ads in a different direction with teaser trailers for its Super Bowl ad, focus group clips showing their reaction to the storyboard concept, and videos of actor Anna Kendrick and NFLer Keyshawn Johnson complaining about how the beer company pulled out of their contracts to be in the ad. Of course no ad existed and the prank essentially created publicity and online commentary worth extensive earned media beyond what any brand advertising during the Super Bowl paid. Resulting increased trial from 60 percent to 72 percent among young consumers indicated a strong showing. Newcastle also spoofed a campaign by Miller Lite. Miller Lite asked consumers for great summer photos that the brand used in its ads, while Newcastle responded by asking for boring photos since it did not have the budget to produce a proper ad campaign.

Other brands looked to April Fool's Day to produce another kind of prank ad. In the past, firms distributed joke messages to media releases and gained publicity when news organizations reported the story. Domino's Pizza advertised its edible pizza box, Scope promoted its bacon-flavoured mouthwash, and Cheetos told everyone about its perfume with a snack-food aroma. WestJet received notoriety with its "Kargo Kids" service where parents could enjoy peace and quiet on a flight by packing their children up and checking them along with their baggage. Experts believe brands can pull off the April Fool's Day humour if they have a good relationship with their audience and if the humour fits with the previous real ads.

[Continued on next page]

[IMC Perspective 8-2 continued]

Sources: Susan Krashinsky, "Humour Virus Infects Online Advertising," *The Globe and Mail*, April 1, 2015, p. B4; Susan Krashinsky, "The Anti Advertising Campaign," *The Globe and Mail*, August 29, 2014, p. B5; Susan Krashinsky, "Bold Charities Learn New Tricks—Prank Ads," *The Globe and Mail*, January 9, 2015, p. B6.

Question:

1. From the point of view of a brand manager, what positive communication effects can be expected from prank video ads?

Audio   The audio element of a video message includes voices, music, and the jingle or sound effects.

Voices   Voices are used in different ways. They may be heard through the direct presentation of a spokesperson or as a conversation among people appearing in the script. A common method for presenting the audio is through a **voiceover**, where the message is delivered or action on the screen is narrated or described by an announcer who is not visible. Advertisers will use a voice that works with the message and brand as the tone provides a distinctive resonance influencing emotional responses.

Music   Music is also an important element that can play a variety of roles.[42] Music acts structurally in an ad, much like grammar in a sentence, and supports the time sequence, motion, repetition, brand identification, and emotion experienced. Music can be a central element as it is used to get attention, break through the advertising clutter, communicate a key selling point, establish an image or position, or add feeling.[43] Music can also create a positive mood that makes the consumer more receptive toward the advertising message.[44] Other research on consumers' cognitive and affective responses to music in advertising found that increased congruity between the music and advertising with respect to variables such as mood, genre, score, image, and tempo contributes to the communication effectiveness of an advertisement by enhancing recall, brand attitude, affective response, and purchase intention.[45]

One new trend is that music houses are placing indie music in ads, following the lead of hit TV shows like *The O.C., Grey's Anatomy,* and *Gossip Girl.* Canadian artist Emilie Mover's song "Made for Each Other" became the key song for the global campaign for Fisher-Price toys. Marketers are looking for a distinctive tone for their ad that is not associated with any other experiences to make the ad more enriching.[46] Hamsters became a hit with the ads for Kia Soul that included popular dance tunes (Exhibit 8-18).

Often music is composed specifically for a campaign. Musicians and composers participate early on in the process of developing the ad; alternatively, the creative specialists who produce the ad look for very specific types of music to support the visuals. For example, a campaign "Kijiji Raps" showcases emerging rappers who wrote songs that described their experiences using the classifieds directory. Eight ads in two languages entertain viewers on YouTube with the goal of driving visits to the Kijiji site for ad placement and purchases. Each rapper produced their own version and style and Kijiji worked with rap engineers to get the right sound for the brand.[47] Finally, advertisers use **needledrop**, which refers to music that is prefabricated, multipurpose, and highly conventional, much like stock photos used in print ads.[48]

Exhibit 8-18   Music and dancing hamsters both played key roles in the Kia Soul ad campaign.

© Kia Motors America

Jingle   Another memorable sound element is a **jingle**, a catchy song about a product or service that delivers the advertising theme and a simple message. For example, "Black's Is Photography" is a jingle that has stood the test of time. Tim Hortons moved to a new jingle, "Always Fresh. Always Tim Hortons," for a while and then picked "It's Time for Tim's." Swiss Chalet reverted to a previous one, "Always So Good for So Little," after trying four different jingles in the past 10 years.[49] Subway garnered lots of mileage with its "Five. Five. Five Dollar. Five Dollar Foot-Long." Sometimes, jingles simply identify a brand and appear at the end of the message. Jingles are often composed by companies that specialize in writing music for advertising. These jingle houses work with the creative team to determine the role music will play in the commercial and the message that needs to be communicated.

Production of Video Messages   The elements of a video message are brought together in a **script**, a written version of a message that provides a detailed description of its video and audio content. The script shows the audio elements—the copy to be spoken by voices, the music, and sound effects. The video portion of the script provides the visual plan—camera actions and angles, scenes, transitions, and other important descriptions. The script also shows how the video corresponds to the audio portion of the commercial.

Once the basic script has been conceived, the writer and art director get together to produce a **storyboard**, a series of drawings used to present the visual plan or layout. The storyboard contains still drawings of the video scenes and descriptions of the audio that accompanies each scene. Like layouts for print ads, storyboards provide those involved in the production and approval with a good approximation of what the final commercial will look like. An animatic (actual video of the storyboard along with the soundtrack) may be produced if a more finished form is needed for client presentations or pretesting. Once the storyboard or animatic is approved, it is ready to move to the production phase, which involves three stages as shown in Figure 8-2. Before the final production process begins, the client must usually review and approve the creative strategy and tactics that will be used for the advertising message.

Figure 8-2   The three phases of production for commercials

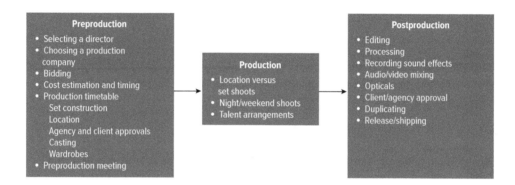

DESIGN FOR AUDIO MESSAGES

Audio messages are mostly delivered through radio, and that is the context for most of the design guidelines; however, digital opportunities make audio messages more prevalent. For example, audio messages can be included in podcasts, and certainly any ad on the Internet (e.g., banner, pop-up) could have an audio equivalent. Imagine listening to an ad while reading the online newspaper. The key elements of an audio message are similar to the audio of video messages, so we concentrate on the verbal and sound elements.

Verbal   Historically, radio has been referred to as the theatre of the mind; the voice(s) speaking to us in these audio messages offer a description or story, like the body copy of a print ad, that allows a visual to take hold. The talking can take many forms—straight announcer, dialogue between two actors, announcer/actor, customer interview—while following any of the executional styles identified earlier in the chapter. Depending on which format is used, a script is written that will attract attention in the opening, communicate the brand's attributes or benefits, and wrap up with a close that includes a call to action, like a store visit, phone number, or website address. The dialogue of the script is critical, much like the voiceover in a video message, but the illuminating words support the theatre idea to maximize the amount of processing time of the message.

With this in mind, it is often easy to hear very silly ideas in radio ads that somehow work because of our natural curiosity to make sense of incongruence. For example, famous actor Gordon Pinsent, who has a perfect radio voice, talked about a new poutine product from NY Fries: "Only the best ingredients coming together for something so perfect, like finding the perfect pair of jeans for your kitten. Little designer ones that sit low on the hips, so that little kitten can work those little designer jeans all sassy-like."[50]

Sound   Audio messages naturally rely on sound due to the lack of a visual. Brands employ unique sound effects to allow the visual to take hold in the receiver's mind. Alternatively, the unique voices of the speakers help create a personality to allow the visual to take hold even more. As seen with video messages, music becomes a key component for audio messages on a number of fronts, such as attracting attention or supporting the message and reinforcing the positioning. Moreover, as seen with video messages, jingles become even more critical as they fit with the format of listening to music. Audio logos are used significantly with audio messages, and are usually the same ones. Astral Media, owner of many different radio formats, uses 11 different versions of its audio logo to fit the genre of music played on the respective station. For example, a guitar riff plays the logo on a rock station followed by the common ending "You're listening to an Astral Media radio station."[51]

Planning Model for Creative Tactics

We highlighted the Rossiter and Percy (R&P) perspective in previous chapters. Another part of their approach concerns recommendations for creative tactics so that the appropriate communication effects will occur with the target audience after processing the message. The R&P model provides guidelines for creative tactics and it contains four distinguishing features: instructions to attain brand awareness, considerations for the type of motivation, suggestions based on the target audience's involvement, and advice on ensuring the tactics generate a balance between cognitive and emotional response.[52] To pull all this together in this section, we review the creative tactics for brand awareness and for brand attitude.

TACTICS FOR BRAND AWARENESS

The first feature is that the R&P model argues that brand awareness is a necessary precursor to brand attitude. According to R&P, brand awareness is a universal communication objective for all circumstances (i.e., one ad, ad campaign, IMC plan). In this view, all marketing communication should strive to achieve awareness in order to make brand attitude operational. R&P have three suggestions for brand awareness:

1. Match the brand stimuli and the type of response behaviour of the target audience so that understanding of the brand in a category is unambiguous.
2. Use a unique brand execution style to connect the brand to the category.
3. Maximize brand contact time in the exposure to reinforce name and category connection.

For awareness to be fully established, the target audience needs to understand the context (brand, behaviour, category), as this illustrates for them how or why the brand exists. If the context is not clear, then the target audience has trouble remembering the brand when it comes time to purchase. A unique execution style helps cut through the clutter. The connection to the category and sufficient exposure is required to make sure that the message is retained. For example, TV ads can sometimes show the package or brand name for too short a time for target audiences to fully grasp where the brand competes in the market.

We also noted that R&P suggest that awareness can be achieved via recognition and/or recall. R&P have two suggestions for recognition that require less media frequency as consumers need only to be familiar with the brand stimuli at the point of purchase:

1. The brand package and name should have sufficient exposure in terms of time or size depending on the media.
2. Category need should be mentioned or identified.

The Dasani ad in Exhibit 8-19 clearly shows the brand name with the large visual of the bottle of water. Its emergence from the plant communicates that the container is made of plant material, and is biodegradable, likely reminding those who stopped consuming the bottled water due to its overreliance on the use of plastic.

Exhibit 8-19   The Dasani ad makes use of a visual to clearly identify the brand.

© The Coca-Cola Company

R&P have six suggestions for this aspect of awareness. Recall also requires high levels of frequency since the brand has to be remembered prior to being at the point of purchase:

1. The brand and the category need should be connected in the primary benefit claim.
2. The primary benefit claim should be short to be easily understood.
3. Within an exposure, the primary benefit claim should be repeated often.
4. The message should have or imply a clear personal reference.
5. A bizarre or unusual execution style can be used if it is consistent with the brand attitude objective.
6. A jingle or similar "memory" tactic should be included.

We have many more specific recommendations for recall since it is a much more difficult mental task for consumers. Advertisers have to help their target audience know their brand prior to purchasing. The ad in Exhibit 8-20 follows many guidelines for improving recall. Thus, all three creative tactics decisions must be considered carefully to ensure that the target audience can retrieve the brand name from long-term memory when the need to purchase a product category arises.

Exhibit 8-20 This Subway ad uses key brand recall guidelines to encourage new consumers.

© Jeff Morgan 05 / Alamy Stock Photo

TACTICS FOR BRAND ATTITUDE

As explained earlier in the book, brand attitude is a universal communication objective, however the route to influencing consumer attitudes will vary depending on many factors. In this section we present four approaches for influencing attitudes, along with corresponding guidelines for creative tactics.

Brand Attitude Grid   The R&P view of consumer attitudes is also framed as a planning grid, with the dimensions of involvement and motivation. For each of these dimensions, R&P argue that their view is an accurate representation of attitude for planning purposes, and the use of these two concepts represents the second and third features.

Low-involvement decision Informational motivation	Low-involvement decision Transformational motivation
High-involvement decision Informational motivation	High-involvement decision Transformational motivation

The involvement dimension ranges from low involvement to high involvement and is specific to the brand as the target audience makes a purchase decision. Further, the high and low involvement levels are also consistent with the central and peripheral routes to persuasion. More precisely, R&P interpret involvement as the degree of risk perceived by the target audience (i.e., new category user or loyal customer) in choosing a particular brand for the next purchase occasion. One extension of this idea, not fully developed by R&P, is that the concept can extend to purchase-related shopping behaviour that we discussed in Chapter 5. For example, how much risk does a person buying a car for the first time take in deciding to visit a particular dealer for a test drive?

The motivation dimension is a continuum from negative motive, or informational-based attitude, to positive motive, or transformational-based attitude. The historical interpretation of an informational-based attitude implies that it is based on careful reasoning that results from the cognitive responses that the target audience has while experiencing advertising messages. However, R&P argue that this is too limiting as attitude is based on both cognition and affect. Accordingly, they suggest that creative tactics for this side of the grid should account for the benefit claims (i.e., cognition) and the emotional portrayal of the motive (i.e., affect). Thus, in order for it to be an informational-based attitude, the emphasis of the benefit claim is stronger than the emotional portrayal of the negative motive.

The notion of transformational-based attitude is partly built on the idea of a transformational ad, defined as "one which associates the experience of using (consuming) the advertised brand with a unique set of psychological characteristics which would not typically be associated with the brand experience to the same degree without exposure to the advertisement."[53] This type of advertising is often used by companies in the travel industry to help consumers envision the experience or feeling they might have when they take a trip such as a cruise or visit a particular destination. Image advertising, which is designed to give a company or brand a unique association or personality, is often transformational in nature. It is designed to create a certain feeling or mood that is activated when a consumer uses a particular product or service. For example, the Lambesis agency has created a unique image for Skyy vodka by creating ads that associate the brand with unique consumption moments (see Exhibit 8-21).

Just as the informational-based attitude is not purely cognitive, the transformational-based attitude is not purely founded on emotion but includes cognitive elements. Intuitively, this makes a lot of sense as some ads with a very strong fear appeal often leave us thinking. Overall, the emphasis of the emotional portrayal is stronger than the benefit claim for transformational-based attitude. Providing information in transformational ads is part of the "Fresh Air" campaign for Newfoundland and Labrador. Much of the message involved breathtaking views of the landscape and a humorous way of conveying the clean air one can breathe along the coastline. Another key component included travel logistics and accommodation information.[54]

Exhibit 8-21   Advertising for Skyy vodka uses an intense theme to create an image for the brand.

Courtesy of Skyy Spirits, LLC

Brand Attitude Grid Tactics   The fourth feature of the R&P model is that its guidelines for creative tactics balance elements in the ad for cognitive and emotional responses that contribute to both aspects of brand attitude. On the emotional side, we are concerned with how the motive is portrayed or conveyed in the ad. To consider this, we have three characteristics: its authenticity, or how real it appears to the target audience; whether the target audience likes the ad; and finally, the target audience's reaction to the execution style. On the informational side, we are concerned with the brand's message with respect to the benefit claims. We also have three characteristics to consider: the number, the intensity, and the repetition of the claims.

While the guidelines for all six characteristics may be a function of all three creative tactics decisions, we can make a stronger connection for certain ones. The authenticity and whether the target audience likes the ad are typically associated with the design elements of the ad. Quite obviously, there is a direct connection between the execution style of the framework and that particular creative tactic decision discussed in this chapter. The benefit claims are mostly a function of the message structure since the latter concerns the details of explaining the product's benefits. It is also a function of the relative balance between a verbal and visual message. We now turn our attention to creative tactics recommendations for the four brand attitude cells.

Low Involvement–Informational Creative Tactics   Ads designed to influence target audiences' attitudes based on low involvement–informational persuasion should have a very obvious benefit claim as shown in Exhibit 8-22. Since the intention is to persuade the target audience so that they automatically learn the connection among the brand, its category, and the benefit, consumer acceptance or rejection of the message is not a factor. Further, the emotion demonstrated in the ad and whether the target audience likes the ad are not necessary as the message is intended to make a creative link among the brand, category, and benefit.

Exhibit 8-22   This ad contains low involvement–informational creative tactics.

© McGraw-Hill Education/John Flournoy

Low Involvement–Informational

Emotional portrayal of motive

Authenticity	Not necessary
Like ad	Not necessary
Execution style	Unusual, problem–solution format

Benefit claim of brand message

Number of benefits	One or two, or one clear group
Intensity of benefit claim	State extremely
Repetition of benefit claim	Few required for reminder

Low Involvement-Transformational Creative Tactics   Three emotional portrayal guidelines are critical for this type of attitude. These points are consistent with transformational ads described above. For example, the representation of the consumption of the brand in the drama or story of the ad must "ring true" with the target audience such that it is perceived as a very enjoyable ad. This characteristic is demonstrated in the Fluevog shoe ad (Exhibit 8-23). In a low-involvement situation, benefit claims are still included but may be indirectly communicated through the story or emotion surrounding the story. Actual acceptance of the benefit claim is not a requirement; however, rejection of the overall message can lead to a reduction in the attitude of the target audience.

Low Involvement–Transformational

Emotional portrayal of motive

Authenticity	Key element and is the single benefit
Like ad	Necessary
Execution style	Unique to the brand

Benefit claim of brand message

Number of benefits	One or two, or one clear group
Intensity of benefit claim	Imply extremely by association
Repetition of benefit claim	Many exposures to build up before trial purchase and reinforce attitude after trial

High Involvement–Informational Creative Tactics   This side of the grid illustrates the importance of information, as *high involvement* implies the requirement of considerable and accurate benefit claims. Many benefits can be claimed here, but they must be organized and presented in a manner that respects the current attitude of the target audience. Since this is an informational-based attitude, the emotional portrayal is important but not the primary consideration. Furthermore, the high-involvement characteristic means that the target audience has to accept the benefit claims. Rejection of the benefit claims may not result in any negative change in attitude if the copy respected the prior attitude of the target audience.

High Involvement–Informational

Emotional portrayal of motive

Authenticity	Key element early in product life cycle and declines as product reaches later stages
Like ad	Not necessary
Execution style	Unusual

Benefit claim of brand message

Number of benefits	Overall claim to summarize multiple (no more than seven) benefits
Intensity of benefit claim	Initial attitude is key reference point
	Very accurate claim; cannot overclaim or underclaim
	Comparative or refutation messages are strong options
Repetition of benefit claim	Many claims within an exposure

Exhibit 8-23 This unique John Fluevog ad captures a particular emotion to encourage store visits.

© John Fluevog Shoes

Exhibit 8-24 Rolex's ad accurately conveys the elegance of the product.

Courtesy of Rolex Watch U.S.A., Inc.

High Involvement–Transformational Creative Tactics   Persuasion through this type of attitude formation requires strong emphasis of the emotion. A positive attitude toward the ad leads to a positive brand attitude. Likewise, the target audience must relate to the execution style and feel like they identify with the product, as shown in the Rolex ad in Exhibit 8-24. The end result is that if the target audience rejects the message because the emotion is not accurate, then the persuasion will not work and may even cause significant attitude reduction. The remaining guidelines illustrate that considerable information is required, similar to what is seen for the high involvement–informational attitude. Once again, this implies that acceptance of the benefit claims is critical for the attitude to take hold with the target audience.

High Involvement–Transformational

Emotional portrayal of motive

Authenticity	Paramount; must reflect lifestyle of target audience
Like ad	Necessary
Execution style	Unique; target audience must identify with product, people, or consumption situation shown

Benefit claim of brand message

Number of benefits	Acceptable number to provide key information
Intensity of benefit claim	Very accurate claim; may overclaim but do not underclaim
Repetition of benefit claim	Many are required to support informational message

IMC Planning: Guidelines for Creative Evaluation

While the creative specialists have much responsibility for determining the message appeal and execution style to be used in a campaign, the marketer must evaluate and approve the creative approach before any ads are produced. A number of people may be involved in evaluating the creative recommendation, including the advertising or communications manager, product or brand managers, marketing director or vice-president, representatives from the legal department, and even senior managers if required.

Top management is involved in selecting an ad agency and must approve the theme and creative strategy for the campaign. Evaluation and approval of individual ads proposed by the agency is often the responsibility of advertising and product managers. The account executive and a member of the creative team present the creative concept to the client's advertising and product managers for their approval before beginning production. A careful evaluation should be made before the campaign actually enters production, since this stage requires considerable time and money. Basic criteria for evaluating the creative approach focus on a number of questions requiring managerial judgment:

- *Is the creative approach consistent with the brand's marketing and advertising objectives?* Advertisers must consider whether the creative strategy and tactics recommended by the agency are consistent with the marketing strategy for the brand and the role advertising and promotion have been assigned in the overall marketing program (i.e., brand image, marketing positioning strategy).

- *Is the creative approach consistent with the communication objectives?* The creative strategy and tactics must meet the established communication objectives. Creative specialists can lose sight of what the advertising message is supposed to be and come up with an approach that fails to execute the advertising strategy. Individuals responsible for approving the ad should ask the creative specialists to explain how the creative strategy and tactics achieve the creative and communications objectives.

- *Is the creative approach appropriate for the target audience?* Careful consideration should be given to whether the creative strategy and tactics recommended will appeal to, be understood by, and communicate effectively with the target audience. This involves studying all elements of the ad and how the audience will respond to them. Advertisers do not want to approve advertising that they believe will receive a negative reaction from the target audience.

- *Does the creative approach communicate a clear and convincing message to the customer?* Most ads are supposed to communicate a message that will help sell the brand. While creativity is important in advertising, it is also important that the advertising communicate information attributes, features and benefits, and/or images that give consumers a reason to buy the brand.

- *Does the creative approach keep from overwhelming the message?* Many creative, entertaining commercials have failed to register the brand name and/or selling points effectively. With advertising clutter, it may be necessary to use a novel creative approach to gain the receiver's attention. However, the creative approach cannot inhibit or limit message delivery to the target audience.

- *Is the creative approach appropriate for the media environment in which it is likely to be seen?* Each media vehicle has its own specific climate that results from the nature of its editorial content, the type of reader or viewer it attracts, and the nature of the ads it contains. Consideration should be given to how well the ad fits into the media environment in which it will be shown.

- *Is the ad truthful and tasteful?* Marketers should consider whether an ad is truthful, as well as whether it might offend consumers. The ultimate responsibility for determining whether an ad deceives or offends the target audience lies with the client. It is the job of the advertising or brand manager to evaluate the approach against company standards. The firm's legal department may review the ad to determine whether the creative appeal, message content, or execution could cause any problems for the company.

The advertising manager, brand manager, or other personnel on the client side can use these guidelines in reviewing, evaluating, and approving the ideas offered by the creative specialists. There may be other factors specific to the firm's advertising and marketing situation. Also, there may be situations where it is acceptable to deviate from the standards the firm usually uses in judging creative output. As we shall see in the next chapter, the client may want to move beyond these subjective criteria and use more sophisticated pretesting research using quantitative and qualitative methods to determine the effectiveness of a particular approach suggested by the creative specialists.

Learning Objectives Summary

LO1 Analyze the creative execution styles that advertisers can use and the situations where they are most appropriate.

Once the creative strategy that will guide the ad campaign has been determined, attention turns to the specific creative tactics that will enhance the cognitive and emotional processing of the message. The creative execution style is the way the advertising appeal is presented in the message and is the first of three creative tactics analyzed in this chapter. A number of common execution techniques were examined, along with considerations for their use. The most appropriate style is a matter of balancing uniqueness in the market against effective communication to achieve the stated objectives. A number of standard approaches are available, like straight sell, slice of life, testimonial, drama, humour, and imagery—all of which can be put in TV commercials, print ads, and radio spots and are now being developed for online video, banner ads, and podcast sponsorships.

LO2 Explain different types of message structures that can be used to develop a promotional message.

The design of the advertising message is a critical part of the communication process and is the second creative tactic discussed. There are options regarding the message structure, including order of presentation of message arguments, conclusion drawing, message sidedness, refutation, and verbal versus visual traits. How these elements are constructed has important implications for enhancing the processing of the message and whether communication effects are achieved with the target audience. Message structure considerations are important for any form of delivery (i.e., video, print, audio) that may be disseminated via traditional or new media.

LO3 Express design elements involved in the creation of print, video, and audio messages.

Attention was also given to tactical issues involved in creating print, video, and audio messages. The elements of a print ad include headlines, body copy, illustrations, and layout. We also examined the video and audio elements of video messages and considerations involved in the planning and production of commercials. Together, these showed the important design decisions that have to be made to complete the creative approach. Finally, we highlighted a couple of key factors in the development of audio messages. These design elements are relevant for producing print, video, or audio ads that can be delivered through a variety of media.

 Apply a planning model for making creative tactics decisions.

We presented a model for creative specialists and marketers to help them make the appropriate decisions for the creative tactics. It provided general and specific suggestions for brand awareness. The model uses the target audience's attitude as the key factor when deciding upon the correct execution style, message structure, and design. These three characteristics ensure that both cognitive and emotional aspects of processing and attitude formation are addressed in the receiver of the message. The model is like a list to double check and know whether the creative execution results have characteristics that influence the target audience's attitude in the way expected.

 Illustrate how clients evaluate the creative work of their agencies and discuss guidelines for the evaluation and approval process.

Creative specialists are responsible for determining the creative strategy and tactics from the marketer's input. However, the client must review, evaluate, and approve the creative approach before any ads are produced or run. A number of criteria can be used by advertising managers, product or brand managers, and others involved in the promotional process to evaluate the advertising messages before approving final production.

Review Questions

1. Identify the difference between a message appeal and a creative execution style. Why is it important to make this distinction?
2. What is meant by a one-sided versus two-sided message? Discuss reasons why marketers may or may not want to use a two-sided message.
3. Are headlines more important for gaining attention or reinforcing awareness?
4. What are the similarities and differences of creative tactics across the four cells of the brand attitude grid of the R&P planning model?
5. Explain how the guidelines for creative evaluation can be applied to ads seen on the Internet.

Applied Questions

1. Look through ads in other chapters and figure out what execution style is used. Do the same for video ads found online.
2. What are the limitations of constructing standard print-format ads for Facebook and billboards?
3. Brands are experimenting with long-form video messages online. Using the design elements discussed in the chapter, contrast this approach with a standard 30-second TV ad. When would a brand use both within its IMC plan?
4. Find an ad for each of the four cells of the R&P framework for creative tactics. Identify the design elements that match the guidelines for each cell.
5. Apply the guidelines for creative evaluation to a campaign for Telus or Bell or Rogers, and conclude whether it fulfills all the criteria sufficiently.

© Chris Ryan/Age Fotostock

CHAPTER NINE

Measuring the Effectiveness of the Promotional Message

LEARNING OBJECTIVES

LO1 Identify the reasons for measuring promotional program effectiveness.

LO2 Describe the measures used in assessing promotional program effectiveness.

LO3 Evaluate alternative methods for measuring promotional program effectiveness.

LO4 Appraise the requirements of proper effectiveness research.

Ad Effectiveness Measurement

Advertising effectiveness measurement is a topic that confounds promotional planners, market researchers, agency personnel, and brand managers alike. Successful advertising seen in awards presentations like Cannes and CASSIES tends to document the resulting communication effects, behavioural influence, and subsequent impact on marketing objectives like sales or market share in addition to providing evidence of the unique creative approach of the message. However, ad effectiveness measurement is also concerned with research at all stages of the creative process so that advertisers can put together the right message prior to releasing it; managers prefer to avoid wasted media costs or wasted time and effort in the case of messages shown in free social media by testing consumer response ahead of time. The problem of figuring out ad effectiveness has remained over many decades; however the research methods have evolved, uncovering new insights.

One research avenue examines why consumers view online video messages (e.g., ads) and why they share the links. About half of all viewers of an online ad visit the brand's Internet site, with 11 percent forwarding the link, so the question of assessing ad effectiveness for digital messaging is similar to a research question that vexed TV advertisers for decades. The input for these messages ranges from digital communication agencies following established processes, to outsourcing to independent contractors (e.g., Tongal), to do-it-yourself activities (e.g., Blendtec). Right now, researchers are investigating how these different creative inputs are influencing ad effectiveness. Distributing the message follows similar outsourcing and do-it-yourself avenues, both of which are concerned with how long viewers watch the message, since online messages often go beyond the TV norm of 30 seconds.

Consumers receive messages from numerous touchpoints—digital through many devices, broadcast, and print media—to go along the various promotional efforts including in-store displays. Newer research looks at how all of these media contribute to the overall impact on the target audience, rather than at isolated influences of each. With unique messages arising from each of these media vehicles, researchers are concerned with both the delivery and the message content effects from all of the touchpoints. From a decision-making point of view, the research is integrated into the planning with a three-step process:

1. Attribution involves the combined and independent effects of each touchpoint.
2. Optimization runs what-if scenarios to consider different combinations of media and messages.
3. Allocation involves the instant adjustment of advertising dollars to the right media and message depending on the scenarios investigated.

From a message standpoint, research over the years has shown that more creative ads result in more focused attention while processing and improved communication effects in terms of stronger brand attitudes, however the link to purchase that aggregates to sales remains elusive. New research investigates different dimensions of creativity: originality, elaboration, synthesis, and artistic value. Originality implies "out of the ordinary" messages, uniqueness, and creative ideas departing from stereotypical thinking. Flexibility looks at different ideas, multiple subjects, and shifting ideas. Elaboration has numerous details, intricate ideas, and higher than expected details. Synthesis means unrelated objects, unusual connections, and bringing unusual things together. Artistic value is visually distinctive, ideas that come alive visually, and artistic production. Their conclusions found varying influences of each type and that elaboration has a stronger impact on sales. Moreover, originality tends to be important but it requires another creative characteristic to be fully influential.

Sources: Thales Teixeira, "How to Profit From Lean Advertising," *Harvard Business Review*, June 2013, pp. 23–25; Wes Nichols, "Advertising Analytics 2.0," *Harvard Business Review,* March 2013, pp. 60–68; Werner Reinartz and Peter Saffert, "Creativity in Advertising," *Harvard Business Review*, June 2013, pp. 106–112.

Question:

1. What part of advertising effectiveness do these research approaches measure?

Measuring the effectiveness of the promotional program is critical since it allows the marketing manager to assess the performance of specific program elements and provide input into the next period's situation analysis. We are concerned with evaluative research to measure the effectiveness of advertising and promotion and/or to assess various strategies and tactics before implementing them. This is not to be confused with planning research used to develop the promotional program, although the two can (and should) be used together.

In this chapter, we identify the reasons for measuring effectiveness. Next we describe key research decisions for evaluative research. Finally, we evaluate research methods and conclude with our IMC planning perspective to appraise the requirement for effectiveness research. Our primary focus is measuring the effects of advertising, because it is well established and other aspects of marketing communication have an advertisement-like message. Thus, most research techniques can be applied or have been adapted for other IMC tools. We highlight methods of measuring effectiveness for these tools in their respective chapters.

 # The Measuring Effectiveness Debate

Employees are generally given objectives to accomplish, and their job evaluations are based on achieving these objectives. Advertising and promotion should be held to the same standard where its performance is measured against the objectives established in the promotional plan, as indicated in Chapter 5. Although this may appear logical, some consider it debatable.

REASONS FOR MEASURING EFFECTIVENESS

Assessing the effectiveness of ads both before they are implemented and after the final versions have been completed and fielded offers a number of advantages.

Avoiding Costly Mistakes   Total advertising topped $14 billion in 2012, and any brand's advertising budget is often a substantial expenditure. Thus, if a program is not achieving its objectives, the marketing manager needs information to know how or where to spend money more effectively. The opportunity loss due to poor marketing communication is just as important. If the advertising and promotions program is not accomplishing its objectives, the potential gain that could result from an effective program is not realized, thereby minimizing the firm's return on its marketing investment.

Evaluating Alternative Strategies   Typically, a firm has a number of strategies under consideration, such as which medium should be used or whether one message is more effective than another. Or the decision may be between two promotional program elements: should money be spent on sponsorships or on advertising? Companies often test alternative versions of their advertising in different cities to determine which ad communicates most effectively. Thus, research may be designed to help the manager determine which strategy is most likely to be effective.

Increasing Advertising Efficiency   The expression "can't see the forest for the trees" is relevant here, since advertisers get so close to the project that they sometimes lose sight of their objectives. They may use technical jargon that not everyone is familiar with. Or the creative department may get too creative or too sophisticated and lose the meaning that needs to be communicated. Conducting research helps companies develop more efficient and effective communications. An increasing number of clients are demanding accountability for their promotional programs and putting more pressure on the agencies to produce.

Determining If Objectives Are Achieved   In a well designed IMC plan, specific communication objectives are established. If objectives are attained, new ones need to be established in the next planning period. An assessment of how program elements led to the attainment of the goals should take place, and/or reasons for less-than-desired achievements must be determined. Research should evaluate whether the strategy delivers the stated objectives and assess the appropriateness of the measures.[1]

REASONS FOR NOT MEASURING EFFECTIVENESS

Companies give a number of reasons for not measuring the effectiveness of advertising and promotion strategies.

Cost   A frequently cited reason for not testing is the expense; good research can be expensive in terms of both time and money. Managers decide that time is critical and they must implement the program while the opportunity is available. Further, money spent on research could go to improved ad production or additional media buys. While the first argument may have merit, the second does not. Imagine the results of a poor campaign that did not motivate the target audience; money would be wasted if the effects could do more harm than good. Spending more money to buy media does not remedy a poor message or substitute for an improper promotional mix.

Research Problems   A second reason cited for not measuring effectiveness is that it is difficult to isolate the effects of promotional elements. Each variable in the marketing mix affects the success of a product or service. Because it is rarely possible to measure the contribution of each marketing element directly, managers become frustrated and decide not to test at all. This argument also suffers from weak logic. While we agree that it is not always possible to determine the dollar amount of sales contributed by promotions, research can provide useful results. Communications effectiveness can be measured and may carry over to sales.

Disagreement on What to Test   The objectives sought in the promotional program may differ by industry, by stage of the product life cycle, or even for different people within the firm. The sales manager may want to see the impact of promotions on sales, top management may wish to know the impact on corporate image, and those involved in the creative process may wish to assess recall and/or recognition of the ad. However, with the proper design, many or even all of the above might be measured. Since every promotional element is designed to accomplish its own objectives, research can be used to measure its effectiveness in doing so.

Objections of Creative Specialists   The marketing manager is ultimately responsible for the success of the product or brand. Given the substantial sums being allocated to advertising and promotion, it is the manager's right, and responsibility, to know how well a specific program, or a specific ad, will perform in the market. However, an age-old industry issue is that creative specialists do not want their work to be tested. They feel that tests are not true measures of ad creativity and effectiveness: applying measures stifles their creativity, and creative ads are more likely to be successful. They want permission to be creative without any limiting guidelines.

 # Decisions for Measuring Effectiveness

We now describe the decisions for measuring the communication effects of advertising. This section considers what elements to evaluate, as well as when and where such evaluations should occur. We cover the issue of how to measure in the next section.

WHAT TO TEST

The focus of the testing is mostly on the creative strategy and creative tactics decisions that the advertiser makes while putting a campaign together for advertising and all IMC tools.

Creative Strategy Decisions   The primary creative strategy decision—the creative theme—can be tested. When a company decides to change its theme or is planning to launch an unusual attention-getting approach, it may want to see the reactions of the target audience prior to investing in the media placement. Similarly, different message appeals can be tested (i.e., rational versus emotional), or different versions of one appeal can be tested. Finally, another important question is whether the spokesperson being used is effective and how the target audience will respond to him or her. A product spokesperson may be an excellent source initially but, owing to a variety of reasons, may lose impact over time in terms of attractiveness or likeability. Thus, all major creative strategy decisions can be tested. IMC Perspective 9-1 summarizes research regarding emotional reactions to creative strategy decisions.

Creative Tactics Decisions   Different execution styles displayed on storyboards can be presented to members of the target audience in focus groups for their reaction. The message structure can be looked at, such as reading the body copy in an interview or another method. Specific design elements, such as the music in a television ad or the headline of a print ad, can also be the focus of research. Overall, advertisers use a variety of research methods to test essentially any creative tactic that they are unsure about or that requires confirmation.

Other Promotional Tools   The other tools we will discuss in this book have an associated creative or message. Many sales promotions have a visual as well as an advertising-like message that reinforces the brand position. Similarly, firms use many creative tactics to gain the attention of media personnel so that their story will obtain exposure through publicity. Thus, while we have examined the creative in the context of advertising, as we noted previously all the decisions are relevant in the other promotional tools, and as expected the same research is possible if the advertiser believes it to be necessary. We review a few specifics in each of the subsequent chapters to measure the effectiveness of other promotional tools.

IMC PERSPECTIVE 9-1

AD EFFECTIVENESS MEASUREMENT THROUGH EMOTIONAL RESEARCH

Imagine sitting in an office wondering how consumers would react to new ads shown as storyboards developed by an advertising agency. Or perhaps consider whether the completed print ads should be placed in magazines for the next campaign. For that matter, if managers are wondering about *any* message to be delivered across any or multiple media, how or what evaluation should be implemented to ensure success? Many approaches toward effectiveness tend to measure consumer knowledge in terms of brand recall or recognition, advertising recall or recognition, and rational thoughts connected to the brand. One promising development involves researchers getting a better read on consumer emotions through a variety of methods.

© Monkey Business Images/Shutterstock

The interest in emotional effects of marketing communication is derived from recent research indicating how intertwined cognition and affect are during human decision making, how and when we process information, and to what extent we remember brand information. At the heart of this is research suggesting that the brain has an intuitive system for making decisions automatically, and another system that rationalizes the intuitive decisions or overrules them so that people will appear more rational. The conclusion of this is that much of decision making is much more emotionally driven than expected, and that our emotional decisions are supported or refuted rationally. From an advertising standpoint, subtle cues in a message can influence emotionally such that consumers automatically prefer aspects of an ad, and quite possibly the brand, as shown in the Chapter 4 models.

Assessing ad effectiveness along the lines of emotional responses is an elusive goal. Typically, consumers have difficulty expressing their emotional attachment to a brand, as they often convey their brand usage in relation to product attributes or benefits. Moreover, self-report measurement through pictorial scales, standard Likert-type scales, and open-ended questions always proves challenging due to validity concerns. Some people express emotions globally while others are more specific, and the very nature of asking about emotions is filtered through the carefully thought out cognitive reply. In short, assessing emotional reactions to ads is a significant measurement issue.

Communication researchers conclude that multiple approaches are warranted. In this case, they suggest three methods to perform data comparisons and make better conclusions so message development can occur. First, in their research they used electrodermal activity, which measures the electrical impulses of the viewer's sympathetic nervous system that are conducted by the perspiration on their skin. Second, they advocate for continuous rating data that viewers indicate with a dial-like joystick throughout the message exposure. The tool allows the respondent to indicate positive or negative feelings easily as they view a message. Third, the standard self-report measures are encouraged for a basis of comparative assessment. Data from their study indicated that all three measurement approaches provided unique and complementary information such that they conclude that one method should not be used, but rather communication planners should consider multiple methods.

Sources: Diana Lucaci, "Emotion vs Logic: How Do You Decide," *Strategy*, March 4, 2014; "Nothing More Than Feelings," *The Economist*, December 7, 2013; Sarah Evans and Joy Hackenbracht, "Implicit Measurement of Emotion Improves Utility of Concept Testing," *Alert Magazine*, Fourth Quarter 2014.

Questions:

1. Why are advertisers so concerned with measuring emotions?

2. Should promotional planners measure emotional responses for other IMC tools, such as sales promotions or direct response?

WHEN TO TEST

Virtually all test measures can be classified according to when they are conducted. **Pretests** are measures taken before the campaign is implemented; **posttests** occur after media exposure of the ad or commercial. Figure 9-1 classifies the pretests and posttests that are available to the marketer, each with its own methodology designed to measure an aspect of the advertising program.

Figure 9-1   Classification of testing methods

Pretests	Lab	Field
Concept	Concept tests	
Rough/copy/commercial	Rough tests	Comprehension tests Reaction tests
	Consumer juries	
Finished print ads	Portfolio	
	Readability	
Finished TV ads	Theatre	
	Physiological	On-air
Posttests		
Finished print ads in magazines		Inquiry tests
		Recognition tests
		Recall tests
		Tracking studies
Finished TV ads on-air		Recall tests
		Comprehensive measures
		Test marketing
		Single-source
		Tracking studies

Pretesting   Pretests may occur at a number of points in the creative process, from as early on as idea generation to rough execution to testing the final version before implementing it. In addition, testing could occur at more than one point in time. For example, concept testing may occur at the earliest development of the ad or commercial, when little more than an idea, basic concept, or positioning statement is under consideration. Later on, layouts of the ad campaign that include headlines, body copy, and rough illustrations are tested along with storyboards and animatics.

The advantage of pretesting is that feedback is relatively inexpensive. Any problems with the concept or the way it is to be delivered are identified before large amounts of money are spent in development. Sometimes more than one version of the ad is evaluated to determine which is most likely to be effective. Since pretesting is generally cheaper than making a mistake public without pretesting, it certainly makes sense to pretest.

The disadvantage is that mock-ups, storyboards, or animatics may not communicate nearly as effectively as the final product. The mood-enhancing and/or emotional aspects of the message are very difficult to communicate in this format. Another disadvantage is time delays. Many marketers believe being first in the market offers them a distinct advantage over competitors, so they forgo research to save time and ensure this position.

Posttesting   In contrast to pretesting, posttesting occurs after placing the marketing communication in a media like broadcast or print, or another communication tool if needed. Posttesting is designed to (1) determine if the campaign is accomplishing the objectives sought and (2) serve as input into the next period's situation analysis. A variety of posttest measures are available, most of which involve survey research promothods.

WHERE TO TEST

In addition to when to test, decisions must be made as to *where*. These tests may take place in either laboratory or field settings.

Laboratory Tests   In **laboratory tests**, people go to a particular location and are shown ads and/or commercials. The testers either ask questions about them or measure participants' responses by other methods (e.g., pupil dilation, eye tracking, galvanic skin response).

The major advantage of the lab setting is *research control*—changes in copy, illustration, formats, or colours can be manipulated inexpensively and the differential impact of each assessed. This makes it much easier for the researcher to isolate the communication effects of each factor.

The major disadvantage is the lack of *realism* that results in **testing bias**. When people go to a lab (even if it has been designed to look like a living room), they may scrutinize the ads more closely than they would at home. A second problem with this lack of realism is that it cannot duplicate the natural viewing situation, complete with the distractions or comforts of home. Looking at ads in a lab setting may not be the same as viewing at home, though testing techniques have made progress in correcting this deficiency. Overall, the control advantage of lab tests probably outweighs the testing bias.

Field Tests   **Field tests** are evaluations of the ad in natural viewing situations, complete with the realism of noise, distractions, and the comforts of home. Field tests account for the effects of repetition, program content, and the presence of competitive messages.

The major disadvantage of field tests is the lack of control. It may be impossible to isolate causes of viewers' evaluations. If atypical events occur during the test, they may bias the results. Field tests usually take more time and money to conduct, so the results are not available to be acted on quickly. Thus, realism is gained at the expense of other important factors. It is up to the researcher to determine which trade-offs to make.

 # Methods of Measuring Effectiveness

Testing may occur at various points throughout the development of an ad or a campaign: (1) concept generation research, (2) rough, prefinished art, copy, and/or commercial testing, (3) finished art or commercial pretesting, and (4) market testing of ads or commercials (posttesting). In this section, we describe methods used for each of these four stages.

CONCEPT GENERATION AND TESTING

Figure 9-2 describes the process involved in advertising **concept testing**, which is conducted early in the campaign development process to evaluate the targeted audience's response to a potential ad or campaign, or alternative advertising strategies. Positioning statements, copy, headlines, and/or illustrations may all be under scrutiny. The material shown is a rough sketch of the ad or a description of a storyboard.

Figure 9-2   Concept testing

Objective:	Explores consumers' responses to various ad concepts as expressed in words, pictures, or symbols.
Method:	Alternative concepts are exposed to consumers who match the characteristics of the target audience. Reactions and evaluations of each are sought through a variety of methods, including focus groups, direct questioning, and survey completion. Sample sizes vary depending on the number of concepts to be presented and the consensus of responses.
Output:	Qualitative and/or quantitative data evaluating and comparing alternative concepts.

A commonly used method for concept testing is a focus group, usually consisting of 8–10 people who are within the ad's target audience. For most companies, the focus group is the first step in the research process. The number of focus groups used varies depending on group consensus, strength of response, and/or the degree to which participants like or dislike the concepts. In general, about 10 are usually needed to test a concept sufficiently. Participants freely discuss the meanings they get from the ads, consider the relative advantages of alternatives, and even suggest improvements or additional themes. They may also be asked to evaluate the ad on a series of rating scales.

The methodology is attractive to marketers since results are easily obtained, directly observable, and immediate. A variety of topics can be examined, and consumers are free to go into depth in any important areas. Also, focus groups don't require quantitative analysis and are more easily accepted and interpreted by managers. Online focus groups (Exhibit 9-1) provide time and cost efficiencies, and their data can be combined with face-to-face focus groups' results. Weaknesses with focus groups are shown in Figure 9-3.

Exhibit 9-1   Online focus groups are used for concept testing.

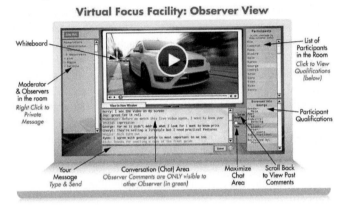

Image provided by InsideHeads.com, conducting online focus groups since 1998

Figure 9-3   Weaknesses associated with focus group research

- The results are not quantifiable.
- Sample sizes are too small to generalize to larger populations.
- Group influences may bias participants' responses.
- One or two members of the group may steer the conversation or dominate the discussion.
- Consumers become instant "experts."
- Members may not represent the target audience.
- Results may be taken to be more representative and/or definitive than they really are.

Another means of gathering consumers' opinions of concepts is to use mall intercepts. Researchers approach consumers who are shopping and ask them to evaluate rough ads and/or copy. Rather than participating in a group discussion, individuals assess the ads via questionnaires that have rating scales, and/or ranking scales to obtain more quantitative descriptive data. Similar individual testing via the Internet occurs as advertisers are able to show concepts simultaneously to consumers throughout Canada to obtain data that can be analyzed almost instantaneously.

ROUGH ART, COPY, AND COMMERCIAL TESTING

Because of the high cost associated with the production of an ad or commercial, advertisers spend more on testing a rendering of the final ad at early stages. Slides of the artwork posted on a screen or animatic and photomatic **rough tests** may be used at this stage. See Figure 9-4 for an explanation of terminology. Rough tests must indicate how the finished commercial would perform, and provide accurate information at a reasonable cost. Past studies demonstrated that these testing methods are reliable and the results typically correlate well with the finished ad.[2] Most of the tests conducted at the rough stage involve lab settings. Popular tests include comprehension and reaction tests and consumer juries.

Figure 9-4   Rough testing terminology

A rough commercial is an unfinished execution that may fall into three broad categories:

1. Animatic Rough

Succession of drawings/cartoons

Rendered artwork

Still frames

Simulated movement: Panning/zooming of frame/rapid sequence

2. Photomatic Rough

Succession of photographs

Real people/scenery

Still frames

Simulated movements: Panning/zooming of frame/rapid sequence

3. Live-Action Rough

Live motion

Stand-in/nonunion talent

Nonunion crew

Limited props/minimal opticals

Location settings

A Finished Commercial Uses

Live motion/animation

Highly paid union talent

Full union crew

Exotic props/studio sets/special effects

Comprehension and Reaction Tests   One concern for the advertiser is whether the message conveys the meaning intended. The second concern is the reaction the ad generates. Obviously, the advertiser does not want an ad that evokes a negative reaction or offends someone. **Comprehension and reaction tests** are designed to assess these responses. Tests of comprehension and reaction employ no one standard procedure. Personal interviews, group interviews, and focus groups have all been used for this purpose, and sample sizes vary according to the needs of the client; they typically range from 50 to 200 respondents.

Consumer Juries   This method uses consumers representative of the target audiences to evaluate the probable success of an ad. **Consumer juries** rate a selection of layouts or copy versions presented in paste-ups on separate sheets. The objectives sought and methods employed in consumer juries are shown in Figure 9-5.

Figure 9-5   Consumer juries

Objective: Potential viewers (consumers) are asked to peruse ads and give their reactions and evaluation. When two or more ads are tested, viewers are usually asked to rate or rank order the ads according to their preferences.

Method: Respondents are asked to view ads and rate them according to either (1) the order of merit method or (2) the paired comparison method. In the former, the respondent is asked to view

[Continued on next page]

[Figure 9-5 continued]

	the ads, then rank them from one to *n* according to their perceived merit. In the latter, ads are compared only two at a time. Each ad is compared to every other ad in the group, and the winner is listed. The best ad is that which wins the most times. Consumer juries typically employ 50 to 100 participants.
Output:	An overall reaction to each ad under construction as well as a rank ordering of the ads based on the viewers' perceptions.

While the jury method offers the advantages of control and cost effectiveness, serious flaws in the methodology limit its usefulness.

- *Self-appointed expert.* One jury method benefit is the objectivity and involvement that the targeted consumer can bring to the evaluation process. However, knowing they are being asked to critique ads, participants sometimes become more expert in their evaluations by paying more attention and being more critical than usual. The result may be an evaluation on elements other than those intended.

- *Number of ads evaluated.* Whether order of merit or paired comparison methods are used, the ranking procedure becomes tedious as the number of alternatives increases. Consider the ranking of 10 ads. While the top two and the bottom two may very well reveal differences, those ranked in the middle may not yield much useful information. In the paired comparison method, 15 evaluations are required for six alternatives. As the number of ads increases, the task becomes even more unmanageable.

- *Halo effect.* Participants may rate an ad as good (bad) on all characteristics because they like (dislike) a few and overlook specific weaknesses (strengths). This tendency, called the **halo effect**, distorts the ratings and defeats the ability to control for specific components.

- *Preferences overshadow objectivity.* Ads that involve emotions or pictures may receive higher ratings or rankings than those employing copy, facts, and/or rational criteria. Even though the latter are often more effective in the marketplace, they may be judged less favourably by jurists who prefer emotional appeals.

Problems noted here can be remedied by the use of ratings scales instead of rankings, but ratings are not always valid either. Thus, while consumer juries have been used for years, questions of bias have led researchers to doubt their validity.

PRETESTING OF FINISHED ADS

At this stage, a finished advertisement or commercial is used; changes can still be made since it has not been presented to the market. Many researchers believe testing the ad in final form provides better information. Several test procedures are available for print and broadcast ads, including both laboratory and field methodologies. Print methods include portfolio tests, analyses of readability, and diagnostic measures. Broadcast tests include theatre tests and on-air tests. Both print and broadcast may use physiological measures.

Pretesting Finished Print Messages   A number of methods for pretesting finished print ads are available. One is described in Figure 9-6. The most common of these methods are portfolio tests, readability tests, and dummy advertising vehicles.

Figure 9-6   Gallup & Robinson's impact system

Objective:	Understand the performance of newspaper or magazine ad executions.
Method:	Interviewers contact respondents door to door or by telephone and screen for qualification.
Output:	Scores include recall, idea communication, persuasion, brand rating, and ad liking. Diagnostics regarding ad reactions and brand attributes are reported.

Portfolio Tests   **Portfolio tests** are a laboratory methodology designed to expose a group of respondents to a portfolio consisting of both control and test ads. Respondents are then asked what information they recall from the ads. The assumption is that the ads that yield the highest recall are the most effective.

Portfolio tests compare alternative ads directly but have two weaknesses that limit their applicability. First, factors other than advertising creativity and/or presentation may affect recall. Interest in the product or product category, the fact that respondents know they are participating in a test, or interviewer instructions may account for more differences than the ad itself. Second, for certain products (those of low involvement) and brands, the ability to recognize the ad when shown may be a better measure than recall.

Readability Tests   The communication efficiency of the body copy in a print ad can be tested with the **Flesch formula** to assess its readability by determining the average number of syllables per 100 words. Human interest, appeal of the material, length of sentences, and familiarity with certain words are also considered and correlated with the educational background of target audiences. Test results are compared to previously established norms for different target audiences. The test suggests that copy is best comprehended when sentences are short, words are concrete and familiar, and personal references are drawn.

This method eliminates many of the interviewee biases associated with other tests and avoids gross errors in understanding. The norms offer an attractive standard for comparison. Disadvantages are also inherent, however. The copy may become too mechanical, and direct input from the receiver is not available. Without this input, contributing elements like creativity cannot be addressed. To be effective, this test should be used only in conjunction with other pretesting methods.

Diagnostic Measures   While above methods are available, their limitations can be overcome by print ad pretesting involving a series of measures. The tests can be used for rough and/or finished ads and are most commonly conducted in the respondents' homes, enabling the researcher to collect multiple measures from many samples. For example, Millward-Brown's link copy test includes measures of emotional responses to ads, assessing metrics such as enjoyment, engagement, likes, and dislikes to address overall emotional response. Ipsos-ASI's methodology also offers multiple measures, as shown in Figure 9-7, and this approach is adapted for assessing online print ads as well.

Figure 9-7   Ipsos-ASI's Next*Print

Objective:	To assist advertisers in copy testing of print advertisements to determine (1) main idea communication, (2) likes and dislikes, (3) believability, (4) ad attribute ratings, (5) overall likability, and (6) brand attribute ratings.
Method:	Tests are conducted in current issues of newsstand magazines. The recall measure consists of 150 responses. Diagnostic measures range from 105 to 150 responses. Highly targeted audiences are available through a version known as the Targeted Print Test.
Output:	Standard scores and specific diagnostics.

Pretesting Finished Broadcast Ads   A variety of methods for pretesting rough and/or broadcast ads are available, such as theatre tests, on-air tests, and physiological measures. Research firms who perform TV testing have expanded for online testing of video messages.

Theatre Tests   In the past, one laboratory method for pretesting finished commercials was **theatre testing**. Participants are invited to view pilots of proposed TV programs. In some instances, the show is actually being tested, but more commonly a standard program is used so that audience responses can be compared with normative responses established by previous viewers. Sample sizes range from 250 to 600 participants. Variations of this method (Figure 9-8) allow for viewing in more convenient locations (e.g., home, office, mall, hotel), with more consumer-friendly data collection devices so the data can be tabulated in manager-friendly reports (Exhibit 9-2).

Figure 9-8   The Ad*Vantage/ACT theatre methodology

AD*VANTAGE/ACT surveys are based on tests carried out in a studio. The number of respondents is typically about *n* = 125, normally composed of category users defined by the client. Each participant is shown a TV program, with commercial breaks that include the test commercial, and then asked questions about the program. The closed- and open-ended questions are recorded via a touch-screen system. Key measures include (1) visibility (Will the commercial be remembered?); (2) branding (Will the brand be remembered?); (3) communications (What visuals and messages will be remembered?); (4) brand enhancement (Does the ad promote a positive feeling toward the brand?); and (5) persuasion (Will the commercial inspire non-users to try the product, and will it enhance brand loyalty among existing customers?). The diagnostics include measures of viewers' awareness, comprehension, uniqueness, and involvement of the commercial. The methodology also allows for scene-by-scene analysis, and can be used to test all traditional forms of advertising as well as digital.

Theatre tests have three notable disadvantages. (1) The environment is artificial, and wiring people for physiological responses takes them too far from a natural viewing situation. (2) The contrived measure of brand preference change seems too phony to believe. Critics contend that participants will see through it and make changes just because they think they are supposed to. (3) The group effect of having others present and overtly exhibiting their reactions may influence viewers who did not have any reactions themselves.

In contrast, theatre tests' three advantages are (1) strong experimental control, (2) that established norms (averages of commercials' performances) indicate how one's commercial will fare against others in the same product class tested previously, and (3) that brand preference measure is supported by actual sales results.

On-Air Tests   Firms conducting theatre tests also may insert the commercials into actual TV programs in certain test markets. Typically, the commercials are in finished form. This is referred to as an on-air test and often includes single-source ad research (discussed later in this chapter). On-air pretesting of finished commercials offers distinct advantages over lab methods, and the realistic test gives an indication of the ad's success when launched. Information Resources, Ipsos-ASI, MSW Group, and Nielsen are well known providers of on-air tests.

Exhibit 9-2   Ad*vantage/Act reports provide detailed analysis of a theatre test.

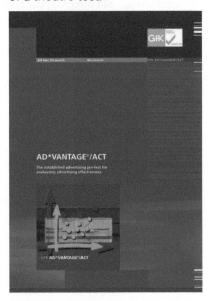

Courtesy of GfK

The most commonly employed metric used in an on-air test is recall—that is, the number of persons able to recall the ad and/or its message. In an examination of real-world advertising tests, one study concludes that recall and persuasion pretests, while often employed, do not fare well in respect to reliability and/or validity. Nevertheless, most of the testing services have offered evidence of both validity and reliability for on-air pretesting of commercials. Both Ipsos-ASI and MSW Group claim their pretest and posttest results yield the same recall scores nine out of 10 times—a strong indication of reliability and a good predictor of the effect the ad is likely to have when shown to the population as a whole. Whether the measures used are as strong an indication as the providers say still remains in question.[3]

Physiological Measures   A less common method of pretesting finished commercials involves measuring physiological responses. These measures indicate the receiver's *involuntary* response (e.g., heartbeat, reflexes.) to the ad, theoretically eliminating biases associated with the voluntary measures reviewed to this point. The particular physiological measures used to test both print and broadcast ads include pupil dilation, galvanic skin response, eye tracking, and brain waves.

Pupil dilation. Research in **pupillometrics** is designed to measure dilation and constriction of the pupils of the eyes in response to stimuli. Dilation is associated with action; constriction involves the body's conservation of energy. Pupil dilation suggests a stronger interest in (or preference for) an ad or implies arousal or attention-getting capabilities. Other attempts to determine the affective (liking or disliking) responses created by ads have met with less success. Because of high costs and methodological problems, the use of pupillometrics has waned over the past decade, but it can be useful in evaluating certain aspects of advertising.

Galvanic skin response (GSR). Also known as **electrodermal response** (EDR), GSR measures the skin's resistance or conductance to a small amount of current passed between two electrodes. Response to a stimulus activates sweat glands, which in turn increases the conductance of the electrical current. Thus, GSR/EDR activity might reflect a reaction to advertising. A review of research in this area concluded that GSR/EDR (1) is sensitive to affective stimuli, (2) may present a picture of attention, (3) may be useful to measure long-term advertising recall, and (4) is useful in measuring ad effectiveness.[4] Another study concluded that GSR is an effective measure and is useful, yet underused, for measuring affect, or liking, for ads.[5]

Eye tracking. A commonly employed methodology is **eye tracking** (Figure 9-9), in which viewers are asked to view an ad while a sensor aims a beam of infrared light at the eye. The beam follows the movement of the eye and shows the exact spot on which the viewer is focusing. The continuous reading of responses demonstrates which elements of the ad are attracting attention, how long the viewer is focusing on them, and the sequence in which they are being viewed. Measurement of Internet advertising has adapted many approaches and eye-tracking has received considerable usage.

Figure 9-9   Eye movement research

Objective:	Tracks viewers' eye movements to determine what viewers read or view in print ads and where their attention is focused in TV commercials, Internet sites, or billboards.
Method:	Fibre optics, digital data processing, and advanced electronics are used to follow eye movements of viewers and/or readers as they process an ad.
Output:	Relationship among what readers see, recall, and comprehend. Scan paths on print ads, billboards, commercials, print materials, and Internet sites.

Eye tracking can identify strengths and weaknesses in an ad. For example, attractive models or background action may distract the viewer's attention away from the brand or product being advertised. The advertiser can remedy this distraction before fielding the ad. In other instances, colours or illustrations may attract attention and create viewer interest in the ad. Eye tracking research is applied to all types of traditional media, outdoor, and Internet, as shown in Exhibit 9-3.

Brain waves. Electroencephalographic (EEG) measures can be taken from the skull to determine electrical frequencies in the brain. EEG research attracted the interest of academic researchers and is now the focus of specialized market research organizations, as shown in IMC Perspective 9-2. The electrical impulses are used in three areas of research: alpha waves, hemispheric lateralization, and indirect methods.

Exhibit 9-3   Eye-tracking is a more commonly used research method.

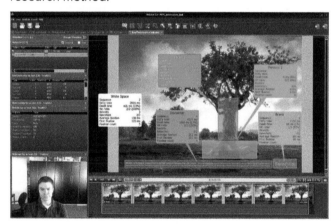

Courtesy of SensoMotoric Instruments (SMI)

- **Alpha activity** refers to the degree of brain activation. People are in an alpha state when they are inactive, resting, or sleeping. The theory is that a person in an alpha state is less likely to be processing information (recall correlates negatively with alpha levels), and that attention and processing require moving from this state. By measuring a subject's alpha level while viewing a commercial, researchers can assess the degree to which attention and processing are likely to occur.

- **Hemispheric lateralization** distinguishes between alpha activity in the left and right sides of the brain. It has been hypothesized that the right side of the brain processes visual stimuli and the left processes verbal stimuli. The right hemisphere is thought to respond more to emotional stimuli, while the left responds to logic. The right determines recognition, while the left is responsible for recall.[6] If these hypotheses are correct, advertisers could design ads to increase learning and memory by creating stimuli to appeal to each hemisphere. However, some researchers believe the brain does not function laterally, and an ad cannot be designed to appeal to one side or the other.

- **Indirect methods** use technologies originally designed for the medical field, such as positron emission tomography (PET) and functional magnetic resonance imaging (fMRI). Neuroscientists have teamed up with marketers to examine physiological reactions to ads and brands through brain scan imaging. PET tracks changes in metabolism while fMRI tracks blood flow, and both provide an indirect measure of brain activity. By monitoring the brain activity, scientists are learning how consumers make up their minds by measuring chemical activity and/or changes in the magnetic fields of the brain as well as how they react to commercials.

MARKET TESTING OF ADS

The fact that the ad and/or campaign has been implemented does not mean there is no longer a need for testing. The pretests were conducted on smaller samples and may have questionable merit, so the marketer must find out how the ad is doing in the field. In this section, we discuss methods for posttesting an ad. Some of the tests are similar to the pretests discussed in the previous section and are provided by the same companies.

Posttests of Print Ads   A variety of print posttests are available, including inquiry tests, recognition tests, and recall tests.

Inquiry Tests   Marketers use **inquiry tests** to measure advertising effectiveness on the basis of target audience contact that is generated from ads appearing in print media. The inquiry may be the number of coupons returned, phone calls generated, or completion of reader cards. Digital inquiries would include emails and social media communication like questions posed on Twitter or Facebook. This is a very simple measure of the ad's or medium's effectiveness; more complex methods may involve (1) running the ad in successive issues of the same medium, (2) running **split-run tests**, in which variations of the ad appear in different copies of the same newspaper or magazine, and/or (3) running the same ad in different media. Each of these methods yields information on different aspects of the strategy. The first measures the cumulative effects of the campaign; the second examines specific elements of the ad or variations on it. The final method measures the effectiveness of the medium rather than the ad itself.

While inquiry tests may yield useful information, weaknesses in this methodology limit its effectiveness. For example, inquiries may not be a true measure of the attention-getting or information-providing aspects of the ad. The reader may be attracted to an ad, read it, and even store the information but not be motivated to inquire at that particular time. Time constraints, lack of a need for the product or service at the time the ad is run, and other factors may limit the number of inquiries. But receiving a small number of inquiries doesn't mean the ad was not effective; attention, attitude change, awareness, and recall of copy points may all have been achieved. At the other extreme, a person with a particular need for the product may respond to any ad for it, regardless of specific qualities of the ad.

IMC PERSPECTIVE 9-2

AD EFFECTIVENESS MEASUREMENT THROUGH TECHNOLOGICAL RESEARCH

In the constant quest to determine the effectiveness of advertising, marketers have turned to MRI machines and heart rate monitors along with changes in the skin and facial muscles to examine physiological responses to advertising messages. The use of neurosciences via an electroencephalography (EEG) machine to test commercials is now both an effective and an efficient option for many advertisers. The methodology places a headset with electrode sensors on people and records their brain waves every two milliseconds while they are watching video messages. Resulting data output indicates at which point in the ad the brain is most active. Measurement involves attention, cognitive responses, emotional responses, and encoding to memory that indicates the development of branded communication effects. Brainsights of Toronto and Neurometrics of Montreal are two market research firms specializing in the application of this technology that provides guidance to marketers looking to adjust their ads.

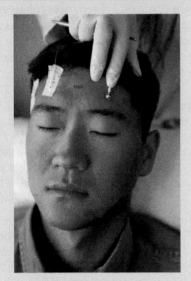
© annedde/Getty Images

An example of a successful application is Brainsight's work with TSN Sportscentre and Molson Coors. The ad tested showed scenes of the on-air personalities bantering about who would win the office fantasy football pool. Encouraging viewers to join the pool appeared to be the most logical objective of the message. The initial version of the ad showed Kate Beirness as the victor with her confident and ambitious approach to go along with her good looks that expectedly would sway the target of 19- to 34-year-old males. However, testing proved otherwise, as viewers preferred Cabbie Richards to win the contest. He came across as an underdog who worked hard and put together a solid roster of players who unfortunately suffered challenges due to injuries, and he proved to be a more appealing winner. The reasoning suggested that younger viewers had stronger emotional responses to Cabbie since they liked stories of individuals unexpectedly succeeding in the face of obstacles. In contrast, the data indicated that Kate appeared to be an entertaining character in the story, but Cabbie's anguish captured the spirit of the pool more accurately.

There are other applications. Research that looks at whether multinational brands should consider locally produced creative messages or use repurposed global creatives is instructive to find the balance across message and whether differences may exist in certain product categories. Research into whether viral ads actually influence brand attitude and brand purchase intention is useful as shared video links may be more indicative of the ads being entertaining but doing little for marketing or branding purposes.

In the case of Neurometric, which worked with the dairy cooperative Natrel, the research tested the product name, a billboard message, and the slogan. The English version of the slogan "Make every day more delicious" appeared fine, but the French version used the word "vachement" meaning "really" instead of the equivalent translation of "more" which would be "plus." Research indicated that respondents keyed on the beginning part of the word—"vache," meaning "cow"—so the French ad slogan changed the word to the exact translation of the English slogan. Neurometric's research is now affordable at about $15,000/study and the online execution makes it very convenient for respondents to participate. A simple download of a Java app makes responding to the print messages as easy as completing an online survey.

Sources: Mark Burgess, "Montreal Firm Takes Neuro-Marketing Online," *Strategy*, January 27, 2016; Jeff Fraser, "Neuro-Marketing Start-Up Plans Brain Experiment of DX3," *Marketing Magazine*, March 10, 2015; Hollie Shaw, "Looking Inside Your Brain," *National Post*, April 18, 2015, p. FP6; Susan Krashinsky, 'Neuro-Marketing Takes Aim at the Mind," *Globe and Mail*, March 6, 2015, p. B7.

Question:

1. Express your feelings on whether you would volunteer as a respondent to this kind of research.

Major advantages of inquiry tests are that they are inexpensive to implement and they provide feedback with respect to the general effectiveness of the ad or medium used. But they are usually not very effective for comparing different versions or specific creative aspects of an ad.

Recognition Tests A common posttest of print ads is the **recognition method**, most closely associated with Roper ASW. The Starch Ad Readership Report lets the advertiser assess the impact of an ad in a single issue of a magazine, over time, and/or across different magazines (see Figure 9-10). Starch claims that (1) the pulling power of the ad can be assessed through the control offered, (2) the effectiveness of competitors' ads can be compared through the norms provided, (3) alternative ad executions can be tested, and (4) readership scores are a useful indication of consumers' involvement in the ad or campaign. The theory is that a reader must read and become involved in the ad before the ad can communicate. To the degree that this readership can be shown, it is a direct indication of effectiveness. An example of a Starch scored ad is shown in Exhibit 9-4.

Exhibit 9-4 A Starch rating scale for an Absolut ad.

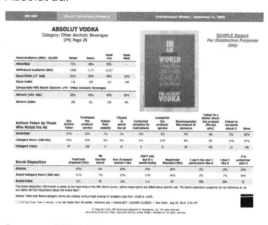

Courtesy of GfK MRI Starch Advertising Research

Figure 9-10   The Starch Ad Readership Report

Objective:	Determining recognition of print ads and providing insight into the involvement readers have with specific ads.
Method:	Personal interviewers screen readers for qualifications and determine exposure and readership. Samples include a minimum of 200 males and females, as well as specific audiences where required. Participants are asked to go through the magazines, look at the ads, and provide specific responses.
Output:	Starch Ad Readership Reports generate three recognition scores: • Noted score—the percentage of readers who remember seeing the ad. • Brand-associated score—the percentage of readers who recall seeing or reading any part of the ad identifying the product or brand. • Read-most score—the percentage of readers who report reading at least half of the copy portion of the ad.

Researchers have criticized the Starch recognition method (and other recognition measures) on the basis of false claiming, interviewer sensitivities, and unreliable scores.

False claiming. Research shows that in recognition tests, respondents may claim to have seen an ad when they did not. False claims may be a result of having seen similar ads elsewhere, expecting that such an ad would appear in the medium, or wanting to please the questioner. Interest in the product category also increases reporting of ad readership. Whether this false claiming is deliberate or not, it leads to an overreporting of effectiveness. On the flip side, factors such as interview fatigue may lead to an underreporting bias—that is, respondents do not report an ad that they did see.

Interviewer sensitivities. Whenever research involves interviewers, there is a potential for bias. Respondents may want to impress the interviewer or fear looking unknowledgeable if they continually claim not to recognize an ad. There may also be variances associated with interviewer instructions, recordings, and so on, regardless of the amount of training and sophistication involved.

Reliability of recognition scores. Starch admits that the reliability and validity of its readership scores increase with the number of insertions tested, which essentially means that to test just one ad on a single exposure may not produce valid or reliable results.

Recall Tests   The best-known tests to measure recall of print ads are the Ipsos-ASI Next*Print test and the Gallup & Robinson Magazine Impact Research Service (MIRS) (described in Figure 9-11). These **recall tests** are similar to those discussed in the section on pretesting broadcast ads, as they attempt to measure recall of specific ads.

Figure 9-11   Gallup & Robinson Magazine Impact Research Service

Objective:	Tracking recall of advertising (and client's ads) appearing in magazines to assess performance and effectiveness.
Method:	Test magazines are placed in participants' homes and respondents are asked to read the magazine that day. A telephone interview is conducted the second day to assess recall of ads, recall of copy points, and consumers' impressions of the ads. Sample size is 150 people.
Output:	Three measurement scores are provided: 1. Proven name registration—the percentage of respondents who can accurately recall the ad. 2. Idea communication—the number of sales points the respondents can recall. 3. Favourable buying attitude—the extent of favourable purchase reaction to the brand or corporation.

In addition to having the same interviewer problems as recognition tests, recall tests have other disadvantages. The reader's degree of involvement with the product and/or the distinctiveness of the appeals and visuals may lead to higher-than-accurate recall scores, although in general the method may lead to lower levels of recall than actually exist. Critics contend the test is not strong enough to reflect recall accurately, so many ads may score as less effective than they really are, and advertisers may abandon or modify them needlessly.

On the plus side, it is thought that recall tests can assess the ad's impact on memory. Proponents of recall tests say the major concern is not the results themselves but how they are interpreted. Studies have shown that the correlation between recall and recognition is very high for print ads.[7]

Posttests of Broadcast Commercials   The most common methods for posttesting broadcast commercials include a combination of day-after recall tests, comprehensive measures, test marketing, and two types of tracking studies.

Day-After Recall (DAR) Tests   This test asks questions over the phone to assess whether a respondent could recall seeing an ad on a TV show from the previous day they claimed to have seen. It proved to be a popular method of posttesting in the broadcasting industry for decades, although its use has waned. The major advantage of day-after recall tests is that they are field tests. The natural setting is supposed to provide a more realistic response profile. These tests also provide norms that give advertisers a standard for comparing how well their ads are performing. In addition to recall, a number of different measures of the commercial's effectiveness are now offered, including persuasive measures and diagnostics.

Although popular, day-after recall tests also had problems, including limited samples, high costs, and security issues (ads shown in test markets could be seen by competitors). Furthermore, DAR tests may favour unemotional appeals because respondents are asked to verbalize the message. Thinking messages may be easier to recall than emotional communications, so recall scores for emotional ads may be lower.[8] Other studies concluded that emotional ads may be processed differently from thinking ones, and ad agencies (e.g., Leo Burnett, BBDO) developed their own methods of determining emotional response to ads.[9]

Comprehensive Measures   As noted in our discussion of pretesting broadcast commercials, a measure of a commercial's persuasive effectiveness is gathered and services offer additional persuasion measures, including purchase-intent and frequency-of-purchase. Copy testing firms also provide diagnostic measures. These measures are designed to garner viewers' evaluations of the ads, and establish how clearly the creative idea is understood and how well the proposition is communicated. Rational and emotional reactions to the ads are also examined. While each of the measures just described provides specific input into the effectiveness of a commercial, many advertisers are interested in more than just one specific input. Thus, companies provide comprehensive approaches in which each of the three measures just described (i.e., recall, persuasion, diagnostics) can be obtained through one testing program. Figure 9-12 describes one such comprehensive program, Ipsos-ASI's Next*TV test (Exhibit 9-5).

Figure 9-12   Ipsos-ASI's Next*TV

Objective:	To assist advertisers in copy testing of their commercials through multiple measures to determine (1) the potential of the commercial for impacting sales, (2) how the ad contributes to brand equity, (3) how well it is in line with existing advertising strategies and objectives, and (4) how to optimize effectiveness.
Method:	Consumers are recruited to evaluate a TV program, with ads embedded into the program as they would be on local prime-time television. Consumers view the recorded program in their homes to simulate actual field conditions. (The option to use local cable television programs with commercial inserts is also provided.)
Output:	Related recall (day-after recall) scores; persuasion scores, including brand preference shifts, purchase intent and frequency, brand equity differentiation, and relevance and communication; and reaction diagnostics to determine what viewers take away from the ad and how creative elements contribute to or distract from advertising effectiveness.

Test Marketing   Companies conduct tests designed to measure their advertising effects in specific test markets before releasing them nationally. The markets chosen are representative of the target audience. For example, a company may test its ads in London, Ontario, Peterborough, Ontario, or Winnipeg, Manitoba, if the demographic and socioeconomic profiles of these cities match the product's market. Many factors may be tested, including reactions to the ads (for example, alternative copy points), the effects of various budget sizes, or special offers. The ads run in finished form in the media where they might normally appear, and effectiveness is measured after the ads run.

The advantage of test marketing of ads is realism. Regular viewing environments are used and the testing effects are minimized. A high degree of control can be attained if the test is designed successfully. The disadvantages of test marketing measures are cost and time. Few firms have the luxury to spend months or years and upwards of a million dollars on such a test. In addition, there is always the fear that competitors may discover and intervene in the research process. Test marketing can provide substantial insight into the effectiveness of advertising if care is taken to minimize the negative aspects of such tests.

Single-Source Tracking Studies   More sophisticated approaches are **single-source tracking methods** that track the behaviours of consumers from the television set to the supermarket checkout counter. Participants in a designated area who agree to participate in the studies are given a card that identifies their household and gives the research company their

Exhibit 9-5   Ipsos-ASI offers a comprehensive testing measure.

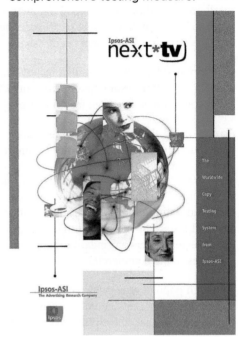

Courtesy of Ipsos-ASI, Inc

demographics. The households are split into matched groups; one group receives an ad while the other does not, or alternative ads are sent to each. Their purchases are recorded from the bar codes of the products bought. Commercial exposures are then correlated with purchase behaviours. The single-source method can be used effectively to posttest ads, allowing for a variety of dependent measures and tracking the effects of increased ad budgets and different versions of ad copy—and even ad effects on sales.[10] After using scanner data to review the advertising/sales relationship for 78 brands, John Jones concluded that single-source data are beginning to fulfill their promise now that more measurements are available.[11]

Tracking Print/Broadcast Ads   A useful and adaptable form of posttesting involves tracking the effects of the ad campaign by taking measurements at regular intervals. **Tracking studies** measure the effects of advertising on awareness, recall, interest, specific copy points, and attitudes toward the ad and/or brand as well as purchase intentions. Personal interviews, phone surveys, mall intercepts, and even mail surveys have been used. Sample sizes typically range from 250 to 500 cases per period (usually quarterly or semiannually). Tracking studies yield perhaps the most valuable information available to the marketing manager for assessing current programs and planning for the future. (See Exhibit 9-6.)

Tracking studies can be tailored to each specific campaign and/or situation. A standard set of questions can track effects of the campaign over time. Tracking studies have also been used to measure the differential impact of varying budget sizes, the effects of flighting, and the effects of each medium and all media combined. Finally, when designed properly, tracking studies offer a high degree of reliability and validity.[12] The problems of recall and recognition measures are inherent in tracking studies as well, since many other factors may affect both brand and advertising recall. Despite these limitations, however, tracking studies are a very effective means of assessing the effects of advertising campaigns.

Exhibit 9-6   Tracking studies provide useful measures.

Decision Analyst

IMC Planning: Program for Measuring Effectiveness

In this section, we offer prescriptions for managers planning evaluative research. Some time ago, the largest U.S. ad agencies endorsed a set of principles aimed at improving the research used in preparing and testing ads.[13] (We include it here due to the U.S. connection of many Canadian agencies.) The principles, called **PACT (Positioning Advertising Copy Testing)**, define *copy testing* as research "which is undertaken when a decision is to be made about whether advertising should run in the marketplace. Whether this stage utilizes a single test or a combination of tests, its purpose is to aid in the judgment of specific advertising executions."[14] The nine principles of good copy testing are shown in Figure 9-13. Adherence may not make for perfect testing, but it goes a long way toward improving the state of the art and providing guidelines for effectiveness research.

Figure 9-13   Positioning Advertising Copy Testing (PACT)

1. Provide measurements that are relevant to the objectives of the advertising.
2. Require agreement about how the results will be used in advance of each specific test.
3. Provide multiple measures (single measures are not adequate to assess ad performance).
4. Be based on a model of human response to communications—the reception of a stimulus, the comprehension of the stimulus, and the response to the stimulus.
5. Allow for whether the advertising stimulus should be exposed more than once.
6. Require that the more finished a piece of copy is, the more soundly it can be evaluated and require, as a minimum, that alternative executions be tested in the same degree of finish.
7. Provide controls to avoid the biasing effects of the exposure context.
8. Take into account basic considerations of sample definition.
9. Demonstrate reliability and validity.

CRITERIA FOR EFFECTIVE RESEARCH

When testing methods are compared to the criteria established by PACT, it is clear that the principles important to good copy testing can be accomplished readily. Principle 1 (providing measurements relative to the objectives sought) and Principle 2 (determining *a priori* how the results will be used) are consistent with DAGMAR (i.e., Chapter 5) and are basic advertising management prescriptions along with Principle 6 (providing equivalent test ads). Principles 3, 5, and 7 are largely in the control of the researcher. Principle 3 (providing multiple measurements) may require little more than budgeting to make sure more than one test is conducted. Likewise, Principle 5 (exposing the test ad more than once) can be accomplished with a proper research design. It might seem that Principle 7 (providing a nonbiasing exposure) would be easy to accomplish, however lab measures are artificial and vulnerable to testing effects while offering control, while field measures are realistic with less control. Research should likely find a balance by using both types over time. Principle 8 (sample definition) requires sound research methodology; any test should use the target audience to assess an ad's effectiveness. If a study is properly designed, and by that we mean it addresses Principles 1 through 8, it should be both reliable and valid. Principle 9 (concern for reliability and validity) includes two critical distinctions between good and bad research, however most of the measures discussed are lacking in at least one of these criteria.

Principle 4—which states the research should be guided by a model of human response to communications that encompasses reception, comprehension, and behavioural response—requires careful consideration because it is the principle least addressed by practising researchers. Even though response models (recall Chapter 4 and 5) have existed for many years, few if any common research methods attempt to integrate them into their methodologies. Models that do claim to measure such factors as attitude change or brand preference change are often fraught with problems that severely limit their reliability. An effective measure must include a relationship to the communications process.

GUIDELINES FOR EFFECTIVE TESTING

Good tests of advertising effectiveness must address the nine principles established by PACT. One of the easiest ways to accomplish this is by following the decision sequence model in formulating promotional plans.

- *Use a consumer response model.* Early in this text we reviewed hierarchy of effects models and cognitive response models, which provide an understanding of the effects of communications and lend themselves to achieving communications goals. We also presented Rossiter and Percy's model for stating communication objectives, which could also be a basis for measurement.

- *Establish communications objectives.* It is nearly impossible to show the direct impact of advertising on sales. The marketing objectives established for the promotional program are not good measures of communication effectiveness. On the other hand, attainment of communications objectives can be measured and leads to the accomplishment of marketing objectives.

- *Use both pretests and posttests.* From a cost standpoint—both actual cost outlays and opportunity costs—pretesting makes sense. It may be the difference between success and failure of the campaign or the product. But it should work in conjunction with posttests, which avoid the limitations of pretests, use much larger samples, and take place in more natural settings. Posttesting may be required to determine the true effectiveness of the ad or campaign.

- *Use multiple measures.* Many attempts to measure the effectiveness of advertising focus on one major dependent variable—perhaps sales, recall, or recognition. As noted earlier in this chapter, advertising may have a variety of effects on the consumer, some of which can be measured through traditional methods, and others that require updated thinking (recall the discussion on physiological responses). For a true assessment of advertising effectiveness, a number of measures may be required.

- *Understand and implement proper research.* It is critical to understand research methodology. What constitutes a good design? Is it valid and reliable? Does it measure what we need it to? There is no shortcut to this criterion, and there is no way to avoid it if you truly want to measure the effects of advertising.

A major study sponsored by the Advertising Research Foundation (ARF) addressed these issues, involving interviews with 12,000 to 15,000 people.[15] While we do not have the space to analyze this study here, note that the research was designed to evaluate measures of copy tests, compare copy testing procedures, and examine the PACT principles. Information on this study has been published in a number of academic and trade journals and by the ARF.

Learning Objectives Summary

 LO1   Identify the reasons for measuring promotional program effectiveness.

This chapter introduced issues and decisions concerning the measurement of advertising and promotion effectiveness. All marketing managers want to know how well their promotional programs are working. This information is critical for planning the next period, since program adjustments and/or maintenance are based on evaluation of current strategies. While the need for understanding how programs are working appears critical, this chapter summarized the debate regarding whether measurement is in fact needed. We conclude that research measuring the effectiveness of advertising is important to the promotional program and should be an integral part of the planning process.

 LO2   Describe the measures used in assessing promotional program effectiveness.

We summarized many types of decisions for advertising research. We identified both creative strategy and creative tactics decisions as being important for testing. We also suggested that most other IMC tools had a key message that required effectiveness testing and that these advertising research methods were applied accordingly. Moreover, research could occur prior to a campaign (i.e., pretesting) or after the campaign (i.e., posttesting), which represents another key decision. Whether a lab or field test is required also should be determined. Lab tests offer greater control but lack a realistic setting, while field tests offer a realistic setting but less control. While there are many choices for research, a comprehensive, yet expensive, evaluation program would test all message variables, before and after a campaign, with both lab and field methods.

LO3   Evaluate alternative methods for measuring promotional program effectiveness.

The chapter described research methods that cover the stages of developing a promotional program. Tests originated with one firm and were later adapted by other firms with companies developing their own testing systems in conjunction with their advertising or communication agency. Concept tests, focus groups, and mall intercepts are used to test initial ideas for creative strategies and promotional messages. Comprehension and reaction tests along with consumer juries appeared useful to testing rough or preliminary examples of print ads and television storyboards.

Finished ads are also tested prior to launching the campaign. Investment in these tests reassures managers so that costly media buys can be avoided. We reviewed portfolio tests, readability tests, and dummy advertising vehicles for evaluating completed print ads. Finished broadcast ads can be examined with theatre tests, on-air tests, and physiological measures. Evaluations after the ads have been launched, known as posttests, offer greater confirmation of the promotion effectiveness. Print ad posttests include inquiry tests, recognition tests, and recall tests. Broadcast posttests include day-after recall tests, comprehensive measures, test marketing, single-source tracking studies, and tracking studies. Single-source research data offer strong potential for improving the effectiveness of ad measures since commercial exposures and reactions may be correlated to actual purchase behaviours.

LO4   Appraise the requirements of proper effectiveness research.

Finally, we reviewed the criteria (defined by PACT) for sound research and suggested ways to accomplish effective studies. It is important to recognize that different measures of effectiveness may lead to different results. Depending on the criteria used, one measure may show that an ad or promotion is effective while another states that it is not. This is why clearly defined objectives, evaluations occurring both before and after the campaigns are implemented, and the use of multiple measures are critical to determining the true effects of an IMC program.

Review Questions

1. What are the reasons why a company should measure the effectiveness of its promotional programs?
2. Discuss the differences between pretesting and posttesting, and lab testing and field testing.
3. Why might a firm use theatre testing, on-air tests, and physiological measures to pretest its finished broadcast ads?
4. Why are the PACT criteria important for testing effectiveness?

Applied Questions

1. Describe how a creative director who worked on an exciting, daring, and provocative ad campaign for months might react if the campaign were to be scrapped prior to launch after preliminary research indicated it did not resonate with audiences tested.

2. Select a popular ad campaign and explain whether it should have tested different creative strategy options or different creative tactics options.

3. Explain why you would or would not want to personally participate in each of the studies described.

4. For any of the print ads located in the previous chapters, design a testing approach based on the final section of this chapter.

© Asif Islam/Shutterstock

CHAPTER TEN

Media Planning and Budgeting for IMC

LEARNING OBJECTIVES

LO1 Illustrate how a media plan is developed.

LO2 Explain the process and identify the decisions for implementing media strategies.

LO3 Explain the process and identify the decisions for implementing media tactics.

LO4 Distinguish among the theoretical and managerial approaches for media budget setting.

LO5 Apply the methods for allocating the media budget to relevant IMC tools and market situations.

YouTube Seeks More Viewers

YouTube's time arrived in Canada during 2015, when *Marketing Magazine* recognized the social media vehicle with its Media Player of the Year Award. As the video-playing Internet site hit its tenth birthday, it looked to make new waves in Canada and marketed its video content more overtly to entice advertisers to spend more with YouTube instead of other social media video sites and TV networks and specialty channels. Armed with data that indicated 70 percent of all Canadians watch YouTube at least monthly, the situation presented a substantial prospect to increase advertising revenue. This especially looked promising as data indicated global viewership grew 50 percent and the world's top 100 brands' ad spending grew 60 percent from 2014 to 2015.

The growth of YouTube spawned unique and wide-ranging content creators for consumer entertainment. Success on YouTube for a show like Montreal's *Epic Meal Time* gave the creators a chance to sign a deal with the FYI TV channel. Furthermore, Toronto's *RachhLoves* moved to TV with the W Network after a few years of YouTube stardom. Similarly, Bell Media introduced Much Digital Studios to reboot the Much Music brand with fresh talent from YouTube. The advertising appeal intensified when research showed that young consumers preferred this new wave of talent over TV and movie stars.

To facilitate this advertising media opportunity, YouTube instituted Google Preferred, a program designed to sway advertisers to place messages within the social media vehicle. The program, established exactly like TV ad buying, assured advertisers that their ads would be shown during the streaming of the most popular YouTube personalities, affectionately known as "YouTubers." Moreover, one Google executive saw the program much like the premium positions (e.g., inside front cover) that magazines hold for their best advertisers. Preliminary results from the U.S. execution indicated success, with the complete ad inventory sold out and YouTube's revenue growing by 70 percent. One early Canadian adopter of the program, Wendy's, obtained significant lifts in ad recall and overall brand awareness.

YouTube garnered publicity for the program with a Fan Fest event at Toronto's Yonge–Dundas Square. This consumer initiative comprised part of an IMC program designed by YouTube to attract more viewers. Growing YouTubers' fan base appeared to be a worthy decision as Facebook was beginning its foray into competing in the social media video domain to complement its social networking presence. YouTube's campaign included online, billboard, and transit ads, and the event coincided with YouTube's significant push to advertisers and media buying agencies by providing them with extensive data on the viewership of each YouTuber celebrity. Building the following of these popular creators also appeared to be an important direction as Facebook undertook similar promotional activities with popular personalities on Instagram.

In another direction, brands' media plans began to change in a new way. Previously, brands would place ads on YouTube after TV broadcasting placement. However, brands began to move toward showing them in social media initially and then placing them on TV or elsewhere. For example, Tim Hortons showed its humorous ads of Sidney Crosby acting as a server at a store on YouTube first, and WestJet premiered its full-length celebratory Christmas messages on YouTube prior to screening the shortened versions in cinemas. These activities and the growth of video ads on the Internet in general give media planners new ways to reach their target audiences with creative messages.

Sources: Chris Powell, "Nearly 70% of Canadians Watch YouTube Monthly," *Marketing Magazine*, November 11, 2015; Russ Martin, "Media Player of the Year 2015," *Marketing Magazine*, February 4, 2016; Susan Krashinsky, "YouTube Set to Launch Canadian Ad Blitz," *The Globe and Mail*, April 6, 2015, p. B3.

Question:

1. In what ways is watching a video show on YouTube similar to watching a regular TV show?

Planning when, where, and how a message will be delivered is a complex and involved process resulting in a media plan. Its purpose is to identify and justify the decisions that will deliver the message to the target audience cost-efficiently and will communicate the product, brand, and/or service message effectively. This chapter illustrates the media planning process, expresses the development of decisions for media strategy and tactics, and distinguishes approaches of setting and allocating an IMC budget. We include budget setting for IMC in this chapter because of the inherent trade-off between media decisions and financial resources.

Media planning has historically been viewed within advertising but it is integrated with and applicable to all IMC tools. For example, advertising media direct visitors to a brand's website or other digital alternatives like unique social media vehicles. In fact, much of the media planning process is consistent with delivering digital messages. Communication of a sales promotion generally requires media delivery so consumers are aware of the offer and can act upon it. Public relations campaigns use media planning principles to encourage visits to events or participation in brand activities. Thus, the media planning and budgeting decisions with reference to advertising described in this chapter are directly used for or transferred to other IMC tools.

 # Media Planning

In this section, we provide an overview of media planning to highlight the context in which messages are delivered, describe the content of a media plan to understand how its content is consistent with other elements of IMC planning, and indicate the unique challenges with media planning not found in other areas of IMC planning.

OVERVIEW

Media planning is the series of decisions involved in delivering the promotional message to prospective purchasers and/or users of the product or brand. Media planning is a process in which the decisions may be altered or abandoned as the plan develops. One primary decision is the type of media selected. Options include mass media such as television, newspapers, radio, and magazines, as well as out-of-the-home media such as outdoor advertising and transit advertising and Internet content publishers and social media (Figure 10-1). Each medium has its own particular strengths and limitations that must be considered in light of the communication problem or opportunity that faces the marketer. This makes the media selection and all other media decisions very difficult. For example, the media planning process becomes even more complicated when the manager has to choose among alternatives within the same medium, like different television stations or shows and different magazine titles.

Figure 10-1   Canadian market data: Net advertising revenues

Media		2008	2009	2010	2011	2012	2013	2014	2015
Television	**Total**	**3,393**	**3,104**	**3,391**	**3,552**	**3,467**	**3,387**	**3,353**	**3,076**
	Conventional	2,345	2,084	2,262	2,302	2,189	2,072	2,081	1,816
	Specialty	1,027	1,001	1,113	1.233	1,263	1,297	1,254	1,244
	Infomercial	22	19	16	17	15	17	18	16
	Online				107	115	123	142	tba
All Television	(with online)	**3,393**	**3,104**	**3,391**	**3,658**	**3,582**	**3,510**	**3,495**	
Daily Newspaper	**Total**	**2,489**	**2,030**	**2,102**	**1,971**	**2,019**	**1,679**	**1,392**	**1,181**
	National	571	406	736	709	804	644	529	401
	Local	1,099	974	631	709	719	592	529	506
	Classified	819	650	462	335	289	249	175	119
	Inserts			273	217	207	173	159	155
	Online	181	186	214	242	235	221	226	228
	Mobile				4	7	10	12	15
Community Newspaper	**Total**	**1,211**	**1,186**	**1,143**	**1,167**	**1,253**	**996**	**932**	**841**
	National			292	131	123	107	110	101
	Local			741	705	798	602	552	484
	Classified			110	113	106	83	74	68
	Inserts				219	226	204	199	188
	Online		27	32	44	35	31	33	40

[Continued on next page]

[Figure 10-1 continued]

Media		2008	2009	2010	2011	2012	2013	2014	2015
All Newspaper	(with online/ mobile)	3,880	3,429	3,491	3,427	3,550	2.936	2,597	2,305
Radio	Total	1,558	1,470	1,517	1,576	1,585	1,600	1,589	1,579
	National	408	376	409	442	454	477	497	509
	Local	1,149	1,094	1,108	1,134	1,131	1,123	1,091	1,070
Online	Total	1,609	1,845	2,279	2,674	3,086	3,418	3,793	4,604
	Search	622	741	907	1,081	1,586	1,802	2,052	2,512
	Display	490	578	688	840	974	1,091	1,274	1,554
	Classified/ Directory	460	467	587	576	249	289	171	162
	Email	18	13	11	13	12	18	19	13
	Video	12	20	37	73	92	208	266	358
	Video Gaming	—	3	2	10	13	11	11	5
	Mobile	7	23	47	81	160	427	903	1,620
Magazine		692	590	606	593	573	558	472	tba
Out-of-Home		463	416	482	485	486	514	521	638
Total Reported		11,415	10,641	11,520	12,017	12,469	12,152	12,053	
Catalogue/Direct Mail		1,542	1,270	1,313	1,243	1,257	1,239	1,181	
Yellow Pages		1,000	815	844	791	811	566	435	
Miscellaneous		500	426	438	428	414	403	341	
Total Unreported		3,041	2,512	2,595	2,462	2,481	2,208	1,957	
Total Advertising		14,456	13,153	14,115	14,479	14,950	14,360	14,010	
Population (Millions)		33.3	33.7	34.1	34.5	35.1	35.2	35.5	35.8
Per Capita Total Advertising		434	390	414	420	426	408	395	

Sources: Television & Radio: CRTC; Daily, Community & Online Newspaper: Newspaper Canada; Internet: Interactive Advertising Bureau Canada; Magazine: Magazines Canada; Out-of-home: Estimate based on Nielsen Media Research Canada; Direct Mail: Canada Post; Yellow Pages: Estimate based on last report by YPG 2014; Miscellaneous: includes estimates for Trade & Other Print from Newspapers Canada; Population: Statistics Canada Mid-Year Population by Year, Media Digest, Canadian Media Director's Council 2015-2016, p. 19.

Internet ad revenue for TV and newspaper is counted within Internet media. All TV and all newspaper summations include online/mobile ads for digital distribution of TV and newspaper media brands.

Mobile ad revenue is counted within Internet advertising formats for 2013, 2014, 2015.

tba = To be announced. These numbers were not available at the time of writing.

A number of decisions must be made throughout the media planning process. The promotional planning model in Chapter 1 identified decisions such as selecting target audiences, establishing objectives, and formulating strategies for attaining them. The development of the media plan and strategies follows a similar path, except that the focus is to determine the best way to deliver the message. Thus, the media plan comprises a short section containing **media objectives**, an explanation of the **media strategy** decisions, and fine-tuning details that are known as media execution or **media tactics**. The activities involved in developing the media plan and the purposes of each are presented in Figure 10-2. Although this simplified template shows a few media for illustrative purposes, the general process is similar for all media and IMC tools.

Figure 10-2   Activities involved in developing the media plan

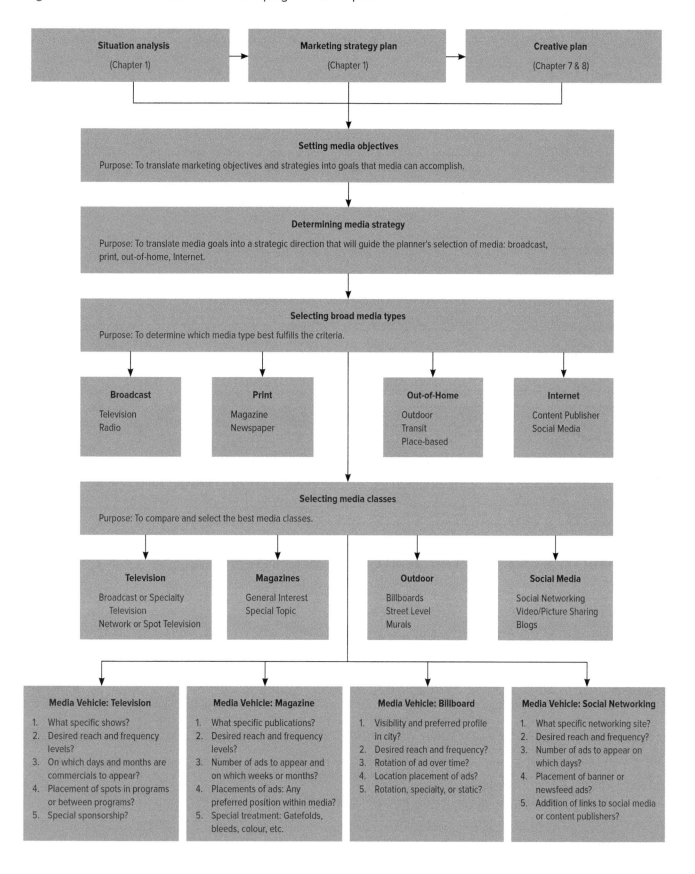

Media planning certainly occurs for advertising, but it is also necessary as part of the decision for other IMC tools as suggested above. Sales promotions often require media expenditure to communicate the offers available or for distribution. Public relations activities use media to communicate corporate activities with respect to sponsorship or community events. A number of media are available for direct marketing, and many aspects of media planning are applicable. In general, the guiding principles for media strategy and media tactics are applicable for the use of media to implement other IMC activities beyond advertising.

Finally, media planning experiences the challenge of developing a plan with limited financial resources, as plans have a prescribed budget that the media planner must respect. All decisions within media planning for advertising face trade-offs to maximize or optimize communication and behavioural objectives. When extended beyond advertising, the promotional planner is faced with the task of allocating expenditures across all IMC tools to achieve broader target audience objectives. In fact, marketing managers are under significant pressure to spend wisely in the promotional domain, as the marketing task has become more financially accountable and firms now calculate their return on marketing investment (ROMI).[1]

MEDIA PLAN

The media plan documents the decisions for finding the best way to get the advertiser's message to the market. In a basic sense, the goal of the media plan is to find the combination of media that enables the marketer to communicate the message in the most effective manner to the largest number of the target audience at the lowest cost. In this section, we review the media plan content regarding media objectives, media strategy, and media tactics.

Media Objectives   Just as the situation analysis leads to establishment of marketing and communication objectives, it should also lead to specific media objectives. The media objectives are not ends in themselves. Rather, they are derived from and are designed to lead to the attainment of communication and behavioural objectives, and contribute to achieving marketing objectives. Media objectives are the goals for the media program and should be limited to those that can be accomplished through media strategies. We now present examples of media objectives that are derived from three communication and two behavioural objectives.

Category Need

- Select media to sufficiently demonstrate how the target audience requires the product category.
- Provide sufficient number of exposures to ensure 80 percent of target audience understands the need for the product category.

Brand Awareness

- Select media to provide coverage of 80 percent of the target audience over a six-month period.
- Provide sufficient number of exposures to ensure 60 percent target audience brand recognition.
- Concentrate advertising during the target audience's peak purchasing time.

Brand Attitude

- Select media to ensure that 40 percent of the target audience have favourable beliefs regarding the brand's benefits and have positive emotions associated with the brand.
- Schedule creative executions over six months to heighten emotions associated with the brand and minimize message fatigue.

Brand Trial

- Select media to allow immediate purchase of brand.
- Schedule sufficient number of opportunities for target audience brand engagement.

Brand Repeat Purchase

- Select media to remind target audience of brand purchase.
- Provide sufficient advertising throughout the year to minimize target audience switching.

The content and exact number of media objectives are at the promotional planner's discretion. These examples merely illustrate the degree to which the link between objectives is not an easy step. The media objectives give direction for the media strategy and tactics decisions. After implementation, marketers need to know whether or not they were successful. Measures of effectiveness must consider two factors: (1) How well did these strategies achieve the media objectives? (2) How well did this media plan contribute to attaining the overall marketing and communications objectives? If the strategies were successful, they should be used in future plans. If not, their flaws should be analyzed.

Media Strategy   As Figure 10-2 indicates, the primary media strategy decision concerns the use of media, moving from a broad perspective to a more specific one. The **medium** is the general category of available delivery systems, which includes broadcast media (like TV and radio), print media (like newspapers and magazines), out-of-home media (like transit, outdoor, place-based), and Internet media (like content publishers and social media). **Media type** refers to the individual media within a medium, so TV is a media type, as is radio, and the term is often shortened to "media." After or during this evaluation, the media planner will consider the relative strengths and limitations of broad **media class** options.

In making the media strategy decisions, a media planner will consider the strategic implications of three concepts. **Reach** is a measure of the number of different audience members exposed at least once to a media vehicle in a given period of time. **Coverage** refers to the potential audience that might receive the message through a vehicle. Coverage relates to potential audience; reach refers to the actual audience delivered. (The importance of this distinction will become clearer later in this chapter.) Finally, **frequency** refers to the number of times the receiver is exposed to the media vehicle in a specified period.

Media Tactics   After the general strategic direction of the media plan has been established, the media planner looks to more specific media decisions like the media vehicle. The **media vehicle** is the specific carrier within a media class. For example, *Maclean's* is a print vehicle; *Hockey Night in Canada* is a television vehicle. As described in later chapters, each vehicle has its own characteristics as well as its own relative strengths and limitations. Specific decisions must be made about the value of each in delivering the message. IMC Perspective 10-1 tells the story of VICE media as it moves from Internet sites to a TV channel.

IMC PERSPECTIVE 10-1

VICE MOVES TO TV

The Voice of Montreal, an upstart newsprint magazine published by Images Interculturelles and started by its new employee Suroosh Avi in 1994, became VICE when it moved to a colour, glossy format in 1996. Since those early days, VICE moved in many directions with up and down results for a period of time until, in the past decade, it hit a

Hand-out/Rogers Communications Inc./Newscom

pinnacle point with the launch of its own TV station entitled Viceland for the Canadian and U.S. markets. For its Canadian TV expansion, VICE partnered with Rogers Media as the former took over the defunct Biography channel. Now valued at $4 billion and based in New York City, the subversively cool media brand finds itself partially owned by large conglomerates like 21st Century Fox and Disney, and a major venture capitalist.

VICE moved from online media with titles and selective interests (kind of like magazines) such as Noisey (music), Thump (electronic music), Broadly (women), Motherboard (technology), Munchies (food), The Creators Project (arts), i-D (fashion), Fightland (pugilism), and VICE News. This appeared to be a significant alteration to its strategy, however Avi claimed it to be a natural extension due to the substantial video content it developed for online purposes in the past decade. Across its vast international empire of online media, VICE produced 6,000 content items daily, each lasting between five and ten minutes. VICE executives saw Viceland as filling a void in the TV landscape for both consumers and advertisers with specialty channels dominated by "redneck reality shows," "pawn stars," and "gator hunters," to name a few! And more importantly, VICE saw this as the incubator of an idea (e.g., network, studio, digital, telecom sponsorship) that could be expanded internationally where all four parts are not fully established.

[Continued on next page]

[IMC Perspective 10-1 continued]

However, a more enlightened view suggested by a Rogers Media executive focused on the need for any major media brand requiring multi-screen exposure to maximize video content distribution and audience reach for advertisers. To further that goal, Viceland planned greater sponsorship of content in contrast to relying on 30-second commercials, a model echoing the early days of TV broadcasts of the 1950s. In contrast, Rogers Media anticipated regular ads and ad messages that provided a "Viceland feel" consistent with the expected millennial audience. And from that perspective, Rogers Media saw the Viceland partnership as the media firm's initial foray into offering a specialized TV vehicle for younger audiences since VICE earned a worldwide designation as an established "millennial brand" that Rogers looked for in specialty channels.

But what exactly is the VICE brand? Some might say it is "edgy" with an inquisitive approach to stories on terrorism, online threats, abandoned communities, and social issues. Online shows featured hosts with interesting personalities who tended to do things their own way and could not get exposure on mainstream media vehicles. In some ways, the original culture of the Voice of Montreal resonates throughout its operations. When launched, it faced competition from two other English cultural papers that are no longer around, a fact Avi finds vindicating.

Despite all of the imagery of a counter brand personality, VICE executives also saw the pragmatic importance of a TV presence as it now brought the brand into more households, and provided their online media advertisers an opportunity to be associated with the VICE media vehicle in a TV environment. Despite fears of millennials "cutting the cord" and not planning to receive TV services any longer, VICE saw this as an opportunity to give them a reason not to leave.

Sources: Kate Wilkinson, "Vice's Growth Officer Talks Viceland Strategy," *Marketing Magazine*, February 29, 2016; Chris Powell, "Viceland to Break the Advertising Programming Mold," *Marketing Magazine*, March 2, 2016; T'cha Dunlevy, "How Vice Built a Global Empire on Gonzo Bravado," *Ottawa Citizen*, March 5, 2016.

Question:

1. How could VICE have leveraged the experiential component of the plan beyond obtaining press coverage?

While making the media vehicle decision, the media planner evaluates the options carefully to maximize coverage, reach, and frequency, and to minimize costs. For example, according to Figure 10-2, once print has been established, the media planner has to decide which specific magazine(s) to select. In addition, certain placement factors need to be carefully evaluated. The tactical decisions include relative cost estimates that may lead to refinements in the allocation of the media dollars. Finally, the complete plan is summarized in a blocking chart. The chart may indicate gaps in media coverage or another concern that would lead the media planner to perform additional evaluation prior to completing the media plan.

MEDIA PLANNING CHALLENGES

Since media planning is a series of decisions, a number of challenges contribute to the difficulty of establishing the plan and reduce its effectiveness. These problems include insufficient information, inconsistent terminologies, need for flexibility, role of media planners, and difficulty measuring effectiveness.

Insufficient Information   While a great deal of information exists about markets and the media, media planners often require more than is available. Some data are just not measured, either because they cannot be or because measuring them would be too expensive. The timing of measurements is also a problem; audience measures are taken only at specific times of the year. This information is then generalized to succeeding months, so future planning decisions must be made on past data that may not reflect current behaviours. Think about planning for TV advertising for the fall season. There are no data on the audiences of new shows, and audience information taken on existing programs may not indicate how these programs will do in the fall as most shows eventually lose their audience. The lack of information is even more of a problem for small advertisers, who may not be able to afford to purchase the information they require and rely on limited or out-of-date data.

Inconsistent Terminologies   Problems arise because of different ways media express their price, and the standards of measurement used to establish these costs are not always consistent. For example, print media may present cost-efficiency data in terms of the cost to reach a thousand people (cost per thousand, or CPM), while broadcast and outdoor media use the cost per ratings point (CPRP). Audience information that is used as a basis for these costs has also been collected by different methods. Finally, terms that actually mean something different (such as *reach* and *coverage*) may be used synonymously, adding to the confusion.

Need for Flexibility   Most media plans are written annually so that all participants are well informed and results can be measured against objectives. However, media planners juggle between requiring a document for action and needing flexibility due to changes in the marketing environment. An opportunity to advertise within a new media vehicle might arise and the planner may shift its expenditure from one medium to another. A competitor may spend more money in certain media and the planner decides a change is required to defend against the threat. Preliminary decisions may not be feasibly implemented in terms of medium availability, thus requiring an adjustment. Poor audience size data in a media vehicle may necessitate a movement of money to another.

Role of Media Planners   Media planners often face a number of expectations from other organizational players. Procurement specialists often put extensive pressure on the media decisions in an effort to save money. Clients request media plans prior to contracting services. Decision makers of all the main IMC tools often look to media planners as implementers instead of key decision-making participants. There also is never-ending debate as to whether media planning buying should be part of an advertising agency or an independent agency.[2]

Difficulty Measuring Effectiveness   Because of the potential inaccuracies of measuring the effectiveness of advertising and promotions, it is also difficult to determine the relative effectiveness of media or media vehicles. While progress has occurred across most media, the media planner must usually balance quantitative data with subjective judgments based on experience when comparing media alternatives. The next section explores how media strategies are developed and ways to increase their effectiveness.

 # Media Strategy Decisions

Having determined what is to be accomplished, media planners consider how to achieve the media objectives. They develop and implement media strategies that consist of five main topics for decision making: media mix, target audience coverage, geographic coverage, scheduling, and reach and frequency.

THE MEDIA MIX

A wide variety of media are available to advertisers. While it is possible that only one might be employed, it is much more likely that a number of alternatives will be used. The behavioural and communication objectives, the characteristics of the product or service, the size of the budget, the target audience, and individual preferences are primary factors that determine the combination of media used. While an evaluation of each medium occurs within the perspective of the communication situation a media planner faces, each medium has varying degrees of use across many segmentation variables.

The context in which the ad is placed may also affect viewers' perceptions, and the creative strategy may require certain media. Therefore, within the media mix a single medium becomes the primary medium where a majority of the budget is spent or the primary effects occur. Because TV provides both sight and sound, it may be more effective in generating emotions than other media. The campaign to attract tourists to Newfoundland and Labrador used TV extensively to convey the experience of actually being in the province while viewing the ad. According to the agency, "Most tourism advertising around the world is an inventory of products, whereas our deep feeling is that the advertising should express and evoke the feeling of the place."[3] Magazines may create different perceptions from newspapers, so we regularly see products in one form of print versus another.

It is possible to increase the success of a product significantly through a strong creative campaign. In some situations, the media strategy to be pursued may be the driving force behind the creative strategy, as the media and creative departments work closely together to achieve the greatest impact with the audience of the specific media. For example, in the case of the "Must Drink More Milk" campaign, six original ads ran on TV but eight cruder and cooler ads with animation ran on YouTube.[4]

As noted at the end of Chapter 5, media planners examine how each medium influences the stages of the consumer decision-making process. For the "All In" campaign for Adidas, the agency viewed its TV and cinema ads and its out-of-home (digital and high impact) as ways of "getting consumers off the couch." The YouTube video and Facebook executions brought all product information together and let consumers enjoy and participate with the "All In" experience. A strong retail presence of display material at Sport Chek and Foot Locker completed the "All In" message.[5]

By employing a media mix, advertisers can add more versatility to their media strategies, since each medium contributes its own distinct advantages. By combining media, marketers can increase coverage, reach, and frequency levels while improving the likelihood of achieving overall communications and marketing goals. Chapters 11, 12, and 13 summarize the characteristics of each medium that make it better or worse for attaining specific communication objectives. We have organized these as media and media-usage characteristics as shown in Figure 10-3.

Figure 10-3

Media Characteristics	Media-Usage Characteristics
Target audience selectivity	Control for selective exposure
Target audience coverage	Attention
Geographic coverage	Creativity for cognitive responses
Scheduling flexibility	Creativity for emotional responses
Reach	Amount of processing time
Frequency	Involvement
Cost efficiency	Clutter
Absolute cost for placement	Media image and production

A summary of the strengths and limitations of the media reviewed in the next three chapters according to these standard media characteristics and media use characteristics is listed in Figure 10-4. We continue with these characteristics for direct marketing and Internet marketing in their respective chapters. With so many competing variables, it becomes clear why media planners spend considerable effort getting the media mix decision right. Finally, keep in mind that these general characteristics guide the media mix decision. Citing them to make a media mix decision is not sufficient. Each strength and limitation needs to be related to the communication situation a specific brand faces, how both types of characteristics will help the brand reach its relevant objectives, and how each medium influences the target audience in the consumer decision-making process. Furthermore, within a given medium there will be variation in the magnitude of the strengths and limitations due to usual examples or the size of the media organization.

Figure 10-4   Strengths and limitations of media characteristics

	Strengths	Limitations
Television	Target audience coverage	Target audience selectivity
	Geographic coverage	Absolute cost
	Scheduling flexibility	Control for selective exposure
	Reach	Amount of processing time
	Frequency	Involvement
	Cost efficiency	Clutter
	Attention	Media image
	Creativity for emotional responses	
	Creativity for cognitive responses	
	Media image	

Radio

Target audience selectivity

Target audience coverage

Geographic coverage

Control for selective exposure

Scheduling flexibility

Attention

Reach

Creativity for emotional responses

Frequency

Amount of processing time

Cost efficiency

Involvement

Absolute cost

Clutter

Creativity for cognitive responses

Media image

Magazines

Target audience selectivity

Target audience coverage

Geographic coverage

Scheduling flexibility

Control for selective exposure

Reach

Attention

Frequency

Creativity for cognitive responses

Absolute cost

Creativity for emotional responses

Cost efficiency

Amount of processing time

Clutter

Involvement

Media image

Newspapers

Target audience coverage

Target audience selectivity

Geographic coverage

Control for selective exposure

Scheduling flexibility

Attention

Reach

Creativity for emotional responses

Frequency

Clutter

Absolute cost

Cost efficiency

Creativity for cognitive responses

Amount of processing time

Involvement

Media image

Outdoor

Geographic coverage

Target audience selectivity

Scheduling flexibility

Target audience coverage

Reach

Absolute cost

Frequency

Creativity for cognitive responses

Cost efficiency

Amount of processing time

Control for selective exposure

Involvement

Attention

Clutter

Creativity for emotional responses

Media image

[Continued on next page]

[Figure 10-4 continued]

	Strengths	Limitations
Transit	Geographic coverage	Target audience selectivity
	Scheduling flexibility	Target audience coverage
	Reach	Attention
	Frequency	Creativity for cognitive responses
	Absolute cost	Creativity for emotional responses
	Cost efficiency	Involvement
	Control for selective exposure	Clutter
	Amount of processing time	Media image

TARGET AUDIENCE COVERAGE

The media planner determines which target audiences should receive the most media emphasis. Developing media strategies involves matching the most appropriate media to this audience by asking, "Through which media and media vehicles can I best get my message to prospective buyers?" The issue here is to get coverage of the audience, as shown in Figure 10-5. The optimal goal is full audience coverage, shown in the second pie chart. Business marketing organizations often get close to full audience coverage due to the small numbers of customers and potential customers. A British Columbia–based firm, 4 Refuel, advertised in trade and industry association publications to attract new customers and obtained considerable leverage for its $100,000. A newsletter offered for publication in the magazines acted as additional publicity and garnered the equivalent of $500,000 in exposure.[6]

Figure 10-5   Marketing coverage possibilities

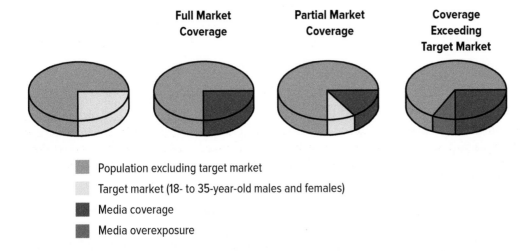

Full Market Coverage   **Partial Market Coverage**   **Coverage Exceeding Target Market**

- Population excluding target market
- Target market (18- to 35-year-old males and females)
- Media coverage
- Media overexposure

More realistically, conditions shown in the third and fourth charts are likely to occur in most marketing situations. In the third chart, the coverage of the media does not allow for coverage of the entire audience, leaving a portion without exposure to the message. In the fourth chart, the marketer is faced with a problem of overexposure (also called **waste coverage**), in which the media coverage exceeds the targeted audience. If media coverage reaches people who are not sought as buyers and are not potential users, then it is wasted. This term is used for coverage that reaches people who are not potential buyers and/ or users. Consumers may not be part of the intended target audience but may still be considered as potential customers—for example, those who buy the product as a gift for someone else.

The goal of the media planner is to extend media coverage to as many members of the target audience as possible while minimizing the amount of waste coverage. The situation usually involves trade-offs. Sometimes one has to live with less coverage than desired; other times, the most effective media expose people not sought. In this instance, waste coverage is justified because the media employed are likely to be the most effective means of delivery available and the cost of the waste coverage is exceeded by the value gained from their use.

The target audience coverage decision relies on primary research and published (secondary) sources. This research can show the number of consumers for a particular product category across many demographic variables and their media consumption habits. We review audience information in Chapters 11, 12, and 13, as each medium has its own method.

When examining these data, media planners are often more concerned with the percentage figures and index numbers than with the raw numbers. This is largely due to the fact that the numbers provided may not be specific enough for their needs, or they question the numbers provided because of the methods by which they were collected. Another key reason is that index numbers and percentages provide a comparative view of the market.

Overall, the **index number** is considered a good indicator of the potential of the market. This number is derived from the formula

$$\text{Index} = \frac{\text{Percentage of users in a demographic segment}}{\text{Percentage of population in the same segment}} \times 100$$

An index number over 100 means use of the product is proportionately greater in that segment than in one that is average (100) or below average (less than 100). Depending on their overall strategy, marketers may wish to use this information to determine which groups are now using the product and target them or to identify a group that is currently using the product less and attempt to develop that segment. While the index is helpful, it should not be used alone. Percentages and product usage figures are also needed to get an accurate picture of the market. A very high index for a particular segment of the population doesn't always mean it is the only attractive segment to target. The high index may be a result of a low denominator (a very small proportion of the population in this segment).

Understanding coverage in a multimedia environment is proving difficult for media planners. Research suggests that consumers frequently consume more than one medium at a time. It suggests that 50 percent use a laptop computer while watching television. Corresponding numbers for other devices include mobile phone (40 percent), game console (25 percent), desktop computer (24 percent), and tablet (12 percent).[7] This is a significant trend since coverage historically implied a reasonably close association with exposure and processing of the advertising message. Clearly, the communication is limited even further if other media are competing for the people's attention. However, communication is intensified for an individual brand if viewers go to a social media site after a TV ad prompt, thereby affecting subsequent TV ads for other brands.

One research study regarding media coverage for a beverage product concluded that TV, gift-packs, in-store displays and outdoor proved to be the right mix since it covered a broad base of category users. It also found that the best coverage for heavy users included public relations, websites, sampling, print, radio, online, and events. Brand growth should avoid media that are associated with heavy category usage. Social media and word-of-mouth proved strong for continued category usage, but not brand growth.[8] These findings imply that both brand and category factors as well as the previous decisions—marketing objectives, target audience, behavioural objectives, and communication objectives—will influence the media mix decision and target audience coverage.

GEOGRAPHIC COVERAGE

The question of where to promote relates to geographic considerations. Should we allocate additional promotional monies to those markets where the brand is already the leader to maintain market share, or does more potential exist in those markets where the firm is not doing as well and there is more room to grow? In the case of the Canadian Tourism Commission, it directed 10 percent of its $57 million budget toward the United States in 2015 since visiting Canada appeared to give good value because of the weaker Canadian dollar.[9] Perhaps the best answer is that the firm should spend advertising and promotion dollars where they will be the most effective—that is, in those markets where they will achieve the desired objectives. Two useful calculations that marketers examine to make this decision are the Brand Development Index and the Category Development Index.

The **Brand Development Index (BDI)** helps marketers factor the rate of product usage by geographic area into the decision process.

$$BDI = \frac{\text{Percentage of brand to total Canadian sales in the market}}{\text{Percentage of total Canadian population in the market}} \times 100$$

The BDI compares the percentage of the brand's total sales in a given market area with the percentage of the total population in the market to determine the sales potential for that brand in that market area. An example of this calculation is shown in Figure 10-6. The higher the index number, the more market potential exists. In the case of this market, the index number indicates a high potential for brand development.

Figure 10-6   Calculating BDI

$$BDI = \frac{\text{Percentage of total brand sales in Ontario}}{\text{Percentage of total Canadian population in Ontario}} \times 100$$

$$= \frac{50\%}{34\%} \times 100$$

$$= 147$$

The **Category Development Index (CDI)** is computed in the same manner as the BDI, except it uses information regarding the product category (as opposed to the brand) in the numerator:

$$CDI = \frac{\text{Percentage of product category total sales in market}}{\text{Percentage of total Canadian population in market}} \times 100$$

The CDI provides information on the potential for development of the total product category rather than specific brands. When this information is combined with the BDI, a much more insightful promotional strategy may be developed. One might first look at how well the product category does in a specific market area. In Alberta, for example, the category potential is low (see Figure 10-7). The marketer analyzes the BDI to find how the brand is doing relative to other brands in this area. This information can then be used in determining how well a particular product category and a particular brand are performing and figuring what media weight (or quantity of advertising) would be required to gain additional market share, as shown in Figure 10-8. In addition to the BDI and CDI considerations, geographic decisions are based on the availability of the product; it may not be prudent to advertise if there is no availability for distribution, however direct marketing applications mitigate this concern.

Figure 10-7   Using CDI and BDI to determine market potential

$$CDI = \frac{\text{Percentage of product category sales in Alberta}}{\text{Percentage of total Canadian population in Alberta}} \times 100$$

$$= \frac{8\%}{11\%} \times 100$$

$$= 73$$

$$BDI = \frac{\text{Percentage of total brand sales in Alberta}}{\text{Percentage of total Canadian population in Alberta}} \times 100$$

$$= \frac{15\%}{11\%} \times 100$$

$$= 136$$

Figure 10-8 Using BDI and CDI indexes

	High BDI	**Low BDI**
High CDI	High market share Good market potential	Low market share Good market potential
Low CDI	High market share Monitor for sales decline	Low market share Poor market potential
High BDI and high CDI	This market usually represents good sales potential for both the product category and the brand.	
High BDI and low CDI	The category is not selling well, but the brand is; probably a good market to advertise in but should be monitored for declining sales.	
Low BDI and high CDI	The product category shows high potential but the brand is not doing well; the reasons should be determined.	
Low BDI and low CDI	Both the product category and the brand are doing poorly; not likely to be a good place for advertising.	

SCHEDULING

Companies would like to keep their advertising in front of consumers at an appropriate level to maintain their behavioural and communications objectives and support their brand positioning strategy. The primary objective of scheduling is to time promotional efforts to coincide with the highest potential buying times and other important brand-building opportunities. For some products, these times are not easy to identify; for others, they are very obvious. Three scheduling methods available to the media planner—continuity, flighting, and pulsing—are shown in Figure 10-9.

Figure 10-9 Three methods of promotional scheduling

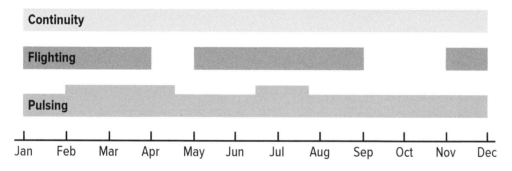

Continuity refers to a continuous pattern of advertising, which may mean every day, every week, or every month. The key is that a regular (continuous) pattern is developed without gaps or non-advertising periods. It is important to note that continuity is entirely predicated on the time period. For example, placing an ad in the newspaper every Monday for a whole year is continuous on a weekly basis, but not continuous on a daily basis. Such strategies might be used for advertising for food products, laundry detergents, or other products consumed on an ongoing basis without regard for seasonality.

A second method, **flighting**, employs a less regular schedule, with intermittent periods of advertising and non-advertising. At some time periods there are heavier promotional expenditures, and at others there may be no advertising. Snow skis are advertised heavily between October and April; less in May, August, and September; and not at all in June and July. The weekly newspaper placement could be viewed as flighting on a daily basis since there is no advertising for the other days of the week.

Pulsing is actually a combination of the first two methods. In a pulsing strategy, continuity is maintained, but at certain times promotional efforts are stepped up. In the automobile industry, advertising continues throughout the year but may increase in April (tax refund time), September (when new models are brought out), and the end of the model year. Advantages and disadvantages to each scheduling method are shown in Figure 10-10.

Figure 10-10   Characteristics of scheduling methods

Continuity	
Advantages	Serves as a constant reminder to the consumer
	Covers the entire buying cycle
	Allows for media priorities (quantity discounts, preferred locations, etc.)
Disadvantages	Higher costs
	Potential for overexposure
	Limited media allocation possible

Flighting	
Advantages	Cost efficiency of advertising only during purchase cycles
	May allow for inclusion of more than one medium or vehicle with limited budgets
Disadvantages	Weighting may offer more exposure and advantage over competitors
	Increased likelihood of wearout
	Lack of awareness, interest, retention of promotional message during nonscheduled times
	Vulnerability to competitive efforts during nonscheduled periods

Pulsing	
Advantages	All of the same as the previous two methods
Disadvantages	Not required for seasonal products (or other cyclical products)

As implied above, advertisers decide on the exact day, week, or months in which to advertise, so a good media plan provides extensive details on the exact timing of the placement. For example, a brand might want a magazine placement during spring months, TV placement could only occur on weekends, and a planner may decide to place Internet display ads only in the morning. Sport Chek decided to use TV during August to December to coincide with back-to-school, hockey, and holiday gift-giving, and used digital throughout the year.[10]

In a battle for market share in the $2 billion market for back-to-school supplies, Staples and Walmart raised the stakes with different approaches. Walmart jump-started the spending spree in July with cinema ads for laptop computers. Thinking that consumers required more time to consider their purchases for more expensive items, the month-earlier beginning coincided with more targeting toward university and college students. The timing also fit with the idea of encouraging consumers to make fewer trips to stores, and of course to visit only one store, Walmart. Faced with the prospect of Walmart having the ability to advertise both school supplies and clothing, Staples responded with a joint effort with Old Navy, offering discounts at the clothing chain with purchases of its supplies. Staples also showed back-to-school ads on its Facebook page in July.[11]

Another scheduling decision involves the order in which each medium occurs when multiple media are in the plan. Which medium should occur first if TV, magazines, and outdoor are used in the campaign? Alternatively, should all media be placed simultaneously? Media placement constraints remove a planner's ability to completely control this decision, but nevertheless, the order is an important consideration. Procter & Gamble releases its ads digitally prior to TV with the aim of consumers forwarding them to others so that more people will attend to the messages when they see them on TV. For its Olympic messages, P&G found one-third of the online viewers shared the video link.[12]

REACH AND FREQUENCY

Advertisers usually must trade off reach and frequency because they face budget constraints when trying to attain objectives. They must decide whether to have the message be seen or heard by more people (reach) or by fewer people more often (frequency). This trade-off requires a complex investigation to answer these two questions for any media, and by extension, the whole media plan and the entire IMC plan.

How Much Reach Is Necessary?   A universal communication objective is product and/or brand awareness. The more consumers are aware, the more they are likely to consider the brand throughout the decision-making process. Achieving awareness requires reach—that is, exposing the target audience to the message. New brands or products need a very high level of reach since the objective is to make all potential buyers aware. High reach is also desired at later purchase-decision stages since a promotional strategy might use a free sample. An objective of the marketer is to reach a larger number of people with the sample in an attempt to make them learn of the product, use it, and develop a favourable attitude toward it that may lead to an initial brand trial purchase.

Reach is the number of target audience individuals exposed at least once to a media vehicle in a specific time period. Media planners use weekly, monthly, or quarterly time periods that are known as *advertising cycles*. The reach number is usually expressed as a percentage provided the number of target audience individuals is clearly identified.

For example, the most watched TV show each week gets about 3.4 million viewers, according to the Bureau of Broadcast Measurement (BBM), and the population of Canada is about 34 million, according to Statistics Canada as reported in the Media Digest. Thus the reach of an ad placed on this show is approximately 10 percent for the advertising cycle of one week.

$$\text{Reach} = \frac{\text{Number of people watching TV ad}}{\text{Number of people in Canada}} = \frac{3.4 \text{ million}}{34 \text{ million}} = 10\%$$

Reach can be compiled over any time period (i.e., week, month, year), geographically (i.e., city, province), or any demographic (e.g., women aged 18–35). Reach can also be considered in terms of the stages of the buyer decision-making process and for any other media used for advertising or other IMC tools that have a media plan component. No matter what audience characteristics the media planner works with, the ratio remains as follows:

$$\text{Reach} = \frac{\text{Number of people in target audience exposed to the media vehicle}}{\text{Number of people in target audience}}$$

The concept of reach gets more complex and complicated going beyond the placement of one ad on one TV show. If one ad is placed on one TV show one time, the number of people exposed is the reach (Figure 10-11A). In order to achieve high levels of reach, brands often use multiple media (e.g., television, Internet). Alternatively, or in addition, brands use multiple media vehicles such as more than one TV station or TV show, or more than one magazine. Thus, it is possible for the target audience to be exposed to an ad more than once with multiple media and multiple media vehicles (Figure 10-11B).

Figure 10-11   Representation of reach and frequency

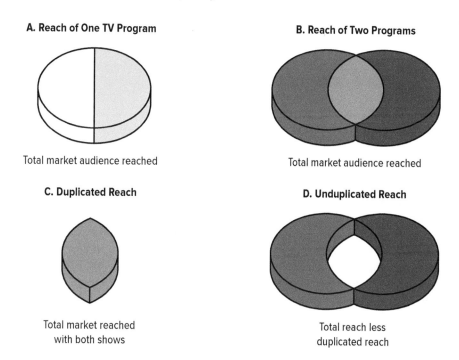

A. Reach of One TV Program

Total market audience reached

B. Reach of Two Programs

Total market audience reached

C. Duplicated Reach

Total market reached
with both shows

D. Unduplicated Reach

Total reach less
duplicated reach

The reach of the two shows, as depicted in Figure 10-11C, includes a number of people who were reached by both shows. This overlap is referred to as **duplicated reach**. If the ad is placed on two shows, the total number exposed **unduplicated reach** (Figure 10-11D). Both unduplicated and duplicated reach figures are important. Unduplica

indicates potential new exposures, while duplicated reach provides an estimate of frequency since some in the target audience saw the ad multiple times. Media plans should account for both unduplicated reach and duplicated reach, or acknowledge which is used, to provide comprehensive reporting of the media buy.

The amount of reach can be estimated through the information contained in the target audience profile regarding customer group (i.e., loyal users or new category users) and other variables like demographics. Based on this information, media planners would know if the required reach is a niche market requiring a selective 10 percent or a broader audience of moving toward 50 percent, in whatever geographic or timing parameters are decided upon. While reach is an important decision, the duplicated reach resulting in a greater number of exposures for a portion of the target audience leads to the next question: What frequency of exposure is necessary for the ad to be seen and to have a communication effect?

What Frequency Level Is Needed?   With respect to media planning, *frequency* carries a particular meaning. **Frequency** is the average number of exposures a target audience individual receives from media vehicles in a specific time period. Frequency is dependent upon how much media target audience individuals consume. It can therefore range substantially, which raises the need to look at average frequency that is derived from a frequency distribution. Continuing with the TV example, ads placed once in each of the top 10 shows in a given week would provide an average frequency of 1.36 (using BBM data from a randomly selected week).

$$\text{Frequency} = \frac{24 \text{ million exposures across 10 TV shows}}{17.6 \text{ million individuals exposed to ad}} = 1.36 \text{ exposures per person}$$

The 24 million exposures are calculated by adding the numbers of people who watched each show. However, some people watch two or more shows, resulting in fewer people actually exposed to the ad. Thus, the 17.6 million individuals exposed to the ad represent the total number of "unduplicated" viewers for all 10 shows who potentially saw the 24 million exposures.

The 17.6 million is *estimated* by adding the unduplicated viewers for each of the 10 shows. The most watched show was 3.216 million. To that number we add the unduplicated numbers of viewers for all the other nine shows. To calculate unduplicated numbers, we adjust the actual ones downward by a percentage of possible repeat viewers.

The second most watched show reached 2.634 million, resulting in 2.384 million unduplicated viewers [i.e., $2.634 \times (34 - 3.216)/34$]. The percentage of people not watching the first show has an equal chance as those watching the second show. These calculations carry on for each subsequent show so that by the tenth show, the unduplicated audience is reduced; 1.946 million watching the tenth show but only 0.975 million new viewers. These calculations can be done for all media individually and combined across all media, but the general calculation remains as follows:

$$\text{Frequency} = \frac{\text{Total number of exposures}}{\text{Total number of unduplicated individuals exposed to media vehicle}}$$

The example with the BBM data is calculated with all viewers, but the data could be refined to a specific demographic and/or other variables used to profile the target audience. The general calculation remains the same, but the numbers will change correspondingly to observe the frequency of exposure for the target audience. Furthermore, actually calculating total exposures to estimate average frequency is generally done by computer software as the complexity intensifies exponentially with multiple media vehicles.

The above discussion suggests frequency is the number of times one is exposed to the media vehicle, not necessarily to the ad itself. While one study has estimated that the actual audience for a commercial may be as much as 30 percent lower than that for the program, not all researchers agree.[13] Most advertisers do agree that a 1:1 exposure ratio does not exist. So while the ad may be placed in a certain vehicle, the fact that a consumer has been exposed to that vehicle does not ensure that it has been seen. As a result, the frequency level expressed in the media plan overstates the actual level of exposure to the ad. This overstatement has led some media buyers to refer to the reach of the media vehicle as "opportunities to see" an ad rather than actual exposure to it.

Having defined and illustrated the calculation of frequency, the question remains of how much frequency is needed within an advertising cycle. Practitioners and academic researchers investigated this question for decades, and Figure 10-12 summarizes their finding. The conclusion that three exposures within an advertising cycle may be sufficient for communication effects to take hold implies that this average is the minimum; however, anyone in the target audience who receives only one or two exposures presumably would not be aware of the brand or understand its performance. Therefore, the average exposure level would have to be higher to ensure sufficient communication for all who were exposed to the message.

Figure 10-12   The effects of frequency

1. One exposure of an ad to a target group within a purchase cycle has little or no effect.
2. Since one exposure is usually ineffective, the central goal of productive media planning should be to enhance frequency rather than reach.
3. The evidence suggests strongly that an exposure frequency of two within a purchase cycle is an effective level.
4. Beyond three exposures within a brand purchase cycle or over a period of four or even eight weeks, increasing frequency continues to build advertising effectiveness at a decreasing rate but with no evidence of decline.
5. Although there are general principles with respect to frequency of exposure and its relationship to advertising effectiveness, differential effects by brand are equally important.
6. Frequency response principles or generalizations do not vary by medium.
7. The data strongly suggest that wearout is not a function of too much frequency; it is more of a creative or copy problem.

To understand this situation further, consider a media buy in which 50 percent of the audience is reached one time, 30 percent of the audience is reached five times, and 20 percent of the audience is reached 10 times. The average frequency of this media buy is 4, which is slightly more than the number established as effective. Yet a full 50 percent of the audience receives only one exposure. Presumably a considerable portion of the money spent on advertising has been wasted because so many in the target audience were not exposed to the message.

Determining Effective Reach and Frequency   Since marketers have budget constraints, they must decide whether to increase reach at the expense of frequency or increase the frequency of exposure but to a smaller audience. A number of factors influence this decision. For example, a new product or brand introduction will attempt to maximize reach, particularly unduplicated reach, to create awareness in as many people as possible as quickly as possible. At the same time, for a high-involvement product or one whose benefits are not obvious, a certain level of frequency is needed to achieve effective reach.

Effective reach represents the percentage of a vehicle's audience reached at each effective frequency increment. This concept is based on the assumption that one exposure to an ad may not be enough to convey the desired message. As we saw earlier, no one knows the exact number of exposures necessary for an ad to make an impact, although advertisers have settled on three as the minimum. Effective reach (exposure) is shown in the shaded area in Figure 10-13 in the range of three to 10 exposures. Fewer than three exposures is considered insufficient reach, while more than 10 is considered overexposure and thus ineffective reach. This exposure level is no guarantee of effective communication; different messages may require more or fewer exposures.

Figure 10-13   Graph of effective reach

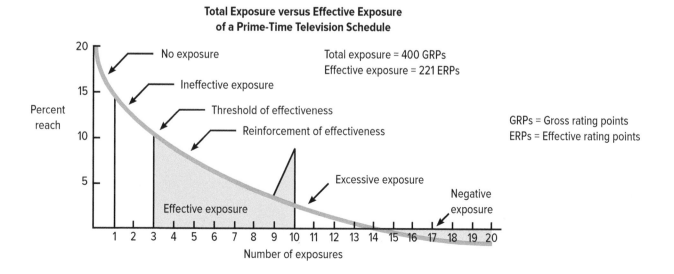

**Total Exposure versus Effective Exposure
of a Prime-Time Television Schedule**

Perhaps the best advice for determining *effective frequency* is offered by Ostrow, who recommended the following:[14] Instead of using **average frequency**, the marketer should decide what minimum frequency goal is needed to reach the advertising objectives effectively and then maximize reach at that frequency level. To determine **minimum effective frequency**, one must consider marketing factors, message factors, and media factors. (See Figure 10-14.) While the idea of minimum effective frequency has been used extensively in the advertising industry, there are some concerns with its use in more recent years.[15] In contrast, with the growth of more media outlets and enhanced syndicated data, minimum effective frequency within and across combinations of media provides opportunity for more efficient and effective use of media expenditures.[16]

Figure 10-14   Factors important in determining frequency levels

Marketing Factors

- *Brand history.* New brands generally require higher frequency levels.
- *Brand share.* The higher the brand share, the lower the frequency level required.
- *Brand loyalty.* The higher the loyalty, the lower the frequency level required.
- *Purchase cycles.* Shorter purchasing cycles require higher frequency levels to attain awareness.
- *Usage cycle.* Products consumed frequently usually require a higher level of frequency.
- *Share of voice.* Higher frequency levels are required with many competitors.
- *Target audience.* The target group's ability to learn and retain messages affects frequency.

Message or Creative Factors

- *Message complexity.* The simpler the message, the less frequency required.
- *Message uniqueness.* The more unique the message, the lower the frequency level required.
- *New versus continuing campaigns.* New campaigns require higher levels of frequency.
- *Image versus product sell.* Image ads require higher levels of frequency than product sell ads.
- *Message variation.* A single message requires less frequency; multiple messages require more.
- *Wearout.* Higher frequency may lead to wearout.
- *Advertising units.* Larger units of advertising require less frequency than smaller ones.

Media Factors

- *Clutter.* More frequency is needed to break through when a media has more advertising.
- *Editorial environment.* Less frequency is needed if the ad is consistent with the editorial environment.
- *Attentiveness.* Media vehicles with higher attention levels require less frequency.
- *Scheduling.* Continuous scheduling requires less frequency than does flighting or pulsing.
- *Number of media used.* The fewer media used, the lower the level of frequency required.
- *Repeat exposures.* Media that allow for more repeat exposures require less frequency.

Using Gross Ratings Points   A summary indicator that combines the reach (duplicated) and the average frequency during an advertising cycle (e.g., one week, or four weeks) and is commonly used for reference is known as a **gross ratings point (GRP)**. The GRP can best be understood by an equation:

$$1 \text{ GRP} = \text{Reach of } 1\% \times \text{Frequency of } 1$$

Like both reach and frequency, GRP calculations are time dependent so that one can plan, calculate, or purchase a GRP on a weekly or monthly basis. We return to a TV placement example to see how this works. If one ad is placed on a top Canadian show with 10 percent reach, then the company has purchased 10 GRPs. If the show happens to be between 60 minutes and three hours (e.g., a sports game), then the number of GRPs could grow to 20 or 30 if the ad is run two or three times, respectively. Of course, this assumes the audience size has remained the same throughout the show.

Extensive amounts of audience data exist and, using computer applications, the planning and scheduling of GRPs is a relatively routine practice. However, most media planners rely on their experience and judgment to complement the quantitative side. GRPs can be calculated for the total population aged 2+, adults 18+, adults 18–34, adults 18–49, or several other measured demographic groups.

Aggregating across multiple shows, media planners can calculate any number of GRPs to achieve their communication objectives. For example, 120 GRPs might be needed in a given week if the planner wants a reach of 30 percent and an average frequency of 4. In this example of 120 GRPs, a media planner would need to run ads on multiple shows and days to achieve these reach and frequency levels.

The purchase of 120 GRPs could mean 60 percent of the audience is exposed twice, or 20 percent of the audience is exposed six times, or 40 percent of the audience is exposed three times, and so on. Thus, for a fixed level of GRPs, there is an inverse relationship between reach and frequency. To know how many GRPs are necessary, the manager chooses the minimum effective frequency and the amount of reach necessary based on the communication and media objectives established from the situation analysis, marketing strategy, and IMC strategy.

The chart in Figure 10-15 illustrates the trade-off between reach and frequency given a fixed number of GRPs. A purchase of 100 GRPs on one network yields a lower reach—just over 30 percent of the target audience, which translates into a frequency of about 3 (100 = 33.3 × 3). The reach climbs to about 40 percent if two networks are used with a frequency of about 2.5 (100 = 40 × 2.5). The reach then climbs to about 50 percent if three networks are used with a frequency of about 2 (100 = 50 × 2). The increase in reach levels off as the incremental growth of adding more exposure does not affect very many new people in the target audience, and in fact the exposure growth begins to increase the amount of frequency as a greater number within the target audience see the ad more often. For example, at 600 GRPs the reach is 60 percent with a frequency of 10 (600 = 60 × 10).

Figure 10-15 Estimates of reach for network GRPs

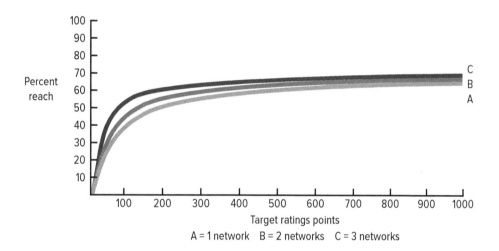

A = 1 network   B = 2 networks   C = 3 networks

LO3 Media Tactics Decisions

Once the initial media strategy has been determined, the marketer addresses three media tactics decisions: media vehicle, relative cost estimates, and blocking chart.

MEDIA VEHICLE

Once the medium or media has been determined, the media planner must consider the most suitable media class and media vehicle. Certain media classes and media vehicles enhance the message because they create a mood that carries over to the communication. The mood is much different on varying classes of TV channels such as sports, comedy, drama, or news. The mood created by magazines like *NUVO, Golf Canada, Canadian Gardening,* and *Style at Home* will vary substantially as well. Each of these special-interest vehicles puts the reader in a particular mood and the promotion of clothing, golf equipment, gardening tools, and home products will be affected.

The message may require a specific media and a certain media vehicle to achieve its objectives. Likewise, certain media and vehicles have images that may carry over to the perceptions of messages placed within them. The explanation of these considerations is the **vehicle source effect**, which is defined as the differential impact that the advertising exposure will have on the same audience member if the exposure occurs in one medium versus another.[17] People perceive ads differently depending on their context.[18] More recent research supported this view and also concluded that "better" advertising content positively influenced attitudes to the media vehicle, thus indicating a symbiotic relationship between advertiser and media vehicle.[19]

Brands look for specific media vehicles when implementing their plans, and Sony's Xperia Ion phone and P&G's Cheer detergent found a good fit with their executions. MTV.ca hosted four episodes of a Sony show that featured artists creating music with unusual items as instruments, all shot with the phone's HD video camera. A little over a half million viewers witnessed the performances and a total of 11 million media impressions ensued. A music video of the band Strange Talk included live links on colourful items (e.g., shirts, leggings); when clicked, users linked to the Cheer Facebook page to win the item and get a free sample, and received the opportunity to read about the product. Cheer managers looked to young consumers, new users in this category, who wore colourful clothes since that fit with the key benefit claim of the brand. The "Dig It! Get It!" campaign lifted purchase intent by 7 percent and claimed 47,000 new Facebook fans.[20]

An extension of this idea is the development of media engagement, where the media experiences of specific vehicles are identified along the global dimensions: inspiration, trustworthy, life enhancing, social involvement, and personal timeout. The purpose of this more detailed investigation of the media experience is to find a more specific link between the media vehicle and communication and behavioural effects.[21]

Related to the idea of directing messages to customers or non-customers, one author recommends finding a fit between the brand users and the media vehicle selected. Through the use of survey and syndicated data, the researcher concluded that demographic matching of target audience and media vehicle is less effective versus a similarity of brand and media vehicle users in terms of values. The author suggests that finding media vehicles that brand users are experiencing is possible for most major media.[22]

Once the media vehicle consideration is resolved, the media planner considers some other fine-tuning. The location within a particular medium (front page versus back page) and size of ad or length of commercial also merit examination. IMC Perspective 10-2 identifies award-winning marketing communications where both media strategy and media tactics contributed to their success.

IMC PERSPECTIVE 10-2

ADVERTISING WITH TECHNOLOGY, MEDIA, AND CONTENT

The AToMiC awards celebrate the achievements of combined efforts in advertising (A), technology (T), media creativity (M), and content (C). Media, digital, or creative agencies can enter their work for the competition presuming it is AToMiC—meaning the marketing communication is innovative by going against conventional thinking and uses elements in all four areas. Although not identified at the time, previous chapters featured a good number of AToMiC winners thus far (e.g., Molson, Ubisoft), as good creative and good media tend to go hand in hand. So, for this vignette, we consider a few other notable winners as examples of innovative use of media.

© Historica Canada

Tim Hortons introduced a new blend of coffee for the first time in 50 years and needed a captivating way of communicating that it carried a new dark roast and encouraging trial. With 78 percent market share of the quick serve restaurant brewed coffee, the iconic brand felt the competitive pressure as consumer tastes evolved and loyal customers branched out seeking other options. The solution focused on a demonstration of the importance of taste. Tim Hortons' agency created a completely dark store with the idea that consumers' taste sensation would be heightened as they sipped the new blend. After people commented on their experience, the lights were turned on to reveal dark coffee, much to their surprise. The filmed responses appeared on YouTube (along with shorter TV versions) and became one of the most viewed productions. Tim Hortons received millions of social media impressions and served over 52 million cups during four months.

Ikea's inventive furniture proved to be the inspiration for thinking outside the box for Montrealers' decorating ideas after the infamous July 1 moving day. With all leases ending on the same day, moving becomes a major headache for all, and Ikea's agency saw this as the perfect opportunity to literally get the message into the hands of those considering new furniture purchases right after changing their residence. Ikea made boxes available for people to use while moving but they looked like no ordinary boxes. Instead, the boxes appeared in the exact size of various furniture pieces with appropriate imagery and lettering on the outside. Once in the new home, consumers visualized how the new furniture could fit in and coordinate with their existing furniture. Success was evident as Ikea ran out of the boxes within hours.

Historica Canada, an independent organization devoted to building awareness of Canadian history, relied on its agency to raise youth awareness of its Memory Project. The initiative used first-hand accounts of veterans to tell the story of Canada's military history. Communicating to young Canadians appeared as a worthy objective to keep the knowledge alive for decades to come. The innovative idea featured a message execution on the Snapchat app, however the instantly disappearing feature of the app sparked the teens' curiosity to encourage Internet site visits. Teens received a 12-second video of a real veteran on Remembrance Day, however the message did not fully play as it replicated the app feature. At this point, a message notified the teens that the veteran's story would vanish for real and that the teen could keep it alive by seeing the rest of it at www.thememoryproject.ca. Interested teens visited the site to see the ending of the hero's World War II story. Visits increased by over 500 percent from the previous year solely due to the message, as no other additional marketing occurred during November 11.

Sources:

http://atomicawards.strategyonline.ca/Winners/Winner/2015/?w=timsdarkstore;

http://atomicawards.strategyonline.ca/Winners/Winner/2015/?w=ikeainspirationbox;

http://atomicawards.strategyonline.ca/Winners/Winner/2015/?w=memoryproject.

Question:

1. Which of these media executions appears to be the most innovative?

RELATIVE COST ESTIMATES

The value of any strategy can be determined by how well it delivers the message effectively to the audience with the lowest cost and the least waste. The media planner strives for optimal delivery by balancing costs associated with each of the media strategy decisions. Media planning is inherently a series of trade-offs between reach and frequency or geographic coverage and scheduling, among others. As these trade-offs are investigated and finalized, the media planner estimates and compares costs. Advertising and promotional costs can be categorized in two ways: in terms of absolute cost and relative cost.

The **absolute cost** of the medium or vehicle is the actual total cost required to place the message. For example, a full-page four-colour ad in *Chatelaine* magazine costs about $42,000. **Relative cost** refers to the relationship between the price paid for advertising time or space and the size of the audience delivered. Relative costs are important because the manager must try to optimize audience delivery within budget constraints. Since a number of alternatives are available for delivering the message, the advertiser must evaluate the relative costs associated with these choices. For example, the media planner could compare the relative cost of reaching a member of the target audience in one magazine versus another. This decision can be influenced by the absolute cost of one magazine having a cheaper back page price versus another magazine. As the number of media alternatives rises, the number of comparisons grows considerably, potentially making this a tedious and difficult process. Media planners typically use two calculations, cost per thousand (CPM) and cost per ratings point (CPRP), to compare both media mix options or media vehicle options.

1. **Cost per thousand (CPM)**. Magazines, and some other media, provide cost breakdowns on the basis of cost per thousand people reached. The formula for this computation is

$$CPM = \frac{\text{Cost of ad space (absolute cost)}}{\text{Circulation}} \times 1,000$$

Figure 10-16 provides an example of this computation for two vehicles in the same medium—*Canadian Living* and *Chatelaine*—and shows that *Canadian Living* is a more cost-efficient buy for a comparable full page ad. However, many might consider the difference not substantial enough to influence the decision on which vehicle to select.

Figure 10-16 Cost per thousand computations: *Canadian Living* versus *Chatelaine*

	Canadian Living	**Chatelaine**
Per-page cost	$52,905	$55,085
Circulation	475,267	440,798
Calculation of CPM	$\frac{\$52,905 \times 1,000}{475,267}$	$\frac{\$55,085 \times 1,000}{440,798}$
CPM	$111.32	$124.97

Like magazines, newspapers now use the cost-per-thousand formula to determine relative costs. As shown in Figure 10-17, the *National Post* costs significantly less to advertise in than does *The Globe and Mail* based on a national advertiser spending $1 million annually.

Figure 10-17 Comparative costs in newspaper advertising

	The Globe and Mail	**National Post**
Cost per page	$56,224	$17,739
Circulation	313,331	188,654
Calculation	$CPM = \frac{\text{Page cost} \times 1,000}{\text{Circulation}}$ $= \frac{\$56,224 \times 1,000}{313,331}$ $= \$179.44$	$\frac{\$17,739 \times 1,000}{188,654}$
CPM	= $179.44	= $94.03

Some media, such as Internet display ads, quote their prices in terms of CPM. So if a display ad placement has a CPM of $30, the media buyer would select the display ad over these magazine and newspaper examples *if cost efficiency is deemed the only decision criterion*. However, virtually all media placement decisions involve multiple criteria beyond pure cost efficiency. In this case, the sizes of the ads are dramatically different, as other factors would be. A simple paid search result in the United Kingdom for Snickers with a link message consistent with its "Hungry" ad campaign produced a CPM of about $5.[23] While this appears impressive, the message is of low quality with a basic text; however, if the click-through rates to a colourful Internet ad proved strong, the CPM and message quality consideration might look more favourable.

2. **Cost per ratings point (CPRP)**. The broadcast media provide a different comparative cost figure, referred to as cost per ratings point or *cost per point (CPP)*, based on the following formula:

$$CPRP = \frac{\text{Cost of commercial time}}{\text{Program rating}}$$

An example of this calculation for a spot ad in a local TV market is shown in Figure 10-18. It indicates that Show A would be more cost-effective than Show B or Show C.

It is difficult to make comparisons across media. What is the broadcast equivalent of cost per thousand? In an attempt to standardize relative costing procedures, the broadcast and newspaper media have begun to provide costs per thousand, using the following formulas:

Figure 10-18   Comparison of cost per ratings point in a local TV market

	Show A	Show B	Show C
Cost per spot ad	$5,000	$10,000	$16,000
Rating	20	10	40
Calculation	$5,000/20	$10,000/10	$16,000/40
CPRP (CPP)	$250	$1,000	$400

$$\text{Television: } \frac{\text{Cost of 1 unit of time} \times 1,000}{\text{Program rating}} \qquad \text{Newspapers: } \frac{\text{Cost of ad space} \times 1,000}{\text{Circulation}}$$

While the comparison of media on a cost-per-thousand basis is important, intermedia comparisons can be misleading. The ability of TV to provide both sight and sound, the longevity of magazines, and other characteristics of each medium make direct comparisons difficult. The media planner should use the cost-per-thousand numbers but must also consider the specific characteristics of each medium and each media vehicle in the decision.

The cost per thousand may overestimate or underestimate the actual cost efficiency. Consider a situation where some waste coverage is inevitable because the circulation exceeds the target audience. If the people reached by this message are not potential buyers of the product, then having to pay to reach them results in too low a cost per thousand, as shown in scenario A of Figure 10-19.

Figure 10-19   Cost per thousand estimates

Scenario A: Overestimation of Efficiency	
Target audience	18–49
Magazine circulation	400,000
Circulation to target audience	65% (260,000)
Cost per page	$15,600

$$CPM = \frac{\$15,600 \times 1,000}{400,000} = \$39$$

$$CPM \text{ (actual target audience)} = \frac{\$15,600 \times 1,000}{260,000} = \$60$$

[Continued on next page]

[Figure 10-19 continued]

Scenario B: Underestimation of Efficiency	
Target audience	All age groups, male and female
Magazine circulation	400,000
Cost per page	$15,600
Pass-along rate	3

$$\text{CPM (based on readers per copy)} = \frac{\text{Page cost} \times 1,000}{260,000 + 3(260,000)} = \frac{\$15,600 \times 1,000}{1,040,000} = \$15.00$$

*Assuming pass-along was valid.

We must use the potential reach to the target audience—the destination sought—rather than the overall circulation figure. A medium with a much higher cost per thousand may be a wiser buy if it is reaching more potential receivers. (Most media buyers rely on **target CPM (TCPM)**, which calculates CPMs based on the target audience, not the overall audience.)

CPM may also underestimate cost efficiency. Sellers of magazine advertising space have argued for years that because more than one person may read an issue, the actual reach is underestimated. They want to use the number of **readers per copy** as the true circulation. This would include a **pass-along rate**, estimating the number of people who read the magazine without buying it. Scenario B in Figure 10-19 shows how this underestimates cost efficiency. Consider a family in which a father, mother, and two teenagers read each issue of *Maclean's*. While the circulation figure includes only one magazine, in reality there are four potential exposures in this household, increasing the total reach.

While the number of readers per copy makes intuitive sense, it has the potential to be extremely inaccurate. The actual number of times the magazine changes hands is difficult to determine. While research is conducted, pass-along estimates are very subjective and using them to estimate reach is speculative. These figures are regularly provided by the media, but managers are selective about using them. At the same time the art of media buying enters, for many magazines' managers have a good idea how much greater the reach is than their circulation figures provided.

A majority of the cost data for media is found with Canadian Advertising Rates and Data (CARD). This subscription service offers extensive information regarding all media. For example, it identifies every media outlet and gives a description of its service and audience. The resource also provides the actual costs of many media for computing the media budget. Data regarding some media are not provided (e.g., TV), while some promotional media costs (e.g., coupon book) are included. Students can typically retrieve this information through the library's computer network or the monthly reports kept in the periodical section of their school's library. We will address specific media costs in each of the subsequent media chapters, but as the past several figures indicate, most media are purchased on a per unit basis: page for print, time for broadcast, and some, like Internet display ads, on a CPM basis.

BLOCKING CHART

The media planning process typically concludes with a blocking chart. The **blocking chart** summarizes many of the media-strategy and media-tactics decisions made thus far, and includes extensive implementation details that guide the media buyers as they attempt to achieve their objectives. An example for Knorr's "What's for Dinner" campaign is shown in Figure 10-20.

Figure 10-20   The Knorr blocking chart shows all media and IMC tools

Knorr	August				September					October				November				December				
	30	6	13	20	27	3	10	17	24	1	8	15	22	29	5	12	19	26	3	10	17	24
	32	33	34	35	36	37	38	39	40	41	42	43	44	45	46	47	48	49	50	51	52	53
Digital:																						
Phase 1 - BARBEQUE - PRE-ROLL																						
Phase 2 - WHAT'S FOR DINNER FOODIE SURGE-HPTOs/TAKEOVERS																						
Phase 3 - WHAT'S FOR DINNER FULL MARKET - DISPLAY																						
WHATS'S FOR DINNER - SOCIAL MEDIA																						
WHATS'S FOR DINNER - SEARCH																						

© CASSIES

A blocking chart is typically formatted according to some type of calendar. While it is often done on a weekly basis, a firm with limited communications may organize it monthly. On the other hand, a firm with extensive communications may produce a blocking chart on a daily basis for all or critical parts of its annual media plan. For example, if a firm launches a new product, daily communications during the first few weeks can be critical and specific media exposure is planned in minute detail.

A synopsis of the media choice decisions with respect to television, print, and out-of-home media may also be contained in the blocking chart. In this age of IMC, the blocking chart can also contain elements of other communication tools such as marketing events, public relations, or direct-response tools. In all likelihood, the blocking chart will break these media choices down by different vehicles and different geographic markets.

Another key detail of the blocking chart is showing the relative weight of media expenditures. For example, it could illustrate the number of GRPs per week for each city. Related to this is a clear indication of the reach and frequency of each media decision.

Because the blocking chart concludes the media planning process, the media expenditures have to be included either in summary form or accompanying the blocking chart. This information allows managers to assess the quality of the media plan and to determine whether any adjustments need to be made during the planning time frame.

While we have briefly highlighted the nature of a blocking chart, it may in fact be more than one chart. If a firm is using multiple media across many months and geographic markets, it may have one summary chart and other supporting charts that break the information down into more readable and action-oriented subsections. Remember that a blocking chart is also a communication tool that has to be organized and presented so that all participants are familiar with all decisions.

 Budget Setting

This section begins with a brief overview of the budget setting process, provides insight into underlying theory with respect to budget setting, discusses how companies budget for promotional efforts, and demonstrates the inherent strengths and weaknesses associated with these theoretical and managerial approaches.

OVERVIEW

Establishing media and communication objectives is an important part of the media planning process; however, the degree to which these objectives can be attained is a function of the media budget or how much the firm wishes to invest in advertising. No organization has an unlimited budget, so objectives must be set with the budget in mind and the budget has to be realistic to achieve any media and communication objectives. However, a longitudinal study with nearly 30 years of data concluded that advertisers consistently overspent in media advertising (e.g., TV, radio, newspaper, magazine, outdoor, Internet) and that the problem worsened over the most recent decade. The data indicated that TV performed the worst by a noticeable amount for just about every year.[24] We discuss many budgeting methods even if they are not recommended. It is important to understand all methods since they are commonly employed by marketers, despite having disadvantages that limit their effectiveness.

In a study of how managers make advertising and promotion budgeting decisions, researchers interviewed 21 managers in eight consumer-product firms and found that the budget-setting process is a perplexing issue and that institutional pressures led to a greater proportion of dollars being spent on sales promotions. The authors concluded that, to successfully develop and implement the budget, managers must (1) employ a comprehensive strategy to guide the process, (2) develop a strategic planning framework that employs an integrated marketing communications philosophy, (3) build in contingency plans, (4) focus on long-term objectives, and (5) consistently evaluate the effectiveness of programs.[25]

Advertising agencies are involved in developing the messages for their clients, but curiously, they are not as involved with the managers of their client organizations when it comes to determining the budget.[26] The authors of this study identify factors inhibiting this opportunity: industry, organizational structure, politics, tradition, compensation system, trust, and length of relationship. They conclude that both agencies and clients could benefit from stronger partnerships on the budget amount. Clients would get a more complete recommendation from communication objectives to message and finally to media purchase, while agencies would better understand the client's business and the pressures faced.

THEORETICAL APPROACHES IN BUDGET SETTING

Most of the approaches used to establish advertising budgets are based on marginal analysis or sales response models. These approaches are viewed as theoretical since academics have long debated the overall effects of advertising on sales, a topic that continually perplexes managers as well.

Marginal Analysis   Figure 10-21 graphically represents the concept of **marginal analysis**. As advertising/promotional expenditures increase, sales and gross margins also increase to a point, but then they level off. Profits are shown to be a result of the gross margin minus advertising expenditures. A marginal analysis theory suggests that a firm would continue to spend advertising/promotional dollars as long as the marginal revenues created by these expenditures exceeded the incremental advertising/promotional costs. As shown on the graph, the optimal expenditure level is the point where marginal costs equal the marginal revenues they generate (point A). If the sum of the advertising/promotional expenditures exceeded the revenues they generated, one would conclude that the appropriations were too high and scale down the budget. If revenues were higher, a higher budget might be in order.

Figure 10-21   Marginal analysis

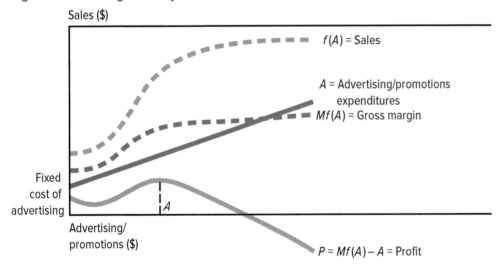

The logic of marginal analysis is weak due to two assumptions. The first is that sales are a direct result of advertising and promotional expenditures and this effect can be measured. In studies using sales as a direct measure, it has been almost impossible to establish the contribution of advertising and promotion.[27] Furthermore, it is generally believed that sales result from the successful attainment of behavioural and communication objectives relevant for the target audience. The second is that advertising and promotion are solely responsible for sales. This assumption ignores the remaining elements of the marketing mix which do contribute to a company's success.

Sales Response Models   The sales curve in Figure 10-21 shows sales levelling off even though advertising and promotion efforts continue to increase. The relationship between advertising and sales has been the topic of much research and discussion designed to determine the shape of the response curve. Almost all advertisers subscribe to one of two models of the advertising/sales response function: the concave-downward response curve or the S-shaped response function.

According to the **concave-downward response curve** (Figure 10-22A), the effects of advertising expenditures on sales quickly begin to diminish. Researchers concluded that the effects of advertising budgets follow the microeconomic law of diminishing returns.[28] That is, as the amount of advertising increases, its incremental value decreases. The logic is that those with the greatest potential to buy will likely act on the first (or earliest) exposures, while those less likely to buy are not likely to change as a result of the advertising. For those who may be potential buyers, each additional ad will supply little or no new information that will affect their decision.

Figure 10-22   Advertising sales/response functions

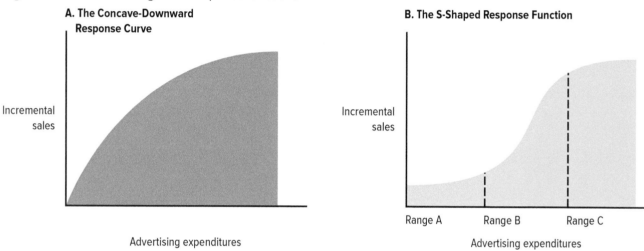

According to the **S-shaped response function** (Figure 10-22B), the effects of advertising expenditures on sales follow an S-shape. Initial outlays of the advertising budget have little impact (as indicated by the essentially flat sales curve in range A). After a certain budget level has been reached (the beginning of range B), advertising and promotional efforts begin to have an effect, as additional increments of expenditures result in increased sales. This incremental gain continues only to a point, however, because at the beginning of range C additional expenditures begin to return little or nothing in the way of sales. The logic is that advertising takes time before its effects (awareness, etc.) take hold.

Even though marginal analysis and the sales response curves may not apply directly, they give managers insight into a theoretical basis of how the budgeting process should work. Empirical evidence indicates that the models may have validity, however the advertising and sales effects may be reversed as we cannot be sure whether the results actually demonstrate the advertising/sales relationship or vice versa.

A weakness in attempting to use sales as a direct measure of response to advertising is the effect of situational factors as shown in Figure 10-23. For a product characterized by emotional buying motives, hidden product qualities, and/or a strong basis for differentiation, advertising would have a noticeable impact on sales. Products characterized as large-dollar purchases and those in the maturity or decline stages of the product life cycle would be less likely to benefit. These factors should be considered in the budget appropriation decision but should not be the sole determinants of where and when to increase or decrease expenditures.

Figure 10-23   Factors influencing advertising budgets

Factor	Relationship of Advertising/Sales	Factor	Relationship of Advertising/Sales
Customer Factors		**Product Factors**	
Industrial products users	—	Basis for differentiation	+
Concentration of users	+	Hidden product qualities	+
Market Factors		Emotional buying motives	+
Stage of product life cycle		Durability	—
Introductory	+	Large dollar purchase	—
Growth	+	Purchase frequency	Curvilinear
Maturity	—	**Strategy Factors**	
Decline	—	Regional markets	—
Inelastic demand	+	Early stage of brand life cycle	+
Market share	—	High margins in channels	—
Competition		Long channels of distribution	+
Active	+	High prices	+
Concentrated	+	High quality	+
Pioneer in market	—	**Cost Factors**	
		High profit margins	+

Note: + relationship indicates a positive effect of advertising on sales; — relationship indicates little or no effect of advertising on sales.

MANAGERIAL APPROACHES IN BUDGET SETTING

This section reviews methods developed through practice and experience for setting budgets and the relative advantages and disadvantages of each. It is important to review many approaches since firms may employ more than one method and budgeting methods also vary according to the size and sophistication of the firm.[29] Based on this research we will indicate its current usage within each description. One approach is **top-down budgeting** because an amount is established at an executive level and then the monies are passed down to the departments (as shown in Figure 10-24). Top-down methods include the affordable method, arbitrary allocation, percentage of sales, competitive parity, and return on investment (ROI). A flaw of these judgmental top-down methods is that top-down budgeting leads to predetermined budget appropriations not linked to the objectives and strategies designed to accomplish them. A more effective budgeting strategy would be to consider the firm's communication objectives and budget for the necessary promotional mix strategies to attain these goals. This is known as **bottom-up budgeting** and we review two approaches: the objective and task method and payout planning.

The Affordable Method   In the **affordable method**, the firm determines the amount to be spent in production and operations (and so on), and then allocates the remainder to advertising and promotion. The task to be performed by the advertising/promotions function is not considered, and the likelihood of under- or overspending is high, as no guidelines for measuring the effects of budgets are established. This approach is found in small firms due to cash flow concerns and non–market-driven large firms and is used 27 percent of the time.

Figure 10-24   Top-down and bottom-up approaches to budget setting

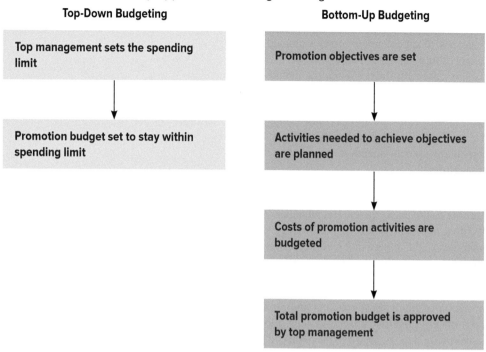

The logic for this approach stems from "We can't be hurt with this method" thinking. That is, if we know what we can afford and we do not exceed it, we will not get into financial problems. While this may be true in a strictly accounting sense, it does not reflect sound managerial decision making from a marketing perspective. Often this method does not allocate enough money to get the product off the ground and into the market. In terms of the S-shaped sales response model, the firm is operating in range A. Or the firm may be spending more than necessary, operating in range C. When the market gets tough and sales and/or profits begin to fall, this method is likely to lead to budget cuts at a time when the budget should be increased.

Arbitrary Allocation   Perhaps an even weaker method than the affordable method for establishing a budget is **arbitrary allocation**, in which virtually no theoretical basis is considered and the budgetary amount is often set by fiat. That is, the budget is determined by management solely on the basis of what is felt to be necessary. The arbitrary allocation approach has no obvious advantages. No systematic thinking has occurred, no objectives have been budgeted for, and the concept and purpose of advertising and promotion have been largely ignored. Other than the fact that the manager believes some monies must be spent on advertising and promotion and then picks a number, there is no good explanation why this approach continues to be used. Yet, about 11 percent of budgets are set this way, and we point out that this method is used—not recommended.

Percentage of Sales   Another method used for budget setting, about 10 percent of the time, is the **percentage-of-sales method**, in which the advertising and promotions budget is based on future sales of the product. Management determines the amount by either (1) taking a percentage of the sales dollars or (2) assigning a fixed amount of the unit product cost to promotion and multiplying this amount by the number of units sold. These two methods are shown in Figure 10-25.

Figure 10-25   Alternative methods for computing percentage of sales

Method 1: Straight Percentage of Sales		
Year 1	Total dollar sales	$1,000,000
	Straight % of sales at 10%	$100,000
Year 2	Advertising budget	$100,000
Method 2: Percentage of Unit Cost		
Year 1	Cost per bottle to manufacturer	$4.00
	Unit cost allocated to advertising	$1.00
Year 2	Forecast sales, 100,000 units	
	Advertising budget (100,000 × $1)	$100,000

The percentage-of-sales method offers advantages. It is financially safe and keeps ad spending within reasonable limits, as it bases spending on the past year's sales or what the firm expects to sell in the upcoming year. Thus, there will be sufficient monies to cover this budget, with increases in sales leading to budget increases and sales decreases resulting in advertising decreases. The percentage-of-sales method is simple, straightforward, and easy to implement. Regardless of which basis—past or future sales—is employed, the calculations used to arrive at a budget are not difficult. Finally, this budgeting approach is generally stable. While the budget may vary with increases and decreases in sales, as long as these changes are not drastic, the manager will have a reasonable idea of the parameters of the budget.

However, the percentage-of-sales method has disadvantages, including the basic premise on which the budget is established: sales. Letting the level of sales determine the amount of advertising and promotions dollars to be spent reverses the cause-and-effect relationship between advertising and sales. It treats advertising as an expense associated with making a sale, rather than as an investment.

Another problem with this approach was actually cited as an advantage earlier: stability. If all firms use a similar percentage, that will bring stability to the marketplace. But what happens if someone varies from this standard percentage? The problem is that this method does not allow for changes in strategy either internally or from competitors. An aggressive firm may wish to allocate more monies to the advertising and promotions budget, a strategy that is not possible with a percentage-of-sales method unless the manager is willing to deviate from industry standards.

The percentage-of-sales method of budgeting may result in severe misappropriation of funds. If advertising and promotion have a role to perform in marketing a product, then allocating more monies to advertising will, as shown in the S-shaped curve, generate incremental sales (to a point). If products with low sales have smaller promotion budgets, this will hinder sales progress. At the other extreme, very successful products may have excess budgets, some of which may be better appropriated elsewhere.

The percentage-of-sales method is also difficult to employ for new product introductions. If no sales histories are available, there is no basis for establishing the budget. Projections of future sales may be difficult, particularly if the product is highly innovative and/or has fluctuating sales patterns.

Finally, if the budget is contingent on sales, decreases in sales will lead to decreases in budgets when they most need to be increased. Continuing to cut the advertising and promotion budgets may just add impetus to the downward sales trend (Figure 10-26). Some argue that more successful companies allocate additional funds during hard times or downturns in the cycle of sales and are rewarded in future years.

A variation on the percentage-of-sales method uses a percentage of projected future sales as a base. This method also uses either a straight percentage of projected sales or a unit cost projection. One advantage of using future sales as a base is that the budget is not based on last year's sales. As the market changes, management must factor the effect of these changes on sales into next year's forecast rather than relying on past data. The resulting budget is more likely to reflect current conditions and be more appropriate. While this appears to be a remedy for some of the problems discussed here, the reality is that problems with forecasting, cyclical growth, and uncontrollable factors limit its effectiveness.

Figure 10-26   Investments pay off in later years

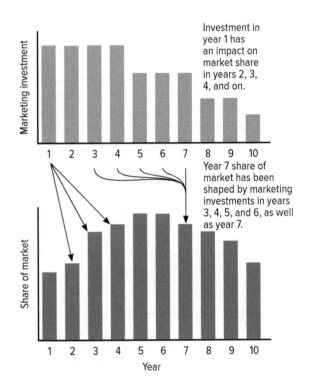

Competitive Parity   Firms having similar advertising expenditures resulting from a competitive analysis occurs 3 percent of the time. Competitors' advertising expenditures are available from market research firms, trade associations, advertising industry periodicals, and media tracking firms. This method is typically used in conjunction with other methods (e.g., percentage-of-sales).

In the **competitive parity method**, managers establish budget amounts by matching the competition's percentage-of-sales expenditures, essentially taking advantage of the collective wisdom of the industry. It also takes the competition into consideration, which leads to stability in the marketplace by minimizing marketing expenditure battles. If companies know that competitors are unlikely to match their increases in promotional spending, they are less likely to take an aggressive posture to attempt to gain market share.

The competitive parity method has disadvantages. First, it ignores the fact that advertising and promotions are designed to accomplish specific objectives by addressing certain problems and opportunities. Second, it assumes that because firms have similar expenditures, their programs will be equally effective. This assumption ignores the success of creative executions, media allocations, and/or promotion. Third, it ignores advantages of the firm itself—some companies simply make better products than others. A study by Yoo and Mandhachitara indicates that a competitive parity strategy must consider the fact that a competitor's advertising can actually benefit one's own firm, and that one competitor's gain is not always the other's loss. As shown in Figure 10-27 there are four different situations to determine how the competitive budgets may impact sales—only one of which involves the zero-sum scenario.[30]

Figure 10-27   Competitors' advertising outlays do not always hurt

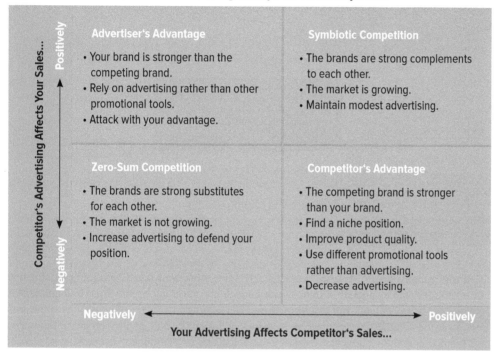

Fourth, there is no guarantee that competitors will continue to pursue their existing strategies. Since competitive parity figures are determined by examination of competitors' previous years' promotional expenditures, changes in market emphasis and/or spending may not be recognized until the competition has already established an advantage. Further, there is no guarantee that a competitor will not increase or decrease its own expenditures, regardless of what other companies do.

Return on Investment (ROI)   In the **ROI budgeting method**, advertising and promotions are considered investments, like plant and equipment. This is consistent with the "advertising causes sales" point in the marginal analysis and S-shaped curve approaches; incremental investments in advertising and promotions lead to increases in sales. The key word here is *investment,* as this approach is seen 12 percent of the time. The budgetary appropriation (investment) leads to certain returns; thus advertising and promotion are expected to earn a certain return.

While the ROI method looks good on paper, the reality is that it is rarely possible to assess the returns provided by the promotional effort—at least as long as sales continue to be the basis for evaluation. Thus, while managers are certain to ask how much return they are getting for such expenditures, the question remains unanswered, and ROI remains a virtually unused method of budgeting.

Objective and Task Method   Objective setting and budgeting should occur simultaneously rather than sequentially; it is difficult to establish a budget without specific objectives in mind, and setting objectives without regard to how much money is available makes no sense. The **objective and task method** of budget setting consists of three steps: (1) defining the communications objectives to be accomplished, (2) determining the specific strategies and tasks needed to attain them, and (3) estimating the costs associated with performance of these strategies and tasks (Figure 10-28). This method is used 26 percent of the time.

1. *Establish objectives.* A company will have marketing and communication objectives to achieve. After the former are established, the firm determines the specific communication objectives needed to accomplish these goals. Communication objectives must be specific, attainable, and measurable, as well as time limited.

2. *Determine required tasks.* A number of elements are involved in the strategic plan designed to attain the objectives established. These tasks may include advertising in media, sales promotions, and/or other elements of the promotional mix, each with its own role to perform.

3. *Estimate required expenditures.* Buildup analysis requires determining the estimated costs associated with the tasks developed in the previous step. For example, it involves costs for developing awareness through advertising, trial through sampling, and so forth.

Figure 10-28   The objective and task method

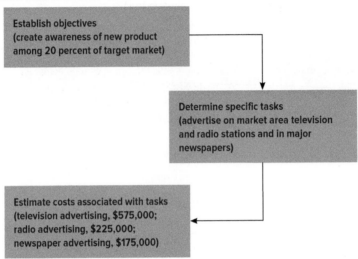

As we saw in Chapter 9 on measuring effectiveness, there are ways to determine how well one is attaining established objectives. Performance should be monitored and evaluated in light of the budget appropriated. Money may be better spent on new goals once specific objectives have been attained. For example, if one has achieved the level of consumer awareness sought, the budget should be altered to stress a higher-order objective such as evaluation or trial. As this suggests, the major advantage of the objective and task method is that the budget is driven by the objectives to be attained. The managers closest to the marketing effort will have specific strategies and input into the budget-setting process.

The major disadvantage of this method is the difficulty of determining which tasks will be required and the costs associated with each. For example, specifically what tasks are needed to attain awareness among 50 percent of the target audience? How much will it cost to perform these tasks? While these decisions are easier to determine for certain objectives—for example, estimating the costs of sampling required to stimulate trial in a defined market area—it is not always possible to know exactly what is required and/or how much it will cost to complete the job. This process is easier if there is past experience to use as a guide, with either the existing product or a similar one in the same product category. For this situation, payout planning is offered as an alternative bottom-up approach.

Payout Planning   The first months of a new product's introduction typically require heavier-than-normal advertising and promotion expenditures to stimulate higher levels of awareness and subsequent trial. Research estimated that the average share of advertising to sales ratio necessary to launch a new product successfully is approximately 1.5:2.0.[31] This means that a new entry should be spending at approximately twice the desired market share, as shown in Figure 10-29. Brand 101 gained a 12.6 percent market share by spending 34 percent of the total advertising dollars in this food product category.

Figure 10-29   Share of advertising/sales relationship (two-year summary)

New Brands of Food Products

Brand	Average share of advertising	Attained share of sales	Ratio of share of advertising to share of sales
101	34%	12.6%	2.7
102	16	10.0	1.6
103	8	7.6	1.1
104	4	2.6	1.5
105	3	2.1	1.4

To determine how much to spend, marketers often develop a **payout plan** that determines the investment value. The basic idea is to project the revenues the product will generate, as well as the costs it will incur, over two to three years. Based on an expected rate of return, the payout plan will assist in determining how much advertising and promotion expenditure will be necessary when the return might be expected. A three-year payout plan is shown in Figure 10-30. The product would lose money in year 1, almost break even in year 2, and finally begin to show substantial profits by the end of year 3.

Figure 10-30   Example of three-year payout plan ($ millions)

	Year 1	Year 2	Year 3
Product sales	15.0	35.50	60.75
Profit contribution (@ $0.50/case)	7.5	17.75	30.38
Advertising/promotions	15.0	10.50	8.50
Profit (loss)	(7.5)	7.25	21.88
Cumulative profit (loss)	(7.5)	(0.25)	21.63

The advertising and promotion figures are highest in year 1 and decline in years 2 and 3, reflecting additional outlays needed to make a rapid impact. For example, retailers expect immediate success, otherwise they will move on to other products needing their limited shelf space. The budget also reflects the firm's guidelines for new product expenditures, since companies generally have set deadlines to establish profitability. Finally, building market share may be more difficult than maintaining it—thus the substantial dropoff in expenditures in later years. When used in conjunction with the objective and task method, payout planning provides a logical approach to budget setting as is seen infrequently at 3 percent of the time.

LO5   IMC Planning: Budget Allocation

Once the overall budget has been determined, the next step is to allocate it. The allocation decision involves determining the relative expenditures across IMC tools and markets while accounting for market-share goals, client/agency policies, and organizational characteristics.

IMC TOOLS

The promotional budget is allocated to broadcast, print, and out-of-home media as suggested in the media plan, and among other IMC tools such as sales promotion, public relations, Internet, and direct marketing. As noted in Chapter 1, firms are increasingly evaluating and employing all IMC tools to achieve their communication and behavioural objectives. For example, Canadian Tire planned to spend $600 million per year from 2015 to 2017 on digital communication across its ecommerce site, advertising, and other communication tools.[32] The degree to which a firm uses more tools to achieve its objectives influences the relative emphasis. Figure 10-31 summarizes examples of traditional media plans and others with evolving IMC tools.[33]

Figure 10-31   Summary of examples of target and media choices

Brand	Target	Media
Newfoundland and Labrador Tourism—$5 million	Sophisticated travellers	TV (Specialty channels), Newspaper (display & insert)
	45+, 25–34 (no-nesting)	Cinema, In-flight video
	Desiring intriguing experiences	Online Rich Media (Weather Network/ Fresh Air)
Nissan Sentra SE-R—$1 million	Auto enthusiasts	YouTube channel, YouTube take-over
	Men	Pre-roll, Page domination (*Sympatico/ Top Gear*)
	Desiring commuter transport	TV teaser ads
Knorr Sidekicks—$4 million	Users of competing product	Pre-launch: Direct mail to current users
	Moms	Wave 1: TV, Magazine, Digital display ad, In-store
	Desiring lower salt product	Wave 2: Wave 1 plus Premium, Social Media

As the macro statistics of Figure 10-1 indicate, firms have a variety of tools and approaches for delivering messages to their target audiences, and careful consideration of the allocation across the tools each year is a central task for IMC planning. The budget allocation across media has been the focus of some research to find the right combination of media, and providing the optimal expenditure levels is a critical decision that has long-lasting communication and financial implications. A study of the SUV market found that the effects of the media mix for the Ford Explorer outperformed the effects of the media mix for the Jeep Grand Cherokee. The authors conclude that balance between image-oriented media versus more tactical media had stronger effects for this set of data.[34] Another study concludes that some media have longer carryover effects versus other media, which should also guide the media allocation decision for advertising.[35] The next research step is to assess the relative effects across different combinations of IMC tools.

MARKET SHARE GOALS

While the budget should be allocated according to the IMC tools needed to accomplish the objectives, the size of the market affects the amount of money invested in promotion. In smaller markets, it is less expensive to reach the target audience and high expenditure in these markets will lead to wasted coverage. In larger markets, the target audience may be more dispersed and thus more expensive to reach. Also, a marketing manager may allocate additional monies to markets that hold higher potential; just because a market does not have high sales does not mean it should be ignored. The key is potential, since a market with low sales and high growth potential may be a candidate for additional appropriations.

Two studies in the *Harvard Business Review* discussed advertising spending with the goal of maintaining and increasing market share.[36] One study compared the brand's share of market with its share of advertising voice (the total value of the main media exposure in the product category) and classified the brands as "profit taking brands, or underspenders" and "investment brands, those whose share of voice is clearly above their share of market." The study indicated that for those brands with small market shares, profit takers are in the minority; however, as the brands increase their market share, nearly three out of five have a proportionately smaller share of voice.

Three factors explained this change. First, new brands generally receive higher-than-average advertising support. Second, older brands received less advertising support when they reached the maturity stage of the product life cycle. Third, there's an advertising economy of scale whereby advertising works harder for well-established brands, so a lower expenditure is required. Thus, for larger brands, it may be possible to reduce advertising expenditures and still maintain market share. Smaller brands, on the other hand, have to continue to maintain a large share of voice. The second study examined the advertising budget in a situation where the marketer wishes to increase market share. Analysis suggested that marketers should be focusing on markets where competition is weak and/or underspending instead of advertising nationally, as shown in Figure 10-32.

Figure 10-32   The share of voice (SOV) effect and ad spending: Priorities in individual markets

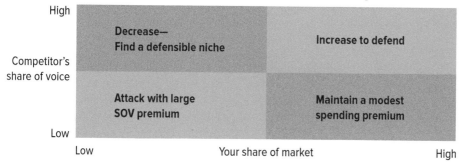

One factor influencing these suggestions is **economies of scale** in advertising. It is argued that larger advertisers can maintain advertising shares that are smaller than their market shares because they get better advertising rates, have declining average costs of production, and accrue the advantages of advertising several products jointly. Some studies presented evidence that firms and/or brands maintaining a large share of the market have an advantage over smaller competitors and thus can spend less money on advertising and realize a better return.[37] Reviewing the studies in support of this position and then conducting research over a variety of small-package products, another researcher concluded otherwise; larger brand share products might actually be at a disadvantage.[38] Results indicated that leading brands spend an average of 2.5 percentage points more than their brand share on advertising. The results of this and other studies suggest there really are no economies of scale to be accrued from the size of the firm or the market share of the brand.[39]

ORGANIZATIONAL FACTORS

A review of how allocation decisions are made between advertising and sales promotion concluded that organizational factors play an important role.[40] The authors noted that the following factors influence the decision: organizational structure, power and politics, use of expert opinions (e.g., consultants), preferences and experiences of the decision maker, approval and negotiation channels, and pressure on senior managers to arrive at the optimal budget.

One example of how these factors influence allocations relates to the level of interaction between marketing and other functional departments, such as accounting and operations. The authors note that the relative importance of advertising versus sales promotion might vary from department to department. Accountants, being dollars-and-cents minded, would argue for the sales impact of promotions, while operations would argue against sales promotions because the sudden surges in demand that might result would throw off production schedules. The marketing department might be influenced by the thinking of either of these groups in making its decision.

The tendencies can also be seen with the agency that may discourage the allocation of monies to sales promotion, preferring to spend them on the advertising area. The agency may take the position that these monies are harder to track in terms of effectiveness and may be used improperly if not under its control. Furthermore, ad agencies are managed by officers who have ascended through the creative ranks and are inclined to emphasize the creative budget, while others may have preferences for a specific medium. Finally, both the agency and the client may favour certain aspects of the promotional program, perhaps on the basis of past successes, that will substantially influence where dollars are spent.

Learning Objectives Summary

 Illustrate how a media plan is developed.

Media planning involves delivering the marketing communications message through different channels such as television, radio, print, and out-of-home, among others. Media planning is required for advertising to deliver the creative strategy but also for any other IMC tool. For example, a sales promotion offer might be communicated over the radio; a charity event that a brand sponsors could be found in a local city newspaper; or a transit ad possibly directs commuters to a firm's website.

A media plan is generally the end result of the media planning process, and it contains sections for objectives, strategy decisions, and tactical decisions. The media plan's objectives must be designed to support the overall marketing objectives and help achieve the behavioural and communication objectives determined for each target audience.

The basic task involved in the development of media strategy is to determine the best matching of media to the target audience, given the constraints of the budget. The media planner attempts to balance reach and frequency and to deliver the message to the intended audience with a minimum of waste coverage. Media strategy development has been called more of an art than a science because, while many quantitative data are available, the planner also relies on creativity and non-quantifiable factors.

 Explain the process and identify the decisions for implementing media strategies.

This chapter discussed five media strategy decisions, including developing a proper media mix, determining target audience coverage, determining geographic coverage, scheduling, and balancing reach and frequency. A summary chart of strengths and limitations of media alternatives was provided. The list provides a starting point for planners who select the right combination of media based on the communication problem or opportunity.

 Explain the process and identify the decisions for implementing media tactics.

The chapter also looked at tactical decisions that fine-tune the media strategy. The media vehicle plays a key part in the media plan as the media planner carefully matches the viewers, listeners, and readers of the media and the profile of the target audience. Relative cost estimates guide the media planner's final decisions for vehicle selection by finding the most cost-efficient placement. Fine-tuning of scheduling details is finalized with the realization of a blocking chart that summarizes all media decisions and costs across relevant time periods and geographic locations.

 Distinguish among the theoretical and managerial approaches for media budget setting.

This chapter summarized theoretical and managerial approaches for budget setting. Theoretical methods feature economic models (i.e., marginal analysis, sales response) that attempt to demonstrate the effects of advertising on sales, often without accounting for the effects of other marketing mix variables. Top-down managerial approaches include affordable, arbitrary allocation, percentage of sales, competitive parity, and return on investment. The methods are often viewed as lacking in any theoretical basis while ignoring the role of advertising and promotion in the marketing mix.

Bottom-up managerial approaches include the objective and task method and payout planning. In particular, the objective and task method connects the cost of advertising and promotion to the communication and behavioural objectives expected for the communication program, as opposed to broader marketing objectives expected for the marketing program. While the objective and task method offers an improvement over the top-down approaches, firms continue to use a combination of approaches to make the budget decision.

 LO5   Apply the methods for allocating the media budget to relevant IMC tools and market situations.

Once the overall budget has been determined, it is allocated to the individual media for advertising and any other IMC tool requiring expenditures. The money for an individual tool may be allocated to certain markets depending on level of the brand's current market share. Sometimes markets are developed requiring a boost in expenditures, while other times markets are in a profit mode and less investment may be forthcoming. Some allocation decisions are affected by unique organizational or interorganizational factors that may be tangential to the primary goals of achieving communication objectives.

Review Questions

1. Explain why media planning involves a trade-off between reach and frequency.

2. Describe what is meant by *waste coverage*. The decision must often be made between waste coverage and undercoverage. Give examples when the marketer might have to choose between the two, and when it may be acceptable to live with waste coverage.

3. What is meant by *readers per copy*? How is this different from CPM? Explain the advantages and disadvantages associated with the use of both.

4. Identify the information resources required to calculate the budget using the objective and task method.

5. What factors influence the budget allocation to different media or different IMC tools?

Applied Questions

1. One long-time advertising agency executive noted that media planning is both an art and a science, with a leaning toward art. Explain what this means and provide examples.

2. Visit the websites for two magazines of the same genre and locate their media kits. Compare how each magazine persuades advertisers to select its media vehicle in terms of editorial content, readership information, customized services for advertising placements, and any other unique features.

3. Calculate the CPM for five or six different media vehicles that are interesting or topical.

4. Assume that a new entry-level car brand wants to achieve 30 percent awareness among graduated students aged 21–24. Calculate how much would have to be in the budget to achieve this objective.

5. For an up-and-coming brand of fashionable jeans, a rebranded local night club for dancing, and an established energy drink, identify the most appropriate media budget allocation (in percentages) to create awareness. Do the same for all three brands with respect to IMC tools.

CHAPTER ELEVEN

Broadcast Media

LEARNING OBJECTIVES

LO1 Describe different types of television advertising, specialty television advertising, alternative time periods and program format, and measurement of television audiences.

LO2 Summarize the strengths and limitations of television as an advertising medium.

LO3 Describe different types of radio advertising, alternative time periods and program format, and measurement of radio audiences.

LO4 Summarize the strengths and limitations of radio as an advertising medium.

LO5 Apply the media knowledge of TV and radio for strategic IMC decisions.

The Good Old Hockey Game—Any Time You Like!

The familiar cry "He shoots! He scores!" sounded more frequently with the NHL and Rogers Media broadcasting deal worth $5.2 billion over 12 years that started in the 2014–2015 season. The deal initially began with discussions between the two parties on whether the NHL would open up a bid for a new Sunday evening broadcast, and the conversation moved to the possibility of the NHL selling "all of it" to one broadcaster. Previously, the NHL partnered with the CBC and TSN in separate deals that ended with the 2013–2014 season. The Rogers Media deal included the Canadian broadcast and multimedia rights to NHL games in all languages and sub-licensing to the CBC and TVA for French broadcasting.

Rogers Media believed the image of its Sportsnet brand through its TV and radio stations, magazine, website, and mobile apps paved the way for the deal to materialize. The executives instrumental in putting the deal together felt it could not be done without a strong media brand and extensive media vehicles. And these executives parlayed their experience with the CBC's *Hockey Night in Canada* and multiple broadcasting deals for the Vancouver and London Olympics to see how the broadcasting could work on Sportsnet's six TV stations, CITY TV, and the CBC network. And with so many stations, Rogers Media planned to show many hockey games, with up to 10 games carried on a Saturday night with the expectation that overall viewership of 1.7–2 million could rise to 1.85–2.3 million.

To make the deal work financially, Rogers Media undertook research to understand how Canadians consume hockey. It needed to attract new viewers who had not watched hockey in the past, like new Canadians and younger Canadians; both of these groups watched other sports, or other programs, or consumed media content elsewhere. For younger Canadians on a second screen while the game aired, the media brand wanted to get a better read on how to link the game experience with social media activity. In addition, Rogers Media needed to ensure that loyal hockey viewers would transition to the new broadcaster and watch hockey on more nights, or watch two games a night more often since the availability increased. Finally, Rogers Media re-established the broadcast in Punjabi that had had a strong run for a while before the CBC pulled back on its broadcast.

Another aspect that made the deal financially viable is that the Sportsnet channels are a specialty network which obtains revenue from brands that want to advertise on TV, and subscription revenue from television service providers who offer the channels in their packages. Profitability of specialty channels continued its margin over conventional networks like the CBC, which lost high profile sports rights like the Grey Cup, the Brier, and finally the NHL. Sportsnet received more than $250 million from cable and other service providers. Coupled with the $120 million sub-licensing revenue from TVA, the deal may look reasonably strong by the end of its life.

When game time arrived, *Rogers Hometown Hockey* emerged as a key feature in the broadcast package to entice the new audiences Rogers Media envisioned. Modelled after the *Hockey Day in Canada* feature the CBC did once a year starting in 2000, the new version had its production crew travel to a different location each week throughout the country for the entire season. For each of the 25 episodes, the broadcast tapped into the joy of hockey by telling the stories of the NHL stars and creating interesting pieces that celebrated the game. And while this certainly worked well with achieving Rogers Media's target objectives, it also helped achieve its CRTC requirements of showing Canadian content of a national interest. Rogers Media generated interest throughout its organization, including at retail outlets and in magazine publications.

Sources: Alicia Androich, "Landing the Holy Grail," *Marketing Magazine*, January/February 2014; Susan Krashinsky and Eric Atkins, "How Do We Watch Hockey," *The Globe and Mail*, February 5, 2014, p. B.5; Susan Krashinsky, "Rogers Ramps Up NHL Ad Buys," *The Globe and Mail*, July 7, 2014, p. B.3; Simon Houpt, "NHL Deal Was Crucial to Survival, Rogers Tells CRTC," *The Globe and Mail*, April 9, 2014, B.6; James Bradshaw, "A Whole New Ball Game," *The Globe and Mail*, October 4, 2014, p. S.1.

Question:

1. How is the new Rogers Media plan for hockey broadcasting a good advertising opportunity for Canadian brands?

TV is in virtually every Canadian household and is a mainstay in most people's lives. The large number of television viewers are important to the TV networks and stations because they can sell time on popular programs to marketers who want to reach that audience with their advertising messages. Moreover, the qualities that make TV a great medium for information and entertainment also encourage creative ads to influence current and potential customers. Radio is also an integral part of people's lives as it is a constant companion in their cars, at home, and even at work for information and entertainment. Radio listeners are an important audience for marketers, just like TV viewers.

In this chapter, we describe the types of TV and radio media that advertisers may select within the media strategy, how advertisers buy TV and radio time, and how audiences are measured and evaluated for each medium. We summarize the specific strengths and limitations of each medium. Finally, we explain how advertisers use TV and radio as part of their advertising and media strategies. We follow this structure for TV and then radio.

 # Television

What is to become of TV viewing? One idea is that it is in fact not dying, but thriving for several reasons. First, people's desire to watch TV shows online actually means that current TV shows are very good. Second, people have no awareness of TV shows until they are on TV first. Third, people are watching TV content on other means of transmission, which is fine for the content producers but not so fine for the future of TV service providers. Fourth, nothing replaces the experience of watching live sports on a big screen except actually being there. Finally, it appears unlikely that the next generation of consumers will forgo buying a big-screen TV after leaving a family home that has one.[1]

A number of options are available to advertisers that choose to use TV as part of their media mix. They can purchase ads on shows that are broadcast across a national or regional network, buy a local or spot announcement in a few cities, or sponsor an entire program. Advertisers can also decide on the degree to which they want to advertise on specialty channels that cater to specific interests (e.g., sports, home). They can purchase advertising in different time periods and program formats that appeal to various types and sizes of audiences. We explore these three decisions in this section. The purchase of TV advertising time is a highly specialized part of the advertising business. Large TV advertisers generally use agency media specialists or specialized media buying services to arrange the media schedule and purchase TV time. We conclude this section with a discussion on measuring TV audiences because it is a critical input for TV advertising decisions.

TYPES OF TELEVISION ADVERTISING

A basic decision for all advertisers is how to allocate their TV media budget to network, local, or spot announcements. Most national advertisers use network schedules to provide national coverage and supplement this with regional or local spot purchases to reach markets where additional coverage is desired. Periodically we see major advertisers do sponsorship advertising as well.

Network Advertising   Advertisers disseminate their messages by purchasing airtime from a **television network**. Canada's television industry features six national networks. The Canadian Broadcasting Corporation (CBC) is a Crown corporation of the federal government of Canada, and its network reaches virtually all English-language homes. Radio-Canada is the CBC cousin for the French-language network, reaching viewers in Quebec and other Canadian provinces and territories. The Canadian Television Network (CTV) and Global both operate as a national English-language service in most Canadian provinces. CITY is a semi-national network in more populated cities in larger provinces of Canada. Finally, TVA, a private French-language network, broadcasts to most Quebec households and a significant number of French-speaking viewers throughout Canada. Many regional commercial networks also dot the Canadian landscape: CBC, CTV, OMNI, CP24, YES TV, V, and Télé-Québec. Figure 11-1 summarizes the Canadian and U.S. networks and independent stations, along with the amount of consumption for each.

A network assembles a series of affiliated local TV stations throughout the country or region, known as **affiliates**, to which it supplies programming and services. There are 134 conventional stations in Canada.[2] These affiliates, most of which are independently owned, contractually agree to pre-empt time during specified hours for programming provided by the networks and to carry the national advertising within the program. The networks share the advertising revenue they receive during these time periods with the affiliates. The affiliates are also free to sell commercial time in non-network periods and during station breaks in the pre-empted periods to both national and local advertisers. TV networks offer their shows online with commercials embedded within them much like regular television viewing. For example, one can visit CTV's website and watch programs that have already aired. The movement of watching "television" programming anytime, anywhere, with any device is expanding TV viewing opportunities and potentially opening up new avenues for advertising as consumers adapt to changing technology.[3] Networks are now offering their shows on mobile apps for viewing on tablets, for example.

Figure 11-1   Share of hours tuned by station group (condensed)

| Station Group | Fall 2014 | | | | |
	2010	2011	*2012	2013	2014
CBC (Total)	5.5	4.9	3.5	4.9	4.6
City			2.7	2.7	2.8
CTV	11.2	10.7	11.0	10.01	9.9
Independent English	7.3	7.1	5.6	5.4	5.3
Global	6.5	6.5	7.3	7.2	7.6
RADIO CANADA (Total)	3.9	3.8	4.3	4.0	4.2
TVA	7.6	7.4	7.3	6.6	7.1
Télé-Québec	0.5	0.6	0.6	0.5	0.5
Quatre Saisons	1.3	1.5	1.5	1.3	1.5
Total CDN Conventional	**43.8**	**42.5**	**43.8**	**42.7**	**43.6**
ABC Affiliates	1.3	1.2	1.4	1.2	1.4
NBC Affiliates	1.1	1.1	1.4	1.4	1.5
CBS Affiliates	2.1	1.9	2.2	1.7	1.5
FOX Affiliates	1.5	1.4	1.4	1.3	1.2
PBS	0.9	0.9	1.1	1.1	1.5
Independent/UPN/WB	1.4	1.4	1.5	1.2	1.2
Total U.S. Conventional	**8.3**	**7.9**	**9.0**	**7.8**	**8.4**
CDN Specialty/Pay	33.3	33.3	34.7	37.2	35.0
U.S. Specialty/Pay	5.0	5.2	6.3	5.2	4.7
VCR, PVR, DVD, Demand	7.3	8.5	2.7	2.8	2.7
Other	1.7	1.8	3.4	4.5	5.7
Total Hours (Millions)	**674.8**	**678.1**	**595.6**	**601.1**	**605.9**

Data from TV Basics 2014–2015, p. 33, Television Bureau of Canada

When an advertiser purchases airtime from a national or regional network, the commercial is transmitted through the affiliate station network. Network advertising truly represents a mass medium, since the advertiser can broadcast its message simultaneously through many affiliates. Advertisers interested in reaching many consumers generally buy time from large networks (e.g., CTV) during the evening prime viewing hours when popular programs are aired. Availability of time can be limited as advertisers compete to obtain network advertising. Traditionally, most prime-time commercial spots, particularly on the programs with a sizable viewership, are sold during the buying period in May/June/July that occurs before the TV season begins. Advertisers hoping to use prime-time network advertising must plan their media schedules and often purchase TV time as much as a year in advance. Demands from large clients who are heavy TV advertisers force the biggest agencies to participate in the upfront market. However, TV time is also purchased during the **scatter market** which runs through the TV season. Network TV can also be purchased on a regional basis, so an advertiser's message can be aired in certain sections of the country with one media purchase.

When using mass media like TV, advertisers are interested in technological adoption for viewing. Figure 11-2 shows that consumers still love TV, as the penetration rates for high-definition TV and high-definition receivers continue to grow, and so does demand for very large televisions! From the actions of TV networks, it appears they do not envision the end of TV either. All major networks are entrenched in the market and owned by major telecommunications firms. Their annual visits to Los Angeles continue with increased intensity as they bid for shows that will attract advertisers. Some TV executives estimate that Canadian networks will try to outbid one another for the top shows as the funnel of good-quality production continues across all the major American producers. Growth in programming expenditures was substantial in the past decade.[4]

Figure 11-2   HD screen and HD receiver penetration

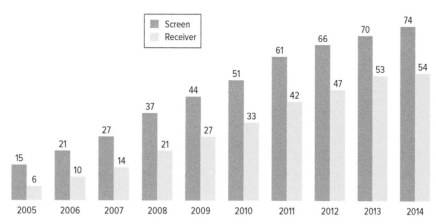

© Media Technology Monitor (MTM)

Figure 11-3 indicates how consumers are connecting their TV sets to the Internet, a phenomenon known as smart TV. The penetration rate of smart TV hit 30 percent in 2015. As these data suggest, the advertising experience for TV viewers is changing. The interactive capabilities may give rise to more interesting creatives to encourage viewership, opportunity for promotional offers, extended branded content or entertainment, or complete avoidance of ads for a percent of viewing time.

Figure 11-3   Access Internet on smart TV

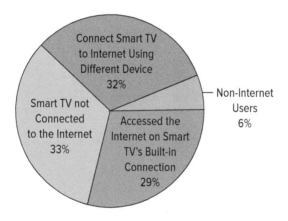

© Media Technology Monitor (MTM)

Spot Advertising   **Spot advertising** refers to commercials shown on local TV stations, with time negotiated and purchased directly from the individual stations or their national station representatives. **Station reps** act as sales agents for a number of local stations in dealing with national advertisers. Spot advertising offers the national advertiser flexibility in adjusting to local market conditions. The advertiser can concentrate commercials in areas where market potential is greatest or where additional support is needed. This ad format is appealing to advertisers with uneven distribution or limited advertising budgets, as well as those interested in test marketing or introducing a product in limited market areas. National advertisers sometimes use spot television advertising through local retailers or dealers as part of their cooperative advertising programs and to provide local dealer support. This attractive option is most prevalent in Canada, with about 60 percent of all TV ads.

Sponsorship Advertising   In the early days of TV, most programs were produced by an identified corporation. Thus, the original concept of a **sponsorship** arrangement occurs when an advertiser produces the content of the program and embeds its own advertising. Today most shows are produced by either the networks or independent production companies that sell them to a network which in turn sells the advertising time to a sponsoring advertiser. For example, CTV received major sponsorship expenditures over the years for its Oscars broadcast from L'Oréal, which aired many ads during the program. Tetley Tea purchased all the advertising time for the TV premiere of *Pitch Perfect*, but instead of playing its ads, it showed clips of its YouTube sponsored show *MsLabelled* in three 10-minute episodes.[5]

As this demonstrates, today's use of sponsorship evolved from its original concept, comes in many forms, and is now linked with social media. Sponsorship is seen with "branded entertainment" or "branded content" that is reminiscent of what occurred decades ago. For example, President's Choice cooked up a reality show, *Recipes to Riches,* in which contestants used the branded products to develop their own recipes. The show attracted over 600,000 viewers and reached the number one most watched video on FoodNetwork.ca. With company chairman Galen Weston as a judge, the show offered contestants an opportunity to demonstrate their culinary flair.[6]

This kind of arrangement is moving toward the Internet with Canada's media conglomerates. A high-profile example occurred with *Canada's Best Beauty Talent,* produced by Rogers Media in association with L'Oréal. The 12-part series showed beauty experts competing to see who was the most talented and appeared only on the Internet, much like watching original-content shows on YouTube.[7] As for whether the sponsorship approach is identified as branded content or branded entertainment, the commercial intention is often understood by the receiver of the message. However, one industry producer believes the intention of branded content is to sell and differs from branded entertainment with its intention to place the brand in a context that has enduring positive effect with its audience.[8]

Within these sponsored segments, the program itself or the branded component invites viewers to interact with social media through voting, viewing online content, or commenting to friends, giving rise to the idea of *social TV*. Figure 11-4 indicates that many Canadians commented about TV programs, including those who are heavy users of "watching TV" on the Internet (i.e., social networkers). A good portion of this communication occurred on shows with hosts. such as sports, entertainment competitions, talk shows, morning programs, news, and the like. IMC Perspective 11-1 describes how social TV is one way TV networks compete against other media for audiences.

Figure 11-4   Canadians used social media to comment about a TV program anytime and during

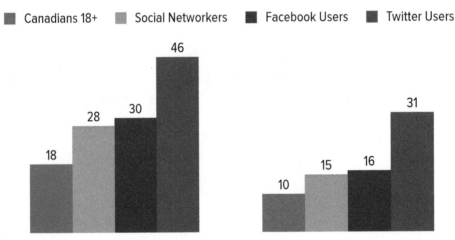

© Media Technology Monitor (MTM)

A company chooses to sponsor a program since it allows the brand to enhance its image by associating it with the prestige of a high-quality program, and the sponsor has control over the number, placement, and content of its ads. Furthermore, its message can be of any length as long as the total amount of commercial time does not exceed network or station regulations. And the message does not in fact count as an ad if it is in the form of branded entertainment or branded content. Finally, the production of this form of influence may require the production expertise of the media company. For example, Canadian Tire partnered with TSN for three years and saw the benefit of being able to access sports stars and teams to produce its branded content pieces that TSN aired and Canadian Tire linked on Twitter and Facebook.[9] As shown in Figure 11-5, about one-third of Canadians use the Internet while watching TV, so immediate communication with the brand can occur beyond the TV ad.

Figure 11-5   Watch TV and access the Internet at the same time.

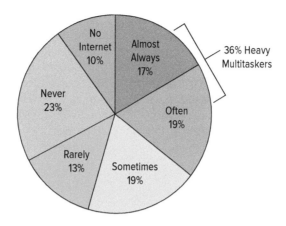

IMC PERSPECTIVE 11-1

SOCIAL TV ARRIVES

What is to become of TV viewing? Television faces a number of questions about the viability of its business model established over 60 years ago; people cancelling television provider services, competition from new content providers like Netflix, viewing on tablets or other mobile devices, and growth of online video sources are problems not to be ignored. Despite this, those in the industry feel TV is responding to the challenge on a number of fronts.

Hand-out/CraveTV/Newscom

The first response is program improvement. Executives believe viewer expectations for higher quality programs arose from new competitors' offerings and that TV improved considerably with many serialized prime-time dramas. In the past, complex storylines with continuing week to week episodes did not work, but conventional TV picked up on the trend and adjusted. Furthermore, they argue that Neflix cannot realistically exist without original television content inventory, indicating the value of TV.

The second response is the transmission of TV programs through digital options for consumers to watch anywhere at any time. Conventional networks developed apps so viewers could see live TV or on-demand programs via mobile phones or tablets. CTV and CITY offered their service to Rogers Media and Bell Media customers respectively. This expanded service complemented the offering of watching the programs online via personal computers. This further evolved with dynamic advertising in which current ads could be inserted into a downloaded show automatically.

The third response is taking advantage of the vertical integration as major networks are affiliated with television service providers, thus allowing them to compete with Netflix offerings with new options like Bell's (CTV) CraveTV and the partnership of Rogers (CITY) and Shaw (Global) offering Shomi. Further to this is that broadcasters are working at acquiring expanded rights for transmitting their purchased content in multiple media. In addition Rogers Media introduced SportsnetNow, where consumers can subscribe to all its sports channels without subscription from a television service provider.

[Continued on next page]

[IMC Perspective 11-1 continued]

The fourth response is the emphasis on live television and the interaction of the program with social media, giving rise to the idea of social TV. Viewers are able to feel like they are part of the program and are on top of pop culture, especially with big events like the Oscars. Sports shows regularly highlight viewers' Twitter messages, and entertainment shows use Facebook to see who is commenting on the show and for contest entries. And here lies the real competition as to which social media vehicle will work best with TV. All of these major social media players are working with TV rather than trying to eradicate it. Twitter views itself as working with TV more strongly with live TV because of its real-time communication capability. Many programs rely on Twitter, making Twitter a strong contender.

However, Facebook counters with the point that it has a larger user base than Twitter, offering greater reach for social TV interactions. Facebook also offers data, and key word searches of its 19 million users on what viewers are saying about a TV program prove invaluable. Integrating TV show activities and social media messages produces greater reach and frequency. For example, a viewer watching *Breakfast Television* sees a coffee ad on TV and comments on the show or the ad with Facebook, and can easily and quickly see an ad for the same coffee brand on Facebook. And while this may seem far-fetched, research indicates that 60 percent of Facebook comments about a TV program occurred while it aired. Canadian Tire experienced this first hand with its "We All Play for Canada" and "Ice Truck" campaigns where extensive Facebook chatter occurred around the ads and the TV program.

Sources: Kristin Laird, "Don't Touch That Dial," *Marketing*, March 2014; Mathew Chung, "The Battle's On," *Marketing*, July 2014; Russ Martin, "Sharing the Wealth on Social TV," *Marketing*, August 2015.

Question:

1. Explain how different types of television programs and advertisers could develop effective marketing communication with viewers using social media at the same time.

SPECIALTY TELEVISION ADVERTISING

Canada has an extensive variety of specialty networks and digital specialty networks that advertisers run commercials on to reach specific target audiences. These specialty networks require consumer adoption of cable, satellite, or Internet technology to access this entertainment. We will briefly review these services and then discuss the advertising on these specialty channels.

Television Service Providers   The expansion of **cable television** represented a historic development in broadcast media. Cable, or CATV (community antenna television), delivers TV signals through coaxial wire rather than the airwaves and, when developed, it provided reception to remote areas that could not receive broadcast signals. Canadians readily accepted cable in the 1970s since it appeared the easiest (or only) method of receiving American channels. Today, cable penetration is about 69 percent, down from 76 percent in 1995.[10]

Direct broadcast satellite (DBS) services emerged in the 1990s. TV and radio programs are sent digitally from a satellite to homes equipped with a small dish. DBS companies marketed their service, superior picture quality, and greater channel choice as subscribers received as many as 200 channels in crisp digital video. The pendulum swung back the other way as cable operators offered digital cable that allowed them to match the number of channels received on satellites. In addition, telecommunication firms (telco) joined the market and offered a digital service via the Internet, commonly identified as IPTV. Total digital satellite, digital cable, and IPTV penetration reached 88 percent in 2014.[11] Combined basic cable and digital services in Canada stands at 93 percent.[12] Figure 11-6 summarizes how Canadians receive television service. As at 2014, almost all cable was digital cable and about half had an HD receiver. Meanwhile, digital satellite and IPTV combined still had not hit the level of digital cable.

Subscribers pay a monthly fee and receive many channels, including the local Canadian and American network affiliates and independent stations, specialty networks, American superstations, and local cable system channels. Operators offer programming that is not supported by commercial sponsorship and is available only to households willing to pay a fee beyond the monthly subscription charge (e.g., The Movie Channel). Program options available to viewers broaden advertisers' options by offering specialty channels, including all-news, pop music, country music, sports, weather, educational, and cultural channels as well as children's programming. Television service providers also offer "on-demand" services where subscribers can access shows not seen during regularly scheduled times.

Figure 11-6   Connected TV in Canada, 2014

Year	Operating Systems	Cable Subs. (000)	Digital Cbl (000)	HDTV Subs (000)	DTH (000)	Telco/IPTV (000)	Total TV Subs (000)
2014	2,212	7,400	6,067	3,551	2,633	1,660	11,718
2010	2,145	8,465	5,359	1,291	2,884	358	11,743
2005	2,097	7,984	2,784		2,597	105	10,686
2000	2,001	8,285	500		1,167		9,452

Data from TV Basics 2014-2015, p. 28, Television Bureau of Canada

Specialty Networks   The proliferation of channels has influenced the nature of television as an advertising medium. Expanded viewing options have led to considerable audience fragmentation. Specialty networks now have about 50 percent of the viewing audience, and much of this audience growth has come at the expense of national and regional networks. Note that a good number of these specialty networks are digital only, meaning a viewer requires a subscription service for access. Specialty networks have become very popular among consumers, leading advertisers to re-evaluate their media plans and the prices they are willing to pay for network and spot commercials on network affiliate stations. Advertising on specialty networks reached $1,263 million in 2012, more than double the amount for 2002, but declined to $1,244 million in 2014. In comparison, conventional television ad revenue reached $2,189 million in 2012, having increased only 11 percent from 2002, and tapered to $2,099 million in 2014.[13]

This change in advertising revenue indicates that advertisers are using specialty networks in order to reach specific target audiences and because of their low cost and flexibility. Advertising rates on specialty networks are much lower than those for the shows on the major networks. This makes TV a much more viable media option for smaller advertisers with limited budgets and those interested in presenting their commercials to a well defined target audience. Also, specialty network advertisers generally do not have to make the large upfront commitments the networks require, which may be as much as a year in advance.

In addition to costing less, specialty networks give advertisers flexibility in the type of commercials. While most network commercials are 30- or 15-second spots, commercials on specialty networks can be longer (e.g., 3 to 30 minutes in length). Direct-response advertisers use longer ads called **infomercials** to describe their products or services and encourage consumers to immediately call in their order. The use of infomercials by direct-response advertisers is discussed in Chapter 16. Finally, specialty network advertising can be purchased on a national or a regional basis. Many large marketers advertise on specialty networks to reach large numbers of viewers across the country with a single media buy. Regional advertising on specialty networks is available but limited. Across all age groups and both languages, Canadians watch between 11 and 13 hours of TV per week on specialty, pay, or digital stations, reaching a substantial portion of the population.

Figure 11-7 shows a summary of 20 out of about 50 highly viewed specialty networks. For example, the average viewer watches TSN an average of 3.8 hours per week and the station reaches about 13 percent of Canadians (4.5/35 million) and is the most watched specialty channel in terms of total hours. Although specialty networks' share of the TV viewing audience has increased significantly, the viewers are spread out among the large number of channels available. Collectively, the specialty networks contribute to greater audience fragmentation as the number of viewers who watch any one cable channel is generally quite low. One media executive estimated that only 10 percent of the 188 specialty channels carried a strong media brand with respectable audience size. The executive forecasted that specialty channels owned by the television service providers like Bell and Rogers would be bundled in future, especially as consumers adjusted the subscriptions with regulatory changes put forth by the CRTC.[14]

Figure 11-7   Average hours watched per week for selected specialty channels

Specialty	Fall 2013 Hours (000)	Fall 2013 Reach (000)	Fall 2013 Avg. Hrs	Fall 2014 Hours (000)	Fall 2014 Reach (000)	Fall 2014 Avg. Hrs
Bravo!	4,414	1,802	2.4	4,170	1,669	2.5
CBC News Network	8,166	5,589	3.2	9,398	2,812	3.3
Comedy Network	3,189	2,000	1.6	3,467	2,148	1.6
CP24	4,357	1,308	3.3	3,960	1,288	3.1
CTV NewsNet	3,160	1,205	2.6	4,154	1,329	2.5
Discovery Channel	5,354	2,748	1.9	6,032	3,039	2.0
Family Channel	7,247	2.008	3.6	6,026	1,622	3.7
Food Network Canada	4,672	2,277	2.0	3,162	1,795	1.8
HGTV Canada	5,565	2,625	2.1	4,491	2,204	2.0
History Television	6,058	2,799	2.2	7,181	3,046	2.4
RDI	4,503	1,103	4.1	4,986	1,220	4.1
Reseau des Sports	10,066	1,899	5.3	7,658	1,715	4.5
Sportsnet	14,011	3,756	3.7	11,431	4,427	2.9
Sportsnet 360	2,175	897	2.4	3,039	1,204	2.5
Showcase	4,936	2,097	2.4	4,189	1,701	2.5
Space	3,890	1,384	2.8	3,412	1,412	2.4
TSN	22,579	5,406	4.2	17,144	4,510	3.8
Vision TV	3,911	1,304	3.0	4,086	1,231	3.3
W Network	5,538	2,480	2.2	5,171	2,139	2.4
YTV	4.996	1,959	2.1	3,581	1,680	2.4

Data from TV Basics 2014–2015, pp. 42–43, Television Bureau of Canada

TIME PERIODS AND PROGRAMS

Another decision in buying TV time is selecting the right time period and program to schedule the advertiser's commercial. The cost of TV advertising time varies depending on the time of day and particular program, since audience size varies as a function of these two factors. As for the particular program, *Hockey Night in Canada* is a popular selection due to the audience size and composition. For these reasons, Red Baron beer, produced by Brick Brewing Co., selected this program to launch its first-ever TV ad after extensive use of radio and out-of-home for many years.[15]

TV time periods are divided into **dayparts** which are specific segments of a broadcast day. Advertising rates differ across these dayparts since audience size and demographic composition vary. The dayparts structure varies as well, but the general format is as follows. Prime time occurs seven days a week between 7:00 p.m. and 11:00 p.m. when front-running shows are aired, leading to the largest audiences. Prime time is the most expensive time slot in which to advertise and is typically dominated by national advertisers. Prime time draws about 40 percent of per capita television consumption. On weekdays, prior to prime time (4:00 p.m. to 7:00 p.m.) and after prime time (11:00 p.m. to 2:00 a.m.) are early and late fringe times respectively, with each daypart drawing about 10 percent per capita television consumption, for a total of 20 percent. On weekdays, early morning (6:00 a.m. to 10:00 a.m.), daytime (10:00 a.m. to 4:00 p.m.), and overnight (2:00 a.m. to 6:00 a.m.) dayparts draw about 20 percent of per capita television consumption. Finally, Saturday and Sunday dayparts (2:00 a.m. to 7:00 p.m.) draw the remaining 20 percent.

Audience size and demographic composition also vary depending on the program. For example, *The Big Bang Theory* peaked as a top-ranked show in Canada and regularly drew 4 million viewers each week. Other top 10 shows typically attracted 1.5 million to 2 million viewers. Other top shows for the past few years include *Grey's Anatomy, The Amazing*

Race, and *Dragons' Den.* As one might expect, the audiences for each of these programs are likely quite different, and as indicated in Chapter 10 an advertiser might want to place a message in all these shows to obtain greater reach. Alternatively, an advertiser might want to place a message in many crime dramas like *Criminal Minds* and *How to Get Away With Murder* to obtain stronger frequency, since these shows likely draw overlapping audiences. Data from the audience measurement system would confirm these or other similar conclusions. As this suggests, selecting the right daypart and the show within the daypart is an important decision, and the variation of the types of programs within the dayparts influences other media decisions significantly.

Given the importance of dayparts and programs for advertisers, Canadian TV networks carefully bid on new programs when they come available and decide on their prime time lineup across each day of the week. In fact, each typically planned an overall strategy for the networks for the week and for each individual evening.[16] For example, networks not airing *Monday Night Football* need to consider what shows to air to attract those not interested in the sport or league. Alternatively, networks may want an evening with programs with a broader audience that may be appealing to advertisers. From another view, a network might want to balance its evening programming for different ages, or for males and females. Strategically, a network may want to insert a new program each evening with the intention of drawing loyal followers of one program to stay on the channel to see the next one. And this idea works for specialty channels as well, with the success of *Orphan Black* which followed the successful *Dr. Who* program on the Space Channel. Ultimately for its time slot, the program became the number one among specialty channels, averaging 330,000 viewers.[17]

MEASURING THE TELEVISION AUDIENCE

As the preceding indicated, audience measurement is critical to advertisers as well as to the networks and stations. Advertisers want to know the size and characteristics of the audience they are reaching when they purchase time on a particular program. And since the rates they pay are a function of audience size, advertisers want to be sure audience measurements are accurate. Audience size and composition are also important to the network or station, since they determine the amount it can charge for commercial time. Shows are cancelled once they fail to attract enough viewers to make their commercial time attractive to potential advertisers. In this section, we examine how audiences are measured and how advertisers use this information in planning their media schedules.

Audience Measurement   Television audiences are measured by Numeris, a not-for-profit broadcast research company based on cooperation among the Canadian Association of Broadcasters, the Association of Canadian Advertisers, and Canadian advertising agencies. Numeris collects TV audience measurement data with two methods: portable people meter (PPM) for national and some local markets, and diary for remaining local markets. Figure 11-8 summarizes data collected by Numeris regarding the amount of TV watched across different groups over the past 20 years. TV viewing remained strong in 2014 despite the prevalence of the Internet, although viewership variation exists across demographic groups.

Figure 11-8   Average weekly hours tuned per capita

Demographic	1995	2000	2005	2010	*2014
All persons 2+	24:36	21:30	24:12	20:24	27:06
Adults 18+	26:06	23:15	26:15	22:18	28:36
Women 18+	28:24	25:28	28:54	24:24	29:48
Men 18+	23:48	20:56	23:36	20:12	27:06
Teens 12–17	18:55	14:04	13:42	10:54	19:24
Children 2–11	19:36	15:27	13:48	12:12	20:24

Data from TV Basics 2014–2015, p. 28, Television Bureau of Canada

Currently, Numeris's portable people meter collects data nationally and in large local markets: Montreal (French and English), Toronto–Hamilton, Calgary, Edmonton, and Vancouver–Victoria. People in the panel wear a device that automatically records a silent audio signal emitted from programming. In fact, the PPM is capable of receiving the signal from other media such as radio, cinema, or any medium that emits a sound. The device records information regarding station, program, and time. Each evening, the device is placed in a docking station and the data are transferred to Numeris. The method offers numerous measurement benefits over the previous technology: it measures unobtrusively since the person does not interact with the device while recording data; it measures on an individual level instead of on a household or television basis; it measures exposure to multiple media for each individual; and it measures exposure of recorded programming from any technology (e.g., PVR).

Criticism of the PPM emerged as specialty channel executives believed the system worked best for measuring audience sizes for large networks. A decline in viewership for children, teens, and young adults appeared in the data, possibly due to the research method since the device needs to be continually worn and placed in the dock each night; some thought that these two actions might not be happening consistently enough with younger members of the sampling panel. Part of the problem lies in the fact that it is chronically difficult to obtain data from young people, and now the pager does not look as "cool" as it used to when first established. A sleeker and wireless version is under development.[18]

Numeris also uses the diary research method for collecting television audience information in 36 local markets. A booklet for each television owned in the household is sent to a representative sample of households. Numeris gathers viewership information from this sample and then projects this information to the total viewing area. The diary method works as follows. Each person aged two years or older records his or her viewing for one week in the booklet. The recordings are based on 15-minute increments from 6:00 a.m. until 2:00 a.m. Viewers write down station call letters, channel numbers, programs, and who is watching. The booklet also contains a number of basic demographic questions. As expected, the diary method is a substantially weaker measurement system than the PPM; the cost efficiencies and ease of use of the PPM will likely lead to expansion to local markets in future.

Numeris provides an extensive array of services, of which we highlight a few. For total Canada and meter markets, advertisers can track the average weekly audience size by demographic, reception type (e.g., satellite, cable, off-air), and station group (e.g., conventional, specialty). Advertisers can observe reach by province, market, station, time period, and program across numerous demographic variables. Numeris offers resources to members regarding research methodology (e.g., sample size and characteristics, data collection, response rates, panel background, geographic boundaries), TV programming (e.g., program listings, technology adoption and use), and day-after viewership data. The EM Stats Card provides detailed viewing information for each market in terms of cable, satellite, and PVR penetration in addition to other similar macro-level data.

Audience Measures   The data collected allow for the calculation of two critical audience measures: program rating and share of audience. A **program rating** is the percentage of people in a geographic area tuned in to a specific program during a specific time period. The program rating is calculated by dividing the number of people tuned to a particular show by the total number of people in the geographic area. A **ratings point** represents 1 percent of all the people tuned to a specific television program and is calculated nationally, regionally, and for each local market. The program rating is the key number for individual stations, networks, and advertisers since the amount of money charged for commercial time is based on it. A 1 percent change in a program's rating during a viewing season can gain or lose substantial dollars in advertising revenue for the media organization or increase or decrease audience size for the advertiser. IMC Perspective 11-2 describes changes with the Super Bowl broadcast that illustrate the importance of audience size.

Another important audience measurement is the **share of audience**, which is the percentage of people watching TV in a specified time period that are tuned to a specific program. Audience share is always higher than the program rating unless all people are watching television (in which case they would be equal). Share of audience is an important performance metric since it indicates how well a program does with the available viewing audience. For example, late at night the size of the viewing audience drops substantially, so the best way to assess the popularity of a late-night program is to examine the share of the available audience it attracts relative to competing programs. Again, share of audience is calculated nationally and for each local market.

Since the data are recorded on a minute-by-minute basis for the PPM and in 15-minute increments for the diary method, the program ratings and share of audience can be examined over different time intervals. In fact, some believe that the ability of new technology to measure audiences with short time intervals on a minute-by-minute basis will provide unexpected research results regarding TV viewing behaviour in the future.[19] Also, since the demographic and other consumer data are recorded, these measures can be investigated in great detail for many target audience profile variables. For example, Figure 11-9 shows the average weekly TV viewing time per capita, which varies by age, indicating that it is a function of the amount of free time people have beyond sleeping, working, or going to school in addition to changes in technological adoption. The sheer complexity and extensiveness of the data makes advanced software and analysis paramount.

Audience Measurement Reporting   The collected television data are analyzed with software applications provided by other organizations. One company, nlogic, is a subsidiary of Numeris and offers numerous solutions for examining the program ratings and share of audience data extensively by time, and by different audience characteristics. Many other third-party processors exist, as it is a competitive market for turning data into valuable media planning information. Some specialize in either diary or meter data, and many offer analysis for both.

Figure 11-9   Average weekly per capita hours by age

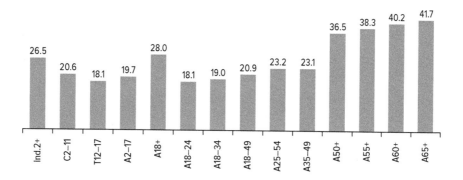

© Courtesy thinktv

Media buying agencies and advertising agencies subscribe to these data and analytic services and use the information for developing media plans for their clients. Advertisers can access some of this aggregate information through ThinkTV, an industry association for television networks, television stations, and firms that sell television advertising time. It offers resources to those in the television industry to demonstrate the value and importance of television as a medium versus competing media (e.g., magazines). It publishes basic facts garnered from the aforementioned sources and conducts primary research through independent market research firms.

IMC PERSPECTIVE 11-2

CANADA GETS U.S. ADS FOR SUPER BOWL

In January 2015, chairman Jean-Pierre Blais of the Canadian Radio-television and Telecommunications Commission (CRTC), announced that Canadians would be able to see American ads during the Super Bowl broadcast starting in 2017. Canadian broadcasters would not be permitted simultaneous substitution (e.g., "simsub") in which they would overlay Canadian ads when airing the Super Bowl on their network. While this appeared to be a win for consumers who annually complained to the CRTC, it essentially turned CTV's investment in broadcast rights worthless. This Super Bowl decision and other simsub changes may have long-term effects for the Canadian media, advertisers, and Canadian culture as we await the results of a court challenge to see what transpires.

© Blend Images/Alamy Stock Photo

The purpose of simsub is to provide Canadian broadcasters advertising revenue when they show an American program on a Canadian network. For example, CTV pays for the rights to broadcast a program in the same time slot as the U.S. broadcast and requires a revenue source for payment in addition to its costs and profits. According to the CRTC, its regulations merely allow broadcasters to request simsub from the television service providers; it is not a regulation that the providers are obligated to follow. However, rarely have Canadians experienced non-simsub broadcasts, so naturally many considered it to be a law of some sort. In fact, one television service provider disclosed incorrect information on Twitter in the face of Super Bowl complaints.

For decades, American brands could have purchased Canadian ad space and shown their ads, and this occurred periodically, but in general it did not appear financially viable. However, the cost per thousand analysis proved otherwise. In the United States, it cost $4.5 million to reach 114 million people, while in Canada it cost $200,000 to reach 8 million, giving a cost per thousand of about $40 and $25 respectively,

[Continued on next page]

[IMC Perspective 11-2 continued]

in favour of the smaller market. And more recently the brands did not see much point as Canadians readily witnessed the clips online. For example, Google research found that more Canadians watched the ads online than actually watched the Super Bowl broadcast! But this did not deter Doritos, which showed its famous "Crash the Super Bowl" user-generated results in Canada.

To spur excitement in the advertising community to develop Canadian must-see ads, CTV offered a contest to creative agencies with a prize of free airing of the winning ad and a trip for two to the Super Bowl. A disappointed broadcaster received only 10 entries after thinking that the contest would obtain a much stronger response. Some international brands made Canadian-only Super Bowl ads, but amortization of production cost over a market of 36 million cannot compare to that of a market with 324 million, a 1:9 ratio!

For the Super Bowl, ad revenue might be approximately $15 million, with $10 million in broadcasting rights given to the NFL along with production costs, giving the broadcaster a healthy profit of a couple of million dollars. With eyeballs moving to a U.S. station to see the ads, one can easily see why Bell Media, the owner of CTV, did not take the decision lightly and naturally received public support from Canadian advertising agencies and media buying agencies who would be out of pocket as well. Other support ensued from a cultural commentator who articulated how Canada's protections, requirements, and subsidies ensured that Canadian TV existed. Bell Media publicly criticized the decision by describing the financial consequences for the television and advertising industries in Canada, took the rare action of writing critically to the CRTC, and challenged the decision in the Federal Court of Appeal to have it overturned. As they say on TV … stay tuned for more information.

Sources: Susan Krashinsky, "Buzz-Worthy Ads to Bypass Canada Again," *The Globe and Mail,* February 1, 2014, p. B.6; Susan Krashinsky, "Don't Blame Us for Super Bowl Signal Swap," *The Globe and Mail,* January 25, 2014, p. B.3; Susan Krashinsky, "A Super Bowl-Sized Challenge for Advertisers," *The Globe and Mail*, January 23, 2015, p. B.47; Susan Krashinsky, "CRTC Clears the Way for U.S. Super Bowl Ads," *The Globe and Mail*, January 30, 2015, p. A.6; Terence Corcoran, "Super Bowl Ads No Victory," *The Globe and Mail,* January 30, 2015, p. A.1; Susan Krashinsky, "P&G's Super Bowl Risk Pays Off," *The Globe and Mail,* February 3, 2015, p. B.7; Katie Taylor, "Where's the Money in CRTC's TV Decisions," *The Globe and Mail,* March 28, 2015, p. R.3; James Bradshaw, "Bell, CRTC Clash Over Super Bowl Call," *The Globe and Mail,* February 3, 2015, p. B.6; Claire Brownell, "Bell to Appeal CRTC Ad Ruling," *National Post,* March 3, 2015, p. FP.1; Christina Pellegrini, "The Second-Last Time You'll Miss the Super Bowl Ads," *National Post,* January 30, 2015, p. FP.1

Question:

1. Do you think the seeing U.S. Super Bowl ads is a one-time change, or is this the end of simsub in Canada?

 # Evaluation of Television

Television is an ideal advertising medium because of its unique mass media characteristics and its ability to combine visual images, sound, motion, and colour. It presents the advertiser with the opportunity to develop creative and imaginative appeals. And while it seems that some people want to watch TV without commercials, evidence suggests that maybe viewers do not mind them and that TV will survive despite some online brands' predictions that it might not. Witness the anticipation for watching new ads during big TV events, the interest in watching programs that show commercials as the content, the YouTube viewing of TV commercials, and the way people share TV ads with one another via email or social media! Despite the positive features of TV, it has characteristics that limit or prevent its use by advertisers.[20]

STRENGTHS OF TELEVISION

TV has numerous strengths compared to other media, including target audience coverage, geographic coverage, scheduling flexibility, reach, frequency, cost efficiency, attention, creativity for cognitive and emotional responses, and media image.

Target Audience Coverage   Marketers selling products and services that appeal to broad target audiences find that TV lets them cover mass markets or large groups of target consumers. Nearly everyone—regardless of age, sex, income, or educational level—watches at least some TV. The average Canadian watches TV 28 hours per week, thereby consuming this medium more than any other. Most people watch on a regular basis: 99 percent of all Canadian households own a TV, and 74 percent have more than one TV. Television advertising makes it possible to ensure that advertisers achieve audience coverage.

As Figure 11-10 indicates, paid TV subscription services in the English language market declined to 77 percent in 2015, down from 82 percent a year earlier and down from 86 percent in 2010 when Netflix entered Canada. Those "watching TV" only through Internet streaming services hit 12 percent (i.e., "TV My Way"); these consumers do not receive live TV channels. Those watching TV with a digital antenna or with one built into the set (i.e., "Off-Air") hit 7 percent (8 percent in 2010); and these viewers may use streaming services as well. Finally, 4 percent do not watch TV through any of the three options and this level has not changed over the years.[21] As this trend indicates, TV's ability to obtain complete coverage is not as strong as in the past.

Figure 11-10   TV distribution, fall 2015, English language market

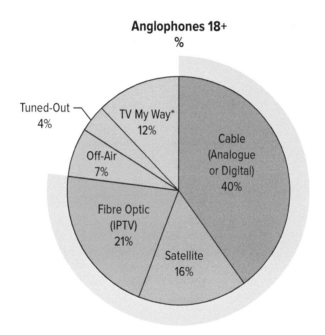

© Media Technology Monitor (MTM)

Geographic Coverage   Advertisers can adjust their media strategies for TV to take advantage of different geographic markets through spot ads in specific market areas. Ads can be scheduled to run repeatedly in more favourable markets. Alternatively, advertisers can obtain national coverage or regional coverage depending upon their marketing objectives. This can be especially useful if promotional planners want to take advantage of information regarding their brand development index or the category development index described in Chapter 10.

Scheduling Flexibility   Television has been criticized for being a nonselective medium, since it is difficult to reach a precisely defined target audience through the use of TV advertising. But some selectivity is possible due to variations in the composition of audiences as a result of broadcast time and program content. For example, Saturday morning TV caters to children; Saturday and Sunday afternoon programs are geared to the sports-oriented male; and weekday daytime shows appeal heavily to homemakers. With the growth of specialty channels, advertisers refine their coverage further by appealing to groups with specific interests such as sports, news, history, the arts, or music. The development of specialty channels allowed for selectivity somewhat similar to magazines on these interests.

Reach   Television viewing is a closely monitored activity such that the size of the audience for a television program is known fairly quickly. Placement of TV ads on certain combinations of shows allows an advertiser to reach as many in its target audience as it deems necessary. As Figure 11-11 shows, TV reaches about 89 percent of Canadians on a daily basis, and virtually everyone on a weekly basis with 98 percent reach.[22] Reach does not vary between males and females, but females watch about 2.5 hours more per week. Also, reach does not vary by language; however French speaking Canadians watch eight hours more per week.[23] In addition, TV continued to reach about 80 percent of young adults aged 18–24 on a daily basis (Figure 11-12). Availability of airtime and amount of budget are the main constraints on allowing an advertiser to reach as large an audience as possible.

Figure 11-11   Daily reach/average weekly per capita hours, adults 18+

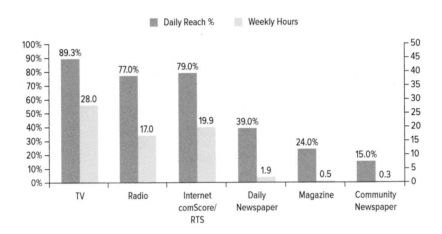

© Courtesy thinktv

Figure 11-12   Daily reach/average weekly per capita hours, adults 18–24

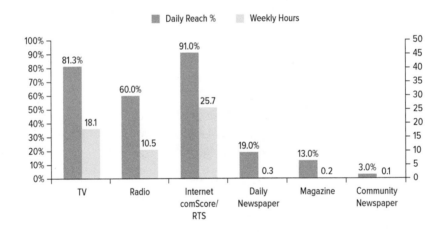

© Courtesy thinktv

Frequency   Scheduling television permits frequency in concentrated blocks throughout a program, evening, week, month, or season. Heightened frequency may be necessary for a new product launch or an effort to obtain switching, while lower levels of frequency may be feasible for advertisers desiring more continuous exposure.

Cost Efficiency   Compared to many other media, the cost to reach individuals by television is reasonably affordable. For example, one of the most expensive placements is an ad shown during the Super Bowl costing $130,000, yet with a viewership of 6.5 million, the average cost per thousand (CPM) is about $20, which is on par with basic banner ad rates.[24] Because of its ability to reach large audiences in a cost-efficient manner, TV is a popular medium among companies selling mass-consumption products. Companies with widespread distribution and availability of their products and services use TV to reach the mass market and deliver their advertising messages at a very low cost per thousand. Television has become indispensable to large consumer packaged-goods companies, car makers, and major retailers. In fact, Hyundai Auto Canada produced its own ad for the Canadian Super Bowl broadcast after a previous poor response from showing the American ad on Canadian TV.[25]

Attention   Television is basically intrusive in that commercials impose themselves on viewers as they watch their favourite programs. Unless we make a special effort to avoid commercials, most of us are exposed to thousands of them each year. This seemingly continuous exposure implies that viewers devote some attention (i.e., selective attention) to many advertising messages. As discussed in Chapter 4, the low-involvement nature of consumer learning and response processes may mean TV ads have an effect on consumers simply through heavy repetition and exposure to catchy slogans and jingles. Research suggests that consumers watching their favourite programs pay greater attention to the program and subsequently to the embedded television commercial.[26] Figure 11-13 indicates that most viewers believe they pay attention to TV ads more than other forms of advertising.

Figure 11-13   Attention to advertising by media

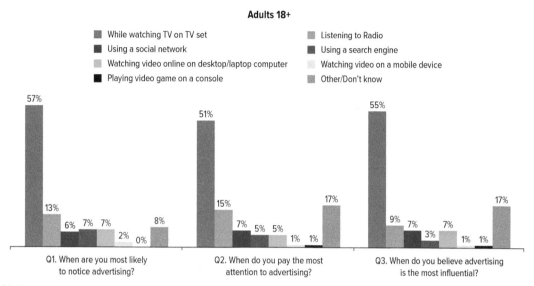

Creativity for Cognitive and Emotional Responses   Perhaps the greatest advantage of TV is the opportunity it provides for presenting the advertising message. The interaction of sight, sound, and motion offers tremendous creative flexibility and makes possible dramatic, lifelike representations of products and services. TV commercials can be used to convey a mood or image for a brand as well as to develop emotional or entertaining appeals that help make a dull product appear interesting. The overall impact of TV's characteristics provides unlimited options for generating optimal cognitive and emotional responses to highly imaginative ads. For example the ads for Newfoundland and Labrador tourism showing fjords in Gros Morne National Park, the province's unique heritage architecture, and L'Anse aux Meadows national historical site all come alive with beautiful cinematography and the directorial skills of Alar Kivilo.[27]

Television is an excellent medium for demonstrating consumption of a product and emphasizing an image. The global advertising campaign for the Italian liqueur brand Campari celebrated its status as the sophisticated choice of upscale drinkers. The campaign commemorated Campari's passionate brand history with iconic high-fashion images used in posterlike print ads and fine art calendars as well as TV commercials featuring actress Jessica Alba. The "Club Campari" campaign ran in over 30 countries in print, television, and outdoor media as well as online. The TV commercial shown in Exhibit 11-1 effectively displays the brand images leading to emotional and cognitive associations the company desired. In fact, the creative agency selected imagery that fit the expectation for each international market.

Media Image   Given the prominence television has with its mass-market characteristic, TV advertising often carries a high degree of acceptability. Television is usually viewed favourably due to the higher costs of placement and production, which demonstrates

Exhibit 11-1   A television ad is an effective means of communicating the passion of drinking Campari.

a level of acceptance or establishment for those who advertise with this medium. Figure 11-14 summarizes data reported by ThinkTV. The evolution of advertisers putting their ads on video hosting sites is a testament to media image. A 60-second ad for the redesigned Subaru Forester featured a collection of sumo wrestlers washing their filthy vehicle. With Forester virtually in every second of the ad, the message "Japanese SUVs just got a little sexier" is humorously communicated with the imagery of the wrestlers engaged in a variety of manoeuvres. So humorous, in fact, that it racked up 700,000 online views and helped spur a 5 percent increase in the Japanese SUV market.[28]

Figure 11-14   Major media comparisons of attitudes, adults 18 to 49

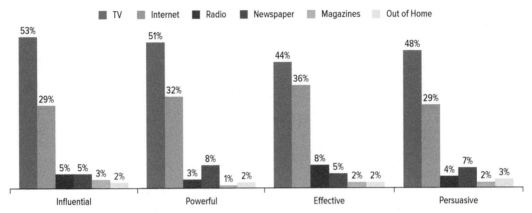

© Courtesy thinktv

LIMITATIONS OF TELEVISION

Although television is unsurpassed from a creative perspective, the medium has several limitations that preclude its use by many advertisers. These problems include target audience selectivity, absolute cost, control for selective exposure, processing time, involvement, clutter, and media image.

Target Audience Selectivity   Selectivity is available in television through scheduling by day, time, or type of program, but advertisers who are seeking a very specific, often small, target audience find the coverage of TV often extends beyond their market. Geographic selectivity can be a problem for local advertisers such as retailers, since a station bases its rates on the total market area it reaches. For example, stations in Ottawa reach viewers in western Quebec and eastern Ontario. The small company whose market is limited to the immediate Ottawa area may find TV an inefficient media buy, since the stations cover a larger geographic area than the merchant's trade area.

Selectivity is possible within a network's portfolio, as Corus Television reaches women with three channels. W Network offers a wide variety of entertainment for women of all ages. Cosmopolitan TV "promises fun, flirty and irreverent entertainment" for women aged 18–34. W Movies is expected to reach women aged 25–54. The flanking strategy of having two niche channels to support the mainstream one is consistent with media vehicle options found with magazines. For example, Transcontinental has *Elle Canada* for women in their twenties, *Canadian Living* and *Homemakers* for women in their thirties and forties, and *More* and *Good Times* for women older than 40.

Absolute Cost   Despite the efficiency of TV in reaching large audiences, it is an expensive medium in which to advertise. The high cost of TV stems not only from the expense of buying airtime but also from the costs of producing a quality commercial. More advertisers are using media-driven creative strategies that require production of a variety of commercials, which drive up their costs. Even local ads can be expensive to produce and often are not of high quality. The high costs of producing and airing commercials often price small and medium-sized advertisers out of the market.

Control for Selective Exposure   When advertisers buy time on a TV program, they are not purchasing guaranteed exposure but rather the opportunity to communicate a message. There is evidence that the size of the viewing audience shrinks during a commercial break for a variety of obvious reasons. Multitasking consumers with their phones are distracted from viewing ads as well (Figure 11-15). Viewers also have selective exposure to television ads resulting from zapping and zipping.

Figure 11-15   Frequency of Canadians using their phone while watching TV

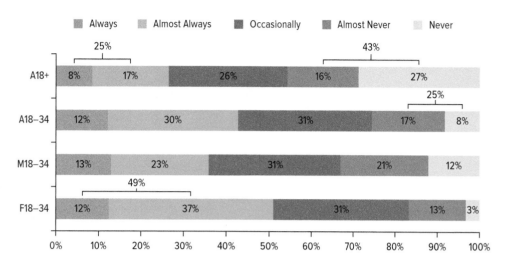

Source: TV Basics 2014-2015, page 21

Zapping refers to changing channels to avoid commercials. An observational study found as much as one-third of program audiences may be lost to electronic zapping when commercials appear.[29] Zapping occurs because commercials are viewed as unbelievable, a poor use of time, and annoying—and TV ads suffer from greater ad avoidance than other media like radio, magazines, and newspapers.[30] Research shows that young adults zap more than older adults, and men are more likely to zap than are women.[31]

A study on zapping behaviour found that people stop viewing TV during a commercial break because they have a reason to stop watching television altogether or they want to find out what is being shown on other channels. The number of people zapping in and out during breaks was not caused by the type of product being advertised or by specific characteristics of the commercials.[32] Research has also shown that zappers recalled fewer of the brands advertised than non-zappers, and that most of the brands recalled by zappers were placed near the end of the commercial break, which is when viewers would be likely to return to a program.[33]

A challenge facing television networks and advertisers is how to discourage viewers from zapping. The networks use certain tactics like previews to hold viewers' attention. Some programs start with action sequences before the opening credits and commercials. Some advertisers believe that producing different executions of a campaign theme is one way to maintain viewers' attention. Others think the ultimate way to zap-proof commercials is to produce creative advertising messages that will attract and hold viewers' attention.

Zipping occurs when customers fast-forward through commercials as they play back a previously recorded program. By 2015, household penetration of PVR technology reached 60 percent in Canada.[34] A Numeris study found that the vast majority of Canadians using PVR were aware of the brands advertised when zipping past commercials and that half stopped zipping and viewed the ads because the brand was of interest to them or they found the ad entertaining.[35] Figure 11-16 shows the distribution of those who watch the ads with a definite skew to those in the 18–24 age range. Finally, the study indicated that only 6 percent of the 26 hours watched is from a PVR. In conclusion, one author suggests that the data showing how and when viewers avoid commercials will provide valued information to make advertising more relevant and efficient.[36]

Processing Time   TV commercials usually last only 30 or 15 seconds and leave nothing tangible for the viewer to examine or consider. Commercials have become shorter as the demand for a limited amount of broadcast time has intensified and advertisers try to get more impressions from their media budgets. Commercials lasting 15 seconds have grown from 13 percent in 1995 to 30 percent in 2012, while 30-second commercials moved from 76 percent to 52 percent as shown in Figure 11-17.

Figure 11-16   Percentage of Canadians who view ads while using a PVR

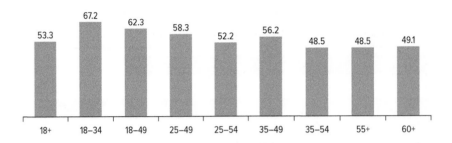

Source: TV Basics 2014–2015, p. 21.

Figure 11-17   Canadian commercial lengths

	5 seconds	10 seconds	15 seconds	30 seconds	60 seconds	120 seconds	Other
2014	0.5%	3.6%	28.9%	47.8%	4.9%	7.8%	6.5%
2010	0.9%	2.5%	29.3%	51.5%	5.7%	4.7%	5.4%
2005	0.2%	1.3%	26.8%	61.8%	5.6%		4.2%
2000	0.5%	2.1%	22.5%	59.9%	8.8%		6.2%
1995			13.4%	76.2%	6.7%		3.7%

Data from TV Basics 2014-2015, p. 19, Television Bureau of Canada

Rising media costs are a factor in the decline in commercial length. A 15-second spot typically sells for about two-thirds the price of a 30-second spot. Since these advertisers believe shorter commercials can deliver a message just as effectively as longer spots, the use of 15-second commercials allows advertisers to run additional spots to reinforce the message through greater frequency, reach a larger audience, or advertise in more purchase cycles.

Involvement   The cumulative effect of the varied television characteristics generally implies that it is a low-involvement medium. While its invasiveness can expose the message to us readily and perhaps hold our attention with significant creative strategies and tactics, the relatively short processing time and clutter make for less effective media for an advertiser to significantly persuade a target audience. While this assertion of television appears historically accurate, some alternative ideas are emerging. For example, some shows attract a devout cohort of viewers who are so engaged or connected with the program that their attention to advertising is heightened.[37] Exhibit 11-2 shows a couple of shots from an exciting ad for HTC that appears able to hold the attention of the target audience for the full 60 seconds. The ad depicted a photography student recording his first fashion shoot while skydiving. HTC deployed the images subsequently in magazine ads to demonstrate the photo quality.

Linking ads with the program content also tries to alleviate this concern. For the Friday night movies on W, Dare Simple Pleasures cookie brand received multiple 5-second billboards, 30-second ads, and 10-second closed-captioning spots from Corus. The station also developed ads for the movies and used a similar "reinvention and transformation" theme

Exhibit 11-2   A television ad is an effective way to communicate the photo quality of the HTC phone.

Made by Mother, www.motherlondon.com

consistent with Dare's message. The ads use an image of the cookie along with images from the movie.[38] As this implies, advertisers create exciting ways to increase the level of involvement with viewers. The dissemination of smart TV and the evolution of multitasking viewers as indicated in Figure 11-18 suggest that TV may overcome some of its involvement limitations.

Figure 11-18 Consumer online activities related to program or ads while watching TV

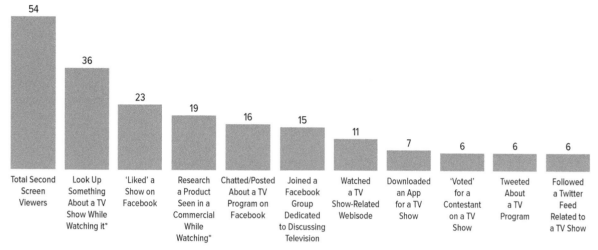

© Media Technology Monitor (MTM)

Clutter   The problems of short TV messages are compounded by the fact that the advertiser's message is only one of many spots and other non-programming material seen during a commercial break, so it may have trouble being noticed. One of advertisers' greatest concerns with TV advertising is the potential decline in effectiveness because of such *clutter*. And this clutter expanded considerably with the use of Internet devices while watching TV, as shown in Figure 11-19.

Figure 11-19 Consumer online activities not related to program or ads while watching TV

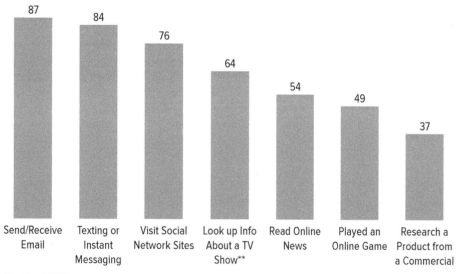

© Media Technology Monitor (MTM)

Imagine counting the number of commercials, promotions for the news or upcoming programs, or public service announcements that appear during a station break and the concern for clutter becomes obvious. With all of these messages competing for target audiences' attention, it is easy to understand why the viewer comes away confused or even annoyed and unable to remember or properly identify the product or service advertised.

One cause of clutter is the use of shorter commercials and **split-30s**, 30-second spots in which the advertiser promotes two different products with separate messages. The Canadian Radio-television and Telecommunications Commission (CRTC), which regulates television, permits 12 minutes of commercials per hour for specialty channels and an unlimited number of minutes for conventional channels. However, when simulcast Canadian commercials are run, there may be extra time since U.S. TV stations often show more commercial minutes. To fill this time, Canadian stations run ads for other shows, public service announcements, or news/entertainment vignettes. Thus, Canadian viewers sometimes experience a different kind of clutter than their American counterparts.

Media Image   To many critics of advertising, TV commercials illustrate everything that is wrong with the industry. Critics often single out TV commercials because of their pervasiveness and the intrusive nature of the medium. Consumers are seen as defenceless against the barrage of TV ads, since they cannot control the transmission of the message and what appears on their screens. Viewers dislike TV advertising when they believe it to be offensive, uninformative, or shown too frequently, or when they do not like its content.[39] Studies have shown that, of the various forms of advertising, distrust is generally the highest for TV commercials.[40] Also, concern has been raised about the effects of TV advertising on specific groups, such as children or the elderly.[41] While these historic concerns are legitimate, TV appears to be the best in terms of receiving video-based messages, as the data show in Figure 11-20.

Figure 11-20   Consumer attitudes toward video-based ads by media, adults 18+

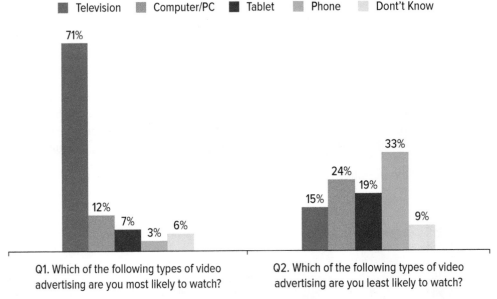

© Courtesy thinktv

 **Radio**

In contrast to television, radio has evolved into a primarily local advertising medium characterized by highly specialized programming appealing to very narrow segments of the population. The pervasiveness of this medium continues as radio advertising revenue modestly grew from $1.468 billion in 2007 to $1.589 billion in 2014.[42] In this section, we show how buying radio time is mostly similar to buying television time. We also review radio's strengths for advertisers to communicate messages to their current and potential customers, and summarize the inherent limitations that affect its role in the advertiser's media strategy.

TYPES OF RADIO ADVERTISING

The purchase of radio time is similar to that of television; advertisers can make either network or spot buys. Since these options were reviewed in the section on buying TV time, we discuss them here only briefly.

Network Radio   Advertising time on radio can be purchased on a network basis. This is a relatively new option for advertisers, who can now run ads on the CHUM radio network, the Team Sports Radio Network, and a few others. Using networks minimizes the amount of negotiation and administrative work needed to get national or regional coverage, and the costs are lower than those for individual stations. However, the number of affiliated stations on the network roster and the types of audiences they reach may vary, so the use of network radio reduces advertisers' flexibility in selecting stations. National advertising revenue topped $497 million in 2014.[43] Syndicated radio operators offer an alternative for radio advertising as they offer packages for advertising across their whole network.

Spot Radio   National advertisers can also use spot radio to purchase airtime on individual stations in various markets. The purchase of spot radio provides greater flexibility in selecting markets, individual stations, and airtime and adjusting the message for local market conditions. Local advertising revenue reached $1.091 billion in 2014.[44] By far the heaviest users of radio are local advertisers; the majority of radio advertising time is purchased from individual stations by local companies. Auto dealers, retailers, restaurants, and financial institutions are among the heaviest users of local radio advertising.

Station Formats   The CRTC lists 1,134 stations, with 807 in English, 224 in French, and 103 in other languages or variations of English or French with another language. It also lists 153 AM stations (118 are commercial, 15 are CBC, 20 are other) and 959 FM stations (590 are commercial, 74 are CBC, 295 are other).[45] Both network and spot advertising is offered across all these format options. Figure 11-21 shows that FM listening is substantially stronger than AM listening.

Figure 11-21   Weekly reach and share hours by station format and demographics

Canada	All (%)	Reach AM (%)	Reach FM (%)	Share AM (%)	Share FM (%)	Misc (%)
Persons 12+	89	26	79	19	80	1
Women 18+	90	25	81	17	82	3
Men 18+	89	31	79	19	78	3
Teens 12–17	74	9	71	5	94	1

Source: Numeris Fall 2013, Media Digest 2014–2015, p. 58.

Many radio stations stream their broadcast online so an Internet listener is exposed to the same ads as the broadcast listener. About one-quarter of all English Canadians listen to a Canadian radio station this way.[46] Figure 11-22 shows that the amount of audio and radio streaming is considerable with English Canadians. Numerous Internet sites compile the links for easy access to these radio broadcasts so that a Canadian can easily listen to radio from anywhere, and Canadians can listen to local, hometown stations while travelling or living abroad. Figure 11-23 indicates that the penetration rate is 19 percent and skewed to younger listeners living in higher income households. Individual audio streaming services that do not broadcast are available as well. Subscription based satellite radio service offers advertising opportunities on a limited basis as well. As this implies, radio advertising options are moving beyond local or national placements.

Figure 11-22   Average weekly hours of streaming audio and radio, English 18+

Streaming Audio		Streaming Radio	
Total	**6.0**	**Total**	**5.4**
Male	5.9	Male	4.1
Female	6.1	Female	7.0
Gen Z (18–25)	6.0	Gen Z (18–25)	2.7
Gen Y (26–34)	9.4	Gen Y (26–34)	5.7

[Continued on next page]

[Figure 11-22 continued]

Streaming Audio		Streaming Radio	
Gen X (35–49)	5.6	Gen X (35–49)	5.6
Younger boomers (50–58)	4.8	Younger boomers (50–58)	7.0
Older boomers (59–69)	3.5	Older boomers (59–69)	7.0
Golden Generation (70+)	2.6	Golden Generation (70+)	7.0

© Media Technology Monitor (MTM)

Figure 11-23   Streaming of personalized audio, English 18+

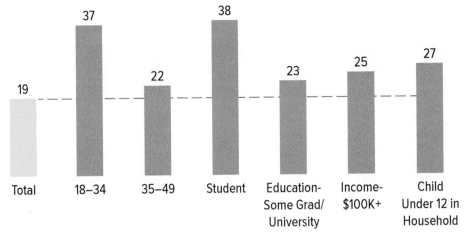

© Media Technology Monitor (MTM)

TIME CLASSIFICATIONS

As with television, the broadcast day for radio is divided into time periods or dayparts. The size of the radio listening audience varies widely across the dayparts, and advertising rates follow accordingly. The largest radio audiences (and thus the highest rates) occur during the early morning and late afternoon drive times. Radio rates also vary according to the number of spots or type of audience plan purchased, the supply of and demand for time available in the local market, and the ratings of the individual station. Rate information is available directly from the stations and is summarized in Canadian Advertising Rates and Data (CARD). Some stations issue grid rate cards. However, many stations do not adhere strictly to rate cards. Their rates are negotiable and depend on factors such as availability, time period, and number of spots purchased. The majority of radio ads are 30 seconds in length; however, stations will book 60-second spots and the majority do not book 15-second spots.

MEASURING THE RADIO AUDIENCE

As noted earlier, Numeris also provides information on radio listenership using the PPM and a diary method similar to television. Surveys are done twice per year in over 130 radio markets. Numeris publishes many reports associated with these surveys. Market reports summarize each radio station's audience by occupation, language, and other important characteristics. Other similar reports with greater aggregation across regions are also published. As seen for television, Numeris provides its members with many supporting documents to understand how to use radio as a communication tool. It also offers many software applications so that advertisers can purchase radio media effectively and efficiently. The three elements in the Numeris reports are similar to those found with TV: the estimated number of people listening, the percentage of listeners in the survey area population, and the percentage of the total estimated listening audience.

These three estimates are further defined by using *quarter-hour* and *cume* figures. The **average quarter-hour (AQH) figure** expresses the average number of people estimated to have listened to a station for a minimum of five minutes during any quarter-hour in a time period. This figure helps to determine the audience and cost of a spot schedule within a particular time period. **Cume** stands for *cumulative audience*, the estimated total number of different people who listened to a station for at least five minutes in a quarter-hour period within a reported daypart. Cume estimates the reach potential of a radio station. The **average quarter-hour rating (AQH RTG)** expresses the estimated number of listeners as a percentage of the survey area population. The **average quarter-hour share (AQH SHR)** is the percentage of the total listening audience tuned to each station. It shows the share of listeners each station captures out of the total listening audience in the survey area.

Audience research data on radio are often limited, particularly compared with TV, magazines, or newspapers. The Numeris audience research measurement mostly focuses on demographics and a handful of lifestyle factors. Most users of radio are local companies that cannot support research on radio listenership in their markets. Thus, media planners do not have as much audience information available to guide them in their purchase of radio time as they do with other media. Figure 11-24 shows an example of breaking down the audience share of listening by location.

Figure 11-24   Percentage of listening audience by location and demographic

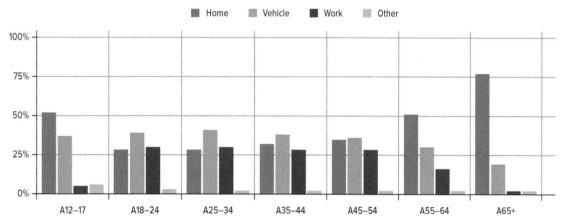

Source: Numeris Fall 2014, Media Digest 2015–16, p. 97.

 # Evaluation of Radio

Radio is an important advertising medium because of its ability to inform consumers of factual information and influence them with rational appeals that often help facilitate their shopping needs. Consumers feel radio keeps them connected: locally with important information, socially with radio personalities, musically with ideas for music not considered, and conveniently with no online search hassles.[47] However, radio does have certain characteristics that limit or even prevent its use by advertisers.

STRENGTHS OF RADIO

Radio has many strengths compared to other media, including target audience selectivity, geographic coverage, scheduling flexibility, reach and frequency, cost efficiency and absolute cost, creativity for cognitive responses, and media image.

Target Audience Selectivity   One major advantage of radio is the high degree of audience selectivity available through the various program formats and geographic coverage of the numerous stations. Radio lets companies focus their advertising on specialized audiences such as certain demographic and lifestyle groups. Most areas have radio stations with formats such as adult contemporary, easy listening, classical music, country, news/talk shows, jazz, and all news, to name a few. Numeris tracks radio listeners across 20 different radio formats. Overlaying radio format listened data with segmentation variables (e.g., demographics) allows advertisers to more accurately target their messages.

Geographic Coverage   Radio is essentially a local medium. In this respect, since all listeners can tune in, it offers excellent coverage within its geographic scope. Radio stations become an integral part of many communities, and the program hosts regularly become popular figures. Advertisers use radio stations and personalities to enhance their involvement with a local market and to gain influence with local retailers. Radio also works very effectively in conjunction with place-based/point-of-purchase promotions. Retailers use on-site radio broadcasts combined with special sales or promotions to attract consumers to their stores and get them to make a purchase. Live radio broadcasts are also used in conjunction with event marketing. Recent Numeris research finds greater radio listening in small and medium sized cities compared to large cities.

Scheduling Flexibility   Radio is probably the most flexible of all the advertising media because it has a very short closing period, which means advertisers can change their message almost up to the time it goes on the air. Radio commercials can usually be produced and scheduled on very short notice. Radio advertisers can easily adjust their messages to local market conditions and marketing situations.

Reach and Frequency   The low cost of radio means advertisers can build more reach and frequency into their media schedule within a certain budget. They can use different stations to broaden the reach of their messages and multiple spots to ensure adequate frequency. Radio commercials can be produced more quickly than TV spots, and the companies can afford to run them more often. Many national advertisers also recognize the cost efficiency of radio and use it as part of their media strategy. Figure 11-25 and Figure 11-26 indicate the degree of reach.

Figure 11-25   Percentage weekly reach by major demographic, by location

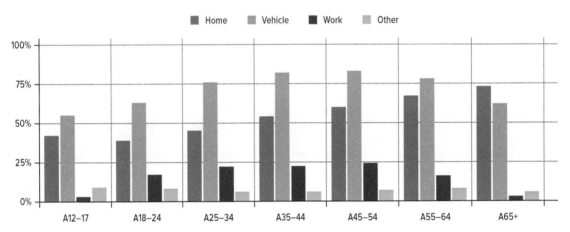

Source: Numeris Survey Media Digest 2015–16, p. 97.

Figure 11-26   Percentage weekly reach and hours tuned by major demographic

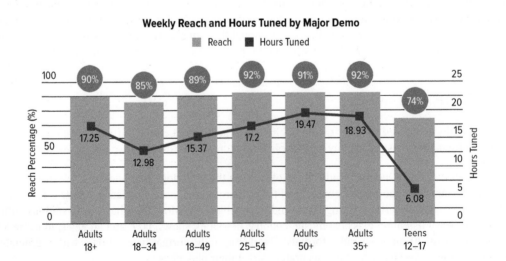

Source: Numeris Fall 2013, Media Digest 2014–15, p. 57.

Cost Efficiency and Absolute Cost   One of the main strengths of radio as an advertising medium is its low cost. Radio commercials are very inexpensive to produce. They require only a script of the commercial to be read by the radio announcer or a copy of a prerecorded message that can be broadcast by the station. The cost for radio time is also low. The low relative costs of radio make it one of the most efficient of all advertising media, and the low absolute cost means the budget needed for an effective radio campaign is often lower than that for other media.

Creativity for Cognitive Responses   The verbal nature of radio ads makes them ideal for long copy to select target audiences who may appreciate greater detailed information for some products. Alternatively, radio ads can also provide more concise brand information in a timely manner. Moreover, both of these factors are highly relevant for those listening in their car, which is a significant percentage of radio listenership. In either case, the informative nature of radio advertising makes it an opportunistic medium to connect with a target audience on a more rational level.

Lay's potato chips used a radio call-in show as the style for its national ad campaign to take advantage of this strength. Farmer Joe Oulton, the same person featured in three TV spots, received calls from people asking for directions. Instead of actually helping them, Joe directed the questioner to the local farm where Lay's grew its potatoes. The 20 ads featured local scenarios—like a lost Calgarian on the Edmonton Trail—to add a bit of folksy humour to the message of authentic home-grown potatoes in every bite.[48]

Media Image   Radio advertising in general has a good media image. Consumers rely on radio for news, weather, and traffic information, not to mention the obvious program content. Listeners enjoy radio media while at work or doing other tasks approximately half the time, and enjoy while not doing any task about a quarter of the time. About half of all listeners report interest and trust in radio ads, and only one-third claim they would like to eliminate radio ads.[49]

LIMITATIONS OF RADIO

Several factors limit the effectiveness of radio as an advertising medium, including target audience coverage, control for selective exposure, listener attention, creativity for emotional responses, amount of processing time, involvement, and clutter. The media planner must consider them in determining the role the medium will play in the advertising program.

Target Audience Coverage   A problem with radio is the high level of audience fragmentation due to the large number of stations. The percentage of the market tuned to any particular station is usually very small. The top-rated radio station in many major metropolitan areas with a number of AM and FM stations may attract less than 10 percent of the total listening audience. Advertisers that want a broad reach in their radio advertising media schedule have to buy time on a number of stations to cover even a local market. With recent media mergers in Canada, syndicated radio stations now provide advertisers with greater coverage, thus reducing this limitation.

Control for Selective Exposure   One environment where radio has a more captive audience is in cars. But getting listeners to expose themselves to commercials can still be difficult. Most people preprogram their car radio and change stations during commercial breaks. One study found large differences between exposure to radio programs and exposure to advertising for listeners in cars. They were exposed to only half of the advertising broadcast and changed stations frequently to avoid commercials.[50]

Listener Attention   Another problem that plagues radio is that it is difficult to retain listener attention to commercials. Radio programming, particularly music, is often the background to some other activity and may not receive the listeners' full attention; thus they may miss all or some of the commercials. This is slightly less of a concern because radio is with consumers throughout the day while doing many activities. Advertisers use creativity in radio ads to minimize the effects of listener attention. For example, Boston Pizza used radio in Quebec for a 13-week campaign to promote its "Mangiare, Mangiare" theme for special meals at $9.95. A popular star, Marc Hervieux, sings opera in Italian for a while until he humorously ends the solo due to his lack of rhyming skills. The 10-second spot's use of Italian intended to break through the clutter and remind consumers that Boston Pizza offered authentic Italian food.[51]

Creativity for Emotional Responses   A major drawback of radio as an advertising medium is the absence of a visual image. The radio advertiser cannot show the product, demonstrate it, or use any type of visual appeal or information. While the creative options of radio are limited, advertisers take advantage of the absence of a visual element to let consumers create their own picture of what is happening in a radio ad. These messages encourage listeners to use their imagination when processing the words, music, and sound effects.

Radio may reinforce a message received from another media such as television. **Image transfer** occurs where the images of a TV commercial are implanted into a radio spot. First, the advertiser establishes the video image of a TV commercial. Then, a similar—or even the same—audio portion is used in the radio spot. The audio could be the exact same speaker, jingle, or music that occurs in both the TV and the radio executions. Receivers of the radio ad recall the images from the TV commercial as the audio portion is recognized and associated with the TV images. While the idea of image transfer originated with a TV to radio sequence, it can be applied for any visual media to any audio media. For example, a video ad message disseminated in social media could have corresponding audio components in an ad message embedded within a podcast.

James Ready Beer successfully transferred its creative concept from outdoor to radio. Long known for its inexpensive price, "Help Us Keep This Beer a Buck," the brewery used only half a billboard, saying that it was saving money so the price of the beer would stay reasonable. The ad invited consumers through other media channels to create the rest of the ad, which culminated in over 100 unique "co-op" messages. For radio, the concept emerged as "Share Our Radio Space," where fans could complete the ending of the radio spots. The ads could be anything from marriage proposals to band gigs, or whatever an individual wanted to market.[52]

Amount of Processing Time   A radio commercial is, like a TV ad, a short-lived and fleeting message that is externally paced and does not allow the receiver to control the rate at which it is processed.

Involvement   Similar to television, radio is generally considered a low-involvement medium since it is faced with the same characteristics of short processing time and clutter. In fact, it may be seen as being less involving because it has the additional limitation of no visual.

Clutter   Clutter is just as much a problem with radio as with other advertising media. Radio stations can play as many minutes of advertising as they like. Most radio stations carry an average of nearly 10 minutes of commercials every hour. During the popular morning and evening rush hours, the amount of commercial time may exceed 12 minutes. Advertisers must create commercials that break through the clutter or use heavy repetition to make sure their messages reach consumers.

IMC Planning: Strategic Use of Broadcast Media

We continue with our IMC planning sections by relating the use of TV and radio with respect to achieving communication and behavioural objectives in general and in terms of the different stages of the consumer decision-making process for the target audience. This builds on our discussions in earlier chapters and highlights the importance of planning creative and media together.

TELEVISION

The creative opportunities associated with the many types of television allow it to play a variety of roles in the decision-making process for the target audience. We link the different types of ads with communication objectives and decision-making processes because the integration of television with other media or tools is predicated upon which types of TV ads will be run. For example, the suggestion to combine TV with Internet advertising, an event sponsorship, or perhaps out-of-home media is contingent on how the two media are planned to influence the target audience. As promotional planners decide upon TV as part of their IMC plan, it is critical to consider its communication objectives in relation to the objectives the other tools will contribute.

Promotional managers can plan for ads to influence their target audience at the prepurchase and need recognition stages. These kinds of ads could focus on one key benefit or consumption experience, and identify the brand sufficiently to contribute to awareness. For example, some car ads fit this role quite nicely, like the commercials positioning the Toyota Corolla as a reliable vehicle. The plan included other media to encourage further progress through the decision-making process. In this case, the Corolla utilized newspaper advertising for additional explanation and support of the reliability (e.g., information search), and transit station posters as a reminder for a test drive (e.g., purchase decision). For Corolla, the media selection, including television, planned a particular role for each selection to encourage all aspects of the decision-making process, each with particular attitudinal communication objectives.

Alternatively, marketers could provide a television message with information to influence their target audience while evaluating alternative brands. WestJet ads communicated the enhanced service level compared to its previous discount offering to encourage Air Canada consumers to switch; this message would be critical at the alternative evaluation stage.

The many executions showed the variety of customer experiences enhanced by the commitment level of the staff to serve its customers in an exemplary manner.

Finally, planners often schedule ads that have more immediate purchase intention or purchase facilitation objectives for the target to take action. An additional type of car ad communicates a promotional event or encourages a dealer visit for a test drive. Virtually all car brands resort to TV ads like this, yet the intensity of the "call to action" and the frequency vary considerably. When these ads are run, car brands typically are not running other types of TV ads but might have instructions to consult the newspaper for additional information. Another example from the social marketing realm is the United Way of Toronto's TV ads that showed a "helping hand" in two different scenarios with a verbal message requesting donations and the Internet address shown visually.

RADIO

While all media are inherently in competition for advertising revenue spent by media planners, radio finds itself with a very significant niche of flexibility that allows it to be in the plans for national brands like Bell and for local advertisers like the pizzeria just around the corner. Moreover, the characteristics of the medium allow planners to integrate radio with virtually any other media or IMC tool.

Whether we are considering a national advertiser like Bell or a local business, often the purchase decision stage is the one where maximum influence occurs. For example, many radio messages have a time frame for encouraging purchase through participation with a price promotion. Retailers use radio extensively for various sales, for instance. Alternatively, other radio messages might remind the target audience of entertainment and leisure activities occurring in the city or province within a time frame requiring more immediate action. In these situations, the key communication objectives attained are brand purchase intention or brand purchase facilitation. As we can see from these points, the scheduling flexibility of radio permits attainment of particular communication objectives or messaging consumers exactly when they are planning to make a purchase decision.

The lower costs associated with radio can contribute to building brand equity or an identifiable positioning through the affordability of repetition. A example of this is the prevalent use of radio by Sleep Country Canada, with owner Christine McGee as the spokesperson. The radio ads give the central positioning as a leading mattress retailer much added frequency beyond its television commercials, thus indicating a natural way to build brands by integrating a consistent message across two broadcast media.

Radio's flexibility and cost implications allow it to support other IMC tools. It can suggest that the target audience visit a brand's Internet site or look for a direct mail piece sent to their home—again, both are action-oriented with a time frame—or with some kind of intention on the part of the receiver of the message. One study found a high percentage of listeners check the Internet, perform a search, type in a web address, or visit the radio station's website after hearing about something on the radio.[53]

As noted above with price promotions, many other sales promotions can be communicated through radio, particularly those affiliated with sponsorship. Radio can be a key integrating medium to generate awareness of the other IMC tools for further communication in the target audience's decision making.

Learning Objectives Summary

 Describe different types of television advertising, specialty television advertising, alternative time periods and program format, and measurement of television audiences.

Television advertising is time dependent rather than space-oriented like print advertising. Advertisers select the time, day, week, and month in which they want their ads to be seen. Television is a system of affiliated stations belonging to a network, as well as individual stations, which broadcast programs and commercial messages. Advertising can be done on national or regional network programs or purchased in spots from local stations. The growth of specialized stations in recent years offers advertisers niche audiences and stronger selectivity than in the past.

Information regarding the size and composition of national and local TV audiences is provided by Numeris Canada. The amount of money a network or station can charge for commercial time on its programs is based on its audience measurement figures. This information is also important to media planners, as it is used to determine the combination of shows needed to attain specific levels of reach and frequency with the advertiser's target audience.

 Summarize the strengths and limitations of television as an advertising medium.

Television is a pervasive medium in most consumers' daily lives and offers advertisers the opportunity to reach vast audiences with very frequent messages. Over the past 60 years, national advertisers (and many local ones) employed TV as their leading medium. No other medium offers its creative capabilities; the combination of sight, sound, and movement gives the advertiser a vast number of options for presenting a commercial message. As a primary medium for these advertisers, the creative opportunities of television contribute to the brand's awareness and help in establishing or maintaining a brand's position. Television also offers advertisers mass coverage at a low relative cost. Variations in programming and audience composition are helping TV offer scheduling opportunities and some audience selectivity to advertisers.

While television is often viewed as the ultimate advertising medium, it has several limitations, including the high absolute cost of producing and airing commercials, low target audience selectivity, short processing time, extensive clutter, high selective exposure, and distrustful image. Despite these concerns, consumers generally appreciate brands more if they are advertised on television because the expenditure signals a stronger and more reputable brand.

 Describe different types of radio advertising, alternative time periods and program format, and measurement of radio audiences.

As with TV, the rate structure for radio advertising time varies with the size of the audience delivered. It differs from television in that purchases are not tied to individual shows or programs. Instead, packages are offered over a period of days, weeks, or months. The primary source of listener information is Numeris. The new PPM technology for television works with radio as well, although the diary method remains for smaller radio markets.

 Summarize the strengths and limitations of radio as an advertising medium.

The role of radio as an entertainment and advertising medium has evolved into a primarily local one that offers highly specialized programming appealing to narrow segments of the market. Radio offers strengths in terms of cost efficiency and absolute cost, reach and frequency, target audience selectivity, geographic coverage, scheduling flexibility, creativity for cognitive responses, and media image. The major drawback of radio is its weak creativity owing to the absence of a visual image. The short and fleeting nature of the radio commercial, the highly fragmented nature of the radio audience, low involvement, and clutter are also problems.

Apply the media knowledge of TV and radio for strategic IMC decisions.

TV and radio still command almost $5 billion in advertising revenue and remain very good media for attaining broad reach and frequency objectives to achieve or maintain brand awareness and establish or reinforce existing brand image perceptions. No doubt these media feel pressure from Internet media and the use of personal devices to listen to music; however, creative advertising in these media with the right connections to digital brand exposure makes them a strong part of major brands' advertising.

Review Questions

1. "Television is a mass medium that offers little selectivity to advertisers." Do you agree with this statement? What are the ways selectivity can be achieved through TV advertising?

2. Discuss the strengths of television as an advertising medium and the importance of these factors to major national advertisers and to smaller local companies.

3. Discuss the methods used to measure radio audiences. Do you think the measurement methods used for each are producing reliable and valid estimates of the viewing audiences?

4. What are the strengths and limitations of advertising on radio? What types of advertisers are most likely to use radio?

5. How can TV best be used to work with social media?

Applied Questions

1. Watch a show on TV and make notes on what ads are shown. Find the equivalent show on the network's website and make notes on what ads are shown. What similarities and differences do you notice?

2. Watch TV or listen to the radio and make note of whether the ads direct the receiver to any aspect of digital media (e.g., a social network).

3. Listen to the radio and make notes on what ads are aired. What similarities and differences do you notice in comparison to TV advertising?

4. Listen to a radio station and pay attention to the ads to assess whether any overcome the limitation of a lack of creativity for emotional responses.

5. How can radio best be used to work with social media?

texture™
by next issue

CHAPTER TWELVE

Print Media

LEARNING OBJECTIVES

LO1 Identify the different types of magazines available for advertising, how circulation and readership levels are determined, how audience size and its characteristics are measured, and the factors that influence advertising rates.

LO2 Evaluate the strengths and limitations of magazines as an advertising medium.

LO3 Identify the types of newspapers offered for advertising, how circulation and readership levels are determined, how audience size and its characteristics are measured, and how advertising rates are determined.

LO4 Evaluate the strengths and limitations of newspapers as an advertising medium.

LO5 Apply the media knowledge of magazines and newspapers for strategic IMC decisions.

Texture Replaces Next Issue

Texture is a premium content subscription service that provides unlimited digital access to nearly 200 worldwide magazines from six publishers—Condé Nast, Hearst Magazines, Meredith, News Corp, Time, and Rogers Media. Launched in 2010 and originally branded as Next Issue, the digital subscription gave access to all the magazines and advertised itself as "the world's greatest newsstand." Picking up on the growth of subscription video (e.g., Netflix) and music (e.g., Spotify) content, the group altered and rebranded its delivery, however the Next Issue name did not work with the improved reading features. The new brand name, Texture, intended to evoke associations with *text* and *culture* and distance itself from the historic idea of reading magazines from cover to cover. Despite the change, the senior vice-president for publishing at Rogers Media indicated the new brand name tested very positively. Even though Texture offered enhanced features, the capability of reading a magazine from cover to cover digitally remained as part of the service, reflective of the original way of reading a magazine.

The new Texture provided features to enhance reading pleasure across all the publications, akin to what consumers experience in other digital sources: "curated collections" organized content articles by theme; "news & noteworthy" brought trending topics together; "search & top stories" let readers find thematic or news content easily; "my collections" let readers save articles; and "first access" let members read articles prior to their hitting the full magazine or paper magazine. The service was offered as an unlimited basic access for 177 titles for $9.99/month or unlimited premium access for 191 titles for $14.99/month.

With the increased features, clearly Rogers Media expected growth beyond its current 100,000+ paid subscribers. Thus far, the majority of the digital subscribers represented new customers for Rogers Media, meaning they did not switch from a print magazine to the digital format. While a shift from print to digital occurred in newspapers, for now it appeared abated with magazines. However, the senior VP at Rogers believed Texture's content and new features appealed to non-magazine readers who almost exclusively consume their reading content on the screen instead of the page. Texture is designed to work on any device rather than being wedded to a particular one, as some digital transitions were. In this sense, Texture faced digital competitors like Apple News and Flipboard.

Canadian acceptance of the new delivery kept ahead of U.S. adoption. The Canadian 100,000+ subscribers topped the level found in the United States. Three titles from Rogers Media—*Chatelaine, Maclean's* and *Hello! Canada*—appeared in the top 10 regularly. Presently, digital readers represent 18 percent of Rogers' circulation. On average, each subscriber reads for three hours per month, at about $5/hour for premium members. Of course the success of the delivery method hinges on whether a critical mass of readers gravitates to digital magazines to attract profitable levels of advertising. Magazines face a challenge of keeping the overall industry ad revenue from declining. Since the start of Next Issue in 2010, magazine ad revenue plummeted from $606 million to $472 million in 2014, not quite as steep a plunge as newspaper revenue saw, but a parallel trend nonetheless.

Sources: Chris Powell, "Next Issue Re-Launching as Texture," *Marketing Magazine*, October 1, 2015; James Bradshaw, "Rogers Revamps Next Issue App to Cater to Digital Reading Habits," *The Globe and Mail*, September 30, 2015; James Cowan, "Netflix for Magazines Service Next Issue Rebrands as Texture," *Canadian Business*, September 30, 2015; "Next Issue Media Announces New Digital Magazine Experience Texture," www.prnewswire.com/news/next+issue+media.

Question:

1. Does this alternative magazine delivery appeal to you or advertisers more than a paper magazine?

Thousands of magazines are published in Canada and throughout the world. They appeal to nearly every consumer interest and lifestyle, as well as to thousands of businesses and occupations. The magazine industry has prospered by becoming a highly specialized medium that reaches specific target audiences. Newspapers are a primary advertising medium in terms of both ad revenue and number of advertisers. Newspapers are particularly important as a local advertising medium for retail businesses and are often used by large national advertisers.

The role of print media differs from that of broadcast media because detailed information can be presented that readers may process at their own pace. Print media are not intrusive like radio and TV, and generally require effort on the part of the reader for the advertising message to have a communication effect. For this reason, magazines and newspapers are often referred to as *high-involvement media*.[1] In fact, the three-month reach for magazines is 80 percent, and 73 percent read a print or digital version of newspapers on a weekly basis.[2] This chapter focuses on these two forms of print media as it identifies important information to determine when and how to use magazines and newspapers in the media plan and examines their unique strengths and limitations.

Magazines

Magazines serve the educational, informational, and entertainment needs of a wide range of readers and are a specialized advertising medium. While certain magazines are general mass-appeal publications, most are targeted to a very specific audience. There is a magazine designed to appeal to nearly every type of consumer in terms of demographics, lifestyle, activities, interests, or fascination. Magazines are targeted toward specific industries and professions as well. Magazine advertising reached $472 million in 2014, down from a peak of $718 million in 2007. Average issue circulation climbed from 63 million to 69 million during the 2004–2011 time period. In this section, we review different types of magazines, circulation and readership information, and magazine advertising rates to understand how to plan for magazine advertising placement.

CLASSIFICATIONS OF MAGAZINES

To gain perspective on the types of magazines available and the advertisers that use them, consider the way magazines are generally classified. Canadian Advertising Rates and Data (CARD), the primary reference source on periodicals for media planners, divides magazines into four broad categories based on the audience to which they are directed: consumer, ethnic, farm, and business publications. Each category is then further classified according to the magazine's editorial content and audience appeal. We also examine the opportunity of foreign publications.

Consumer Magazines   Consumer magazines are bought by the general public for information and/or entertainment. CARD divides 772 domestic consumer magazines into 46 classifications, among them general interest, women's, city/regional, entertainment, and sports, as seen in Figure 12-1. Figure 12-2 shows that the majority of all magazines have circulations below 50,000 and only 23 publications (3 percent) have circulations above 500,000. Magazines can also be classified by frequency—weekly, monthly, and bimonthly are the most common—and by distribution—subscription, store distribution, or controlled (free). Consumer magazines are suited to marketers interested in reaching a wide variety of consumers. For example, the ad in Exhibit 12-1 could be found in general magazines to encourage people to consider Australia as a destination early in their vacation plans.

Exhibit 12-1   Tourism Australia's ad appeals well in general consumer magazines.

WELCOME TO THE WORLD'S MOST SCENIC RUNWAY

THERE'S NOTHING LIKE AUSTRALIA

DISCOVER THE GREAT BARRIER REEF AT AUSTRALIA.COM

Courtesy Australian Tourist Commission ™ © The Brand Australia Trademark is the subject of copyright and is a trademark of the Australia Tourist Commission, 2013

Figure 12-1   Top editorial category circulation

Rank	Editorial Category	2014 Circulation (000's)		
		Total	English	French
1	General Interest	9,399	7,844	1,554
2	Homes/Gardening	6,459	5,018	1,441
3	Travel	5,627	4,741	885
4	Women's	4,525	3,470	1,054
5	Lifestyle	4,695	4,616	790
6	Food and Beverage	4,182	3,320	861
7	Entertainment	3,467	2,581	886
8	City and Regional	3,365	2,708	656
9	Business and Finance	2,191	1,916	274
10	Senior/Mature Market	1,874	1,375	499

Source: CARD, Magazines Canada Fact Book 2015, page 11.

Figure 12-2   Circulation distribution

Circulation Size	Number of Titles	Percent of Total Titles	Group Circulation	Percent of Total Circulation
1 million+	6	0.7	9,501,508	14.8
500,000 to 999,999	17	2.2	11,783,223	18.3
250,000 to 499,999	25	3.2	9,291,283	14.5
100,000 to 249,999	90	11.6	13,262,537	20.6
50,000 to 99,999	153	19.8	10,864,044	16.9
20,000 to 49,999	235	30.4	7,054,242	11.0
1 to 19,999	240	31.0	2,450,053	3.8

Source: MPA, Magazines Canada Fact Book 2015, page 12

National advertisers tend to dominate consumer magazine advertising in terms of expenditures in many large circulation magazines. Consumer magazines are important to smaller companies selling products that appeal to specialized markets and reach consumers with special-interest magazines. These publications assemble consumers with similar lifestyles or interests and offer marketers an efficient way to reach these people with little wasted coverage or circulation. For example, a manufacturer of ski equipment (e.g., Salomon) might find *Ski Canada* magazine to be the best vehicle for advertising to serious skiers. Not only are these specialty magazines of value to firms interested in reaching a specific market segment, but their editorial content often creates a very favourable advertising environment for relevant products and services. For example, the TaylorMade ad in Exhibit 12-2 might fit better in a specialty golf magazine for someone at the information search or alternative evaluation stage of their decision-making process.

As described in the opening vignette, digital expansion of magazines provides greater overall reach for individual magazine titles. With the transition to another media format, new advertising decisions emerged but many advertising placement decisions in a digital magazine are consistent with a published paper magazine. Magazines with digital presence reported stronger overall readership as duplication levels across the website or app versus the printed version appeared minimal. Magazines that have made this transition successfully include *Toronto Life, Fresh Juice, The Walrus, Alberta Venture,* and *The Hockey News.*[3]

The growth of free, customized magazines from retailers on a **controlled-circulation basis** (i.e., free) is an interesting trend. For example, about 500,000 copies of *Food & Drink* are distributed in Ontario liquor stores. Some customized retail magazines are now online; *Chill* is published by Ontario's The Beer Store and is only available in a digital format. Harry Rosen's *Harry* magazine is distributed to the chain's top customers and features many pages of paid advertising from selective advertisers like Bugatchi, Versace, Armani, and Hugo Boss.

Exhibit 12-2   TaylorMade ads appeal well in specialty golf magazines.

Ethnic Publications   CARD currently lists 124 magazines directed to persons with many backgrounds based on ethnicity. The majority of these are written in English (67), French (20), and Arabic (18), with many other languages (Chinese, German, Greek, Punjabi, Romanian, Russian, Spanish, Urdu) in the range of four to six publications each. Some of these publications have low circulation figures or do not have an authenticated circulation. Thus, the cost of advertising in these publications is currently very low.

Farm Publications   The third major CARD category consists of all the magazines directed to farmers and their families. About 88 publications are tailored to nearly every possible type of farming or agricultural interest (e.g., *Ontario Milk Producer, Ontario Produce Farmer*). CARD groups farm publications into general, livestock, crops, dairy, and community. A number of farm publications are directed at farmers in specific provinces or regions, such as *Alberta Beef.* Farm publications are not classified with business publications because historically farms were not perceived as businesses.

Business Publications   Business publications are those magazines or trade journals published for specific businesses, industries, or occupations. CARD lists almost 700 business magazines and trade journals, and breaks them into about 80 categories. The major categories include:

- Magazines directed at specific professional groups, such as *Canadian Lawyer* for lawyers and *Canadian Architect* for architects.

- Industrial magazines directed at businesspeople in manufacturing and production industries—for example, *Process Equipment and Control News* and *Heavy Construction.*

- Trade magazines targeted to wholesalers, dealers, distributors, and retailers, among them *Canadian Grocer.*

- General business magazines aimed at executives in all areas of business, such as *Canadian Business.*

The numerous business publications reach specific types of professional people with particular interests and give them important information relevant to their industry, occupation, and/or career. Business publications are important to advertisers because they provide an efficient means of reaching the specific types of individuals who constitute their target market. Much marketing occurs at the trade and business-to-business level, where one company sells its products or services directly to another.

Foreign Publications   Canadian magazines face competition from foreign publications, particularly American consumer magazines that account for about 90 percent of newsstand sales for foreign publications. These U.S. print vehicles are another means for Canadian advertisers to reach Canadian consumers. Current legislation allows for foreign publications to accept advertising space from Canadian advertisers for magazines sold in Canada. In addition, foreign publications can accept greater amounts of advertising if the majority of editorial content is Canadian.[4] Figure 12-3 shows circulation for the top U.S. publications; the opportunity for Canadian advertisers is to a degree limited in comparison to Canadian titles. Figure 12-4 shows that the spillover of American magazines declined substantially over many decades, thus indicating the strength of Canadian publications. Figure 12-5 shows the corresponding growth of Canadian magazines during the same time period. It also indicates that U.S. publications rebounded after a steady decline, although the resurgence has not spilled over.

Figure 12-3   U.S. magazines with a circulation of 100,000+ in Canada

Magazine Name	Total Paid Canadian Circulation
National Geographic	235,699
Cosmopolitan	144,276
People	129,231
Prevention	110,908
Women's Health	107,199
O, The Oprah Magazine	100,056

Source: Alliance for Audited Media; Media Digest 2015–2016, p. 141

Figure 12-4   U.S. spill trends

Year	Total Spill Circulation (000s)	Index	Average Circulation/Title	Index
1983	10,705	100	26,303	100
1989	9,969	93	21,031	80
1998	9,155	86	16,203	62
2002	8,160	76	15,396	59
2006	7,666	72	13,664	52
2010	6,349	59	14,235	54
2014	4,749	45	13,136	50

Source: ABC. Magazines Canada Fact Book 2015, page 13.

Figure 12-5   Canada continues to outpace the United States in magazine title growth

| Year | Canada | | United States | |
	Number of Titles	Index	Number of Titles	Index
1997	818	100	7,712	100
2001	961	117	6,336	82
2005	1,160	142	6,325	82
2009	1,276	156	7,110	92
2013	1,311	160	7,240	94

Source: Magazines Canada; Comparison of Canada and USA 2014, page 9.

MAGAZINE CIRCULATION AND READERSHIP

Two important considerations in deciding whether to use a magazine in the advertising media plan are the size and characteristics of the audience it reaches. Media buyers evaluate magazines on the basis of their ability to deliver the advertiser's message to as many people as possible in the target audience. To do this, they must consider the circulation of the publication as well as its total readership, and match these figures against the audience characteristics they are attempting to reach.

Circulation   Circulation figures represent the number of individuals who receive a publication either through subscription or store purchase, or on a controlled-circulation basis. Given that circulation figures are the basis for a magazine's advertising rates and one of the primary considerations in selecting a publication for placement, the credibility of circulation figures is important. Most major publications are audited by the Alliance for Audited Media (AAM), a North America–wide organization founded in 1914 and sponsored by advertisers, agencies, and publishers. AAM collects and evaluates information regarding the subscriptions and sales of magazines and newspapers to verify their circulation figures. Figure 12-6 shows some of the top magazines by circulation for both print and digital editions.

Figure 12-6   Top English-language Canadian magazines by circulation

Publication	Print Circulation (June 2014)	Digital (December 2013)
Chatelaine	534,294	5,590
Canadian Living	497,641	5,015
Reader's Digest	326,968	12,707
Maclean's	294,016	7,807
Canadian House & Home	220,455	11,045
Coup de Pouce	201,924	3,613
Moneysense	149,638	5,148
Hello!	133,914	4,401
Hockey News	95,380	3,533

Source: Based on data from Alliance for Audited Media

AAM provides media planners with reliable figures regarding the size and distribution of a magazine's circulation, which helps them evaluate its worth as a media vehicle. The AAM statement also provides detailed circulation information that gives a media planner an indication of the quality of the target audience. For example, it shows how the subscription was sold, the percentage of circulation sold at less than full value, the percentage of circulation sold with an incentive, and the percentage of subscriptions given away. Many advertisers believe that subscribers who pay for a magazine are more likely to read it than are those who get it at a discount or for free. Media buyers are generally skeptical about publications whose circulation figures are not audited and will not advertise in unaudited publications. Circulation data, along with the auditing source, are available from CARD or from the publication itself.

AAM recently added a new category of magazine circulation with the growth of unlimited access programs like Texture. Overall digital circulation hit just over 400,000 and represented 6 percent of the overall circulation of nearly 7 million. Planned measurement included the average number of total requests by paid subscribers and average number of times issues were opened, among others. The digital subscription would be counted as a paid subscription, accurately reflecting the media consumption.[5]

Readership   Advertisers are often interested in the number of people a publication reaches as a result of secondary, or pass-along, readership. **Pass-along readership** can occur when the primary subscriber or purchaser gives a magazine to another person or when the publication is read in doctors' waiting rooms or beauty salons, on airplanes, and so forth.

Advertisers generally attach greater value to the primary in-home reader than the pass-along reader or out-of-home reader, as the former generally spends more time with the publication, picks it up more often, and receives greater satisfaction from it. Thus, this reader is more likely to be attentive and responsive to ads. However, the value of pass-along readers should not be ignored since they can expand a magazine's reach.

The **total audience**, or **readership**, of a magazine is calculated by multiplying the **readers per copy** (the total number of primary and pass-along readers) by the circulation of an average issue. For example, a magazine with a circulation of 150,000 and 10 readers per copy has a total audience of 1.5 million. The readers per copy is estimated from market research data. Since it is an estimate, media planners are advised to assess its accuracy when deciding how much actual reach is attained with total readership.

Magazines Canada is an industry association representing hundreds of titles. It provides extensive information services for its members, and promotes magazines to advertisers as worthy media for advertising placement. A few figures of this chapter rely on just a fraction of the data available, and interested students may pursue additional resources at its website (MagazinesCanada.ca). One may find readership data there or on the websites or media kits of individual magazine titles. A campaign devoted to increasing magazine readership featured a couple in a magazine shop communicating with each other by picking up and showing different magazine covers, a very clever execution! Various magazines offered in-kind media exposure, and a Valentine's Day contest with a vacation as a prize completed the IMC integration of the message.[6]

MAGAZINE ADVERTISING RATES

Magazine rates are primarily a function of circulation; the greater the circulation, the higher the cost of the ad. Ads in controlled-circulation magazines (i.e., free) are generally cheaper than ads in paid circulation magazines. Advertising space is generally sold on the basis of space units, such as full-page, half-page, quarter-page, or double-page spread (two facing pages); a greater cost is incurred for ads requiring more space.

Rates for magazine ad space can also vary according to the number of times an ad runs and the amount of money spent during a specific period. The more often an advertiser contracts to run an ad, the lower the space charges. Volume discounts are based on the total space purchased within a contract year, measured in dollars or number of insertions. The following table from CARD shows the cost per colour ad (i.e., known as full-page four colour or FP4C) per month by size and the number of times inserted (i.e., ti) for *Ski Canada Magazine,* which publishes four issues per year.[7]

	1 ti	2 ti	3 ti	4 ti
Full page	$4,990	$4,745	$4,242	$3,990
2/3 p.	$4,142	$3,935	$3,520	$3,106

	1 ti	2 ti	3 ti	4 ti
1/2 p.	$3,393	$3,224	$2,884	$2,545
1/3 p.	$2,246	$2,133	$1,909	$1,684
1/6 p.	$1,098	$1,043	$933	$823
1/12 p.	$749	$711	$636	$561

Other variables that increase the cost of an ad include the colours used, its position in the publication, the particular editions (geographic, demographic) chosen, any special mechanical or production requirements, and the number and frequency of insertions. *Ski Canada Magazine* charges an additional 15 percent, 10 percent, and 25 percent for ad placement on inside front cover (IFC), inside back cover (IBC), and outside back cover (OBC), respectively.

Ads can be produced or run using black and white, black and white plus one colour, or four colours. The more colour used in the ad, the greater the expense because of the increased printing costs. Colour ads are so prominent in magazines that many do not even quote a non-colour cost in their CARD listing. Recall and action taken are stronger with colour ads versus non-colour ads.[8] Larger ads produce stronger recall and action taken. For example, a full-page ad can have 20 percent stronger communication effects.[9] Ads placed inside the front cover, inside the back cover, and outside the back cover yield 15 percent, 10 percent, and 20 percent stronger recall than a regularly placed ad.[10]

Finally, the CARD listing for *Ski Canada Magazine* shows an audited circulation of about 27,000, broken down as individual subscription 8,500, sponsored placement for in-room reading at hotels and ski resorts 8,500, sponsored individually addressed delivery to ski associations and ski travel companies 8,000, and sponsored distribution to ski retailers 2,000. The cost per thousand (CPM) is about $185 for a one-page ad (i.e., $4,990/27), but the CPM per reader is much lower with the placement in public locations. At three readers per copy, the CPM approaches $60 (i.e., $185/3). For its online version, *Ski Canada Magazine* charges a monthly rate for each type of display ad. In contrast, other online titles sell their ad space on a cost-per-thousand basis.

Evaluation of Magazines

Magazines have a number of strengths and limitations in comparison to other media. We review each of these according to the criteria of Chapter 10. Astute readers will acknowledge that each evaluation represents a generalization across all classifications of magazines. As such, exceptional anomalies may be found, thereby opening the assessment up to debate.

STRENGTHS OF MAGAZINES

Magazines have a number of characteristics that make them attractive for advertisers. Strengths of magazines include their target audience selectivity, geographic coverage, control for selective exposure and attention, creativity for cognitive and emotional responses, amount of processing time and reader involvement, and media image.

Target Audience Selectivity   One main advantage of using magazines is their **selectivity**, or ability to reach a specific target audience. Magazines are the most selective of all media except direct communication where the receiver's identity is known (e.g., addressed direct mail). Most magazines are published for readers with very specific reading requirements. The magazines reach all types of consumers and businesses and allow advertisers to target their advertising to groups that are consistent with their segmentation strategies along the lines of demographics, socioeconomics, and lifestyle (e.g., activities and interests). For example, *PhotoLife* is targeted toward camera buffs, while *Exclaim!* appeals to those with an avid interest in music.

One Canadian success story is the lifestyle magazine *Nuvo,* a refined publication (non-paid circulation) catering to the very affluent who appreciate a refined lifestyle of luxury. It claims to be Canada's premier lifestyle magazine with an audited circulation hitting 50,000.[11] Another successful interest magazine is *Hello!,* which features photos of and articles about celebrities. The uniquely Canadian edition found a niche where its focus on celebrities did not follow old ways of telling the stories but used a distinctive voice.[12] Homeowners interested in decoration and renovation ideas can select *Canadian House and Home,* with an audited circulation of 220,000. This is one of Canada's largest special-interest magazines with a paid circulation. A readership of 2.4 million implies 10 readers per copy, resulting in a CPM per reader just under $9, a good balance of selectivity and cost efficiency for advertisers of household decor.[13]

In addition to providing selectivity based on interests, magazines provide advertisers selectivity by other means. *Demographic selectivity,* or the ability to reach specific demographic groups, is available in two ways. First, most magazines are, as a result of editorial content, aimed at fairly well defined demographic segments. *Canadian Living* and *Chatelaine* (Exhibit 12-3) are read predominantly by women; *The Hockey News* is read mostly by men. Older consumers can be reached through publications like *FiftyPlus.* Second, selectivity can be applied effectively by tailoring the message by language since Canada naturally has magazines written in both English and French. Furthermore, publications in other languages permit additional targeting capabilities. *Geographic selectivity* occurs with magazines that offer a *geographic split run* where one region receives one message and another receives a different message.

Two technological developments—selective binding and ink-jet imaging—allow *individual selectivity* so advertisers can deliver personalized messages to targeted audiences. **Selective binding** is a production process that allows a magazine to send different editorial content and/or advertising messages within the same publication issue to groups of subscribers. **Ink-jet imaging** reproduces a message by projecting ink onto paper and makes it possible to personalize an advertising message. These innovations permit advertisers to target their messages more finely and let magazines compete more effectively with direct mail and other direct-marketing vehicles.

Loulou customized its magazine with different versions for Centre à la Mode customers who fit into three groups based on their shopping behaviour as derived from its database: impulsive, thoughtful, and habitual. Eight unique pages of clothing matched the three profiles so that consumers could visit the location with just the right shopping plans. Databases played an important role for Curel in working with *Reader's Digest* and *Selection* magazines, which wrote editorials about dry skin and sent emails using addresses from their subscription lists to those who had indicated having skin concerns. Combined with emails from an Environics list, the communication achieved 190,000 unique visits.[14]

Geographic Coverage   One way to achieve specific geographic coverage is to use a vehicle that is targeted toward a particular area, such as city magazines. *Toronto Life, Vancouver Magazine,* and *Montréal Scope,* to name a few, provide residents of these areas with articles concerning lifestyle, events, and the like in these cities and their surrounding metropolitan areas (Exhibit 12-4). Toronto enjoyed an expansion of titles much like what occurred 30 years ago due to an energized street scene, new inexpensive publishing technology, and post-recession optimism.[15]

Another way to achieve selective geographic coverage in magazines is through purchasing ad space in specific geographic editions of national or regional magazines. A number of publications (e.g., *Maclean's, Chatelaine*) divide their circulation into groupings based on regions or major metropolitan areas and offer advertisers the option of concentrating their ads in these editions.

Exhibit 12-3   *Chatelaine* allows for demographic selectivity.

Hand-out/Chatelaine/Newscom

Exhibit 12-4   City magazines such as *Toronto Life* offer advertisers high geographic selectivity.

© Toronto Life

CARD lists the consumer magazines offering geographic editions. Regional advertisers can purchase space in editions that reach only areas where they have distribution, yet still enjoy the prestige of advertising in a major national magazine. National advertisers can use the geographic editions to focus their advertising on areas with the greatest potential or those needing more promotional support. They can also use regional editions to test-market products or alternative promotional campaigns in regions of the country.

Ads in regional editions can also list the names of retailers or distributors, thus encouraging greater local support from the trade. The trend toward regional marketing is increasing the importance of having regional media available to marketers. The availability of regional and demographic editions can also reduce the cost per thousand for reaching desired audiences.

Control for Selective Exposure and Attention   With the exception of newspapers, consumers are more receptive to advertising in magazines than in any other medium. Magazines are generally purchased because the information they contain interests the reader, and ads provide additional information that may be of value in making a purchase decision. For example, magazines such as bridal or fashion publications are purchased as much for their advertising as for their editorial content. Figure 12-7 shows that magazines hold readers' attention better than other media.

Figure 12-7   Consumers' ratings of how well various media hold their attention

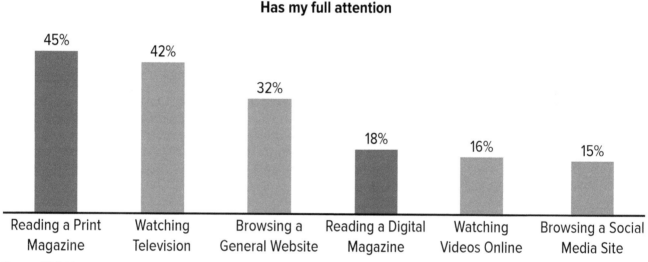

Has my full attention

| 45% | 42% | 32% | 18% | 16% | 15% |
| Reading a Print Magazine | Watching Television | Browsing a General Website | Reading a Digital Magazine | Watching Videos Online | Browsing a Social Media Site |

Source: ABC. Magazines Canada Fact Book 2015, page 13.

Creativity for Cognitive and Emotional Responses   A valued attribute of magazine advertising is the reproduction quality of the ads. Magazines are generally printed on high-quality paper stock and use printing processes that provide excellent reproduction in black and white or colour. And, the reproduction quality of most magazines is far superior to that offered by newspapers. Second, magazines are a visual medium in which a photographic image or illustration is the dominant part of an ad designed to generate emotional reactions like joy or pleasure, or allow receivers to carefully consider the argument put forth in the message. For example, Asics' global advertising campaign called "The Cleansing Power of Sport" used exercise, and more specifically running, as a cleansing metaphor. As shown in Exhibit 12-5, the brand executed the creative theme by showing a runner sprinting through walls of water as words such as *fear,*

Exhibit 12-5   Striking visuals in Asics' global campaign evoked emotional responses.

anima sana in corpore sano

© Asics Corporation

stress, insecurity, and *doubt,* rendered in various languages, fall away from his body. This campaign worked because the visually iconic images took advantage of magazines' major strength. Figure 12-8 presents evidence of the emotional importance of magazines.

Figure 12-8   Percentage of people expressing emotion when consuming media

Half Hours When Each Medium Was Used	Print Magazines	Digital Magazines	TV	Radio/Audio	Computer*	Mobile	Tablet*
Happy	36	39	27	30	22	30	28
Confident	19	30	7	10	8	7	11
Excited	15	23	5	7	5	8	5
Hopeful	17	14	5	6	4	6	7
Interested	25	30	5	4	5	5	9

Source: Magazines Canada Fact Book 2015, p. 50.

In addition to their excellent reproduction capabilities, magazines also offer advertisers options in terms of the type, size, and placement of the advertising material. Good magazines offer (often at extra charge) a variety of special opportunities to enhance the creative appeal of the ad such as gatefolds, bleed pages, inserts, and creative space buys.

Gatefolds enable an advertiser to make a striking presentation by using a third page that folds out and gives the ad an extra-large spread. Gatefolds are typically found at the inside cover of large consumer magazines and are especially useful for a new product introduction or new ad creative campaign for the brand. Advertisers use gatefolds to make a very strong impression and gain stronger recall scores.[16] **Bleed pages** are those where the advertisement extends all the way to the end of the page, with no margin of white space around the ad. Bleeds give the ad an impression of being larger and make a more dramatic impact.

Inserts used in magazines are designed for promotion, and can include recipe booklets, coupons, and even product samples. Cosmetics companies use scented inserts to introduce new fragrances, and others use them to promote products for which scent is important (e.g., deodorants, laundry detergents). Cost-effective technologies enhance the reading of advertising messages through options like anaglyphic images (three-dimensional materials that are viewed with coloured glasses); lenticular (colour) images printed on finely corrugated plastic that seem to move when tilted; and pressure- or heat-sensitive inks that change colour on contact. **Creative space buys** allow advertisers to purchase space units in certain combinations to increase the impact of their media budget.

Magazines work well with other media and promotional tools to contribute to strong responses. Digital technology integration with a print ad is possible; as shown in Exhibit 12-6, the Lexus ad becomes animated—the engine revs, the headlights flash, the wheels spin, and the background pulses with colour, all to a musical soundtrack—when placed over an iPad that has a Lexus microsite loaded. *Fashion* magazine helped with the launch of the new Calvin Klein fragrance Beauty by offering a contest via its magazine's website. *Fashion* invited its Twitter and Facebook followers to submit a photo that represented beauty and to explain what beauty meant to them. The communication involved 5,300 readers who commented on the photos and who subsequently received a sample. *Canadian Living* worked with P&G to identify possible leads from the former's reader panel for a Herbal Essences promotion. Participants provided online feedback in social media that proved to be

Exhibit 12-6   This Lexus ad becomes animated when placed over an iPad with a microsite loaded.

Photographer: John Higginson, Associate Creative Director: Fabio Simoes Pinto/Molly Grubbs, Art Producer: Lisa Matthews. Agency: Team One Advertising

useful content for future testimonial advertising. While these opportunities appear fruitful, research indicated a stronger preference remains for printed magazines for their emotional association.[17] IMC Perspective 12-1 describes new approaches for digital magazines.

Amount of Processing Time and Reader Involvement   A distinctive strength offered by magazines is that they are generally read over several days. TV and radio are characterized by fleeting messages that have a very short life span. Readers devote about 44 minutes to reading a magazine with a high degree of interest.[18] Figure 12-9 highlights the behavioural effects of the longer processing time and high reader involvement for health care products. Magazines are retained in the home longer than any other media and are referred to on several occasions; nearly 73 percent of consumers retain magazines for future reference.[19] One benefit of the longer life of magazines is that reading occurs at a less hurried pace and there is opportunity to examine ads in considerable detail. This means ads can use longer and more detailed copy, which can be very important for complex products or services. The permanence of magazines also means readers can be exposed to ads on multiple occasions and can pass magazines along to other readers.

Figure 12-9   Behavioural effects of high involvement processing of magazines

Actions Taken (indexed 12 month data)	Magazine Media	Internet*	TV	Radio	Newspapers
Returned a free sample card	236	83	191	24	172
Called a toll-free number to get additional information	234	102	180	139	155
Visited a pharmaceutical company's website	210	104	131	129	142
Switched to a different brand	208	115	156	121	150
Referred to a book, journal, or magazine to get additional information	192	101	116	119	124
Asked your doctor for a product sample of a prescription drug	179	95	145	111	125
Consulted a pharmacist	178	79	134	115	130
Discussed an ad with a friend or relative	176	120	135	147	134
Used a coupon	176	89	128	130	136
Asked your doctor to prescribe a specific drug	152	100	131	95	132
Purchased a nonprescription product	140	93	121	115	117
Called for a prescription refill	136	74	132	106	114
Made an appointment to see doctor	132	81	114	104	112
Took medication	126	87	121	112	113

Source: Magazines Canada Fact Book 2015, p. 162

Media Image   Another positive feature of magazine advertising is the prestige the product or service may gain from advertising in publications with a favourable image. Companies whose products rely heavily on perceived quality, reputation, and/or image often buy space in prestigious publications with high-quality editorial content whose consumers have a high level of interest in the advertising pages. For example, *Flare* covers young women's fashions in a very favourable environment, and a clothing manufacturer may advertise its products in these magazines to enhance the prestige of its lines. *Canadian Geographic* provides an impressive editorial environment that includes high-quality photography. The magazine's upscale readers are likely to have a favourable image of the publication that may transfer to the products advertised on its pages. Media planners rely on their experiences to assess a magazine's prestige and reader opinion surveys in order to select the best magazine title. Data in Figure 12-10 indicate how much consumers enjoy advertising in magazines.

Figure 12-10   Magazines offer a good media image for advertisers

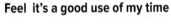
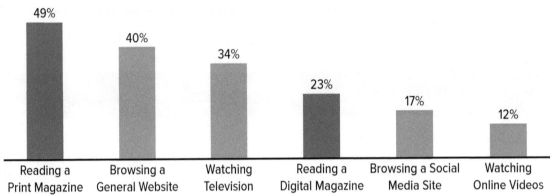
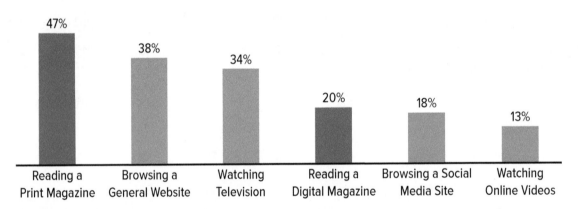
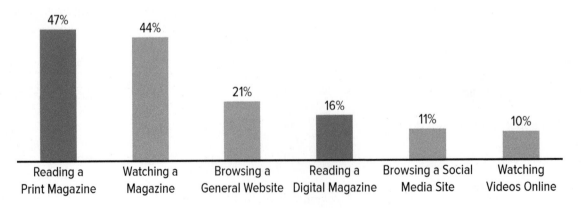

Has information I trust

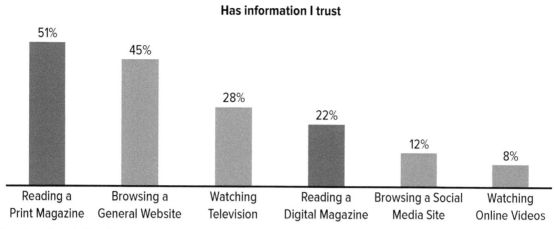

| 51% | 45% | 28% | 22% | 12% | 8% |
| Reading a Print Magazine | Browsing a General Website | Watching Television | Reading a Digital Magazine | Browsing a Social Media Site | Watching Online Videos |

Source: Magazines Canada Fact Book 2015, pp. 56–59

IMC PERSPECTIVE 12-1

MAGAZINES GO DIGITAL AND GO BEYOND

New results about magazines indicated that digital magazines continued to gain traction, with nearly 5 million Canadians reading them in 2015, up from just under 2 million two years earlier, with one-quarter reading digital magazines exclusively. The 5 million are divided on their preferred delivery, with one-third each liking the web edition, tablet option, or print version. Digital readers are well educated, urban, young adults employed in a professional/managerial job. And they read digital magazines like a printed magazine, reading on the couch (96 percent) or in bed (73 percent). Readers answered that they attend to digital magazine ads; they enjoy digital ads more than ads on digital

© baranq/Shutterstock

newspapers, social networking sites, and digital TV sites; and they are more likely to take action (71 percent to 59 percent) after seeing a digital magazine ad. For example, 83 percent visited the advertiser's Internet site, 53 percent recommended the brand, and 51 percent purchased the product. Digital magazines are all encompassing, with 79 percent having a Facebook page, 77 percent owning an Internet site, 67 percent sending enewsletters, 61 percent posting on a blog, 52 percent setting up a LinkedIn profile, and 46 percent creating video content. Clearly, magazines are in a new world of communication and we look at how three media companies reacted.

Given the above, it is no surprise to see that Montreal-based TVA entered the market with its digital magazine subscription Molto as an alternative to Texture by Next Issue, marketed by Rogers Media. Molto is "abundance" in Italian, and the brand name seemed an apt descriptor of the 400 titles available for reading for a fee of $8.49/month. Molto offered two themed packages for food and home décor for $5.49/month each and planned additional packages in future. It also planned to evaluate adding non-TVA publications to the mix, including book publishers. TVA developed Molto in association with miLibris, a French company with experience in bringing print titles together digitally.

Another magazine publisher—St. Joseph Communications, Media Group—did not plan to offer a competing subscription service but did move one of its key titles to a digital only version. *Canadian*

[Continued on next page]

[IMC Perspective 12-1 continued]

Family, a parenting magazine, had its readership decline and the publisher moved its content to an Internet site, Pinterest, and Facebook, and grew its audience respectably to complement its enewsletters. Amidst the overall print magazine ad revenue decline, certain categories of titles felt the pressure of advertisers' disinterest more significantly, such as parenting. Prior to going digital only, its initial foray to digital increased readership, but generated insufficient revenue and no profitability for a number of years.

Although faced with the same media environment of declining ad revenue, another media company expanded and moved its titles into a new realm with apparent success. Blue Ant is a Toronto-based media company that manages 10 media brands. With media vehicles moving beyond their traditional base, the terminology of *media brand* emerged. One of Blue Ant's successful print magazine titles, *Cottage Life*, got a new lease on life with movement into video with the Cottage Life TV channel that shows many related programs like *Brojects, Man Made Home,* and *Cabin Pressure*. Similar expansion of digital content moved to YouTube with the Cottage Life Magazine social media channel. The innovative development of Blue Ant as a multimedia producer of content and media delivery contributed to its being recognized as Media Player of the Year by *Marketing Magazine* in 2014. Blue Ant's next big step focused on international expansion by purchasing the Omnia multi-channel network on YouTube, which registers 60 million subscribers and 848 million monthly views.

Sources: Chris Powell, "TVA Group Launches Digital Subscription Service," *Marketing Magazine*, April 18, 2016; Chris Powell, "Digital Magazine Readership Tops 5 Million," *Marketing Magazine*, November 18, 2015; Chris Powell, "Started Small Going Global," *Marketing Magazine*, February/March 18, 2015; John Greenwood, "*Canadian Family* Ends Print Run," *National Post*, June 11, 2014.

Question:

1. How is the experience of reading a print magazine similar to or different from a digital version of the same title?

In addition to their relevance, magazine ads are likely to be received favourably by consumers because, unlike broadcast ads, they are nonintrusive and can easily be ignored. The majority of magazine readers welcome ads; only a small percentage have negative attitudes toward magazine advertising. Consumers generally enjoy magazines over other media along many measures such as advertising receptivity, inspirational, trustworthy, life-enhancing, social interaction, and personal timeout. Furthermore, readers believe advertising contributes to the enjoyment of reading a magazine more strongly than other media and they have stronger attitudes to magazine ads versus ads in other media.[20]

Advertisers take advantage of this strength with clever creative tactics. For example, Audi and *Maclean's* teamed up to put an ad on the magazine cover that looked entirely normal except for a discreetly placed "open here" message. Readers lifted a small flap to reveal the car ad—which proclaimed the AQ was foxy compared to a generic "boxy" competitor.[21] *Vice* magazine managed to put a BMW ad on its cover that could be seen only in the dark. The publisher distributed copies to nightclubs, where the ad would become visible.[22]

LIMITATIONS OF MAGAZINES

Although the strengths offered by magazines are considerable, they have certain drawbacks too. These include weak target audience coverage, the long lead time required in placing an ad leading to poorer scheduling flexibility, their limited reach and frequency, the absolute cost of advertising and its efficiency, and the problem of clutter.

Target Audience Coverage   The flipside of the strength of target audience selectivity is the limitation of magazines in providing extensive target audience coverage. Even though a magazine may draw an audience with a particular interest—for example, hockey with *The Hockey News*—the number of people reading the publication versus the number of people who actually play hockey is substantially disproportionate. The ability to achieve coverage with young adults aged 18–24 is limited as purchase and subscription levels are quite low; however, one study finds that young adults are vastly more receptive to reading print versions of magazines versus digital versions and prefer ads in magazines over digital ads.[23] And one expert sees great opportunity for continued development for magazines—and subsequently advertisers—with the growth of tablets, as long as the content resonates with the young audience.[24]

Scheduling Flexibility   Another drawback of magazines is the long lead time needed to place an ad, thus reducing scheduling flexibility. Most major publications have a 30- to 90-day lead time, which means space must be purchased and the ad must be prepared well in advance of the actual publication date. No changes in the art or copy of the ad can be made after the closing date. This long lead time means magazine ads cannot be as timely as other media, such as radio or newspapers, in responding to current events or changing market conditions.

Reach and Frequency   Magazines are generally not as effective as other media in offering reach and frequency. While adults in Canada read one or more consumer magazines each month, the percentage of adults reading any individual publication tends to be much smaller. As Figure 12-2 showed, the circulation of 80 percent of all titles is below 100,000. An ad in a magazine with this circulation reaches less than half a percent of all households.

Advertisers seeking broad reach must make media buys in a number of magazines, resulting in greater costs with multiple transactions. For a broad reach strategy, magazines are used in conjunction with other media. Since most magazines are monthly or at best weekly publications, the opportunity for building frequency through the use of the same publication is limited. Using multiple ads in the same issue of a publication is an inefficient way to build frequency, although a product category like fashion finds success with this approach as volume discounts are offered.

Despite these concerns from an individual title's viewpoint, total magazine reach is as impressive as any other media. About 8 out of 10 Canadians (aged 12–64) read magazines within the most recent three months.[25] As for frequency, while magazines cannot compete on this compared to broadcast media, placing an ad in consecutive months (e.g., five or more) provides measurably stronger awareness levels compared to placements for fewer months.[26]

Absolute Cost and Cost Efficiency   The cost of advertising in magazines varies according to size of audience reached and selectivity. Advertising in large mass-circulation magazines like *Maclean's* can be very expensive. For example, a full-page, four-colour ad in *Maclean's* national edition (circulation 362,000) had a cost of $37,000. Popular positions such as the back cover cost even more.

Magazines must be considered not only from an absolute cost perspective but also in terms of relative costs. Most magazines emphasize their efficiency in reaching specific target audiences at a low cost per thousand. Media planners generally focus on the relative costs of a publication in reaching their target audience. However, they may recommend a magazine with a high cost per thousand because of its ability to reach a small, specialized market segment. Of course, advertisers with limited budgets will be interested in the absolute costs of space in a magazine and the costs of producing quality ads for these publications. Strong brands or companies with large advertising budgets (e.g., car companies) are regularly in publications where the absolute cost is not a substantial deterrent for ad placement.

Clutter   Advertising clutter is not a serious issue for print media, as data show strong communication effects even with a competitor's ad in the same issue.[27] Consumers are more receptive to and tolerant of print advertising and control their exposure to a magazine ad simply by turning the page; however, the many pages of ads in a magazine raise an issue of concern when planning print ad placement. And this issue is a paradox for magazines since successful titles attract more advertising pages, potentially leading to greater clutter. Magazine publishers control clutter by maintaining a reasonable balance of editorial pages to advertising. Advertisers control the clutter with the use of strong visual images, catchy headlines, and other creative techniques to gain a reader's attention. In fact, new creative executions in magazines over many issues minimize ad wear-out, another factor contributing to issues of clutter.[28]

Newspapers

Newspapers are another form of print media and are one of the largest of all advertising media in terms of total dollar volume despite a recent and noticeable decline. In 2014, $1.4 billion was spent on daily newspaper advertising, or about 10 percent of the total advertising expenditures in Canada. Community newspapers hit $925 million or 7 percent, and online newspapers came in at almost $273 million but this amount is counted as Internet advertising revenue. The total of $2.6 billion dropped nearly $1 billion from 2012 to 2014 with no gain for online newspaper ad revenue. Newspapers are an especially important advertising medium for local advertisers, local and national retailers, and national advertisers of goods and services. In this section, we review different types of newspapers, types of newspaper advertising, newspaper circulation and readership, and finally newspaper advertising rates.

TYPES OF NEWSPAPERS

The traditional role of newspapers has been to deliver prompt news information and features that appeal to readers. In short, they provide detailed coverage of news, events, and issues concerning the local area as well as business, sports, and other relevant information and entertainment. The vast majority of newspapers are daily publications. However, community, national, Internet, and special-audience newspapers and newspaper supplements have special characteristics that can be valuable to advertisers.

Daily Newspapers   Daily newspapers, which are published each weekday, are found in cities and larger towns across the country. Some areas have more than one daily paper and are known as competitive markets, while the vast majority of smaller Canadian cities and towns have one publication. In 2014, there were 104 daily newspapers in Canada; of these, 91 were English-language papers and 13 were French-language papers, with a total circulation of 5.3 million. Most daily newspapers charge a price (or subscription fee); however, free dailies emerged on the market and represent substantial circulation and advertising revenue. There are 13 free daily newspapers in eight markets under the *Metro* or *24 Hours* or *Epoch Times* banner.[29] Figure 12-11 provides overview statistics of the number of daily newspapers and markets served.

Figure 12-11   Daily newspaper circulation by size of market

	1MM+	500M–1MM	100M–500M	50M–100M	Under 50M	Total
Number of Dailies	28	6	25	18	27	104
Daily Circulation	3,606,259	546,017	749,875	232,870	180,696	5,315,718
Weekly Circulation	21,305,858	3,522,114	4,525,632	1,379,164	1,032,688	31,765,434

© Newspapers Canada 24/7 Study, January 2016

Community Newspapers   Most community newspapers publish weekly and originate in small towns where the volume of news and advertising cannot support a daily newspaper. Canada had about 1,100 community newspapers in 2015 with a total circulation of 21 million. Community newspapers also dot the suburbs of many larger Canadian cities. These papers focus primarily on news, sports, and events relevant to the local area and usually ignore content covered by the city-based daily newspaper. Community newspapers appeal primarily to local advertisers because of their geographic focus and lower absolute cost. Most national advertisers avoid community newspapers because of their duplicate circulation with daily papers in the large metropolitan areas.

National Newspapers   Newspapers in Canada with national circulation include the *National Post* and *The Globe and Mail*. Both are daily publications and have editorial content with a national appeal. The *National Post* has a weekday print circulation of about 163,000 and a Saturday circulation of almost 167,000, and its corresponding print readership figures are 384,000 and 451,000 respectively.[30] *The Globe and Mail* has a weekday print circulation of about 347,000 and a Saturday circulation of approximately 416,000.[31] National newspapers appeal primarily to large national advertisers and to regional advertisers that use specific geographic editions of these publications.

Internet Newspapers   Major Canadian daily newspapers, the two national newspapers, and community newspapers offer an Internet version of their publications. Regular newspapers charge for subscriptions or for individual papers at newsstands, and rely on advertising revenue to support the distribution of editorial content. Internet versions are similar in this respect; the publishing firms have experimented with different combinations of fees and ads. Newspapers raced to develop apps so readers could consume their media on new reading and mobile devices, and this growth of digital media permitted accurate tracking of reader consumption. Consumers are readily adopting digital newspaper editions. Newspapers package online and print ads for advertisers, and larger media companies embed TV ads within their digital editions. However, as one industry executive suggested, "We need to think more about selling our audiences, because that is something that is sincere and heartfelt and resonates with advertisers."[32]

Most Canadian newspapers remain quite strong as readers continue to seek out information, which keeps readership levels steady. Further, readers seek content from a credible and trusted source like a newspaper in the face of less credible sources found on the Internet. Newspapers have found a growing niche in readers getting news through different digital avenues, which raises a significant concern about having to charge for "free" online service. However, some inventive techniques for both content and advertising may hold off the pay-for-service model for a while.

Furthermore, social media is now an important place for reporters to be on the scene for changes in stories, thereby giving content a new meaning of importance as readers are letting publishers know what stories are relevant; this approach should permit stronger reader interest in the long run. Continuing with this idea is that publishers are trying to stay more connected with the community to ensure local stories are covered more thoroughly.[33]

Special-Audience Newspapers   A variety of papers offer specialized editorial content and are published for particular groups, including labour unions, professional organizations, industries, and hobbyists. Many people working in advertising and marketing read *Marketing Magazine*. Specialized newspapers are also published in areas with large foreign-language-speaking ethnic groups, among them Chinese. Newspapers targeted at various religious and educational groups compose another large class of special-interest papers. A trend has arisen with the establishment of local business newspapers.

Newspaper Supplements   Although not a category of newspapers as such, papers include magazine-type supplements. For example, *The Globe and Mail* publishes a glossy *Report on Business* magazine at the end of each month. Newspapers are also in the game of custom publishing magazine supplements for advertisers. This is a relatively new field for this media as titles look to replace lost advertising revenue with classified ads shifting to digital vehicles. In contrast, as noted in the magazine section, this kind of activity occurred with great frequency in that media, but newspapers struggle with the balance of journalistic integrity and the need to please advertisers. One example is Sunnybrook Hospital's twice-yearly publication, *Sunnybrook Magazine*, put together by *The Globe and Mail*. This publication provides extensive information regarding all of the hospital's activities and is a key tool for generating donations as it is sent to 50,000 *Globe and Mail* subscribers and 30,000 donors.[34]

TYPES OF NEWSPAPER ADVERTISING

The ads appearing in newspapers can also be divided into different categories. The major types of newspaper advertising are display and classified. Other special ads and preprinted inserts also appear in newspapers.

Display Advertising   **Display advertising** is found throughout the newspaper and generally uses illustrations, headlines, white space, and other visual devices in addition to the copy text. The two types of display advertising in newspapers are local and national (general).

Local advertising refers to ads placed by local organizations, businesses, and individuals who want to communicate with consumers in the market area served by the newspaper. Supermarkets and department stores are among the leading local display advertisers, along with numerous other retailers and service operations such as banks and travel agents.

National or general advertising refers to newspaper display advertising done by marketers of branded products or services that are sold on a national or regional level. These ads are designed to create and maintain demand and to complement the efforts of local retailers that stock and promote the advertiser's products. Major retail chains, auto makers, and airlines are heavy users of newspaper advertising.

Classified Advertising   **Classified advertising** provides newspapers with revenue; however, online classifieds and search ads have completely eroded this from $846 million in 2007 to $175 million in 2014 . These ads are arranged under subheads according to the product, service, or offering being advertised. While most classified ads are just text set in small type, newspapers also accept classified display advertising.

Special Ads   Special advertisements in newspapers include government and financial reports and public notices of changes in business and personal relationships. Other types of advertising in newspapers include political or special-interest ads promoting a particular candidate, issue, or cause. Newspapers like *The Globe and Mail* offer sponsorship opportunities in which, for a few days each week, they will focus on a particular topic (e.g., tax planning, luxury travel, Olympics) that provides interested advertisers with an opportunity to customize messages or focus their spending knowing a certain audience will read featured content.

Preprinted Inserts   **Preprinted inserts** do not appear in the paper itself; they are printed and inserted before delivery. Retailers use inserts such as free-standing inserts (FSI), circulars, catalogues, or brochures in specific circulation zones to reach shoppers in their particular trade areas. "Inserts" advertising revenue is now presented as a separate line item in the Media Digest report on Canadian advertising revenue (see Figure 10-1 in Chapter 10). Canadian Tire spends more than $10 million per year on flyers.[35] While still a significant print communication, digital newspapers and other online locations display digital flyers that look exactly like the printed version. In time, we may see a higher proportion of online retail flyers as companies look for cost savings and consumers' media habits change.

A trend is for creative inserts; car companies periodically include poster-like inserts that people may choose to keep. Belairdirect insurance used inserts that looked like file folders similar to what consumers would use while researching this purchase. For the holiday season, a Molson insert looked like a beer fridge; upon opening, consumers would see cases on flaps that could be opened to reveal promotional information underneath, such as PIN codes for an online contest to win a beer fridge.[36] One media planner suggested ads in retail flyers could be a good alternative to magazine ads since they offer a low CPM and data indicated that half of all Canadians regularly used a grocery store flyer and readers spend an average of 20 minutes reading flyers.[37]

NEWSPAPER CIRCULATION AND READERSHIP

The media planner must understand the size and reader characteristics of the audience reached by a newspaper when considering its value in the media plan. As with other media, advertisers are concerned with the size of the audience reached through a particular vehicle. Thus, the circulation, or number of readers, is an important statistic. And while the audience size is important, advertisers are also interested in the amount of reading occurring and similar reader usage statistics prior to making their decision regarding newspapers.

Circulation   The basic source of information concerning the audience size of newspapers comes from circulation figures available through CARD, discussed earlier in this chapter. The Alliance for Audited Media (AAM) verifies circulation figures for many newspapers, as illustrated in the magazine media section. Advertisers using a number of papers in their media plan may find CARD to be the most convenient source.

Newspaper circulation figures are generally broken down into three categories: the city zone, the retail trading zone, and all other areas. The **city zone** is a market area composed of the city where the paper is published and contiguous areas similar in character to the city. The **retail trading zone** is the market outside the city zone whose residents regularly trade with merchants within the city zone. The "all other" category covers all circulation not included in the city or retail trade zones. Sometimes circulation figures are provided only for the primary market, which is the city and retail trade zones combined, and the "all other" area. Both local and national advertisers consider the circulation patterns across the various categories in evaluating and selecting newspapers.

Readership   Circulation figures provide the media planner with the basic data for assessing the value of newspapers and their ability to cover market areas. However, the media planner also wants to match the characteristics of a newspaper's readers with those of the advertiser's target audience. Media planners may seek additional readership information (e.g., demographics), including the number of readers per copy, about a particular newspaper title on their website or within their media kit. For example, the *Globe and Mail* website lists extensive information about its readership. As an example of useful newspaper readership data, Figure 12-12 shows that weekly readership remained strong with print and digital access combined. In fact, about one-quarter read the actual print version and all three digital editions.

Figure 12-12   Weekly newspaper readership by platform access

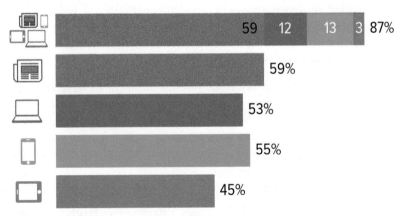

© Newspapers Canada 24/7 Study, January 2016

The Canadian Newspaper Association (CNA) and the Canadian Community Newspapers Association (CCNA) jointly execute research for newspaper audience measurement through their joint organization, Newspapers Canada. Each organization retains its own board of directors and many organizational functions are done as one. CNA promotes the benefits of advertising in newspapers, both daily and community, to advertisers, agencies, media planners, and newspapers themselves through research and information. In the past, Newspapers Canada performed community newspaper research; however, cost considerations and the infrequency of community newspaper publication required a change in the methodology. The most recent data collection in 2013 surveyed 200 respondents in five regions: Alberta, Saskatchewan, Manitoba, Northern Ontario, and Nova Scotia. The following results demonstrate the significance of community newspapers: 73 percent read a community newspaper (weekend or weekday), females exhibit higher readership at 76 percent, readership is higher with older Canadians, and there is no variation with different income levels.[38]

NEWSPAPER ADVERTISING RATES

Advertisers are faced with a number of options and pricing structures when purchasing newspaper space. The cost of advertising space depends on the circulation, and whether the circulation is controlled (free) or paid. It also depends on factors such as premium charges for colour in a special section, as well as discounts available. National rates can be about 15 percent higher than local rates, to account for agency commission.

Newspaper space is sold by the **agate line** and **column width**. A line (or agate line) is a unit measuring one column wide and 1/14-inch deep. One problem with this unit is that newspapers use columns of varying width, from 6 columns per page to 10 columns per page, which affects the size, shape, and costs of an ad. (Note that these columns are not the actual columns viewed while reading the newspaper.) This results in a complicated production and buying process for national advertisers that purchase space in a number of newspapers.

Advertisers need to know the number of lines and number of columns on a newspaper page in order to calculate the cost of an ad. For example, the following calculation is for the weekday cost of a full-page ad in the national edition of the *National Post*. The paper has 301 lines and 10 columns per page, and the open cost per line is $17.69. (Results of all calculations are rounded to the nearest dollar.)

$$10 \text{ columns} \times 301 \text{ lines} \times \$17.69/\text{line per column} = \$53,247$$

This calculation could be done differently with the same result when the entire length of the paper is known (301 lines/14 agate lines per column inch).

$$10 \text{ columns} \times 21.5 \text{ inches} \times 14 \text{ agate lines per column inch} \times \$17.69 \text{ per agate line} = \$53,247$$

This principle can be used to calculate the cost of ads of various sizes. For example, for an ad that is 5 columns wide and 6 inches deep, the calculation would then be the following:

$$5 \text{ columns} \times 6 \text{ inches} \times 14 \text{ agate lines per column inch} \times \$17.69 \text{ per agate line} = \$7,430$$

Newspaper rates for local advertisers continue to be based on the column inch, which is 1 inch deep by 1 column wide. Advertising rates for local advertisers are quoted per column inch, and media planners calculate total space costs by multiplying the ad's number of column inches by the cost per inch.

Most newspapers have an **open-rate structure**, which means discounts are available. These discounts are generally based on frequency or bulk purchases of space and depend on the number of column inches purchased in a year. The above calculations used the most expensive cost based on a one-time ad. The maximum discount puts the cost per line at $11.82, about one-third less expensive. A full-page ad would drop from $53,247 to $35,578, a saving of $17,669.

Newspaper space rates also vary with an advertiser's special requests, such as preferred position or colour. The basic rates quoted by a newspaper are **run of paper (ROP)**, which means the paper can place the ad on any page or in any position it desires. While most newspapers try to place an ad in a requested position, the advertiser can ensure a specific section and/or position on a page by paying a higher **preferred position rate**. Colour advertising is also available in many newspapers on an ROP basis or through preprinted inserts or supplements.

With the decline of newspaper advertising revenue, Postmedia signed a three-year advertising payment deal with Mogo, an online financial service targeted to younger adults. Postmedia provided advertising across its 200 media properties in exchange for a percentage of Mogo's revenue and the option to buy shares. The arrangement worked out to $50 million in advertising based on posted ad rates and allowed for a two-year extension.[39] Time will tell if this is a one-time experiment or a new wave of the future for print media and maybe all media.

Evaluation of Newspapers

Newspapers have a number of strengths and limitations in comparison to other media. We review each of these according to the criteria of Chapter 10. Newspapers present unique opportunities for ad placement that affect their strengths and limitations, as does the use of national, city, or community publications. Despite this, the generalizations are reasonably consistent no matter the situation.

STRENGTHS OF NEWSPAPERS

Newspapers have a number of characteristics that make them popular among both local and national advertisers. These include target audience coverage, geographic coverage, scheduling flexibility, reach and frequency, absolute cost and cost efficiency, amount of processing time and reader involvement, creativity for cognitive responses, and media image.

Target Audience Coverage   Coverage of a specific target audience is argued to be a limitation for the newspaper in comparison to its print cousin, the magazine. However, placement of ads in certain newspaper sections that recur every day (e.g., sports, business, entertainment) or once a week (e.g., food, cars, finance) can be advantageous for marketers.

Geographic Coverage   Newspapers generally offer advertisers targeted geographic or territorial coverage. Advertisers can vary their coverage by choosing a paper—or combination of papers—that reaches the areas with the greatest sales potential. National advertisers take advantage of the geographic coverage of newspapers to concentrate their advertising in specific areas they can't reach with other media or to take advantage of strong sales potential in a particular area. For example, more expensive automobile manufacturers advertise in Toronto newspapers that reach the greater Toronto area and beyond with their wide distribution.

A number of companies use newspapers in their regional marketing strategies. Newspaper advertising lets them feature products on a market-by-market basis, respond and adapt campaigns to local market conditions, and tie in to more retailer promotions, fostering more support from the trade.

Local advertisers like retailers are interested in geographic coverage within a specific market or trade area. Their media goal is to concentrate their advertising in the areas where most of their customers are. Many newspapers now offer advertisers geographic areas or zones for this purpose.

Scheduling Flexibility   Another strength of newspapers is the flexibility they offer advertisers in terms of requirements for producing and running the ads. Newspaper ads can be written, laid out, and prepared in a matter of hours. For most dailies, the closing time by which the ad must be received is usually only 48 hours before publication (although closing times for supplements and for special ads, such as those using colour, are longer). The short production time and closing times or dates make newspapers very suitable for responding to current events or presenting timely information to consumers.

Reach and Frequency   One of the primary strengths of newspapers is the high degree of market coverage they offer an advertiser. In most areas, 40–50 percent of households read a daily newspaper each day, and the reach figure hits the higher end among households with higher incomes and education levels. Most areas are served by one or two daily newspapers. The extensive penetration of newspapers makes them a truly mass medium and provides advertisers with an excellent opportunity for reaching all segments of the population. Also, since many newspapers are published and read daily, the advertiser can build a high level of frequency into the media schedule.

Absolute Cost and Cost Efficiency   Newspapers assist small companies through free copywriting and art services. Small advertisers without an agency or advertising department often rely on the newspaper to help them write and produce their ads. Production costs of ads are reasonable since many are simple copy with a standard image or photo-stock visual. The creative flexibility of newspapers in terms of size and format of the ad makes it difficult to exactly conclude the cost implications of this medium. Small and local businesses can run a small ad with a reasonable cost per thousand compared to magazines.

Amount of Processing Time and Reader Involvement   Another important feature of newspapers is consumers' level of acceptance for and involvement with papers and the ads they contain. The typical newspaper reader spends considerable time each day reading. Most consumers rely heavily on newspapers not only for news, information, and entertainment but also for assistance with consumption decisions. Figure 12-13 gives an idea of how much news reading occurs throughout the day for different ways to access the information. As expected, reading via phone devices peaks throughout the day, thereby giving newspapers the opportunity to adjust content and give advertisers direction for targeting. And the remaining access points are relatively consistent.

Figure 12-13   Newspaper access types by time of day

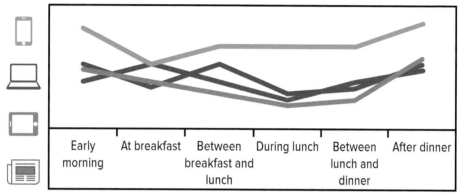

© Newspapers Canada 24-7 Study, January 2016

Consumers also typically rely on a newspaper because of the advertising it contains. Consumers use retail ads to determine product prices and availability and to see who is having a sale. One aspect of newspapers that is helpful to advertisers is readers' knowledge about particular sections of the paper. For example, the weekly food section in newspapers is popular for recipe and menu ideas as well as for the grocery store ads and promotional offers, and financial services ads are found in the business section.

Creativity for Cognitive Responses   Newspapers offer the opportunity for extremely long copy, perhaps a thousand words extolling the attributes and benefits of a product. The option of considerable explanation of a product could be quite important for marketers looking to persuade consumers who are at the information search stage of the decision-making process. Furthermore, newspapers offer numerous creative options as ads can be run in different sizes, shapes, and formats to persuade the reader. Magazine innovations described earlier are adapted to newspapers as well.

Media Image   The value of newspaper advertising as a source of information has been shown in several studies. One study found that consumers look forward to ads in newspapers more than in other media. In another study, 80 percent of consumers said newspaper ads were most helpful to them in doing their weekly shopping. Newspaper advertising has also been rated the most believable form of advertising in numerous studies. IMC Perspective 12-2 reflects on interesting changes in newspapers to attract greater advertising revenue.

IMC PERSPECTIVE 12-2

NEWSPAPERS FACE READERSHIP DECLINES

The downfall of newspapers' advertising revenue continued as the total (including Internet) dropped from $3.7 billion in 2010 to $2.6 billion in 2014. After giving away free journalistic content online for 10–15 years with no subscription fee and minimal support from Internet advertising revenue at $273 million in 2014, industry players faced their unprofitable business and realized they were at the crossroads in deciding their future. Recently, many newspapers gravitated to fees to access news online and three notable examples of interesting decisions—*The Globe and Mail*, Postmedia's *Ottawa Citizen*, and *La Presse*—illustrate changes in the industry.

© Asia Images Group/Getty Images

[Continued on next page]

[IMC Perspective 12-2 continued]

A significant change *for The Globe and Mail* featured video content for presenting news information, with the newspaper thereby acting more like a news broadcaster. It hit 3 million unique streams per month. An important component included *Globe Now*, a daily news show presented at noon every Monday to Friday featuring 60- to 90-second clips on business, technology, lifestyle, and arts. The show led with a thought piece or discussion point based on current issues rather than breaking news. Viewers continued to return, with metrics indicating higher repeat visits lasting longer than established norm measures and video preroll completion rates hitting 86 percent. These three data points looked favourable to advertisers who targeted affluent and influential audiences. *Globe Now* also offered content to other publisher partners to reach an additional 10 million readers and viewers. Another development is refinement in the development of customer publications through its Custom Content Group. The look is different from regular content to indicate that it is promotional in nature, but it is based on the journalistic quality of the regular reporting staff. For example, twice a year it produces a magazine-quality publication (*Sunnybrook Magazine*) for Sunnybrook Hospital for its fundraising activities.

Postmedia owns 45 newspaper titles and selected the *Ottawa Citizen* as the first of many to be revamped since the publication in the nation's capital had begun the process already. Claiming Postmedia's stance as a "news media company" rather than a newspaper company, the progression of the *Ottawa Citizen* included the paper version, a website version, tablet edition, and smart phone edition. Each delivery method featured news and ads created and designed to take advantage of the respective unique strengths. Postmedia based the change on extensive research, having surveyed 17,000 Canadians in eight markets to understand their reading habits throughout the day with all delivery methods. Data indicated differences in age and past experience with newspaper reading. As part of the plan, the larger metro region newspapers would take on new operational procedures and share news content.

In Montreal, *La Presse* took an entirely different direction than the other two. It spent $40 million in development and introduced a free digital edition of its paper version entitled *La Presse+* specifically designed to be used on an iPad, with an Android version to be added later. Executives believed younger consumers are too used to receiving journalistic content for free to reverse the trend, especially for a non-international publication. In contrast, a large player like *The New York Times* successfully relaunched its pay system. After starting, *La Presse* hit 400,000 installed apps and 300,000 weekly readers. Each reader spends more than 30 minutes on weekdays and more than an hour on weekends. The edition is loaded at 5:30 a.m. every day, featuring text, interactive images, videos, photo galleries, and scrolling screens. Interactive ad units provide new ways of communicating with consumers for brand advertising. All ads are hyperlinked to a brand's Internet site. *La Presse* claimed 70 percent of its readers like the digital ads. Readership skewed to high-income young adults, dramatically different from the skew of its print years.

Sources: Chris Powell, "Paper Tigers," *Marketing Magazine*, January/February 2014; "Post Media Roll Out New Model," *National Post*, May 20, 2014; "*The Globe*'s Recipe for Killer Custom Content," *Strategy*, December 2014, "*Globe and Mail*'s Aggressive Video Push Pays Off in Upscale Audience," *Strategy*, July 2014.

Question:

1. Why are digital newspapers a stronger or weaker alternative as an advertising medium compared to other digital alternatives?

LIMITATIONS OF NEWSPAPERS

While newspapers have strengths, they also have limitations that media planners must consider as with other media. The limitations of newspapers include their target audience selectivity, control for selective exposure and attention, creativity for emotional responses, and clutter.

Target Audience Selectivity   While newspapers can offer advertisers geographic selectivity, they are not selective in terms of demographics or lifestyle characteristics. Most newspapers reach broad and very diverse groups of consumers, which makes it difficult for marketers to focus on narrowly defined market segments. For example, manufacturers of fishing rods and reels will find newspapers very inefficient because of the wasted circulation that results from reaching all the newspaper readers who don't fish. Thus, they are more likely to use special-interest magazines. Any newspaper ads for their products will be done through cooperative plans whereby retailers share the costs or spread them over a number of sporting goods featured in the ad.

Control for Selective Exposure and Attention   Unlike magazines, which may be retained around the house for several weeks, a daily newspaper is generally kept less than a day. So an ad is unlikely to have any impact beyond the day of publication, and repeat exposure is very unlikely. Compounding this problem are the short amount of time many consumers spend with the newspaper and the possibility they may not even open certain sections of the paper. Media planners can offset these problems somewhat by using high frequency in the newspaper schedule and advertising in a section where consumers who are in the market for a particular product or service are likely to look. Another approach puts together different kinds of front pages that are in fact ads on the actual newspaper, known as "front page wraps," to obtain reader attention. Some are concerned that this detracts from the delivery of the news product, but others are finding success. Other inventions—like "belly bands," which are advertising strips surrounding the paper like a belt, and "French doors," which are section wraps split down the middle—are making headway as well.

Creativity for Emotional Responses   A significant limitation of newspapers for advertising is their poor reproduction quality. The coarse paper stock used for newspapers and the absence of extensive colour limits the quality of most newspaper ads. Newspapers have improved their reproduction quality, and colour reproduction has become more available. Also, advertisers desiring high-quality colour in newspaper ads can turn to such alternatives as freestanding inserts or supplements. However, these are more costly and may not be desirable to many advertisers. As a general rule, if the visual appearance of the product is important, the advertiser will not rely on newspaper ads. Ads for food products and fashions generally use magazines to capitalize on their superior reproduction quality and colour.

Clutter   Newspapers, like most other advertising media, suffer from clutter. Because a substantial amount of the average daily newspaper in Canada is devoted to advertising, the advertiser's message must compete with numerous other ads for consumers' attention and interest. Moreover, the creative options in newspapers are limited by the fact that most ads are black and white. Thus, it can be difficult for a newspaper advertiser to break through the clutter without using costly measures such as large space buys or colour. Advertisers use creative techniques like island ads—ads surrounded by editorial material. Island ads are found in the middle of the stock market quotes on the financial pages of many newspapers.

IMC Planning: Strategic Use of Print Media

In Chapter 11, we ended with a discussion of the use of broadcast media to achieve strategic IMC objectives. In this IMC planning section, we investigate the use of magazines and newspapers to achieve communication and behavioural objectives at different stages of the target audience's decision-making process.

MAGAZINES

The selectivity and creativity options for magazines allow promotional planners a multitude of opportunities for establishing and maintaining very unique brand positions across all potential target audiences. For example, if research reveals a high proportion of non-users in certain lifestyle publications, the promotional planner can develop print ads with extensive copy to build category need as well as sufficient brand coverage for awareness while communicating the most appropriate brand benefit message for persuasion. Alternatively, research in other publications might indicate strong brand development and a high proportion of current customers, thus allowing the promotional planner the opportunity to use messages that maintain the strong brand equity. This might suggest a more emotional message with enticing visuals for low-involvement processing.

While the decision to offer more customized messages to each audience is met with a certain amount of risk, this is mitigated by the consistency in the creative theme and creative tactics such as the design elements (e.g., layout). This possible scenario for promotional planners suggests that ads directed toward non-users could be developed to influence the prepurchase and need recognition stages, whereas the ads for the customer could attempt to influence the purchase decision stage, as the brand would be encouraging a repeat purchase objective.

Extending this argument geographically is another strategic opportunity for promotional planners. For example, if the brand has a low brand development index in one part of the country, more persuasive switching messages directed to consumers at the purchase decision stage might be considered through regional or city editions. Alternatively, other regional editions could be examined if the brand has a high brand development index and the promotional planner concentrates on brand maintenance messages that focus, for example, on postpurchase satisfaction.

As the use of these key strengths of magazines implies, promotional planners can use magazines to attain virtually any of the communication objectives with any type of target audience and create the unique brand positions desired. Magazines are also strong for attaining purchase intention objectives and shopping objectives; ads generate action or planned action in 50–60 percent of respondents.[40] Magazine ads are useful for prompting Internet searches and website visits, with 26–36 percent of respondents reporting such behaviour.[41] Granted, certain costs are associated with this strategic use of magazines; the promotional planner can schedule the placements over time so as not to break the budget.

These strengths of magazines allow print to work with other media and IMC tools. Visuals can be the same as those from TV commercials to enhance message frequency. Headlines can be consistently used across out-of-home media and print ads. Sales promotions can be added to the message, like coupons or Internet site links to register for samples. Brand-building charity sponsorship or events can be communicated if they especially resonate with the readership audience. In short, magazines offer a degree of potential integration in the IMC plan.

NEWSPAPERS

The strategic use of newspapers is similar to radio in that national and local advertisers design messages with related objectives. National advertisers employ newspapers for brand-building messages they wish to disseminate across the country or in select regions. These ads take a few general forms. One kind of ad builds awareness and benefit beliefs at the prepurchase and need recognition stages due to the broad reach of newspapers. With the majority of Canadian households reading newspapers on a regular basis, brands naturally reach their target audience and those who may not be in the market for such products. Other types of ads contribute at the information search stage for the target audience. The involved nature of the messages that can be creatively communicated in a more rational manner to fit the editorial context permits promotional planners to persuade their audience via high-involvement, informational brand attitude. One limitation with the opportunity is that the number of consumers actually in the market at this stage is smaller, thus making the purchase less cost-efficient. Finally, national advertisers utilize newspapers for executing information regarding sales promotions. For example, automobile manufacturers and large retailers are the largest advertisers who communicate their price and other promotions in newspapers to influence consumers at the purchase decision stage.

As noted in the cost implications discussion, newspapers offer local advertisers and small businesses (e.g., retailers, services) a tremendous opportunity for reaching an entire city for a reasonable cost. These advertisers can design ads to meet any communication objectives. A perusal of the local newspaper will identify ads that are clearly trying to build awareness and communicate certain brand benefits. However, the daily/weekly time frame of newspapers reveals that many ads have stronger purchase intention objectives.

Like magazines, newspapers offer good potential for integrating with other media and IMC tools. Television and radio commercials frequently suggest that consumers "see newspaper for details." In this case, the initial ads are influencing the target audience at the need recognition stage and the newspaper is influencing the information search stage. Many public relations activities (such as sponsorship of charity events in the local community) are conveyed in newspapers since they act as a planning resource for things to do in one's city.

Learning Objectives Summary

 LO1 Identify the different types of magazines available for advertising, how circulation and readership levels are determined, how audience size and its characteristics are measured, and the factors that influence advertising rates.

Magazines are a very selective medium and are valuable for reaching specific types of customers and market segments. The four broad categories of magazines are consumer, ethnic, farm, and business publications. Each of these categories can be further classified according to the publication's editorial content and audience appeal. Foreign publications compete with Canadian magazines also.

Circulation and readership are verified with an audit function so advertisers are confident that the number claimed by the individual title is accurate. Extensive information about magazine readers is available.

Advertising space rates in magazines vary according to a number of factors, including the size of the ad, position in the publication, particular editions purchased, use of colour, and number and frequency of insertions. Rates for magazines are compared on the basis of cost per thousand, although other factors such as the editorial content of the publication and its ability to reach specific target audiences must also be considered.

 LO2 Evaluate the strengths and limitations of magazines as an advertising medium.

The strengths of magazines include their target audience selectivity, geographic coverage, control for selective exposure and attention, creativity for cognitive and emotional responses, amount of processing time and reader involvement, and media image. Limitations of magazines include their weak target audience coverage, the long lead time required in placing an ad leading to poorer scheduling flexibility, their limited reach and frequency, the absolute cost of advertising and its efficiency, and the problem of clutter.

 LO3 Identify the types of newspapers offered for advertising, how circulation and readership levels are determined, how audience size and its characteristics are measured, and how advertising rates are determined.

A variety of newspapers are available for advertisers, including daily, community, national, Internet, and special-audience newspapers and newspaper supplements. Newspapers offer great flexibility regarding the type of ad, including display, classified, special, and inserts. Extensive research is conducted to ensure that the number of readers is accurate. Additional research of newspaper readers provides a detailed profile of their characteristics.

Newspaper ads are sold as a full page or any partial page the advertiser desires. The line and column characteristics of newspapers allow nearly unlimited sizes, although most ads follow conventional sizes of half-page, quarter-page, and so on, with smaller advertisers selecting smaller spaces. Advertising rates are determined by the size of the ad and the circulation.

 LO4 Evaluate the strengths and limitations of newspapers as an advertising medium.

Newspapers are a very important medium to local advertisers, especially retailers. Newspapers are a broad-based medium and reach a large percentage of households in a particular area. Newspapers' other advantages include target audience coverage, geographic coverage, scheduling flexibility, reach and frequency, absolute cost and cost efficiency, amount of processing time and reader involvement, creativity for cognitive responses, and media image. Limitations of newspapers include their target audience selectivity, control for selective exposure and attention, creativity for emotional responses, and clutter. The use of special inserts and supplements allows advertisers to overcome these limitations to a degree. However, newspapers face increasing competition from Internet media as the World Wide Web continues to grow as an information resource for consumers.

Apply the media knowledge of magazines and newspapers for strategic IMC decisions.

Print media are important for IMC plans as their potential for long-form copy, lengthy reading, and selectivity for magazines and coverage for newspapers makes expenditures worthwhile for certain product categories or for when consumers are in the information or purchase decision stage. Given their importance for providing information, print media are readily linked with other media as ads may suggest connection to digital media or follow-up on messages found in broadcast or out-of-home media that have broader coverage.

Review Questions

1. Discuss how circulation figures and readership composition are used in evaluating magazines as part of a media plan and setting advertising rates.
2. Discuss the strengths and limitations of magazines for advertising. How do magazines differ from television and radio as advertising media?
3. Discuss how circulation figures and readership composition are used in evaluating newspapers as part of a media plan and setting advertising rates.
4. Discuss the strengths and limitations of newspapers for advertising. How might the decision to use newspapers in a media plan differ for national versus local advertisers?
5. How do magazines and newspapers help achieve brand behavioural and communication effects?

Applied Questions

1. Explain why advertisers of products such as cosmetics or women's clothing would choose to advertise in magazines such as *Flare, Elle Canada,* or *Chatelaine*.
2. Select an enjoyable print ad from a magazine and apply the earlier text material. Identify the target audience, behavioural objectives, communication objectives, brand positioning strategy, and creative strategy and tactics decisions, and associate these points with the key strengths of magazines as an advertising medium.
3. Explain why advertisers of products such as smart phones or men's clothing would choose to advertise in newspapers such as *The Globe and Mail, Vancouver Sun,* or *Metro*.
4. What differences might one conclude exist between national newspapers and community newspapers regarding the strengths and limitations of newspapers?
5. Identify how newspapers and magazines can be used for each stage of the consumer decision-making process for automobile purchases.

© Andres Garcia Martin/Shutterstock

CHAPTER THIRTEEN

Out-of-Home and Support Media

LEARNING OBJECTIVES

LO1 Identify the options within out-of-home media for developing an IMC program and for audience measurement, and their strengths and limitations.

LO2 Apply the concepts of out-of-home media to promotional products and product placement to construct support programs within an IMC plan.

LO3 Show how out-of-home and support media are important elements of IMC planning.

Billboards Go Digital

The growth of digital billboards changed the game for marketers and contributed to the 15 percent growth in advertising revenue for outdoor media during the first quarter of 2015, and rivalled the growth in mobile advertising worldwide. Media companies installed the first digital billboard about a decade ago and other outdoor and indoor applications ensued, most notably in transit shelters. However, the sheer size and number of billboards drove attracted advertisers to place their brand messages throughout our cities. In addition, research unearthed constructive findings; 60 percent of Canadian shoppers noticed digital billboards and 73 percent of smart phone owners noticed digital billboards. Consumers who recall out-of-home ads are more likely to use their device for shopping activities like store location and research for features and price, a boon for those using digital billboards and transit shelter ads.

Key features of digital outdoor media are the lower production cost, improved scheduling flexibility, and faster installation. The message can be live immediately after the creative message contained in an electronic file is complete, rather than waiting for a paper display to be printed and installed that has to last for four weeks to gain economies of scale for all parties. Recent intensification of installations improved the ability of marketers to target audiences by location, time of day, or other variables like weather.

In fact, the creative message can change as often as an advertiser desires throughout the day. For example, McDonald's implemented the technology on a billboard on the highway between Vancouver and Whistler, British Columbia. Depending on the snow conditions, the message focused on a particular beverage, advertising McCafé Latte on light snowfall days, McCafé Cappuccino on moderate snowfall days, and McCafé Deluxe Hot Chocolate on heavy snowfall days. Carrying this further, a quick service restaurant could advertise its breakfast menu in the morning, lunch menu at midday, and dinner menu in the evening.

Digital outdoor media also includes wireless near-field communication so that it works with consumers' mobile devices and offers considerable message customization comparable to mobile ads. And more importantly, the combined effect of both out-of-home media and mobile media message offers advertisers an optimal message delivery approach. An example of the new implementation of technology for outdoor media is JUICE Mobile's proximity network across all outdoor media. Users who are close to billboard or transit media will receive an advertising message or promotional offer with an opportunity to accept or decline. The company expects strong consumer adoption as the majority of Canadians are willing to receive a notification on their phone if they perceive it to be an offer of value. The system also promises accurate reporting of the numbers of consumers passing by the message and of those accepting the message. Data supports this belief, indicating that the majority of consumers plan to take action after interacting with an outdoor ad.

Sources: "JUICE Mobile Technology to Provide the Missing Link Between Mobile and OOH Media," *Strategy*, September 2014; "Astral-Out-of-Home Drives Campaign Success With Digital Technology and New Formats," *Strategy*, September 2014; "The New OOH Front: Dynamic, Interactive and Immediate," *Strategy*, September 2014; Chris Powell, "Digital Puts the Awe Into OOH," *Marketing Magazine*, May 2014; Chris Powell, "Digital Outdoor Gets Noticed," *Marketing Magazine*, June 10, 2015; Chris Powell, "The McSnow Report," *Marketing Magazine*, February 17, 2016.

Question:

1. Why are advertisers turning toward mobile messages delivered by digital billboards?

Every time we step out of the house, we encounter media directing an advertising message to us. Often we see ads while travelling, and many places we go to for leisure have advertising. **Out-of-home media** is quite pervasive as it delivers advertising messages that we experience while moving throughout our town or city while accomplishing our day-to-day activities. Some are new to the marketplace, and others have been around a while. In this chapter, we review three broad categories of out-of-home media: outdoor, transit, and place-based media, which generated $521 million in advertising revenue in 2014. The term *out-of-home media* is adopted because it encompasses media that are located in public spaces.

We also encounter messages from **support media**. These media are used to reach those in the target audience that primary media may not, or to reinforce the message contained in primary media. We conclude this chapter by summarizing two types: promotional products and product placement. The term *promotional media* might be more appropriate; however, the notion of support media has existed for a while and remains relatively accurate. Its function as a public dissemination of a brand's messages is similar to out-of-home media, allowing this chapter to have a consistent theme. Finally, for each out-of-home and support medium, we offer a summary of strengths and limitations; these are generalizations, however, and advertisers can certainly find exceptions as these media continue to flourish and innovate.

Outdoor Media

Outdoor media are pervasive, and it appears that we are surrounded. However, the amount spent on this medium is but a portion of the $521 million spent on out-of-home media. In contrast, advertising on the Internet is about seven times larger than out-of-home. Despite this paradox of both large and small scale, the growth of outdoor media options and the medium's contribution to sales may be a key factor in its continued appeal to advertisers. For example, a study showed that outdoor advertising can have a significant effect on sales, particularly when combined with a promotion.[1] We now describe outdoor media options, their audience measurement, and their strengths and limitations as an advertising medium.

OUTDOOR MEDIA OPTIONS

A variety of outdoor media options are available, as shown in Figure 13-1. **Posters** describe the typical billboard, which can be horizontal (e.g., 3 metres by 6 metres) or vertical (e.g., 5 metres by 4 metres). These displays are front lit for visibility at night and are located in areas with high vehicle traffic (see Exhibit 13-1). They may be purchased on an individual basis or for a certain level of GRPs in cities such as Toronto or in smaller markets such as Timmins, Ontario. As the name implies, **backlit posters** are posters of generally the same size that have a light behind them so that they are more clearly illuminated (see Exhibit 13-2). These units are located at major intersections or high-traffic-volume areas in or near major cities in Canada.

Exhibit 13-1 Example of a poster ad.

© OUTFRONT Media Inc.

Exhibit 13-2 Example of a backlit poster.

© OUTFRONT Media Inc.

Figure 13-1 Out-of-home media

Outdoor	Transit	Place-Based
Horizontal/vertical poster	Interior horiz./vert. poster	Bar, restaurant, hotel
Backlit poster	Exterior bus poster	Mall, cinema
Superboard, spectacular	Superbus, bus mural	Airport poster/video display
Video/electronic display	Station video display	Arena, stadium
Street level/transit shelter poster	Station poster	Golf, ski, fitness centre
Wall banner, mural	Station domination	Office building
Mobile signage	Taxi	University, college
Aerial, bench, receptacle, parking lot, bike rack	In-flight video/magazine	Washroom, elevator

Creativity is possible with billboards; one located near a subway track featuring a photo of a model advertising hair care products contained an interactive feature where her hair blew as the train arrived. Of course the ad did not actually change, but a video projected upon the billboard gave the effect of visually experiencing the product benefit.[2]

Larger billboards, known as **bulletins, superboards,** or **spectaculars**, are larger displays (two to three times larger) that have a variety of sizes depending upon the media company (see Exhibit 13-3). These displays are sold on a per location basis due to their size and the low number of options available in major Canadian markets. *Trivisions* and *permanents* are two specialized forms of bulletins. Trivisions are horizontal or vertical posters with rotating blades that allow three different ads to be shown. Permanents feature unique sizes and formats and are erected in specific locations permanently.

Research on billboards is lacking in comparison to other media, but one study on why billboards are used found that managers rated visibility and media efficiency as more influential than local presence and tangible results (e.g., sales). The most critical factors for billboard success included name identification, location, readability, and clarity. A secondary set of factors suggested IMC and visuals, while the third group indicated creative and information. This implies that allowing the target audience to clearly read the brand identification at the right place is paramount over the most creative or informative ad.[3]

Smaller backlit displays, known as **street-level posters** and measuring about 2 metres by 1 metre, are available across the country and are also posted in **transit shelters**. Industry people also refer to this as "street furniture"; a couple of examples are shown in Exhibits 13-4 and 13-5. Innovation in transit shelters features interactive communication with people's phones and is described in IMC Perspective 13-1. A study conducted in Europe makes a number of conclusions regarding outdoor advertising's usefulness:[4]

- Clear branding and inclusion of new-product information enhances product recognition.
- Large amounts of text and pictures of people delay product recognition.
- Lengthy, large headlines, information cues, and humour delay brand recognition.
- Short headlines, longer body text, and a product shot enhance the creative appeal.
- Specifying a brand name in the headline or providing price information reduces appeal.

A number of innovative outdoor tools have emerged in Canada, with firms setting up large video-display units that have full animation and colour. For example, Dundas Square, near the Eaton Centre in downtown Toronto, features a 12-metre-wide by 9-metre-high full-colour video screen in addition to eight display faces and Canada's largest neon sign, at 18 metres in diameter. With its high-profile location, Dundas Square is ideal for brands looking to extend their reach (Exhibit 13-6). As another example, a billboard for Cadbury's Creme Eggs relied on precipitation to completely reveal a gooey adventure for all to see in person or online. A pendulum-like device with a giant egg at one end and a box that collected snow and rain at the other eventually tilted so that the egg made contact with a fan. The ensuing contact broke the egg and released the faux cream filling upon the billboard.[5]

Exhibit 13-3   Example of a superboard.

© OUTFRONT Media Inc.

Exhibit 13-4   Example of a transit shelter poster.

© OUTFRONT Media Inc.

Exhibit 13-5   Example of a street poster.

© Lukas Davidziuk / Shutterstock.com

Electronic message signs offer short ads (e.g., 10 seconds) on a two- or three-minute rotation. As expected, both of these displays are located in high-traffic locations in a few large urban markets, with various sizes and packages available depending on the media firm. The growth of outdoor video displays is such that the firms offer network services, thereby reaching many viewers across the country. Murals and wall banners are sold in a few major markets in Canada (e.g., Toronto, Vancouver) with varying sizes (Exhibit 13-7).

The Media Merchants of Vancouver projected video images onto building walls in Montreal, Toronto, Calgary, and Vancouver using a hand-held projector with ads for a Burger King promotion connected to the movie *Transformers: Revenge of the Fallen.* Operators handed out coupons and carried the speakers in backpacks. The technology allowed advertising at night in places where outdoor ads do not exist and vehicle ads cannot reach.[6]

A number of firms offer **mobile signage** by placing displays on trucks or vehicles. These are sold by the number of vehicles and the number of months. And mobile messages with advertising-wrapped cars are driving into Canada, after growing substantially in the United States in the past decade. CityFlitz offers a fleet of 35 Minis with a cost of $4,500 per month for the advertiser. With a claimed exposure of at least 50,000 people, the CPM clicks in at a mere $3, far cheaper than static billboards located in the same place for one month. In addition, the cars are Wi-Fi equipped, offering additional opportunity for inventive marketers. The logistics of driving are covered by members who join the company and rent the car for only $1 per day.[7] Finally, we find outdoor media in unusual outdoor locations. Signage is placed on benches, bicycle racks, and garbage receptacles, in parking lots, and in the air through aerial advertising on airplanes or hot-air balloons. It seems that no matter where we turn outside, there will be a form of advertising message directed toward us.

Exhibit 13-6 Advertising at Dundas Square in Toronto.

© rmnoa357 / Shutterstock.com

Exhibit 13-7 Murals are part of the outdoor landscape.

© Leonard Zhukovsky / Shutterstock.com

The major outdoor operators are shown in Figure 13-2. These companies can present examples of past outdoor campaigns producing awareness and other communication effects. The examples can be for a product category or for individual campaigns. The operators can also provide maps to illustrate the locations and other relevant data (e.g., demographics). The aforementioned outdoor options are typically purchased for four weeks and provide anywhere from 25 GRPs to 150 GRPs per day, depending upon the number of displays or showings chosen within a local market. Recall from Chapter 10 that one GRP represents 1 percent of the market exposed to the ad once. Thus, buying 50 GRPs possibly implies that the marketer reaches 50 percent of the market once per day. The costs for placing outdoor advertising are not readily available with CARD any longer; however, the locations and other basic data are still offered.

Application of digital technology for out-of-home media reached new heights with movement on three significant fronts. Digital signage is a small portion of the facings in Canada, but media companies are moving toward greater penetration. Secondly, Bluetooth technology used with billboard ads directs messages to the smart phones of passersby. Finally, considerable adaptations of Bluetooth and other technology to various types of displays permit enhanced communication. Industry specialists estimate that about 9,000 advertising faces in Canada are digital, about 5 percent of the overall total. Pattison, one of the leaders with 10,000 advertising faces (digital and non-digital), is the largest digital firm with its acquisitions and new placements. Other firms like Astral and Lamar Outdoor are converting their static outdoor ads to digital, which means the media landscape will certainly grow beyond the 5 percent level in the coming years. A similar trend is occurring with Newad, which is converting to digital for many of its place-based ads in restaurants, bars, and fitness centres.[8]

Figure 13-2   Share of COMB-approved outdoor advertising faces in Canada

	2008	2009	2010	2011	2012
Outfront Media	37.6%	37.4%	36.8%	37.1%	36.4%
Pattison Outdoor	41.9%	42.3%	43.6%	42.4%	43.1%
Astral Out-of-Home	15.8%	15.5%	16.9%	17.7%	17.9%
All Others	4.7%	4.8%	2.7%	2.8%	2.6%

Source: COMB data reports 2008–2012.

IMC PERSPECTIVE 13-1

TRANSIT SHELTERS GO DIGITAL

Technology advances similar to those we saw earlier with billboards have occurred with transit shelters in major Canadian cities; notably, there has been a transition to digital message delivery and the opportunity to take advantage of near field communication. Outdoor media companies Astral and Quebecor both made other advances in their respective markets of Toronto and Montreal/Quebec City. In time, we may see downtown core and other high traffic areas using only digital transit shelters as the technology advances and advertisers learn how to customize messages.

© Sam Dao / Alamy Stock Photo

Quebecor signed a 20-year deal for the 2,700 advertising faces in Montreal and initially equipped 50 shelters with large screens and planned many more in the coming years. The company reached a similar deal in Laval and instituted digital technology in some shelters as well. The shelters all featured near field technology and Quebecor planned to add beacons for additional interaction allowing consumers to receive messages. Other advanced features with Quebecor's transit shelters included a code to scan to receive news, weather, and live bus schedule information, and touch screen and gesture recognition to offer creative message delivery for advertisers. In an example of implementing a campaign with the new Quebecor transit shelters, Febreze ran a message requesting people to select words and then played corresponding music to create an ambient environment within the shelter. Another brand displayed a virtual catalogue of winter coats.

Down the Trans-Canada highway in Toronto, Astral Media signed a deal with the city government and initially installed large digital screens in 40 transit shelters and planned to add 120 more over the next three years. The locations are busy, commercial areas in regions of high interest to advertisers with clear sight-lines and continuous power. Short eight-second ads run in a 48-second loop, keeping the creative message fresh for all those passing by. As part of the deal, Astral reserved a small portion of the time for city and emergency messages. Commenting on the change, Astral indicated that the new media offered advertisers a unique approach to message delivery and that future technological innovations may enrich the message even further. With heightened resolution, the imagery appeared to be a giant step beyond ink and paper. The next step for Astral involved an installation of smaller, portable screens in 10 other transit shelters, allowing viewers to interact and receive movie trailers, car information, concert listings, and financial tools. Testing indicated acceptance, with 90 percent agreeing to greater availability.

Mark's presents another example of the creative messages with digital transit shelters; the image posted a discount corresponding to the temperature—consumers received a 20 percent discount on a day when the temperature was 20 degrees below zero! The ad headline proclaimed, "The colder it gets, the more you save" as a way to attract attention to the new approach to communicate a sales promotion. The idea worked well, as Mark's market research attributed 30 percent of its sales to weather-related changes. Primary media of TV and flyers did not lend themselves to up-to-the-minute approaches for ad execution, and Internet and social media did not build reach and frequency quickly enough, so digital transit shelters offered a useful complement to the existing media strategy. Executives believed the digital message simultaneously offered brand building communication ability and quick tactical pricing information. Mark's managers envisioned similar ideas applied to other cities, such as keying discounts to rainfall in Vancouver or snowfall elsewhere. The Mark's example impressed Astral Media, allowing the retailer to win a Carte Blanche award for innovative use of outdoor media.

Sources: "Quebecor Transit Shelters Are Upping Interactivity That Grabs Consumer Attention," *Strategy,* September 2014; Chris Powell, "Toronto Transit Shelters Forecast Savings at Mark's," *Marketing Magazine,* February 4, 2015; Chris Powell, "Astral to Introduce 40 Digital TSAs in Toronto," *Marketing Magazine,* October 24, 2014; Chris Powell, "Astral Launches TSA Interactive," *Marketing Magazine,* October 28, 2014; Mira Shenker, "Astral Announces Carte Blanche Winners for Toronto and Montreal," *Marketing Magazine,* May 1, 2014.

Question:

1. Why are advertisers turning toward mobile messages delivered by digital transit shelters?

Mac's and Couche-Tard introduced a network of mobile antennae from iSign Media Corporation in their 1,500 convenience stores to push advertising messages to those within 100 metres who had a phone with Bluetooth technology. Consumers received a "tile" pop-up on their phone screen and would authorize receiving the message, giving permission if any information were to be tracked and recorded. Generally the message would contain a promotional offer to ensure the acceptance. The technology allowed the stores to feature specific products and allowed consumers a more useful exposure beyond flyers and radio ads.[9]

AUDIENCE MEASUREMENT

COMB   Audience measurement is done by the Canadian Out-of-Home Measurement Bureau (COMB), an independent organization comprising members from advertisers, advertising agencies, and media firms. Founded in 1965, its members provide guidance, funding, and oversight of the measurement process. COMB maintains a national database of all products for outdoor and place-based media firms in order to compile the audience measurement data. COMB publishes circulation and market data for approximately 80,000 out-of-home facings in about 280 markets.

COMB's methodology to determine advertising exposure (impressions) of out-of-home media is comprehensive with its unbiased, accurate, and independently collected quantitative data; however, the methodologies for outdoor and place-based are customized to a degree to account for the unique travel patterns of each media type. Important characteristics of the research are the visibility criteria which identify the number of people who have a reliable opportunity to see the message within a standardized distance for each advertising format, the use of sound statistical procedures, the inclusion of market-specific data, and reliable data collection procedures.

For the outdoor research, COMB begins with data from municipalities for road planning purposes, which is then assessed on how it can be used for measuring the regular traffic flow. This data is adjusted for the visibility criteria, the average number of people in the vehicle, and the number of hours an ad is illuminated. This is augmented with pedestrian data that also meets the visibility criteria in order to calculate the average daily circulation per face. As might be expected, all of this data is examined with advanced mapping technologies to visually see the volume of people potentially exposed to an advertising message.

These circulations are applied to each poster along a certain part of the road called a link. The numbers are adjusted to account for time-of-day variations throughout the week to arrive at an adjusted circulation. An important refinement of the data is the use of GPS technology that tracks traffic moving into a Census Metropolitan Area (CMA) in Canada's five larger cities, which accounts for commuters who are exposed to advertising messages.

From this data, COMB calculates the number of people (aged 5+) who have a reasonable opportunity to see an ad and estimates reach and frequency levels with sophisticated mathematical models. Advertisers confidently purchase the advertising space knowing that rigorous standards and exceptional research methodology provide accurate exposure levels. To facilitate their planning, COMB offers two planning software tools. The COMB Data Report is a comprehensive system for identifying all of the 80,000 facings with a number of reporting options. The COMBNavigator® allows planners to select media vehicles to attain reach and frequency levels for various target audience profiles.

OMAC   The Out-of-Home Marketing Association of Canada (OMAC), formed in 2005, is a membership among five founding media companies—Astral Media Outdoor, Newad, Pattison Outdoor, CBS Outdoor, and Zoom Media—and four others that have joined—Lamar Transit, Metromedia Plus, OBN, and Titan 360. OMAC's mission is to develop the market for this medium, implement new industry initiatives, establish guidelines, and act on behalf of the industry on any issues. Like other organizations that represent a particular medium, OMAC commissions research to demonstrate its effectiveness that acts as key information for decision makers. Finally, OMAC statistics indicate that advertising revenue in the industry is about 20 percent higher due to some media companies not reporting to Nielsen Media Research (e.g., $600 million for 2014 versus the reported $500 million).

OMAC undertook two "Day in the Life" (DIL) studies. The first, DIL I, investigated time spent inside/outside home, out-of-home exposure, commuting habits, and related shopping behaviour. Based on telephone interviews with 2,500 Canadians aged 12+ in major markets, the study found that the average person spends 55 percent of the day (while awake) out of the home and 33 percent in the home. On a typical weekday, urban Canadians spend as much time exposed to out-of-home media (3.8 hours) as to television and the Internet (Figure 13-3). The typical urban Canadian drives nearly 130 kilometres a week, with commuting to and from work accounting for half this distance and taking 65 minutes. Many urban workers (73 percent) use a vehicle to get to work, with the incidence of travelling by vehicle increasing significantly among suburbanites.

Figure 13-3   Time exposed to various media

	Average Time Exposed per Day (Hours)		
	Weekday	Saturday	Sunday
Out-of-Home Stimulus	3.8	4.7	4.7
Radio	2.2	1.3	1.1
Internet	3.6	2.6	2.4
Newspapers	0.5	0.6	0.4
Magazines	0.4	0.3	0.2
Television	3.8	3.1	3.1

Source: Out-of-Home Marketing Association of Canada (OMAC)

Figure 13-4 shows when people do their shopping: more than 50 percent shop on their way to work or home. From a measurement standpoint, advertisers can be confident that out-of-home media reach a substantial portion of the population while they are planning to shop or actually shopping. In fact, 87 percent shop either closer to work, closer to home, or somewhere equally close to both places. Out-of-home advertising also wields considerable influence on purchase decisions. The study found that in the past three months, 30 percent of people visited a specific website after seeing it promoted on out-of-home advertising; 25 percent learned about a store/product/sale that motivated them to visit a specific store; and 17 percent were prompted to purchase or seek information about a new product. The second Day in the Life study, DIL II, investigated the relevance and impact of out-of-home media versus other media. Figure 13-5 suggests that consumers do not believe there is too much out-of-home advertising compared to other media.[10]

Another source of measurement is technology that tracks a driver's eye movement to assess which ads are actually seen while driving. OMAC commissioned the Outdoor Advertising Consumer Exposure Study (OACES) to investigate the usefulness of this research. The study used 27 randomly selected drivers and passengers from Ottawa and Montreal, who were asked to drive a predetermined route that passed by outdoor advertising products and consisted of different driving conditions. The route was driven at different times of day, respondents' eye movements were tracked using a headband eye camera, and the entire visual interaction was also video recorded. An outdoor ad was considered "seen" if a driver or passenger fixated on it for at least 200 milliseconds. The study found that 55 percent of the ads selected for analysis were seen by the 27 drivers and passengers tested. Passengers, unsurprisingly, were more likely to see them (73 percent, versus 52 percent of drivers who saw them). Those people who looked at advertising looked at an ad an average of 2.04 times on a single drive-by. Out-of-home ads with three rotating faces were looked at more often, 2.46 times, compared with 1.9 times for a standard poster. In total, 535 outdoor exposures were eye-tracked during the study. Neither drivers nor passengers knew the study was related to advertising, with most of them thinking it was something to do with the transport ministry.[11]

Figure 13-4 Time of day when workers shop

Source: Out-of-Home Marketing Association of Canada (OMAC)

Figure 13-5 Perceptions of amount of advertising by medium

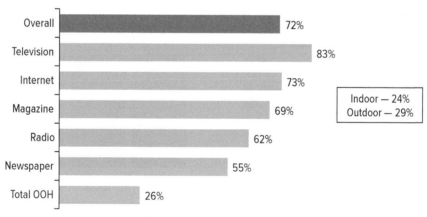

Source: Out-of-Home Marketing Association of Canada (OMAC)

STRENGTHS OF OUTDOOR MEDIA

Geographic Coverage   Outdoor media can be placed along highways, near stores, or on mobile billboards, almost anywhere that the law permits. Local, regional, or even national markets may be covered.

Scheduling Flexibility   Modern technologies have reduced production times for outdoor advertising to allow for rapid turnaround time. Placement can be done on a monthly basis assuming availability exists.

Reach   With proper placement, a broad base of exposure is possible in a given market, with both day and night presence. A 100 GRP **showing** (the percentage of duplicated audience exposed to an outdoor poster daily) could yield exposure to an equivalent of 100 percent of the marketplace daily! This level of coverage is likely to yield high levels of reach. Behavioural responses toward outdoor media are considerable, with extensive reach possibilities as documented in Figure 13-6.

Figure 13-6   Behavioural responses to outdoor ads in past six months

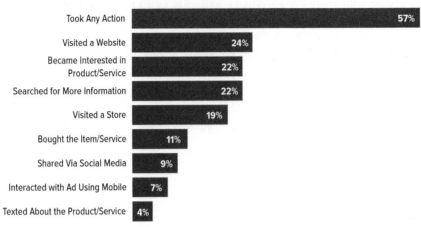

Source: Out-of-Home Marketing Association of Canada (OMAC)

Frequency   Because purchase cycles for outdoor media are typically for four-week periods, consumers are usually exposed a number of times, resulting in high levels of frequency. The importance of frequency is substantiated with the results of a study shown in Figure 13-7.

Figure 13-7   Out-of-home ads support other media when part of the budget

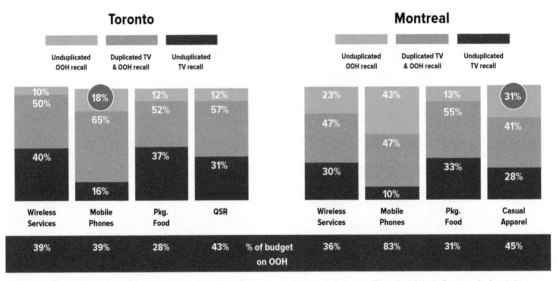

The bar chart shows the unduplicated and duplicated recall of TV and OOH among those who recalled seeing TV and/or OOH ads. For example, for wireless in Toronto: 10% recalled OOH only, 50% recalled both OOH and TV, and 40% recalled TV only.

Source: Out-of-Home Marketing Association of Canada (OMAC)

Cost Efficiency   Outdoor ads usually have a very competitive CPM when compared to other media. The average CPM of outdoor ads is less than that of radio, TV, magazines, and newspapers.

Control for Selective Exposure   On the one hand, outdoor ads are difficult for consumers to avoid since they are so pervasive. Moreover, a consumer has little control as with television or radio to change the channel or station. On the other hand, consumers can deliberately ignore outdoor ads; however, the high profile of the ads makes this a difficult task at times.

Attention   The ads' sheer size, strategic placement, and creative elements of colour make outdoor advertising an attractive medium to draw the attention of the target audience.

Creativity for Emotional Responses   As shown in Exhibits 13-1 and 13-2, outdoor ads can be very creative. Large print, colours, and other elements attract attention and tend to generate short emotional responses that connect the target audience to the brand. Presumably this emotional involvement contributes to the strong brand building leading to strong follow-up behaviour for continued shopping due to out-of-home media as shown in Figure 13-8.

Figure 13-8   Behavioural effects of out-of-home advertising

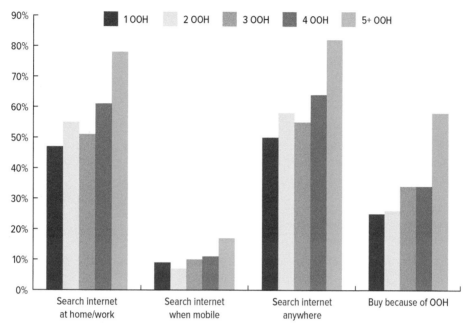

Source: Out-of-Home Marketing Association of Canada (OMAC)

LIMITATIONS OF OUTDOOR MEDIA

Target Audience Selectivity   Reaching a specific target audience is challenging due to the broad exposure of outdoor media in general. However, strategic use can overcome this limitation, for example by using reminder ads for a type of product near the retail outlets.

Target Audience Coverage   With the broad base reach of outdoor advertising, it is difficult to ensure that the specific target audience coverage is sufficient. While it is possible to reach an audience with select location placement, in many cases the purchase of outdoor ads results in a high degree of waste coverage. It is not likely that everyone driving past a billboard is part of the target audience.

Absolute Cost   A basic level of 25 GRPs per day over four weeks in ten—or even three—major cities can be quite prohibitive for many advertisers. For smaller businesses, selecting a few strategic locations in a local market could overcome this limitation.

Creativity for Cognitive Responses   Lengthy appeals are not physically possible in many instances, and if they were, they would have less likelihood of complete comprehension. Thus, it is expected that outdoor ads suffer from their inability to fully persuade consumers with an involved message.

Amount of Processing Time   Because of the speed with which most people pass by outdoor ads, exposure time is short, so messages are limited to a few words and/or an illustration. Despite this concern, there appears to be sufficient processing for consumers to text a response (Figure 13-9).

Figure 13-9   Likelihood* of texting in response to digital OOH advertising by age

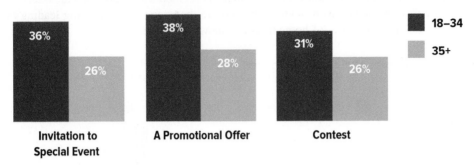

Invitation to Special Event   A Promotional Offer   Contest

18–34
35+

*Very/Somewhat likely

Source: Out-of-Home Marketing Association of Canada (OMAC)

Involvement   The overall effect of the short repeated message is that outdoor ads tend to be considered a low-involvement media.

Clutter   By their very nature, outdoor ads have competing messages. At any streetscape or location where outdoor ads are featured, it is very likely that other messages will be also vying for consumer attention, as seen in Exhibit 13-8.

Media Image   Outdoor advertising has suffered image problems and disregard among consumers. This may be in part due to fatigue of the high frequency of exposures that may lead to wearout—people are likely to get tired of seeing the same ad every day.

Exhibit 13-8   Competing messages present a challenge with outdoor media.

© Luciano Mortula / Shutterstock.com

Transit Media

Another form of out-of-home advertising is **transit advertising**. While similar to outdoor in the sense that it uses posters, digital, and video messages, transit is targeted at the millions of people who are exposed to commercial transportation facilities, including buses, subways, light-rail trains, and airplanes. Transit ad revenue is a noticeable but small portion of overall transit revenue. For example, the Toronto Transit Commission reported $19 million in advertising revenue and well over $900 million in fares annually. It looked to increase its advertising revenue to $27 million per year for 12 years in a deal with Pattison.[12] We now describe transit media options available, and their strengths and limitations as an advertising medium.

TRANSIT MEDIA OPTIONS

Common transit ads viewed are **interior transit cards** placed above the seating. Ads are positioned in backlit units above windows and along both sides of the bus, streetcar, subway, or light-rail transit cars (see Exhibit 13-9). **Interior door cards** are available in major markets where there is subway-like transit. These cards are placed on both sides of the doors and are about 50 percent larger than the aforementioned interior transit cards. **Exterior posters** may appear on the sides, backs, and/or roofs of buses, taxis, trains, subways, and streetcars (see Exhibit 13-10). Various sizes are available depending on the media company and the transit vehicles; however, the two most common are "seventies" (0.5 metres by 1.8 metres, but named because the width of 1.8 metres is equal to 70 inches) and "king" (0.75 metres by 3.5 metres), which are seen on buses and so on.

Transit offers creative opportunities with innovative thinking. For example, a rejuvenated campaign for the Caramilk "Secret" featured 50 interactive audioboards in the Toronto subway system among other media like TV, print, and online. A series of interpretive reveals of the secret kept the mystery and discovery experience exciting for consumers. Cadbury promoted consumption with a Chocolate Couture Fashion Show where fashion designers and chocolate artists teamed up to create an outfit made of chocolate.[13]

Station posters are of varying sizes and forms that attempt to attract the attention of those waiting for a subway-like ride. The most common size is 1 metre by 2 metres. As Exhibit 13-11 shows, station posters can be very attractive to gain attention. Similar-sized posters are found at bus or streetcar **transit shelters** and often provide the advertiser with expanded coverage where other outdoor boards may be restricted. Many of these are sold by outdoor media companies as they are identical to street-level posters, but others are listed in transit. Larger station posters are available as well; Metromedia offers super vertical subway posters and platform posters, for example.

Innovations in transit media include the superbus, where an advertiser "owns" the bus and places a vinyl ad on its entire surface. This is often done for a longer-term contract of a half- or full year because of the application on the bus (see Exhibit 13-12). The new TTC streetcars appeared in Toronto with a Volvo wrap to celebrate the Volvo XC90 being voted as truck/utility vehicle of the year for 2016. The longer "Flexity" streetcar allowed for a 30-metre wrap that looked as impressive as a wall mural ad, according to one media expert.[14] On a less grand scale in a few select markets, smaller bus murals can be applied to the side or tail for a shorter period of time. Similar wraps are also possible for subway cars. And in Vancouver, where wireless competition intensified, a few Telus wrapped buses also offered free Wi-Fi, with riders being directed to the brand's network splash page.[15]

The Toronto and Montreal subway systems have featured station domination, where a single advertiser can be the sole sponsor of all points of communication within that station. This could include wrapping a number of different parts of the infrastructure and erecting sizable murals and posters. **Subway online** is located in the 10 busiest subway stations in Toronto. It features digital news centres with video capabilities that deliver news, sports, and weather highlights with 20-second ads. Video applications are coming to taxis where screens show 15-minute video clips, of which five minutes are advertising. Play Taxi had installed screens in 4,000 vehicles by 2012, and major advertisers looked to use the interactive features creatively by offering ads consumers wanted to see, games, and promotions.[16]

The Toronto group of Venture Communications transformed the stairway of Toronto's Union Station from street level to track level with a virtual trek down a ski hill with wall-to-wall images of the Alberta Rockies. "We felt our ski messaging would have a large impact on the quarter-million commuters who frequent the station on a daily basis," commented a director of Travel Alberta. Other media complemented the initial eye-opener and included store kiosks, direct mail, and a website (SkiCanadianRockies.com) where visitors could experience video clips of the hills and plan a vacation.[17]

Exhibit 13-9   Example of interior transit ad.

© Pattison Outdoor Adversiting

Exhibit 13-10   Example of exterior transit ad.

© Pattison Outdoor Adversiting

Exhibit 13-11   Station posters can be used to attract attention.

© Pattison Outdoor Adversiting

Transit media are sold in select markets on a four-week basis with a certain desired level of GRPs. The range of GRPs is quite varied, going from a low of 5 GRPs to a high of 100 GRPs. Other purchases of transit media are based on the number of showings. For example, if an operator has the rights to 400 buses or subway cars, then an advertiser could typically buy displays in varying numbers (i.e., 25 percent, 50 percent, 75 percent, 100 percent) over a four-week time period. Unlike outdoor advertising, there is no industry association to document circulation or authenticate reach and frequency levels despite their use in pricing of the media purchase. However, information is gained from the research conducted by BBM so that rough estimates of exposure are possible. OMAC's DIL research also touches on transit to a degree, as shown in Figure 13-10 where most people find transit advertising acceptable.

Exhibit 13-12   Example of a bus wrap on a streetcar.

© Pattison Outdoor Adversiting

Figure 13-10   Perceived amount of advertising by outdoor medium

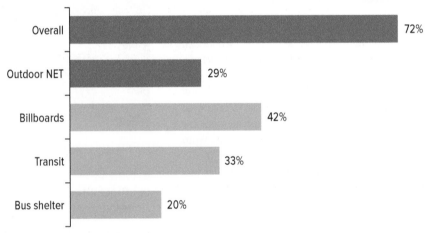

Overall	72%
Outdoor NET	29%
Billboards	42%
Transit	33%
Bus shelter	20%

Source: Out-of-Home Marketing Association of Canada (OMAC)

Transit media viewed while travelling *between* cities and towns presents similar transit and terminal (i.e., airport, train or bus station) options. Free magazines are published by travel operators (see Exhibit 13-13) and in-flight videos are common on longer flights. For example, Air Canada sells different packages depending on the type of show (e.g., news, movie) and these commercial messages can last up to three minutes. Listening to in-flight radio is a pleasant way to pass the time while flying, and offers another opportunity for advertisers to deliver an audio message beyond standard radio. Ads can be placed on collateral material such as boarding passes, ticket jackets, and meal trays. The design of these media is important as both Air Canada and WestJet put considerable effort into their in-flight magazines to reflect their positioning. Air Canada's looks more like a sophisticated lifestyle magazine with luxurious full-page ads, fitting with its international and business clientele, while WestJet's is a more utilitarian offering with functional travel tips.[18]

Exhibit 13-13   In-flight magazines are available on most carriers.

©2016 Air Canada enRoute

STRENGTHS OF TRANSIT MEDIA

Geographic Coverage   For local advertisers in particular, transit advertising provides an opportunity to reach a very select segment of the population. A purchase of a location in a certain neighbourhood will lead to exposure to people of specific ethnic backgrounds, demographic characteristics, and so on.

Scheduling Flexibility   The capacity available for transit ads makes it fairly good for placement. Ads can be produced quickly and inserted internally or externally.

Reach   Transit advertising benefits from the absolute number of people exposed. Millions of people ride mass transit every week, providing a substantial number of potential viewers that can be reached.

Frequency   Because our daily routines are standard, those who ride buses, subways, and the like are exposed to the ads repeatedly. If a commuter rode the same subway to work and back every day, in one month the person would have the opportunity to see the ad 20 to 40 times. The locations of station and shelter signs also afford high frequency of exposure.

Absolute Cost and Cost Efficiency   Transit advertising tends to be one of the least expensive media in terms of both absolute and relative costs. An ad on the side of a bus can be purchased for a very reasonable CPM.

Control for Selective Exposure   Similar to outdoor advertising, transit ads are quite pervasive for those using the service and consumers have little control over the use of the media.

Amount of Processing Time   Long length of exposure to an ad is a major strength of indoor forms. The audience is essentially a captive one, with nowhere else to go and nothing much to do. As a result, riders are likely to read the ads—more than once.

LIMITATIONS OF TRANSIT MEDIA

Target Audience Selectivity   While a strength of transit advertising is the ability to provide exposure to a large number of people, this audience may have certain lifestyles and/or behavioural characteristics that are not true of the target audience as a whole. For example, in rural or suburban areas mass transit is limited or nonexistent, so the medium is not very effective for reaching these people.

Target Audience Coverage   While geographic selectivity may be an advantage, not everyone who rides a transportation vehicle or is exposed to transit advertising is a potential customer. For products that do not have specific geographic segments, this form of advertising incurs a good deal of waste coverage. Another problem is that the same bus may not run the same route every day. To save wear and tear on the vehicles, transit companies alternate city routes (with much stop and go) with longer suburban routes. Thus, a bus may go downtown one day and reach the desired target group but spend the next day in the suburbs, where there may be little market potential.

Attention   The smaller size and location of interior transit ads make it difficult to use the creative elements to attract attention. The movement of transit vehicles makes it difficult to perceive the message.

Creativity for Emotional and Cognitive Responses   It may be very difficult to place colourful and attractive ads on cards, thus limiting their emotional content. And while much copy can be provided on inside cards, the short copy on the outside of a bus provides less rational persuasion.

Involvement   Like outdoor advertising, with shorter copy and seemingly fleeting messages, transit ads are generally considered to be low-involvement media.

Clutter   Inside ads suffer from clutter of competing ads and outside ads feel the pressure of other street-level ads. Furthermore, the environment is cluttered in another sense as sitting or standing on a crowded subway may not be conducive to reading advertising, let alone experiencing the mood the advertiser would like to create.

Media Image   To many advertisers, transit advertising does not carry the image they would like to represent for their products or services. Thus, advertisers may think having their name on the side of a bus or in a bus does not reflect well on the firm.

Place-Based Media

The variety of out-of-home media continues to increase, and the idea of bringing an advertising medium to consumers wherever they may be underlies the strategy behind place-based media. In this section we summarize a few of the more prevalent options that include both print and video messages and highlight their strengths and limitations.

PLACE-BASED MEDIA OPTIONS

As Figure 13-1 indicated at the start of this chapter, advertising messages reach consumers in numerous locations. Many of these options occur where consumers enjoy leisure or recreational activities, while others are where consumers work or study. Figure 13-11 shows that Canadians are aware of many forms of place-based advertising. Many of these media occur indoors (*indoor advertising* is a term that is also used). The main media companies offering place-based media are Newad and Pattison. In all of these locations there are poster or print messages, and in many there are video or digital applications. There is also growth in these locations that allows consumers to interact with their hand-held mobile device. Given the interaction with websites and text messages after viewing ads (Figure 13-12 and Figure 13-13), it appears that this "on-the-spot" follow-up to messages will be a new evolution in advertising and consumer response behaviour.

Figure 13-11   Awareness of place-based media

	Total %	18–34 %	35+ %
Shopping Malls	48	58	45
Outdoor	47	53	45
Airport	28	30	27
Public Transit	25	36	21
Restaurants	25	36	20
Medical Waiting Rooms	21	23	20
Bars/Nightclubs	18	28	14
Office Elevators	12	16	10
Health/Fitness Clubs	9	17	6

Source: Out-of-Home Marketing Association of Canada (OMAC)

Figure 13-12   Percentage visiting a website within past three months after seeing indoor/outdoor ad

	DITL 1	DITL 2
Toronto	29.5	36.9
Montreal	27.8	37.7
Vancouver	27.6	38.3
Females	29.5	38.5
Males	29.0	35.7

Source: Out-of-Home Marketing Association of Canada (OMAC)

Figure 13-13   Percentage sending a text message within past three months after seeing indoor/outdoor ad

	DITL 1	DITL 2
Toronto	4.8	4.7
Montreal	3.2	6.0
Vancouver	3.2	6.9
Females	2.7	4.3
Males	4.4	6.5

Source: Out-of-Home Marketing Association of Canada (OMAC).

An original example of place-based media is the mall poster (Exhibit 13-14). It is often backlit, like the transit shelter or transit-station poster, and is located throughout a shopping mall. The key feature of the mall poster is that it is in the shopping environment and therefore one step closer to the actual purchase. These posters are sold in most markets across the country similarly to outdoor posters with individual spot buys and varying levels of GRPs. Firms also sell various sizes of mall posters for branding or interaction purposes. Advertisers use these posters for interaction purposes by including QR codes so consumers can use their smart phone and receive additional information. Video or digital displays are growing in retail locations as well.

An example of video messages occurring out-of-home at a specific location is cinema or movie theatre ads. Since the commercials last 60 to 90 seconds, advertisers have a unique opportunity to communicate for a longer period of time than with a typical TV ad. In fact, many of the theatre ads are also shown on television, albeit in a shortened format. Cinema ads lead other public video media as they report audience measurement information. Cineplex reported $134 million in media revenue in 2014, comprising cinema advertising and its digital advertising networks in retail locations.[19] IMC Perspective 13-2 highlights aspects of Cineplex's advertising media opportunities that have grown substantially over the years. Beyond this, Cineplex also partnered with Sony Computer Entertainment Canada on the "Cineplex WorldGaming Canadian Tournament Presented by PlayStation." This offered significant advertising opportunities for Sony, which also controlled who sponsored and advertised during the event.[20]

Exhibit 13-14   Backlit poster ads encourage further digital communication.

© Pattison Outdoor Adversiting

Research on consumer attitudes toward cinema ads in general found a number of sources of negativity in terms of restriction (e.g., less communication, captive, delayed gratification, minimizing escapism) and equity (unfair, time-waster, payment); however, many people enjoy the experience of specific ads (entertaining, liking the ad, involved, ad congruent with movie) as long as it is not shown too many times. It appears that this, like other media, has a tension of both positive and negative reactions.[21] Despite this mixed view, Toyota developed an ad specifically for cinema with a scene set in a car at a drive-in movie theatre. The movie showed a montage of Toyota vehicles over the past 20 years to reinforce the message that 80 percent of all Toyotas sold in the past 20 years are still on the road. A creative director for the agency commented, "Toyota likes cinema. We get good recall results from it. Those ads create good drama for the brand."[22]

Exhibit 13-15   While picking up luggage, airport travellers viewed an ad encouraging them to consider certain services.

© rmnoa357/Shutterstock

Airport terminals have extensive signage since they are similar to a mall with shopping concourses and restaurant areas and high volumes of consumers passing by. Displays are available ranging from smaller backlit posters in the terminal to superboards near the terminal and other types of displays depending upon the media company and terminal (Exhibit 13-15).

An exploratory study of airport terminal advertising reports the following conclusions.[23]

1. Ads are more likely to be processed when in the main concourse or near retail outlets.
2. The situational variable of the person's activity influences their degree of processing.
3. Repetition of a simple message is necessary, but with less frequency.
4. Elements of the ad influence recall and recognition differently, thus necessitating decisions on design and communication objective.
5. Frequent flyers' responses are strong up to a point then taper off after receiving a repetitious message.

Lexus innovated with a touch screen attached to the window of its new luxury crossover vehicle. The screen allowed consumers to interact with the vehicle's advanced features. A high-contrast rear-projection film adhesive located inside allowed the touch screen to be seen from the outside. Lexus used the message "Reinventing the vehicle that invented it all" and placed the RX in Toronto's major airport for 13 weeks to obtain 64,000 interactions and 1.3 million envious glances.[24]

A number of place-based media are outdoor media brought into a particular environment. Backlit posters, superboards, electronic message signs, and video displays are used in leisure locations such as movie theatres, hotels, restaurants and bars, and sports stadiums or arenas, and athletic venues such as golf, ski, or fitness centres. The OMAC DIL research estimates that the average Canadian spends 1.3 hours per weekday and 2.2 hours per weekend day on leisure. For example, 55 percent visited a restaurant or bar four times per month for an average of two hours, and 24 percent visited a health club eight times per month for an average of 1.4 hours. Advertising with these media in office buildings or convention centres or similar venues also reaches those who are at work. Firms reach younger consumers on university and college campuses with indoor posters that are standard and non-standard. Research confirms the average student's experience as each campus visit averages five hours—plenty of exposure time for messages in various university/college buildings. And to reach virtually anyone, print and video ads are placed in elevators or washrooms (Exhibit 13-16), and print ads on floors or escalator handrails. Another media is closed-circuit television that typically reaches workers in office towers, travellers in hotels, or patients in medical waiting rooms. Despite the prevalence of place-based media, Canadians do not believe it is too much (Figure 13-14).

Place-based media became experiential as marketers presented their brands in public places. Moving beyond ads, sales promotions, and even digital communication, brands saw the need to allow consumers to participate in a demonstration of product usage to fully enjoy what it has to offer. For example, Nivea opened a temporary pop-up shop in Toronto called Nivea Haus that included interactive skin tests, personalized skin care suggestions, photo shoots, product shots, and an Xbox Kinect game. Nivea designed the experiential effort to communicate how one's skin is an important part of one's physical and emotional well-being. Axe's "Hair Action" campaign featured a Virtual Hair Play Van where men received the touch of a woman as she attended to his hair, all in a virtual simulation of course. The van visited numerous locations including campuses and events such as the Warped Tour and Montreal Jazz Festival. Photos of the experience gave the participants the opportunity to upload pictures to their Facebook account where friends could "like" it and give the guy a chance to win a $10,000 prize.[25] Exhibit 13-17 shows how Budweiser brings the red light to consumers in public locations.

As identified earlier with outdoor ads, digital communication within these place-based locations occurs. For example, an Ontario health organization delivered its message to the smart phones of those in medical waiting rooms. People received the ads based on their acceptance of mobile apps for games, news, or maps. And applying this to all of the above locations is certainly possible, however executives feel the message and location context are paramount for acceptance.[26] Finally, portable outdoor-like digital screens for message display can be set up in trade shows, conferences, stores, and marketing events. With Wi-Fi connection, the display analytically tracks consumers' behaviour with respect to the message. The system is fully customizable in various sizes and configurations depending on requirements for the location.[27]

Exhibit 13-16   Ads in unusual locations provide a unique vehicle for advertising.

© NEWAD

Exhibit 13-17   Budweiser takes its TV imagery to the streets for consumers to see.

© rmnoa357/Shutterstock

Figure 13-14   Perceived amount of advertising by indoor medium: percentage having "too much" advertising

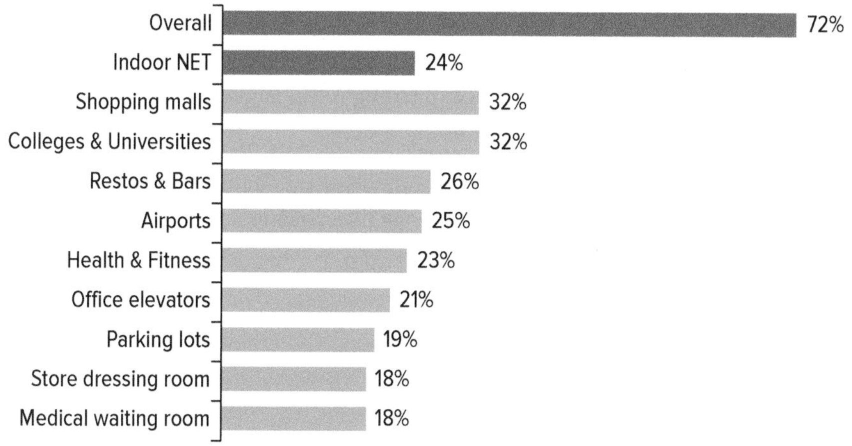

Source: Out-of-Home Marketing Association of Canada (OMAC)

STRENGTHS OF PLACE-BASED MEDIA

Target Audience Selectivity   The main purpose of place-based media is to reach a specific target audience or to reach the target audience while closer to the purchase decision in terms of time and space. For example, ads in fitness clubs could contain messages for athletic gear, mall posters could have ads for food outlets that are located in the mall food court, and movies could attract a certain crowd who fit with particular brands more than others.

Absolute Cost and Cost Efficiency   The absolute cost and CPM are generally reasonable compared to other media options.

Control for Selective Exposure   Since many of these media options have captive or nearly captive audiences, the opportunity for consumers to avoid the ads or direct their attention elsewhere is minimal compared to other media. For example, ads on the walls of restaurants, bars, gyms, etc., will be noticeable by customers enjoying the service.

Attention and Involvement   With the above strengths of many place-based media options, the collective conclusion suggests that the target audience may be more involved with the advertising message than similar media in different contexts. The growth of video and digital messages in many locations offers greater opportunity to gain attention, and with a degree of target audience selectivity the creative can be customized with appropriate headlines for print messages.

Creativity for Cognitive and Emotional Responses   Because the target and place are intertwined, the message may generate more in-depth cognitive responses or stronger emotional responses. For example, creative lifestyle messages can be prominent in poster ads located in clubs or bars. Large-scale spectaculars have been used to create fantastic visual effects to generate positive feelings. The special mood created in the movie theatre compared to at-home consumption makes the experience richer, and advertisers use theatre ads as an emotional spike that can transfer to the product more readily, especially if the theatre is located next to a mall or store where the product may be sold.

LIMITATIONS OF PLACE-BASED MEDIA

Target Audience and Geographic Coverage   The logistical availability of these types of media makes full target audience coverage difficult or quite challenging to implement, and it is nearly impossible to get complete geographic coverage.

Scheduling Flexibility   While not a complete or comprehensive limitation, the logistics of changing place-based media, which is done on a monthly basis, put certain restrictions on an advertiser for scheduling a timely message. Placement for cinema ads generally requires eight weeks, and category exclusivity in certain distribution outlets further limits the availability and scheduling ease with this media option.

Reach and Frequency   Place-based media plays more of a supporting role to other media since it is very difficult to ensure high levels of either reach or frequency. Exceptions can be considered, but in general media planners will look for other media to maximize these two factors.

Amount of Processing Time   For the most part, place-based media suffer from very short messages to target audiences that are more likely preoccupied with other tasks. Evidence of strong recall suggests that the processing may be stronger for more creative executions, where additional processing occurs.

Clutter   The clutter that consumers perceive while watching television may be similar as the video displays generally play a block of commercials, although this can be lessened in options like cinema ads where one or two video ads could play. Similarly, locations have multiple posters of varying sizes, thus giving a similar clutter experience as reading a newspaper or magazine.

Media Image   Often, place-based media are exposed to consumers when they do not expect a selling message to occur, which may cause displeasure. Consumers appear to be generally accustomed to ads in malls since they are so similar to the store signage. Cinema ads, in contrast, provoked negative reaction when first introduced.[28] However, we find mixed research results; one study reports a high percentage of viewers claiming not to mind this form of advertising.[29] Other research suggests that a negative image remains concerning how the ad infringes upon patrons' time prior to the movie, removes control for avoidance, delays movie enjoyment, minimizes the feeling of escapism associated with being in the theatre, makes too much money for the theatre, steals personal time, and represents an unwarranted cost.[30] We have provided additional details for cinema ads as research exists compared to other media, and suggest that certain points may be relevant for other place-based media.

IMC PERSPECTIVE 13-2

SEE ADS AT THE MOVIES

Moviegoers are an attractive market with promising consumption behaviour for advertisers. They tend to be well educated with higher incomes, use social media, and combine their movie experience with shopping or eating. Moreover, 62 percent are happy and 29 percent are excited when going to the movies, a mood situation that no other media vehicle can claim. Cinema ads combined with TV messages produce strong communication numbers, providing strong incentive for advertisers to add this to their mix. With a 55-foot screen and superior video and audio capability, it is no wonder that Cineplex's Show Time ads attain 70 percent awareness, 88 percent brand association, and 40 percent ad entertainment scores.

© Cineplex Entertainment LP

Cineplex's Pre-Show numbers attain similar levels, albeit with lower audience size. The Pre-Show features entertainment clips, quizzes, and the like, all supported with ads. Another Pre-Show option is an interactive game patrons play with their phone. Cineplex signed a deal to expand its Timeplay capability from 231 screens to 725. The trivia-like games (based on movies, of course) embed ads or offer branded prizes and attain better results: 86 percent awareness, 96 percent brand association, and 51 percent ad entertainment. Cineplex sees its early traffic increasing so people can play the game before the movie starts.

Cineplex Media offers message delivery opportunities in its theatres beyond on-screen ads. Large digital lobby signage in 157 locations shows movie clips and advertising with 71 percent reach. A total of 438 digital backlit posters in 135 locations similar to those found in digital transit shelters show full-motion HD quality video ads on a three-minute loop. Digital lobby HD screens located above box offices and concession stands play ads within a 10-minute loop. Cineplex's interactive media zone in 44 theatres presents four high resolution screens with touch capability and gesture and skeletal tracking. It also allows users to create content for sharing on social media. Services include custom creative support, scheduling flexibility by theatre, city or national exposure, and processing analytics by capturing a user's use by a camera.

While waiting in various locations throughout the theatre, a movie fan can be one of the 3.7 million *Cineplex Magazine* monthly readers to catch up on the latest about movie stars or upcoming releases. A total of 750,000 free publications regularly garner five readers per copy. Print ads are within the magazine and brands place messages both in print and on-screen, even across all media options depending on frequency requirements. The magazine provides higher reach than other magazines, and considerable unduplicated reach beyond other popular publications.

Cineplex Media extended its communication to all facets of the movie experience and branched out beyond. It offers massive digital posters with its Oxford Malls Network that features large HD screens showing ads within its own channel. Its shopping media includes other standards like regular sized digital backlit posters, activation signage, and elevator and escalator wraps in 10 locations. Cineplex Media established TimsTV in over 2,300 coffee outlets for national and regional ad opportunities. Follow-up research demonstrated that the network reached substantial numbers, provided higher brand recall numbers, and enjoyed considerable positive reaction from consumers. A similar TV option is available in 10 major Canadian business centres with its Concourse Network, and the company offers advertising options in Ontario at 20 highway rest stop buildings containing restaurants.

With all its growth beyond an initial foray into showing ads before a movie, Cineplex still believes that the movie experience is important as part of its overall package. It recently launched a heart-warming ad of its own shown prior to the movie. The touching story traced the life from childhood to adulthood of Lily, who sort of lost her way and saw "The Big Picture" by both seeing a movie on a large screen and taking the time to enjoy life. Cineplex planned to continue showing Lily's character and carry on the story in other exposures across all of its media options, much like advertising clients.

Sources: Susan Krashinsky, "Small Screen Strategy, Big Ambition," *The Globe and Mail*, March 25, 2014, p. B.3; Jim Middlemis, "Navigating Digital Media World," *National Post*, June 20, 2014, p. SR.2; Shane Schick, "Cineplex Urges Busy Canadian to Make Time for Entertainment," *Marketing Magazine*, December 17, 2015; Cineplex Media Kit 2016.

Question:

1. In what way is advertising through Cineplex effective?

Promotional Products

Promotional products are useful and/or symbolic items that are implemented in marketing communication programs as a promotion or message vehicle, or a combination of both. Promotional products include advertising specialty, premium/gift, and incentive/reward. An advertising specialty contains brand identification on a useful item and is given away for free in numerous marketing communication situations, most often for awareness purposes. As will be seen in Chapter 14, promotional products retain a promotional element as a premium or gift typically given for brand equity or goodwill purposes. They also may be given to employees as an incentive or reward to recognize their work or achievement.[31]

As this suggests, promotional products are seen as advertising and sales promotion media. We treat promotional products as advertising media in the IMC program since they communicate or represent the brand and its positioning. For example, IKEA offered a gift bag at an event that fit perfectly with the brand; it contained a USB key, a Jansjo lamp, an ice cube tray, Kort design cards, and a sewing kit, all useful household items that communicate the style and functionality IKEA is known for.[32] The ultimate promotional product finds its way into the swag bag given to the Academy Awards' Oscar nominees. For example, Montreal-based Rouge Maple provided 70 baskets, each containing $300 worth of maple syrup products. And the cost did not end there as it also paid a $4,000 participation fee. In addition, a booth in the gifting suite at the Oscars costs $5,000 to $40,000. At the American Music Awards backstage gifting suite in 2014, Halifax-based Miss Foxine Jewellery handed out 150 custom pieces and ultimately doubled its sales after the event due to the notoriety of artists and media receiving the gift.[33]

The promotional product industry in Canada is substantial and the Canadian trade association is known as the Promotional Product Professionals of Canada (PPPC) (see www.promocan.com). The industry is divided into suppliers (e.g., manufacturers, importers, printers) and distributors (i.e., communication agencies, catalogues, operators). PPPC compiles research information across both groups, and we briefly highlight a few relevant distributor facts. Distributor revenue hit about $2 billion in 2012 (most recent data). To put this figure into perspective, it is comparable to Internet search advertising of $2 billion in 2014. Figure 13-15 shows the percentage of sales by product category; wearables/apparel (32 percent), writing instruments (9 percent), and calendars (7 percent) accounted for the top three and represented nearly half of all sales.[34]

Figure 13-15   Distribution product category breakdown

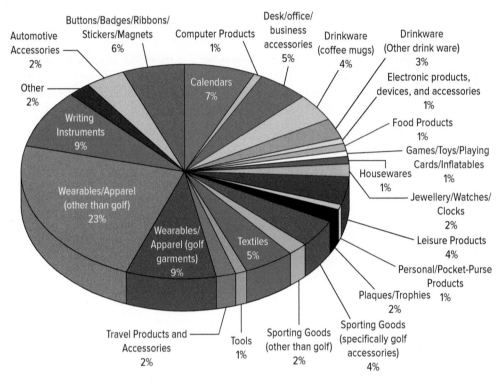

Source: Promotional Product Professionals of Canada

As the figure indicates, numerous promotional products exist—pens, mugs, glassware, key rings, calendars, T-shirts, and USB flash drives. Unconventional specialties such as plant holders, wall plaques, and gloves with the advertiser's name printed on them also promote a company or its product. The variety of promotional products makes it a virtual certainty that a manager will be able to strengthen consumer attitudes with an item that represents the brand appropriately. Often, promotional products are used to thank customers for patronage and encourage repeat purchasing. Furthermore, many of the items summarized in Figure 13-15 are appropriate for rewarding employees. Promotional products support other IMC tools like sales promotion or public relations, so they contribute substantially to the overall promotional mix. In summary, companies use promotional products as a means to fully communicate with their customers, suppliers, employees, and the general public. The benefits of promotional products are strong and research over many years commissioned by the Promotional Products Association International (PPAI) illustrates numerous strengths.[35]

STRENGTHS OF PROMOTIONAL PRODUCTS

Media Characteristics   Because promotional products are generally distributed directly to target customers, the medium offers a high degree of target audience selectivity and coverage. The communication is distributed to the desired recipient, reducing waste coverage. Most promotional products are designed for consumers to keep possession of them for a period of time. Key chains, calendars, and pens remain with the potential customer for a long time, providing repeat exposures to the advertising message at no additional cost. One set of statistics suggests 50 percent of all promotional products are kept for a year or longer and contribute to extensive frequency. Promotional products can be expensive in terms of absolute cost (e.g., leather goods), but most are affordable to almost any size organization. While they are costly on a CPM basis when compared with media, the high number of repeat exposures drives the relative cost per exposure of this medium downward for respectable cost efficiency.

Media Usage Characteristics   As the variety of promotional products demonstrates, this medium offers a high degree of message flexibility contributing to positive cognitive and emotional responses. A message as simple as a logo or as long as is necessary can be distributed through a number of means. Both small and large companies can employ this medium, limited only by their own creativity. With such opportunity, it is possible to use promotional products to achieve particular beliefs about the brand. Promotional products are perhaps the only medium that generates goodwill in the receiver. Because people like to receive gifts and many of the products are functional, consumers are grateful to receive them. Attention, processing and involvement may vary, but all would be considered strengths of promotional products assuming the recipient appreciates the actual item. Certainly the selection of the item in question will heavily influence consumer reaction.

LIMITATIONS OF PROMOTIONAL PRODUCTS

Media Characteristics   An advertiser hoping to expand its market through wider reach would likely find promotional products a weaker choice. As a support medium, it thrives on assisting existing media that have reach as their strength. While promotional products can be distributed essentially anywhere, the cost implications would severely curtail significant geographic distribution for most advertisers. Finally, the lead time required to put together a promotional products message can be longer than that for most other media due to supply and printing requirements.

Media Usage Characteristics   Recipients of promotional products are in complete control of whether they choose to keep or display the item. It is entirely possible that a tremendous investment could receive no or very minimal exposure to the intended target audience. While most forms of promotional products are received as friendly reminders of the brand name, the firm must be careful in choosing the item. The company image may be cheapened by a chintzy or poorly designed advertising form. A problem of clutter may arise if other organizations use this advertising medium. While one can always use another pen, the value to the receiver declines if replacement is too easy, and the likelihood that one will retain the item or even notice the message is reduced. The more unusual or unique the promotional product, the more value it is likely to have to the receiver.

PROMOTIONAL PRODUCTS RESEARCH

Owing to the nature of the industry, promotional products have no established ongoing audience measurement system. Research conducted to determine the impact of this medium is archived with PPAI (www.ppai.org) and shows the pronounced communication effect of promotional products when combined with media. The results of one experiment shown in Figure 13-16 illustrate the stronger impressions that occur when a promotional product is combined with TV and print ads for a local pizzeria. Another survey of more than 550 business travellers at a U.S. airport found that 71 percent had received a promotional product within the past 12 months; 34 percent actually had the item with them at the time of the survey; and 76 percent recalled the brand name. A field experiment at a trade show indicated that visits to a firm's booth increased significantly when a modest promotional product (i.e., magnet) and a promise to receive a more valuable item (i.e., T-shirt) were mailed to registrants prior to the show compared with a simple invitation. Finally, research shows that recipients have strong brand recall and keep and use the promotional product for up to two years. Most recipients were current customers or received the item as they were in the process of becoming a customer.[36]

Product Placement

Product placement occurs when a brand name, a logo, the actual product, or an ad for it is part of a movie, TV show, or video game. Product placement is considered a sales promotion rather than advertising at times, but this distinction is not a critical one and we have decided to treat product placement as a form of advertising. We review a few key product placement decisions and their corresponding strengths and limitations.

Figure 13-16   Respondents' evaluation of a brand or product

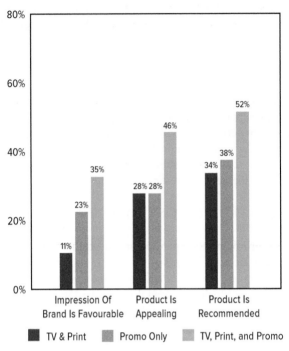

Source: Promotional Product Professionals of Canada

PRODUCT PLACEMENT OVERVIEW

The global market for product placement reached about $10 billion in 2011, with three countries accounting for close to 80 percent: the United States at $6 billion, Brazil at $1 billion, and Mexico at $1 billion. Historically, other strong countries include Australia, Japan, France, the United Kingdom, and Italy. TV and movies represented 90 percent of the amount spent, as estimated by PQMedia.[37] The media tracking firm calculated the total based on actual financial transactions and excluded non-paid placements for in-kind exposure. The high-level deal-making environment of this decision makes it difficult to develop accurate reporting; however, developments have improved the situation.[38]

Much of the logic behind product placement is that since the placement is embedded in the script or program setting it cannot be avoided, thereby increasing exposure. Given the lack of intrusiveness of the placement, consumers may not have the same negative reactions to it as they may to a commercial. Assuming a marketer selected the right movie or TV vehicle, product placement contributes to higher awareness by its sheer volume of exposure. Product placement appears promising, but its greatest strength may lie in maintaining existing loyalty of current customers who see the product they favour actually consumed by a character in a situation they can relate to. Research into product placement finds that it contributes to brand attitude and awareness and that consumers do not mind the prevalence of product placement.[39] Other research concluded that product placement in movies led to higher rates of return on stock prices, indicating that product placement benefits both advertiser and content producer.[40] However, another study concluded that the maximum rate of return for product placement hit its peak a couple of decades ago, indicating that consumers do not notice the placements as much as in the past.[41]

Product placement on Canadian television is not of the same magnitude as in the United States. One executive noted, "If you're a U.S. network getting a $200,000 fee for placement, that kind of money is worth the trouble. But as a Canadian broadcaster charging one-tenth of that, $20,000 just isn't worth it." Despite this concern, product placement has grown in Canada. However, producers of one hit show find the product placement proposals far too blatant and uninspired and avoid the concept altogether. Although they are open to the idea, a commercial-like premise of the placement cannot be a natural fit with the characters. Another concern is the time delay where the show's production may not coincide with the advertising schedule and message evolution. Some are also concerned with the ability to accurately measure the effects in comparison to established procedures in advertising.[42]

Interestingly, products are placed in shows as part of the story and character without fees from the brand. Don Draper, a character in the hit show *Mad Men*, regularly drinks Canadian Club whisky. When the vintage bottle looked fatigued after a few seasons, the distiller Beam Inc. gladly provided an update—the first time any contact between the show and the company occurred.[43] So, technically, if there is no fee involved it is not product placement and more akin to publicity via a non-news medium.

PRODUCT PLACEMENT DECISIONS

A summary of product placement research identifies seven execution decisions that influence processing effects such as involvement, communication effects such as brand awareness, brand attitude, and behavioural effects like purchase intention and brand usage: program type, execution, amount of processing time, message structure, brand priming, type and amount of information, and brand relevance.[44] Individual factors also influence these effects, however this section is primarily concerned with identifying the decisions.

Program Type   A primary issue to decide concerns the source as represented by the type of movie or TV show. Much like there are media vehicle source effects upon the receiver's mood, the right entertainment selection creates a positive mood effect for the brand. Many TV programs feature product placement as data indicate that it occurs every three minutes, with storied shows having the fewest and game shows and news shows having the most.[45]

Execution   The placement can be an actual product filmed or digitally embedded afterward or added via overlay for live sports. Growth of this has occurred in sports broadcasts, however league organizers are not adopting the concept as quickly as suppliers had hoped. These virtual products are added to the background or foreground of a scene. But transition shots—usually outdoor city images—provide a blank canvas on which to plaster ads.[46]

Amount of Processing Time   TV ads are most frequently 30 seconds long, and other media have corresponding processing times. Thus, the amount of time the product is featured and how many different vehicles a marketer wants to be exposed in represent a decision. While a marketer and its agent obviously try to negotiate the most favourable situation on these issues, they are also dependent upon the director's final artistic decision. TV show exposure averaged about five seconds, with many of the incidents being simple "plugs" where the brand is mentioned.[47]

Message Structure   Much like the structure of advertising messages described in Chapter 8, the message can be visual or verbal or a combination of both, and a dual approach is generally hypothesized to improve effects. For example, the creative use of the product profoundly impacts the experience, ranging from a central role in the scene to a mere showing of the product to having a central character use or talk about the product. Most ads are visual or verbal, with a dual approach rarely occurring.[48]

Brand Priming   Related to message structure of the product placement is priming the message via advertising, social media, or media publicity, or not priming the existence of the product placement ahead of time. This decision regarding priming could be visual, verbal, or both.

Type and Amount of Information   Generally, product placements are more concerned with brand exposure, as the opportunity to transfer in-depth, meaningful information is limited to the plot, scene, and character development. However, related to message structure, the type and amount of information presented is an important decision. Furthermore, its selection can provide transformational experiences beyond information.

Brand Relevance   Finally, the brand personality and its positioning must "fit" with the characters, story, editorial content, and media vehicles. Much like message and source congruence found with other messages, product placements must make sense to the receiver; otherwise, the placement faces rejection like any other promotional message. Chapter 7 highlighted the importance of brand to consumer relevance within the advertising creativity section. Therefore, an optimal alignment of the brand within the placement contributes to its being relevant to the intended audience.

As a support medium, product placement needs to work with other marketing communication tools to achieve its maximum contribution. One expert suggests that product placement needs to be linked with other aspects of the marketing communication plan, and the communication effect can take time, much like with other IMC tools, so brand managers need to be patient before seeing their investments pay off.[49] Finally, one study tested the effects of entertainment, information, and irritation characteristics on product placement value and advertising value. Entertainment and information more strongly predicted advertising value compared to predicting product placement value. However, the irritation factor had a stronger negative prediction to product placement value compared to no link to advertising value. These findings support the media role of product placement that, if not done well, it could potentially cause damage to the brand.[50]

PRODUCT PLACEMENT GROWTH

Innovation in product placement occurred on a few fronts, but they are all a partial return to historical activities. Advertisers insert ads for brands that naturally fit in a storyline. For example, if the story has a restaurant scene, then an ad for a restaurant could play immediately thereafter. One network that tested the idea found improved measures of overall effectiveness and brand resonance.[51] Additionally, content sponsorship occurs when an advertiser sponsors a specific program and receives product placement, brand integration into the story, and other promotional considerations in return.

As noted in Chapter 11, this is somewhat of a return to the early days of television when advertisers sponsored TV shows. An equivalent in this age is seen with HGTV's *Home to Win* program. The 10-part series includes many stars from other shows from this specialty channel, such as Mike Holmes and Sarah Richardson. The reality-based show takes viewers through the story of designing a dream home, which one of the viewers who enters the contest wins. The renovation stars highlight many brands such as Leon's, KitchenAid, Maytag, Samsung, Tempur-Pedic, Toyota, Benjamin Moore, Moen, and Jeld-Wen as they search for decorating items, design, and build the prize winning home.[52]

Another approach is the use of "advertainment," which is the creation of video and/or music content by an advertiser in an attempt to entertain viewers while advertising their products. All of these innovations are sometimes referred to as "branded entertainment," signalling a blurring of the promotional message and the original creative content. In this respect, these promotional activities circumvent advertising laws as the distinction between the advertising message and the editorial content is strictly adhered to for TV shows and TV commercials, and print ads in magazines and newspapers.

Product placement invaded the gaming world, and research found that when people select avatars for simulation games, they often select clothing they wear or aspire to wear—giving an unusual opportunity for clothing companies to place an identity that people can virtually purchase with points, and purchase for real as they buy virtual currency to adjust their swag. Xbox Live users have made 290 million customization adjustments to their avatars! Clothing brands adapted by users for their avatar grew awareness by 44 percent, and purchase intent by 31 percent. With such success, it is no wonder that Billabong updates the virtual lineup as often as its in-store selection![53]

Avatar clothing is but one of many options for in-game placements. Embedding brands within big-name games produced by Electronic Arts (EA) is one avenue that used to be quite expensive with a long lead time. However, programming changes make this cheaper and easier with gaming networks. In-game product placement hit $1 billion in 2010 in North America. With 172 million consoles worldwide and about 5 million in Canada, the reach and frequency potential is strong. Dynamic in-game placement is a new and popular option, with Gatorade obtaining a 24 percent increase in sales with one usage and the Canadian Armed Forces finding a 200 percent increase in military career interest.[54]

STRENGTHS OF PRODUCT PLACEMENT

Media Characteristics   The potential for geographic coverage is substantial as a top movie or television show could have national or international coverage. We emphasize the importance of this qualifying aspect, as entertainment viewers can be fickle. A large number of people see movies each year, providing reasonable reach. The average film is estimated to have a life span of 3.5 years, and most of these moviegoers are very attentive audience members. When this is combined with home rentals, movies on demand, specialty movie channels, and finally network viewing, the potential exposure for a product placed in a movie is enormous. A similar logic holds true for TV shows that are available with similar distribution intensities. Depending on how the product is used in the movie or program, there may be ample opportunity for repeated exposures for greater frequency due to those who like to watch a program or movie more than once. While the cost of placing a product may range from free samples to millions of dollars, the CPM can be very low because of the high volume of exposures it generates.

Media Usage Characteristics   A theatre audience member needs to physically avoid the product placement by leaving the theatre, so has little control for selective exposure. Similarly, it is unlikely that many viewers at home will skip a product placement while enjoying the drama, action, or comedy of a movie or program. We previously discussed the advantage of source identification that occurs with a creative message. When consumers see their favourite movie star wearing Oakley sunglasses, drinking Gatorade, or driving a Mercedes, this association may lead to a favourable product image. Most of those involved in product placement believe that association with the proper source is critical for success. A product placement done properly has direct relevance for the character or situation and is almost a transformational experience emotionally for the audience member who is paying full attention to the entertainment. With category exclusivity rights within the media vehicle and the fact that any show or movie has only a few product placements, the potential for clutter is very low. However, the plot, scenes, and dialogue act as a form of clutter that can be overcome with creative use of product placement.

LIMITATIONS OF PRODUCT PLACEMENT

Media Characteristics   By its very nature of being cast in a movie, the potential for exposure beyond a brand's target audience is enormous. Although a certain amount of target audience selectivity is viable through the type of movie or show, there is likely considerable wasted coverage. Movie attendance is historically strong; however, in many cases it will be difficult to attain a substantial portion of one's target audience coverage with a single movie. Similarly, even a hit television show may reach only a portion of a brand's target audience. In many movies, the advertiser has no say over when and how often the product will be shown, providing minimal scheduling flexibility. While the CPM may be very low for product placement in movies, the absolute cost of placing the product may be very high, pricing advertisers out of the market.

Media Usage Characteristics   Product placement in a movie or TV show has an attitudinal impact due to the vehicle source effect; there is no guarantee viewers will notice the product. Product placements vary in whether they are conspicuous or not. When the product is not featured prominently or lasts for only a few seconds, the advertiser runs the risk of not being seen or being thought inconsequential. The appeal that can be made in this media form is limited. There is no potential for discussing product benefits or providing detailed information. Rather, appeals are limited to source association, use, and enjoyment. The endorsement of the product is indirect, and the flexibility for product demonstration is subject to its use in the film, contributing to minimal cognitive processing. TV viewers and moviegoers can be put off at the idea of placing ads in programs or movies. These viewers want to maintain the barrier between program content and commercials. If the placement is too intrusive, they may develop negative attitudes toward product placement as a media, ultimately affecting brand image.

AUDIENCE MEASUREMENT FOR PRODUCT PLACEMENT

Research studies and companies attempting to monitor and measure the impact of product placement have not resulted in an accepted industry standard like TV has; however, companies offer service in this area. Nielsen Media Research, the TV ratings company in the United States, currently tracks product placement on network television. Nielsen-IAG Research maintains a panel where 5,000 daily viewers take an online quiz about the previous night's prime-time programs, the commercials, and product placements therein. The information is used to determine which ads work best; what shows, spots, and placements are being remembered; and viewers' attitudes toward the same. An advertising agency and product placement valuation company, Deutsch and iTVX, combined their efforts to measure effects. Their method values the quality of each hundredth of a second of a placement, and then translates the data into a product placement/commercial cost ratio and compares it to the value of a commercial. Two studies have demonstrated the potential effectiveness of product placement. One showed that prominently displayed placements led to strong recall.[55] Another study indicated that viewers are accepting of promotional products and in general evaluate them positively, though certain products (alcohol, guns, cigarettes) are perceived as less acceptable.[56] As measurement systems develop, planners can rely on this preliminary information and may still make decisions based on their own creative insights or rely on the attractiveness and credibility of the source.

IMC Planning: Strategic Use of Out-of-Home and Support Media

Previously, the strategic use of out-of-home and support media might have been considered an oxymoron, as both types appeared in promotional planners' budgets after money had been allocated to other more "valuable" media. An IMC perspective toward media selection provides a new look at how these types of opportunities can achieve communication and behavioural objectives, primarily at the pre-purchase and purchase decision stages.

OUT-OF-HOME MEDIA

For the most part, outdoor, transit, and place-based media tend to have two primary objectives. The first is awareness, as these media share common strengths of cost efficiency with extensive reach and frequency levels in the geographic areas in which the media are located or placed. The ability to use clever images and headlines or very short-copy messages permits these messages to have emotional relevance to help ensure brand recognition or recall. Moreover, these two design elements can be consistent with creative messages from other media to ensure additional message frequency with the intention to build awareness more strongly.

In general, these media are limited in their ability to build category need or influence brand attitudes beyond maintaining the current attitude of the target audience. Many brands will use these media as an inexpensive, yet cost-effective means of communicating simple brand preference messages directed toward current customers or messages to reinforce the general market position of the brand to all potential consumers. Given the limited nature of these media to influence attitudes extensively with short messages, they typically are good for building communication effects at the pre- and post-purchase stages.

Most place-based media typically offer the opportunity for promotional planners to achieve a second objective: brand purchase intention. Since the messages for place-based media are context-dependent in terms of location or time, they can provide the right situational motive to spur on a store visit or more immediate sale. Particular place-based media, like movie theatres, are vehicles for additional exposure of the more traditional broadcast and print media ads and thus permit strong brand positioning strategy opportunities. As noted in the chapter, movie theatres can show longer and more specialized ads that brands may be reluctant to show in a broadcast environment.

Given the broad reach and public nature of these media, often they are more general and have a less clear behavioural objective. However, given that many messages are reinforcing existing attitudes, it appears a substantial number of these ads attempt to influence repeat purchasing. Application of out-of-home messages including connections to mobile hand-held devices suggests greater opportunity for brand switching for trial purchases.

From an integration perspective, out-of-home or transit media provide additional frequency of a creative message that has been placed in broadcast or print media. Typically, we do not see advertisers using these media for executing sales promotions except in poster locations. This medium is also used for public relations activities, and we infrequently observe any connection to direct marketing or Internet applications.

SUPPORT MEDIA

The size and growth of support media such as promotional products and product placement is almost hidden given the degree to which it fits into our everyday life or our normal TV, movie, and video game consumption habits. In this regard, they are similar to out-of-home media that are a part of our everyday experiences. However, for these two support media, the exposure is both more widespread and more narrow. Promotional products are more widespread as we are selectively observing them virtually everywhere depending on the product. Given that a high percentage of products are wearable, we witness brand names on shirts, hats, and so on almost constantly. Product placement is clearly narrower, as it is limited within the time frame and scope of the vehicle it is delivered in. These characteristics suggest that both are excellent for building awareness, much like out-of-home media, and could be especially useful for all stages of the target audience's decision-making process.

Promotional products and product placement offer brand-building capabilities much like specialized place-based media such as movie theatres. The vehicle with which the brand is associated provides an additional source effect that puts significant context around the brand experience. For example, observing a particular brand in a movie approximates an endorsement from both the character and the actor. This is consistent with viewing a television commercial with the same actor, but even more so as the emotion and involvement with the movie compounds the positive effect. Given this more profound viewing experience, it is no wonder that advertisers are willing to pay substantial parts of their budget to have the brand featured in a few seconds of a popular movie.

The independence of these kinds of media suggests more limited opportunity for integration, but opportunities are pursued. Public relations activities are often used to connect the brand and its product placement in a movie or television show. For example, for blockbuster placements, like showing a new car model in a movie, news media will report the appearance in both traditional versions and on the Internet. News media have reported upon the placement of brands in video games. Naturally, the Internet offers a wide variety of information content, and a brand can highlight its placement on its own site.

Learning Objectives Summary

Identify the options within out-of-home media for developing an IMC program and for audience measurement, and their strengths and limitations.

This chapter introduced three types of out-of-home media available to marketers: outdoor, transit, and place-based. Within each, there are numerous options for promotional planners to use to achieve their objectives. Many provide the opportunity to creatively express the brand message in a very appropriate location depending on where people live, work, or play.

Outdoor advertising audience measurement is very strong in Canada. The industry association COMB has established a strong research methodology for ensuring accurate estimates of exposure levels. This research has expanded to place-based media such as those found in restaurants and hotels as well as health and fitness outlets. Documentation for transit audiences is less thorough, although a degree of assessment is possible.

Collectively, the three outdoor media offer consistent strengths. For the most part, the public nature of these media leads to high numbers of people reached, which in turn suggests relatively positive cost efficiency, allowing advertisers to extend their frequency levels. Also, each medium allows for creativity for either emotional or cognitive responses. In addition, many of the media discussed here have effectively demonstrated their power to obtain positive communication and business effects. Perhaps the major weakness is the lack of audience measurement and verification for transit and place-based media in comparison to out-of-home; however, the developments in out-of-home advertising offer potential development in the transit and place-based media in the future.

Apply the concepts of out-of-home media to promotional products and product placement to construct support programs within an IMC plan.

Support media include promotional products and product placement. All of these media are public displays of brand messages that are more fitting with the unique situation in which they are delivered. Research of audience size for the support media of promotional products and product placement is mixed. Clearly, product placements in movies and TV shows rely on movie ticket sales (and later video purchase and rentals) and audience size estimates for television viewing. Similarly, marketers know the number of promotional product items given out since they pay the bill, and could estimate pass-along rates and readership rates much like is done in magazines. But in both cases, estimates of exposure level and subsequent achievement of objectives are incomplete or mixed.

Show how out-of-home and support media are important elements of IMC planning.

In many instances, IMC planners require broad exposure levels for the brand name and basic positioning message to be reinforced for many consumers. Out-of-home and support media are very good at achieving these tasks, and with the development of digital communication, these media are contenders for initiating consumer contact for product information or participation with various kinds of brand experiences or sales promotions. As such, their potential for moving into the realm as a primary medium continually improves over time.

Review Questions

1. Explain how out-of-home ads can be creative and foster emotional responses. Why would brands use outdoor ads for this purpose?
2. What are promotional products? List the advantages and disadvantages of this medium. Provide examples where the use of this medium would be appropriate.
3. How do out-of-home media and support media help achieve awareness objectives?

Applied Questions

1. While travelling through a town or city, look for the most unusual place-based ad and decide whether it represents effective advertising.
2. Watch a movie or TV show and try to figure out which brands potentially used product placement. Then do an Internet search to see if there was an actual payment from the brand to the producers of the entertainment.
3. Explain how out-of-home and support media might be used as part of an IMC program. Take any three of the media discussed in the chapter and explain how they might be used in an IMC program for automobiles, smart phones, and Internet services.

All Tim Hortons trademarks referenced herein are owned by Tim Hortons. Used with permission.

CHAPTER FOURTEEN

Sales Promotion

LEARNING OBJECTIVES

LO1 Explain the role of sales promotion in a company's integrated marketing communications program and examine why it is increasingly important.

LO2 Identify the objectives, strategy, and tactical components of a sales promotion plan.

LO3 Describe consumer sales promotion strategy options and evaluate the factors to consider in using them.

LO4 Describe trade sales promotion strategy options and evaluate the factors to consider in using them.

LO5 Apply key IMC issues related to sales promotion decisions.

RRRoll Up With Timmies

Tim Hortons' "RRRoll Up the Rim to Win" contest reached its 30th anniversary in 2016, shortly after the company's 50th anniversary in 2014. The 2016 edition saw 40 grand prizes of a Honda Civic sedan, 120 LG 4K OLED TVs, 100 $5,000 CIBC prepaid cards, 25,000 $100 TimCards, and millions of coffee and doughnut prizes. After giving away 500 million prizes, the company made novel changes in the past couple of years to keep the momentum going. "RRRoll Up Replay!" allowed consumers to participate online with the chance of winning an additional 250,000 prizes in 2016, similar to those in the main contest. "RRRoll Up at Home" included purchases made for home brewing as consumers took a photo of their receipt and uploaded it to the contest site for a chance of winning from 10,000 additional prizes. They also experimented one year with a cup that rolled up two times and gave customers a chance to double their winnings. The contest remained supported with heavy media advertising, and participants used social media in clever ways to show their victories or their participatory spirit.

The enriched "RRRoll Up the Rim to Win" contest may be intended to ward off the competitive threat of a lower priced McDonald's and better selection offering at Starbucks as Tim Hortons received fewer patrons the past few years. Other concerns included longer delivery times as the menu expanded, something the new CEO viewed as a critical challenge to overcome. In addition, Tim Hortons lagged behind other quick service restaurants in store redesign features that encourage customers to linger, such as couches and gas fireplaces. Some critics observed that the menu might require revision despite significant growth in this area over the years. No matter what service changes are in store, "RRRoll Up the Rim to Win" remains a key feature.

As part of the 50th anniversary, Tim Hortons conducted research to understand consumers' technique when rolling up the rim; 50 percent tried the slow and steady thumb rolling approach—possibly resulting from lingering imagery of a TV ad decades ago, 24 percent preferred to use their teeth for the roll, and 12 percent believed in the "flatten and roll" style. Looking at the participation from another angle, 38 percent claimed the cup should be empty before rolling, 13 percent rolled up the same way all the time, and 8 percent purchased from the same location every time! And to think, all of this started when one cup company tried to secure more business from Tim Hortons with its innovative feature of a rim that could roll up!

This fun approach to the contest remained consistent from a couple of years ago when Tim Hortons introduced the "pre-cup agreement" to settle any disputes about who wins after receiving a coffee from a friend. Guidelines on the roles of the "well-wisher" (giver) and "happy-roller" (receiver) clarified who should get what if the cup turned out to be a winner. An informal poll found that two-thirds of all receivers should keep the cup. Of course the instructions concluded that the protocol was not legally binding, but the jaunty tone provided another enjoyable moment during the annual promotional event.

Sources: "Rolling Up a Winner," *Strategy*, May 2014; Rebecca Harris, "Tim Hortons Enhances 'Roll Up the Rim' Ahead of Q4," *Marketing Magazine*, February 18, 2014; Andrew Ryan, "Tim Hortons Adds Pre-Cup Agreement to Annual 'Roll Up the Rim to Win' Promotion," *The Globe and Mail*, February 18, 2014; David Friend, "Tim Hortons Set to Unveil New Strategy, Revamps 'Roll Up the Rim' to Take on Rivals," *National Post*, February 17, 2014; "Rituals Reign During Tim Hortons 'RRRoll Up the Rim to Win,'" *Canada Newswire*, February 3, 2016.

Question:

1. What changes would you suggest for future "RRRoll Up the Rim to Win" events?

Advertising alone may not be enough to convince consumers to switch brands, try a new product category, or return to the same brand purchased previously. Companies also use sales promotion methods targeted at both consumers and the wholesalers and retailers that distribute their products to stimulate demand. Most IMC programs include consumer and trade promotions that are coordinated with advertising, direct marketing, and publicity/public relations campaigns as well as salesforce efforts.

This chapter focuses on the role of sales promotion in a firm's IMC program. We explain how marketers use both consumer and trade promotions to influence the purchase behaviour of consumers and wholesalers and retailers, respectively. We identify the objectives of sales promotion programs and describe the types of sales promotion tools that can be used at both the consumer and trade level. We also consider how sales promotion can be integrated with other elements of the promotional mix, and look at problems that can arise when marketers become overly dependent on consumer and trade promotions.

Sales Promotion Planning

Of all the IMC tools available to a promotional planner, sales promotion potentially allows brands to achieve multiple objectives or provides the opportunity to enhance an IMC plan due to the nature of its characteristics and the many types that are available. We review these two topics in this section and highlight the reasons why sales promotion has grown so tremendously, thus indicating the relative strengths of sales promotion.

CHARACTERISTICS OF SALES PROMOTION

Sales promotion is a direct inducement within an action-focused marketing event that offers an extra value or incentive for the product to the salesforce, distributors, or the ultimate consumer with the primary objective of influencing customer and potential customer behaviour which may include an immediate purchase.[1] This definition indicates two distinguishing features of sales promotion.

First, sales promotion involves an inducement that provides an *extra incentive* to buy. This incentive is usually the key element in a promotional program: it may be purely financial (i.e., coupon, price reduction, refund, or rebate), emotionally based (i.e., opportunity to enter a contest or sweepstakes, gift or premium), value-oriented (e.g., extra amount of product, sample a free product), or experiential (i.e., attend a marketing event). The financial incentive can be seen as extrinsic while the intrinsic non-financial incentives are hedonic in nature, demonstrating entertainment, personal exploration, and value expression.[2] One study investigated consumer reactions to online promotions and found slightly stronger recall levels for non-financial offers.[3] Furthermore, sales promotions also reinforce consumers' feelings about themselves, as finding deals is seen as an achievement and a personal reward for being a good shopper, thereby increasing the frequency of purchases.[4]

Second, sales promotion is essentially an *acceleration tool,* designed to speed up the buying process of consumers and maximize sales volume.[5] By providing an extra incentive, sales promotion techniques can motivate consumers to purchase a larger quantity of a brand or shorten the purchase cycle of consumers by encouraging them to take more immediate action. Companies also use limited-time offers such as price-off deals or a coupon with an expiration date to accelerate the purchase process.[6] Sales promotion attempts to maximize sales volume by motivating customers who have not responded to advertising. The ideal sales promotion program generates sales that would not be achieved by other means. However, sales promotion offers may end up being used by current users of a brand rather than attracting new users.

TYPES OF SALES PROMOTION

Sales promotion activities can be *targeted to different audiences* in the marketing channel. As shown in Figure 14-1, sales promotion can be directed to consumers and trade members. Activities involved in **consumer sales promotion** include samples, coupons, premiums, contests and sweepstakes, refunds and rebates, bonus packs, price-offs, programs, and event marketing. These promotions are directed at consumers, the end purchasers of goods and services, and are designed to induce them to purchase the marketer's brand. Consumer promotions are also used by retailers to encourage consumers to shop in their particular stores. Sales promotion can also be directed to intermediaries like wholesalers, distributors, and retailers, known as trade members. **Trade sales promotion** includes dealer trade allowances, point-of-purchase displays, cooperative advertising, contests and incentives, sales training programs, trade shows, and potentially other programs designed to motivate organizations in the distribution channel to carry and merchandise a product.

Marketing programs usually include both trade and consumer promotions, since motivating both groups maximizes effectiveness. Programs designed to persuade the trade to stock, merchandise, and promote a manufacturer's products are part of a **promotional push strategy**. The goal of this strategy is to push the product through the channels of distribution with promotional activities. A push strategy tries to convince resellers that they can make a profit on a manufacturer's product and to encourage them to order the merchandise and communicate and promote the brand to their customers. Company sales representatives call on resellers to explain the product, discuss the firm's plans for building demand among ultimate consumers, and describe and offer the trade promotion programs. The company may use **trade advertising**, generally publications that serve the particular industry, to generate reseller interest.

Companies also employ a **promotional pull strategy**, spending money on sales promotion efforts directed to the ultimate consumer with the goal of creating demand among consumers. Effort directed toward the end-user encourages the reseller to stock and promote the product. Thus, stimulating demand at the end-user level pulls the product through the channels of distribution.

Figure 14-1   Types of sales promotion activities

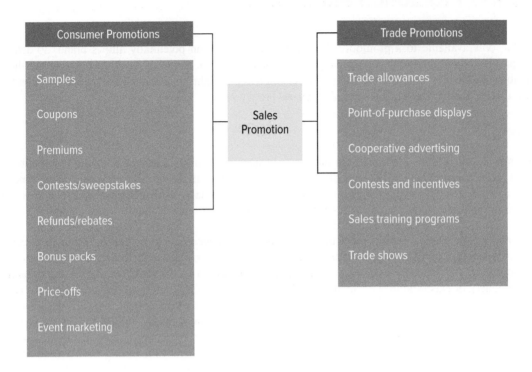

Whether to emphasize a push or a pull strategy depends on a number of factors, including the company's relations with the trade, its promotional budget, and demand for the firm's products. Companies that have favourable channel relationships may prefer to use a push strategy and work closely with channel members. A firm with a limited promotional budget may not have the funds for sales promotion that a pull strategy requires and may find it more cost-effective to build distribution and demand by working closely with resellers. When the demand outlook for a product is favourable because it has unique benefits, is superior to competing brands, or is very popular among consumers, a pull strategy may be appropriate. Companies often use a combination of push and pull strategies, with the emphasis changing as the product moves through its life cycle.

GROWTH OF SALES PROMOTION

Historically, advertising received the major budget allocation for most consumer-products companies' plans. Over time, the proportion of the marketing budget allocated to sales promotion rose sharply, mostly due to increased trade promotion but also due to more attractive and creative consumer promotions. Thus, sales promotion now takes an important strategic role in an IMC program. Many factors usually found in a situation analysis influenced this evolution: strategic importance, reaching a specific target audience, promotional sensitivity, declining brand loyalty, brand proliferation, short-term focus, accountability, power of retailers, and competition.

Strategic Importance   Previously, sales promotion specialists participated in planning after key strategic branding decisions were made to develop a promotional program that could create a short-term increase in sales. However, companies now include promotional specialists as part of their strategic brand-building team, and promotional agencies offer integrated marketing services and expertise to enhance brand equity (see Exhibit 14-1). Critics contend that if the trend toward spending more on sales promotion at the expense of media advertising continues, brands may lose the equity that advertising helped create. However, not all sales promotion activities detract from the value of a brand, as the next example illustrates.

Exhibit 14-1   Aspen Marketing Services touts its IMC capabilities.

Courtesy of Aspen Marketing Services

Nivea coordinated a contest with its pop-up store and other promotional tools to celebrate its 100th anniversary (see Exhibit 14-2). "We know from our proprietary research that our consumer is totally interested in educating themselves about skin care," commented one executive. As such, after a visit to the pop-up store and a skin care consultation, consumers received a branded bag containing their after-effects photo, samples, and coupons, and were offered a chance to win a $10,000 "body and soul regimen for two" featuring the services of a beauty and well-being expert, a Nivea skin care expert, a massage therapist, a fashion stylist, a personal trainer, a chef, and a nutritionist. One hundred gift sets rounded out the prize list. Other promotion of the contest included direct mail, national magazine ads in both languages, and a microsite.[7]

Exhibit 14-2 Nivea implemented a comprehensive sales promotion program.

© Vittorio Zunimo Celotto/Stringer/Getty Images

Reaching a Specific Target Audience   Marketing efforts focus on specific market segments, and firms use sales promotions to reach geographic, demographic, psychographic, and customer or non-customer audiences. Sales promotion programs can also be targeted to specific user-status groups such as customers or non-customers, as well as non-category users or light versus heavy users. Sales promotion tools have become one of the primary vehicles for geographic-based programs tied into local flavour, themes, or events.

Promotional Sensitivity   Marketers use sales promotion in their marketing programs because consumers respond favourably to the incentives it provides. Since the incentive can be financial, emotionally based, value-oriented, or experiential, it seems likely that consumers for most goods and services typically look for a little extra, which is consistent with economic theory. Buying a product with a sales promotion is a routine response behaviour for promotion-sensitive consumer segments who only buy when there is a "deal."

Declining Brand Loyalty   Consumers are always willing to buy their preferred brand at full price without any type of promotional offer. However, consumers can also be loyal coupon users and/or are conditioned to look for deals when they shop. They may switch back and forth among a set of brands they view as essentially equal. These brands are all perceived as being satisfactory and interchangeable, and favourable brand switchers (discussed in Chapter 3) purchase whatever brand is promoted.

Exhibit 14-3   A premium offer is used to provide extra incentive to purchase Lucky Charms.

© The McGraw-Hill Companies/Mark Dierker, photographer

Brand Proliferation   New brands entering mature product categories may lack significant advantages that can be communicated in an advertising campaign. Thus, these companies may depend on sales promotion to encourage consumers and trade members to try or to adopt these brands. Marketers also rely on sales promotion tools to achieve consumer trial of their brand's extensions (Exhibit 14-3). Marketers face competitive pressure to obtain shelf space for new products in stores as retailers favour new brands with strong sales promotion support.

Short-Term Focus   Marketing plans and reward systems are geared to short-term performance measures of quarterly and yearly market share and sales volume. Critics believe the packaged-goods brand management system has contributed to marketers' increased dependence on sales promotion at the expense of brand building activities. Marketing or brand managers use promotions to help them move products into the retailers' stores at the request of the salespeople, who also face short-term quotas or goals.[8] Managers view consumer and trade promotions as the most dependable way to generate short-term sales, particularly when they are price-related.

Accountability   Senior management puts pressure on marketing or brand managers and the salesforce to produce an acceptable return on investment of marketing expenditures. In companies struggling to meet their sales and financial goals, top management is demanding measurable, accountable ways to relate promotional expenditures to sales and profitability. Managers held accountable to produce results use sales promotions since they produce a quick and easily measured jump in sales as compared to advertising, which takes longer to show impact and the effects are more difficult to measure.

Power of Retailers   Marketers also feel pressure from the trade as retailers demand sales performance from their brands. Real-time data available from computerized checkout scanners makes it possible for retailers to monitor promotions and track the results they generate on a daily basis. With optical checkout scanners and sophisticated in-store computer systems, retailers estimate how quickly products turn over, which sales promotions are working, and which products make money. Retailers use this information to analyze sales of manufacturers' products and then demand discounts and other promotional support from manufacturers of lagging brands. Companies that fail to comply with retailers' demands for more trade support may have their shelf space reduced or even have their product dropped.

Competition   Manufacturers rely on trade and consumer promotions to gain or maintain competitive advantage. Exciting, breakthrough creative ideas are difficult to achieve on a regular basis, so there can be an overreliance on sales promotion. Companies tailor their trade promotions to key retail accounts and develop strategic alliances with retailers that include both trade and consumer promotional programs to achieve differentiation. A major development is **account-specific marketing**, whereby a manufacturer collaborates with an individual retailer to create a customized promotion that accomplishes mutual objectives.

LO2   Sales Promotion Plan

In this section, we examine the various parts of a sales promotion plan. First, we consider objectives marketers have for sales promotion programs. Next, we illustrate why the sales promotion decisions are strategic options. Finally, we discuss the key tactics that are critical for all sales promotions. We focus on the consumer market to illustrate these ideas. Application to the trade market is readily done once the concept is understood.

OBJECTIVES OF CONSUMER SALES PROMOTION

Marketers plan consumer promotions by conducting a situation analysis and determining a sales promotion's specific role in the IMC program. They decide what the promotion is designed to accomplish and to whom it should be targeted. Setting clearly defined objectives and measurable goals for sales promotion programs is consistent with the planning process of Chapter 1. While the goal is to induce brand purchase, the marketer may have different objectives for new versus established brands or new versus current customers, such as trial, repeat purchase, consumption, and brand equity that are consistent with the behavioural and communication objectives of Chapter 5.

Trial Purchase   An important use of sales promotion is to encourage consumers to try a new product or service. New products introduced to the market may fail within the first year due to a lack of the promotional support needed to encourage initial brand trial by enough consumers. Also, new versions of an existing brands that do not offer additional unique benefits may flounder without promotions that induce trial. Thus, sales promotion is important for new brand introduction strategies; the level of initial trial can be increased through techniques such as samples, coupons, and refund offers (see Exhibit 14-4).

A trial purchase objective is also relevant for an established brand that uses a sales promotion to attract non-users of the product category, which can be difficult, as these consumers may not see a need for the product. Sales promotions can appeal to non-users by providing them with an extra incentive to try the product, but a more common strategy for increasing sales of an established brand is to attract consumers who use a competing brand. This can be done by giving them an incentive to switch, such as a sample, coupon, premium offer, bonus pack, or price deal.

Exhibit 14-4   Gillette used a sample and coupon to promote trial.

© The McGraw-Hill Companies, Inc./Mark Dierker, photographer

Repeat Purchase   The success of a new brand depends not only on getting initial trial but also on inducing a reasonable percentage of people who try the brand to repurchase it and establish ongoing purchase patterns. Promotional incentives such as coupons or refund offers are included with a sample to encourage repeat purchase after trial. For example, when Peek Freans introduced its Lifestyle Selections brand of cookie, it distributed free samples along with a 50-cent coupon and a contest offer with the winner receiving a trip to Las Vegas. The samples allowed consumers to try the new cookie, while the coupon provided an incentive to purchase it.

A company can use sales promotion techniques in several ways to retain its current customer base through continued repeat purchases. One way is to load them with the product, taking them out of the market for a certain time. Special price promotions, coupons, or bonus packs can encourage consumers to stock up on the brand. This not only keeps them using the company's brand but also reduces the likelihood they will switch brands in response to a competitor's promotion.

Consumption   Marketing managers responsible for established brands competing in mature markets, against established competitors, where consumer purchase patterns are well set, try to ensure continued or increased consumption. Awareness and brand trial of an established brand is generally high after cumulative advertising effects, and sales promotion can generate new interest in an established brand. One way to increase product consumption is by identifying new uses for the brand. Sales promotion tools like recipe books or calendars that show ways of using the product often can accomplish this. One of the best examples of a brand that has found new uses is Arm & Hammer baking soda. Exhibit 14-5 shows a clever freestanding insert (FSI) coupon that promotes the brand's new fridge–freezer pack, which absorbs more odours in refrigerators and freezers. Sales promotion also can stimulate consumption of the existing household stock of product. For example, the Bud Red Light, a premium installed in people's homes, shines when their home team scores, which possibly reminds loyal drinkers to head to the fridge for another round.

Brand Equity   A final objective for consumer promotions is to enhance or support the brand's IMC effort. Although maintaining or building brand equity and image has traditionally been viewed as being accomplished by media advertising, it has also become an important objective for sales promotions. Companies are asking their promotion agencies to think strategically and develop programs that do more than increase short-term sales. They want promotions that require consumer involvement with their brands. Sales promotion techniques such as contests or sweepstakes and premium offers are often used to draw attention to an ad, increase involvement with the message and product/service, and help build relationships with consumers.

Exhibit 14-5   Arm & Hammer used this freestanding insert to promote a specific use for the product.

© Church & Dwight Co., Inc. Use of image is with the express written permission of Church & Dwight Co., Inc. Princeton, New Jersey

CONSUMER SALES PROMOTION STRATEGY DECISIONS

Strategic decisions for sales promotions fall into three broad categories: sales promotion strategy options, application across product lines, and application across geographic markets.

Sales Promotion Strategy Options   Our view of sales promotions is that the options identified in Figure 14-1 are important strategic choices for a marketer. Essentially, the key strategic decision for a marketer concerns the most appropriate sales promotion option that will best achieve the behavioural objective for the target audience. Two characteristics of sales promotions help guide the strategic direction of the sales promotion plan: the degree to which the sales promotion is "franchise building," and whether the incentive of the sales promotion is immediate or delayed.

Franchise-Building Characteristic   Sales promotion activities that communicate distinctive brand attributes and contribute to the development and reinforcement of brand identity are **consumer franchise-building (CFB) promotions**.[9] Consumer sales promotion efforts cannot make consumers loyal to a brand that is of little value or does not provide them with a specific benefit. But they can make consumers aware of a brand and, by communicating its specific features and benefits, contribute to the development of a favourable brand attitude. Consumer franchise-building promotions are designed to build long-term brand preference and help the company achieve the ultimate goal of full-price purchases that do not depend on a promotional offer. Specialists in the promotional area stress the need for marketers to use sales promotion tools to build a franchise and create long-term continuity in their promotional programs. Well-planned CFB activities can convert consumers to loyal customers.

For years, franchise or image building was viewed as the exclusive realm of advertising, and sales promotion was used only to generate short-term sales increases. But now marketers are recognizing the image-building potential of sales promotion and realizing its CFB value. The Peek Freans contest mentioned earlier contributed to building the brand as it reinforced the image of the cookie as being better for the consumer (e.g., healthier). Since the cookie was good, the winner had to go to "Sin City in order to be bad."

Nonfranchise-Building Characteristic   **Nonfranchise-building (non-FB) promotions** are designed to accelerate the purchase decision process and generate an immediate increase in sales. These activities do not communicate information about a brand's unique features or the benefits of using it, so they do not contribute to the building of brand equity and image. Price-off deals, bonus packs, and rebates or refunds are examples of non-FB sales promotion techniques. Short-term non-FB promotions have their place in a firm's promotional mix, particularly when competitive developments call for them since they can switch customers from other brands. But their limitations must be recognized when a long-term marketing strategy for a brand is developed.

Trade promotions are mostly viewed as being nonfranchise-building. First, promotional discounts and allowances given to the trade are passed on to consumers intermittently. Second, trade promotions that are forwarded through the channels reach consumers in the form of lower prices or special deals and lead them to buy on the basis of price rather than brand benefits. Like consumer sales promotions, a franchise-building characteristic can be built into the trade promotion program with activities that do not have a price focus.

Incentive Characteristic   Sales promotions provide consumers with an extra incentive or reward to influence their behaviour, such as purchasing a brand. For certain sales promotion tools the incentive that the consumer receives is immediate, while for others the reward is delayed and not realized immediately. Using their situation analysis, marketers decide the relative balance between immediate and delayed incentives. The decision is based on the target audience(s) and the intended behavioural objective(s). The chart in Figure 14-2 outlines which sales promotion tools can be used to accomplish behavioural objectives and identifies whether the extra incentive or reward is immediate or delayed.[10] Some of the sales promotion techniques are listed more than once because they can be used to accomplish more than one objective with both immediate and delayed incentives, and with trial and repeat purchase behaviour.

Figure 14-2   Consumer sales promotion tools for various objectives

Consumer Reward Incentive	Communication and Behavioural Objectives		
	Trial purchase	Repeat purchase/ customer loading	Support IMC program/ build brand equity
Immediate	• Sampling • Instant coupons • In-store coupons • In-store rebates	• Price-off deals • Bonus packs • In- and on-package free premiums	• Events • In- and on-package free premiums
Delayed	• Media- and mail-delivered coupons • Mail-in refunds and rebates • Free mail-in premiums • Scanner- and Internet-delivered coupons	• In- and on-package coupons • Mail-in refunds and rebates • Loyalty programs	• Self-liquidating premiums • Free mail-in premiums • Contests and sweepstakes

One explanation for how sales promotion incentives work lies in the theory of **operant conditioning**. Individuals act on an aspect of the environment that reinforces behaviour. In a promotion context, if a consumer buys a product with a sales promotion and experiences a positive outcome, the likelihood that the consumer will use this product again increases. If the outcome is not favourable, the likelihood of buying the product again decreases. Two aspects of reinforcement relevant to sales promotion strategies are schedules of reinforcement and shaping.

Different **schedules of reinforcement** result in varying patterns of learning and behaviour. Learning occurs most rapidly under a *continuous reinforcement schedule,* in which every response is rewarded—but the behaviour is likely to cease when the reinforcement stops. This implies promotional offers like earning points in an online branded game should carry on indefinitely so that customers would not switch. Learning occurs more slowly but lasts longer when a *partial or intermittent reinforcement schedule* is used and only some of the individual's responses are rewarded. This implies that an IMC program should have a sales promotion with partial reinforcement schedule. The firm does not want to offer the incentive every time (continuous reinforcement), because consumers might become dependent on it and stop buying the brand when the incentive is withdrawn. A study that examined the effect of reinforcement on bus ridership found that discount coupons given as rewards for riding the bus were as effective when given on a partial schedule as when given on a continuous schedule.[11] The cost of giving the discount coupons under the partial schedule, however, was considerably less.

Reinforcement schedules can also be used to influence consumer behaviour through a process known as **shaping**, the reinforcement of successive acts that lead to a desired behaviour pattern or response.[12] In a promotional context, shaping procedures are used as part of the introductory program for new products. Figure 14-3 provides an example of how samples and discount coupons can be used to introduce a new product and take a consumer from trial to repeat purchase. Marketers must be careful in their use of shaping procedures: if they drop the incentives too soon the consumer may not establish the desired behaviour, but if they overuse them the consumer's purchase may become contingent on the incentive rather than the product or service.

Figure 14-3   Applications of shaping procedures for sales promotion

Behaviour Change	Type of Sales Promotion
Induce product trial	Free samples distributed; large discount coupon
Induce purchase with little financial obligation	Discount coupon prompts purchase with little cost; coupon good for small discount on next purchase enclosed
Induce purchase with moderate financial obligation	Small discount coupon prompts purchase with moderate cost
Induce purchase with full financial obligation	Purchase occurs without coupon assistance

Application Across Product Lines   Another part of the strategic sales promotion decision is the degree to which each sales promotion tool is applied to the range of sizes, varieties, models, or products. Overall, there are three important product decisions for sales promotions. The first concerns whether the sales promotion should be run on the entire line or on individual items. If the latter option is selected (i.e., selective application), the second decision concerns which specific items. The marketer could run a promotion on either the more or less popular items. Similarly, the marketer could focus on higher or lower price points. Sometimes, a sales promotion is offered on a unique product format or size instead of the regular product. For example, Kellogg's bundled three brands of cereal with plastic in one sales promotion in which each size was not the standard size typically distributed. Thus, the third strategic issue concerns whether the sales promotion is run on the "regular" stock or another special version.

Application Across Geographic Markets   Sales promotions can be run nationally or in select markets. Local or regional market conditions, with respect to consumer demand and competitive intensity, tend to dictate the degree of tailoring of sales promotions for each geographic market. Intuitively, it appears that marketers would be faced with situations where offering unique sales promotions for each geographic market would achieve optimal communication and behavioural effects; however, there are three factors that marketers need to consider. First, a regional focus requires additional managerial commitment in planning and implementation. Second, achieving objectives more specifically may result in greater expense, thus necessitating a cost–benefit analysis. Third and finally, national accounts may not be too receptive, with different types of sales promotions in one province versus another.

CONSUMER SALES PROMOTION TACTICS DECISIONS

A coupon can be received with a value anywhere from 50¢ to $2.00 for many consumer products, early in the year or later in the year, often or not so often, or from any number of outlets (e.g., direct mail, magazine). As this implies, for each sales promotion option, the marketer faces a number of key tactical decisions: value of the incentive, timing, and distribution. We briefly describe each of these in order to put together a comprehensive sales promotion plan.

Value of Incentive   Whether the marketer is offering a price discount or a consumer franchise-building sales promotion such as a premium, eventually the marketer has to decide the value of the sales promotion. For example, should the coupon be the equivalent of a 10 percent or a 20 percent discount? This decision is contingent upon the threshold at which consumers will respond to a sales promotion and the number of potential consumer responses; each will contribute to the total cost of the sales promotion. Similarly, if a beer company is offering a premium, a strategic decision has to be made as to the relative value of the premium: for example, a T-shirt worth $10 to $15, or perhaps a "cozy" worth a couple of dollars.

Timing   The time element of the sales promotion is important in a few directions that are mutually dependent. A marketer has to decide during which months, weeks, or days the sales promotion will be offered. Seasonal or some other consumption pattern discovered through market research or the situation analysis may guide this choice. In addition, sales promotions can be offered for one day, one week, a few weeks, or even a few months. Target audience and behavioural objectives typically guide this duration decision. The frequency of the sales promotion is a final timing consideration. If coupons have been chosen, the marketer needs to decide whether one will be offered every six months or perhaps two every six months.

Distribution   For most sales promotions, there is a logistical consideration as to how the promotion will get to the consumer or how the consumer will get to the sales promotion. There are many choices for sales promotions, such as coupons (e.g., direct mail, in-ad), while for others, such as premiums, the choices may be limited. We discuss the distribution options for each sales promotion in the next section, where we describe each sales promotion and its strengths and limitations. In addition, IMC Perspective 14-1 in the next section identifies new ways to distribute discounts digitally.

 Consumer Sales Promotion Strategy Options

A number of consumer sales promotions that managers may select from to develop a strategic sales promotion plan were identified in Figure 14-1. Each of these options can assist the promotional planner in achieving the objectives just discussed. We now review each of these options by describing their characteristics, distribution methods, and strengths and limitations.

SAMPLING

Sampling involves a variety of procedures whereby consumers are given an amount of a product for no charge to induce trial. Sampling is generally considered the most effective way to generate trial, although it is also the most expensive. Sampling is used to introduce a new product to the market and can be used for an established product; however, it may not induce satisfied users of a competing brand to switch and may simply reward the firm's current customers who would buy the product anyway.

Sampling can have strong consumer franchise–building strength if supported within the IMC program. McDonald's initiated its free coffee offer with extensive advertising: TV, billboard, and out-of-home spectaculars. The ads conveyed that it was a premium roast coffee made with 100 percent Arabica beans, hand-picked and fire-roasted for a full-bodied flavour—a clear reason to enjoy the sample even more and increase the likelihood of actual purchase with a change in consumer attitude.[13]

Packaged goods (e.g., food, health care) producers are heavy users of sampling since their products meet the three criteria for an effective sampling program. The products are of relatively low unit value, so samples do not cost too much. The products are divisible, which means they can be broken into small sizes that are adequate for demonstrating the brand's features and benefits. The purchase cycle is relatively short, so the consumer will consider an immediate purchase. One of the cleverest samples that seems to satisfy these criteria occurred within four subway ads in Toronto. Commuters plugged their headphones into an audio jack to hear book excerpts, much like sampling music online or in a store. The recording ended with "HarperCollins: We tell the world's greatest stories."[14]

Strengths of Sampling   In general, managers expect samples to yield strong prospective consumer participation and subsequent trial purchase behaviour. Researchers of in-store food sampling found that it effectively stimulated trial in general, provided an incentive for category users to switch brands, and even encouraged consideration among non-category users.[15] No wonder we see so many sampling stations set up in Costco! Getting people to try a product is a second benefit of sampling: consumers experience the brand directly, gaining a greater appreciation for its benefits. This can be particularly important when a product's features and benefits are difficult to describe through advertising. Food, beverage, and cosmetic products have subtle features that are most appreciated when experienced directly.

Limitations of Sampling   While samples are an effective way to induce trial, the brand must have some unique or superior benefits for a sampling program to be worthwhile. Otherwise, the sampled consumers revert back to other brands and do not become repeat purchasers. The costs of a sampling program can be recovered only if the program gets a number of consumers to become regular users of the brand at full retail price.

Another possible limitation to sampling is that the benefits are difficult to gauge immediately, and the learning period required to appreciate the brand may require supplying the consumer with larger amounts of the brand than are affordable. An example would be an expensive skin cream that is promoted as preventing or reducing wrinkles but has to be used for an extended period before any effects are seen.

Sampling Methods   One decision the promotional manager must make is how to distribute the sample. The sampling method chosen is important not only in terms of costs but also because it influences the type of consumer who receives the sample. The best sampling method gets the product to the best prospects for trial and subsequent repurchase. Promotional planners are not limited to one method. In fact, multiple methods for sample requests and delivery can occur. We now review the distribution options available.

Door-to-door sampling, in which the product is delivered directly to the prospect's residence, is used when it is important to control where the sample is delivered. This distribution method is very expensive because of labour costs, but it can be cost-effective if the marketer has information that helps define the target audience and/or if the prospects are located in a well-defined geographic area.

Sampling through media distributes goods through print media as they are delivered to residences. Newspapers use bags with advertising on the outside and the sample is tucked inside with the reading material, or an extension is put on the bag allowing greater visibility of the promotional offer. Magazines have similar capabilities but for smaller products. Companies use Internet media for consumers to sample their products. Software, information, or entertainment products can easily be delivered electronically in the digital age. Samples that are physical goods can be delivered to consumers, who can easily make a request using the Internet.

Sampling through the mail is common for small, lightweight, non-perishable products. This gives the marketer control over where and when the product will be distributed and can target the sample to specific market areas. Marketers use information from geodemographic target marketing programs to better direct their sample mailings. Sampling requests obtained from various sources (e.g., phone, Internet, mail) are usually mailed to consumers. The main drawbacks to mail sampling are postal restrictions and costs.

In-store sampling occurs when the marketer hires temporary demonstrators who set up a table or booth, prepare small samples of the product, and pass them out to shoppers. This approach can be very effective for food products, since consumers get to taste the item and the demonstrator can give them more information about the product while it is being sampled. Demonstrators may offer a financial incentive for the sampled item to encourage immediate trial purchase. This sampling method can be very effective with direct product experience but it requires greater investment, extensive planning, and retailer cooperation.

On-package sampling, where a sample of a product is attached to another item (see Exhibit 14-6), can be very cost-effective, particularly for multiproduct firms that attach a sample of a new product to an existing brand's package. A drawback is that since the sample is distributed only to consumers who purchase the item to which it is attached, the sample will not reach non-users of the carrier brand. Marketers can expand this sampling method by attaching the sample to multiple carrier brands and including samples with products not made by their company.

Event sampling occurs at venues such as concerts, sporting events, and cultural festivals and the brand's event marketing activities. Marketers use sampling programs that are part of integrated marketing programs that feature events, media tie-ins, and other activities that provide consumers with a total sense of a brand rather than just a few tastes of a food or beverage or a trial size of a packaged-goods product.

Location sampling allows companies to use specialized sample distribution services that help the company identify consumers who are non-users of a product or users of a competing brand and develop appropriate procedures for distributing a sample to them. For example, university and college students receive sample packs at the beginning of the semester that contain trial sizes of such products as mouthwash, toothpaste, headache remedies, and deodorant.

COUPONS

The oldest and most widely used sales promotion is the coupon. These characteristics are a function of options with its tactical considerations: the variability in discount offered (e.g., $0.50, $1.00), time flexibility in terms of offer and expiration (e.g., limited, unlimited), and how it is distributed (e.g., media, direct, package, retailer), allowing it to fit in many of the cells of Figure 14-2. Research indicates that the average Canadian household receives about 200 coupons per year and uses about eight coupons, a 4 percent redemption rate.[16] Extensive research on coupons in Canada is not available; however, Figure 14-4 shows data from the United States. Consumer use of "extreme couponing" demonstrated on TV shows is not possible in Canada due to retailers' acceptance of only one coupon per purchase and their reluctance to offer "double-up" redemptions; however, consumers find great savings with effort and plan their shopping accordingly.[17] Digital distribution of coupons occurred on Internet sites years ago, and new approaches with convenient smart phone apps have now emerged to go along with the historic media, home, and store delivery.

Exhibit 14-6   Armor All uses on-package samples for related products.

ArmorAll Products Corporation

Figure 14-4   U.S. coupon facts

	2013
Value distributed	$513 billion
Quantity distributed	329 billion
Quantity redeemed	2.9 billion
Average face value coupons *distributed*	$1.56
Average face value coupons *redeemed*	$1.27
Average valid period	2.2 months
Consumer savings	$3.7 billion

Based on Inmar 2014 Coupon Trends Report

Strengths of Coupons   Coupons' strengths make them effective for both new and established products, and for potential and current customers. First, coupons make it possible to offer a price reduction only to those consumers who are price-sensitive. Such consumers generally purchase because of coupons, while those who are not as concerned about price buy the brand at full price. Second, coupons make it possible to reduce the retail price of a product without relying on retailers for cooperation, which can often be a problem. Third, coupons are generally regarded as second only to sampling as a promotional technique for generating trial since they reduce the consumer's perceived risk associated with trial of a newly launched brand. Fourth, coupons can encourage repeat purchase after initial trial as new products might include a coupon inside the package to encourage a subsequent buy. Fifth, coupons can be useful promotional devices for established products by encouraging non-users to try a brand and encouraging repeat purchase among current users.

Limitations of Coupons   There are a number of problems with coupons. First, there is potential that coupons will not achieve their intended objective. Coupons intended to attract new users to an established brand can be and are redeemed by consumers who already use the brand. Rather than attracting new users, coupons can end up reducing the company's profit margins among consumers who would probably purchase the product anyway. Due to the incentive, conditions, and expiry date, coupons remain less effective than sampling for inducing initial product trial in a short period.

Second, it can be difficult to estimate how many consumers will use a coupon and when. Response to a coupon is rarely immediate; it typically takes anywhere from two to six months to redeem one. A study of coupon redemption patterns found that coupons are redeemed just before the expiration date rather than in the period following the initial coupon drop.[18] Marketers are attempting to expedite redemption by shortening the time period before expiration. The uncertainty in knowing the redemption rate and timing makes for more difficult financial planning for coupons.

A third problem with coupons involves low redemption rates and high costs. Couponing program expenses include the face value of the coupon redeemed plus costs for production, distribution, and handling of the coupons. Figure 14-5 shows the calculations used to determine the costs of a couponing program using a freestanding insert (FSI) in the newspaper and a coupon with an average face value of one dollar. The marketer should track costs closely to ensure that the promotion is economically feasible.

Figure 14-5   Calculating couponing costs

Cost per Coupon Redeemed: An Illustration	
1. Distribution cost 5,000,000 circulation × $15/M	$75,000
2. Redemptions at 2%	100,000
3. Redemption cost 100,000 redemptions × $1.00 face value	$100,000
4. Retailer handling cost and processor fees 100,000 redemptions × $0.10	$10,000
5. Total program cost (Items 1 + 3 + 4)	$185,000
6. Cost per coupon redeemed (Cost divided by redemptions)	$1.85
7. Actual product sold on redemption (misredemption estimated at 10%) 100,000 × 90%	90,000
8. Cost per product moved (Program cost divided by amount of product sold)	$2.06

A final problem with coupon promotions is mistakes during redemption through the wrong product format or incorrect size, or redemption without product purchase. Instances of coupon fraud have occurred at times through store personnel (e.g., redemption by salesclerks in exchange for cash, manager collecting coupons without selling product, etc.).

Coupon Distribution   Coupons can be disseminated to consumers in a number of ways, including newspaper freestanding inserts, direct mail, newspapers (either in individual ads or as a group of coupons in a cooperative format), magazines, packages, and the Internet. Figure 14-6 summarizes a few relevant U.S. coupon redemption rates.

Figure 14-6   U.S. coupon redemption rates, 2013

Media (FSI, newspaper, magazine)	0.5%
Direct Mail	4.0%
Regular In-Pack	3.5%
Regular On-Pack	12.9%
In-Pack Cross-Ruff	1.7%
On-Pack Cross-Ruff	3.0%
On-Shelf (paper, electronic)	11.0%
Handout	2.0% to 5.0%
Internet	9.0%

Based on Inmar 2014 Coupon Trends Report

Freestanding inserts (FSIs) are distributed through newspapers and are used for a number of reasons, including their high-quality four-colour graphics, competitive distribution costs, national same-day circulation, and market selectivity, and the category exclusivity given by the FSI company. Because of their consumer popularity and predictable distribution, coupons distributed in FSIs are also a strong selling point with the retail trade. On the other hand, FSIs suffer from a low redemption rate and their widespread distribution may lead to a clutter problem.

Newspaper and *magazine* distribution of coupons offers a print media alternative. The advantages of newspapers include market selectivity, shorter lead times with timing to the day, cooperative advertising opportunities that can lead to cost efficiencies, and promotional tie-ins with retailers. Other advantages of newspaper-delivered coupons are the broad exposure and consumer receptivity. Consumers actively search the newspaper for coupons, especially on "food day" (when grocery stores advertise their specials). This enhances the likelihood of the consumer at least noticing the coupon. Magazine distribution takes advantage of the selectivity of the publication to reach specific target audiences, along with enhanced production capabilities and extended copy life in the home. One feature of these print options is that the distribution cost is not a factor if the advertiser was planning to run a print ad in the first place.

Direct mail coupons are sent by local retailers or through co-op mailings where a packet of coupons for different products is sent to a household. Direct mail couponing has several advantages. First, the mailing can be sent to a broad audience or targeted to specific geographic or demographic segments. Second, firms that mail their own coupons through addressed mail can be quite selective about recipients. Third, direct-mail coupons can also be combined with a sample, greatly enhancing communication and behavioural effects. Finally, the above strengths generally give this method a redemption rate higher than FSI. The major disadvantage of direct-mail coupon delivery is the expense relative to other distribution methods. The cost per thousand for distributing coupons through co-op mailings ranges from $10 to $15, and more targeted promotions can cost $20 to $25 or even more. Also, the higher redemption rate of mail-delivered coupons may result from the fact that recipients are already users of the brand who take advantage of the coupons sent directly to them. Some companies even produce and distribute their own coupon books, as demonstrated by Procter & Gamble in Exhibit 14-7.

Placing coupons either *inside* or on the *outside of the package* has virtually no distribution costs and a much higher redemption rate than other couponing methods. An in/on pack coupon that is redeemable for the next purchase of the same brand is known as a **bounce-back coupon**. Bounce-back coupons are often used with product samples to encourage the consumer to purchase the product after sampling. They

Exhibit 14-7   P&G produces and distributes its own coupon book.

© The McGraw-Hill Companies, Inc./Mark Dierker, photographer

may be included in or on the package during the early phases of a brand's life cycle to encourage repeat purchase, or they may be a defensive manoeuvre for a mature brand that is facing competitive pressure and wants to retain its current users. The main limitation of bounce-back coupons is that they go only to purchasers of the brand and thus do not attract non-users. A bounce-back coupon placed on the package for a Kellogg's cereal bar is shown in Exhibit 14-8.

Another type of in/on pack coupon is the **cross-ruff coupon**, which is redeemable on the purchase of a different product, usually one made by the same company but occasionally through a tie-in with another manufacturer. Cross-ruff coupons can be effective in encouraging consumers to try other products or brands. Yet another type of package coupon is the **instant coupon**, which is attached to the outside of the package so that the consumer can rip it off and redeem it immediately at the time of purchase. These can be selectively placed in terms of promotion timing and market region.

In-store coupons are distributed to consumers while shopping via tear-off pads, handouts, on-shelf dispensers, and electronic dispensers. These in-store coupons can reach consumers when they are ready to make a purchase, increase brand awareness on the shelf, generate impulse buying, encourage product trial, and provide category exclusivity. Extending this idea, coupons are distributed essentially in any place-based location by simply handing them out.

Coupon distribution also occurs online. Couponclick.ca distributes coupons that can be instantly downloaded and printed. Each voucher contains a code tracked to the individual consumer for measurement effectiveness and security purposes. Two websites, Coupons.com and Save.ca, allow consumers to print or receive coupons in the mail, respectively. The famous blue Valpak, distributed to households through the mail system, is now available online. Another step in the digitization of coupons is the capability of using them with mobile devices as described in IMC Perspective 14-1. A significant advantage of digital distribution is a higher redemption rate since consumers are seeking out a desired brand when shopping.

Exhibit 14-8   Kellogg Company uses an on-package coupon to encourage repurchase.

© The McGraw-Hill Companies/Jill Braaten, photographer

IMC PERSPECTIVE 14-1

COUPONS APPS ABOUND

An alternative for consumers to clipping coupons from various print or packaging options is their smart phone. Many new competitors entered the Canadian market with varying electronic features with mobile apps, and some are being bought out by larger organizations to complement their digital promotional offers.

Tapped Mobile partnered with Shazam to distribute digital coupons. Canadians know and use the Shazam app for its music-identification features that send information such as the artist and song back to the user. About 3.5 million Canadians use Shazam annually for 15 million downloads. The company introduced a visual recognition software feature that allows a user to read specially marked print materials (e.g., magazine ads, poster ads, packaging) to access information from an advertiser. The user opens the app and camera icon and uses the device by scanning it across the ad to access the digital coupon. The system works with existing in-store technology for easy consumer redemption. Research indicated potential acceptance as

© Serg Pilipencos/Shutterstock

[Continued on next page]

[IMC Perspective 14-1 continued]

younger consumers tended to download coupons to their phone, and there was a general trend toward stronger coupon use and digital flyer use. The concept appealed to advertisers for the data as coupon requests and redemptions appeared instantly in their database. Advertisers could track shopping behaviour and better measure the promotional results.

Another system, Groupon, is affiliated with 800 stores with plans to increase by a few hundred more. Consumers install the app on their phone, select a store where they shop, and receive weekly offers automatically. When at the store, the shopper scans the codes and then presents their phone at the checkout to receive the offer. The average consumer uses the app seven times per month. In future, the company plans to use its beacon technology where consumers will get alerts of promotional offers when they enter certain areas of the store. In fact the accuracy of the technology is astounding, as the system will know the demographics of the use and the exact location and where the phone is located, thus indicating what the shopper is looking at. So a promotional offer for a competing brand could be sent right when the consumer is evaluating a brand. For stores with a loyalty program, the company is integrating the promotional offer.

The app for Checkout 51 works as follows. Consumers buy the products that have cash-back offers, communicated via the app or Internet site. Afterward, the consumer photographs their receipt to redeem the coupon and receives a cheque upon accumulating $20. The app currently has 1 million users in Canada and 3 million in the United States and consumers have received a total of $15 million over the past couple of years. The app looked promising as News America Marketing purchased the organization so it could offer a stronger line-up of digital promotional tools. Groupon also expanded its horizons by purchasing SnapSaves, yet another company offering a coupon app. It works similarly to Checkout 51's app, with consumers taking a picture of their receipt and then receiving a cheque in the mail after hitting a threshold. Groupon desired more digital offerings to go along with its initial strategy of discounts and its existing Freebies digital coupons.

Sources: Danny Kucharsky, "Toronto Firm Aims to Revolutionize Coupon Cutting," *Canadian Grocer,* August 21, 2015; Drew Hasselback, "Canadian Online Coupon Startup Checkout 51 Bought by News Corp Unit," *National Post*, July 2015; Rebecca Harris, "Tapped Mobile Launches Shazamable Mobile Coupons," *Marketing Magazine*, November 24, 2015; David Friend, "Canadian Grocery App SnapSaves Sells to Deals Site Groupon," *The Globe and Mail*, June 23, 2014.

Question:

1. How attractive are these coupon options, and which one would you likely use?

PREMIUMS

A **premium** is an offer for a small gift item or merchandise or service either free or at a low price that is an extra incentive for purchasers. Premiums are usually in a product package, given out at a retail location, or sent to consumers who mail in a request along with a proof of purchase. For example, in/on-package free premiums for cereal products include toys, trading cards, or other items, as well as samples of one product included with another. Marketers seek value-added premiums that reflect the quality of the product and are consistent with its image and positioning in the market and try to avoid gimmicks. A research study concluded that surprising consumers with an unknown gift for more emotionally driven purchases produced stronger interest and more positive purchase intentions, but this approach faltered with more cognitively driven purchases.[19]

Strengths of Premiums   Package-carried premiums are advantageous as they immediately provide an extra incentive to buy the product as a key distinguishing feature. For example, McDonald's is a leader in the restaurant market for giving free premiums with its Happy Meal for children (Exhibit 14-9). As this example shows, premiums build or reinforce a brand image and work with co-branding, another key feature. Premiums also have high impulse value that can lead to frequent purchases. Research concluded that premium usage is a function of deal-proneness, compulsive buying tendency, and variety-seeking tendency.[20]

A fourth benefit of premiums is their ability to work with the rest of the IMC program effectively to build the brand image. For example, Kraft Canada supported its ad that told the story of the Kraft peanut butter teddy bear's life with its owner from a young girl to a woman by offering a plush version available to buy with the purchase of the product. Kraft opted to promote a higher quality version of the teddy bear, manufactured by Gund, than it had in past iterations of premium offers. The emotional ad warranted a more plush and huggable teddy bear for long lasting memories as exhibited in the message.[21]

Finally, premiums can also encourage trade support and gain in-store displays for the brand and the premium offer. CocaCola's "Share a Coke" campaign featured various sizes and formats of cans and bottles of its famous beverage adorned with individual names written in the stylized font of the popular brand. In addition to being supported with other IMC activities as noted above, retailers accepted additional units and promoted the initiative with signage to attract customers.[22]

Exhibit 14-9   McDonald's Happy Meal uses toys to help attract children.

© urbanbuzz / Alamy Stock Photo

Limitations of Premiums   There are limitations associated with the use of premiums. First, there is the cost factor, which results from the premium itself as well as from extra packaging that may be needed. Finding desirable premiums at reasonable costs can be difficult, particularly for adult markets, and using a poor premium that costs less may do more harm than good. A solution to this is to offer **self-liquidating premiums** requiring the consumer to pay a portion or all of the cost of the premium. The marketer usually purchases items used as self-liquidating premiums in large quantities and offers them to consumers at lower-than-retail prices. The goal is not to make a profit on the premium item but rather just to cover costs and offer a value to the consumer. A newer solution is an **embedded premium** where a brand donates money to a worthy social cause for every purchase made by consumers. Research concluded that this sales promotion is an efficient use of marketing dollars and contributes to strengthening the brand.[23] A second limitation is that offers usually require the consumer to send in more than one proof of purchase to receive the premium. This requires effort from the consumer and money for the mailing and does not offer an immediate reinforcement or reward. A third limitation is that the marketer faces the risk of poor acceptance and is left with a supply of items with brand identification (e.g., a logo) that makes them hard to dispose of. Thus, it is important to test consumers' reaction to a premium incentive and determine whether they perceive the offer as valuable. Another option is to use premiums with no brand identification, but that detracts from their consumer franchise-building value.

CONTESTS AND SWEEPSTAKES

Contests and sweepstakes are an increasingly popular consumer sales promotion since they seem to have an appeal and glamour that other promotions lack. A **contest** is a promotion where consumers compete for prizes or money on the basis of skills or ability. The company determines winners by judging the entries or ascertaining which entry comes closest to predetermined criteria. Contests usually provide a purchase incentive by requiring a proof of purchase or an entry form that is available from a dealer or advertisement. Some contests require consumers to read an ad or package or visit a store display to gather information. Marketers must be careful not to make their contests too difficult to enter, as doing so might discourage participation among key prospects in the target audience.

A **sweepstakes** is a promotion where winners are determined purely by chance; it cannot require a proof of purchase as a condition for entry. Entrants need only submit their names for the prize drawing. While there is often an official entry form, handwritten entries must also be permitted. One form of sweepstakes is a **game**, which also has a chance element or odds of winning. Scratch-off cards with instant winners are a popular promotional tool. Some games occur over a longer period and require more involvement by consumers. Promotions where consumers must collect game pieces are popular among retailers and fast-food chains as a way to build store traffic and repeat purchases. For example, McDonald's has used promotions based on the game Monopoly several times.

Because they are easier to enter, sweepstakes attract more entries than do contests. They are also easier and less expensive to administer, since every entry does not have to be checked or judged. Choosing the winning entry in a sweepstakes requires only the random selection of a winner from the pool of entries or generation of a number to match those held by sweepstakes entrants. Experts note that the costs of mounting a sweepstakes are also very predictable. Companies can buy insurance to indemnify them and protect against the expense of awarding a big prize. In general, sweepstakes present marketers with a fixed cost, which is a major advantage when budgeting for a promotion. Exhibit 14-10 shows an ad for a sweepstakes where the prize and brand are closely aligned to build brand equity, another key feature of these promotions.

Strengths of Contests/Sweepstakes   Sales can be enhanced by trial and repeat purchases through a sweepstakes advertised via in-store ad-pads. A 12-week experiment of 20 mass-merchandiser outlets—10 test and 10 control stores—revealed that a major household product increased its sales by 70 percent in the test stores during the four-week test period compared to the previous four-week period that featured no advertising or promotion. Furthermore, during the posttest four-week period that had no ad-pad, sales hit a 30 percent increase.[24] Clearly, either non-customers recalled the sales promotion and ad message, or new or existing customers returned for a repeat purchase. In either case, the improved communication and behavioural effects of the promotion make it useful for both manufacturers and retailers.

Contests and sweepstakes can involve consumers with a brand by making the promotion product relevant or by connecting the prizes to the lifestyle, needs, or interests of the target audience. Part of Honda's marketing communication for its compact car is the Civic Nation, an approach to building strong feeling through driving the vehicle and a way for individual consumers to customize their experience with a mass-marketed product. The "United We Drive" theme took a new direction with a contest where musical souls could create an "Anthem for a Nation" using samples of music from hip-hop artist Saukrates. Multimedia directed those interested to a website (CivicNation.ca) where they developed a 30-second electronica, hip-hop, or electropop track. After voting, the winning selections played as the intro for a radio show. The second and third phases of the campaign culminated in a full Civic Nation anthem.[25]

Courtesy of Levi's

The Canadian division of LG conceived the inaugural LG "Life's Good" Film Festival, where aspiring filmmakers from all over the world could submit a high-definition film up to five minutes in length that expressed an uplifting message consistent with the brand's slogan. LG partnered with Google, YouTube, and Film.com and a dedicated website (LGFilmFest.com) to announce the contest and allow viewership. Categories included animation, sports, narrative, and fashion and music, with three category winners receiving $10,000 and a fourth overall winner receiving $100,000.[26]

Limitations of Contests/Sweepstakes   Sweepstakes and/or contest promotions rarely contribute to consumer franchise building for a product or service and may even detract from it. The sweepstakes or contest often becomes the dominant focus rather than the brand, and little is accomplished other than giving away substantial amounts of money and/or prizes. Promotional experts question the effectiveness of contests and sweepstakes. The following example raises this question, although executives accepted the results.

Using Facebook, Absolut invited Vancouver's artists, writers, visual artists, musicians, curators, filmmakers, and gallery owners to create artwork, series, or educational programs that reflected the brand's values of "engaging," "visionary," "bold," and "perfection." The best effort received an award of $120,000. The popular vodka maker obtained only 30 entries, with about half worthy of serious evaluation. Given the historical close connection of Absolut and artists, the low number appears startling, yet executives were satisfied because the task demanded excellence in order to find a long-lasting artistic partner to portray the brand. In fact, for complete success the artistic work had to demonstrate a partnership with the brand and its values.[27]

Numerous legal considerations affect the design and administration of contests and sweepstakes.[28] But companies must still be careful in designing a contest or sweepstakes and awarding prizes. Most firms use consultants that specialize in the design and administration of contests and sweepstakes to avoid any legal problems, but they may still run into problems with promotions. IMC Perspective 14-2 tells the story of a simple contest that did not go as expected.

A final problem with contests and sweepstakes is participation by professionals or hobbyists who submit entries but have no intention of purchasing the product or service. Because it is illegal to require a purchase as a qualification for a sweepstakes entry, people can enter as many times as they wish. Professional players sometimes enter one sweepstakes several times, depending on the nature of the prizes and the number of entries the promotion attracts. There are even newsletters that inform them of all the contests and sweepstakes being held, the entry dates, estimated probabilities of winning, how to enter, and solutions to any puzzles or other information that might be needed. The presence of these professional entrants not only defeats the purpose of the promotion but also may discourage entries from consumers who think their chances of winning are limited.

IMC PERSPECTIVE 14-2

ON A MISALIGNED ROUTE FOR PROMOTION

A thirsty traveller who left Parliament Hill and took a short one-kilometre stroll down O'Connor Street, and then turned right on Somerset, would be at the door of Union Local 613, one of the best bars in Canada according to Air Canada's inflight *enRoute* magazine published by Spafax Canada. The only troubling aspect of this claim is how short lived it was, after the bar owner requested a delisting from the magazine's ranking. While most bars and restaurants—indeed most businesses for that matter—welcome positive exposure through unexpected publicity, which would likely enhance their reputation, co-owner Ivan Gedz saw the situation much differently. However, this story all started with a contest leading to a series of unanticipated events.

© Media Style and Union Local 613

enRoute enlisted the help of its readers to vote on the best bar from the magazine's initial list of 100, and entered each voter into the contest with a chance to win dinner and drinks at a nominated bar closest to their residence. The initiative mirrored a similar promotional activity previously executed by *enRoute* to discover Canada's best restaurant. Coincidentally, Union Local 613 made it to the restaurant list the previous year without any controversy and remained on the list. However, the recognition prompted Gedz to consider the purpose of such lists and who benefits.

The publisher for Air Canada's magazine saw the restaurant and bar lists, and subsequent voter results, as an important service for the airline's customers who travel to many cities and for those living in the cities to become familiar with new alternatives. In fact, the editor-in-chief of Spafax claimed that the restaurant list obtained overwhelming positive support from the restaurant industry, which allowed the magazine to forge strong relationships with chefs to create well-received editorial content.

After seeing the success of the restaurant contest, Rickards beer (owned by Molson Coors) contacted *enRoute* to implement the best bar contest with Rickards as a key sponsorship partner. From the publisher's perspective, the editorial content of the bars' profiles fit well with the readers and the marketing association for Rickards. However, Gedz took exception to being associated with the *enRoute* and Rickards brands, especially considering the establishment did not stock any Molson Coors products and only sold craft beer. In his view, the entire promotion and story amounted to an advertorial message that blurred the lines between editorial content and promotion.

When asked to, *enRoute* publishers immediately retracted Union Local 613's listing, however the editor and VP appeared perplexed by the request, as were other industry commentators. However, Gedz summed up his view succinctly: "We have no interest in being affiliated with Molson Coors. We don't sell any of their products. Why would we lend our brand and be affiliated with the contest itself that they're using as advertising? We took exception to the fact that they felt that it was a privilege to be associated with their brands without asking us if we wanted our brand to be associated with that."

Our traveller, leaving Union Local 613 slightly less thirsty and walking a little more slowly up O'Connor Street, might wonder what would happen if the winner of the contest happened to be from Ottawa. Since the winner could go to a bar near their home, would the Ottawa winner have been permitted to claim their prize at the withdrawn alternative? That might have created another unanticipated series of events!

Sources: Michelle Dipardo, "Air Canada and Rickard's Seek Canada's Top Bars," *Marketing Magazine*, July 11, 2014; Rebecca Harris, "Ottawa Bar Balks at Rickard's Branded Content," *Marketing Magazine*, August 8, 2014; "Thanks, But No Thanks," *Ottawa Citizen*, August 6, 2014; Robert Bostelaar, "Contest Not Cool Enough," *National Post*, August 8, 2014, p. A1.

Questions:

1. Do you agree or disagree with the decision of the co-owner of the bar?
2. Are the contest and the editorial content of the magazine's articles sufficiently distinct?

REFUNDS AND REBATES

Refunds (also known as rebates) are offers by the manufacturer to return a portion of the product purchase price, usually after the consumer supplies proof of purchase. Consumers are generally very responsive to rebate offers, particularly as the size of the savings increases. Rebates are used by makers of all types of products like packaged goods, appliances, vehicles, and car care items (Exhibit 14-11). Consumers may perceive the savings offered through a cash refund as an immediate value that lowers the cost of the item, even though those savings are realized only if the consumer redeems the refund or rebate offer. Redemption rates for refund offers typically range from 1–3 percent for print and point-of-purchase offers to 5 percent for in/on-package offers.

Strengths of Refunds/ Rebates   Marketers use refund offers for all types of behavioural objectives. They can be used to induce trial of a new product which encourages users of another brand to switch, or non-category users to try the brand. Refund offers can also encourage repeat purchase since they may require consumers to send in multiple proofs of purchase. The size of the refund offer may even increase as the number of purchases gets larger. Secondly, rebates offer a temporary price reduction in the face of competition to spur consumers who are at the decision stage. The rebate may be perceived as an immediate savings even though consumers do not follow through on the offer. This perception can influence purchase even if the consumer fails to realize the savings, so the marketer can reduce price for much less than if it used a direct price-off deal. Finally, rebates can influence the timing of a purchase, as seen in vehicle rebates offered toward the end of the model year.

Exhibit 14-11   Pennzoil uses a refund offer that is tied to a future purchase.

Used with permission from Penzoil/Quaker State Company

Limitations of Refunds/Rebates   Limitations are associated with refunds and rebates since not all consumers are motivated by a refund offer because of the delay and the effort required to obtain the savings (e.g., completing forms and mailing receipts). A study of consumer perceptions found a negative relationship between the use of rebates and the perceived difficulties associated with the redemption process.[29] The study also found that consumers perceive manufacturers as offering rebates to sell products that are not faring well. Non-users of rebates were particularly likely to perceive the redemption process as too complicated and to suspect manufacturers' motives. This implies that companies using rebates must simplify the redemption process and use other promotional elements such as advertising to retain consumer confidence in the brand.

When small refunds are being offered, marketers may find other promotional incentives such as coupons or bonus packs more effective. They must be careful not to overuse rebate offers and confuse consumers about the real price and value of a product or service. Also, consumers can become dependent on rebates and delay their purchases, or purchase only brands for which a rebate is available.

BONUS PACKS

Bonus packs offer the consumer an extra amount of a product at the regular price by providing larger containers or extra units (Exhibit 14-12). Bonus packs result in a lower cost per unit for the consumer and provide extra value as well as more product for the money.

There are several advantages to bonus pack promotions. First, they give marketers a direct way to provide extra value without having to get involved with complicated coupons or refund offers. The additional value of a bonus pack is generally obvious to the consumer and can have a strong impact on the purchase decision at the time of purchase. Second, due to the simplicity of the presentation of a percentage of extra quantity, consumers generally prefer a bonus pack over an equivalent price discount.[30] Third, bonus packs can also be an effective defensive manoeuvre against a competitor's promotion or introduction of a new brand. By loading current users with large amounts of its product, a marketer can often remove these consumers from the market and make them less susceptible to a competitor's promotional efforts. Fourth, bonus packs may result in larger purchase orders and favourable display space in the store if relationships with retailers are good.

A limitation is that bonus packs usually require additional shelf space without providing any extra profit margins for the retailer, so the marketer can encounter problems with bonus packs if trade relationships are not good. A second limitation is that bonus packs may appeal primarily to current users who probably would have purchased the brand anyway, or to promotion-sensitive consumers who may not become loyal to the brand.

PRICE-OFF DEALS

Another consumer sales promotion tool is the direct **price-off deal**, which reduces the price of the brand. Price-off reductions are offered right on the package through specially marked price packs, as shown in Exhibit 14-13. Typically, price-offs take 10–25 percent off the regular price, with the reduction coming out of the manufacturer's profit margin, not the retailer's. Keeping the retailer's margin during a price-off promotion maintains its support and cooperation.

Marketers use price-off promotions for several reasons. First, since price-offs are controlled by the manufacturer, it can make sure the promotional discount reaches the consumer rather than being kept by the trade. Second, price-off deals present a readily apparent value (e.g., much like a bonus pack) to shoppers, especially when they have a reference price point for the brand and thus recognize the value of the discount.[31] Third, communication of price-offs attracts attention and the amount saved can be a strong influence at the point of purchase when price comparison shopping and evaluation occurs. Finally, price-off promotions can also encourage consumers to purchase larger quantities, pre-empting competitors' promotions and leading to greater trade support.

A limitation is that price-off promotions may not be favourably received by retailers, since they can create pricing and inventory problems. Another limitation concerns retailer acceptance of packages with a specific price shown, thereby taking price decision-making control away from retailers. Also, price-off deals appeal primarily to regular users instead of attracting non-users, much like bonus packs. Finally, the federal government has regulations regarding the conditions that price-off labels must meet and the frequency and timing of their use.

Retailers offer price-offs and, due to the flexible implementation of price-offs within their stores, they need to adhere to laws regarding the timing of price-offs. The Competition Bureau periodically investigates retail price discounts, and one recent case involved major department stores not offering mattresses at a regular price for a substantial period of time before putting them on sale. The retail marketing of this product category is known for extensive price competition and careful inventory logistics to manage profit margins. In this case, both retailers cooperatively provided information to resolve the investigation.[32]

Services offer discounts, as seen with the Milestones "Wednesday Date Night" promotion. The casual dining chain offered patrons dinner for two for $50 when ordering off a special menu. Radio communicated the promotion and the dating theme prevailed in the execution. Management saw the promotion as a way of distinguishing the brand from competitors like The Keg and Moxies.[33] Electronic products are discounted, and the ebook market experienced fierce discounting since publishers only paid royalties on paper editions. Publishers discounted

Exhibit 14-12   Bonus packs provide more value for consumers.

ArmorAll Products Corporation

Exhibit 14-13   Examples of price-off packages.

KAO Brands Company

ebooks to $10 when selling hardcover equivalents for $30.[34] Vehicles are discounted via money reduced from the manufacturer or from the retail dealer. The offer is a straight discount or a special finance rate that is regularly scheduled or used to clear inventory. The Honda Civic, Canada's number one selling car for many years in a row, faced aggressive marketing efforts of numerous brands that coveted the title. In response, Honda immediately increased its advertising and provided a low-interest financing option to retain its market share.[35]

Swiss Chalet found an innovative way to bypass fees to promotion brokers like Groupon by inventing the Rotisserie Channel on Rogers, where viewers could watch chicken roasting. The channel offered promotional codes that could be redeemed for deals at the restaurant's Internet site and Facebook page. Chicken orders rose 30 percent and 13,000 coupons were downloaded in the first week; the number of Facebook fans grew 12,000 from a base of 70,000 in a month; Rogers claimed 1 million households watched the channel for an average of eight minutes; and the media placement won a Cannes Silver Lion![36]

EVENT MARKETING

It is important to make a distinction between *event marketing* and *event sponsorships,* as the two terms are often used interchangeably yet refer to different activities. **Event marketing** is a promotion where a company or brand is linked to an event or where a themed activity is developed for the purpose of creating experiences for consumers and promoting a brand. Pepsi associated its Mountain Dew brand with various action sports (Exhibit 14-14) . Event marketing allows marketers to develop integrated marketing programs including promotional tools that create experiences for consumers in an effort to associate their brands with certain lifestyles and activities. Marketers use events to distribute samples as well as product information,

Exhibit 14-14   Pepsi established the AST Dew Tour.

Courtesy of Mountain Dew, © 2009 PepsiCo, Inc. Used with permission.

or to let consumers actually experience the product. Data from one study indicated that stronger brand attitude and brand equity resulted from experiences with marketing events.[37] Some events provide experiential elements associated with the brand with some experimenting with virtual reality. For example, the *Game of Thrones* exhibit at the South by Southwest music festival placed viewers on the 700-foot ice wall of Castle Black.[38]

An **event sponsorship** is an integrated marketing communications activity where a company develops actual sponsorship relations with a particular event (e.g., concert, art exhibition, cultural activity, social change initiative, sports event) and provides financial support in return for the right to display a brand name, logo, or advertising message and be identified as a supporter of the event. Part of the confusion between these two promotions arises from the fact that event marketing takes place as part of a company's event sponsorship. We describe examples of event marketing here and address event sponsorship in Chapter 15 as it relates more closely to public relations activities.

Perrier fans who signed up online (SocietePerrier.ca) received a special PIN code that allowed them to attend "soirees" at upscale nightclubs. These exclusive parties occurred in branded VIP areas and offered a free Perrier cocktail, a taxi voucher, and complimentary Perrier all evening. Each club displayed bar mats, coasters, stir sticks, candles, and tent cards describing the three cocktails. Brand reps gave out business cards to invite registrations, and other communication occurred with wild postings via email, Facebook, and Twitter.[39]

Red Bull Crashed Ice (RBCI) is a marketing event established by the sports energy drink marketer 15 years ago that features a new sport, ice cross downhill, which combines downhill skiing, hockey, and boardercross (a snowboard competition). Competitors decked out with full hockey gear race in groups of four to the bottom of the track, with the top two moving on to the next round. A series of events in North America and Europe culminates with the world champion being crowned at the final competition. With cheering spectators along the walls of the track drinking Red Bull and big-screen viewing available, the electric atmosphere is a true party for all who attend. Red Bull attracts and provides considerable digital media coverage throughout the season. RBCI is one of many events the brand created beyond advertising that "Red Bull Gives You Wings." With worldwide distribution, the energy drink creates or sponsors events in other sports, games, and music to promote the brand. So it is not too surprising to find RBCI primarily featured in the land of snow and ice where hockey rules.[40]

Fido sponsored a series of underground artsy events/parties called Fido Sessions that centred on art, culture, design, and fashion in areas where young, hip people live, work, and play. The location and the events remained a mystery until two giant dolls eventually joined after eight days of getting closer together. The four-storey, white, featureless dolls had no identity except for a text shortcode where people could learn about the events. A team of people dressed as mini dolls deployed the message as well through wild postings, chalk art, night projections, tree hangers, and flying cloud logos. The lack of branding fit with the underground nature of the events—although participants could order drinks with Fido phones.[41]

 # Trade Sales Promotion

Trade sales promotions that managers may select from to develop a strategic sales promotion plan were identified in Figure 14-1. Each of these options can assist the promotional planner in achieving the objectives with resellers. The objectives are similar to those of consumer sales promotions since the promotion acts as a behavioural incentive. We now review objectives and strategic options for trade sales promotions.

OBJECTIVES OF TRADE SALES PROMOTION

Like consumer promotions, sales promotion programs targeted to the trade should be based on well defined objectives and measurable goals and a consideration of what the marketer wants to accomplish. Typical objectives for promotions targeted to marketing intermediaries such as wholesalers and retailers include obtaining distribution for new products, maintaining trade support for established brands, building retail inventories, and encouraging retailers to display established brands.

Obtain Distribution for New Products   Trade promotions are often used to encourage retailers to give shelf space to new products. Essentially, this translates into a trial purchase objective like we saw with consumer promotions. Manufacturers recognize that only a limited amount of shelf space is available in supermarkets, drugstores, and other major retail outlets. Thus, they provide retailers with financial incentives to stock new products. While trade discounts or other special price deals are used to encourage retailers and wholesalers to stock a new brand, marketers may use other types of promotions to get them to push the brand. Merchandising allowances can get retailers to display a new product in high-traffic areas of stores, while incentive programs or contests can encourage wholesale or retail store personnel to push a new brand.

Maintain Trade Support for Established Brands   Trade promotions are often designed to maintain distribution and trade support for established brands. Clearly, this objective is akin to a repeat purchase objective that we saw with consumer sales promotion. Brands that are in the mature phase of their product life cycle are vulnerable to losing wholesale and/ or retail distribution, particularly if they are not differentiated or face competition from new products. Trade deals induce wholesalers and retailers to continue to carry weaker products because the discounts increase their profit margins. Brands with a smaller market share often rely heavily on trade promotions, since they lack the funds required to differentiate themselves from competitors through media advertising. Even if a brand has a strong market position, trade promotions may be used as part of an overall marketing strategy.

Build Retail Inventories   Manufacturers often use trade promotions to build the inventory levels of retailers or other channel members, another form of repeat purchasing. There are several reasons why manufacturers want to load retailers with their products. First, wholesalers and retailers are more likely to push a product when they have high inventory levels rather than storing it in their warehouses or back rooms. Building channel members' inventories also ensures they will not run out of stock and thus miss sales opportunities.

Manufacturers of seasonal products offer large promotional discounts so that retailers will stock up on their products before the peak selling season begins. This enables the manufacturer to smooth out seasonal fluctuations in its production schedule and pass on the inventory carrying costs to retailers or wholesalers. When retailers stock up on a product before the peak selling season, they often run special promotions and offer discounts to consumers to reduce excess inventories.

Encourage Retailers to Display Established Brands   Another objective of trade-oriented promotions is to encourage retailers to display and promote an established brand. This could be analogous to increased consumption as seen with consumer sales promotion objectives, since the retailer demonstrates increased commitment. Marketers recognize that purchase decisions are frequently made in the store and promotional displays are an excellent way of generating sales. An important goal is to obtain retail store displays of a product away from its regular shelf location. A typical supermarket has numerous display areas (e.g., end of aisle, checkout counter) and marketers want their products displayed in these areas to increase the probability of shopper exposure. Manufacturers often use multifaceted promotional programs to encourage retailers to promote their products at the retail level. For example, a manufacturer will combine its advertising and consumer sales promotions and offer them at the same time as the trade promotion. For example, Exhibit 14-15 shows a promotion calendar that WD-40 provides to retailers showing all facets of the IMC plan for the year.

TRADE SALES PROMOTION STRATEGY OPTIONS

Manufacturers use a variety of trade promotion tools as inducements for wholesalers and retailers. Next we examine the most often used types of trade promotions and factors that marketers must consider in using them. These promotions include trade allowances, point-of-purchase displays, cooperative advertising, contests and incentives, sales training programs, and trade shows.

Exhibit 14-15   Example of WD-40's trade promotion and media support calendar.

Courtesy of the WD-40 Company

Trade Allowances   Probably the most common trade promotion is some form of **trade allowance**, a discount or deal offered to retailers or wholesalers to encourage them to stock, promote, or display the manufacturer's products. Types of allowances offered to retailers include buying allowances, promotional or display allowances, and slotting allowances.

Buying Allowances   A buying allowance is a deal or discount offered to resellers in the form of a price reduction on merchandise ordered during a fixed period. These discounts are often in the form of an **off-invoice allowance**, which means a certain per-case amount or percentage is deducted from the invoice. A buying allowance can also take the form of *free goods*; the reseller gets extra cases with the purchase of specific amounts (for example, one free case with every 10 cases purchased).

Promotional (Display) Allowances   Manufacturers often give retailers allowances or discounts for performing certain promotional or merchandising activities in support of their brands. These merchandising allowances can be given for providing special displays away from the product's regular shelf position, running in-store promotional programs, or including the product in an ad. The manufacturer generally has guidelines or a contract specifying the activity to be performed to qualify for the promotional allowance. The allowance is usually a fixed amount per case or a percentage deduction from the list price for merchandise ordered during the promotional period.

Slotting Allowances   Retailers often demand a special allowance for agreeing to accept a new product. *Slotting allowances* (also called *stocking allowances, introductory allowances,* or *street money*) are fees retailers charge for providing a slot or position to accommodate the new product. Slotting fees range from a few hundred dollars per store to $50,000 or more for an entire retail chain. Manufacturers that want to get their products on the shelves nationally can face substantial slotting fees. Retailers charge slotting fees because of their power and the limited availability of shelf space in supermarkets relative to the large numbers of products introduced each year. Large manufacturers with popular brands are less likely to pay slotting fees than smaller companies that lack leverage in negotiating with retailers.

A study examined the views of manufacturers, wholesalers, and grocery retailers regarding the use of slotting fees. Their findings suggest that slotting fees shift the risk of new product introductions from retailers to manufacturers and help apportion the supply and demand of new products. They also found that slotting fees lead to higher retail prices, are applied in a discriminatory fashion, and place small marketers at a disadvantage.[42]

Strengths of Trade Allowances   Buying allowances are used for several reasons. They are easy to implement and are well accepted, and sometimes expected, by the trade. They are also an effective way to encourage resellers to buy the manufacturer's product, since they will want to take advantage of the discounts being offered during the allowance period. Manufacturers offer trade discounts expecting wholesalers and retailers to pass the price reduction through to consumers, resulting in greater purchases.

Promotional allowances provide brands that sell in retail stores the opportunity to have specialized displays to feature their product. Promotional allowances also permit a brand to obtain a favourable end-of aisle location or another prominent place where high traffic occurs, thus ensuring greater exposure. Brands would like to reproduce the imagery from their commercials or any other advertising vehicle where brand recognition at the point of sale is required. Extensive and elaborate displays would also reinforce the positioning strategy of the brand and contribute to its overall brand development. Thus, retailers prefer to merchandise a brand that has a consistent and well thought out strategy so that they will not be stuck with inventory unsold due to a lack of in-store communication.

Limitations of Trade Allowances   Marketers give retailers these trade allowances so that the savings will be passed through to consumers in the form of lower prices, but companies claim that only one-third of trade promotion discounts actually reach consumers because one-third are lost in inefficiencies and another one-third are pocketed by the trade. Moreover, marketers believe that the trade is taking advantage of their promotional deals and misusing promotional funds.

For example, retailers and wholesalers do **forward buying**, where they stock up on a product at the lower deal or off-invoice price and resell it to consumers after the marketer's promotional period ends. Another common practice is **diverting**, where a retailer or wholesaler takes advantage of the promotional deal and then sells the product purchased at the low price to a store outside its area or to an intermediary that resells it to other stores.

In addition to not passing discounts on to consumers, forward buying and diverting create other problems for manufacturers. They lead to huge swings in demand that cause production scheduling problems and leave manufacturers and retailers always building toward or drawing down from a promotional surge. Marketers also worry that the system leads to frequent price specials, so consumers learn to make purchases on the basis of what's on sale rather than developing any loyalty to their brands.

Point-of-Purchase Displays   Point-of-purchase (POP) displays are an important promotional tool because they can help advertisers obtain more effective in-store merchandising of products. In one sense, a display acts as a "medium" since it is an important method of transmitting an advertising-like message when consumers are making a purchase decision. We put *medium* in quotes because often displays do not appear to be typical media; in fact, however, a display shares similar characteristics with place-based media (discussed in Chapter 13). A display is also viewed as a sales promotion since the messages include a sales promotion and most require the participation of retailers that necessitates a payment from the advertiser that is often recorded as a trade promotion expense in the budget.

Figure 14-7 identifies different types of point-of-purchase displays. Exhibit 14-16 shows an award-winning POP display created by E-B Display Co. to promote the SeaKlear family of pool and spa treatments. The display holds 16 different pool and spa products and the unique octagonal shape allows for 360 degrees of display availability in a relatively small footprint. The display also has large graphic areas to educate consumers regarding specific uses and applications and help them make their purchase decisions.

The Point of Purchase Advertising Institute (POPAI) is an organization serving marketers and retailers worldwide with research information and examples of successful display innovations. Its main study classifies purchases into four groups, as shown in Figure 14-8, with the following breakdown: specifically planned, 24 percent; generally planned, 15 percent; substitutes (i.e., brand switch), 6 percent; and unplanned, 55 percent. The top two reasons provided by respondents on why an unplanned purchase occurred were that they remembered they needed or wanted an item once in the store, and that they took advantage of a sale.[43] These results suggest the importance of displays as they prompt existing beliefs through recognition at the point of purchase.

Exhibit 14-16   This award-winning point-of-purchase display plays an important role in the merchandising of SeaKlear pool and spa treatments.

Courtesy of SeaKlear

Figure 14-7   Types of point-of-purchase displays

On-premise sign	Pre-assembled display	Display card	TV display
Window display	Display shipper	Shelf sign	LED board
Modular display rack	Wall display	Stand-up rack	End-of-aisle display

Figure 14-8   Classification of purchases for POPAI research

Specifically Planned	Purchases the shopper specifically identified by name in a pre-shopping interview and bought.
Generally Planned	Purchases that were referred to generically in a pre-shopping interview and bought on impulse.
Substitutes	Purchases that were specifically identified by name in a pre-shopping interview, but actual purchase reflected a substitute of brand or product.
Unplanned	Purchases that were not mentioned in the pre-shopping interview and bought on impulse.

Strengths of Point-of Purchase Displays   It is easy to see why advertisers use point-of-purchase displays extensively. The main purpose is to reach the target audience while they are making the brand choice, so naturally a message or promotion attempting to influence a decider appears imperative. Indeed, deterministic benefits can be communicated just prior to purchase as these benefits may become salient only during the final choice decision. Innovations in point-of-purchase options—such as video screens at cash registers—attempt to bring the emotion of television commercials to the store environment so that consumers feel the same way just prior to purchasing the product. Since consumers are in the process of shopping, point-of-sale media have a tremendous opportunity for attracting the attention of the target audience. In general, consumers are seeking additional information or sensory experience as they consider the product selection. Coverage objectives also can be achieved by distributing point-of-purchase displays across the country through retail chains. For example, a brand could have displays in virtually all grocery stores at the same time with placement agreed among personnel at a few head offices. A key strength of point-of-sale display is that it is communicating to virtually all people who are considering purchasing in a particular category except those going direct through the Internet or catalogues. It may be difficult to suggest that point-of-purchase displays are universally involving. However, it appears reasonable to suggest that if the target audience has not avoided a certain part of the store and also paid attention to a display, then the potential is strong that the relevant messages will resonate such that a sufficient amount of consideration will be given. And finally, the absolute cost and CPM are generally reasonable compared to other media options.

Limitations of Point-of Purchase Displays   Despite these strengths, point-of-purchase displays have limitations. One source of discontent for a consumer is that the shopping experience may be hindered by numerous promotional messages. Consumers have complete control over where they want to look in a store, how much time they prefer to stay in one area, and whether they want to look at any form of in-store communication. If an advertiser desires to be there, so does the competition. The clutter consumers feel while watching television or reading a magazine may be felt in the purchase environment. Processing of point-of-sale media requires a consumer's presence in the retail environment. So, except for circumstances where a consumer is entering an establishment repeatedly, the likelihood of an advertiser achieving sufficient frequency through this medium is quite limited. Finally, a marketer is reliant on the retailer, who may not install or set up the display correctly and also requires payment.

Cooperative Advertising   A trade promotion that has consumer effects like point-of-purchase display is **cooperative advertising**, where the cost of advertising is shared by more than one party. There are three types of cooperative advertising. Although the latter two are not exactly trade promotion, they involve the trade at times and are consistent with cooperative advertising.

The most common form of cooperative advertising is **vertical cooperative advertising**, in which a manufacturer pays for a portion of the advertising a retailer runs to promote the manufacturer's product and its availability in the retailer's place of business. Manufacturers generally share the cost of advertising run by the retailer on a percentage basis (usually 50/50) up to a certain limit. Major manufacturers threatened to withdraw this funding to retailers who discounted the manufacturer's brand too substantially. Fierce price competition led retailers to market well-known brands as discounted loss leaders, much to the dismay of the brand managers who felt it significantly cheapened the brand image.[44]

The amount of cooperative advertising the manufacturer pays for is usually based on a percentage of dollar purchases. If a retailer purchases $100,000 of product from a manufacturer, it may receive 3 percent, or $3,000, in cooperative advertising money. Large retail chains often combine their co-op budgets across all of their stores, which gives them a larger sum to work with and more media options.

Cooperative advertising can take on several forms. Retailers may advertise a manufacturer's product in a newspaper ad or a flyer insert featuring a number of different products, and the individual manufacturers reimburse the retailer for their portion of the ad. Or the ad may be prepared by the manufacturer and placed in the local media by the retailer. Research supports the value of retail ads like these as advertised products are purchased in greater numbers and dollar amounts.[45] Exhibit 14-17 shows a cooperative ad format that retailers can use by simply inserting their store name and location.

Horizontal cooperative advertising is advertising sponsored in common by a group of retailers or other organizations providing products or services to the market. For example, automobile dealers who are located near one another often allocate some of their ad budgets to a cooperative advertising fund. **Ingredient-sponsored cooperative advertising** is supported by raw materials manufacturers; its objective is to help establish end products that include the company's materials and/or ingredients. Perhaps the best known, and most successful, example of this type of cooperative advertising is by Qualcomm (Exhibit 14-18).

Contests and Incentives Manufacturers may develop contests or special incentive programs to stimulate greater selling effort and support from reseller management or sales personnel. Contests or incentive programs can be directed toward managers who work for a wholesaler or distributor as well as toward store or department managers at the retail level. Manufacturers often sponsor contests for resellers and use prizes such as trips or valuable merchandise as rewards for meeting sales quotas or other goals.

Manufacturers devise contests or special incentives that are targeted to the sales personnel of the wholesalers, distributors/dealers, or retailers. These trade promotions are typically tied to product sales, new account placements, establishing promotional programs, or merchandising efforts (e.g., displays). These salespeople are an important link in the distribution chain because they are familiar with the market, frequently in touch with the customer (whether it be another reseller or the ultimate consumer), and more numerous than the manufacturer's own sales organization. In sales contests, salespeople can win trips or valuable merchandise for meeting certain goals established by the manufacturer. The incentive programs may involve cash payments made directly to the retailer's or wholesaler's sales staff to encourage them to promote and sell a manufacturer's product. These payments are known as **push money** or *spiffs*. For example, an appliance manufacturer may pay a $25 spiff to retail sales personnel for selling a certain model or size.

While contests and incentive programs can generate reseller support, they can also be a source of conflict between retail sales personnel and management. Retailers want to maintain control over the selling activities of their sales staff. They don't want their salespeople devoting an undue amount of effort to trying to win a contest or receive incentives offered by the manufacturer, or becoming too aggressive in pushing products that serve their own interests instead of the product or model that is best for the customer.

Sales Training Programs   Products sold at the retail level may require knowledgeable salespeople who provide consumers with information about the features and benefits of various brands and models (e.g., cosmetics, appliances, computers). Manufacturers provide assistance to retail salespeople through training sessions so that retail personnel can increase their knowledge of a product line and understand how to sell the manufacturer's product. A manufacturer's salesforce also provides sales training assistance to retail employees. The reps provide ongoing sales training as they come into contact with retail sales staff on a regular basis and can update them on changes in the product line. Sales reps often provide resellers with sales manuals, product brochures, reference manuals, videos, and product-use demonstrations. These selling aids are also presented to customers.

Exhibit 14-17   This Bridgestone Golf ad is an example of vertical cooperative advertising.

Courtesy of Bridgestone Golf Inc.

Exhibit 14-18   Qualcomm uses ingredient sponsored advertising for its Snapdragon processor.

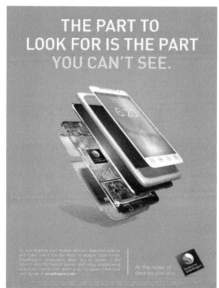

©2013 QUALCOMM Incorporated

Trade Shows   A forum where manufacturers display their products to current as well as prospective consumers and resellers is a **trade show**. Similar shows are also directed to consumers. According to the Center for Exhibition Industry Research, nearly 107 million people attend over 13,000 trade and consumer shows each year in the United States. Mexico, and Canada, and the number of exhibiting companies reached 1.9 million.[46] Trade shows are a major opportunity to display one's product lines and interact with customers. They are often attended by important management personnel from large retail chains as well as by distributors and other reseller representatives.

A number of promotional functions can be performed at trade shows, including demonstrating products, identifying new prospects, gathering customer and competitive information, and even writing orders for a product. Trade shows are particularly valuable for introducing new products, because resellers are often looking for new merchandise to stock. Shows can also be a source of valuable leads to follow up on through sales calls or direct marketing. The social aspect of trade shows is also important. Companies use them to entertain key customers and to develop and maintain relationships with the trade. An academic study demonstrated that trade shows generate product awareness and interest and can have a measurable economic return.[47] The International Consumer Electronics Show (CES) is a forum for launching all sorts of technological products (Exhibit 14-19).

Exhibit 14-19   The CES is a very popular trade show.

© Consumer Electronics Association

IMC Planning: Strategic Use of Sales Promotion

Rather than being seen as separate activities competing for a firm's promotional budget, advertising and sales promotion should be viewed as complementary tools. When properly planned and executed to work together, advertising and sales promotion can have a persuasive communication effect that is greater than the unique strengths of each promotional mix element operating independently. Successful integration of advertising and sales promotion requires decisions concerning the allocation of the budget to each area, the coordination of the ad and sales promotion creative themes, the brand equity implications of sales promotion, and the measurement of sales promotion effectiveness.

BUDGET ALLOCATION

It is difficult to say just what percentage of a firm's overall promotional budget should be allocated to advertising versus consumer and trade promotions. The allocation will likely vary according to a brand's stage in the product life cycle as there are different promotional objectives. In the introductory stage, a large amount of the budget may be allocated to sales promotions (e.g., sample, coupon) to induce trial. In the growth stage, however, the budget may be used primarily for advertising to stress brand differences for positioning purposes and heighten brand awareness with sales promotion taking on a lesser role.

When a brand moves to the maturity stage, advertising is primarily a reminder for brand awareness with sales promotion taking on a stronger role. Consumer sales promotions may be needed periodically to maintain consumer loyalty, attract new users, and protect against competition. Trade promotions are needed to maintain shelf space and accommodate retailers' demands for better margins as well as encourage them to promote the brand. When a brand enters the decline stage, most of the promotional support will probably be removed and expenditures on sales promotion are unlikely.

Some brands never move on to the decline stage as their equity remains for decades or even longer. In this situation, promotional managers examine the competitive dynamics of new entrants or old foes who may attempt to steal share, and plan accordingly with appropriate allocations based on the objectives determined to ward off the threat. Alternatively, long-standing brands remain so as they periodically encourage new cohorts of consumers to try the brand with the right balance of advertising and sales promotion initially, and then retain them with an alternative ratio as these consumers remain loyal to the newfound brand.

CREATIVE THEMES

To integrate the advertising and sales promotion programs successfully, the theme of consumer promotions should be tied in with the advertising and positioning theme wherever possible. Sales promotion tools should attempt to communicate a brand's unique attributes or benefits and to reinforce the sales message or campaign theme. In this way, the sales promotion effort contributes to the consumer franchise-building effort for the brand.

At the same time, media advertising and other IMC tools should be used to draw attention to a sales promotion program. An excellent example of this is the award-winning "Win 500 Flights" sweepstakes that was developed by MasterCard and its promotional agency. The sweepstakes was developed under the umbrella of MasterCard's "Priceless" campaign theme and thus was designed to deliver on the brand promise that MasterCard understands what matters most to consumers—in this case travelling for any reason at all. The primary objective of the integrated marketing campaign was to drive MasterCard use during the summer travel season. Consumers using their MasterCard were automatically entered in the sweepstakes for a chance to win 500 airline tickets to anywhere, which could be shared with family and friends. Media advertising—including television, print, out-of-home, and online banner ads—was used to promote the sweepstakes, along with an extensive public relations campaign. Exhibit 14-20 shows one of the print ads used to promote the "Win 500 Flights" sweepstakes.

Exhibit 14-20   MasterCard used media advertising to promote its sweepstakes.

Courtesy of MasterCard

MEDIA SUPPORT

Media support for a sales promotion program should be coordinated with the media program for the ad campaign since it is used to deliver sales promotion materials (e.g., coupon, contest entry form, premium offer). It is also needed to inform consumers of a promotional offer as well as to create awareness and favourable attitudes toward the brand. By using advertising in conjunction with a sales promotion program, marketers can make consumers aware of the brand and its benefits and increase their responsiveness to the promotion. Consumers are more likely to redeem a coupon or respond to a price-off deal for a brand they are familiar with than one they know nothing about.

Using a promotion without prior or concurrent advertising can limit its effectiveness and risk damaging the brand's image. If consumers perceive the brand as being promotion dependent or of lesser quality, they are not likely to develop favourable attitudes and long-term loyalty. Conversely, the effectiveness of an ad can be enhanced by a sales promotion as well for a reciprocal effect. Dove's Men+Care launch relied on multiple IMC tools requiring coordination for success (Exhibit 14-21). To coordinate their sales promotion programs and media exposure effectively as in cases like Dove, companies get their sales promotion agencies significantly involved throughout the advertising and promotional planning process.

Exhibit 14-21   Dove Men+Care coordinated advertising, sales promotion, and other IMC tools for its launch.

Courtesy of Unilever

BRAND EQUITY

The increasing use of sales promotion led to concerns that sales promotion can be offered with too much frequency or with too valuable an economic offering. In short, a constantly promoted brand may lose perceived value. Consumers purchase a brand because they pay less, they get a premium, or they have a coupon, rather than basing their decision on a favourable attitude developed over time. Ultimately, they switch to another brand when the promotional incentive is not available. Competitive situations with extensive sales promotion suggest that managers should consider balancing equity building and non-equity building promotions during the year.

One study examined whether price promotions affect pretrial evaluations of a brand.[48] The study found that offering a price promotion is more likely to lower a brand's evaluation when the brand has not been promoted previously compared to when it has been frequently promoted; that price promotions are used as a source of information about a brand to a greater extent when the evaluator is not an expert but does have product or industry knowledge; and that promotions are more likely to result in negative evaluations when they are uncommon in the industry. The findings suggest that marketers must be careful in the use of price promotions as they may inhibit trial of a brand in certain situations.

Marketers must consider both the short-term impact of a promotion and its long-term effect on the brand. The ease with which competitors can develop a retaliatory promotion and the likelihood of their doing so should also be considered, as shown in Figure 14-9. Marketers must be careful not to damage the brand franchise with sales promotions or to get the firm involved in a promotional battle that erodes the brand's profit margins and threatens its long-term existence. Marketers are tempted to resort to sales promotions to deal with declining sales and other problems when they should examine such other aspects of the marketing program as channel relations, price, packaging, product quality, or advertising.

Figure 14-9   Competitive dynamic of sales promotion

	Our Firm	
All Other Firms	**Cut back promotions**	**Maintain promotions**
Cut back promotions	Higher profits for all	Market share goes to our firm
Maintain promotions	Market share goes to all other firms	Market share stays constant; profits stay low

MEASURING SALES PROMOTION EFFECTIVENESS

Elizabeth Gardener and Minakshi Trivedi offer a communications framework to evaluate sales promotion strategies on specific criteria. Borrowing from advertising applications, and using four communications goals—attention, comprehension (understanding), persuasion, and purchase—the researchers showed the impact of four promotional tools and everyday low pricing (EDLP) on each goal.[49] A tabulation of the results is shown in Figure 14-10, and an implication is that the framework we summarized in Chapter 5 is applicable for evaluating sales promotion, and other IMC tools.

Figure 14-10   Conceptual framework analysis

		Communication Factors			
		Attention/ Impression	Communication/ Understanding	Persuasion	Purchase
Sales	FSI coupons	✓✓	✓✓✓	✓✓	✓✓
Promotions	On-shelf coupons	✓✓✓	✓✓✓	✓✓✓✓	✓✓✓
	On-pack promotions	✓	✓	✓✓✓	✓
	Bonus packs	✓✓✓	✓✓	✓✓	✓✓
	EDLP	✓	✓✓	✓✓	✓
Promotional tendency to fulfill factor: ✓✓✓ = Strong; ✓✓ = Moderate; ✓ = Weak					

Many of the advertising research methods and measures discussed in Chapter 9 are also applied to sales promotions. For example, pre- or post-surveys can be used to assess brand awareness or brand attitude (i.e., attribute or benefit beliefs) associated with the sales promotion. Furthermore, assessment of attention, cognitive, and emotional responses of the promotional offer can also be measured with the appropriate method. From a behavioural standpoint, measurement of switching and loyalty is assessed with scanner data. Other aspects of behaviour can be measured by counting the number of inquiries or coupon redemptions. Sales promotions communicated and executed online and within social media—such as contest entries or participation with premiums—are readily tracked. Tracking of commentary in social media provides guidance of attitudinal effects of the promotional offer and potential resulting equity effects upon the brand.

Learning Objectives Summary

LO1   Explain the role of sales promotion in a company's integrated marketing communications program and examine why it is increasingly important.

Sales promotion is an incentive and an acceleration tool that is offered as value to any person or organization within the overall marketing system, such as consumers and any trade members like wholesalers and retailers. Marketers have been allocating more of their promotional dollars to sales promotion to influence purchasing behaviour. Reasons for this shift include the strategic importance of sales promotions, reaching a specific target audience, promotional sensitivity, declining brand loyalty, brand proliferation, short-term focus of managers and accountability of promotional managers, and power of retailers and the competition.

LO2   Identify the objectives, strategy, and tactical components of a sales promotion plan.

The objectives of sales promotion are often stated in terms of brand behaviour such as trial, re-trial, and repeat purchases, or product category trial or re-trial. Sales promotions can be characterized as either consumer franchise-building (CFB) promotions or nonfranchise-building (non-FB) promotions. The former contribute to the long-term development and reinforcement of brand identity and image; the latter are designed to accelerate the purchase process and generate immediate increases in sales. Sales promotions can also be looked at in terms of their incentive characteristic, which can be immediate or delayed. Tactical considerations for sales promotion include the amount of the incentive, the timing of the promotion in terms of schedule and duration, and the distribution of the sales promotion.

LO3   Describe consumer sales promotion strategy options and evaluate the factors to consider in using them.

A number of consumer sales promotion techniques were examined, including sampling, coupons, premiums, contests and sweepstakes, refunds and rebates, bonus packs, price-off deals, and event marketing. The characteristics of these promotional tools were discussed, along with their strengths and limitations. Promotional planners can select any combination of these tools for their IMC plans to achieve trial and repeat purchasing objectives and execute them with appropriate tactics to reinforce brand communication effects. The selection of the right combination reinforces the direction of the plan to influence both customers and non-customers.

LO4   Describe trade sales promotion strategy options and evaluate the factors to consider in using them.

The chapter identified trade promotions including trade allowances, point-of-purchase displays, cooperative advertising, contests and incentives, sales training programs, and trade shows. These have different terminology and are similar to consumer sales promotion, but are intended for resellers who are in a similar buying process with more business-like objectives instead of personal objectives. Strategic and tactical decisions for each sales promotion are as critical here as they are with consumer promotions.

 LO5   Apply key IMC issues related to sales promotion decisions.

Advertising and sales promotion should be viewed as complementary tools. When planned and executed properly, advertising and sales promotion can produce a strong communication and behavioural effect that is greater than the response generated from either promotional mix element alone. To accomplish this, marketers coordinate budgets, advertising and promotional themes, media scheduling and timing, and target audiences. Extensive sales promotion can result in diminished brand equity when marketers become too dependent on the use of sales promotion techniques and sacrifice long-term brand position and image for short-term sales increases. Many industries experience situations where competitors use promotions extensively and it becomes difficult for any single firm to cut back on promotion without risking a loss in sales. Overuse of sales promotion tools can lower profit margins and threaten the image and even the viability of a brand.

Review Questions

1. What are the differences between consumer and trade sales promotion? Discuss the role of each in a marketer's IMC program.
2. Discuss how sales promotion can be used as an acceleration tool to speed up the sales process and maximize sales volume.
3. Post-secondary educational institutions do not usually use sales promotions. Consider which ones could be used and identify the target audience in which they could be effective.
4. Explain why a brand might devote more of its budget to trade sales promotions than to consumer sales promotions.
5. Explain why it is important for sales promotion to contribute to brand equity. In what circumstances will brand equity enhancement not be a priority?

Applied Questions

1. Explain how the consumer sales promotions identified in Figure 14-1 can be executed with Internet media.
2. What are the differences between consumer franchise-building and nonfranchise-building promotions? Find an example of a promotional offer you believe contributes to the equity of a brand and explain why.
3. Phone service providers do not offer premiums all that often. Identify good ones for different brands.
4. Consider all the trade sales promotions that a major brand like Tassimo would use and explain how they would be effective or ineffective for increasing sales of the machine and the coffee discs.
5. Why does the Red Bull Crashed Ice event not use the imagery from the advertising with the slogan "Red Bull Gives You Wings"?

CHAPTER FIFTEEN

Public Relations

LEARNING OBJECTIVES

LO1   Recognize the role of public relations in the promotional mix.

LO2   Explain how to compile a public relations plan.

LO3   Examine how public relations is generated through media publicity and argue the strengths and limitations of media publicity·

LO4   Illustrate how public relations is managed through corporate advertising.

LO5   Apply the ideas of public relations within the development of an IMC plan.

Brand Activation at TIFF

Usually the red carpet at the Toronto International Film Festival (TIFF) is reserved for the movie stars, but TIFF executives rolled out an impressive recruitment drive for sponsors. TIFF is held in September and it is the largest film festival in the world after the famous Cannes festival held in May each year. TIFF is a non-profit organization and it doubled its sponsorship revenue the past five years and hit $13 million with a concerted effort to attract lucrative brands for which TIFF could fulfill sponsorship requirements. Despite the drive for more sponsors, satisfied brands have returned, such as Visa for 18 years, RBC for eight years, Moët & Chandon for eight years, L'Oréal for four years, McDonald's for four years (as the official coffee!), and brands like Bell, Hugo Boss, and Jackson-Triggs for an undisclosed number of years. The recent trend is toward innovative on-site brand activation strategies by these brands.

L'Oréal's beauty team prepped the celebrities, offered tips to fans on social media, and put together a video montage featuring people using their new product line. L'Oréal also set up a location where consumers could use the brand's virtual reality app to test out different make-up looks they could apply on themselves. L'Oréal claimed its sales grow noticeably after a TIFF sponsorship. Visa established the Visa Screening Room at the Elgin Theatre where fans who asked question to stars on Twitter could hear the replies from the stars. The theatre featured the Infinite and Infinite Privilege private lounges for cardholders. It also enabled fans to have their photo taken, to be shown later on the giant on-location screen and shared by fans on social media. Finally, Visa opened a story-telling game in its Infinite Story Booth where fans could contribute after the initial premise was begun by actor Morgan Freeman. Visa expected that consumers would find the experiences unique and hoped the activities would contribute to greater acceptance of its new Infinite line of credit cards.

Bell created a four-storey building featuring a spa, technology demonstrations, an interactive green screen, and a DJ performing on the rooftop that overlooks the red carpet. One year, RBC set up a prize-cube of LED panels that showed TIFF content, RBC social media, and promotional gifts. Another year, RBC set up its "Someday Studio" consistent with its current advertising. The studio allowed people to have their photo taken for social media and to enjoy additional interaction with the stars, and facilitated private screenings that were offered as contest prizes. Hugo Boss offered a pocket square for $45 as a fundraiser for lower income youth to attend TIFF and learning programs.

McDonald's created a fun immersive experience where consumers waved their mobile device on specially marked products to access video that showed parodies of movies that featured coffee beans with titles, such as *Beanheart; Lawrence of Arabica; The Grinding; The Good, The Bad, and the Brewed*; and *Donnie Darkroast*. TIFF gave Moët & Chandon the title of "the champagne of cinema" since it offered a glass to all the stars prior to their film debut. It put forth a nine litre bottle, had celebrities sign it, and subsequently auctioned it off with proceeds going to TIFF. Finally, newcomer Samsung promoted its latest gadgets and let consumers give them a spin by creating user-generated content. It also created the Samsung TIFF Emerging Directors Showcase in which young directors, after receiving guidance from famous directors, received a gadget to make a short film that would be streamed to the brand's billboard in Dundas Square. It sure looks like TIFF has a blockbuster in its new recruitment efforts.

Sources: Susan Krashinsky, "TIFF Gives Sponsors the Hollywood Treatment," *The Globe and Mail*, September 12, 2014; Josh Kolm, "Going Bigger With Activations: TIFF's Repeat Sponsors," *Strategy*, September 8, 2014; Josh Kolm, "Visa's Infinite Social Push at TIFF," *Strategy*, September 8, 2014; Sonya Fatah and Val Maloney, "Brands Get Red Carpet Ready," *Strategy*, September 14, 2015; Rebecca Harris, "McDonald's Beans Hit the Small Screen for Toronto Film Fest," *Marketing Magazine*, September 11, 2015; Michelle Dipardo, "Samsung and TIFF Put Festival-Goers in the Centre of the Action," *Marketing Magazine*, September 10, 2015; Danny Kucharsky, "Moet & Chandon Uncorks Media Opportunities at TIFF," *Marketing Magazine*, September 24, 2015.

Question:

1. Why are Tiff sponsors interested in brand activation at this cultural event?

Public relations, publicity, and corporate advertising all have promotional program elements that may be of great benefit to marketers. They are integral parts of the overall promotional effort that must be managed and coordinated with the other elements of the promotional mix. However, these three tools do not always have the specific objectives of product and service promotion, and often involve other methods of reaching their target audiences. Typically, these activities are designed more to change attitudes toward an organization or issue than to promote specific products or affect behaviours directly. Aspects of these tools assist the marketing of products periodically for firms with a new view of the role of these tools. This chapter explores the domain of public relations, its related topic of publicity generated by news media, corporate advertising, the strengths and limitations of each, and the process by which they are planned and implemented.

Public Relations

What is public relations (PR)? How does it differ from other elements of marketing communication discussed thus far? Perhaps a good starting point is to define what the term *public relations* has traditionally meant, to introduce its new role, and to compare it to publicity.

TRADITIONAL VIEW OF PR

Public relations is the management function that evaluates public attitudes, identifies the policies and procedures of an organization with the public interest, and executes a program of action and communication to earn public understanding and acceptance.[1] In this definition, public relations requires a series of stages: the determination and evaluation of public attitudes, the identification of policies and procedures of an organization with a public interest, and the development and execution of a marketing communication program designed to achieve public understanding and acceptance. An effective public relations program continues over months or even years as it builds public trust between citizens and the organization.

This definition reveals that public relations involves marketing communication activities beyond advertising and promotion that are designed to influence consumers to buy a product. The PR program may also involve promotional program elements previously discussed but use them in a different way. For example, a press release may announce a new product launch or an organizational change, a special event may be organized to create goodwill in the community, and advertising may be used to state the firm's position on an issue. In addition, the *management* aspect means that public relations is not limited to business management but extends to other types of organizations, including government and non-profit institutions.

While the tools of public relations have changed significantly over the past two decades with digital media, practitioners believe the fundamental purpose remains consistent over time with the PR function being required to align corporate communications with the organization's goals. However, the digital media clutter and demand for timely messages puts pressure on PR professionals to deliver top-notch writing with visual storytelling. One avenue where this is especially important is the social media image and presence of the corporate leaders as their personal brand becomes the face of the corporate brand. The changes contribute to the significance of marketing and PR working in tandem.[2]

NEW ROLE OF PR

An increasing number of marketing-oriented companies have established new responsibilities for public relations. PR takes on a broader (and more marketing-oriented) perspective, designed to promote the organization as well as its products and/or services. For example, McDonald's continued its efforts at eroding Tim Hortons' hold on the coffee market by sponsoring minor hockey, a long-time sponsorship activity of the leading coffee retailer in the quick service market.[3] Big events like the Grey Cup allow brands to present their public image (Exhibit 15-1).

The way companies and organizations use public relations might best be viewed as a continuum. On one end of the continuum is the use of PR from a traditional perspective, where it is viewed as a non-marketing function whose primary responsibility is to maintain mutually beneficial relationships between the organization and its publics. In this case, customers or potential customers are only part of numerous publics—employees, investors, neighbours, special interest groups, and so

Exhibit 15-1 The Grey Cup stage offered a venue for public relations activities.

© Valentino Visentini/Alamy

on. Marketing and public relations are separate departments; if external agencies are being used, they are separate agencies. At the other end of the continuum, public relations is considered primarily a marketing communications function. Public relations reports to marketing and all non-customer relationships are perceived as necessary only in a marketing context.[4] Thus, in these organizations, the PR becomes much closer to a marketing function than a traditional PR function.

In the new role of public relations, strong marketing and PR departments work closely together, blending their talents to provide the best overall image of the firm and its product or service offerings. In fact, marketing and public relations are complementary functions; each makes unique contributions that are mutually supportive to building and maintaining the many relationships essential for achieving organizational goals.[5] This position is consistent with our perspective that public relations is an important part of the IMC process, contributing in its own way but also in a way consistent with marketing goals.

PUBLICITY

Publicity is the generation of news about a person, good, service, idea, or organization that appears in broadcast or print media, and now on the Internet. It often seems that publicity and public relations occur at the same time or in close proximity. For example, Maple Leaf Foods faced the absolute worst experience in its long history when consumers perished or became severely ill from eating its contaminated meat products. In response, CEO Michael McCain took a strong leadership role in reassuring Canadians. Maple Leaf Foods used extensive public relations activities at varying stages of the identification and solution of the problem to address the situation such that consumers were exposed to both publicity (i.e., information coming from the media) and public relations (i.e., information coming from Maple Leaf Foods itself). McCain met with journalists on a regular basis at press conferences and acted as the main spokesperson in corporate advertising messages that communicated the actions the company had undertaken to prevent further problems. Maple Leaf's message reached some Canadians on TV while others viewed it on YouTube. By all accounts, Maple Leaf Foods regained its image as a strong Canadian brand (see Exhibit 15-2).

Exhibit 15-2 Maple Leaf Foods responded well to a crisis and the brand remains strong.

© Ryan Remiorz/The Canadian Press

In other instances, it seems that publicity is the end result or effect of the public relations effort. Because marketers like to have as much control as possible over the time and place where information is released, they often provide the news media with pre-packaged material. One way to do this is with a **video news release (VNR)**, a piece produced by publicists so that stations can air it as a news story. Print media publications also receive material from brands with the intention of getting an editorial story written. Internet bloggers receive similar communication and follow-up with published stories. In all cases, the media source presents and endorses the message, giving it more credibility, and consumers may see it as publicity for the originating organization.

Given the above scenarios, there are two significant characteristics that distinguish the unique role and effects of public relations and publicity.

1. Publicity typically lasts for a short period of time. The communication effect of an article in the newspaper about a new product may last for a few weeks. Positive or negative publicity communicated by consumers in social media can recede a few days later. In both cases, the long-term communication effects can be minimal. Alternatively, public relations is a concerted program, with several exposures extending over a period of time with the intention of establishing lasting communication effects.
2. Public relations is usually controlled by the firm or its agent and designed to provide positive information. Companies or brands use many different tools with an attempt to influence public opinion. Publicity, on the other hand, is not always positive and is not always under the control of, or paid for by, the organization.

Negative publicity arising within the news occurs when brands are accurately or inaccurately criticized, often by a special interest group. For example, Greenpeace brought to light P&G's use of palm oil in a product and linked the company to issues of deforestation. The consumer products giant immediately responded with a new deforestation policy. Observing this situation, one expert highlighted three steps brands should take: (1) prepare by examining the critic's public communication (e.g., newsletter, website, social media), (2) take corrective action by informing stakeholders with relevant facts, and (3) counterattack if necessary with opinion leaders (e.g., academics, scientists) and a customized message delivered with the most optimal media given the problem.[6]

On the other hand, positive publicity arises and brands can take advantage of these unexpected events. For example, while pretending to be an employee working at the drive-through, one loyal Tim Hortons customer proposed to his fiancée, who was ordering. The slick video production placed in social media looked completely professional but the coffee chain's involvement amounted to giving permission for the recording to occur. And in case the romantic side of you was wondering, she said "Yes" with considerable Tim Hortons branding all around the happy couple![7]

IMC Perspective 15-1 identifies the positive publicity the fundraising activities for ALS received, resulting in significant financial gains.

ALS ICE BUCKET CHALLENGE PUBLICITY

During the hot summer of 2015, millions of people worldwide cooled off by dumping a bucket of ice water on their heads—go figure! It all started with the first dunk by Peter Frates, a former captain of the Boston College baseball team who suffered from amyotrophic lateral sclerosis, or ALS as most people know it. After Peter dumped his bucket, he challenged famous sports figures to do the same in his online video. From there it took off as many others joined in by challenging their friends and family; and as more and more people saw the videos of people dousing themselves, the donations started rolling in.

Companies jumped in as well, with one notable challenge from Volvo Canada executives who performed the feat and challenged their competitors at BMW, Mercedes-Benz, and Audi. Volvo received an invitation from ALS Canada and enjoyed its first-mover advantage as one of the first Canadian companies to join in. According to a Volvo Canada marketing executive, the company has a loyal social media following that is strongly interested in the social causes the company supports.

Despite its being a wonderful feel-good story with money raised for further research, critics chimed in with their opinion that "It's a gimmick since the task is too silly for a serious disease"—which one author quickly dispelled, countering that most everyday people needed a very enjoyable way of

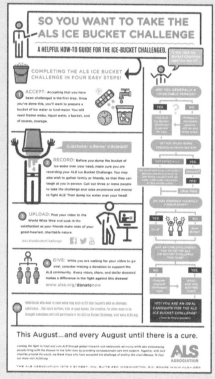

© The ALS Association

participating. When critics said, "It's too simple for commitment," he responded with the point that something easy to understand gets people to participate more. When they argued that, "It's too narcissistic—people should donate quietly in private," he pointed out the importance of sharing information and experiences to generate greater funds. Finally, to the claim that the success of the ALS Ice Bucket Challenge deprived other charities of money, he responded that instead it had expanded the donation market and gained new donors.

One commentator summarized a number of lessons from the ALS Ice Bucket Challenge for similar organizations to learn from.

1. Time it right. The combination of relaxed summertime and warmer temperatures made everyone want to give it a try.

[Continued on next page]

[IMC Perspective 15-1 continued]

2. Make it personal. Having the challenge start with one individual suffering from ALS gave it a personal tone everyone could believe in.

3. Add celebrities. Famous people added some source attractiveness to the message that everyone accepted.

4. Keep it simple. The task's simplicity made it possible for anyone.

5. Make it real. The "schoolyard tease" prompted everyone to want to lay down the gauntlet to their friends and family.

6. Focus on the goal. The call to action kept the focus on encouraging donations while doing the challenge.

7. Reputation is key. While the ALS Society kept a low profile in the past, it had no negatives to hold it back once the publicity exploded.

The Ice Bucket Challenge proved to be a resounding success from a financial standpoint as the ALS Society of Canada raised $17 million. Facebook counted over 28 million who posted content, or commented on or liked others' posts about the Challenge, and individuals uploaded 2.4 million campaign videos worldwide. Other research showed that Facebook accounted for 28 percent of all fundraising referrals. Clearly, publicity is a powerful motivator for participation and donations once the winning formula is discovered.

Sources: Susan Krashinsky, "Ice Bucket Challenge," *The Globe and Mail*, August 22, 2014, p. B5; Mathew Chung, "Brands Grab Hold of Ice Buckets," *Strategy*, August 21, 2014; Phillip Haid, "Stop Throwing Water on the Ice Bucket Challenge," *Marketing Magazine*, August 21, 2014; Steve Olenski, "Seven Marketing Lessons From the ALS Ice Bucket Challenge," *Forbes*, August 22, 2014.

Question:

1. How might other charities be able to build momentum for fundraising like the ALS Ice Bucket Challenge?

 ## Public Relations Plan

Public relations is an ongoing process requiring formalized policies and procedures for dealing with problems and taking advantage of opportunities. A public relations plan is required, as with an advertising plan or a sales promotion plan. Moreover, the public relations plan needs to be integrated into the overall marketing communications program. A public relations plan can be structured like the other IMC tools we have discussed thus far. It starts with a situation analysis and includes decisions with respect to target audiences, behavioural objectives, communication objectives, strategy, and tactics. Once the plan is written, marketers should ask themselves the questions inFigure 15-1 to determine whether their public relations plan is complete. Given the broad nature of public relations, there are options for each part of the plan that we now discuss.

SITUATION ANALYSIS

Elements of the situation analysis from the marketing plan or IMC plan are also in the public relations plan. An additional key piece of information is a current assessment of people's attitudes toward the firm, its product or service, or specific issues beyond those directed at a product or service. Why are firms so concerned with the public's attitudes? One reason is that these attitudes may affect sales of the firm's products. Also, no one wants to be perceived as a bad citizen. Corporations exist in communities where their employees work and live. Negative attitudes carry over to employee morale and may result in a less-than-optimal working environment internally and in the community.

Organizations planning for PR typically survey public attitudes for a few reasons. First, initial public attitudes become the starting point in the development of programs designed to maintain favourable positions or change unfavourable ones. Second, these initial attitudes might signal a significant potential problem, which allows the firm to handle it proactively.

Third, it will be much easier for the PR team to gain the support it needs to address this problem. Fourth and finally, optimal communication can occur if the firm understands a problem completely.

Figure 15-1   Ten questions for evaluating public relations plans

1. Does the plan reflect a thorough understanding of the company's business situation?
2. Has the PR program made good use of research and background sources?
3. Does the plan include full analysis of recent editorial coverage?
4. Do the PR people fully understand the product's strengths and weaknesses?
5. Does the PR program describe several cogent, relevant conclusions from the research?
6. Are the program objectives specific and measurable?
7. Does the program clearly describe what the PR activity will be and how it will benefit the company?
8. Does the program describe how its results will be measured?
9. Do the research, objectives, activities, and evaluations tie together?
10. Has the PR department communicated with marketing throughout the development of the program?

DETERMINE RELEVANT TARGET AUDIENCES

The target audiences for public relations efforts vary, and as we saw earlier each will have unique behavioural and communication objectives. These audiences may be internal or external to the firm. **Internal audiences** are connected to the organization and include the employees of the firm, shareholders and investors, local community members, and suppliers and customers. **External audiences** are those people who are not closely connected with the organization (e.g., the public at large), and may include the media, educators, civic and business organizations, and governments. It may be necessary to communicate with both groups on an ongoing basis for a variety of reasons and it is likely that those who are not in the target audience will in fact receive the message, like we observe with product advertising.

Employees of the Firm   Maintaining morale and showcasing the results of employees' efforts are often prime objectives of the public relations program. Organizational newsletters, notices on intranet resources, mail/email, and annual reports are methods used to communicate with these groups. Personal methods of communicating may be as formal as an established grievance committee or as informal as an office party. Other social events such as corporate sports teams, picnics, or cause-related or community activities are also used to create goodwill. Home Depot's employees readily supported the company's commitment to helping with youth homelessness with repair projects and development programs. In total, employees devoted 60,000 volunteer hours to 285 projects in one year.[8]

Shareholders and Investors   An annual report like the one in Exhibit 15-3 provides shareholders and investors with financial information regarding the firm. While this is one purpose, annual reports are also a communications channel for informing this audience about why the firm is or is not doing well, future plans, and other information that goes beyond numbers. In addition to current shareholders, potential investors, financial advisers, and lending institutions may be relevant target audiences for annual reports and other related corporate information to keep them abreast of new developments since they offer the potential for new sources of funding. By creating a favourable image and goodwill in the financial community, the firm makes itself attractive to potential share purchasers and investors, leading to investments for working capital and research and development. Other means of communication include meetings, video presentations, direct mail, and digital media.

Exhibit 15-3   Annual reports serve a variety of purposes.

Courtesy of GE

Community Members   People who live and work in the community where a firm is located or doing business are often the target of public relations efforts. Such efforts may involve ads informing the community of activities that the organization supports, like cleaning up water supplies. Demonstrating to people that the organization is a good citizen with their welfare in mind may also be a reason for communicating to these groups. BMO supported local community soccer when it saw data indicating that the participation level for soccer is 33 percent, double the rate of hockey. The growth of soccer in this country, the link between the Canadians who play soccer and BMO customers, and the fact that the bank is present in most communities motivated BMO to devote 20 percent of its corporate marketing to soccer activities, with 40 percent directed toward sponsorship.[9] For over two decades, Boston Pizza has celebrated Valentine's Day by selling heart-shaped pizza (Exhibit 15-4) with proceeds going to worthy causes. Currently, the proceeds go to Boston Pizza Foundation Future Prospects, which donates funds to organizations like Big Brothers Big Sisters, which offers mentoring programs and whose members act as strong role models for children.[10]

Exhibit 15-4   Boston Pizza's community oriented efforts help children.

Hand-out/Boston Pizza International Inc./Newscom

Suppliers and Customers   An organization wishes to maintain *goodwill* with its suppliers as well as its consuming public. Consumers likely demonstrate loyalty with a company that is socially conscious. For example, "Extraordinary, Authentic Nourishment for All" is Campbell Canada's contribution with an emphasis to alleviate hunger, prepare better meals, and eat nutritious food. The company worked with the Food Bank and donated 1 million pounds of food each year and agreed to provide additional funds, supplies, and personnel support in the future. A new ambitious task is Campbell's product, Nourish, a complete meal in an easy-open can requiring no heating or water for preparation, which is suitable for food banks and disaster relief situations. The product features a protein-rich grain developed by federal government scientists and is the result of committed Campbell's employees who wanted the company to do more for hunger. Campbell's placed ads in multiple media and used public relations to encourage Canadians to participate in the cause by sharing on Facebook, tweeting on Twitter, or watching the "Story of Nourish" on YouTube, with each step leading to a donation of one can of Nourish. After five weeks, the campaign achieved a total of 85,000 additional cans donated. Campbell's placed additional funds into the food system with each can sold to consumers, who were also encouraged to buy and donate to food banks.[11]

The Media   Perhaps one of the most critical external publics is the media, which determine what is read in a newspaper or seen on TV, and how this news will be presented. Because of the media's power, they should be informed of the firm's actions. Companies issue press releases and communicate through conferences, interviews, and special events. The media are generally receptive to such information so long as it is handled professionally; reporters are always interested in good stories. Tesla relied on communicating only with the media for consumers to receive news stories about the electric car company for many years as it grew from a startup to selling 25,000 cars globally. One recent approach included a tour across the United States to feature its network of charging stations, thinking news media would feature the story. Executives expected that regular advertising would be warranted in future as sales grew.[12]

Educators   A number of organizations provide educators with information regarding their activities. The Canadian Marketing Association and the Promotional Products Association of Canada, among others, keep educators informed in an attempt to generate goodwill as well as exposure for their causes. These groups and major corporations provide information regarding innovations, state-of-the-art research, and other items of interest.

Civic and Business Organizations   Local non-profit civic organizations also serve as gatekeepers of information. Companies' financial contributions to these groups, speeches at organization functions, and sponsorships are all designed to create goodwill. Corporate executives' service on the boards of non-profit organizations also generates positive public relations. Home Depot's Orange Door project enlisted the assistance of numerous community groups with expertise on the needs of homeless youth. Home Depot is significantly involved with Volunteer Canada.

Governments   Public relations often attempts to influence government bodies directly at both local and national levels. Successful lobbying may mean immediate success for a product, while regulations detrimental to the firm may cost it millions. For example, Tweed Marijuana Inc. is based near Ottawa in Smiths Falls and is licensed by Health Canada to grow medical marijuana. It argues that regulated firms such as itself should be the only ones legally permitted to sell the product to recreational users if usage laws are revised in future. Tweed's position originated from the growth of illegal outlets in Canada and the experiences of American states.[13]

BEHAVIOURAL OBJECTIVES

The framework for behavioural objectives discussed in Chapter 5 is readily applicable for public relations. Recall that behavioural objectives are trial purchase, repeat purchase, shopping, or consumption. No matter what target audiences are selected in the prior step, an astute marketer will know that it is important to understand the type of behaviour desired as a result of the communication. The idea of a "purchase" seems incongruous for certain public relations situations, so the marketer may have to view this as the target audience "buying into the idea" or another specific behaviour in order to carefully define the objectives. The RBC Blue Water Project encourages considerable involvement of citizens to actively improve Canada's water supply, such as drinking less bottled water and volunteering with watershed cleanups. The initiative includes social media where citizens discuss water issues and raise awareness.[14]

Similarly, Bell pledged money in support of mental health and initiated the "Let's Talk" idea to communicate the importance of mental health. Bell invited Canadians to talk about mental health by talking to or texting loved ones, with $0.05 going to the cause for every form of communication. Widespread support for the cause included TV, radio, before-and-after print ads, in-store, billboard, out-of-home digital, digital at the Bell Centre, rink boards, banner ads, Internet site (LetsTalk.Bell.ca), and public relations via many TV shows. Messages featured notable celebrity spokespersons who had publicly communicated their personal stories. For 2016, Canadians hit 126 million calls, texts, tweets and shares that contributed $6.3 million to mental health.[15]

COMMUNICATION OBJECTIVES

The communication objectives of Chapter 5 can similarly be used for public relations. Communication objectives include category need, brand awareness, brand attitude, and purchase intention. Each of these can be the focus of the public relations plan, although slight modifications are needed. For example, the "brand" may in fact be the corporation itself or a new product that is talked about in a press release. In addition, the notion of a "category" has to be adjusted. Some target audiences want to be affiliated with "good corporate citizens" that are responsible to the community, the environment, or another issue. Often, the "category" will be related to the particular topic or the public relations message content.

Awareness is critical for a brand and is important for the organization. Organizations support social causes because the exposure of their name will enhance the general public's recall and recognition at a later point in time. For example, Cisco created a social networking site (OneMillionActsOfGreen.com) focused on environmental sustainability (Exhibit 15-5). The site fit the technology company's global "Human Network" campaign and allowed Canadians to post their "green" ideas such as riding a bike to work. Cisco partnered with the CBC for outreach to encourage participation by having the program featured on *Hockey Night in Canada* and *The Hour*. Extensive direct communication occurred with online video, newsletters, and email. Organizations jumped onboard by encouraging employee involvement. At the time of the award, the site had hit 1.3 million acts from 33,000 registered users, with 186,000 unique visitors having spent an average of 17 minutes on the site. Positive publicity through numerous articles in media and comedians spoofing the initiative proved such remarkable acceptance that this Canadian idea went global.[16]

Exhibit 15-5   Cisco's distinctive corporate imagery is the face of many of its public relations activities.

© Caro/Alamy

We started off by highlighting the importance of existing attitudes of the target audiences. Clearly, then, the public relations plan should have a specific section that outlines the attitude change or modification desired. It should also illustrate the key motives addressed and what attributes or benefits of the firm or product the message should focus on. Automobile firms are good examples of where positive publicity via news media is desired and encouraged. New product launches include media releases and feature interviews for articles appearing in the car section, a weekly feature in national and most large daily newspapers. Further positive press occurs with trade shows that occur in major cities, which typically get coverage resulting in framing initial consumer attitudes about a vehicle model.[17]

STRATEGY

The strategy decisions for public relations are twofold, as we saw with advertising: message and media. The primary message decisions concern the degree to which the message will have a marketing or corporation focus, and the creative associated with the message. We will briefly describe issues related to this decision in this section. Like advertising, there are a number of options to disseminate the message—news media, advertising media, and events. We will discuss these in more detail in the next major section.

Message Content   Public relations activities designed to support marketing objectives are referred to as **marketing public relations (MPR)** functions.[18] Marketing objectives that may be aided by public relations activities include raising awareness, informing and educating, gaining understanding, building trust, giving consumers a reason to buy, and generating consumer acceptance. These points are consistent with the behavioural and communications objective of our framework. Marketing public relations can be used effectively in the following ways: building marketplace excitement before media advertising breaks, creating news about a new advertising or promotional campaign, introducing a product with little or no advertising, providing information to influential opinion leaders, defending products at risk with a message of reassurance, and constructively promoting a product.

IKEA Canada's innovative activities successfully increase media exposure and exemplify marketing public relations. In fact, a key source of zany ideas originated from its consumer surveys—shopping at IKEA was seen as a bit stressful for couples so it hosted relationship seminars on Valentine's Day. IKEA's Relax event noted the fact that Canadians found relaxing to be more naughty than sex. This prompted IKEA to issue instructions for making a restful home along with an "IKEA Adrenaline Index" on the website featuring humorous questions to assess people's stress levels. Store openings and catalogue launches both host ambitious events to ensure the media cover the story. IKEA sees the value of these activities and invests heavily, with a 50 percent budget increase and each event receiving a $500,000 allotment.[19]

The historical role of public relations is one of communicating a favourable image of the corporation as a whole. The domain of this image, or reputation management, concerns every facet of how the organization interacts with its social, economic, political, and charitable constituents, in addition to the general public locally, nationally, and internationally. For example, during GM's difficulties during the recession, the U.S. division moved toward the "Rebirth of the American Car" message in its ads to restore its corporate reputation, but the Canadian version of the ad made no reference to the bankruptcy and did not have American imagery (i.e., the U.S. flag). Instead, a message of reinvention that highlighted the strong brands and models emphasized a more positive and future-oriented direction. According to the advertising director for GM Canada, "We are thinking it is coming across in the right tone and manner—acknowledging the situation we are in and moving forward in a positive direction."[20]

Given the two broad directions of the actual message, marketing versus corporate, an organization has to decide the relative degree of the message's impact over the course of a year or even longer, as public relations tends to have a lasting communication effect. Too much of a focus in either direction and the organization loses the opportunity to communicate fully. As concluded earlier, a balance between using public relations for marketing purposes and corporate purposes appears to be a viable approach for many organizations.

Message Creativity   We will discuss the tools for public relations shortly; however, in deciding what message to communicate, the marketer is faced with the decision as to whether the creative strategy of advertising or other IMC tools should be adopted for public relations. On the one hand, there is the argument that all communications should have a common look and feel to them. To counter this, one could argue that unique target audiences with a specific message should have an appropriate associated creative.

Honda developed the "Blue Skies for Our Children" theme and directed messaging to children with TV, print, online banner, POS ads, elevator wraps, and digital brochures as part of an Earth Day launch of Honda's long-standing commitment to the environment. Its website (HondaBlueSky.ca) contained three sections—Yesterday, Today, and Tomorrow—with the latter showing interviews of children to symbolically show what Honda plans to do beyond its current Insight vehicle.[21]

Message Delivery   In the course of defining public relations and publicity, and explaining the content of a public relations plan, we have generally described two mechanisms for the delivery of the message. News media outlets are available and the media have the choice of publishing or not publishing the materials that organizations submit for their consideration. Alternatively, organizations can turn to other options where they control the dissemination of the message through different types of corporate advertising opportunities in which the organization is responsible for the costs, much like regular product advertising we have covered thus far.

During Toyota's major recall a few years ago, the U.S. division halted sales of the affected models and its advertising response to the negative publicity focused on its reputation for quality. The managing director for Toyota Canada released a four-minute online video that clarified the situation in Canada. Since the problem of the gas pedal sticking affected only one Canadian model, the extensiveness of the problem was not as severe. However, Toyota Canada did offer a "voluntary safety improvement campaign," where it replaced the parts on models recalled only in the United States even though the parts on the Canadian versions were manufactured with different materials and would not cause problems. Toyota Canada executives also appeared on television news shows. Extensive communication occurred on the company's website, and Toyota directly contacted all owners to explain the solution and how it planned to resolve the problem (Exhibit 15-6).[22]

Exhibit 15-6   Toyota's brand remains strong after handling its PR challenge

© JuliusKielaitis/Shutterstock

TACTICS

The choice of news media or corporate advertising dictates the types of tactics employed. When using news media, a marketer would need to know how to make a media presentation, whom to contact, how to issue a press release, and what to know about each medium addressed, including TV, radio, newspapers, magazines, and direct-response advertising. In addition, decisions have to be made regarding alternative media such as news conferences, seminars, events, and personal letters, along with insights on how to deal with government and other legislative bodies. Because this information is too extensive to include as a single chapter in this text, we suggest students peruse additional resources for further insight.

For corporate advertising, numerous considerations have been addressed in the advertising message chapters (Chapters 7 and 8) and the media chapters (Chapters 10 to 13). We can see an application of this with a recent effort by McDonald's, which publicly emphasized its commitment to Ronald McDonald House Charities (RMHC) Canada to increase people's knowledge of the charity's mission and inspire greater donations. The creative showed how Ronald McDonald Houses provided a place for families to stay while their children received treatment. The storyline showed the point of view of each parent and the child with emotional scenes that evoked heightened empathy. Media included TV, cinema, print, radio, out-of-home and in-store. The combination of paid and donated media yielded 13 million impressions. Both measures improved with a 59 percent lift in understanding and a 72 percent lift in donations. [23]

PUBLIC RELATIONS EFFECTIVENESS

As with the other promotional program elements, it is important to evaluate the effectiveness of the public relations efforts. In addition to determining the contribution of this program element to attaining communications objectives, the evaluation tells management how to assess what has been achieved through public relations activities, measure public relations achievements quantitatively, and judge the quality of public relations achievements and activities.

In measuring the effectiveness of PR, one author suggests three approaches: (1) media content analysis that systematically and objectively identifies the messages appearing in the media and analyzes the content to determine trends and perceptions relevant to the product or brand, (2) survey research that quantitatively assesses consumers' attitudes toward the product or brand, and (3) marketing mix modelling that draws data from multiple sources and integrates them to provide insight into the process.[24] Figure 15-2 summarizes a number of exposure measures that may be used to assess the effects of PR programs through news media that are consistent with the first step.

Others suggest comprehensive approaches like we have seen with advertising. Walter Lindenmann says three levels of measures are involved: (1) the basic, which measures the actual PR activities undertaken; (2) the intermediate, which measures audience reception and understanding of the message; and (3) the advanced, which measures the perceptual and behavioural changes that result.[25] As a reminder, this approach is entirely consistent with the exposure, processing, and communications effects model described in Chapter 4. Finally, from another point of view regarding effectiveness, Home Depot did not publicize its Orange Door Project beyond in-store displays and its Internet site, and viewed effectiveness in terms of how well it contributed to eradicating the homelessness problem.

Figure 15-2   Criteria for measuring the effectiveness of PR

A system for measuring the effectiveness of the public relations program has been developed by Lotus HAL. The criteria used in the evaluation process follow:

1. Total number of impressions over time
2. Total number of impressions on the target audience
3. Total number of impressions on specific target audiences
4. Percentage of positive articles over time
5. Percentage of negative articles over time
6. Ratio of positive to negative articles
7. Percentage of positive/negative articles by subject
8. Percentage of positive/negative articles by publication or reporter
9. Percentage of positive/negative articles by target audience

Media Publicity

In this section, we discuss how organizations can achieve public relations communication objectives through publicity generated through the media. We refer to this as *media publicity*; that is, publicity that the firm attempts to control by influencing the media to report an organization's story to the public. In this section, we review different ways to reach the media and consider the strengths and limitations of this option. When considering the significance of this assessment, keep in mind that consumers receive the message through all the media discussed thus far, so the effects can be varied.

MEDIA OPTIONS

A number of media options are available for communicating with the media, including press releases, press conferences, exclusives, and interviews. Of course, this effort could be for naught if the media decides not to report the information and the message would not reach the intended target audience.

Press Releases   One of the most important publics is the press, and information delivered must be factual, true, and of interest to the medium as well as to its audience. The source of the **press release** can do certain things to improve the likelihood that the "news" will be disseminated, such as ensuring that it reaches the right target audience, making it interesting, and making it easy to pass along. The information in a press release won't be used unless it is of interest to the users of the medium it is sent to, so financial institutions should issue press releases to business trade media and to the editor of the business section of a general-interest newspaper, for example. Press releases are typically a simple one-page text summary of the story a company wishes to be published in news media, along with background and contact information. Digital transmission of these includes a photo and links to other digital resources.

Additional information and presentation material may accompany the press release, making the whole presentation appear to be a complete ad campaign to influence the media. Companies release studies and will provide copies of the report and supporting links to associated data. They may also provide collateral material in both print and digital formats with video and still images. For example, Fairmont Hotels owns many historic properties and views their ownership as an important stewardship. Fairmont released a study indicating the value travellers place on visiting luxury accommodations and its responsibility in maintaining the historical authenticity of its properties. Exhibit 15-7 shows the cover of the document illustrating the classic architecture. The digital press release included a standard text summary, a short video clip, stunning photos, and other useful information supporting Fairmont's stewardship positioning.[26]

Exhibit 15-7   Fairmont publicly acknowledges its responsibility regarding its historic properties

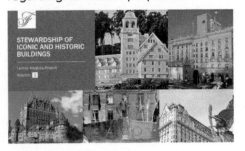

© FRHI Hotels & Resorts

Press Conferences We are all familiar with **press conferences** held by political figures. While used less often by organizations and corporations, this form of delivery can be very effective as scenes of corporate spokespeople will be viewed on television. The topic must be of major interest to a specific group before it is likely to gain coverage. Companies often call press conferences when they have significant news to announce, such as the introduction of a new product or advertising campaign. On a local level, community events, local developments, and the like may receive coverage. Sports teams use this tool to attract fan interest when a new star is signed. The development of technology has allowed the delivery of press conferences to occur remotely where reporters receive the presentation and participate in the follow-up question and answer session.

Exclusives Although most public relations efforts seek a variety of channels for distribution, an alternative strategy is to offer one particular medium exclusive rights to the story if that medium reaches a substantial number of people in the target audience. Offering an **exclusive** may enhance the likelihood of acceptance, and sometimes the media actually use these exclusives to promote themselves.

Interviews Interviews occur on a variety of news or information shows. Usually, someone will raise specific questions and a spokesperson provided by the firm will answer them. Often, the president or owner will give interviews when there is important news about the firm.

STRENGTHS OF MEDIA PUBLICITY

Credibility Public relations communication through media publicity is not perceived in the same light as advertising. Consumers understand that most advertising is directly paid for by the sponsoring organization. Obviously exceptions occur, such as public service announcements heard on the radio, for example. The fact that the media are not being compensated for providing the information may lead receivers to consider the news more truthful and credible. For example, an article in a newspaper or magazine discussing the virtues of ibuprofen may be perceived as much more credible than an ad for a particular brand of ibuprofen. And while firms present the media with news releases or press kits and incur a cost, consumers generally perceive the media source to be reasonably trustworthy with its reporting expertise.

Endorsement Information from media publicity may be perceived as an endorsement by the media vehicle in which it appeared. Automotive awards presented in magazines such as *Motor Trend* carry clout with potential car buyers, and car companies often advertise their achievements. A number of auto manufacturers advertised their high customer satisfaction ratings reported by J.D. Power & Associates, an independent research firm specializing in satisfaction research. Taken together, the credibility and endorsement effects constitute a significantly positive media image.

Cost In both absolute and relative terms, the cost of media publicity is very low, especially when the possible effects are considered. While a firm can employ public relations agencies and spend millions of dollars, for smaller companies, this form of communication may be the most affordable alternative available. Public relations programs require little more than the time and expenses associated with putting the program together and getting it distributed, yet they still accomplish their objectives.

Avoidance of Clutter Because they are typically perceived as news items, media publicity messages are not subject to the clutter of ads. A story regarding a new product introduction or breakthrough is treated as a news item and is likely to receive attention.

Reach Specific Audiences Because certain products appeal only to small market segments, it is not feasible to implement advertising and/or promotions to reach them. If the firm does not have the financial capabilities for promotional expenditures, the best way to communicate to these groups is through media publicity.

Image Building Effective public relations helps to develop a positive image for the organization. The examples discussed thus far have indicated strong image-building capabilities with proactive public relations. News about a product may in itself serve as the subject of an ad. Exhibit 15-8 demonstrates how General Mills used favourable publicity from a variety of sources to promote the importance of whole grains in a healthy diet and promote the use of whole grains in its cereal.

Exhibit 15-8   General Mills capitalizes on positive publicity.

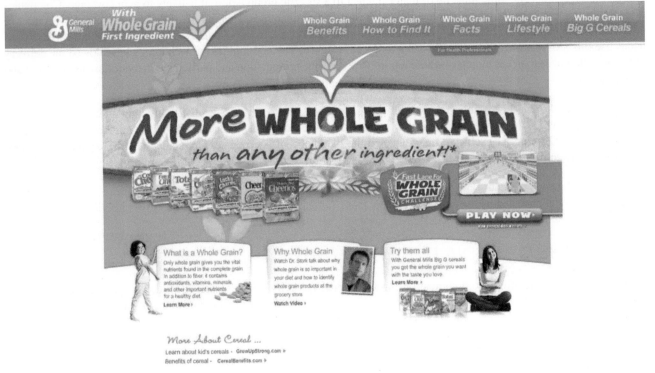

Used with permission of General Mills Marketing Inc. (GMMI)

Frequency Potential   Another strength of publicity is the frequency of exposure it generates. For example, a successful public relations activity could generate exposure in multiple media (i.e., broadcast, print, Internet).

LIMITATIONS OF MEDIA PUBLICITY

Brand/Corporate Identification   Perhaps the major disadvantage of media publicity is the potential for not completing the communications process. While these messages can break through the clutter of advertising messages, the receiver may not make the connection to the brand or corporate source.

Inconsistent Message   Media publicity may also misfire through mismanagement and a lack of coordination with the marketing department. When marketing and PR departments operate independently, there is a concern of inconsistent communications or redundancies in efforts.

Timing   Timing of media publicity is not always completely under the control of the marketer. Unless the press thinks the information has very high news value, the timing of the exposure of the press release content to the public is entirely up to the media—if it gets released at all. Thus, the information may be released earlier than desired or too late to achieve communication effects.

Accuracy   The information contained in a press release can get lost in translation—that is, it is not always reported the way the provider wishes it to be. As a result, inaccurate information, omissions, or other errors may result.

Corporate Advertising

For the purposes of this text, we use the term **corporate advertising** for marketing communication implemented for the direct benefit of the corporation rather than its products or services. This method of delivery is selected over media publicity since the firm exerts complete control over the communication process rather than relying on the media acceptance for publicity to occur. Marketers seek attainment of corporate advertising's objectives by implementing image advertising, cause-related advertising, and sponsorship. Cause-related advertising and sponsorship have moved to the product level in communications strategy, so the distinction has blurred. We cover these three topics in this section, but first we look at the purpose of corporate advertising, namely the management of corporate reputation.

CORPORATE REPUTATION

Earlier in this text we suggested that the communications framework described for advertising can be applied to other communication tools, and previously in this chapter we highlighted that it can be used for public relations tools. This thought is echoed with a summary of the planning process used by executives of a leading public relations firm, FleishmanHillard Canada, in its efforts to assist clients with reputation management:[27]

- Gain a detailed, forward-looking understanding of corporate business objectives, competitive positioning, and the desired corporate reputation or corporate brand. This is best accomplished through interviews with senior corporate and business unit executives.

- Define the key audience, and derive audience-specific behavioural and attitudinal objectives and audience-specific corporate positioning attributes.

- Assess current perceptions of the company held by each key stakeholder group or audience on each of the key reputational attributes.

- Implement reputation-management programs throughout the corporation.

- Establish an ongoing plan to measure and monitor corporate reputation, and use reputation measurement to refine communications programs.

We highlight the issue of *corporate reputation*, a term that is used in public relations to convey the idea of corporate image, since a key outcome of corporate advertising is to influence overall perceptions of the organization. Clearly, the notion of corporate reputation is attitudinal, thus indicating that the general framework suggested in this text can be applied to all IMC tools. Furthermore, all methods described in Chapter 9 (e.g., focus groups, interviews, surveys) are readily applied for measuring corporate advertising effectiveness. News organizations publish polls that ask Canadians their opinion about corporations. Figure 15-3 summarizes the findings from the 2015 corporate reputation survey by *Marketing Magazine*/Leger.[28]

Figure 15-3   The top 10 companies in the 2015 *Marketing Magazine*/Leger Corporate Reputation Survey

Rank	Company
1	Google
2	Tim Hortons
3	Canadian Tire
4	Shoppers Drug Mart
5	Heinz
6	Kraft
7	Samsung
8	Kellogg
9	Staples
10	Campbell

© *Marketing Magazine*, June/July 2015

Other entities beyond big brands look to develop their reputation. For example, cities often are looking to promote themselves in a positive light for reasons related to tourism, business investment, and overall citizen goodwill. Vancouver and Calgary sought to enhance their reputations with both domestic and international audiences. Tourism Vancouver needed a quick response to the post-hockey-playoff difficulties and worked with the theme of "This Is Our Vancouver," undertaking extensive activity in social media. "Calgary: Be Part of the Energy" tried to develop an image and build people's interest in moving to the city for employment as labour demand continued to mount.[29]

IMAGE ADVERTISING

One form of corporate advertising is devoted to promoting the organization's overall image. **Image advertising** may accomplish a number of objectives by creating a position for the company, creating goodwill both internally and externally through sponsorship, and specifying a firm's perspective on an issue by advocacy.

Positioning   Firms, like products, need to establish a position in the marketplace, and corporate image advertising activities are one way to accomplish this objective. A well positioned product is much more likely to achieve success than is one with a vague image or none at all. The same holds true of the firm. Companies with strong positive corporate images have an advantage over competitors that may be enhanced when they promote any aspect of their organization or products. As shown in Exhibit 15-9, ads are often designed to create an image of the firm in the public mind. The exhibit shows how Toyota is attempting to create an image of itself as an innovator and leader in responsible car manufacturing by explaining how its vehicles emit less carbon dioxide.

Television Sponsorship   A firm often runs corporate image advertising on TV programs or specials. By associating itself with high-quality or educational programming, the firm hopes for a carryover effect that benefits its own image. IBM acted as the sponsor (i.e., sole advertiser) for a number of newscasts on CBC and Canwest that addressed seven major themes, such as "The Smart City" and "Building Sustainable Value." As part of IBM's "Smarter Planet" brand positioning, the effort encouraged the media partners to investigate the themes within their existing news programs. For instance, the CBC investigated the topics on *The Nature of Things* and *Mansbridge One on One,* while Canwest linked in its *Global News* and *Financial Post* properties.[30]

Exhibit 15-9   Toyota uses image advertising.

© The Advertising Archives

Advocacy   Firms often take positions on certain social, business, or environmental issues that influence their image and the public's perception. Such **advocacy advertising** is concerned with propagating ideas and elucidating controversial social issues of public importance in a manner that supports the interests of the sponsor.

While still portraying an image for the company or organization, advocacy advertising does so indirectly, by adopting a position on a particular issue rather than promoting the organization itself. The ads may be sponsored by a firm or by a trade association and are designed to tell readers how the firm operates or management's position on a particular issue. The reason for the advertising can be due to the firm's negative publicity or the firm's inability to place an important message through public relations channels, or because the firm just wants to get certain ideas accepted or have society understand its concerns. Renewable energy producers like Samsung devote a considerable portion of their website to communicating the environmental advantages of wind turbines to fulfill future energy needs. The rationale is to build an understanding of the potential benefits and likely to thwart the efforts of protesters who have health, safety, and economic criticisms (Exhibit 15-10).[31]

Exhibit 15-10   Citizens protest the development of wind turbines, citing numerous concerns.

© igor kisselev/Shutterstock

CAUSE-RELATED ADVERTISING

An increasingly popular method of image building is **cause-related marketing**, in which companies link with charities or non-profit organizations as contributing sponsors. The company benefits from favourable publicity, while the recipient receives much-needed funds or in-kind support. Companies also take the opportunity to communicate their involvement (Exhibit 15-11), giving rise to the idea of **cause-related advertising**. Both of these ideas fall within **corporate social responsibility**, defined as the broad voluntary activities undertaken by a company to operate in an economically, socially, and environmentally sustainable manner. Proponents of cause-related marketing say that association with a cause may differentiate one brand from another, increase consumer acceptance of price increases, generate favourable publicity, and even win over skeptical officials who may have an impact on the company.[32]

For example, the Bell "Let's Talk" campaign (Exhibit 15-12) mentioned earlier took a different road when one of its famous spokespersons toured Canada on a bicycle. Clara Hughes, a six-time Canadian Olympic medallist, covered 11,000 kilometres to build on the momentum of the cause and increase awareness, acceptance, and action toward mental health. Clara's Big Ride gained support from Bell and many other corporations as she visited 105 communities in five months before gliding to Parliament Hill on Canada Day. Extensive media coverage ensued, which encouraged 150,000 to visit an event and 1 million to watch the documentary about the ride.[33]

Cause-related marketing activities historically took a variety of forms: making outright donations to a non-profit cause, having companies volunteer for the cause, donating materials or supplies, or running public service announcements. Research found that 80 percent of Canadians engage with a cause-related campaign; the same number say they would switch to another brand due to its cause-related activity presuming price and quality parity; and 60 percent want to hear about the cause-related marketing activities through periodic ads.[34] Accordingly, brands look for unique opportunities to facilitate the communication process effectively and efficiently with innovations in three ways: committing to a cause represented by an existing organizational partner with a complete IMC plan, creative fundraising, and inventing causes to fit their brand.

Becel has supported the Heart & Stroke Foundation for decades with a variety of activities. Exhibit 15-13 shows cyclists participating in Becel's Heart & Stroke Ride for Heart. It moved in a new direction as the founding sponsor for the Foundation's "Heart Truth" campaign designed to inform the public that heart disease is the leading cause of death among women. The key message focused on how supporters could help save the life of a woman they loved (e.g., mother, sister, friend). TV ads and sponsorship of women's shows heightened awareness during February's Heart Month. Print and PR communicated the Foundation's Red Dress Fashion Show featuring Canadian celebrities and benefit concerts. After three months, awareness of heart disease increased from 13 percent to 23 percent, and Becel's sales grew by 9 percent. Becel also sponsored a two-minute film entitled *The Heart* that premiered during the Academy Awards. The message artistically encouraged women to think of themselves and their heart health. A montage of images of a woman's life as she cared for her family ensued as heartfelt music kept pace. Pre-broadcast publicity occurred with *eTalk Daily* host Tanya Kim and stories placed in print and broadcast media. Post-broadcast messaging with *eTalk* continued along with placement of the film in Cineplex movie theatres and online placements in social media.[35]

These next two activities show examples where a brand creatively fundraises for a non-profit organization and receives a marketing communication benefit in return. Virgin Mobile's Re*Generation program raised money for clothing for at-risk and homeless youth and donated the money to non-profit organizations like the Broadway Youth Resource Centre in Vancouver. One fundraising activity saw Lady Gaga perform at a Toronto nightclub, while another featured contributions for every Samsung Re*Generation phone sold.[36] And Food Banks Canada received a total of $2.5 million from Kraft over the past few years in a matching donations program. Kraft extended the idea with a recipe program that included a partnership with American Greetings. For every recipe ecard forwarded to a friend, Kraft donated $2, up to a maximum of $50,000.[37]

Exhibit 15-11   Whirlpool supports the effort for affordable housing.

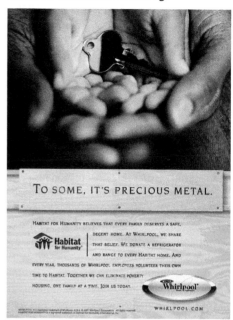

To some, it's precious metal.

Exhibit 15-12   Bell's "Let's Talk" cause-related activities supported mental health.

© Bell Canada

Exhibit 15-13   Becel supports the Heart & Stroke Foundation with sponsorship events.

Michael Stuparyk/Toronto Star via Getty Images

Companies also become involved in causes that reinforce their brand or corporate mandate by establishing a worthy cause themselves rather than working with an existing organization as described above. Indigo, Cadbury Canada, and Canadian Tire all experienced significant success by positioning their cause-marketing in a domain that fits their business mandate and consumer basis, creating a beneficial relationship for both sides.

Indigo established the Love of Reading Foundation and donated $7.5 million to 70 schools in support of library renovations and book purchases (Exhibit 15-14). It teamed up with a publisher of children's books to contribute a portion of sales to the fund. A 60-second public service announcement and other media advertised the initiative, which also helped the publisher expand its franchise to a new merchandising product line based on a book character.[38]

Exhibit 15-14   Indigo's support of reading fits the image of the brand perfectly.

© TheStoreGuy/Alamy

An international chocolate brand established the Cadbury's Cocoa Partnership, a 10-year, $80 million program to help cocoa farmers in countries where its beans are purchased. The Canadian division launched a Bicycle Factory program to send 5,000 bicycles to Ghana, allowing children to travel to school. Cadbury featured promotional activities designed to get Canadian consumers involved; a website allowed consumers to enter the code on its package to "buy" one part for a bike. Each bike requires 100 parts, so after 500,000 chocolate bars the collaboration achieved its mandate.[39] A later continuation of the program included a light unit that generated its power from the school trips, allowing students to travel and study in the evening at home where no electricity existed.[40]

Canadian Tire's Jumpstart charity partnered with the Hockey Canada Foundation (HCF) to launch "The Big Play," an initiative to provide 30,000 lower family income children with the opportunity to play minor hockey. The program worked with the World Junior Championship and in particular Team Canada. Each player's home town received funding to support five children for a total of $250,000. A national public service announcement of the program occurred on the Boxing Day launch, with Jumpstart kids being surprised with game tickets! The message encouraged families to visit online to learn more about the program and to get involved. Additional funding occurred for every social media retweet of TSN's "Big Play" highlight. Jumpstart awareness hit 95 percent, website traffic increased 30 percent, and an additional $45,000 fundraising resulted with higher than average social media communication.[41]

While all these examples look great, not all cause-related marketing is guaranteed to succeed. Cause-related marketing requires more than just associating with a social issue, since these examples show that it takes time and effort to organize a meaningful activity that will be accepted and gain participation. It is also possible to waste money by associating with a cause that offers little relation to their brand, with firms discovering that their customers and potential customers have little interest in the cause. Finally, the results of cause-marketing efforts can be hard to quantify. Despite these cautions, one practitioner commented that good cause-related marketing gave people something to do that was simple, rewarding, and interesting.[42]

SPONSORSHIP

Corporate sponsorship of different events plays a major role in the public relations plans of organizations. While companies sponsor specific events with primarily traditional public relations objectives in mind, a separate and more marketing-oriented use of sponsorships is also on the increase; event sponsorship occurs for product-level brands compared to corporate brands. In either case, the decisions involved are comparable—we turn to these in this section, beginning with a brief overview.

Overview   Activities where a fee is paid in exchange for marketing communication benefits for an organization are known as **event sponsorship**. An organization agrees to sponsor an event since it provides exposure to a selective audience, and potentially a larger audience with television coverage or photos or video posted on the Internet. A further benefit includes the ability to have the organization associated with the event, thus providing additional development of the corporate or product brand. Overall, sponsorship offers the potential to achieve multiple objectives: awareness, brand positioning, and trial or repeat purchases through merchandising and promotional offers with the ultimate goal of increasing loyalty and distancing a brand from its competitors.[43]

A survey of managers found that sponsorship contributes to brand differentiation and financial success provided that advertising and sales promotion supported the initiative.[44] Furthermore, academic research conducted in lab experiments suggests that sponsorship contributes to brand recall and stronger brand attitudes, and initial field research supports this conclusion as well.[45] However, factors like too many sponsors, controversial co-sponsors, a poor product association with the event, and weak initial brand attitude can all contribute to less desirable outcomes regarding brand attitude among others.[46] A longitudinal study of a major sponsor for the United European Football League concluded that awareness measures of recall and recognition grew over time, indicating that brands should view sponsorship as a long-term investment and sign multi-year contracts.[47]

Sponsorship occurs in many forms, as shown inFigure 15-4. Sports sponsorship is the overwhelming leader, and Molson's deal with the NHL confirms the importance of hockey for selling beer. The seven-year deal worth $375 million breaks out as $100 million for the rights, $100 million for guaranteed advertising buys, $100 million for events and special promotions, and $75 million for unreported marketing activities.[48] In response to sponsorship growth, industry members began the Sponsorship Marketing Council of Canada to demonstrate sponsorship's communication value by establishing best practices and measurement tools to validate sponsorship investment.[49] The Council annually recognizes the best sponsorship in four categories: arts and culture, sports, causes, and events and festivals. Sponsorship beyond these forms can occur, and CIBC is the official financial sponsor of the Greater Toronto Airports Authority and the new UP Express train from the Pearson airport to downtown. As part of the deal, CIBC pays for the baggage carts and lets everyone know about it with a decorative sculpture (Exhibit 15-15). CIBC enjoys exclusivity for ATMs, foreign exchange, and specialized hospitality services.[50]

Exhibit 15-15   CIBC is a sponsor at Toronto's Lester B. Pearson International Airport.

© Jill Morgan / Alamy Stock Photo

Figure 15-4   Annual sponsorship spending in North America by property ($ billions)

	2002	2006	2009	2012	2015
Sports	$6.43	$8.94	$11.28	$13.01	$14.98
Entertainment	0.87	1.38	1.64	1.93	2.13
Festivals, fairs, events	0.83	0.61	0.76	0.83	0.86
Causes	0.83	1.30	1.51	1.70	1.92
Arts	0.61	0.74	0.82	0.89	0.86
Associations/membership organizations	____	0.40	0.50	0.55	0.59
Total	$9.57	$13.37	$16.51	$18.91	$21.34

Promo, June 1, 2002; Promo Xtra, January 24, 2007; Promo, January 28, 2010, Sponsorship.com 2012, 2015.

One example of a successful sponsorship with many partners is Kraft's Hockeyville. The initiative allowed communities to compete to be named the country's best hockey town, with the winner announced on *Hockey Night in Canada* after online fan voting. Leading up to this, Kraft narrowed down the towns and cities to a final list. The winner received $100,000 in rink upgrades, and the four runners-up received $25,000 each. The promotion continued yearly with sales up noticeably during the eight-week campaign. Several brand measures were strong, like "Kraft has great community spirit," and Kraft "actively cares and supports my community." These results are what Kraft looked for when the promotion began, as its research indicated that most Canadians' lives revolved around the local community centre with a rink for hockey, figure skating, public skating, ringette, and sledge hockey—the assistance to improve the facilities appeared a natural fit for a company that makes family products (Exhibit 15-16).[51]

Exhibit 15-16 Kraft's Hockeyville celebrates with the NHL.

© Francis Vachon/TCPI/The Canadian Press

As expected, a number of decisions are associated with event sponsorship, including the types of sponsorship, target audience fit, target audience exposure, and brand positioning. We explore these important sponsorship decisions in the context of sports sponsorship for illustrative purposes because it represents the dominant expenditure—more than $15 billion in North America in 2015. Each idea can be readily adapted to other domains, for example entertainment or arts festivals. Sports sponsorship can be successful with clear objectives, a good positioning strategy, adequate budget, the appropriate sporting vehicle, and key tactical implementation—characteristics we have seen in other types of promotional plans. IMC Perspective 15-2 describes the growth of sports sponsorships and Scotiabank's relationship with the NHL.

IMC PERSPECTIVE 15-2

SPORTS SPONSORSHIPS LEAD ALL OTHERS

Sports sponsorship deals exist internationally with the Olympics, nationally with the NHL, and locally with companies supporting things like minor soccer, and recent statistics indicate that the Canadian sponsorship industry is worth about $1.7 billion. Companies spend about one-quarter of their marketing budget on this IMC tool and the average amount spent on their largest sponsorship expenditure is $2.2 million. Of this, pro-sports account for two-thirds and amateur sports account for just under a quarter, and in the end, 90 percent of all primary sponsorship goes to sports, according to a sample from the Sponsorship Landscape Study conducted each year. However, from the perspective of overall dollar amount spent, sports accounts for 60 percent of all sponsorship.

© Gerry Thomas/NHLI via Getty Images

However we look at the data, sports sponsorship is big business in Canada. And according to other research, Canada's Most Valuable Property study, not surprisingly The Grey Cup and each of the seven NHL teams are the best in the pro-sports market with the Canadian Olympics being the strongest for amateur sports. This research examined emotional variables, including personal involvement, creating memorable experiences, and sponsor fit. A third study, the Sports Brand Equity Index, found that the top three sports brands are the Montreal Canadiens, the Toronto Maple Leafs, and the Saskatchewan Roughriders, on the measures of first team that comes to mind, respect for team, most loyal fans, team popularity, and atmosphere at venue.

Scotiabank sponsored hockey significantly and earned the reputation as "Canada's hockey bank" over the past decades. It began with a sponsorship of the Ottawa Senators in 2003, and eventually expanded to all Canadian teams and then to the NHL. The deal permitted the bank to use the league logo and all 30 team logos for its ScotiaHockey Visa and debit cards. According to executives, the process took considerable time to build relationships with each team and make arrangements for a sponsorship deal that worked for each team and the bank. With Rogers' new TV deal with the NHL, Scotiabank negotiated a six-year broadcast contract for *Scotiabank Wednesday Night Hockey* and is the presenting sponsor of *Rogers Hometown Hockey*. Scotiabank's results are impressive as executives claimed increased brand familiarity, opinion, and impression to go with higher purchase consideration and likelihood to recommend.

Scotiabank's sponsorship worked well with the NHL's drive to increase the number of properties available. The league created events like the Heritage Classic, the Winter Classic, The Molson Canadian NHL Faceoff, Because It's the Cup, and the NHL draft. This propelled the NHL to attract $400 million in sponsorship investment, up from $327 million in 2010 and not too far behind the $700 million for the NBA. Major sponsors appreciated the growth and partnership with the NHL since the league proved very interested in building the league image as well as the image of its sponsors.

At lower levels of hockey, the bank committed support of minor hockey with its Scotiabank Community Hockey and won the Best in Show award from the Sponsorship Marketing Council of Canada. Overall, the program garnered 47 million impressions, $2.4 million in advertising value, and significant results in media relations.

Sources: Rebecca Harris, "Which Sponsorship Partners Are Tops With Canadians," *Marketing Magazine*, July 7, 2015; Chris Powell, "Tim Hortons Among the Top Sports Sponsor Brands," *Marketing Magazine*, July 8, 2015; Chris Powell, "Ahead in the Game," *Marketing Magazine*, November/December, 2014; Sponsorship Landscape Study, 2014.

Question:

1. In what ways does Scotiabank's sponsorship strategy with the NHL fit the brand?

Types of Sponsorship   Sports sponsorship involves endorsement deals or sponsoring a team, league, event, athlete, or organization, along with stadium naming or broadcast rights. The goal is to associate a brand with its target audience's entertainment consumption or lifestyle, thus enriching the overall brand experience. One thought on the topic suggested three levels of sponsorship:[52]

1. *Proprietary* has little or no external sanctioning or partnerships; Nike's Run TO featured a running event throughout the entire city of Toronto (Exhibit 15-17).

2. *Affiliated advertising* utilizes the assets of a sponsorship or association; the Esso Legends of Hockey brings together the Hockey Hall of Fame, NHL, NHL Players' Association, and NHL Alumni.

3. *Programming* lives within a larger event or sponsorship; Powerade's "Thirst for Soccer" visits youth soccer tournaments across Canada.

Working with an athletic sponsorship is similar to sponsorship with a team, but with a few unique issues. Foremost is ensuring a fit between the athlete and the company or brand. Exposure arrangements regarding an athlete's identity (i.e., name, image, and

Exhibit 15-17   Participants in the Nike Run TO event.

Lucas Oleniuk/Toronto Star via Getty Images

likeness), amount and type of service, and corporate logo placement need to be established. Rounding out the arrangement is the strategic communication use of an athlete in advertising, public relations, or sales promotion and conditions for the sponsor to protect its investment (e.g., an ethics clause). A significant sponsorship agreement between Sport Chek and Kyle Lowry of the Raptors emerged when the star signed a four-year contract extension. It appeared to be a great match for promoting the retailer in Toronto, especially as the popularity of basketball exploded in the past few years.[53]

Brand Positioning   Companies are attracted to event sponsorships because effective IMC programs can be built around them and promotional tie-ins can be made to local, regional, national, and even international markets. Companies are finding event sponsorships an excellent platform from which to build equity and gain affinity with target audiences, as well as a good public relations tool for the corporation in general.

While the overall market position of the brand may be well established throughout the marketing plan, sport sponsorship permits a brand positioning strategy to a unique and well defined target audience toward which the brand has specific communication and behavioural objectives. For example, a sports sponsorship could enable a brand to establish awareness and new brand associations as it reaches new customers to develop trial purchases.

However, brands should be prepared to spend accordingly to achieve their objectives, as the initial sponsorship investment requires additional advertising or sales promotion expenditures. As the foundation is critical, brands should ensure that the rights and benefits of the sports sponsorship allow the brand to achieve its objectives and positioning. For example, sponsorship in hockey can have limits without the clearance from its stakeholders (e.g., NHL, NHL Players' Association, and Hockey Canada). Finally, picking the right sponsorship that has the right profile at the right time and a partner that is receptive to making the deal work is paramount for successful implementation.

Target Audience Fit   Most companies focus their marketing efforts on specific market segments and are always looking for ways to reach these target audiences. Marketers are finding that event sponsorships are very effective ways to reach specific target audiences based on geographic, demographic, psychographic, and ethnic characteristics. For example, golf tournaments are a popular event for sponsorship by marketers of luxury automobiles and other upscale products and services. The golf audience is affluent and highly educated, and marketers believe that golfers care passionately about the game, leading them to form emotional attachments to brands they associate with the sport. Alternatively, brands will look to similar venues to reach a consistent target audience that fits. For example, Pepsi signed a deal with the NBA and reached the pinnacle of sports sponsorship by owning all four major North American sports leagues: MLB, NFL, NHL, and NBA. Industry observers felt the youthful, pop-culture audience of Pepsi blended well with the fans of all four sports.[54] The Telus World Ski and Snowboard Festival allowed the national telecommunications firm to reach its youth market with its sponsorship investment (Exhibit 15-18).

Exhibit 15-18   A competitor on the half-pipe at the Telus Festival.

© Christian Kober 1/Alamy

Target Audience Exposure   Marketers are attracted to event sponsorship because it gets their company and/or product names in front of consumers. By choosing the right events for sponsorship, companies can get visibility among their target audience. Clearly this appears to be a key reason why Molson spent its money sponsoring the NHL as it anticipates that hockey viewers are also beer drinkers. Curiously, sponsorship deals raise interesting questions as to the target audience exposure of a sponsorship message, as shown in Exhibit 15-19. While exposure is no doubt important, the degree to which the sponsorship is noticed is a concern for managers since most events offer varying exposure levels for different amounts of dollars invested. Thus, the risk of potential clutter due to the prominence of a major sponsor can inhibit the exposure of secondary sponsors.

An additional exposure issue is the perceived infringement or "ambush" of non-sponsors upon a sponsor's property. In this case, a non-sponsor's marketing communication gives the impression that it is a sponsor through its imagery or promotional activities. This issue arises during the Olympics, and the Canadian Olympic Committee (COC) took exception to North Face's launch of its "International Collection" of clothing that featured the Canadian flag or symbolic references to Sochi or Russia. In addition, North Face ran a contest featuring a trip to Sochi to attend a major international sports competition for the winner. Ultimately, the COC filed a lawsuit against North Face.[55] Similarly, Budweiser continued its Red Light promotion during the Olympics by encouraging Canadians to post a picture of the light in support of Team Canada. Once again the COC took exception to this despite the beer brand's disclaimer that it did not sponsor the Olympics, the COC, or Hockey Canada.[56]

Exhibit 15-19   Zurich Insurance saw a connection between its target audience and viewers of beach volleyball.

© Caro/Alamy

Brand Activities   Most sponsored properties include guidelines on what level of marketing the brand's support permits in terms of the number and size of signs, for example. Sponsored properties allow extensive brand activation to occur, while others place significant limitations on the type of brand activities permitted during the exposure. *Brand activation* is a catch-all term that describes various promotional activities such as sampling, demonstration, and interaction both personally and technologically that provides interesting experiences for consumers. Essentially, it is marketing communication with a goal of bringing consumers closer to purchase intention while in their decision-making process. The TIFF example at the start of the chapter captured innovative activations for cultural sponsorship, and sports sponsorship is very similar. For example, Crankworx is a mountain bike festival held annually in Whistler, British Columbia, that attracts significant sponsorship levels. As shown in Exhibit 15-20, Crankworx offers substantial brand activation promotional activities as part of the deal. Its Internet site lists its numerous partners and many exhibitors who showcase their products with clear and colourful brand identification. One study found positive brand communication effects of both anticipating and experiencing brand activation experiences at a sponsored event.[57]

Exhibit 15-20   Crankworx draws sponsors for its bike events.

© Dan Galic/Alamy

Measuring Sponsorship Effectiveness   As we have seen with other communication tools, sponsorship planning follows a general framework of performing a situation analysis with relevant consumer and competitive research, establishing objectives (i.e., marketing, communication, behavioural), developing strategy and tactics, and outlining the criteria and measures of effectiveness to assess whether objectives have been met. A major issue that faces the event sponsorship industry is incomplete research. As marketers become interested in targeted audiences, they will want more evidence that event sponsorship is effective and a good return on their investment.

Despite this concern, the growth in sponsorship investments has led to a corresponding emergence of measuring the effectiveness of sponsorships. While each of these measures has its advantages and disadvantages, we suggest using several in assessing the impact of sponsorships. Essentially, measures of sponsorship effectiveness can be categorized as exposure-based methods or tracking measures:[58]

- *Exposure-based methods.* Exposure-based methods can be classified as those that monitor the quantity and nature of the media coverage obtained for the sponsored event and those that estimate direct and indirect audiences. These measures have been commonly employed by corporations, but heavily criticized by scholars. Pham argues that media coverage is not the objective of sponsorships and should not be considered a measure of effectiveness. He argues that the measures provide no indication of perceptions, attitude change, or behavioural change and should therefore not be considered as measures of effectiveness.[59]

- *Tracking measures.* These measures are designed to evaluate the awareness, familiarity, and preferences engendered by sponsorship based on surveys. A number of empirical studies have measured recall of sponsors' ads, awareness of and attitudes toward the sponsors and their products, and image effect including brand and corporate images. Moreover, the tracking measures could be done for current customers, potential customers, and the general public before, during, and after the event to get a complete picture of the sponsorship.

Finally, at the conclusion of investigating numerous studies of the persuasion effects of sponsorship, the researcher makes a number of managerial prescriptions based on the findings. Sponsorship content should be visible. An organizer should clearly thank the sponsor at the event; this can be implemented in the media as well. Planners should avoid multiple-sponsor events. The sponsorship should offer true value to the audience, who should perceive it as being distinct from brand advertising.[60]

LO5   IMC Planning: Strategic Use of PR

As discussed in this chapter, public relations activities often communicate infrequently to a broader population and attempt to persuade the target audience on more global or abstract attributes of the company and its brand. With this in mind, public relations generally does not influence the decision-making process because the activities are not sequenced to match the purchase and consumption behaviour of consumers, as they are in advertising or sales promotion. For that matter, it is unlikely that a single public relations activity would coincide exactly with decision making for any other stakeholder that might be a target audience for the organization.

For example, CIBC is the title sponsor for Run for the Cure, an annual event to raise funds for the Canadian Breast Cancer Foundation (Exhibit 15-21). The late-September event features considerable lead-up media exposure funded by CIBC; however, this timing does not necessarily fit for all customers and non-customers of CIBC since financial products and services are purchased year-round. Presumably, CIBC expects this sponsorship activity to have a broad, long-term benefit associated with the corporate brand that consumers and all other internal and external stakeholders would retain during the year and until the event returns. After two decades of support, CIBC wanted to stand out from the clutter of charity fundraising events by recording a first-person account of breast cancer treatment. The video contributed to significant increases in post-event attitudinal measures (e.g., inspiring, moving, hopeful).[61]

Exhibit 15-21   CIBC's Run for the Cure draws enthusiastic supporters.

© Photo courtesy of the Canadian Breast Cancer Foundation

However, the growth of cause-related marketing activities and the resulting data shown in this chapter indicate that programs by major brands may be contributing to stronger overall attitudes.

Advertising and PR often reinforce one another. The launch of a new advertising campaign is helped with additional exposure through news media in the form of announcements in the newspaper, clips shown on television, or information and complete ads posted on the Internet. Sometimes, brands take advantage of favourable publicity and make note of this in their advertising or make it a central theme in a particular message. Alternatively, if the corporation involved itself with sponsorship of arts, a cause, or sports, the advertising can make reference to this for regular brand messages beyond advertising messages dedicated to communicating information about the sponsorship. For these reasons, it is no wonder we have seen extensive proliferation of public relations expenditures.

Telus funded $1 million over four years to WWF-Canada by selling Telus branded pandas, essentially a self-liquidating premium. Media exposure included TV and Internet ads, and additional exposure of the initiative included social media participation (#hometweethome) with $1 donated to the fund for every social media posting to go along with significant media publicity. Overall, impressive participation and website traffic numbers helped Telus be recognized by *Strategy* as a leading cause-marketing program.[62] Internet sites for corporations are a primary vehicle for communicating basic facts, especially the corporation's social and community interests, and for disseminating common public relations tools. For example, firms regularly put copies of their press releases on their sites and also include video clips of corporate activities like speeches or annual shareholder meetings. The ability of virtually anyone to obtain basic company information through the Internet makes it a desirable tool for firms to project their best image with timely content to ensure strong reputation management. However, the darker side of the Internet appears in the form of unwarranted negative publicity for brands. Even the average person may try to sabotage organizations that have appropriate corporate missions, sell legitimate products, and follow the laws of the land.

Learning Objectives Summary

 Recognize the role of public relations in the promotional mix.

This chapter examined the role of public relations. Public relations is typically accomplished through publicity generated through news media and corporate advertising. We noted that these areas are significant to the marketing communication effort and are usually considered differently from the other promotional elements. The reasons for this special treatment stem from the facts that (1) they are typically not designed to promote a specific product or service, and (2) in many instances it is harder for the consumer to make the connection between the communication and its intent.

PR is often a separate department operating independently of marketing; in others, it is considered a support system. Many large firms have an external public relations agency, just as they have an outside ad agency. Thus, public relations is useful with its traditional responsibilities; however, increasingly more marketing-oriented firms use this tool at the brand or product level for enhanced communication efforts.

 Explain how to compile a public relations plan.

Like all aspects of IMC, a public relations plan begins with a situation analysis, in particular an evaluation of public attitudes to the firm through a survey methodology in order to gauge an accurate reading. Influencing the right audience is another critical element as the organization must decide to communicate with groups such as employees, investors, community members, suppliers, customers, media, educators, and any other relevant societal stakeholder. Objectives need to be set, consistent with the behaviour and communication ideas suggested earlier in this book.

An appeal of sorts is also established for public relations, much like we saw in advertising examples: it is a clear message with a focus that often has creative elements. The delivery of the message can occur through established media channels discussed already, and through the media to generate publicity. Finally, tactical considerations and effective measures need to be established for full implementation.

 Examine how public relations is generated through media publicity and argue the strengths and limitations of media publicity.

News about a person, product, service, or organization that appears in broadcast or print media or on the Internet is known as publicity. It can occur through a story a journalist decides to write. In this case, publicity can be positive or negative and the firm is in more of a reactionary mode; preparedness for this scenario is certainly possible and recommended. Alternatively, a firm can seek media coverage for important news by communicating with the media through tools with the planned intention of receiving positive stories. Firms use press releases, press conferences, exclusives, interviews, and community involvement, and may use other creative means to persuade journalists to cover them.

Messages about a company that consumers receive through the media have strengths, including credibility, endorsement, low cost, less clutter, ability to reach specific audiences, image building, and frequency potential. Limitations include whether the brand is actually stronger, and a lack of control leading to an inconsistent message, poor timing, and possible inaccuracy.

LO4   Illustrate how public relations is managed through corporate advertising.

Corporate advertising involves the reputation management of the firm through advertising and promotional activities designed to put the firm in the most favourable public position. *Corporate advertising* is a general term to cover all marketing communication that usually includes image advertising, cause-related advertising, and sponsorship. Corporate advertising can be controversial because sometimes the source of the message is top management, who may have their own intentions and motivations. This element of communication definitely has its place in the promotional mix but should follow the planning suggestions outlined in this chapter in order to be effective.

LO5   Apply the ideas of public relations within the development of an IMC plan.

Public relations is an integral part of an IMC program as PR potentially reaches so many different constituents in the general public and those immediately connected to the organization. Furthermore, public relations both supports and can lead other IMC tools like advertising, sales promotion, and digital communication. As such, the execution of public relations should be carefully planned with objectives, strategies, and tactics much like any other aspect of marketing communication.

Review Questions

1. Identify the key differences between public relations and media publicity. In what ways are the two interdependent?
2. Describe the reasons why firms use public relations in an IMC program. Provide an example of an appropriate use of public relations in this mix.
3. Many companies are now trying to generate as much media publicity as they can. Cite examples, and discuss the advantages and disadvantages associated with this strategy.
4. Companies are now taking the position that their charitable contributions should lead to something in return—for example, sales or increased visibility. Discuss the pros and cons of this position.
5. Explain how public relations activities and media publicity can be executed with Internet media.

Applied Questions

1. Some marketers and PR people believe public relations should replace advertising as the primary tool for introducing new products. Explain why this would or would not be a good plan.
2. Who are the target audiences for the ALS Ice Bucket Challenge described in the chapter?
3. How do music artists take advantage of media publicity? Which strengths do they predominantly use? How do they minimize the limitations of media publicity?
4. Identify the sponsors of different concerts or entertainment activities you have attended and make a conclusion as to why this type of sponsorship may be successful.
5. Explain why a company like RBC would use the tools described in the chapter, including media publicity, corporate image advertising, cause-related advertising, and sponsorship.

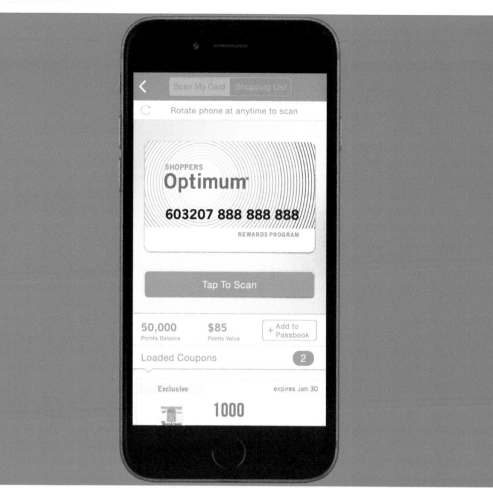

Hand-out/SHOPPERS DRUG MART CORPORATION/Newscom

CHAPTER SIXTEEN

Direct Marketing

LEARNING OBJECTIVES

LO1 Define direct marketing and summarize the importance of a database for direct marketing communication decisions.

LO2 Express the decisions of a direct-marketing plan.

LO3 Describe the content of a loyalty program.

LO4 Evaluate the strengths and limitations of direct marketing.

LO5 Apply the ideas of direct marketing within the development of an IMC plan.

An Optimal Loyalty Program

Shoppers Drug Mart launched its Optimum loyalty program many years ago and became the second largest loyalty program after Air Miles, making it the largest single brand loyalty program, just ahead of PC Points at 9 million. Its members are mostly women (i.e., above 70 percent) with a slight skew to the 45–65 age bracket. For a period of time Shoppers communicated with existing members using direct mail and email, providing general promotional offers to all customers that fostered greater use of the loyalty program and increased purchases. Later Shoppers personalized the email message with considerable success, as these types of messages enjoyed an opening rate 10 percent higher than non-personalized messages and yielded stronger purchase levels. In total, 2 million of the 10 million loyalty program members opted-in to receive emails and they received coupons based on their past purchase history.

The results surpassed executives' expectations regarding the participation rate of redeeming coupons, however the printing of the coupon proved to be a significant obstacle. "We know from our research that a certain amount of people just didn't participate because they didn't have a printer or it was a hassle," commented one manager. Despite this concern, it proved to Shoppers decision-makers that consumers desired personalization. In fact, it appeared that consumers accepted the exchange of providing their personal information to be stored in the database for customized offers and incentives. And while 90 percent of all Canadians are enrolled in a loyalty program, many industry players remained concerned that loyalty programs did not increase the amount, rate, or frequency of repeat buying, and that program members may not be any more loyal than non-program customers.

As part of a long-term plan to offer greater personalization, Shoppers Drug Mart launched a digital version of its Optimum loyalty program in the spring of 2015. Entitled "My Optimum—My Rewards," the new version allowed members to receive points and offers via mobile, email, or the web (MyOptimum.ca). A new app allowed users to load coupons and other offers directly to their smart phone. The offers remained targeted based on purchase history, just as in the past with the email version. Features of the program included the ability to scan a digital Optimum card directly from a mobile device to earn and redeem points, check balance, transfer points, browse flyers, create shopping lists, manage prescriptions, and locate stores.

However, the app contained many other features that active smart phone users would appreciate such as the ability to collect points, use the digital card at the point of purchase, and donate points to charity. A previous app could not allow consumers to collect points or receive offers, so the new digital version looked like a winner for many. On the other hand, many consumers continued to use the new technology while still using the older technology by going to the website for updates, or carried on using the actual plastic cards. Shoppers continues significant brand marketing with an emphasis on beauty and innovation so as not to lose sight of its mission.

Sources: Hollie Shaw, "Shoppers Optimum Goes Digital," *National Post*, May 28, 2015; Jered Stuffco, "The Evolution of Shoppers Drug Mart's Loyalty Program," *Marketing Magazine*, September 15, 2015; Chris Powell, "Shoppers Drug Mart Ushers Loyalty Program Into Digital," *Marketing Magazine*, June 8, 2015, Matthew Chung, "Shoppers Takes Personalized Deals National," *Strategy*, April 22, 2013.

Question:

1. Do you agree that giving up personal information and shopping behaviour data to a retailer in order to receive promotional offers is a good deal?

Direct marketing includes programs that use direct-response media such as direct mail, catalogues, telephones, TV infomercials, and newer methods of digital communication. In essence, it uses the media identified thus far and others, but with a more immediate behavioural objective in addition to communication objectives. We begin with an overview of direct marketing, describing the development of a database and two important uses of database marketing. We then identify key decisions for direct-marketing programs including target audience, objectives, direct-response media, and effectiveness. A loyalty program is identified as a main direct marketing program and its characteristics and consumer adoption are explored. The chapter concludes with a summary of the strengths and limitations of this marketing tool and an IMC application.

Direct Marketing

While companies rely on promotional mix elements such as advertising and sales promotion to move their goods and services through intermediaries, they also market directly to the consumer. Advertising and sales promotion are viewed as effective in creating brand image, conveying information, and/or creating awareness. However, going direct with these same tools can generate an immediate behavioural response that makes direct marketing a valuable part of the integrated communications program. For this section we briefly define the purpose of direct marketing, illustrate how to develop a database, and summarize two implementation uses of a database: targeting and customer relationship management (CRM).

DEFINING DIRECT MARKETING

As noted in Chapter 1, **direct marketing** is the interactive use of advertising media to stimulate an immediate behaviour modification in such a way that this behaviour can be tracked, recorded, analyzed, and stored on a database for future retrieval and use.[1] Direct marketing involves marketing research, segmentation, strategic and tactical decisions, and evaluation as shown in our planning model in Chapter 1. For the execution, direct marketing uses **direct-response media**, including direct mail, telephone, interactive TV, print, the Internet, mobile devices, and other media to reach both customers and prospective customers. Exhibit 16-1 shows how advertising encourages direct communication and purchasing via the Internet.

The use of direct-response media differs depending on whether the identity of an individual within the target audience is known. For example, direct mail can be addressed, where the person's name and address is on the communication sent to the home (or business) location. In contrast, unaddressed mail reaches homes and is delivered in bulk to selected geographic areas, or to areas determined through the use of another segmentation variable chosen by the promotional planner. In either case, an important element of direct media selected is the development of a database. We briefly examine the content and use of a database for the purpose of marketing communication. This general approach is applicable for all direct-response media described in this chapter and for Internet media discussed in Chapter 17.

DEVELOPING A DATABASE

As noted throughout the text, market segmentation and targeting are critical components of any promotional program. Direct-marketing programs employ these principles significantly since their success is tied to reaching a very specific target audience. Direct marketers use a **database**, a listing of customers and/or potential customers, to identify and profile their target audience. This database is a tool for **database marketing**—the use of specific information about individual customers and/or prospects to implement effective and efficient marketing communication. In this section we look at the content of a database, database use for targeting, and database use for CRM.

Exhibit 16-1   Bose uses multiple methods to promote its products.

Courtesy of Bose ® Corporation

Database Content   The database contains names, addresses, and postal codes; more sophisticated databases include information on demographics and psychographics, purchase transactions and payments, personal facts, neighbourhood data, and even credit histories (see Figure 16-1). With the development of electronic communication, databases may also contain email addresses and consumers' social media identification. For example, Facebook developed an app that automatically generates a contact form that feeds into an advertiser's database.[2] Canada's privacy legislation places limitations on what marketers can do with database information; refer to www.privcom.gc.ca for a complete guide. Companies are very concerned with protecting this data from hackers after significant media stories over the past decade, and are responsible about how they use the data. In fact, one trend is that companies will "de-identify" the data to avoid any potential breaches of privacy.[3]

Figure 16-1 Contents of a database for direct marketing

Consumer Database	Business-to-Business Database
Name	Name of company, name and title of contact
Address/postal code	Address/postal code
Telephone number	Telephone number
Email, social media coordinates	Email, social media coordinates
Age	Credit history
Gender	Industrial classification
Marital status	Size of business
Family	Revenues
Education	Number of employees
Income	Time in business
Occupation	Source of order/inquiry or referral
Transaction history	Purchase history
Promotion history	Promotion history
Inquiry history	Inquiry history
Unique identifier	Unique identifier

Organizations compile their own database and regularly update it through transaction information or through past marketing communication activities. Other sources of data include warranty cards, surveys, consumer/trade shows, inbound communication, and Internet browsing behaviour especially through social media. A key success factor of a customer database is that it must be kept current, purged of old and/or inactive customers, and updated frequently. The **RFM scoring method** is used to see the **r**ecency, **f**requency, and **m**onetary transactions between the company and the customer. Data need to be entered each time there is a transaction so that the company can track how recently purchases have been made, how often they are made, what amounts of money are being spent, and which products and/or services are purchased.

Database marketing has become ubiquitous as companies have established comprehensive databases on existing and potential customers; people are now concerned about their privacy. Direct marketers are concerned as well. The Canadian Marketing Association (CMA) and the Canadian Advertising Foundation (CAF) have asked members to adhere to ethical rules of conduct in their marketing efforts. For example, companies who collect data ask for consent from consumers prior to communicating, and reassure their customers that the data will not be sold to a third party. In contrast, research shows that about half of all Canadians willingly share personal information if they receive promotional offers in return; however two-thirds are uncomfortable at receiving the offers on their smart phone.[4] And another somewhat reassuring point is that managers admit that they have too much data at times and not enough time to analyze the data for their decision-making.[5]

There are numerous outside sources of information for buying or renting a database. Census data from Statistics Canada provides information on almost every Canadian household in Canada (e.g., size, demographics, income). Canada Post provides information on a postal code level for both household and business locations, and also offers comprehensive mailing lists for rent. Other list service organizations exist, such as Info Canada, which offers numerous types of business and consumer lists that the company builds from many sources. Large market research organizations conduct annual studies of customers and compile the information on total orders placed, types of products purchased, demographics, and purchase satisfaction. Loyalty programs contain significant amounts of information on consumer purchase patterns, and this data is shared with marketing partners. Finally, any company that collects consumer data is a potential source of data for purchase, provided the company disclosed this to its customers.

Database Use for Targeting   Marketing decisions require information, and the database compiled for direct marketing purposes provides detailed facts for two managerial concerns in this section. As noted earlier, profiling a target audience with precision provides greater marketing communication effectiveness and efficiency, and CRM practices require considerable data for implementing customized promotional offers. The database permits extensive and advanced statistical analysis to identify specific audiences for which a customized and/or personalized message or promotional offer can be delivered through a direct-response medium. For example, Knorr entered the frozen food category and delivered direct-mail pieces, also containing a coupon, to households according to demographic and purchase behaviour potential along 10 different characteristics. Those most likely to respond included past Knorr consumers of other product categories who were interested in the frozen food category and who had sufficient disposable income to afford a premium product. The various combinations of the 10 characteristics provided opportunities to reach different target audiences ranging from very low to extremely high levels of audience attractiveness. The results indicated a 10 percent response rate, substantially higher than the projected 3 percent. One of the more attractive target audiences attained a response rate of 50 percent.

As this Knorr example illustrates, certain consumers are more likely to be potential purchasers than others. By analyzing the characteristics of the database, a marketer like Knorr can target potential audiences that have a stronger likelihood of responding to the offer (e.g., use coupon, trial purchase) and the database serves as the foundation to profile the target audience who will likely make a trial purchase.[6] Finally, this example shows how brands cross-sell by offering new products or related products to customers who have bought in another product category.

Similarly, the database is used to target customers to help encourage repeat purchases. Once an initial purchase occurs, the customer's name and other information may be entered into the database. These people are proven users who offer high potential for repurchase. Magazines, for example, routinely send out renewal letters and/or call subscribers before the expiration date. Companies like lawn care services and car dealers build a base of customers and contact them when they are "due" to repurchase. These activities are examples where the timing of repeat purchasing is important, as identified in Chapter 5. Costco mails promotions to members regularly to encourage return visits (Exhibit 16-2), which likely improves the frequency objective identified in Chapter 5.

Exhibit 16-2   Costco mails promotional offers to its members.

Courtesy of Costco Wholesale

Database Use for CRM   Another aspect of repeat purchasing occurs through customer relationship management (CRM), where marketers develop and maintain a significant amount of information about their clients. The aim is to establish and maintain a relationship with customers through personalized communication and customized product/service offerings. CRM relies on software technology and an extensive database specifically designed to implement the management of customer relationships. For example, Exhibit 16-3 shows brands that have a loyalty program, a key part of CRM since it provides an incentive for repeat purchase. And loyal buyers are open to receiving regular communication from previously purchased brands; about 60 percent of consumers are interested in personalized promotional offers or product recommendations for items like groceries, entertainment, health/beauty, electronics, and clothing.[7]

Exhibit 16-3   The databases for these brands help facilitate CRM.

© Tracy Leonard

Timely communication and appropriate promotional offers that fit with the customer's past purchase behaviour are the hallmark of CRM, of which a database and direct-response media are imperative. The Canadian division for American Express promotes the credit card to its members as a tool for enhanced service with its "Front of the Line" program. It expanded the offering with faster security clearance and taxi service in a sponsorship arrangement with Toronto's Lester B. Pearson International Airport. As part of the package, AMEX sponsored free Wi-Fi and entertainment to all waiting passengers.[8] As this example indicates, a company can identify trends and buying patterns that will help it establish a better relationship with its customers by more effectively meeting their needs through analysis of the data.

Despite this promise, research suggests that up to two-thirds of all organizations did not experience the full benefit of CRM initiatives. Collectively, they spent about $220 billion from 2000 to 2005 and have achieved a return of only $50 billion in the intervening years to date. Criticism focused on the fact that even though companies bought leading-edge call centres, databases, software, hardware, and Internet sites, they did not appropriately adjust how they operated or trained personnel to build these relationships. The researchers suggested that business moved too quickly to expand the program rather than being patient and learning with a smaller base of customers prior to full implementation.[9] In contrast to this opinion, one commentator claimed Nespresso's product introduction strength resided in the "Club" that registered every single customer. Its benefits comprised an online magazine, product alerts, a loaner machine when required, and opportunity to order capsules for delivery.[10]

LO2   Direct-Marketing Plan

To successfully implement direct-marketing programs, companies must make a number of decisions. As in other marketing programs, they must determine (1) whom to target by using a database; (2) what the program's objectives will be; (3) what direct-response media strategy will be employed; and (4) how to measure direct-marketing effectiveness.

TARGET AUDIENCES FOR DIRECT MARKETING

As the database description suggested, direct marketing is especially useful to target current customers. Well managed firms have extensive records of their customers in terms of their purchases and other relevant characteristics, allowing for much more meaningful communication as it can be personalized and customized. Alternatively, the database section identified other sources from which to compile a database of non-customers. Businesses are often expanding geographically or along another dimension (e.g., demographic, socioeconomic) where an accurate database and direct marketing could generate trial among prospects. As the earlier Knorr example showed, other segmentation variables are used to accurately profile the target audience for the marketing communication.

Targeting with direct marketing to other known individuals is a key strength of this IMC tool. The agency Target Marketing and Communications won Best in Show honours and Direct Mail Gold with its execution for its client the Canadian Sea Turtle Network (CSTN) at the ICE Awards. The agency arranged to have an issue of *National Geographic* dedicated to CSTN's efforts to save leatherback turtles; the magazine included a handwritten note from the executive director of the CSTN and was wrapped in an actual fishing net. The recipients, journalists, and bloggers with environmental and conservation backgrounds, who had the most potential to be key influencers, had to physically cut the net to read the magazine and card.[11]

Thus far we have discussed direct marketing and the use of databases with the idea that the identity of the receiver is known. While this is true, direct marketing is also used with broader media (i.e., television) and with media that allow for delivery without identity (i.e., unaddressed direct mail). In these situations, databases are (or should be) used to identify the most relevant profile variables to ensure the highest response rate possible. A planner can use census data and postal codes to select attractive regions within a vicinity for unaddressed direct mail. For example, Nubody's Fitness targeted its unaddressed monthly mail drop of 190,000 pieces with key demographic variables, leading to stronger retail visits and phone inquiries.[12] In rare situations, an addressed direct mail piece is sent to "resident" since the company's database indicates the household is not a customer. Fido (Exhibit 16-4) is an example of a brand that could send promotional pieces to postal codes where it has low sales penetration, or to

Exhibit 16-4   A brand like Fido could use direct response media to entice switching.

© Martin Good / Shutterstock.com

addresses where its database indicates it has no current customer. The high level of brand switching behaviour in the mobile phone service market potentially makes this direct-marketing decision effective and profitable.

A third idea for targeting occurs through profiling current customers and using the information to select prospective customers from an alternative database. Working with Canada Post, the Canadian Cancer Society followed this approach with an experiment. They identified four different groups: (1) profiled postal code and receive mail, (2) profiled postal code and receive no mail, (3) non-profiled postal code and receive mail, and (4) non-profiled postal code and receive no mail. The results found a 13.5 percent higher response rate for profiled segments, with net revenue being 19.2 percent higher.[13]

DIRECT-MARKETING OBJECTIVES

The direct marketer seeks an immediate behavioural response, and behavioural objectives identified in Chapter 5—brand trial, re-trial, switching, or category trial—become more salient. A database of consumers' past purchase history information helps identify those who have not previously purchased the brand. For databases containing current customer purchase history, the direct marketer can attempt to influence the rate, amount, or timing of purchases. Often, direct marketing attempts to bring consumers along in their decision-making process. Thus, shopping behaviour can be an objective through retail visits that manifest in ways such as test driving cars or trying on shoes and clothes, requests for service such as obtaining free estimates, or experiencing other marketing communication. Repeat consumption is also an objective with current customers. For example, financial-service firms can use direct marketing to encourage additional visits by customers for yearly financial planning advice. Exhibit 16-5 shows an ad for a car inviting customers to take a test drive at an exclusive club.

A behavioural response is not the only objective for direct marketing. All communication objectives and how the message and offers influence attitudes are still very relevant for direct marketing. As we noted in Chapter 5, brand objectives (i.e., awareness, attitude) are considerations for all pieces of marketing communication. In fact, direct marketers are very innovative, with clever creative approaches to attract attention and encourage processing the message so that a communication effect occurs even if the receiver declines the call to action. A typical objective of perhaps a 2–3 percent response rate suggests that communication objectives are as valuable here as in other marketing communication tools.

DIRECT-RESPONSE MEDIA

Direct-response media include media like direct mail, catalogue, broadcast, and telemarketing. To help achieve the previously identified objectives, these media generally follow a couple of approaches. In the **one-step approach**, the medium is used directly to obtain an order. For example, TV commercials for products such as workout equipment urge viewers to phone a toll-free number to place an order immediately. The **two-step approach** involves the use of more than one medium. The first effort is designed to screen, or qualify, potential buyers. The second effort generates the response. For example, business marketing companies use telemarketing to screen on the basis of interest, then follow up to interested parties with more information designed to achieve an order or use personal selling to close the sale.

Exhibit 16-5   Acura invites new customers to take a test drive.

Courtesy of Pinehurst and Acura

Direct Mail   Direct mail and catalogue distribution advertising revenue hit $1.2 billion in 2014, down from a peak of $1.6 billion in 2007.[14] This amount is equivalent to the amount spent on Internet display ads for 2014. As an example, the material shown in Exhibit 16-6 is just one piece that was sent by Maserati to market its Quattroporte automobile, which indicates that high-end brands see considerable value in this direct-response medium. As noted, a successful direct mail program relies on a database that may be a purchased **mailing list** comprising relevant market information regarding geography, demographics, socioeconomics, and lifestyles. Lists are now very selective for improved effectiveness and very current to minimize waste coverage and maximize efficiency. For example, a Canadian company like www.cleanlist.ca offers many different types of lists to acquire, retain, and cross-sell customers and claims it has very current information for all of its lists.

Exhibit 16-6   Maserati used direct mail to introduce its new automobiles.

Courtesy of Maserati North America, Inc.

Canada Post has a strong interest in developing the market for direct mail and provides extensive research and service to facilitate this goal, especially for small businesses concerned with reaching their customers and prospects with a low-cost option. Canada Post research shows that:

- Receiving mail is meaningful due to the ritual of retrieving and sorting through the mail in the same home location each day. The ritual is more significant in a consumer's life compared to the fluid routine of scanning email or social media messages. In fact, 70 percent are curious to find out what is in their mailbox.

- Direct mail advertising obtains strong exposure levels; 74 percent always or sometimes notice direct mail advertising to go along with the fact that 85 percent will open mail if it looks interesting, and 81 percent read their mail the same day they receive it.

- Direct mail messages contribute to ad recall; 80 percent remember seeing or reading mail sent to them in the past four weeks, and 60 percent say that really good ad mail helps to keep the sender's brand name top of mind.

- Many direct mail ads remain in the household for a good amount of time, leading to continued exposure and potential action, as Figure 16-2 indicates.

- Direct ad mail drives behaviour, with 64 percent visiting an Internet site, 47 percent visiting a store, and 54 percent interacting with social media. And surprisingly, Canadians prefer mail over email from businesses marketing their products.[15]

Figure 16-2   Length of time consumers retain direct mail ads

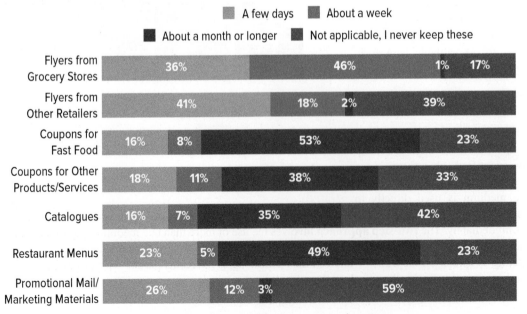

Source: "Breaking Through the Noise," White Paper published at www.canadapost.ca.

Creativity is possible with direct mail, as Grey Advertising won a Gold Lion at the 2010 Cannes Awards with its innovative execution for its client, GGRP, a premier sound design house located in Vancouver. GGRP needed a message to rejuvenate its image for creativity in sound to existing and new North American clients who truly appreciated the audio art the company could produce. The idea picked up on the love audiophiles have for vinyl, an expressive medium for sound that has resurged in popularity. The direct-mail piece featured a cardboard record player that also acted as the envelope along with a vinyl 45. Users spun the record with a pencil and the cardboard naturally amplified the vibrations going through the needle. A response rate of almost 100 percent resulted, as all recipients either talked about it or wanted more copies. It also became an Internet hit, with hundreds of blog reports, extensive YouTube hits on the video showing how to set up the record player, and 70,000 hits to the GGRP website.[16]

Direct mail works well as the first step in the two-step approach for message delivery. Tourism Yukon's direct-mail initiative obtained a 20 percent response rate for website visits versus 5 percent for its online ads presenting the same message. Bear Mountain Resort delivered brochures to two selective markets that encouraged online registration to view its new condominiums and garnered a 37 percent response versus a 14 percent response for past newspaper ads.[17]

Catalogues   Certain companies rely solely on catalogue sales. For example, Yves Rocher is a firm that markets botanical beauty care products for women. It expanded into Canada with its small catalogues and sells directly to consumers. Lee Valley Tools of Ottawa began as a mail-order catalogue company years ago, but has branched out to retail stores across the country and online sales. Exhibit 16-7 is an example of a catalogue for RoadRunner, a brand that eventually moved to physical retail locations.

Companies also use catalogues in conjunction with their retail sales outlets and other promotional tools. For example, Canadian Tire sells directly through catalogues but also uses them to inform consumers of product offerings available in the stores. Canadian Tire revamped its catalogue and presented it online with a much different look than its Internet site. Entitled "The Canadian Way," the virtual presentation featured four sections—living, fixing, playing, and driving—with customized options. Executives saw it as directed toward families with young children with its colour photos and demonstration-like presentation.[18] About 350,000 visitors read more than 4 million pages within the first six months, one-third returned more than one time, and the average time spent lasted six minutes—twice the amount compared to its Internet site; culminating in the retailer winning a bronze in *Strategy*'s Shopper Innovation Award.[19] Moreover, Canadian Tire achieved its best quarterly sales ever by generating 2 percent growth and won a bronze Cassie Award.[20]

Exhibit 16-7   RoadRunner offers both catalogue and in-store sales.

Courtesy of Road Runner Sports-World's Largest Running Store.

IKEA delivers millions of catalogues to Canadian homes each summer, introducing new products, styles, and décor ideas, and the catalogue is a main marketing tool to encourage consumers to visit a retail outlet or the Internet site. The catalogue is a strong brand-building tool to demonstrate how IKEA's products can improve the homes of millions of consumers. With sales lagging slightly, IKEA advertised and promoted the catalogue as a planning vehicle for redecorating when consumers perceived changes in their life.[21] IKEA also developed a mobile app to allow consumers to interact with the catalogue by looking behind closed doors or altering decorative items.[22] IKEA moved into social media communication regarding the catalogue by encouraging consumers to makes posts on #IKEAPageForThat. This carried the idea that people used the catalogue much like a fashion magazine for the home.[23]

Email   Direct mail on the Internet is essentially an electronic version of regular mail; it is highly targeted, relies heavily on lists, and attempts to reach consumers with specific needs through targeted messages. Consumers can opt to have specific types of email sent to them and other types not sent. Figure 16-3 summarizes the reasons why Canadian consumers are interested in receiving email messages from companies. Consumers also receive unwanted emails, referred to as **spam**. However, legitimate and enlightened marketers accept the practice of permission-based marketing. Canada's anti-spam law requires any organization to obtain the receiver's consent, identify their organization, and provide an unsubscribe option with every electronic communication delivered (for more information, see http://fightspam.gc.ca). The changeover required extensive upgrades in information technology and legal costs for organizations to comply.[24]

Figure 16-3   Reasons why Canadians receive email messages.

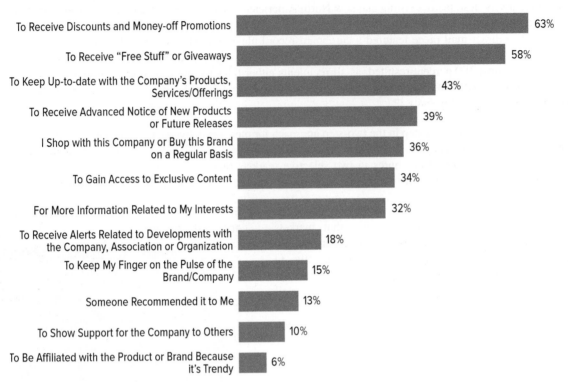

Based on data from ExactTarget, 'Subscribers, Fans & Followers #21: The Digital North,' June 13, 2013

Consumers receive email from publication subscriptions and from loyalty programs. A detailed and sophisticated database is developed from consumers agreeing to opt in since they provide segmentation-like information. Two successful sites (thrillist.com, urbandaddy.com) send out publications to men that are consistent with the regular content not sent digitally. Each publication has a growing email list and sends customized content that is quite distinct with unique positioning approaches.[25] Best Buy enhanced its Reward Zone loyalty program in an email (with clickable link) where consumers could participate in a contest. Click-through rates hit about 20 percent as Best Buy customized the message for different demographics. Customers normally received monetary reward certificates for qualifying purchases that approximated a 1 percent rebate, and other improvements were gifts like show tickets, free movie rentals, and private shopping events for program members only.[26]

Research investigated two of the behavioural responses to receiving email: visiting the brand's website, and forwarding the email to a friend. In a study for cosmetic and body care products sold in retail stores, more useful permission-based email messages yielded fewer website visits, presumably because the information satisfied consumer requirements. However, more useful, more interesting, and more frequent email messages resulted in more store visits, presumably to examine or buy the product. Consumers perceived useful emails as offering sales promotion information, or information about new products.[27]

In a sample of 1,259 forwarded emails from 34 participants, a study found extraordinary dispersion in the number forwarded during the one-month time frame. One person forwarded 177 messages and two others forwarded more than 100, while three people sent one each. Overall, participants forwarded about 40 percent of the emails received, which ranged from 0 percent to 100 percent. The implication of finding a "lead sender" for an email forwarding campaign appears critical for success, much like a lead user in a diffusion of innovation. Additional qualitative research in the study finds that participants experienced substantial positive and negative emotional responses when receiving forwarded email.[28]

It is important to note that the pass-along of email is an outcome and not a strategy. It is a manifestation of the cognitive and emotional responses of the receiver to the message. The similarity to a TV ad would be to recall the ad and tell someone about it, or to call out to a family member ("Hey Dad, come check out this ad on TV"). Secondly, email can experience extensive pass-along yet have minimal benefit for the brand since it entails a single exposure of a brand message for many of the receivers, who simply delete it after viewing.[29]

Broadcast Media   Two broadcast media are available to direct marketers: television and radio. While radio was used quite extensively in the 1950s, its use and effectiveness have dwindled substantially. Thus, the majority of direct-marketing broadcast advertising now occurs on TV. Direct-response TV encompasses direct-response TV spots, infomercials, and home shopping shows (teleshopping).

TV Spots   Referred to in the direct-marketing industry as *short-term programs,* these spots include direct-response commercials for products such as health and beauty, fitness, and household goods. In **direct-response advertising**, the product or service is offered and a sales response is solicited through either the one- or two-step approach. Toll-free phone numbers are included so that the receiver can immediately call to order and companies run direct-response television commercials to encourage website visits.

Infomercials   An **infomercial** is a long commercial that ranges from 3 to 60 minutes. Infomercials are usually produced by the advertisers and are designed to be viewed as regular TV shows. As the name implies, *infomercial* is a shorter way of saying *informational commercial* (Exhibit 16-8). Relatively speaking, infomercials in Canada are less significant in terms of expenditures, with only $18 million in revenue for 2014, a decline of $6 million since peaking in 2007.[30] One study compared the communication effects of a one-minute ad, 15-minute infomercial, 30-minute infomercial, and direct experience (i.e., interacting with the product). The authors concluded that infomercials provided results more closely related to direct experience than a one-minute ad, presumably because both messages allow for extensive cognitive and emotional processing for a longer duration.[31]

Exhibit 16-8   Mini uses an infomercial-like video to attract buyers.

© Adriano Castelli / Shutterstock.com

Thane Direct, with world headquarters located in Toronto, operates in over a dozen countries and controls 250,000 half-hour time slots and 500,000 short-time-frame slots globally, demonstrating strong commitment to direct TV ads and infomercials. Specific targeting at a low cost is possible with more TV options via specialty channels. And despite Internet growth where consumers are actively searching, advertising responses when consumers are passively watching TV is still a fruitful channel according to Thane's CEO: "The message has to be clear, concise, it has to solve a real problem which the consumer is experiencing. It has to provide the consumer with instant gratification, be a good price point, provide value, and be demonstratable."[32]

The decline of Canadian infomercial ad revenue suggests that the video capabilities of the Internet may diminish infomercials in the future. Brands can place the equivalent of an infomercial on their website, or on video sites like YouTube. Brands now produce long messages of the same length as an infomercial, however the content is more story-like rather than being purely informational. These ads are shown both on TV and in Internet media vehicles. For example, Mini (Exhibit 16-8) produced a 360 degree virtual reality story, to be used with a smart phone, that provided a cinematic experience of driving the car. We suggest that a long form ad of a brand such as this might be described as a transformational commercial compared to an informational commercial, which is consistent with the two consumer purchase motivations identified in Chapter 6.

Home Shopping   The Shopping Channel (TSC) is Canada's broadcast retailer available on all delivery formats (cable, satellite) across the country. It claims a reach of 6.5 million households, viewership of 1.5 million Canadians each week, and a 70:30 female–male ratio. TSC recruits its audience like other channels, via direct mail and email, broadcast ads, print ads, paid Internet search, and social media. The lines of communication get blurred a little as TSC is available in catalogue form and on the Internet.[33]

Telemarketing   Communication resulting in sales via the telephone is known as **telemarketing**. There are two types of telemarketing. *Outbound telemarketing* refers to calls made by a company or its sponsor to a potential buyer or client, soliciting the sale of products, services, donations, votes, or any other "value" issue. *Inbound telemarketing* occurs when a company has advertised its toll-free number or its website address, for example asking the customer to call the number, visit the store, or log on to the website. Both for-profit and charitable organizations have employed this medium effectively in one- and two-step approaches.

Data on call centres in Canada show that most call centres are well managed. The majority communicate clearly if the interaction is recorded, follow the laws governing telemarketing, and work with their employees to ensure appropriate interactions.[34] The Canadian Marketing Association's Code of Ethics and Standards of Practice provides extensive guidelines for telemarketing, among many other marketing practices, to ensure that Canadians are treated fairly and responsibly using legitimate marketing practices.[35] However, while telemarketing may have a negative media image due to annoying cold-calls, it also receives negative media image effects when fraudulent and deceptive activities are executed by phoning unsuspecting victims; in this case it is most definitely not telemarketing but rather a crime.

DIRECT-MARKETING EFFECTIVENESS

For direct-marketing programs that do not have an objective of generating an immediate behavioural response, traditional measures of advertising effectiveness can be applied. In those situations requiring a direct response, measuring the effectiveness should include specific behavioural measures in addition to the communication measures. Using the *cost per order (CPO)*, advertisers can evaluate the relative effectiveness of an ad in only a few minutes based on the number of calls generated. By running the same ad on different stations, a direct marketer can determine the relative effectiveness of the medium itself. For example, if the advertiser targets a $5 return per order and a broadcast commercial (production and print) costs $2,500, the ad is considered effective if it generates 500 orders. Similar measures have been developed for print and direct mail ads.

Another measure of effectiveness is **Customer Lifetime Value (CLTV)**. CLTV calculates potential profitability the company can generate from a customer associated with the brand over the course of the long-term relationship. The value is used to determine whether or not a customer should be acquired and what service level to provide to existing customers. Companies use CLTV to assist them in assessing future revenues and profit streams from the customer, so that they can focus more on the satisfaction and retention of their more profitable customers. Thus, the company can focus its promotional budget on profitable customers while spending less on those with a lower CLTV score.

Loyalty Programs

One significant direct-marketing program is a *loyalty program* designed to reward customers for their repeat purchases. Companies track transactions in a database and provide cash, preferential treatment, goods, or services in return for continued patronage. These programs are common with airlines, car rental companies, hotel chains, and retailers (e.g., grocery, department, home centres, bookstores). Canadian retailers account for about half of all loyalty memberships.[36] Numerous other names are used, such as *rewards program, frequency program,* and *continuity program*; however, a literature review concluded that the term *loyalty program* is most useful.[37] In this section we explain the purpose of loyalty programs, describe loyalty program characteristics, review consumer attitudes toward and usage of loyalty programs, and discuss digital communication with program members.

PURPOSE OF LOYALTY PROGRAMS

Marketers view loyalty programs as a means of encouraging consumers to buy their products or services on a continual basis and as a means for developing strong customer loyalty. Companies realize the importance of customer retention and understand that the key to retaining and growing market share is building relationships with loyal customers. Loyalty programs provide marketers with the opportunity to develop databases containing valuable information on their customers that can be used to better understand their needs, interests, and characteristics as well as to identify and track a company's most valuable customers.

These databases can also be used to target specific programs and offers to customers to increase the amount they purchase and/or to build stronger relationships with them. Careful management of databases is

Exhibit 16-9 The WD-40 FanClub is a popular customer loyalty program.

Courtesy of WD-40 Company

necessary to identify and track valuable customers and their purchase history and to make strategic use of targeted loyalty rewards. For example, the WD-40 FanClub is a loyalty program for the brand that provides members with product information, usage tips, newsletters, game downloads, and other benefits (Exhibit 16-9).

The growth of loyalty programs suggests that their implementation now goes beyond a reward mechanism offered by organizations. One view is that a loyalty program is now an important competitive strategic characteristic on which companies differentiate themselves. In short, brands compete on design characteristics since they could be a significant factor in consumer decision making. For example, 45 percent believe that a loyalty program could be replaced with a competitor's program. In fact, research suggests that it may be one of the main drivers of consumer satisfaction after overall quality, leading the research company to suggest that loyalty programs may be the fifth "P" in the marketing mix.[38]

Academic studies echo some of this managerial thinking. One study of a convenience store loyalty program found that the program increased the dollar amount of goods purchased by light and medium volume purchasers. Heavy volume consumers did not alter their purchase patterns.[39] Another study found that the monetary, social, and entertainment benefits predicted a more positive view of the loyalty program, which in turn predicted customer brand loyalty, thereby supporting practitioners' view of the effectiveness of loyalty programs.[40]

LOYALTY PROGRAM CHARACTERISTICS

As the above example suggests, loyalty programs have identifiable characteristics that distinguish them from sales promotions. Figure 16-4 shows five characteristics of loyalty programs based on a substantial review of the topic.[41] The most significant point separating a loyalty program from a sales promotion is the enrollment, since registration requires information that builds the database to track purchases and allows direct follow-up communication. Exhibit 16-10 shows a fan of Canadian Tire's original and iconic promotional activity that encouraged repeat purchases. IMC Perspective 16-1 highlights the characteristics of Canadian Tire's loyalty program, which features significant digital communication.

Exhibit 16-10 Canadian Tire money represents an iconic loyalty incentive.

© Photo by David Cooper/Toronto Star via Getty Images

Figure 16-4   Characteristics of loyalty programs

Characteristic	Customer Effect
Strategic with goals	Maintains strong brand attitude
	Encourages purchase frequency, purchase amount, purchasing timing
Structured	Customer formally enrolls as a member
Long-term	Customer participates continually over time
Rewarding	Purchases recognized via goods/services, preferential treatment, or financial gain
Ongoing	Receives regular communication and offers

IMC PERSPECTIVE 16-1

CANADIAN TIRE MONEY GOES DIGITAL

In the fall of 2014, Canadian Tire launched its digitally based loyalty program entitled My Canadian Tire 'Money.' Consumers who purchased with their Canadian Tire Options MasterCard, loyalty card, or the app accumulated 'Money' for redemption for purchases online and at Canadian Tire stores, including automotive and home services. Accumulated 'Money' could be donated to Canadian Tire's Jumpstart program designed to fund sports participation for less fortunate children. Purchased goods from other retailers within the corporate umbrella (i.e., Mark's, Sport Chek, PartSource, L'Équipeur) also qualified for 'Money.' While over $1 billion of the Canadian Tire 'Money' hit the wallets of its customers over the years since 1958, most expected the iconic promotion to wane over time.

Hand-out/CANADIAN TIRE CORPORATION, LIMIT/Newscom

The new loyalty program appeared much like the original but with at least two important differences: (1) the program required customers to register, and (2) customers received a payback of 4 percent of sales as a reward if they used the credit card. Previously, the retailer distributed Canadian Tire 'Money' anonymously for cash purchases with a reward of one-tenth of the generous 4 percent which would continue with non-credit card purchases. Canadian Tire accommodated those wishing to trade in the paper money for digital money.

Canadian Tire tested the new loyalty program for a few years in Nova Scotia to ensure a flawless national rollout. The company discovered many logistical details that it needed to address and ended up spending considerable dollars per customer to get the system up and running. The resulting data indicated that some consumers spent their 'Money' reward immediately while others saved it for a big purchase. The data also showed that members visited the store more often but did not purchase more per trip than non-members.

Canadian Tire planned exclusive promotional offers sent directly to loyalty program members' online account. The smart phone app allowed members to collect, redeem, and manage their 'Money' and receive bonus offers. Moreover, the app acted as a transaction hub to review transactions and initiate product returns. Executives expected the data from the loyalty program would provide great insight into shoppers' habits and allow the retailer to direct more relevant messages to members with personalized and customized communication.

According to the chief operating officer, "With the information received through the program, we'll better understand how and when customers shop and what they're buying. That means we can be more relevant to our customers by ensuring our products, services, and promotions reflect their shopping preferences. Knowing our customers better means we can offer them so much more and will enable us to turn our digital flyer into a tool that is specific to each individual customer."

Some may feel saddened by the eventual elimination of paper Canadian Tire 'Money,' and there may be those devoted to the tangible paper option over the next decade or so, much like those who relish the sound of vinyl records. However, actual Canadian currency moved from paper to polymer over the past decade with great acceptance, so it seems likely most Canadians will sway toward the digital option as shopping with a smart phone gains greater traction.

Sources: Kristin Laird, "Canadian Tire Introduces Enhanced Loyalty Program," *Marketing Magazine,* September 9, 2014; Francine Kopun, "Canadian Tire Launches New Loyalty Program," *Toronto Star,* September 9, 2014; Linda Nguyen, "Canadian Tire to Roll Out New Digital Loyalty Program," *The Globe and Mail,* September 9, 2014; Matt Semansky, "Canadian Tire Pilots New Loyalty Program in Nova Scotia," *Marketing Magazine,* February 15, 2012.

Questions:

1. Who would be most attracted to the features of Canadian Tire's loyalty program?
2. How competitive is Canadian Tire's loyalty program compared to other loyalty programs?

A review of loyalty programs concludes that loyalty programs influence consumers in three ways. The *points-pressure mechanism* occurs when consumers earn points and then realize they are close to achieving a reward level and make additional purchases to achieve it. The *rewarded-behaviour mechanism* occurs after reward redemption as this process contributes to positive attitudinal and behavioural responses. The *personalized marketing mechanism* occurs with the use of the database marketing activities. The design of the loyalty programs affects each of these mechanisms. Design includes the structure in terms of the time frame and whether the reward is based on frequency or tiered customer groups. Another characteristic is whether the program is a single brand or a partnership. A third design consideration is whether the rewards are monetary vs. non-monetary, or brand vs. non–brand related. Finally, the reward could be immediate or delayed.[42]

The popular Air Miles loyalty program offers an example of these design decisions. Air Miles is a partnership approach where shoppers collect points while buying goods and services at retail locations or online, among others, like using a credit card. Air Miles offers tiered customer groups with its gold level for those who collect a certain number of points from a minimum number of brands. Air Miles originally offered non-monetary rewards when consumers redeemed points for goods and services, including air travel. For many items, it would require a time delay to collect points and redeem them. Air Miles currently offers consumers the option of using points collected as cash when making purchases at a point of sale. While a minimal delay is incurred, it is substantially less so since the minimum $10 purchase can be made with 95 points, a level someone could accumulate in a month.[43]

Air Miles also retains the characteristics of a loyalty program. It is a major strategic initiative for its participating brands. For example, Shell Canada offers Air Miles and regularly promotes additional offers to encourage repeat visits. Shell recently sent a direct-mail piece that contained a card designed to be kept in one's wallet to receive a bonus when buying Shell gas. Air Miles is clearly structured as members enroll, receive a card, and track point totals on their online account. The accumulation of points takes time, and monetary and non-monetary rewards are a strong incentive. Consumers regularly receive direct mail and email notifications of offers to accumulate additional points.

Loyalty programs are at varying levels of sophistication, so a number of prescriptions have emerged to guide successful implementation. A primary one concerns customer information within the database to allow behavioural (level, amount purchased) and attitudinal (brand associations and feeling) segmentation. Second, customized and personalized communication is critical as a one-size-fits-all approach is not viable even though companies pursue it. Third, marketers should consider moving beyond direct mail and email for communication within the loyalty program and augment with social media to forge a stronger relationship with consumers who have connected with the brand (e.g., Facebook fan pages). Finally, greater smart phone penetration allows loyalty programs to adjust their offerings or communicate ways to earn rewards more immediately through the use of location-based apps.[44]

CONSUMER ATTITUDES AND USAGE

Virtually all Canadians are enrolled in a loyalty program; on average each of us is a member of about 11 programs but we regularly use only seven of them. A number of attitudinal measures demonstrate the appeal of loyalty programs; 75 percent feel loyalty programs are worth the effort, 77 percent claim continued transactions with brands they participate in, 67 percent say the program forms a part of their relationship with a company, 71 percent modify when and where they shop, and 65 percent modify the brands purchased to maximize loyalty benefits. While consumers feel good about loyalty programs, about one-third believe they do not increase the dollar amount of purchase once enrolled in a program.[45]

Overall, about two-thirds are "very" or "somewhat" satisfied with their loyalty program. Functional satisfaction with loyalty programs is strongly associated with the following: appeal of rewards/benefits, ability to reach desired rewards/benefits in a timely manner, number of ways rewards/benefits can be earned, amount accumulated per $1 spent, and the time it takes to receive your redeemed rewards/benefits. Experience–brand satisfaction with loyalty programs is due to its being worth the effort of participating, the program was enjoyable to participate in, and that the program meets needs, is trustworthy, and is a personalized experience.[46]

While the success of loyalty programs appears strong, marketers are faced with the continued issue of whether the program merely rewards behaviour that would have occurred anyway since consumers generally sign up for programs with brands that they are already emotionally attached to and have a purchase history with. For example, 30 percent would not be loyal to the brand if the loyalty program did not exist, and 45 percent believe that a loyalty program could be replaced with a competitor's program. Research suggests that hard benefits of financial rewards in terms of discounts, cash, or merchandise are critical; softer rewards with respect to privilege, access, and information are very important for fostering strong loyalty over time. Furthermore, consumers become attached to brands with loyalty programs for regular purchases and are more likely to use the brand once again for infrequent larger purchases.

The experience of being in a loyalty program is also a strong consideration as consumers value seeing the rewards accumulating over time. Furthermore, the experience of "cashing in" for a big-ticket item is seen as an important consumption event that helps strengthen the relationship with the brand. In fact, one-quarter of all Canadians "splurge" with their rewards claim. And this loyalty is seen in the 40 percent of major loyalty program members who have stayed with a program for over 10 years, especially since many "save up" for big-ticket items.

DIGITAL COMMUNICATION

Communication with existing members and providing promotional offers is a value-enhancing approach to foster increased use of the loyalty program and greater purchases. While loyalty programs still work with direct mail and email to administer and communicate with members, more are moving toward social media, mobile, and Internet site interactions to permit timely or customized offers.[47] Many of the improvements are designed to provide an experience that is similar to buying and consuming the brand. For example, members of the Jack Astor's loyalty program can design a unique identity on Facebook and receive text messages and promotions.[48]

Industry experts consider the possibility that these channels might permit brands to bring their loyalty programs "in-house," away from plans like Air Miles or Aeroplan, while others envision much more personalized and customized offerings, or perhaps profile sites where consumers share their profile to select brands rather than signing up for multiple loyalty cards.[49] In turn, Air Miles is testing an enhancement of its offerings through a mobile app allowing members to visit a participating retailer's site and earn promotional incentives with more frequent visits. Shoppers Drug Mart instituted a game to create a friendly online experience associated with the program.[50]

The Scene card allows its members to collect reward points by attending movies, using products associated with Scotiabank (e.g., a Scene debit or credit card), buying goods at the concession stand, and ordering tickets in certain ways (e.g., online). Consumers also receive discounts and special promotion offers and contests, and can spend their rewards on free tickets or on restaurants, music, or magazines. Scene augmented its loyalty program by giving more points if members formed online groups and attended movies together. It also offered a mobile app and text alerts for keeping in touch and improving services.[51]

My Starbucks Rewards gives "stars" to customers with their purchases and offers rewards along three collection levels. At the Welcome level, consumers get a drink for their birthday; at the Green level, consumers can get a free refill with five stars; and at the Gold level, consumers receive free food or drink once they hit 30 stars within a year and obtain status with a gold card. Many tweeted a positive response to the gold card as recognition for their high volume of purchases. A new smart phone app allows consumers to track their stars in a fun way consistent with the brand image. Members can interact with one another for ideas on improving the Starbucks experience.[52] Managers attributed Starbucks' sales growth and increased number of store visits to its rewards program and improved digital communication with its members. In fact, its rewards program is linked directly with the mobile payment system from the customer's smart phone, and this encouraged stronger mobile payment uptake well ahead of other retailers.[53]

Evaluation of Direct Marketing

We presented strengths and limitations of direct marketing thus far, but summarize these factors in a concluding section as we have done in previous chapters. Given that direct marketing employs different media, each with its own characteristics, these conclusions are generalizations in which variation can be expected.

STRENGTHS OF DIRECT MARKETING

Direct marketing has many strengths, including target audience selectivity, target audience coverage, frequency, creativity for cognitive and emotional responses, scheduling flexibility, and costs.

Target Audience Selectivity   Marketers can purchase lists of recent product purchasers (e.g., car buyers), and these lists may allow segmentation on the basis of geographic area, occupation, demographics, and job title. Combining this information with the geocoding capabilities of PRIZM C2 (discussed in Chapter 3), marketers can develop effective segmentation strategies. In fact, a personalized or customized message can be sent in situations where the identity of the person is known. Car owners are mailed letters congratulating them on their new purchase and offering accessories. Computer purchasers are sent software solicitations. With the ability of direct marketing to personalize and customize messages through a relevant direct-response medium, we suggest that fairly strong attention and involvement of the message occurs in these situations.

Target Audience Coverage   Direct marketing lets the advertiser reach a high percentage of the selective target audience and reduces waste coverage. Since the database allows precise target audience profiles, the direct-response medium selected can achieve a strong level of hits. For example, while not everyone drives on highways where there are billboards or pays attention to TV commercials, virtually everyone receives mail. A good list allows for minimal waste, as only those consumers with the highest potential are targeted. For example, a political candidate can direct a message at a very select group of people (those living in a certain postal code, or members of McGill University Alumni, or the Royal Vancouver Yacht Club).

Frequency   Depending on the medium used, it may be possible to build frequency levels. The program vehicles used for direct-response TV advertising are usually the most inexpensive available, so the marketer can afford to purchase repeat times. Frequency may not be so easily accomplished through the mail, since consumers may be annoyed to receive the same mail repeatedly.

Creativity for Cognitive and Emotional Responses   Direct marketing can take on a variety of creative forms. Direct-mail pieces allow for detailed copy that provides a great deal of information. The targeted mailing of DVDs containing product information has increased dramatically, as companies have found this to be a very effective way to provide potential buyers with product information.

Scheduling Flexibility   While some media require long-range planning and have long closing dates, direct-response advertising can be much more timely. Direct mail, for example, can be put together very quickly and distributed to the target population. TV programs typically used for direct-response advertising are older, less sought-after programs that are likely to appear on the station's list of available spots. Another common strategy is to purchase available time at the last possible moment to get the best price.

Costs   While the CPM for direct mail may be high, its ability to specifically target the audience and eliminate waste coverage reduces the actual CPM. Email costs are generally very affordable. The ads used on TV for infomercials are among the lowest-priced available. A second factor contributing to the cost-efficiency of direct-response advertising is the cost per customer purchasing. Because of the low cost of media, each sale generated is very inexpensive.

LIMITATIONS OF DIRECT MARKETING

As with all things, direct marketing has limitations to balance out its benefits. These include media image, control for selective exposure, and reach.

Media Image   Generally, people believe unsolicited mail promotes undesired products, and others dislike being solicited. Likewise, direct-response ads on TV are often low-budget ads for lower-priced products, which contributes to the image that somewhat less than the best products are marketed in this way. Some of this image is being overcome by the home shopping channels, which promote very expensive products. Telemarketing is found to be irritating to consumers, as is spam email.

Control for Selective Exposure   While target audience selectivity attempts to address this factor, consumers exert tremendous control with respect to direct marketing. It is easy to simply toss a direct-mail piece into one's paper recycling bin. As seen in the discussion for television, consumers can readily zip or zap a direct message, and consumers usually have to actively seek and select an infomercial. In contrast to this point, those who are in fact interested in the offer are expected to devote considerable levels of time to processing the message, irrespective of the limitations of the direct-response media selected.

Reach   The selectivity of direct marketing and the cost associated with it suggest that achieving high levels of reach is neither feasible nor even a realistic characteristic of the purpose of this marketing approach. Similarly, the costs associated with complete geographic coverage are expected to be prohibitive in most direct marketing programs.

LO5 IMC Planning: Strategic Use of Direct Marketing

Direct marketing is now an important component of the integrated marketing programs of organizations. In some cases it is used as a tool for an immediate response, and in other cases it plays a key role in building the brand by moving through the target audience's decision-making process. In addition, direct-marketing activities support and are supported by other elements of the promotional mix.

DECISION-MAKING PROCESS

As described in this chapter, direct-marketing tools are typically employed to persuade immediate consumer action. At this point, it is critical that the promotional manager plan for a specific action in order to select the most appropriate direct-response media. In Chapter 5 we reviewed different types of behavioural objectives for promotional communication, which we will use to develop IMC planning prescriptions. Trial and repeat purchasing objectives suggest that much of direct marketing involves influence at the purchase decision stage.

Trial objectives require a broader-based direct-response medium, much like what is seen in advertising media decisions. Typically, wide-ranging direct-mail pieces targeted by census track and income dispersions allow firms to reach as many potential consumers as possible. In this situation, the database used relies on more public sources, and a manager may use unaddressed drop-offs. Alternatively, for more targeted messages, brands may rely upon the list services and provide addressed mailings. Alternatively, with a database of existing customers, cross-selling of other products is now a trial purchase for the promotional planner's brand in a new product category. This trial purchase may be relatively new and be viewed as a purchase within the product category, thus requiring a direct-response medium providing considerable information.

We mentioned that existing customer databases are used for repeat purchases. Repeat purchasing objectives involve the timing, amount, and rate of consumer purchases. These different options suggest other criteria for evaluating the different direct-media options. For example, repeat purchasing objectives for specific timing might suggest telemarketing if the managers have current databases and permission to call upon the company's current customers. A favourite direct-response medium is bill inserts delivered monthly to enhance frequency and thus improve the amount and rate of purchase. Thus, the opportunity of promotional planners to match the specific objectives with the right direct-response medium requires full consideration.

Shopping behaviour objectives frequently involve influencing consumers at earlier stages in their decision making. For example, direct-mail pieces may be delivered to encourage need recognition and prompt the target audience to make a sales inquiry at the retail location or over the telephone, or to visit the Internet site for further understanding of the brand during the information search stage. Alternatively, telephone calls can be made to follow up after the sales inquiry to ensure that the brand is seriously considered at the alternative evaluation stage.

DIRECT MARKETING AND IMC TOOLS

Obviously, direct marketing is in itself a form of advertising. Whether through mail, print, or TV, the direct-response offer is an ad. It usually contains a contact number, a form that requests mailing information, or a link to an Internet site. Sometimes the ad supports the direct-selling effort. Direct-response ads or infomercials are also referred to in retail outlet displays.

Public relations activities often employ direct-response techniques. Private companies may use telemarketing activities to solicit funds for charities, or co-sponsor charities that use these and other direct-response techniques to solicit funds. Likewise, corporations and/or organizations engaging in public relations activities may include contact numbers or Internet addresses in their ads or promotional materials.

Telemarketing and direct selling are two methods of personal selling. Non-profit organizations such as charities often use telemarketing to solicit funds. For-profit companies are also using telemarketing with much greater frequency to screen and qualify prospects (which reduces selling costs) and to generate leads. Direct-mail pieces are often used to invite prospective customers to visit auto showrooms to test-drive new cars; the salesperson then assumes responsibility for the selling effort.

Direct mail is often used to notify consumers of sales promotions like sales events or contests. Ski shops regularly mail announcements of special end-of-season sales. Whistler Ski Resort and Intrawest constantly mail out promotions to their customer database announcing promotional and seasonal vacation packages, room rates, and lift ticket specials. Consumer packaged-goods firm Garnier used both addressed (5 percent redemption) and unaddressed mail (1.5 percent redemption) with extensive profiling to deliver a sample and coupon offer for its Long and Strong brand.[54] Hudson's Bay, Sears, and other retail outlets call their existing customers to notify them of special sales promotions. In turn, the sales promotion event may support the direct-marketing effort since databases are often built from the names and addresses acquired from a promotion, permitting other direct-marketing follow-up.

Learning Objectives Summary

 Define direct marketing and summarize the importance of a database for making marketing communication decisions.

Direct marketing includes a variety of methods and media that seek to obtain an immediate behavioural response from the target audience. Its success is predicated on a database that contains information for each customer or prospect in terms of demographic variables. More thorough databases contain additional variables on purchase history, socioeconomic characteristics, media exposure, and any other relevant segmentation variables the marketer believes to be necessary. Direct marketing is a valuable promotional tool for targeting audiences and for managing CRM activities despite its intrusiveness toward consumers and the challenges and investment requirements of databases.

 Express the decisions of a direct-marketing plan.

Direct marketing involves careful target audience profiling through the use of the database. Direct marketers can target lapsed customers in an attempt to generate re-trial. Alternatively, they can target current customers and try to encourage repeat purchasing of the brand, but with additional products (i.e., cross-selling). Databases garnered from other means can be compiled to develop stronger trial among non-category users or non-brand users. Thus, a critical part of the direct-marketing plan is profiling the target audience and selecting the corresponding objective, since this guides the promotional offer and the selection of the most appropriate direct-response media.

Direct marketing is executed with a variety of direct-response media including direct mail, catalogues, broadcast, telemarketing, and new digital applications. We summarized the former ones in this chapter and examine the latter in the next chapter. These media are used in a specific manner to encourage consumers to take action in terms of a purchase or getting involved with another medium or another IMC tool such as sales promotion.

 Describe the content of a loyalty program.

An important part of a direct-marketing plan is a loyalty program designed to maintain continued repeat purchasing from consumers who enroll and become members. Most of these consumers are behaviourally and attitudinally loyal; however, others join to collect points to earn rewards and might readily switch to an alternative provider if they did not have so much invested in the program. Despite this limitation, consumers are quite satisfied with these programs and Canada has one of the highest participation rates in the world.

 Evaluate the strengths and limitations of direct marketing.

Advantages of direct marketing include target audience selectivity that permits personalization in direct-response media like direct mail leading to stronger attention and involvement, target audience coverage, frequency, creativity for cognitive and emotional responses, scheduling flexibility, and affordable absolute cost and efficiency. At the same time, a number of disadvantages are associated with the use of direct marketing, including media image, control for selective exposure, and reach implying limited geographic scope for some direct-response media.

Apply the ideas of direct marketing within the development of an IMC plan.

Direct marketing is one activity in marketing where activities are clearly demarcated with respect to targeting potential customers with a message to ensure a trial purchase or targeting existing customers to continue purchasing. The source of information for sending the message and offer is a database of leads or current customers, so the most appropriate approach is possible, unlike with other forms of marketing communication. Direct marketing acts as the delivery mechanism for other IMC tools like sales promotion. As seen in some of the loyalty programs, promotional offers to members can enhance their experience. Similarly, public relations activities can be tied with direct marketing for stronger communication effect or cost efficiencies.

Review Questions

1. Explain how companies use database marketing. How is the information derived from the database used to target audiences?

2. What is the difference between the one- and two-step approaches to direct marketing? Give examples of companies that pursue both methods.

3. Why are loyalty programs considered to be direct-marketing programs rather than sales promotions?

4. One of the disadvantages associated with direct-marketing media is the high cost per exposure. Some marketers feel that this cost is not really as much of a disadvantage as is claimed. Argue for or against this position.

5. How does direct marketing influence each stage of the consumer decision-making process as it works with other IMC tools?

Applied Questions

1. Construct a list of variables that a fashion brand might desire in its database to market to students in college or university.

2. Collect any direct mail delivered to your household and evaluate whether it is effective.

3. Read up online about an interesting loyalty program and apply Figure 16-4 to identify the characteristics and give an assessment of the program's value.

4. How might a smart phone service improve its marketing communication with the use of direct marketing?

5. Provide examples for both consumer goods and services of how companies might use direct marketing as part of an IMC program.

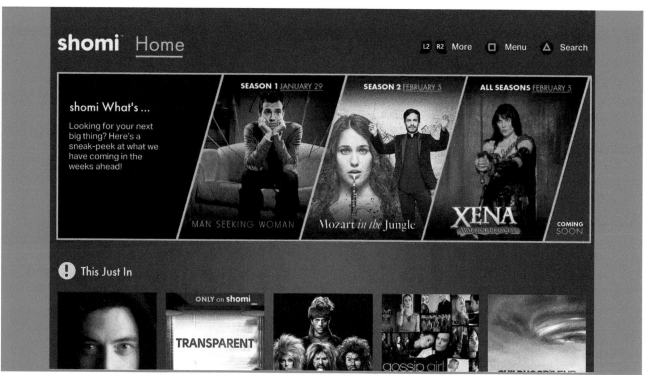

Hand-out/shomi Partnership/Newscom

CHAPTER SEVENTEEN

Internet Media

LEARNING OBJECTIVES

LO1   Describe the general characteristics of Internet users and explain website communication.

LO2   Identify the advertising formats of Internet media.

LO3   Illustrate how to use social media in an IMC plan.

LO4   Define measures of Internet media effectiveness.

LO5   Evaluate the strengths and limitations of Internet media.

LO6   Apply the ideas of Internet media within the development of an IMC program.

Show Me Shomi Winning the Award

Marketing Magazine recognized Shomi as its Marketer of the Year for 2015 after a successful launch in the Streaming Video on Demand (SVOD) market. The Rogers and Shaw joint venture went up against the established Netflix and Bell Canada's up-and-coming CraveTV with a sweet digital presence, a solid line-up of content, an entertaining campaign, and the right media and IMC mix to establish the new brand with Canadians. Acting as a standalone brand from both parent organizations, the entrepreneurial company showed no brand imagery from Rogers or Shaw and differentiated the Shomi brand with its service-oriented human side by responding to consumer feedback, interacting on social media, and allowing content artists to organize and curate the content line-up rather than relying on an algorithm.

Shomi's messaging played on its catchy name with phrases like, "Shomi something funny," and "Shomi what's good," to help create its brand image as fun and personable. Visual images and entertaining creatives fostered the playful tone as well. In fact, the creative changed quickly to keep interest high and make it feel like one has changed the show they are watching as it focused on eight key TV shows. According to the senior marketing director, "We're in the business of entertainment, and when marketing stops being entertaining, then we have a challenge on our hands." Overall, the marketing balanced building the brand and conveying the line-up of programs to watch.

Media placement included TV, in-cinema activations, and out-of-home in 20 markets. The Shomi brand featured its logo on spectaculars, wall murals, billboards, and transit shelters, and took over Toronto's Yonge–Dundas Square. One could not miss the spectacular purple throughout the cities, and the frequent TV rotation ensured strong exposure, leading to 76 percent awareness in one year compared to 90 percent for Netflix after four years, closely followed by CraveTV with 69 percent. Other communication featured Twitter quiz cards, contests, brand placement within a TV show and a portable "stream machine" for demonstrations. It also provided a sample by posting a full episode of *The Enfield Haunting* on Facebook. Sharing the link led to a successful number of views and subsequent leads to follow up for sales.

Later on, Apple TV added both Shomi and CraveTV to its service. With 1.1 million Canadian subscribers, about half of whom do not subscribe to any of the three companies' TV service, Apple TV allowed these brands to gain revenue from an ever growing number of "cord-cutters." Data showed that up to 1.4 million Canadian households do not use a television service provider. However, as things change, and as Apple TV brands its service, it seems the very definition of a TV service provider is changing even if the service is delivered via Internet media. Penetration of SVOD services hit nearly 50 percent in Canada, showing that consumers are seeing value with both types of subscriptions, for now. Many in the industry expect that substantial advertising will eventually migrate to these new services that keep evolving as well. For example, the NFL tested a live stream of a game (and other sports are following suit), and in another direction, Rogers' Sportsnet channel began offering a digital stream by subscription, thereby letting customers avoid having to pay for Rogers cable.

Despite Shomi's promising future, Rogers and Shaw announced the demise of the new service in the latter part of 2016 due to their continued financial losses. Research indicated 83 percent awareness of the service, however only 4 percent of Canadian households actively viewed Shomi's collection of movies and programs. Industry observers suggested the video-streaming market could not support Netflix and two Canadian brands.

Sources: Kristin Laird, "Marketer of the Year: Shomi" *Marketing Magazine,* February 4, 2016; Matthew Chung, "Creating for the Next Generation," *Strategy,* December 2014; Shane Dingman, "Made-in-Canada Streaming Services CraveTV, Shomi Added to Apple TV," *The Globe and Mail,* May 2015; Chris Powell, "Canadians Abandoning Pay TV for OTT Services," *Marketing Magazine,* November 2015; James Bradshaw, "Video-Streaming Service Shomi to Shut Down at End of November," *The Globe and Mail,* September 26, 2016.

Question:

1. What advertising opportunities do you foresee for CraveTV's video-streaming service?

The chapter opener illustrates that Internet media continue to change, potentially giving brands new advertising and promotion opportunities to reach a target audience. In this chapter we discuss Internet media from a communication perspective. First we describe general characteristics of Internet media users and explain website communication. Next, we identify the advertising formats that promotional planners place in virtually any location within Internet media. We then illustrate how social media can be planned within an IMC program, as an approach for directly communicating with audiences, as a media vehicle for ad placement, and as a means for consumers to see and contribute user-generated content from customers and non-customers. To conclude, we define the options for measuring Internet media communication effectiveness, evaluate its key strengths and limitations, and apply the ideas of Internet media within an IMC program.

Internet Communication

The **Internet** and the **World Wide Web (WWW)** allow for marketers and consumers to conduct transactions for goods and services; however, our focus is to consider these digital tools as media for communication and facilitation of the promotional program. In the academic literature, many digital marketing domains are investigated beyond advertising.[1] Our particular interest is Internet advertising research that examines the effectiveness of Internet media advertising, interactivity, how advertising works, attitude to Internet media ads (including websites), and finally comparisons to other media.[2] As this suggests, the Internet connects consumers—both current customers and potential customers—and marketers seeking or greeting both types of consumers through advertising and other tools. In this section, we describe Canadian Internet media users and explain the primary purpose of website marketing communication.

INTERNET USERS

Approximately 92 percent of all Canadians accessed Internet media at any location in 2015 (Figure 17-1). After a couple of decades of Internet use, we now see consistency across demographic groups except for those with less household income and older consumers. However, older consumers' usage grew from 54 percent to 74 percent over 2007–2015, and we can expect Canadian Internet usage to be close to universal by 2020. Usage proved very consistent provincially, by city/town size and in each major Canadian city.

Figure 17-1   Past month Internet use by demographics, fall 2015, anglophones 18+

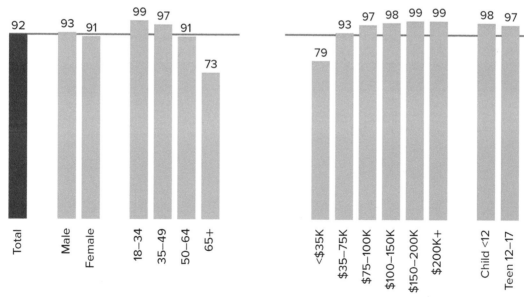

© Media Technology Monitor (MTM)

Mobile access to Internet media via smart phones has continued to grow, and hit 77 percent in 2015 (Figure 17-2). Similar data variation with age and incomes occurred here as well. And some disparity existed geographically, as Atlantic Canada and communities with fewer than 100,000 residents had slightly lower penetration levels. Other 2015 Internet media facts included an 84 percent on home Wi-Fi access and 50 percent on penetration for tablets and for Internet connected TVs. Clearly, these numbers confirm the penetration of Canadian Internet media use.

Figure 17-2   Penetration of smart phones by demographics, fall 2015, anglophones 18+

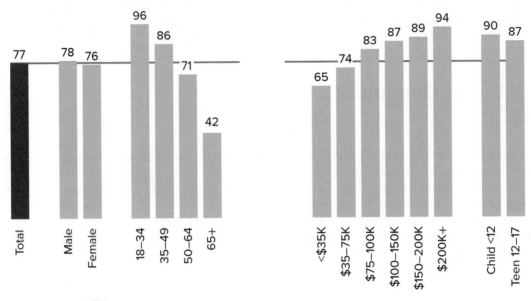

© Media Technology Monitor (MTM)

Figure 17-3 illustrates that Internet media reached 81 percent of Canadians on a weekly basis, lower than broadcast media and higher than print media. However, the growth is noticeable; it moved up from half the population 15 years ago. The amount of time Canadians consumed Internet media reached just over 20 hours per week, compared to 29 hours for TV. And a significant difference between Internet and TV media consumption by age emerged for younger and older people, while the proportions were consistent for those aged 35–54. Furthermore, Canadians who are more active in social media consumed greater Internet media.

Figure 17-3   Internet exposure vs. other media

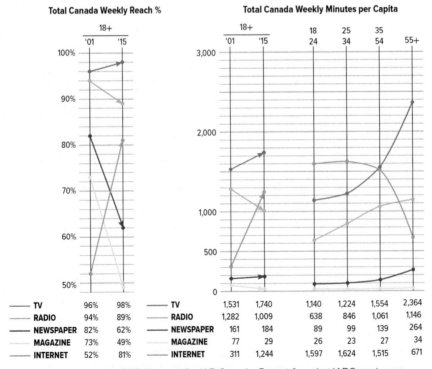

Source: Canada's Media Landscape, prepared by PHD Network for IAB Canada, Report found at IABCanada.com

Figure 17-4 summarizes the types of usage during the past month uncovered by Media Technology Monitor. These overview statistics indicate that Internet media facilitated many different types of consumer experiences. Taken together with the reach level and time spent consuming, Internet media attained the status of a regular day-to-day media for most Canadians, leading to advertisers spending over $4 billion in advertising for 2015.

Figure 17-4   Internet activity, fall 2015, anglophones 18+

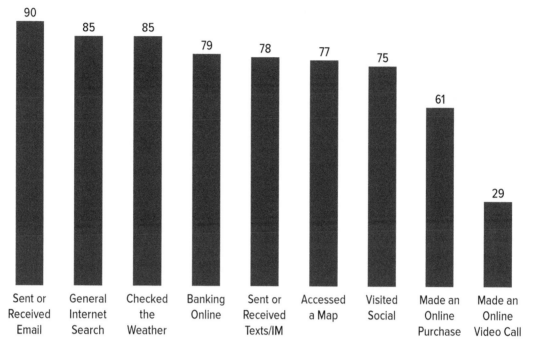

© Media Technology Monitor (MTM)

Figure 17-5 shows the varying entertainment activities Canadians enjoyed with Internet media in 2015. Clearly, the extensive activities Canadians experience on the Internet allow advertisers opportunities to reach specific customer groups, lifestyles, or virtually any marketing segmentation variable. In fact, some opportunities may be *very* good—the Internet appears to have spurred greater consumption of news when adding up the total exposure from traditional and digital media as shown in Chapter 12 statistics. Furthermore, the development of user-generated content—such as product reviews, forum or journal posts, blogs, websites, wikis, audio files, video files, and podcasts—contributes to an enormous amount of word-of-mouth communication. One study documented how certain types of psychographic groups relied on these different Internet media sources of information when making purchase decisions.[3] With these variations within Internet media, we can conclude that some aspects will present advertising opportunities with mass exposure potential like TV, selective reach like magazines, and interactive capabilities unique to Internet media. At present, Procter & Gamble, maker of Crest toothpaste (Exhibit 17-1), is one of Canada's leading Internet media advertisers. In fact, how advertisers will allocate the more than $4 billion in expenditures across the many Internet media vehicles will continue to be an important media decision, much like in past decades with older media.

Exhibit 17-1   Procter & Gamble is one of the largest advertisers in Canada using Internet media.

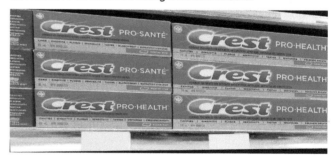

© rmnoa357 / Shutterstock.com

Figure 17-5   Internet entertainment activity, fall 2015, anglophones 18+

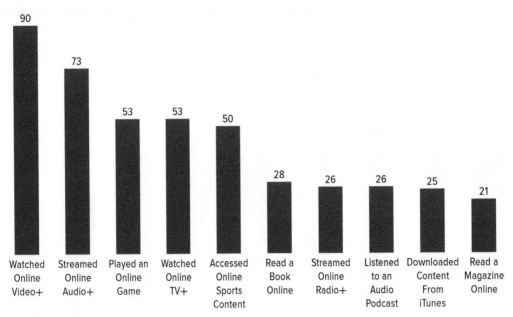

© Media Technology Monitor (MTM)

WEBSITE COMMUNICATION

We investigate website communication since digital marketing communication tools direct users to many different types of websites. One role of a **website** is to provide information to Internet users. To attract visitors to the site—and to have them return—requires a combination of creativity, updated information, and the use of digital and other media to direct consumers. A second role of a website is to provide more creative with video, still images, audio, and graphic design; brands create unique messages and digital experiences unlike any consumers had previously experienced with other advertising media. A third website role is to facilitate communication and interaction among consumers using the capability of two-way communication features. From a communication standpoint, websites typically achieve four broad communication objectives: develop awareness, disseminate information, build a brand image, and facilitate interaction. These latter three are attitudinal in nature and are consistent with earlier chapters.

Develop Awareness   Communicating on a website enhances or creates awareness of an organization as well as its specific product and service offerings. Websites for well established products offer additional interactive exposure of the brand in terms of its key messages and typical signature (e.g., logo, slogan, colours). The website for Red Bull creates a fun experience for consumers to enjoy the brand and keep awareness strong. Its brand image is reinforced on its site much like at public events (Exhibit 17-2). For small companies with limited budgets, a website is an opportunity to create awareness well beyond what might be achieved through other media. Internet media may not be optimal for awareness in these situations due to its limited reach without other communication to direct consumers to the website; however, these consumers are often in the information search stage of their decision making and are very good prospects for ensuring they do not forget about the brand when making a final decision, or for when they want to buy on their next purchase occasion.

Exhibit 17-2   Red Bull offers many reasons to visit its website.

© arindambanerjee / Shutterstock.com

Disseminate Information   A primary communication objective for a website is to provide information about a company's products and services. With increased health interest, Canadians rely on food company websites for more in-depth facts than might be seen in other media or at the point of sale. For example, Kraft Canada's website presents ingredient and nutritional information for its salad dressing (Exhibit 17-3). In most markets, a website is a necessity since buyers, both consumer and business-to-business, expect that a company will have a site providing them with detailed information about its offerings and where to buy. In fact, considerable current market research indicates that most Canadians "window shop" or browse the Internet for information on goods or services in general, and similar numbers arise for specific activities like getting medical and travel information and banking online. In the public sector, all levels of government use Internet media to provide citizens with a wide range of information on services.

Build a Brand Image   Websites are designed to reflect the image a company wants to portray. Interestingly, marketers have had difficulty creating a brand image on the Internet. While some companies have been successful, others have not fared as well and realize that branding and image-creating strategies must be specifically adapted to the medium. Websites also provide a transformational experience, with video, animation, and social media-like tools to make the brand experience truly unique and interactive beyond what consumers experience with other media. Guess is a good example, as it links all of its social media to its website (Exhibit 17-4).

A study by the marketing research firm Millward Brown published in the *Journal of Advertising Research* concludes that Internet media is capable of building a brand like other established advertising media, although certain caveats seen elsewhere remain. For example, ensuring that the right message is communicated within the appropriate media vehicle is critical, a key conclusion that we have seen with more established media.[4] Since then, it is clear that Internet sites are a critical component of any brand's ability to project its image to customers, non-customers, and any other stakeholders. A few great Canadian examples include MAC Cosmetics, BlackBerry, Lululemon, Canada Goose, NRML, and Harry Rosen—check them out!

Facilitate Interaction   Companies set up websites to interact with an audience on a regular basis, and may use a membership component to obtain personal information with permission and communicate afterward (e.g., email). For example, the Canadian website for Alfa Romeo achieves all three previous objectives and its splash page invites visitors to sign up for a newsletter, obtain a brochure, go to a dealer, or build and price a model (Exhibit 17-5). From another perspective, Mazda and its agency JWT created a smart phone app that viewers used in a Cineplex movie theatre to simulate a car test drive. The app synchronized with the big screen video and users tried to match the driving, while the app measured their success. The app ended with an invitation for a real test drive and 9,000 signed up, a 5 percent hit rate. A similar event occurred a year earlier for the Mazda3 that simulated a race car game where participants and winners received concession product or movie tickets. The competition app garnered 6,000 test drive requests.[5]

Exhibit 17-3   Kraft provides ingredient and nutrition information on its website.

© rmnoa357 / Shutterstock.com

Exhibit 17-4   The website for Guess builds its brand much like its storefronts.

© Martin Good / Shutterstock.com

Exhibit 17-5   Alfa Romeo offers many ways for potential customers to interact with the company.

© meunierd / Shutterstock.com

Interaction also occurs during the execution of sales promotions. The Coors Light "Search+Rescue" contest required consumers to find 880 "hidden" branded boxes containing prizes (e.g., party invites, gift cards, sports equipment). Consumers visited the website with an interactive map to find the location. After finding, the lucky contestant tweeted their selfie with the box and then received the skill-testing question from the company to open up their winnings. The promotional event ended with a "Base Camp Party" in nine major cities. Negative publicity ensued when Toronto traffic snarled when police received notice of a "suspicious package" attached to a downtown railing. The company experienced a "human error" when the person placed the box in an incorrect location. The brand took significant precautions and placed the boxes away from transit, schools, and tourist areas, however they scrapped the public placement after the incident.[6]

WEBSITE STRATEGY

As noted, some websites are designed for informational purposes only, while others approach the market with transformational purposes as they become a valuable resource for important life experiences. And firms use more than one site to achieve their objectives. Wind Mobile used two websites when it entered the Canadian market. It had a branded site (WindMobile.ca) and a website (WirelessSoapbox.com) that continued the dialogue with consumers after a series of ads that illustrated the state of Canada's wireless industry and demonstrated the need for increased choice for consumers.[7] It subsequently closed the latter and moved its content and communication to Twitter and Facebook since they offered stronger reach and interaction features.[8] In this sense, a brand's page within a social media vehicle is essentially an extension of its website strategy since clicking (or touching!) from page to page within a website is not very different from linking to its branded social media page.

The Dove brand (Exhibit 17-6) has a website that is an example of a newer trend, with multiple capabilities and an extensive array of text, video, graphics, and photos. Having started decades ago as a beauty cream bar differentiated from soap, the brand has now been placed on other products for women (body wash, hair care, deodorant), similar products for men, and a few for babies. Its main menu offers four selections: Products; Men+Care; Tips, Topics & Tools; and Our Mission. Its first two sections provide factual information for each type of product with expected imagery. The third section offers articles, advice, and videos on a number of topics for health and beauty. Finally, Our Mission ties in Dove's "Campaign for Real Beauty," which supports self-esteem and further, offers information for specific individuals (e.g., girls, mothers, educators). Surrounding the content displayed for each menu item are "banner ad-like" boxes for multiple products. As this state-of-the-art example from Dove demonstrates, a website can be an effective marketing tool to achieve any or all communication objectives, and in fact to achieve different types of behavioural objectives (identified in Chapter 5) for multiple audiences at varying stages of the decision-making process (identified in Chapter 3). Other brands with interesting approaches for website communication include EveryCup.ca, Fora.MTV.ca, and HavanaCultura.com.

A consumer interacting with a website raises the question of what is meant by *interactivity*. **Interactivity** is the extent to which an actor involved in a communication episode perceives

Exhibit 17-6   A beauty bar like Dove uses many transformational features on its website.

© chris brignell / Alamy Stock Photo

the communication to be reciprocal, responsive, speedy, and characterized by the use of nonverbal information.[9] Applying this idea, a website is *reciprocal* when it offers multiple opportunities for the consumer to act, such as with links, buttons, or connections to other utilities like social media. It is *responsive* if every action produces a relevant and appropriate outcome. Quick response suggests that the website is *speedy*. It is *characterized by the use of nonverbal information* if it makes extensive use of pictures, sounds, and animation. Notably absent from this definition is the notion of control, since it is a media usage characteristic of both interactive media and non-interactive media as described in Chapter 10. Empirical findings supported this definition of interactivity, which was also found to be a strong predictor of attitude to the website and media involvement. Furthermore, preliminary research indicated that more interactive websites generated deeper information processing and message believability, leading to stronger attitudes to the brand and website.[10]

This attitudinal communication effect is another source of findings where researchers investigate what design factors lead to a consumer's positive attitude to the website.[11] Additionally, research investigated the impact of attitude to the website on brand attitude or company attitude.[12] This effect has been investigated for both high/low involvement and informational/transformational brand attitudes, previously discussed in Chapter 8.[13] Research also examined the attitudinal effects on purchase intentions.[14] Building on this and consistent with earlier ad research, a paper with two studies investigated design factors on specific cognitive and affective responses to the website, and attitude to the website to a greater number of behaviourial outcomes.[15]

Figure 17-6 summarizes these ideas, which are similar to the models described in Chapter 4. Several of the advertising principles established in other media are investigated with Internet media, and it remains to be seen whether their application will be completely similar or show variation. In the end, however, the notion of Internet advertising is now common terminology. Finally, consumers develop an affinity for or are very loyal to their favourite Internet sites for their information or entertainment needs. More loyal users tend to spend more time at these sites and have much more positive attitudes toward the sites' relevance, content, and features. This is consistent with other media, where people have their favourite TV show or radio station.

Figure 17-6   Model of website advertising effects

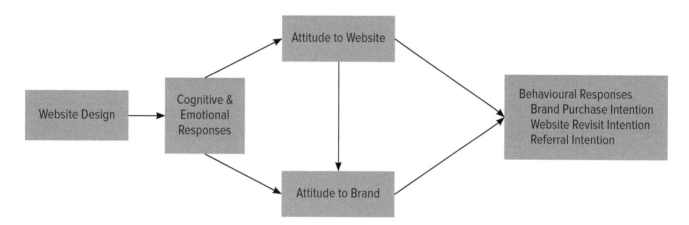

But how do brands motivate consumers to visit their website? While we saw the use of broadcast and print media in earlier chapters to direct viewers, brands also use Internet media advertising. And its growth spawned recognition in the form of Webby Awards. Liberté Blueberry Greek Yogurt used a tablet-based mobile ad, located on the lower part of the page, where users played a game trying to put the blueberries on the banner ad back in the container by tipping and turning the device. Locating the ad at the bottom of the page reinforced the attribute of the berries at the bottom of the container and reinforced the brand's natural positioning. On an automotive shopping website, BMW (Exhibit 17-7) created the world's longest banner ad—which expanded when touched by the cursor to reveal a witty story that "people could not put down" as the average time spent with the ad reached three minutes![16]

Exhibit 17-7   BMW is one of many automotive brands using Internet media for advertising.

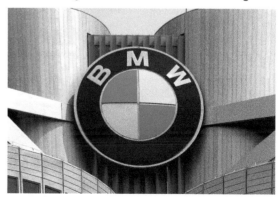

In addition to Internet media advertising, brands rely on social media for communication and also encourage consumers to visit their social media pages, two topics we also examine in this chapter. For example, Sephora (Exhibit 17-8) lists seven different social media sites on its website for visitors to consider checking out. Practitioners refer to each of these IMC tools as "owned" media (e.g., website), "paid" media (e.g., banner ad), and "earned" media (e.g., user-generated content). While this handy vocabulary works well to a degree, it does limit the innovativeness and creativity of a plan, as we shall see. Finally, as we turn to these topics, keep in mind that Canadian consumers indicated discomfort with many Internet media ads in a survey by Advertising Standards Canada (Figure 17-7).

Exhibit 17-8   Sephora provides a consistent image across all social media vehicles

© Goran Bogicevic / Shutterstock.com

Figure 17-7   Comfort of advertising by Canadians

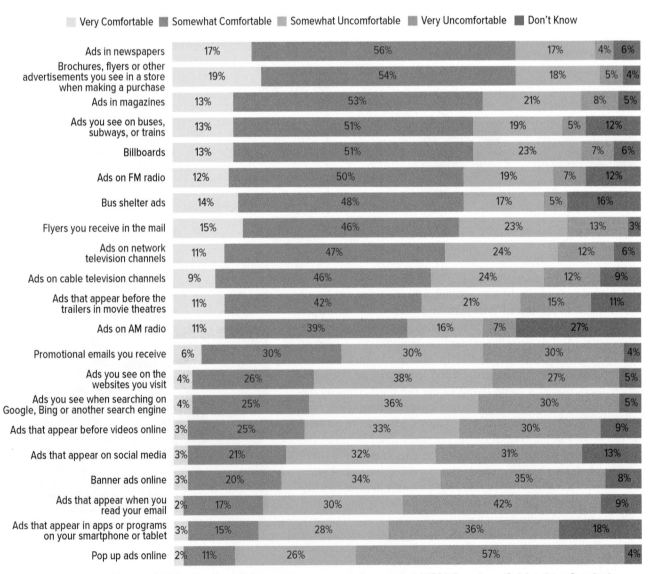

Source: Study conducted in early 2016 by The Gandalf Group with a representative sample of 1,564 Canadians. © Advertising Standards Canada, Consumer Perspectives on Advertising, 2016.

LO2 Advertising

The Interactive Advertising Bureau (IAB) of Canada estimated that Internet advertising revenue reached $4.6 billion in 2015 (Figure 17-8). Compared to 2014 data for other means of advertising, this is higher than the $3.4 billion spent on television, lower than total broadcast at $5 billion, and ahead of total print at $3 billion. Internet advertising revenue accounted for 27 percent of the total estimated advertising revenue and 31 percent of the total reported advertising revenue in Canada for 2014. Advertising in the French language gradually declined as a percentage of total Canadian Internet advertising revenue, from 21 percent over 2005–2009 to an average of 19 percent during 2010–2014.

Figure 17-8 shows that IAB reports online advertising revenue of ads directed to desktop computers and laptops, and mobile advertising revenue of ads directed to phones and tablets. Consumer adoption and use of mobile devices attracted increasing advertising dollars, growing tenfold from $160 million in 2012 to $1.6 billion in 2015. In contrast, online ad revenue stabilized at about $2.9 billion for each year during 2012–2015.

Figure 17-8   Total Canadian Internet advertising revenue ($ millions)

	2010	2011	2012	2013	2014	2015
Online (desk/laptop)	2,232	2,593	2,925	2,991	2,890	2,984
Percent growth/year	23	16	13	2	–3	3
Mobile (phone/tablet)	47	81	160	427	903	1,620
Percent growth/year	105	72	98	167	111	79
Total (online and mobile)	2,279	2,674	3,085	3,418	3,793	4,604
Percent growth/year	24	17	15	11	11	21

Source: IAB Canada, Canadian Internet Advertising Revenue Survey, 2016

Expenditures of advertising formats are shown in Figure 17-9 During the early years of mobile advertising (e.g., 2010–2012), the method of estimating advertising revenue by ad format evolved. Thus, the ad revenue breakdown by format for these three years is for online only. Alternatively, the ad revenue breakdown by format during 2013–2015 is for both online and mobile. The ad formats identified in Figure 17-9 are described in this section and are used as headings to organize the presentation of this topic.

Figure 17-9   Canadian Internet advertising revenue ($ million), by advertising format

	2010	2011	2012	2013	2014	2015
Search	907	1,081	1,586	1,802	2,052	2,512
Display	688	840	974	1,091	1,274	1,554
Classified/Directory	587	576	249	289	171	162
Video	37	73	92	208	266	358
Email	11	13	12	18	19	13
Video Gaming	2	10	13	11	11	5
Subtotal (online)	2,232	2,593	2,926			
Total (online and mobile)	2,279	2,674	3,085	3,418	3,793	4,604

Source: © IAB Canada, Canadian Internet Advertising Revenue Survey, 2016

DISPLAY ADS

Display advertising revenue hit $1,554 million in 2015, more than doubling since 2010, and accounted for one-third of total Internet media advertising ad revenue. The original use of display ads occurred in print media and so it is not too surprising that Internet media ads look like the ads found in those media as well. Display ads are placed on virtually any Internet site, including social media Internet sites and within email messages. Figure 17-10 shows where advertisers place display ads across different types of Internet media. As expected, advertisers are keenly interested in placing display ads on social media sites and these accounted for a substantial portion.

Figure 17-10   Ad impressions by type of Internet media

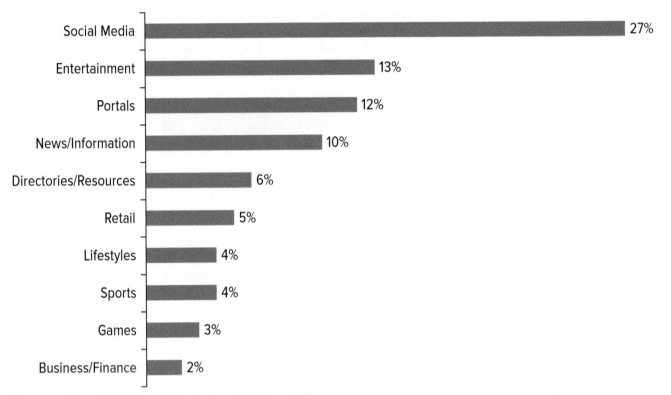

Source: comScore, Digital Future in Focus, Canada 2015, page 47.

The top Internet advertisers in Canada for 2014 (by billions of display ad impressions) were General Motors (5.6), Microsoft (4.9), Procter & Gamble (4.6), TD Bank (4.5), AMEX (4.4), and RBC (4.0). As expected from this list, the top advertising product categories by ad impressions were finance, retail, automotive, consumer goods, and computer/technology. Within consumer goods, the top three were health and beauty (37 percent), household (15 percent) and food/grocery (11 percent).[17] The types of products advertised on the Internet in 2014 by ad revenue are shown in Figure 17-11.

Display ad formats follow industry standardization; extensive demonstrations of these formats and their technical requirements are available (see IAB.net and IABCanada.com). A major adjustment to the standardized formats occurred in 2012 with the deletion of old formats and the addition of new ones to take advantage of technological innovations. We now review the different ad formats that advertisers place in Internet media vehicles.

Figure 17-11   Distribution of online revenue by major product category, 2014

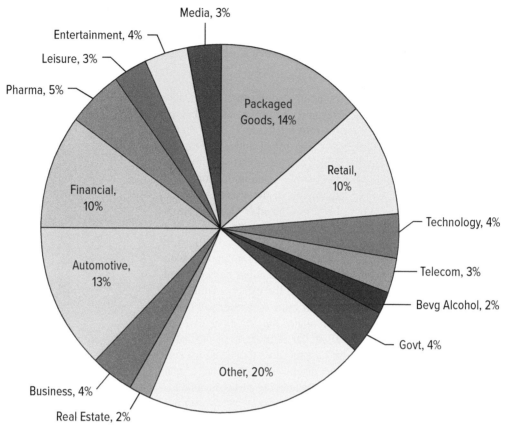

Source: © IAB Canada, Canadian Internet Advertising Revenue Survey, 2015.

Banner Ad   A common advertising format is a **banner ad**. Banner ads take their name and format from ads found in newspapers. A banner ad is now referred to as Universal Ad Package (UAP; CAUP in Canada), with four formats: rectangle, medium rectangle, skyscraper, and leaderboard. Other ad units are available, like super leaderboard, half page, button 2, and micro-bar. Various page locations are available for these ad units, with limitations due to industry standardization. Figure 17-12 identifies adoption level of UAP in Canada for 2014.

Figure 17-12   Distribution of advertising creative size, 2014

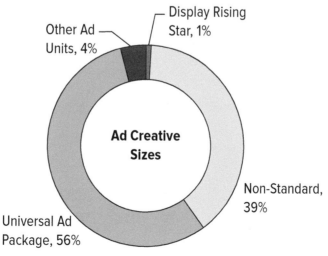

Source: comScore, Digital Future in Focus, Canada 2015, page 43.

Banner ads are found in all sorts of Internet media vehicles, and this revenue total includes ads also found in social media outlets like Facebook. Naturally, banner ads have a link embedded allowing users to move to another digital location, usually a brand or company website or a branded page on a social network, and developments allow for different interactive features. The historic average click-through rate in Canada and the United States is 0.10 percent, meaning one in 1,000! Variation exists depending on size, location on page, use of an image, and use of flash technology, however the rate does not grow significantly. Variation due to Internet media vehicle and device use is observed, with slightly stronger rates in social media and mobile.[18]

Since banner ads are the original marketing communication found in Internet media and account for extensive advertising revenue, a number of academics have investigated their usefulness. Much of this research built on other media studies with an interest in predicting awareness (i.e., recall and recognition), attitude to the brand, attitude to the ad, attitude to the advertising format, purchase intention, and click-through rates—all communication and behavioural effects discussed earlier. One study looked at the effects of forced exposure; that is, whether the user had control to avoid the ad.[19] Other research has shown the importance of congruence between the website (i.e., media vehicle) or the search engine keywords inputted and the brand advertised.[20] Another inquiry looked at whether the audience was familiar or unfamiliar with the advertised brand, a key factor in advertising planning that has been covered extensively in this book.[21] Other research investigated the effects of message content design elements and format of the ads on both communication and behavioural effects.[22] For example, research investigated the effects of different shapes, like vertical banner ads (Exhibit 17-9) similar to those in print media. Furthermore, media scheduling and duration of exposure of the banner ads replicated findings of advertising from other media. For example, longer exposure and repetition are generally important in achieving desired effects.[23] And, while existing research uncovered how banner ads work, some banner ads will instantly turn into an interactive microsite without redirection that allows the downloading of promotional items (e.g., a coupon). Subsequently, these ads will include provisions for feedback (e.g., sign-up) and transactions.[24]

Exhibit 17-9   An example of a skyscraper banner ad.

© Hallmark

Rich Media   Rich media ads are display ads that use computer software technology offering greater creativity options, and permit user interaction such as expansion of the ad, additional product description, or movement that appears video-like. Ads that occur within a video player are measured as digital video ads, not rich media.[25] Figure 17-13 identifies adoption level of rich media in Canada for 2014, clearly a strong opportunity not realized thus far by promotional planners. Click-through rates for these ads attained up to 0.5 percent, or five in 1,000.

Figure 17-13   Distribution of advertising creative types, 2014

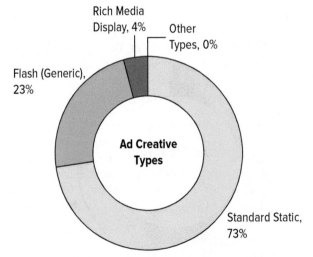

Source: comScore, Digital Future in Focus, Canada 2015, page 43.

A major addition to the roster of ad formats is collectively referred to by IAB as Rising Stars Display Ad Units and includes six different presentations: billboard, filmstrip, portrait, pushdown, sidekick, and slider. Research found that consumers were 2.5 times more likely to interact with these ads and spent twice as much time interacting with the ads than standard banner ads. Consumers found the ads more enjoyable and claimed stronger website impressions for those using the new format.[26] Exhibit 17-10 shows a filmstrip ad unit where the sequence of the ad is user-controlled by moving the cursor over each part.

Advertisements that appear on the screen with a message are known as **pop-ups**. Pop-ups are usually larger than banner ads but smaller than a full screen. **Pop-unders** are ads that appear underneath the Internet page and become visible only when the user leaves the site. These ads have been delisted by IAB, but some websites do not adhere to IAB standards. **Floating ads** move along in front of the website's page. In contrast, one academic study concludes that these ads may be welcomed when users are in an entertainment-minded mood, the ads are relevant, or the ads provide value.[27] The frequency and effectiveness of these ads have been greatly reduced given the opportunity for Internet users to use an application that blocks the ads before they appear on the screen.

Interstitials are ads that emerge on the screen while a site's content downloads. Although advertisers believe that interstitials are irritating and more of a nuisance than a benefit, one study found that only 15 percent of those surveyed felt that the ads were irritating (versus 9 percent for banner ads) and that 47 percent liked the ads (versus 38 percent for banners). Perhaps more importantly, while recall of banner ads was approximately 51 percent, recall of interstitials was much higher, at 76 percent. A new form of interstitial is in-person ads, where a person begins speaking to the user, so the effect is similar to experiencing a presentation from a salesperson.

A preliminary page that precedes the homepage of an Internet site is known as a **splash page**. Ads in this format typically disappear after a few seconds and permit the viewer to skip them. One clever splash page

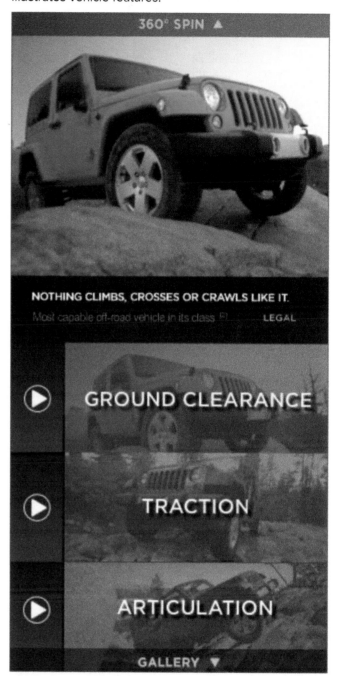

Exhibit 17-10   This IAB Rising Stars filmstrip ad illustrates vehicle features.

© IAB

shows a hand with a scalpel that cuts the page open to reveal the homepage and a display ad requesting donations for Sunnybrook Hospital in Toronto. As this example shows, captivating creative executions are possible with short messages to enhance further exposure and processing. Research that compared standard display ads to full screen take-over, large display, and splash page wraps yielded stronger brand recognition and recall, and higher ratings for entertainment, education, and brand value.[28] All of these display ads and video ads are bought and sold with a system undergoing change, as shown in IMC Perspective 17-1.

IMC PERSPECTIVE 17-1

EXCHANGES FOR DISPLAY ADS

Ad networks place ads for advertising clients across millions of potential Internet sites that publish content efficiently and effectively. Hundreds of ad networks operate globally, with big names like Google commanding significant market share. The ad network provider obtains ad placement inventory from multiple Internet sites that publish content, forecasts the inventory for the coming time frame (e.g., month), and organizes the inventory across multiple segmentation variables adhering to advertiser requirements. Second, the network negotiates and sells the ad placements to advertising clients. And finally, the network facilitates delivery of the ads from the advertiser to the publisher.

© Ariel Skelly/Blend Images LLC

When a network needs to manage its inventory of ads (buying or selling), it turns to an ad exchange that operates much like a stock exchange. The publisher provides information and requests an ad from the exchange. The exchange submits the request to advertisers. An advertiser then bids on the ad impression against other advertisers. The ad exchange selects the best bid and sends the ad to the publisher. The publisher completes the process, submitting the ad. The entire process is completed one ad at a time yet takes milliseconds!

Ad exchanges are beneficial since fewer parties involved results in less overall commission and greater dollars invested in advertising. Logistically, the whole process is simpler for all parties. The pricing mechanisms offer less risk to the publisher receiving minimal amounts of money for its space. Research suggests publishers stand to make more money. Advertisers know exactly where their ad will appear, thus avoiding any negative media vehicle source effects. This takes care of the problem of ads for wholesome brands with respectable images appearing in unsavory Internet locations. Finally, the instantaneous bidding permits dynamic allocations of the advertising budget.

The interaction between ad networks and ad exchanges is a feature of the complex system of ad transactions that is known as programmatic buying. Most marketers are unaware of the system, partly out of ignorance and partly because it is contracted to their media agencies. However, the difficulties emerging with the system should get marketers interested in a hurry. Foremost is that the layers of complexity of buyers and sellers within the system disrupt the benefit of knowing where the ads are being placed. Big name brands find their ads on websites that host pirated movies, TV shows, and music. Quality branded products see their ads on websites containing shady content (e.g., violence, hate speech, pornography). In short, the foundation of vehicle source effect has become seriously detrimental.

Another outcome of too many players in the system is significant fraud. Unscrupulous ad networks conduct transactions within the ad exchange representing publishing websites that do not actually have any visitors, or the few visitors are vastly overstated. The source of this is computers infected with malware and other assorted nefarious software that mimics human behaviour, commonly known as *bots*, short for *robots*. Some estimate that 25–50 percent of Internet ads are potentially fraudulent, which hurts everyone. Advertisers are wasting money, a portion of which is potentially going to major organized crime outfits. And the money wasted could have funded legitimate media instead, such as magazines and newspapers which are struggling. Consumers own computers that run more slowly since a portion of their power is busy pretending to be a human on many websites. Specialized software tries to seek out the fraudulent websites and initiatives are beginning to qualify participants in the system to weed out the bad players.

Sources: Chris Powell, "It's About Real Time," *Marketing Magazine*, August 13, 2012, pp. 36–41; David Brown, "Exchange Is Good," *Marketing Magazine*, November 14, 2011; "Ad Networks vs. Ad Exchanges: How They Stack Up," *OpenX Whitepaper*, July 2010;

"Digging Into the Data," *Marketing Magazine,* November/December 2014; Susan Krashinsky, "Bots, Consumers and Budgets: The Growing Threat of Ad Fraud," *The Globe and Mail,* August 8, 2014, p. B.1; Susan Krashinsky, "A New Player in the Fight Against Piracy," *The Globe and Mail,* October 10, 2014, p. B.5.

Question:

1. Does the threat of poor advertising delivery through this complex system threaten digital advertising in the future?

PAID SEARCH ADS

A substantial form of advertising on the Internet is **paid search**, or search engine advertising in which advertisers pay only when a consumer clicks on their ad or link from a search engine page (Exhibit 17-11). Other payment methods are also available depending on the search engine and other factors. Paid search ads in a link format are essentially primitive display ads received by the searcher who at that point in time has a particular target audience characteristic. Visually, link ads are text-only ads and are the most basic form of display ad, containing no visual and no or minimal copy. Click-through rates are 1.5–2.0 percent depending on the device used. Search advertising revenue reached $2,512 million in Canada for 2015, accounting for 55 percent of all Internet advertising.

Google is the dominant provider, accounting for two out of every three searches. Google's application of AdSense and AdWords is an example of this form of advertising (Exhibit 17-12). Link ads with AdSense on an Internet site provide additional information and/or related materials at another site, much like the original link in the paid search. Almost all the company's revenue comes from selling advertisements associated with search keywords. A keyword-targeted advertising program called AdWords uses short text-only ads to maintain an uncluttered page design and to maximize page loading speed. These text ads are identified as "sponsored links" that appear at the top or far right side of the search results page and are separated for clear user distinction. Online advertisers compete for the privilege of having their ads displayed with the results of a particular keyword search in a higher position than their competitors' ads. Advertisers pay only when an ad is clicked (called cost-per-click, or CPC), which in turn takes the web surfer to the advertiser's website. AdWords runs a specialized auction to decide which ads to show on the basis of (1) each advertiser's CPC bid and (2) the advertiser's *quality score,* which is a measure of the *relevance* of how well an ad matches a user's search query. The

Exhibit 17-11   A familiar student activity is to Google it!

© Your Design / Shutterstock.com© Your Design / Shutterstock.com

Exhibit 17-12   Google's AdWords provides links for advertisers to do search engine advertising.

© Mon's Images / Shutterstock.com

AdWords pricing system is designed to reward more relevant ads and keywords by showing them higher in the search results. Google does this by decreasing the amount that relevant ads must bid per click to beat their competition. This means that Google can display the advertisements that are the most targeted and relevant to a Google user's *search query,* which draws more users and click-throughs and thus generates more revenue for Google.[29]

In an effort to more specifically target customers who may be interested in their offerings, advertisers employ search engine optimization (SEO). SEO is the process of improving the volume of traffic driven to one's site by a search engine through unpaid results as opposed to paid inclusions. The belief is that the higher a site appears on the search results list, the more visitors it will receive. SEO considers how search engines work and edits its HTML and coding to increase its relevance to keywords and to remove barriers to the indexing activities of search engines. SEO is an integral part of an Internet marketing strategy of companies and organizations of all sizes.

Jeff Quipp, CEO of Toronto-based Search Engine People, makes the following recommendations for search success:

1. The titles for the pages should be labelled and unique, and the text should not be embedded in visuals.
2. Content should be unique and valuable so that designers of other sites will see value and include a link on their site.
3. To increase a ranking on search, pay the extra money for the search terms and do what is necessary in messaging to ensure strong click-through rates.
4. Optimize customization through past search history.[30]

CLASSIFIED AND DIRECTORY ADS

Classified and directory ads are found on Internet sites where consumers search for information when comparison shopping or where consumers are planning a purchase and looking to complete a transaction. One noteworthy example of this is Kijiji; while the average Canadian can post an ad for free to sell used items, Kijiji offers display ad options and paid search capabilities for advertisers such as dealerships to sell new and used vehicles. For the most part, Kijiji sells its ad space on a CPM basis, ranging from $2 to $18. Similarly, Auto Trader lets private sellers post ads for free and generates revenue from auto dealers who try to attract those who are searching for a new car in the free postings. And employment directories like Workopolis charge a set fee for a job posting ad with varying levels of service and exposure.

All of the targeting options described above are possible with these online directories, giving this opportunity for advertising extensive sophistication over traditional newspaper advertising. In fact, it appeared as if a direct substitution effect from newspaper to online occurred, with online stealing a significant portion of revenue from newspaper for a period of time. However, IAB reported only $171 million in ad revenue in 2014 due to a decline of ad revenue of $100 million for one company and a categorization of another company to paid search. Consequently, classified and directory advertising dropped from $576 million in 2011, indicating perhaps a general shift in advertising beyond the two extraordinary circumstances cited. The level of ad revenue stayed consistent with a slight decline to $162 million in 2015.

VIDEO AND AUDIO ADS

Video streaming penetration rose from 69 percent in 2011 to 80 percent in 2014 and varies by age and income (Figure 17-14). The number of hours of video streaming viewed per person hit 8 hours per week in 2014, double the 4 hours seen in 2011. Streaming by devices in 2014 showed 75 percent by computer, 47 percent by smart phone, 31 percent by tablet, and 23 percent by Internet connected TV. Beyond movie and program watching via Netflix, where there is no advertising, viewing news content rose to 51 percent and watching sports rose to 40 percent in 2015.

Figure 17-14 Internet video viewers, fall 2014, anglophones 18+

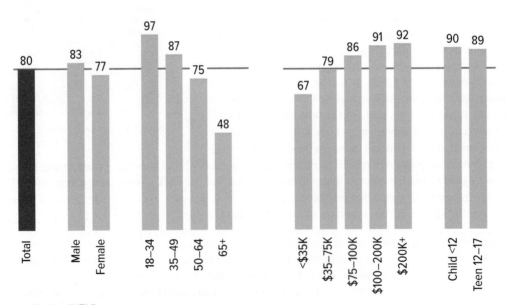

Video ads on Internet media have made great strides, as advertising revenue hit $358 million in 2015. There are two perspectives for video: ones that appear on video hosting sites like YouTube, for which there is no placement fee, and placement of ads prior to seeing a content video that could be on a video hosting site or any content publisher of video material. As noted in Figure 10-1, online TV ads accounted for $142 million of the $266 million spent in 2014. Figure 17-15 identifies the type of online video viewing where a portion of video ads are placed and indicates that video streaming reached 90 percent in 2015.

Figure 17-15   Internet video activities, fall 2015, anglophones 18+

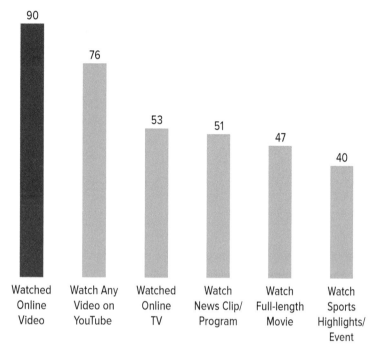

© Media Technology Monitor (MTM)

The growth of mobile advertising means that brands determine on which device to place a video ad. Recent statistics found that ad impressions achieved the following distribution: 46 percent for desk/laptop only; 33 percent for desk/laptop and mobile; 12 percent for desk/laptop, mobile, and Internet TV; and 7 percent for mobile only. Fifty-seven percent of the ads lasted 15 seconds and 56 percent featured consumer packaged goods or automotive products. Advertisers purchased 90 percent on a guaranteed CPM basis.[31]

Online Video Ads   The increased penetration of broadband into households and mobile has increased the use of streaming video advertising messages. The equivalent of traditional television commercials, online commercials are appearing on Internet media vehicles. Some companies create new video messages for the Internet, while others run the same spots they show on TV. Companies have also been successful in blending the two media, showing the commercial on TV and then directing interested viewers to their Internet site if they wish to see it again or to view longer versions. These viewings on a company's Internet site are usually hosted on YouTube or an equivalent video hosting service. Goodlife Fitness (Exhibit 17-13) puts training videos on its website that are hosted by Vimeo.

Exhibit 17-13   Goodlife makes use of video to communicate on its website.

© rmnoa357 / Shutterstock.com

Digital Video Ads   Online video versions of entertainment activities or shows (which include ads or are sponsored) are also available through the Internet. For example, CTV website visitors can watch free TV programs along with embedded commercials, similar to the existing television model. Viewership hit nearly 50 percent in 2014 with similar variation with age and income (Figure 17-16). The future of advertising through streamed television shows is a new and promising opportunity for promotional planners, even though the innovation is in the early stages of development for the sender and the receiver. All major TV broadcasters offer varying options for ad placement for the majority of their shows. Much of the targeting potential and fit of audience of a show is now possible via online video.

Figure 17-16   Internet TV viewers, fall 2014 anglophones 18+

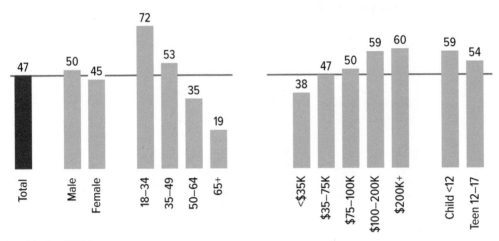

© Media Technology Monitor (MTM)

Looking for even more revenue, YouTube offers the potential to see ads before viewing the intended video. Some have the option for viewers to skip the ad, while others are controlled so the viewer must watch the ad, much like the experience with television. Other media vehicles like news sites offer video ads prior to seeing the intended news video clip. These options are priced using CPM methods to account for instances when viewers do not watch the complete message. Future Internet media ad placement may move toward pricing and planning with GRPs like other media as advertisers look toward intermedia comparisons.[32]

Podcasting   **Podcasting** is a medium that uses Internet media to distribute video and audio files for learning or entertainment purposes, and contains ad and sponsorship messages (Exhibit 17-14). For example, Volvo sponsored a podcast for $60,000 that was downloaded 150,000 times, while other initial sponsorships garnered $25 per thousand. In addition, metrics for understanding the audience size emerged similar to other media (e.g., Podtrac.com). One study investigated podcasting and found an average of 2.4 ads per podcast with an average length of 16 seconds, consistent with a length seen on television and ads shown prior to video clips on news or portal sites. The majority of the ads (i.e., 75 percent) preceded or ended the podcast with a sponsorship message, much like the early days of television in the 1950s. The specificity of the podcast content allowed for very targeted ads (60 percent), such as automobile brands sponsoring a car-care podcast; thus, we see a very strong media vehicle source effect much like magazines.[33] It appears a familiar advertising model with a sponsorship approach will continue to grow; however, the content of

Exhibit 17-14   Audiences for podcasts represent a useful audio advertising opportunity.

© Ryan McVay/Getty Images

a podcast is also a message with possible commercial intent. For example, in order to increase demand for fine wine consumption, a podcast describing the nuances of grapes, vintages, tasting, and so on could act as a means of switching consumers who currently purchase less premium brands. Frank and Oak, a men's online clothing retailer, found success with one- to three-minute podcast ads that described their home try-on program and tracking system. They also found that this worked well with Tumblr since it displayed the imagery of the product line.[34]

MOBILE ADS

As noted earlier in the chapter, smart phone penetration reached 77 percent and tablet penetration reached 53 percent of the population in 2015. Mobile ad revenue accounts for messages delivered to either device and topped $1,620 million in 2015. As seen in Figure 17-8, IAB Canada separates its ad revenue statistics by online (desk/laptop) and mobile (phone/tablet). While accessing Internet media via mobile technology differs, Figure 17-9 indicates that IAB Canada tracks advertising expenditures with the same advertising formats—display, paid search, directory, video, email, and gaming. However, a breakdown of mobile ad revenue data for 2015 showed $631 million for display, $871 million for paid search, $106 million for video, and $10 million for other. For both online and mobile, paid search accounted for 55 percent of all ad revenue expenditures.

Most of the points raised earlier about these ad formats are relevant for mobile, however mobile's effectiveness remains to be seen. Does a video ad on a smart phone with a much smaller screen influence consumers the way a TV ad might with a large screen? How could a student possibly pay attention to a smart phone ad while passing people, dodging cars and skateboarders, and avoiding absent-minded professors? These questions and others are relevant as brands offer rewards and discounts so that users will view mobile ads at the conclusion of a call.[35] A preliminary study found mobile display ads ineffective for the most part, and only effective for high involvement–utilitarian purchases.[36] Due to the similarity of ad formats, we do not provide information on these topics for mobile. Instead, we present a few specific points regarding mobile device usage, mobile applications, and short message service.

Mobile Device Usage   How Canadians use their devices is summarized in Figure 17-17 for smart phones and Figure 17-18 for tablets, indicating both similarities and differences. Data such as these can be used by promotional planners to know how to reach their target audience much like other media. Variation in Internet media activities reminds us of the importance of applying all media planning principles described in Chapter 10 accordingly.

Figure 17-17   Frequency of Internet media activities using smart phones, fall 2015, anglophones 18+

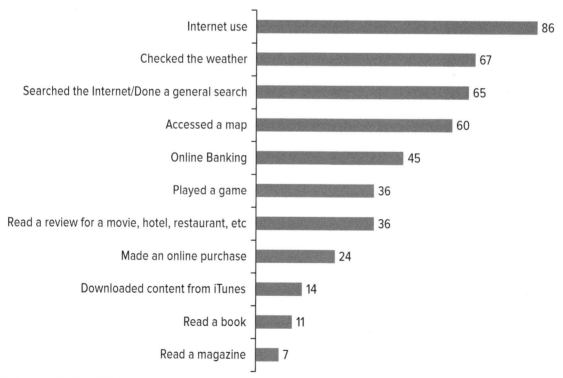

© Media Technology Monitor (MTM)

Figure 17-18   Frequency of Internet media activities using tablets, fall 2015, anglophones 18+

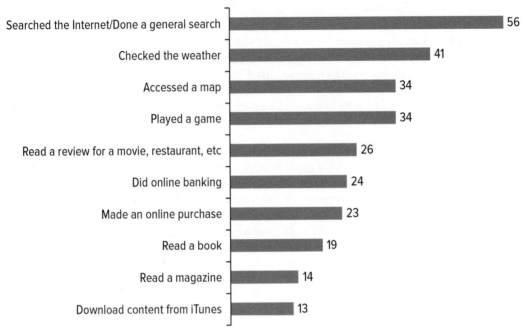

© Media Technology Monitor (MTM)

Figure 17-19 and Figure 17-20 indicate that Canadians use each mobile device somewhat differently for communication activities and content sharing. Whether this leads to the potential for adjusting their promotional message content or delivery remains to be seen. For example, while at a sports event, most fans would likely have their phone and not their tablet, and a promotional offer might best be sent on Twitter rather than other social media vehicles as people respond to what is happening during the event. In contrast, since tablet adoption trails smart phone adoption, these data may eventually even out over time. Thus, the more important consideration for promotional planners may be differences in their promotional plans for online versus mobile. The final consideration may be that all display and video messages may be viewed similarly, whether online or mobile, since the Internet activities may be quite alike over time.

Figure 17-19   Communication activities on smart phones and tablets, fall 2015, anglophones 18+

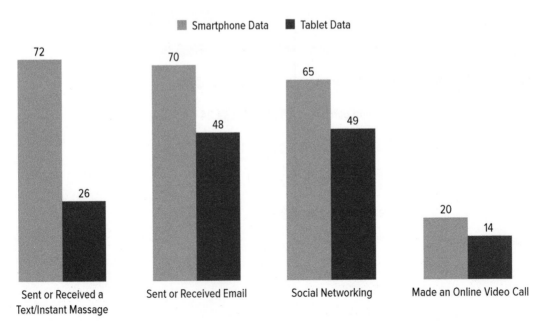

© Media Technology Monitor (MTM)

Figure 17-20   Content creation on smart phones and tablets, fall 2015, anglophones 18+

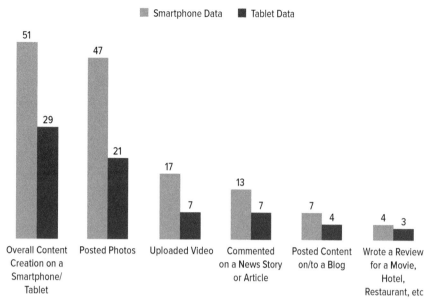

As discussed in Chapter 11, TV broadcasters are interested in social TV where viewers interact with a program with their mobile device, notably through social media. Figure 17-21 and Figure 17-22 indicate the kinds of Internet media activities consumers take part in when watching TV. These data indicate opportunities for advertisers with TV programs that may have product placement or sponsorship activities occurring. In particular, live sports regularly encourage consumer feedback or participation in promotional offers while the game is on. For example, during the Raptors' playoff drive, the announcers invited viewers to use both Twitter and Snapchat. Similar activities occur with NHL hockey and during the Blue Jays' playoffs. Oreo jumped to the task with instant Twitter messages during the women's gold medal hockey game at the Olympics. After the victory, one tweet proclaimed, "Recipe for gold: 1 part skill, 1 part heart, 1 part awesome comeback." An earlier example when witty and timely Oreo tweets generated 280 million ad impressions after the Super Bowl blackout a few years ago set the stage for the cookie brand to be ready at all times to send out similar messages during big events.[37]

Figure 17-21   Second screen activities with smart phones, fall 2015, anglophones 18+

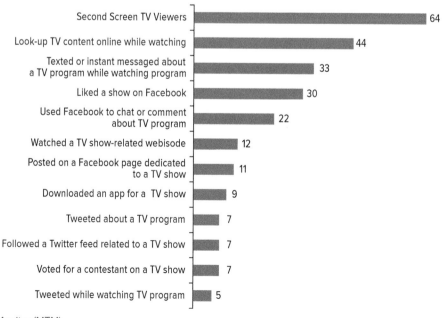

Figure 17-22 Second screen activities with tablets, fall 2015, anglophones 18+

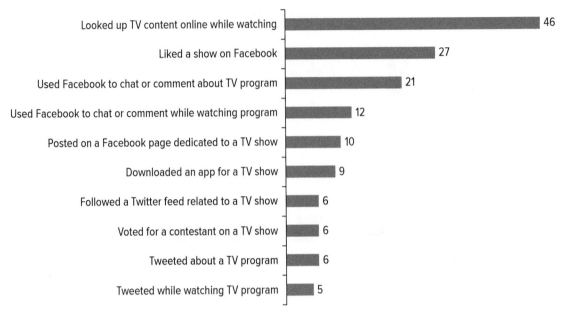

© Media Technology Monitor (MTM)

Mobile Applications Known as "apps" for short, these small programs are downloaded to a mobile device for many purposes. They act as ads since they generally carry brand identification and a brand experience. For example, according to one co-founder of Frank and Oak, "With the app on a phone's home screen you see our logo twenty times a day. That's great marketing for us." In fact, the company finds that consumers with the app (e.g., current customers) tend to buy more.[38] Fundamentally, the use of a mobile device to participate in marketing communication is not a regular activity for most consumers, but that is changing as statistics presented in the chapter attest. Advertising and most promotional tools are passive exposures that interrupt people's lives and are for the most part tolerated. However, apps and increasingly interactive digital communication are wonderful from the marketer's point of view since consumers will spend more time processing brand information. However, consumers generally do not share the same perspective, at least not for every brand at all times, as we showed in Figure 17-7. But, a signal that things are changing is that Cannes added a Mobile Lion to its prize list in 2012, with the Hospital for Sick Children's app announced as the winner.

Mobile location apps (e.g., Foursquare) are increasingly being used by marketers and consumers alike. Brands like HarperCollins, Molson, the NHL, Metro News, and the Toronto International Film Festival have all used these kinds of apps for advertising and sales promotion purposes to achieve attitudinal and trial objectives. And the apps themselves offer reward points for continued use of the app![39] Companies take advantage of the apps section on Facebook and mobile platforms by offering games with point or badge systems to encourage continued patronage to the site.[40] Mobile apps are also a driving force behind the successful implementation of group buying or group discount activities in social media vehicles as well, which suggests that handheld devices will be a main marketing communication tool if consumers desire to interact with brands in this manner.[41] TV broadcasters are developing apps for a second-screen experience for viewers while watching TV shows. Their rationale is to foster enhanced viewer participation in the show's content by commenting on it via social media or enrolling in promotions, and to develop new advertising revenue sources.[42]

Apps appear to be for everything and anything, but Figure 17-23 tracks the growth of apps in various product categories. We see growth on the practical shopping side with retail and banking, and entertainment with sports. The growth of newspapers may be expected since we described the growth in digital reading of this media.

Figure 17-23   App growth among smart phone users

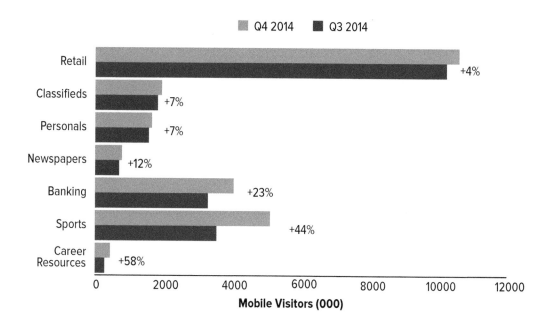

Source: comScore, Digital Future in Focus, Canada 2015, page 29.

Consumers perform many shopping related activities using apps, as shown in Figure 17-24. The mobile characteristics of smart phones make them ideal for consumers to rely on while shopping. Companies can use data like this to configure apps more usefully and design them with key advertising messages. An example of the pervasiveness of shopping related apps is Poynt, a popular Canadian app that allows users to find restaurants, movies, people, and businesses based on their location. The app allows consumers to book an appointment or reservation, save it in the calendar, and access all the contact information without even exiting the app. The next step appears to be features that will deliver promotional offers to users based on their location and user profile. As it works with data suppliers and other third-party developers, the app is a handy tool for consumers shopping virtually anywhere.[43] One study found that apps provided strong brand effects, and that shopping related apps led to stronger purchase intentions than experiential brand-building apps.[44] As this indicates once again, advertising researchers continue to use established methods and ad theories to test digital marketing communication.

Short Message Service   Sending a text message is the most common activity when using a smart phone (as shown in Figure 17-19), offering a number of opportunities for new communication and promotional offers. Coca-Cola put forth a promotion with under-the-cap personal identification numbers and SMS codes that offered discounts for cellphone bills. In hindsight, the incentive did not completely fit the teen target audience, who usually did not pay their own cellphone bill; however, the new approach gave the soft drink brand strong results for future implementation that included iTunes downloads and a contest to win concert tickets. Air Miles sends permission-based text alerts customized by transaction activity to encourage shopping at affiliated sponsors; response rates of up to 8 percent have occurred. Opt-in geolocation SMS provides offers to consumers who have not previously visited a store. Additionally, mobile users can now collect reward points via their device with innovative approaches for those interested in continued brand patronage.[45] Consumers can send messages to select what will be viewed in digital display networks in malls and transit stations, or on large screens in public locations.[46]

As the above suggests, these promotional messages have content much like other forms of marketing communication with a particular source and message structure. A study investigated the effects of these variables in an experiment of short messages sent to gamers during a local area network (LAN) party. The source was either a brand or a member of the party, while the message structure was either normal advertising language or shorthand text language, similar to what is sent in short text messages by users on a daily basis.[47] Thus, while this new "medium" is an alternative for sending the message, the principles discussed thus far in terms of positioning and advertising messages remain relevant for understanding attitudinal responses and purchase intentions. Furthermore, while searching with the mobile device occurs as in other computer environments, the GPS feature on smart phones gives retailers and event marketers a greater opportunity to persuade consumers. The coordinates signalled from the device are tracked, allowing brand information to be placed higher in the search.

Figure 17-24   Retail activities via smart phone app and browser

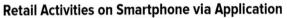
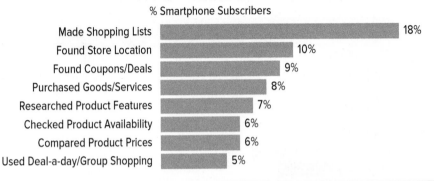

Retail Activities on Smartphone via Application

% Smartphone Subscribers

Activity	%
Made Shopping Lists	18%
Found Store Location	10%
Found Coupons/Deals	9%
Purchased Goods/Services	8%
Researched Product Features	7%
Checked Product Availability	6%
Compared Product Prices	6%
Used Deal-a-day/Group Shopping	5%

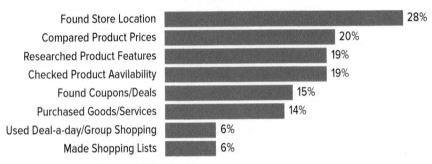

Retail Activities on Smartphone via Browser

Activity	%
Found Store Location	28%
Compared Product Prices	20%
Researched Product Features	19%
Checked Product Aavilability	19%
Found Coupons/Deals	15%
Purchased Goods/Services	14%
Used Deal-a-day/Group Shopping	6%
Made Shopping Lists	6%

Source: comScore, Digital Future in Focus, Canada 2015, page 25.

A communication related to apps and SMS codes is 2D (two-dimensional) barcode, also known as a QR (quick response) code. Consumers scan the code—from an out-of-home ad, for example—and their browser locates the programmed destination (e.g., brand's website, promotional offer, social media). Labatt tested the idea with a tie-in to film festivals and received about 1,000 interested users for its Stella Artois beer. With consumers opting in at 20 percent, the software is picking up detailed exposure information on number of scans, who is scanning, and where.[48] However, data suggest that consumers are not positive on the use of QR codes, with minimal usage levels reported in market studies. Even though the idea of making static out-of-home ads becomes more exciting with handheld interactive features, one critique finds the idea unpalatable; the images are unattractive, they distract from the main ad message, and there is no motivating reason to scan the code.[49] No wonder consumers are reluctant to get more involved.

INTERNET MEDIA VEHICLES

The advertising formats can be placed on virtually any Internet site to target a brand's audience. Promotional planners need guidance on how to structure this decision even though targeting on different Internet media types is similar to targeting in other media types. Figure 17-25 applies the media terminology of Chapter 10 and compares broadcast and Internet. The Internet is a medium much like broadcast (i.e., TV and radio) is a medium. Since there are two types of broadcast, it is plausible to group Internet media along the same lines. Pre-existing Internet sites that consisted of content publishers and entertainment venues (i.e., early non–social media that continue to exist) provide opportunity for the placement of ads. We also have social media that accept ads as well; however, the membership characteristics, ability for interaction, and facility for contributing user-generated content provide a new way of planning brand messaging.

Figure 17-25   Comparison of mediums

Medium	Internet	Internet	Broadcast	Broadcast
Media Type	Social media	Content publisher	Television	Radio
Media Class	Social networking	News and information	Sports	Modern rock
Media Vehicle	Facebook	Yahoo	TSN (World Jr. Hockey)	Live 88.5 (Ottawa)

This implies that ads can be placed in a specific media class within social media and a specific media class within content publishers. For example, a social networking Internet site would be a media class within social media. Carrying on, Facebook, Google+, and LinkedIn would be avenues for placing an ad and would be the equivalent of a media vehicle, much like an ad placed on TSN's broadcast of the World Jr. Hockey tournament or placing an ad on a particular kind and name of radio station. For Internet content publishers, we see Yahoo as a media vehicle within the media class of news and information.

However, the targeting capabilities are much different even though the idea of a media vehicle is similar. An advertiser can be very precise on a number of segmentation variables to direct an ad in these social media environments for a particular time frame. In contrast, the TV advertiser reaches an expected group of hockey fans during the game, with certain characteristics based on historical audience profile data.

We present this perspective to convey the importance and pervasiveness of social media and to understand that the avenues for placing a message via a display ad or within the social media itself offer many vehicles to select from. This is much like what occurs in other aspects of Internet media, like established content publishers such as Yahoo and content publishers from existing print media like *Maclean's* or *The National Post,* and content streamers like CTV. Furthermore, it is an extension of the idea of media vehicles in existing broadcast and print media.

As such, the notion of a media vehicle is critical for targeting in any medium and this is true for any aspect of Internet media since media vehicles assist promotional planners in directing their message to their target audience. Targeting is fundamental to many applications for directing display ads through an ad network or ad exchange to any other Internet site or through a social networking site like Facebook. This would necessitate understanding how media vehicle options are classified. Advertising on a particular Internet site based on its content is known as **contextual targeting**, and this concept is essentially an extension of the concept of a media vehicle. For example, an advertiser places an airline ad on a travel site, or a golf club ad on a golf site, or even in or near a story about golf on another site. This is much like putting an ad for tools on HGTV during a Mike Holmes renovation show. Exhibit 17-15 shows RBC ads for unique audiences that would be placed at the most appropriate Internet sites.

Exhibit 17-15   RBC targets different audiences in unique Internet media vehicles.

All segmentation variables identified in Chapter 3 can be applied for targeting with Internet media. The Advertising Research Foundation suggests behaviour, geography, and time of day as additional critical variables given the technical capabilities of Internet media.[50] **Behavioural targeting** lets advertisers target consumers according to their Internet viewing. By compiling clickstream data and Internet protocol (IP) information, segments of potential buyers can be identified and ads directed specifically to them. For example, by tracking an individual's visits to a number of automobile websites, an ad for cars or a dealership could be served to that individual. Since the consumer behaviour implies interest in a topic or brand, this form of targeting is also known as *interest-based targeting*, or *interest-based advertising*.

In response to concerns about these forms of targeting, the Digital Advertising Alliance of Canada instituted the AdChoices programs in conjunction with similar organizations worldwide. This organization is a self-regulatory body comprising major advertisers, media companies, and industry organizations (e.g., IAB, Ad Standards Canada). Consumers can see the blue triangle icon on ads and click it for information on why the ad is placed on the website they are visiting, choose to opt out of receiving ads from the company listed (generally an ad server), and obtain information about the ad server's privacy policy. Issues of privacy and the legal and ethical use of contextual and behavioural targeting emerged with notable concerns as described in IMC Perspective 17-2.

Geographic targeting lets advertisers adjust their brand messages depending upon where the user is located. This information can be determined technologically and with the user's voluntary declaration of residence (e.g., country, city, etc.). For example, different versions of travel websites (e.g., Travel Alberta) can emerge depending upon where the information seeker is living. Local display ads are presented even if the viewer is on a website without a local connection.

Time of day targeting lets advertisers direct a message to consumers when they are consuming certain Internet media vehicles. This consumer variation in media usage is akin to what occurs in television and radio media consumption. Television viewership composition and frequency vary across the day (e.g., early morning, daytime, prime-time). Similarly, radio's audience size and composition varies considerably, especially considering commuters driving to and from work. Internet media are following a similar pattern, with groups of working people accessing Internet media during the day for business purposes, primarily in the morning. Usage declines during the afternoon and at dinner time and then peaks once again during the evening for leisure purposes.

IMC PERSPECTIVE 17-2

PRIVACY MATTERS TO CANADIANS

A ruling by the office of Canada's privacy commissioner seemed at odds with Canadians' willingness to sell their privacy for the right price, but that's the story line with the Personal Information Protection and Electronic Documents Act (PIPEDA) and Google's behavioural targeting of its digital ads via AdSense. It all started when a man searched for medical devices for his sleep apnea (a condition in which sleeping people stop breathing), then began receiving ads from companies that sell devices that treat this condition. He complained, and eventually the privacy commissioner decided in his favour since the information tracked about his web viewing pertained to health, something deemed as sensitive information under the Act.

© Nejron Photo/Shutterstock

While the Act does not mention specifically what *sensitive information* means, the commissioner put the onus on companies to know what it means in their industry, especially for health and financial factors. Even Google's own policies consider health information as sensitive along with many other types, yet somehow this occurred, possibly with some of Google's ad network partners not subscribing to the rules. As restitution, Google promised to improve staff oversight and its monitoring practices. One commentator suggested the source of the problem may have been that breathing devices to address sleep apnea are listed as consumer electronic—not medical—devices in the United States.

The incident raised questions about how much behavioural targeting should occur, but given that the participants based the whole programmatic system on behavioural targeting, it seemed that incidents like this might continue. However, the industry's development of the AdChoices program suggested that better days were ahead for Canadian consumers. And after the ruling, the Interactive Advertising Bureau of Canada released a reminder to its members to participate in the program. Other marketing organizations like the Association of Canadian Advertisers and the Canadian Marketing Association worked with privacy advocates as part of the establishment of the Digital Advertising Alliance of Canada responsible for the AdChoices program.

As the industry players get onboard with AdChoices, a survey of 9,000 respondents worldwide by Microsoft concluded that many are interested in selling their data for rewards. The data indicated that Canadians more strongly favoured the idea than Americans, at 45 percent compared to 33 percent. From a money standpoint, 32 percent said that they would sell their data for money, and when the study asked for how much, the average amount was over $2,000! One expert in the field raised concerns about whether health data should be sold, what could be the effect on vulnerable people, and whether someone was selling their own data. Another raised the question as to how companies would profile those who chose not to sell their data. One-third identified the power of consumers rising in the Internet age as more of them realized the value of their information.

And so the issue remains muddled. On the one hand, consumers are concerned about behavioural targeting, but on the other hand, they realize that their data is in play and that if they get free media, or free service online, then the trade is fair and they are okay with it. We live in interesting times, as one counterapproach is to install software on one's computer to make it appear like one is browsing in many places to disrupt the profile data being collected, sort of like installing your own bot on your own device—go figure.

Sources: Susan Krashinsky, "Data Ad Nauseam: A Plan to Overload Marketers," *The Globe and Mail,* November 7, 2014, p. B.5; Susan Krashinsky, "Canadians Open to Selling Their Online Data, Microsoft Finds," *The Globe and Mail,* January 30 2014, p. B.4; Susan Krashinsky, "Life After Privacy," *The Globe and Mail,* March 1, 2014, p. F.4; Susan Krashinsky, "Google Broke Canada's Privacy Laws With Targeted Health Ads, Watchdog Says," *The Globe and Mail,* January 15, 2014, p. A.1; Susan Krashinsky, "Advertisers Scramble to Reassure Public After Google Ruling," *The Globe and Mail,* January 17, 2014, p. B.1; Matt Hartley and Armina Ligaya, "Google's Health Ads Run Afoul of Watchdog," *National Post,* January 16, 2014, p. A.1.

Question:

1. Do you think the AdChoices program will be effective?

Social Media

Without question, the most significant media trend is the consumer adoption of social media. Approximately half of all Canadians regularly use social media—media that did not even exist less than a decade ago. Moreover, they are using social media with multiple hardware avenues like TVs, personal computers, smart phones, game consoles, and tablets, and whatever future technology that may be available. In this section we review different classes of social media. While it is impossible to address all of them, we provide guidance on the major ones that may generalize to others for marketing communication purposes.

SOCIAL MEDIA CLASSIFICATION

Social media is an Internet-based application that allows the creation and exchange of user-generated content resulting in six social media classes: collaborative projects (e.g., wikis, social bookmarking), blogs, content communities (e.g., YouTube), social networking sites (e.g., Facebook), virtual game worlds, and virtual social worlds.[51] For our purposes in this chapter, we investigate the first four of these six social media classes in this section. Virtual game world advertising is more closely aligned with product placement (see Chapter 13), and advertising implications of virtual social worlds remain open for further development. Figure 17-26 identifies numerous social media brands spanning different social media classes and illustrates differences in the percentages of consumers visiting the sites.

Figure 17-26   Usage of social media during the past month, fall 2014, anglophones 18+

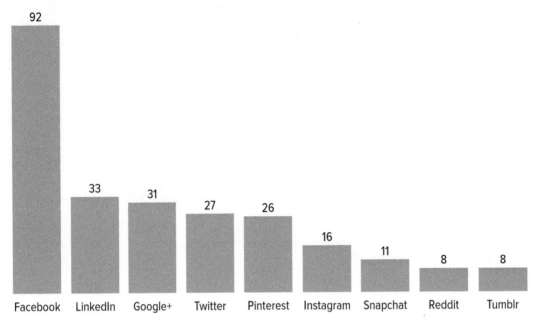

© Media Technology Monitor (MTM)

User-generated content is the key distinguishing feature of social media, and further research expanded this idea and defined *consumers' online brand-related activities (COBRAs)* as being consuming, contributing, and creating. All three of these occur in social networking sites as the penetration rate grows in Canada (Figure 17-27). *Consuming* includes watching a brand video, listening to brand audio, viewing brand pictures, following brand threads in a forum, reading brand social network pages, reading product reviews, playing branded games, and downloading branded material (e.g., widgets). *Contributing* involves rating products, joining a brand social network page, participating in brand conversations in a forum, and commenting in brand blogs. *Creating* involves behaviours like publishing a brand blog; uploading brand video, audio, or pictures; writing brand articles; and writing product reviews.[52]

Figure 17-27   Social networking usage during the past month, fall 2014, anglophones 18+

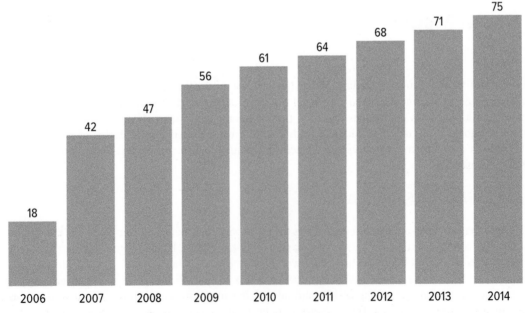

© Media Technology Monitor (MTM)

Another perspective suggests that there are 25 social media classes, as indicated in Figure 17-28, illustrating the pervasiveness of social media and where all aspects and different types of COBRAs occur. Although one might question such a broad view, and though some classes have stronger social dynamic characteristics than others, the point remains that social media is a significant media type with multiple classes and multiple vehicles within each class. As both the Internet and social media mature, the significance of this will be more valuable as targeting precision strengthens.

Figure 17-28 Main social media classes

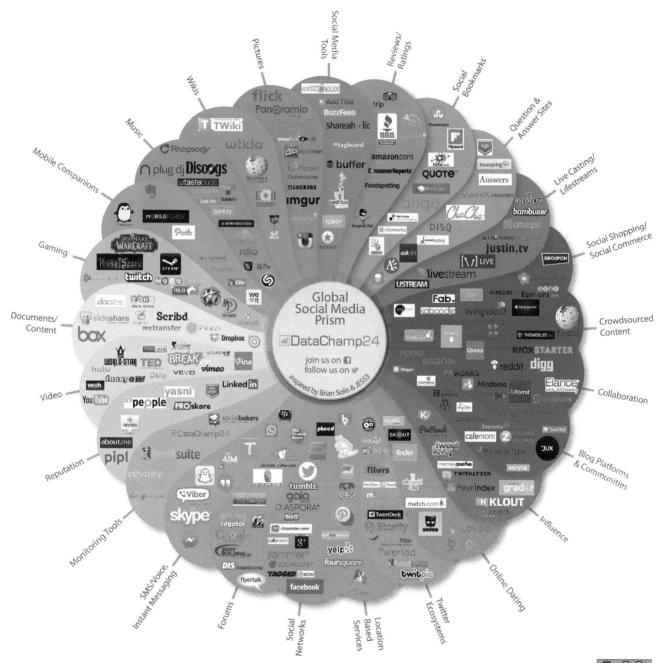

Source: © ethority GmbH & Co. KG 2016. All Rights Reserved.

Marketing communication of brands occurs within the social media itself. For example, branded Facebook pages are unique extensions of the brand image promoted and undoubtedly resemble "owned" media—much like the brand's website, and other "owned" media that has existed for decades before the Internet. As we know, ads are displayed in social media like Facebook, which means "paid media" occurs here. And finally, consumers visit a branded page within Facebook, "like" it, and communicate positive and negative consumption experiences in a variety of ways. These activities are COBRAs and indicate user-generated content, a unique feature of social media leading to the designation of "earned" media.

Figure 17-29 shows that some social media vehicles are used more frequently than others, which suggests that they will have considerably different media plans. Thus, when we say we are going to use social media in an IMC plan, the promotional planner needs to carefully consider whether the plan is addressing one, two, or all three of these aspects. Clearly all are connected to a degree, but promotional planners want to influence optimally to achieve objectives and should consider how it will work prior to investing time and money. Furthermore, preliminary research across social media vehicles found different user-generated content. The researchers found user-generated content on YouTube to be akin to self-promotion, on Twitter to be seen as brand information delivery, and on Facebook to be in between these two endpoints of the spectrum.[53] This implies that unique COBRAs within a social media vehicle provide a different exposure context, suggesting this as an important media planning consideration.

Figure 17-29   Frequency of social media usage, fall 2014, anglophones 18+

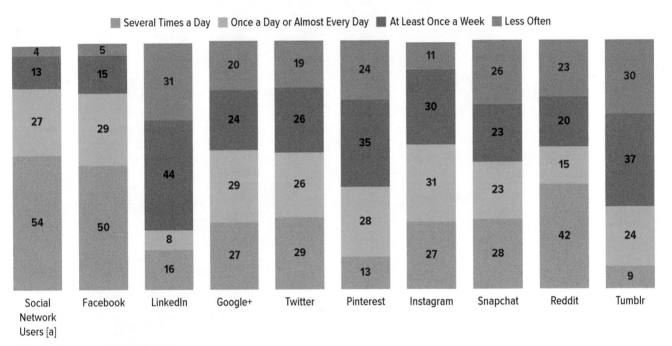

© Media Technology Monitor (MTM)

The three approaches for message delivery in social media occur with all other major players. Followers subscribe to a Twitter feed of their favourite brand, are exposed to paid messages, and converse with people whom they do not even know. Consumers witness a brand's video on YouTube, see ads for the brand on other videos, and forward links to others, comment on videos, or produce a response video. Consumers keep in touch with brands on blogs, see ads alongside the blog, and correspond seemingly as with a beloved friend as they respond to postings. Consumers use a wiki (a social bookmarking page) to creatively express their relationship to a brand, see paid ads, and understand something of a brand from the basic information provided. As all these behaviours imply, consumers digitally involve themselves in several ways with a brand; this section explores how communication occurs within social media among users, the placement of display ads within social media, and how brands convey the message they control. The result of this is that we see variation in the amount of time spent with each social media vehicle (Figure 17-30), which will once again have significant implications for media decisions.

Figure 17-30   Amount of time on social media, fall 2015, anglophones 18+

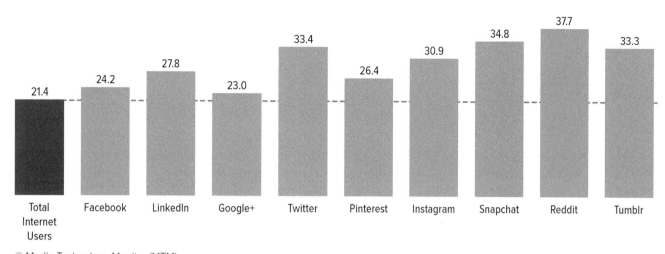

© Media Technology Monitor (MTM)

The significance of social media and the resulting consumer participation can be seen with Mars Canada's campaign with its famous M&Ms candy treat that won a Cannes award. Using Google Street View, Foursquare, Twitter, and Facebook, the brand sent people on a scavenger hunt to locate three oversized red M&M candies hidden in Toronto and captured by Google's cameras. Winners drove away with a red Smart Car. While the uniqueness of the adventure is appealing, managers wondered what the significance of looking for the candy meant in terms of brand communication effects.[54] And here is the rub: with technology at our fingertips—for both planner and consumer alike—which direction should a brand take with social media, and how can it marry the three approaches successfully? Furthermore, which social media should it use for which kinds of ad messages, and which IMC tools should a brand work with as usage levels change over time (Figure 17-31)?

Figure 17-31   Social media vehicle use by time, fall 2015, anglophones 18+

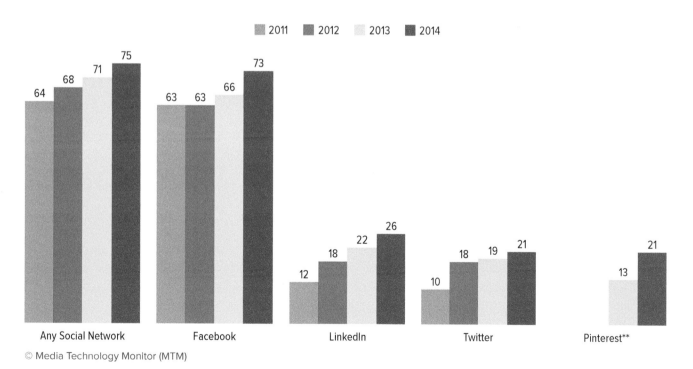

© Media Technology Monitor (MTM)

SOCIAL NETWORKING

Social media have exploded in popularity; social networking sites are a prominent destination for many Canadians who visit on a regular basis, as the past few figures have summarized. In fact, social networking users tend to be heavy Internet media consumers (i.e., spend more time, watch more online video, listen to more online audio) compared to non-social networking users. The top social networking sites attract numerous visitors each month, with Facebook at 1.1 billion, Twitter at 310 million, LinkedIn at 255 million, and Google+ at 120 million. Although critics might not agree that all are pure social networking sites, this ranking and others measure the visits and see sufficient similarity to group them together. For example, users create a personal profile and connect with others to digitally share content for all of these media.[55] We take a look at Facebook and Twitter, a couple of popular ones.

Facebook   From an advertising standpoint, Facebook is a media vehicle much like a specific magazine or television show. There is placement of a print or video message within a content environment (or via a link). These messages are similar to the ads described above, such as a banner ad with a link to a brand's website or video messages created by the brand. While a whole book could be written about Facebook, we highlight a couple of communication similarities to other media, along with its unique features.

The targeting abilities of Facebook as a media vehicle make it a very attractive advertising opportunity, allowing for complete choice and substantial precision among all segmentation variables summarized in Chapter 3. For example, Ben and Jerry's wanted to remind ice cream consumers who had savoured their brand in the past to consider eating their seven classic flavours once again. Using data from people's postings and other data, the brand increased sales from this target audience by 8 percent.[56] Facebook provides guidelines on how the targeting and costing operates, and for the most part the steps are similar to what we have seen for other media but with simpler, "point and click" options as opposed to other more involved logistical arrangements.

The ability to target exceedingly precisely on key variables places a premium on this media vehicle, provided people pay attention to the ads. One decision facing advertisers is whether to place a promotional message in a newsfeed or on the right-hand side; each has different cost implications and click-through rates, but in either case Facebook tracking indicates from which ad the user went to the advertiser's website.[57] However, the newsfeed is cluttered with both ads and content from friends, making it more difficult to ensure that a step beyond exposure occurred. Empirical research also confirmed that Facebook advertising can be as cluttered a media environment as TV.[58]

And Facebook is trying to make the ads it delivers in the newsfeed as interesting as the social content a person receives from friends. This becomes more critical as more advertising occurs through mobile devices, but especially for smart phones since there is less screen space for banner ads. The end result is that advertisers now receive fewer impressions but pay higher rates.[59] In particular, Facebook moved into YouTube's territory by offering autoplay video ads arising from the newsfeed. Canadian Club is one brand accepting the idea and playing its 15-second ads both on TV and digitally, likely with greater emphasis on mobile.[60]

In another sense these media are completely unique, with the development of "brand pages" that allow an instant connection to exciting brand content, making the whole page a commercial experience in which the user may not even perceive (or may not be concerned about) the advertising due to pervasive brand loyalty. This idea of content on a branded Facebook page is not the same as content found in broadcast or print media where the content is a TV program, a radio show, a newspaper article on a topic like youth unemployment, or a magazine piece on how university and college students can live away from home economically. Much of the content presented by a brand on a Facebook brand page is a form of advertising or another kind of marketing communication message.

Support for this idea is found in research that tested the effects of a brand's posting on the brand page. The study examined the factors that led to consumers "liking" the posting or commenting on the posting. The results found that high vividness ranging from no visual to photo to video produced higher levels of "likes" for video only, but did not garner more comments. Interactivity produced higher levels of "likes" with contest links, but not for website links, voting links, calls to action, or questions. Information and entertainment value did not produce "likes" or more comments. In contrast, the positional location of the brand post and the positive comments of others produced higher levels of "likes" and more comments.[61]

Fan pages offer virtually any marketing communication tool depending on the brand's objective. For example, during the summer of 2010 the Molson Canadian Facebook page featured about 430,000 fans who could watch six Molson videos and 32 videos posted by fans or other consumers. Similarly, Molson posted six photo albums, while fans posted about 1,300 photos. Concert information and links to buy tickets for the Molson Canadian Amphitheatre could be found, as could locations of bars to attend. True fans could read about and participate in the "Seize the Summer" promotion by earning badges for their summer experiences (much like a child's summer camp experience) that could be recorded on a personal page. This final step required the permission of the user, who had to agree to let Molson do the following four things: "(1) access my basic information (i.e., name, profile picture, gender, networks, user ID, list of friends, and any other information I've shared with everyone); (2) send me an email (i.e., Molson Canadian Seize the Summer may email me directly at . . .); (3) post to my wall (i.e., Molson Canadian Seize the Summer may post status messages, notes, photos, and videos to my wall); (4) access my data any time (i.e., Molson Canadian Seize the Summer may access my data when I'm not using the application)."

The implications of giving this kind of access to a company are interesting. The data could, over time, be compiled into a database and act as a resource for other marketing activities. For example, for a product like a beer brand, a sophisticated marketer might want to figure out when a group of friends are planning to go to a particular bar, and then send out a promotional team to the same bar. Additional direct digital marketing activities may be developed such that a group of friends could be invited to an event.

Facebook encourages extensive brand promotion in its literature (Exhibit 17-16), which is designed to educate businesspeople that Facebook advertising is quite consistent with advertising elsewhere.[62] The page has a cover photo, a visually attractive brand presentation much like a print ad in a magazine. The profile picture gives a prime location for brands to present their logo or any other identifying image, once again adapting a long-established advertising principle found in other media. The filmstrip-like row of activities that includes apps provides additional promotional experiences. The ability to include brand information or photos in the pinned posts offers extended reading or viewing opportunities, and the experience is akin to reading feature magazine articles about a brand. But the distinction about content made earlier suggests that these posts are more like copy found in catalogues or other collateral material. Communications regarding sales promotions like contests or discounts are certainly familiar as they occur in all other types of media as well.

However, another important attribute that is distinctive for this social media is the part of the page where fellow Facebookers describe their buying and consumption experiences as a message to consumers. While these messages are not controlled by the advertiser like the initial photos and messages are, their content can be influenced by the brand since they can be reactions to what the brand initially posted. Nevertheless, a degree of brand influence clearly occurs from the social dynamic of people conversing—the extent, however, is open for investigation.

Kraft Dinner presents a friendly example of a popular brand using Facebook to maintain a fascinating attachment with Canadians. Since the product's name south of the border is Kraft Macaroni and Cheese, KD (as it is known here) retains its unique identity with home-grown advertising featuring the famous "Gotta Be KD" slogan, invented by a consumer more than 10 years ago during the brand's cross-country promotional tour. Playing on the sense of ownership Canadians feel with KD, the Facebook page presented challenges for its fans—including photo bombing with KD, making a KD .gif, putting captions on photos of KD, and "Make It Epic" recipe battles. TV ads with humorous battle scenes between two roommates drove traffic to Facebook. The campaign pumped up the fan roster from 120,000 to 270,000, an especially impressive result considering the challenges did not reward winners with prizes like most contests. Instead, winners received social media glory as KD victors![63]

Exhibit 17-16   Facebook provides information on advertising using the social media platform.

© Ingvar Bjork / Shutterstock.com

Twitter   Twitter self-identifies as a "real-time information network" on its Internet site.[64] This contributes to difficulty in classifying it, since "networking" implies it is similar to entities like Facebook, however "real-time information" implies a blog or micro-blog. However, the messages distributed are much like the newsfeed feature on Facebook, so it remains in the social networking domain. Twitter established an office in Canada and expanded services previously available only in the United States. Its managing director moved over from TV and sees Twitter as marrying with TV rather than being in competition.[65] Canadian Twitter users are evenly split between men and women; 44 percent are aged 18–34, are active second screen users, and spend eight more hours using Internet media than the average social networker.

To some degree, Twitter is entirely free—any brand or person (e.g., performing artist, athlete) can set up an account and send messages to followers, who will ultimately be influenced by such communication. The messages can be simple phrases and, if desired, can include links to whatever digital content the author would like to associate, including video. In this manner, brands can distribute a controlled message to anyone who is following or motivated to seek out the messages, much like other Internet media that is owned. With so many users and so many messages there is considerable clutter, which led to Twitter offering advertising options for fees, otherwise moving into a world of paid media (Exhibit 17-17).

Twitter's ad products for marketing communication include promoted accounts, promoted tweets, and promoted trends.[66] Promoted accounts are identified by the brand name, like Cirque du Soleil, and are featured in the "Who to follow" account recommendation search engine. Cirque du Soleil wanted to announce tour dates and new shows to potential customers who can find this branded account among others. So this works much like a short link ad from a search engine to encourage repeat exposures to brand messages.

Exhibit 17-17   Twitter use is strong with smart phones.

© dolphfyn / Shutterstock.com

Promoted tweets are brand messages much like specific advertising messages found in other online media where consumers willingly seek brand information (i.e., Internet sites). They are also similar to brand messages placed in non-digital media like magazines. For one promoted tweet, Cirque requested followers to communicate their experience while seeing a show. In this respect, the social media message from a customer (i.e., source of the message) acts as a testimonial so that potential customers vicariously experience the spectacle. The customer testimonial is the unique contribution of social media; this personal content acts as a brand message yet shares similar qualities since there is an identifiable source characteristic regarding similarity (see Chapter 7).

The message often has a link to the Internet site or any other type of digital communication the brand planned. Cirque made use of promoted tweets that include sales promotions for discounted tickets that linked to its Facebook page. Naturally, the links could go to a brand's Internet site, which Gongshow Gear successfully employed, or to a YouTube video for continued brand exposure, like Porsche did for its launch of the 911 model. Promoted trends are listed in a designated trends section on Twitter, which acts as an automated search designed to encourage continued exposure to other messages. Again, this operates much like a link ad from a search engine. For example, Porsche initially established its hashtag in a promoted tweet and then listed the same hashtag in the promoted trends.

Twitter operates like any other media, offering an opportunity for brand exposure for fees. As of early 2013, a promoted trend cost $200,000 per day. Advertisers pay when people follow a promoted account, or when people retweet, reply, favourite, or click on a brand's promoted tweet. The cost for these two ad products is based on a bidding system and ranges from $0.50 to $2.50 per follower for the former and $0.50 to $1.50 per action for the latter.[67] The minimum price works out to a CPM of $500, a very expensive proposition compared to other media. Other agencies figured out a way to make money from Twitter by using it as a medium for celebrity endorsements. Brands pay the celebrity (with a cut to the agency) to talk about a product and the digital response is substantial with links to Internet sites.[68]

From a social marketing standpoint, brands encourage lots of interaction with fun activities like Twestivals, which raise funds for a worthy cause the brand sponsors; TweetUps, where people who follow a brand can meet up and socialize face-to-face; and Twitter parties, where consumers continually talk about a brand with multiple comments.[69] These and any other follow-up messages from consumers are the height of social media, with user-generated content (e.g., earned media). While these can have positive impact, there is tremendous risk for negative communication as the company loses control, something most brands historically have not desired. Figure 17-32 is a summary of statistics indicating the degree to which Twitter users perform a few COBRAs. For example, Ford Canada claimed Twitter success with anecdotal stories of consumers reporting they purchased a Ford after seeing the company's Twitter presence or responses. Furthermore, the brand uses Twitter as a listening post to act upon negative experiences with a direct call once contact information is ascertained. A whole team constantly monitors the account, providing responses 24/7.[70]

Figure 17-32 Content creators of Twitter users, fall 2014, Canadians 18+

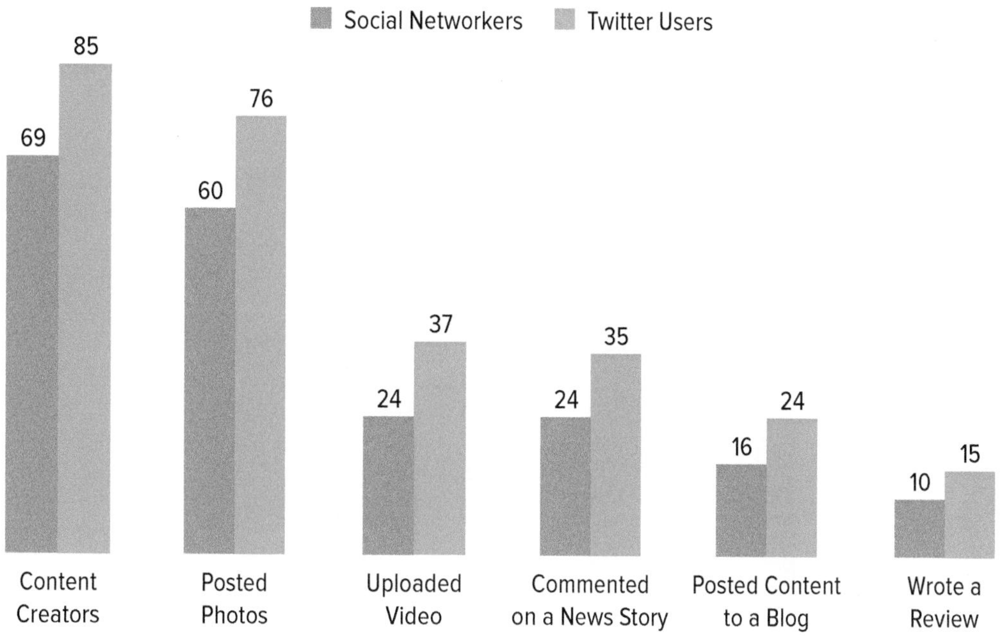

■ Social Networkers   ■ Twitter Users

	Content Creators	Posted Photos	Uploaded Video	Commented on a News Story	Posted Content to a Blog	Wrote a Review
Social Networkers	69	60	24	24	16	10
Twitter Users	85	76	37	35	24	15

© Media Technology Monitor (MTM)

However the implementation of Twitter messages remains a concern for brands that are grappling with questions much like any other media when it first arrived.[71] What message should be sent via Twitter? When should the messages be sent? How frequently should the messages be sent? Molson moved toward posting less frequently but with higher quality images and brand messages due to the value of shared tweets; in contrast, during the World MasterCard Fashion week, the sponsor tweeted 60 times per day to share the runway photos![72] Where should the brand digitally direct the user via its links? Why is someone motivated to receive our brand's Twitter feed? Canadian companies like Tim Hortons and Harvey's understand that their tone needs to fit within Canadian culture and be humble, sincere, and friendly. Canadian divisions of American brands like Denny's opened a separate Canadian Twitter feed so the message resonated with Canadians.[73] The Canadian Football League worked Twitter into its plan to present the action on the field and the players as part of its Grey Cup communications directed to younger fans less interested in nostalgia.[74]

Finally, who in the organization should be sending the message? PR executives feel strongly that Twitter responses and all social media communication are in their domain, since these professionals are trained and experienced with continual messaging with the press and the public as issues and topics emerge over time. On the other side, digital agencies believe they should be in charge since they have the technical skills and are stronger resources in our technological era.[75]

A number of criticisms and challenges face Twitter despite its appeal. One criticism is the usefulness of the format—a stream of tweets that viewers typically do not backtrack to see, thereby limiting actual exposure. Coupled with this is a problem that messages are cluttered.[76] In terms of concerns, the user base growth is not meeting expectations and a noticeably small portion of users are active tweeters, with the remainder acting as quiet bird-watchers. In addition, the frequency of actually tweeting from the active users is not as strong as hoped for by advertisers liking to invest their budget.[77] To counter these issues, Twitter introduced "conversational" ad formats where consumers answer to a branded tweet by touching a ready-made response in which they can also add their own comments. Samsung Canada tested the concept to promote its smartwatch Gear S2 and claimed good success by obtaining exposure and response from 53,000 consumers over four days.[78]

CONTENT COMMUNITIES

Content communities exist for users to share video, photo images, and audio media. We concentrate on the first two for this section; there is no documented revenue stream for audio advertising revenue, and video advertising revenue hit $358 million in Canada for 2015. For video, we concentrate on YouTube since it is the industry leader in advertising practices and retains a strong market position.

YouTube   As expected, YouTube (with 1 billion monthly visits) has a strong lead over remaining contenders like Vimeo at 130 million, Yahoo Screen at 130 million, and Daily Motion at 125 million.[79] Figure 17-33 summarizes usage statistics and, while most students visit YouTube monthly, the average is certainly not universal. Like any other Internet site, YouTube generates revenue by selling display ads such as standard banner ads (including masthead ads with options) and rich media ads, and also offers in-video overlay display ads and specialized options for homepage ads. These types of ads are available for mobile delivery as well, demonstrating that YouTube is a paid media Internet media option.

Figure 17-33   Percentage watching YouTube by demographics, fall 2014, Canadians 18+

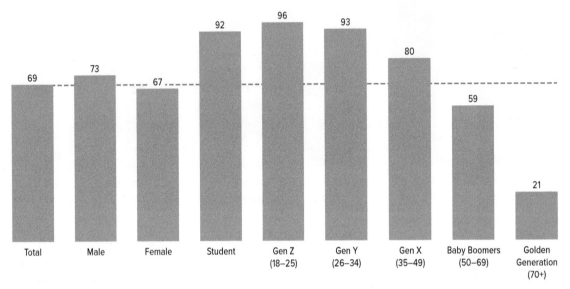

© Media Technology Monitor (MTM)

Of course, companies can put video on YouTube as owned media, and this is great for any kind of growing business. Martell Home Builders, a small and enterprising construction startup in Moncton, stumbled upon using YouTube with a video clip of industry tradespeople endorsing the owner to potential customers. With quick distribution of the video link within the real estate industry, Pierre Martell was in business. Subsequent videos describe the customized house building process so well that the owner can now close a sale in two hours, down from eight hours, because the video answers so many preliminary questions.[80]

Brands became very creative with YouTube to establish owned media in different ways. Schick funded a series entitled *MsLabelled* featuring Ella, a young employee working at a fashion magazine with aspirations to be a fashion blogger. Ella came to life with her own accounts on Instagram, Tumblr, and Twitter. The brand saw similarity between Ella's character—who is fun and flirty—and their target audience. Although Schick did not promote its involvement substantially, the company received more visits to its website and strong traffic on Ella's social media.[81]

YouTube offers the opportunity for channels—designated repositories of whatever videos a brand may want to post for viewers—including ads appearing on TV, on another Internet location, or specifically customized. User channels are cost-free with the same functionality as for any other user. Thus, a YouTube channel retains the idea of owned media for brands desiring to host video messages. Brand channels are cost-free and offer additional avenues for brand identification and enhanced viewer experience. Custom brand channels offer interactive applications, user-generated submission, live streaming, and client services for fees. Given the considerable amount of video available, the frequency of use shown in Figure 17-34 is completely expected.

Figure 17-34   Frequency of watching YouTube, fall 2014, Canadians 18+

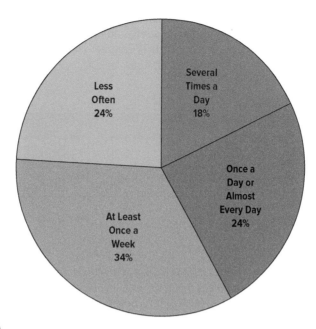

© Media Technology Monitor (MTM)

In some respects, the use of channels on YouTube is a wonderful opportunity for advertisers to initiate further social media communication among their viewers (e.g., owned media). Viewers might want to comment on Koodo and its advertising after experiencing the game. Similarly, the Skittles use of YouTube described in Chapter 8 presents ample opportunity for consumers to respond to the brand, much like the sensation with Old Spice a few years ago. And, for some unknown reason, consumers may decide to create tribute ads for brands they love. One enterprising former student created his own "BlackBerry There Then There Now—Z10 Commercial" on YouTube and had picked up nearly 58,000 views by late 2016. As Figure 17-35 summarizes, YouTube users participate in a good number of COBRAs.

Figure 17-35   Usage of YouTube, fall 2014, Canadians 18+

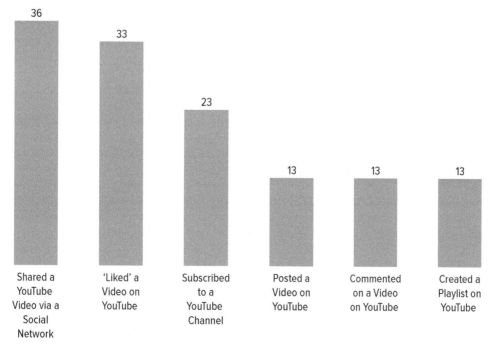

© Media Technology Monitor (MTM)

Growth in consumer interaction may be on the horizon. Major Canadian brand channels for vehicle brands had low subscription rates in 2013, as shown in Figure 17-36, but most of them had achieved a tenfold increase by 2016. However, brands can see razor sharp returns—like Dollar Shave Club, with over 10 million views! And it seems that the old adage—familiar from media before Internet video—is that creativity, no matter where it is located or viewed, gets notoriety. A brand's video message in social media is passed along if it is original and creative, much like we see in all facets of advertising.[82]

Figure 17-36   YouTube subscriber statistics

	Ford	Chevrolet	Chrysler	Honda	Toyota	Nissan
2013 Subscribers	1,239	2,413	54	920	751	1,311
2016 Subscribers	13,228	21,478	545	3,547	6,512	8,051

Source: Compiled by observation on June 4, 2013, May 21, 2016.

As an alternative to YouTube, brands can move to lesser known video hosting vehicles beyond the most dominant player. For Molson Canadian's "The Code" campaign, Molson put together an online video launch to reflect the unwritten rules of "guy social conduct" for targeted beer drinkers aged 19–24. The videos filmed at sporting and music events with comedian Nicole Arbour interviewed audience members with questions like, "What do you do if you spill someone's beer?" or "Do you have a six-pack or a mega-keg?" Viewers streamed the nine videos on Heavy.com a total of 7 million times and could really identify with what their peers were saying and instantly made a link to the brand.[83] As this example suggests, even though YouTube has a dominant position, others are interested in gaining share of a growing market, as seen in Exhibit 17-18.

In commenting on the success of brand messages on video hosting sites, experts suggest that a positive return on investment is achieved if a clip reaches the 1 million mark. For example, a video that costs $50,000 to produce results in a CPM of $50. This is a different cost comparison based on production since there is no media cost, for now. Canadian advertisers are taking creative risks by placing ads on these sites that they might not normally place on TV. For example, Lululemon posted a video mocking its very own customers in a humorous version of "stuff yogis say" as a take-off on other pop-culture examples.[84] Of course, the 1 million mark only happens if the video link ricochets throughout social media, another example of how the same ad units discussed in the previous section work in social media as well. And the media cost for distribution is free, since ordinary consumers are doing the work that brands would normally pay media companies to do.

Exhibit 17-18   Popular YouTube faces competition as the market grows.

© dolphfyn / Shutterstock.com

Streaming ads operate much like TV, showing a message while viewing a content video, with options. True View ads permit viewers to skip the ad after five seconds, and YouTube offers four versions: in-stream ads, in-slate ads, display, and search. Standard in-stream ads occur before, during, or after a video and do not have the skip feature. First Watch plays a brand's ad first no matter what video the viewer watches.

YouTube original channels offer similar media vehicles much like TV. There are a host of genres of shows in terms of sports, comedy, lifestyle, and others. Ads can be selectively placed on any of these channels. Alternatively, advertisers can select placement on regular videos based on profiling characteristics seen in previous media placement.

Photo Images   Instagram with 100 million monthly visitors leads Imgur at 88 million, Flickr at 80 million, and Photobucket at 60 million. Flickr and Photobucket have relinquished the lead over the past three years to Instagram and Imgur, a cautionary reminder for both Internet media and companies advertising to keep abreast of the media with a larger audience much like has been done with older media historically. Figure 17-37 totals up the content creation of Instagram users much like we saw for Twitter. Sixty percent of Instagram users are women; 68 percent are in the age range of 18–34, are active second screen users, and spend six more hours using Internet media than the average social networker.

Figure 17-37   Instagram and social networkers content creation, fall 2014, Canadian, 18+

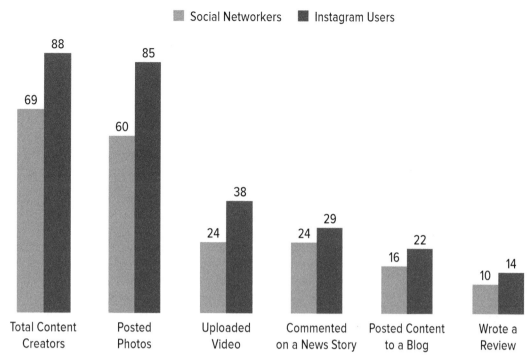

© Media Technology Monitor (MTM)

All four of these organizations, and others, accept advertising placements. Instagram offers numerous avenues for advertising with photo, video, and carousel ads. Many of the targeting features found with Facebook are available here as well since Facebook owns Instagram. And Instagram pushes ads through the newsfeed similarly, with ads having the same look as the media content. For its Canadian launch, Instagram worked with Hudson's Bay, Target, Sport Chek, Air Canada, and Travel Alberta as the initial advertisers. The advertisers readily accepted this format since most Instagram use occurred on smart phones where display ads cannot work with the smaller screen.[85] Yahoo owns Flickr and so placement in this media vehicle yields numerous options as it is part of the broad advertising tools available across all digital media. In contrast, Photobucket provides very basic information on its Internet site for advertising placement, with a request to call or email them.

The brand development in this social media class appears enormous for different types of advertisers. For example, for experiential products, like travel, entertainment, and so on—essentially, any product category that has a transformational motive—the images contribute to existing positive attitudes or begin to build new ones for non-users. If Canada wanted to foster more travel, what better way than to sprinkle photos or videos among the social media vehicles that people from other countries might see? Or, to take advantage of the user-generated concept of social media, the travel organizations can merely seek out the photo/video postings of ordinary citizens and create a means for consumers to find them, like a social bookmarking site. Exhibit 17-19 indicates that the creative potential of sequencing images for owned and earned media is strong with Instagram. For example, Mazda posted batches of three to six photos or videos periodically for about four months to get the feel of driving their vehicle and experience the brand during a virtual road trip.[86]

Exhibit 17-19   Instagram photo images provide opportunity for owned and earned media exposure.

© ArthurStock / Shutterstock.com

BLOGS

A **blog** (short for *weblog*) is a publication consisting primarily of periodic articles, normally presented in reverse chronological order. Blogs reflect the writings of an individual, a community, a political organization, or a corporation. A blog set up for brand presentation is akin to a website in that it is owned media. Blogs also present the opportunity for ad placement (e.g., paid media). And the ability of consumers to participate with responses and by adding user-generated content permits both positive and negative brand communication. Thus, this social media vehicle is a multifaceted brand communication tool, like other social media. Blog sites where writers can set up their own blogs with varying levels of visitors include WordPress and Blogger. The top branded blogs with their monthly views include Huffington Post at 110 million, TMZ at 30 million, Business Insider at 30 million, and Mashable at 24 million.

Companies have experimented with corporate or brand blogs to present a friendly public relations face to the general public and allow some interactions. These can be within the corporate website or as a standalone. The imagery and tone of blogs provide a less formal approach for communication, so companies look to blogs as a way of appearing friendly and opening dialogue. Brands can also look to blogs to address issues or ideas related to consumers who are more committed to the brand by virtue of their participation in viewing and interacting with the blog.

Blogs offer advertisers a potential way to reach their target audience at a small cost since they are specialized vehicles for placing display and video ads, as described in the previous section. WordPress does not facilitate the placement of ads; however, Blogger, owned by Google, is associated with its system of ad placements. Individual blogs offer their own media kit for ad prices that are consistent with previous descriptions. For example, BlogTO, a blog about Toronto, offers different banner ad options with a CPM of $10 to $20, along with other customized options.[87] A Vancouver-based blog entitled Scout sells ads to small local businesses on a per placement basis in its "Locals We Recommend" section.[88] Extreme fragmentation occurs, with literally millions of blog media vehicles available in which an advertiser might place its ad. This problem supports the need for digital ad placement firms.

Personal bloggers often find themselves as key influencers for consumers while describing their product experiences. For certain consumers, a blogger has a strong source credibility effect. In this respect, bloggers are acting similarly to journalists who feature product stories in newspapers or magazines. Marketers are also starting to recognize that mothers who blog are particularly successful in this role, as mothers seem to trust other mothers considerably. Blogs directed to foodies (Exhibit 17-20) are popular and provide good opportunity for food companies to influence consumers.

Advertisers also sponsor personal blogs, or an individual blog that is part of a collection of blogs such as the YummyMummyClub.ca. Erica Ehm, a famous media host, documented a trip to Alberta on her blog, which included photos taken with a Sony camera. One page of the blog ended with the brand prominently displayed with a sponsorship notice that provided full disclosure of the relationship between the blogger and the brand. Some are critical of this process and suggest that it circumvents the "idea" of a blog, while others are concerned that bloggers do not communicate the advertiser's exact financial contribution. In defence, bloggers cite industries (e.g., fashion, travel) where free goods are routinely passed along for endorsement.

Exhibit 17-20   Bloggers post photo images on their sites and provide opportunity for earned media exposure for brands.

© Stock-Asso/Shutterstock

Currently, Advertising Standards Canada, the self-regulatory body for marketers, plans significant changes for its code for advertisers with bloggers and other similar influencers in social media.[89] Full description of their practices occurs in Chapter 18, however in March 2016 they put forth amendments that clearly address situations in which advertising persuasion occurred that consumers may not be fully aware of. Essentially, any blogger or someone within social media who has any "material connection" to an advertiser and acts as an endorser, reviewer, or influencer is viewed as an "advertiser" and is expected to adhere to the code. And, anyone in social media who does not have any "material connection" is not considered as such.

Blogs that are personal expressions exist with interested followers. For example, Justyna Baraniecki's fashion blog (Chameleonic) shows photographs of herself modelling the clothing of brands she enjoys wearing for her own personal style.

Readers vote their "likes" or appreciate how she puts her collection together through comments. Justyna says, "Everyone has their own way of speaking through their clothes," and suggests fashion blogs are good for young girls learning their style rather than reading celebrity magazines.[90]

COLLABORATIVE PROJECTS

This type of social media includes wikis and social bookmarking Internet sites. Both of these share a common characteristic of having extensive user-generated content. Wikis permit users to add, remove, or change text-based content, and social bookmarking sites allow users to collect links to Internet sites and rate their quality. The top reference site is Wikipedia with 475 million monthly visitors followed by Yahoo Answers at 150 million, About at 100 million, and Answers at 95 million. Some of these do not completely reflect wikis, but their format resembles the idea of a collaborative project for the most part since users respond and converse on a multitude of topics.

Wikipedia does not accept advertising and encourages an active debate on its merits.[91] Answers.com offers extensive placement options and provides a thorough media kit describing the standard and custom formats; this is similar to other social media and Internet sites that are not social media, as discussed in the advertising section.[92] These kinds of collaborative question and answer sites appear conducive for both positive and negative brand communication effects as consumers are in a role of communicating a testimonial by contributing their consumption experiences, which may or may not resonate with readers.

Top social bookmarking sites are Pinterest at 250 million monthly visitors, Tumblr at 110 million, and Reddit at 32 million. What social media vehicles to include on this list demonstrates the difficulty with exact classification given their overlapping features with other social media, however the bookmarking feature is the most noteworthy and these social media vehicles are identified as the main ones. The drop-off in visitors relative to the other social media lists implies that this avenue for placing ads is less useful for promotional planners beyond a few vehicles. Reddit provides instructions for how would-be advertisers can place ads alongside the content, while others appear not to offer advertising at all. Reddit users are active at creating content as well (Figure 17-38). Providing further support that each social media vehicle attracts a particular audience like other media, research into the conversation from the website indicated three psychological traits for Reddit users: individualism, innovation, and fairness.[93] Seventy-five percent of Reddit users are men; 70 percent are in the age range of 18–34, are active second screen users, and spend 18 more hours using Internet media than the average social networker.

Figure 17-38   Reddit and social networkers content creation, fall 2014, Canadian, 18+

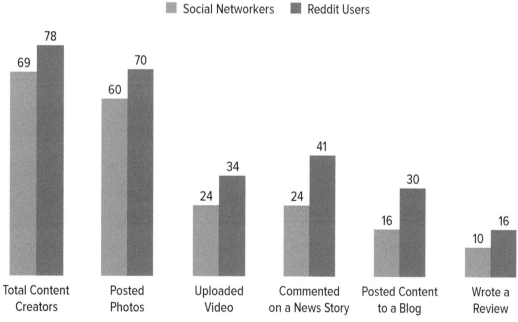

The user-generated content is quite fascinating from a marketing communication standpoint. For example, extensive lists of bookmarks of Internet sites on a site like Delicious appear very similar to a list of links from a search engine. Additionally, one might construe it as a list of link ads such that the whole site is merely a collection of ads. Alternatively, one could even view it along the same lines as a directory. In either of these cases, the user-generated content appears as if it were advertising of sorts, placed by the advertisers. However, since this "content" was placed by regular people known as "users," this would constitute non-advertising. Of course, all of this gets terribly complicated if the regular person is in fact paid by the advertiser, or its agent, to make the posting.

A site like Pinterest permits all kinds of repurposing of Internet content by users through a simple process of "pinning" images that retain the original link. Eighty percent of Pinterest users are women; 36 percent are in the age range of 18–34, are marginally active second screen users, and spend two more hours using Internet media than the average social networker. Users spend an average of 16 minutes on the site—versus 3 and 12 minutes for Twitter and Facebook, respectively—and experts see it as a useful social media for expressive and transformational brands.[94] What more could a brand ask than for its customers to select photos from the Internet and comment to show others how great the product is? Figure 17-39 highlights the content creation of Pinterest users.

Figure 17-39   Pinterest and social networkers content creation, fall 2014, Canadian 18+

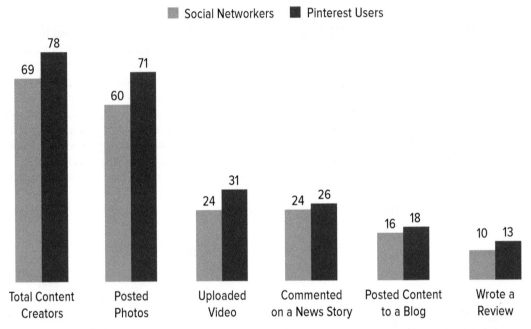

© Media Technology Monitor (MTM)

In its literature to explain how businesses can use this social media, Pinterest cites the example of Sephora, where the retailer noticed that consumers selected pictures from its company Internet site and "pinned" them—which, of course, encouraged others to visit its site.[95] This is another example where "advertising material" became "social media content" as users moved it from one digital location to another. Sephora took advantage of this by adjusting its site with "Pin It" buttons to foster further postings in the social media and sent emails to encourage registered customers to do more pinning. As this suggests, certain aspects of brand messages in social media occur because of consumer initiative, while others are responses to concerted marketing communication efforts by the brand. In either case, Pinterest imagery appears to be a good way to establish owned and earned media (Exhibit 17-21).

Exhibit 17-21   Pinterest photo images provide opportunity for stylish brand expression.

© Bloomua / Shutterstock.com

SOCIAL MEDIA INCENTIVES

Promotional planners offer incentives (e.g., sales promotions) to consumers via Internet media. Most of the sales promotions are identical to the ones described in Chapter 14; as discussed in that chapter, Internet media is the delivery or execution mechanism instead of a store or delivery to the home. As mentioned, a coupon can be printed or digitally saved, or clipped from a newspaper flyer. Incentives are also used in Internet media to encourage continued media consumption, and this especially occurs in social media. Because of the interactive nature of social media, promotional planners continue to explore ways to ensure that users will try certain aspects of social media and, importantly, continue using social media.

In social media environments, members often receive digital treats. Loyal customers are rewarded with related electronic items provided to them—such as ringtones, wallpapers, emoticons, skins, winks, and pictures for instant message services. In this sense, these services have become digital "gifts" or "premiums," as described in Chapter 14 on sales promotion. Although the non-virtual world usually considered tangible goods to be the premium, the digital age has spawned the concept of intangible gifts that become highly valued.

Another example occurs where various types of points systems allow repeat customers to generate even further rewards—a virtual continuity program for avid Internet media users who are brand loyal. Also, brands offer *advergames*—skill-challenging endeavours that keep customers amused while offering brand messages during play. Like other aspects of Internet media, games are associated with mobile apps, and brands like Foursquare offer status badges for continued use of their service.[96] Molson established the "Seize the Summer" app with Foursquare where users collected badges for activities accomplished to share on Facebook, which translated to a 20 percent growth in fans. The NHL connected with Foursquare to get fans interested in the game with prizes to be won after collecting badges and demonstrating greater use of hockey's social media.[97] Thus, Internet media allow previously intangible sales promotions to create value through intangible benefits for continued usage.

Finally, one of the most significant rewards for loyal customers has been the delivery of enhanced content in terms of information or entertainment. Loyal customers are rewarded with exclusive video for their participation. To give thanks, advertisers provide enhanced levels of information where this is deemed valuable. In this sense, the content is not the product witnessed as it is perceived as a bonus—something fitting the original definition of a sales promotion.

 # Measuring Internet Effectiveness

Understanding how to measure the effectiveness of Internet media is an involved topic requiring perhaps a whole chapter to fully appreciate its complexity, but we will provide a brief overview for direction. As expected, numerous measures, or metrics as they are often known, are electronically recorded with digital communication. These data, and data from other methods similar to those described in Chapter 9, are analyzed to assess whether all facets of marketing communication described in this chapter are effective. Consistent with measurement in other media, we initially comment on audience information measures (demographics, psychographics, and so on) for Internet media. We then apply the communication model adapted through earlier chapters: exposure, processing, communication effects, and action.

AUDIENCE MEASURES

The electronic recording of Internet user behaviour allows advertisers to investigate a multitude of ways of understanding what has been looked at on a website and for how long, along with user characteristics.[98] When Internet media first developed its own audience size measures, concerns with the research methods led to a slower adoption rate by traditional media buyers. In an attempt to respond to criticism of the audience metrics used, as well as to standardize the measures used to gauge effectiveness, the Interactive Advertising Bureau (IAB)—the largest and most influential trade group—formed a task force consisting of global corporations involved in advertising and research. The final reports of the task force are available from IAB.net and contain both American and international guidelines (see also IABCanada.com).

The basic problem facing Internet media concerns a standardized method for determining the size of the audience. The report identified the technical procedures for accurately reporting whether an ad impression has occurred. This answers the fundamental expectation of advertisers as to whether the receiver of the message actually experienced an opportunity to see the ad (i.e., degree of exposure to the message). Another aspect concerns the accepted procedures for auditing the data, much like we see in traditional print media. Another key part of the report included guidelines for presenting data in terms of time of day, week, and month, much like we see in broadcast media. Finally, industry representatives agreed upon substantial guidelines for disclosure of research methodology, again consistent with all major media described in previous chapters. In future, advertisers can look forward to more authentic data to assess the viability of committing increased resources to Internet communication. Firms now use methods similar to those found in other media (e.g., Vividata) to measure demographics, psychographics, location and method of Internet access, media usage, and buying habits.

COMMUNICATION MODEL MEASURES

A significant development on this topic is a summary of 197 metrics (shortened from an initial list of 350) for websites, mobile, social media, and email published by the Advertising Research Foundation (ARF).[99] The 197 metrics are catalogued into nine categories: advertising, audience/traffic, site navigation/site performance, media consumption, engagement/ interaction, amplification/endorsement, conversion, ecommerce, and ad effectiveness. The metrics are also cross-listed by four marketing stages: capture (86 metrics), connect (90), close (18) and keep (3). Neither of these listing methods is exactly consistent with the communication approach of this book, but the marketing stage view is simpler to consider, with only four marketing stages. The numbers indicate that the vast majority of the metrics are capture and connect, and for the most part these metrics address exposure, or act as a proxy for processing since they are time- (e.g., number of minutes on website per visit) or incident-based (e.g., did the viewer watch the complete video). Many of the close metrics address aspects of ecommerce purchases, and some are general measures of conversion of any online behaviour that an advertiser wishes to track. Keep in mind that there are minimal measures of communication effects since these are knowledge-based and attitudinally based, in contrast to the electronic records of people's Internet media consumption. And there are no brand-based measures for trial or repeat purchasing.

As noted, there are numerous exposure metrics, such as: How many unique visitors came to our website? How many impressions did our page generate virally? How many times did a person see a specific ad or other piece of content? How many unique people did our video reach? And, there are many processing measures, such as: What percentage of people who downloaded our app are using it? How long is a specific page viewed? How many of our brochures were downloaded? How many things were pinned from our website? These selective examples provide an overview of many metrics that can be tracked across all the different communications occurring in Internet media. For a shorter and cheaper investigation, consult a journal article that gives a concise description.[100] While this work is substantial and very useful for promotional planners, concern still remains about fraud, the reliability of the metrics, the poor representation of advertisers within the automatic buying system, and the resiliency of the resolution mechanisms when disputes arise within this complicated system.[101]

The movement for comprehensive communication effects measurement reveals that the Internet has its own set of criteria for measuring effectiveness and is also borrowing from traditional measures. Companies that provide research information in traditional media now extend their reach to Internet media. Academics publish articles related to measuring communication effectiveness with Internet media, such as consumers' attitudes toward a site or consumers' attitudes to an ad (e.g., banner ads).[102]

A number of companies use traditional measures of recall and retention to test their Internet ads. The same measures have been used to pretest online commercials as well. Survey research, conducted both online and through traditional methods, is employed to determine everything from site usage to attitudes toward a site. Companies now provide information on specific communication measures like brand awareness, message association, brand attitude, and purchase intention.

One of the more extensive attempts to measure the effectiveness of integrating interactive and traditional media is through IAB's *cross-media optimization studies (CMOST)*. These studies are designed to determine the optimal mix of online and offline advertising media vehicles, in terms of frequency, reach, and budget allocation for a given campaign to achieve its marketing goals. Examples of these studies are regularly published on the IAB website. A recent one featured a Tetley Tea campaign using magazines and two expandable rich media ads and a video preroll. Results indicated the importance of both media with varying communication effects (awareness, message retention, purchase intention) at different stages of the consumer decision-making process, as shown in Chapter 5.[103] What makes these studies important is that they provide insight into (1) the relative contributions of each medium in the mix, (2) the combined contribution of multiple media, (3) optimal media budget allocations, and (4) actionable media mix strategies.

Finally, social media may require its own set of metrics based on its "owned" media characteristics. Reviewing the theoretical and practical literature, authors of one review article conclude with nine guidelines for implementing a measurement system. One significant guideline suggests unique metrics for different social media vehicles and unique metrics within different parts of a given social media vehicle. Another identifies the importance of focusing on the quality of the information rather than the quantity of social media activities.[104] As these two points imply, revised social media metrics will likely give greater insights into attitudinal brand effects.

LO5 Evaluation of Internet Media

As we have done for other media thus far in the text, we summarize the strengths and limitations of Internet media for delivering a message.

STRENGTHS OF INTERNET MEDIA

Target Audience Selectivity   A major strength of Internet media is the ability to target very specific groups of individuals with a minimum of waste coverage. Internet sites are tailored to meet consumers' needs and wants through personalization and other targeting techniques. As a result of precise targeting, messages can be designed to appeal to the specific needs and wants of the target audience. The interactive capabilities of Internet media make it possible to carry on personalized and customized marketing communication with increased success. Social media vehicles are available for any taste in any of life's domains, permitting brands to set up a presence, put up display ads, or encourage or receive any type of COBRAs.

Involvement and Processing Time   Because Internet media is interactive, it provides strong potential for increasing customer involvement and almost immediate feedback for buyers and sellers. A main objective of most websites is to provide significant brand information or rich transformational experiences. By its very definition, the user-generated content requires extensive involvement and processing, as do even the most basic levels identified with the COBRAs.

Control for Selective Exposure   Perhaps the greatest strength of Internet media is its availability as an information source. Internet users can find a plethora of information about almost any topic of their choosing merely by conducting a search. Once they have visited a particular site, users can garner a wealth of information regarding product specifications, costs, purchase information, and so on. Links will direct them to even more information if it is desired. Moreover, this control is very quick compared to all other media.

Creativity   Creatively designed sites can enhance a company's image, lead to repeat visits, and positively position the company. Technological advances have made Internet media as enjoyable to use as broadcast and print media for both cognitive and emotional responses. Social media and interesting ways for consumers to involve themselves with a brand open the door for unlimited creative potential.

Costs   Internet media enables smaller companies with limited budgets to gain exposure to potential customers. For a fraction of the investment that would be required using traditional media, companies can gain national and even international exposure in a timely manner. A creative approach in social media can generate considerable consumer response, providing a significant return on investment for both small and large organizations.

LIMITATIONS OF INTERNET MEDIA

Target Audience Coverage   In the past, one of the greatest limitations of Internet media was the lack of reliability of the research numbers generated. A quick review of forecasts, audience profiles, and other statistics offered by research providers will demonstrate a great deal of variance—leading to a concern about validity and reliability. The actions by IAB to standardize metrics will help reduce these concerns. Tremendous improvement has occurred in the more than 20 years since the first banner ad was placed online.

Clutter   As ads proliferate, the likelihood of one ad being noticed drops accordingly. The result is that ads may not get noticed, and consumers may become irritated by the clutter. Studies already show that banner ads may be losing effectiveness for this very reason, while others show consistently declining click-through rates. Kantar Media reports an average of two display ads per page on Canadian Internet sites.[105] Certain social media vehicles contain vast amounts of information or video or pictures, leading to a great difficulty in getting consumers to notice ads competing for viewer attention. Moreover, the blurring between advertising messages and actual content limits consumers' perception and may heighten clutter.

Reach   While Internet media numbers are growing, the ability to reach vast numbers with a placement of a few ad messages, or the ability to attract large numbers to a brand's website, raises strong concern about its ability to generate significant reach levels compared to TV. As a result, Internet media works well with traditional media to achieve reach and awareness goals.

Media Image   A poor media image is due to annoying characteristics, deception, and privacy concerns. Numerous studies have reported on the irritating aspects of Internet tactics—like spam, pop-ups, and pop-unders—that deter visitors from repeat visits. Attempts by advertisers to target children with subtle advertising messages have proven to be a significant concern. In addition, data collection without consumers' knowledge and permission, hacking, and credit card theft are problems confronting the Internet. Like direct marketing, Internet marketers must be careful to respect users' privacy. Again, IAB has issued guidelines to alleviate this concern. In contrast to these early Internet media issues, many consumers enjoy the abundance of social media experiences and find shopping with Internet media very useful for planning all sorts of purchases. In this respect, Internet media is looked upon more favourably, and we might say that it is a paradox in simultaneously having both a strong media image and a poor media image.

LO6 IMC Planning: Strategic Use of Internet Media

The text, video, and audio characteristics of Internet media—along with various types of applications (e.g., websites, banner ads, streaming video, sponsorship, promotions, social networks, apps, etc.)—position it as being capable of communicating with customers and non-customers to achieve all communication and behavioural objectives, and to influence consumers at every stage of their decision-making process. The challenge for promotional planners is to select the correct application that fits the target audience and allows for the achievement of the most relevant objective along with the most appropriate message that supports the brand-positioning strategy. This is not an easy task, as there are multiple combinations of digital media opportunities for consideration.

One Canadian Google manager suggested that marketers will need to think about planning issues similar to those found in other media, like how to break through the clutter and how to deliver messages digitally across a wide spectrum of vehicles. At the same time, marketers will have to figure out a way to tap into the resources of the many online connections consumers have through their friends on social networking applications.[106] While this appears to be a solid recommendation, some brands seem to use every conceivable option for Internet media communication.

A second planning issue concerns how Internet media may or may not be better than other media for advertising purposes. Early research investigated whether Internet or TV produced better results and found that the former appeared stronger for high-involvement purchases only.[107] Other research compared the same ad delivered via print media to Internet media and found similar communication effects; however, ads with promotional messages (i.e., discounts) delivered better in print.[108]

A third planning issue pertains to how Internet media are integrated with other media for advertising purposes. One early study concluded that offline advertising increased awareness and subsequent website visits, while online ads contributed to website visits. Neither affected the brand equity, as the actual visit to the website played more strongly in that regard.[109] Another study found that a combined TV–Internet message performed better in terms of processing and stronger communication effects versus two TV messages or two Internet messages.[110] The conclusions of a print and Internet study recommended that print ads convey clear reasons to motivate readers to visit the website versus merely placing the website address in the ad.[111]

A fourth planning issue is how Internet media are increasingly part of a complete IMC program. Advertising and social media messages are regularly coordinated and integrated. Sales promotions are executions on mobile devices and have supporting messages in ads. Research uncovered a significant communication effect of direct-response media through mobile devices after viewers received advertising or promotional TV messages that prompted continued interaction.[112] The list is endless, as essentially any combination of tools can be used with and within Internet media.

Internet media often work with other IMC tools. Promotional planners using print, broadcast, or out-of-home media would need to investigate the degree to which the advertising campaign in these media would be directly transferred to Internet advertising. This is commonly done and there are many examples. Alternatively, Internet advertising could take a substantially different direction—some microsites, for example, have allowed brands to take a more experiential or informational track and have a substantially different role and message compared to what is more publicly available. Finally, Internet media is consumed with other media, notably TV, and the communication effects of simultaneous brand exposure via a brand's TV ad and social media are promising avenues for future development, especially for heavy multitasking users who tend to be younger.

Internet advertising supports sales promotion activities designed to encourage trial and repeat purchases with banner ads or sponsored search links that direct consumers to contests or price promotional offers. Internet advertising is used successfully for public relations activities, as links to corporate websites are found on relevant Internet sites (e.g., financial information sites) and other mechanisms are available to direct consumers to corporate information to influence appropriate stakeholders. Finally, Internet advertising assists in direct-response marketing as it facilitates communication to the websites for conducting transactions.

Internet media as sales promotion is a new opportunity for marketers, with brands having success. This can work very well with media advertising and sales promotions, as seen in the decorative options delivered to computer users. These fun activities are consistent with both the brand image and consumer experience, with sales promotions offering additional exposure and increasing meaningful brand experiences.

Internet media as public relations supports considerable advertising for consumer packaged goods and food products. Broadcast and print ads for such products create images and persuade consumers with an appropriate brand-positioning strategy. However, consumers may desire more information on usage, or would like to know the exact ingredients in more detail. The Internet site for Becel margarine offers a wonderful array of information for consumers desiring a more involved message about the brand, and acts as a tremendous public relations resource by presenting a comprehensive and honest assessment of the brand.

Internet media for direct-response advertising works very well for Belairdirect. The insurance company's print and radio ads suggest that consumers visit its Internet site to compare quotes from Belairdirect and up to five competitors. In this sense, Internet media function beyond mere communication like a regular informational website, especially considering that for a few years the focus of all the ads has been to encourage a direct response via the Internet.

In short, Internet media is capable of communicating all facets of the IMC program, and all aspects of Internet media can work with any other existing advertising media to achieve a brand's objectives. Careful planning is required like any other promotional decision, but the potential for positive results is limitless.

Learning Objectives Summary

 LO1   Describe the general characteristics of Internet users and explain website communication.

Internet communication is relatively common for a vast majority of the population. While older segments of the population rely on these media less than younger groups do, the fact that the average hourly per capita consumption reached significant levels suggests that Internet communication will be the significant media of the future. This appears especially true as consumers perform shopping activities online on company websites.

Website communication is used for any and all communication objectives described in this book. Websites contribute to building brand awareness, disseminating information, building a brand image, and fostering interaction between consumers and the company. The unlimited creativity we have witnessed with websites is remarkable, and something that many might not have dreamed possible two decades ago. This creativity has given rise to consumers, practitioners, and academics referring to website communication as website advertising or Internet advertising. They apply existing models to understand how attitudes to the website and brand attitude are influenced by strategic and tactical design elements, much like what occurs with print and broadcast media.

 LO2   Identify the advertising formats of Internet media.

Advertising formats of Internet media include display ads that involve various types of "banner" ads and rich media ads, link ads, paid search ads, and video ads including online commercials, video-on-demand, and podcasts. Internet media permits targeting of these ad formats across all segmentation variables described in Chapter 3 and, in particular, in terms of behaviour, geography, and time of day. Targeting occurs through the appropriate selection of the right Internet media vehicle. Whether that may be a news or entertainment portal, established media published from print or broadcast, new forms of publications found on the Internet, or many social media such as social networking, social bookmarking, blogging, etc., successful placement of ads in any of these media vehicles requires an understanding of the receivers or participants. Virtually all of these opportunities can express their audience or provide guidance in directing messages to the most appropriate target audience characteristics.

 LO3   Illustrate how to use social media in an IMC plan.

Social media includes collaborative projects, blogs, content communities, social networking sites, virtual game worlds, and virtual social worlds; this chapter investigated the first four. Social media provides three ways of garnering positive brand communication. It demonstrated that there is opportunity for brands to present their image with a degree of control much like they have on their websites. For example, a Facebook page for a brand contains numerous pieces of brand information, photos, and videos.

The chapter concluded that each is a media vehicle for placing any type of ad unit. Most of the specific titles give detailed information on their audience and explain how to place an ad in their media, much like other media have done for decades. Social networking sites with vast amounts of individual information allow specific targeting much like direct marketing. In this respect, social media are very closely aligned with how advertising has operated historically.

More significantly, social media gives its participants the opportunity to publish user-generated content in any of the four venues described. In some instances, this is true user-generated content, where people make videos or post their photos or write their thoughts. In other instances, the user-generated content is repurposed and is in fact someone else's content. An example of user-generated content is content from a brand, otherwise known as advertising. The end result is that planning brand communication in social media is a delicate situation as brands encourage positive reactions and interactions with current and potential customers.

Define measures of Internet media effectiveness.

Like with other media, we concentrated on different measures of effectiveness for each stage of the communication process. Measures are obtained for exposure, processing, and communication effects and behavioural responses. The majority of these are tracked digitally; however, communication effects require direct measurement or a proxy.

 Evaluate the strengths and limitations of Internet media.

We viewed the Internet as a means for communicating with audiences (much like other media), and for delivering a message and interacting with current and potential customers. With this in mind, Internet media currently offers numerous strengths. Advertisers can direct tailored messages to very selective target audiences. And with technological advances, the creative messages can be richly experienced both cognitively and emotionally for considerable amounts of time as the users themselves decide what they would like to receive and not receive. Finally, this incredible messaging ability is possible at a reasonably low absolute and relative cost.

There are limitations, however. It is unclear to marketers to what degree the target audience can be covered and reached. Internet media can be viewed as tremendous clutter as users move among websites and social media worlds. And, finally, severe problems regarding advertising delivery, illegal activities, and privacy concerns remain significant drawbacks.

 Apply the ideas of Internet media within the development of an IMC program.

Internet media has been the most rapidly adopted medium of our time. It holds great potential for communicating with all groups of consumers, and customers and non-customers alike. Moreover, it is useful for implementing all aspects of the IMC program including sales promotion, public relations, and direct marketing. Other stakeholders are potential audiences as well, making Internet media unlimited in its ability to persuade. However, contrary to popular belief, the Internet is not a standalone medium. Its role in an integrated marketing communications program strengthens the overall program as well as the effectiveness of Internet media itself.

Review Questions

1. How has Internet media threatened other media? How has Internet media assisted other media?
2. Explain the different advertising formats that advertisers use with Internet media. Discuss the advantages and disadvantages associated with each.
3. Explain the three ways in which a promotional planner can achieve positive marketing communication effects in social media.
4. Describe the ways that marketers measure the effectiveness of their use of Internet media. How do these measures relate to more traditional measures?
5. Review the limitations of Internet media and assess whether these are as weak as the limitations of other media.
6. Discuss the advantages of Internet media. For which types of advertisers is Internet media best suited? Why?

Applied Questions

1. Select a favourite Internet site for a brand and investigate how it achieves the objectives outlined in this chapter.
2. Visit a number of Internet media vehicles and evaluate the effectiveness of the display ads in terms of creativity, message, and ability to reach the intended target audience.
3. Investigate the social media use, in as many vehicles as possible, of a favourite brand, and assess which social media appears most effective for that brand.
4. What measures of marketing communication effectiveness are relevant for each of the four types of social media investigated in this chapter?
5. Given the strengths and limitations of Internet media, how would a promotional planner use all the Internet media options to optimize a digital media plan?
6. Select a product of interest and explain how each of the four types of social media described in this chapter can be integrated effectively with other broadcast, print, and out-of-home media.

CHAPTER EIGHTEEN

Regulatory, Ethical, Social, and Economic Issues for IMC

LEARNING OBJECTIVES

LO1 Describe the advertising regulation system in Canada.

LO2 Evaluate the ethical perspectives of advertising.

LO3 Explain the social effects of advertising.

LO4 Examine the economic role of advertising and its effects on consumer choice, competition, and product costs and prices.

Social Benefits With Advertising

Advertising provides considerable benefit in many facets of society despite criticism it faces across multiple domains. Critics claim that advertising contributes to obesity since it encourages people to eat too much non-nutritious food, encourages consumers to drink alcohol excessively leading to a myriad of problems, or sways people to buy goods that they do not really need. Despite the potential for this possibly occurring, advertising and the system of advertising effectively contribute to significant issues as we see in the following examples.

In British Columbia, Vancouver police and provincial health officials launched a campaign to raise awareness about the dangers of fentanyl, an opioid substantially more potent than morphine. Authorities found the prescription drug responsible for one-quarter of the province's 336 overdoses, mostly affecting men aged 20–49. Police believed that the users did not fully know what they were taking as the enforcement professionals found fentanyl laced within other drugs like heroin, marijuana, and cocaine. Habitual drug users appeared aware of the issue from harm-reduction sites, so this communication program targeted unaware recreational drug users in the general public and delivered its message on a website (KnowYourSource.ca) and with Facebook ads. Furthermore, the public relations side of marketing communication worked as well since news articles provided guidelines on how to take drugs to prevent an overdose and described the symptoms of a fentanyl overdose for proper identification.

In the aftermath of Rehtaeh Parsons' bullying-related death, her father established a project entitled "No Place to Hide" to prevent bullying by collecting submissions on Facebook. This development intrigued the chief creative officer of Taxi, who organized a presentation at Advertising Week in New York City to encourage broader participation across many marketing communication professionals. And they stepped up big time with the founder of One Laptop Per Child, Twitter's event marketing manager, Google's chief creative officer, and Facebook's director of global creative solutions all joining to pitch in their ideas. Other communication initiatives emerged recently and, together, many in the industry saw changes in the positive direction with greater involvement.

The Ontario government launched a campaign targeting bystanders who witness sexual assault with a message that they could do something to prevent it from occurring. A series of scenes showed an assault occurring with the perpetrator thanking the viewer for not doing anything. The message then played, "When you do nothing, you're helping him. But when you do something, you help her." Subsequently, the scenes changed so that the potential victim thanked the viewer for taking action and prevented any occurrence. The video ad played on TV, in cinemas, and online, with print and out-of-home ads following up. After one year, YouTube listed 3 million views, and the message achieved world dissemination with user translations due to social media.

Finally, worthy causes would not achieve their financial donation goals without advertising. Campaigns act as reminders for loyal donors and encourage new donors who may feel the need to participate. Lately, charities have moved toward the idea of premiums or gifts as part of the message to give the donation a stronger tangible feel. A famous Canadian actor recently recorded an ad for Plan Canada in which he played a goat encouraging people to buy creatures like him for children in developing countries, ending his spiel by shouting "Shop today!" The message resonated well to propel the fundraising activity for the charity as consumers flocked to buy from its Gifts of Hope catalogue specific items that children abroad needed. Unicef requested the services of YouTube channel host Lewis Hilsenteger for its online fundraising activity. Lewis is famous for unboxing technological products and reviewing them to his nearly 2 million subscribers. The host unboxed various Unicef aid products it sends worldwide so people could understand what their money would be used for.

Source: Susan Krashinsky, "Anti-Bullying Initiative Solicits Strategies on Facebook," *The Globe and Mail*, February 4, 2014, p. A.7; Susan Krashinsky, "Donors' Gift Giving a Charitable Success," *The Globe and Mail*, December 12, 2014, p. B.4; Maura Forrest, "Campaign Aims to Make Public Aware of Fentanyl Risk," *The Globe and Mail*, March 3, 2015, p. S.1; Josh Kolm, "Making Sexual Violence Everyone's Problem," *Strategy*, April 2015, p. A.10; Plan Canada, https://youtu.be/8qY3JsODhQM.

Question:

1. Which of these appear to offer significant social benefit by the target audience believing and acting upon the message?

Not everyone shares the positive view regarding the role of marketing communication in today's society that our text illustrates thus far. Our perspective looks at advertising and other promotional tools as marketing activities used to convey information to consumers and influence their behaviour in an appropriate manner to facilitate a mutually satisfying exchange. Advertising and promotion are the most visible of all business activities and face scrutiny from scholars, economists, politicians, sociologists, government agencies, social critics, special-interest groups, and consumers, who criticize advertising for its excessiveness, the way it influences society, the methods it uses, its exploitation of consumers, and its effect on our economic system.

Advertising is a very powerful force, and this text would not be complete without a look at the criticisms regarding its ethical, social, and economic effects as well as defences against these claims.

Exhibit 18-1 Some magazines refused to run this Benetton ad.

© Fotogramma/Ropi/ZUMAPRESS.com/Newscom

Before we entertain this debate, we review the regulations affecting advertising in Canada. The perspectives presented in this chapter reflect judgments of people with different backgrounds, values, and interests. Some students may see nothing wrong with advertising, while others may oppose some ads on moral and ethical grounds (Exhibit 18-1). We attempt to present the arguments on both sides of these controversial issues and allow individuals to draw their own conclusions.

LO1 Advertising Regulation in Canada

Regulation of advertising in Canada occurs through both government regulation and self-regulation, and we review both topics in this section. With respect to government regulation, we focus on four prevalent domains. The Canadian Radio-television and Telecommunications Commission (CRTC) is responsible for laws and regulations concerning broadcasting and telecommunications, so its role in advertising is relevant. The *Competition Act* regulates misleading or deceptive ads. Finally, the Quebec government has strong regulations with respect to advertising to children. In the other direction, Advertising Standards Canada (ASC) acts as the self-regulation body for the advertising industry. Responsibility for many of the federal laws regarding the content of advertising messages for specific product categories has been transferred to ASC by the request of the federal government.

CANADIAN RADIO-TELEVISION AND TELECOMMUNICATIONS COMMISSION (CRTC)

The CRTC is an administrative tribunal within the federal government. It is responsible for regulating and supervising Canada's communication system derived from the *CRTC Act*, the *Bell Canada Act*, the *Broadcasting Act,* and the *Telecommunications Act*. The broad objective of these acts ensures that all Canadians receive broadcasting and telecommunications services. Beyond this public service mandate, the CRTC balances the needs of citizens, industries, and interest groups with respect to Canadian content programming, technological considerations, and many communication issues. CRTC organizes its responsibilities across Phone, Internet, TV & Radio, and Business & Licensing domains. Extensive research occurred recently where the CRTC invited Canadians to offer their opinions. In its current three-year plan, the CRTC planned to focus on three themes: create—by ensuring quality, diverse, and compelling content; connect—by ensuring quality, choice, and innovative communication services; and protect—by ensuring access to safe communication systems.

For the purposes of this chapter, we concentrate on broadcasting since we highlighted telephone (e.g., Chapter 16) and Internet (e.g., Chapter 17) regulatory points previously, and the licensing does not primarily affect IMC decisions directly. The CRTC regulates media organizations (i.e., television, cable distribution, AM and FM radio, pay and specialty television, direct-to-home satellite systems, multipoint distribution systems, subscription television, and pay audio) and is responsible for granting the licences for these media and ensuring that they comply with the *Broadcasting Act*. The CRTC undertakes significant activities to ensure that Canadian content occurs in Canadian media. Its most recent direction is to emphasize quality over quantity. This is beneficial for advertisers trying to reach audiences viewing uniquely Canadian programming. The CRTC is involved significantly in two ad broadcasting topics that are relevant for advertising: advertising time limits and signal substitution.

Advertising Time Limits   The CRTC regulates the amount of advertising in a few circumstances. Specialty TV services carry 12 minutes per hour of advertising during the broadcast day, which lasts 18 hours beginning at 6:00 a.m. The CBC radio network is prohibited from advertising except for special sponsorship. CBC Escape Music and CBC 2 are permitted 4 minutes of advertising per hour. Similar 4- and 12-minute limits occur with different community-based services as well. Note that public service announcements, political ads, and "ads" for Canadian TV shows are not counted in this total, nor is product placement or virtual ads placed within shows. Pay TV services have no advertising, while conventional TV and radio stations have no limits.

Signal Substitution   Signal substitution occurs when a television service provider temporarily replaces the entire signal of one TV channel with another channel that is showing the same program at the same time. Most times this occurs when a Canadian signal replaces an American signal. This protects the interests of the broadcasters who have paid for the rights to show the program in Canada. It also promotes local broadcasting and content creation by allowing these media to retain their audience. Finally, it keeps advertising revenue within the Canadian market.

While this appears acceptable to many Canadians most of the time, football viewers are not satisfied when U.S. ads are not part of the domestic feed for the Super Bowl. Although some are bought for domestic media, most Canadians resort to seeing the Super Bowl ads online after the game. Other problems occur when a live event (e.g., sport) runs overtime, late programming changes happen, or poor quality occurs. The CRTC reviewed this practice and plans to be more active in resolving the problems and potentially intervening upon media companies. And the good news is that the Super Bowl will not be subjected to signal substitution any longer.

COMPETITION ACT

The federal *Competition Act* prevents false or misleading advertising. Significantly revised in 1999, most of the act contains civil provisions to ensure compliance with the act rather than to seek punishment. In this situation, the goal is not so much to prove deliberate intent, but rather to remedy the situation with the most appropriate solution, such as a cease-and-desist order. Some criminal provisions still exist for the most serious offences, where false advertising occurred knowingly. Enforcement of the act falls under the jurisdiction of the Competition Bureau of Industry Canada. Some examples of what is not permissible are shown in Figure 18-1.[1] In 2009, the *Competition Act* underwent revision with respect to deceptive marketing, items pertaining to pricing, and some other amendments. In particular, the fines for misleading representation in advertising increased substantially for non-criminal offences.[2] Some questioned whether the changes were constitutional or whether the expanded situations of misrepresentation were clearly identified; nevertheless, the laws are currently in place.[3] Industry people expected strong enforcement and the following examples proved them correct.

Figure 18-1   Advertising and marketing law in Canada

Guideline	Advertising Claim	Misleading Content
Cannot make false claims	Buy this vacuum and get a year's supply of vacuum bags absolutely free	There is a $12 administration fee for the vacuum bags
Even if claim is true, do not give false impression	Drive away in a Corvette for just $39,000	The visual display is a version with a sport package and costs $50,000
Avoid double meanings	Number one in the category	Best in sales, but not in quality
Disclaimers should not contradict headlines or body copy	Don't pay a cent until 2018	Fine-print says except for taxes and $750 freight

Source: Adapted from *Advertising and Marketing Law In Canada,* Brenda Pritchard and Susan Vogt, LexisNexis, Butterworths, 2006.

The Competition Bureau levied a $10 million penalty on Bell for misleading advertising over the course of three and a half years. Rogers faced the same penalty of $10 million previously for claiming that it was a more reliable service than its competitor Wind Mobile. The Bureau found that Bell charged higher prices than advertised for many of its services since it added mandatory fees hidden from consumers in fine-print disclaimers. As support for its ruling, the Bureau cited one example of an ad that claimed $69.90/month, yet the price rose to $80.27 with the required mandatory fees, a 15 percent increase. In making the decision, the Bureau identified the geographic scale and the length of time the marketing message occurred as critical factors in the size of the fine.

The impetus for the investigation stemmed from consumer complaints to the Bureau, and it appears the fines did not stem the tide as growing consumer complaints emerged with these two competitors and others. The Bureau sought an additional $10 million from Bell, Rogers, and Telus for misleading wireless consumers about the cost of third-party premium text services such as trivia questions, ringtones, and games, and sought $1 million from the Canadian Wireless Telecommunications Association. The Bureau also looked to stop ads that do not disclose the cost of premium-rate digital content and to ensure that consumers received a refund for the costs they did not expect to incur. In response, the wireless carriers claimed they only do the billing for third-party digital providers and are not responsible for the charges or the communication of the charges. The wireless carriers had previously sought guidance from the Competition Bureau on how to handle the situation and appeared at a loss as to why the Bureau deemed it necessary to pursue the charges.[4] Ethical Perspective 18-1 describes more recent details on this situation and others for consideration.

ETHICAL PERSPECTIVE 18-1

Competition Bureau Steps Up

The Competition Bureau's new mandate continues to promote the best interests of Canadian consumers. For years, the many parts of the federal government moved toward serving citizens' needs more thoroughly, as demonstrated by the improvements at Passport Canada. The CRTC involved itself in consumer issues with its "Let's Talk" TV initiative. And now the serious problems Canadians face with advertising are being addressed and the Bureau has produced results, as seen in the following examples.

A few years after opening an investigation, the Competition Bureau successfully fined Rogers, Bell Canada Enterprises,

© Marc Bruxelle/Shutterstock

and Telus $10 million each and the industry association—the Canadian Wireless Telecommunications Association—$1 million. The Bureau claimed the wireless providers profited by as much as $40/month from customers who unwittingly signed up for services—by playing a game, for example. As part of the settlement, Rogers planned to reimburse current customers on their bill and directed past customers to an Internet site to resolve their claim, at an estimated cost of over $5 million. Furthermore, Rogers would not pay the money to the Bureau, but rather the rest of the fine would be devoted to improved employee training and awareness advertising regarding the improved service. Rogers admitted to not handling the premium services effectively, and had made substantial changes to its premium services prior to disbanding the offering. The Bureau thanked Rogers for cooperating with the issue, and continued its efforts with Bell, Telus, and the industry organization a few years after starting the investigation.

The Bureau's next target was the car rental business, as it sought a $30 million fine from Avis and Budget for their misleading advertising regarding price information. The Bureau claimed that each car agency advertised that it charged extra fees on behalf of the government, but the Bureau saw the message as misleading advertising since the extra charges amounted to covering normal business costs. Eight different charges over the course of 10 years for things like air conditioning excise tax, premium location surcharges, and tire management fees raised the price of renting a vehicle significantly above the advertised price. The penalty represented the largest fine the Bureau ever attempted as part of its renewed mandate for improved monitoring for Canadian consumers, and it did not let up, as seen by its next target.

[Continued on next page]

[Ethical Perspective 18-1 continued]

Bauer Canada agreed to amend the claims for its RE-AKT hockey helmet and to donate $500,000 to a youth sports charity and pay for the cost of the investigation. The Bureau concluded that the ads "contained words, images and videos" to give "the impression that the product would offer hockey players protection from concussions caused by rotational impacts." Although Bauer did not agree that the ads gave the adjudicated impression, it fully cooperated with the investigation and agreed with the corrective action. In discussing the ruling, Bauer cited its research with a university medical team whose testing indicated a reduction in "brain stress" with a "rotational impact." A complicating factor in this issue is the lack of established standards regarding concussions.

Finally, as seen in the above examples, the Competition Bureau takes action when it receives complaints and, at this stage, that is all that occurred with computer manufacturer Lenovo. Disgruntled consumers raised the issue when the brand cancelled their online purchases due to incorrect pricing information. The source of dissatisfaction mounted when the system only alerted the buyers after the completed transaction with credit card information processed. While mistakes do happen, as Lenovo claimed, the future will tell if this is true or whether it is an example of bait and switch.

Source: Jeff Gray, "Rogers Settles Misleading Advertising Allegations Over Premium Text Services," *The Globe and Mail*, March 17, 2015, p. B.61; Susan Krashinsky, "Lenovo Gaffe Brings Complaints of Bait and Switch," *The Globe and Mail*, May 28, 2014, p. B.5; Greg Keenan and Jeff Gray, " Competition Bureau Raps Avis, Budget for Misleading Prices," *The Globe and Mail*, March 12, 2015, p. B.1; Jeff Gray, "Bauer Agrees to Stop Concussion Claims," *The Globe and Mail*, November 14, 2014, p. B.3.

Question:

1. As a consumer, are you in agreement with the Competition Bureau's effort to penalize companies?

REGULATIONS ON ADVERTISING TO CHILDREN

Although no federal laws specifically regulate advertising to children, the Broadcast Code for Advertising to Children acts as an important guide to ensure that children are not easily manipulated with exaggerated claims. In contrast, the province of Quebec provides strict regulations. According to the *Consumer Protection Act of Quebec,* it is illegal to direct commercial advertising messages to persons younger than 13 years of age. Specific provisions determine whether or not an ad is directed to children regarding the product, the ad presentation, and the ad time and placement.

To apply the law, the Quebec government provides summary guidelines for advertisers to follow, and it also provides screening services for advertisers if they are uncertain whether an item contravenes the law. The purpose of the guidelines is to ensure that advertisers fully understand and correctly interpret the law. The guidelines precisely describe the types of advertising appeals that are not permitted, clearly define what is meant by a children's TV program, and state exactly the percentage of children in the audience that constitutes a children's TV program. The guidelines include the degree to which messages can be directed toward children depending upon whether the product is exclusively for children (i.e., candy), partially for children (i.e., cereal), or not for children. There are also specific guidelines for public service announcements directed to children, even though there is no commercial message.

Vachon, maker of the Jos Louis and Passion Flakie treats, pushed the limits of these laws. It created a cartoon character named Igor to represent its chocolate-filled, gorilla-shaped muffins. Vachon placed the imagery on CDs, DVDs, and other materials for daycare centres to use when entertaining the children. Vachon tested the laws in three ways—the product, the message, and the time and place—and faced a $44,000 fine. It appears that the Quebec government is getting tougher with not-so-healthy products with the higher incidence of child obesity. However, there are indications that brands of healthier products, or a corporate initiative to encourage children to stay active, might not be as scrutinized. So while there are laws governing advertising to children in Quebec, the consistent application appears murky given the ethical implications.[5]

ADVERTISING STANDARDS CANADA (ASC)

ASC is a not-for-profit, self-regulatory industry body with a mandate to create and maintain community confidence in advertising. ASC represents advertisers, media organizations, and advertising industry suppliers and has more than 200 corporate members. Its Standards Division administers the industry's self-regulatory codes (i.e., *Canadian Code of*

Advertising Standards, Gender Portrayal Guidelines), handles complaints about advertising, and administers any disputes that arise between advertisers. Its Advertising Clearance Division previews advertisements in five industry categories, as well as ads directed toward children, ensuring that advertisers will follow applicable legislation, regulatory codes, and industry standards. An example of one of its public service ads is shown in Exhibit 18-2.

Canadian Code of Advertising Standards   The Code, as it is known, describes what is not acceptable advertising. According to ASC, "Advertising is defined as any message (the content of which is controlled directly or indirectly by the advertiser) expressed in any language and communicated in any medium to Canadians with the intent to influence their choice, opinion or behaviour." The Code pertains to the content of ads only. It does not limit the promotion of legal products or the demonstration of products for their intended purpose. The intention of the Code is to provide standards so that responsible and effective advertising results without minimizing the right of firms to advertise. It does not supersede any laws or regulations. In early 2016, ASC proposed notable revisions to the definition of *advertiser* and *advertisement*, presumably with the growth of digital communication via social media.

The Code provides the criteria to assess whether a complaint is legitimate or not, and ASC is very clear in how it uses the Code to resolve complaints. "The context and content of the advertisement and the audience actually, or likely to be, or intended to be, reached by the advertisement, and the medium/media used to deliver the advertisement, are relevant factors in assessing its conformity with the Code." The Code is supported by all member organizations as it sets the standard for advertising with respect to honesty, truth, accuracy, fairness, and propriety. Members are expected to follow the Code both in letter and in spirit and are expected to substantiate any advertised claims when requested. The Code contains 14 clauses:

1. Accuracy and Clarity
2. Disguised Advertising Techniques
3. Price Claims
4. Bait and Switch
5. Guarantees
6. Comparative Advertising
7. Testimonials
8. Professional or Scientific Claims
9. Imitation
10. Safety
11. Superstitions and Fears
12. Advertising to Children
13. Advertising to Minors
14. Unacceptable Depictions and Portrayals

Exhibit 18-2   This ad by ASC communicates its purpose.

© Advertising Standards Canada

As part of the 2016 proposed revision, ASC suggested revisions for Clauses 1 and 14. Clause 1 changes provided greater clarity on the meaning of *deceptive and misleading ads*. Clause 14 changes identified additional characteristics that could not be the basis of personal discrimination. In 2003, ASC updated Clauses 6, 10, and 14 as part of its ongoing mandate to ensure that the Code reflects current practices and fairness. While on the surface the 2003 changes were just a few words for each clause, the meaning permitted a more reasonable and flexible interpretation.

ASC Interpretation Guidelines ASC released "interpretation guidelines" over the years so that members could understand how ASC will evaluate ads in terms of specific codes or advertising trends.[6] The first and fourth guidelines concern Clauses 10 and 14 with respect to humour/fantasy and motor vehicle advertising respectively. The second guideline provides extensive documentation on advertising to children pertaining to Clause 12. Environmental claims and how they are related to Clause 1, the Competition Bureau, and the Canadian Standards Association are the topic of the third guideline.

As part of the second guideline, ASC acts as the administrator for the Canadian Children's Food and Beverage Advertising Initiative (CAI).[7] Canada's largest food and beverage marketers have committed to not advertising directly to children under 12 years of age, although some committed to advertising only "better-for-you" products to children. The initiative is in response to the growing obesity problem among children. In doing so, the marketers agreed to five core principles for advertising directed to children under 12 years of age:

1. Devote 100 percent of television, radio, print, and Internet advertising to furthering the goal of promoting healthy dietary choices and/or healthy active living.

2. Incorporate only products that represent healthy dietary choices in interactive games primarily directed to children under 12 years of age.

3. Reduce the use of third-party licensed characters in advertising for products that do not meet the CAI's product criteria.

4. Do not pay for or actively seek to place food and beverage products in program/editorial content of any medium.

5. Do not advertise food or beverage products in elementary schools.

The principles apply to other avenues of communication directed to children under 12, such as micro-sites, early childhood (EC) video/computer games, DVDs, mobile devices, and word-of-mouth. ASC monitored the performance of all 19 organizations committed to CAI in 2011 and concluded in its report that all companies complied with all guidelines in all media and promotional vehicles.[8]

The just released fifth interpretation guideline pertains to testimonials, endorsements and reviews. Any endorser, reviewer, influencer, or person making a representation must disclose any "material connection" between themselves and the entity (e.g., advertised brand). In this case, ASC is concerned with various activities in social media where the influencer, etc., is sending messages with an advertising intent but it is not completely clear to the receiver that it is in fact an ad without the disclosure. An example of this is a Federal Trade Commission decision in the United States in which it fined Lord & Taylor, a division of the Hudson's Bay Company, for not disclosing its advertising intent in social media. The fashion retailer paid 50 popular Instagram users and gave them a dress; the users then posted a photo in which they wore the new outfit. The FTC ruled that consumers have a right to know when they are seeing paid advertising, which is consistent with what occurred in other media for decades.[9] Finally, while not an interpretation guideline, ASC drew attention in the 2014 complaints report to the importance of distinguishing journalistic content and advertising within Clause 2 (e.g., disguised advertising techniques) due to the growing use of "branded content," "sponsored content," or "native advertising." A few complaints along these lines also proved important for the proposed 2016 revisions.[10]

Gender Portrayal Guidelines The guidelines, based on a previous CRTC task force, attempt to ensure that women and men are portrayed appropriately and equally in advertising. ASC presents the guidelines as the direction of areas or topics from which complaints or issues have arisen over the past 30 years. There are six overall clauses, pertaining to authority, decision making, sexuality, violence, diversity, and language. For example, some might find the passionate theme of Calvin Klein ads as conveying overt sexuality (Exhibit 18-3, Exhibit 18-4).

When interpreting the guidelines, ASC has four suggestions that advertisers should consider. The overall impression of the ad should not violate the spirit of gender equality; there are clauses specifically addressed toward women, as men are at less risk of being negatively portrayed. History and art should not be used as an excuse for violating a clause. Finally, certain products and how they are advertised are amenable to more appropriate media.

Exhibit 18-3 Calvin Klein ads depict women in sexual poses.

© Sorbis/Shutterstock

Complaint Process   The Standards Division handles complaints in three streams. **Consumer complaints** are those from ordinary citizens who believe that an ad is unacceptable. ASC receives these complaints directly as well as through government departments and agencies at all levels, such as the Better Business Bureau, the CRTC, and the Canadian Broadcast Standards Council. **Special interest group complaints** are those from a demonstrated organization that expresses a unified viewpoint. Complaints from other advertisers are known as **advertiser disputes**. While there are distinct complaint processes for consumers and special interest groups, the general procedures for each have a degree of similarity that we will touch upon. One difference, however, is that ASC first determines that the special interest group complaint is not a disguised trade dispute.

Exhibit 18-4   Calvin Klein ads depict men in sexual poses.

© Lars A. Niki

The initial complaint is authenticated to make sure that it is, in fact, a consumer or special interest group complaint and not an advertiser dispute. From there, the complaint is evaluated to determine whether it legitimately violates a Code provision or whether it is not a legitimate complaint. Reasons for a complaint not being legitimate include that the complaint did not identify a specific advertiser, that the ad was no longer current, and that the communication was not advertising. If the complaint is valid, the advertiser is contacted and has an opportunity to respond to the complaint before the Council makes a formal ruling. On the other hand, the advertiser can take an appropriate action to remedy the complaint as part of the response. In these cases, the advertiser would not be identified in the ASC complaints report. An advertiser who responds and does not remedy the situation can be identified in the report if the Council upholds the complaint.

While the above general approach existed for many years, and still does, ASC instituted a couple of revisions for certain clauses in 2012. For Clauses 10 and 14, ASC acts as an intermediary between the complainant and the advertiser so that both can see one another's point of view for resolution prior to the Standards Council involvement. For Clauses 1 and 3, ASC administratively resolves these concerns as sometimes they are due to minor human error than can easily be corrected.

The Council for Canadians filed a special interest group complaint against Nestlé for a claim that "most water bottles avoid landfill sites and are recycled" in a *Globe and Mail* ad. Its complaint cited a statement from Nestlé's annual report stating the contrary. And while this appeared to be a complaint with merit, ASC dismissed the case since the Council went public with its complaint, thereby contravening the confidentiality requirement of the proceedings.[11] Sierra Club Canada filed a special interest complaint concerning a Canwest piece that stated, "in partnership with Shell Canada." The oil company put the advertorial series together as a public relations information source for the media, the government, and the general public. An editor with the media organization stated that the layout of the ad was not consistent with the editorial content and that "readers would realize the pages are advertisements for Shell." However, the executive director of Sierra Club concluded they appeared like neither advertising nor editorial.[12]

For trade disputes, there is a formal adjudication procedure where each party represents its point of view at a hearing if an initial first-stage resolution is unsuccessful. An appeal of the decision is possible, but eventually there is a resolution if an advertiser is found in violation. As members of ASC, they follow the recommendations of ASC similar to the consumer and special interest process. However, a situation emerged where for the first time ever an advertiser did not follow ASC's decision. Rogers disputed a Bell advertising claim and ASC upheld the complaint, suggesting Bell amend the ad or stop showing it. Bell did not participate in the hearing or comply with the decision since it was not a member and continued running the ad. In turn, and for the first time, ASC asked media companies to refrain from airing the ad.[13]

Complaints Report   ASC publishes a comprehensive annual report that includes the identification of advertisers and the details of all complaints. Figure 18-2 shows a capsule summary of the past few years. For each statistic, the first data point is the number of complaints, while the second in parentheses is the number of ads those complaints represent. The ratio of the number of complaints to the number of ads indicates that the number of complaints per ad is fewer than two. This underscores the fact that the content of the complaint is justification for investigating an ad. The source of the most complaints in 2015 occurred with Clause 1 (accuracy and clarity) and Clause 3 (price claims) that combined for 717 complaints, Clause 14 (unacceptable portrayal and depictions) for 453 complaints, and Clause 8 (professional and scientific claims) for 109. Complaints by media showed television (672), Internet (348), direct marketing (248), and out-of-home media (221). We now briefly review ads that achieved notoriety over the past decade, summarized from past reports found at the ASC website.

Figure 18-2   Summary of complaints from Advertising Standards Canada's annual complaints report

	2013		2014		2015	
Number of Complaints (ads)						
Received by ASC	1,286	(1,075)	1,274	(864)	1,774	(1,135)
Met code acceptance criteria	823	(678)	817	(589)	1,268	(776)
Administratively resolved by staff	45	(45)	96	(64)	134	(122)
Evaluated by Council	100	(71)	135	(62)	291	(77)
Upheld by Council	79	(50)	80	(36)	242	(50)

Sources: http://www.adstandards.com/en/ConsumerComplaints/2015adComplaintsReport.pdf;
http://www.adstandards.com/en/ConsumerComplaints/2014adComplaintsReport.pdf;
http://www.adstandards.com/en/ConsumerComplaints/2013adComplaintsReport.pdf

Complaints for Debate   One of the most controversial rulings occurred in 2001. A Ford Motor Company TV ad showed a young female shoving a male store clerk into the hatchback of her car and driving away with him. This ad received nine complaints, and the Council upheld the complaints, citing Clause 14 as the ad depicted an abduction, which is an unlawful activity. Ford appealed the decision; however, the Appeal Panel confirmed the original decision. Ford's post-appeal statement makes this example an interesting debate:

> Ford of Canada did not intend to offend any segment of the population in this particular advertisement; rather the aim of the ad was to show the attributes of the Focus. The identical advertisement shown in Quebec (both in English and in French) was determined not to contravene the *Code* by the Consumer Response Council and Appeal Panel in Quebec. Particulars of this complaint were provided to the press by a consumer complainant even though this process is intended to be confidential. Subsequent to the Appeal Decision, Margaret Wente, in a lengthy *Globe and Mail* article dated January 31, 2002, gave strong positive support for the ad. However, in light of the decision of the ASC Appeal Panel, Ford of Canada will withdraw the current English advertisement.[14]

In early 2004, a television ad for an alcohol beverage depicted two women engaging in a passionate kiss. The 113 complaints indicated that the scene was inappropriate for family viewing programming. Council upheld this complaint, stating, "the commercial displayed obvious indifference to conduct or attitudes that offended standards of public decency prevailing among a significant segment of the population." Council concluded that the ad in question did not contravene the code providing it was shown later than 9:30 in the evening.

A Kia Canada television commercial caused controversy during 2007 and received 77 complaints from individuals and those in the law-enforcement profession. The advertised vehicle contained two adults "making out," after which the woman returned to a police car wearing an officer's uniform. Council upheld the complaint citing Clause 14(c) and concluded that the ad demeaned female officers in particular and all law-enforcement officials in general. Kia responded to the complaint with the following statement:

> As a responsible advertiser, Kia Canada Inc. [Kia] is aware of Advertising Standards Canada [ASC] guidelines, of which its media service agencies are members, and strives to adhere to the spirit of which they have been written. While not in agreement with the Council's final decision, Kia respects it and the process by which it was achieved. Kia believes it has responded to the subject of the complaints by making revisions to the commercial in question, and in adherence to the ASC's Advertising Standards Code.[15]

However, Kia's concern became more public when it ran an edited version of the ad that did not show the woman leaving the car. Instead, words on the screen announced a more suitable ending to the commercial for all audiences. The final scene featured a goat eating in a meadow for 10 seconds while light-hearted music played. We leave the interpretation of this revised ending for interested students to debate![16]

Also in 2007, the council determined that certain Dairy Queen ads showed an unsafe act and reinforced bullying behaviour as the TV ad characters restrained others while eating Dairy Queen ice cream. The response from managers of the brand appears to suggest caution to advertisers with co-branding messages:

> Dairy Queen is all about creating smiles and stories for families and often uses irreverent, off-beat humour in its commercials. The Kit Kat commercial was meant to accentuate this in a humorous way how families interact in a playful manner. Although we are not in agreement with the Council's decision, we are respectful of the process.[17]

An ad from Auto Trader, part of an overall campaign that compared buying a used car online to meeting another person with an online dating service, received only six complaints. However, the complaint, the council decision, and the advertiser statement cover new ground:

> In a television commercial, a man and a woman met in a coffee shop for the first time. After exchanging names, the woman asked the man if she could "take a quick peek". The man obliged by lowering his pants so the woman could look at his private parts from various angles. In the audio portion of the commercial the announcer said that "You can do that on Auto Trader—where you can research your car before you buy it."[18]

The complaint alleged that the ad depicted a demeaning portrayal of men and offended standards of public decency. However, the council agreed with the latter point but concluded that the ad denigrated both men and women. Auto Trader's rebuttal statement takes into account the media time frame and media vehicle, two critical points that ASC highlighted in previous rulings for more acceptable adult messages. And its inclusion as part of a television show makes this case another one for debate:

> Trader Corporation is not condoning the behaviour in the commercial "Research". We believe it is clear to anyone viewing that the actions in the commercial are exaggerated and, via the copyline "You can do that on AutoTrader.ca", clearly portrayed as behaviour that is not socially acceptable. Rather these actions are used in a humourous and entertaining manner to support the campaign message—It is easier to find your perfect "match" (car) with Auto Trader. Our belief that most people understand the humour is supported not only by positive reviews by the advertising press for its empowering message to female car buyers but also by quantifiable market research that indicates that the commercial performed significantly above industry norms on scores such as 'enjoyable' and 'appropriate and fits my lifestyle'. We have also tried to put it into adult-oriented television programs which match the content of the ads realizing that the commercial is somewhat risqué for Canadian standards. It is also interesting to note that the commercial was recently selected for the U.S.-based show *World's Funniest TV Commercials*.[19]

We summarized these cases from the complaints reports as they illustrate significant milestones during the history of ASC decisions. They show disagreement between ASC administrators (i.e., Ford), one of the most complaints ever (i.e., alcohol beverage), the most unexpected reaction from an identified advertiser (i.e., Kia), a difficulty with co-branding (i.e., Dairy Queen), and a substantial rebuttal (i.e., Auto Trader). Exhibit 18-5 shows an ad from ASC to encourage consumer awareness of truthfulness in advertising.

Clearance Process   ASC provides clearance services for ads for many product categories and ads directed toward children for all jurisdictions except Quebec.

- *Alcohol.* ASC adheres to the CRTC *Code for Broadcast Advertising of Alcoholic Beverages*. The CRTC disbanded clearance services in 1997. This code gives 17 precise guidelines on what is not permitted in alcohol ads. Some of the guidelines pertain to not attracting underage drinkers, non-drinkers, or problem drinkers. Many other guidelines focus on the message with respect to the type of consumption motivation, consumption situation, source, and appeal. ASC will review all TV and radio ads across the country as well as print and out-of-home ads in British Columbia.

- *Cosmetics.* Health Canada transferred the clearance for cosmetic product ads to ASC in 1992, although clearance is not an absolute requirement. ASC follows the *Guidelines for Cosmetic Advertising and Labelling Claims*. The most recent version is a joint publication of ASC, Health Canada, and the Canadian Cosmetic, Toiletry and Fragrance Association, and was published in 2000. The guidelines list acceptable and unacceptable claims for two types of hair care products, nail products, and five types of skin care products. Another set of guidelines list unacceptable and acceptable claims for toothpaste, deodorant, mouthwash, perfumes/fragrances/colognes, sun-care products, vitamins, and aromatherapy products. Finally, the same is done for different benefit claims, such as anti-wrinkle, healthy ingredients, nourishment, relaxation, respiration, revitalization, therapy/treatment, and lifting.

- *Non-prescription drugs.* Health Canada also transferred the clearance of non-therapeutic aspects of non-prescription drug ads directed toward consumers to ASC in 1992. ASC ensures that broadcast and print copy comply with Health Canada's *Consumer Drug Advertising Guidelines* and the *Food and Drugs Act and Regulations.* Health Canada has also given ASC the responsibility for resolving any complaints of advertising for this category. To facilitate this change, Health Canada has published a document that describes its role, ASC's role, and the claims that can be made in ads directed to consumers. Most of the guidelines in this document focus on the need for advertisers to provide factual information about the product's attributes and benefits, and require that the claims be scientifically valid.

Exhibit 18-5   An ASC ad humorously shows how truth in advertising is important.

- *Ads directed to children.* ASC uses the *Broadcast Code for Advertising to Children (Children's Code),* published by the Canadian Association of Broadcasters in cooperation with ASC, to assess whether ads directed toward children are appropriate. The code takes into account the unique characteristics of children to ensure adequate safety and has nine guidelines concerning factual presentation, product prohibitions, avoiding undue pressure, scheduling, source or endorser of the message, price, comparison claims, safety, and social values. The code also gives seven instructions on clearance procedures, such as when clearance is required or not, when ads can be directed to children, and during which programs ads can be directed to children.

- *Food.* ASC evaluates broadcast ads with respect to the *Food and Drugs Act and Regulations* and the *Guide to Food Labelling and Advertising.* Its policy guidelines make a distinction between food claims that are exempt from clearance and those that require clearance in four categories: general advertising, occasion–greeting advertising (e.g., Christmas), promotional advertising, and sponsorship advertising. In addition, the ASC guidelines for the use of comparative advertising in food commercials outline six principles for appropriate executions of this presentation style. Finally, the ASC guidelines on claims based on research and survey data have requirements pertaining to all aspects of the research design (i.e., sample, data collection).

In conclusion, Advertising Standards Canada self-regulates advertising in Canada based on Canadian laws. However, as the name indicates, it is responsible only for advertising. Other brand messages arising from more innovative communication tools are not covered by these guidelines. For example, product reviews found on Internet sites or brand evaluations on blogs are not considered advertising, even though the actual effect may be quite similar in terms of awareness or influencing consumer opinion.

 ## Ethical Effects of Advertising

While many laws and regulations determine what advertisers can and cannot do, not every issue is covered by a rule. Marketers must often make decisions regarding appropriate and responsible actions on the basis of ethical considerations rather than on what is legal or within industry guidelines. **Ethics** are moral principles and values that govern the actions and decisions of an individual or group.[20] Advertising and promotion are areas where a lapse in ethical standards or judgment can result in actions that are highly visible and often very damaging to a company, so ethical considerations are imperative when planning IMC decisions. Much of the controversy over advertising stems from the ways companies use it as a selling tool and from its impact on society's tastes, values, and lifestyles. Specific techniques used by advertisers are criticized as untruthful or deceptive, offensive or in bad taste, and exploitative of certain groups, such as children. We discuss each of these criticisms, along with advertisers' responses.

ADVERTISING AS UNTRUTHFUL OR DECEPTIVE

One complaint about advertising is that many ads are misleading or untruthful and deceive consumers. A number of studies have shown a general mistrust of advertising among consumers.[21] A historic study found that consumers felt that less than one-quarter of TV commercials are honest and believable.[22] Another older survey to determine current attitudes toward and confidence in advertising found that consumers generally do not trust advertising, although they tend to feel more confidence in advertising claims when focused on their actual purchase decisions.[23]

Advertisers should have a reasonable basis for making a claim about product performance and may be required to provide evidence to support their claims. However, deception can occur more subtly as a result of how consumers perceive the ad and its impact on their beliefs.[24] The difficulty of determining just what constitutes deception, along with the fact that advertisers have the right to use puffery and make subjective claims about their products, tends to complicate the issue. **Puffery** has been legally defined as "advertising or other sales presentations which praise the item to be sold with subjective opinions, superlatives, or exaggerations, vaguely and generally, stating no specific facts."[25] But a concern of many critics is the extent to which advertisers are *deliberately* untruthful or misleading.

This puffery or possibly misleading issue cropped up with food advertising. Food product ingredients are a concern for many people since these affect our bodies so significantly. With many words and phrases used to convey authentic quality, the term "natural" appeared important for brands to use—and the practice underwent criticism. Processed meats emerged as one particular target since many brands claimed to be using all-natural ingredients to distance themselves from the unhealthy image these foods have typically received. And, in particular, Schneiders Country Naturals took heat from critics when it claimed that its processed meats are "made with natural ingredients and no artificial additives or preservatives." Debate ensued when critics pointed out that one of the natural ingredients acted like a preservative that had unhealthy consequences. Schneiders disputed the claim; nevertheless, the issue of what exactly "natural" means remained with consumers.[26]

Sometimes advertisers make overtly false or misleading claims, however, these cases usually involve smaller companies and a tiny portion of the billions of dollars spent on advertising and promotion each year. Most advertisers do not design their messages with the intent to mislead or deceive consumers. Not only are such practices unethical, but the culprits would damage their reputation and risk prosecution by regulatory groups or government agencies. National advertisers in particular invest large sums of money to develop loyalty to, and enhance the image of, their brands. These companies are not likely to risk hard-won consumer trust and confidence by intentionally deceiving consumers. Some companies test the limits of industry and government rules and regulations to make claims that will give their brands an advantage in highly competitive markets. Ethical Perspective 18-2 highlights concerns with alcohol advertising regarding issues identified in this section.

ETHICAL PERSPECTIVE 18-2

Alcohol Advertising Effects

An old joke says that the legal drinking age is merely a suggestion; however those who see the outcome of underage drinking see the situation differently and view alcohol ads as one of the main instigators. An editorial on the *Canadian Medical Journal* Internet site concluded that exposure to alcohol ads contributed to girls as young as 13 beginning to drink, which led to adverse health effects. It cited research indicating that girls see as many alcohol ads as do women who are of legal age, and other research that indicated those who saw more ads experience more serious drinking problems a few years later while in high school. Similarly, a Canadian Community Health Survey found that the rate of

© Jacob Lund/Shutterstock

underage drinking among girls climbed from 18 percent to 21 percent, while the rate remained stable for boys at 30 percent. Some suggest that packaging should convey warnings; however the Association of Canadian Distillers believes that warnings are not necessary and that Canada's laws are strict, and even

[Continued on next page]

[Ethical Perspective 18-2 continued]

stronger than those in other countries. The Brewers Association of Canada suggested that peers and parents remain as the primary influencers of drinking behaviour and that attractive people in attractive situations being shown in ads holds true for many products beyond alcohol.

Sensing a change in consumers prompted Diageo Canada, distiller of Smirnoff vodka, to augment its brand positioning strategy. Researching Canadian consumers led to a Canada-specific focus on the more common situations in which they consume alcohol: with meals, during house parties, at cottages, and at bonfires. This represented a clear departure from the club imagery of everyone having the most epic time of their life that of course only happens occasionally. The impetus for the new strategy focused on the need to introduce the brand to younger drinkers aged 19–24, but also to become a consideration for consumers in the 25–39 age bracket who might tend to gravitate away from the party scene as they settle down. The campaign used TV and print to go with its promoted Twitter messages and hashtag #thisishappening. As all of this implies, this is imagery that is conducive to encouraging situational consumption rather than enticing teens.

Despite an example like Smirnoff, a U.S. study found a link between higher levels of magazine ads and underage alcohol consumption. The researchers claimed that the brands most loved by underage people had higher exposure levels in magazines that draw a younger audience. They also claimed that if similar research completed for TV produced similar results, then there would be causal evidence for putting greater regulatory control on alcohol ads. However, other academics questioned the validity of the exposure behaviour model without any analysis of actual decision-making. In Canada, regulations already exist for there being no alcohol advertising in media with a demonstrated younger audience, and Advertising Standards Canada rarely receives an alcohol complaint.

Diageo Canada's marketing communication of other brands tended to show responsible messages directed to older consumers. For example, 10 percent growth in the ready-to-drink canned drink market prompted the distiller to launch Jeremiah Weed Spiked Iced Tea. The digital and radio ads took a "food-for-thought" theme by offering interesting quizzes targeted to those in the legal drinking age to 29 demographic. To launch a new premium brand of vodka, Crioc, Diageo Canada created a completely different campaign than the international one since it relied on a celebrity who would be considered a role model for underage consumers. Instead, the company sponsored the Toronto International Film Festival to retain the exclusivity positioning established abroad, a clear departure from what underage consumers would seek.

Sources: Susan Krashinsky, "Half Empty," *The Globe and Mail*, July 11, 2014, p. B.5; Susan Krashinsky, "Alcohol Ads Push Underage Girls to Drink More, Research Finds," *The Globe and Mail*, June 13, 2013; Josh Kolm, "Smirnoff Comes Down to Earth," *Strategy*, February 2, 2015; Harmeet Singh, "Diageo's Domestic Plan," *Strategy*, July 2, 2015.

Question:

1. What is your opinion regarding the effects of advertising on underage consumption?

Periodically, we find advertising that some may claim to be deceptive or unethical. Labatt Breweries of Canada advertised its "Hockey Playoff Payoff: Hockey Tickets for Life" during the NHL playoffs. The prize featured tickets for 20 games per year over 50 years, with the fine print stating that the winner could take the money instead. The fine print also acknowledged that the brand, Budweiser, was not an official sponsor of the NHL as Labatt had lost that title a year previously. One sponsorship agency executive publicly criticized Labatt for crossing the ethical line since the promotion could damage the brand rights of Molson.[27]

While many critics of advertising would probably agree that most advertisers are not out to deceive consumers deliberately, they are still concerned that consumers may not be receiving enough information to make an informed choice. They say advertisers usually present only information that is favourable to their position and do not always tell consumers the whole truth about a product or service.

Many believe advertising should be primarily informative in nature and should not be permitted to use puffery or embellished messages. Others argue that advertisers have the right to present the most favourable case for their products and services and should not be restricted to just objective, verifiable information.[28] They note that consumers can protect themselves from being persuaded against their will and that the industry and government regulations suffice to keep advertisers from misleading consumers. Figure 18-3 shows the advertising principles of the Association of Canadian Advertisers, which advertisers may use as a guideline in preparing and evaluating their ads.

Figure 18-3 Advertising principles of the Association of Canadian Advertisers

1. *Advertisers must behave responsibly.* ACA believes:
   - Industry self-regulation is in the best interests of all Canadians. Self-regulatory policy exists to ensure that Canadians' fundamental rights and social values are not only acknowledged, but also protected.
   - Advertisers already demonstrate their responsibility by endorsing the Canadian Code of Advertising Standards—the principal instrument of self-regulation for the advertising industry in Canada.
   - The Code of Advertising Standards is only one of many industry codes and guidelines. For example, there are guidelines for gender portrayal, advertising to children, and food labelling, to name just a few.

2. *Advertisers have a right to freedom of speech.* Specifically:
   - The ACA does not believe it is reasonable for a government to allow companies to manufacture and sell legal products, and collect taxes, and then restrict them from telling anyone about it.
   - The ACA remains vigilant in ensuring advertisers' commercial freedom of speech.
   - Advertising, including advertising of products we may not like, is an aspect of free speech, and that free speech is one of society's highest values.

3. *Advertisers make an important contribution to the Canadian economy and culture.* Specifically:
   - Advertising is important to the economic and cultural life of Canadians.
   - In all its forms, advertising is estimated to represent an annual $10 billion investment in the Canadian economy.
   - Advertising revenues fuel the Canadian broadcasting system. Advertisers pay for the production and delivery into Canadian homes of programs that entertain, inform, and educate. Advertising also funds newspapers, magazines, and even movies and Internet sites.
   - Commercials reflect our life. They are a powerful tool and means of passing along our values, traditions, and lifestyles to new citizens and the next generation.
   - Locally produced commercials contribute to our sense of identity and promote national unity.

4. *Advertisers support a vibrant, competitive economy.* The ACA believes:
   - An increased reliance on market forces does not mean that a strong and enriched local and Canadian identity cannot be maintained.
   - Our ability to protect culture by limiting access to communications vehicles is becoming increasingly difficult. A prime example is the Internet.
   - In the rapidly changing world of communications, market conditions, not protectionism, should prevail.

Based on The Association of Canadian Advertisers, www.aca-online.com.

ADVERTISING AS OFFENSIVE OR IN BAD TASTE

Another common consumer criticism of advertising is that ads are offensive, tasteless, irritating, boring, or obnoxious. Studies have found that consumers sometimes feel offended by advertising or that advertising insults their intelligence and that many ads are in poor taste.[29] Consumers can be offended or irritated by advertising in a number of ways, such as product type, fear appeals, sexual appeals, and shock appeals.

Product Type Consumers object when certain products—like personal hygiene products or contraceptives—are advertised at all; however, the objections vary over time. Historically, media did not accept ads for condoms, but they reconsidered with the emergence of AIDS; currently, these ads do not register the same level of concern as in the past. A study of prime-time TV commercials found a strong product class effect (i.e., some personal care products) with respect to the types of ads consumers perceived as distasteful or irritating.[30] Another study found that consumers are more likely to dislike ads for products they do not use and for brands they would not buy.[31] ASC's 2015 annual report identified a number of complaints pursued for product categories, with non-commercial (273), retail (210), cars (141), service (106), food (104), and leisure services (103) leading the way and accounting for 74 percent of all complaints (637/1,268). These data suggest that some general categories are more concerning for consumers, although these groupings are very broad compared to individual personal care products. Some products, such as snack foods and sugared beverages, as shown in Exhibit 18-6, may experience consumer objection by encouraging consumption. However, the development of the Canadian Children's Food and Beverage Advertising Initiative, as noted earlier in this chapter, may reassure consumers that the advertising is more appropriate for healthy living.

One product came under fire when it planned a campaign featuring a streetcar's exterior wrapped with the slogan, "Life Is Short. Have an Affair." The slogan is used by Ashley Madison, a married dating service. The phrase would also be placed in all other advertising slots and extended to 10 streetcars, for total revenue of $200,000 for the Toronto Transit Commission (TTC). A day after the Ashley Madison controversy hit the news, the TTC's advertising review committee decided not to run the ads. According to one voter, "When it's a core fundamental value around cheating or lying, we're not going to let those kinds of ads go on. It's not about sexuality, it's about cheating. We would not have accepted an ad that said 'Life is short, cheat on your exams.' It's frankly a no-brainer."[32] In the future, Canadians may see ads for another product they previously did not expect: marijuana. Producers of medical marijuana lobbied for greater ability to communicate their product after the federal government instituted increased restrictions and levied fines to non-compliant growers.[33]

Fear Appeals   Another way in which advertising can offend consumers is by the type of appeal or the manner of presentation. For example, many people object to appeals that exploit consumer anxieties. Fear appeal ads—especially for products such as deodorants, mouthwash, and dandruff shampoos—are criticized for attempting to create anxiety and using a fear of social rejection to sell these products. The idea of fear is embodied with suicide, which became the central message of a campaign. Toronto's Virgin Radio 99.9 created three ads showing a radio resting at the edge of a bridge, sitting beside a bathtub, and standing at the edge of a subway platform—all with the impression of the radio about to commit suicide—with the copy "Give Your Radio a Reason to Live." Virgin Radio was stopped in its tracks when the Toronto Transit Commission denied the "subway platform" ad to be placed on bus shelters, even though the first two ads had appeared on bus shelters for the previous six weeks. Interestingly, ownership of the shelters and the placement of the ads is the domain of Astral Media, not the TTC; however, a contract stipulates that any TTC request for removal of ads must be honoured by Astral. Public reaction to this theme is consistent as ads depicting suicide have been previously rejected. In 2001, a potato impaled itself on a fork after discovering an empty Imperial margarine container, which required Unilever to pull the ad. In 2007, a robot jumped off a bridge after dropping a screw while assembling a GM vehicle, which required GM to revise the ad.[34]

Sexual Appeals   The advertising appeals that have received the most criticism for being in poor taste are those using sexual appeals and/or nudity. These techniques are often used to gain consumers' attention and may not even be appropriate to the product being advertised. Even if the sexual appeal relates to the product, people may be offended by the nudity or sexual suggestiveness in the advertising message, such as with the image shown in Exhibit 18-7. Another common criticism of sexual appeals is that they can demean women or men by depicting them as sex objects.

Exhibit 18-6   Advertisers for certain products may experience consumer objections.

© McGraw-Hill Education/John Flournoy

Exhibit 18-7   Abercrombie and Fitch received criticism for its ad conveying a sexual appeal.

© Kumar Sriskandan/Alamy

The use of sex in advertising is a polarizing issue as attitudes and opinions vary depending upon the individual's values and religious orientation, as well as across demographic characteristics including age, education, and gender. A study found major differences between men and women in their attitudes toward sex in advertising.[35] As shown in Figure 18-4, while almost half of men said they liked sexual ads, only 8 percent of women felt the same way. Most men (63 percent) indicated that sexual ads have high stopping power and get their attention, but fewer women thought the same (28 percent). Also, most women (58 percent) said there is too much sex in advertising, versus only 29 percent of the men. Women were also much more likely than men to say that sexual ads promote a deterioration of moral and social values and that they are demeaning of the models used in them.

Figure 18-4   Attitudes toward sex in advertising, men vs. women

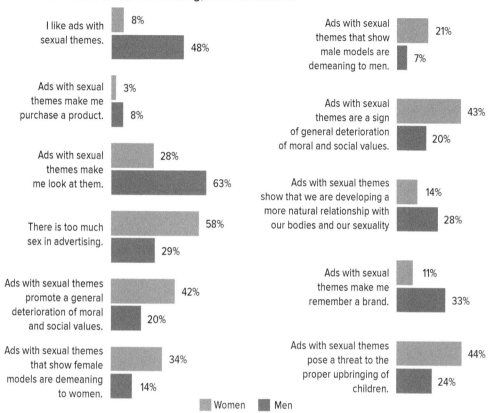

I like ads with sexual themes. — Women 8%, Men 48%

Ads with sexual themes make me purchase a product. — Women 3%, Men 8%

Ads with sexual themes make me look at them. — Women 28%, Men 63%

There is too much sex in advertising. — Women 58%, Men 29%

Ads with sexual themes promote a general deterioration of moral and social values. — Women 42%, Men 20%

Ads with sexual themes that show female models are demeaning to women. — Women 34%, Men 14%

Ads with sexual themes that show male models are demeaning to men. — Women 21%, Men 7%

Ads with sexual themes are a sign of general deterioration of moral and social values. — Women 43%, Men 20%

Ads with sexual themes show that we are developing a more natural relationship with our bodies and our sexuality — Women 14%, Men 28%

Ads with sexual themes make me remember a brand. — Women 11%, Men 33%

Ads with sexual themes pose a threat to the proper upbringing of children. — Women 44%, Men 24%

☐ Women ☐ Men

Critics are particularly concerned about sexual appeals that glorify the image of alcohol consumption. Skyy Spirits used provocative, sexually oriented ads to promote its popular namesake vodka brand. Some of its ads using stylized images that place the brand's distinctive blue bottle in suggestive situations have received criticism (Exhibit 18-8). However, a company spokesperson has responded to the criticisms by noting, "Style is a maker of interpretation and like with all art we appreciate all points of view."[36] A review of sexual imagery in six mainstream American magazines for the years 1983, 1993, and 2003 across 18 product categories found that use of sexual imagery increased from 15 percent in 1983 to 27 percent in 2003. Most of the growth occurred in low involvement product categories of alcohol, entertainment, and beauty, although product categories with the highest use included health/hygiene (38 percent), beauty (36 percent), drugs/medicine (29 percent), and clothing (26 percent).[37]

Exhibit 18-8   Ads are often criticized for being sexually suggestive.

Courtesy of Skyy Vodka and Lambesis

Shock Appeals   Because of advertising clutter, brands continue to use sexual appeals that may offend people but catch the attention of consumers and possibly generate publicity. Heightened emotional intensity occurs with a shock appeal in which marketers use startling or surprising images of nudity, sexual suggestiveness, or other unexpected aspects of society. A shock appeal is not new; Benetton (Exhibit 18-9) used this approach in ads for many years, yet it remains an interesting example and continues to intrigue students today. Advertising experts argue that what underlies the use of shock appeals is the pressure on marketers and their agencies to do anything to attract attention. However, critics argue that the more advertisers use the appeal, the more shocking the ads have to be to achieve this objective. How far advertisers can go with this appeal will probably depend on the public's reaction. When advertisers have gone too far, they are likely to pressure the advertisers to change their ads and the media to stop accepting them. Exhibit 18-10 shows a more current Benetton ad for which the company returned to its controversial ways after a hiatus. While marketers and ad agencies often acknowledge that their ads push the limits with regard to taste, they also complain about a double standard that exists for advertising versus editorial television program content. They argue that even the most suggestive commercials are bland compared with the content of many television programs.

ADVERTISING AND CHILDREN

One historical review of advertising to children concluded that television is an important source of information for children about products.[38] However, it is a long-standing concern that children, particularly young ones, are especially vulnerable to advertising because they lack the experience and knowledge to understand and critically evaluate the purpose of persuasive advertising appeals. Research has shown that preschool children cannot differentiate between commercials and programs, do not perceive the selling intent of commercials, and cannot distinguish between reality and fantasy.[39] Research has also shown that children need more than a skeptical attitude toward advertising; they must understand how advertising works in order to use their cognitive defences against it effectively.[40] Because of children's limited ability to interpret the selling intent of a message or identify a commercial, some believe that advertising to them is inherently unfair and deceptive and should not be permitted (like we see in Quebec), or should be severely restricted.

Exhibit 18-9   Benetton's "Death Row" ads created a major controversy.

Courtesy Cannes Lions International Advertising Festival

Exhibit 18-10   Benetton's advertising continues with controversial images.

© ROPI/ZUMAPRESS/Newscom

At the other extreme is the point that advertising is a part of life and children must learn to deal with it in the **consumer socialization process** of acquiring the skills needed to function in the marketplace.[41] In this respect, existing restrictions may be adequate for controlling advertising directed to children. One study provided support for socialization as it found that adolescents developed skeptical attitudes toward advertising that were learned through interactions with parents and peers. They also found that marketplace knowledge played an important role in adolescents' skepticism toward advertising. Greater knowledge of the marketplace gave teens a basis by which to evaluate ads and made them more likely to recognize the persuasion techniques used by advertisers.[42]

The *Children's Code* and the Canadian Children's Food and Beverage Advertising Initiative discussed earlier recognize the above debate explicitly to find a balance between these two points of view. A study comparing the attitudes of business executives and consumers regarding children's advertising found that marketers of products targeted to children believe advertising to them provides useful information on new products and does not disrupt the parent–child relationship. However, the general public did not have such a favourable opinion. Older consumers and those from households with children had particularly negative attitudes toward children's advertising.[43] Clearly, companies communicating directly to children need to be sensitive to the naïveté of children as consumers to avoid potential conflict with those who believe children should be protected from advertising.

However, this balance becomes even more critical with children using digital media such that the issues are increasingly complex, with new ideas for protection and groups making suggestions on how marketers should abide by the spirit of the laws prescribed for existing media. Despite this positive trend, marketers remain intrusive within the everyday lives of children. For example, 90 percent of popular children's Internet sites contain advertising, and many are really advertising disguised as content in the form of games or activities associated with toys, TV characters, or other brand identification. An interpretation guideline of federal laws by Advertising Standards Canada is a good start; however, it does not contain guidance for digital sources although the general message is certainly applicable. As well, the Canadian Children's Food and Beverage Advertising Initiative provides strong guidance that includes measures for digital communication, but adherence remains voluntary. Experts in the field expect direction and regulation soon in the aftermath of recent hearings by the Office of the Privacy Commissioner regarding online tracking and behavioural advertising.[44]

In the meantime, it appears reasonable for marketers to consider the following suggestions. (1) Even if there are no guidelines for online, advertisers should just use the broadcast code instructions and the interpretation guidelines for digital since they are readily adaptable. (2) Advertisers should involve parents as much as possible. (3) Advertisers should have an understanding from a moral perspective on blurring the lines between advertising and content since the receiver should always know and understand that advertising has occurred. (4) Advertisers should be respecting children's privacy and treating data in the same way as is done with adults. (5) Advertisers should apply the standard found in other media for online communication. (6) Advertisers should assess whether advertising to children is actually financially viable, as they have no income and do not make purchases.[45]

Despite these suggestions for improvements, advertisers continue to look for ways of influencing children. Another attempt in this direction occurred with the placement of TVs in schools as a pilot project to keep students informed of schedules, events, activities, and student content. To support the cost, the TVs had messages for "good" products such as milk, government, and higher education institutions. Reactions were initially positive, however conflict arose over a planned expansion toward more minutes of advertising per day, with some stakeholders being concerned that this would be the start of messages that many would not welcome in schools. Further, some did question why even "good" advertising messages should be in the school in the first place.[46]

 ## Social Effects of Advertising

Concern is expressed over the impact of advertising on society, particularly on values and lifestyles. While a number of factors influence the cultural values, lifestyles, and behaviour of a society, the overwhelming amount of advertising and its prevalence in the mass media lead many critics to argue that advertising plays a major role in influencing and transmitting social values. While there is general agreement that advertising is an important social influence agent, opinions as to the value of its contribution are often negative. Advertising is criticized for encouraging materialism, manipulating consumers to buy things they do not really need, perpetuating stereotypes, and controlling the media.

ADVERTISING ENCOURAGES MATERIALISM

Critics claim advertising has an adverse effect on consumer values by encouraging **materialism**, a preoccupation with material things rather than intellectual or spiritual concerns. Critics contend that an ad like the one shown in Exhibit 18-11 can promote materialistic values. In summary, they contend that advertising seeks to create needs rather than merely show how a product or service fulfills them; surrounds consumers with images of the good life and suggests the acquisition of material possessions leads to contentment and happiness and adds to the joy of living; and suggests material possessions are symbols of status, success, and accomplishment and/or will lead to greater social acceptance, popularity, sex appeal, and so on.

This criticism of advertising assumes that materialism is undesirable and is sought at the expense of other goals, but some believe materialism is acceptable. For example, some consumers believe their hard work and individual effort and initiative allows for the accumulation of material possessions as evidence of success. Others argue that the acquisition of material possessions has positive economic impact by encouraging consumers to keep consuming after their basic needs are met. Many believe economic growth is essential and materialism is both a necessity and an inevitable part of this progress.

It has also been argued that an emphasis on material possessions does not rule out interest in intellectual, spiritual, or cultural values. Defenders of advertising say consumers can be more interested in higher-order goals when basic needs have been met. Raymond Bauer and Stephen Greyser point out that consumers may purchase material things in the pursuit of non-material goals.[47] For example, a person may buy an expensive stereo system to enjoy music rather than simply to impress someone or acquire a material possession.

Even if we assume materialism is undesirable, there is still the question of whether advertising is responsible for creating and encouraging it. While critics argue that advertising is a major contributing force to materialistic values, others say advertising merely reflects the values of society rather than shaping them.[48] They argue that consumers' values are defined by the society in which they live and are the results of extensive, long-term socialization or acculturation.

The argument that advertising is responsible for creating a materialistic and hedonistic society is addressed by Stephen Fox in his book *The Mirror Makers: A History of American Advertising and Its Creators.* Fox concludes that advertising has become a prime scapegoat for our times and merely reflects society.[49] Advertising does contribute to our materialism by portraying products and services as symbols of status, success, and achievement and by encouraging consumption, but as Richard Pollay says, "While it may be true that advertising reflects cultural values, it does so on a very selective basis, echoing and reinforcing certain attitudes, behaviours, and values far more frequently than others."[50]

ADVERTISING AND PERSUASION

A common criticism of advertising is that it manipulates and exploits consumers by persuading them to buy things they do not need. Critics say advertising should just provide information useful in making purchase decisions and should not persuade. They view information advertising (which reports price, performance, and other objective criteria) as desirable, but persuasive advertising (which plays on consumers' emotions, anxieties, and psychological needs and desires such as status, self-esteem, and attractiveness) as unacceptable. Persuasive advertising is criticized for fostering discontent among consumers and encouraging them to purchase products and services to solve deeper problems.

Defenders of advertising offer three rebuttals to these criticisms. First, they point out that a substantial amount of advertising is essentially informational in nature.[51] Also, it is difficult to separate desirable informational advertising from undesirable persuasive advertising. Shelby Hunt, in examining the *information–persuasion dichotomy,* points out that even advertising that most observers would categorize as very informative is often very persuasive.[52] Hunt says, "If advertising critics really believe that persuasive advertising should not be permitted, they are actually proposing that no advertising be allowed, since the purpose of all advertising is to persuade."[53]

Second, defenders of advertising also take issue with the argument that it should be limited to dealing with basic functional needs. In our society, most lower-level needs recognized in Maslow's hierarchy—such as the needs for food, clothing, and shelter—are satisfied for most people. It is natural to move from basic needs to higher-order ones such as self-esteem and status or self-actualization. Consumers are free to choose the degree to which they attempt to satisfy their desires, and wise advertisers associate their products and services with the satisfaction of higher-order needs. While this is true, fulfillment of lower-level needs continue to benefit from advertising (Exhibit 18-12).

Exhibit 18-11   Critics argue that advertising contributes to materialistic values.

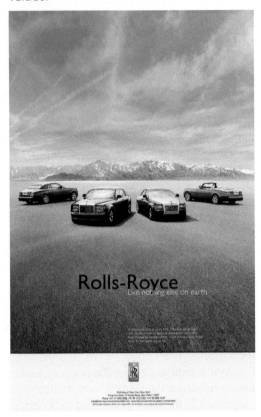

© Rolls Royce Motor Cars New Delhi

Exhibit 18-12   Viagra reminds Canadian consumers to talk to their doctor with this colourful street ad.

© Marc Bruxelle / Shutterstock.com

Third, this criticism attributes too much power to advertising and assumes consumers have no ability to defend themselves since it ignores the fact that consumers have the freedom to make their own choices when confronted with persuasive advertising. While they readily admit the persuasive intent of their business, advertisers are quick to note that it is extremely difficult to make consumers purchase a product they do not want or for which they do not see a personal benefit. If advertising were as powerful as the critics claim, we would not see products with multimillion-dollar advertising budgets failing in the marketplace. The reality is that consumers do have a choice, and they are not being forced to buy. Consumers ignore ads for products and services they do not really need or that fail to interest them.

ADVERTISING AND STEREOTYPING

Advertising is often accused of creating and perpetuating stereotypes through its portrayal of women and visible minorities.

Women   The portrayal of women in advertising is an issue that has received a great deal of attention through the years.[54] Advertising has received much criticism for stereotyping women and failing to recognize the changing role of women in our society. Critics have argued that advertising often depicts women as preoccupied with beauty, household duties, and motherhood, or shows them as decorative objects or sexually provocative figures. The research studies conducted through the years show a consistent picture of gender stereotyping that has varied little over time. Portrayals of adult women in American television and print advertising have emphasized passivity, deference, lack of intelligence and credibility, and punishment for high levels of effort. In contrast, men have been portrayed as constructive, powerful, autonomous, and achieving.[55]

Research on gender stereotyping in advertising targeted to children has found a pattern of results similar to that reported for adults. A study found sex-role stereotyping in television advertising targeted at children in the United States as well as in Australia.[56] Boys are generally shown as being more knowledgeable, active, aggressive, and instrumental than girls. Nonverbal behaviours involving dominance and control are associated more with boys than girls. Advertising directed toward children has also been shown to feature more boys than girls, to position boys in more dominant, active roles, and to use male voiceovers more frequently than female ones.[57]

While stereotyping still exists, advertising's portrayal of women is improving in many areas as advertisers now show women realistically. Researchers argue that the transformed social positioning of women in North American society is perhaps the most important social development of this century.[58] They note that as women have crossed the boundary from the domestic sphere to the professional arena, expectations and representations of women have changed as well. For example, magazines incorporate and appeal to the sociocultural shifts in women's lives. Advertisers depict women in a diversity of roles that reflect their changing place in society. The stereotypical character traits attributed to women have shifted from weak and dependent to strong and autonomous.[59] The ad for Network Solutions shown in Exhibit 18-13 is an example of how advertisers portray women in their ads. However, brands like Axe continue to depict women in an entirely different manner, raising criticism toward the parent company, Unilever, which portrayed women naturally in its famous Dove "Campaign for Real Beauty." A Canadian advertising agency executive responsible for the Axe account claimed the ads reflected a "fun and cheeky" brand personality, and that the product helped in facilitating girls and guys to come together.[60]

This trend is seen in the 2015 annual report published by Advertising Standards Canada (ASC). It received a total of 453 complaints regarding 152 ads associated with Clause 14 (unacceptable depictions and portrayals). However, most of these concerned personal taste or preference, and the council ultimately upheld 92 complaints for 7 ads. In comparison, ASC received 717 complaints for Clause 1 (accuracy and clarity) and Clause 3 (price claims) combined and upheld 167 complaints for 43 ads.[61] While the statistics are a positive indication, the issue of digitally altering photographic images is a concern. An illustration of this occurred with a Polo Ralph Lauren ad, where one astute viewer commented, "Dude, her head's bigger than her pelvis." Upon investigation, Polo apologized and claimed the mistake would not occur in future.[62]

Exhibit 18-13   Many advertisers now portray women in powerful roles.

It should be noted that portrayal and depiction problems occurring in advertising are not necessarily reflected in the statistics, as advertising gets amended or withdrawn prior to anyone making a complaint to ASC. In the case of a Loblaws flyer featuring Joe Fresh ads for women's underwear and night clothes, the retailer immediately pulled its flyers once a few consumers complained directly and a media story questioned whether the images should be displayed in such a public manner. One vice-president for the brand noted, "We stand by the flyer. We think the photography is beautiful, and we have definitely seen a positive reflection in our sales since the flyer went out."[63] The issue of ad images that are criticized for being in public display is raised periodically, and ads such as the one shown in Exhibit 18-14 may elicit objections or complaints.

Finally, the shoe is on the other foot, so to speak, as one advertising professional observed that some ads portray a stereotype of men as dumb, goofy, or inept. Deborah Adams, senior vice-president of Harbinger Communications, a consultancy firm that focuses on marketing to women, recounted a comment from a woman on their market research panel: "You know, if you want to make inroads with me, if you want to resonate with me, you really shouldn't be showing my husband as an idiot."[64] This is precisely the reason why the ASC guidelines on depictions and portrayal include both women and men. In addition, other criticisms of ads focused on men and their role as fathers in unflattering portrayals. Huggies came under fire for an ad that showed fathers being incapable of leaving the TV to tend to the diaper changing needs of their infants. Consumers' criticism resulted in the brand altering the ad to include a more palatable conclusion.[65] A study by Microsoft and its agency Omnicom concluded that advertisers might want to reconsider how men are portrayed in ads, and their data found that high percentages of men declared themselves to be interested in cooking, nutrition, and personal care and grooming. Men indicated significant involvement in shopping for durables, consumables, and their own clothing, thereby challenging marketers' belief that women made most purchase decisions.[66]

Visible Minorities   Several U.S. academic studies in the late 1980s and early 1990s examined the incidence of visible minorities in advertising. A study conducted in 1987 found that 11 percent of the people appearing in commercials were African-Americans.[67] Another study conducted two years later found that African-Americans appeared in 26 percent of all ads on network TV that used live models but Hispanics appeared in only 6 percent of the commercials with live models. The researchers also found that TV ads in which black people appeared were overwhelmingly integrated and that black people were likely to have played either minor or background roles in the majority of the ads.[68] A study conducted in 1995 found that 17 percent of prime-time network TV ads featured African-Americans as dominant characters and the majority of commercials featured them in minor roles.[69] A study by Corliss L. Green found that ads targeting African-Americans through racially targeted media, especially with race-based products, benefit from featuring African-American models with a dominant presence in the ad.[70]

A study of U.S. prime-time TV commercials found that Asian male and female models are overrepresented in terms of their proportion of the U.S. population (3.6 percent), appearing in 8.4 percent of the commercials. However, Asian models were more likely than members of other minority groups to appear in background roles, and Asian women were rarely depicted in major roles. The study also found that portrayals of Asian-Americans put more emphasis on their work ethic and less on other aspects of their lives.[71]

It may be difficult to generalize these findings to Canada; however, Canadians are exposed to American ads when watching U.S. television programs that do not simulcast Canadian commercials or when reading American magazines. So, to a degree, Canadian consumers will experience and perceive some amount of imbalance through this exposure. However to counter this, one recent study of 2,000 ads shown in prime time on CBC, Global, and CTV found that 79 percent of the characters in the ads were Caucasian, and a corresponding 21 percent were non-Caucasian. In the 2011 census, about 6.25 million Canadians identified themselves as visible minorities, about 19 percent of the population of 33.5 million. Thus, based on this one sample, we can see a roughly equal representation.[72] And the outcomes of Cheerios ads that showed an interracial couple in the United States and Canada are revealing. The American ads shown during 2013 and 2014 received racist commentary in social media; however an interracial couple shown in a Canadian Cheerios ad execution aired three years earlier produced no racial commentary, and therefore seeing the U.S. ad did not surprise the Canadian executives as being unexpected.[73]

Exhibit 18-14   This Triumph lingerie ad may be inappropriate for public display to some consumers.

© Philippe Hays/Alamy Stock Photo

ADVERTISING AND THE MEDIA

The fact that advertising plays such an important role in financing the media has led to concern that advertisers may influence or even control the media. It is well documented that *economic censorship* occurs, whereby the media avoid certain topics or even present biased news coverage in acquiescence to advertiser demands.[74] Having the media in Canada supported by advertising means we can enjoy them for free or for a fraction of what they would cost without advertising. The alternative to an advertiser-supported media system is support by users through higher subscription costs for the print media and a fee or pay-per-view system with TV. Although not perfect, our system of advertising-supported media provides the best option for receiving information and entertainment, however the points on both sides of the issue have merit.

Critics charge that the media's dependence on advertisers' support makes them susceptible to influence, including exerting control over the editorial content of magazines and newspapers; biasing editorial opinions to favour the position of an advertiser; limiting coverage of a controversial story that might reflect negatively on a company; and influencing the program content of television. A survey of 147 daily newspapers found that more than 90 percent of editors have been pressured by advertisers and more than one-third of them said advertisers had succeeded in influencing news at their papers.[75] Thus, a newspaper may be reluctant to print an unfavourable story about a local business upon whose advertising it depends. For TV, programming decisions are made largely on the basis of what shows will attract the most viewers and thus be most desirable to advertisers. Critics say this results in lower-quality television as educational, cultural, and informative programming is sacrificed for shows that get high ratings and appeal to the mass markets.

Media executives cite two reasons why advertisers do not exert undue influence over the media. First, it is in the media's best interest not to be influenced by advertisers. To retain public confidence, media must report the news fairly and accurately without showing bias or attempting to avoid controversial issues. The vast array of topics media cover and their investigative reporting is evidence of their objectivity. Second, media executives note that an advertiser needs the media more than the media need any individual advertiser, particularly when the medium has a large audience or does a good job of reaching a specific market segment. Many publications and stations have a very broad base of advertising support and can afford to lose an advertiser that attempts to exert too much influence.

ADVERTISING AND SOCIAL BENEFIT

It is important to note that advertising and other IMC tools play an important role in many activities that provide tremendous social benefit in a number of ways. Companies use advertising in their sponsorship or cause-related activities that encourage participation to help raise money for important causes. For example, communicating to the thousands who participated in CIBC's Run for the Cure and Becel's Ride for Heart efforts would not be possible without advertising—and, more importantly, would not occur without the existing advertising industry and infrastructure.

Organizations dealing with social problems, such as alcohol-impaired driving, use advertising to influence attitudes and behaviour. Exhibit 18-15 identifies one organization that uses advertising and other marketing communication tools to achieve these objectives. The messages try to persuade those at risk not to engage in the behaviour and to take precautions if they do. One study reviewing the effects of mass media campaigns found a 13 percent decline in alcohol-related crashes and concluded that the social benefit of the advertising clearly outweighed the cost of the advertising.[76] Furthermore, advertising attempts to influence social norms by giving friends and family the courage to intervene. A multimedia ad campaign from the provincial distributor of alcohol in Ontario supported this idea. Its research indicated that consumers often feel embarrassed or awkward when stopping someone from drinking and driving. An interactive website (DeflateTheElephant.com) allowed users to practise, with the elephant shrinking as they achieved success.[77]

Non-profit organizations that raise funds for their worthy causes rely on advertising as well. The United Way campaigns are certainly successful, with thousands of volunteers; however, the whole campaign requires some assistance with advertising. To facilitate the delivery of government services or implementation of policy, advertising is used extensively. Transit systems, generally a part of most city governments, rely on advertising to communicate routes, and so on. Provincial governments encourage visitors from other provinces to plan a vacation. Advertising for health care service resulted in positive results. Flu shot advertising in Ontario contributed to raising the participation rate from 14 percent to 34 percent. Informing Ontario consumers about health-care options lowered the number of non-emergency visits to emergency rooms by 13 percent.[78]

One interesting criticism is that agency creative specialists take pro bono work for charities that are seeking increased donations with ads that are emotionally involving and creative so that the agency can win awards beyond its roster of paying clients of established products who rely on more rational messages that have less creative latitude. This issue resulted in Cannes not permitting pro bono work to be submitted for its categories, allowing it to compete only in the "Grand Prix for Good" category. In fact, agencies arrive at creative ideas and actively seek out non-profit organizations and pitch the ideas for increased business.[79]

Exhibit 18-15 The Alberta Gaming and Liquor Commission encourages people to drink responsibly.

Alberta Gaming and Liquor Commission

Economic Effects of Advertising

Advertising develops consumer awareness of products and services by providing people with information for decision making; however, it affects the functioning of our entire economic system. Advertising can encourage consumption and foster economic growth; facilitate entry into markets for a firm or a new product or brand; and lead to economies of scale in production, marketing, and distribution, thereby increasing the standard of living. In contrast, critics view advertising as detrimental since it fails to perform its basic function of information provision adequately, adds to the cost of goods and services, and discourages competition and market entry, leading to industrial concentration and higher prices for consumers. To resolve this debate we turn to economists who take a macroeconomic perspective as they consider the economic impact of advertising on an industry or on the economy. Our examination focuses on advertising's effects on consumer choice, competition, and product costs and prices.

EFFECTS ON CONSUMER CHOICE

Critics say advertising hampers consumer choice, as large advertisers use their power to limit our options to a few well-advertised brands. Economists argue that advertising is used to achieve (1) **differentiation**, whereby the products or services of large advertisers are perceived as unique or better than competitors', and (2) brand loyalty, which enables large national advertisers to gain control of the market, usually at the expense of smaller brands. Larger companies often charge a higher price and achieve a more dominant position in the market than smaller firms that cannot compete against them and their large advertising budgets. When this occurs, advertising not only restricts the choice alternatives to a few well-known, heavily advertised brands, but also becomes a substitute for competition based on price or product improvements.

Heavily advertised brands dominate the market in certain product categories (e.g., soft drinks).[80] But advertising defenders claim it generally does not create brand monopolies and reduce the opportunities for new products to be introduced to consumers. In most product categories, a number of different brands are on the store shelves and thousands of new products are introduced every year. The opportunity to advertise gives companies the incentive to develop new brands and improve their existing ones. When a successful new product such as a smart phone is introduced, competitors quickly follow and use advertising to inform consumers about their brand and attempt to convince them it is superior to the original.

EFFECTS ON COMPETITION

Critical economists argue that power in the hands of large firms with huge advertising budgets creates a **barrier to entry**, which makes it difficult for other firms to enter the market. This results in less competition and higher prices. Economists note that smaller firms already in the market find it difficult to compete against the large advertising budgets of the industry leaders and are often driven out of business. Large advertisers clearly enjoy a competitive advantage through **economies of scale** in advertising, particularly with respect to factors such as media costs. Firms such as Procter & Gamble, which spends millions of dollars per year on advertising and promotion, are able to make large media buys at a reduced rate and allocate them to their various products. Large advertisers usually sell more of a product or service, which means they may have lower production costs and can allocate more money to advertising, so they can afford the costly but more efficient media like network television. Their large advertising outlays also give them more opportunity to differentiate their products and develop brand loyalty. To the extent that these factors occur, smaller competitors are at a disadvantage and new competitors are deterred from entering the market.

While advertising may have an anticompetitive effect on a market, there is no clear evidence that advertising alone reduces competition, creates barriers to entry, and thus increases market concentration. High levels of advertising are not always found in industries where firms have a large market share as there is an inverse relationship between intensity of product class advertising and stability of market share for the leading brands.[81] These findings run contrary to many economists' belief that industries controlled by a few firms have high advertising expenditures, resulting in stable brand shares for market leaders. Defenders of advertising say it is unrealistic to attribute a firm's market dominance and barriers to entry solely to advertising. Industry leaders often tend to dominate markets because they have superior product quality and the best management and competitive strategies, not simply the biggest advertising budgets.[82] While market entry against large, established competitors is difficult, companies with a quality product at a reasonable price often find a way to break in. Moreover, they usually find that advertising actually facilitates their market entry by making it possible to communicate the benefits and features of their new product or brand to consumers.

EFFECTS ON PRODUCT COSTS AND PRICES

Critics such as consumer advocates argue that advertising increases the prices consumers pay for products and services. First, they say the large sums of money spent advertising a brand constitute an expense that must be covered and the consumer ends up paying for it through higher prices. Several studies show that firms with higher relative prices advertise their products more intensely than do those with lower relative prices.[83]

A second way in which advertising can result in higher prices is by increasing product differentiation and adding to the perceived value of the product in consumers' minds. Paul Farris and Mark Albion note that product differentiation occupies a central position in theories of advertising's economic effects.[84] The fundamental premise is that advertising increases the perceived differences between physically homogeneous products and enables advertised brands to command a premium price without an increase in quality. Critics point to the differences in prices between national brands and private-label brands that are physically similar as evidence of the added value created by advertising. They see consumers' willingness to pay more for heavily advertised national brands rather than purchasing the lower-priced, non-advertised brand as wasteful and irrational.

Proponents of advertising acknowledge that advertising costs are at least partly paid for by consumers. But advertising may help lower the overall cost of a product more than enough to offset its costs. For example, advertising may help firms achieve economies of scale in production and distribution by providing information to and stimulating demand among mass markets. These economies of scale help cut the cost of producing and marketing the product, which can lead to lower prices—if the advertiser chooses to pass the cost savings on to the consumer.

Advertising can also lower prices by making a market more competitive, which usually leads to greater price competition. A study found that prices of eyeglasses were 25–30 percent higher in states that banned eyeglass advertising than in those that permitted it.[85] One researcher of the toy industry concluded that advertising resulted in lower consumer prices and that curtailment of TV advertising would drive up consumer prices for toys.[86] Economist James Ferguson argues that advertising cannot increase the cost per unit of quality to consumers because, if it did, consumers would not continue to respond positively to advertising.[87] He believes advertising lowers the costs of information about brand qualities, leads to increases in brand quality, and lowers the average price per unit of quality. Finally, advertising is a means to market entry rather than a deterrent and helps stimulate product innovation, which makes markets more competitive and helps keep prices down.

SUMMARIZING ECONOMIC EFFECTS

Albion and Farris suggest that economists' perspectives can be divided into two principal schools of thought that make different assumptions regarding the influence of advertising on the economy.[88] Figure 18-5 summarizes the main points of the "advertising equals market power" and "advertising equals information" perspectives.

Advertising Equals Market Power   The belief that advertising equals market power reflects traditional economic thinking and views advertising as a way to change consumers' tastes, lower their sensitivity to price, and build brand loyalty among buyers of advertised brands. This results in higher profits and market power for large advertisers, reduces competition in the market, and leads to higher prices and fewer choices for consumers. Proponents of this viewpoint generally have negative attitudes regarding the economic impact of advertising.

Figure 18-5   Two schools of thought on advertising's role in the economy

Advertising = Market Power		Advertising = Information
Advertising affects consumer preferences and tastes, changes product attributes, and differentiates the product from competitive offerings.	Advertising	Advertising informs consumers about product attributes but does not change the way they value those attributes.
Consumers become brand loyal and perceive fewer substitutes for advertised brands.	Consumer buying behaviour	Consumers become more price sensitive and buy best "value." Only the relationship between price and quality affects elasticity for a given product.
Potential entrants must overcome established brand loyalty and spend relatively more on advertising.	Barriers to entry	Advertising makes entry possible for new brands because it can communicate product attributes to consumers.
Firms are insulated from market competition and potential rivals; concentration increases, leaving firms with more discretionary power.	Industry structure and market power	Consumers can compare competitive offerings easily and competitive rivalry increases. Efficient firms remain, and as the inefficient leave, new entrants appear; the effect on concentration is ambiguous.
Firms can charge higher prices and are not as likely to compete on quality or price dimensions. Innovation may be reduced.	Market conduct	More informed consumers pressure firms to lower prices and improve quality; new entrants facilitate innovation.
High prices and excessive profits accrue to advertisers and give them even more incentive to advertise their products. Output is restricted compared with conditions of perfect competition.	Market performance	Industry prices decrease. The effect on profits due to increased competition and increased efficiency is ambiguous.

Advertising Equals Information   The belief that advertising equals information takes a more positive view of advertising's economic effects. This model sees advertising as providing consumers with useful information, increasing their price sensitivity (which moves them toward lower-priced products), and increasing competition in the market. Advertising is viewed as a way to communicate with consumers and tell them about a product and its major features and attributes. More informed and knowledgeable consumers pressure companies to provide high-quality products at lower prices. Efficient firms remain in the market, whereas inefficient firms leave as new entrants appear. Proponents of this model believe the economic effects of advertising are favourable and think it contributes to more efficient and competitive markets. Exhibit 18-16 shows an ad from the International Advertising Association used to support this positive role of advertising.

A Final Thought   The debate over the economic effects of advertising will likely continue; however, the point of view expressed by Leo Burnett many years ago seems relevant today with the growth of mobile devices and other innovations (Figure 18-6). While many advertising and marketing experts agree that advertising and promotion play an important role in helping to expand consumer demand for new products, not everyone would agree that this is desirable.

Exhibit 18-16   This ad promotes the value of advertising in building strong brands.

Courtesy of the American Advertising Federation

Figure 18-6 The positive economic effects of advertising

To me it means that if we believe to any degree whatsoever in the economic system under which we live, in a high standard of living and in high employment, advertising is the most efficient known way of moving goods in practically every product class.

My proof is that millions of businessmen have chosen advertising over and over again in the operations of their business. Some of their decisions may have been wrong, but they must have thought they were right or they wouldn't go back to be stung twice by the same kind of bee.

It's a pretty safe bet that in the next 10 years many Americans will be using products and devices that no one in this room has even heard of. Judging purely by past performance, American advertising can be relied on to make them known and accepted overnight at the lowest possible prices.

Advertising, of course, makes possible our unparalleled variety of magazines, newspapers, business publications, and radio and television stations.

It must be said that without advertising we would have a far different nation, and one that would be much the poorer—not merely in material commodities, but in the life of the spirit.

— Leo Burnett

These excerpts are from a speech given by Leo Burnett on the American Association of Advertising Agencies' 50th anniversary. April 20, 1967.

Learning Objectives Summary

LO1   Describe the advertising regulation system in Canada.

Various levels of government regulate different aspects of Canadian advertising; however, self-regulation of these laws is quite prominent in Canada. This self-regulation occurs through Advertising Standards Canada (ASC), a non-profit organization of advertising industry members. ASC responds to all complaints with respect to advertising and publishes an annual report that summarizes the complaints it receives each year. ASC is also responsible for clearing ads prior to their airing for a number of products. Some of ASC's responsibilities have been given to it as the federal government has withdrawn services with the belief that industry is sufficiently responsible.

LO2   Evaluate the ethical perspectives of advertising.

Even though there appears to be sufficient control of advertising, it is a very powerful institution that has been the target of considerable criticism regarding its ethical, social, and economic impact. The criticism of advertising concerns the specific techniques and methods used as well as its effect on societal values, tastes, lifestyles, and behaviour. Critics argue that advertising is deceptive and untruthful; that it is often offensive, irritating, or in poor taste; and that it exploits certain groups. Many people believe advertising should be informative only and advertisers should not use subjective claims, puffery, embellishment, or persuasive techniques.

Advertising often offends consumers by the type of appeal or manner of presentation used; sexually suggestive ads and nudity receive the most criticism. Advertisers say their ads are consistent with contemporary values and lifestyles and are appropriate for the target audiences they are attempting to reach. Advertising to children is an area of particular concern, since critics argue that children lack the experience, knowledge, and ability to process and evaluate persuasive advertising messages rationally.

Explain the social effects of advertising.

The pervasiveness of advertising and its prevalence in the mass media have led critics to argue that it plays a major role in influencing and transmitting social values. Advertising has been charged with encouraging materialism, manipulating consumers to buy things they do not really want or need, and perpetuating stereotypes through its portrayal of certain groups such as women and visible minorities.

Examine the economic role of advertising and its effects on consumer choice, competition, and product costs and prices.

Advertising has also been scrutinized with regard to its economic effects. The basic economic role of advertising is to give consumers information that helps them make consumption decisions. Some people view advertising as a detrimental force that has a negative effect on competition, product costs, and consumer prices. Economists' perspectives regarding the effects of advertising correspond to two basic schools of thought: the "advertising equals market power" model, and the "advertising equals information" model. Arguments consistent with each perspective were considered in analyzing the economic effects of advertising.

Review Questions

1. Explain why you agree or disagree with the rulings of Advertising Standards Canada presented in this chapter regarding the Ford Focus and Kia automobile ads.
2. Evaluate the arguments for and against advertising to children. Do you feel that restrictions are needed for advertising and other forms of promotion targeted to children?
3. Discuss how attitudes toward the use of sex in advertising differ between men and women. Discuss the implications of these attitudinal differences for marketers who are developing ads for each gender.
4. Describe the differences between the two major perspectives of the economic impact of advertising: "advertising equals market power" versus "advertising equals information."

Applied Questions

1. Why are the laws for advertising regulation not applied to sponsorship and some other IMC tools?
2. Find the most offensive ad possible and express why it is so offensive. Apply the ASC code to determine which guidelines it violates.
3. Explain which position you agree with and why: "Advertising determines Canadian consumers' tastes and values and is responsible for creating a materialistic society," or "Advertising is a reflection of society and mirrors its tastes and values."
4. Do you believe that advertising power has ever restricted your personal choice in buying products?

ENDNOTES

CHAPTER ONE

1. "AMA Board Approves New Marketing Definition," *Marketing News*, March 1, 1985, p. 1.

2. Richard P. Bagozzi, "Marketing as Exchange," *Journal of Marketing*, 39 (4), October 1975, pp. 32–39.

3. Kristin Laird, "Dinner Time Is Prime Time for Maple Leaf Foods," *Marketing Magazine*, June 16, 2011.

4. Kristin Laird, "Art Is Joyful for BMW," *Marketing Magazine*, May 8, 2009.

5. Joseph Brean, "World War Pink Comes to Canada," *National Post*, January 27, 2014, p. A1.

6. Rebecca Harris, "Nice Package," *Marketing Magazine*, September 4, 2012.

7. Kevin Lane Keller, "Conceptualizing, Measuring, and Managing Customer Based Brand Equity," *Journal of Marketing*, 57 (1), January 1993, pp. 1–22.

8. Sreedhar Madhavaram, Vishag Badrinarayanan, and Robert E. McDonald, "Integrated Marketing Communication (IMC) and Brand Identity as Critical Components of Brand Equity Strategy," *Journal of Advertising*, 34 (4), Winter 2005, pp. 69–80.

9. Brand Finance, "Canada 100 2015: The most valuable Canadian brands of 2015," http://brandirectory.com/league_tables/table/canada-100-2015.

10. Ipsos Reid, " ICA and Ipsos Reid Announce Top 10 Most Influential Brands in Canada," http://www.ipsos-na.com/news-polls/pressrelease.aspx?id=6735.

11. Susan Krashinsky, "Growth in Brand Value of Canadian Firms Slowing," *The Globe and Mail*, May 27, 2014, p. B3.

12. J. Josko Brakus, Bernd H. Schmitt, and Lia Zarantonello, "Brand Experience: What Is It? How Is It Measured? Does It Affect Loyalty?", *Journal of Marketing*, 73 (3), May 2009, pp. 52–68.

13. C. Whan Park, Deborah J. MacInnis, Joseph Priester, Andreas B. Elsingerich, and Dawn Iabucci, "Brand Attachment and Brand Attitude Strength: Conceptual and Empirical Differentiation of Two Critical Brand Equity Drivers," *Journal of Marketing*, 74 (6), November 2010, pp. 1–17.

14. Rajeev Batra, Aaron Ahuvia, and Richard P. Bagozzi, "Brand Love," *Journal of Marketing*, 76 (3), March 2012, pp. 1–16.

15. Grant Surridge, "MOY: Duncan Fulton Retells Sport Chek's Story," *Strategy*, December 7, 2012.

16. Paul W. Farris and David J. Reibstein, "How Prices, Ad Expenditures, and Profits Are Linked," *Harvard Business Review*, November–December 1979, pp. 172–84.

17. Tamsin McMahon, "Mortgage Broker's Low Rate Has Downside," *The Globe and Mail*, March 27, 2015, p. B3.

18. Daniel J. Howard and Roger A. Kerin, "Broadening the Scope of Reference Price Advertising Research: A Field Study of Consumer Shopping," *Journal of Marketing*, 70 (4), October 2006, pp. 185–204.

19. Dhruv Grewal, Kent B. Monroe, and R. Krishnan, "The Effects of Price-Comparison Advertising on Buyers' Perceptions of Acquisition Value, Transaction Value, and Behavioral Intentions," *Journal of Marketing*, 62 (2), April 1998, pp. 46–59.

20. Roger A. Kerin, Steven W. Hartley, Eric N. Berkowitz, and William Rudelius, *Marketing*, 8th ed. (Burr Ridge, IL: Irwin/McGraw-Hill, 2006).

21. Kevin Lane Keller, "Brand Equity Management in a Multichannel, Multimedia Retail Environment," *Journal of Interactive Marketing*, 24 (2), 2010, pp. 58–70.

22. https://www.ama.org/AboutAMA/Pages/Definition-of-Marketing.aspx

23. Michael L. Ray, *Advertising and Communication Management* (Englewood Cliffs, NJ: Prentice Hall, 1982).

24. Ralph S. Alexander, ed., *Marketing Definitions* (Chicago: American Marketing Association, 1965), p. 9.

25. Numeris, Weekly Top 30 Programs.

26. "Analysis of the Economics of Canadian Television Programming." Study performed by Nodicity Group Ltd., March 2009.

27. Arjun Chaudhuri, "How Brand Reputation Affects the Advertising–Brand Equity Link," *Journal of Advertising Research*, 42 (3), May–June 2002, pp. 33–43.

28. Amit Joshi and Dominique M. Hanssens, "The Direct and Indirect Effects of Advertising Spending on Firm Value," *Journal of Marketing*, 74 (1), January 2010, pp. 20–33.

29. Kristin Laird, "Broil King Heats Up Advertising for Summer," *Marketing Magazine*, May 5, 2009.

30. Kristin Laird, "Products of the Year," *Marketing Magazine*, May 2014, pp. 42–43.

31. Megan Hayes, "Marketers of the Year: Sandra Sanderson Keeps Shoppers Fabulous," *Strategy*, December 7, 2012.

32. H. Frazier Moore and Bertrand R. Canfield, *Public Relations: Principles, Cases, and Problems*, 7th ed. (Burr Ridge, IL: Irwin, 1977), p. 5.

33. Kristin Laird, "Tim Hortons Is Turning Green," *Marketing Magazine*, June 1, 2009.

34. Qasim Mohammad, "After Years in the Slow Lane, Canada's e-Commerce Ecosystem is Booming," *Canadian Business*, February 22, 2016.

35. Russ Martin, "Influential Partners," *Marketing Magazine*, September 2014.

36. Emily Wexler, "Driving Away a Winner," *Strategy*, February 1, 2011.

37. John R. Rossiter and Larry Percy, "How the Roles of Advertising Merely Appear to Have Changed," *International Journal of Advertising*, 32 (3), 2013, pp. 391–398.

38. Michaela Draganska, Wesley R. Hartmann, and Gena Stanglein, "Internet Versus Television Advertising: A Brand-Building Comparison," *Journal of Marketing Research*, 51 (5), October 2014, pp. 578–590. Issac M. Dinner, Harald J. Van Heerde, and Scott A. Neslin, "Driving Online and Offline Sales: The Cross-Channel Effects of Traditional, Online Display, and Paid Search Advertising," *Journal of Marketing Research*, 51 (5), October 2014, pp. 527–545.

39. David Brown, "Rogers Media," *Marketing Magazine*, November 14, 2011.

40. Don E. Schultz, "Integrated Marketing Communications: Maybe Definition Is in the Point of View," *Marketing News*, January 18, 1993, p. 17.

41. Don Shultz and Philip Kitchen, "Integrated Marketing Communications in US Advertising Agencies: An Exploratory Study," *Journal of Advertising Research*, 37 (5), September–October 1997, pp. 7–18.

42. Tom Duncan and Sandra E. Moriarty, "A Communication-Based Model for Managing Relationships," *Journal of Marketing*, 62 (2), April 1998, pp. 1–13.

43. Joep P. Cornelissen and Andrew R. Lock, "Theoretical Concept or Management Fashion? Examining the Significance of IMC," *Journal of Advertising Research*, 40 (5), September–October 2000, pp. 7–15.

44. Philip J. Kitchen, Joanne Brignell, Tao Li, and Graham Spickett Jones, "The Emergence of IMC: A Theoretical Perspective," *Journal of Advertising Research*, 44 (1), March 2004, pp. 19–30.

45. Don E. Schultz, "IMC Receives More Appropriate Definition," *Marketing News*, September 15, 2004, pp. 8–9.

46. Dong Hwan Lee and Chan Wook Park, "Conceptualization and Measurement of Multidimensionality of Integrated Marketing Communications," *Journal of Advertising Research*, 47 (3), September 2007, pp. 222–236.

47. Mike Reid, Sandra Luxton, and Felix Mavondo, "The Relationship Between Integrated Marketing Communication, Market Orientation, and Brand Orientation," *Journal of Advertising*, 34 (4), Winter 2005, pp. 11–23.

48. George Low, "Correlates of Integrated Marketing Communications," *Journal of Advertising Research*, 40 (3), January–February 2000, pp. 27–39.

49. Cornelissen and Lock, "Theoretical Concept or Management Fashion?"

50. Harlan E. Spotts, David R. Lambert, and Mary L. Joyce, "Marketing Déjà Vu: The Discovery of Integrated Marketing Communications," *Journal of Marketing Education*, 20 (3), December 1998, pp. 210–218.

51. Kitchen, Brignell, Li, and Jones, "The Emergence of IMC: A Theoretical Perspective."

52. Chris Powell, "Time for a Marketing Makeover at Canada's Big Banks?" *Marketing Magazine*, August 2014, pp. 20–24.

53. Alicia Androich, "Why McDonald's Bare-Bones Marketing Approach Works," *Marketing Magazine*, October 1, 2012; Kristin Laird, "2012 Marketers of the Year Shortlist: McDonald's Canada," *Marketing Magazine*, November 20, 2012; Kristin Laird, "Marketer of the Year 2012," *Marketing Magazine*, January 23, 2013; Susan Krashinsky, "From Twitter to TV, McDonald's Offers Answers," *The Globe and Mail*, October 2, 2012.

54. Leonard L. Berry, "Relationship Marketing of Services—Growing Interest, Emerging Perspectives," *Journal of the Academy of Marketing Science*, 23 (4), Fall 1995, pp. 236–245; Jonathan R. Capulsky and Michael J. Wolfe, "Relationship Marketing: Positioning for the Future," *Journal of Business Strategy*, 11 (4), July–August 1991, pp. 16–26.

55. B. Joseph Pine II, Don Peppers, and Martha Rogers, "Do You Want to Keep Your Customers Forever?" *Harvard Business Review*, March–April 1995, pp. 103–114.

56. Adrian Payne and Pennie Flow, "Strategic Framework for Customer Relationship Management," *Journal of Marketing*, 69 (4), October 2005, pp. 167–176.

57. Megan Haynes, "MOY: Marie-Josée Lamothe's Digital Domination," *Strategy*, December 7, 2012.

58. Anthony J. Tortorici, "Maximizing Marketing Communications Through Horizontal and Vertical Orchestration," *Public Relations Quarterly*, 36 (1), 1991, pp. 20–22.

59. Mike Reid, "Performance Auditing of Integrated Marketing Communication (IMC) Actions and Outcome," *Journal of Advertising*, 34 (4), Winter 2005, pp. 41–54; Sandra Luxton, Mike Reid, and Felix Mavondo, "Intergrated Marketing Communication Capability and Brand Performance," *Journal of Advertising*, 44 (1), Winter 2015, pp. 37–46.

60. Eve Lazarus, "Tourist Contraction," *Marketing Magazine*, November 28, 2011.

61. Cassies.ca. http://cassies.ca/Entry/viewcase/17506

CHAPTER TWO

1. Alvin J. Silk, "Build It, Buy It Or Both? Rethinking the Sourcing of Advertising Services," Working Paper, Harvard Business School, 2015.

2. Sharon Horsky, Steven C. Michael, and Alvin J. Silk, "The Internalization of Advertising Services: An Inter-Industry Analysis," Working Paper, Harvard Business School, 2008.

3. Sharon Edelson, "Target Drops Wieden + Kennedy as Lead Ad Agency," *Women's Wear Daily*, January 9, 2012; http://target-creative.com/

4. Kristin Laird, "Joe Fresh," *Marketing Magazine*, November 28, 2011, p. 29.

5. M. Louise Ripley, "What Kind of Companies Take Their Advertising In-House?" *Journal of Advertising Research*, 31 (5), October/November 1991, pp. 73–80.

6. Horsky, Michael, and Silk, "The Internalization of Advertising Services: An Inter-Industry Analysis."

7. http://www.icacanada.ca/aarc/Publications%20and%20Studies.aspx

8. Susan Krashinsky, "The Animals Will Stay, But Telus's Ad Business is Changing Hands," *The Globe and Mail*, June 27, 2014.

9. Megan Haynes, "DDB's Partner Quest," *Strategy*, November 2014, p. A.48.

10. Jeromy Lloyd, "A New Kind of MARCOM," *Marketing Magazine*, August 31, 2009.

11. www.r3ww.com

12. Susan Krashinsky, "Vision 7 Paves Inroad to Asia With Sale of Cossette, Citizen," *The Globe and Mail*, December 2, 2014, p. B4.

13. Susan Krashinsky, "Global Firm Havas Looks to Double Its Size in Canada," *The Globe and Mail*, December 16, 2014, p. B5.

14. Alvin J. Silk and Charles King III, "How Concentrated Is the U.S. Advertising and Marketing Services Industry? Myth Versus Reality," *Journal of Current Issues & Research in Advertising*, 34 (1), 2013, pp. 166–193.

15. Susan Krashinsky, "Ad Agency Young & Rubicam to Operate Under Taxi Canada Name," *The Globe and Mail*, July 6, 2015.

16. Melinda Mattos, "Canadian Agencies Go Global," *Strategy*, June 3, 2011, p. 8; David Brown, "Sid Lee vs. The World," *Marketing Magazine*, January 16, 2012; Bertrand Marotte, "Sid Lee's Texas Office Builds on Its Global Ambitions," *The Globe and Mail*, May 5, 2011.

17. Chris Powell, "NO, Canada," *Marketing Magazine*, June 13, 2011, pp. 31, 32, 34, 36, 37.

18. "Brilliant Ad Creative," *Strategy*, June 2014.

19. Jennifer Horn, "2014 Agency of the Year Shortlists Revealed," *Strategy*, August 22, 2014.

20. Eve Lazarus, "Rising in the West," *Marketing Magazine*, December 12, 2011, pp. 23–25, 27, 29.

21. Bill Currie, "Tiny Ad Agency Gains Tories' Favour," *The Globe and Mail*, January 21, 2012, p. A13.

22. Jeromy Lloyd, "Creativity Built Upon the Rock," *Marketing Magazine*, October 24, 2011, p. 12.

23. Tanya Kostiw, "John St.'s Appetite for Acceleration," *Strategy*, November 2014, p. A.28.

24. Jon Steel, *Truth, Lies & Advertising: The Art of Account Planning* (New York: Wiley, 1998).

25. Jeromy Lloyd, "Rumbles in the Jungles," *Marketing Magazine*, February 28, 2011, pp. 22–23, 25–26, 28–29. A video format of this material is on marketingmag.ca published in February 2011.

26. Susan Krashinsky, "Two Ad Agencies Become One," *The Globe and Mail*, July 16, 2012, p. B3.

27. Jennifer Horn, "From A to Zulu," *Strategy*, November 2014, p. A.42.

28. Josh Kolm, "Planning for Success at PHD," *Strategy*, November 2014, p. A.44.

29. Val Maloney, "OMD Turns Up the Heat on Tech," *Strategy*, November 2014, p. A.32.

30. Lloyd, "Rumbles in the Jungles."

31. Tanya Kostiw, "Narrative Fashions Its Own Storyline," *Strategy*, November 2014, p. A.46.

32. Val Maloney, "MEC's Ground-Breaking Year," *Strategy*, November 2014, p. A.52.

33. Simon Houpt, "Beyond Advertising," *Strategy*, June 3, 2011, p. 39.

34. Susan Krashinsky, "What's an Ad Worth? How Canada's Mad Men and Women Get Paid," *Globe and Mail*, August 22, 2013.

35. Susan Krashinsky, "What's an Ad Worth? How Canada's Mad Men and Women Get Paid," *Globe and Mail*, August 22, 2013.

36. Susan Krashinsky, "What's an Ad Worth? How Canada's Mad Men and Women Get Paid," *Globe and Mail*, August 22, 2013.

37. George Nguyen, "Saying No to Pitches," *Strategy*, April 2014, p. 10.

38. http://www.icacanada.ca/

39. Susan Krashinsky, "What's an Ad Worth? How Canada's Mad Men and Women Get Paid," *Globe and Mail*, August 22, 2013.

40. Fred Beard, "Marketing Client Role Ambiguity as a Source of Dissatisfaction in Client–Ad Agency Relationships," *Journal of Advertising Research*, 36 (5), September/October 1996, pp. 9–20; Paul Michell, Harold Cataquet, and Stephen Hague, "Establishing the Causes of Disaffection in Agency–Client Relations," *Journal of Advertising Research*, 32 (2), March–April 1992, pp. 41–48; Peter Doyle, Marcel Corstiens, and Paul Michell, "Signals of Vulnerability in Agency–Client Relations," *Journal of Marketing*, 44 (4), Fall 1980, pp. 18–23; Daniel B. Wackman, Charles Salmon, and Caryn C. Salmon, "Developing an Advertising Agency–Client Relationship," *Journal of Advertising Research*, 26 (6), December 1986/January 1987, pp. 21–29.

41. Mukund S Kulkarni, Premal P. Vora, and Terence A. Brown, "Firing Advertising Agencies," *Journal of Advertising*, 32 (3), Fall 2003, pp. 77–86.

42. Matt Semansky, "A Tighter Grip," *Marketing Magazine*, February 23, 2009.

43. "Whither the Full-Service Agencies?" *Marketing Magazine*, February 28, 2011, p. 9.

44. Matthew Chung, "Veritas Expands Its Influence, *Strategy*, November 2014, p. A.54.

45. Russ Martin, "Porsche Canada Selects Red Urban and Canadian AOR," *Marketing Magazine*, March 17, 2014.

46. www.Lg2boutique.com.

47. Jonathan Paul, "MAOY Gold: MediaCom's Innovation Evolution," *Strategy*, November 10, 2011; Chris Powell, "Bell, MediaCom Take Optimistic But Cautious Approach With New Multi-Screen Tech," *Marketing Magazine*, August 24, 2012; Alicia Androich, "Neale Named Managing Partner at MediaCom Canada," *Marketing Magazine*, January 12, 2012.

48. Danny Kucharsky, "Worldly Experience," *Marketing Magazine*, July 2014, pp. 8–9.

49. Prema Nakra, "The Changing Role of Public Relations in Marketing Communications," *Public Relations Quarterly*, 36 (1), Spring 1991, pp. 42–45.

50. Emily Wexler, "North Strategic Does It Their Way," *Strategy*, November 2014, p. A.36.

51. Emily Wexler, "PR AOY Gold Cases," *Strategy*, November 2014, p. A.38.

52. Megan Haynes, "Think Like an Agency, Act Like Lg2," *Strategy*, November 2014, p. A.25.

53. Hy Haberman, "Walking the Talk on Integration," *Marketing Magazine*, February 9, 2004.

54. Philip J. Kitchen and Don E. Schultz, "A Multi-Country Comparison of the Drive for

IMC," *Journal of Advertising Research, 39* (1), January/February 1999, pp. 21–38; William N. Swain, "Perceptions of IMC After a Decade of Development: Who's at the Wheel and How Can We Measure Success?" *Journal of Advertising Research, 44* (1), March 2004, pp. 46–67.

55. David N. McArthur and Tom Griffin, "A Marketing Management View of Integrated Marketing Communications," *Journal of Advertising Research, 37* (5), September/October 1997, pp. 19–26.

56. http://www.ana.net/content/show/id/enhancing-relationships.

57. Megan Haynes, "The Creative Wild West," *Strategy*, June 2014, p. 16.

CHAPTER THREE

1. David Court, Dave Elzinga, Susan Mulder, and Ole Jorgen Vetvik, "The Consumer Decision Journey," http://www.mckinsey.com/insights/marketing_sales/the_consumer_decision_journey.

2. "Are You Ready for the Mobile Consumer?" *Strategy*, November 2014, p. A.6.

3. Manjit S. Yadav, Kristine de Valck, Thorsten Hennig-Thurau, Donna L. Hoffman, and Martin Spann, "Social Commerce: A Contingency Framework for Assessing Marketing Potential," *Journal of Interactive Marketing*, 27 (4), November 2013, pp. 311–323.

4. A. H. Maslow, "'Higher' and 'Lower' Needs," *Journal of Psychology*, 25 (1948), pp. 433–436.

5. For a historic review of memory and consumer behaviour, see James R. Bettman, "Memory Factors in Consumer Choice: A Review," *Journal of Marketing*, 43 (2), Spring 1979, pp. 37–53.

6. David Thomas, "Getting Social With Automobiles," *Marketing Magazine*, August 2014, pp 18–19.

7. Amar Cheema and Purushottam Papatla, "Relative Importance of Online Versus Offline Information for Internet Purchases: Product Category and Internet Experience Effects," *Journal of Business Research*, 63, 2010, pp. 979–985.

8. Todd Powers, Dorothy Advincula, Marnila S. Austin, Stacy Graiko, and Jasper Snyder, "Digital and Social Media in the Purchase Decision Process," *Journal of Advertising Research*, 52 (4), December 2012, pp. 479–489.

9. Jonathan Paul, "Digital Hits the Aisles," *Strategy*, March 1, 2011.

10. Manjit S. Yadav, Kristine de Valck, Thorsten Hennig-Thurau, Donna L. Hoffman, and Martin Spann, "Social Commerce: A Contingency Framework for Assessing Marketing Potential," *Journal of Interactive Marketing*, 27 (4), November 2013, pp. 311–323.

11. Jonathan Paul, "Digital Hits the Aisles," *Strategy*, March 1, 2011.

12. Gordon W. Allport, "Attitudes," in *Handbook of Social Psychology*, ed. C. M. Murchison (Winchester, MA: Clark University Press, 1935), p. 810.

13. Robert B. Zajonc and Hazel Markus, "Affective and Cognitive Factors in Preferences," *Journal of Consumer Research*, 9 (2), September 1982, pp. 123–131.

14. Alvin Achenbaum, "Advertising Doesn't Manipulate Consumers," *Journal of Advertising Research*, 10 (2), April 1970, pp. 3–13.

15. William D. Wells, "Attitudes and Behavior: Lessons From the Needham Lifestyle Study," *Journal of Advertising Research*, 25 (1), February–March 1985, pp. 40–44; and Icek Ajzen and Martin Fishbein, "Attitude–Behavior Relations: A Theoretical Analysis and Review of Empirical Research," *Psychological Bulletin*, 84 (5), September 1977, pp. 888–918.

16. Jonathan Paul, "Digital Hits the Aisles," *Strategy*, March 1, 2011.

17. Manjit S. Yadav, Kristine de Valck, Thorsten Hennig-Thurau, Donna L. Hoffman, and Martin Spann, "Social Commerce: A Contingency Framework for Assessing Marketing Potential," *Journal of Interactive Marketing*, 27 (4), November 2013, pp. 311–323.

18. Joel B. Cohen, Paul W. Minniard, and Peter R. Dickson, "Information Integration: An Information Processing Perspective," in *Advances in Consumer Research*, vol. 7, ed. Jerry C. Olson (Ann Arbor, MI: Association for Consumer Research, 1980), pp. 161–170.

19. Peter L. Wright and Fredric Barbour, "The Relevance of Decision Process Models in Structuring Persuasive Messages," *Communications Research*, 2 (3), July 1975, pp. 246–259.

20. James F. Engel, "The Psychological Consequences of a Major Purchase Decision," in *Marketing in Transition*, ed. William S. Decker (Chicago: American Marketing Association, 1963), pp. 462–75.

21. Richard L. Oliver, *Satisfaction: A Behavioral Perspective on the Consumer* (New York: McGraw-Hill, 1997).

22. John A. Howard and Jagdish N. Sheth, *The Theory of Consumer Behavior* (New York: John Wiley & Sons, 1969).

23. Lyman E. Ostlund, *Role Theory and Group Dynamics in Consumer Behavior: Theoretical Sources*, ed. Scott Ward and Thomas S. Robertson (Englewood Cliffs, NJ: Prentice Hall, 1973), pp. 230–275.

24. James Stafford and Benton Cocanougher, "Reference Group Theory," in *Perspective in Consumer Behavior*, ed. H. H. Kassarjian and T. S. Robertson (Glenview, IL: Scott, Foresman, 1981), pp. 329–343.

25. Harmeet Singh, "Mattel's Girl Power," *Strategy*, April 2015, p. A.8.

26. Jagdish N. Sheth, "A Theory of Family Buying Decisions," in *Models of Buying Behavior*, ed. Jagdish N. Sheth (New York: Harper & Row, 1974), pp. 17–33.

27. Robert Fulford, "From Gen X to Gen Z: The Absurd Alphabetification of Society," *National Post*, June 21, 2014, p. A.16.

28. David Booth, "The New Harley-Davidson: We Are Everyone," *National Post*, March 9, 2012, p. DT2.

29. Michael R. Solomon, *Consumer Behavior: Buying, Having, and Being*, 8th ed. (Pearson Prentice Hall, 2009).

30. Chris Daniels, "The Visible Majority," *Marketing Magazine*, March 12, 2012.

31. Jeromy Lloyd, "Bet on Black," *Marketing Magazine*, March 28, 2011.

32. For an excellent discussion of social class and consumer behaviour, see Richard P. Coleman, "The Continuing Significance of Social Class to Marketing," *Journal of Consumer Research*, 10 (3), December 1983, pp. 265–280.

33. Russell Belk, "Situational Variables and Consumer Behavior," *Journal of Consumer Research*, 2 (3), December 1975, pp. 157–164.

34. Larry Percy and Richard Rosenbaum-Elliot, *Strategic Advertising Management*, 4th ed. (Oxford University Press, 2012). The first OUP edition (2001) included Rossiter as an author.

35. Mary Maddever, "Media," *Strategy*, June 2009, p. 44.

36. John Rossiter and Larry Percy, *Advertising Communications and Promotion Management* (New York: McGraw Hill, 1996). An updated version is Larry Percy and Richard Rosenbaum-Elliot, *Strategic Advertising Management*, 4th ed. (Oxford University Press, 2012). The first OUP edition (2001) included Rossiter as an author.

37. Susan Krashinsky, "Losing Loyalty," *The Globe and Mail*, June 6, 2014, p. B.5.

38. Stephen Beatty, "How to Win Back Your Customers, Toyota-Style," *Marketing Magazine*, May 16, 2011, pp. 22–23.

39. Susan Krashinsky, "RIM's Marketing Challenge: Revive the CrackBerry Addiction," *The Globe and Mail*, January 25, 2012, p. B1.

40. Thomas J. Reynolds and Carol B. Phillips, "In Search of True Brand Equity Metrics: All Market Share Ain't Created Equal," *Journal of Advertising Research*, 45 (2), June 2005, pp. 171–186.

41. Susan Krashinsky, "Loblaw Targets Foodies in Ad Overhaul," *The Globe and Mail*, September 18, 2014, p. B.4.

42. Melita Kuburas, "Initiative's Meaghan Stafford: Savvy Hyper-Targeter Hits Her Mark," *Strategy*, June 2009, p. 25.

43. Theresa Wood, "Design," *Strategy*, June 2009, p. 48.

44. Simon Houpt, "Trying on a Younger, Hipper Image," *The Globe and Mail*, August 5, 2011, p. B7.

45. "Interactive IMC: The Relational–Transactional Continuum and the Synergistic Use of Customer Data," *Journal of Advertising Research*, 46 (2), June 2006, pp. 146–159.

CHAPTER FOUR

1. Wilbur Schram, *The Process and Effects of Mass Communications* (Urbana: University of Illinois Press, 1955).

2. Ibid.

3. David G. Mick, "Consumer Research and Semiotics: Exploring the Morphology of Signs, Symbols, and Significance," *Journal of Consumer Research, 13* (2), September 1986, pp. 196–213; Edward F. McQuarrie and David Glen Mick, "Figures of Rhetoric in Advertising Language," *Journal of Consumer Research, 22* (4), March 1996, pp. 424–438.

4. "Megan Hayes, "Brand Storytelling Gets Seriously Tech-ified," *Strategy*, August 29, 2012.

5. Chris Powell, "Subaru Canada Sizzles With New Campaign," *Marketing Magazine,* July 6, 2012; Jeromy Lloyd, "2012 Marketers of the Year Shortlist: Subaru," *Marketing Magazine,* November 14, 2012; Alicia Androich, "Holy Holograms! *The Grid* Gets Special Cover Treatment," *Marketing Magazine,* June 20, 2012.

6. Emily Jackson, "Shopper Marketing Techs Up," *Strategy,* August 29, 2012.

7. Gian M. Fulgoni and Andrew Lipsman, "Digital Word of Mouth and Its Offline Amplification," *Journal of Advertising Research, 55* (1), March 2015, pp. 18–21; Dee T. Allsop, Bryce R. Bassett, and James A. Hoskins, "Word-of-Mouth Research: Principles and Applications," *Journal of Advertising Research, 47* (4), December 2007, pp. 398–411; Barry L. Bayus, "Word of Mouth: The Indirect Effect of Marketing Efforts," *Journal of Advertising Research, 25* (3), June/July 1985, pp. 31–39; Robert E. Smith and Christine A. Vogt, "The Effects of Integrating Advertising and Negative Word-of-Mouth Communications on Message Processing and Response," *Journal of Consumer Psychology, 4* (2), 1995, pp. 133–151.

8. Kate Niederhoffer, Rob Mooth, David Wiesenfeld, and Jonathon Gordon, "The Origin and Impact of CPG New-Product Buzz: Emerging Trends and Implications," *Journal of Advertising Research, 47* (4), December 2007, pp. 420–426.

9. Tralee Pearce, "Word of Mom: Publicity Money Can't Buy," *The Globe and Mail,* November 18, 2011, p. L2.

10. Michael Trusov, Anand V. Bodapati, and Randolph E. Bucklin, "Determining Influential Users in Internet Social Networks," *Journal of Marketing Research, 47* (3), August 2010, pp. 643–658.

11. Tao Sun, Seounmi Youn, Guohua Wu, and Mana Kuntaraporn, "Online Word-of-Mouth (or Mouse): An Exploration of Its Antecedents and Consequences," Journal of Computer Mediated Communication, *11,* 2006, pp. 1104–1127.

12. Pranjal Gupta and Judy Harris, "How e-WOM Recommendations Influence Product Consideration and Quality of Choice: A Motivation to Process Information Perspective," *Journal of Business Research, 63* (9/10), September 2010, pp. 1041–1049.

13. Emily Wexler, "Dove's Online Song and Dance," *Strategy,* April 1, 2011, p. 10.

14. Larry Yu, "How Companies Turn Buzz Into Sales," *MIT Sloan Management Review,* Winter 2005, pp. 5–6.

15. John E. Hogan, Katherine N. Lemon, and Barak Libai, "Quantifying the Ripple: Word-of-Mouth and Advertising Effectiveness," *Journal of Advertising Research, 44* (3), September 2004, pp. 271–280; Jeffrey Graham and William Havlena, "Finding the Missing Link: Advertising's Impact on Word of Mouth, Web Searches, and Site Visits," *Journal of Advertising Research, 47* (4), December 2007, pp. 427–435.

16. Ed Keller and Brad Fay, "The Role of Advertising in Word-of-Mouth," *Journal of*

17. Ed Keller and Brad Fay, "Word-of-Mouth Advocacy," *Journal of Advertising Research, 52* (4), December 2012, pp. 459–464.

18. Robert Allen King, Pradeep Racherla, and Victoria D. Bush, "What We Know and Don't Know About Online Word-of-Mouth: A Review and Synthesis of the Literature," *Journal of Interactive Marketing, 28* (3), August 2014, pp. 167–183.

19. Simon Houpt, "Budding Filmmakers Need Not Apply," *The Globe and Mail,* July 14, 2011.

20. Colin Campbell, Leyland F. Pitt, Michael Parent, and Pierre R. Berthon, "Understanding Consumer Conversations Around Ads in a Web 2.0 World,"*Journal of Advertising, 40* (1), Spring 2011, pp. 87–102.

21. Emily Wexler, "Roundtable: Surviving the Social Revolution," *Strategy,* October 2009, p. 17.

22. E. K. Strong, *The Psychology of Selling* (New York: McGraw-Hill, 1925), p. 9.

23. Jonathan Paul, "Value Targeting: Top Youth Brands' Niche Connection Plans," *Strategy,* April 1, 2011, p. 34.

24. Robert J. Lavidge and Gary A. Steiner, "A Model for Predictive Measurements of Advertising Effectiveness," *Journal of Marketing, 24* (4), October 1961, pp. 59–62.

25. Jonathan Paul, "Value Targeting: Top Youth Brands' Niche Connection Plans," *Strategy,* April 1, 2011, p. 34.

26. William J. McGuire, "An Information Processing Model of Advertising Effectiveness," in *Behavioral and Management Science in Marketing,* ed. Harry J. Davis and Alvin J. Silk (New York: Ronald Press, 1978), pp. 156–180.

27. "Canada's Most Trusted Brands in 2011," *Marketing Magazine,* May 16, 2011, pp. 17–21.

28. Anthony G. Greenwald and Clark Leavitt, "Audience Involvement in Advertising: Four Levels," *Journal of Consumer Research, 11* (1), June 1984, pp. 581–592; Judith L. Zaichkowsky, "Conceptualizing Involvement," *Journal of Advertising, 15* (2), 1986, pp. 4–14.

29. Michael L. Ray, "Communication and the Hierarchy of Effects," in *New Models for Mass Communication Research,* ed. P. Clarke (Beverly Hills, CA: Sage, 1973), pp. 147–175.

30. Robert E. Smith, "Integrating Information From Advertising and Trial: Processes and Effects on Consumer Response to Product Information," *Journal of Marketing Research, 30* (2), May 1993, pp. 204–219.

31. DeAnna S. Kempf and Russell N. Laczniak, "Advertising's Influence on Subsequent Product Trial Processing," *Journal of Advertising, 30* (3), Fall 2001, pp. 27–38.

32. Herbert E. Krugman, "The Impact of Television Advertising: Learning Without Involvement," *Public Opinion Quarterly, 29* (3), Fall 1965, pp. 349–356.

33. Scott A. Hawkins and Stephen J. Hoch, "Low-Involvement Learning: Memory Without Evaluation," *Journal of Consumer Research, 19* (2), September 1992, pp. 212–225.

34. Emily Wexler, "Fiona Stevenson: P&G's Cover Girl Blasts the Competition," *Strategy,* October 2009.

35. Jerry C. Olson, Daniel R. Toy, and Phillip A. Dover, "Mediating Effects of Cognitive Responses to Advertising on Cognitive Structure," in *Advances in Consumer Research,* ed. H. Keith Hunt (Ann Arbor, MI: Association for Consumer Research, 1978), pp. 72–78.

36. Anthony A. Greenwald, "Cognitive Learning, Cognitive Response to Persuasion and Attitude Change," in *Psychological Foundations of Attitudes,* ed. A. G. Greenwald, T. C. Brock, and T. W. Ostrom (New York: Academic Press, 1968); Peter L. Wright, "The Cognitive Processes Mediating Acceptance of Advertising," *Journal of Marketing Research, 10* (1), February 1973, pp. 53–62; Brian Wansink, Michael L. Ray, and Rajeev Batra, "Increasing Cognitive Response Sensitivity," *Journal of Advertising, 23* (2), June 1994, pp. 65–76.

37. Peter Wright, "Message Evoked Thoughts, Persuasion Research Using Thought Verbalizations," *Journal of Consumer Research, 7* (2), September 1980, pp. 151–175.

38. Morris Holbrook and Rajeev Batra, "Assessing the Role of Emotions as Mediators of Consumer Responses to Advertising," *Journal of Consumer Research, 14* (3), December 1987, pp. 404–420.

39. Raffi Chowdhury, Douglas Olson, John Pracejuc, "Affective Responses to Images in Print Advertising," *Journal of Advertising, 37* (3), Fall 2008, pp. 7–18.

40. Scott B. Mackenzie, Richard J. Lutz, and George E. Belch, "The Role of Attitude Toward the Ad as a Mediator of Advertising Effectiveness: A Test of Competing Explanations," *Journal of Marketing Research, 23* (2), May 1986, pp. 130–143; Rajeev Batra and Michael L. Ray, "Affective Responses Mediating Acceptance of Advertising," *Journal of Consumer Research, 13* (2), September 1986, pp. 234–249.

41. Tim Ambler and Tom Burne, "The Impact of Affect on Memory of Advertising," *Journal of Advertising Research, 39* (3), March/April 1999, pp. 25–34.

42. Abhilasha Mehta, "Advertising Attitudes and Advertising Effectiveness," *Journal of Advertising Research, 40* (3), May–June 2000, pp. 67–72.

43. David J. Moore and William D. Harris, "Affect Intensity and the Consumer's Attitude Toward High Impact Emotional Advertising Appeals," *Journal of Advertising, 25* (2), Summer 1996, pp. 37–50; Andrew A. Mitchell and Jerry C. Olson, "Are Product Attribute Beliefs the Only Mediator of Advertising Effects on Brand Attitude?" *Journal of Marketing Research, 18* (3), August 1981, pp. 318–332.

44. David J. Moore, William D. Harris, and Hong C. Chen, "Affect Intensity: An Individual Difference Response to Advertising Appeals," *Journal of Consumer Research, 22* (2), September 1995, pp. 154–164; Julie Edell and Marian C. Burke, "The Power of Feelings in Understanding Advertising Effects," *Journal of Consumer Research, 14* (3), December 1987, pp. 421–433.

45. Richard E. Petty and John T. Cacioppo, "Central and Peripheral Routes to Persuasion: Application to Advertising," in *Advertising and Consumer Psychology,* ed. Larry Percy and Arch Woodside (Lexington, MA: Lexington Books, 1983), pp. 3–23.

46. David A. Aaker, Rajeev Batra, and John G. Myers, *Advertising Management,* 5th ed. (Upper Saddle River, NJ: Prentice Hall, 1996).

47. Gerald J. Gorn, "The Effects of Music in Advertising on Choice: A Classical Conditioning Approach," *Journal of Marketing, 46* (1), Winter 1982, pp. 94–101; James J. Kellaris, Anthony D. Cox, and Dena Cox, "The Effect of Background Music on Ad Processing: A Contingency Explanation," *Journal of Marketing, 57* (4), Fall 1993, p. 114.

48. Richard E. Petty, John T. Cacioppo, and David Schumann, "Central and Peripheral Routes to Advertising Effectiveness: The Moderating Role of Involvement," *Journal of Consumer Research, 10* (2), September 1983, pp. 135–146.

49. Demetrios Vakratsas and Tim Ambler, "How Advertising Works: What Do We Really Know?" *Journal of Marketing, 63* (1), January 1999, pp. 26–43.

50. John Rossiter and Larry Percy, *Advertising Communications and Promotion Management* (New York: McGraw Hill, 1996). An updated version is Larry Percy and Richard Rosenbaum-Elliot, *Strategic Advertising Management,* 4th ed. (Oxford University Press, 2012). The first OUP edition (2001) included Rossiter as an author.

51. William M. Weilbacher, "Point of View: Does Advertising Cause a 'Hierarchy of Effects'?" *Journal of Advertising Research, 41* (6), November/ December 2001, pp. 19–26; Thomas E. Barry, "In Defense of the Hierarchy of Effects: A Rejoinder to Weilbacher," *Journal of Advertising Research, 42* (3), May/ June 2002, pp. 44–47; William M. Weilbacher, "Weilbacher Comments on 'In Defense of the Hierarchy of Effects'," *Journal of Advertising Research, 42* (3), May/June 2002, pp. 48–49; William M. Weilbacher, "How Advertising Affects Consumers," *Journal of Advertising Research, 43* (2), June 2003, pp. 231–234; Stephen D. Rappaport, "Lessons From Online Practice: New Advertising Models," *Journal of Advertising Research, 47* (2), June 2007, pp. 135–141.

52. Weilbacher, "How Advertising Affects Consumers."

53. Figure 4-8 is a shorter adaptation from William J. McGuire, "An Information Processing Model of Advertising Effectiveness," in *Behavioral and Management Science in Marketing,* ed. Harry J. Davis and Alvin J. Silk (New York: Ronald Press, 1978), pp. 156–180.

CHAPTER FIVE

1. http://cassies.ca/content/caselibrary/winners/2011_Hellmanns.pdf.

2. Hollie Shaw, "Data Overload: Marketers Not Ready for Digital Influx," *National Post,* October 28, 2011, p. FP7.

3. Donald S. Tull, "The Carry-Over Effect of Advertising," *Journal of Marketing, 29* (2), April 1965, pp. 46–53.

4. Darral G. Clarke, "Econometric Measurement of the Duration of Advertising Effect on Sales," *Journal of Marketing Research, 23* (4), November 1976, pp. 345–357.

5. Gerard J. Tellis, *Effective Advertising* (Thousand Oaks, California: Sage Publications Inc., 2004).

6. Russell H. Colley, *Defining Advertising Goals for Measured Advertising Results* (New York: Association of National Advertisers, 1961).

7. Stewart H. Britt, "Are So-Called Successful Advertising Campaigns Really Successful?" *Journal of Advertising Research,* 9 (2), June 1969, pp. 3–9.

8. Steven W. Hartley and Charles H. Patti, "Evaluating Business-to-Business Advertising: A Comparison of Objectives and Results," *Journal of Advertising Research,* 28 (2), April/ May 1988, pp. 21–27.

9. Study cited in Robert F. Lauterborn, "How to Know If Your Advertising Is Working," *Journal of Advertising Research,* 25 (1), February/March 1985, pp. RC 9–11.

10. John Rossiter and Larry Percy, *Advertising Communications and Promotion Management* (New York: McGraw Hill, 1996). An updated version is Larry Percy and Richard Rosenbaum-Elliot, *Strategic Advertising Management,* 4th ed. (Oxford University Press, 2012). The first OUP edition (2001) included Rossiter as an author.

11. Jennifer Wells, "Cossette Duo's Tricks Are a Treat," *The Globe and Mail,* May 8, 2009, p. B8; Jonathan Paul, "McDonald's Big Bean Blitz," *Strategy,* June 2009, p. 21; Lesley Ciarula Taylor, "McD's Goes Free to Counter Tim Hortons," *Toronto Star,* March 2, 2010.

12. Kristin Laird, "Canadian Blood Services Gets Personal," *Marketing Magazine,* May 5, 2009.

13. Susan Krashinsky, "To Catch Coke, Pepsi Dusts Off an Old Trick," *The Globe and Mail,* May 17, 2012, p. B3.

14. Eric Lam, "Curtain Still Rises," *National Post,* June 4, 2011, p. FP6.

15. Alicia Androich, "Around and Around We Go," *Marketing Magazine,* June 4, 2012.

16. "Shopper Marketing," *Marketing Magazine,* October 24, 2011, p. 29.

17. Michelle Warren, "Engagement Marketing: The Back-to-School Edition," *Marketing Magazine,* September 12, 2011, pp. 40–43.

18. Brian Wansink and Michael Ray, "Estimating an Advertisement's Impact on One's Consumption of a Brand," *Journal of Advertising Research, 40* (6), November–December 2000.

19. Susan Krashinsky, "Stalking the Elusive Millennial Male," *The Globe and Mail,* July 20, 2012, p. B5.

20. Susan Krashinsky, "A Fresh Twist on Tried-and-True Brews," *The Globe and Mail,* May 18, 2012, p. B6.

21. Susan Krashinsky, "Natural Selection: McDonald's, Coke Hit by Healthy Habits," *The Globe and Mail,* October 22, 2014, p. B1.

22. http://cassies.ca/entry/viewcase/7522

23. http://cassies.ca/entry/viewcase/7111

24. http://cassies.ca/content/caselibrary/winners/2011_Activia.pdf.

25. Kristin Laird, "Everything You Want in a Drug Store," *Marketing Magazine,* December 2012.

26. Carly Weeks, "How Green Is Your Wallet?" *The Globe and Mail,* March 15, 2011, p. L1.

27. Jeremy Cato, "Mazda Needs the BMW Blueprint," *The Globe and Mail,* March 9, 2012, p. D10.

28. Melinda Mattos, "BC Hydro Regenerates," *Strategy,* April 1, 2011, p. 27.

CHAPTER SIX

1. Susan Krashinsky, "Air Canada Unveils a Global Brand Makeover," *The Globe and Mail,* May 19, 2014, pp. B1.

2. Jonathan Paul, "Sobeys Takes a Fresh Approach," *Strategy,* March 1, 2011, p. 21.

3. Russ Martin, "Do You Want Beer With That?" *Marketing Magazine,* September 2014, p. 8.

4. Megan Haynes, "Birks Regains Its Lustre," *Strategy,* December 2014, p. A14.

5. Usage data observed from University of Ottawa subscription of Print Measurement Bureau. Data collection questions for brand and usage are publicly available at PMB.ca.

6. Charles Blankson, Stavros P. Kalafatis, Julian Ming-Sung, and Costas Hadjicharalambous, "Impact of Positioning Strategies on Corporate Performance," *Journal of Advertising Research, 48* (1), March 2008, pp. 106–122; Charles Blankson and Stavros P. Kalafatis, "Congruence Between Positioning and Brand Advertising," *Journal of Advertising Research, 47* (1), March 2007, pp. 79–94.

7. Jack Trout, "Branding Can't Exist Without Positioning," *Advertising Age,* March 14, 2005, p. 25.

8. Al Ries and Jack Trout, *Positioning: The Battle for Your Mind,* McGraw-Hill, 2001.

9. John Rossiter and Larry Percy, *Advertising Communications and Promotion Management* (New York: McGraw Hill, 1996).

10. David Aaaker, Rajeev Batra, and John Myers, *Advertising Management,* 4th ed. (Englewood Cliffs, NJ: Prentice Hall, 1992); Larry Percy and Richard Elliot, *Strategic Advertising Management,* 4th ed. (Oxford University Press, 2012).

11. Larry Percy and Richard Elliot, *Strategic Advertising Management,* 4th ed. (Oxford University Press, 2012); Orville Walker Jr., John Mullins, Harper Boyd Jr., and Jean-Claude Larreche, *Marketing Strategy: A Decision-Focused Approach,* 8th ed. (McGraw-Hill Irwin, 2006).

12. Jeremy Cato, "The Changing Face of Luxury Cars," *The Globe and Mail,* December 16, 2011.

13. Based on a case study available at www.cassies.ca.

14. Based on a case study available at www.cassies.ca.

15. Hollie Shaw, "Sinking Roots in Canada," *National Post,* June 10, 2011, p. FP12.

16. Chris Powell, "Reebok Gets Fired Up in New Hockey Campaign," *Marketing Magazine,* February 5, 2013.

17. http://cassies.ca/winners/2011/cassies.ca/winners/2011Winners/2011_winners_Activia.html

18. Jonathan Paul, "Dentsu's Min Ryuck: Driving Interactive Digital," *Strategy,* June 2009, p. 24.

19. Susan Krashinsky, "The Food Industry's Real Message," *The Globe and Mail,* February 24, 2012, p. B6.

20. Chris Powell, "Tassimo Touts Barcode Technology in New Campaign," *Marketing Magazine,* May 18, 2012.

21. Simon Houpt, "How About a History Lesson With That Lager?" *The Globe and Mail,* May, 12, 2011.

22. Jonathan Paul, "Molson Paints It Black," *Strategy,* April 1, 2011, p. 14.

23. Susan Krashinsky, ""Nestlé Urges Workaholics to Take a Break," *The Globe and Mail*, March 10, 2014.

24. Brian Wansink and Jennifer Marie Gilmore, "New Uses That Revitalize Old Brands," *Journal of Advertising Research, 39* (2), April 1999, pp. 90–98.

25. Paul Brent, "Craft Brewers Carve Out a Niche," *National Post*, June 29, 2011, p. AL7; Tanya Kostiw, "Cracking the Craft Beer Category," *Strategy*, July 2014, p. 12.

26. Josh Kolm, "Anheuser–Busch's New Brews," *Strategy*, May 2015, p. A11.

27. Megan Haynes, "General Mills Quests for Men," *Strategy*, July 23, 2014.

28. "Blizzard Menu Ever," *Strategy*, May 2015, p. A 41.

29. Chris Powell, "Time for a Marketing Makeover at Canada's Big Banks?" *Marketing Magazine*, August, 2014, pp. 20–24.

30. Hollie Shaw, "Loblaw's Recipe to Brand Building," *National Post*, April 17, 2014, p. FP. 7.

31. Matt Semansky, "Yves Rocher Plants New Brand, Store, Concept in Montreal," *Marketing Magazine*, May 22, 2009.

32. Theresa Wood, "Lay's Calls on Local Spuds," *Strategy*, March 2009, p. 17.

33. Russ Martin, "Concerts Kick Off Samsung Galaxy S4 Possibilities," *Marketing Magazine*, April 26, 2013.

34. Russ Martin, "Molson Brings Back 'I Am Canadian' for Canada Day," *Marketing Magazine*, June 24, 2013.

35. Melinda Mattos, "Gatorade Primes for G Series," *Strategy*, March 1, 2011, p. 14; Matt Semansky, "Gatorade to Go Beyond Beverages With G Series," *Marketing Magazine*, August 18, 2010; Jonathan Paul, "Gatorade's Sport Chek Nutrition Centre Scores," *Strategy*, January 17, 2012; Susan Krashinsky, "Building a Brand When the Brand Is a Person," *The Globe and Mail*, June 2012, p. B3.

36. For a review of multiattribute models, see William L. Wilkie and Edgar A. Pessemier, "Issues in Marketing's Use of Multiattribute Models," *Journal of Marketing Research, 10* (4), November 1983, pp. 428–441.

37. David Thomas, "Tims in Transition," *Marketing Magazine*, April 2014.

38. Joel Rubinson and Markus Pfeiffer, "Brand Key Performance Indicators as a Force for Brand Equity Management," *Journal of Advertising Research, 45* (3), June 2005, pp. 187–197.

39. Based on a case study available at www.cassies.ca.

40. Based on a case study available at www.cassies.ca.

41. Based on a case study available at www.cassies.ca.

42. Rebecca Harris, "Molson Coors," *Marketing Magazine*, November 28, 2011, pp. 31, 36; Simon Houpt, "How Green Is Your Beer?" *The Globe and Mail*, August, 11, 2011.

43. Krashinsky, "The Food Industry's 'Real' Message."

44. Hollie Shaw, "Duelling Couches," *National Post*, July 24, 2009, p. FP10; Jonathan Paul, "Bell & Rogers: Couch Wars," *Strategy*, September 2009, p. 24; Scott Deveua, "Telus Sues Rogers Over 'Fast' Claims," *National Post*, November 19, 2009, p. FP1; Simon Houpt, "Telus, B.C. Judge on Same Wavelength," *The Globe and Mail*, November 25, 2009, p. B1; Simon Houpt, "B.C. Judge Tells Rogers: Tear Down Those Billboards," *The Globe and Mail*, December 1, 2009, p. B1; Simon Houpt, "Rogers Suit Turns the Tables on Competition," *The Globe and Mail*, December 2, 2009, p. B1.

45. Chris Powell, "ING Adopts New Positioning, Unveils New Marketing," *Marketing Magazine*, April 24, 2013.

46. Chris Powell, "Mobilicity Targets Wireless Big 3 in New Campaign," *Marketing Magazine*, January 13, 2012; Simon Houpt, "Disconnecting From Discontent," *The Globe and Mail*, July 2011, p. B6.

47. Chris Powell, "Van Houtte Explores Coffee Culture in New Video Series," *Marketing Magazine*, March 21, 2013.

48. Jonathan Paul, "Mr. Lube Is a Homewrecker," *Strategy*, February 1, 2011, p. 14.

49. Kristin Laird, "Cassies Target Newfoundland Tourism Campaign," *Marketing Magazine*, January 24, 2012.

50. Hollie Shaw, "'Wellthy' Trending: Brands Such as Adidas Link Good Health to Status," *National Post Magazine*, April 27, 2012, p. FP6.

51. Susan Krashinsky, "KD's New Pitch," *The Globe and Mail*, July 2014, p. B3.

52. Stefania Moretti, "An Empire State of Mind," *Canadian Business*, March 12, 2013.

CHAPTER SEVEN

1. Mary Teresa Bitti, "Future Ad Execs?" *National Post*, April 14, 2009, p. FP14.

2. Jaafar El-Murad and Douglas C. West, "The Definition and Measurement of Creativity: What Do We Know?" *Journal of Advertising Research, 44* (2), June 2004, pp. 188–201.

3. Robert E. Smith, Scott B. MacKenzie, Xiaojing Yang, Laura Buchholz, William K. Darley, and Xiaojing Yang, "Modeling the Determinants and Effects of Creativity in Advertising," *Marketing Science, 26* (6), November–December 2007, pp. 819–833.

4. Robert E. Smith and Xiaojing Yang, "Toward a General Theory of Creativity in Advertising: Examining the Role of Divergence," *Marketing Theory, 4* (1/2), June 2004, pp. 29–55.

5. Visit http://www.absolutad.com to see examples of the campaign.

6. Jeff Cioletti, "In a Changing World, There's Only One Absolut," *Beverage World*, July 2007, pp. 20–25; Stuart Elliott, "In an 'Absolut World,' a Vodka Could Use the Same Ads for More Than 25 Years," *The New York Times*, April 27, 2007, p. C3.

7. Sheila L. Sasser and Scott Koslow, "Desperately Seeking Advertising Creativity," *Journal of Advertising, 37* (4), Winter 2008, pp. 5–19.

8. Leonard N. Reid, Karen Whitehall, and Denise E. DeLorme, "Top-Level Agency Creatives Look at Advertising Creativity Then and Now," *Journal of Advertising, 27* (2), Summer 1998, pp. 1–16.

9. Anonymous, "Envisioning the Future of Advertising Creativity Research," *Journal of Advertising, 37* (4), Winter 2008, pp. 131–149.

10. Daniel W. Baack, Rick T. Wilson, and Brian D. Till, "Creativity and Memory Effects," *Journal of Advertising, 37* (4), Winter 2008, pp. 85–94; Brian D. Till and Daniel Baack, "Recall and Persuasion," *Journal of Advertising, 34* (3), Fall 2005, pp. 47–57.

11. Elizabeth C. Hirschman, "Role-Based Models of Advertising Creation and Production," *Journal of Advertising, 18* (4), 1989, pp. 42–53.

12. Edith G. Smit, Lex Van Meurs, and Peter C. Neijens, "Effects of Advertising Likeability: A-Year Perspective," *Journal of Advertising Research, 46* (1), March 2006, pp. 73–83.

13. Karolien Poel and Siegfried Dewitte, "Getting a Line on Print Ads," *Journal of Advertising, 37* (4), Winter 2008, pp. 63–74.

14. Micael Dahlen, Sara Rosengren, and Fredrick Torn, "Advertising Creativity Matters," *Journal of Advertising Research, 48* (3), September 2008, pp. 19–26.

15. Charles Young, "Creative Differences Between Copywriters and Art Directors," *Journal of Advertising Research, 40* (3), May–June 2000, pp. 19–26.

16. Alisa White and Bruce L. Smith, "Assessing Advertising Creativity Using the Creative Product Semantic Scale," *Journal of Advertising Research, 41* (6), November–December 2001, pp. 27–34; Douglas C. West, Arthur J. Kover, and Alber Caruana, "Practitioner and Customer Views of Advertising Creativity," *Journal of Advertising, 37* (4), Winter 2008, pp. 35–45.

17. Robert E. Smith, Jiemiao Chen, and Xiaojing Yang, "The Impact of Advertising Creativity on the Hierarchy of Effects," *Journal of Advertising, 37* (4), Winter 2008, pp. 47–61.

18. Smith, MacKenzie, Yang, Buchholz, Darley, and Yang, "Modeling the Determinants and Effects of Creativity in Advertising."

19. Swee Hoon Ang, Yih Hwai Lee, and Siew Meng Leong, "The Ad Creativity Cube: Conceptualization and Initial Validation," *Journal of the Academy of Marketing Science, 35* (2), Summer 2007, pp. 220–232; Arthur J. Kover, Stephen M. Goldenberg, and William L. James, "Creativity vs. Effectiveness? An Integrative Classification for Advertising," *Journal of Advertising Research, 35* (6), November/December 1995, pp. 29–38.

20. Smith, MacKenzie, Yang, Buchholz, Darley, and Yang, "Modeling the Determinants and Effects of Creativity in Advertising."

21. David Ogilvy, *Confessions of an Advertising Man* (New York: Atheneum, 1963); Hanley Norins, *The Compleat Copywriter* (New York: McGraw-Hill, 1966).

22. Hank Sneiden, *Advertising Pure and Simple* (New York: ANACOM, 1977).

23. Scott Koslow, Sheila L. Sasser, and Edward A. Riordan, "Do Marketers Get the Advertising They Need or the Advertising They Deserve?" *Journal of Advertising, 35* (3), Fall 2006, pp. 81–101.

24. "Residence Inn by Marriott Breaks Out of the Box With New Ad Campaign Featuring Exotic Acrobatic Performers," *PR Newswire*, July 19, 2007.

25. Kasey Windels and Mark Wilson Stuhlfaut, "Confined Creativity: The Influence of Creative Code Intensity on Risk Taking in Advertising Agencies," *Journal of Current Issues & Research in Advertising, 35*, 2014, pp. 147–166.

26. James Webb Young, *A Technique for Producing Ideas*, 3rd ed. (Chicago: Crain Books, 1975), p. 42.

27. W. Glenn Griffin, "From Performance to Mastery: Development Models of the Creative Process," *Journal of Advertising, 37* (4), Winter 2008, pp. 95–108.

28. Arthur J. Kover, "Copywriters' Implicit Theories of Communication: An Exploration," *Journal of Consumer Research, 21* (4), March 1995, pp. 596–611.

29. Sasser and Koslow, "Desperately Seeking Advertising Creativity."

30. Jon Steel, *Truth, Lies and Advertising: The Art of Account Planning* (Wiley, 1998).

31. Eric Haley, Ronald Taylor, and Margaret Morrison, "How Advertising Creatives Define Excellent Planning," *Journal of Current Issues & Research in Advertising, 35,* 2014, pp. 167–189.

32. Sandra E. Moriarty, *Creative Advertising: Theory and Practice* (Englewood Cliffs, NJ: Prentice Hall, 1986).

33. Bruce MacDonald, "The Art of the Brief," *Marketing Magazine,* October 27, 2003.

34. "Facebook Fans to Drive Volkswagen Ad," *National Post,* July 22, 2011.

35. Susan Krashinsky, "For Tough Times, A Sobering Sell," *The Globe and Mail,* January 26, 2012, p. B3; Hollie Shaw, "Need Your Bank Say More?" *National Post,* February 10, 2012, p. FP12.

36. John O'Toole, *The Trouble With Advertising,* 2nd ed. (New York: Random House, 1985), p. 131.

37. Harvey Schachter, "Don't Sell a Brand. Tell a Story," *The Globe and Mail,* March 16, 2015, p. B5.

38. Rosser Reeves, *Reality in Advertising* (New York: Knopf, 1961), pp. 47, 48.

39. Susan E. Morgan and Tome Reichert, "The Message Is in the Metaphor: Assessing the Comprehension of Metaphors in Advertisements," *Journal of Advertising, 28* (4), Winter 1999, pp. 1–12; Barbara J. Phillips and Edward F. McQuarrie, "Impact of Advertising Metaphors on Consumer Belief," *Journal of Advertising, 38* (1), Spring 2009, pp. 49–61.

40. Margo van Mulken, Andreu van Hooft, and Ulrike Nederstigt, "Finding the Tipping Point: Visual Metaphor and Conceptual Complexity in Advertising," *Journal of Advertising, 43* (4), pp. 333–343.

41. Martin Mayer, *Madison Avenue, U.S.A.* (New York: Pocket Books, 1958).

42. Susan Krashinsky, "An Edge-of-Your-Seat Approach to Ads," *The Globe and Mail,* March 13, 2015, p. B6.

43. Susan Krashinsky, "Sport Chek Feeds Off Raptors' 'We the North' Campaign," *The Globe and Mail,* January 19, 2015, p. B3.

44. Susan Krashinsky, "SickKids Hopes Intimacy Will Drive Charity," *The Globe and Mail,* November 8, 2014, p. A7.

45. Al Ries and Jack Trout, *Positioning: The Battle for Your Mind* (McGraw-Hill, 2001).

46. Timothy R. V. Foster, "The Art & Science of the Advertising Slogan," 2001, www.adslogans.co.uk

47. Russ Martin, "Kobo Launches First John St. Campaign," *Marketing Magazine,* May 1, 2013; Carly Lewis, "Understanding the YOLO Generation," *Marketing Magazine,* April 22, 2013; Chris Powell, "Tassimo Touts Barcode Technology in New Campaign," *Marketing Magazine,* May 18, 2012; Rebecca Harris, "Hawaiian Punch Comes Back to Canada With a Smash," *Marketing Magazine,* March 14, 2013; David Brown, "Autotrader Refinances Brand Position," *Marketing Magazine,* March 4, 2013; Carly Lewis, "Corona Targets Adventurous Millennials in New Campaign," *Marketing Magazine,* March 20, 2013; Marina Strauss, "Canadian Tire Waves the Flag in New Campaign," *The Globe and Mail,* March 17, 2011, p. B3.

48. Chiranjeev Kohli, Sunil Thomas, and Rajneesh Suri, "Are You in Good Hands? Slogan Recall: What Really Matters," *Journal of Advertising Research, 53* (2), March 2013, pp. 31–42.

49. Matt Semansky, "Koodo Ditches Spandex for New Language," *Marketing Magazine,* March 16, 2009.

50. Simon Houpt, "How Nature Can Nurture Our Brand Appreciation," *The Globe and Mail,* October 2, 2009, p. B5; Kristin Laird, "Hippos Make TELUS Big and Fast," *Marketing Magazine,* March 5, 2009.

51. Emily Wexler, "Labatt's Kristen Morrow: Beer Drinkers' Best Bud," *Strategy,* July 2009, p. 10.

52. Carey Toane, "Creating a New Connection," *Strategy,* January 2009, p. 30.

53. Michael Adams, *Fire and Ice* (Penguin, 2003).

54. http://www.environicsinstitute.org/uploads/news/michael%20adams%20fire%20and%20ice%20revisited%20-%20eag%20user%20conference%20keynote%20-%20presentation%20nov%204-2013.pdf.

55. Susan Krashinsky, "Maytag Comes Up With a New Canadian Spin Cycle," *The Globe and Mail,* March 2012, p. B6.

56. William M. Weilbacher, *Advertising,* 2nd ed. (New York: Macmillan, 1984), p. 197.

57. William L. Wilkie and Paul W. Farris, "Comparative Advertising: Problems and Potential," *Journal of Marketing, 39* (4), October 1975, pp. 7–15.

58. For a review of comparative advertising studies, see Cornelia Pechmann and David W. Stewart, "The Psychology of Comparative Advertising," in *Attention, Attitude and Affect in Response to Advertising,* eds. E. M. Clark, T. C. Brock, and D. W. Stewart (Hillsdale, NJ: Lawrence Erlbaum, 1994), pp. 79–96; Thomas S. Barry, "Comparative Advertising: What Have We Learned in Two Decades?" *Journal of Advertising Research, 33* (2), March–April 1993, pp. 19–29.

59. Stuart J. Agres, "Emotion in Advertising: An Agency Point of View," in *Emotion in Advertising: Theoretical and Practical Explanations,* eds. Stuart J. Agres, Julie A. Edell, and Tony M. Dubitsky (Westport, CT: Quorom Books, 1991).

60. Susan Krashinsky, "Google Puts Fizz Back in Classic Coke Ad," *The Globe and Mail,* April 13, 2012, p. B6.

61. Susan Krashinsky, "Getting Emotional," *The Globe and Mail,* May 23, 2014, p. B7.

62. Clair Cain Miller, "Google Advertising 'About Emotion' Love, Babies," *National Post,* January 3, 2012, p. FP2.

63. Hamish Pringle and Peter Field, *Brand Immortality, How Brands Can Live Long and Prosper* (London: Kogan Page Limited), 2009.

64. Susan Krashinsky, "Food Makers Put Their Faith in Nostalgia," *The Globe and Mail,* April 3, 2015, p. B4.

65. Susan Krashinsky, "A New Generation of Moms Meets an Old Favourite," *The Globe and Mail,* April 3, 2018, p. B7.

66. Edward Kamp and Deborah J. MacInnis, "Characteristics of Portrayed Emotions in Commercials: When Does What Is Shown in Ads Affect Viewers?" *Journal of Advertising Research, 35* (6), November/ December 1995, pp. 19–28.

67. For a review of research on the effect of mood states on consumer behaviour, see Meryl Paula Gardner, "Mood States and Consumer Behavior: A Critical Review," *Journal of Consumer Research, 12* (3), December 1985, pp. 281–300.

68. Kristin Laird, "Women Feel Good in Lusty Ads for Second Clothing," *Marketing Magazine,* November 2009.

69. Dacher Keltner and Jennifer S. Lerner, "Emotion," *Handbook of Social Psychology,* eds. Susan T. Fiske, Daniel T. Gilbert, and Gardner Lindzey (John Wiley & Sons, 2010).

70. Susan Krashinsky, "Tugging at Our Glowing Heart Strings," *The Globe and Mail,* January 3, 2014, p. B3.

71. Michael L. Ray and William L. Wilkie, "Fear: The Potential of an Appeal Neglected by Marketing," *Journal of Marketing, 34* (1), January 1970, pp. 54–62.

72. Brian Sternthal and C. Samuel Craig, "Fear Appeals Revisited and Revised," *Journal of Consumer Research, 1* (3), December 1974, pp. 22–34.

73. Punam Anand Keller and Lauren Goldberg Block, "Increasing the Persuasiveness of Fear Appeals: The Effect of Arousal and Elaboration," *Journal of Consumer Research, 22* (4), March 1996, pp. 448–460.

74. John F. Tanner, Jr., James B. Hunt, and David R. Eppright, "The Protection Motivation Model: A Normative Mode of Fear Appeals," *Journal of Marketing, 55* (3), July 1991, p. 45.

75. Ibid.

76. Herbert Jack Rotfeld, "The Textbook Effect: Conventional Wisdom, Myth and Error in Marketing," *Journal of Marketing, 64* (2), April 2000, pp. 122–127.

77. Hollie Shaw, "Sell It With a Laugh," *National Post,* March 2009, p. FP12.

78. For a discussion of the use of humour in advertising, see C. Samuel Craig and Brian Sternthal, "Humor in Advertising," *Journal of Marketing, 37* (2), October 1973, pp. 12–18.

79. Harlan E. Spotts, Marc G. Weinberger, and Amy L. Parsons, "Assessing the Use and Impact of Humour on Advertising Effectiveness: A Contingency Approach," *Journal of Advertising, 26* (3), Fall 1997, pp. 17–32.

80. Yong Zhang, "Response to Humorous Advertising: The Moderating Effect of Need for Cognition," *Journal of Advertising, 25* (1), Spring 1996, pp. 15–32; Marc G. Weinberger and Charles S. Gulas, "The Impact of Humor in Advertising: A Review," *Journal of Advertising, 21* (4), December 1992, pp. 35–59.

81. Marc G. Weinberger and Leland Campbell, "The Use of Humor in Radio Advertising," *Journal of Advertising Research, 30* (6), December 1990–January 1991, pp. 44–52.

82. Thomas J. Madden and Marc C. Weinberger, "Humor in Advertising: A Practitioner View,"

Journal of Advertising Research, 24 (4), August/September 1984, pp. 23–26.

83. David Ogilvy and Joel Raphaelson, "Research on Advertising Techniques That Work and Don't Work," *Harvard Business Review,* July/August 1982, p. 18.

84. Susan Krashinsky, "MasterCard`s New Plan to Keep Cardholders Swiping," *The Globe and Mail,* March 19, 2014, p. B4.

85. Garine Tcholakian, "Kia Gets Soul-ful," *Media in Canada,* February 9, 2009; Jonathan Paul, "Kia Incites Vehicular Voyeurism," *Strategy,* March 2009, p. 16; Kristin Laird, "Kia Bares Its Soul," *Marketing Magazine,* February 10, 2009.

86. Herbert C. Kelman, "Processes of Opinion Change," *Public Opinion Quarterly, 25* (1), Spring 1961, pp. 57–78.

87. William J. McGuire, "The Nature of Attitudes and Attitude Change," in *Handbook of Social Psychology,* 2nd ed., eds. G. Lindzey and E. Aronson (Cambridge, MA: Addison-Wesley, 1969), pp. 135–214; Daniel J. O'Keefe, "The Persuasive Effects of Delaying Identification of High- and Low-Credibility Communicators: A Meta-Analytic Review," *Central States Speech Journal, 38,* 1987, pp. 63–72.

88. Roobina Ohanian, "The Impact of Celebrity Spokespersons' Image on Consumers' Intention to Purchase," *Journal of Advertising Research, 31* (1), February/March 1991, pp. 46–54.

89. Erick Reidenback and Robert Pitts, "Not All CEOs Are Created Equal as Advertising Spokespersons: Evaluating the Effective CEO Spokesperson," *Journal of Advertising, 15* (1), 1986, pp. 35–50; Roger Kerin and Thomas E. Barry, "The CEO Spokesperson in Consumer Advertising: An Experimental Investigation," in *Current Issues in Research in Advertising,* eds. J. H. Leigh and C. R. Martin (Ann Arbor: University of Michigan, 1981), pp. 135–148.

90. A. Eagly and S. Chaiken, "An Attribution Analysis of the Effect of Communicator Characteristics on Opinion Change," *Journal of Personality and Social Psychology, 32* (1), 1975, pp. 136–144.

91. For a review of these studies, see Brian Sternthal, Lynn Phillips, and Ruby Dholakia, "The Persuasive Effect of Source Credibility: A Situational Analysis," *Public Opinion Quarterly, 43* (3), Fall 1978, pp. 285–314.

92. Brian Sternthal, Ruby Dholakia, and Clark Leavitt, "The Persuasive Effects of Source Credibility: Tests of Cognitive Response," *Journal of Consumer Research, 4* (4), March 1978, pp. 252–260; Robert R. Harmon and Kenneth A. Coney, "The Persuasive Effects of Source Credibility in Buy and Lease Situations," *Journal of Marketing Research, 19* (2), May 1982, pp. 255–260.

93. For a review, see Noel Capon and James Hulbert, "The Sleeper Effect: An Awakening," *Public Opinion Quarterly, 37* (3), 1973, pp. 333–358.

94. Darlene B. Hannah and Brian Sternthal, "Detecting and Explaining the Sleeper Effect," *Journal of Consumer Research, 11* (2), September 1984, pp. 632–642.

95. H. C. Triandis, *Attitudes and Attitude Change* (New York: Wiley, 1971).

96. J. Mills and J. Jellison, "Effect on Opinion Change Similarity Between the Communicator and the Audience He Addresses," *Journal of*

Personality and Social Psychology, 9 (2), June 1968, pp. 153–156.

97. Ben Kaplan, "A&W Guys Are the New Apple Guys," *National Post,* November 19, 2009, p. AL1.

98. Matt Semansky, "Harry Rosen Keeps It Real," *Marketing Magazine,* February 2009.

99. For an excellent review of these studies, see Marilyn Y. Jones, Andrea J. S. Stanaland, and Betsy D. Gelb, "Beefcake and Cheesecake: Insights for Advertisers," *Journal of Advertising, 27* (2), Summer 1998, pp. 32–51; W. B. Joseph, "The Credibility of Physically Attractive Communicators," *Journal of Advertising, 11* (3), 1982, pp. 13–23.

100. Michael Solomon, Richard Ashmore, and Laura Longo, "The Beauty Match-Up Hypothesis: Congruence Between Types of Beauty and Product Images in Advertising," *Journal of Advertising, 21* (4), December 1992, pp. 23–34; M. J. Baker and Gilbert A. Churchill, Jr., "The Impact of Physically Attractive Models on Advertising Evaluations," *Journal of Marketing Research, 14* (4), November 1977, pp. 538–555.

101. Robert W. Chestnut, C. C. La Chance, and A. Lubitz, "The Decorative Female Model: Sexual Stimuli and the Recognition of the Advertisements," *Journal of Advertising, 6* (4), Fall 1977, pp. 11–14; Leonard N. Reid and Lawrence C. Soley, "Decorative Models and Readership of Magazine Ads," *Journal of Advertising Research, 23* (2), April/May 1983, pp. 27–32.

102. Amanda B. Bower, "Highly Attractive Models in Advertising and the Women Who Loathe Them: The Implications of Negative Affect for Spokesperson Effectiveness," *Journal of Advertising, 30* (3), Fall 2001, pp. 51–63; Amanda B. Bower and Stacy Landreth, "Is Beauty Best? Highly Versus Normally Attractive Models in Advertising," *Journal of Advertising, 30* (1), Spring 2001, pp. 1–12.

103. Kristin Laird, "The Real Impact of Real Beauty," *Marketing Magazine,* September 2014, pp. 20–23.

104. Susan Krashinsky, "Dove Beauty Campaign Loses Its Glow," *The Globe and Mail,* April 10, 2015, p. B6.

105. George E. Belch and Michael A. Belch, "A Content Analysis Study of the Use of Celebrity Endorsers in Magazine Advertising," *International Journal of Advertising, 32 (3),* pp. 369–389.

106. B. Zafer Erdogan, Michael J. Baker, and Stephen Tagg, "Selecting Celebrity Endorsers: The Practitioner's Perspective," *Journal of Advertising Research, 41* (3), May–June 2001, pp. 39–48; B. Zafer Erdogan and Tanya Drollinger, "Endorsement Practice: How Agencies Select Spokespeople," *Journal of Advertising Research, 48* (4), December 2008, pp. 573–582.

107. Matt Semansky, "Brand Nash," *Marketing Magazine,* September 14, 2009.

108. Jasmina Illicic and Cynthia M. Webster, "Eclipsing: When Celebrities Overshadow the Brand," *Psychology and Marketing, Vol 31 (11),* November 2014, pp. 1040–1050.

109. Susan Krashinsky, "The Negotiator William Shatner's Alter Ego Comes to Canada," *The Globe and Mail,* September 14, 2014, p. B5.

110. Valerie Folkes, "Recent Attribution Research in Consumer Behavior: A Review and New Directions," *Journal of Consumer Research, 14* (4), March 1988, pp. 8–65; John C. Mowen and Stephen W. Brown, "On Explaining and Predicting the Effectiveness of Celebrity Endorsers," in *Advances in Consumer Research,* vol. 8 (Ann Arbor, MI: Association for Consumer Research, 1981), pp. 437–441.

111. Charles Atkin and M. Block, "Effectiveness of Celebrity Endorsers," *Journal of Advertising Research, 23* (1), February/March 1983, pp. 57–61.

112. Grant McCracken, "Who Is the Celebrity Endorser? Cultural Foundations of the Endorsement Process," *Journal of Consumer Research, 16* (3), December 1989, pp. 310–321.

113. Clinton Amos, Gary Holmes, and David Strutton, "Exploring the Relationship Between Celebrity Endorser Effects and Advertising Effectiveness," *International Journal of Advertising, 27* (2), pp. 209–234.

114. Michael A. Kamins, "An Investigation Into the 'Match-Up' Hypothesis in Celebrity Advertising," *Journal of Advertising, 19* (1), Spring 1990, pp. 4–13.

115. McCracken, "Who Is the Celebrity Endorser? Cultural Foundations of the Endorsement Process."

CHAPTER EIGHT

1. Gerald J. Gorn and Charles B. Weinberg, "The Impact of Comparative Advertising on Perception and Attitude: Some Positive Findings," *Journal of Consumer Research, 11* (2), September 1984, pp. 719–727.

2. "If You Don't Like This Ad, You're Simply Not Subaru Material," *National Post,* November 20, 2009, p. FP10.

3. Kristin Laird, "Scotiabank Redefines Richer Campaign," *Marketing Magazine,* January 23, 2012.

4. David Brown, "Big Data Made Beautiful," *Marketing Magazine,* April/May 2015.

5. Judith A. Garretson and Scot Burton, "The Role of Spokescharacters as Advertisement and Package Cues in Integrated Marketing Communications," *Journal of Marketing, 69* (4), October 2005, pp. 118–132.

6. David Brown, "The Birth of a Freedom Farter," *Marketing Magazine,* May 16, 2011, p. 13.

7. Hollie Shaw, "Aliens 'Natural Fit' for Mobilicity," *National Post,* July 22, 2011, p. FP12.

8. Barbara B. Stern, "Classical and Vignette Television Advertising: Structural Models, Formal Analysis, and Consumer Effects," *Journal of Consumer Research, 20* (4), March 1994, pp. 601–615; John Deighton, Daniel Romer, and Josh McQueen, "Using Drama to Persuade," *Journal of Consumer Research, 15* (3), December 1989, pp. 335–343.

9. Susan Krashinsky, "Christmas Comes Early for Apple's Marketing Team," *The Globe and Mail,* August 19, 2014, p. B3.

10. Susan Krashinsky, "We Interrupt This Ad to Bring You…Another Ad," *The Globe and Mail,* March 9, 2012, p. B7.

11. "BBDO Pushes Skittles to Top of Cheese-o-Meter," *National Post,* March 30, 2012, p. FP14.

12. Susan Krashinsky, "Creative Ad Campaign Gives Boston Pizza a Boost," *The Globe and Mail,* April 9, 2012, p. B4.

13. Paul van Kuilenbury, Menno D.T. de Jong, and Thomas J.L. van Rompay, "That Was Funny, But What Was the Brand Again?" *International Journal of Advertising, 30* (5), pp. 795–814.

14. Herbert E. Krugman, "On Application of Learning Theory to TV Copy Testing," *Public Opinion Quarterly, 26* (4), 1962, pp. 626–639.

15. Susan Krashinsky, "An Edge-of-Your-Seat Approach to Ads," *The Globe and Mail,* March 13, 2013, p. B6.

16. William E. Baker, Heather Honea, and Cristel Antonia Russell, "Do Not Wait to Reveal the Brand Name: The Effect of Brand-Name Placement on Television Advertising Effectiveness," *Journal of Advertising, 33* (3), Fall 2004, pp. 77–85.

17. C. I. Hovland and W. Mandell, "An Experimental Comparison of Conclusion Drawing by the Communicator and by the Audience," *Journal of Abnormal and Social Psychology, 47* (3), July 1952, pp. 581–588.

18. Alan G. Sawyer and Daniel J. Howard, "Effects of Omitting Conclusions in Advertisements to Involved and Uninvolved Audiences," *Journal of Marketing Research, 28* (4), November 1991, pp. 467–474.

19. George E. Belch, "The Effects of Message Modality on One- and Two-Sided Advertising Messages," in *Advances in Consumer Research, 10,* eds. Richard P. Bagozzi and Alice M. Tybout (Ann Arbor, MI: Association for Consumer Research, 1983), pp. 21–26.

20. Robert E. Settle and Linda L. Golden, "Attribution Theory and Advertiser Credibility," *Journal of Marketing Research, 11* (2), May 1974, pp. 181–185; Edmund J. Faison, "Effectiveness of One-Sided and Two-Sided Mass Communications in Advertising," *Public Opinion Quarterly, 25* (3), Fall 1961, pp. 468–469.

21. Martin Eisend, "Two-Sided Advertising: A Meta-Analysis," *International Journal of Research in Marketing, 23,* June 2006, pp. 187–199.

22. Susan Krashinsky, "For Buckley's, It's All About Being Frank," *The Globe and Mail,* April 11, 2011, p. B7.

23. Alan G. Sawyer, "The Effects of Repetition of Refutational and Supportive Advertising Appeals," *Journal of Marketing Research, 10* (1), February 1973, pp. 23–37; George J. Szybillo and Richard Heslin, "Resistance to Persuasion: Inoculation Theory in a Marketing Context," *Journal of Marketing Research, 10* (4), November 1973, pp. 396–403.

24. Andrew A. Mitchell, "The Effect of Verbal and Visual Components of Advertisements on Brand Attitudes and Attitude Toward the Advertisement," *Journal of Consumer Research, 13* (1), June 1986, pp. 12–24; Julie A. Edell and Richard Staelin, "The Information Processing of Pictures in Advertisements," *Journal of Consumer Research, 10* (1), June 1983, pp. 45–60; Elizabeth C. Hirschmann, "The Effects of Verbal and Pictorial Advertising Stimuli on Aesthetic, Utilitarian and Familiarity Perceptions," *Journal of Advertising, 15* (2), 1986, pp. 27–34.

25. Jolita Kisielius and Brian Sternthal, "Detecting and Explaining Vividness Effects in Attitudinal Judgments," *Journal of Marketing Research, 21* (1), February 1984, pp. 54–64.

26. H. Rao Unnava and Robert E. Burnkrant, "An Imagery-Processing View of the Role of Pictures in Print Advertisements," *Journal of Marketing Research, 28* (2), May 1991, pp. 226–231.

27. Susan E. Heckler and Terry L. Childers, "The Role of Expectancy and Relevancy in Memory for Verbal and Visual Information: What Is Incongruency?" *Journal of Consumer Research, 18* (4), March 1992, pp. 475–492.

28. Michael J. Houston, Terry L. Childers, and Susan E. Heckler, "Picture–Word Consistency and the Elaborative Processing of Advertisements," *Journal of Marketing Research, 24* (4), November 1987, pp. 359–369.

29. Hollie Shaw, "The Elephant in the Room," *National Post,* December 18, 2009, p. FP10.

30. William F. Arens, *Contemporary Advertising,* 6th ed. (Burr Ridge, IL: Irwin/McGraw-Hill, 1998), p. 284.

31. W. Keith Hafer and Gordon E. White, *Advertising Writing,* 3rd ed. (St. Paul, MN: West Publishing, 1989), p. 98.

32. Surendra N. Singh, V. Parker Lessig, Dongwook Kim, Reetina Gupta, and Mary Ann Hocutt, "Does Your Ad Have Too Many Pictures?" *Journal of Advertising Research, 40* (1/2), January–April 2000, pp. 11–27.

33. Susan Krashinsky, "As Seen on TV, A Lot," *The Globe and Mail,* June 29, 2012, p. B5.

34. Matt Semansky, "2008 Marketer of the Year: Quality Kraft-Manship," *Marketing Magazine,* December 8, 2008.

35. Simon Houpt, "Building a Better World, One Cup at a Time," *The Globe and Mail,* July 8, 2011, p. B6.

36. Hollie Shaw, "It's a New Reality," *National Post,* May 15, 2009, p. FP10.

37. Matt Semansky, "Kokanee Says It's Time to Move Beyond Ranger," *Marketing Magazine,* May 28, 2009.

38. Debora V. Thompson and Prashant Malaviya, "Consumer-Generated Ads: Does Awareness of Advertising Co-Creation Help or Hurt Persuasion?" *Journal of Marketing, 77* (3), May 2013, pp. 33–47.

39. Alicia Androich, "Microsoft Releases Results For NUads Format," *Marketing Magazine,* January 8, 2013; Rebecca Harris, "Subway Tries Interactive TV With Microsoft XBOX Ad," *Marketing Magazine,* September 26, 2012.

40. Tsai Chen and Hsiang-Ming Lee, "Why Do We Share? The Impact of Viral Videos Dramatized to Sell," *Journal of Advertising, 54* (3), September 2014, pp. 292–303.

41. Thales Teixeira, Rosalind Picard, and Rana el Kaliouby, "Why, When, and How Much to Entertain Consumers in Advertisements? A Web-Based Facial Tracking Field Study," *Management Science, 33* (6), November–December 2014, pp. 809–827.

42. David Allan, "A Content Analysis of Music Placement in Prime-Time Advertising," *Journal of Advertising Research, 48* (3), September 2008, pp. 404–414.

43. Russell I. Haley, Jack Richardson, and Beth Baldwin, "The Effects of Nonverbal Communications in Television Advertising," *Journal of Advertising Research, 24* (4), August–September 1984, pp. 11–18.

44. Gerald J. Gorn, "The Effects of Music in Advertising on Choice Behavior: A Classical Conditioning Approach," *Journal of Marketing, 46* (1), Winter 1982, pp. 94–100.

45. Steve Oakes, "Evaluating Empirical Research Into Music in Advertising: A Congruity Perspective," *Journal of Advertising Research, 47* (1), March 2007, pp. 38–50.

46. Susan Krashinsky, "Changing Their Tune," *The Globe and Mail,* July 13, 2012, p. B6.

47. Chris Powell, "Kijiji Puts the Raps on New Campaign," *Marketing Magazine,* October 7, 2015.

48. Linda M. Scott, "Understanding Jingles and Needledrop: A Rhetorical Approach to Music in Advertising," *Journal of Consumer Research, 17* (2), September 1990, pp. 223–236.

49. Jeromy Lloyd, "Swiss Chalet Blasts Back From the Past," *Marketing Magazine,* September 23, 2009.

50. Simon Houpt, "Poutine, Pussycats and Political Messages," *The Globe and Mail,* March 25, 2011, p. B6.

51. Chris Powell, "Astral Media Expands Its Audio Identity," *Marketing Magazine,* April 2009.

52. John Rossiter and Larry Percy, *Advertising Communications and Promotion Management* (New York: McGraw-Hill, 1996).

53. Christopher P. Puto and William D. Wells, "Informational and Transformational Advertising: The Different Effects of Time," in *Advances in Consumer Research, 11,* eds. Thomas C. Kinnear (Ann Arbor, MI: Association for Consumer Research, 1984), p. 638.

54. www.cassies.ca

CHAPTER NINE

1. Spike Cramphorn, "What Advertising Testing Might Have Been, If We Had Only Known," *Journal of Advertising Research, 44* (2), June 2004, pp. 1–2.

2. John M. Caffyn, "Telepex Testing of TV Commercials," *Journal of Advertising Research, 5* (2), June 1965, pp. 29–37; Thomas J. Reynolds and Charles Gengler, "A Strategic Framework for Assessing Advertising: The Animatic vs. Finished Issue," *Journal of Advertising Research, 31* (5), October/ November 1991, pp. 61–71; Nigel A. Brown and Ronald Gatty, "Rough vs. Finished TV Commercials in Telepex Tests," *Journal of Advertising Research, 7* (4), December 1967, p. 21.

3. Ye Hu, Leonard Lodish, Abba Krieger, and Babk Hayati, "An Update of Real-World TV Advertising Tests," *Journal of Advertising Research, 49* (2), June 2009, pp. 201–206.

4. Paul J. Watson and Robert J. Gatchel, "Autonomic Measures of Advertising," *Journal of Advertising Research, 19* (3), June 1979, pp. 15–26.

5. Priscilla A. LaBarbera and Joel D. Tucciarone, "GSR Reconsidered: A Behavior-Based Approach to Evaluating and Improving the Sales Potency of Advertising," *Journal of Advertising Research, 35* (5), September/ October 1995, pp. 33–40.

6. Flemming Hansen, "Hemispheric Lateralization: Implications for Understanding Consumer Behavior," *Journal of Consumer Research,* 8 (1), June 1988, pp. 23–36.

7. Jan Stapel, "Recall and Recognition: A Very Close Relationship," *Journal of Advertising Research,* 38 (4), July/August 1998, pp. 41–45.

8. Hubert A. Zielske, "Does Day-After Recall Penalize 'Feeling Ads'?" *Journal of Advertising Research,* 22 (1), February/March 1982, pp. 19–22.

9. Arthur J. Kover, "Why Copywriters Don't Like Advertising Research—And What Kind of Research Might They Accept," *Journal of Advertising Research,* 36 (2), March/April 1996, pp. RC8–RC10.

10. Dave Kruegel, "Television Advertising Effectiveness and Research Innovations," *Journal of Consumer Marketing,* 5 (3), Summer 1988, pp. 43–52.

11. John Philip Jones, "Single-Source Research Begins to Fulfill Its Promise," *Journal of Advertising Research,* 35 (3), May/June 1995, pp. 9–16.

12. James F. Donius, "Marketing Tracking: A Strategic Reassessment and Planning Tool," *Journal of Advertising Research,* 25 (1), February/March 1985, pp. 15–19.

13. "Positioning Advertising Copy-Testing," *Journal of Advertising,* 11 (4), 1982, pp. 3–29.

14. Ibid.

15. Russell I. Haley and Allan L. Baldinger, "The ARF Copy Research Validity Project," *Journal of Advertising Research,* 31 (2), April/May 1991, pp. 11–32.

CHAPTER TEN

1. William A. Cook and Vijay S. Talluri, "How the Pursuit of ROMI Is Changing Marketing Management," *Journal of Advertising Research,* 44 (3), September 2004, pp. 244–254; Joan Fitzgerald, "Evaluating Return on Investment of Multimedia Advertising With a Single-Source Panel: A Retail Case Study," *Journal of Advertising Research,* 44 (3), September 2004, pp. 262–270.

2. Chris Powell, "Talking Heads," *Marketing Magazine,* March 23, 2009.

3. Jennifer Wells, "Finding the There, There," *The Globe and Mail,* January 23, 2009, p. B6.

4. Carey Toane, "Integrated," *Strategy,* June 2009, p. 51.

5. Jonathan Paul, "Adidas Goes All In," *Strategy,* April 1, 2011, p. 12.

6. Mary Teresa Bitti, "Manage Your Message," *National Post,* July 7, 2009, FP7.

7. Jeromy Lloyd, "'Cough Sir' Redefined," *Marketing Magazine,* March 12, 2012.

8. Jenni Romaniuk, Virginia Beal, and Mark Uncles, "Achieving Reach in a Multi-Media Environment," *Journal of Advertising Research,* 53 (2), June 2013, pp. 221–230.

9. "Canada Increases Budget for Advertising to U.S. Tourists," *The Globe and Mail,* April 2, 2014, p. S2.

10. Kristin Laird, "Agencies Collaborate to Make Sport Chek More Inspiring," *Marketing Magazine,* August 29, 2012.

11. Marina Strauss, "Back-to-School Marketing Hits the Books Early," *The Globe and Mail,* August 10, 2009, p. B3.

12. Susan Krashinsky, "Advertisers Compete for the Online Podium," *The Globe and Mail,* July 2012, p. B6.

13. Michael J. Naples, *Effective Frequency: The Relationship Between Frequency and Advertising Effectiveness* (New York: Association of National Advertisers, 1979).

14. Joseph W. Ostrow, "Setting Frequency Levels: An Art or a Science?" *Journal of Advertising Research,* 24 (4), August/September 1984, pp. 9–11.

15. Hugh M. Cannon, John D. Leckenby, and Avery Abernethy, "Beyond Effective Frequency: Evaluating Media Schedules Using Frequency Value Planning," *Journal of Advertising Research,* 42 (6), November–December 2002, pp. 33–47.

16. William Havlena, Robert Cardarelli, and Michelle De Montigny, "Quantifying the Isolated and Synergistic Effects of Exposure Frequency for TV, Print, and Internet Advertising," *Journal of Advertising Research,* 47 (3), September 2007, pp. 215–221.

17. David A. Aaker and Phillip K. Brown, "Evaluating Vehicle Source Effects," *Journal of Advertising Research,* 12 (4), August 1972, pp. 11–16.

18. Joel N. Axelrod, "Induced Moods and Attitudes Toward Products," *Journal of Advertising Research,* 3 (2), June 1963, pp. 19–24; Lauren E. Crane, "How Product, Appeal, and Program Affect Attitudes Toward Commercials," *Journal of Advertising Research,* 4 (1), March 1964, p. 15.

19. Sara Rosengren and Micael Dahlen, "Judging a Magazine by Its Advertising," *Journal of Advertising Research,* 53 (1), March 2013, pp. 61–70.

20. Jennifer Horn, "AToMiC Awards: Brands Join the Band," *Strategy,* May 29, 2013.

21. Max Kilger and Ellen Romer, "Do Measures of Media Engagement Correlate With Product Purchase Likelihood?" *Journal of Advertising Research,* 47 (3), September 2007, pp. 313–325.

22. Kazuya Kusumot, "Affinity-Based Media Selection: Magazine Selection for Brand Message Absorption," *Journal of Advertising Research,* 42 (4), July–August 2002, pp. 54–65.

23. Susan Krashinsky, "Why Google Is Wooing Canada's Ad Agencies," *The Globe and Mail,* January 24, 2014, p. B5.

24. Yunjae Cheong, Federico de Gregorio, and Kihan Kim, "Advertising Spending Efficiency Among Top U.S. Advertisers From 1985 to 2012: Overspending or Smart Managing?" *Journal of Advertising,* 43 (4), 2014, pp. 344–358.

25. George S. Low and Jakki Mohr, "Setting Advertising and Promotion Budgets in Multi-Brand Companies," *Journal of Advertising Research,* 39 (1), January/February 1999, pp. 667–678.

26. Jody Harri and Kimberly A. Taylor, "The Case for Greater Agency Involvement in Strategic Partnerships," *Journal of Advertising Research,* 43 (4), December 2003, pp. 346–352.

27. Frank M. Bass, "A Simultaneous Equation Regression Study of Advertising and Sales of Cigarettes," *Journal of Marketing Research,* 6 (3), August 1969, p. 291; David A. Aaker and James M. Carman, "Are You Overadvertising?"

Journal of Advertising Research, 22 (4), August/September 1982, pp. 57–70.

28. Julian A. Simon and Johan Arndt, "The Shape of the Advertising Response Function," *Journal of Advertising Research,* 20 (4), August 1980, pp. 11–28.

29. Douglas West, John B. Ford, and Paul W. Farris, "How Corporate Cultures Drive Advertising and Promotion Budgets," *Journal of Advertising Research,* 54 (2), June 2014, pp. 149–162.

30. Boonghee Yoo and Rujirutana Mandhachitara, "Estimating Advertising Effects on Sales in a Competitive Setting," *Journal of Advertising Research,* 43 (3), August 2003, pp. 310–320.

31. James O. Peckham, "Can We Relate Advertising Dollars to Market Share Objectives?" in *How Much to Spend for Advertising,* ed. M. A. McNiven (New York: Association of National Advertisers, 1969), p. 30.

32. Hollie Shaw, "Canadian Tire Gets Aggressive on Digital," *National Post,* October 10, 2014, p. FP4.

33. http://cassies.ca/entry/viewcase/4468; http://cassies.ca/content/caselibrary/winners/2011_KNORR.pdf; http://cassies.ca/content/caselibrary/winners/2011_NISSAN.pdf.

34. Demetrios Vakratsas and Zhenfeng Ma, "A Look at the Long-Run Effectiveness of Multimedia Advertising and Its Implications for Budget Allocation Decisions," *Journal of Advertising Research,* 45 (2), June 2005, pp. 241–254.

35. David Berkowitz, Arthur Allaway, and Giles d'Souza, "The Impact of Differential Lag Effects on the Allocation of Advertising Budgets Across Media," *Journal of Advertising Research,* 41 (2), March/April 2001, pp. 27–36.

36. John P. Jones, "Ad Spending: Maintaining Market Share," *Harvard Business Review,* January/February 1990, pp. 38–42; James C. Schroer, "Ad Spending: Growing Market Share," *Harvard Business Review,* January/February 1990, pp. 44–48.

37. Randall S. Brown, "Estimating Advantages to Large-Scale Advertising," *Review of Economics and Statistics,* 60 (3), August 1978, pp. 428–437.

38. Kent M. Lancaster, "Are There Scale Economies in Advertising?" *Journal of Business,* 59 (3), 1986, pp. 509–526.

39. Johan Arndt and Julian Simon, "Advertising and Economics of Scale: Critical Comments on the Evidence," *Journal of Industrial Economics,* 32 (2), December 1983, pp. 229–241; Aaker and Carman, "Are You Overadvertising?"

40. George S. Low and Jakki J. Mohr, "The Budget Allocation Between Advertising and Sales Promotion: Understanding the Decision Process," *1991 AMA Educators' Proceedings,* Chicago, Summer 1991, pp. 448–457.

CHAPTER ELEVEN

1. John Doyle, "Watch How You Want: TV Is Still the Future," *The Globe and Mail,* May 21, 2012, p. R3.

2. TV Basics 2014–2015, Television Bureau of Canada website (www.tvb.ca), p. 28.

3. Kristin Laird, "Shaw Across the Bow," *Marketing Magazine,* March 14, 2011, p. 12.

4. Jamie Sturgeon, "Building Outside the Box," *National Post,* May 14, 2011, p. FP1.

5. Chris Powell, "Tetley Introduces *Pitch Perfect* Campaign," *Marketing Magazine,* December 4, 2015.

6. Hollie Shaw, "Yum, Yum: Loblaw Cooks Up Some Branding Subtleties," *National Post,* December 2, 2011, p. FP12.

7. Steve Ladurantaye, "Rogers' New Reality Show: Canada's Next Broadcast Strategy," *The Globe and Mail,* April 6, 2012, p. B1.

8. Jim Kiriakakis, "Branded Entertainment Is Not an Ad," *Strategy,* July 2014.

9. Val Maloney, "The New Partners," *Strategy,* July 2014.

10. TV Basics 2014–2015, Television Bureau of Canada website (www.tvb.ca), p. 29.

11. TV Basics 2014–2015, Television Bureau of Canada website (www.tvb.ca), p. 30.

12. TV Basics 2014–2015, Television Bureau of Canada website (www.tvb.ca), p. 30.

13. Media Digest 2015–2016, Canadian Media Director's Council, p. 19.

14. "Choose Your Own Adventure: Specialty TV Edition," *Strategy,* July 2014.

15. Kristin Laird, "Brick Puts Red Baron on TV for First Time," *Marketing Magazine,* January 5, 2010.

16. Val Maloney, "Prime Time Face Off," *Strategy,* July 2014; "Shaw Media Gets Dramatic," *Strategy,* July 2014.

17. Emily Wexler, "The Little Orphan That Could," *Strategy,* July 2014.

18. Simon Houpt, "Where Did the Kids Go?" *The Globe and Mail,* June 16, 2012, p. R12.

19. Robert J. Kent, "Second-by-Second Looks at the Television Commercial Audience," *Journal of Advertising Research, 42* (1), January–February 2002, pp. 71–78.

20. John Doyle, "In Praise of Commercials, Sort Of," *The Globe and Mail,* July 25, 2012, p. R3.

21. Media Technology Monitor, Off-Air and Tuned Out, April 2016.

22. TV Basics 2014–2015, Television Bureau of Canada website (www.tvb.ca), p. 29.

23. ThinkTV, Reach and Time Spent by Age, Broadcast Year 2015.

24. Susan Krashinsky, "Why Most Super Bowl Ads Get Stopped at the Border," *The Globe and Mail,* February 3, 2012, p. B8.

25. Ibid.

26. Kate Lynch and Horst Stipp, "Examination of Qualitative Viewing Factors of Optimal Advertising Strategies," *Journal of Advertising Research, 39* (3), May–June 1999, pp. 7–16.

27. Stephen Stanley and Carey Toane, "NFLD Tourism: Target Truly Transports You," *Marketing Magazine,* June 2009, p. 50.

28. Stephen Stanley and Carey Toane, "Subaru: DDB's Sumos Get Sexy," *Marketing Magazine,* June 2009, p. 50.

29. John J. Cronin, "In-Home Observations of Commercial Zapping Behavior," *Journal of Current Issues and Research in Advertising, 17* (2), Fall 1995, pp. 69–75.

30. Paul Surgi Speck and Michael T. Elliot, "Predictors of Advertising Avoidance in Print and Broadcast Media," *Journal of Advertising, 26* (3), Fall 1997, pp. 61–76.

31. Carrie Heeter and Bradley S. Greenberg, "Profiling the Zappers," *Journal of Advertising Research, 25* (2), April/May 1985, pp. 9–12; Fred S. Zufryden, James H. Pedrick, and Avu Sandaralingham, "Zapping and Its Impact on Brand Purchase Behavior," *Journal of Advertising Research, 33* (1), January/February 1993, pp. 58–66.

32. Lex van Meurs, "Zapp! A Study on Switching Behavior During Commercial Breaks," *Journal of Advertising Research, 38* (1), January/February 1998, pp. 43–53.

33. Alan Ching Biu Tse and Rub P w. Lee, "Zapping Behaviour During Commercial Breaks," *Journal of Advertising Research, 41* (3), May/June 2001, pp. 25–29.

34. TV Basics 2014–2015, Television Bureau of Canada website (www.tvb.ca), p. 21.

35. TV Basics 2014–2015, Television Bureau of Canada website (www.tvb.ca), p. 21.

36. Kenneth C. Wilbur, "How the Digital Video Recorder (DVR) Changes Traditional Television Advertising," *Journal of Advertising, 37* (1), Spring 2008, pp. 143–149.

37. Cristel Antonia Russell and Christopher P. Puto, "Rethinking Television Audience Measures: An Exploration Into the Construct of Audience Connectedness," *Marketing Letters, 10* (4), August 1999, pp. 393–407.

38. Kristin Laird, "Corus Begins Simple Pleasures Campaign for Dare," *Marketing Magazine,* July 20, 2009.

39. Linda F. Alwitt and Parul R. Prabhaker, "Identifying Who Dislikes Television Advertising: Not by Demographics Alone," *Journal of Advertising Research, 32* (5), September–October 1992, pp. 30–42.

40. Banwari Mittal, "Public Assessment of TV Advertising: Faint Praise and Harsh Criticism," *Journal of Advertising Research, 34* (1), January–February 1994, pp. 35–53; Ernest F. Larkin, "Consumer Perceptions of the Media and Their Advertising Content," *Journal of Advertising, 8* (2), Spring 1979, pp. 5–7.

41. Lucy L. Henke, "Young Children's Perceptions of Cigarette Brand Advertising Symbols: Awareness, Affect, and Target Market Identification," *Journal of Advertising, 24* (4), Winter 1995, pp. 13–28.

42. Media Digest 2015–2016, Canadian Media Director's Council, p. 19.

43. Ibid.

44. Ibid.

45. http://www.crtc.gc.ca/eng/tv_radio.htm.

46. Media Technology Monitor, Audio Streaming, Anglo, April 2015.

47. Radio Engagement in Canada, October 2012, Vision Critical, radioahead.ca

48. Emily Wexler, "Radio," *Strategy,* June 2009, p. 46.

49. Magazines Canada, Consumer Magazine Fact Book 2015.

50. Avery Abernethy, "Differences Between Advertising and Program Exposure for Car Radio Listening," *Journal of Advertising Research, 31* (2), April/May 1991, pp. 33–42.

51. Brian Dunn, "Boston Pizza Promotes Specials With Radio Spots," *Marketing Magazine,* April 13, 2009.

52. Carey Toane, "James Ready Shares the Radio Waves," *Strategy,* June 2009, p. 8.

53. Ibid.

CHAPTER TWELVE

1. Herbert E. Krugman, "The Measurement of Advertising Involvement," *Public Opinion Quarterly, 30* (4), Winter 1966–67, pp. 583–596.

2. Media Digest 2015–2016, pp. 119 and 137.

3. Jeff Hayward, "Gloss Leaders," *Marketing Magazine,* June 4, 2012, pp. 30–36.

4. Magazines Canada, A Comparison of Canada and USA 2014, page 9.

5. Chris Powell, "Alliance for Audited Media to Measure Multi-Platform Media," *Marketing Magazine,* February 3, 2016.

6. Chris Powell, "Magazines Canada Wants Canadians to Share the Love," *Marketing Magazine,* March 1, 2016.

7. http://www.cardonline.ca/listings/14058.jsf.

8. Magazines Canada, Consumer Magazine Fact Book 2015, p. 32.

9. Ibid.

10. Magazines Canada, Consumer Magazine Fact Book 2015, p. 30.

11. http://cardonline.ca/listings/14345.jsf.

12. Chris Powell, "*Hello!*'s Rising Star," *Marketing Magazine,* April 6, 2009.

13. http://cardonline.ca/listings/13639.jsf; Media Digest, Canadian Media Director's Council, 2012–2013, p. 70.

14. Alica Androich, "Canada's Magazines Aren't Doomed," *Marketing Magazine,* May 16, 2011, pp. 26–29, 31–32.

15. Doug Bennet, "How Many City Magazines Does Toronto Actually Need?" *Marketing Magazine,* May 16, 2011.

16. Magazines Canada, Consumer Magazine Fact Book 2015, p. 32.

17. Magazines Canada, Consumer Magazine Fact Book 2015, p. 49.

18. Magazines Canada, Consumer Magazine Fact Book 2015, p. 25.

19. Magazines Canada, Consumer Magazine Fact Book 2012, p. 48.

20. Magazines Canada, Consumer Magazine Fact Book 2012, p. 45.

21. Chris Powell, "*Maclean's* Opens Up for Audi," *Marketing Magazine,* April 1, 2009.

22. Jonathan Paul, "Cundari's Camo *Vice* Cover Ad," *Strategy,* June 2009, p. 47.

23. "Crunch," *Marketing Magazine,* May 16, 2011, p. 46.

24. Tom Gierasimczuk, "Where the Young Readers Are," *Marketing Magazine,* May 16, 2011, p. 30.

25. Magazines Canada, Consumer Magazine Fact Book 2015, page 21.

26. Magazines Canada, Consumer Magazine Fact Book 2015, p. 38.

27. Magazines Canada, Consumer Magazine Fact Book 2012, p. 38.

28. Magazines Canada, Consumer Magazine Fact Book 2012, p. 39.

29. Media Digest, Canadian Media Director's Council, 2015–2016, p. 118.

30. http://mediakit.nationalpost.com/newspaper/reaching-your-audience/

31. http://globelink.ca/readership/.

32. Steve Ladurantaye, "Slow Online Ad Sales Hurt Publishers," *The Globe and Mail,* May 10, 2012, p. B6.

33. Susan Krashinsky and Simon Houpt, "The Battle for the Digital Newsstand," *The Globe and Mail,* February 26, 2011, p. B6.

34. Chris Powell, "Custom Takes Off," *Marketing Magazine*, June 4, 2012.

35. Marina Strauss, "Canadian Tire on Top of Digital Game," *The Globe and Mail*, May 9, 2014, p. B.9.

36. Kristin Laird, "Molson Is in the Fridge for Christmas Promo," *Marketing Magazine*, December 11, 2009.

37. Jason Dubroy, "In Defence of the Flyer," *Strategy*, May 2015.

38. Newspapers Canada, Connecting to Canadians With Community Newspapers 2013.

39. Chris Powell, "Postmedia Announces Strategic Partnership With Mogo," *Marketing Magazine*, January 25, 2016.

40. Magazines Canada, Consumer Magazine Fact Book 2012, pp. 59, 60.

41. Magazines Canada, Consumer Magazine Fact Book 2012, pp. 73, 74.

CHAPTER THIRTEEN

1. Mukesh Bhargava and Naveen Donthu, "Sales Response to Outdoor Advertising," *Journal of Advertising Research*, 39 (4), August 1999, pp. 7–18.

2. Rae Ann Fera, "Apotek: Interactive Billboard," *Marketing Magazine*, May 2014.

3. Charles R. Taylor, George R. Franke, and Hae-Kyong Bang, "Use and Effectiveness of Billboards," *Journal of Advertising*, 35 (4), Winter 2006, pp. 21–34.

4. Lex Van Meurs and Mandy Aristoff, "Split-Second Recognition: What Makes Outdoor Advertising Work?" *Journal of Advertising Research*, 49 (1), March 2009, pp. 82–92.

5. Chris Powell, "Dundas Square to Get Creamed by Cadbury," *Marketing Magazine*, February 25, 2009.

6. Jonathan Paul, "Media Merchants Ninja," *Strategy*, July 2009, p. 7.

7. Hollie Shaw, "Driving the Message," *National Post*, March 20, 2009, p. FP12.

8. Chris Powell, "Out-of-Home Run," *Marketing Magazine*, April 24, 2011, p. 11.

9. Susan Krashinsky, "Ads That Reach Out to the Passing Pedestrians," *The Globe and Mail*, February 28, 2012, p. B3.

10. Day in the Life Study accessed at omaccanada.ca

11. David Chilton, "Eying Outdoors," *Marketing Magazine*, October 26, 2006.

12. Jeromy Lloyd, "Next Stop," *Marketing Magazine*, August 1, 2011, p. 7.

13. Emily Wexler, "Getting Cadbury More Face Time," *Strategy*, March 1, 2009, p. 20.

14. David Brown, "Pattison Debuts Flexity Streetcar Ad for Volvo," *Marketing Magazine*, March 16, 2016.

15. Brenda Bouw, "Telus Gives B.C. Bus Commuters Free Wi-Fi," *Marketing Magazine*, August 21, 2014.

16. Susan Krashinsky, "An Advertising Concept Takes Viewers for a Ride," *The Globe and Mail*, July 3, 2012, p. B3.

17. Emily Wexler, "Travel Alberta's Subway Slopes," *Strategy*, January 2009, p. 8.

18. Jeromy Lloyd, "In-Flight Magazine Smack-Down," *Marketing Magazine*, November 28, 2011, p. 15.

19. Cineplex Annual Report 2014.

20. Chris Powell, "Cineplex Gets Its Game Face On," *Marketing Magazine*, January 12, 2016.

21. Joanna Phillips and Stephanie M. Noble, "Simply Captivating: Understanding Consumers' Attitudes Toward the Cinema as an Advertising Medium," *Journal of Advertising*, 36 (10), Spring 2007, pp. 81–94.

22. Jeromy Lloyd, "Toyota's Cinema Spot 20 Years in the Making," *Marketing Magazine*, December 22, 2009.

23. Rick T. Wilson and Brian D. Till, "Airport Advertising Effectiveness," *Journal of Advertising*, 37 (1), Spring 2008, pp. 59–72.

24. Jonathan Paul, "Lexus RX's Touch Screen Touchdown at Airport," *Strategy*, June 2009, p. 22.

25. Theras Wood, "See Me, Touch Me, Feel Me," *Strategy*, June 3, 2011, p. 34.

26. Susan Krashinsky, "Targeted Ads to Be Shown at Health-Care Facilities," *The Globe and Mail*, February 18, 2015, p. B.7.

27. Jeff Fraser, "Big Digital Wants to Make Event Signage Beautiful," *Marketing Magazine*, April 20, 2015.

28. Michael A. Belch and Don Sciglimpaglia, "Viewers' Evaluations of Cinema Advertising," Proceedings of the American Institute for Decision Sciences, March 1979, pp. 39–43.

29. "Catch a Commercial at the Movies," *Center for Media Research*, October 29, 2007.

30. Phillips and Noble, "Simply Captivating."

31. http://www.promocan.com

32. Kristin Laird, "Sweetish," *Marketing Magazine*, September 12, 2011, p. 14.

33. Suzanne Dansereau, "How Some Canadian Entrepreneurs Are Using Red Carpet Celebrity Events as a Powerful Marketing Tool," *National Post*, February 22, 2015.

34. 2013 Promotional Products Industry Sales Volume Study, Promotional Products Association of Canada, November 2013.

35. http://www.ppai.org/

36. http://www.ppai.org/inside-ppai/research/research-summaries

37. http://www.pqmedia.com/about-press-20150615.html

38. Michael Belch and Cristel A. Russell, "A Managerial Investigation Into the Product Placement Industry," *Journal of Advertising Research*, 45 (1), March 2005, pp. 73–92.

39. Carrie La Ferle and Steven M. Edwards, "Product Placement," *Journal of Advertising*, 35 (4), Winter 2006, pp. 65–89.

40. Michael A. Wiles and Anna Danielova, "The Worth of Product Placement in Successful Films: An Event Study Analysis," *Journal of Marketing*, 73 (4), July 2009, pp. 44–63.

41. Ekaterina V. Karniouchina, Can Uslay, and Grigori Erenburg, "Do Marketing Media Have Life Cycles? The Case of Product Placement in Movies," *Journal of Marketing*, 35 (3), May 2011, pp. 27–48.

42. Simon Houpt, "Why Timbits Aren't Likely to Drive the Plot of *The Border*," *The Globe and Mail*, August 21, 2009, p. B4.

43. Susan Krashinsky, "*Mad Men* Serves Canadian Club a Bracer," *The Globe and Mail*, April 20, 2012, p. B7.

44. Siva K. Balasubramanian, James A. Karrh, and Hemant Patwardhan, "Audience Response to Product Placements," *Journal of Advertising*, 35 (3), Fall 2006, pp. 115–141.

45. Carrie La Ferle and Steven M. Edwards, "Product Placement," *Journal of Advertising*, 35 (4), Winter 2006, pp. 65–89.

46. Susan Krashinsky, "He Shoots—and the Advertisers Score!" *The Globe and Mail*, April 21, 2011.

47. La Ferle and Edwards, "Product Placement."

48. Ibid.

49. Kristin Laird, "Beam Me Up, Bombardier," *Marketing Magazine*, December 12, 2011, p. 11.

50. Harsha Gagadharbatla and Terry Daugherty, "Advertising Versus Product Placements: How Consumers Assess the Value of Each," *Journal of Current Issue & Research in Advertising*, 34 (1), 2013, pp. 21–38.

51. Jennifer Wells, "The Right Breaks at the Right Time," *The Globe and Mail*, May 29, 2009, p. B5.

52. Chris Powell, "Shaw Announces Brand Sponsors For Home Show to Win," *Marketing Magazine*, September 17, 2016.

53. Kristin Laird, "Money for Nothing," *Marketing Magazine*, September 12, 2011, p. 11.

54. Peter Nowak and Jeromy Lloyd, "Press Start," *Marketing Magazine*, January 24, 2011, pp. 24, 26, 28, 31–32.

55. Pola Gupta and Kenneth Lord, "Product Placement in Movies: The Effect of Prominence and Mode on Audience Recall," *Journal of Current Issues and Research in Advertising*, 20 (1), Spring 1998, pp. 1–29.

56. Pola B. Gupta and Stephen J. Gould, "Consumers' Perceptions of the Ethics and Acceptability of Product Placements in Movies: Product Category and Individual Differences," *Journal of Current Issues and Research in Advertising*, 19 (1), Spring 1997, pp. 40–49.

CHAPTER FOURTEEN

1. Robert C. Blattberg and Scott A. Neslin, *Sales Promotion: Concepts, Methods and Strategies*, (Englewood Cliffs, New Jersey, Prentice Hall, 1990).

2. Pierre Chandon, Brian Wansink, and Gilles Laurent, "A Benefit Congruency Framework of Sales Promotion Effectiveness," *Journal of Marketing*, 64 (4), October 2000, pp. 65–81.

3. Esmeralda Crespo-Amendros and Salvador Del Barrio-Garcia, "The Quality of Inter-User Recall," *Journal of Advertising Research*, 54 (1), March 2014, pp. 56–70.

4. Judith A. Garretson and Scot Burton, "Highly Coupon and Sales Prone Consumers: Benefits Beyond Price Savings," *Journal of Advertising Research*, 43 (3), June 2003, pp. 162–172.

5. Scott A. Nielsen, John Quelch, and Caroline Henderson, "Consumer Promotions and the Acceleration of Product Purchases," in *Research on Sales Promotion: Collected Papers*, ed. Katherine E. Jocz (Cambridge, MA: Marketing Science Institute, 1984).

6. J. Jeffrey Inman and Leigh McAlister, "Do Coupon Expiration Dates Affect Consumer Behavior?" *Journal of Marketing Research*, 31 (3), August 1994, pp. 423–428.

7. Melinda Mattos, "Nivea Pops Up for 100th Anniversary," *Strategy,* May 1, 2011, p. 10.

8. Leonard M. Lodish and Carl F. Mela, "If Brands Are Built Over Years, Why Are They Managed Over Quarters?" *Harvard Business Review,* July–August 2007, pp. 104–112.

9. Robert C. Blattberg and Scott A. Neslin, *Sales Promotion: Concepts, Methods and Strategies,* (Englewood Cliffs, New Jersey, Prentice Hall, 1990).

10. Adapted from Terrence A. Shimp, *Advertising, Promotion, and Supplemental Aspect of Integrated Marketing Communication,* 4th ed. (Fort Worth, TX: Dryden Press, 1997), p. 487.

11. Brian C. Deslauriers and Peter B. Everett, "The Effects of Intermittent and Continuous Token Reinforcement on Bus Ridership," *Journal of Applied Psychology, 62* (4), August 1977, pp. 9–75.

12. Michael L. Rothschild and William C. Gaidis, "Behavioural Learning Theory: Its Relevance to Marketing and Promotions," *Journal of Marketing, 45* (2), Spring 1981, pp. 70–78.

13. Kristin Laird, "McDonald's Serves Up Fresh, Free Coffee for All," *Marketing Magazine,* April 20, 2009.

14. Jonathan Paul, "HarperCollins Opens Eyes and Ears," *Strategy,* November 2009, p. 80.

15. Carrie Heilman, Kyryl Lakishyk, and Sonya Radas, "An Empirical Investigation of In-Store Sampling Promotions," *British Food Journal, 113* (10), 2011, pp. 1252–1266.

16. Jerry Langton, "Economics of the Humble Coupon," *Toronto Star,* July 7, 2008.

17. "Fine Print: Extreme Couponing as a Canadian Sport," *Sympatico,* November 12, 2011.

18. Inman and McAlister, "Do Coupon Expiration Dates Affect Consumer Behavior?"

19. Juliano Laran and Michael Tsiros, "An Investigation of the Effectiveness of Uncertainty in Marketing Promotions Involving Free Gifts," *Journal of Marketing, 77* (March), 2013, pp. 112–123.

20. Gerard P. Prendergast, Derek T. Y. Poon, Alex S. L. Tsang, and Ting Yan Fan, "Predicting Deal Proneness," *Journal of Advertising Research, 48* (2), June 2008, pp. 287–296.

21. Susan Krashinsky, "Sticky Symbols," *The Globe and Mail,* October 17, 2014.

22. Susan Krashinsky, "What's in a Name? Sales, Coke Hopes," *The Globe and Mail,* July 1, 2014, p. B5.

23. Ty Henderson and Neeraj Arora, "Promoting Brands Across Categories With a Social Cause: Implementing Effective Embedded Premium Programs," *Journal of Marketing, 74* (November), 2010, pp. 41–60.

24. Wayne Mouland, "Sweeping Up Additional Sales," *Marketing Magazine,* October 6, 2003.

25. Garine Tcholakina, "Honda Drives Civic Nation Mix-Off," *Strategy,* November 2009, p. 40.

26. Jonathan Paul, "Life's Good, But LG Thinks It's Better in HD," *Strategy,* September 2009, p. 8.

27. Denise Ryan, "Can You Brand the West Coast?" *National Post,* November 16, 2009, p. B16.

28. Brenda Pritchard and Susan Vogt, *Advertising and Marketing Law in Canada* (LexisNexis, Butterworths, 2006).

29. Peter Tat, William A. Cunningham III, and Emin Babakus, "Consumer Perceptions of Rebates," *Journal of Advertising Research, 28* (4), August/September 1988, pp. 45–50.

30. Haipeng Chen, Howard Marmorstein, Michael Tsiros, and Akshay R. Rao, "When More Is Less: The Impact of Base Value Neglect on Consumer Preferences for Bonus Packs Over Price Discounts," *Journal of Marketing, 76* (July), 2012, pp. 64–77.

31. Edward A. Blair and E. Lair Landon, "The Effects of Reference Prices in Retail Advertisements," *Journal of Marketing, 45* (2), Spring 1981, pp. 61–69.

32. Marina Strauss and Jeff Gray, "Mattress Discounts at Sears, Hudson Bay Under Review," *The Globe and Mail,* February 23, 2015, p. B1.

33. Kristin Laird, "Milestones Wants to Make Dates," *Marketing Magazine,* April 28, 2009.

34. James Adams, "Who Gets the Biggest Piece of the Digital Pie?" *The Globe and Mail,* February 28, 2009.

35. Greg Keenan, "Saving the Civic," *The Globe and Mail,* February 15, 2011, p. B1.

36. Katie Bailey, "Swiss Chalet Roasts With Rogers," *Strategy,* May 1, 2011, p. 9.

37. Lia Zarantonello and Bernd H. Schmitt, "The Impact of Event Marketing on Brand Equity," *International Journal of Advertising, 32* (5), pp. 255–280.

38. Rae Ann Fera, "Get the Most Out of VR," *Marketing Magazine,* January 2015.

39. Kristin Laird, "Perrier Goes Clubbing in Toronto," *Marketing Magazine,* November 27, 2009.

40. http://www.newswire.ca/en/story/1024845/ ice-cross-downhill-charges-into-canada-with -two-races-in-the-true-north; http://www.newswire.ca/en/story/1130527/ switzerland-s-derek-wedge-takes-ice-cross- downhill -win-in-quebec-city-in-season-finale; http://www.newswire.ca/en/story/1066133/ ice-cross-downhill-crashes-into-niagara-falls -for-a-thrilling-2013-season-opener; http://www.redbull.com.

41. Jonathan Paul, "Promotion," *Strategy,* June 2009, p. 443.

42. Paul N. Bloom, Gregory T. Gundlach, and Joseph P. Cannon, "Slotting Allowances and Fees: Schools of Thought and Views of Practicing Managers," *Journal of Marketing, 64* (2), April 2000, pp. 92–108.

43. http://www.popai.com/engage/docs/ Media-Topline-Final.pdf

44. Marina Strauss, "The Fight to Set Prices," *The Globe and Mail,* March 7, 2014, p. B1.

45. Scot Burton, Donald R. Lichtenstein, and Richard G. Netemeyer, "Exposure to Sales Flyers and Increased Purchases in Retail Supermarkets," *Journal of Advertising Research, 39* (5), September–October 1999, pp. 7–14.

46. http://www.ceir.org/ ceir-breaking-news-2015-exhibition-industry- census-now-available

47. Srinath Gopalakrishna, Gary L. Lilien, Jerome D. Williams, and Ian K. Sequeria, "Do Trade Shows Pay Off?" *Journal of Marketing, 38* (3), July 1995, pp. 75–83.

48. Priya Raghubir and Kim Corfman, "When Do Price Promotions Affect Pretrial Brand Evaluations?" *Journal of Marketing Research, 36* (2), May 1999, pp. 211–222.

49. Elizabeth Gardner and Minakshi Trivedi, "A Communications Framework to Evaluate Sales Promotion Strategies," *Journal of Advertising Research, 38* (3), May/June 1998, pp. 67–71.

CHAPTER FIFTEEN

1. Raymond Simon, *Public Relations, Concept and Practices,* 2nd ed. (Columbus, OH: Grid Publishing, 1980), p. 8.

2. Mary Teresa Bitti, "The New Mad Men: PR's Makeover," *National Post,* December 29, 2014, p. FP.7.

3. John Heinzl, "Tims v. Mickey D's," *The Globe and Mail,* November 30, 2011, p. B15.

4. Scott M. Cutlip, Allen H. Center, and Glen M. Broom, *Effective Public Relations,* 11th ed. (Upper Saddle River, N.J.: Prentice Hall, 2012).

5. Cutlip, Center, and Broom, *Effective Public Relations.*

6. Tanya Kostiw, "Battle Strategies for Besieged Brands," *Strategy,* April 28, 2014.

7. Susan Krashinsky, "Marriage Proposal Video a Boon for Tim Hortons," *The Globe and Mail,* May 29, 2014.

8. "Home Depot Keeps It Close to Home," *Strategy,* April 2015.

9. Simon Houpt, "BMO Finds Fertile Sponsorship Ground on the Soccer Pitch," *The Globe and Mail,* March 31, 2011.

10. http://www.marketwired.com/press-release/ have-a-heart-this-valentines-day-at- boston-pizza-1988608.htm, February 4, 2015.

11. Melinda Mattos, "Bringing CSR Into Focus," *Strategy,* May 1, 2011, p. 20.

12. Wing Sze Tang, "Selling Eco Creed," *Marketing Magazine,* April 2014.

13. Daniel Leblanc, "Medical Pot Grower Lobby Ottawa to Shut Down Post Dispensaries," *The Globe and Mail,* January 21, 2016.

14. Carol Neshevich, "Royal Bank of Canada," *Marketing Magazine,* November 28, 2011, pp. 35, 40.

15. Emily Wexler, "Bell Tackles Tough Topic," *Strategy,* May 1, 2011, p. 31; www.letstalk.bell.

16. Carey Toane, "Overall Winner: Cisco's One Million Acts of Green," *Strategy,* May 2009, p. 30.

17. Susan Krashinsky, "Fantasy Cars for Real-Life Drivers," *The Globe and Mail,* February 17, 2012, p. B6.

18. Thomas L. Harris, "How MPR Adds Value to Integrated Marketing Communications," *Public Relations Quarterly, 38* (2), Summer 1993, pp. 13–18.

19. http://www.ikea.com/ms/en_CA/about_ikea/ press_room/press_release/national/ sleep_newsrelease.html

20. Hollie Shaw, "GM Reinvented," *National Post,* June 26, 2009, p. FP10.

21. Jonathan Paul, "Childlike Fascination Insightful for Honda," *Strategy,* May 2009, p. 19.

22. "Toyota Launches Ad Blitz to Reassure Customers," *Marketing Magazine,* February 1, 2010; "*Marketing's* Q&A: Toyota Boss Talks Brand Re-Building After Massive Recall," *Marketing Magazine,* February 2, 2010;

"Toyota Canada Launches Campaign to Distance Itself From U.S. Problems," *Marketing Magazine,* February 23, 2010.

23. Jennifer Horn, "Cause + Action Awards 2014," *Strategy,* May 2014, p. A24.

24. Mark Weiner, "Marketing PR Revolution," *Communication World,* January/February 2005, pp. 1–5.

25. Walter K. Lindenmann, "An Effectiveness Yardstick to Measure Public Relations Success," *Public Relations Quarterly, 38* (1), Spring 1993, pp. 7–10.

26. http://www.multivu.com/players/English/7782651-fairmont-luxury-insights/

27. Linda Smith, "When the Trust Begins to Rust," *Marketing Magazine,* March 1, 2004.

28. Chris Daniels, "Best Brand Reputation in 2015," *Marketing Magazine,* June/July 2015.

29. Siri Agrell, "Ads Aim to Win Hearts, Change Minds," *The Globe and Mail,* June 22, 2011, p. A6.

30. Kristin Laird, "IBM's Smart Conversation With CBC, CANWEST," *Marketing Magazine,* September 15, 2009.

31. Claudia Cattaneo, "Gas Industry on Fracking Offensive," *National Post,* May 28, 2011, p. FP3; Mark Hume, Enbridge Ads Intensify Pipeline Battle," *The Globe and Mail,* May 30, 2012, p. S1.

32. Harvey Meyer, "When the Cause Is Just," *Journal of Business Strategy, 20* (6), November/December 1999, pp. 27–31.

33. Jennier Horn, "Cause + Action Awards 2015," *Strategy,* April 2015, pp. A22.

34. Josh Kolm, "Cause Engagement by the Numbers," *Strategy,* April 2015, p. A9.

35. Katie Bailey, "Becel to Debut *The Heart* at Oscars," *Strategy,* February 25, 2010; Emily Wexler, "Becel's Margaret McKellar: Marketing With Heart," *Strategy,* June 2009, p. 18; Carey Toane, "Top Health Awareness Program: Becel's Heart Truth," *Strategy,* May 2009, p. 37.

36. Emily Wexler, "Virgin Re*Generates," *Strategy,* January 2009, p. 8.

37. Kristin Laird, "Kraft Has a Recipe for Joy," *Marketing Magazine,* December 18, 2009.

38. Emily Wexler, "Indigo Fights Illiteracy With Squirrel Power," *Strategy,* November 2009, p. 90.

39. Carey Toane, "For the Creative Good," *Strategy,* June 3, 2011, p. 24; Emily Wexler, "Cadbury Cycles Change," *Strategy,* May 1, 2011, p. 28.

40. Mathew Chung, "Cadbury's Light-Generating Bikes," *Strategy,* June 2014, p. 8.

41. Jennier Horn, "Cause + Action Awards 2015," *Strategy,* April 2015, p. A22.

42. Phillip Haid, "Stop Telling Me to Be Good," *Strategy,* April 2015, p. A48.

43. IEG's Guide to Sponsorship accessed at www.sponsorship.com.

44. T. Bettina Cornwall, Donald P. Roy, and Edward A. Steinard II, "Exploring Managers' Perceptions of the Impact of Sponsorship on Brand Equity," *Journal of Advertising, 30* (2), Summer 2001, pp. 41–51.

45. Kirk L. Wakefield, Karen Becker-Olsen, and T. Bettina Cornwell, "I Spy a Sponsor," *Journal of Advertising, 36* (4), Winter 2007, pp. 61–74.

46. Julie A. Ruth and Bernard L. Simonin, "Brought to You by Brand A and Brand B," *Journal of Advertising, 32* (3), Fall 2003, pp. 19–30; Julie A. Ruth and Bernard L. Simonin, "The Power of Numbers," *Journal of Advertising, 35* (4), Winter 2006, pp. 7–20.

47. Merel Walraven, Tammo H. A. Bijmolt, and Ruun H. Koning, "Dynamic Effects of Sponsoring: How Sponsorship Awareness Develops Over Time," *Journal of Advertising, 43* (2), Summer 2014, pp. 142–154.

48. Simon Houpt and David Shoalts, "For Molson, Hockey's a Springboard to U.S.," *The Globe and Mail,* July 13, 2011, p. B1.

49. http://www.sponsorshipmarketing.ca/50; Susan Krashinsky, "Planes, Trains, and Banking Machines," *The Globe and Mail,* February 13, 2015, p. B4.

50. Susan Krashinsky, "Planes, Trains, and Banking Machines," *The Globe and Mail,* February 13, 2015, p. B4.

51. Simon Houpt, "BMO Finds Fertile Sponsorship Ground on the Soccer Pitch," *The Globe and Mail,* March 31, 2011.

52. Mark Harrison, "Own Alone," *Marketing Magazine,* February 23, 2004.

53. Rachel Brady, "Lowry Embraces the North With Sport Chek Sponsorship," *The Globe and Mail,* February 10, 2015.

54. Susan Krashinsky, "MLB, NHL, NFL and NBA: Pepsi's Pro-Sport Domination," *The Globe and Mail,* April 14, 2015.

55. Susan Krashinsky, "Olympic Committee Looks to Force the North Face Out of the Village," *The Globe and Mail,* January 17, 2014, p. B1.

56. Susan Krashinsky, "Olympic Committee Takes Issue With Labatt Hockey Ad," *The Globe and Mail,* February 10, 2014, p. B5.

57. Angeline G. Close and Russell Lacey, "How the Anticipation Can Be as Great as the Experience: Explaining Event Sponsorship Exhibit Outcomes via Affective Forecasting," *Journal of Current Issues & Research in Advertising, 35,* pp. 209–224.

58. Bettina Cornwell and Isabelle Maignan, "An International Review of Sponsorship Research," *Journal of Advertising, 27* (1), Spring 1998, pp. 1–21.

59. Michel Tuan Pham, "The Evaluation of Sponsorship Effectiveness: A Model and Some Methodological Considerations," *Gestion 2000, 8* (4), July–August 1991, pp. 47–65.

60. Bill Harvey, Stu Gray, and Gerald Despain, "Measuring the Effectiveness of True Sponsorship," *Journal of Advertising Research, 46* (4), December 2006, pp. 398–409.

61. Jennifer Horn, "Cause + Action Awards 2015," *Strategy,* April 2015, p. A22.

62. Jennifer Horn, "Cause + Action Awards 2014," *Strategy,* May 2014, p. A24.

CHAPTER SIXTEEN

1. Bob Stone and Ron Jacobs, *Successful Direct Marketing Methods* (New York, McGraw-Hill, 2010).

2. Jeff Fraser, "Leads Can Now Sign Up for More Info Within Facebook Ads," *Marketing Magazine,* October 13, 2015.

3. Erin Anderssen, "You Can Run From Big Data...," *The Globe and Mail,* October 3, 2014, p. L1.

4. Susan Krashinsky, "Big Data Rewards Come With Tricky Set of Risks," *The Globe and Mail,* November 3, 2014, p. B3.

5. Rebecca Harris, "Knowing What They'll Do Next," *Marketing Magazine,* October 2014, pp. 12–13.

6. Sarah Dobson, "Knorr Says 'Frozen' Doesn't Have to Be a Bad Word," *Marketing Magazine,* April 11, 2006; Canadian Marketing Association Awards Magazine, November 16, 2007.

7. Rebecca Harris, "Knowing What They'll Do Next," *Marketing Magazine,* October 2014, pp. 12–13.

8. Susan Krashinsky, "AMEX, Pearson Team Up on Perks," *The Globe and Mail,* June 18, 2012, p. B3.

9. Stan Maklan, Simon Knox, and Joe Peppard, "Why CRM Fails—and How to Fix it," *National Post,* October 25, 2011, p. FE7.

10. Mark Tungate, "It's Not Just Coffee, It's a Lifestyle," *Marketing Magazine,* June 29, 2014.

11. Jeromy Lloyd, "Target Nets Top ICE Award for Turtle Campaign," *Marketing Magazine,* October 29, 2009.

12. The Goldstein Group, "Acquisition Marketing in a Multi-Channel World: The Resilient Principles of Successful Direct Mail." Report published at www.canadapost.ca.

13. Ibid.

14. Media Digest 2014–2015.

15. "Breaking Through the Noise," White Paper published at www.canadapost.ca.

16. Emily Wexler, "Cannes Lions: Grey Canada Wins Direct Gold," *Strategy,* June 21, 2010; www.canneslions.com

17. Goldstein Group, "Acquisition Marketing in a Multi-Channel World."

18. Chris Powell, "Canadian Tire Launches 'The Canadian Way' Catalogue Online," *Marketing Magazine,* April 10, 2013.

19. "Canadian Tire's Digital Catalogues, ," *Strategy,* March 4, 2014.

20. "Canadian Tire Takes Its Canadianness to Digital," *Strategy,* February 19, 2015.

21. "Ikea Breathes Inspiration Into Catalogue Pages," *Strategy,* February 19, 2015.

22. Kristin Laird, "IKEA's Mobile-Enabled Catalogue Goes Live in Canada," *Marketing Magazine,* August 13, 2012.

23. Val Maloney, "Ikea Promotes Its Pages," *Strategy,* August 29, 2013.

24. Susan Krashinsky, "The Cost of a World With No Spam," *The Globe and Mail,* June 20 2014, p. B4.

25. Basil Katz, "Email Newsletters Aim for Men's Inbox, Wallet," *National Post,* September 2009, p. FP10.

26. Alicia Androich, "The Loyalty Treatment," *Marketing Magazine,* December 3, 2012, pp. 33–39.

27. Brett A.S. Martin, Joel Van Durme, Mika Raulas, and Marko Merisavo, "E-mail Advertising: Exploratory Insights From Finland," *Journal of Advertising Research, 43* (3), September 2003, pp. 293–300.

28. Joseph E. Phelps, Regina Lewis, Lynne Mobilio, David Perry, and Niranjan Raman, "Viral Marketing or Electronic Word-of-Mouth Advertising: Examining Consumer Responses and Motivations to Pass Along Email," *Journal*

of Advertising Research, 44 (4), December 2004, pp. 333–348.

29. Alexandra Lopez-Pacheco, "Nirvana Is the Exception," *National Post*, July 14, 2009, p. FP7.

30. Media Digest 2014–2015.

31. Mandeep Singh, Siva K. Balasubramanian, and Goutan Chakraborty, "A Comparative Analysis of Three Communication Formats: Advertising, Infomercial, and Direct Experience," *Journal of Advertising*, 29 (4), Winter 2000, pp. 59–75.

32. Simon Houpt, "Call Now to Take Advantage of This Special TV Advertising Offer," *The Globe and Mail*, December 16, 2011, p. B5; http://www.thaneinc.com

33. www.theshoppingchannel.com

34. Canadian Marketing Association 2014 Fact Book.

35. https://www.the-cma.org/regulatory/code-of-ethics

36. Harmeet Singh, "Loyalty Programs Begin Turnaround," *Strategy*, February 13, 2015.

37. Tammo Bijmolt, Matilda Dorotic, and Peter Verhoef, "Loyalty Programs: Generalizations on Their Adoption, Effectiveness and Design," *Foundations and Trends in Marketing, 5* (4), 2010, pp. 197–258.

38. Josh Kolm, "Are Loyalty Programs the Fifth P of Marketing?" *Strategy*, April 27, 2016.

39. Yuping Liu, "The Long-Term Impact of Loyalty Programs on Consumer Purchase Behavior and Loyalty," *Journal of Marketing, 71* (4), October 2007, pp. 19–35.

40. Hye-Young Kim, Ji Young Lee, Dooyoung Choi, Juanjuan Wu, and Kim K. P. Johnson, "Perceived Benefits of Retail Loyalty Programs: Their Effects on Program Loyalty and Customer Loyalty," *Journal of Relationship Marketing, 12* (2), June 2013, pp. 95–113.

41. Bijmolt, Dorotic, and Verhoef, "Loyalty Programs: Generalizations on Their Adoption, Effectiveness and Design."

42. Ibid.

43. www.airmiles.ca

44. Alicia Androich, "Secrets of Canada's Top Loyalty Programs," *Marketing Magazine*, March 28, 2011.

45. Bond Loyalty Report, 2015. Report published at www.bondbrandloyalty.com.

46. Bond Loyalty Report, 2015. Report published at www.bondbrandloyalty.com.

47. Matt Semansky, "Threats and Opportunities in the Loyalty Game," *Marketing Magazine*, March 28, 2011, pp. 26–27.

48. Matt Semansky, "Jack Astor's Triples the V in VIP," *Marketing Magazine*, August 26, 2011.

49. Semansky, "Threats and Opportunities in the Loyalty Game."

50. Alicia Androich, "Get in the Game," *Marketing Magazine*, August 29, 2011, pp. 54–56.

51. Alicia Androich, "Scene Gamifies, Gets Mobile to Keep Movie Buffs Loyal," *Marketing Magazine*, December 22, 2011.

52. Alicia Androich, "The Loyalty Treatment," *Marketing Magazine*, December 3, 2012.

53. Rebecca Harris, "Why Starbucks Is Winning at Loyalty," *Marketing Magazine*, July 28, 2015.

54. Goldstein Group, "Acquisition Marketing in a Multi-Channel World."

CHAPTER SEVENTEEN

1. Chang Hoan Cho and Hyoung Koo Khang, "The State of Internet-Related Research in Communications, Marketing, and Advertising: 1994–2003," *Journal of Advertising*, 35 (3), Fall 2006, pp. 143–163.

2. Juran Kim and Sally J. McMillan, "Evaluation of Internet Advertising Research," *Journal of Advertising, 37* (1), Spring 2008, pp. 99–112.

3. Cate Riegner, "Word of Mouth on the Web: The Impact of Web 2.0 on Consumer Purchase Decisions," *Journal of Advertising Research, 47* (4), December 2007, pp. 436–447.

4. Nigel Hollis, "Ten Years of Learning on How Online Advertising Builds Brands," *Journal of Advertising Research, 45* (2), June 2005, pp. 255–268.

5. Rebecca Harris, "Mazda Accelerates In-Cinema Gaming With Cineplex, JWT," *Strategy*, November 2013; Jennifer Horn, "B!G Bronze; JWT and Mazda Reinvent the Test Drive," *Strategy* October 30, 2014.

6. Michelle Dipardo, "Coors Light Wants to Save You From an Average Summer," *Marketing Magazine*, July 4, 2014; Michelle Dipardo, "What Happens Now With Coors Light Search and Rescue?" *Marketing Magazine*, July 8, 2014.

7. Simon Houpt, "Wind Finally Gets Its Moment in the Sun," *The Globe and Mail*, December 18, 2009, p. B7.

8. Rebecca Harris, "Why Wind Moved Its Soapbox Into Social Media," *Marketing Magazine*, July 30, 2012.

9. Grace J. Johnson, Gordon C. Bruner II, and Anand Kumar, "Interactivity and Its Facets Revisited," *Journal of Advertising*, 35 (4), Winter 2006, pp. 35–52.

10. Maria Sicilia, Salvador Ruiz, and Jose L. Munuera, "Effects of Interactivity in a Web Site," *Journal of Advertising*, 34 (3), Fall 2005, pp. 31–45; Alex Wang, "Advertising Engagement: A Driver of Message Involvement on Message Effects," *Journal of Advertising Research*, 46 (4), December 2006, pp. 355–368.

11. Qimei Chen and William Wells, "Attitude Toward the Site," *Journal of Advertising Research*, 39 (5), September–October 1999, pp. 27–38; Qimei Chen, Sandra J. Clifford, and William Wells, "Attitude Toward the Site II: New Information," *Journal of Advertising Research, 42* (2), March–April 2002, pp. 33–45.

12. Gary L. Geissler, George M. Zinkhan, and Richard T. Watson, "The Influence of Home Page Complexity on Consumer Attention, Attitudes, and Purchase Intent," *Journal of Advertising*, 35 (2), Summer 2006, pp. 69–80.

13. Micael Dahlen, Alexandra Rasch, and Sara Rosengren, "Love at First Site? A Study of Website Advertising Effectiveness," *Journal of Advertising Research*, 43 (1), March 2003, pp. 25–33.

14. Julie S. Stevenson, Gordon Bruner II, and Anand Kumar, "Webpage Background and Viewer Attitudes," *Journal of Advertising Research*, 40 (1/2), January–April 2000, pp. 29–34; Gordon Bruner II and Anand Kumar, "Web Commercials and Advertising Hierarchy-of-Effects," *Journal of Advertising*

Research, 40 (1/2), January–April 2000, pp. 35–42.

15. Guda van Noort, Hilde A.M. Voorveld, and Eva A. van Reijmersdal, "Interactivity in Brand Web Sites: Cognitive, Affective, and Behavioural Responses Explained by Consumers' Online Flow Experience," *Journal of Interactive Marketing, 26* (4), November 2012, pp. 223–234.

16. Susan Krashinsky, "The Wild, Wacky, Weird World of Webby Advertising," *The Globe and Mail*, April 2, 2012, B7.

17. http://www.comscore.com/Insights/Presentations_and_Whitepapers/2015/2015_Canada_Digital_Future_in_Focuscomscore

18. http://www.smartinsights.com/internet-advertising/internet-advertising-analytics/display-advertising-clickthrough-rates/

19. Chang-Hoan Cho, Jung-Gyo Lee, and Marye Tharp, "Different Forced-Exposure Levels to Banner Advertisements," *Journal of Advertising Research*, 41 (4), July–August 2001, pp. 45–56.

20. Prem N. Shamdasani, Andrea J. S. Stanaland, and Juliana Tan, "Location, Location, Location: Insights for Advertising Placement on the Web," *Journal of Advertising Research*, 41 (4), July–August 2001, pp. 7–21; Wenyu Dou, Randy Lim, and Sixian Yang, "How Smart Are 'Smart Banners'?" 41 (4), July–August 2001, pp. 31–43.

21. Micael Dahlen, "Banner Advertisement Through a New Lens," *Journal of Advertising Research*, 41 (4), July–August 2001, pp. 21–30.

22. Kelli S. Burns and Richard J. Lutz, "The Function of Format: Consumer Responses to Six On-line Advertising Formats," *Journal of Advertising*, 35 (1) Spring 2006, pp. 53–63; Robert S. Moore, Claire Allison Stammerjohan, and Robin A. Coulter, "Banner Advertiser—Web Site Context Congruity and Color Effects on Attention and Attitudes," *Journal of Advertising*, 34 (2) Summer 2005, pp. 71–84; Ritu Lohtia, Naveen Donthu, and Edmund K. Hershberger, "The Impact of Content and Design Elements on Banner Advertising Click-Through Rates," *Journal of Advertising Research*, 43 (4), December 2003, pp. 410–418.

23. Peter J. Danaher and Guy W. Mullarkey, "Factors Affecting Online Advertising Recall: A Study of Students," *Journal of Advertising Research, 43* (3), September 2003, pp. 252–267; Idil Yaveroglu and Naveen Donthu, "Advertising Repetition and Placement Issues in On-Line Environment," *Journal of Advertising*, 37 (2), Summer 2008, pp. 31–43.

24. Jonathan Paul, "ICE Widget Activates Ads," *Strategy*, February 2009, p. 26.

25. IAB Internet Advertising Revenue Report, 2015 Full Year Results.

26. http://www.iab.net/about_the_iab/recent_press_releases/press_release_archive/press_release/pr-020226_adportfolio

27. Steven M. Edwards, Hairong Li, and Joo-Hyun Lee, "Forced Exposure and Psychological Reactance: Antecedents and Consequences of the Perceived Intrusiveness of Pop-Up Ads," *Journal of Advertising*, 31 (3), Fall 2002, pp. 83–95.

28. Shawn D. Baron, Caryn Brouwer, and Amaya Garbayo, "A Model for Delivering Branding

Value Through High-Impact Digital Advertising," *Journal of Advertising Research,* September 2014.

29. http://www.google.com/adwords; http://www.google.com/adsense

30. "Getting Search Right," *Marketing Magazine,* March 1, 2010.

31. Chris Powell, "Cross-Screen Video Advertising on the Rise; Videology," *Marketing Magazine,* March 2, 2016.

32. Alicia Androich, "The Future Is Data," *Marketing Magazine,* August 13, 2012, p. 14.

33. Daniel M. Haygood, "A Status Report on Podcast Advertising," *Journal of Advertising Research, 47* (4), December 2007, pp. 518–523.

34. Kristin Laird, "What Men Want," *Marketing Magazine,* April 2014.

35. Hollie Shaw, "Wind Mobile–MyScreen Partnership Gives Customers Rewards and Discounts," *National Post,* January 7, 2011, p. FP12.

36. Yaknv Bart, Andrew T. Stephen, and Miklos Sarvary, "Which Products Are Best Suited to Mobile Advertising? A Field Study of Mobile Display Advertising Effects on Consumer Attitudes and Intentions," *Journal of Marketing Research, 51* (3), June 2014, pp. 270–285.

37. Susan Krashinsky, "Inside Oreo's Olympics War Room," *The Globe and Mail,* February 21, 2014, p. B.5

38. Susan Krashinsky, "An Ad for Every Flavour," *The Globe and Mail,* April 25, 2014, p. B.5.

39. Jonathan Paul, "It's Still All About Location, Location, Location," *Strategy,* February 1, 2011, p. 20.

40. Simon Houpt, "It's All Fun and Games—Until Someone Bonds With a Brand," *The Globe and Mail,* January 2, 2011, p. B1.

41. Matt Semansky, "Location-Based Marketing for the Rest of Us," *Marketing Magazine,* August 1, 2011, pp. 16–21.

42. Alicia Androich, "Ready to Get More Social With Your TV?" *Marketing Magazine,* April 12, 2013.

43. Jameson Berkow, "No Magic Formula," *National Post,* January 17, 2011; Marina Strauss and Omar El Akkad, "A Handheld Way Retailers Are Fighting Online Store Wars," *The Globe and Mail,* December 20, 2011.

44. Steven Bellman, Robert F. Potter, Shiree Treleaven-Hassard, Jennifer A. Robinson, and Duane Varan, "The Effectiveness of Branded Mobile Phone Apps," *Journal of Interactive Marketing, 25* (4), November 2011, pp. 191–200.

45. Chris Daniels, "Rewards for the Mobile Masses," *Marketing Magazine,* August 29, 2011, pp. 51–53.

46. Grant Buckler, "From Your Smartphone to the Big Screen," *The Globe and Mail,* November 23, 2011, p. B18.

47. Jacque Natel and Yasha Sekhavat, "The Impact of SMS Advertising on Members of a Virtual Community," *Journal of Advertising Research, 48* (3), September 2008, pp. 363–374.

48. Simon Houpt, "Why Click When You Can Scan Your Way to Ad Messages?" *The Globe and Mail,* October 2009, p. B8.

49. Ivor Tossell, "Wave of the Future, or Just Annoying?" *The Globe and Mail,* August 16, 2011, p. L2.

50. Joe Plummer, Steve Rappaport, Taddy Hall, and Robert Barocci, *The Online Advertising Playbook,* 2007 (John Wiley & Sons, Hoboken, NJ).

51. Andreas M. Kaplan and Michael Haenlein, "Users of the World, Unite! The Challenges and Opportunities of Social Media," *Business Horizons,* 2010, 53, pp. 59–68.

52. Daniel G. Muntinga, Marjolein Moorman, and Edith G. Smit, "Introducing COBRAs: Exploring Motivations for Brand-Related Social Media Use," *International Journal of Advertising,* 30 (1), 2011, pp. 13–46.

53. Andrew N. Smith, Eileen Fischer, and Chen Yongjian, "How Does Brand-Related User-Generated Content Differ Across YouTube, Facebook and Twitter," *Journal of Interactive Marketing,* 26 (2), May 2012, pp. 102–113.

54. Simon Houpt, "The Tweet Taste of Success," *The Globe and Mail,* September 6, 2012, p. B9.

55. Kaplan and Haenlein, "Users of the World, Unite!"

56. Susan Krashinsky, "An Ad for Every Flavour," *The Globe and Mail,* April 25, 2014, p. B.5.

57. Eilene Zimmerman, "Facebook Goes Toe-to-Toe With Google on Ads," *National Post,* January 27, 2014, p. FP8.

58. Karen Nelson-Field, Erica Riebe, and Byron Sharp, "More Mutter About Clutter," *Journal of Advertising Research,* June 2013.

59. Susan Krashinsky, "Mobile Ads Fuel Facebook Revenue Surge," *The Globe and Mail,* July 24, 2014, p. B.8.

60. Susan Krashinsky, "Will the Video Platform Kill the TV Spot?" *The Globe and Mail,* October 24, 2014, p. B.6.

61. Lisette de Vries, Sonja Gensler, and Peter S.H. Leeflang, "Popularity of Brand Posts on Brand Fan Pages: An Investigation of the Effects of Social Media Marketing," *Journal of Interactive Marketing,* 26 (2), May 2012, pp. 83–91.

62. http://fbrep.com//SMB/Pages_Product_Guide.pdf

63. Hollie Shaw, "Catering to the Kraft Dinner Cult," *National Post,* March 23, 2012, p. FP12.

64. https://business.twitter.com

65. Alicia Androich, "Twitter Canada Talks Targeting, Engagement at Official Launch," *Marketing Magazine,* June 14, 2013.

66. https://business.twitter.com/

67. http://searchenginewatch.com/article/2190651/Twitter-Advertising-Guide

68. Matt Hartley, "The Revolution Will Be Monetized," *National Post,* March 19, 2011, p. FP1; Christina Rexrode, "How Twitter Changed #endorsements," *The Globe and Mail,* November 4, 2009, p. L2.

69. "Where's the Party?" *Marketing Magazine,* October 10, 2011, p. 31.

70. Kristin Laird, "Accelerating Social Media," *Marketing Magazine,* October 10, 2011, pp. 28–29.

71. Kristin Laird, "The Very Necessary Twitter Guide for Canadian Marketers," *Marketing Magazine,* October 10, 2011, pp. 24–27.

72. Russ Martin, "Quality Over Quantity," *Marketing Magazine,* November/December 2014.

73. Claire Brownell, "Engaged vs. Edgy; Brands Walk the Fine Line in Retweet Game," *National Post,* January 26, 2015.

74. Rebecca Harris, "The Blitz Begins for Tomorrow's Fans," *Marketing Magazine,* November/December 2014, pp. 9–10.

75. "Who Should Own a Client's Social Media Duties?" *Marketing Magazine,* February 28, 2011, pp. 30–31.

76. Matthew Braga, "To Go Mainstream, Twitter Needs to Kill the Stream," *National Post,* February 8, 2014, p. FP3.

77. Omar El Akkad, "Different Circles," *The Globe and Mail,* November 26, 2014.

78. Russ Martin, "How Samsung Is Using Twitter's New Conversational Ads," *Marketing Magazine,* January 13, 2016.

79. Statistics for all social media vehicles are retrieved from http://www.ebizmba.com.

80. Ivor Tossell and John Lorinc, "Social Media Superstars," *The Globe and Mail,* April 25, 2012, p. 11.

81. Megan Haynes, " Risky Business," *Strategy,* June 2015; Susan Krashinsky, "Schick Launches YouTube Web Series to Reach Younger Consumers," *The Globe and Mail,* March 25, 2015.

82. Simon Houpt, "What Makes a Video Go Viral?" *The Globe and Mail,* May 26, 2011.

83. Melita Kuburas, "Updating Molson's Social Media Status," *Strategy,* May 1, 2009, p. 25.

84. Susan Krashinsky, "Lululemon Ad Pokes Fun at Own Customers—and Goes Viral," *The Globe and Mail,* January 13, 2012, p. B5.

85. Susan Krashinsky, "Brand-Building, One Instagram Post at a Time," *The Globe and Mail,* November 10, 2014, p. B.3.

86. Rae Ann Fera, "Mazda; The Long Drive Home," *Marketing Magazine,* July 2014.

87. http://www.blogto.com/blogto-mediakit.pdf

88. Chris Koentges, "The Hypest of the Hyperlocal," *Marketing Magazine,* June 4, 2012, pp. 21–22.

89. https://adstandards.com/en/Standards/Proposed-Code-Changes-EN.pdf

90. Angela Hickman, "In Blogs They Trust," *National Post,* August 20, 2011, p. WP5.

91. http://en.wikipedia.org/wiki/Wikipedia:Advertisements

92. https://s3.amazonaws.com/answ-img/AnswersMediaKit_20130201.pdf

93. Megan Haynes, "Reddit Knows What Canadians Want," *Strategy,* July 2014, p. 10.

94. Kristin Laird, "Pinterest Rate," *Marketing Magazine,* April 9, 2012, pp. 8–10.

95. http://business.pinterest.com/case-study-sephora/

96. Houpt, "It's All Fun and Games—Until Someone Bonds With a Brand."

97. Paul, "It's Still All about Location, Location, Location."

98. Subdh Bhat, Michael Bevans, and Sanjit Sengupta, "Measuring Users' Web Activity to Evaluate and Enhance Advertising Effectiveness," *Journal of Advertising, 31* (3), Fall 2002, pp. 97–106.

99. Stephen D. Rappaport, The Digital Metrics Field Guide, *The Advertising Research Foundation,* 2014.

100. Stephen D. Rappaport, "Lessons Learned From A Field Guide to Digital Metrics," *Journal of Advertising Research,* March 2014.

101. Benjamin Edelman, "Pitfalls and Fraud in Online Advertising Metrics," *Journal of Advertising Research*, June 2014.

102. Alexa Bezjian-Avery, "New Media Interactive Advertising vs. Traditional Advertising," *Journal of Advertising Research, 38* (4), August 1998, pp. 23–32; Qimel Chen and William D. Wells, "Attitude Toward the Site," *Journal of Advertising Research, 39* (5), September–October 1999, pp. 27–38; Kim Bartel Sheehan and Sally J. McMillan, "Response Variation in E-Mail Surveys," *Journal of Advertising Research, 39* (4), July–August 1999, pp. 45–54; John Eighmey, "Profiling User Responses to Commercial Websites," *Journal of Advertising Research, 37* (3), May–June 1997, p. 66.

103. http://iabcanada.com/files/IABCanada_CMOST_TetleyRedTeaReport_FINAL_English.pdf

104. Kay Peters, Yubo Chen, Andreas M. Kaplan, Bjorn Ognibeni, and Koen Pauwels, "Social Media Metrics—A Framework and Guidelines for Managing Social Media," *Journal of Interactive Marketing, 27* (4), November 2013, pp. 281–298.

105. Kanter Media-Canadian Online Advertising Trends Analysis, March 2012.

106. Anonymous, "Internet Marketing: Daunting," *National Post*, November 11, 2009, p. FP3.

107. Sung-Joon Yoon and Joo-Ho Kim, "Is the Internet More Effective Than Traditional Media? Factors Affecting the Choice of Media," *Journal of Advertising Research, 41* (6), November–December 2001, pp. 53–60.

108. Katherine Gallagher, K. Dale Foster, and Jeffrey Parsons, "The Medium Is not the Message: Advertising Effectiveness and Content Evaluation in Print and on the Web," *Journal of Advertising Research, 41* (4), July–August 2001, pp. 57–70; Katherine Gallagher, Jeffrey Parsons, and K. Dale Foster, "A Tale of Two Studies: Replicating 'Advertising Effectiveness and Content Evaluation in Print and on the Web'," *Journal of Advertising Research, 41* (4), July–August 2001, pp. 71–81.

109. Johanna S. Ilfeld and Russell S. Winer, "Generating Website Traffic," *Journal of Advertising Research, 42* (5), September–October 2002, pp. 49–61.

110. Yumiin Chang and Esther Thorson, "Television and Web Advertising Synergies," *Journal of Advertising, 33* (2), Summer 2004, pp. 75–84.

111. Ali M. Kanso and Richard Alan Nelson, "Internet and Magazine Advertising: Integrated Partnerships or Not?" *Journal of Advertising Research, 44* (4), December 2004, pp. 317–326.

112. Robert Davis and Laszlo Sajtos, "Measuring Consumer Interactivity in Response to Campaigns Coupling Mobile and Television Media," *Journal of Advertising Research, 48* (3), September 2008; Randolph J. Trappey III and Arch G. Woodside, "Consumer Responses to Interactive Advertising Campaigns Coupling Short-Message-Service Direct Marketing and TV Commercials," *Journal of Advertising Research, 45* (4), December 2005, pp. 382–401.

CHAPTER EIGHTEEN

1. Brenda Pritchard and Susan Vogt, *Advertising and Marketing Law in Canada*, Fifth Edition (LexisNexis, 2015).

2. A Guide to the Amendments of the Competition Act, Competition Bureau Canada, April 22, 2009.

3. Hollie Shaw, "Bogus Ads," *National Post*, May 22, 2009, p. FP12.

4. Scott Deveau, "Aitken Wages War on Pricing's Fine Print," *National Post*, June 30, 2011, p. FP3; Jamie Sturgeon, "Bell Hit for $10M Over Misleading Advertising," *National Post*, June 29, 2011, p. FP1; Canadian Press, "Competition Bureau Sues Canada's 3 Wireless Giants Over Texting Advertising," *Marketing Magazine*, September 14, 2012; Chris Koentges, "United by Telco Animosity," *Marketing Magazine*, January 15, 2013.

5. Jean-Francois Ouellet, "Vachon's Igor Crossed the Line in Quebec," *National Post*, March 10, 2009, p. FP13.

6. Canadian Code of Advertising Standards Interpretation Guidelines, http://www.adstandards.com/en/ASCLibrary/interpretationGuidelines.pdf

7. http://www.adstandards.com/en/childreninitiative

8. http://www.adstandards.com/en/childreninitiative/2011ComplianceReport.pdf

9. "Lord & Taylor Settles Charges of Deceptive Instagram Posts," *Marketing Magazine*, March 15, 2016.

10. Susan Krashinsky, "Ad Watchdog Warns Against Disguised Marketing Attempt," *The Globe and Mail*, March 26, 2015, p. B.4.

11. Jeromy Lloyd, "Hot Water," *Marketing Magazine*, April 20, 2009.

12. Jeromy Lloyd, "Shell Advertorials Spurn Complaint to Ad Standards Council," *Marketing Magazine*, February 11, 2010.

13. Matt Semansky, "Bell Ignores ASC Ruling," *Marketing Magazine*, February 23, 2009.

14. http://adstandards.com/en/standards/complaints_report/2001ascReportEn.pdf, accessed December 12, 2007.

15. http://www.adstandards.com/en/-standards/adComplaintsReports.asp?periodquarter=1&periodyear=2007, accessed December 12, 2007.

16. David Brown, "Kia Gets the Goat," *Marketing Magazine*, February 27, 2007.

17. http://www.adstandards.com/en/Standards/adComplaintsReports.asp?periodquarter=2&periodyear=2007

18. http://www.adstandards.com/en/standards/adComplaintsReports.asp?periodquarter=2&periodyear=2008

19. Ibid.

20. Eric N. Berkowitz, Roger A. Kerin, Steven W. Hartley, William Rudedius, et al., *Marketing*, 5th ed. (Burr Ridge, IL: Irwin/McGraw-Hill, 1997), p. 102.

21. Stephanie O'Donohoe, "Attitudes to Advertising: A Review of British and American Research," *International Journal of Advertising, 14* (3), Fall 1995, pp. 245–261.

22. Banwari Mittal, "Public Assessment of TV Advertising: Faint Praise and Harsh Criticism," *Journal of Advertising Research, 34* (1), January–February 1994, pp. 35–53.

23. Sharon Shavitt, Pamela Lowery, and James Haefner, "Public Attitudes Toward Advertising; More Favorable Than You Might Think," *Journal of Advertising Research, 38* (4), July/August 1998, pp. 7–22.

24. Gita Venkataramini Johar, "Consumer Involvement and Deception From Implied Advertising Claims," *Journal of Marketing Research, 32* (3), August 1995, pp. 267–279; J. Edward Russo, Barbara L. Metcalf, and Debra Stephens, "Identifying Misleading Advertising," *Journal of Consumer Research, 8* (2), September 1981, pp. 119–131.

25. Ivan L. Preston, *The Great American Blow-Up: Puffery in Advertising and Selling* (Madison: University of Wisconsin Press, 1975), p. 3.

26. Carly Weeks, "Bad. Good?" *The Globe and Mail*, October 17, 2011, p. L1.

27. Bruce Dowbiggin, "TV Beer Battle Comes to a Head," *The Globe and Mail*, May 18, 2012, p. S5.

28. Shelby D. Hunt, "Informational vs. Persuasive Advertising: An Appraisal," *Journal of Advertising, 5* (3), Summer 1976, pp. 5–8.

29. Mittal, "Public Assessment of TV Advertising: Faint Praise and Harsh Criticism"; J. C. Andrews, "The Dimensionality of Beliefs Toward Advertising in General," *Journal of Advertising, 18* (1), 1989, pp. 26–35; Shavitt, Lowery, and Haefner, "Public Attitudes Toward Advertising; More Favorable Than You Might Think."

30. David A. Aaker and Donald E. Bruzzone, "Causes of Irritation in Advertising," *Journal of Marketing, 49* (2), Spring 1985, pp. 47–57.

31. Stephen A. Greyser, "Irritation in Advertising," *Journal of Advertising Research, 13* (1), February 1973, pp. 3–10.

32. Kenyon Wallace, "TTC Flirts With Online Adulterers," *National Post*, December 11, 2009, p. A1; Kenyon Wallace, "Pro-Adultery Agency Loses TTC Ad Bid," *National Post*, December 12, 2009, p. A21.

33. Andrea Woo, "Ad Policy Impedes Doctors, Growers Say," *The Globe and Mail*, January 13, 2015, p. S.2.

34. Chris Powell, "Astral Campaign Gives Radio Hope," *Marketing Magazine*, March 5, 2009; "Toronto Unhappy About Virgin Suicides," *Marketing Magazine*, April 17, 2009; Jeff Gray, "Suicide Ad Irks Transit Authority," *The Globe and Mail*, April 17, 2009, p. A3.

35. Tim Nudd, "Does Sex Really Sell?" *Adweek*, October 17, 2005, pp. 14–17.

36. James B. Arndorfer, "Skyy Hit the Limit With Racy Ad: Critics," *Advertising Age*, February 7, 2005, p. 6.

37. Tom Reichert, Courtney Carpenter Childers, and Leonard N. Reid, "How Sex in Advertising Varies by Product Category: An Analysis of Three Decades of Visual Sexual Imagery in Magazine Advertising," *Journal of Current Issues and Research in Advertising, 33* (1), January 2012, pp. 1–19.

38. Scott Ward, Daniel B. Wackman, and Ellen Wartella, *How Children Learn to Buy: The Development of Consumer Information Processing Skills* (Beverly Hills, CA: Sage, 1979).

39. Thomas S. Robertson and John R. Rossiter, "Children and Commercial Persuasion: An Attribution Theory Analysis," *Journal of Consumer Research, 1* (1), June 1974, pp. 13–20; Scott Ward and Daniel B. Wackman, "Children's Information Processing of Television Advertising," in *New Models for Communications Research*, eds. G. Kline and

P. Clark (Beverly Hills, CA: Sage, 1974), pp. 81–119.

40. Merrie Brucks, Gary M. Armstrong, and Marvin E. Goldberg, "Children's Use of Cognitive Defenses Against Television Advertising: A Cognitive Response Approach," *Journal of Consumer Research, 14* (4), March 1988, pp. 471–482.

41. For a discussion on consumer socialization, see Scott Ward, "Consumer Socialization," *Journal of Consumer Research, 1* (2), September 1974, pp. 1–14.

42. Tamara F. Mangleburg and Terry Bristol, "Socialization and Adolescents' Skepticism Toward Advertising," *Journal of Advertising, 27* (3), Fall 1998, pp. 11–21.

43. Robert E. Hite and Randy Eck, "Advertising to Children: Attitudes of Business vs. Consumers," Journal of Advertising Research, 27 (5), October/ November 1987, pp. 40–53; Ann D. Walsh, Russell N. Laczniak, and Les Carlson, "Mothers' Preferences for Regulating Children's Television," *Journal of Advertising, 27* (3), Fall 1998, pp. 23–36.

44. Dakshana Bascaramurty, "The Fine Line Between a Pokemon Ad and Entertainment," *The Globe and Mail*, November 15, 2011, p. L1.

45. Joanna Pachner and Alicia Androich, "Kids in Play," *Marketing Magazine*, March 14, 2011, pp. 27–28, 30–31.

46. Kate Hammer, "Advertising on School TV Screens Raises Alarm?" *The Globe and Mail*, March 9, 2011, p. A14.

47. Raymond A. Bauer and Stephen A. Greyser, "The Dialogue That Never Happens," *Harvard Business Review*, January/February 1969, pp. 122–128.

48. Morris B. Holbrook, "Mirror Mirror On the Wall, What's Unfair in the Reflections on Advertising," *Journal of Marketing, 51* (3), July 1987, pp. 95–103; Theodore Levitt, "The Morality of Advertising," *Harvard Business Review*, July/August 1970, pp. 84–92.

49. Stephen Fox, *The Mirror Makers: A History of American Advertising and Its Creators* (New York: Morrow, 1984), p. 330.

50. Richard W. Pollay, "The Distorted Mirror: Reflections on the Unintended Consequences of Advertising," *Journal of Marketing, 50* (2), April 1986, p. 33.

51. Jules Backman, "Is Advertising Wasteful?" *Journal of Marketing, 32* (1), January 1968, pp. 2–8.

52. Hunt, "Informational vs. Persuasive Advertising."

53. Ibid., p. 6.

54. Alice E. Courtney and Thomas W. Whipple, *Sex Stereotyping in Advertising* (Lexington, MA: Lexington Books, 1984).

55. Daniel J. Brett and Joanne Cantor, "The Portrayal of Men and Women in U.S. Television Commercials: A Recent Content Analysis and Trends of 15 Years," *Sex Roles, 18* (9/10), 1998, pp. 595–608; John B. Ford and Michael La Tour, "Contemporary Perspectives of Female Role Portrayals in Advertising," *Journal of Current Issues and Research in Advertising, 28* (1), Spring 1996, pp. 81–93.

56. Beverly A. Browne, "Gender Stereotypes in Advertising on Children's Television in the 1990s: A Cross-National Analysis," *Journal of Advertising, 27* (1), Spring 1998, pp. 83–96.

57. Richard H. Kolbe, "Gender Roles in Children's Advertising: A Longitudinal Content Analysis," in *Current Issues and Research in Advertising*, ed. James H. Leigh and Claude R. Martin, Jr. (Ann Arbor: University of Michigan, 1990), pp. 197–206.

58. Steven M. Kates and Glenda Shaw-Garlock, "The Ever Entangling Web: A Study of Ideologies and Discourses in Advertising to Women," *Journal of Advertising, 28* (2), Summer 1999, pp. 33–49.

59. Basil Englis, Michael Solomon, and Richard Ashmore, "Beauty Before the Eyes of Beholders: The Cultural Encoding of Beauty Types in Magazine Advertising and Music Television," *Journal of Advertising, 23* (2), June 1994, pp. 49–64.

60. Hollie Shaw, "Axe Kicks It Up a Notch," *National Post*, September 9, 2011, p. FP12.

61. www.adstandards.com/en/consumercomplaints/2015adcomplaintsreport.pdf

62. Nathalie Atkinson, "Picture-Perfect Manipulation," *National Post*, October 10, 2009, p. A3.

63. Kristin Laird, "Loblaw Stands by Sexy Joe Fresh Underwear Flyer," *Marketing Magazine*, April 7, 2009; Kelly Egan, "Sexualized Ads Signal Disturbing Trend," *Ottawa Citizen*, April 3, 2009.

64. Jeromy Lloyd, "Shell Advertorials Spurn Complaint to Ad Standards Canada," *Marketing Magazine*, February 11, 2010.

65. Susan Krashinsky, "You've Come a Long Way, Dad," *The Globe and Mail*, May 4, 2012, p. B7; Seth Stevenson, "The Reign of the Doltish Dad," *National Post*, March 29, 2012, p. A18.

66. Susan Krashinsky, "Time to Adapt Ads for Modern Men," *The Globe and Mail,* July 9, 2014, p. B.8.

67. James Stearns, Lynette S. Unger, and Steven G. Luebkeman, "The Portrayal of Blacks in Magazine and Television Advertising," in *AMA Educator's Proceedings*, eds. Susan P. Douglas and Michael R. Solomon (Chicago: American Marketing Association, 1987).

68. Robert E. Wilkes and Humberto Valencia, "Hispanics and Blacks in Television Commercials," *Journal of Advertising, 18* (1), 1989, pp. 19–26.

69. Julia Bristor, Renee Gravois Lee, and Michelle Hunt, "Race and Ideology: African American Images in Television Advertising," *Journal of Public Policy and Marketing, 14* (1), Spring 1995, pp. 48–59.

70. Corliss Green, "Ethnic Evaluations of Advertising: Interaction Effects of Strength of Ethnic Identification, Media Placement, and Degree of Racial Composition," *Journal of Advertising, 28* (1), Spring 1999, pp. 49–64.

71. Charles R. Taylor and Barbara B. Stern, "Asian-Americans: Television Advertising and the 'Model Minority' Stereotype," *Journal of Advertising, 26* (2), Summer 1997, pp. 47–61.

72. Susan Krashinsky, "The Mismatch of Race in TV Ads," *The Globe and Mail*, May 7, 2014,

B.4; https://www12.statcan.gc.ca/nhs-enm/2011/as-sa/99-010-x/99-010-x2011001-eng.cfm.

73. Tanya Kostiw, "Normalizing Today's Normal," *Strategy*, April 2015, p. A.16.

74. Jef I. Richards and John H. Murphy, II, "Economic Censorship and Free Speech: The Circle of Communication Between Advertisers, Media and Consumers," *Journal of Current Issues and Research in Advertising, 18* (1), Spring 1996, pp. 21–33.

75. Lawrence C. Soley and Robert L. Craig, "Advertising Pressure on Newspapers: A Survey," *Journal of Advertising, 21* (4), December 1992, pp. 1–10.

76. Randy W. Elder, Ruth A. Shults, David A. Sleet, James L. Nichols, Robert S. Thompson, and Warda Rajab, "Effectiveness of Mass Media Campaigns for Reducing Drinking and Driving and Alcohol-Involved Crashes," *American Journal of Preventative Medicine, 27* (1), July 2004, pp. 57–65.

77. Kristin Laird, "LCBO Is Deflating Elephants," *Marketing Magazine*, December 9, 2009.

78. Hollie Shaw, "Campaign Brings Home Hard Reality About Health Care," *National Post*, January 28, 2011, p. FP6.

79. Jeromy Lloyd, "A Prize at What Price?" *Marketing Magazine*, September 12, 2011, pp. 38–39; David Brown, "The Ethics Talk," *Marketing Magazine*, September 12, 2011, p. 27.

80. For a discussion of monopolies in the cereal industry, see Paul N. Bloom, "The Cereal Industry: Monopolists or Super Marketers?" *MSU Business Topics*, Summer 1978, pp. 41–49.

81. Lester G. Telser, "Advertising and Competition," *Journal of Political Economy*, December 1964, pp. 537–562.

82. Robert D. Buzzell, Bradley T. Gale, and Ralph G. M. Sultan, "Market Share—A Key to Profitability," *Harvard Business Review*, January/February 1975, pp. 97–106.

83. Robert D. Buzzell and Paul W. Farris, *Advertising Cost in Consumer Goods Industries*, Marketing Science Institute, Report No. 76, August 1976, p. 111; Paul W. Farris and David J. Reibstein, "How Prices, Ad Expenditures, and Profits Are Linked," *Harvard Business Review*, November/ December 1979, pp. 173–184.

84. Paul W. Farris and Mark S. Albion, "The Impact of Advertising on the Price of Consumer Products," *Journal of Marketing, 44* (3), Summer 1980, pp. 17–35.

85. Lee Benham, "The Effect of Advertising on the Price of Eyeglasses," *Journal of Law and Economics, 15* (October 1972), pp. 337–352.

86. Robert L. Steiner, "Does Advertising Lower Consumer Price?" *Journal of Marketing, 37* (4), October 1973, pp. 19–26.

87. James M. Ferguson, "Comments On 'The Impact of Advertising on the Price of Consumer Products,'" *Journal of Marketing, 46* (1), Winter 1982, pp. 102–105.

88. Farris and Albion, "The Impact of Advertising."

Name and Company Index

Subject Index